PEARSON ASE TEST PREPARATION GUIDE
A1–A8 AND L1

Prentice Hall
Upper Saddle River, New Jersey
Columbus, Ohio

Editor in Chief: Vernon Anthony
Acquisitions Editor: Wyatt Morris
Editorial Assistant: Chris Reed
Production Coordination: Andrea Shearer, GGS Book Services PMG
Project Manager: Holly Shufeldt
Operations Specialist: Laura Weaver
Art Director: Candace Rowley
Interior Design: Candace Rowley
Cover Designer: Rachel Hirschi
Cover image: Courtesy of iStockphoto
Director of Marketing: David Gesell
Marketing Assistant: Les Roberts

This book was set in Minion by GGS Book Services PMG and was printed and bound by Courier. The cover was printed by Phoenix Color Corp.

Pearson Prentice Hall™ is a trademark of Pearson Education, Inc.
Pearson® is a registered trademark of Pearson plc
Prentice Hall® is a registered trademark of Pearson Education, Inc.

Pearson Education Ltd., London
Pearson Education Singapore Pte. Ltd.
Pearson Education Canada, Inc.
Pearson Education—Japan

Pearson Education Australia Pty. Limited
Pearson Education North Asia Ltd., Hong Kong
Pearson Educación de Mexico, S.A. de C.V.
Pearson Education Malaysia Pte. Ltd.

Prentice Hall
is an imprint of

www.pearsonhighered.com

10 9 8 7 6 5 4 3 2 1
ISBN-13: 978-0-13-504025-6
ISBN-10:   0-13-504025-6

CONTENTS

A1 ENGINE REPAIR

CHAPTER ONE

GENERAL ENGINE DIAGNOSIS

CHAPTER OBJECTIVES

- The technician will complete the ASE task list on General Engine Diagnosis.
- The technician will be able to answer 15 questions dealing with the Diagnosis section of the A1 ASE test.

ENGINE INSPECTION AND DIAGNOSIS

Before you begin any engine repair, it is necessary to identify, as closely as possible, the defects involved. This chapter explains the tests that are performed to identify problem areas, while the engine is still in the vehicle and in operating condition.

The most important aspect of engine diagnosis is listening to the customer. Let the customer describe the symptoms and clue you in to the problem. This will give you a fairly good idea of where to begin your search. Then, conduct a visual inspection of the vehicle and verify the complaint by experiencing the symptoms during a test drive.

Preliminary Inspection

A quick inspection before your test drive can often isolate the problem's source. Before you drive the vehicle and begin engine testing, do the following:

- Check all drive belts to make sure none are cracked, frayed, loose, or slipping, figure 1-1
- Check electrical harnesses and connectors for loose contacts, brittle insulation, and broken wires
- Check all engine-mounted components for loose or missing bolts, worn bushings, and loose or broken support brackets
- Check all hoses to make sure none are soft, brittle, kinked, or otherwise damaged, figure 1-2

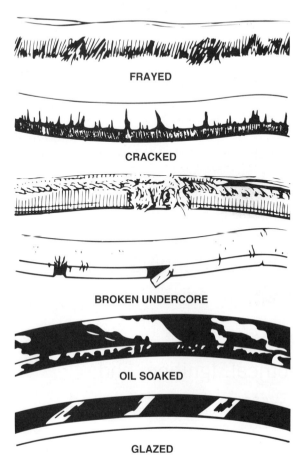

FRAYED

CRACKED

BROKEN UNDERCORE

OIL SOAKED

GLAZED

Fig.1-1. Inspect drive belts for wear and damage.

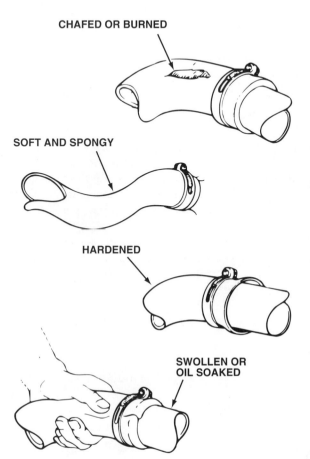

CHAFED OR BURNED

SOFT AND SPONGY

HARDENED

SWOLLEN OR OIL SOAKED

Fig.1-2. Check hoses for damage.

- Check all fuel lines, hoses, and fittings for leakage, loose connections, and damage
- Check the battery; look for corrosion on the terminals, proper electrolyte level, and missing or damaged hold-down assemblies
- Check the secondary ignition cables for damaged insulation, corrosion, and loose connections
- Check the air cleaner filter element for dirt or blockage
- Check emission control systems for brittle, burned, or damaged hoses and loose fittings

If the engine exhibits any of the following symptoms, refer to Chapter 5 for additional information and troubleshooting procedures.

- No-crank
- Cranks but will not start
- Hard starting (long crank times)

If no obvious problems are found and the engine starts normally, continue your evaluation by making a test drive.

Test Drive

Whenever possible, let your customer accompany you on the test drive. The customer knows the vehicle and can point out sounds, vibrations, and other annoyances that you might assume to be normal or overlook.

Conduct a thorough road test; one quick lap around the block is not enough. The engine must be brought to normal operating temperature, and your test should include a stop-and-go city driving cycle and a period of cruising at highway speed. If the car has air conditioning, operate it during the test drive. If a hilly stretch of road is available, include it in your route. It's best to have one, or several, predetermined routes that include a variety of driving conditions.

Unusual Engine Noises

Engine noises can be divided into two general categories: those that originate in the top end of the engine, and those that originate in the bottom end of the engine. Begin engine noise diagnosis by determining where in the engine the noise is coming from. Bottom end, or crankcase, noises occur at crankshaft speed, so they tend to produce a high-frequency knock or rumble. Top end, or valve train, noises occur at a lower frequency because these parts operate at one-half crankshaft speed.

A stethoscope is a handy tool for isolating noises. You can also use a timing light to determine whether a noise is from the top or bottom end of the engine. Connect the timing light and listen. If the engine noise cycles in time with the flashing light, the sound is coming from the bottom end. Sounds that are audible with every other flash of the timing light originate in the top end of the engine.

Top-End Noises

The top end of a healthy engine produces a high-pitched, whirring noise with a very rapid and much fainter sewing-machine-like clicking coming from the valves. The more valves the engine has, and the higher the idle speed, the more the individual clicks will blend into a constant drone. Any deviation is abnormal and indicates a problem. Listen for:

- An irregular clacking or knocking noise caused by excessive camshaft endplay
- An irregular slapping or thumping at the front of the engine caused by a loose timing belt. A tight timing belt makes a whirring, whining, hum that rises and falls in pitch with rpm
- A single, clear clack whenever a particular valve opens can be a collapsed lifter or a broken valve spring
- A loud, cycling, valve rattle that you can hear over the normal valve noise can indicate either worn valve guides or rocker arm pivots
- Low pressure or restricted oil flow will produce an excessively loud, rhythmic clatter

Bottom-End Noises

Healthy engines produce an evenly pitched, rapid, whirring sound and nothing else. Knocking or thumping noises are signs that something is wrong. In general, bottom-end noise can be caused and indicated by:

- An irregular knock at idle that can be made louder or fainter by playing with the clutch pedal indicates too much crankshaft endplay
- A sharp clattering knock that may be continuous at idle or only appear when the throttle closes suddenly can indicate a bad connecting rod bearing. The noise will diminish if the spark plug for the offending cylinder is grounded
- A hollow metallic clatter that is loudest when the engine is cold may be piston slap caused by too much piston to cylinder wall clearance. Grounding the spark plug of the affected cylinder will often make piston slap louder because it eliminates the cushioning of the extra gas pressure pushing on the piston
- A sharp knocking that stands out most at idle can indicate a **wrist pin** that is loose in its bore. Grounding the spark plug of the affected cylinder makes the knock audible at top dead center as well as bottom dead center. Retarding the spark decreases wrist pin noise
- A rapid, steady dull pounding that increases with load is typical of worn main bearings

Insight

Noises from the exhaust tail pipes or air intake system can indicate possible problems with intake or exhaust valve sealing!

Unusual Exhaust Color and Odor

Although a healthy catalytic converter can do a good job of cleaning up the exhaust, you can tell something about the internal engine condition by checking for unusual smoke or smells:

- Black exhaust smoke. This is caused by a rich air-fuel mixture, and is often accompanied by the "rotten-egg" smell of an overworked catalytic converter
- Blue exhaust smoke indicates excessive oil burning, which gives off a pungent odor

A1

Wrist Pin: The cylindrical or tubular metal pin that attaches the piston to the connecting rod (also called the piston pin).

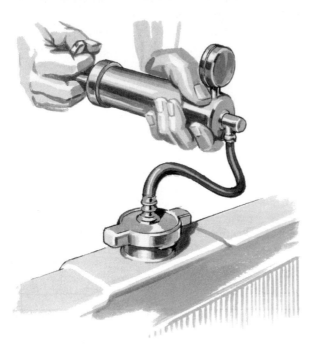

Fig. 1-3. Attach the pressure tester to the filler neck.

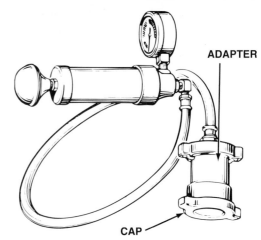

Fig. 1-4. Radiator cap pressure test.

- Cloudy white exhaust is often the result of engine coolant leaking into the combustion chamber. Burning coolant also produces a distinctive chemical odor. Check the temperature gauge for overheating

Keep in mind that oil vapor odors are not always the result of an internal engine problem. A clogged or malfunctioning positive crankcase ventilation (PCV) system can not only produce a burning-oil smell, but can also cause excessive crankcase vapor and increase oil consumption. Always check all external sources before you condemn the engine.

Inspecting for Fluid Leaks

Fluid leaks, especially engine oil, are often difficult to locate because the leaking fluid has spread over a large area before the problem is detected. Therefore, it is often advantageous to steam clean or pressure wash the engine before you try to isolate the source of a leak.

Coolant Leaks

The quickest way to find an external coolant leak is by pressure testing the cooling system. Perform the test on a cold engine using a hand pump with a pressure gauge as follows:

1. Remove the pressure cap and attach the radiator pressure tester to the filler neck
2. Pump the tester until the gauge reading matches the specified system pressure, figure 1-3
3. Observe the gauge; the reading should remain steady
4. If the gauge shows a pressure loss, pump the tester to maintain pressure and check for leaks. External leaks should be obvious as pressure forces the coolant out
5. If there is no sign of leakage, there may be an internal leak and additional testing is required

Your next step is to pressure test the radiator pressure cap by using the system pressure tester and an adapter, figure 1-4. Proceed as follows:

1. Attach the cap to one end of the adapter, then connect the opposite end to the tester
2. Pump the tester until the gauge reading matches the pressure rating of the cap
3. Observe the gauge; it should hold steady within 1 or 2 pounds per square inch (psi) of the rating for at least 10 seconds, then gradually decrease. If the gauge reading drops too fast or too far, the cap is bad; replace it
4. If the reading does not drop at all, continue applying pressure until the cap vents. The cap should vent when pressure exceeds the rating of the cap by 1 to 3 pounds

Internal coolant leaks, generally the result of head gasket failure or casting cracks, are more difficult to detect. To check for leakage into the crankcase, remove the dipstick. If the oil on the dipstick looks milky or thickened, it may be contaminated by coolant.

There are several methods to check for coolant in the combustion chambers. Remove the radiator cap, start the engine, and bring it to operating temperature. A major leak will reveal itself by creating bubbles in the coolant. These bubbles rise to the surface and are visible at the filler neck. Small leaks can be detected using a chemical test kit or an exhaust gas analyzer. With chemical testing, vapors that collect above the coolant in the radiator are passed through a test fluid. The fluid is sensitive to exhaust gases and will change color if there are exhaust gases present in the radiator.

To use an exhaust gas analyzer, hold the wand over the filler neck. Never allow coolant to be drawn into the machine. Any exhaust gases in the system will register on the meters.

Insight

A spark plug or two adjacent cylinder plugs could be clean, indicating coolant leaking into the combustion chambers because of a blown head gasket.

Fuel Leaks

Fuel leaks are generally easy to locate simply because the system is under pressure whenever the engine is running. In addition, fuel injection systems continue to hold pressure after the engine is shut down.

Visually inspect the system. Check all fuel lines or the fuel rail and fuel injectors for signs of gasoline leaks. Also, check pump and fuel tank fittings.

Oil Leaks

If an oil leak is severe, the source is usually obvious. Severe oil leaks generally are under pressure and come from the following locations:

- Oil sending unit
- Oil filter and gasket
- Camshaft and plug
- Crankshaft seals
- External oil lines

Engine oil leaks that are not under pressure are more difficult to trace. The oil pan, timing cover, and valve cover gaskets are prime suspects. Check for signs of seepage along the sealing flanges. Leaks may be caused by normal wear or overtightening, but they can also be caused by too much pressure in the crankcase forcing oil past seals and gaskets. For this reason, thoroughly check the PCV system for proper operation.

Oil leaks that are difficult to find can be pinpointed by dye testing. A fluorescent dye is added to the oil and allowed to circulate in a running engine. After running, inspect the engine using a black light. The treated oil will glow brightly when exposed to the black light.

Excessive Oil Consumption

All engines burn oil during normal operation, but how much oil consumption is too much? This is always a judgment call. In general, if the engine consumes more than about 1 quart of oil every 500 miles, it needs attention. At that level, the oil burning in the combustion chamber forms significant deposits on the intake valve, piston crown, cylinder head, and spark plug.

If an engine burns oil, the spark plugs will have whitish-gray ash deposits on the electrodes. If the engine is burning a lot of oil, the plugs will be covered in liquid oil when you remove them. Oil normally enters the combustion chamber by either seeping past worn piston rings or by running down loose valve guides. An engine pulling oil through the valve guides will often have deposits built up on the intake port side of the spark plug only. Oil passing the piston rings will generally be spread more evenly on the end of the plug.

ENGINE TESTING

Specific internal mechanical problems on a running engine can be located by performing several basic tests. The tests that you will perform on a running engine include:

- Manifold vacuum
- Cylinder power balance
- Cylinder compression
- Cylinder leakage

Manifold Vacuum Tests

As a piston moves downward in the cylinder, it draws air with it to create a pressure drop in the intake manifold. A vacuum gauge connected to the intake manifold is used to measure the difference between **atmospheric pressure** and **manifold pressure**. Vacuum gauges are usually calibrated in inches of mercury (in-Hg). Vacuum gauge readings can pinpoint:

- Intake manifold gasket and vacuum line leaks
- Valve and valve guide problems
- Retarded ignition and valve timing
- Exhaust system restrictions
- Poor combustion chamber sealing

All vacuum readings decrease with increases in elevation, figure 1-5. Manufacturers provide specifications for testing at sea level, and it is up to you to correct these specifications for the altitude at which you are testing. As a rule of thumb, subtract 1 inch for every 1000 feet above sea level.

Normal engine vacuum at idle is 15 and 21 in-Hg, figure 1-6. Vacuum decreases as the throttle opens. At steady part-throttle cruising, engine vacuum should run between 10 and 15 in-Hg. During full throttle acceleration, manifold vacuum will drop to near zero.

Vacuum tests measure intake manifold vacuum, so the gauge must be connected downstream of the throttle plates.

ALTITUDE	INCHES OF VACUUM
Sea level to 1000 ft.	18 to 22
1000 ft. to 2000 ft.	17 to 21
2000 ft. to 3000 ft.	16 to 20
3000 ft. to 4000 ft.	15 to 19
4000 ft. to 5000 ft.	14 to 18
5000 ft. to 6000 ft.	13 to 17

Fig. 1-5. Vacuum gauge readings are corrected for altitude.

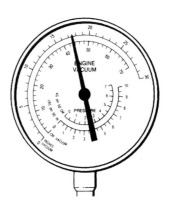

Fig. 1-6. Engine in good condition. Needle steady.

A1

Atmospheric Pressure: Weight of air at sea level, about 14.7 pounds per square inch (101 kPa), decreasing at higher altitudes.
Manifold Pressure: Vacuum, or low air pressure, in the intake manifold of a running engine, caused by the descending pistons creating empty space in the cylinders faster than the entering air can fill it.

Look for a port on the intake manifold to make the gauge connection, or tap into a vacuum line and install a tee-fitting. Avoid tapping into the canister or exhaust gas recirculation valve lines. These usually carry vacuum signals which are lower than manifold vacuum. Also, avoid lines that contain a vacuum control valve or restrictor.

Interpreting Test Results

Most tests are conducted with the engine idling. Interpret manifold vacuum gauge readings as follows:

- A steady reading 3 to 9 inches below normal indicates internal leakage around the piston rings, late ignition timing, or intake manifold leakage, figure 1-7

- A reading with the gauge needle fluctuating 3 to 9 inches below normal indicates a vacuum leak in the intake system, figure 1-8
- A leaking head gasket will cause the needle to vibrate as it floats through a range from slightly below to slightly above normal, figure 1-9
- An **oscillating** needle 1 or 2 inches below normal could indicate an incorrect fuel mixture, figure 1-10
- A rapidly vibrating needle at idle that steadies as engine speed increases indicates worn valve guides, figure 1-11
- If the needle regularly drops 1 to 2 inches from the normal reading, one of the engine valves is burned or not seating properly, figure 1-12

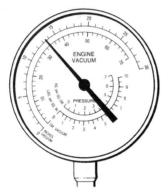

Fig. 1-7. Internal leakage or late timing. Needle steady, low reading.

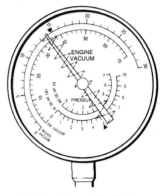

Fig. 1-10. Incorrect fuel mixture. Oscillating needle, low reading.

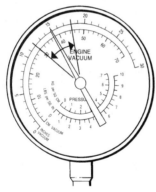

Fig. 1-8. Vacuum leak in the intake system. Needle fluctuating, low reading.

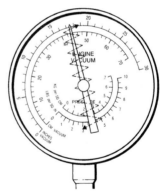

Fig. 1-11. Worn valve guides. Vibrating needle at idle, steadies at speed.

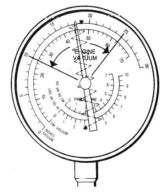

Fig. 1-9. Leaking head gasket. Vibrating needle floating low to high.

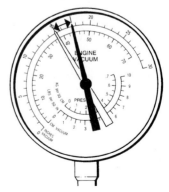

Fig. 1-12. Burned valve or valve not seating. Needle drops regularly below normal.

Oscillating: A swinging, steady, up-and-down or back-and-forth motion.

- An irregular drop of 1 or 2 inches from a normal reading indicates sticking valves, figure 1-13
- Weak valve springs will produce a normal reading at idle, but the needle will fluctuate rapidly between 12 and 24 inches as engine speed increases, figure 1-14
- A steady reading that drops 2 to 3 inches when the engine is brought off idle indicates retarded ignition timing, figure 1-15
- A steady reading that rises 2 to 3 inches when the engine is brought off idle indicates too much ignition timing advance, figure 1-16
- A needle that drops to near zero at high rpm, then rises slightly to stabilize at a reading below that of a normal idle indicates an exhaust restriction, figure 1-17

Cylinder Power Balance Test

The cylinder power balance test informs you whether an individual cylinder, or a group of cylinders, is not producing its share of power. During the test, you short out the suspected spark plug, or plugs, so that there are no power strokes from the cylinder being tested. You measure results in terms of engine rpm drop, manifold vacuum drop, or a combination of these two factors. Most engine analyzers have the capability of performing a power balance test.

Perform a cylinder power balance test as follows:

1. Check the service manual of the vehicle being tested for any specific requirements
2. Connect the engine analyzer
3. If the engine has an EGR system, disconnect and plug the EGR valve vacuum line
4. If the engine has electronic controls, the test should be performed while in **open-loop** operation

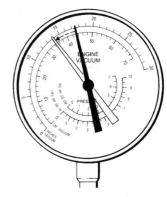

Fig. 1-15. Retarded ignition timing. Needle drops when brought off idle.

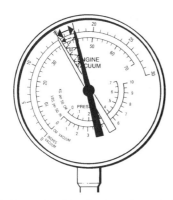

Fig. 1-13. Sticking valve. Needle drops irregularly below normal.

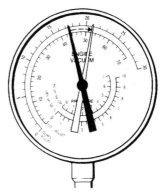

Fig. 1-16. Advanced ignition timing. Needle rises when brought off idle.

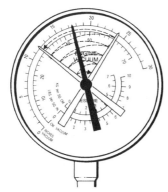

Fig. 1-14. Weak valve springs. Needle fluctuates when brought off idle.

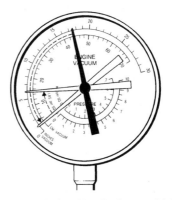

Fig. 1-17. Exhaust restriction. Needle drops at high rpm, then rises slightly.

A1

Open-loop: An operational mode in which the engine management computer adjusts the system to function according to predetermined instructions and does not respond to feedback signals from system input sensors.

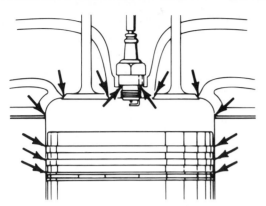

Fig. 1-18. A compression test checks how well a cylinder is sealed.

5. Start and run the engine to bring it up to normal operating temperature
6. Hold engine speed at a fast idle, about 1,000 to 1,500 rpm, or at another test speed as specified
7. Press the button to kill one cylinder. Note and record the engine rpm drop and manifold vacuum drop. Release the button
8. Repeat the test for each cylinder

Insight
In today's fuel injection systems, a power balance test should be performed by incapacitating the fuel injector(s) so the catalytic converter is not damaged.

Interpreting Test Results
Compare test results for all cylinders. If the changes in engine rpm and manifold vacuum are about the same for each cylinder, the engine is in good mechanical condition. If the changes for one or more cylinders exceed 10 percent, the engine has a problem. The fault may be mechanical, or it may be in the ignition or fuel systems.

Cylinder Compression Test
A compression test reveals how well each cylinder is sealed by the piston rings, valves, cylinder head gasket, and spark plug, figure 1-18. **Compression pressure** is measured in pounds per square inch (psi) or kilopascal (kPa) using a compression gauge. The gauge measures the amount of air pressure that a cylinder is capable of producing. Vehicle manufacturers provide compression specifications for their engines in the service manual. Specifications are usually stated in one of two ways. Some require the lowest-reading cylinder to be within a certain percentage of the highest cylinder. Others are a minimum value, with an allowable variation between the cylinders.

Performing a Compression Test
For optimum results, the engine should be at normal operating temperature during testing. Remove all spark plugs before testing and block the linkage to hold the throttle in wide-open

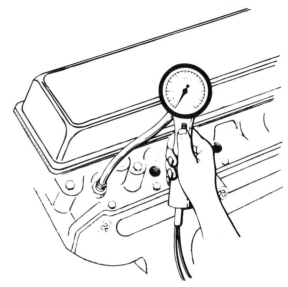

Fig. 1-19. Connect the compression gauge to the No. 1 cylinder spark plug hole.

position. Make sure the battery is fully charged. Check compression as follows:

1. Connect the compression gauge to the No. 1 cylinder spark plug hole, figure 1-19
2. Crank the engine for four complete compression strokes on the cylinder being tested. Watch the gauge and record readings for the first and fourth strokes
3. Disconnect the gauge and check compression for all other cylinders

Insight
Caution! Removing spark plugs from an engine with warm aluminum cylinder heads could damage the threads.

Interpreting Test Results
Compare the reading for each cylinder with those specified by the manufacturer. Interpret as follows:

• Compression is normal when the gauge shows a steady rise to the specified value with each compression stroke
• If the compression is low on the first stroke and builds up with each stroke, but not to specifications, the piston rings are probably worn
• A low compression reading on the first stroke that builds up only slightly on the following strokes indicates sticking or burned valves
• Two adjacent cylinders with equally low compression readings indicate head gasket leakage between the two cylinders
• A higher than normal reading usually means excessive carbon deposits in the combustion chamber

When compression is low, a wet test can be performed to isolate valve and piston ring problems. Squirt about 1 tablespoon of engine oil through the spark plug opening of each low-reading cylinder and retest compression. The oil acts as a temporary seal

---

Compression Pressure: The total amount of air pressure developed by a piston moving to TDC with both valves closed.

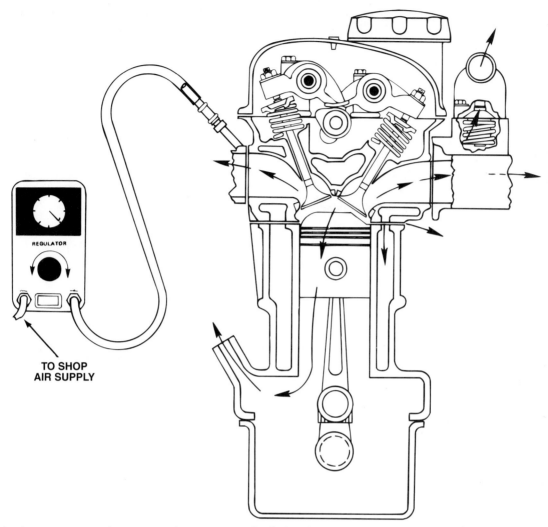

**TO SHOP
AIR SUPPLY**

Fig. 1-20. Leakage testers use air pressure to locate compression leaks.

between the cylinder wall and the rings but has no effect on leaking valves or a blown head gasket. If compression increases on the wet retest, the piston rings or cylinder walls are worn. If compression does not increase on a wet test, the low compression is the result of a valve or head gasket problem.

Cylinder Leakage Test

A cylinder leakage tester, or leak-down tester, gives even more detailed results than a compression test. A leakage test can reveal:

- The exact location of a compression leak
- How serious the leak is in terms of a percentage of total cylinder compression

Leakage testers force air into the combustion chamber through the spark plug hole. A gauge installed in the air line indicates how much pressure leaks out of the combustion chamber, figure 1-20. The gauge scale is marked from 0 to 100 percent. Cylinder leakage testers differ slightly by equipment manufacturer; you must calibrate the gauge before each test and follow the procedures for the particular unit being used.

Performing a Cylinder Leakage Test

The following is a general procedure that will work for most equipment:

1. Start and run the engine to bring it up to normal operating temperature, then shut the engine off
2. Remove all spark plugs, disable the ignition, block the throttle in a wide open position, disconnect the PCV hose from the crankcase, and remove the cooling system pressure cap
3. Calibrate the tester according to instructions provided by the manufacturer
4. Rotate the crankshaft by hand until the cylinder to be tested is at top dead center (TDC) on the compression stroke; both valves must be closed
5. Install the tester adapter in the spark plug hole, then connect the tester to the adapter
6. Connect the air hose to the tester and pressurize the cylinder
7. Note the percentage of air leakage on the gauge

Insight

Caution! Removing spark plugs from an engine with warm aluminum cylinder heads could damage the threads.

Use the following table to interpret cylinder leakage tester gauge readings:

Leakage %	Condition
0-10%	Good
10-20%	Fair
20-30%	Poor
30-100%	Dead!

Interpreting Test Results

If the cylinder has more than 20 percent leakage, pinpoint the cause of the leaks as follows:

- Listen for air escaping through the air intake; this indicates a leaking intake valve

- Listen for air escaping through the exhaust pipe; this indicates a leaking exhaust valve
- Listen for air escaping through the crankcase and PCV system; this indicates worn or damaged piston rings, worn cylinder walls, or a worn or cracked piston
- Watch for air bubbles in the coolant; this indicates a leaking head gasket or a crack in the engine block or cylinder head casting
- If two adjacent cylinders have high leakage readings, the head gasket is leaking between them, or the head or block is cracked

CHAPTER QUESTIONS

1. After receiving a repair order:
   Technician A says to begin diagnostic
   testing. Technician B says to verify the
   driver's complaint. Who is right?
   a. A only
   b. B only
   c. Both A and B
   d. Neither A nor B

2. The technician is completing a
   cranking vacuum test. Good cranking
   vacuum test readings will normally be:
   a. 1 to 3 inches Hg
   b. 5 to 15 inches Hg
   c. 17 to 22 inches of Hg
   d. 29 to 31 inches of Hg

3. Technician A uses fluorescent dye to
   locate oil leaks. Technician B uses
   fluorescent dye to locate coolant leaks.
   Which technician uses the dye
   correctly?
   a. A only
   b. B only
   c. Both A and B
   d. Neither A nor B

4. While using a pressure tester on the
   cooling system: Technician A says to
   apply 30 psi of pressure to the radiator
   cap. Technician B says if the gauge
   reading drops check the system for
   the leak. Who is right?
   a. A only
   b. B only
   c. Both A and B
   d. Neither A nor B

5. An engine produces a sharp clattering
   knocking sound, but grounding a
   spark plug lead quiets the noise down.
   The most likely cause would be:
   a. Worn main bearings
   b. A loose wrist pin
   c. A worn connecting rod bearing
   d. A broken valve spring

6. In a cylinder compression test, if the
   compression is low on the first stroke
   and increases on following strokes but
   never reaches specifications, it
   probably means:
   a. Cylinder compression is okay
   b. Rings may be worn or valves may
      be sticking
   c. Head gasket may be leaking
   d. Excessive carbon build-up

7. The engine exhaust gives off white
   smoke. Technician A says the
   head gasket could be the cause.
   Technician B says after the repair
   the oxygen sensor must be replaced.
   Who is right?
   a. A only
   b. B only
   c. Both A and B
   d. Neither A nor B

8. Black smoke could be caused by:
   a. Leaky fuel injector
   b. Worn exhaust valve guide
   c. Head gasket leak
   d. Fuel rail leak

9. A cylinder compression test will detect
   all of the following problems
   EXCEPT:
   a. Valve not seating
   b. Worn valve guide
   c. Broken piston rings
   d. Leaking head gasket

10. High compression readings, good
    cylinder leakage test results, and good
    power balance can be the result of:
    a. Incorrect valve timing
    b. Exhaust restriction
    c. Carbon deposits on the pistons
    d. Leaking valve guide seals

A1

CHAPTER TWO

CYLINDER HEAD AND VALVE TRAIN DIAGNOSIS AND REPAIR

CHAPTER OBJECTIVES

- The technician will complete the ASE task list on Cylinder Heads and Valve Train Diagnosis and Repair
- The technician will be able to answer 15 questions dealing with the Cylinder Head and Valve Train sections of the A1 ASE test.

This chapter covers inspection, measurement, and repair of the cylinder head and the **valve train**.

CYLINDER HEAD GASKET REPLACEMENT

When cylinder head gasket leakage is indicated, keep in mind that head gasket failure is generally the result of another problem. Check the cylinder head and the block for warpage, cracking, and other conditions that may have led to gasket failure.

Cylinder Head Removal

The engine must be cold to remove the cylinder head. Loosening head bolts on a warm engine can warp the head casting. The following cylinder head removal guidelines apply to most engines:

- Always disconnect the battery to avoid accidental shorting
- For overhead camshaft (OHC) engines, the timing chain or belt must be removed from the camshaft. Secure the tensioner to prevent it from overextending.
- Air-conditioning compressors and power steering pumps can generally be unbolted from their brackets and moved aside without disconnecting lines and hoses
- Relieve residual pressure before disconnecting fuel lines and plug the lines to prevent contamination
- For overhead valve (OHV) engines, leave the rocker arms attached. Loosen them just far enough to free the pushrods. Be sure to keep pushrods in order.
- Break the cylinder head bolts loose in the reverse order of the tightening sequence. Loosen all the bolts, then remove them.
- If the head will not lift off the engine block, use a pry bar inserted into one of the ports. Do not pry on machined surfaces.

Cleaning and Inspection

Head gasket surfaces must be clean, free of scratches or surface damage, and flat within specified limits. Check the head for leakage and surface warp.

Checking for Leakage

Before cleaning the sealing surface, inspect it for signs of combustion, coolant, and oil leakage.

- Combustion leaks are usually obvious because they burn away pieces of the gasket and leave a trail of carbon on the head and block surfaces
- Coolant chemically reacts when it comes in contact with combustion. Look for traces of coolant flow etched into the metal
- Oil leakage does not always leave a visible mark. Carefully inspect the gasket for signs of seepage and check the oil galleries for cracking and distortion

Cleaning Surfaces

Both sealing surfaces, cylinder head and block, must be clean before a new gasket is installed.

Use a gasket scraper to remove traces of the head gasket from cast-iron surfaces. If the gasket has left an impression etched into the metal, clean it off with a block of wood or a file wrapped with emery cloth. A scraper can easily gouge aluminum surfaces. When cleaning aluminum cylinder heads, use only the block and emery cloth. You can also clean an aluminum gasket surface with nylon-mesh pads that chuck into a drill motor. Exercise caution not to allow the pad to remove metal from the surface.

Checking for Warpage

To check a surface for flatness, place a straightedge across it, figure 2-1. Try to slip a feeler gauge under the straightedge to determine if the head is warped. Check the casting horizontally, vertically, and by opposing corners in an "X" pattern, figure 2-2. Warpage is equal to the largest feeler gauge that will slip under the straightedge without lifting it.

CYLINDER HEAD AND GASKET INSTALLATION

If the cylinder head is in sound condition, it is ready to be installed. If problems are found, recondition or replace the cylinder head.

Cleaning Threaded Holes and Bolts

Use a bench grinder with a wire wheel to clean head bolts. Thoroughly clean the threaded portion and the seating area on the underside of the bolt head.

Valve Train: The assembly of parts that transmits force from the cam lobe to the valve.

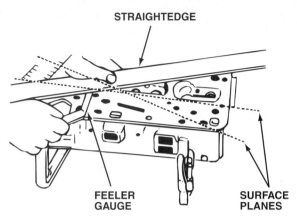

Fig. 2-1. Check surface flatness with a straightedge.

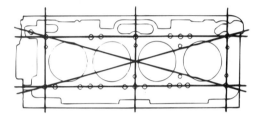

Fig. 2-2. Reposition the straightedge several times to get an accurate picture of surface condition.

Run a thread chaser or a bottoming tap down the threads of each bolt hole. Remove the tool and clear any residual debris out of the hole with a blast of compressed air.

Installing the Head Gasket

Many head gaskets are marked "Top" or "Front" to indicate which way they install. Make sure any directional markings are properly oriented.

Check fit the gasket. Be sure all locating dowels are in position. Then, fit the gasket over the dowels and onto the block. Head gaskets install without sealer unless otherwise specified by the engine manufacturer.

Installing the Cylinder Head

Slowly lower the cylinder head straight down onto the block to engage the dowels and lock it in place. Install the head bolts and run them in finger tight, then tighten incrementally and in sequence according to specified **torque**.

Torque-to-yield bolts, also known as stretch bolts, may be used to attach the cylinder head. Most torque-to-yield bolts are not reusable and must be replaced whenever they are removed. Torque-to-yield bolts generally have a reduced diameter shank, unusual head configuration, or other distinctive characteristics to make them recognizable, figure 2-3.

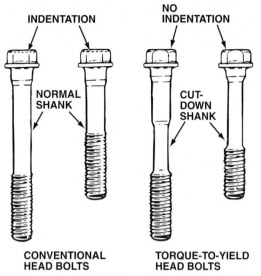

Fig. 2-3. Torque-to-yield bolts have distinguishing characteristics for easy identification.

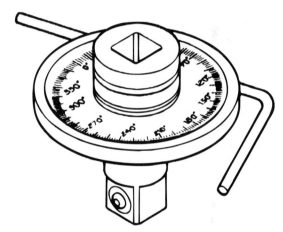

Fig. 2-4. A torque angle gauge gives accurate degree readings for final tightening.

Torque-to-yield bolts are brought to torque, then tightened additionally by a specific number of degrees. A torque angle gauge is used to measure degrees during final tightening, figure 2-4.

CYLINDER HEAD DISASSEMBLY, CLEANING, AND INSPECTION

Installed height is the distance from the spring seat, or cylinder head casting, to the bottom of the spring retainer, figure 2-5. Before removing the valves, measure the original valve spring **installed height**, so you can restore proper spring tension and correct rocker arm angle on reassembly.

Installed Height: The distance from the valve spring seat to the bottom of the spring retainer, also called assembled height.
Torque: A measurement of the twisting force required to rotate a fastener.
Torque-to-Yield: A method of tightening a fastener utilizing an initial torque plus an added rotation measured in degrees.

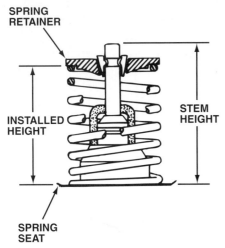

Fig. 2-5. Measure valve installed height before disassembling the cylinder head.

Removing Valves, Springs, and Keepers

An accumulation of varnish and sludge forms between the valve stem, keepers, and spring retainer as a normal result of engine operation. This causes the parts to stick together and can make them difficult to remove. Lightly tapping the top of the valve spring with a hammer will generally loosen the parts.

Use a valve spring compressor to depress the valve spring, then remove the keepers. A small magnet works well for lifting the keepers off of the valve stem. Once the keepers are removed, release the valve spring compressor and lift off the valve spring, retainer, and shims. Then, remove the valve and valve stem seal. Set the parts aside, but keep them in order for inspection and reassembly.

Cylinder Head Cleaning

Most cleaning methods require that all cover plates, sending units, core plugs, and other attachments be removed from the cylinder head. In addition, some or all of the manifold studs may have to come off if resurfacing is required. Strip the head to a bare casting to prepare for cleaning.

Cleaning Methods

Cylinder heads can be cleaned using a variety of methods. Common cleaning equipment includes:

- Hot tanks
- Spray booths
- Glass bead blaster
- Airless shot blaster
- Thermal ovens

After cleaning, some carbon will probably still cling to the cylinder head and back sides of the valves. Use a rotary wire brush that chucks into a drill motor to finish cleaning the ports and combustion chambers.

Scale deposits that build up in the coolant passages can be broken loose with a thin flexible scraper and cleaned out with a small wire brush. Flush the passages with solvent, then clear and dry with compressed air.

Run a rifle brush completely through the oil galleries to remove any built-up deposits and trapped debris.

Evaluating Head Condition

Once the cylinder head casting is clean, inspect it for warpage, casting cracks, and other signs of damage.

Checking for Warpage

The procedure for checking the head gasket surface was detailed previously. Recheck now that the head is clean. Surface warpage, if not too severe, can be corrected by machining. Flatness and finish can be restored either by **surface grinding** or by **milling**.

Warped aluminum heads can be straightened by heat treating. The head is bolted to a surface plate with shim stock strategically placed between the head and plate. The assembly is then heated and cooled in an oven to relieve tension in the casting.

The alignment of the camshaft-bearing journals should be checked on an overhead cam cylinder head. Lay a straight-edge across all of the camshaft-bearing journals. It should rest firmly in place and contact each of the journals. If not, use a feeler gauge to measure the warpage. Most heads will bow up in the center when they warp. Actual warpage will equal one half the thickness of the largest feeler gauge that will fit between the straightedge and bearing saddle.

Inspecting for Cracks

Several methods are available for locating casting cracks. These include:

- Magnetic particle inspection
- Pressure testing
- Dye penetrant testing

Magnetic Particle Inspection

Magnetic particle inspection can be used only on ferrous metals (cast iron), and will reveal cracks only on visible surfaces of the casting. There are two types of magnetic particle test medium; dry powder and fluorescent liquid. Both mediums are magnetic. However, the powder is visible to the naked eye, while the liquid must be viewed under a black light.

The particle inspection process works by magnetizing a section of the casting. The test medium is then applied to the magnetized area. Any crack on, or near, the surface will interrupt the magnetic field. This causes the test medium to accumulate along the crack, making it visible, figure 2-6.

Insight

For a crack to attract the test medium and become visible, it must cross the magnetic field. The test medium does not

---

Milling: The process of using a multiple-tooth cutting bit to remove metal from a workpiece.
Surface Grinding: The process of using a power-driven abrasive stone to remove metal from a casting to restore the surfaces.

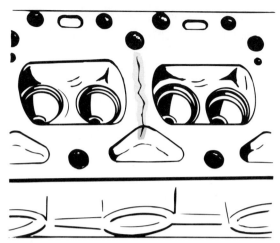

Fig. 2-6. Magnetic particles accumulate along a crack to make it more visible.

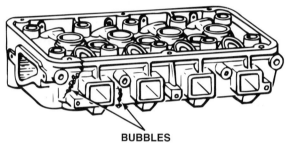

Fig. 2-7. Pressure testing will cause the soap solution to bubble when air escapes.

Fig. 2-8. Apply the dye penetrant and allow it to soak in.

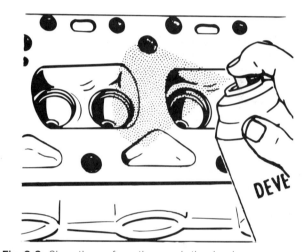

Fig. 2-9. Clean the surface, then apply the developer.

A1

accumulate along a crack that runs parallel to the magnetic field. To eliminate this possibility, rotate the magnet 90 degrees and repeat the test on the same area.

Pressure Testing

Pressure testing can be used for both ferrous (cast-iron) and non-ferrous metals (such as aluminum). The test is performed by sealing off all of the coolant passages, then charging the water jackets with compressed air. Cracks are revealed by escaping air. Two types of equipment are available

- Universal pressure testers
- Submersible pressure testers

Both methods will reveal surface and internal cracks that are not readily visible.

With a universal tester, the head is mounted to a bench, and adjustable pads are used to seal the passages. Compressed air is supplied through a coupling installed into one of the pads. A detergent solution is sprayed on the casting and any escaping air will cause the solution to bubble, figure 2-7.

Submersible testers require a variety of sealing plates to close off the coolant passages. An air hose is connected to one of the plates, and the head is lowered into a water tank. Cracks are revealed by a series of bubbles that rise to the surface of the water.

Dye Penetrant Testing

Dye penetrant testing is a chemical technique that will work for both ferrous and non-ferrous metals. This process reveals

cracks only on visible surfaces of the casting. Different manufacturers have somewhat different procedures. Most use a dye penetrant, a dye remover, and a developing agent. Follow these general steps:

1. Clean the surface to be checked with a non-residual solvent
2. Apply the dye penetrant to the surface and allow it to soak for several minutes, figure 2-8
3. Apply the remover and wipe the remover and the excess penetrant from the surface
4. Apply the developer and allow it to dry, figure 2-9

As the developer dries, it draws the dye penetrant out of the cracks and reacts with it to make it visible, figure 2-10.

VALVE SPRING INSPECTION

Visually inspect valve springs thoroughly. Look for nicks, pitting, corrosion, and cracks that might cause the spring to break while in service. Once the springs pass a visual inspection, check them for:

- Free height
- Squareness
- Tension

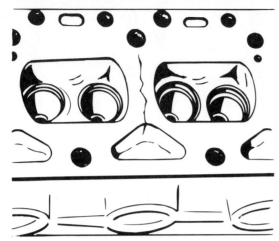

Fig. 2-10. As the developer dries, dye remaining in a crack becomes visible.

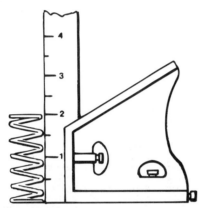

Fig. 2-11. Valve springs must be square and of equal height.

Free Height Comparison

Arrange the springs in a line and lay a straightedge across their tops. Look for variations in length. All of the springs should stand at approximately the same height. Replace any that are not within 1/16 inch of the others.

Checking for Squareness

To test for squareness, place a spring next to a square, then rotate the spring, figure 2-11. Squareness should not vary by more than 1/32 inch at any location along the circumference of the spring.

Testing Tension

Spring tension is measured with a special gauge, figure 2-12. Specifications are generally provided for the two extremes, open pressure and seat pressure, at which the spring operates. Open pressure indicates spring tension with the spring compressed and the valve fully open. Seat pressure indicates spring tension with the spring at its installed height and the valve resting on its seat.

To test a spring, place it on the table, pull the lever down to the specified height, and observe the indicator. If tension is not within 90 percent of specifications at each length, discard the spring and install a new one.

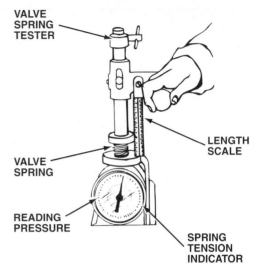

Fig. 2-12. Valve spring tension gauge.

VALVE SPRING KEEPERS AND RETAINERS

Check the fit of each keeper onto the valve stem. If a keeper does not fit securely to the valve or you notice any scoring, pitting, or other signs of wear, replace it. Visually inspect the lock grooves machined into the valve stem. The groove must be clean, smooth, and well defined. Replace the valve if any sign of deformation is present.

Inspect shims, retainers, seats, and any other parts for signs of wear. If valve rotators are used, be sure they allow free movement without binding.

VALVE STEM SEAL SERVICE

Valve stem seals are installed to minimize oil flow down the valve guide and into the combustion chamber. Seal failure will increase oil consumption and cause heavy deposits to form on the back side of the valve. Valve stem seals will be one of three designs:

- O-ring
- Umbrella
- Positive lock

Stem seals are routinely replaced when servicing the valves and can also be fitted without removing the cylinder head from the engine.

On-Vehicle Seal Replacement

Special tools are required to replace valve stem seals without removing the cylinder head. To replace the seal, the valve spring must be removed. In order to do this, the valve must be held firmly against its seat. This can be accomplished by charging the cylinder with compressed air while the intake and exhaust valves are closed.

To perform the operation, position the piston in the cylinder to be serviced at TDC on the firing stroke. Insert an air fitting into the spark plug hole and attach an air line to it. The air pressure will hold the valve against its seat, so that keepers and spring can be removed without the valve falling into the cylinder. The piston must be exactly at TDC or the air pressure will rotate the crankshaft.

Once the cylinder is pressurized, a special valve spring compressor is used to remove the valve spring. Remove and replace the seal. Then, reinstall the valve spring, retainer, and keepers.

On-Bench Seal Replacement

O-ring and umbrella seals fit snugly to the valve stem. To install, lubricate the seal and slide it over the valve stem. Umbrella seals are fitted before the valve spring is installed. O-ring seals are installed after the valve spring, while the spring is compressed.

Positive-lock seals seat on the outside diameter of the valve guide and must be installed before the valve is fitted. Use a seal installation tool to press the seal onto the valve guide, figure 2-13. Then, lubricate the valve stem, fit the valve into the guide, and carefully push it through the seal.

VALVE GUIDE INSPECTION AND SERVICE

Valve guides may be either the "**integral**" or "insert" type. Integral guides are machined directly into the cylinder head casting, while the insert guide is a separate piece that is press-fit into the head casting. Aluminum cylinder heads always have insert-type valve guides. Valve guides are wear items that demand attention whenever cylinder head repairs are performed.

Residual pockets of carbon or gum often remain in the guides after the cylinder head has been cleaned. Therefore, it is important to clean the guides before measuring them. Use brushes and scrapers designed specifically for valve guide cleaning.

Measuring Valve Guides

To evaluate valve guide condition, two measurements are required:

- Valve guide height
- Stem-to-guide clearance

Valve Guide Height

Valve guide height is the distance the guide protrudes from the valve spring side of the cylinder head. Valve guide height can be measured with a machinist's scale.

Stem-to-Guide Clearance

Valve guides wear to a bell-mouth shape at each end, figure 2-14. Measure the inside diameter at the top, bottom, and center of the guide to get an accurate picture of guide condition.

There must be a minimal amount of clearance between a valve guide and the valve stem, generally 0.001 to 0.002 inch. To determine this clearance, measure the inside diameter of the guide and the outside diameter of the valve stem. The difference

between these two readings is the clearance. Measure the guide inside the diameter using a:

- Valve guide dial bore gauge
- Small hole gauge and outside micrometer
- Dial indicator

The dial bore gauge will provide the most accurate results. A fixture is used to zero the gauge to the valve stem diameter. Insert the calibrated gauge into the valve guide and clearance will register on the dial face.

To use a small hole or split-ball gauge, insert the gauge into the valve guide, figure 2-15. Adjust the thumb screw so the fingers contact the guide, then lock the tool to hold the setting. Remove the tool and use an outside micrometer to measure across the gauge, figure 2-16. Subtract valve stem diameter from guide inside diameter to calculate clearance.

Using a dial indicator is the least accurate method of checking guide clearance. Place a new valve in the guide and attach a dial indicator to the cylinder head, so the indicator plunger touches the edge of the valve. Rock the valve to get a reading on the dial indicator. A new valve must be used to eliminate recording wear on the valve stem.

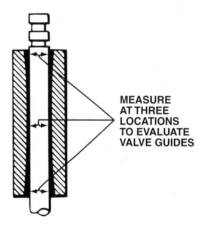

MEASURE AT THREE LOCATIONS TO EVALUATE VALVE GUIDES

Fig. 2-14. Valve guide wear is greatest at each end; take three measurements.

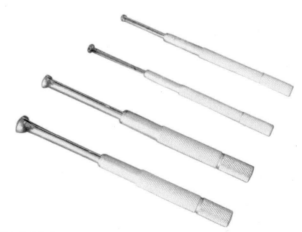

Fig. 2-15. Small-hole gauges are available in a number of sizes.

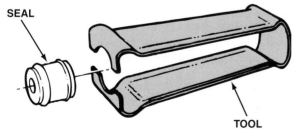

SEAL

TOOL

Fig. 2-13. Positive-lock valve seal installation tool.

Integral: A part that is formed into a casting.

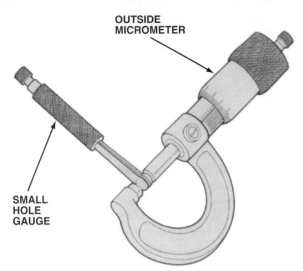

Fig. 2-16. Measure a valve guide with a small-hole gauge, then measure the gauge with an outside micrometer.

Integral Valve Guide Repair

Worn integral valve guides can be repaired with:

- Valves with oversized stems
- Knurling
- Thin-wall liners
- False guides
- Coil wire inserts

Oversized Valve Stems

Valves with oversized stems are of limited availability. To fit the valves, the inside diameter of the valve guide is bored to accept the larger diameter valve stem.

Knurling

Knurling is a repair that can be used only if the excess valve guide clearance is less than 0.005 inch. A special threaded arbor is fed through the guide to knurl it. The threads of the arbor push their way into the guide, forcing metal out into the bore to create a smaller inside diameter.

After knurling, a valve guide **reamer** is used to bring the guide to final size. Final size should provide one-half the minimum specified clearance. The small clearance is necessary to provide as much service life as possible.

Thin-Walling

Installing thin-wall liners is a method of restoring worn valve guides back to standard diameter. Most liners are made of bronze and have a wall diameter of about 0.010 inch. Thin-wall liners are used when guide wear is within 0.020 inch of specification.

The original valve guide bore is opened up with a piloting drill. The liner is pressed or driven into the bore, then the top is cut flush with the head using a special trimming tool. An **expander broach** is run through the insert to firmly seat it in the head. The inside of the insert is reamed to final size.

False Guides

Integral valve guides worn beyond 0.020 inch can be repaired by installing a "false guide." False guides resemble the guide inserts used with aluminum heads and can be made of either cast-iron or bronze.

When installing false guides, a special fixture is used to align the drill bit and retain the centerline of the original guide. The bore is drilled slightly smaller than the outside diameter of the new guide, then opened with a reamer to obtain an interference fit. The false guide is pressed, or driven into the head, and the inside diameter is reamed to size.

Coil Wire Inserts

Coil wire inserts resemble the helical inserts used to repair damaged threads. The installed insert has a spiralled internal finish. The spiral helps retain oil so valves can be fitted with about one-half the clearance required by solid wall guides. Installation procedures are similar to those used for thread repair.

Insert Valve Guide Replacement

All aluminum cylinder heads use valve guide inserts. These are serviceable items and should always be replaced whenever valve work is performed.

Valve guide inserts install with an interference fit, usually about 0.001 to 0.002 inch. Preheating the head makes removal and installation easier. Remove inserts using a valve guide driver. Measure the bore to determine the proper size for the new guide. Some standard replacement inserts are as much as 0.008 inch oversized and the bore may have to be opened up to accept them.

Install the new insert into the head using the guide driver. Measure the height of the installed guide. It must have the exact same amount of protrusion as the original. Ream the inside diameter to obtain the proper oil clearance.

VALVE INSPECTION AND SERVICE

Remove any carbon deposits from the valves by using a bench grinder with a soft-wire wheel. Perform a visual inspection to check for:

- Burning
- Guttering or channeling
- Necked valve stem
- Cracks
- Valve face wear
- Valve stem wear

Inspecting for Wear and Damage

Burning, guttering, and channeling are caused by excessive valve temperatures, figure 2-17. This condition is a result of pre-ignition, poor seating, deposit accumulation, or metal erosion.

Valves do not always burn through from overheating. Sometimes the heat-softened valve will deform as it is forced into its seat by the springs and combustion pressure. The head of the valve will pull down in the center to form a cup.

Expander Broach: A tool used to seat a bushing and form the outside diameter of the bushing to the irregular surface of the bore.
Reamer: A side cutting tool used to finish a drilled hole to an exact size.

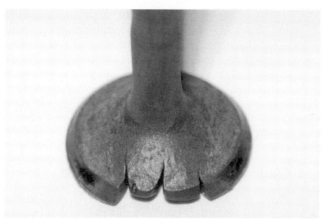

Fig. 2-17. Valve burning and guttering results from overheating.

Fig. 2-19. Uneven cooling causes hoop stressing, which can cause a valve to crack.

A1

Fig. 2-18. Necking refers to a narrow area on the valve stem caused by the stretching.

Necking occurs when the head of the valve pulls away from the valve stem, stretching the metal just above the head and causing it to thin, figure 2-18. Necking is caused by overheating or too much valve spring pressure.

Cracks often result from "hoop stressing," a common overheating failure. Valves exposed to temperatures higher than they are designed to withstand cool unevenly. The outer edge of the valve cools quickly and contracts around the hot center. This temperature differential can stress the valve to the breaking point, figure 2-19.

1. Look the valve face over for signs of wear. Normal operating conditions will wear an even groove around the middle of the valve face where it makes seat contact. Check for signs of hot spots, peening from debris, and recession caused by high seating forces
2. Check the valve stems for signs of galling, scoring, and binding. High seating forces and uneven seat pressure can

Fig. 2-20. Check for scoring or galling on the valve stem and for signs of stress at the tip end.

develop stress cracks in the stem just above the valve head, figure 2-20. Excessive valve lash and guide clearance, worn rocker arms, and weak springs can cause wear at the tip of the stem near the keeper seats. Check the valve tip for mushrooming and other deformities

3. Next, measure the valves to ensure they are in usable condition. Take three micrometer readings along the valve stem to check for wear and taper. Overall stem diameter must be within factory specifications. Taper should not exceed 0.001 inch. Check for bent stems using V-blocks and a dial indicator. Use a vernier caliper to verify **valve margin**. There must be at least ¹⁄₃₂ inch of margin after grinding the valve face

---

Valve Margin: The distance on a valve from the top of the machined face to the edge of the valve.

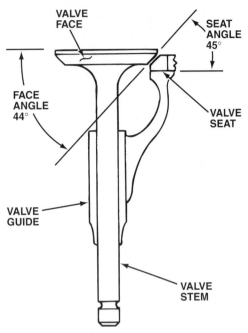

Fig. 2-21. An interference angle, different angles on the valve face and seat, improves valve seating on initial startup.

Grinding Valve Faces

The valve face is reconditioned using a valve grinding machine. Procedures will vary slightly between types of equipment. However, the basic operations are the same, regardless of the valve grinder being used.

Most valves are finished at a 45-degree angle, although some intake valve faces are ground to 30 degrees. Some manufacturers call for an **interference angle**, figure 2-21. This technique:

- Promotes positive seating on initial startup
- Improves valve sealing at high engine speeds and temperatures
- Helps to prevent carbon build-up

Although the interference angle can be machined into either the valve face or the seat, most machinists prefer to grind interference into the valve. A half degree of interference is generally sufficient, but common practice is to provide 1 degree of interference. For 1 degree of interference, the valve face is ground to 44 degrees and the seat to 45 degrees.

Keep these tips in mind when reconditioning valves:

- The chuck should grip the valve just above the wear area on the stem and as close as possible to the fillet to prevent wobble
- Keep the grinding stone well dressed to ensure a good finish, and occasionally rotate the diamond tip to equalize wear when dressing
- Switch on the spindle motor and visually check valve runout before taking a cut
- Allow a constant stream of coolant to flow over the valve while grinding

- Advance the stone feed wheel until the stone contacts the valve face, and begin stroking the valve across the stone immediately
- Never allow any part of the valve face to pass beyond either edge of the stone while you stroke it
- To get a clean, smooth, concentric face on the valve, advance the stone slowly. Never feed the stone in more than about 0.001 to 0.002 inch at a time. Wait for sparks to dissipate before advancing the stone further
- After grinding the valve, remeasure the margin and replace the valve if the margin is less than ½ inch

Once the face cleans up, back off the stone feed. Never back the valve away from the stone. Moving the valve off of the stone will distort the edge of the valve.

Grinding Valve Stems

Resurfacing, or **tipping,** the valve stem end provides a smooth, flat, square surface for the rocker arm or cam follower to contact. In addition, removing metal from the valve stem compensates for the valve sinking into the head as a result of valve and seat reconditioning.

With some valve grinders, the tip must be ground before the face to eliminate mushrooming and provide a true surface for the spindle chuck to grip. Tipping the valve to correct assembled height must be done after the valve seat has been reconditioned.

Usually, grinding 0.003 inch from the stem provides an adequate surface. To finish the valve, grind a 45-degree chamfer on the edge of the stem.

VALVE SEAT INSPECTION AND SERVICE

Valve seats can be either integral (cast into the head) or inserts (press-fit into the head); both types can be reconditioned and replaced.

Inspecting for Wear and Damage

Most integral valve seats are induction-hardened to provide longer service life. A drawback to induction-hardening is that it creates stress in the casting and makes the valve seats prone to cracking. Inspect valve seats for cracks, burned areas, recession, and other damage. Minor damage can be repaired by grinding or cutting new seating angles. A head with extensive seat damage can often be salvaged by boring out the old seat and installing an insert-type replacement seat.

Insert-type seats are inspected for cracks, burns, and other damage. Also, look for erosion on the cylinder head around the outside circumference of the seat. Check for looseness by gently prying up on the seat. If movement is detected, the seat must be replaced. Seats that are solidly mounted in the head can be reconditioned.

Restoring Valve Seats

Three different angles must be established to recondition a valve seat. Most automotive valves use a 45-degree seating angle,

---

Interference Angle: The difference between the angle at which the valve face is ground and the angle at which the valve seat is ground.
Tipping: Term for grinding the stem end of a valve to maintain correct stem height after grinding the valve face.

figure 2-22. The seat width and position is corrected by grinding 30-degree, figure 2-23, and 60-degree, figure 2-24, angles. For intake valve seats with a 30-degree face angle, use 15-degree and 45-degree correction angles to restore the seat.

All valve guide repairs must be performed before the seats are restored because the valve guide is used to center the pilot for seat reconditioning equipment. If the guide is not in good condition, the seat will not be concentric to the guide, and the valve will not seal.

Seat Grinding

The key to successful seat grinding is to select the proper stone and keep it well dressed to get a good surface finish. Stones are available in different harnesses for working different metals. Use a stone that is slightly larger in diameter than the seat but will not contact surrounding areas of the head.

To prepare for grinding, dress the stone, insert a pilot into the valve guide, and fit a lifting spring over the pilot. To grind a valve seat:

1. Grind the 45-degree angle to establish the seat. Work the stone into the seat with short, momentary contacts
2. Remove the pilot and install the valve to check the fit. The seat must contact the valve face evenly along the entire circumference of the port
3. Grind a 30-degree "**topping**" angle to lower the seat contact and position it on the valve face
4. Grind a 60-degree "**throating**" angle to narrow the seat and move it up the valve face
5. Recheck contact and position. If the contact patch is too wide, alternately top and throat until the desired width is achieved, figure 2-25
6. If topping and throating make the seat too narrow, correct by taking another light cut with the 45-degree stone

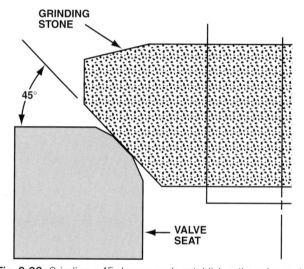

Fig. 2-22. Grinding a 45-degree angle establishes the valve seat.

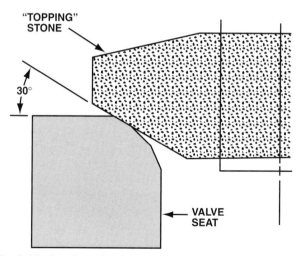

Fig. 2-23. Grinding a 30-degree angle removes metal from the top of the seat to lower and narrow the seat in the cylinder head.

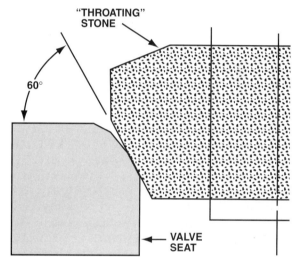

Fig. 2-24. Grinding a 60-degree angle removes metal from the bottom of the seat to raise and narrow the seat in the cylinder head.

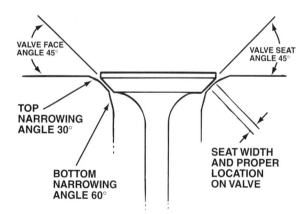

Fig. 2-25. Three-angle valve seat grinding positions the contact patch on the valve face for proper sealing.

A1

Throating: Term for raising a valve seat in the cylinder head and narrowing the valve-to-seat contact patch by grinding an angle 15 degrees greater than the seating angle.
Topping: Term for lowering a valve seat in the cylinder head and narrowing the valve-to-seat contact patch by grinding an angle 15 degrees smaller than the seating angle.

Seat Cutting

Seat cutting uses a carbide cutting bit, rather than a stone, to remove metal from the seat, figure 2-26. Cutting works well on bronze seat inserts that are difficult to grind and hard on stone life, soft seats that clog grinding stones to cause galling, and replacement seats that require excessive removal of metal. Another advantage of cutters is that they do not require dressing and always cut a true angle.

Most seat cutters form one angle at a time and operate similarly to seat grinders. Establish the seat, then correct the height and width by topping and throating. Single point cutting, a recent development, uses three blades on the same head to machine all three seat angles at once.

Replacing Valve Seats

Both integral and insert valve seats can be replaced if wear or damage is severe. For integral seats, a counterbore is cut into the old seat, then a new insert-type seat is press-fit into place. With insert seats, the old seat is removed and a new one is fitted.

When replacing integral seats with inserts, keep these points in mind:

- Bore a hole 0.005 to 0.008 inch smaller than the new seat insert to provide an interference fit
- Bore to the exact depth of the new insert so the seat will fit flush to the head. Double check the depth before installing the insert
- Chilling the seat in a refrigerator or freezer, or heating the cylinder head, will help overcome the interference and allow the seat to go in easier
- To ensure that the seat does not come out, stake it in place after it is installed in the head

There are several methods to remove original equipment insert seats. Some can be driven out with a long punch through the ports. Others can be lifted out with a pry bar. To remove difficult seats, weld a narrow bead around the inside of the seat. This will cause the seat to shrink and simplify its removal.

Valve-to-Seat Contact

Proper valve-to-seat contact is critical for efficient engine operation. The following checks are made during the machining process to ensure good contact: checking valve-to-seat contact and checking valve seat concentricity.

Checking Valve-to-Seat Contact

A common practice for checking seat contact is to apply a light coating of Prussian blue to the valve face. Install the valve stem in the valve guide. Hold the valve about an inch above the seat, then gently lower it until the valve face contacts the valve seat. Do not rotate the valve while it is on the seat. Remove the valve and examine the impression on the valve face.

The contact patch should be about $1/16$ to $3/32$ inch wide, with a minimum of $1/32$ inch overhang between the top of the seat and the edge of the valve face, figure 2-27. As a general rule, it is better to leave a wider seat on the exhaust valve because it runs hotter than the intake valve. Although a narrow seat provides better sealing, it also limits heat transfer.

Checking Valve Seat Concentricity

Special dial indicating fixtures are available for checking valve seat **concentricity**. The tool fits a pilot into the valve guide and the plunger rests on the valve seat. The indicator is zeroed, then slowly rotated around the seat. The dial will register runout. Ideal runout is within 0.001 inch, although up to 0.002 inch is generally acceptable. Correct high spots by grinding or cutting.

VALVE AND VALVE SPRING ASSEMBLY

It is important to give the cylinder head a final cleaning before the valves are installed. All traces of abrasive dust and metal chips from machining must be removed. Any core plugs that fit to the head are installed at this time. Then, final checks and adjustments can be made.

Measuring Valve Stem Height

To measure valve stem height, fit the valve and hold it tightly to its seat. Then, measure the distance from the tip of the stem to the spring seat, figure 2-28. Compare this measurement to the one taken before reconditioning.

If the valve stem is too high, it can be corrected by tipping the valve as described earlier in this chapter. When valve stem height is too low, correct it by grinding the valve seat.

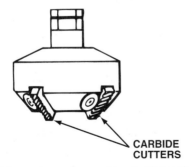

Fig. 2-26. Valve seats can be machined with special carbide cutting bits.

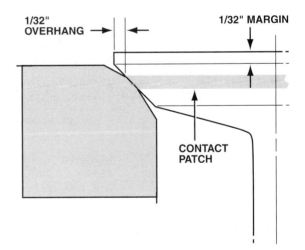

Fig. 2-27. A properly seated valve has an even seat contact patch with adequate overhang and margin.

Concentricity: Having the same center, such as two circles drawn around a common center point. A valve guide and valve seat must be concentric, or have centers at the same point.

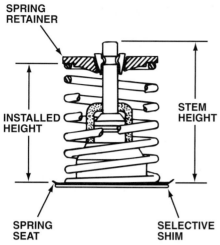

Fig. 2-28. Selective shims are used to correct valve installed height during assembly.

Measuring Valve Spring Assembled Height

Spring assembled height, or installed height, is the distance from the spring seat to the bottom of the spring retainer. With the valve in place, install the retainer and keepers, without the spring, and measure with a telescoping gauge or machinist's scale.

If the assembled height is too great, shims can be placed under the spring to reduce it. Correct insufficient assembled height by grinding either the valve seat or the valve face.

Shim Selection and Installation

Valve spring shims to correct installed height are available in three sizes:

- 0.015 inch
- 0.030 inch
- 0.060 inch

Shims that are serrated on one side install with the serration facing down, toward the cylinder head.

Assembling Valves to the Cylinder Head

Generously lubricate the valve stem and guide with engine oil. If positive-lock seals are used, they must be installed before the valves are fitted. Slip the valve into the guide and hold it against its seat. Install umbrella-type valve guide seals before fitting the spring. Slide the seal down over the valve stem until it contacts the guide. Fit the shims, springs, and retainer, then compress the spring. O-ring seals are installed with the valve spring compressed. Fit the keepers securely into the groove on the valve stem. Slowly release spring tension and remove the valve spring compressor.

Some engines use **variable-pitch springs**. These have coils wound closer together at one end of the spring than at the other end. The tightly coiled end of a variable-pitch spring always installs toward the cylinder head, figure 2-29.

PUSHROD AND ROCKER SERVICE

Pushrods, rocker arms, and related parts are all wear items that must be closely inspected whenever they are removed from the

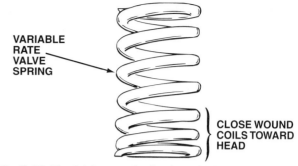

Fig. 2-29. The tightly wound coils of a variable-pitch valve spring install toward the cylinder head.

A1

engine. These items are non-serviceable items and are replaced rather than repaired.

Pushrod Service

Pushrods are cleaned, inspected for excessive wear, and checked for straightness. Wash pushrods with solvent and run a length of wire through the bore of hollow pushrods to dislodge any trapped debris.

Look over the ends of the pushrods. If you find nicks or grooves, a rough surface finish, any deformation, or signs of excessive wear, replace the part. Inspect the oil drill holes of hollow pushrods. If the oil hole is oval shaped, the pushrod is worn out and must be replaced. Look at the sides of the pushrod for signs of rubbing and scuffing and replace it if any metal has been rubbed away.

A quick and easy way to check the straightness of a pushrod is to roll it across a surface plate, thick piece of glass, or other perfectly smooth surface. Straight pushrods will roll smoothly across the surface, while bent rods will tend to hop as they roll. Pushrod runout can also be checked using a special fixture or a dial indicator and V-blocks. As a general rule, runout should be less than 0.003 inch.

Stud-Mounted Rocker Arm Assemblies

Wash the rocker arm parts in solvent and dry with compressed air to prepare them for inspection. Check rocker arms for wear on the valve stem contact area, the pushrod seat, and the pivot area. If valve stem wear is off-center or shows grooves, pits, scores, or other irregularities, replace the rocker arm. Look for a ridge built up around the circumference of the pushrod seat. Also, check for galling, pitting, scoring, or indications of the pushrod hammering against the rocker arm. Inspect the sides of the rocker around the stud opening for stress cracks and uneven wear.

Inspect the face of pivot balls and fulcrums for scoring, galling, or pitting. Some pivots and fulcrums are relieved to direct oil flow. Replace the part if wear is to the bottom of any relief machined into the contact surface.

Shaft-Mounted Rocker Arm Assemblies

The rocker shaft assembly on most engines can be unbolted and lifted off the engine as a unit, then disassembled on the bench. Always loosen and tighten the retaining bolts in small

---

Variable-pitch Spring: A spring that changes its rate of pressure increase as it is compressed. This is achieved by unequal spacing of the spring coils.

GALLED

NOT ROTATING

CHIPPED AND PITTED

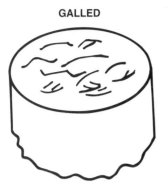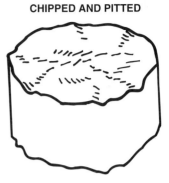

Fig. 2-30. Typical valve lifter wear patterns.

increments and in sequence. This will equalize valve spring pressure on the shaft to prevent bending the shaft.

Remove the cotter pin, roll pin, or any other fastener that holds the shaft assembly together. Then, slide the rocker arms, springs, spacers, and other parts off the shaft. Wash all components in solvent and lay them out in order on the work bench for inspection.

Inspect the shaft. The shaft surface should be smooth and free of any galling, scoring, or signs of excessive wear. Normal wear patterns will be greatest on the underside of the shaft, facing the cylinder head, due to spring pressure. Techniques previously detailed for inspecting stud-mounted rocker arms also apply to shaft-mounted arms. In addition, examine the shaft bore and replace the rocker if any deformation is found. Check for broken springs or any signs of bending, binding, or cracking. Spacers should spin freely on the shaft. Look for indications of binding, galling, or scoring on the internal bore and signs of undercutting on the end faces of the rockers.

VALVE LIFTER AND CAM FOLLOWER SERVICE

Valve lifters, also known as tappets or cam followers, are cylindrical parts that ride directly on the camshaft to open and close the valves. All engines use some type of lifter. Designs and service techniques will vary.

Overhead-Valve Engine Lifter Service

Virtually all modern OHV automotive engines are fitted with hydraulic lifters. The hydraulic lifter uses engine oil pressure to take up slack in the valve train, so the valves operate with zero lash.

The pushrods must be removed to access the lifters. Because of the varnish build-up at the lower end of lifter bodies, you may have to soak the bores with penetrating oil to get them out. Once free of varnish, the valve lifters can be lifted from their bores by hand or with a special tool. Keep valve lifters in order, so they can be reinstalled into the same bore.

Inspect valve lifters for wear on the base. If wear is normal, the lifter base will be worn from a slightly convex surface to a concave surface. However, the wear pattern should never extend all the way to the edge of the lifter face. Pitting on the surface indicates excessive wear. Varnish build-up may cause valve lifters to stop rotating in their bores. Figure 2-30 shows

typical wear patterns. The lifter base must have a slight crown. Check with a straightedge. If the straightedge lies flat, the lifter is worn out and must be replaced. Examine the sides of the lifter for signs of scoring and galling. Check the pushrod seat for indications of excessive wear and hammering.

Hydraulic lifters can be disassembled by removing the snap ring holding the pushrod seat, figure 2-31. Remove the internal parts, wash in clean solvent, and inspect for wear and damage. Internal lifter parts are not available individually, and you must replace the entire lifter if any damage is found.

Clean the valve lifter bores thoroughly to ensure free valve lifter rotation. In some engines, it is possible to use a brake cylinder hone to deglaze the bores.

Hydraulic valve lifters should be leak-down tested before installation. Test procedures are detailed later in this chapter.

Fill hydraulic lifters with oil and purge any trapped air before installation. This can be done without special tools by submerging the valve lifters in motor oil and depressing the plunger several times. When you install the valve lifters, oil the bores and check for free rotation. Lifters should slip in easily and rotate by hand.

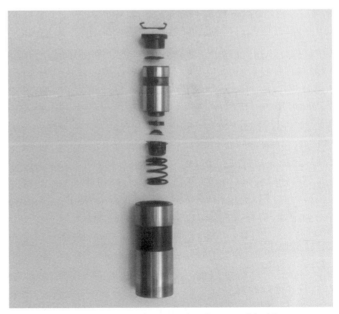

Fig. 2-31. Most hydraulic lifters can be disassembled for cleaning and inspection.

Overhead Cam Engine Lifter Service

Overhead cam engines use two basic cam follower designs: the bucket type that fits between the cam lobe and the valve stem, and the finger type that opens the valve through lever action, figure 2-32. Valve lash with either type may be mechanically or hydraulically adjusted.

Bucket-Type Lifter Removal and Inspection

The camshaft must be removed to access bucket lifters. With the camshaft out of the way, simply lift the buckets out. Keep them in order so they can be returned to the same location.

Inspect the lifters for signs of scoring and galling, and replace any defective units. Hydraulic bucket followers are not serviceable items. Defective units must be replaced. Store hydraulic buckets upside down in a container of clean engine oil to prevent hydraulic bleed-down.

Finger-Type Lifter Removal and Inspection

Finger-type cam followers are similar in design to the rocker arms of an OHV engine. Often, they can be removed with the camshaft installed by relieving spring pressure on the valve. The lifter for most finger followers is a remote pivot that fits a bore machined into the head casting, figure 2-33.

Service procedures for finger-type hydraulic lifters are similar to those previously detailed for OHV lifters. With most designs, they can be disassembled, cleaned, inspected, and leak-down tested.

Hydraulic Lifter Testing

New and used hydraulic lifters should be tested before installation. The best way to check lifters is with a leak-down test.

Leak-Down Testing

Leak-down testing checks the ability of a lifter to hold hydraulic pressure. A special tester is used, figure 2-34. The lifter is submerged in a test fluid, a weighted arm is placed on the pushrod seat, and the time it takes for the lifter to fully compress is recorded. Manufacturers provide leak-down rates for their lifters; normal leak-down time ranges from 20 to 90 seconds.

Kick-Back Testing

A kick-back test checks for internal binding. Hold the lifter upright and press down on the pushrod seat with your finger. Quickly release the lifter, and it should snap back into a fully extended position immediately.

VALVE LASH ADJUSTMENT

Typical valve lash clearance specifications range from 0.004 inch to 0.03 inch for solid lifter cams to a specified preload on

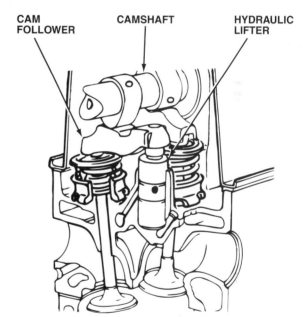

Fig. 2-33. Some OHC engines use finger followers that pivot on a remote hydraulic lifter.

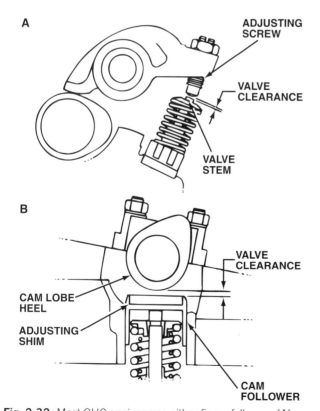

Fig. 2-32. Most OHC engines use either finger followers (A) or bucket followers (B).

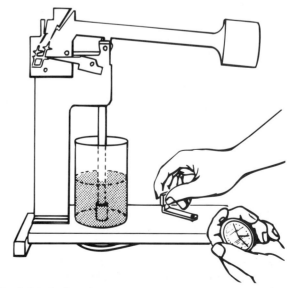

Fig. 2-34. Performing a leak-down test on a hydraulic lifter.

A1

hydraulic lifter designs. Exhaust valves generally run with slightly more clearance than the intake valves. There are three common valve adjustment mechanisms:

- An adjustment nut holding the rocker to the rocker stud
- An adjustment screw on the rocker arm
- Selectively sized adjustment shims

For more information on valve adjustment procedures, refer to the applicable service manual or book eight of this series.

CAMSHAFT DRIVE SERVICE

Both OHC and OHV engines drive the camshaft through a gear set, a chain and sprockets, or a belt and sprockets. The camshaft drive is accessible for repairs on the front of the engine. Gear-to-gear setups are primarily used to drive the camshaft in heavy-duty OHV engines. Timing chains are common in OHV engines and are also used on some OHC engines. Timing belts are found on many OHC engines.

Disassembly, Inspection, and Measurement

To access the timing cover, the belts, fan, radiator, water pump, alternator, air-conditioning compressor, crankshaft pulley, harmonic balancer, and other items that attach to the front of the engine may need to be removed. Gear and chain systems will have either a stamped steel or a cast aluminum timing cover. Timing belts often have a lightweight plastic cover.

Remove stamped steel covers by removing the bolts and then gently prying the cover away from the block. Cast aluminum covers often bolt to the front of the block and to the oil pan and cylinder head as well. Most of the oil pan bolts may need to be loosened to lower the pan and allow the timing cover to be removed. Belt covers usually unbolt and remove easily.

With the cover removed, rotate the crankshaft so that all of the timing marks are correctly aligned. The valve spring load on the camshaft must be removed to get accurate measurements. Remove the valve cover and loosen the rocker arms, or lash adjusters.

OHV Gear Drive Systems

Camshaft and crankshaft timing gears might be pressed onto their shafts and require a puller to remove, although most are a slip fit. Before removing the gears, check backlash, runout, and camshaft endplay.

Measuring Runout

To measure **runout**:

1. Set up and zero a dial indicator with the plunger resting on the face of the gear just inside the teeth, figure 2-35
2. While watching the dial indicator, rotate the crankshaft through one complete revolution. Turn the crankshaft by hand; motion should be smooth and slow
3. Note the maximum dial indicator readings, both positive and negative, while the gear is turning
4. Add the two maximum dial indicator readings together to determine total gear runout

Compare the runout to specifications for the engine being checked. Typical tolerance will be 0.004 to 0.005 inch for the camshaft gear and 0.003 to 0.005 inch for the crankshaft gear. If there is too much runout, check for debris caught between the gear and the shoulder of the shaft behind it. Excessive runout can also be caused by a bent gear or shaft.

Measuring Backlash

To measure **backlash**:

1. Attach a dial indicator to the engine so that its plunger tip is in line with the edge of the gear and resting on the edge of a gear tooth, figure 2-36

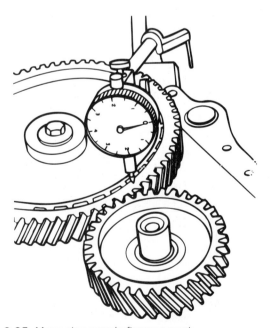

Fig. 2-35. Measuring camshaft gear runout.

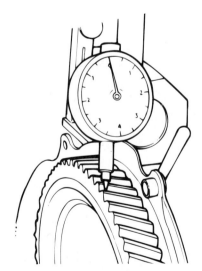

Fig. 2-36. Using a dial indicator to check timing gear backlash.

Backlash: Clearance between two gears, resulting in a lag between when one gear moves and when it engages the other.
Runout: Side-to-side deviation in the movement of a rotating assembly.

2. Take all the backlash out of the gear mesh by rotating the crankshaft slightly. Then, zero the dial indicator
3. Slowly rotate the crankshaft in the opposite direction just enough to take up all free play
4. Note and record total backlash as displayed on the dial indicator
5. Repeat this procedure on at least six gear teeth equally spaced around the camshaft gear

Average the results of the six readings to get an accurate picture of gear backlash. Compare the results to backlash specifications listed in the service manual. Typically, specifications will be between 0.002 and 0.006 inch. If there is too much backlash, replace the gears.

Backlash can also be measured using a feeler gauge. To use a feeler gauge, take the backlash out of the gear mesh and insert a feeler gauge between the gear teeth of the slack side. Backlash will be equivalent to the thickness of the largest feeler gauge blade that will fit between the gears. Be aware, feeler gauge readings will not be as accurate as those with a dial indicator.

Measuring Camshaft Endplay

To measure camshaft **endplay**:

1. Attach a dial indicator to the engine so its plunger is resting directly on the end of the fixing bolt, or on a machined surface near the center point of the gear, figure 2-37
2. Push the camshaft toward the rear of the engine to take up all the clearance, then zero the dial indicator
3. Insert two screwdrivers or pry bars under opposite sides of the gear. Gently pry out on the gear, then release tension on the screwdrivers
4. The reading on the dial indicator reflects total camshaft endplay

Compare findings to specifications from the manufacturer. Acceptable endplay is generally between 0.001 and 0.007 inch. If the endplay is outside limits, check the camshaft spacers or thrustplate for wear or damage.

OHV Chain Drive Systems

Before removing the timing chain and gears, check chain slack as follows:

1. Rotate the crankshaft counterclockwise just enough to take all slack out of the left side of the chain, without turning the camshaft
2. Mark a reference point on the block face in line with the midpoint of the tensioned side of the chain. Then, measure from the reference point to the chain, figure 2-38
3. Without turning the camshaft, rotate the crankshaft clockwise just enough to transfer the chain tension to the opposite side
4. Push the slack portion of the chain towards the reference point and measure the distance from the reference point to the chain, figure 2-39
5. Total chain deflection is the difference between the two measurements

Compare your measurement to the specifications provided in the service manual. As a general rule, chain slack should be less than ½ inch.

To remove the chain and gear assembly, remove the bolt holding the camshaft gear and gently tap the edge of the gear to loosen it. The crankshaft sprocket is sometimes pressed in and must be removed with a puller. Slip both gears and the chain off of the engine.

Arrange the new timing chain and sprockets so that the timing marks align, and then simultaneously slip the sprockets over the camshaft and crankshaft snouts. Install the retaining bolts and draw the camshaft sprocket onto the camshaft by gradually tightening to specified torque. Check the camshaft

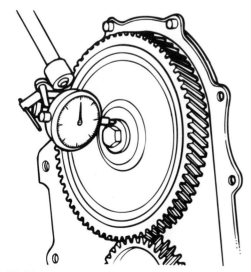

Fig. 2-37. Measuring camshaft endplay.

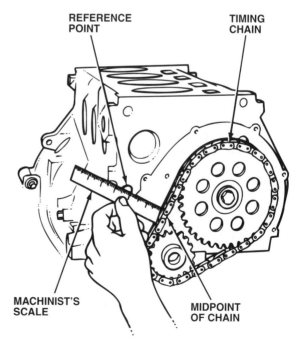

Fig. 2-38. Mark a reference point with all slack taken out of the chain.

Endplay: Movement along, or parallel to, the centerline of a shaft. Also called end thrust or axial play.

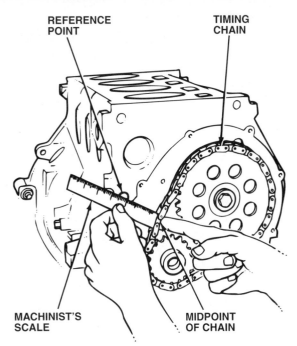

Fig. 2-39. Rotate to transfer slack to the opposite side, then measure chain deflection.

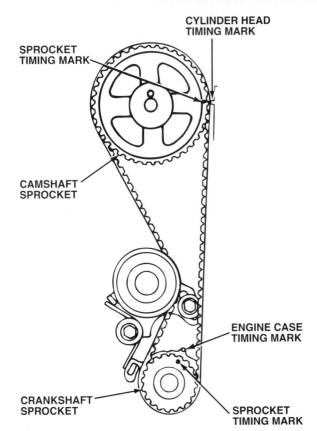

Fig. 2-40. Timing belt slack must be on the tensioner side when all of the timing marks are aligned.

endplay as previously described. Turn the crankshaft two complete revolutions in the normal direction of rotation, and check that the timing marks on both gears line up again.

OHC Chain Drive Systems

OHC engines require a specialized chain tensioning device to take up slack in the long chain run. Chain tensioners, whether mechanical or hydraulic, are wear items normally replaced along with the chain. In addition, an intermediate gear may be used to drive the distributor or fuel pump. Ensure that all timing marks, including those on the intermediate gear, are aligned properly.

OHC Belt Drive Systems

With the timing cover removed, slowly rotate the crankshaft with a wrench as you inspect the entire length of the belt. Watch for:

- Dirt, coolant, and oil-soaked areas
- Hardened or cracked outer surface
- Separating cloth and rubber layers
- Worn, cracked, or missing teeth
- Wear or cracks on the side or back of the belt

Also, inspect the crankshaft and camshaft sprockets, the tensioner, and any idler sprockets and pulleys for wear or damage.

To replace the belt, rotate the engine so all timing marks align. Loosen the tensioner and slip off the sprockets, figure 2-40. Check the tensioner assembly for wear and free movement. Slip the new belt over the notches in the crankshaft sprocket, then fit it onto the camshaft sprocket. Keep the drive side of the belt as tight as possible. Turn the crankshaft slightly in the normal direction of rotation to take up any slack, then adjust the tensioner. Slowly turn the engine two complete revolutions and check to ensure that all the timing marks line up.

Due to the many variations of OHC engine design, refer to the OEM procedures for checking camshaft endplay and gear/sprocket runout.

CAMSHAFT INSPECTION

The camshaft must be removed from the engine to check it for wear, damage, and straightness. When a new camshaft is installed, the lifters must also be replaced. Check camshaft:

- Surface finish and condition
- Straightness
- Journal diameter
- Lobe configuration and runout

Inspecting for Wear and Damage

Look for wear patterns on the camshaft lobes. A normal wear pattern is wide on the nose, narrow on the base, and will not extend to the edges of the lobe, figure 2-41. Pitting, scoring, or rounding of the camshaft lobes are immediate signs of extreme wear which will affect **valve duration** and lobe lift. Replace the camshaft if extreme wear is found.

Checking Camshaft Straightness

A dial indicator and a set of V-blocks are used to check camshaft straightness. Support the shaft in the V-blocks by the front and rear bearing journals. Position the dial indicator so its plunger rests on the center bearing journal, and zero the gauge. Watch the dial indicator as you slowly rotate the shaft through one

---

Valve Duration: The number of crankshaft degrees that a valve remains open.

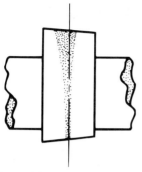

Fig. 2-41. Normal cam lobe wear creates a pattern that is wide on the nose and narrow on the heel.

complete revolution. The difference between the highest and the lowest dial indicator readings is the total camshaft runout. As a general rule, runout should be less than 0.002 inch.

Measuring the Camshaft

Both the bearing journal diameters and the lobe heights are measured to determine overall camshaft condition. All measurements can be taken with an outside micrometer.

Journal Diameter

Be aware that each camshaft bearing journal is a different diameter on an OHV engine. The smallest journal is at the rear of the engine, and the largest is at the front. This allows you to easily fit the shaft through the bearings when installing it into the engine block. On an OHC engine, the bearing journals are usually all the same size when the camshaft is held in place by bearing caps.

On any camshaft, journal diameter can be quickly and accurately measured with an outside micrometer. Measure each journal at least twice in different locations around the circumference. Also, measure at both ends of the journal to check for taper. Compare your findings to specifications to determine if the camshaft is within tolerance.

Base Circle

Measure across the cam lobe to determine the **base circle** diameter. Measure the base circle diameter on all of the lobes; readings should be identical. An outside micrometer can be used for most camshafts. However, the ramps on some high-performance cams begin below the base circle center line. These cannot be measured with a micrometer.

Cam Lobe Height

Cam lobe height is the distance from the heel to the nose of the lobe, figure 2-42. Use an outside micrometer to measure the height of all the cam lobes, and take readings in the center and at both edges of the lobe. Expect to see up to about 0.002 inch of taper across the nose of a cam lobe. This can be considered normal and is machined into the lobe to help rotate the lifter in its bore.

Calculating Camshaft Lift

Camshaft lift is the distance that the cam lobes raise the lifters. Calculate lift by subtracting the base circle diameter from the

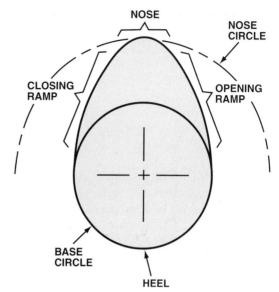

Fig. 2-42. Camshaft lobe nomenclature.

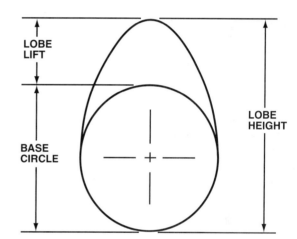

Fig. 2-43. Camshaft lobe lift is the lobe height minus the base circle diameter.

lobe height, figure 2-43. Lift can also be measured with a dial indicator. Install the dial indicator so that its plunger rests on the heel of a lobe. Zero the dial face, then rotate the shaft until the plunger is on the nose. The total dial indicator reading is equal to the cam lobe lift.

Base Circle Runout

Base circle runout, or concentricity, is measured with a dial indicator while the camshaft is supported in V-blocks. Position the dial indicator with the plunger resting on the heel of a cam lobe and zero the dial face. Slowly rotate the camshaft to the point where the gauge reading is lowest. Rotate the shaft in the opposite direction, so the plunger crosses the heel, to reach the lowest reading on the other side. The difference from side-to-side is the total base circle runout. Typically, the base circle runout should not exceed 0.001 inch.

Base Circle: An imaginary circle drawn on the profile of a cam lobe that intersects the very bottom of the lobe. It is the lowest point on the cam lobe in relation to the valve train.

CAMSHAFT BEARING AND BORE SERVICE

Inspect the camshaft bearings for signs of excessive wear and damage. Measure the inside diameter of the bearings with an inside micrometer or dial bore gauge. Measure camshaft bearing journals with an outside micrometer. Measure in several positions across the face to determine taper, and check at several points around the circumference to determine out-of-round. Determine the clearance by subtracting the journal diameter from the bearing inside diameter.

Removing and Installing Camshaft Bearings

The camshaft bearings on OHV engines are press fit to the engine block and must by removed using a special tool, figure 2-44.

Aluminum OHC cylinder heads often do not have bearings, as the camshaft rides directly on journals machined into the head. However, split-shell camshaft bearing inserts, similar to those used for crankshaft main and connecting rod bearings, are used on some OHC designs. Other OHC engines use one-piece bearings that are press-fit into the head. These must be removed and installed with a forcing screw-type puller similar to those for an OHV engine.

New camshaft bearings are installed in an OHV engine using the same tool used to remove the old ones. Bearings must be checked for location because it is common to find different bearing diameters down the length of the camshaft. Generally, large bearings are to the front and small bearings to the rear. Also, check the bearings for alignment so that the oil holes in the bearings will line up with the oil holes in the block. Install the bearings dry and fit them in order, working from the back of the engine toward the front.

CAMSHAFT INSTALLATION

Double-check the bearing oil hole alignment, then lubricate the bearings with engine oil. Coat the camshaft lobes with

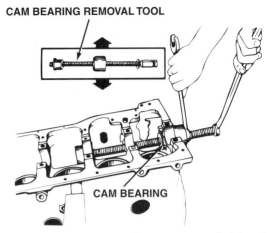

CAM BEARING REMOVAL TOOL

CAM BEARING

Fig. 2-44. Special tools are used to remove camshaft bearings.

special high-pressure camshaft lubricant before installing the camshaft.

Feed the camshaft slowly and carefully through the bearing bores. Avoid scraping the soft bearing faces with the cam lobes. Once installed, the camshaft should spin freely by hand. If binding occurs, remove the shaft and dress any burrs or high spots on the bearings with a bearing scraper. Install the camshaft thrust plate, if used. Also, install the core plug behind the rear cam bearing.

Checking Camshaft Timing

Check the camshaft endplay and install the camshaft drive gears, or sprockets and chain, as previously detailed. Remember, the position in which the camshaft drive is installed determines **valve timing**. This usually consists of aligning marks on the gears. Turn the engine two complete revolutions and check that the marks are once again in alignment. Lubricate the new chain, tensioner, and gears with engine oil before installing the timing cover.

Valve Timing: A method of coordinating camshaft rotation and crankshaft rotation, so that the valves open and close at the right times during each of the piston strokes.

CHAPTER QUESTIONS

1. Which of the following operations is **NOT** required when replacing a cylinder head gasket?
   a. Checking for warpage
   b. Checking for squareness
   c. Checking for leakage
   d. Cleaning the bolt holes

2. Cylinder head gasket failure may be due to all of the following **EXCEPT:**
   a. Coolant leaks
   b. Compression leaks
   c. Oil leaks
   d. Vacuum leaks

3. Which of the following should be checked before disassembling the cylinder head?
   a. Rocker arm alignment
   b. OHC cam bore alignment
   c. Valve spring installed height
   d. Surface warpage

4. Internal cracks on a cast-iron cylinder head can be located by which of the following methods?
   a. Magnetic particle testing
   b. Pressure testing
   c. Dye penetrant testing
   d. All of the above

5. Valve springs are bench tested for all of the following **EXCEPT:**
   a. Installed height
   b. Free height
   c. Tension pressure
   d. Squareness

6. When removing the cylinder head: Technician A says to loosen the head bolts in a reverse tightening sequence. Technician B says a torque-to-yield bolt should be reused. Who is right?
   a. A only
   b. B only
   c. Both A and B
   d. Neither A nor B

7. When getting ready to torque the head bolts: Technician A says to clean and oil them for proper torque. Technician B says to use a torque angle gauge instead of a torque wrench. Who is right?
   a. A only
   b. B only
   c. Both A and B
   d. Neither A nor B

8. When checking a valve spring for free height a straightedge is laid across the springs and the height should not vary more than:
   a. $\frac{1}{16}$"
   b. $\frac{3}{32}$"
   c. $\frac{1}{8}$"
   d. $\frac{5}{32}$"

9. After a valve job, the spring assembled height is too great. It can be corrected by:
   a. Grinding the seat
   b. Installing new springs
   c. Installing shims
   d. Tipping the valve

10. Valve margin must be at least:
    a. $\frac{1}{8}$ inch
    b. $\frac{1}{16}$ inch
    c. $\frac{1}{32}$ inch
    d. $\frac{1}{64}$ inch

11. Umbrella-type valve guide seals are installed:
    a. Before the valve
    b. Before the spring
    c. With the spring compressed
    d. On the guide

12. A concave face on the base of a hydraulic lifter is an indication of:
    a. Overheating
    b. Lack of rotation
    c. Lack of lubrication
    d. Normal wear

13. Which of the following items must be removed in order to remove hydraulic lifters from an OHV engine?
    a. The camshaft
    b. The rocker arm
    c. The pushrod
    d. The cylinder head

14. Excessive camshaft endplay can be caused by:
    a. Worn timing gears
    b. A worn thrust plate
    c. Debris behind the thrust plate
    d. Worn timing chain

15. Camshaft lift is the difference between:
    a. Base circle diameter and lobe height
    b. Journal diameter and lobe height
    c. Camshaft runout and base circle diameter
    d. Base circle runout and lobe height

A1

CHAPTER THREE

ENGINE BLOCK DIAGNOSIS AND REPAIR

CHAPTER OBJECTIVES

- The technician will complete the ASE task list engine block diagnosis and repair.
- The technician will be able to answer 10 questions dealing with the engine block diagnosis section of the A1 ASE test.

Most engine block repairs require that the engine be removed from the vehicle, although some repairs, such as replacing crankshaft seals, oil pans, and timing covers, can be performed with the engine in the chassis. This chapter covers only the engine block operations performed on the bench.

ENGINE BLOCK DISASSEMBLY

To make disassembly easier and prevent overlooking hidden fasteners, steam clean or pressure wash the engine before you begin tearing it down. Watch for clues as to what caused the engine to fail as you disassemble it. Look for:

- Damaged or worn-out parts
- Asymmetric wear patterns
- Non-stock components and internal marks
- Mistakes made during previous engine work

Remove all accessories, brackets, and mounts that bolt to the engine block. This includes the distributor, dipstick tube, and oil-sending unit. Remove the intake and exhaust manifolds, cylinder heads, and camshaft drive assembly as described in the previous chapter.

Remove the oil pan bolts and take the oil pan off; remove and discard the pan gasket. Remove the oil pickup, oil pump, and pump drive. Look the engine over to be sure nothing is left in place that can interfere with removing the internal parts.

Inspect all covers and the oil pan for distortion or damage to the sealing surface. Minor distortion at the bolt holes can be repaired by placing the area on a flat metal surface and lightly tapping with a ballpeen hammer to restore the surface. Badly damaged covers and oil pans should be discarded.

Marking Bearing Caps

Before the pistons and crankshaft can be removed, the bearing caps and connecting rods must be marked so they can be reassembled in proper order. Use an electric engraver to make the identification markings. Never use a punch, number stamp, scribe or file to mark the connecting rod caps. Many connecting rods today are manufactured using the **powdered metal** process and will be damaged if they are marked with any of these methods.

Main bearing caps are often numbered at the factory, but connecting rods and caps are not. Mark the connecting rods and caps of an inline engine so the marks all face the same side of the engine. Markings on a V-type engine should all face the outside of the block.

Cylinder Wall Ridge Removal

The next step is to remove the ridge at the top of each cylinder bore to allow the pistons to come out without damage. A **ridge reamer** is used to cut away the ridge, figure 3-1. Turn the

CYLINDER RIDGE REAMER

Fig. 3-1. Using a reamer to remove the cylinder ridge.

Powdered Metal: A forging procedure in which the steel alloy is placed into a mold as a powder and is heated in a forge to melt the contents.

Ridge Reamer: A hand-operated cutting tool used to remove the wear ridge at the top of a cylinder bore.

crankshaft to position the piston at bottom dead center (BDC), then fit the ridge reamer in the bore and adjust the blade to take a light cut. Turn the reamer with a wrench to remove the ridge. Lead the cutting blade with the wrench by a few degrees. This helps smooth the cut and prevents undercutting or gouging. Clean all metal chips out of the cylinder after reaming the ridge.

Removing Piston Assemblies

Remove the bearing cap retaining nuts and lift off the cap. Slip protective covers or a small length of hose over the exposed ends of the rod bolts to prevent damaging the crank journal. Place the end of a hammer handle on the bottom of the piston and push the piston out of the bore. Remove both halves of the bearing shell. Keep the bearings in order for later inspection. Loosely re-install the bearing cap onto the connecting rod.

Removing the Crankshaft

Remove the main bearing caps and lift the crankshaft free of the saddles. The flywheel may need to be removed first. However, on most engines, the flywheel can be removed with the crankshaft. Set the crankshaft aside. Always store crankshafts in an upright position to prevent bending. Remove the main bearing inserts, keeping them in order for inspection. Then, reinstall and tighten the bolts to specified torque.

ENGINE BLOCK INSPECTION

Examine the engine block casting for obvious indications of damage. Carefully check around **core plugs** for signs of leakage, then remove the plugs. Any caps or plugs installed at the ends of the oil galleries must also be removed. Check to make sure the block has been stripped down to a bare casting; then, clean it thoroughly, using one of the methods discussed in the previous chapter.

Water Passages and Oil Galleries

Once the block is clean and dry, run a rifle brush completely through the oil galleries to remove any residual sludge or trapped debris. After brushing, clear the passages with a blast of compressed air. Also, clean water jackets with a brush or scraper and compressed air to remove any scale or corrosion.

Inspect the Oil Filter

Remove the oil filter and drain the contents into a clean pan. Look for signs of contamination, such as metal filings, dirt, or coolant contamination. If in doubt, carefully cut the shell from the filter and inspect the **filter media** for additional contamination.

Insight
Do not confuse the filings from the saw cut as engine debris.

Crack Inspection

Carefully inspect the engine block for signs of damage. Check the block for casting cracks, using magnetic particle inspection or a dye penetrant test. Both methods were discussed in Chapter Two of this book. Note any stripped or pulled threads that need to be repaired before reassembly.

Deck Warpage and Surface Condition

Examine the surface for excessive scoring, corrosion, erosion, threads pulling up around bolt holes, cracks, dents, and scratches. Check for warpage, using a straightedge and feeler gauge. Surface grinding will usually repair deck surface irregularities.

A1

REPAIRING DAMAGED THREADS

Inspect all of the threaded holes in the block for damage. Threads that are in good shape get cleaned with a thread chaser or bottoming tap as previously discussed for cylinder heads. Damaged internal threads can be repaired by:

- Drilling and tapping to oversize
- Installing a **helical insert**
- Installing an insert bushing

Drilling and tapping to oversize can be used only in non-critical areas. A larger bolt installed in a critical area will not properly tighten to specified torque and can cause problems.

Helical inserts, better known by their trademark name Helicoil®, restore threaded holes to their original size. When correctly installed, a helical insert is often stronger than the original threads, especially in aluminum castings.

Insert bushings are tubular, case-hardened, solid-steel wall pieces that are threaded inside and outside. The inner thread of the insert is sized to fit the original fastener of the hole to be repaired. Several types are available. All require the hole to be drilled considerably larger than the original, then tapped to the external thread size of the insert. Fasteners with damaged external threads should always be replaced rather than repaired.

CYLINDER INSPECTION AND MEASUREMENT

Under normal conditions, a cylinder will develop two distinct wear patterns: taper and out-of-round. When the piston changes direction at the top of its stroke, combustion forces it into the cylinder wall. As a result, wear will be greatest near the top of the bore. This is known as taper, figure 3-2. Reciprocating motion causes the connecting rod to push the piston to the side, perpendicular to the rod, as it moves in the cylinder bore. This causes the cylinder to wear more on the sides than on the front and rear. Eventually, the cylinder bore wears to an oval shape, which is known as out-of-round.

Core Plug: A metal cup inserted into the engine block to seal holes left by manufacturing. Also called a freeze plug or expansion plug.
Filter Media: The paper material that actually filters the oil within the assembly.
Helical Insert: A precision-formed coil of wire used to repair damaged threads.

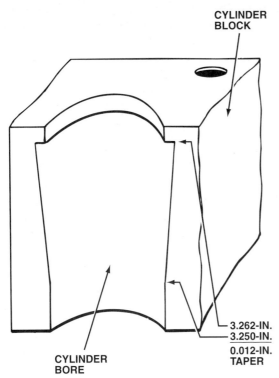

Fig. 3-2. Cylinder taper is the difference in diameter between the top and bottom of the bore.

Fig. 3-3. A telescoping gauge used with an outside micrometer can be used to measure cylinder diameters.

Begin your inspection by checking the cylinder bores for major damage, such as cracks, gouges, scoring, and broken cylinder walls. Next, measure the cylinder bore, using precision instruments to evaluate wear damage.

Measuring Cylinders

Cylinders are measured using a dial bore gauge, an inside micrometer, or a telescoping gauge and an outside micrometer. A dial bore gauge gives the most accurate readings. A telescoping gauge is the least accurate tool for measuring a cylinder bore, figure 3-3. Regardless of what type of tool you are using, several measurements are required to determine cylinder condition.

Checking for Overbore

The first check determines whether the cylinders were bored oversize during a previous rebuild. Measure bore diameter near the bottom of the cylinders below the ring travel area. Take readings perpendicular to, and parallel to, the crankshaft in a non-wear area.

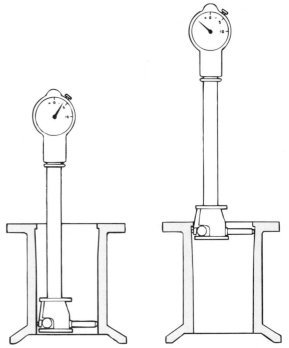

Fig. 3-4. Using a dial bore gauge to measure cylinder diameters and determine taper.

Measuring for Taper

Two measurements are taken to check for taper. Measure cylinder diameter near the top of the bore just below the ridge and at the bottom in the unworn portion of the cylinder, figure 3-4. Taper is equal to the difference between the two measurements. A realistic limit for cylinder wall taper on gasoline engines is about 0.005 inch. The limits for diesel engines are much lower, usually about 0.003 inch. To repair excessive taper requires boring to oversize or installing a sleeve in the cylinder.

Measuring for Out-of-round

Determining out-of-round also requires two measurements. Measuring cylinder diameter is similar to checking for overbore; one measurement is taken in line with the crankshaft centerline, and the other is taken at a right angle to the crankshaft. However, these measurements are taken toward the top of the cylinder slightly below the ridge line. The difference between the two diameters equals cylinder out-of-round. A realistic limit for cylinder out-of-round, for both diesel and gasoline engines, is about 0.001 inch.

CYLINDER WALL RECONDITIONING

If the cylinders are out of specifications for either taper or out-of-round, the bore should be opened up to a standard oversize. If cylinder wear is within specification, you can deglaze the cylinder walls and install new rings on the old pistons.

Cylinders can be oversized by either boring or honing. Both methods are discussed below. **Hypereutectic** aluminum blocks must be honed to oversize. Attempting to bore a

---

Hypereutectic: A casting process that combines aluminum with small silicon particles. The silicon particles provide a durable surface finish.

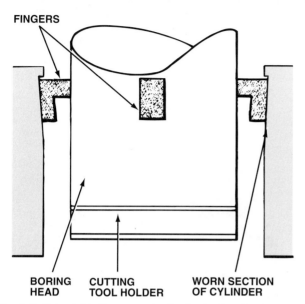

Fig. 3-5. Extendable fingers center the boring head in the cylinder.

hypereutectic aluminum block can gouge the cylinder wall and cause irreparable damage.

Boring Cylinders

All boring equipment operates on the same principle. A single-point cutting bit clamps into a boring head at the bottom of a heavy, steel sleeve. The boring head is centered in the bore using extendable fingers, figure 3-5. The boring machine rotates the cutting bit, as it simultaneously feeds the boring head down through the cylinder to cut an oversized hole.

The surface in a freshly bored cylinder is too rough and irregular to seat piston rings correctly. Therefore, the tool bit is set to cut a diameter not quite as large as the final size. The cylinder is then brought out to the final size by honing to prepare the surface for new piston rings.

Boring can remove a considerable amount of metal with one pass. In order to bore a cylinder to 0.030 inch oversize, the boring head can be set to cut about 0.027 inch of metal from the wall. The remaining 0.003 inch of metal is removed by honing, which ensures a good surface finish for positive ring seating, figure 3-6.

Honing Cylinders

Honing machines use abrasive stones to remove metal from the cylinder bore. The stones mount in a honing head and are adjusted to cut an exact diameter. The head mounts to the machine and rotates as it moves up and down through the bore. Different grit stones are available for rough and finish cutting.

Cylinders can be oversized completely by honing. However, most machinists prefer to bore the cylinders first, then hone them to final size.

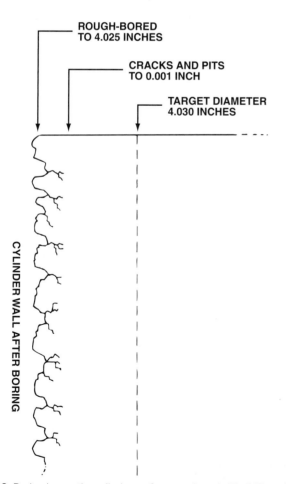

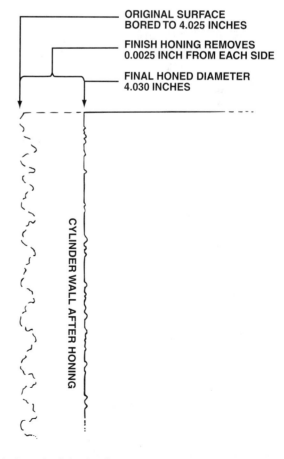

Fig. 3-6. Boring leaves the cylinder surface rough and pitted. Then, it must be honed to bring it to final size and provide an adequate finish.

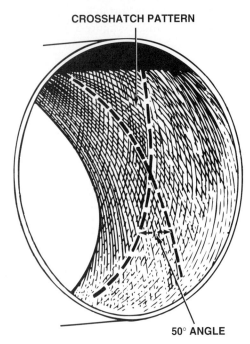

Fig. 3-7. Proper honing technique leaves a crosshatch pattern on the cylinder wall.

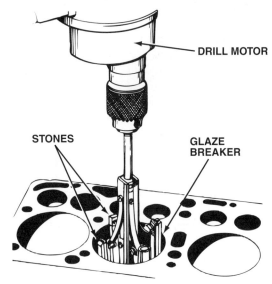

Fig. 3-8. A glaze breaker deglazes cylinder walls to promote piston ring seating.

Unlike boring, honing leaves a **plateau surface** that can support an oil film for the rings and piston skirts. Honing also establishes a **crosshatch** pattern on the cylinder walls, figure 3-7. The speed of the vertical and rotational movement of the honing head through the cylinder bore determines the angle of the crosshatch pattern. The crosshatch retains oil long enough to lap the piston rings to the cylinder walls, so they form a gas-tight seal.

After the cylinders are brought out to final size by honing, the bore reconditioning process is finished by grinding a 45-degree **chamfer** on the top edge of the bore.

Deglazing Cylinder Walls

Cylinder deglazing is a cylinder wall reconditioning method only used when the cylinder walls and the pistons are in good condition. Deglazing roughens the surface of the cylinders without significantly changing their overall diameter. The rough wall surface is necessary to break in new rings and allows the rings to conform exactly to the cylinders, creating an effective seal.

A glaze breaker is used to deglaze the cylinders. The glaze breaker chucks into a drill motor and uses abrasive stones to prepare the cylinder walls, figure 3-8. The drill is operated at low speed, between 200 and 500 rpm, and stroked up and down in the cylinder bore. Stroking the tool creates the required crosshatch pattern on the cylinder wall.

When deglazing cylinders, lubricate the stones with a lightweight oil to keep particles in suspension and prevent heat build-up. Avoid using solvents or other chemical agents.

Cleaning Cylinder Walls

Wash freshly machined cylinders with hot soapy water. Never use solvents or any other type of cleanser as these leave a residue on the cylinder wall. Any trace of dirt left behind can cause hot spots and prevent ring seating. Contaminants in the engine turn the soapy water gray. Continue cleaning until the soap suds no longer change color. Use fresh, clean water to rinse off all the detergent. Dry the bores using compressed air and immediately spray the machined surfaces with a light lubricant to prevent corrosion.

CAMSHAFT BEARING SERVICE

Servicing the camshaft bearings was covered in detail in the previous chapter and will only be highlighted here.

Visually inspect the bearings and bores for wear and damage. Measure the bores for out-of-round and misalignment. Damaged cam bearing bores on an overhead valve (OHV) engine can be line bored and fitted with oversized bearing inserts. Most overhead cam (OHC) engines fitted with camshaft bearing caps can be repaired back to standard size.

To restore OHC camshaft bearings to standard size, remove the bearing caps and grind a small amount of metal off the parting faces. This reduces the inside diameter of the bearing bores. Reinstall the bearing caps and open the bores to standard size by line boring.

CRANKSHAFT INSPECTION

Crankshaft inspection begins with a visual check for surface cracks and other damage. The reluctor ring for the engine speed sensor is an integral part of some crankshafts, and on

---

Chamfer: A beveled edge.
Crosshatch: A multi-directional surface finish left on a cylinder wall after honing. The crosshatch finish retains oil to aid in piston ring seating.
Plateau Surface: A finish in which the highest points of a surface have been honed to flattened peaks.

some, it is a separate part that attaches to the crankshaft. With either design, carefully inspect the reluctor ring. Look for cracked, chipped, and missing teeth, as well as any other signs of damage. Once the crankshaft passes a visual inspection, it is checked for straightness, then the journals are measured for diameter, taper, and out-of-round. Bent crankshafts can be straightened by pressing, peening, or heat stress-relieving. Damaged journals are restored to serviceable condition by grinding them to a standard undersize.

Crankshaft journals are generally reground to an undersize of 0.010 inch, 0.020 inch, or 0.030 inch. Oversized rod and main bearings are readily available in these increments for most engines. Normal practice is to grind all rod journals or all main journals to the same undersize, even when only one is damaged. Crankshaft journals that are within limits can be micropolished to improve the surface finish. **Micropolishing** simply restores the surface finish and will not correct for taper or out-of-round.

Surface Cracks and Damage

Examine the shaft for signs of cracking. Magnetic particle testing can be used to verify a crack. Cast-iron crankshafts usually self-destruct when a crack develops, so you will seldom find a cracked cast-iron crankshaft in a running engine. Forged-steel shafts are stronger, and you may occasionally remove a cracked one from a running engine.

Inspect the journal areas of the crankshaft. A slight discoloration is normal. Excessive discoloration, scoring, or pitting indicate problems. Check the snout for keyway damage and the flange for pilot-bearing bore damage and stripped threads.

Check crankshaft straightness using a dial indicator and V-blocks. Position the indicator plunger on a main journal and rotate the shaft one complete revolution. Crankshaft bend equals one-half of total indicated runout.

Cleaning Oil Passages

If the crankshaft has threaded sludge trap plugs that seal the ends of the oil drillways, remove them to clean the oil passages. Wash the shaft with solvent and use a brush to clean the oil passages.

Measuring Crankshaft Journals

Bearing journals are measured with an outside micrometer. Check for diameter, taper, and out-of-round. To get an accurate picture of wear, it is important to measure each journal at three locations; near the front and rear fillet radii and at the midpoint of the journal, figure 3-9. In addition, take at least two readings at each location. The second measurement should be taken 90 degrees around the circumference of the journal from the first.

The maximum diameter reading is used to determine oil clearance and will reveal if the crankshaft was reground to undersize previously. Compare the readings taken 90 degrees apart to determine out-of-round. The three measurements across the

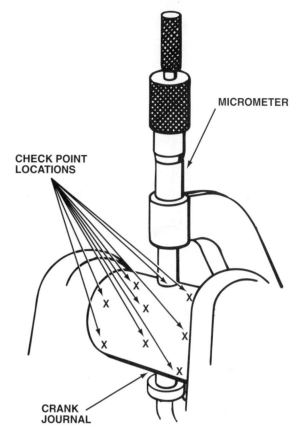

Fig. 3-9. Several outside micrometer measurements are taken to evaluate wear on a crankshaft journal.

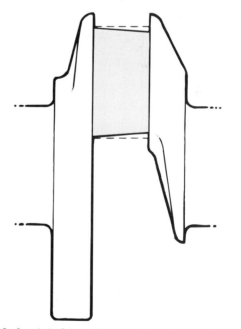

Fig. 3-10. Crankshaft journal wear with end-to-end taper.

journal determine taper. Three common bearing journal wear patterns are:

* End-to-end taper, figure 3-10
* Hourglass taper, figure 3-11

Micropolishing: A machining technique that uses an abrasive belt to restore mild crankshaft journal damage while removing minimal amounts of metal.

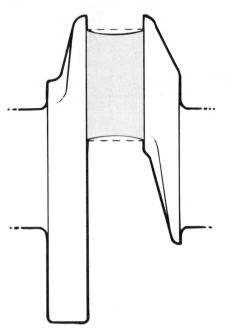

Fig. 3-11. Crankshaft journal wear with hourglass taper.

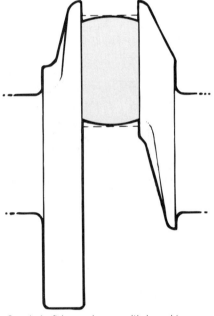

Fig. 3-12. Crankshaft journal wear with barrel taper.

- Barrel taper, figure 3-12

Compare your findings to manufacturer specifications. Crankshaft tolerances for taper and out-of-round are usually very tight. Modern engines often allow only 0.0002 to 0.0005 inch. In addition, any wear that reduces the diameter to 0.001 inch below standard requires the journal to be ground to an undersize.

MAIN AND CONNECTING ROD BEARING INSPECTION

Evaluating the main and rod bearing insert wear helps determine which areas of the block and crankshaft, and which connecting rods, will require close examination. Also, bearing wear patterns often provide insight into the cause of engine failure.

Evaluating Wear Patterns and Damage

Wipe the bearing shells clean with a rag and examine them. Line inserts pair up in the order they fit the engine. There should not be any scratches, embedded particles, or pieces of metal flaking off of the bearing shells. The internal surface of the bearing shells should be uniformly gray and smooth. Wear should be greatest toward the center of the bearing and minimal near the **parting line** at the sides of the bore.

Look for asymmetric wear patterns on the bearings. Localized, smeared areas on the bearing indicate that dirt particles were trapped between the bearing shell and the saddle. Flaking or wear at the edges of the shell can indicate that a shell is too wide for the journal, the bearing riding on the **fillet**, or a bent connecting rod. Connecting rod bearing wear at opposite sides and opposite ends of the two shells also indicates a bent rod.

Main bearing wear on apparently random areas across the various bearings can indicate a warped block. Wear in a short arc on the bearing face indicates partial contact caused by excessive clearance. Even scoring across the bearing face indicates a poor finish on the crankshaft. A bent crankshaft is indicated by severe wear on the bearings at the center of the engine and a minimum amount of wear on the bearing shells that were installed at either end of the engine.

Turn the bearing shells over and inspect their backs. If the backs of the bearings show any scoring, unusual patterns, or appear highly polished, the bearings have spun in the bores. When this type of damage is found, the bearing bores will need to be reconditioned.

Calculating Oil Clearance

Proper bearing oil clearance is critical to engine service life. To calculate oil clearance, you need to know:

- Housing bore diameter
- Insert thickness
- Bearing inside diameter
- Journal outside diameter

Housing bore diameter is the diameter across a bearing bore without the bearing inserts installed, figure 3-13. Measure housing bore diameter using a dial bore gauge, inside micrometer, or telescoping gauge and outside micrometer.

Insert thickness is the true thickness of the bearing insert or shell. It is not the same as the nominal oversize or undersize.

Fillet: A curve of a specific radius machined into the edges of a crankshaft journal. The fillet provides additional strength between the journal and the crankshaft cheek.

Parting Line: The meeting points of two parts or machined pieces, such as the two halves of a split shell bearing.

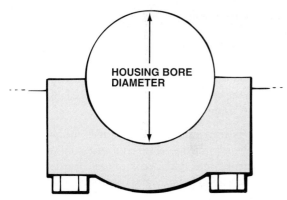

Fig. 3-13. Housing bore diameter is the distance across a bore without the bearings installed.

Oversize inserts have a larger outside diameter to fit an over-sized bore. Undersize inserts have a smaller inside diameter to fit a reground journal. Both are thicker than standard-sized bearings. A special outside micrometer with a ball-shaped anvil is used to measure bearing insert thickness. A standard micrometer will give a false reading because of the bearing's arch.

Bearing inside diameter is the diameter across the hole for the journal, with the bearing inserts in place and the cap tightened to specified torque, figure 3-14. You can install the bearings and measure the inside diameter or you can calculate it by adding twice the insert thickness to the housing bore diameter.

Crankshaft journal diameter is the maximum distance across the journal. Measuring crankshaft journal diameter was detailed previously in this chapter.

To determine the oil clearance, subtract the journal diameter from the bearing inside diameter. An alternative method for checking oil clearance is to measure it using **Plastigauge®**.

A strip of the plastic is placed between the bearing and the journal, and the cap is tightened to final torque, then carefully removed. Because the diameter of the gauging material is exact,

tightening the cap crushes the Plastigauge® a specific amount. The amount of crush can be measured to determine oil clearance using a scale on the Plastigauge® package.

There are three important precautions to keep in mind when using Plastigauge®:

- The plastic material is not compatible with engine oil. Both bearing and journal must be perfectly dry
- When measuring main bearing clearance with the engine in the vehicle, support the crankshaft's weight with a jack to prevent the shaft's weight from causing an inaccurate reading
- Never turn the crankshaft with Plastigauge® installed. This can smear the plastic and skew your results

Installing Main Bearings

Fit all of the bearing inserts to the block first, then to the caps. The block-side insert must have a drilled hole that aligns with the oil gallery opening in the saddle. Some manufacturers machine a relief into the upper shell that directs oil flow to the parting line at either side of the bearing. Be sure these bearing halves are installed into the engine block, not into the cap.

Bearing inserts assemble to the block and caps dry; do not lubricate them before you install them. Also, wipe the backside of the bearing shells clean before you fit them. Install the bearing shells in order, working from one end of the block to the other, then fit the bearing shells to the caps. If the engine has separate thrust-bearing inserts, fit them last. A couple of dabs of assembly lube on the outside edge of the thrust insert help hold it in place. Avoid getting any lubricant behind the thrust bearings. Finish by wiping off the bearings' working surface, then lubricate them with a thin film of engine oil.

Crankshaft Oil Seals

Lip-type oil seals are used where movement occurs against the seal surface, figure 3-15. These seals have a definite lip which should face the lubricant. A spring garter is generally used

A1

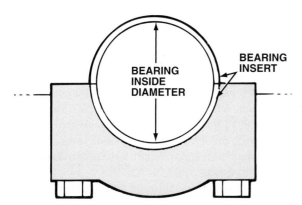

Fig. 3-14. Bearing inside diameter is the distance across a bore with the bearings installed.

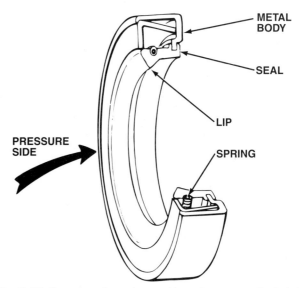

Fig. 3-15. One-piece lip seal assembly makes an excellent shaft seal because oil pressure pushes the sealing lip into the shaft.

Plastigauge®: A string-like piece of plastic manufactured to a precise diameter used for measuring bearing clearance.

behind the lip to maintain pressure and improve sealing. Coat the outer edge of the seal with gasket sealer to prevent oil leaks around the outside and lubricate the seal lip with engine oil before installing it.

Insight

Do not lubricate teflon type oil seals. They must be installed dry, as any oil on the surface interferes with the "burn-in" required of this style seal.

Wick-type oil seals are impregnated with a graphite lubricant. The rear, main oil seal is an example. The seal is installed in a groove in the block and in a groove in the bearing cap or bearing seal, figure 3-16. The seal is seated in place, and the excess length is trimmed flush with the parting line.

Installing the Crankshaft

The crankshaft journals must be perfectly clean; wipe down before you place the crank into the block. Refer to the OEM guidelines for the correct lubricant to coat the journals and shells with, before installation. If no OEM information is available, apply a thin coat of engine oil to both surfaces. Do not use grease on these surfaces.

Keep the crankshaft parallel to the bearing bores as you slowly lower it straight down into position. Make sure the crankshaft does not gouge the soft surface of the thrust bearings as you lower it. Make sure that separate thrust bearing inserts remain fully seated as you install the crank.

Once in place, the crankshaft must fit squarely and be solidly supported by the main bearings in the saddles. The shaft must rotate freely and easily without resistance; if it does

not, there is a problem. Binding may be caused by a bent shaft, misaligned bearing bores, incorrectly installed bearing shells, or defective or incorrectly sized bearings. Correct any problems now. Do not install the bearing caps if the crankshaft does not spin smoothly when resting in the block saddles.

Secure the crankshaft in the block by installing the main bearing caps using the following steps:

1. Fit the bearing caps over the journals and push down to mate them to the saddles. If you staggered the rear main seal parting line, add a drop of gasket sealer to the seal ends. Be sure to fit both ends of the seal precisely into the grooves
2. Lubricate the bolt threads as required, then install the bolts and draw them up hand tight
3. Rotate the crankshaft as you lightly tap the sides of each cap with a soft-face hammer to seat it. This is an important step, as it squares the cap in the saddle
4. Draw the bolts up as far as you can by hand
5. Place a large screwdriver between a cap and crankshaft cheek and pry the crankshaft back and forth to align the thrust bearing. Do not pry on the cap that holds the thrust bearing
6. Rotate the crankshaft at least one complete revolution to check for free movement
7. Follow the OEM's procedure for torquing the bolts in the correct sequence

Insight

Some manufacturers now use torque-to-yield fasteners requiring special tightening procedures. Some of these new fasteners cannot be reused or **re-torqued**. Refer to the applicable shop manual for further information.

PISTON AND CONNECTING ROD SERVICE

Worn and damaged pistons cannot be repaired; they must be replaced. On older engines, connecting rods can generally be reconditioned and returned to service, unless they are severely damaged. On late model engines, the connecting rod and piston are often replaced as a unit and cannot be repaired if damaged.

Cleaning and Measuring Pistons

Carefully remove any heavy deposits on the tops of the pistons with a gasket scraper. Do not scrape down to the metal because the piston tops are easily damaged. Clean remaining deposits by soaking the pistons in solvent such as carburetor cleaner or washing them with safety solvent. Pistons must never be cleaned by bead blasting, sand blasting, or wire brushing. These methods will damage the **ring lands** and/or the special coating on the piston and will embed abrasive materials in the surface of the piston.

A critical operation is cleaning the piston ring grooves so that the new rings will slide freely when installed. For this job,

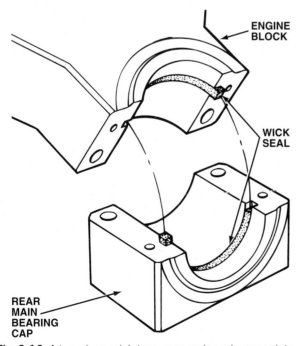

ENGINE BLOCK

WICK SEAL

REAR MAIN BEARING CAP

Fig. 3-16. A two-piece, wick-type, rear, main seal presses into grooves on the bearing cap and engine block.

Re-torque: To torque again as in reusing a fastener.
Ring Lands: The part of a piston between the ring grooves. The lands strengthen and support the ring grooves.

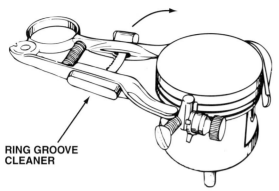

Fig. 3-17. A piston ring groove cleaner scrapes carbon, varnish, and other debris from the ring grooves of a piston.

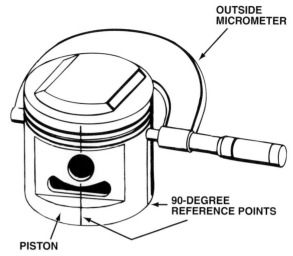

Fig. 3-18. Measuring piston diameter with an outside micrometer.

A1

special ring groove scrapers are available, figure 3-17. Use the tool carefully and do not allow it to gouge the ring land or remove any metal from the piston. Check the oil drain holes located at the back of the oil control ring groove to make sure that they are clear.

Inspecting and Measuring Pistons

Examine the entire piston, keeping a close eye out for unusual wear patterns on the skirts, ring lands, and wrist pin bosses. Inspect the wear patterns on the piston thrust faces for indications of a bent connecting rod. Wear patterns should be straight up and down, perpendicular to the wrist pin. An angled pattern indicates a bent rod. Check the ring lands. Replace the piston if you find any scuffing, hairline cracks, or chips. Check the wrist pin bosses for signs of cracking and metal fatigue on the inside of the piston.

Three measurements are taken to evaluate overall piston condition. They are:

- Piston diameter
- Piston skirt diameter
- Ring groove side clearance

Measure the piston diameter using an outside micrometer. Diameter is generally measured on the thrust surface at the centerline of the pin bore and perpendicular, at a 90-degree angle, to the wrist pin, figure 3-18. Most automotive pistons will measure 0.001 to 0.003 inch less than the cylinder bore diameter.

Check for collapsed skirts by measuring across the thrust surfaces at the bottom of the skirt with an outside micrometer. Compare this figure to the piston diameter. The piston should be about 0.0015 inch wider at the skirt bottom.

A new piston ring is required to calculate ring groove side clearance. Typical side clearance for automotive engines is in the 0.001 to 0.003 inch range. There are two methods of measuring ring groove side clearance. One uses a ring wear gauge and micrometer and the other uses a blade-type feeler gauge. A ring wear gauge is a type of feeler gauge designed specifically to measure the ring groove width, figure 3-18. Measure the ring groove width with the wear gauge and

measure the new ring's thickness with an outside micrometer. Then, subtract the ring width from the groove width to calculate side clearance.

To measure side clearance with a feeler gauge, simply fit the new ring backward into the groove. Then, slip the feeler gauge blades between the ring and the groove, figure 3-19. The largest feeler gauge blade that will fit between the ring and the side of the groove equals the side clearance.

Checking Connecting Rod Alignment

The connecting rod bore centerline at each end must be parallel to within approximately 0.001 inch for each six inches of connecting rod length, figure 3-20. If bore centerlines are out of parallel as viewed from the edge of the rod, the condition is called **bend**. If bore centerlines are out of parallel as viewed

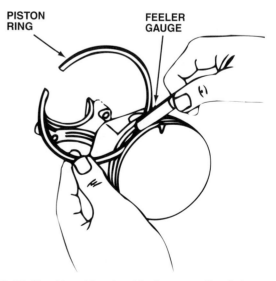

Fig. 3-19. Checking piston ring side clearance with a feeler gauge.

Bend: On a connecting rod, the condition of the two bores being out-of-parallel when viewed from the edge of the rod.

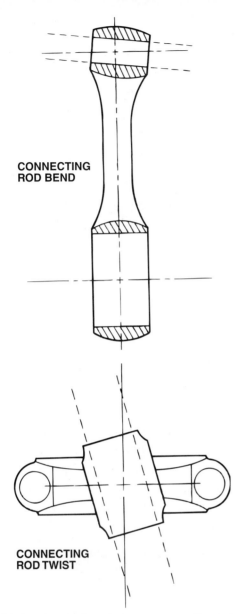

CONNECTING
ROD BEND

CONNECTING
ROD TWIST

Fig. 3-20. Bend and twist are common connecting rod alignment problems.

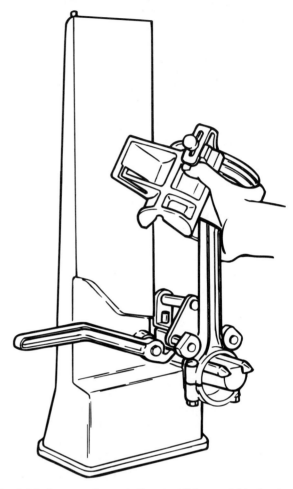

Fig. 3-21. A connecting rod alignment fixture quickly checks a rod for bend, twist, and offset.

from the top, the condition is called **twist**. If the bore center-lines lie on different planes when the rod is viewed from its edge, the condition is called **offset**.

Connecting rod alignment can be checked using an alignment fixture, figure 3-21. Most fixtures allow you to check alignment either with or without the piston attached to the rod. Different adapters are used to check bend, twist, and offset.

Rod alignment problems can be corrected by cold bending the rod back into position using special tools.

Damaged connecting rod bearing bores can be reconditioned by honing.

Separating Pistons and Connecting Rods

Two types of wrist pin, press-fit and full-floating, are commonly used on automotive engines. Press-fit pins are installed with an interference fit of about 0.001 inch. Full-floating pins are installed without interference and are held in place by snap rings that fit into machined slots on the pin bore of the piston, figure 3-22.

Removing and Measuring Press-Fit Wrist Pins

Press-fit wrist pins are removed with a press. Special adapters are used to support the piston and prevent damaging it while the pin is being removed. The pin is pressed out of the piston and rod with an arbor.

Once the pin is removed, the diameter of the wrist pin, the bore on the small-end of the connecting rod, and the pin bore on the piston are measured. Wrist pin diameter can be measured using an outside micrometer. The piston pin bore and connecting rod bore are measured using a special precision bore gauge, figure 3-23. The precision bore is generally an accessory item that attaches to a rod honing machine.

Offset: On a connecting rod, the condition of the two bores being out-of-parallel when viewed from the side.
Twist: On a connecting rod, the condition of the two bores being out-of-parallel when viewed from the top.

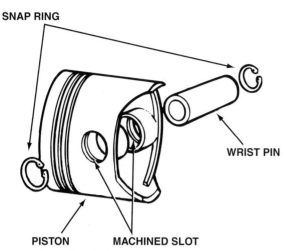

Fig. 3-22. Snap rings hold a full-floating wrist pin in the piston.

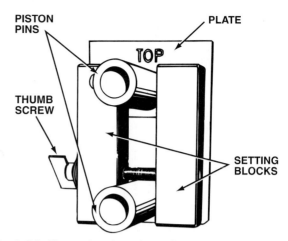

Fig. 3-24. Piston pins clamp into a fixture to measure them on a precision bore gauge.

Fig. 3-23. A precision bore gauge is used to measure piston pin and bore diameters.

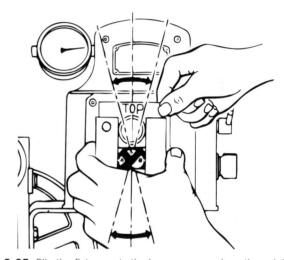

Fig. 3-25. Slip the fixture onto the bore gauge and gently rock it to get an accurate reading on the dial indicator.

To measure pin bores with a precision bore gauge, it must be calibrated using a pin gauge setting fixture. Clamp two wrist pins into the setting fixture, figure 3-24. Then, fit the setting fixture onto the bore gauge and adjust the dial gauge to read the correct clearance, figure 3-25. Once the gauge is set, it can be used to check clearance in rod bushings or in piston bores.

When measurements are out of tolerance, oversized wrist pins can be installed. However, a considerable amount of machining is required, and it is more common to simply replace the piston and wrist pin with new ones.

Installing Press-Fit Wrist Pins

Press-fit pins are installed using either a press or connecting rod heater. Press fitting is basically the reverse of removal, using an arbor and adapters. A connecting rod heater warms the small end of the connecting rod. This expands the pin bore and makes the pin fit easier. With either method, it is important to get the pin properly centered in the bores.

Removing and Measuring Full-Floating Wrist Pins

Disassembling full-floating pins is easy and requires no special tools. Remove both snap rings and push the wrist pin free. When built-up varnish tends to stick the pin in the bore, use a drift and light hammer taps to free it.

Most full-floating pins ride on a soft metal bushing that is press-fit into the small-end bore. Inspect the bushing for damage. Full-floating piston pins require a slight amount of clearance between the pin and the rod and piston bores. This clearance is generally only a few ten-thousandths of an inch. Measure the pin, piston bores, and bushing inside diameter as described for press-fit pins.

Pin bushings have a tendency to wear to a taper, figure 3-26, or develop a bell-mouthed shape, figure 3-27. If either condition exists, replace the bushings.

Installing Full-Floating Wrist Pins

Full-floating wrist pins should slip easily into the bores if the parts are properly cleaned and there is adequate clearance. Double check measurements to verify clearance, lubricate the parts, and slip the pin into position. Install the snap rings and

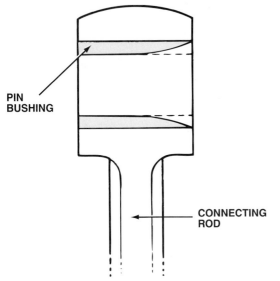

Fig. 3-26. Pin bushing taper wear results from rod misalignment and is corrected by straightening the rod and installing a new bushing.

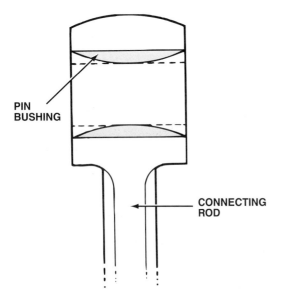

Fig. 3-27. Pin bushing bell-mouth wear is a result of too much pin clearance.

make sure they seat firmly into the grooves. The open portion of the snap ring should face down, toward the crankshaft.

Connecting-Rod Reconditioning

Unless there is serious damage, older model connecting rods can be reconditioned and returned to service. Connecting-rod reconditioning can include straightening the rod, reducing and honing the big-end bore, and replacing bushings in the small-end bore. Check for straightness using an alignment fixture and measure the bores as described below to evaluate overall connecting-rod condition.

Fig. 3-28. A precision bore gauge can be used to measure connecting rod bores.

Measuring the Bearing Bore

The bearing, or big-end, bore of a connecting rod is subject to **stretch** and must be measured for diameter and out-of-round. Although an inside micrometer can be used, this is not a satisfactory way to check the very close tolerances specified for new connecting rods. A better way is to use a dial-indicating device designed specifically for measuring bearing bores or a precision bore gauge, figure 3-28. Always take readings at several locations whenever you measure a bearing bore, and never measure directly across the parting lines, figure 3-29.

Two specialized machine tools, a connecting-rod grinder and a connecting-rod hone, are used to restore the bearing bore. The rod grinder removes precise amounts of metal from the parting faces of the rod and bearing cap. This reduces the inside diameter of the bore to less than standard size. Once the bore is reduced, the hone is used to open up bore and bring it back to standard size.

The connecting rod hone is also used to replace wrist-pin bushings on full-floating rods. The old bushing is pressed out, and a new bushing is pressed into the bore. An expander broach expands the bushing into the bore. Excess bushing material is trimmed away with a facing cutter. After the new bushing is installed, it is finish-honed to bring it out to final size and provide the correct amount of clearance.

PISTON RING SERVICE

The first step in installing new piston rings is to read the instructions provided with the ring set. These instructions contain key points specified by the manufacturer that often vary from the original equipment rings. Do not expect all piston ring sets to look the same or to install the same way. Compression rings are often marked to indicate which side the ring faces. Although some rings are stamped "top," others use a different type of marking, such as a dot or an arrow, to indicate which way they install. As a general rule, if the inside edge of the ring has a bevel or counterbore, it faces up, and if the counterbore is on the outside edge of the ring, it installs facing down. If only one compression ring has a bevel or counterbore on the inside, it generally goes in the top ring groove. Remember to check instructions supplied with each set of piston rings to avoid problems.

Stretch: An extreme out-of-round condition on a bearing bore.

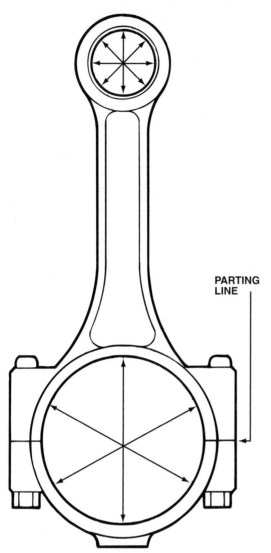

PARTING
LINE

Fig. 3-29. Measuring a connecting rod bore at several locations to get accurate readings. Never measure directly across the parting lines.

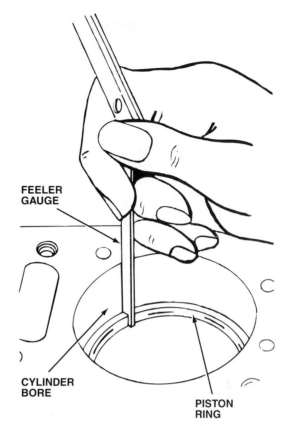

FEELER
GAUGE

CYLINDER
BORE

PISTON
RING

Fig. 3-30. Checking piston ring end gap with a feeler gauge.

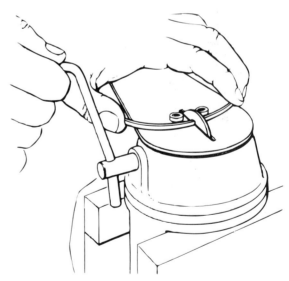

Fig. 3-31. Correcting piston ring end gap by filing on a special ring grinder.

A1

Piston Ring End Gap

Check piston ring end gap before installing the rings on the pistons. Place the piston rings squarely in the cylinder, in the bottom of worn cylinders, or near the top, below the ridge area, of freshly reconditioned cylinders. Use a feeler gauge to check the end gap, figure 3-30. The correct end gap is approximately 0.003 to 0.004 inch for each inch of cylinder diameter, with a maximum of about 0.025 inch.

If the gap you measure is too small, file the ends of the ring to obtain the correct gap. Special ring grinders are available to open up the end gap, figure 3-31. An alternative is to use a fine-toothed file. Clamp the file in a vise and draw the ring across the file. File in one direction only, then dress any rough edges on the sides, face, and back of the ring. Recheck end gap frequently to avoid removing too much ring material.

Installing Rings on the Piston

Double check the ring side gap as described earlier, then install the rings onto the piston. Piston rings must be fitted so that the end gaps are offset from each other on the piston,

figure 3-32. If the gaps are aligned vertically, serious oil consumption and blowby problems can result.

Work from the bottom to the top as you install the rings on the piston. Install the oil control ring first, then fit the bottom compression ring, and install the top compression ring last. Three-piece oil control rings also install in a particular order:

1. Spring expander
2. Top rail
3. Bottom rail

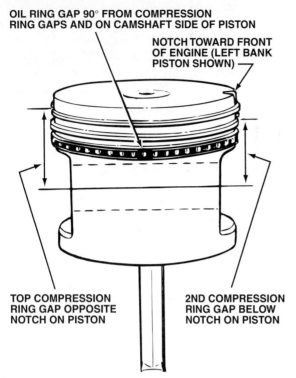

OIL RING GAP 90° FROM COMPRESSION
RING GAPS AND ON CAMSHAFT SIDE OF PISTON

NOTCH TOWARD FRONT
OF ENGINE (LEFT BANK
PISTON SHOWN)

TOP COMPRESSION
RING GAP OPPOSITE
NOTCH ON PISTON

2ND COMPRESSION
RING GAP BELOW
NOTCH ON PISTON

Fig. 3-32. Stagger piston ring end gaps to ensure good compression sealing on startup.

Be sure to hold the expander securely, with the ends butted together, when fitting the rails. Never allow the ends of the expander to overlap. This will damage the cylinder wall.

Coat the ring grooves and the rings with engine oil for easier installation. Use a ring expander tool to expand compression rings so they clear the piston crown, figure 3-33. Piston rings are brittle, and an expansion tool is used to avoid breaking them.

Installing Rods and Pistons in the Engine

Before installation, the piston rings and cylinder walls must be well oiled. Use a ring compressor tool to compress the rings so the piston will slide into the cylinder, figure 3-34.

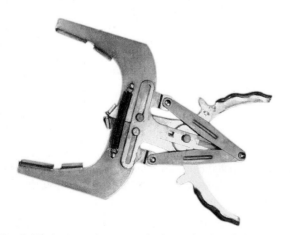

Fig. 3-33. A piston ring expander is used to install rings on the piston.

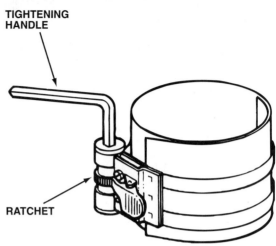

TIGHTENING
HANDLE

RATCHET

Fig. 3-34. A piston ring compressor squeezes the rings so the piston will fit into the cylinder bore.

Remove the rod bearing cap and wipe off the bearing bore. It must be perfectly clean and dry. Place the bearing inserts into position in the rod and rod cap, making sure any lock tabs and grooves are aligned. Fit protective covers over the ends of the rod bolts to prevent accidental damage to the crankshaft journal, figure 3-35. Make sure the rod and piston are both correctly assembled and positioned in the cylinder, so they both face the proper direction.

A notch or arrow on the piston top will generally point toward the front of the engine. Connecting rods usually have a directional indicator, but it is often subtle, and you must know what to look for.

Install the rod and piston assembly by fitting it into the cylinder and pushing down on the piston top with a hammer handle. Ensure that the rod slips over the crankshaft in the normal position for assembly. Coat the bearings with a thin film

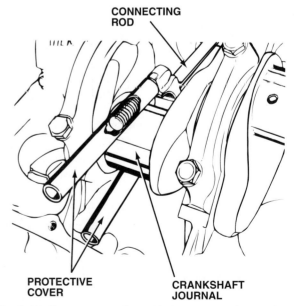

CONNECTING
ROD

PROTECTIVE
COVER

CRANKSHAFT
JOURNAL

Fig. 3-35. Fit covers over the rod bolts to protect the crankshaft journal during piston installation.

of assembly lube or engine oil. Then, install the rod cap and torque to the proper specifications, referring to the OEM specifications for the correct procedure and values.

After all of the piston and rod assemblies are installed, check the connecting-rod side clearance.

Measuring Connecting-Rod Side Clearance

Side clearance is the distance between the crankshaft cheek and the side of the connecting rod, or the space between the two connecting rods that share a journal on a V-type engine. Manufacturers provide side-clearance requirements in their specification data. The largest feeler gauge that fits into the gap between the rod and crankshaft, or two adjacent rods, equals the side clearance.

Before proceeding with the final assembly of the cylinder block, rotate the engine several times to ensure there are no problems. Before proceeding with assembly, refer to the OEM's timing procedure and set the timing gears at the correct location. If no information is available rotate the engine until the timing marks align on an OHV engine. For an OHC engine place cylinder number one at TDC.

REASSEMBLE REMAINDER OF ENGINE

Install the oil pan and any other covers for the cylinder block.

Gaskets and Sealers

Cork, rubber, or composite material gaskets are used where surfaces may not be perfectly flat and where considerable crush is required. Oil pans, valve covers, and timing covers generally use cork, rubber, or composite gaskets. Cork gaskets change shape with the humidity in the air, and they may not fit properly when first removed from the package. They can be made to grow by soaking them in warm water, and made to shrink by drying them over a warm surface. Gasket sealer may be used on the sheet metal side of the gasket to hold it in place during installation. Flatten the sheet metal sealing surfaces with a ball peen hammer before you install the gaskets.

Gasket Sealants

Many cork and rubber gaskets can be installed without sealants, and a thin coating of sealant is all that is required to seal a paper gasket. There is a wide variety of products available to do the job. Generally, only non-hardening gasket sealants should be used in automotive repair. Since these sealants remain pliable, the seal is not compromised by different rates of metal expansion during operation.

A gasket may not conform to all the channels and ridges of the flange. Using a formed-in-place sealant will fill these irregularities. There are two types of this sealant—aerobic and anaerobic.

Aerobic, or room-temperature vulcanizing (RTV), sealant cannot be used on the exhaust system because it cannot withstand such high temperatures. You must fit the parts together within 10 minutes of applying the sealant because it will harden.

Anaerobic sealants cure only after the mating parts are bolted together, which excludes air from the joint. This sealant is thinner than RTV compound and is not practical for flexible covers. It is recommended for machined surfaces only.

Be aware that the electronic controls on some engines can be affected by certain gasket sealing compounds. Sealants cure in a running engine and as they do, spent chemicals are emitted. These contaminants can circulate in the engine and cause faulty signals from various sensors. Oxygen sensors are especially vulnerable to certain RTV silicone sealers. Use the correct type of sealant, and use it only where specified.

HARMONIC BALANCER SERVICE

The harmonic balancer, or vibration damper, is removed using a special puller. Using any other tool can damage the balancer.

Inspect the harmonic balancer for damage to the keyway and for wear to the hub caused by the timing cover seal. If the wear groove from the seal is too deep, you can usually press on a repair sleeve rather than replace the entire balancer, figure 3-36. Repair sleeves are available from gasket manufacturers. If the balancer has a rubber bonding ring, examine it carefully. These bonding rings deteriorate eventually and can cause the assembly to break apart dramatically on a running engine. Look for cracks and pieces of the ring breaking loose. Replace the balancer if any signs of damage are found.

Also inspect the crankshaft snout. Look for signs of scoring, gouging, and other damage on the shaft, keyway, and key.

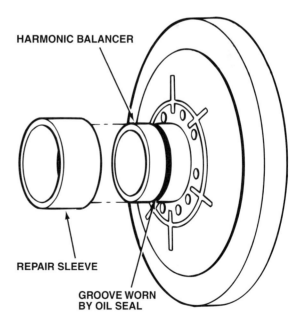

Fig. 3-36. A repair sleeve can often salvage a harmonic balancer that has a groove worn into it from an oil seal.

Aerobic: Curing in the presence of oxygen.
Anaerobic: Curing in the absence of oxygen.

Dress any minor damage with a fine file, emery cloth, or stone. Replace damaged keys.

Install the harmonic balancer by aligning the key and keyway, then slipping the balancer over the snout. Use a large, open drift and hammer to seat the balancer to the crankshaft.

FLYWHEEL SERVICE

Three areas of the the flywheel must be inspected to ensure good service life, the:

- Ring gear
- Clutch seating surface
- Mounting flange

Check the ring gear for worn or missing teeth as a result of poor starter motor engagement. The ring gear is a shrink-fit on many flywheels and can be replaced easily. This is done by heating the gear, but not the body of the flywheel, with a torch flame to expand the metal. Once the gear is hot enough, it will simply drop off of the flywheel. Heat is also used to expand and install the new ring gear; a few careful raps with a hammer will guarantee a good seat.

Inspect the clutch seating surface for hard spots, heat checks, and cracks. A damaged surface can be restored by turning on a lathe or by grinding with a surface grinder. Lathe cutting will not remove hard spots. Surface grinding will, so grinding is a more common practice.

Look the mounting flange over for any nicks, chips, or burrs that will prevent the flywheel from seating onto the crankshaft. Also, check the end of the crankshaft. Correct any minor damage by dressing with a file or hand stone. Check the bolt holes for distortion. Replace the flywheel if any bolt hole distortion is found. Make sure the threaded holes on the crankshaft and flywheel are in good condition.

Flywheel Installation

The flywheel must be installed in its original position to maintain engine balance. Fit the flywheel to the crankshaft flange. Install the retaining bolts, and tighten them in a star pattern to bring them to specified torque. Once it is installed, check the flywheel runout and crankshaft endplay.

Checking Flywheel Runout

Check flywheel runout with a dial indicator. Attach the indicator to the engine block and position its plunger so that it rests on the clutch surface of the flywheel, figure 3-37. Use a large screwdriver or prybar to pry the flywheel away from the block, then zero the indicator dial. Keep the screwdriver in place to prevent the shaft from floating as you rotate the crankshaft one complete revolution. The highest reading on the dial indicator is total runout.

Checking Crankshaft Endplay

To check crankshaft endplay, attach a dial indicator to the front of the engine so that the plunger rests on the end of the crankshaft snout. Move the crankshaft as far back in the block as possible by prying with a screwdriver between the flywheel and block. Zero the dial indicator, then push the crankshaft forward in the block. The dial indicator will read total endplay.

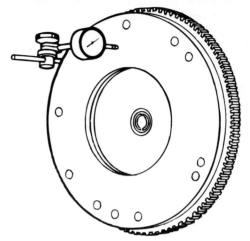

Fig. 3-37. Check flywheel runout with a dial indicator.

PILOT BEARING OR BUSHING SERVICE

Pilot bearings are one of two types; a solid bushing or a sealed bearing. Bearing-type pilots are usually held in place with a snap ring. Remove the snap ring and the bearing will usually come out of the crankshaft easily. Bushings are removed using a slide hammer fitted with a blind bearing puller, figure 3-38. Bushings are installed with an interference fit and can require a considerable amount of force to remove.

Before installing a pilot bearing or bushing, inspect the crankshaft bore. The bore must be clean and free of any burrs, chips, or gouges. Check the internal bore on the bearing or bushing by sliding it onto the transmission input shaft.

All pilots, whether bearing or bushing, are installed using a special driver. For additional information on pilot bearings and bushings, refer to book three of this series.

AUXILIARY ENGINE SHAFT SERVICE

Many engines are fitted with auxiliary shafts. These include balance, intermediate, idler, counterbalance, or silencer shafts.

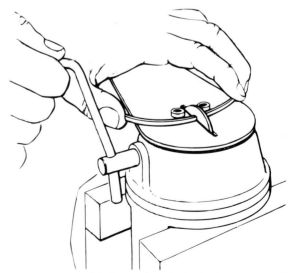

Fig. 3-38. Using a slide hammer and adapter to remove a pilot bushing.

Auxiliary shafts must be removed and inspected during engine rebuilding. In an inline engine, auxiliary shafts are generally driven by the crankshaft through a timing chain or belt. In V-type engines, auxiliary shafts are gear driven by the camshaft. Be sure timing marks align before disassembling.

Remove the shafts, then inspect and measure the bearing journals. Check for diameter, taper, and out-of-round as previously described. Check shaft straightness using V-blocks and a dial indicator. Auxiliary shafts may use split shell bearings or press-fit insert bearings. Inspect, measure, and replace bearings, as necessary, using techniques described earlier in this book.

To reinstall the shaft, be sure all timing marks align, and fit the parts following the procedures provided by the engine manufacturer. Rotate the crankshaft two complete revolutions, and recheck to make sure all of the timing marks align.

A1

CHAPTER QUESTIONS

1. Connecting rods are marked:
   a. After removal
   b. With a scribe
   c. Before removal
   d. On the bottom of the cap

2. After cleaning the block in a hot tank, you should:
   a. Remove the ring ridge
   b. Brush clean the oil galleries
   c. Remove the core plugs
   d. Mark the bearing caps

3. Cylinders are measured near the top and near the bottom to determine:
   a. Diameter
   b. Out-of-round
   c. Taper
   d. Oversize

4. While measuring the main bearing the Plastigauge is wider the specified: Technician A says you will have insufficient oil clearance. Technician B says you will have excessive oil clearance. Who is right?
   a. A only
   b. B only
   c. Both A and B
   d. Neither A nor B

5. After the cylinder walls are honed, they are cleaned with:
   a. Solvent
   b. Soap and Water
   c. A hot tank
   d. Air Hose

6. Technician A says deck clearance is to check for a warped block deck. Technician B says the deck clearance is to check for bent connecting rods. Who is right?
   a. A only
   b. B only
   c. Both A and B
   d. Neither A nor B

7. The cylinder ridge is formed because:
   a. Oil is burnt as it escapes past the rings
   b. The area above the top piston ring travels
   c. Too rich a fuel mixture
   d. Cylinder glaze build up

8. If the block and rods are in good shape, main and rod bearing insert wear will be:
   a. Even across the bearing face
   b. Concentrated on apparently random areas of the bearing faces
   c. In a short arc near the fillet
   d. Greatest in the center and minimal at the parting line

9. Damaged internal threads can be repaired by:
   a. Drilling and taping oversize
   b. Installing a helical insert
   c. Installing an insert bushing
   d. All of the above

10. The technician uses a telescoping gauge with an outside micrometer to measure:
    a. Cylinder diameter
    b. Cylinder out of round
    c. Cylinder taper
    d. All of the above

11. The crankshaft journal is measured in the same direction at opposite ends. Technician A says it is being checked for taper. Technician B says it is being checked for out of round. Who is right?
    a. A only
    b. B only
    c. Both A and B
    d. Neither A nor B

12. New rings are installed in an engine. If the ridge is not removed:
    a. The ridge does not make a difference.
    b. The top ring and land may be broken
    c. The top of the piston will hit the ridge
    d. The top ring seats faster

13. Piston ring end gap is checked on:
    a. The piston
    b. Top of the cylinder
    c. Middle of the cylinder
    d. Bottom of the cylinder

14. When assembling the connecting rod onto a piston:
    a. The rod can be installed in either direction
    b. The rod can be installed in one direction only
    c. The piston pin must be installed in the connecting rod first
    d. The piston notch is always to the rear of the engine

15. Install rods and pistons:
    a. By tapping with a ball peen hammer
    b. By pushing gently with a wooden hammer handle
    c. Clean and dry
    d. With rod caps reversed

CHAPTER FOUR

LUBRICATION AND COOLING SYSTEM DIAGNOSIS AND REPAIR

CHAPTER OBJECTIVES

- The technician will complete the ASE task list on Lubrication and Cooling System Diagnosis and Repair.
- The technician will be able to answer 8 questions dealing with the Lubrication and Cooling System Diagnosis and Repair section of the A1 ASE test.

This chapter details the various inspections, tests, and repair procedures for engine. lubrication and cooling systems.

LUBRICATION SYSTEM

Besides changing the oil and oil filter at regular intervals, lubrication system service generally consists of:

- Locating and repairing leaks
- Testing the oil pressure
- Servicing the oil pump

Oil Pressure Testing

The following tests or diagnostic inspections may be performed on assembled engines in the vehicle to locate the cause of low oil pressure or noises. Excessive clearance or leakage anywhere in the lubrication system can cause a loss of oil pressure, figure 4-1.

Checking Oil Pressure

Engines that indicate low oil pressure on the instrument cluster can be tested more precisely by connecting a mechanical oil pressure gauge. With the engine running, the gauge will display the true oil pressure the engine is producing.

Another test requires removing the oil pan, connecting an outside source of oil pressure, and turning the engine slowly by hand.

While the engine is turning, carefully watch the oil flow through all pressure-fed bearings, including the camshaft

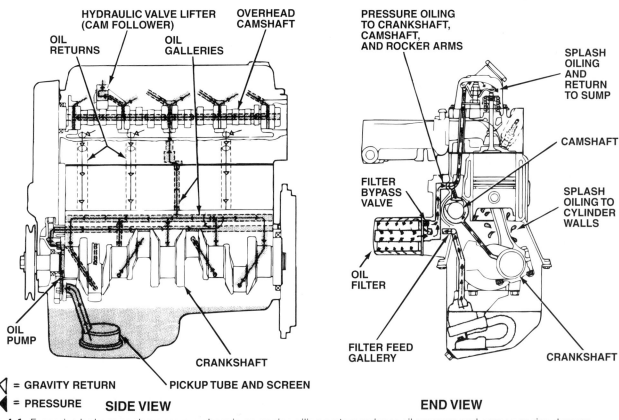

Fig. 4-1. Excessive leakage or clearance anywhere in an engine oiling system reduces oil pressure and causes engine damage.

bearings. If excessive flow is found, rotate the crankshaft 45 to 90 degrees in either direction and recheck. A false indication of excessive flow can occur if the crankshaft oil holes and the engine block **oil gallery** drillings are aligned, allowing unrestricted flow. If rotating the engine causes the flow to decrease, this alignment is probably the cause of the excessive flow. Also, check the oil pump pressure relief valve to see if it is stuck in the open position.

Oil Pump Service

There are two basic oil pump designs:

- Gear type, figure 4-2
- Rotor type, figure 4-3

Gear-type pumps generally bolt to the engine block or to a main bearing cap. These pumps are driven by a shaft that is geared to the camshaft or an idler gear. Some rotor-type pumps are driven by the camshaft. Others mount to or inside the timing cover and are driven directly by the crankshaft.

An oil pump must be removed from the engine and cleaned before it can be inspected. In most cases, the oil pan must be removed to access the oil pump. With a crankshaft-driven pump, the timing cover must be removed to access the pump.

Once the oil pump is removed from the engine, disassemble it, thoroughly clean the parts with solvent, dry with compressed air, then inspect the components for wear and damage. It is especially important that oil pressure relief valves and oil passages be free of **sludge** and **varnish**, so the valve can move freely in its bore and operate normally. Also, thoroughly clean and carefully inspect the pickup screen for damage before reinstalling it.

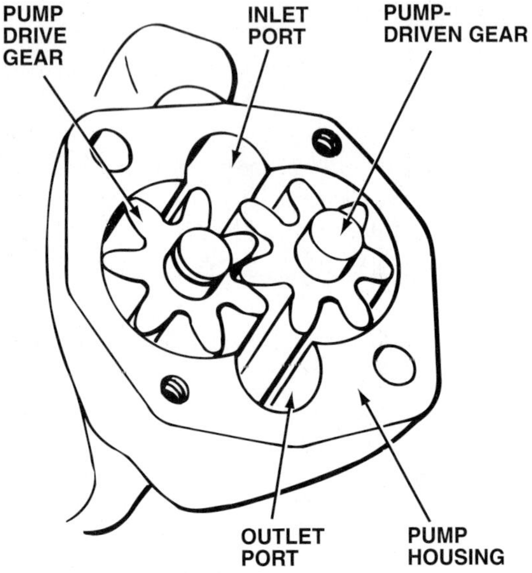

If the pump is shaft-driven, begin your inspection by examining the driveshaft. Look for signs of twisting, bending, or other distortion. Replace the shaft if anything appears questionable. The end of the shaft must fit snugly into the pump with virtually no free play. If the end is worn or rounded off, install a new driveshaft.

All oil pumps use a pickup tube and screen to filter large particles out of the intake oil. Any debris that can pass through the screen are small enough to pass through the pump without locking up the gears or rotors. The pickup may be bolted, threaded, or pressed onto the pump body or engine block. Remove the pickup assembly, wash it in solvent, and inspect the screen. If the screen shows any sign of damage, replace it.

Gear-Type Oil Pumps

Gear-type pumps use the meshing of two gears, a drive gear and an idler gear, to provide pressurized oil flow to the engine.

The gears fit into the pump housing and are held in place by the end cover. Remove the end cover to access the gears. Make sure there are clear index marks on the gears before you remove them from the pump body. If the gears are reused during assembly, these marks must be realigned for the best results.

Inspection and Measurement

Two measurements are used to determine if a gear pump is in serviceable condition:

- End clearance
- Gear-to-housing clearance

End Clearance

End clearance is the distance from the gear faces to the end cover. It is measured with a feeler gauge and a straightedge.

Place the pump on the workbench with the gears facing up and lay the straightedge across the pump. Clearance is equal to

Fig. 4-2. A gear pump uses the mesh of two straight-cut gears to pick up, pressurize, and deliver oil to the engine.

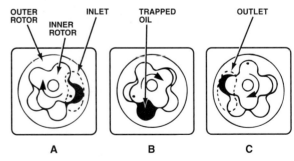

Fig. 4-3. A rotor pump uses lobes to pick up oil from the inlet port (A), trap it between the two rotors (B), then compress and push it through the outlet under pressure (C).

Oil Gallery: Pipes or drilled passages in the engine block that are used to carry engine oil from one area to another.
Sludge: Black, moist deposits that form in the interior of the engine. A mixture of dust, oil, and water whipped together by the moving parts.
Varnish: A hard, undesirable deposit formed by oxidation of fuel and motor oil.

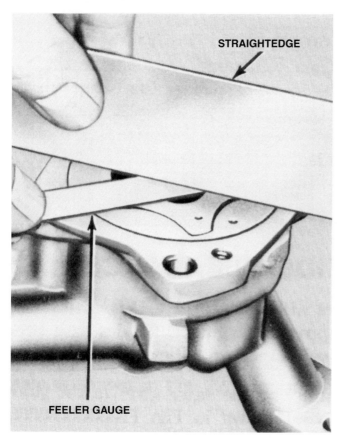

Fig. 4-4. Checking oil pump end clearance with a straightedge and feeler gauge.

the largest feeler gauge that fits between the gear faces and the straightedge, figure 4-4. In general, end clearance should be less than 0.003 inch.

Gear-to-Housing Clearance

Gear-to-housing clearance equals the largest feeler gauge that fits between a gear tooth and the housing. Measure both gears at several locations and rotate the gears to get readings on different teeth. Typically, gear-to-housing clearance should not exceed 0.005 inch.

Remove the gears and examine, for signs of wear, all of the contact surfaces of the:

- Gears
- Pump body
- End cover

Replace the pump if you find any deep scoring, chips, cracks, or other deformation. If the pump body is in good condition, you can install a rebuild kit and return the unit to service.

A rebuild kit includes:

- New gears
- Pressure relief valve spring
- Seals
- Gaskets

The pump housing's end plate develops a wear pattern and slight scoring from contacting the rotors under normal operating conditions. You can resurface the end plate if scoring is less than 0.003 inch deep.

Resurface the plate by lapping on a flat surface using wet or dry sandpaper lubricated with engine oil.

Rotor-Type Oil Pumps

All rotor pumps work on the same principle, but there are a number of different rotor designs in use.

With a rotor pump, an inner rotor is positioned off-center in the pump body and driven by an external power source, such as a driveshaft or the crankshaft. The outer rotor fits around, and is driven by, the inner rotor. The clearance between the two rotors is constantly changing. Oil is carried from large to small clearance areas between the rotors, then forced from the pump outlet under pressure.

Most rotor pumps can be readily disassembled for inspection. If the pump body is in good condition, install a rebuild kit and return the unit to service. A rebuild kit includes:

- New rotors
- Pressure relief valve spring
- Seals
- Gaskets

Remove the end cover to access the rotors. Check for index marks on the rotor faces. Although the rotors do not have to be aligned with each other on assembly, they both must face their original direction.

Inspection and Measurement

Three measurements are required on a rotor pump:

- End clearance
- Rotor-to-rotor clearance
- Rotor-to-housing clearance

All measurements are taken with a feeler gauge. End clearance is the distance from the rotor faces to the end cover and is measured using a straightedge as described for gear-type pumps.

To check rotor-to-rotor clearance, position the rotors so that a lobe on the inner rotor faces a lobe on the outer rotor, then measure between the lobes with a feeler gauge, figure 4-5. As a general rule, rotor-to-rotor clearance should be less than 0.010 inch.

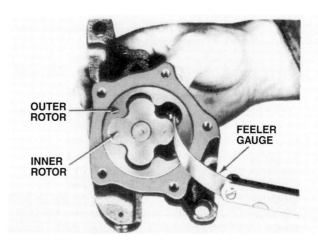

Fig. 4-5. Align inner and outer lobe tips and check oil pump rotor-to-rotor clearance with a feeler gauge.

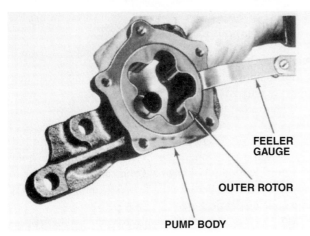

Fig. 4-6. Remove the inner rotor to check oil pump rotor-to-housing clearance with a feeler gauge.

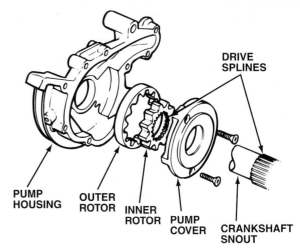

Fig. 4-7. The oil pump inner rotor splines to the crankshaft, and the pump assembles behind the timing cover on some engines.

Remove the inner rotor to measure rotor-to-housing clearance. Then, insert feeler gauge blades between the outer rotor and the pump body to measure the clearance, figure 4-6. Rotor-to-housing clearance equals the thickest feeler gauge blade that will fit the gap. If clearance exceeds 0.012 inch, replace the pump or install a rebuild kit.

Check all parts for scoring, chips, cracks, or other deformation and install a rebuild kit or replace the pump if any are found. You can resurface the end plate as previously described for gear pumps.

Crankshaft-Driven Oil Pumps
Crankshaft-driven pumps are rotor-type pumps that mount to the engine timing cover. The inner rotor slips over the crankshaft snout and is secured to the shaft by splines. The outer rotor fits into a pocket on the inside of the timing cover, and the pump assembly is held in place by a cover plate that bolts to the timing cover, figure 4-7. The service procedures for crankshaft-driven pumps are similar to those outlined for rotor pumps. However, tolerances are generally tighter.

Inspection and Measurement
It is often impossible to measure end clearance using a straightedge because the pump assembly is recessed into the front cover. Check end clearance, also known as rotor drop, using a depth micrometer. Position the micrometer so that it rests on the cover-mounting flange and straddles the opening, figure 4-8. Run the micrometer spindle down until the anvil contacts the rotor face, then take a reading. Acceptable tolerance is generally in the 0.001- to 0.004-inch range.

Measure rotor-to-rotor and rotor-to-housing clearances as previously described. Expect rotor-to-rotor clearance, also known as tip clearance, readings in the 0.004- to 0.009-inch range. Rotor-to-housing, or side clearance, should be slightly more, with an upper limit of about 0.015 inch.

Oil Pressure Relief Devices
The pressure relief valve is a component that is common to all oil pumps. Usually, a spring-loaded plunger bleeds off excess oil to maintain optimum pressure to the engine. The relief valve, which may be installed in the pump housing, timing

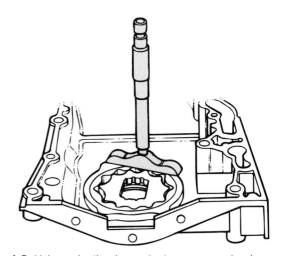

Fig. 4-8. Using a depth micrometer to measure rotor drop on a crankshaft-driven oil pump.

cover, or oil filter flange, is held in place by a threaded plug, cotter pin, roll pin, snap ring, cover plate, or other fastener.

Remove the fastener that holds the relief valve in place, then withdraw the plunger and spring from the bore. Pay close attention to how the pieces are assembled; installing them incorrectly can result in no oil pressure or excessive oil pressure. Wash the parts in clean solvent and inspect for signs of scoring or excessive wear. Clean the bore with a suitable brush. Measure the spring length and tension, compare to specifications, and replace as necessary.

Oil Pump Installation
When assembling an oil pump, remember that the gasket that seals the end housing to the pump body is manufactured to a specific thickness to provide the proper end clearance. Do not substitute any other gasket. Excessive end clearance results in an oil pressure loss, while insufficient clearance can cause binding and premature failure. Install the gasket without sealant. Using sealant can alter clearance. In addition, excess sealer can be drawn into the pump, restrict oil flow, and lead to engine damage.

You must prime the oil pump before you install it. If not primed, the pump will not circulate oil immediately on startup or it may not be able to pick up oil at all. Submerge the pump pickup in a container of clean engine oil and spin the rotors or gears by hand until the pump discharges a good stream of oil. Prime the pump with engine oil only. Do not pack a pump with grease, assembly lube, or other heavy lubricant unless specifically instructed to do so by the engine manufacturer.

After the pump is installed, the pickup screen must be positioned parallel to the bottom of the oil pan, with about ¼ to ⅜ inch of clearance between the screen and the pan. Measure clearance by taking two readings with a ruler.

Measure from the screen opening to the block pan rails, then from the floor of the sump to the flange on the oil pan. The difference between the two measurements is the clearance.

Always change the engine oil and replace the oil filter after servicing the oil pump. If engine contamination is suspected, inspect the filter as described in Chapter Two.

Oil Cooler Service

Some turbocharged and high performance engines are equipped with an engine oil cooler to reduce oil operating temperature. Engine oil coolers may be located in several locations.

- Inside the cylinder block (internal)
- Attached to the cylinder block (external)
- In the lower radiator tank
- In front of the radiator core

Oil Cooler Inspection

Before inspecting the oil cooler, ensure that the engine is cool. Never try to service the cooler on a hot engine, as injury or fire could result. External coolers should be visually inspected for signs of fluid leakage. Systems that use the engine coolant to cool the oil may show signs of cross-contamination of oil in the coolant and/or coolant in the oil if the cooler leaks.

Oil Cooler Leak Testing

If external leakage is not detected, remove the cooler and perform a pressure test:

1. Drain the coolant before removing the cooler
2. Remove the cooler and drain oil from the assembly
3. Clean the cooler by flushing with solvent and drying with compressed air
4. Cap or plug the oil passage outlet and apply 15 psi compressed air to the inlet port
5. Submerge the cooler assembly in a pan of water, completely covering the cooler assembly
6. Watch for bubbles, which indicate that air is escaping from the cooler
7. If no leak is observed, gradually increase the air pressure while continuing to watch for leakage. Do not exceed 75 psi during the test
8. If a leak is detected, replace the cooler assembly
9. If no leak is observed, reinstall the cooler using new gaskets or o-rings as required

COOLING SYSTEM SERVICE

Basic cooling system service consists of:

- System inspection
- System and component testing
- System cleaning
- Component replacement

Cooling System Inspection

To maintain normal operating temperatures, all of the cooling system components must be in good condition. Listening while the engine is running will often reveal cooling system problems. Listen for:

- An engine thump at normal temperature caused by a restriction in the **water jacket** or an incorrectly installed head gasket
- A screeching noise caused by a loose drive belt
- A buzz or whistle caused by a poor pressure cap seal or vibrating radiator fan shroud
- A ringing or grinding noise from a worn or damaged water pump bearing or loose drive belt pulley
- A gurgling from the radiator caused by a plugged radiator or air in the coolant

With the engine off, evaluate system condition by performing the following checks:

- The water pump drive belt must be correctly tensioned and free of any glazing, deterioration, or other damage
- Look at all hoses for hardness, cracks, or brittleness, softness or interior damage, and loose connections or leakage
- Look for signs of leakage around the core plugs, figure 4-9
- Inspect the radiator for oil, rust, or scale inside the filler neck, leakage at the tank seams, kinked or damaged

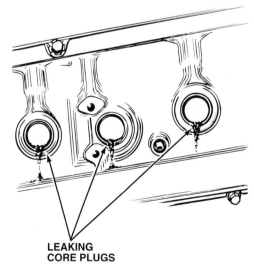

**LEAKING
CORE PLUGS**

Fig. 4-9. Check for signs of coolant leakage at the core plugs on the sides of the engine block.

A1

Water Jacket: The area in the block and head around the cylinders, valves, and spark plugs that is left hollow so the coolant can circulate.

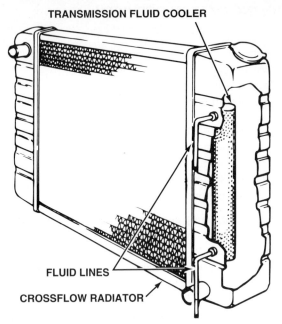

Fig. 4-10. Check for automatic transmission fluid cooler leakage and signs of damage to the lines and fittings while inspecting the radiator.

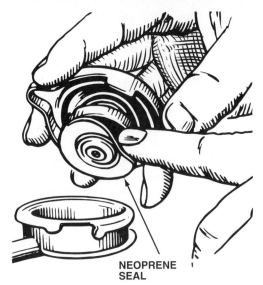

Fig. 4-11. Make sure the seal on the radiator cap is soft and pliable.

overflow tubes, and damage around the automatic transmission cooler lines, figure 4-10
• Inspect the radiator cap; it must fit securely on the filler neck. Also, check for a brittle cap seal, insufficient spring action, and correct pressure rating, figure 4-11
• Inspect the heater core for signs of leakage and loose connections
• Inspect the water pump for leakage at the shaft seal, bleed hole, and gasket. Check the pump for wobble, binding, or looseness when turned by hand
• Look for cooling fan blade misalignment or damage
• Check fan clutches for fluid leakage, noise or roughness when turned by hand, and excessive shaft endplay
• Check electric cooling fans for loose electrical connections and damaged wiring

Cooling System Testing

Cooling system tests generally include the coolant and performing system and radiator cap pressure tests. You may also want to test the thermostat's operation.

Coolant Checks

One aftermarket problem is that there is no way of knowing what kind of antifreeze is in a customer's cooling system when it comes into the shop. It may be the factory-fill coolant, an aftermarket coolant, a **propylene glycol** coolant, or a mixture of several different types of coolants. If you don't keep this in

mind, a simple coolant check with a **hydrometer** may provide a false indication of the coolant's strength. A **refractometer** is a better tool to use because it doesn't measure specific gravity; instead, it determines how the liquid bends light based on the liquid's density.

Chemical test strips are available to check the coolant's concentration and condition. But test strips designed for conventional green coolants won't give an accurate indication of the coolant's condition if used with some other types of coolant.

Testing Ethylene Glycol-Based Coolant

The concentration of **ethylene glycol** in the coolant and its relative protection against freezing and boil-over effectiveness is tested with a cooling system hydrometer. For accurate results, the coolant should be hot when tested. Before doing the test, draw a coolant sample into the hydrometer and return it to the radiator a few times to stabilize the hydrometer's internal thermometer. Test as follows:

1. Hold the hydrometer straight and draw enough coolant to raise the float, figure 4-12. The float should not touch the sides of the hydrometer
2. Take the reading at eye level, watching the top of the letter on the float that is touched by the coolant
3. Find this letter on the hydrometer scale and read down the column under the letter until you are opposite the thermometer reading
4. The number shown at this point is the degree of protection given by the coolant in the system

---

Ethylene Glycol (EG): A chemical solution used as an antifreeze and anti-boil agent. It reduces the freezing point of water and increases its boiling point.
Hydrometer: A device used to measure a fluid's specific gravity.
Propylene Glycol (PG): A less toxic chemical used for some coolant blends.
Refractometer: Tool used to accurately test coolant mixtures more accurately than traditional testers, through a liquid's ability to bend light.

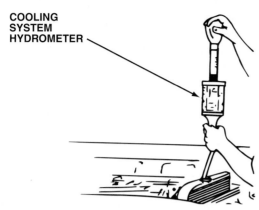

COOLING SYSTEM HYDROMETER

Fig. 4-12. A hydrometer checks the concentration and effectiveness of the coolant in the system.

Testing Propylene Glycol-Based Coolant

The best way to determine the concentration of PG in uncontaminated coolant (no EG present) is to use a refractometer; the specific gravity of PG increases up to about a 70% concentration, then falls off. Consequently, a 100% PG solution will read the same as a 45% solution on a hydrometer.

Organic Additive Technology

The latest corrosion-inhibiting additives are based on a different chemistry called "**Organic Additive Technology**" (**OAT**). Antifreeze with OAT corrosion inhibitors contains organic acid salts of mono- and dicarboxylic acids such as sebasic and octanoic acids, plus tolytriazole. The coolant is less alkaline and protects with a pH reading of only about 8.3. OAT coolant contains an orange dye to distinguish it from other coolants with conventional additive packages.

The main advantage of OAT technology is extended service life: up to five years or 150,000 miles. But to achieve this length of service, the OAT coolant must not be mixed with any other type of antifreeze. If the system is topped off with ordinary green antifreeze, the corrosion protection will be reduced to that of a conventional coolant, according to some coolant manufacturers.

Coolant Test Strips

Another method of testing a coolant's concentration is the use of a test strip. These strips are available through several suppliers. The strips test both ethylene and propylene glycol-based coolants, even mixtures of the two. Refer to the instructions provided with the strips. If none are available follow these steps:

1. Run the test in a well lit area (natural light if possible)
2. Antifreeze coolant sample should be between 40° and 110° F
3. Follow the enclosed test procedure on the back of the color chart
4. Dip the reactive (pad) end of the test strip into the antifreeze coolant

5. Compare the color of the test strip pad and the chart provided after one, but not more than three, minutes. (The pad's color will continue to change as the pad dries)
6. Below 50° F, read the color after two, but not more than five, minutes

Cooling System Pressure Test

A pressure test is performed on a cold engine that is not running. Remove the pressure cap to test the cooling system and the cap. Test procedures are detailed in Chapter One of this book.

Heater Core Testing

If the engine coolant level is low but the cooling system is not leaking, check the heater core. Coolant may leak from pinholes in the heater core in the form of steam, which enters the passenger compartment along with the heated air. When this air condenses against the cold windows, the coolant deposits there, forming a sticky, sweet-smelling residue. To pressure-test the heater core on the vehicle:

1. Drain the coolant
2. Disconnect the heater hoses from the heater core inlet and outlet tubes
3. Use adapters to connect a cooling system pressure tester to one heater core tube
4. Fill the heater core with water and seal off the other tube
5. Apply specified pressure with the hand pump and watch the gauge for at least three minutes:

   - If pressure holds for three minutes, the heater core is not leaking
   - If pressure drops, double-check the connection between the tester and heater core; if the leak is not there, remove the heater core for bench testing

Heater Core Bench Test

Removing the heater core from the vehicle may require considerable disassembly of the heating, ventilation, and air conditioning system plenum or ductwork. Once removed, bench test the core to locate the leak:

1. Drain the coolant and plug one heater core tube with a suitable stopper
2. Seal the other tube using a fitting with an air valve
3. Use a hand pump or low-pressure compressed air and charge the heater core to the recommended pressure
4. Submerge the pressurized heater core in a water bath and watch for a stream of bubbles from the leak

Some heater cores can be repaired by a radiator shop, while others must be replaced if a leak is found.

On-Car Thermostat Test

Thermostat opening temperature can be checked without removing the thermostat. Perform the test on a cold engine. Remove the radiator pressure cap and check and correct the coolant level. Then, test the thermostat as follows:

1. Place a thermometer, or a temperature-registering label, in the filler neck of the radiator

---

Organic Additive Technology (OAT): An additive with organic corrosion inhibiters.

2. Start the engine and monitor the thermometer as the engine warms up
3. Watch the coolant that is visible at the filler neck. As the thermostat opens and you see the coolant swirling around, note the thermometer reading

If the thermostat opened above or below its temperature rating, the unit is defective and should be replaced.

Electric Fan Test

An electric cooling fan that fails to engage is often the result of a defective **coolant temperature sensor** or switch. On most late model vehicles, the electric cooling fan is controlled by the **PCM**. Testing the control circuit can best be accomplished by following the manufacturer's troubleshooting procedures utilizing the appropriate **scan tool**. Most ECT failures will cause the PCM to set a **Diagnostic Trouble Code (DTC)** and illuminate the **Malfunction Indicator Lamp (MIL)**.

If the system does not control the fan with the PCM, check the switch as follows:

1. With the engine cold, disconnect the electrical connector from the coolant temperature switch. Connect an ohmmeter, or a self-powered test lamp. Most switch circuits are open when cold
2. Reconnect the switch connector. Start the engine and run it to normal operating temperature
3. If the fan does not engage, switch off the engine. Disconnect the switch connector and retest the circuit. If an open circuit is found, replace the switch

The fan motor can be checked quickly using a fused jumper wire. Disconnect the electrical connector from the coolant temperature switch and connect the jump wire across the connector's terminals. Switch on the ignition and the fan should run.

Note: On systems using the coolant temperature sensor, do not perform this test, as damage to the PCM may result.

Viscous Fan Clutch Test

The operation of a **viscous fan clutch** can be checked using a timing light and tachometer. Perform this procedure on a cold engine. Attach a thermometer to the engine side of the radiator so you can watch it during testing to prevent overheating. Perform the test as follows:

1. Connect the timing light and tachometer, then start the engine

2. Aim the timing light at the fan blades; they should appear to move slowly
3. Block the radiator to restrict air flow and promote rapid heat buildup. Keep an eye on the thermometer and do not allow the engine to overheat
4. When the thermometer indicates the fan clutch engagement point, remove the radiator cover and aim the timing light at the fan blades. Fan speed should increase as the clutch engages and the blades will appear to move faster in the timing light beam
5. Continue to watch the fan blades with the timing light as the coolant temperature drops. Fan speed should decrease once the temperature falls below the engagement point

Replace the fan clutch if it fails to engage or if it engages and disengages at an incorrect temperature.

Cooling System Cleaning

The cooling system should be completely drained and flushed once a year to prevent internal damage. If the system is regularly serviced and only light contamination is present, the system can be flushed with clean water.

1. Drain the old coolant by opening the radiator and engine drain plugs or by disconnecting the lower radiator hose
2. Remove the cap from the coolant recovery reservoir and use a suction gun to empty the contents
3. Remove the thermostat and reinstall the thermostat housing
4. Place a hose in the radiator filler neck and adjust the water flow to keep the water level at the top of the radiator while water is flowing out of the drains
5. Flush the system for 10 minutes. Run the engine at idle for a more thorough flushing
6. Reinstall the thermostat and close all the drains or reconnect the lower radiator hose
7. Fill the system with the recommended amount of coolant to the correct level
8. Refill the coolant reservoir to the "Cold" mark on the side
9. Start the engine and allow it to reach operating temperature
10. Check the entire system for leaks
11. Operate the heater to eliminate all air in the system

If the system is badly contaminated, it will need to be flushed with a chemical cleaner. Various methods and equipment may

---

Coolant Temperature Sensor: Often designated as the Engine Coolant Temperature (ECT) Sensor. A variable resistance sensor threaded into the engine coolant passage. Changes resistance as temperature varies.

Diagnostic Trouble Code: A numerical or alphanumerical code related to a specific system malfunction. DTCs are accessed or read with a scan tool.

Malfunction Indicator Lamp: Also known as the Check Engine Lamp. Illuminates to indicate a malfunction in the powertrain control system.

PCM: Powertrain Control Module. An OBD II term for the electronic computer that controls the engine and transmission.

Scan Tool: An electronic test device allowing the user to monitor computer controlled circuits and clear trouble codes.

Viscous Fan Clutch: A temperature sensing fan drive filled with a silicone fluid. As the temperature of the air passing the clutch increases, the internal valving in the clutch allows the fluid to flow into the coupling and increases the speed of the fan blade.

be used to flush the system. If using special equipment such as a back-flusher, follow the manufacturer's instructions.

If no flushing equipment is available, follow these steps to clean the cooling system.

1. Drain the system; refill with clean water and add chemical cleaner
2. Run the engine at fast idle for about 30 minutes. Do not allow the coolant to boil
3. Stop the engine and drain the system while the engine is still warm
4. Allow the engine to cool
5. Close the drains and fill the system with the recommended amount of **neutralizer** and water
6. Run the engine at fast idle for about 10 minutes, then stop the engine and drain the system completely
7. Disconnect all hoses from the coolant reservoir. Remove the reservoir and pour out any fluid. Scrub and clean the inside of the reservoir with soap and water
8. Reinstall the thermostat and fill the system, including the coolant recovery reservoir

Using either of the methods may also clean the internal passages of the heater core(s). Some vehicles require that the heater controls be placed in the "Heat" position to allow flow through the core. Feel the hoses leading to the heater(s) to ensure coolant is flowing during the flushing procedure.

If coolant does not flow through the heater core during the flushing procedure, follow the procedure under "Heater core flushing" in this chapter for more information.

Many late-model vehicles require bleeding to remove all of the trapped air when the cooling system is drained and refilled. These procedures vary by manufacturer, model, and engine. Check the appropriate service manual. Failure to properly bleed a cooling system can result in overheating.

Heater Core Flushing
A heater core can collect sediment or scale that insulates the heater core metal from the coolant and reduces the amount of heat available for the passenger compartment. Backflushing, which sends water through the heater core in the opposite direction from the normal coolant flow, removes this sediment without removing the heater core from the vehicle. To backflush:

1. Remove the heater hoses
2. Connect a drain hose to the inlet tube
3. Attach a hose and nozzle to the outlet and spray pressurized water through the heater core

Chemicals such as oxalic acid can also remove deposits. The acid breaks up oily, scaly deposits in the system that water cannot dissolve.

Component Replacement
Cooling system components that may periodically need replacement include:

- Drive belts
- Hoses and thermostat

Fig. 4-13. Checking drive belt tension by deflection.

- Core plugs
- Water pump
- Radiator
- Viscous fan clutch
- Electric fan motor
- Coolant temperature sensor or switch
- Air dam and seals
- Fan shroud

Replacing Drive Belts
Never force or pry a belt over pulley flanges. If the belt cannot be run into the grooves by rotating the pulley, move the driven accessory to obtain closer centers. With the belt removed, examine the pulleys for damage and misalignment. Replace pulleys as required and install the new belt.

Belts must be properly tensioned. A loose belt will slip, and a tight belt can damage bearings. Adjust tension to specifications by either the deflection method, figure 4-13, or using a tension gauge, figure 4-14. Tighten retaining bolts securely to maintain proper adjustment. Start the engine and watch how the belt rides in the pulley grooves. Ideally, the belt should be flush with, or not more than 1/16 inch above, the top of the pulley grooves. If it is too high, the belt sides will wear excessively. If it is too low, the belt will bottom on the grooves, wear prematurely, glaze, and eventually slip. Make sure the belt cross-section conforms to the angle of the pulley grooves. If it does not, recheck to ensure that the correct belt was installed.

Visually inspect pulleys for signs of damage and rotate them with the belt removed to check for free movement of the bearings. Replace the pulley or bearings if any damage is found, or if there is binding on rotation. Also, check for proper alignment between the pulleys. Pulley alignment is especially critical for serpentine belts. Incorrect pulley alignment loads the sides of a belt and leads to premature failure.

On engines that have an automatic belt tensioning device, inspect the tensioner whenever the belt is removed. Make sure the bearing is in good condition and allows the

---

Neutralizer: A chemical compound added to the cooling system to reduce the alkaline chemicals in the flushing solution.

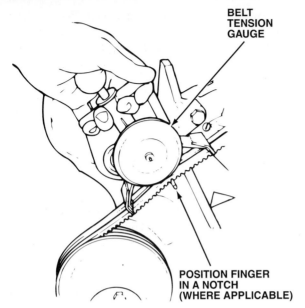

Fig. 4-14. Checking drive belt tension with a gauge.

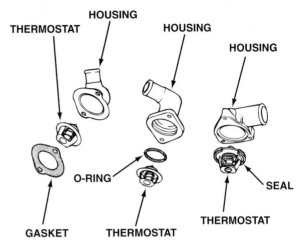

Fig. 4-15. Always replace the gasket or seal with a new one when installing a thermostat.

tensioner to rotate smoothly. Look for nicks, dings, or scratches that might damage the belt. With the belt installed, check belt tension to make sure the spring assembly is applying enough pressure to keep the belt taut.

After installing a new drive belt, allow the engine to run for at least 10 to 15 minutes. Switch the engine off, then recheck and adjust belt tension using "used" belt specifications.

Radiator and Heater Hose Service
Replace any brittle, cracked, or swollen hose. A hose that has defects on its outer surface will probably also be defective inside. Be sure the replacement hose is the same configuration as that of the original one. Trim the new hose to the proper length as needed. The installed hose must be free of kinks and twists. Draw the hose clamps up tight, but do not overtighten them to the point where they cut into the hose.

Thermostat Service
To access the thermostat, disconnect the radiator hose, remove the thermostat housing, and lift out the thermostat. Thermostats seal with either a gasket, O-ring, or rubber seal, figure 4-15. The seal, no matter which type is used, is always replaced when the thermostat is removed. Scrape off all traces of old gasket and sealant from both sealing surfaces. Once removed, the thermostat can be bench-tested as follows:

1. Suspend the thermostat and a thermometer in a heat-proof container and fill the container with water
2. Heat the water. Note the temperature when the thermostat begins to open and the temperature when it is fully open
3. Turn off the heat source. Note the temperature at which the thermostat is fully closed

The thermostat should begin to open when the temperature is about 3 to 9 degrees below the rated temperature. The

thermostat should be fully open when coolant temperature matches the rating. As it cools down, the thermostat should be fully closed when the coolant reaches the same temperature where opening began. Replace the thermostat if it did not perform as described.

Removing and Replacing Core Plugs
Any signs of moisture, rust, or coolant stains around a core plug indicate seepage. The plug should be replaced. A pressure test of the cooling system is an effective leakage test. If pressure bleeds down but you cannot spot a leak, feel for dampness around the core plugs.

Core plugs can be removed using a punch and hammer. Place the end of the punch on the edge of the plug and strike the punch with the hammer to turn the plug sideways in the bore. Be careful not to gouge or damage the sides of the plug bore with the punch. Once the plug is sideways, you can pry it out with a screwdriver or pull it free with a pair of pliers. Clean the sides of the bore with emery paper.

Cup-type plugs have two different shoulder heights; deep cup and shallow cup. The two designs cannot be interchanged. To select the correct depth, measure the thickness of the core holes.

Before installation, coat the sides of the core plug with gasket sealer. The plug is driven into the bore using a special installation tool. The cup must fit squarely in the bore. When properly installed, the edges of the cup will be slightly recessed into the engine block.

Water Pump Service
Here are some general tips to remember when replacing a water pump:

- First, drain the coolant
- Note the locations of bolts of different lengths. These must be returned to their original position, figure 4-16
- Use thread sealant when reinstalling bolts
- Make sure the pump gasket is aligned so that coolant bypass holes are not blocked

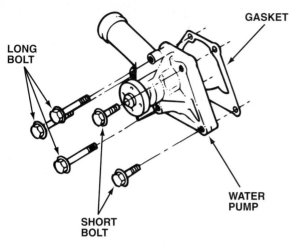

Fig. 4-16. Water pumps often attach to the block with different length bolts. Be sure to install them correctly.

- Be sure all mating surfaces are perfectly clean and use only non-hardening sealants
- Compare the old pump to the replacement before installing it. Be sure the pulley is correctly positioned to maintain belt alignment

Water pump replacement often requires a considerable amount of disassembly to access the pump. Ensure that all the parts that were removed are reinstalled and properly secured.

Viscous Fan Clutch Replacement
Viscous fan clutch replacement normally does not require removing the radiator. In many cases the fan shroud must be detached from the radiator and positioned as far rearward as possible to facilitate access to the fan and clutch attaching fasteners. Follow the appropriate service manual when replacing the clutch assembly.

Electric Fan Drive Motor Replacement
To replace the electric fan drive motor, make sure the ignition key is in the off position. Most fan motors are serviced by first removing the **cooling fan module** from the vehicle. One the module is removed, the motor can be serviced. Follow the appropriate service manual when performing fan motor service.

Engine Coolant Temperature Sensor (ECT) Replacement
To replace the coolant temperature sensor or switch, you first need to drain the coolant below the level of the sensor. Use the appropriate six-point deep socket to prevent damage to the sensor during the process. Depending on the system

the replacement sensor may have a sealant applied to the threaded portion. Do not add sealer to the threads of grounding type sensors or switches as they may rely on the electrical connection between the sensor and the engine to function correctly.

After installation, operate the vehicle and check for proper operation of the engine cooling fan and ensure that no DTCs are present.

Radiator Removal and Replacement
Radiators generally need repairs or replacement only after years of service or neglect. Infrequent cooling system flushing can cause built-up sediment and contaminants to block the internal passages of the radiator and restrict coolant flow. A clogged radiator must be removed and disassembled to be repaired. Normally, **rodding** the passages is sufficient to return the unit to service. In extreme cases, the radiator core will need to be replaced. Both services are generally performed at a specialty shop.

When installing radiators, ensure that all rubber mounts are in good condition. Transmission cooler tubes and hoses must be securely attached with all the mounting brackets in place. Also, check all hose and transmission cooler connections for tightness. Check for leakage after running the engine.

Air Dam and Seal Service and Replacement
Many vehicles are equipped with **air dams** and/or seals designed to prevent air from bypassing the radiator core. Missing or damaged components may cause the vehicle to overheat. Refer to the applicable service or body shop manuals for the location of these components.

Fan Shroud Service and Replacement
Inspect the **fan shroud** to ensure it is correctly installed and undamaged. The shroud has two major functions. First, it creates a safety barrier between the rotating fan blades and anyone servicing underhood components. Second, it seals the area between the fan and the radiator, preventing air from bypassing the core. In many vehicles, overheating will result if the shroud is damaged or missing.

Damaged shrouds on rear wheel drive vehicles may be the result of excessive engine movement. Check the engine mounts to ensure the engine is not allowed to move far enough for the fan blades to contact the shroud. Replace the mounts if required.

When installing the shroud, make sure that all fasteners are installed correctly. Before starting the engine, rotate the fan blade by hand to ensure sufficient clearance between the fan blades and the shroud.

A1

Air Dam: Body component designed to control or direct the flow of air through or around the vehicle. In the cooling system, it is designed to force air to pass through the radiator core to improve cooling.
Cooling Fan Module: Refers to the combination of the fan drive motor, fan blade, and the housing or shroud.
Fan Shroud: Housing located around the fan for the purpose of utilizing the full drawing power of the fan.
Rodding: A method of repairing a radiator by running a drill bit through the internal passages of the core.

CHAPTER QUESTIONS

1. The cause of an overheating engine with an automatic transmission: Technician A says that engine timing could be the problem. Technician B says that a vehicle pulling a heavy trailer could be the cause. Who is right?
   a. A only
   b. B only
   c. Both A and B
   d. Neither A nor B

2. A false indication of excessive oil flow can occur if:
   a. The oil galleries in the block and the oil holes in the bearings are aligned
   b. There is excessive valve lash
   c. The warning lamps or indicators are malfunctioning
   d. Oil dilution has occurred from a rupture in the fuel pump diaphragm

3. When installing an oil pump, it should be primed with:
   a. Assembly lube
   b. Petroleum jelly
   c. Motor oil
   d. High-pressure lubricant

4. Oil pump tip clearance is the same as:
   a. Rotor drop clearance
   b. End clearance
   c. Rotor-to-housing clearance
   d. Rotor-to-rotor clearance

5. An oil pressure relief may be located in any of the following locations, **EXCEPT:**
   a. Oil pump housing
   b. Oil filler neck
   c. Oil filter flange
   d. Timing cover

6. With the engine running, an engine thump at normal temperature can mean:
   a. A loose drive belt
   b. A poor pressure cap seal
   c. A restriction in the water jacket
   d. A worn water pump

7. A V-type drive belt that rides too low and bottoms in the pulley groove causes:
   a. Premature wear, glazing, and slippage
   b. The belt sides to wear excessively and split
   c. High belt tension that can lead to bearing damage
   d. The belt to bind, seize, and eventually break

8. The rated temperature of a thermostat indicates:
   a. The temperature where it begins to open
   b. The temperature where it is fully open
   c. The temperature where it fully closes
   d. The thermostat bypass temperature

9. A thermometer, timing light, and tachometer can be used to check the operation of:
   a. The cooling system
   b. The thermostat
   c. An electric fan
   d. A fan clutch

10. A pressure tester can be used to:
    a. Test thermostats
    b. Test radiators, pressure caps, and hoses
    c. Test for exhaust leaks into the cooling system
    d. Test the coolant

CHAPTER FIVE

FUEL, ELECTRICAL, IGNITION, AND EXHAUST SYSTEMS INSPECTION AND SERVICE

CHAPTER OBJECTIVES

- The technician will complete the ASE task list on Fuel, Electrical, Ignition and Exhaust Systems Inspection and Service.
- The technician will be able to answer 7 questions dealing with the Fuel, Electrical, Ignition and Exhaust Systems Inspection and Service section of the A1 ASE test.

This chapter discusses various components of the subsystems that are required on a running engine. Many of these systems are addressed in other ASE certification examinations, and successfully passing the A1 test requires only general or basic knowledge of these systems. Therefore, the following discussions are brief and do not cover all aspects of each system. For additional information, refer to the appropriate volume in this series.

FUEL SYSTEM TESTING AND SERVICE

A constant flow of clean, pressurized fuel and filtered air must be supplied to ensure proper combustion. These requirements are handled by the fuel and air supply systems. A fuel pump must deliver enough fuel at the correct pressure to the engine in order to maintain efficient combustion. Two types of fuel pumps are used:

- Mechanical
- Electric

Both types can usually be checked for pressure and volume.

Mechanical Pump Testing

Mechanical fuel pumps are used on many older carburetor-equipped engines. A mechanical fuel pump is checked for delivery pressure and volume.

Pressure Test

Pressure testing is performed using a pressure gauge normally calibrated for a range of 0-30 psi. To test:

1. Remove the air cleaner and connect a tachometer to the engine
2. Disconnect the fuel inlet line at the carburetor and install a tee in the line. Connect the ends of the tee to the supply line and the third port to the gauge, figure 5-1
3. Start and run the engine at the specified rpm. Compare the pressure reading to specifications
4. Stop the engine. Pressure should hold for several minutes

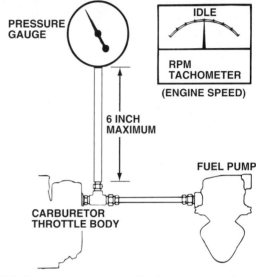

Fig. 5-1. Pressure gauge connection for pressure testing a mechanical fuel pump.

Volume Test

To check fuel pump volume:

1. Disconnect the fuel supply line at the carburetor and attach a length of fuel hose, figure 5-2. If a fuel filter is used, do not remove it
2. Place the free end of the tubing into a graduated container
3. Start the engine and run it at 500 rpm for 15 seconds while monitoring the fuel level in the container
4. Note the fluid level at 15 seconds, then multiply by four to get a one-minute reading

Most mechanical fuel pumps can deliver approximately 1 quart or liter of fuel in one minute or less.

Low volume is often caused by a restriction somewhere in the supply line. Check the fuel filter and replace if needed. Also, look for bent, kinked, dented, or leaking fuel lines and hoses. If you suspect that the fuel pump pickup is clogged by contamination in the fuel tank, clear the pickup by applying a short blast of low-pressure compressed air through the fuel-feed line, then repeat the volume test.

Other causes of low fuel pump volume include a worn or broken pump **eccentric**, pushrod, rocker arm, or linkage.

Eccentric: Off center or out of round. A shaft lobe which has a center different from that of the shaft.

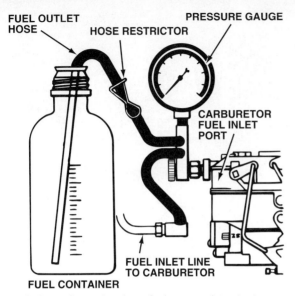

Fig. 5-2. Setup for performing a fuel pump volume test.

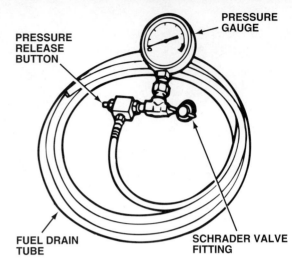

Fig. 5-3. Fuel injection system pressure testing requires a high-pressure gauge.

Replace the pushrod or pump, then repeat the test. If volume is still low, the eccentric is worn and the camshaft needs replacement.

Electric Pump Testing

Pressure and volume test procedures are identical for a carburetor-equipped engine, whether it has a mechanical or electric fuel pump. If testing the pump with the engine not running, bypass the pump control wiring and supply battery voltage directly to the pump. Many late model vehicle fuel pumps can be actuated utilizing a scan tool. Refer to the appropriate service manual for the procedure. In addition to pressure and volume testing, check the pump electrical circuits for:

- System voltage
- Good ground connections
- All other electrical connections

The electric pumps used on fuel-injection systems operate at higher pressures, and the test gauge must be able to register pressures that are higher than the system maximum. Typically, a low-pressure, throttle-body, injection system operates on 10 to 15 psi of pressure, while most electronic fuel-injection systems require 35-50 psi of fuel pressure. Many of the newer returnless fuel-injection system pumps provide up to 75 psi of pressure. Always check the specifications and use a test gauge that can register more than the maximum, figure 5-3.

Almost all fuel injection systems retain pressure in the fuel lines when the engine is off. As a safety precaution, relieve fuel system pressure before opening fittings to connect the test gauge or make repairs.

Relieving Fuel Pressure

There are several methods of relieving fuel pressure; follow the recommendations of the vehicle manufacturer. You may have to:

- Apply vacuum to the fuel pressure regulator using a hand-vacuum pump, figure 5-4

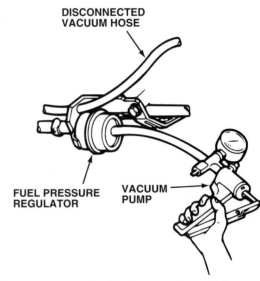

Fig. 5-4. Relieving residual fuel pressure by applying vacuum to the pressure regulator.

- Attach a special pressure gauge to a **Schrader valve** on the throttle body or fuel rail
- Remove the fuel pump fuse and run the engine until it dies
- Remove the wiring harness connector from a fuel injector, then jump one of the injector terminals to ground and apply battery voltage to the other

Pressure Test

Specifications are usually given for the system-regulated pressure supplied to the injectors. Excess pressure produced by the pump is returned to the fuel tank. A vacuum pump may be required to take readings with and without vacuum applied to the pressure regulator.

Attach the gauge as instructed by the manufacturer to test system pressure. Start the engine and make sure the pressure is

---

Schrader Valve: A service valve that uses a spring-loaded pin and internal pressure to seal a port; depressing the pin will open the port.

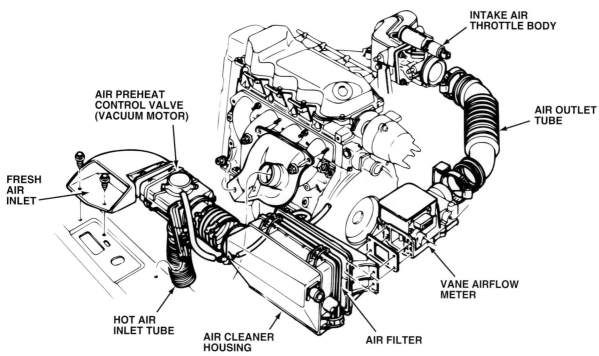

Fig. 5-5. Inspect the entire air intake ductwork for signs of leakage and damage.

within specifications at all speeds and conditions. When specifications for rest, or **residual pressure**, are provided, shut the engine off and leave the gauge attached. Check the gauge reading after waiting the recommended time.

Low system pressure readings may be caused by a faulty fuel pump, accumulator, pressure relief valve, or clogged fuel filter. Low residual pressure is generally the result of a defective pump check valve.

Volume Test
When a pump volume test is specified, it is measured at the fuel return line. Disconnect the return line, attach a piece of fuel hose to the line fitting, and route the open end of the hose into a suitable container. Start the engine and confirm that the specified amount of fuel is delivered within the time allowed.

Fuel System Service
Replacing the fuel filter is generally the only routine service performed on the fuel system. Replace the filter at the recommended interval.

Carburetor-equipped engines may have an inline filter installed in the fuel supply line with hose clamps. Some use a filter that installs into the fuel inlet on the carburetor. Remove the supply line fitting with a flare-nut wrench to access the filter.

Fuel injection systems use an inline filter. It may be located in the engine compartment, or underneath the vehicle near the fuel pump. Some injection filters use flare-nut fittings to attach to the lines. Relieve residual pressure before disconnecting the filter.

AIR INDUCTION SYSTEM
The air induction system supplies the engine with a steady stream of fresh air, which is blended with the fuel to create a combustible mixture. The air induction system consists of:

- Air intake ductwork
- Air cleaner and filter element
- Intake preheat system
- Manifold heat control valves
- Intake manifold

In addition, the air induction system on some engines includes a **turbocharger** or **supercharger** to boost the power output of the engine. The positive crankcase ventilation (PCV) system can also be considered part of the induction system, because the crankcase vapors vent into the intake charge.

AIR INTAKE DUCTWORK
A typical air intake system is a complex system of ducts, filters, meters, valves, and tubes, figure 5-5. Intake ductwork must be airtight to prevent entry of contaminants and potential loss of air volume to the engine. On a fuel-injected engine, air leakage downstream of the **airflow sensor** can create a lean condition and affect performance. Replace components as needed to maintain system integrity.

Air Filter Service
Carburetor-equipped and throttle-body injected engines have the air filter mounted directly to the carburetor or throttle body.

Airflow Sensor: A sensor used to measure the rate, density, temperature, or volume of air entering the engine.
Residual Pressure: A constant pressure held in the fuel system when the pump is not operating.
Supercharger: A crankshaft-driven compressor that delivers an air-fuel mixture to the engine cylinders at a pressure greater than atmospheric pressure.
Turbocharger: A compressor device that uses exhaust gases to turn a turbine that forces the air-fuel mixture into the cylinders.

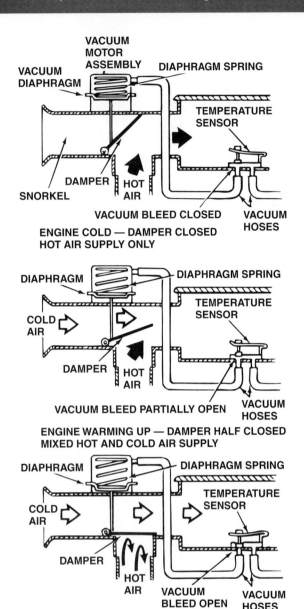

Fig. 5-6. Vacuum-actuated hot air control valve uses a temperature-sensitive switch to open and close a blend door.

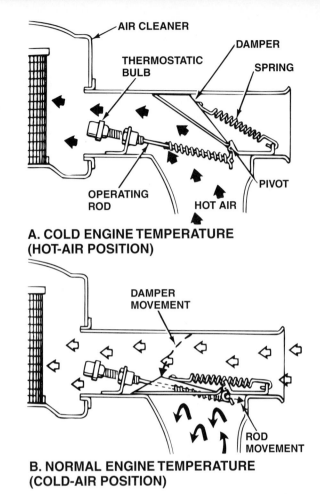

A. COLD ENGINE TEMPERATURE (HOT-AIR POSITION)

B. NORMAL ENGINE TEMPERATURE (COLD-AIR POSITION)

Fig. 5-7. A thermostatic bulb responds to temperature changes to open and close a blend door.

To replace the filter element, remove the fasteners holding the housing cover, lift off the cover, and take out the element. Check top and bottom seals for dust leakage and check the filter material for breaks. A paper element cannot be cleaned and must be replaced if it is dirty or torn.

Most fuel-injected engines use a flat filter element installed in a remote air cleaner housing. Some of the ductwork may have to be disconnected and moved aside or removed to access the filter housing. Unfasten the clips holding the housing together, then lift out the element. Replace the element if it is dirty or torn.

INTAKE AIR PREHEAT SYSTEMS

Some vehicles utilize air cleaners designed to control the temperature of the intake air. This speeds warm up and reduces the amount of **hydrocarbon** (HC) and **carbon monoxide** (CO) emissions on a cold running engine. There are three basic tests for these systems:

- Vacuum diaphragm test
- Temperature sensor test
- **Thermostatic bulb** test

The vacuum diaphragm and temperature sensor tests are used to check systems with vacuum-actuated hot air control valves, figure 5-6. The third test is for systems that use the hot air damper controlled by a thermostatic bulb, figure 5-7.

Carbon Monoxide: An odorless, colorless, tasteless, poisonous gas. A pollutant produced by an internal combustion engine.
Hydrocarbon: A chemical compound of hydrogen and carbon. A major pollutant from an internal combustion engine. Gasoline itself is a hydrocarbon compound.
Thermostatic Bulb: A device that automatically responds to changes in temperature to actuate a damper in the intake passage.

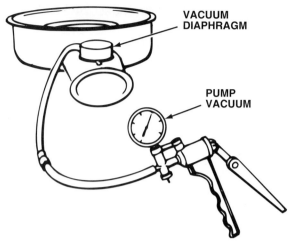

Fig. 5-8. Use a handheld vacuum pump to test the diaphragm on a vacuum motor.

Vacuum Motor Test

Vacuum motor function is tested with a hand-held vacuum pump as follows:

1. Inspect all hoses for correct routing and connections
2. Note the cold damper position with the engine off. It should cover the hot air passage and allow only cool air into the air cleaner
3. Disconnect the hose and attach the hand-operated pump to the vacuum motor, figure 5-8
4. Apply nine inches of mercury (in-Hg) to the vacuum, and the damper should close off the cool air and allow only hot air from the exhaust manifold
5. With vacuum applied, clamp the line from the vacuum source. The damper should stay closed

Sensor Test

Test the temperature sensor by placing a thermometer inside the air cleaner near the sensor. Then, start and run the engine while watching the damper door. As soon as the damper begins to open, note the air on the thermometer. Continue watching and note the temperature at which the damper door is fully open. If either reading is not within specifications, replace the sensor.

Thermostatic Bulb Test

A bench test is performed to check the function of a thermostatic bulb, and the entire air cleaner assembly must be removed from the vehicle. To test:

1. Disconnect and remove the intake duct and damper assembly from the air cleaner housing
2. Place the duct assembly in a hot water bath; water temperature should be about 100°F
3. Allow to soak for five minutes, then check the damper position. It should close off the cool air duct
4. Heat the water to maintain a temperature between 130° and 150°F
5. Soak for five minutes and recheck the damper position. It should now close off the hot air inlet. If it does not, the bulb is defective

INTAKE MANIFOLD

Intake manifolds seal to the cylinder head with a gasket to provide airtight passages to the combustion chambers. Engine coolant circulates through most intake manifolds, and the intake manifold on a V-type engine seals to the engine block to seal off the lifter valley. Therefore, manifold-to-engine sealing must prevent air, coolant, and oil leakage.

Manifold sealing surfaces must be clean, flat, and in good condition. Inspect all of the surfaces before you install the manifolds, and check for warpage using a straightedge and feeler gauge. Be sure the ports and all passageways are free of carbon and any other deposits. Check-fit the gaskets to make sure they will seal properly and all of the openings line up.

A1

Installation

Intake manifold gaskets normally install dry, without any sealer. Some engines use small, O-ring seals for the coolant passages in addition to the manifold gasket. If not, a thin bead of RTV silicone around coolant passages prevents coolant leakage. A small dab of silicone sealant is also recommended at the corners of the end seals on a V-type engine to prevent oil leakage. Although the exact procedure varies by engine, the following installation guidelines apply to any intake manifold:

- Check all of the sealing surfaces on the manifold, cylinder heads, and engine block. Make sure they are clean and free from any old gasket material and sealer
- Position the manifold on the engine, then install all of the retaining bolts hand-tight. Make sure bolts are in the correct location; several different length bolts may be used
- Check that all brackets, ground cables, and other attachments that are held in place by the manifold bolts are correctly positioned
- Tighten bolts to recommended torque in sequence as specified by the manufacturer. Tighten the bolts evenly in stages

TURBOCHARGER SERVICE

A turbocharger is an exhaust-driven compressor used to increase an engine's power output. The system requires no maintenance other than more frequent engine oil and filter changes. Turbocharger malfunctions usually fall into one of the following categories:

1. Lack of proper lubrication caused by the wrong type of oil, a restricted oil supply line, or a worn engine that develops low oil pressure
2. Dirty or contaminated oil system caused by infrequent oil changes, or failure of an engine bearing, piston ring, or other internal component, or an oil filter bypass valve stuck open
3. Contamination in the air intake or exhaust systems caused by a leaking air duct or missing air cleaner, or a damaged catalytic converter (when installed between the turbocharger and the exhaust manifold)

LACK OF POWER OR EMITS BLACK EXHAUST SMOKE

POSSIBLE CAUSE	CORRECTION
Damaged or disconnected air cleaner ducting	Inspect and correct
Restricted air filter element	Replace air filter
Intake or exhaust manifold leak	Check turbocharger installation for air or exhaust leak
Turbocharger damage	Check turbocharger rotating assembly for binding or dragging
Exhaust system restriction	Check exhaust system; check manifold heat control valve
Carburetor or fuel injection problem	Inspect and correct
Incorrect ignition timing, advance–or other ignition problem	Inspect and correct
EGR problem	Inspect and correct
Lack of compression or other engine wear	Inspect and correct
Low boost pressure	Check boost pressure and wastegate operation; adjust or replace as required

Fig. 5-9. Turbocharger black smoke/lack of power troubleshooting chart.

HIGH OIL CONSUMPTION OR EMITS BLUE EXHAUST SMOKE

POSSIBLE CAUSE	CORRECTION
Excessive blowby or PCV problem	Check for engine wear; service PCV system
Engine oil leakage	Inspect and correct
Worn engine rings, cylinders, valves, valve guides	Check for engine wear; check for low compression and cylinder leakage
Leaking turbocharger oil seals*	Replace turbocharger
Restricted turbocharger oil return or too much oil in center housing	Check oil return line for restrictions and blow out with compressed air; check center housing for sludge; clean as required
Carburetor or fuel injection problem	Inspect and correct
Incorrect ignition timing, advance, or other ignition problem	Inspect and correct
EGR problem	Inspect and correct

*Smoke and detonation indicate a leak on the compressor side; smoke alone indicates a leak on the turbine side.

Fig. 5-10. Turbocharger high oil consumption/blue smoke troubleshooting chart.

Troubleshooting

Turbocharger problems are generally revealed by: a lack of power or heavy black smoke from the tailpipe, figure 5-9, high oil consumption or blue smoke from the tailpipe, figure 5-10, or abnormal sounds, figure 5-11. Use the troubleshooting charts to isolate the cause of turbocharger malfunctions.

TURBOCHARGER PROBLEMS

SOUND	CAUSE
Louder than normal noise that includes hissing	Exhaust leak
Uneven sound that changes in pitch	Restricted air intake from a clogged air cleaner filter, bent air ducting, or dirt on the compressor blades
Higher than normal pitch sound	Intake air leak
Sudden noise reduction, with smoke and oil leakage	Turbocharger failure
Uneven noise and vibration	Possible shaft damage, damaged compressor or turbine wheel blades
Grinding or rubbing sounds	Shaft or bearing damage, misaligned compressor or turbine wheel
Rattling sound	Loose exhaust pipe or outlet elbow, damaged wastegate

Fig. 5-11. Turbocharger abnormal sounds troubleshooting chart.

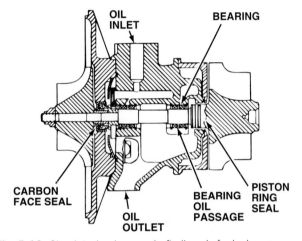

Fig. 5-12. Check turbocharger shaft oil seals for leakage.

Inspection and Service

Perform a preliminary turbocharger inspection as follows:

1. Check that the air cleaner is in place and that there are no loose connections or leaks, restrictions, or broken ducting
2. Examine the exhaust system for burned areas, leakage, and loose connections
3. Disconnect the turbocharger air inlet and exhaust outlet and inspect the turbine and compressor with a flashlight and a mirror. Look for bent or broken blades and wear marks on the blades or housing
4. Turn the wheel by hand. Listen and feel for binding or rubbing. Move both ends of the shaft up and down. There should be little, if any, movement
5. Check the shaft seal areas, figure 5-12, for signs of oil leakage

Turbocharger service consists of testing the **boost pressure** and checking the **wastegate** operation. A turbocharger can be

---

Boost Pressure: The amount of air pressure increase above atmospheric pressure provided by a turbocharger.
Wastegate: A diaphragm-actuated bypass valve used to limit turbocharger boost pressure by limiting the speed of the exhaust turbine.

disassembled, internal components replaced, and clearances set with a dial indicator. However, common practice is to simply replace a defective unit.

Checking Turbocharger Boost Pressure

Boost pressure can be checked during a road test, or on a chassis dynamometer, using a pressure gauge. Connect the gauge to a pressure port on the compressor side of the turbo, or tee it into the line running to the warning lamp pressure switch. Test with the engine at normal operating temperature. Accelerate from zero to 40 or 50 mph and note the gauge reading under load. Repeat several times and compare results to specifications.

Checking the Wastegate Actuator

The wastegate is a pressure relief device that protects the system from overcharging. Test the wastegate actuator as follows:

1. Connect a hand-operated pressure pump and gauge to the actuator
2. Apply about five psi of pressure. If pressure drops below two psi after one minute, the actuator diaphragm is leaking
3. Clamp or mount a dial indicator on the turbocharger housing so the plunger contacts the actuator rod
4. Apply the specified boost pressure to the actuator diaphragm and note the amount of rod movement shown on the indicator. If not within specifications, generally less than 0.015 inch, repair or replace the actuator
5. Remove the fastener that holds the rod to the wastegate arm or link, then move the arm. It should travel freely through a 45-degree arc. If not, replace the wastegate

SUPERCHARGER SERVICE

A supercharger is a crankshaft-driven, positive-displacement pump that supplies an excess volume of intake air to the engine. The supercharger boosts the pressure and density of the intake air charge to increase engine output. A typical supercharger consists of two lobed rotor shafts supported by bearings in a cast housing. The two shafts are geared together, so they rotate in opposite directions. One of the shafts is driven off the crankshaft by a belt.

The supercharger supplies boost whenever the engine is running. Most units use a vacuum-operated bypass valve to bleed off excess boost pressure during idle and low-speed operation.

With the exception of belt inspection and adjustment, a supercharger does not require maintenance. Bearings are lubricated by a self-contained oiling system. Some systems allow you to check the oil level; a low oil level indicates an internal problem. Typical problems include:

- Incorrect boost
- Poor response and fuel economy
- Excessive noise
- Oil leakage

Many problems result from a malfunctioning boost control or bypass valve. Valve operation can quickly be checked using a hand-operated vacuum pump. On some systems, you can check boost using a pressure gauge. Boost pressure will vary from about 3.5 to 11 psi, depending on test speed; check specifications for the unit being tested. For the most part, internal components are not serviceable. If a problem is detected, replace the assembly.

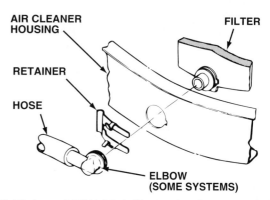

Fig. 5-13. Inspect PCV inlet air filters and replace as needed.

A1

POSITIVE CRANKCASE VENTILATION (PCV) SYSTEM

The PCV system is relatively simple and most problems are the result of built-up deposits that restrict or prevent air flow. A blocked PCV system may cause:

- Increased oil consumption
- Diluted or dirty oil from sludge, water, or acid in the crankcase
- Escaping blowby vapors from the dipstick tube, oil fill tube, valve-cover gasket areas, and other openings to the crankcase
- Uneven or rich fuel mixture at idle and low speed

Inspection and Testing

Service the PCV system by looking at it, operating it, and replacing defective parts. To inspect:

1. Check all hoses for proper connections, cracks, and clogging
2. Remove the air cleaner cover and check the filter element. Crankcase blowby can clog the filter with oil
3. Check the crankcase inlet air filter, if equipped. The filter may be in the air cleaner or air hose, figure 5-13, or in the valve cover or oil fill cap
4. Check for deposits that clog the passages in the manifold

Vacuum Test

Several testers are available to check overall PCV system operation. Some measure pressure in the crankcase. Others test the flow rate at engine idle speed.

When a PCV tester is not available, hold a small piece of stiff paper over the oil fill opening with the engine idling. Crankcase vacuum should pull the paper down against the opening if the system is working properly. If not, or if the paper is blown upward, the system is not working right.

Engine Speed Drop Test

Use the following method to test the PCV system when you do not have a PCV tester, or when the results of the vacuum test are not conclusive:

1. Connect a tachometer and start the engine
2. Disconnect the PCV valve and the line from the crankcase
3. Place a finger over the valve and watch the tachometer
4. Engine speed should drop by 40 rpm or more if the system is working correctly

PCV Valve Test

As a general rule, PCV valves are replaced at recommended service intervals. Replace the valve more often if it fails any test or inspection check. To test a PCV valve:

1. Disconnect the PCV valve from the valve cover or manifold
2. Run the engine at idle. The valve should make a hissing noise as air passes through it
3. Put a finger over the end of the PCV valve. You should feel a strong vacuum. If not, check for a clogged valve or restricted hose
4. Shut off the engine and remove the valve. Shake the valve and listen for the rattle or clicking of the needle in the valve. If not, the valve is bad

PCV SYSTEM SERVICE

Service of the PCV system usually consists of cleaning or replacing the system air filter, or replacing the connecting hoses or the valve itself.

Filter Replacement

On some engines, the PCV inlet air is filtered through the engine air filter. Simply replace the element at the recommended interval. The same is true of separate polyurethane foam filter elements that mount in the air cleaner housing. If a wire screen filter is used, clean it in solvent and allow it to dry.

Filters installed in the oil filler cap are usually made of wire mesh. Remove the filler cap and soak the complete cap and filter in solvent. Allow it to drain and dry in the air. Do not use compressed air to dry these filters because the air pressure will damage the wire mesh.

Hose Replacement

Any damaged or deteriorated hoses must be replaced to ensure proper system operation. Use only hoses designed for PCV and fuel system applications. Standard heater hoses will not withstand the blowby vapors.

PCV Valve Replacement

A PCV valve cannot be distinguished by its appearance; internal valve characteristics are specifically calibrated for each application. Always refer to the part number when you replace a valve. To replace a valve, simply install the new part in place of the old one. Make sure the valve is installed with the arrow indicating the direction of flow pointing toward the intake manifold. If the valve is mounted in a rubber grommet, make sure it is a snug fit. If the grommet is hardened or cracked, replace it.

ELECTRICAL SYSTEM INSPECTION AND SERVICE

The field of engine repair includes tasks that would normally be considered part of the electrical system. The following discussion provides general guidelines for evaluating, removing, replacing, and servicing the battery and starter motor. For more detailed information, see book six of this series.

Battery Service

When working near, or servicing, a battery, follow these safety rules:

- Keep area clear of sparks, smoking materials, and open flame
- Operate charging equipment only in well-ventilated areas
- Never short across the battery terminals or cable connectors
- Never connect or disconnect charger leads while the charger is on
- Remove watches, rings, or other jewelry before working on, or near, the battery or electrical systems
- Use a battery carrier to lift and carry batteries

Inspection

The **electrolyte** level should be above the tops of the plates or at the indicated level within the cells. Add distilled or mineral-free water to refill. Inspect the battery case, terminals, connectors, and holddown tray for rust, corrosion, and damage. Check the battery for cracks, loose terminal posts, or other damage, and replace the battery if defective.

Clean the battery with a solution of baking soda and water. Be careful to keep corrosion off painted surfaces and rubber parts. Rinse the battery and cable connections with fresh water. Disconnect and clean the terminal connections.

For post-type terminals, use connector-spreading pliers to open the connector, then clean the inside of the connectors and the posts with a brush or reamer. On side-terminal batteries, remove the bolts and clean the threads and contact surfaces with a wire brush. Inspect for damage and corrosion; replace the terminal ends or the cables as required.

State of Charge Testing

If the battery has removable vent caps, the state of charge can be checked using a hydrometer to test **specific gravity**. Remove the cell caps, insert the hydrometer into a cell, and draw electrolyte into the tester, figure 5-14. Gently shake or tap the hydrometer to keep the float from touching the sides of the tube. Hold the hydrometer at eye level and read specific gravity on the indicator. Return the electrolyte to the cell, then check the remaining cells.

Specific gravity readings for a fully charged battery should be 1.265, figure 5-15. Specific gravity is based on an electrolyte temperature of 80°F. Four points (0.004) should be added or subtracted to the readings for each 10°F difference in temperature. If corrected readings are below 1.225, recharge the battery. The battery should be replaced if readings vary by more than 50 points (0.050) between cells.

Battery Charging

Batteries can be charged at rates from 3 amperes (slow charging) to 50 amperes (fast charging). Generally, any battery in

---

Electrolyte: The chemical solution, generally sulfuric acid and water, in a battery that conducts electricity and reacts with the plate materials.

Specific Gravity: The weight of a volume of liquid divided by the weight of the same volume of water at a given temperature and pressure. Water has a specific gravity of 1.000.

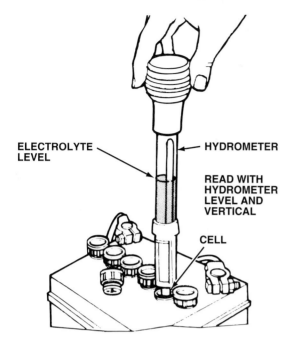

ELECTROLYTE LEVEL

HYDROMETER

READ WITH HYDROMETER LEVEL AND VERTICAL

CELL

Fig. 5-14. Check the specific gravity of a battery with a hydrometer.

ELECTROLYTE SPECIFIC GRAVITY	BATTERY STATE OF CHARGE
1.265	100%
1.225	75%
1.190	50%
1.155	25%
1.120	Discharged

Fig. 5-15. Battery state of charge is determined by the specific gravity of the electrolyte.

good condition can be charged at any current rate if electrolyte gassing and spewing do not occur, and the electrolyte temperature stays below 125°F. Never fast charge a battery that is sulfated or has plate or separator damage. If time allows, a slow rate of 5 to 15 amperes is preferable.

To charge a battery, the electrolyte level should be 0.25 inch above the separators in each cell. Leave the cell caps in place during charging, but be sure the vent holes are open. When charging a sealed, maintenance-free battery, follow the directions of the battery manufacturer for charging rate and time. Charge a battery as follows:

1. Disconnect both battery cables and connect the charger cables to the battery with the correct polarity
2. Set the charger for the desired rate, then switch it on
3. Periodically check the specific gravity, electrolyte temperature, and voltage across the battery terminals during charging
4. If voltage rises above 15.5 volts at any time, lower the charging rate
5. The battery is fully charged when all cells are gassing freely and specific gravity does not increase for three hours

After charging, wash and dry the battery top to remove any acid from electrolyte gassing. Check the electrolyte level;

replenish if needed. Reconnect the positive cable first, then the ground cable.

Cranking System Service

The cranking system includes the battery, ignition switch, safety switch, starter relay, solenoid, and starter motor, as well as the circuitry that links everything together. A failure at any point of the system can prevent the engine from starting.

Troubleshooting

When an engine fails to crank, perform these preliminary checks:

- Inspect the battery. Check for loose or corroded terminals and cable connections, frayed cables, and damaged insulation
- Inspect the ignition switch. Check for loose mounting, damaged wiring, sticking contacts, and loose connections
- Inspect the safety switch. Check for proper adjustment, loose mounting and connections, and damaged wiring
- Inspect the solenoid. Check for loose mounting, loose connections, and damaged wiring
- Inspect the starter motor. Check for loose mounting, proper pinion adjustment, and loose or damaged wiring or connections

Use the troubleshooting table in figure 5-16 to assist in diagnosing the problem and to determine the possible cure.

System Testing

To test the starter, the battery must be fully charged and in good condition. Most starting system tests are made while the starter motor is cranking the engine. The engine must not start and run during the tests or the readings will be inaccurate. To keep the engine from starting, bypass the ignition switch with a remote starter switch and turn the ignition key off. Alternative methods include disabling the fuel pump, the ignition system, or both. Do not crank the starter motor for more than 15 seconds at a time while testing. Allow two minutes between tests for the motor to cool in order to prevent damage.

Cranking Voltage Test

Connect the positive lead of a voltmeter to the starter terminal that is energized by the ignition switch, and attach the negative lead to a good ground. Crank the engine and observe the voltmeter. Readings should be over 9.6 volts and the starter should crank freely.

Low readings can be caused by a weak battery, high circuit resistance, or low starter pinion rpm due to high mechanical engine resistance. If readings are good but the starter cranks poorly, there is an internal starter problem.

Current Draw Test

An ammeter is used to perform this test. The test measures the amperage the circuit requires to crank the engine. Starter current draw specifications are provided by the vehicle manufacturer.

With an inductive ammeter, simply clamp the inductive pickup to the positive battery cable and crank the engine for 15 seconds while observing the meter. Compare readings to specifications.

A1

STARTING SYSTEM TROUBLESHOOTING TABLE		
SYMPTOM	POSSIBLE CAUSE	CURE
Nothing happens when ignition switch is turned to START.	1. Battery discharged 2. Open in control circuit 3. Defective starter relay or solenoid 4. Open starter motor internal ground	1. Recharge or replace 2. Check control circuit continuity, repair or replace components as necessary 3. Replace relay or solenoid 4. Replace starter
Solenoid contacts click or chatter but starter does not operate, OR moveable pole shoe starter chatters or disengages before engine has started	1. Battery discharged 2. High resistance in system 3. Open in solenoid or moveable pole shoe hold-in winding 4. Defective starter	1. Recharge or replace 2. Test voltage drop, replace components as necessary 3. Replace solenoid or replace moveable pole shoe starter 4. Replace starter
Starter motor operates but does not turn engine	1. Defective starter drive assembly 2. Defective ring gear	1. Replace starter drive 2. Replace ring gear
Starter motor turns the engine over slowly or unevenly	1. Battery discharged 2. High resistance in system 3. Defective starter 4. Defective ring gear 5. Poor flywheel to starter engagement	1. Recharge or replace 2. Test voltage drop, replace components as necessary 3. Replace starter motor 4. Replace ring gear 5. Adjust starter position if possible
Engine starts but motor drive assembly does not disengage	1. Defective drive assembly 2. Poor flywheel to starter engagement 3. Shorted solenoid windings 4. Shorted control circuit	1. Replace starter drive. 2. Adjust starter position if possible 3. Replace solenoid 4. Test circuit, repair and replace components as needed.

Fig. 5-16. Starting system troubleshooting table.

For an ammeter that has mechanical hookups, a voltmeter and carbon pile are required. Test as follows:

1. Refer to figure 5-17 for test connections
2. Set the carbon pile to its maximum resistance (open)
3. Crank the engine and watch the voltmeter reading
4. With the starter motor off, adjust the carbon pile until the voltmeter reading matches the reading taken in step 3
5. Note the ammeter reading and set the carbon pile back to open. Then, compare the ammeter reading to specifications

Interpret test results as described for the cranking voltage test.

Circuit Resistance Tests

The starting system is composed of three circuits:

- Insulated circuit; all high current cables and connections between the battery and starter
- Ground circuit; the return path from the starter motor to the battery
- Control circuit; the low current wiring, switches, and relays used to energize the starter motor

Resistance tests on all three circuits can be performed with a voltmeter. One voltmeter lead is connected to the battery terminal and the other to various connections in the circuit.

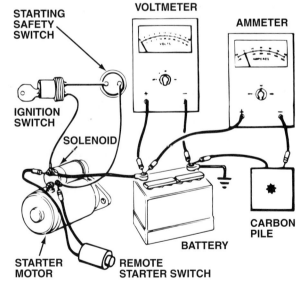

Fig. 5-17. Test meter hookup for performing a starter motor current draw test.

Manufacturers recommend different specific test points for their vehicles. The engine is cranked and the voltmeter observed. As a general rule, the maximum drop should not exceed 0.1 volt per connection.

Starter Motor Removal and Replacement

You may have to remove, loosen, or relocate heat shields, support brackets, or exhaust pipes to access the starter motor. Always begin by disconnecting the battery ground cable at the battery.

After gaining access to the starter motor, disconnect all of the wires from the starter motor or solenoid. Remove the mounting bolts securing the starter motor to the engine, then remove the starter motor.

Once the starter is removed, inspect the ring gear. Look for any chipped, broken, missing, or excessively worn teeth. Turn the engine over by hand to examine the entire ring gear. If damage is found, replace the ring gear.

Bolt the new starter motor to the engine. Check the flywheel/starter engagement. Some designs require shims to provide correct engagement of the starter pinion with the flywheel. Add or remove shims until the engagement is correct. Connect all wires to the solenoid or motor terminals and replace all items removed on disassembly. Reconnect negative battery cable.

IGNITION SYSTEM INSPECTION AND SERVICE

Ignition system service is limited to component inspection, replacement, and adjustment in this book. For more specific information on ignition system diagnosis, testing, and repair, refer to book eight of this series.

Primary Wiring and Connectors

Primary wiring and connectors are a potential source of high **resistance**, as well as open or grounded circuits that can prevent an engine from starting. This type of problem can be found with simple voltmeter and ohmmeter tests. Check for correct supply voltage first. If voltage is present, check for a **voltage drop** using a voltmeter. When voltage drop indicates high or low resistance, verify with an ohmmeter. Many problems can easily be solved by cleaning connectors or repairing wiring.

Ignition Signaling Devices

Electronic ignition systems use one of several types of **signal generators** to trigger spark plug firing. These sensors tell the ignition module or PCM the speed and position of the crankshaft.

Magnetic Pulse Generator

These devices produce an alternating current (AC) signal from the movement of a metal tooth past a pickup coil. On many, the air gap between the pickup coil and trigger wheel is adjustable. Some systems couple two generators together for information about crankshaft position and speed, figures 5-18 and 5-19. Gap has no affect on the dwell period; dwell is determined by the control module. The air gap must be set to a specific clearance when a new pickup unit is installed. During

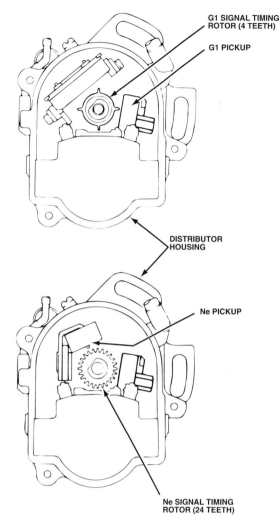

Fig. 5-18. Some distributors use two pickup coils. This Toyota distributor provides two position signals to the PCM.

use, the air gap should not change. However, it should be checked before performing troubleshooting tests.

The air gap between the trigger wheel and the pickup coil can change because of worn distributor bushings. With a conventional distributor, the gap can also change because of breaker plate and vacuum advance mechanism wear.

Check and adjust the air gap using a nonmagnetic (brass) feeler gauge, figure 5-20. The pickup coil magnet will attract a steel gauge, causing an inaccurate adjustment. Air gaps differ between manufacturers, as well as between models. You must have the correct specifications.

To check and adjust the air gap:

1. Rotate the engine to align one trigger wheel tooth with the pickup coil
2. Place a nonmagnetic feeler gauge of the specified thickness between the wheel tooth and the pickup coil. The feeler gauge should just barely make contact on both sides

Resistance: Opposition to electrical current measured in ohms.
Signal Generator: An electrical device that creates a voltage pulse that changes frequency or amplitude, or both, in relation to rotational speed.
Voltage Drop: The measurement of the loss of voltage caused by the resistance of a conductor or a circuit device.

Ne AND G SIGNAL VARIATIONS

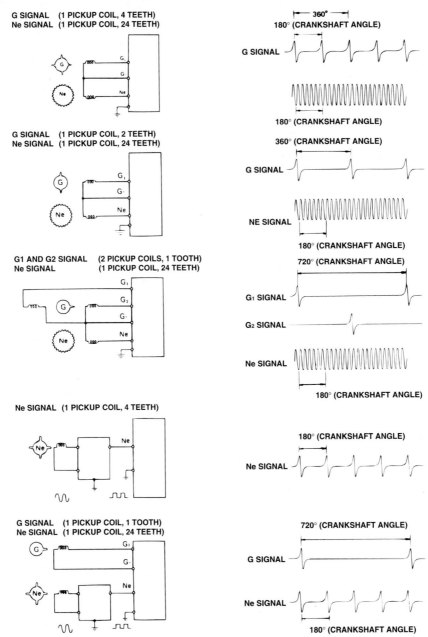

Fig. 5-19. The size, shape, and number of teeth on the reluctor wheel determines the timing and shape of the signal waveform.

3. If adjustment is necessary, loosen the lockscrew and use a screwdriver blade to shift the pickup plate. Tighten the lockscrew. If force is required to remove the feeler gauge, the adjustment is too tight

4. Apply vacuum to the advance diaphragm as you watch the breaker plate move through its full travel. Be sure the pickup coil does not hit the trigger wheel tooth. Release vacuum and recheck the air gap. If the pickup plate is loose, the distributor should be overhauled

Hall-Effect Switch

Many ignition systems use a **Hall-effect switch**, which produces a digital signal by blocking and exposing a magnetic field to the base of the Hall-effect element, figure 5-21. These devices require a reference voltage to operate and are more accurate than magnetic generators.

A Hall-effect switch requires no maintenance or adjustment, and its condition cannot be determined by a visual inspection. Verify the signal using a digital multimeter, oscilloscope, or logic probe, and replace as necessary.

Optical Sensor

An optical sensor uses a light-emitting diode (LED), a shutter wheel, and a phototransistor to produce a digital signal that changes **frequency** in proportion to rotational speed. Like a Hall-effect switch, an optical sensor is maintenance- and

---

Hall-effect Switch: A semiconductor that produces a voltage in the presence of a magnetic field. This voltage can be used to cycle a transistor on and off to produce a variable-frequency digital signal.

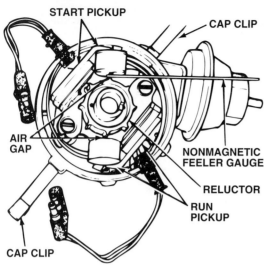

Fig. 5-20. Adjusting the reluctor-to-pickup coil air gap on a Chrysler dual-pickup distributor.

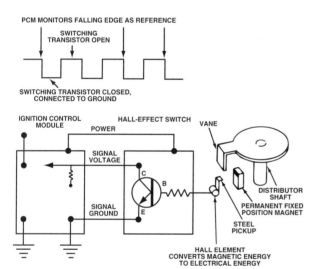

Fig. 5-21. A Hall-effect switch requires an external power source to generate a digital signal voltage that changes frequency in proportion to speed.

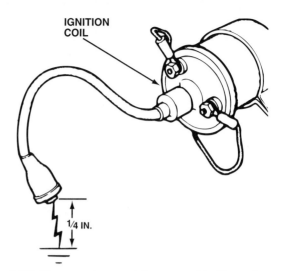

Fig. 5-22. The secondary spark from a good ignition coil can bridge a considerable gap.

A1

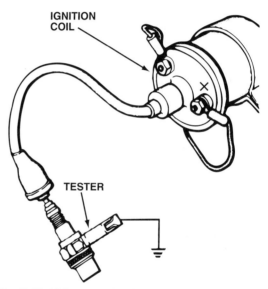

Fig. 5-23. Using a spark plug simulator to check for secondary voltage.

adjustment-free. Check sensor operation with the appropriate test equipment and replace the unit as needed.

Secondary Voltage Check

Often, it is useful, when diagnosing a no-start condition, to verify that secondary voltage is available from the coil by performing a spark test. Begin by disconnecting a spark plug cable from the plug or removing the coil cable at the distributor cap. Hold the end of the disconnected cable about ¼ inch (6 mm) from a good ground, and watch for a spark while cranking the engine, figure 5-22. A bright, blue spark should be clearly visible. Be aware that this creates high open-circuit voltage that causes damage on some electronic systems. The preferred method is to use a spark plug simulator, figure 5-23.

Distributor Cap and Rotor Replacement

Never clean cap electrodes or the rotor terminal by filing. If electrodes are burned or damaged, replace the part. Filing changes the rotor air gap and increases resistance. Most caps are replaced by simply unsnapping two spring-type clips, L-shaped lug hooks, or holddown screws. Lift the old cap off and install a new one. When replacing the cap, be sure to install the spark plug cables in correct firing sequence.

Rotors may be retained by holddown screws or may simply slip-fit onto the shaft. Rotors also use one or more locating lugs to correctly position them on the distributor shaft, figure 5-24. Ensure that the rotor is fully seated. If not, it can strike the cap when the engine is started.

Frequency: The number of periodic voltage oscillations, or waves, occurring in a given unit of time, usually expressed as cycles per second, or Hertz.

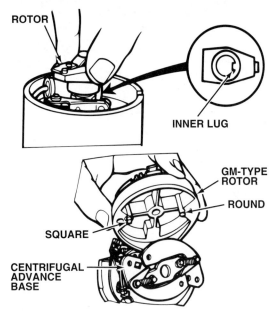

Fig. 5-24. Alignment lugs hold the rotor in position on the distributor shaft.

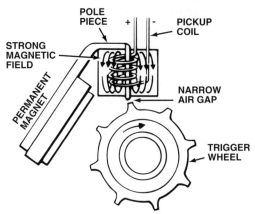

Fig. 5-25. Align a trigger wheel tooth with the pole piece when static timing an engine that uses a pickup coil.

Use caution when installing caps on distributors with the coil inside the distributor. The carbon brush in the cap may break if the cap is pushed into place after it is seated. Align the components before installing the distributor cap.

Ignition Timing

Ignition timing on older engines with a conventional distributor may be mechanically adjusted. However, the timing on most late-model engines is electronically regulated and cannot be adjusted. Timing advance is also electronically controlled on newer systems, while a conventional distributor advances timing in relation to engine speed using mechanical weights, a vacuum diaphragm, or a combination of both.

Mechanical Ignition Timing

Ignition timing can be advanced within the distributor centrifugally and with vacuum. Engine speed governs centrifugal advance, its load, and vacuum advance. As speed increases, so does the timing advance. Also, light load operating conditions will advance timing to decrease fuel consumption.

Dual diaphragm distributor units can either use one diaphragm for advance and the other for retard, or use one for low advance and the other for high advance. The advance/retard unit uses **ported vacuum** to advance the timing, and manifold vacuum to allow the timing to retard further in the absence of ported vacuum.

The advance/advance unit uses manifold vacuum through a thermal vacuum switch to advance the timing on cold engines for better driveability. Ported vacuum is typically used to advance the timing during driving under load. When testing

an ignition system with a dual diaphragm, it is important to know which system you have.

Static Timing Procedure

The following procedure can be used to statically time an electronic ignition system:

1. Rotate the engine until the crankshaft timing mark aligns with the proper timing specification and the number one cylinder is on the compression stroke
2. Loosen the distributor holddown clamp and bolt
3. Rotate the distributor housing in the direction of rotor rotation until the trigger wheel tooth is aligned with the pole piece, and the rotor is pointed toward the number one plug wire in the distributor cap, figure 5-25
4. Tighten the holddown bolt
5. Check and adjust the dynamic timing

Dynamic Timing

Dynamic timing is adjusted by rotating the distributor housing while the engine is running at idle and is at normal operating temperature. Most manufacturers specify that the distributor vacuum lines be disconnected and plugged. Precise spark timing is important to ensure correct engine performance and to reduce vehicle emissions:

1. Connect a timing light and tachometer to the engine
2. Disconnect and plug distributor vacuum lines to prevent unwanted vacuum advance
3. Slightly loosen the distributor holddown bolt
4. Start the engine. Adjust idle speed to specifications to prevent unwanted centrifugal advance
5. Point the timing light toward the timing marks. Carefully sight the marks at a right angle, figure 5-26. Looking at the marks from an incorrect position can result in an initial timing error of as much as 2 degrees
6. Rotate the distributor housing until the proper marks are aligned, figure 5-27
7. When the timing is set to specifications, carefully tighten the distributor holddown bolt. Recheck the timing

Ported Vacuum: The low-pressure area, or vacuum, located just above the intake air throttle plates of an engine.

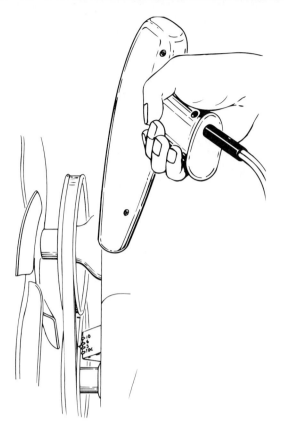

Fig. 5-26. Observing timing marks with a stroboscopic timing light.

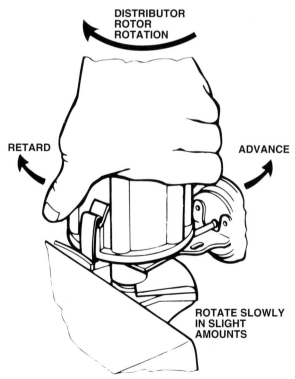

Fig. 5-27. Slowly rotate the body of a conventional distributor to adjust ignition timing.

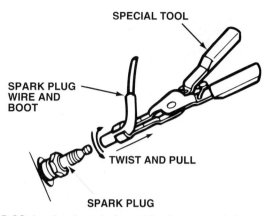

Fig. 5-28. Insulated spark plug cable pliers prevent shock and protect cables.

Electronic Timing Control

The ignition module or power control module (PCM) calculates ignition timing on most late-model vehicles. The PCM receives inputs from sensors, such as engine temperature, engine rpm, load, vehicle speed, throttle position, amount of EGR, barometric pressure, and possible detonation.

Typically, setting the base timing involves disabling the computer from controlling timing. Follow the procedure on the engine decal or check other sources if the decal does not specify. This operation can be done by disconnecting a wire or coolant sensor, jumping between two wires, or jumping the connectors in the **data link connector** (DLC). It is important to follow the correct procedure.

Spark Plug Replacement

Spark plug access is limited on many late-model engines, due to a maze of air conditioning and emission control plumbing and engine-driven accessory mounting. Engine accessories may have to be loosened from their mountings and moved to get to the plugs. Air conditioning compressors, air pumps, and power steering pumps are frequent candidates for relocation during plug service. Whenever you must move one of these accessories, be careful of its plumbing and wiring. The spark plugs on some engines are most easily reached from underneath the engine.

Spark Plug Removal

To remove the spark plugs:

1. Disconnect cables at the plug by grasping the boot and twisting gently while pulling. Do not pull on the cable. Insulated spark plug pliers will provide a better grip and are recommended when working near hot manifolds, figure 5-28
2. Loosen each plug one or two turns with a spark plug socket, then blow dirt away from around the plugs with compressed air
3. Remove the plugs, keeping them in cylinder number order for inspection
4. When removing gasketed plugs, be sure the old gasket comes out with the plug

Data Link Connector: An electrical connector that allows a scan tool to communicate with the powertrain control module (PCM).

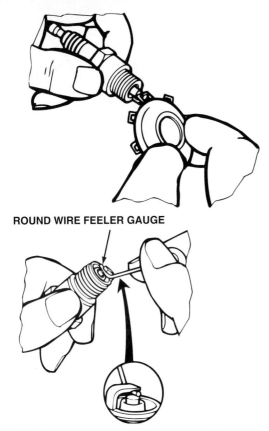

Fig. 5-29. Check spark gap with a round wire feeler gauge.

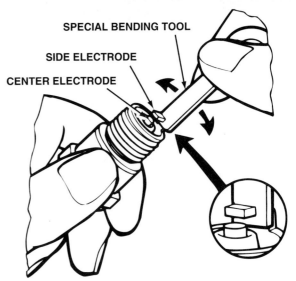

Fig. 5-30. Carefully bend the electrode with a special tool to adjust spark plug gap.

PLUG TYPE	CAST-IRON HEAD		ALUMINUM HEAD	
	Foot-Pounds	Newton-Meters	Foot-Pounds	Newton-Meters
14-MM Gasketed	25-30	34-40	13-22	18-30
14-MM Tapered Seat	7-15	9-20	7-15	9-20
18-MM Tapered Seat	15-20	20-27	15-20	20-27

Fig. 5-31. Always tighten spark plugs to specified torque.

Spark Plug Installation

Spark plugs, both new and used, must be correctly gapped before they are installed. Although a wide variety of gapping tools are available, a round wire feeler gauge is the most efficient for used plugs, figure 5-29. A flat feeler gauge should not be used because the measurement will be inaccurate. Adjust the gap by carefully bending the ground electrode, figure 5-30. Set the gap to specifications provided by the engine manufacturer:

- Do not assume that new plugs are correctly gapped
- Do not try to set a wide-gap plug (electronic ignition) to a small-gap specification. This will damage the electrode
- Do not try to set a narrow-gap plug (breaker-point ignition) to a wide-gap specification. This will result in misaligned electrodes
- Do not make gap adjustments by tapping the electrode on a workbench or other solid object. This can cause internal plug damage

Cleaning the threaded plug holes in the cylinder head with a thread chaser will ensure easy spark plug installation. With aluminum heads, use the tool carefully to avoid damaging the threads.

Some manufacturers recommend using an antiseize compound or thread lubricant on the plug threads. Thread lubricant recommendations are rare. Use only when specified by the manufacturer. Antiseize compound is commonly used when installing spark plugs in aluminum cylinder heads. Use the specific compound recommended by the manufacturer. Not all compounds are compatible with aluminum. Whenever thread lubricant or antiseize is used, reduce the tightening torque slightly.

Once the plug gap has been properly set, install as follows:

1. Wipe any dirt and grease from the cylinder head plug seats with a clean cloth
2. Check that gaskets used on the plugs are in good condition and properly installed
3. Install the plugs in the engine and run them in by hand
4. Tighten the plugs to specification with a torque wrench. General torque values are listed in figure 5-31

EXHAUST SYSTEM SERVICE

When servicing the exhaust system, keep in mind that it is necessary to inspect all system components for leaks, noises, missing parts, configuration, and routing.

Exhaust Manifold Inspection and Service

Before installing an exhaust manifold, check the sealing surfaces, gasket fit, and hardware condition. Examine the mating surface on the cylinder head for any problems, such as pulled or damaged threads.

Carefully inspect the manifold for signs of cracking or other damage. Magnetic particle testing, as explained in chapter two, works well for locating hairline cracks on a cast-iron manifold. Check the straightness of the manifold flanges.

A quick, easy way to do this is to run a file straight across each flange. If flat, the file will scuff the entire surface area. You can take the surface down with the file if the flange is slightly warped.

Exhaust manifolds seal to the head with either a single gasket, an individual gasket for each port, or a combination intake/exhaust gasket. Some gaskets are stainless steel on one side and a composition material on the other. These are installed with the steel side toward the manifold.

Replace all exhaust manifold mounting hardware, studs, nuts, and bolts with new pieces. The extreme temperatures these fasteners are exposed to result in corrosion and a loss of tensile strength. Over time, the metal becomes brittle and will break easily. Always use brass or copper-plated nuts. These will not bind on the threads as the metals expand and contract.

Once everything passes inspection, install the exhaust manifold and gasket. Start all of the nuts or bolts, and run them up hand-tight. Be sure any brackets or shrouds that attach with the manifold are in place. Then bring the fasteners up to specified torque in stages.

Exhaust System Tests

Exhaust System Restriction Testing

In addition to a good visual inspection, you may need to have an assistant use a leather glove to temporarily cover the end of the exhaust pipe, which will build enough pressure to find small leaks.

To test for a restricted exhaust system, take the following steps:

1. Connect a vacuum gauge to the engine's intake manifold
2. Operate the engine until it reaches operating temperature
3. Accelerate the engine to 3000 rpm and allow the speed to stabilize
4. If the exhaust system is not restricted, the manifold vacuum should stabilize around 18 inches of mercury
5. If the system is restricted, the vacuum will drop sharply and then rise to a few inches below normal

Refer to Chapter One for additional information on using the vacuum gauge for testing the engine.

Test gauges are also available for testing exhaust restriction. To use, a small hole must be drilled in the exhaust pipe close to the manifold. A special fitting is used to connect the gauge while the test is being performed. Once the test is complete, a small rivet is driven into the test hole or it can be brazed to seal the system.

Heat Riser Valve Testing

The **heat riser valve**, also known as the **Early Fuel Evaporation (EFE)** system, is found on many older vehicles. Regardless of the design, the system is designed to aid in quick engine warm-up and lower exhaust emissions.

Check the valve in the exhaust manifold to ensure it rotates freely and that the spring (when equipped) is not damaged. If the valve is damaged, it must be replaced. If lubrication is necessary, use only a graphite based lubricant. Do not use petroleum products as they will burn on the shaft of the valve and may form carbon deposits, which will cause further problems with rotation.

Muffler and Catalytic Converter Testing

If a restricted muffler or **catalytic converter** is suspected, the most effective diagnosis requires removal from the vehicle. Once removed, shake the muffler or converter, listening for loose pieces inside. Shine a light into the inlet and outlet, looking for restrictions or signs of damage.

Exhaust System Mounting Hardware Inspection

Inspect the entire exhaust system, looking at the condition of all hangers, supports, flange hardware, and clamps. Tighten all loose connections and replace any damaged or missing components.

A1

Catalytic Converter: An exhaust-mounted device designed to reduce pollutants in the exhaust system.
Early Fuel Evaporation (EFE): A system using a heat riser valve to warm the combustion chamber faster to eliminate excessive unburned fuel emissions and promote better cold engine performance.
Heat Riser Valve: A device in the exhaust system that directs exhaust gases through passages in the intake manifold to speed engine warmup and reduce exhaust emissions.

CHAPTER QUESTIONS

1. A battery is being tested. Technician A says the open circuit voltage should be above 9.6 volts. Technician B says when load testing a battery the load should be the CCA Rating for 15 seconds. Who is right?
   a. A only
   b. B only
   c. Both A and B
   d. Neither A nor B

2. A typical electronic multi-port injection system operates at a system pressure of about:
   a. 25 psi
   b. 35 psi
   c. 45 psi
   d. Over 50 psi

3. Low system pressure on an engine with electronic fuel injection can be caused by all of the following *EXCEPT*:
   a. Defective fuel pump
   b. Faulty fuel pressure regulator
   c. Clogged fuel filter
   d. Defective fuel pump check valve

4. Voltage drop is measured at 2 volts between the positive battery terminal and positive battery cable. Technician A says this is within specifications. Technician B says to clean the negative battery terminal.
   a. A only
   b. B only
   c. Both A and B
   d. Neither A nor B

5. Technician A says to replace the catalytic converter that rattles during operation. Technician B says a defective oxygen sensor may cause the catalytic converter to set a code. Who is right?
   a. A only
   b. B only
   c. Both A and B
   d. Neither A nor B

6. Most turbocharger failures are caused by:
   a. Excessive high-speed operation
   b. Exhaust temperatures too high
   c. Dirt and contamination
   d. Operation with leaded gasoline

7. To check the boost pressure of a turbocharger, a pressure gauge is installed:
   a. On the compressor side of the turbocharger
   b. On the turbine side of the turbocharger
   c. At the wastegate port of the turbocharger
   d. In the intake air plenum

8. To bleed off excess boost pressure during idle and low speed operation, most supercharger engines use a(n):
   a. Vacuum-operated bypass valve
   b. Pressure-controlled wastegate
   c. Electric cut-out switch
   d. Pop-off valve

9. A clogged PCV system can cause all of the following *EXCEPT*:
   a. Increased oil consumption
   b. Lean fuel mixture
   c. Oil dilution
   d. Oil leaks

10. When doing an engine speed drop test of the PCV system, the engine idle speed should drop by at least:
    a. 20 rpm
    b. 40 rpm
    c. 60 rpm
    d. 80 rpm

11. The specific gravity of a fully charged battery with an electrolyte temperature of 80°F will be about:
    a. 1.225
    b. 1.245
    c. 1.265
    d. 1.285

12. The preferred rate for charging an automotive battery is:
    a. Less than 5 amps
    b. 5 to 15 amps
    c. 15 to 25 amps
    d. More than 25 amps

13. Low readings on a starter motor cranking voltage test can be caused by all of the following *EXCEPT*:
    a. Weak battery
    b. High circuit resistance
    c. Low starter pinion speed
    d. Internal starter problem

14. Which of the following is *NOT* one of the starting system circuits?
    a. Control circuit
    b. Isolated circuit
    c. Insulated circuit
    d. Ground circuit

15. Starter circuit resistance tests are performed with a(n):
    a. Ammeter
    b. Oscilloscope
    c. Ohmmeter
    d. Voltmeter

16. Which of the following signal generating devices produces an alternating current (AC) signal to let the PCM know how fast the crankshaft is turning?
    a. Hall-effect switch
    b. Magnetic pulse generator
    c. Optical sensor
    d. All of the above

17. To check base timing on a late-model computer-controlled engine, it may be necessary to:
    a. Disconnect the oxygen sensor
    b. Bypass the idle air control valve
    c. Disable computer controlled timing
    d. Disconnect the throttle position sensor

18. On a conventional distributor, the air gap between the trigger wheel and the pickup coil can change because of:
    a. Incorrect base timing setting
    b. Incorrect timing advance
    c. Worn distributor bushings
    d. Worn distributor cap and rotor

19. Spark plug gap is checked using a:
    a. Round wire feeler gauge
    b. Flat blade feeler gauge
    c. Non-magnetic feeler gauge
    d. All of the above

20. How do exhaust manifold gaskets that are stainless steel on one side and a composition material on the other install?
    a. With the steel side toward the cylinder head
    b. With the steel side toward the manifold
    c. Either way
    d. Depends on the engine

SAMPLE TEST

Test Taking Advice

This sample test can help you review your knowledge of this entire book. The format of the questions is similar to the certification tests given by the National Institute for Automotive Service Excellence. Generally, the questions here are more difficult than the chapter review questions you answered as you read the technical material in this book.

Read these sample test questions carefully, then read all the possible answers before making your decision. Always select the best possible answer. In some cases, you may think all the answers are partially correct, or you may feel that none is exactly right. But in every case, there is a **best** answer; that is the one you should select.

Answers to the questions in this sample test will be found after this test. If you answer at least 30 of these questions correctly, then you can be confident of your knowledge of the subjects covered in this book and in the ASE Certification Test A1 Engine Repair. If you answer fewer than 30 correctly, you should reread the text and take another look at the illustrations. Also, check the glossary as you review the material.

A1

1. A compression test was performed on a four-cylinder engine with the following results: cylinder #1 = 138 psi, cylinder #2 = 127 psi, cylinder #3 = 115 psi, cylinder # 4 = 135 psi. Technician A says low compression in cylinders 2 and 3 indicates that the cylinder head gasket is leaking between these two cylinders. Technician B says the compression test is not conclusive enough to determine the problem. Uneven readings may be caused by burnt, sticking, or improperly adjusted valves or carbon deposits on the valve faces.
Who is right?
   a. A only
   b. B only
   c. Both A and B
   d. Neither A nor B

2. A vacuum gauge is connected to an engine. The gauge reads 18 in-Hg at idle. When engine speed is increased, the gauge momentarily drops to near zero, then slowly rises and stabilizes at 9 in-Hg. The likely cause of these readings would be:
   a. Weak piston rings
   b. Incorrect fuel mixture
   c. Restricted exhaust
   d. Retarded ignition timing

3. Manifold vacuum, compression, cylinder leakage, and cylinder power balance test results are all within specification, but the engine suffers from high oil consumption, even though the valve guide seals were recently replaced.
Technician A says that the problem may be caused by a clogged PCV valve or worn valve guides. Technician B says clogged oil drainback passages or worn pushrod tips can increase oil consumption.
Who is right?
   a. A only
   b. B only
   c. Both A and B
   d. Neither A nor B

4. A cylinder leakage test is being performed on a 4-cylinder engine. When testing the number 2 cylinder, air escapes from the number 3 spark plug hole.
Technician A says that a leaking head gasket could be the problem. Technician B says that the number 2 intake valve not seating could be the problem.
Who is right?
   a. A only
   b. B only
   c. Both A and B
   d. Neither A nor B

5. A cylinder compression test reveals fairly even compression, but lower than specification. A second wet test results in higher readings on all cylinders. These results indicate:
   a. Poor valve seating
   b. Worn valve guides
   c. Worn piston rings
   d. Leaking head gasket

6. The needle of a vacuum gauge rapidly vibrates between 14 and 18 in-Hg with the engine running at idle. As engine speed increases, the gauge stops vibrating and stabilizes. These readings are most likely caused by:
   a. Weak piston rings
   b. Incorrect fuel mixture
   c. Worn valve guides
   d. Weak valve springs

7. Which of the following is the proper procedure for performing a cylinder balance test?
   a. Run the engine at idle, short the spark plugs one at a time, and note any rpm drop
   b. Run the engine at 1500 rpm, short the spark plugs two at a time, and note any rpm drop
   c. Run the engine at idle speed, shorting all but two spark plugs, and note any rpm drop
   d. Run the engine at 1500 rpm, short the spark plugs one at a time, and note any rpm drop

8. An engine has a hollow, metallic clatter when started cold. The noise diminishes and eventually goes away as the engine warms up to operating temperature.
Technician A says the noise could result from low oil pressure caused by worn main bearings. Technician B says the noise could be piston slap caused by too much piston-to-cylinder wall clearance.
Who is right?
   a. A only
   b. B only
   c. Both A and B
   d. Neither A nor B

9. The needle on a vacuum gauge oscillates back and forth when the engine is run at idle. This generally indicates which of the following?
   a. Late valve timing
   b. Poor air-fuel mixture
   c. A blown cylinder head gasket
   d. An air leak in the intake manifold

10. Technician A says that grinding the valve face will increase valve spring installed height. Grinding the valve

tip will correct installed height. Technician B says that grinding the valve face will decrease valve spring installed height. Installing shims under the spring will correct installed height.

Who is right?

a. A only
b. B only
c. Both A and B
d. Neither A nor B

11. After facing, valves must have a margin of at least?

a. ¹⁄₆₄ inch
b. ¹⁄₃₂ inch
c. ¹⁄₁₆ inch
d. ¹⁄₈ inch

12. Resurfacing an OHC cylinder head will?

a. Increase valve lift
b. Alter cam timing
c. Change valve lash
d. Lower compression

13. Valve spring installed height is measured from?

a. Spring seat to valve tip
b. Valve guide top to valve keeper groove
c. Valve retainer top to valve stem end
d. Spring seat to valve retainer

14. Which of the following tools will give the most accurate measurements when calculating valve guide wear?

a. Split-ball gauge
b. Inside micrometer
c. Dial indicator
d. Dial bore gauge

15. Which of the following methods is **NOT** used for detecting cracks in a cast-iron cylinder head?

a. Dye penetrant testing
b. Pressure testing
c. Magnetic particle testing
d. Leak-down testing

16. Technician A says that it is a good practice to replace torque-to-yield cylinder head bolts with new ones whenever they are removed. Technician B says that torque-to-yield cylinder head bolts can be reinstalled if you torque them to specification, then tighten them an additional 90 degrees.

Who is right?

a. A only
b. B only
c. Both A and B
d. Neither A nor B

17. Technician A says the close-wound end of a variable-pitch valve spring should be installed up, with the tight coils at the tip end of the valve. Technician B says the close-wound end of a variable-pitch valve spring should be installed down, with the tight coils at the spring seat of the cylinder head.

Who is right?

a. A only
b. B only
c. Both A and B
d. Neither A nor B

18. A cylinder bore measures 3.067 inches below ring travel at the bottom and 3.077 below the ridge at the top. The standard factory bore is 3.065. What would be the proper repair?

a. Deglaze the cylinder walls and install the old pistons with new cast-iron rings
b. Bore and hone the cylinder to 3.097 inches and install 0.030 inch oversize pistons with new rings
c. Bore and hone the cylinder to 3.075 inches and install knurled pistons with new rings
d. Bore and hone the cylinder to 3.095 inches and install 0.030-inch oversized pistons with new rings

19. Technician A says a full-floating wrist pin should be checked for clearance fit. Technician B says a press-fit wrist pin should be checked for interference fit.

Who is right?

a. A only
b. B only
c. Both A and B
d. Neither A nor B

20. Two cylinder bore measurements are taken: one perpendicular (at a right angle) to the crankshaft and the other in line with the crankshaft. These two measurements are used to determine:

a. Cylinder out-of-round
b. Cylinder taper
c. Cylinder warpage
d. Cylinder ridge

21. When installing a piston assembly, the notch on the head of the piston will generally face toward:

a. The rear of the engine
b. The major thrust side
c. The front of the engine
d. The minor thrust side

22. Before installing pistons into freshly honed cylinder bores, the cylinders should be cleaned using:

a. Clean solvent
b. Hot soapy water
c. Water soluble oil
d. Carbon tetrachloride

23. Failure to remove the cylinder ridge before removing the piston and connecting rod assemblies from the engine block can result in:

a. Scored cylinder walls
b. Bent connecting rods
c. Broken piston skirts
d. Damaged piston ring lands

24. In a high mileage engine, cylinder wear is normally the greatest at the:

a. Top of the cylinder measured parallel to the crankshaft
b. Top of the cylinder measured at right angles to the crankshaft
c. Bottom of the cylinder measured parallel to the crankshaft
d. Bottom of the cylinder measured at right angles to the crankshaft

25. A diagonal, or angled, wear pattern on the thrust surface of a piston is an indication of:

a. A bent connecting rod
b. Too much piston pin clearance
c. An out-of-round cylinder bore
d. A collapsed piston skirt

26. During an oil pressure test, low oil pressure is noted only at low engine speeds, and there are no abnormal engine noises. These findings may indicate:

a. Faulty hydraulic valve lifters
b. Pressure-oiled rocker arm shaft assembly wear
c. Badly worn engine bearings
d. An open oil pump pressure relief valve

27. A cooling system pressure tester is connected to the radiator and pumped up to the proper pressure. The engine is started, and after a while, the

pressure begins to rise. What could be the cause of the problem?
a. The thermostat is bad
b. The bypass hose is blocked
c. The tester is being used incorrectly
d. The head gasket is leaking

28. Which of the following may be a cause of low oil pressure?
a. Worn piston rings
b. Excessive valve guide clearance
c. Excessive main bearing clearance
d. Stretched timing chain

29. Technician A says that two measurements, end clearance and rotor-to-housing clearance, are taken to evaluate a rotor-type oil pump. Technician B says that three measurements, end clearance, gear-to-gear clearance, and gear-to-housing clearance, are taken to evaluate a gear-type oil pump. Who is right?
a. A only
b. B only
c. Both A and B
d. Neither A nor B

30. High or low resistance in the primary ignition circuit can be located by:
a. Current draw testing
b. Checking available voltage
c. Voltage drop testing
d. State of charge testing

31. A Hall-effect switch on a computer-controlled engine triggers spark plug firing through the use of:
a. A light-emitting diode and a reluctor plate
b. A semiconductor and a permanent magnet
c. A pickup coil and a trigger wheel
d. A magnetic pulse generator and an armature

32. A voltage loss in the primary circuit may be caused by all of the following **EXCEPT**:
a. High circuit resistance
b. Insufficient battery voltage
c. Low charging system output
d. Excessive starter motor current draw

33. While the engine is running, a technician pulls the PCV valve out of the valve cover and puts his thumb over the valve opening. There are no changes in engine operation. Technician A says the PCV valve could be stuck in the open position. Technician B says the hose between the intake manifold and the PCV valve could be plugged. Who is right?
a. A only
b. B only
c. Both A and B
d. Neither A nor B

34. Residual fuel pressure reads low on an engine with electronic fuel injection. The most likely cause is:
a. A defective fuel pump
b. A faulty fuel-pressure regulator
c. A clogged fuel filter
d. A defective fuel pump check valve

35. Black exhaust smoke from a turbocharged engine can indicate:
a. Coolant leakage into the cylinders
b. Leaking oil seals in the turbo
c. Clogged intake air filter
d. High boost pressure

36. Insufficient system pressure in a port fuel-injection system can be caused by all of the following **EXCEPT**:
a. A defective fuel-pressure regulator
b. A sticking fuel pump check valve
c. A clogged fuel filter
d. A faulty fuel accumulator

37. The thermostatically controlled air cleaner should:
a. Close hot air passage during warm-up
b. Open hot air passage during warm-up
c. Provide hot air at all times
d. Provide cool air at all times

38. When slow-charging a battery, the electrolyte temperature should not rise above:
a. 112°F
b. 115°F
c. 125°F
d. 135°F

39. Which of the following circuits is **NOT** part of the cranking system?
a. Ignition switch
b. Engine speed sensor
c. Starter relay
d. Battery

40. To correct specific gravity readings taken at a temperature of 90°F:
a. Add 0.004 to the hydrometer reading
b. Add 0.006 to the hydrometer reading
c. Add 0.008 to the hydrometer reading
d. Add 0.010 to the hydrometer reading

A1

ANSWERS

GLOSSARY

Aerobic: Curing in the presence of oxygen.

Air Dam: Body component designed to control or direct the flow of air through or around the vehicle. In the cooling system, it is designed to force air to pass through the radiator core to improve cooling.

Airflow Sensor: A sensor used to measure the rate, density, temperature, or volume of air entering the engine.

Anaerobic: Curing in the absence of oxygen.

Atmospheric Pressure: Weight of air at sea level, about 14.7 pounds per square inch (101 kPa), decreasing at higher altitudes.

Backlash: A lack of mesh between two gears, resulting in a lag between when one gear moves and when it engages the other.

Base Circle: An imaginary circle drawn on the profile of a cam lobe that intersects the very bottom of the lobe. It is the lowest point on the cam lobe in relation to the valve train.

Bend: On a connecting rod, the condition of the two bores being out-of-parallel when viewed from the edge of the rod.

Boost Pressure: The amount of air pressure increase above atmospheric pressure provided by a turbocharger.

Carbon Monoxide: An odorless, colorless, tasteless poisonous gas. A pollutant produced by an internal combustion engine.

Catalytic Converter: An exhaust-mounted device designed to reduce pollutants in the exhaust system.

Chamfer: A beveled edge.

Compression Pressure: The total amount of air pressure developed by a piston moving to TDC with both valves closed.

Concentricity: Having the same center, such as two circles drawn around a common center point. A valve guide and valve seat must be concentric, or have centers at the same point.

Coolant Temperature Sensor: Often designated as the Engine Coolant Temperature (ECT) Sensor. A variable resistance sensor threaded into the engine coolant passage. Changes resistance as temperature varies.

Cooling Fan Module: Refers to the combination of the fan drive motor, fan blade, and the housing or shroud.

Core Plug: A shallow, metal cup inserted into the engine block to seal holes left by manufacturing. Also called a freeze plug or expansion plug.

Crosshatch: A multi-directional surface finish left on a cylinder wall after honing. The crosshatch finish retains oil to aid in piston ring seating.

Data Link Connector: An electrical connector that allows a scan tool to communicate with the powertrain control module (PCM).

Diagnostic Trouble Code: A numerical or alphanumerical code related to a specific system malfunction. DTCs are accessed or read with a scan tool.

Early Fuel Evaporation (EFE): A system using a heat riser valve to warm the combustion chamber faster to eliminate excessive unburned fuel emissions and promote better cold engine performance.

Eccentric: Off center or out of round. A shaft lobe which has a center different from that of the shaft.

Electrolyte: The chemical solution, generally sulfuric acid and water, in a battery that conducts electricity and reacts with the plate materials.

Endplay: Movement along, or parallel to, the centerline of a shaft. Also called end thrust or axial play.

Ethylene Glycol (EG): A chemical solution used as an antifreeze and anti-boil agent. It reduces the freezing point of water and increases its boiling point.

Expander Broach: A tool used to seat a bushing and form the outside diameter of the bushing to the irregular surface of the bore.

Fan Shroud: Housing located around the fan for the purpose of utilizing the full drawing power of the fan.

Fillet: A curve of a specific radius machined into the edges of a crankshaft journal. The fillet provides additional strength between the journal and the crankshaft cheek.

Filter Media: The paper material that actually filters the oil within the assembly.

Frequency: The number of periodic voltage oscillations, or waves, occurring in a given unit of time, usually expressed as cycles per second, or Hertz.

Hall-effect Switch: A semiconductor that produces a voltage in the presence of a magnetic field. This voltage can be used to cycle a transistor on and off to produce a variable-frequency digital signal.

Heat Riser Valve: An exhaust manifold-mounted butterfly valve designed to restrict exhaust flow from the engine and force it up through special ports in the cylinder heads to help the engine warm up faster.

Helical Insert: A precision-formed coil of wire used to repair damaged threads, or to reduce the internal diameter of a bored hole.

Hydrocarbon: A chemical compound of hydrogen and carbon. A major pollutant from an internal combustion engine. Gasoline itself is a hydrocarbon compound.

Hydrometer: A device used to measure the specific gravity of a fluid.

Hypereutectic: A casting process that combines aluminum with small silicon particles. The silicon particles provide a durable surface finish.

Installed Height: The distance from the valve spring seat to the bottom of the spring retainer; also called assembled height.

Integral: A part that is formed into a casting.

Interference Angle: The difference between the angle at which the valve face is ground and the angle at which the valve seat is ground.

Malfunction Indicator Lamp: Also known as the Check Engine Lamp. Illuminates to indicate a malfunction in the powertrain control system.

Manifold Pressure: Vacuum, or low air pressure, in the intake manifold of a running engine, caused by the descending pistons creating empty space in the cylinders faster than the entering air can fill it.

Micropolishing: A machining technique that uses an abrasive belt to restore mild crankshaft journal damage while removing minimal amounts of metal.

Milling: The process of using a multiple-tooth cutting bit to remove metal from a workpiece.

Neutralizer: A chemical compound added to the cooling system to reduce the alkaline chemicals in the flushing solution.

Offset: On a connecting rod, the condition of the two bores being out-of-parallel when viewed from the side.

Oil Dilution: Oil thinned or diluted by unburned fuel that gets past the piston rings and into the crankcase. Oil dilution also can result from water condensation in the crankcase.

Oil Galleries: Pipes or drilled passages in the engine block that are used to carry engine oil from one area to another.

Open-loop: An operational mode in which the engine management computer adjusts the system to function according to predetermined instructions and does not respond to feedback signals from system input sensors.

Organic Additive Technology (OAT): An additive with organic corrosion inhibiters.

Oscillating: A swinging, steady, up-and-down or back-and-forth motion.

Parting Line: The meeting points of two parts or machined pieces, such as the two halves of a split shell bearing.

PCM: Powertrain Control Module. An OBD II term for the electronic computer that controls the engine and transmission.

Plastigauge®: A string-like piece of plastic manufactured to a precise diameter used for measuring bearing clearance.

Plateau Surface: A finish in which the highest points of a surface have been honed to flattened peaks.

Ported Vacuum: The low pressure area, or vacuum, located just above the intake air throttle plates of an engine.

Positive Displacement Pump: A pump that delivers the same volume of fluid with each revolution regardless of speed.

Powdered Metal: A forging procedure in which the steel alloy is placed into a mold as a powder and is heated in a forge to melt the contents.

Propylene Glycol (PG): A less toxic chemical used for some coolant blends.

Reamer: A side-cutting tool used to finish a drilled hole to an exact size.

Refractometer: Tool used to accurately test coolant mixtures more accurately than traditional testers, through a liquid's ability to bend light.

Residual Pressure: A constant pressure held in the fuel system when the pump is not operating.

Resistance: Opposition to electrical current.

Re-torque: To torque again, as in reusing a fastener.

Ridge Reamer: A hand-operated cutting tool used to remove the wear ridge at the top of a cylinder bore.

Ring Lands: The part of a piston between the ring grooves. The lands strengthen and support the ring grooves.

Rodding: A method of repairing a radiator by running a drill bit through the internal passages of the core.

Runout: Side-to-side deviation in the movement of a rotating assembly.

Scan Tool: An electronic test device allowing the user to monitor computer controlled circuits and clear trouble codes.

Schrader Valve: A service valve that uses a spring-loaded pin and internal pressure to seal a port; depressing the pin will open the port.

Signal Generator: An electrical device that creates a voltage pulse that changes frequency or amplitude, or both, in relation to rotational speed.

Sludge: Black, moist deposits that form in the interior of the engine. A mixture of dust, oil, and water whipped together by the moving parts.

Specific Gravity: The weight of a volume of liquid divided by the weight of the same volume of water at a given temperature and pressure. Water has a specific gravity of 1.000.

Stretch: An extreme out-of-round condition on a bearing bore.

Supercharger: A crankshaft-driven compressor that delivers an air-fuel mixture to the engine cylinders at a pressure greater than atmospheric pressure.

Surface Grinding: The process of using a power-driven abrasive stone to remove metal from a casting to restore the surfaces.

Thermostatic Bulb: A device that automatically responds to changes in temperature to actuate a damper in the air intake passage.

Throating: Term for raising a valve seat in the cylinder head and narrowing the valve-to-seat contact patch by grinding an angle 15 degrees greater than the seating angle.

Tipping: Term for grinding the stem end of a valve to maintain correct stem height after grinding the valve face.

Topping: Term for lowering a valve seat in the cylinder head and narrowing the valve-to-seat contact patch by grinding an angle 15 degrees smaller than the seating angle.

Torque: A measurement of the twisting force required to rotate a fastener.

Torque-to-Yield: A method of tightening a faster utilizing an initial torque plus an added rotation measured in degrees.

Turbocharger: A compressor device that uses exhaust gases to turn a turbine that forces the air-fuel mixture into the cylinders.

Twist: On a connecting rod, the condition of the two bores being out-of-parallel when viewed from the top.

Valve Duration: The number of crankshaft degrees that a valve remains open.

Valve Lash: The gap between the rocker arm or the cam follower and the tip of the valve stem when the valve is closed. Also called valve clearance.

Valve Margin: The distance on a valve from the top of the machined face to the edge of the valve.

Valve Timing: A method of coordinating camshaft rotation and crankshaft rotation so that the valves open and close at the right times during each of the piston strokes.

Valve Train: The assembly of parts that transmits force from the cam lobe to the valve.

Variable-pitch Spring: A spring that changes its rate of pressure increase as it is compressed. This is achieved by unequal spacing of the spring coils.

Varnish: A hard, undesirable deposit formed by oxidation of fuel and motor oil.

Viscous Fan Clutch: A temperature sensing fan drive filled with a silicone fluid. As the temperature of the air passing the clutch increases, the internal valving in the clutch allows the fluid to flow into the coupling and increases the speed of the fan blade.

Voltage Drop: The measurement of the loss of voltage caused by the resistance of a conductor or a circuit device.

Wastegate: A diaphragm-actuated bypass valve used to limit turbocharger boost pressure by limiting the speed of the exhaust turbine.

Water Jacket: The area in the block and head around the cylinders, valves, and spark plugs that is left hollow so the coolant can circulate.

Wrist Pin: The cylindrical or tubular metal pin that attaches the piston to the connecting rod (also called the piston pin).

A1

A2

AUTOMATIC TRANSMISSIONS AND TRANSAXLES

CHAPTER ONE

GENERAL TRANSMISSION/TRANSAXLE DIAGNOSIS

CHAPTER OBJECTIVES

- The technician will complete the ASE task list on General Transmission/Transaxle Diagnosis.
- The technician will be able to answer 25 questions dealing with the General Diagnosis.

TRANSMISSION/TRANSAXLE INSPECTION AND DIAGNOSIS

This book uses the term transmission and transaxle interchangebly. Unless specifically noted either term applies to both type assemblies. To troubleshoot automatic transmission or transaxle problems, you must know the symptoms. Get a detailed description of the symptoms from the customer before you begin. Keep in mind that what your customer feels is an internal transmission/transaxle problem may actually be caused by poor engine performance, incorrectly adjusted linkage, or an emission control system malfunction. You must know:

- Exactly what the concern is
- The circumstances under which it occurs
- When the problem first occurred

Problems that develop gradually usually indicate an internal disorder, such as a clogged filter, a pressure loss, or fluid contamination. Problems that develop suddenly suggest an external disorder, such as a ruptured cooler line, or a large internal failure, such as a broken **band**. If the symptoms began after other work was performed on the vehicle, the cause may simply be an incorrect idle speed, linkage adjustment, or fluid level.

MECHANICAL & HYDRAULIC SYSTEMS

Preliminary Inspection

Check the vehicle over and verify that all of the following are in working order and properly adjusted:

- Ignition system components
- Ignition timing
- Fuel and air filters
- Engine **manifold vacuum** lines and components
- Positive crankcase ventilation system
- Cylinder compression
- Exhaust system

If all of the engine systems are in good condition, check the transmission for:

- Proper fluid level and condition
- Signs of fluid leakage
- Proper shift and kickdown linkage adjustment
- Loose or damaged electrical connections and wiring
- Broken or disconnected vacuum lines and hoses

Road Testing the Transmission

Road test the vehicle once you have performed the preliminary inspection.

Before the road test, look up the shift speed specifications, also called shift points, in the Service Manual. Be aware that shift points differ according to engine, transmission, axle, tire size, and model year combination. Make sure specifications are an exact match for the vehicle being tested. During the road test, record the exact shift points for comparison. Also have a clutch and band application chart with you, so you can determine which devices are active at any given time, figure 1-1. Depending upon the symptoms, you may also want to connect a pressure gauge to the transmission to monitor hydraulic pressure while driving.

During the road test, check for:

- Slippage
- Early, late, or erratic shift timing
- Poor shift quality
- Unusual noise or vibrations
- Torque converter clutch operation

A lightly traveled road is ideal for conducting a road test. Take advantage of any natural features, such as hills and curves, which might emphasize the problem the customer complained about.

Performing the Road Test

Begin a road test from a standing start with gear selector in drive or overdrive, if so equipped. Accelerate the vehicle moderately. Record all the upshift points.

When cruising in top gear, quickly open the throttle partway to test the part throttle downshift. Repeat, opening the throttle fully, to test the full throttle downshift. With a lockup torque converter, you should also be able to feel the converter clutch release during a downshift. Check for a coasting, or closed throttle, downshift by decelerating to a stop.

Selector Position / Gear	Park	Reverse	Neutral	D 1st	D 2nd	D 3rd	D 4th	3 1st	3 2nd	3 3rd	2 1st	2 2nd	1 1st
1-2, 3-4 Shift Solenoid	ON	ON	ON	ON	OFF	OFF	ON	ON	OFF	OFF	ON	OFF	ON
2-3 Shift Solenoid	ON	ON	ON	ON	ON	OFF	OFF	ON	ON	OFF	ON	ON	ON
Fourth Clutch	—	—	—	—	—	—	A	—	—	—	—	—	—
Reverse Band	—	A	—	—	—	—	—	—	—	—	—	—	—
Second Clutch	—	—	—	—	A	A	A	—	A	A	—	A	—
Third Clutch	—	—	—	—	—	A	A*	—	—	A	—	—	A
Third Sprag	—	—	—	—	—	H	O	—	—	H	—	—	H
Input Clutch	A*	A	A*	A	A*	—	—	A	A*	A	A	A*	A
Input Sprag	H*	H	H	H	O	—	—	H	O	H	H	O	H
2-1 Manual Band	—	—	—	—	—	—	—	—	—	—	A	A	A
1-2 Support Roller Clutch	—	—	—	H	H	O	O	H	H	O	H	H	H
Forward Band	—	—	—	A	A	A*	A*	A	A	A*	A	A	A

ON = the solenoid valve is energized.
OFF = the solenoid valve is de-energized.
A = Applied
H = Holding
O = Overrun
* = applied, or holding, with no load (not transmitting torque).

Fig. 1-1. Four speed automatic transaxle clutch, band, and solenoid application chart.

To check operation of manual third, manual second, or manual 1 (low), accelerate from start with the gear selector in the proper range. Check the manual downshift quality by operating the vehicle at a moderate cruising speed or speed recommended by the manufacturer. Release the accelerator pedal, then move the gear selector from Drive or Overdrive to manual third. Repeat, shifting the gear selector to manual second, and then manual first or low.

Test the TCC (Torque Converter Clutch) during the road test by lightly tapping the brake while observing the engine RPM.

A scan tool can be used on newer vehicles to perform this test. A technician can manually engage and disengage the TCC while monitoring the scan tool data. On some scan tools there is also a TCC slip percent/count data for diagnosing TCC.

Finally, stop the vehicle and place the gear selector in reverse. Check the transmission/transaxle operation in reverse at both part-throttle and full-throttle openings.

NOISE, VIBRATION, HARSHNESS, AND SHIFT QUALITY DIAGNOSIS

Noise and Vibration

When road testing the vehicle notice when and in what gear range the noise and/or vibration occurs. A noise and/or vibration in lower gear ranges could point to the planet pinion gears. In direct drive the planet gears are not turning.

A whine noise may indicate a low transmission fluid level. Check and adjust the fluid level as necessary.

A whine noise in all gear ranges which may be load or RPM sensitive or ceases when the TCC engages may be caused by the torque converter. A torque converter noise will increase under load.

A whine or growling noise that increases and fades with vehicle speed and is most noticeable under light throttle may be caused by the transaxle drive link assembly.

A high pitch whine noise in all gear ranges which intensifies with engine rpm or is oil pressure sensitive may be caused by the transmission oil pump system. An increase in oil pressure will vary an oil pump noise.

A popping noise in all gear ranges which sounds like popcorn popping may be caused by transmission oil pump cavitation, a transmission fluid strainer seam leak, or a damaged or improperly positioned transmission fluid strainer seal.

A buzz or high frequency rattle sound may be caused by binding or contact of the transmission cooler pipes.

A ratcheting noise may indicate a weak, damaged or misassembled parking pawl return spring.

A hum or final drive noise which is most noticeable under light throttle acceleration and/or turns may be caused by the transaxle final drive gear set.

A light metallic rattle noise which is most noticeable under coast or drive operation may be caused by a damaged clutch pack, excessive clutch pack clearance, or excessive clutch plate to case clearance.

A rattle noise that occurs at idle or low speed may indicate loose flex plate mounting bolts.

A squealing noise at low speed may indicate a defective speedometer gear.

A whine noise in park and vibration in reverse may indicate broken oil pump vane rings.

A vibration in a neutral run-up may point to a cracked or out of balance flex plate. Internal or external engine balancing components could also show up in a neutral run-up. This type of a vibration is sometimes difficult to isolate.

Vibration may be caused by loose or damaged transmission and/or engine mounts. Vibration may also be caused by loose or worn drivetrain components, loose or worn suspension components, tire imbalance, or loose or worn wheel bearings.

Harshness and Shift Quality

A clutch and band application chart lets you know which components are active in which gears. The chart is a handy reference for analyzing the symptoms you experience during a road test.

For example assume there is slippage in second gear on a vehicle with a three speed Hydra-Matic 3T40 transaxle. The clutch and band application chart, figure 1-2, shows how the forward clutch and intermediate band apply in drive second and manual second. In all other forward gears, the forward clutch is used but not the intermediate band. Therefore if the transmission slips only in second, an intermediate band failure is likely at fault. A forward clutch problem would cause the transmission to slip in low and high gears as well.

Slippage in reverse with the Hydra-Matic 3T40 transaxle can be caused by either a direct clutch or low-reverse band failure. But, if the direct clutch is at fault, there should be slippage in third gear as well as reverse, but not in any other forward gears. A low-reverse clutch failure results in a lack of engine braking on deceleration in manual low, as well as slippage in reverse. Consider that the low roller clutch locks up to prevent noticeable slippage if the low-reverse band begins to slip when under acceleration in manual low. However, the low roller clutch freewheels on deceleration and does not provide engine braking. The low-reverse band stays applied during both acceleration and deceleration to provide engine braking. Therefore, a faulty low-reverse band will slip in reverse and during deceleration in manual low.

During the road test, with manual third selected, there will be a 1-2 shift at a specified speed and a 2-3 shift at a specified speed. The transmission will not upshift again regardless of speed. With manual second selected, there will be a 1-2 upshift

RANGE	GEAR	DIRECT CLUTCH	INTERMEDIATE BAND	FORWARD CLUTCH	LOW ROLLER CLUTCH	LOW-REVERSE CLUTCH
P-N						
D	1st			APPLIED	HOLDING	
D	2nd		APPLIED	APPLIED		
D	3rd	APPLIED		APPLIED		
2	1st			APPLIED	HOLDING	
2	2nd		APPLIED	APPLIED		
1	1st			APPLIED	HOLDING	APPLIED
R	REVERSE	APPLIED				APPLIED

Fig. 1-2. A clutch and band application chart, which tells you which devices apply to achieve the different gear ranges, is an indispensable diagnostic tool. The chart above is for a Hydra-Matic 3T40 transaxle.

at the specified speed for most transmissions. Once in second gear, the transmission will not upshift again, regardless of speed, and provides engine braking on deceleration. However, some transmissions start and stay in second gear when the gear selector lever is in manual second. When manual low is selected, most transmissions will remain in low gear and provide engine braking on deceleration. Again there are exceptions, as some transmissions will upshift to second to prevent damage to the transmission or engine.

During the road test, when moving the gear selector lever from Drive or Overdrive to manual third at moderate cruising speed, or a speed specified by the manufacturer, the transmission should downshift from 4-3. Observe the shift quality and check for engine braking. The torque converter clutch should also release.

When moving the gear selector lever from Drive or Overdrive to manual second at moderate cruising speed, or a speed specified by the manufacturer, the transmission should downshift from 4-2. Observe the shift quality and check for engine braking. The torque converter clutch should also release.

When moving the gear selector lever from Drive or Overdrive to manual first or low at moderate cruising speed, or a speed specified by the manufacturer, many transmissions will shift into second when manual first or low is selected if the vehicle speed is too high, then downshift into first once the speed drops low enough to prevent damage. Observe the shift quality and check for engine braking. The torque converter clutch should also release.

If initial engagement is delayed when the transmission is placed in gear, then the check valve in the oil pump may be faulty. This condition, known as converter drain back, allows fluid to drain into the transmission pan from the torque converter while the vehicle is not being operated, figure 1-3.

To diagnose converter drain back, perform a road test and check the transmission fluid level. Park the vehicle for several hours, and then recheck the fluid level before starting the engine. If the fluid level is extremely high on the dipstick, fluid has drained back into the pan. Remove the transmission and repair or replace the check valve in the pump.

The cause of harsh engagement and/or harsh shifts may be:

- Incorrect transmission fluid level
- Misadjusted throttle linkage
- Misadjusted band

- Missing valve body check balls
- Damaged band, clutch, or planetary component
- Faulty torque converter clutch

Once the faulty component has been identified, adjust or replace as necessary.

Checking Fluid Level and Condition

When checking the automatic transmission fluid (ATF) level, it is important to follow the procedure recommended by the manufacturer. Most require that the level be checked when the fluid is at normal operating temperature, the vehicle is on a level surface, and the engine is running at idle. Dipsticks are often marked for taking readings at different fluid temperatures, figure 1-4. Always follow the prescribed procedure.

The transmission fluid that clings to the dipstick can often be used to help determine internal transmission conditions. Analyze the fluid by looking for:

- Unusual color
- Strong odors
- Particles of metal, friction material, and other debris

Unusual Fluid Color

Most ATF contains red dye to make identification easy. As the fluid ages, the color will change to a reddish brown. This discoloration is normal for some fluids, such as DEXRON III, Dexron VI, and Mercon®. Color change is not a cause for concern in itself as long as the fluid is not burnt. If the color on the dipstick is hard to detect, wipe the fluid onto a clean white cloth or paper towel. This allows the fluid to reflect its true color. Unusual color conditions will include:

- Dark brown with a pungent odor—brown discoloration may be normal, but the odor indicates overheating, and the fluid should be changed
- Dark gray or black—this indicates excessive friction material in the fluid. The particles will separate from the fluid when wiped onto a rag
- Milky pink or milky brown—this is an indication of water or coolant contamination. Severe damage will result if the leak is not repaired
- Foamy red or reddish-brown—this indicates fluid aeration, often the result of overfilling

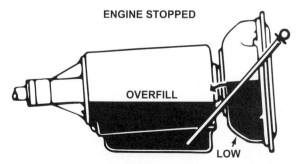

Fig. 1-3. Torque converter drain back, which causes delayed engagement on initial start up, is the result of a faulty oil pump check valve or bushing.

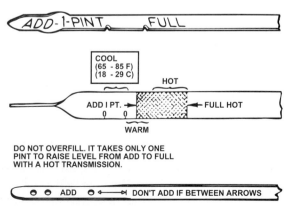

Fig. 1-4. Fluid temperature must be considered to get an accurate dipstick reading.

A2

Unusual Fluid Odor

Fresh ATF is odorless. Burned or overheated fluid may retain its red coloration but will give off a pungent, foul smell. To determine odor, rub a small amount of fluid between two fingers and smell it. Burnt fluid that is chemically broken down must be drained and replaced to avoid band and clutch failures.

Particles in the Fluid

When particles are found on the dipstick, drain the transmission and remove the oil pan for closer inspection. It is common to find dirt, as well as tiny flakes of aluminum, brass, and bronze in the pan. These are of no concern unless the pieces are large. Friction material wear creates a fine dust that can collect into a grayish-black sludge that settles in the bottom of the pan. Heavy deposits or large particles indicate the bands and clutches need replacement.

Checking for Fluid Leakage

Fluid leaks, a common cause of low fluid levels, are often difficult to locate because the air passing under the vehicle tends to spread the fluid around. To find a leak, first clean off the transmission case; use degreaser or steam cleaning if necessary. Warm the transmission up to operating temperature, lift the vehicle on a hoist, and check for leaks with the engine running. Next, shut the engine off and watch for leaks caused by drain back. Look for leakage at the:

- Oil pan gasket
- Oil cooler lines and fittings
- Fluid filler and vent tubes
- Speedometer and throttle valve cable connections
- Output shaft and torque converter seals
- Governor cover
- Downshift control lever shaft and manual shaft seals
- Pressure tap plugs
- Vacuum modulator

With certain transmissions, a leak may result from case porosity. The pressurized fluid actually works its way through the metal of the casting at certain places. Some porosity leaks can be repaired by applying a special epoxy to the affected area of the case.

Checking Linkage Adjustment

Many transmissions use mechanical linkage to select the desired gear range, figure 1-5.

This shift linkage must be properly adjusted. Incorrect adjustment can cause:

- Creeping in park or neutral
- Delayed engagement in any gear
- Failure to start in park or neutral
- Failure to lock in park
- Low **mainline pressure** and premature clutch and band wear

In addition, some transmissions use mechanical linkage to control **throttle pressure**. Since throttle pressure affects shift timing, an incorrect accelerator linkage setting can cause shifting problems, figure 1-6.

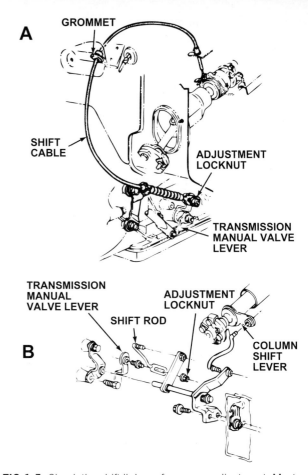

FIG.1-5. Check the shift linkage for proper adjustment. Most linkages, whether cable (A) or rod (B) actuated, adjust at the manual valve lever.

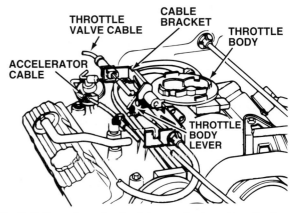

Fig. 1-6. Correct accelerator linkage adjustment is critical on transmissions that use mechanical linkage to position the throttle valve.

Inspect the shift linkage for correct positioning and movement. Adjustment procedures are covered in Chapter Two of this book.

Checking Vacuum Controls

Some transmissions use engine manifold vacuum to modulate shifting. Check the vacuum supply hose; repair or replace the hose as required. Details for testing the **vacuum modulator** diaphragm and vacuum source can be found in Chapter Three of this book. Also, check and repair any vacuum hoses, valves, and connections used in the torque converter lockup system.

TRANSMISSION TESTING

A road test can help you to identify which **apply device** is not working right, but it cannot always determine the actual cause of the malfunction. Simply replacing the bad part may only temporarily solve the problem. Failure can reoccur if the condition that first caused it is not corrected. A hydraulic pressure test is the most accurate way to pinpoint a problem.

Hydraulic Pressure Testing

Many automatic transmissions and transaxles are equipped with pressure test ports that allow you to tap into the hydraulic system. The test gauge must be capable of registering at least 50 psi more than what is expected on the circuit. For most applications, a gauge that will register up to 300 psi of pressure is adequate. Typically, tests must be made at a specific engine speed and vacuum level, so a tachometer and vacuum gauge are also required. Combination testers that contain one or two pressure gauges, plus a tachometer and a vacuum gauge, figure 1-7, are available.

Electronic pressure analyzers, a recent development of the tool industry, work well for testing transmissions, figure 1-8. These tools use transducers to convert pressure to a voltage signal. A wiring harness carries the voltage signal to the analyzer that displays pressure on a digital readout. Current models can process up to four signals simultaneously and, because the tool will register both positive and negative pressure, you do not need an additional vacuum gauge.

Hydraulic pressure specifications often vary for the same transmission in different model years or for different vehicle and engine combinations. Specifications for the exact make, model, and year of transmission and vehicle being tested are essential. The automatic transmission uses three types of hydraulic pressure to actuate components and regulate shifting:

- Mainline pressure
- Throttle pressure
- Governor pressure

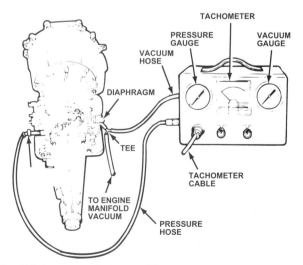

Fig. 1-7. A pressure tester combines a pressure gauge, vacuum gauge, and tachometer into a single cabinet.

Fig. 1-8. Electronic pressure analyzers display transmission pressures as a digital readout.

Mainline Pressure

Mainline pressure is developed by the transmission pump and controlled by a pressure-regulating valve at the pump output. Mainline pressure, also known as control pressure or drive oil, is used to hold, activate, and drive **planetary gearset** members to provide different gear ratios. Mainline pressure provides the source for all other hydraulic pressures in the transmission.

Throttle Pressure

Throttle pressure is developed from mainline pressure at the throttle valve. The throttle valve is connected to the engine by mechanical linkage or a vacuum modulator. Throttle pressure, also known as modulator pressure, increases with engine load and throttle opening and interacts with governor pressure to control shift points.

Governor Pressure

Governor pressure increases with the vehicle road speed and works in conjunction with throttle pressure to control shift points. The governor, a centrifugally operated valve driven off the transmission or transaxle output shaft, develops governor pressure from mainline pressure.

Hydraulic Pressure Test Procedures

A pressure test is performed with the transmission at normal operating temperature. Remove the appropriate test-port plug from the transmission case and connect the pressure gauges. Screw the pressure gauge hose fitting into the port and tighten snugly with a wrench. Do not overtighten. Where the gauge connections are made varies with transmission design. You must tap into the correct port to get accurate results.

Preliminary Checks

Run the engine long enough to bring ATF temperature into the normal operating range. Then, check the following:

- Fluid level
- Fluid condition
- Transmission electrical connections
- Shift linkage adjustment

Also, verify that the engine is in sound mechanical condition and in a good state of tune. A poor-running engine can have low manifold vacuum, which can cause pressure problems on transmissions that use a vacuum modulator.

Securely support the vehicle on a hoist with the drive wheels free to rotate. When testing a front-wheel drive (FWD) vehicle, place jack stands or some other type of support under the lower control arms to prevent damage to the drive axles.

As you monitor pressure, look for readings to meet specifications and note how much time it takes pressure to build up. Hydraulic pressures should respond and build to peak levels quickly—generally in less than one second. Slow build-up indicates a problem that can affect shift quality.

Mainline Pressure Test

Set the parking brake, apply the service brakes, and shift the gear selector into park.

Test mainline pressure as follows:

1. Watch the gauges as you start the engine. Look for:

   - An immediate line pressure rise to about 50 to 75 psi
   - A stable idle speed
   - A steady 15 to 21 in-Hg of manifold vacuum

This test checks the pump circuit. Be aware that some transmission units do not produce true line pressure in park, so do not be alarmed if there is no reading on the gauge. Simply repeat this step with the gear selector in neutral to isolate and check the pump circuit.

2. Allow the engine to idle, apply the brakes, and shift the transmission through all gear ranges. Pause long enough in each gear for conditions to stabilize, then record the gauge reading. For most applications, expect:

   - Line pressure in all forward ranges to be similar to readings taken in park or neutral. Manual low pressure may be slightly higher than other readings
   - Reverse line pressure higher than any of the other readings
   - Vacuum above 15 in-Hg during the entire test sequence

3. Conditions for taking the next set of readings will vary greatly by the transmission being tested. Choices include:

   - Hold engine speed at fast idle, 1000 to 1200 RPM, while you repeat step two
   - Allow the drive wheels to freewheel or drive the vehicle to check shift speeds
   - Conduct a stall test and record the pressure for each gear range at stall speed

Performing a stall test at this point provides you with maximum line pressure readings and the pressure test sequence is complete. If a stall test is not recommended, continue to determine maximum line pressures.

4. Use one of the following methods to ensure that the throttle valve remains wide open:

   - Disconnect the throttle valve linkage at the transmission, move the throttle valve to the wide-open position, and lock it in place
   - Disconnect the vacuum hose at the modulator and plug the end of the hose to prevent a vacuum leak

5. Run the engine at idle, or other specified speed, apply the brakes, and record gauge readings as you shift through all gear ranges. Full-throttle pressure varies greatly by transmission and you must have specifications on hand.

6. You now know the minimum and maximum line pressure. Your final check is to see how pressure responds to throttle input. Reconnect the throttle valve linkage or modulator vacuum.

7. With the engine at idle and the gear selector in drive range, slowly depress the accelerator pedal as you watch for a rise in pressure. The response should be almost immediate. Less than ¼ inch of pedal travel, or a 3 in-Hg drop in manifold vacuum, should cause pressure to rise.

8. Continue to slowly depress the accelerator. Pressure build-up should be steady until you reach the maximum pressure previously established. Release the throttle and allow the engine to return to idle. Generally, you will see maximum pressure at about 75-percent throttle; it should always occur before full throttle.

This completes the mainline pressure test sequence. Allow the engine to idle down and run unloaded for about one minute to cool the fluid and lower transmission temperature before you switch it off.

Governor Pressure Test

Some transmissions have a separate governor test port on the transmission, figure 1-9. You test others by watching for line pressure to cutback, or drop off, under certain operating conditions.

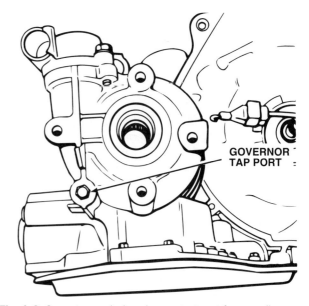

GOVERNOR TAP PORT

Fig. 1-9. Some transmissions have a test port for sampling governor pressure.

If the transmission has a governor pressure test port, the factory Service Manual should provide a specification table for comparing pressure readings at various road speeds. Test by installing a pressure gauge and either driving the vehicle or operating it on a hoist with the drive wheels freewheeling.

To check for line pressure cutback, leave the gauge installed in the line pressure port. Select drive range and slowly accelerate as you watch the gauge. If the governor is working properly, line pressure will momentarily drop as road speed reaches about 10 to 20 MPH. If the transmission has a vacuum modulator, disconnect and plug the vacuum line. Connect a hand-operated vacuum pump and apply 10 in-Hg of vacuum to the modulator. Slowly accelerate and watch for cutback to occur between 10 to 20 MPH. Next, apply 2 in-Hg of vacuum to the modulator and repeat the test. With lower vacuum, cutback should occur at a higher speed—usually around 30 to 50 MPH. If cutback does occur, the problem most likely lies in the **valve body**.

Evaluating Line Pressure Test Results

Compare your test readings with the specification ranges provided by the manufacturer to determine whether pressure is too low, too high, or within range for all facets of the test. In general:

- The initial reading, in park or neutral with the engine at idle, isolates the pump. Readings outside specifications indicate a defective pump or a problem on the pickup side of the pump
- Incorrect pump pressure will affect pressure readings for all other test phases
- Two or more readings that are either too high or too low are the result of a common problem, not an indication of multiple problems

Refer to the pressure diagnosis chart in the Service Manual to identify the offending circuit. To fully evaluate pressure test results, you need to know how hydraulic pressure is routed through the transmission. The best source for this information is the fluid flow diagrams that the manufacturers provide in their Service Manuals, figure 1-10.

Air Pressure Testing

Air pressure testing substitutes compressed air for fluid pressure to check the operation of clutches and servos. Although you can perform an air test without removing the transmission from the vehicle, you do have to remove the oil pan, filter, and valve body to access the hydraulic passages in the transmission case. Testing some transmissions requires an adapter plate that bolts onto the case in place of the valve body. You apply air pressure to the hydraulic passages through holes on the face of the plate, figure 1-11.

From a diagnostic standpoint, an air pressure test is the last step before removing the transmission or making repairs. This procedure is a follow-up to hydraulic pressure testing and a thorough road test. The pressure test lets you know if you have a pressure loss on a circuit, and the air test pinpoints the leak.

Air Test Procedure

Always wear eye protection to perform an air test, and allow sufficient time for the ATF to completely drain after you remove the pan, filter, and valve body. You must be able to identify the hydraulic passages in the transmission case to conduct an air test. Manufacturers provide passage identification charts in the Service Manual, figure 1-12.

To check a circuit, apply 25 to 30 psi of air pressure to the passage. Hold the air on for several seconds as you listen and watch. Expect to hear a dull thud, the sound of the clutch piston moving, as you first apply air. If you cannot hear the piston move, place your fingertips on the clutch drum or input shell and reapply air pressure. You should be able to feel piston movement if the clutch is operating.

Observe the operation of the bands by watching them tighten and loosen around the drums as you apply and release air pressure. Hold the air applied to check for leaks; leaks produce a hissing noise. Applying air to the governor creates a sharp whistling, clicking, or buzzing noise.

Stall Testing

A stall test checks engine performance, converter stator **one-way clutch** operation, and the holding ability of the clutches and bands. The test reveals the stall speed, the highest engine RPM obtainable at full throttle with the rear wheels locked and the transmission in gear.

Perform a stall test only if it is recommended by the manufacturer. Stall testing vehicles with electronic control systems can create false trouble codes and cause component damage. In addition, considerable damage to the engine, transmission, and brakes results if the test is not done correctly. Clutches and bands that are in marginal condition before testing can be destroyed from the strain of the test.

Stall Test Procedures

Transmission fluid and engine coolant levels must be correct and at normal operating temperature. To conduct a stall test:

1. Connect a tachometer to the engine.
2. Block the wheels securely.
3. Start the engine, fully apply the parking and the service brakes, and shift into the range being tested.
4. Depress the accelerator to full throttle and hold it until the tachometer reading stabilizes. Do not keep the throttle open longer than five seconds.
5. Release the accelerator immediately if the engine speed exceeds the maximum limit specified. This indicates clutch or band slippage.
6. Record the maximum RPM shown on the tachometer.
7. Shift the transmission into neutral. Run the engine at a fast idle RPM for 60 seconds to cool the fluid.
8. Repeat the procedure for each driving range.

Interpreting Test Results

Compare the maximum RPM readings obtained during the stall test with specifications provided by the manufacturer. In general, results can be interpreted as follows:

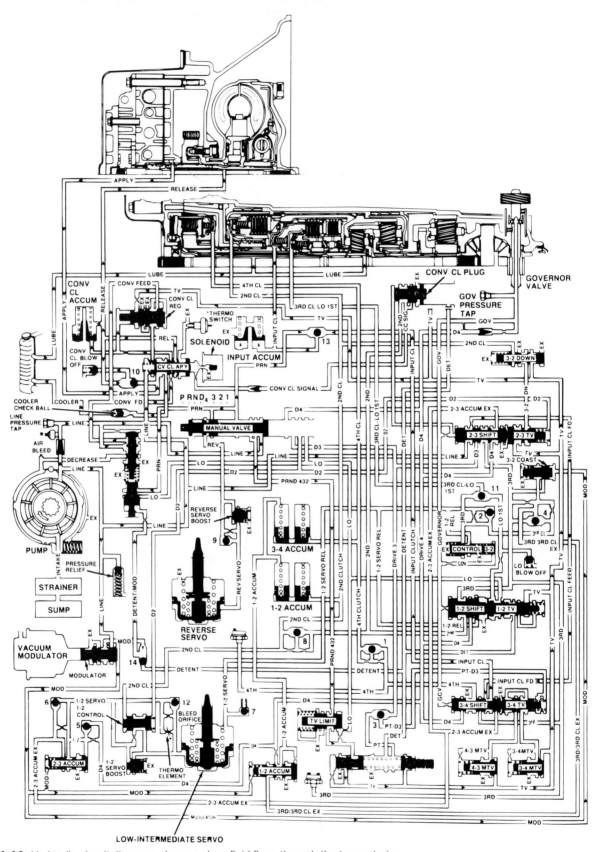

Fig. 1-10. Hydraulic circuit diagrams show you how fluid flows through the transmission.

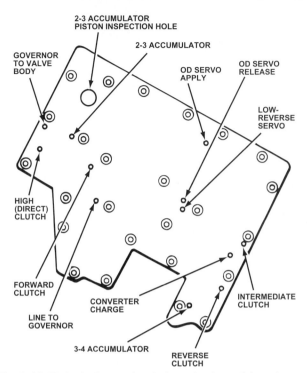

Fig. 1-11. Typical adapter plate bolts on in place of the valve body for air testing an automatic transmission or transaxle.

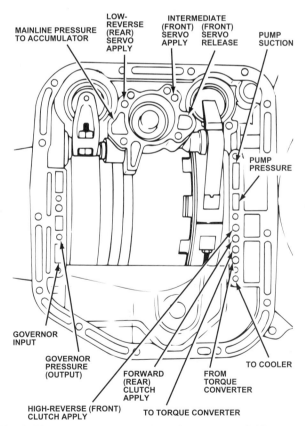

Fig. 1-12. You must be able to identify the correct fluid passage to perform an air test.

Stall speed too high

A stall speed more than 200 RPM above the maximum specified speed indicates possible clutch or band slippage. Use a clutch and band application chart to determine which components are applied.

Stall speed too low

A stall speed 250 to 350 RPM below the minimum specified by the manufacturer indicates torque converter problems, often a failed one-way clutch. Confirm the condition with a road test. If the vehicle operates satisfactorily at cruising speed, but has poor low-speed acceleration, replace the torque converter.

Stall speed within specifications

Double check a normal stall speed by a road test. If low-speed acceleration is normal but highway speeds require a high throttle opening, the stator is probably locked up. In this case, the transmission also runs hotter than normal. Check the exhaust system for restrictions. A partially blocked exhaust system can produce the same symptoms as a locked stator clutch.

Stall speed noise

Fluid flow causes a harsh whine during a stall test. If you also hear a loud metallic noise, the torque converter may be bad. Operate the vehicle on a hoist at light throttle with the transmission in drive and then in neutral. If you hear a noise from the torque converter housing, replace the converter.

A2

TORQUE CONVERTER TESTING

The torque converter couples the engine to the geartrain and multiplies engine torque. Conventional torque converters consist of an impeller, a turbine, and a stator, figure 1-13. Lockup torque converters also include a clutch assembly that, when applied, mechanically links the engine to the geartrain, figure 1-14. In some lockup converters, clutch application is electronically controlled. Torque converter problems can result in the following conditions:

- Acceleration from a standstill is slow in all ranges
- Acceleration is normal, but high speed performance is poor
- The transmission overheats

Converter functions can be checked by pressure testing, stall testing, and road testing.

Stator Testing

The torque converter stator and its one-way clutch may develop two malfunctions. The stator may:

- Freewheel in both directions
- Remain locked up at all times

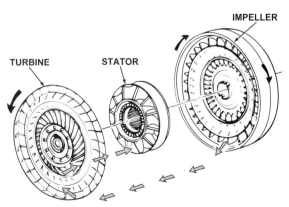

Fig. 1-13. The main components of a torque converter are the impeller, stator, and turbine.

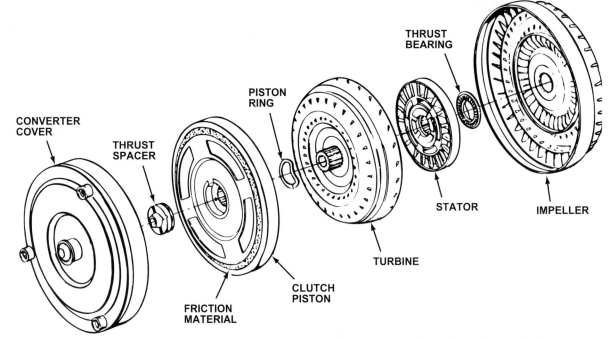

Fig. 1-14. Lockup torque converters use a clutch assembly to eliminate slippage between the engine and transmission.

Both problems tend to show up during a road test. When the clutch is not locking up the stator, the vehicle accelerates slowly at speeds below about 30 or 35 MPH, while at higher road speeds it accelerates normally. A stator that is constantly locked restricts engine RPM and vehicle speed. Often, the vehicle cannot go faster than about 50 MPH.

When the vehicle accelerates poorly at lower road speeds, inspect the exhaust system for restrictions and check the state of tune of the engine. Place the transmission in neutral and press the accelerator. If the engine accelerates to high RPM without difficulty, the engine and exhaust system are both normal.

A vehicle in which the stator is constantly locked up accelerates normally but is likely to overheat. The only way to verify the condition of the stator clutch is to check it with the torque converter removed from the transmission.

ELECTRONIC CONTROL SYSTEMS

Modern transmissions use an electronic control system to regulate torque converter clutch (TCC) application, gear changes, and mainline pressure. Although electronic controls reduce the number of moving parts in a transmission and eliminate the source of some failures, they create a whole new transmission subsystem that requires a unique diagnostic approach.

On earlier model vehicles, the electronic control system does not monitor or control the entire powertrain. Late-model vehicle engine and transmission systems are completely electronically controlled.

Mechanical systems and components, both transmission and engine, must all be inspected before troubleshooting the electronic control system. Transmission and engine control system functions are interrelated and cannot be separated. The two systems share information, often rely on the same sensors, and may operate using a single computer, figure 1-15.

Therefore, when an electronic failure is indicated, it is important to check the operation of both the engine and the transmission control systems.

ELECTRONIC SYSTEMS

Preliminary Inspection

During the preliminary inspection, verify that:

- Charging system output is within specifications
- The battery is in good condition
- Battery terminal connections are clean and tight

Next, check for good circuit connections and continuity. Inspect connectors for signs of damage, corrosion, or pushed out pins.

DIAGNOSTIC TROUBLE CODE (DTC) CHECKS

Always check both transmission and engine codes, even if the vehicle has only engine data parameters available. On many models, a Malfunction Indicator Lamp or warning lamp will illuminate when a DTC has been detected by the control module. Make sure the system is not operating in limp home mode, or the results of any test you perform may be inconclusive. Some manufacturers' limp home mode will not allow the transmission to either upshift or downshift from the current gear range that it is operating. If the engine is shut down, while in limp home mode, the Powertrain Control Module (PCM) or Transmission Control Module (TCM) may not allow any gear to engage after restarting. Some systems display codes by a lamp on the instrument panel or gear shift indicator, but the best way to read codes is with a scan tool.

Scan tools communicate with the vehicle control modules through a diagnostic connector. Since the inception of onboard electronic controls manufacturers have used a variety of diagnostic connectors to access their control systems. However, with

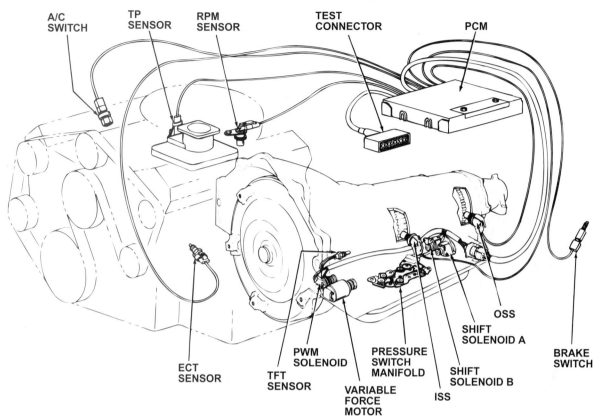

Fig. 1-15. Electronic controls for the Hydra-Matic 4L80E transmission. Note: A single PCM regulates both engine and transmission functions.

the introduction of Onboard Diagnostics II (OBD II) all late model vehicles use a standard SAE Data Link Connector (DLC) for control system testing, figure 1-16. Refer to the appropriate Service Manual for location of the correct diagnostic connector in non-OBD II vehicles.

Control Module Flash and Programming Updates
Always check the vehicle Service Manual and Service Bulletins for information on control module flash and programming updates before performing diagnostic procedures.

Road Testing the Transmission
Road test the vehicle once you have performed the preliminary inspection.

Before the road test, look up the shift speed specifications, also called shift points, in the Service Manual. Be aware that shift points differ according to engine, transmission, axle, tire size and model year combination. Make sure specifications are an exact match for the vehicle being tested. During the road test, record the exact shift points for comparison. Also have a clutch, band, and shift solenoid application chart with you, so you can determine which devices are active at any given time, figure 1-1, and an automatic transmission electronic control system wiring diagram.

During the road test, check for:

- Slippage
- Early, late, or erratic shift timing
- Poor shift quality
- Unusual noise or vibrations
- Torque converter clutch operation

A lightly traveled road is ideal for conducting a road test. Take advantage of any natural features, such as hills and curves, which might emphasize the problem the customer complained about.

Performing the Road Test
Connect a scan tool to the vehicle data link connector, figure 1-16. Refer to the appropriate Service Manual for location of the correct diagnostic connector in non-OBD II vehicles.

Begin the road test by placing the transmission gear selector in Park and setting the parking brake. Start the engine and verify the scan tool data can be obtained and is functioning properly.

Monitor the brake switch signal by depressing and releasing the brake pedal. The scan tool should indicate when the brake pedal switch is closed or opened.

Apply the brake pedal and move the gear selector lever through each of the selector positions, pausing a few seconds in each gear position. The gear engagements should be immediate and not harsh, soft or delayed.

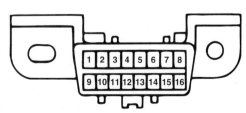

Fig. 1-16. The 16-pin OBD-II data link connector is standard on all late-model vehicles.

Many PCMs and TCMs calculate upshift points based on throttle angle and vehicle speed. When the control module determines that conditions are met for an upshift to occur, the control module commands the shift by opening or closing the ground circuit for the appropriate solenoid.

Place the transmission gear selector in Overdrive or Drive, then accelerate the vehicle using the specified throttle angle for the vehicle being tested and note the vehicle speed at which each upshift occurs. Each upshift should be immediate and not harsh, soft, or delayed. Note any slipping or noise or vibration. Also note the Torque Converter Clutch engagement.

When cruising in top gear, quickly open the throttle partway to test the part throttle downshift. Repeat, opening the throttle fully, to test the full throttle downshift. You should also be able to feel the torque converter clutch release during a downshift. Check for a coasting, or closed throttle, downshift by decelerating to a stop.

To check operation of manual third, manual second, or manual 1 (low), accelerate from start with the gear selector in the proper range. Check the manual downshift quality by operating the vehicle at a moderate cruising speed or speed recommended by the manufacturer. Release the accelerator pedal, then move the gear selector from Drive or Overdrive to manual third. Repeat, shifting the gear selector to manual second, and then manual first or low.

Testing the TCC (Torque Converter Clutch) during a road test can be done by lightly tapping the brake while observing the engine RPM.

The scan tool can be used on newer vehicles to perform this test. A technician can manually engage and disengage the TCC while monitoring the scan tool data. On some scan tools there is also a TCC slip percent/count data for diagnosing TCC.

Finally, stop the vehicle and place the gear selector in reverse. Check the transmission/transaxle operation in reverse at both part-throttle and full-throttle openings.

Check the scan tool for any Diagnostic Trouble Codes (DTCs) that may have set during the road test. Also check for abnormal scan tool readings and data. Refer to the vehicle Service Manual for Diagnostic Trouble Code (DTC) interpretation.

Pressure Test

A scan tool should be used along with a hydraulic transmission pressure gauge when performing the pressure test. When performing the pressure test, refer to the vehicle Service Manual for test procedure and specifications.

For example, on a vehicle equipped with a Hydra-Matic 4T65-E, connect a scan tool to the vehicle data link connector, figure 1-16. Refer to the appropriate Service Manual for location of the correct diagnostic connector in non-OBD II vehicles. Start the engine and use the scan tool to check for any stored Diagnostic Trouble Codes (DTCs). If DTC(s) are present, refer to the vehicle Service Manual for DTC interpretation. Make the required repairs before proceeding with the pressure test. Turn off the engine and remove the oil pressure test plug. Connect an oil pressure test gauge to the oil pressure test hole. Place the transmission gear selector in Park and apply the vehicle parking brake. Start the engine and allow the engine to warm up. Access the pressure control solenoid test on the scan tool.

Increase the pressure control solenoid actual current from 0.0 amps to 1.0 amps in 0.1 amp intervals. Allow the pressure to stabilize for a few seconds after each pressure change and note the pressure gauge reading. The total running test time should not exceed two minutes to avoid damage to the transmission. Compare the pressure gauge reading to the vehicle Service Manual specifications and perform necessary repair procedures as needed.

Torque Converter Clutch Test

For many models the Torque Converter Clutch (TCC) is hydraulically operated and controlled by the Powertrain Control Module (PCM) or Transmission Control Module (TCM). The PCM or TCM adjusts hydraulic fluid pressure by controlling a Pulse Width Modulated (PWM) solenoid valve which is located inside the automatic transmission assembly.

Testing the TCC (Torque Converter Clutch) during a road test can be done by lightly tapping the brake while observing the engine RPM.

The scan tool can be used on newer vehicles to perform this test. A technician can manually engage and disengage the TCC while monitoring the scan tool data. On some scan tools there is also a TCC slip percent/count data for diagnosing TCC.

Basic Checks

Begin by verifying system voltage. Minimum battery open-circuit voltage is 12.4 volts for proper cranking; most electronic systems require at least 10 volts to conduct a diagnostic sequence.

Check all of the electrical connections to be sure they are clean and tight. Inspect the wiring harness and repair any damage. Check the resistance on suspected circuits by voltage drop testing, figure 1-17.

Next, test for voltage drop at the battery ground cable while cranking. Readings over 0.2 volt indicate high circuit resistance that could cause electronic control problems.

Examine the electrical connectors carefully, check for proper contact and for correct routing of the wires. Also, inspect all related wires and harnesses. Look for burned, melted, cut, or broken insulation and any other signs of damage. Repair as needed before continuing.

Circuit Testing

The most important tool for locating circuit faults is accurate service information for the specific vehicle you are working on. This includes:

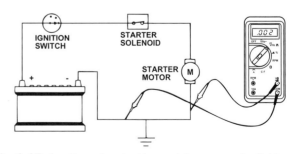

Fig. 1-17. A voltage drop test is a quick, easy, and reliable way to check for high resistance on the ground side of any electrical circuit.

- DTC troubleshooting flowcharts
- Wiring diagrams
- Pin voltage charts
- Connector pin charts

When using DTC troubleshooting flowchart, or pinpoint, tests, always complete each step of the procedure. Skipping steps can lead to inconclusive results. Test individual circuits and components as instructed by the flowchart using a **digital multimeter** (DMM), lab scope, or in many cases the scan tool.

Using Serial Data

Serial data are transmitted on the **data stream** and allow you to monitor **sensor**, **actuator**, and circuit voltages to determine how well the system is performing. Be aware: Data being read on the scan tool could actually be a default value that the transmission control module (TCM) substitutes to compensate for possible circuit failures. Also, serial data transmitted by the TCM to the scan tool are an interpretation of what the TCM thinks it is seeing. The true readings may be different. You can confirm actual signal values by testing the circuit with a DMM or lab scope.

Operating Range Tests

Some sensors develop an erratic signal, or dropout, at one point in the signal range as the unit ages or wears, figure 1-18. A loose or corroded ground connection for a sensor can also force the signal out of range, but not far enough to set a DTC.

You can check the operation of many sensors by using the operating range charts provided by the manufacturer. These charts list signal range specifications for voltage, resistance, **frequency**, or temperature that the sensor provides under varying conditions.

Using a DMM, take initial readings at the sensor connector, then, if necessary, at the main harness connector to the TCM. You can backprobe sensor connectors or install jumper wires to provide connection points for your meter. If possible, operate the sensor through its full range and check the signal at several points to make sure it does not drop out.

Input Sensors and Signals

Electronic automatic transmissions depend upon a complex network of input sensing devices and circuitry. The TCM uses

these to determine the operational status of transmission, engine, chassis, and body components. Some sensors transmit signals only to the TCM. Others feed information to both the transmission and engine computers.

Switch

Switches are **digital** sensors commonly used to provide signals that indicate:

- Throttle position (at or off idle)
- Basic high or low temperature (above or below the switch set point)
- Gear selector lever position
- Transmission gear ratio
- Power steering and air conditioning pressure

When used as sensors, switches generally install on the ground side of a circuit. The switch receives either system voltage from the vehicle electrical system or a **reference voltage** from the computer. As the switch opens and closes the circuit to ground, the voltage provided by the computer changes state; it switches from low to high or high to low. Both normally opened and closed switches are used as input sensors.

With a switch installed on the ground side of a circuit, the computer monitors circuit voltage on the power side, also known as the high, battery, or B+ side of the circuit, figure 1-19. To test, monitor the switch circuit voltage on the computer side of the switch with DMM.

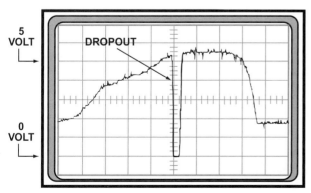

Fig. 1-18. Signal dropout is apparent on this lab scope trace of a throttle position sensor, but often it occurs so rapidly that the PCM overlooks it and does not set a trouble code.

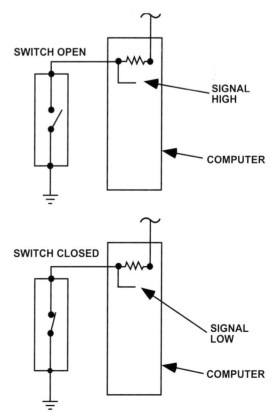

Fig. 1-19. When used as a sensor, a switch provides a digital high or low signal to the computer.

Potentiometer

A **potentiometer** is a variable resistor that senses motion or position and transmits an **analog** voltage signal. A potentiometer has three terminals:

- Reference voltage
- Signal voltage
- Ground

The computer applies a reference voltage, usually 5 volts, to the terminal at one end of the resistor. A terminal at the opposite end of the resistor connects it to ground. The third terminal, located between the other two, attaches to a movable wiper that sweeps back and forth across the resistor. This is the terminal that sends the variable signal voltage back to the computer. The wiper mechanically attaches to the device being monitored. Most automotive control systems use a potentiometer as a throttle position (TP) sensor.

Signal voltage from a potentiometer will vary between high and low, depending on whether the movable wiper is near the supply or ground end of the resistor, figure 1-20. Most units install so the wiper is in the low-voltage (high-resistance) position when the linkage they connect to is at rest. For example, when the throttle is closed, the potentiometer signal voltage will be at its lowest, which is about 0.2 volt. As the linkage moves to a fully open position, signal voltage will rise to its highest level, which is about 4.6 volts.

Thermistor

A **thermistor** is a solid-state, variable resistor, usually with two connector terminals. The resistance of a thermistor changes as temperature changes, thereby making it an ideal analog temperature sensor. There are two types of thermistors:

- Negative temperature coefficient (NTC)
- Positive temperature coefficient (PTC)

The resistance of an NTC thermistor decreases as temperature increases, while the resistance of a PTC thermistor increases as temperature increases, figure 1-21. In automotive applications,

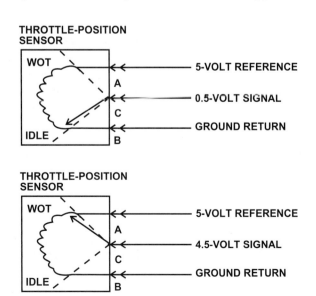

Fig. 1-20. The signal voltage of a potentiometer varies according to the position of the movable wiper.

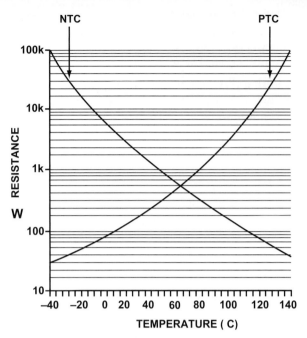

Fig. 1-21. The resistance of a thermistor changes according to temperature. Resistance of an NTC thermistor decreases as temperature increases, and the resistance of a PTC thermistor inreases as temperature increases.

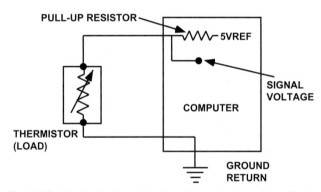

Fig. 1-22. A typical automotive thermistor circuit applies a 5-volt reference to the sensor through a pull-up resistor.

NTC thermistors are commonly used as transmission fluid temperature (TFT), engine coolant temperature (ECT), and air temperature sensors. Although automotive use of a PTC thermistor is rare, they are found as ECT sensors on a few early systems.

When used as a temperature sensor, the computer applies a reference voltage, usually 5 volts, through a pull-up resistor to the thermistor. The computer then monitors the voltage drop across the pull-up resistor and interprets any change in voltage as a signal of changing temperature, figure 1-22. When cold, NTC thermistor resistance is high, so signal voltage will be high as well. Resistance decreases as the NTC thermistor warms up. Because there is less resistance in the circuit, the reference signal has a more direct path to ground, and the signal voltage decreases in response.

Piezoresistive Sensor

When pressure is applied to a piezoresistive crystal, the crystal changes its resistance. If a reference voltage is applied to the

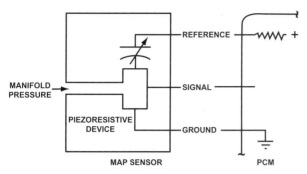

Fig. 1-23. The signal voltage of a piezoresistive MAP sensor, which changes in response to intake manifold vacuum, is used by the PCM to determine engine load.

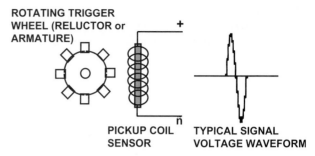

Fig. 1-24. A magnetic pickup coil produces an AC signal that varies in amplitude and frequency.

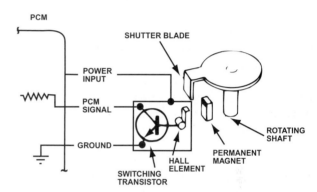

Fig. 1-25. The signal from a Hall-effect switch changes from high to low as a shutter blade passes between the Hall element and a permanent magnet.

A2

piezoresistive crystal, this voltage will also vary in response to pressure changes that alter resistance.

Some manifold absolute pressure (MAP) sensors consist of a bridge network of four piezoresistive resistors on a silicon wafer. One side of the wafer is a sealed reference, and the other side is connected to an intake manifold vacuum source. The wafer flexes in response to the changes in manifold vacuum. This causes the resistance of the resistors to change too, producing an analog output signal based on an applied voltage.

Since the MAP signal is proportional to manifold vacuum, it can be used to calculate engine load, figure 1-23. The TCM uses MAP sensor input to adjust shift scheduling, torque converter lockup, and line pressure value to meet the demands of operating conditions.

Typically, MAP sensor signal voltage is high when there is no vacuum. Expect to see about 4.75 volts on your DMM with the key on and engine off. When manifold vacuum is high, MAP signal voltage should be low. The MAP signal should be approximately 0.5 volt with the engine running at idle. Voltage should gradually increase as the throttle opens and vacuum drops off. Some MAP sensors, primarily those used by Ford, work under the same principle but produce a frequency instead of an analog voltage. In this case, frequency is high with low vacuum and low with high vacuum.

Speed Sensor

A number of speed inputs are provided to the TCM by a number of different sensors. These may include engine speed, vehicle speed, transmission input speed, and transmission output speed. These signals are generally transmitted by one of the following types of sensor:

- Pickup coil
- Hall-effect switch
- Optical sensor

Pickup coil

Pickup coil sensors, also called variable reluctance sensors or permanent magnet generators, are voltage generating sensors. These are composed of a pickup coil wound around a permanent magnet and a trigger wheel. As the teeth of a rotating trigger wheel pass by the magnet, the magnetic field expands and collapses to generate an **alternating current** (AC) voltage, figure 1-24. As the speed of the trigger wheel increases, so does the frequency and **amplitude** of the signal voltage.

Hall-effect switch

A Hall-effect switch uses a microchip to switch a transistor on and off and generate a digital signal that is transmitted to the PCM. As a shutter wheel passes between the Hall-effect element and a permanent magnet, the magnetic field expands and collapses to produce an analog signal. A Hall-effect switch does not generate its own voltage; power must be provided for the device to work, figure 1-25.

Hall-effect operation requires a three-wire circuit—power input, signal output, and ground. The Hall element receives an input voltage from either the ignition switch or the PCM to power it. Activity from the magnetic field and shutter blade opens and closes a switch to ground on the input signal. Be aware that the output signal voltage is not always the same as the input signal voltage. Therefore, you must have accurate specifications for the unit being tested.

The Hall-effect switch produces a square-wave voltage signal that ranges from 0 volts to the level of the input voltage. The frequency of the signal varies with the speed of the shutter wheel.

Optical sensor

An optical sensor uses a light-emitting diode (LED), a shutter wheel, and a phototransistor to produce a digital signal that changes frequency in proportion to rotational speed. Like a Hall-effect switch, an optical sensor uses a three-wire circuit. One wire carries power to operate the LED, one is the signal generated by the transistor to the PCM, and the third provides a common ground path, figure 1-26.

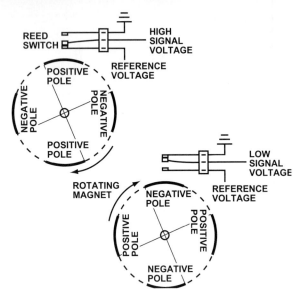

Fig. 1-26. The light-emitting diode (LED), shutter wheel, and phototransistor of an optical sensor produce a variable frequency digital signal.

Signal voltage, which is usually 5 volts, switches on and off as the rotating shutter passes between the phototransistor and LED to switch the ground circuit. When the shutter allows light to shine on the phototransistor, the base of the transistor switches, causing the signal voltage to change state. When the reflector plate blocks the light to the phototransistor, the base of the transistor switches again, and signal voltage changes as well.

Optical sensors are more expensive to manufacture and more delicate than a magnetic pickup or Hall-effect switch. Therefore, they are the least common of the three. Typically, optical sensors are used as vehicle speed sensors and engine speed sensors because their high-speed data rate is more accurate than other sensor designs for high RPM applications.

Output Actuators and Circuits

Actuators are the output devices the computer controls by switching internal driver circuits on and off. The actuators respond to voltage commands, which, in turn, control other circuits or convert electrical energy into mechanical work.

Most automotive actuators contain an induction coil. Since these devices are electrical components that perform a mechanical action, they can fail as a result of either a mechanical or electrical problem. In addition, certain hydraulic failures can mimic a solenoid malfunction.

Relay

A relay is a switch that uses electromagnetism in the control coil to close the relay power circuit contacts, figure 1-27. Typically, relays supply current to devices that draw a considerable amount of current. Because most electronic transmission controls draw only a small amount of current, the need for relays is limited.

Some manufacturers use a transmission control relay to route battery voltage to the solenoid pack on its electronic transmissions. The solenoid pack is a unit that contains all of the solenoids and pressure switches for the transmission. Most other

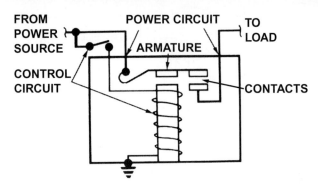

Fig. 1-27. A relay uses a low-current control circuit to operate an electromagnetic coil and switch a high-current power circuit on and off.

manufacturers do not use dedicated transmission relays. However, relays on other circuits, such as the ignition switch, starter, fuel pump, and main power, may also be linked to the TCM and play either a direct or indirect role in transmission operations.

Relays are easy to troubleshoot, as they either do or do not flow current. Be aware that a relay can also be used to interrupt current in the power circuit, so it is important to know how the unit is designed to operate. Check with a DMM.

Solenoid

A **solenoid** is a direct-current electromechanical device that uses magnetism to move an iron core. Electronic transmissions use three types of solenoids as output control devices:

- Two-position
- Pulse-width modulated
- Variable force

Two-position solenoids

A two-position solenoid can be in only one of two states: opened or closed, figure 1-28. These devices, often called an ON/OFF solenoid, typically install in the valve body of the transmission where they direct fluid flow to activate and deactivate apply devices. When used in this manner, these units are referred to as the shift solenoids. This type of solenoid is also used to engage the TCC on some transmissions.

Two-position solenoids may normally be either opened or closed when at rest. When the TCM sends an output signal to a solenoid, it changes state. As shift valves change state, they either direct fluid flow to pressurize passages, or exhaust fluid to the sump and relieve pressure in certain passages. Because these devices can only be either fully on or off, they do not alter fluid pressure; they simply turn fluid flow on or off.

Pulse-width modulated solenoids

All solenoids are, in fact, two-position solenoids, as they can only be fully on or off. However, if the TCM rapidly pulses the circuit that energizes a solenoid on and off, the position of the mechanical device the solenoid controls can be varied. This is called **pulse-width modulation** (PWM). Pulsing the signal at a specific number of cycles per second, or **hertz**, allows the device to regulate pressure as well as flow. Most late-model transmissions use a PWM solenoid to engage and release the TCC.

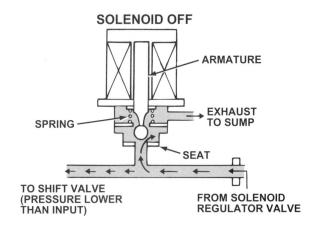

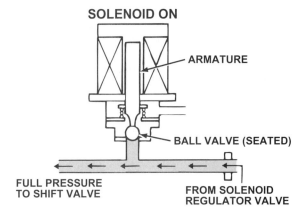

Fig. 1-28. Two-position solenoids, which are on/off switches, are often open and close passages to direct fluid flow in the transmission.

The complete operating cycle of a pulsed solenoid is the sequence from off to on to off again. Depending on design and use, an actuator solenoid can operate at any number of cycles per second, or frequency. Solenoids used in transmission controls generally operate at a fixed frequency. The TCM regulates fluid flow and pressure by varying the ratio of "on-time" to "off-time."

Some manufacturers provide pulse-width specifications for their solenoids, while others list **duty cycle** in their service information. These represent two methods of evaluating a pulsed solenoid; both specifications provide similar information.

Pulse width is the amount of time that a solenoid is energized, or the "on" part of the cycle, which is measured in thousandths of a second, or milliseconds (ms). Most systems that transmit a data stream provide pulse-width parameters for the pulsed solenoids. In order to sample pulse width in milliseconds, you need a high-quality DMM. However, if you know the frequency of the solenoid, you can calculate pulse width from the duty cycle.

Duty cycle is the percentage of the complete off-on-off cycle during which the solenoid is energized, figure 1-29. For example, a solenoid operating at a 25-percent duty cycle is energized for 25 percent of the total off-on-off cycle time and switched off the remaining 75-percent of the cycle. A 75-percent duty cycle means that the solenoid energizes for 75 percent of the cycle and switches off the remaining 25 percent. At a 0-percent duty cycle, the solenoid is fully off. Conversely, at 100 percent, the solenoid is fully on. Most digital multimeters have a setting for reading duty cycle.

Variable-Force Solenoids

A variable-force solenoid (VFS), figure 1-30, is a type of PWM solenoid used to regulate mainline pressure on some transmissions. Manufacturers apply different names to their line pressure solenoids; some call it an electronic, pressure-control (EPC) solenoid while others refer to it as either the pressure-control solenoid (PCS) or simply the force motor. Regardless of the name, all variable-force solenoids operate in a similar fashion.

A VFS uses an integral spool-type regulator valve to control how much fluid pressure from the oil pump enters the

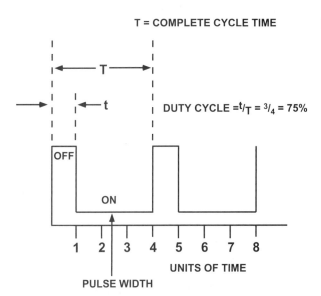

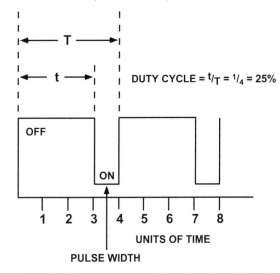

Fig. 1-29. Pulse width is the amount of time a solenoid is switched on, and duty cycle is the percentage of time the solenoid is switched on compared to the complete cycle.

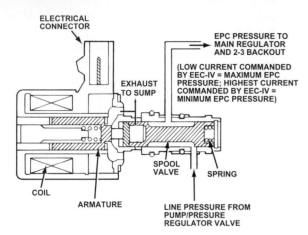

Fig. 1-30. A variable-force motor, which positions a spool valve to control how much fluid pressure from the oil pump enters the transmission, regulating mainline pressure.

transmission. The solenoid must overcome spring force before it can move the spool valve. The TCM positions the regulator valve by varying **amperage** to the solenoid and by adjusting the pulse width of the signal.

When there is no current in the circuit, internal pressure and spring force hold the regulator valve in. This allows maximum line pressure into the transmission. As the TCM increases current to the solenoid, the solenoid piston overcomes spring force and moves the spool valve to close off the fluid passages, reducing line pressure. Line pressure decreases proportionately as current applied to the solenoid increases.

The primary input for VFS regulation is throttle position, and the two act as opposites. At closed throttle, the duty cycle and current draw of the VFS should be at their maximum. When monitoring a VFS, expect both duty cycle and amperage to drop to near zero as you approach full throttle.

TCM REPLACEMENT

Vehicle computers do fail, but not with great frequency or regularity. Too often, the TCM is replaced simply because someone thought it might be the problem. However, from time to time, manufacturers release revised computers to correct specific vehicle problems. Most newer control modules can be

"flash" programmed to electronically update the internal programming, rather than physically replacing the TCM.

Check these items before replacing the TCM:

1. Battery voltage supply to the TCM and main system ground—Be sure the battery is fully charged and provides at least 9.6 to 10 volts during cranking. Be sure the charging system is maintaining correct battery charge. Most control systems receive battery voltage through a fuse, fusible link, or both. Be sure that battery voltage is available at the specified terminal of the main harness connector. Most systems are grounded remotely through a wire in the harness. Trace and check the ground connection to ensure good continuity.

2. Operation of a system power relay—The power to the TCM may be supplied through a system power relay; if so, check the relay.

3. Sensor reference voltage and ground circuits—Many sensors share a common reference voltage supply from the TCM and a common ground. Incorrect or erratic reference voltage or a bad common ground can affect operation of several sensors simultaneously. The symptoms may appear as if the TCM has a major internal problem. A simple wiring connection repair may correct the problem.

4. Resistance and current flow through all controlled solenoids and relays—Every output device controlled by the TCM has a minimum resistance specification. Actuator resistance limits the current through the TCM output control circuit. If the actuator is shorted, current can exceed the maximum safe resistance and internally damage the TCM. In most cases, current through a controlled output device should not exceed 0.75 ampere (750 milliamperes). The notable exception would be a VFS that can draw up to about 1.0 ampere at closed throttle. Before replacing a TCM, check all output circuits for shorts or low resistance that could cause internal damage to the computer.

As a general rule, the TCM should be at the bottom of the list of things to replace. It can fail, but a sensor, actuator, faulty wiring, poor connection, or mechanical or hydraulic failure is more likely the cause of a problem, figure 1-31.

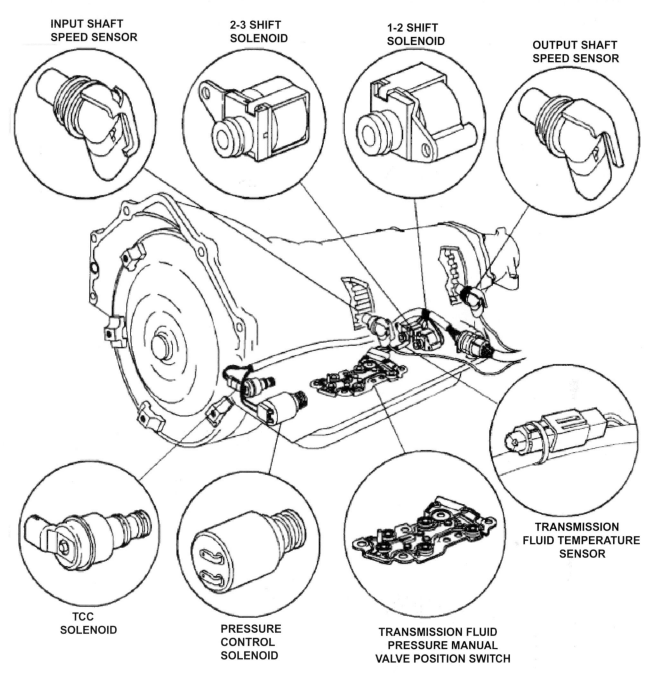

INPUT SHAFT
SPEED SENSOR

2-3 SHIFT
SOLENOID

1-2 SHIFT
SOLENOID

OUTPUT SHAFT
SPEED SENSOR

A2

TRANSMISSION
FLUID TEMPERATURE
SENSOR

TCC
SOLENOID

PRESSURE
CONTROL
SOLENOID

TRANSMISSION FLUID
PRESSURE MANUAL
VALVE POSITION SWITCH

Fig. 1-31. Typical layout of input sensors and output actuators in an electronically controlled automatic transmission.

CHAPTER QUESTIONS

1. The transmission is losing fluid with no visible leakage. Technician A says the Transmission cooler is leaking. Technician B says the vacuum modulator. Who is right?
   a. A only
   b. B only
   c. Both A and B
   d. Neither A nor B

2. The vehicle will not start in park. Technician A says to check shift linkage adjustment. Technician B says to check for a broken transmission mount. Who is right?
   a. A only
   b. B only
   c. Both A and B
   d. Neither A nor B

3. Milky pink ATF generally indicates:
   a. Clutch or bearing failure
   b. Clogged filter
   c. Water contamination
   d. Low fluid level

4. Which of the following conditions would best describe severely overheated transmission fluid?
   a. Dark gray or black with particle contamination
   b. Dark brown with a pungent odor
   c. Foamy red or reddish-brown with a pungent odor
   d. Dark brown with particle contamination

5. Throttle linkage adjustment has a direct effect on:
   a. Mainline pressure
   b. Governor pressure
   c. Control pressure
   d. Throttle pressure

6. When performing a voltage drop test at the battery ground terminal, readings over which of the following voltages would indicate high circuit resistance that could cause electronic control problems?
   a. 2 volts
   b. 0.2 volt
   c. 0.02 volt
   d. 0.002 volt

7. Technician A says torque converter drain back causes delayed initial engagement on start up when the transmission is placed in gear. Technician B says torque converter drain back may be caused by a faulty oil pump check valve or bushing. Who is right?
   a. A only
   b. B only
   c. Both A and B
   d. Neither A nor B

8. The best method for determining the cause of a transmission malfunction would be to perform a:
   a. Pressure test
   b. Stall test
   c. Road test
   d. Teardown evaluation

9. Which of the following is a centrifugally operated valve driven off the transmission output shaft?
   a. Throttle valve
   b. Vacuum modulator
   c. Governor valve
   d. Pressure-regulating valve

10. During a stall test, high RPM readings may indicate:
    a. Clutch slippage
    b. Torque converter problems
    c. Vacuum modulator malfunction
    d. Poor engine performance

11. A torque converter defect can cause all of the following symptoms **EXCEPT**:
    a. Slow acceleration from a stop
    b. Erratic shifting
    c. Poor high speed performance
    d. Overheating

12. Technician A says poor mechanical engine condition could produce poor transmission operation. Technician B says crack in a vacuum hose could produce poor shift quality. Who is right?
    a. A only
    b. B only
    c. Both A and B
    d. Neither A nor B

13. Which of the following items is not needed when performing a comprehensive road test?
    a. Clutch and band application chart
    b. Stall speed chart
    c. Shift speed chart
    d. None of the above

14. If initial engagement is delayed when the transmission is first placed in gear, the most likely cause is:
    a. A worn pump bushing or leaky seal
    b. A stuck converter drain-back valve
    c. Severely worn clutches and bands
    d. A defective oil pump or pump check valve

15. Which of the following tools is **NOT** needed to conduct a pressure test?
    a. Pressure gauge
    b. Vacuum pump
    c. Tachometer
    d. Vacuum gauge

16. Control pressure is another name for:
    a. Mainline pressure
    b. Throttle pressure
    c. Modulator pressure
    d. Governor pressure

17. The hydraulic pressure that increases and decreases in response to changes in road speed is called:
    a. Mainline pressure
    b. Throttle pressure
    c. Control pressure
    d. Governor pressure

18. An air pressure test is used to:
    a. Pinpoint hydraulic leaks
    b. Check a vacuum modulator
    c. Check for pressure cutback
    d. See how well clutches and bands hold

19. In a computer controlled transaxle the TCC torque converter clutch locks up at 25 mph instead of the specified 45 mph. Technician A says the map sensor is at fault. Technician B says the VSS sensor is malfunctioning.
    a. A only
    b. B only
    c. Both A and B
    d. Neither A nor B

20. The resistance of an NTC thermistor:
    a. Decreases as temperature increases
    b. Decreases as temperature decreases
    c. Decreases as pressure increases
    d. Decreases as pressure decreases

21. Most late-model transmissions use which type of solenoid to engage and release the converter clutch?
    a. Two-position
    b. Pulse-width modulated
    c. Variable force
    d. Pressure control

22. Hunting between gears during a road test might be caused by:
    a. Incorrect band adjustment
    b. Defective torque converter clutch
    c. Incorrect shift solenoid adjustment
    d. Incorrect throttle valve linkage adjustment

CHAPTER TWO

IN-VEHICLE TRANSMISSION/TRANSAXLE MAINTENANCE AND REPAIR

CHAPTER OBJECTIVES

- The technician will complete the ASE task list on In-Vehicle Transmission/Transaxle Maintenance and Repair
- The technician will be able to answer 12 questions dealing with the In-Vehicle Transmission/Transaxle Maintenance and Repair section of the A2 ASE test.

Routine maintenance service for an automatic transmission generally includes frequent fluid level checks and an occasional fluid and filter change. Some manufacturers specify a regular mileage interval for fluid replacement. Others recommend fluid replacement only when a major overhaul is performed, or when the vehicle is operated under severe service conditions. Severe service conditions are most often defined as:

- Constant operation in a hot and dusty climate
- Frequent hauling of heavy loads or trailer towing
- Constant stop-and-go driving in heavy traffic

Other maintenance operations that are performed in conjunction with a fluid change include:

- Band adjustments
- Linkage adjustments
- Electronic circuitry checks

Not all transmissions require band and linkage adjustments, and specific procedures vary greatly from one transmission to another. The procedures for checking and adjusting linkages in this chapter are included as general guidelines only.

In addition to routine maintenance items, a considerable number of automatic transmission repairs can be made without removing the unit from the chassis. These would include external repairs such as repairing fluid leaks, servicing the fluid cooler, and replacing the modulator. Internal repairs such as overhauling the valve body, servos, accumulator, and governor can often be performed while the transmission is in the vehicle.

LINKAGE ADJUSTMENT

There are four types of linkage involved in transmission operation:

- Accelerator linkage
- Throttle valve linkage
- Downshift linkage
- Gearshift linkage

Not every transmission uses all four types of linkage. Usage depends on the transmission and the vehicle in which it is installed. Symptoms of misadjusted transmission control linkages include:

- Early or late shifts
- Hunting between gears
- Harsh or slipping shifts

Before adjusting, check linkages for binding or bent parts and loose retaining nuts. Adjustment procedures vary; follow instructions provided by the manufacturer. The procedures presented here are general guidelines that apply to most linkage adjustments.

Accelerator Linkage

The linkage from the accelerator pedal to the engine must be adjusted correctly on all vehicles. This is especially true on transmissions that use mechanical linkage to control the **throttle valve** and provide forced downshifts. The procedures for checking and adjusting accelerator linkage differ between manufacturers. However, there are two important points to remember for all vehicles:

1. When the accelerator is depressed all the way to the floor, the throttle plates should be wide open, with the throttle lever against the wide-open throttle stop.
2. When pressure on the accelerator is released, the linkage must return freely and immediately to the idle position.

To check a throttle cable, inspect the adjustment bracket on the engine. As a general rule, clearance between the end of the outer cable and the cable stopper should be between zero and 0.040 inch. To adjust the cable, fully depress the accelerator, loosen the adjusting nuts, and reposition the cable as required.

Throttle Valve Linkage

Automatic transmissions use throttle pressure to control mainline pressure and regulate upshifts and downshifts according to the engine throttle position. The throttle valve in the valve body must move in direct proportion to the throttle opening of the engine. This is achieved either mechanically through linkage or cables, or by intake manifold vacuum acting on a vacuum modulator. Mechanical systems, both linkage and cable, are usually adjustable. Most vacuum operated systems do not need adjustments.

In general, throttle valve linkage adjustments are made with both the engine and transmission at operating temperature. The fast-idle cam or any cold enrichment or idle-boost devices must be in the off position, and idle speed must be adjusted to specifications. Adjustments are made by removing all **backlash** from the linkage or cable. Adjust with the engine off while holding the throttle in a wide-open position.

Typical linkage adjustments are made by means of an adjustable swivel, figure 2-1, or movable trunnion, figure 2-2. Loosen the adjusting screw, push the linkage toward the engine to remove backlash, then tighten the screw to specified torque.

Cable adjustments are generally made by repositioning the cable in its housing. The cable may be held in place by snap lock or a threaded collar placed at either end of the assembly. Before adjusting, check all of the supporting brackets for looseness, bending, and other damage, and repair and tighten as needed. Inspect the cable routing and reposition to remove any sharp bends. To adjust a typical cable linkage with a snap lock mechanism:

1. Disconnect the cable from the lever at the throttle body.
2. Make sure the throttle plates are in the closed position and the lever at the transmission is in the rest position.
3. Press and hold the lock button to release the cable in the adjuster head, figure 2-3.
4. Adjust the length so the cable end is centered on the attachment stud at the throttle body.
5. Release the button to lock in the adjustment, then reconnect the cable to the lever.

The above adjustment procedure is for a Chrysler transmission. Adjusting Ford, figure 2-4, and General Motors, figure 2-5, snap lock throttle valve linkage is similar.

The throttle valve cable on some transaxles has a threaded shank for adjusting the free length. The spring seat is a split ring design that you open up to compress the spring and retract the shank. Some spring seats can be spread open by hand. Others will require a screwdriver, or similar tool, to pry them open. Once the threaded shank is retracted, move the primary throttle lever to the wide-open position as you watch the shank. The threaded shank should ratchet out of the grip jaws to take up slack. If not, replace the cable.

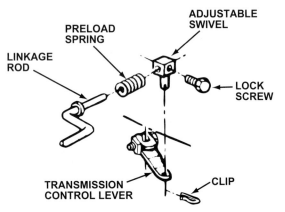

Fig. 2-1. The throttle valve linkage is adjusted by repositioning a swivel on the linkage rod of this transmission.

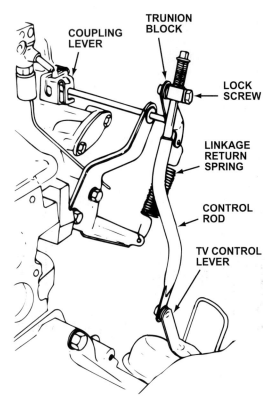

Fig. 2-2. A sliding trunion block is used to adjust throttle valve linkage on some transmissions with rod-type linkages.

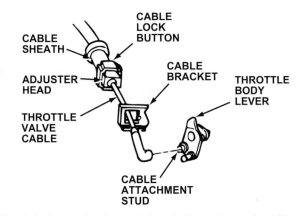

Fig. 2-3. Depressing the cable lock button releases the adjuster head for removing the slack from a throttle valve cable.

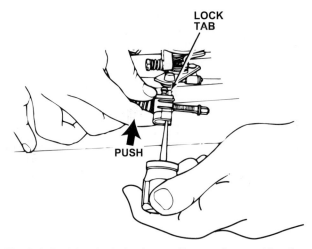

Fig. 2-4. Pushing the lock tab out with a small screwdriver frees the adjuster block on many throttle valve cables.

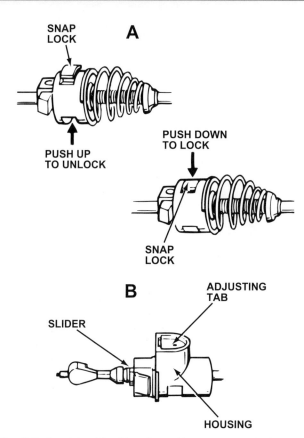

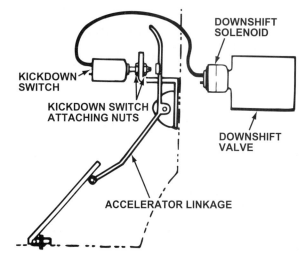

Fig. 2-6. An electric switch at the accelerator pedal energizes a solenoid to force downshifts on some transmissions.

A2

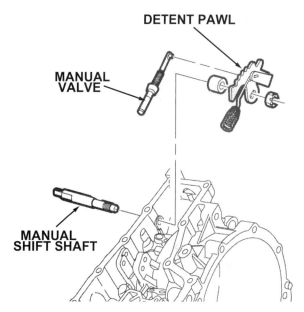

Fig. 2-7. Typical detent pawl and shift shaft.

Fig. 2-5. A variety of throttle valve cables use a snap lock adjuster (A), others have a self-adjusting cable assembly (B).

Downshift Linkage

Downshift linkage, which is also called kickdown linkage, is used on some transmissions. Generally, a rod-type linkage is used to connect the **downshift valve** in the valve body to the accelerator pedal. The rod forces downshifts at wide-open throttle when the accelerator is depressed to the maximum. You can check the kickdown shift points by depressing the accelerator through the **detent** at the appropriate speed during a road test. Kickdown shift points are an indication of how the downshift valve is working. Be sure the accelerator linkage is correctly adjusted. Then, check and adjust the downshift linkage as follows:

1. Block the throttle open against its wide-open stop.
2. Depress the downshift rod until the downshift valve is forced against its stop in the valve body. Hold the downshift rod in this position.
3. Check the clearance between the throttle lever and the end of the kickdown adjusting screw. Adjust the screw to obtain the specified clearance.
4. Return the downshift rod to its normal position and release the throttle from its blocked-open position.

Some transmissions use an electric kickdown switch operated by the accelerator pedal, figure 2-6. The kickdown switch is electrically connected to a downshift solenoid in the transmission. The solenoid operates the downshift valve on command from the switch.

When correctly positioned, the kickdown switch closes just before the throttle lever reaches the wide-open stop. Closing the switch energizes the solenoid, activates the solenoid plunger, and moves the downshift valve in the valve body.

Gearshift Linkage

The gearshift linkage, also called manual valve linkage, positions the **manual valve** in the transmission valve body to direct fluid to the correct circuits for the driving range selected. If the shift linkage is out of adjustment, fluid can leak past the manual valve and cause erratic transmission operation. Under normal circumstances, the gearshift linkage does not need adjustment. Adjustment is required when a transmission is removed and reinstalled or when repairing or replacing worn or damaged linkage components. On some transmissions, the shift lever and its linkage must be removed to provide room for band adjustment, and the linkage will need adjusting on reassembly.

Control of the manual valve is basically the same for both steering column and floor-mounted gear selector levers. An arm of the manual valve lever engages a groove in the end of the manual valve that protrudes from the valve body, figure 2-7. The lever has notches for each gear selector position. These are engaged by a spring-located detent ball in the valve body. The detent ball and **pawl** hold the manual valve in its various positions.

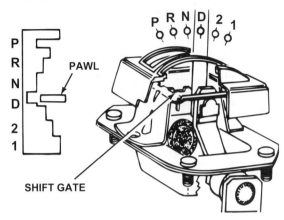

Fig. 2-8. Gate stops on the gear selector mechanism correspond to the notches on the manual valve detent pawl.

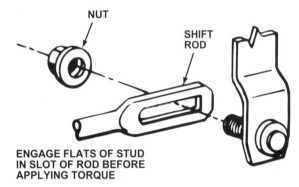

Fig. 2-9. Some shift linkage adjustments are made by loosening a locknut and repositioning the shift rod.

The gear selector has a shift gate with notches, or stops, that correspond to the notches in the pawl of the manual valve lever, figure 2-8. The manual valve detents must be synchronized with the gear selector gate stops for the transmission to operate correctly.

Shift linkage designs, as well as adjustment procedures, vary widely. Those using cables are relatively simple. Others which use a series of rods can be more complicated. Some manufacturers specify that adjustment be made with the transmission in drive; others recommend adjusting with the selector in park. Most linkages can be adjusted satisfactorily in either position. However, you must know the proper direction in which to move the manual lever at the transmission, so its detent position will coincide with that of the gear selector lever. The following general procedures can be used to adjust most gearshift linkage:

1. Move the selector lever to the drive position, with the lever pawl against the shift gate stop.
2. Raise the car on a hoist to a comfortable working height and locate the adjustment device. Look for a locknut that holds the shift rod or cable to the manual valve lever, figure 2-9, or an adjustment swivel with a lockscrew, figure 2-10.
3. Loosen the locknut or screw.
4. Shift the manual valve lever into the appropriate detent to position the manual valve in drive.
5. Torque the adjusting nut or swivel lockscrew to specifications. Be sure that any flats on the stud are aligned with the flats on the cable end before applying torque.

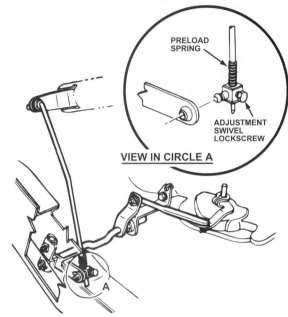

Fig. 2-10. A lockscrew holds the spring-loaded adjustment swivel in position on this shift linkage.

6. Check transmission operation for all selector lever detent positions. There should be little or no movement of the selector with the detents engaged.

Transmission Range Sensor (TRS)

The Transmission Range Sensor (TRS) communicates shift lever position to the powertrain control module (PCM) or transmission control module (TCM) as a combination of open and closed switches. Each shift lever position has an assigned combination of switch states (open/closed) that the PCM/TCM receives from four sense circuits. The TCM interprets this information and determines the appropriate transmission gear position and shift schedule. The TRS can also provide for Park/Neutral only starter operation and back-up lamp operation. On most vehicles the TRS is mounted on the valve body inside the transmission.

Park/Neutral Position Switch

The park/neutral position switch is installed in series between the starter relay coil ground terminal and ground. This normally open switch prevents the starter relay from being energized and the starter motor from operating unless the automatic transmission gear selector is in the Neutral or Park positions.

To test the switch, remove the wiring connector. Continuity should exist only when the transmission is in PARK or NEUTRAL.

CASE SERVICE

Fluid leaks are a common automatic transmission problem that can often be repaired without removing the unit.

Oil Seal Service

Three main types of seals are used in automatic transmissions:

- Lip seals
- O-ring and square-cut seals
- Sealing rings

Lip Seals

On most transmissions, the front pump drive, output shaft, and manual valve shaft are sealed with a metal-clad lip seal, figure 2-11. The seal itself is synthetic rubber. In high-pressure applications, some sealing faces have spiral ribs. The seal and ribs redirect fluid back into the transmission case. A garter-type spring helps maintain lip seal tension. With the exception of the front seal, these can be replaced with the transmission in the car.

Special tools should be used to remove lip seals, figure 2-12. The tool uses expandable jaws that grip the inside of the seal to prevent damage to the case and shafts. Small lip seals, such as those used on manual valve shafts, can usually be removed with a screwdriver and pliers. Always check the bore for damage after removing a seal in this way.

Install the new seal with a seal driver, figure 2-13. The driver supports the inside of the seal to keep the spring in place and distributes force equally around the entire shoulder of the seal. Before installing, lubricate the lip of the seal with clean transmission fluid. Place the seal on the head of the seal driver with its lip facing the lubricant or pressure side, and position the seal and driver in the seal bore. Press or drive the seal into place until it is fully seated.

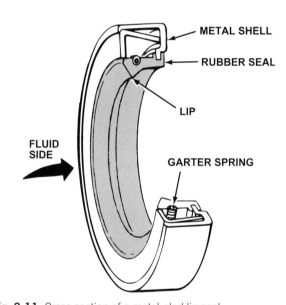

Fig. 2-11. Cross section of a metal-clad lip seal.

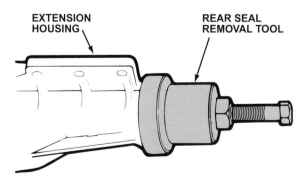

Fig. 2-12. A seal removal tool grips the inside of the seal to prevent damage to the case and shaft.

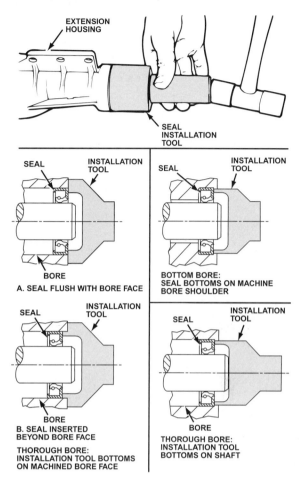

Fig. 2-13. Different seal driver designs are available to drive a variety of seal shapes and sizes into their bore without damage.

A2

O-Rings and Square-Cut Seals

O-ring and square-cut seals, figure 2-14, can be used to seal either low-pressure or high-pressure areas. Both types of seal allow for **axial movement** but cannot be used to seal rotating parts. The square-cut, also called lathe-cut, design permits greater movement, as it has less tendency to roll as the parts move. Both designs can harden, flatten, or crack with age. When this happens, they lose their sealing ability, resulting in leaks and pressure loss. The problem is most apparent when a vehicle is cold. O-ring and square-cut seals are used on clutch and servo pistons, speedometer driven gear units, vacuum modulators, and oil pumps.

To remove an O-ring or square-cut seal, apply pressure on opposite sides of the seal. This causes it to bulge slightly in the center. Grasp the bulge with your fingers and twist the seal off.

If the O-ring or seal has hardened, or otherwise is difficult to remove by hand, carefully slip a small screwdriver blade under the ring. Twist the screwdriver and revolve its blade around the outside of the component. This draws the seal from its groove for easy removal.

Install new O-rings or seals by fitting one side in the groove and working the remainder of the ring over the component. Do not stretch the new seal more than is absolutely necessary or it may distort. Make sure it fits snugly into its groove around the entire circumference of the component.

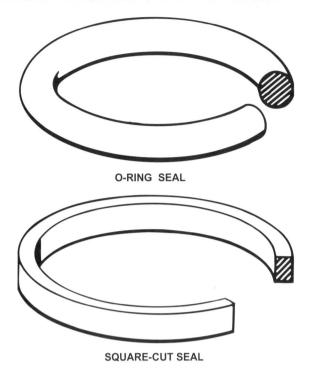

O-RING SEAL

SQUARE-CUT SEAL

Fig. 2-14. O-ring and square-cut seals are similar but have a different cross section.

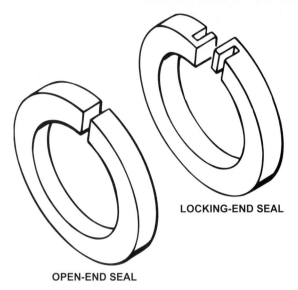

OPEN-END SEAL

LOCKING-END SEAL

Fig. 2-15. Open-end and locking-end metal seal rings contain fluid to direct flow, but do not form a fluid-tight seal.

SCARF-CUT SEAL

Fig. 2-16. The ends of a scarf-cut Teflon® seal ring butt on installation to minimize fluid seepage.

Sealing Rings

Many transmission pieces use metal or Teflon® oil rings as seals. Sealing rings are effective where axial and rotational movement is present. Oil seal rings hold automatic transmission fluid (ATF) under pressure, but are designed to allow a controlled amount of leakage. In addition to acting as a seal, oil rings may also control the direction of fluid flow necessary to apply a clutch or servo.

Rings used on servo pistons and the governor support shaft can often be replaced with the transmission installed. Others, such as those on the oil pump cover, can be serviced only on the bench.

Metal seal rings may have open, butt, or locking ends, figure 2-15. Teflon® seal rings are either solid, which requires special tooling to replace, or a scarf-cut design that can be installed by hand, figure 2-16. Removal and replacement procedures differ according to the type of ring used.

Open-End Ring Replacement

These oil seal rings use square-cut ends which do not touch. To remove an open-end ring, insert the tips of a pair of snapring pliers between the ends of the ring. Expand the ring ends enough to slide the ring off the shaft. New rings are expanded with the pliers and slipped over the shaft and into the proper groove.

Butt-End Ring Replacement

The square-cut ends of this type of ring touch, or butt against each other. They are removed by prying one end free from the groove with a small screwdriver blade. Pull the remainder of the ring from the groove as you would an O-ring and remove it from the shaft. New rings are installed in the same way as open-end rings.

Locking-End Ring Replacement

This type of seal ring may have angled ends which butt together, or hooked ends which connect. Both types are removed by prying one end free and pulling the ring from the groove. When reinstalling locking-end seal rings, make certain that the ring ends contact each other, or they cannot do their job. The term "locking ring" refers to a metal ring, while the term "scarf-cut ring" refers to one made of Teflon®.

Solid Teflon® Ring Replacement

Solid Teflon® seal rings are soft and resilient, so they tend to return to their original size after being stretched to fit over the shaft and into the groove. Teflon® seals cannot be reused, so the best way to remove them is to cut them. Stretch and pull the ring out of the groove either by hand or with a small screwdriver, then cut it with a sharp knife and remove it.

Fitting a solid Teflon® seal requires three special tools: an installer, pusher, and sizer, figure 2-17. The installer is cone-shaped to stretch the seal, as the pusher guides it onto the shaft and the sizer helps shrink the seal back to size. Each size seal requires a separate set of installation tools. Always install the

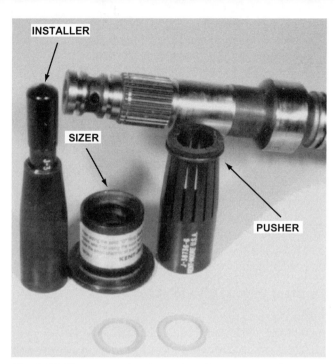

Fig. 2-17. Three special tools—an installer, pusher, and sizer—are used to install solid Teflon® seal rings.

farthest seal first, then work toward the end of the shaft. To install a solid seal ring:

1. Attach the installer to the shaft with its leading edge aligned with the top of the seal ring groove.
2. Fit the new seal ring onto the small end of the pusher.
3. Slip the pusher onto the installer and apply firm, even pressure to the top of the pusher.
4. Guide the ring into the groove when the pusher reaches the end of the installer.
5. Repeat to install the remaining seals.
6. Carefully fit the sizer over all the seals, making sure it is facing the correct direction.

Gasket Service

Flat surfaces on the transmission are sealed with a gasket. Gaskets are used to seal between the transmission case and housings, the oil pan, and the valve body. A gasket must be able to withstand heat and pressure to prevent fluid leakage between the surfaces. Always replace an old gasket with a new one whenever the gasket seal has been broken. Gaskets tend to take a set and harden in use. You cannot depend on them to provide a satisfactory seal when reused.

Clean sealing surfaces with solvent and carefully remove all remaining gasket material with a gasket scraper. Make sure the mating surfaces are clean, free of scratches or surface damage, and flat within specified limits. You cannot expect a new gasket to seal properly unless these conditions are met.

Gasket sealant, or cement, is a common item in all shops, but use it with caution on an automatic transmission. If sealant gets into the hydraulic system, it can clog a filter or a valve body. A cellulose-type, or paper, oil pan gasket is the only transmission gasket that requires the use of sealant. In this case, use nonhardening sealant and apply a thin, even coat to the pan

side of the gasket. If necessary, you can hold gaskets in place during assembly with a thin coating of petroleum jelly or assembly lubricant.

When you disassemble a transmission, save all the old gaskets until you complete the overhaul. Most overhaul kits contain two or three gaskets for the same part. This is particularly true of valve body and pump gaskets. Providing several alternative gaskets allows manufacturers to sell one overhaul kit for different versions of the same transmission. Match the old gaskets to the alternative gaskets to select the right one. Be sure that all the holes in the new gaskets match all the holes in the old one.

DRIVELINE

Slip Yoke

A driveshaft slip yoke generally does not require routine service because the yoke splines and outside surfaces are lubricated by transmission fluid. However, some do require periodic lubrication and grease to their splines. Check the Service Manual specifications for proper grease type and recommended service intervals. Leaks around the output shaft can be caused by a worn seal or output shaft bushing or by damage to the yoke surface.

Universal Joints

Most factory installed U-joints cannot be lubricated unless they are disassembled. Some factory installed and most aftermarket U-joints have grease fittings, commonly called zerk fittings, figure 2-18. Grease should be pumped into the joint until fresh lube appears at each cap. If lube does not appear at each cap, disassemble the joint and inspect for damage or contamination.

When replacing universal joints, you may need to know which of two basic types of Cardan U-joint you have. One type is held in place by internal snaprings that fit into grooves at the outer ends of the yokes. The other type is held in place by "C" clips or snaprings that fit into grooves in the bearing cups, figure 2-19.

If you anticipate reinstalling a U-joint when you remove it, mark the position of each bearing, cross and yoke for proper reassembly. If snaprings are used, loosen them by driving one bearing cup slightly inward. The bearing cups on some universal joints are held in the yokes by molded plastic

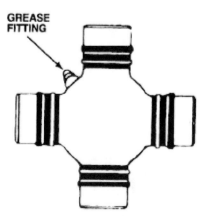

Fig. 2-18. Some U-joints have grease fittings to permit periodic lubrication.

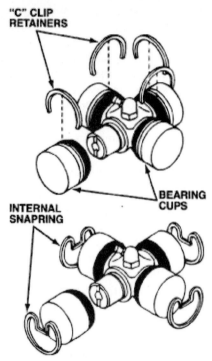

Fig. 2-19. Two types of retainer, "C" clips and snaprings, are used to hold a Cardan U-joint in place.

rings. These will shear when the bearing cup is forced from the yoke. Replacement U-joints will have special bearing caps with internal grooves for snapring installation and bearing cup installation.

If a special removal tool is not available, place the joint in a bench vise with a large socket, bigger in diameter than the bearing cup, against the yoke and a smaller socket against the opposite bearing, figure 2-20. Closing the vise drives the bearing from the yoke into the larger socket. If this procedure does

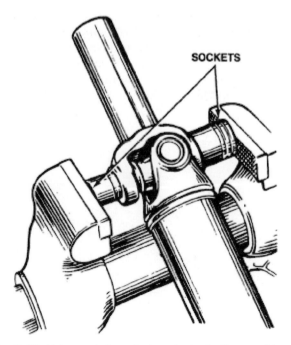

Fig. 2-20. Using sockets and a bench vise to disassemble a Cardan U-joint.

not force the bearing all the way out, clamp the exposed portion in the vise and drive upward on the yoke with a rubber mallet. Inspect the cross, bearings, and bearing cup assemblies for wear. Replace the entire joint if any wear is found.

To reassemble the joint, insert the cross in its original position inside the yoke. When installing a new U-joint with the zerk fitting, assemble it so that the fitting faces the driveshaft. Make sure all the needle bearings are in position in the cup and lightly coated with grease. Position the bearing cups in the yoke bores and press them into position with a bench vise and suitably sized sockets. Use new snaprings to secure the U-joints in place.

On double Cardan U-joints, figure 2-21, be careful to install the centering ball correctly to maintain U-joint alignment. Also make sure the spring in the linking yoke is in good condition and properly centered.

Constant Velocity (CV) Joint

Inspection
A modern CV joint can be expected to last about 100,000 miles (160,000 km), but without proper lubrication, it will wear much faster. Most CV joint failures are due to lack of lubrication and/or contamination caused by a torn boot. Always check CV joint boots for damage to ensure that lubricant remains in the joint.

Outer CV joints, at the wheel end of the axle shaft, usually wear more quickly than the inner joints because they are subject to a variety of axle shaft operating angles. The shaft at the outer CV joint may move as much as 40 degrees to compensate for suspension and steering angles. Normal operating angles at the inner CV joint are only about 10 to 20 degrees.

When checking CV joint boots, raise the vehicle on a hoist and use a trouble light. Wipe grease and dirt from the boot so that you can see any small tears or punctures. Check that the boot clamps are secure. Also, check to be sure that oil or coolant is not leaking on the boots, since this contaminates the rubber, making the boots weak and prone to tears. Also look for cracking, flaking, and other signs of rubber deterioration.

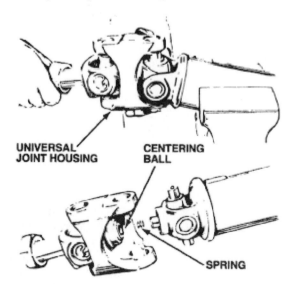

Fig. 2-21. The centering ball and spring must be correctly positioned to maintain alignment on a double Cardan U-joint.

Usually, if the boot is damaged, then the CV joint is worn. This is because, as a CV joint turns, centrifugal force pushes grease outward, forcing it through even the tiniest of openings in the boot. This lack of lubrication, coupled with the constant movement of the joint, quickly leads to CV joint failure. In addition, a damaged boot allows dirt, water, and other contaminations into the joint.

If the boot is damaged, remove it. You may have to remove the axle shaft first. Place a small amount of grease from inside the boot between your fingertips and rub your fingers together. If the grease feels gritty, replace the CV joint as described in this chapter. If the grease feels smooth, you may have caught the problem before any damage was done to the joint. If this is the case, pack the joint with grease and install a new boot.

Replacement

If the CV joints are worn and can be separated from the axle shaft, use the following procedure as a guide to remove and replace them. On some vehicles, you must replace the CV joints and axle shaft as a unit.

1. Clamp the axle shaft assembly in a soft-jaw vise.
2. Remove the boot clamps and cut away the boots. Never reuse old boots.
3. Locate the snap ring that holds the CV joint in place and remove it using snap ring pliers.
4. Separate the CV joint from the axle shaft. Gently tap CV joint housing with a soft-faced hammer to drive it from the shaft if necessary.
5. Inspect the splines on the end of the axle shaft. If they are chipped or worn, replace the axle shaft.
6. Before installing a new CV joint match it up to the old one and check the part number to be sure that it is the correct replacement.
7. Wrap tape around the axle shaft splines. This prevents the splines from ripping the new boot as you install it onto the shaft.
8. Slip the new CV joint boot on the shaft, and then remove the tape from the axle shaft splines.

9. Fit the new CV joint onto the axle shaft splines. Tap the joint onto the axle with a soft-face hammer until you hear a click as the snapring drops into the groove. Tug on the joint to make sure the snapring has engaged.
10. Pack the CV joint using the correct amount of recommended grease. The incorrect grease may contaminate the boot. Often the CV joint boot kit comes with grease. Never mix greases. Use the quantity of grease supplied with the boot, and do not over pack the joint.
11. Slip the boot end over the joint housing and install the clamps to secure it to the housing and the axle.
12. Install the axle shaft/CV joint assembly in the vehicle.
13. Check wheel alignment after replacing CV joints.

Be aware that some vehicles use boots manufactured of special materials. Special replacement clamps and pliers are required when installing these boots to be sure they seal properly.

There are two-piece or "split" replacement boots available for some CV joint applications. However, these are not recommended by most vehicle manufacturers. Split boots are bolted or glued together and the glue must cure for two to four hours. Bolt-together boots, if not properly installed, will allow CV joint contamination. Single-piece CV joint boots are the best choice, although you must remove the axle shaft to install this type of boot.

Oil Cooler Service

A transmission fluid cooler, located in the radiator tank, is used to reduce internal operating temperatures. Two lines connect the transmission and the cooler, figure 2-22. One of the lines carries hot fluid to the cooler from the torque converter circuit. Heat carried by the fluid is transferred to the engine coolant and dissipated by the radiator. The other line returns the cool fluid to the transmission lubrication circuit to lubricate the moving parts.

For the transmission fluid cooler to operate efficiently, the engine cooling system must be in good condition. Any defect in the radiator or cooling system reduces the ability of the coolant to transfer heat from the transmission fluid.

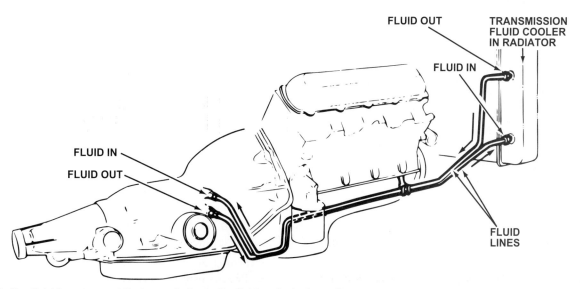

Fig. 2-22. Two fluid lines connect the transmission to the fluid cooler in the radiator.

When inspecting the fluid cooler, also include a general check of the complete cooling system. To check:

1. Inspect the fluid lines and fittings between the transmission and the cooler for looseness, wear, damage, or leakage. Tighten or replace any leaking fittings, and replace any damaged lines.

2. Inspect the coolant in the radiator. If you find transmission fluid in the coolant, the cooler is leaking.

3. Check the transmission dipstick for signs of engine coolant. If the fluid has a milky pink color, the radiator or cooler is leaking internally.

Repairing Lines, Fittings, and Hoses

A cooler line is generally a single length of steel tubing with a double-flare fitting at each end. On some vehicles, a short length of flexible hose connects the tubing to the cooler fitting.

Damaged cooler lines should be replaced rather than repaired. Replacement lines should be made either from seamless or double-wrapped and brazed steel tubing. Do not use copper or aluminum tubing. Normal vibration causes flexing that turns soft, alloy tubing brittle, causing cracks and leaks. To fabricate a new line:

1. Measure the damaged length of tubing as accurately as possible.
2. Use a tubing cutter and cut a section of new tubing to the length measured in Step One.
3. Use a tubing bender to form the new tubing to the shape of the damaged line. Trim the length of the new tubing if necessary.
4. Ream the ends of the tubing to remove any burrs, then install the necessary fitting on each end.
5. Use a flaring tool to form a double-flare at each end of the tubing.
6. Position the new line loosely under the existing clamps on the engine or chassis. Connect each end of the line and torque the fitting to specifications. Then, tighten the mounting clamps.
7. Run the engine at idle and check for leaks.

When replacing a damaged section of flexible hose, use a high-grade, high-temperature, reinforced hose that matches the specifications of the old hose. Cut the hose to the proper length and install it with new clamps. Fit the new hose flush against the radiator at one end and extend it at least two inches over the tubing at the other.

Cooler Flushing

The transmission fluid cooler should be flushed clean whenever there has been an internal transmission failure. Metal and friction material particles, varnish, and burned fluid tend to collect in the cooler. When the engine is started, fluid from the cooler flows directly to the internal mechanism of the transmission to provide lubrication. If not removed, this debris can cause serious damage. To clean the fluid cooler, use the following procedure:

1. Connect a piece of hose to the cooler inlet, with the free end draining into a container.

2. Apply short blasts of compressed air to the outlet fitting, keeping air pressure below 25 psi.
3. Pump a pint of ATF into the cooler through the outlet fitting.
4. Continue applying short blasts of air to the outlet fitting until no more fluid drains out. Remove the hose.

When sludge has built up in the cooler, the above procedure might not remove it. A special flushing machine is required to remove heavy sludge. The machine is connected to the cooler and pumps solvent through it with compressed air. Several different flushing machines are available. When using a flushing machine, follow the specific instructions provided by the manufacturer.

VALVE BODY SERVICE

The valve body is a high-precision hydraulic component that should be disassembled, thoroughly cleaned, and carefully inspected whenever internal transmission repairs are made. With the oil pan and filter screen removed from the transmission, the valve body is readily accessible. Avoid distortion when removing the valve body by loosening and removing retaining bolts in increments and in sequence. Drop the unit straight down from the transmission case and place it on the bench for disassembly.

Valve Body Disassembly

The work area must be spotlessly clean. A small particle of dirt that finds its way into the valve body can result in failure. Also, be sure there is adequate room to spread parts out while keeping them in order. Be aware, correct reassembly is vital. Installing the wrong spring on a valve or installing a spool valve backward can make a valve inoperative.

Disassemble the valve body by removing the screws holding the lower housing to the upper housing. Carefully separate the two housings, do not pry or hammer, and lift off the separator plate. Avoid losing any check balls or springs. Remove the cover plates that retain the valve assemblies and slip the valves from their bores. Keep all of the parts in order for reassembly, and save any old gaskets to match with the new ones.

Valve body designs vary greatly from transmission to transmission. Although many are composed of two main housings, some have three separate housings, while others have some of the valve body passages cast into the transmission case. Some transaxles, such as the Hydra-Matic 4T80-E, have two valve bodies: one that bolts up to the side of the transaxle and another that attaches to the bottom of the case.

Clean all parts in fresh solvent or carburetor cleaner to remove gum, varnish, dirt, and grease. After cleaning, rinse the parts in hot, running water. Then, immerse them in fresh solvent to separate water from the clean parts. Dry parts with low-pressure, filtered, compressed air to prepare them for inspection.

Inspecting Valve Body Components

Once all the parts are clean, inspect the valve body and its components for the following defects:

- Scored, cracked, or burred plugs and valves
- Broken, bent, or worn springs
- Scored or rusted bores

- Plugged or restricted fluid passages
- Bent or rusted separator plate
- Stuck check valves
- Bent manual valve
- Cracked castings and distorted or nicked mating surfaces

Many valve body parts are not sold separately, so you may have to replace the entire valve body if any parts fail inspection. Shiny areas on **valve lands** indicate friction between the **spool valve** and the body. These areas can be lightly polished with crocus cloth. Be careful not to round any edges of valve lands when polishing. Rewash and dry any valves that require polishing.

Solenoids and sensors that attach to the valve body in an electronically controlled transmission are serviced at this time as well. The magnetic field of a solenoid tends to attract metallic particles and other debris circulating in the transmission fluid. This contamination can prevent, delay, or restrict plunger movement, leading to a loss of apply pressure. Clean internal solenoid passages by solvent washing, then check winding resistance using an ohmmeter. Replace a solenoid if varnish build-up remains after cleaning, or if resistance readings are out of specification. Also, clean and inspect any filter screens that install in the hydraulic supply passages for the solenoids. Replace screens that are torn or damaged.

Valve Body Assembly and Installation

Match the old gaskets with the new ones to ensure that replacements are correct. Then install the valve assemblies. Lubricate each spool valve with ATF and slide it into its bore. A valve should slide back and forth of its own weight, without sticking or hesitation. Install the valve retaining plates, and tighten to specified torque. Position check balls in the correct passages of the valve body, figure 2-23. Fit the separator plate and assemble the upper and lower valve body castings. Working from the center outward, tighten all

screws to the specified torque values. Use a torque-limiting screwdriver or an accurate inch-pound torque wrench.

Fit the assembled valve body to the transmission case and loosely install the retaining bolts. Check to make sure the manual valve linkage and parking pawl are properly engaged and indexed. Tighten the bolts to specified final torque following the sequence prescribed by the manufacturer. For transmissions with electronic controls, be sure all sensors, solenoids, switches, and harnesses are correctly positioned and secured before installing the filter and oil pan.

SERVO AND ACCUMULATOR SERVICE

All transmissions with bands use a servo to convert hydraulic pressure to mechanical force to apply and release bands. An **accumulator** is used on some transmissions to stabilize the hydraulic pressure acting on the servo. Servos and accumulators may be mounted to the side of the transmission case, on the bottom of the transmission, or incorporated into the valve body. All are serviceable items that can generally be accessed without removing the transmission from the vehicle.

Servo Service

A servo is a piston and cylinder assembly that actuates the band with an operating rod. A spring on the back side of the piston returns the servo to its off position when hydraulic pressure is released, figure 2-24. Some designs use a combination of spring pressure and offsetting hydraulic pressure to release the servo.

Servos are held in place by a cover that attaches to the transmission either with a snapring or bolts. To remove a servo with a bolt-on cover, loosen and remove the bolts in sequence, lift off the cover, and pull the piston straight out of the bore, figure 2-25. If a snapring is used, depress the cover and use snapring pliers to remove the retaining ring. Lift off the cover and remove the piston, figure 2-26.

Remove all sealing rings and gaskets, wash the parts, including the bore, in clean solvent, dry with compressed air, and inspect the parts. Look for:

- Cracked or scored servo bore
- Nicked, scored, burred, or worn piston and piston rod

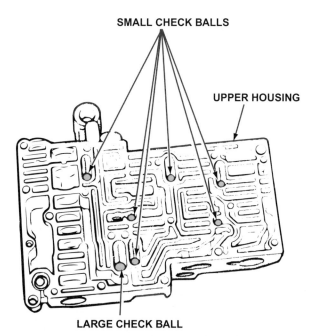

SMALL CHECK BALLS

UPPER HOUSING

LARGE CHECK BALL

Fig. 2-23. Valve body check balls must all be in their correct location for the transmission to shift properly.

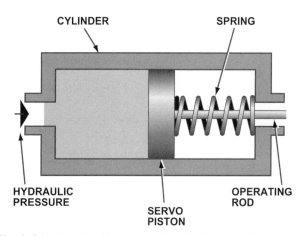

CYLINDER   SPRING

HYDRAULIC
PRESSURE   OPERATING
                  ROD
         SERVO
         PISTON

Fig. 2-24. As hydraulic pressure builds, the servo piston moves and the operating rod tightens the band around the drum. When hydraulic pressure drops, spring force retracts the piston and rod to release the band.

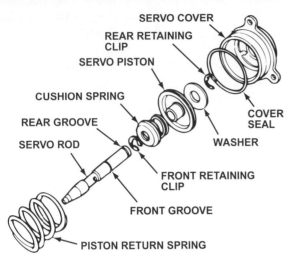

Fig. 2-25. A bolt-on cover may hold the overdrive servo assembly in the transmission/transaxle case.

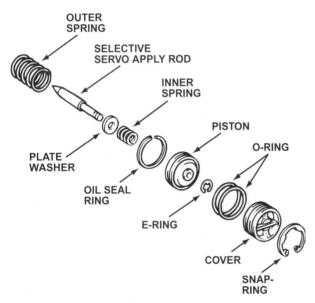

Fig. 2-26. The second coast servo assembly is held in the case by a snapring in transmissions/transaxles.

- Cracked or distorted servo spring
- Obstructed or restricted fluid passages
- Damaged or distorted cover gasket sealing surface
- Faulty spring action
- Burred or distorted body-to-case mating surfaces

Replace any damaged parts and reassemble the unit using new seals. Liberally coat all parts with ATF or assembly lubricant, then install the servo.

Some transmissions use a plastic piston with Teflon® oil seal rings. These oil seal rings cannot be satisfactorily removed from the plastic piston. When seal replacement is necessary, install a new piston and seal assembly.

Accumulator Service

Accumulators can be either the independent piston-type, integral piston-type, or the valve-type. All serve the same purpose—to absorb hydraulic shock and smooth the action of the servo for progressive band application.

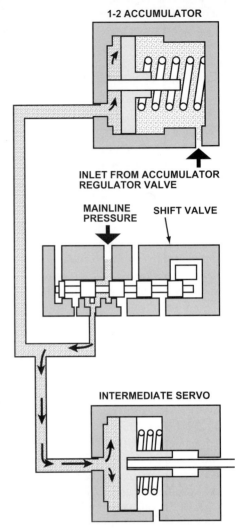

Fig. 2-27. An independent piston accumulator, which resembles a servo, installs in its own bore.

Independent piston-type accumulators operate in a dedicated bore remotely mounted from the servo, figure 2-27. To service, follow the techniques detailed for servos.

An integral piston-type accumulator is installed in the same bore as a servo piston, figure 2-28. However, the accumulator piston is generally a part of the apply circuit for a servo other than the one with which it is combined. For example, the accumulator piston installed in the low-reverse servo regulates pressure when the intermediate band is applied. These units are serviced along with, and in the same manner as, the servo.

Valve-type accumulators use a spool valve and a metered orifice to stabilize pressure for smooth band application, figure 2-29. The accumulator valves are generally incorporated into the valve body and can be serviced as described earlier in this chapter.

GOVERNOR SERVICE

The **governor** is a valve that develops governor pressure from mainline pressure through **centrifugal force.** Governor pressure builds in relation to vehicle speed and opposes throttle pressure to regulate shift points. Most governors are driven by the transmission output shaft. However, some transaxles drive

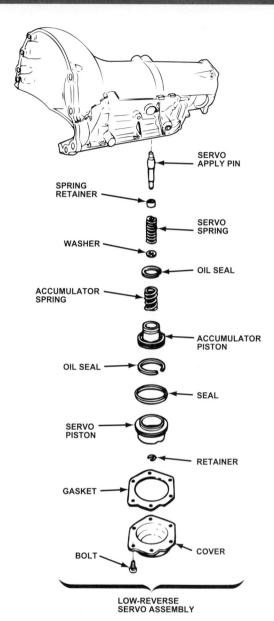

Fig. 2-28. An integral piston accumulator installs into the same bore as a servo assembly.

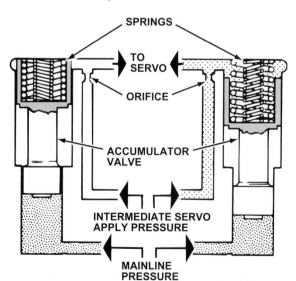

Fig. 2-29. A valve-type accumulator uses a spool valve to cushion hydraulic apply fluid acting on the servo piston.

the governor with the transfer shaft. The governor may be shaft mounted and driven by splines, or remotely mounted and gear-driven by the shaft.

There are three common governor designs:

- Gear-driven with spool valve
- Gear-driven with check balls
- Shaft-mounted with spool valve

On a shaft-mounted governor, the entire assembly rotates along with the shaft, and spool valve movement is controlled by centrifugal force acting on spring-loaded weights, figure 2-30. Gear-driven governors fit into a case bore and are driven by the transmission output shaft. Some gear-driven units use a spool valve to regulate pressure, figure 2-31; others use check balls, figure 2-32. Gear-driven governors are accessed by

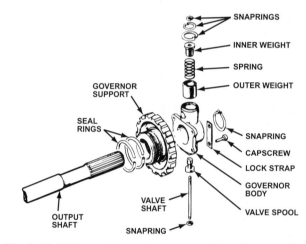

Fig. 2-30. With a shaft-mounted governor the entire assembly rotates along with the shaft.

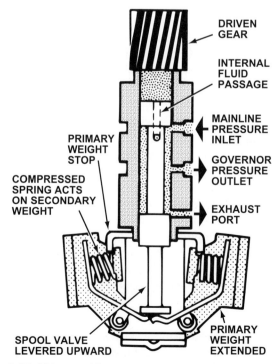

Fig. 2-31. This gear-driven governor uses centrifugal force acting on weights to move a spool valve and direct governor pressure through the transmission.

A2

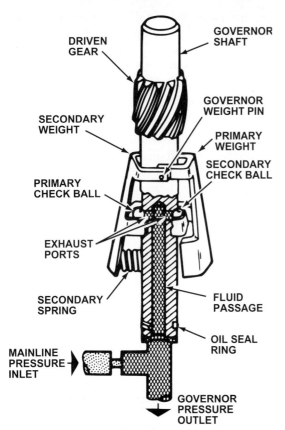

Fig. 2-32. Check balls open or close passageways to control governor pressure flow to the transmission on this gear-driven governor design.

removing the governor cover from the transmission case. The cover may be bolted on or held in place by a wire bail. With the cover removed, the governor assembly can be withdrawn from its bore. To access a shaft-driven governor, the extension housing must be removed from the transmission. The valve bolts onto the governor support, and the entire assembly is located on the shaft with a snapring.

The governor assembly usually consists of a shaft, a spool valve or check balls, two weights, two springs, and various snaprings and attaching parts. Disassemble the governor and clean all the parts in solvent. Inspect for the following:

- Scored or rusted valve bore
- Scored, nicked, or rusted spool valve
- Damaged or plugged governor screen. The screen may be located in the case or in the main valve body
- Damaged or distorted mating surfaces
- Binding, sticking, or damaged weights
- Broken or distorted springs
- Cut, distorted, or loose seals
- Broken snaprings and damaged ring grooves
- Plugged or restricted fluid passages in the case or the output shaft
- Damaged gears

When reassembling a shaft-driven governor, the weights and the spool valve must slide freely on the shaft and in the valve bore. Lubricate all parts with ATF or assembly lubricant during installation. Install the governor using new O-rings, seals, and gaskets.

SPEEDOMETER DRIVE GEAR SERVICE

Speedometer gears and/or speedometer sensors are mounted on the output shaft of RWD transmissions, figure 2-33. In a transaxle the speedometer drive gear or sensor reluctor are generally mounted on the governor shaft of the RH axle shaft. Most drive gears are attached to the output shaft with a spring clip or pin. Inspect all components of the drive gear assembly for signs of excessive wear or damage. If the gear requires replacement make sure to use the correct replacement part; otherwise speedometer calibration will be affected.

Vehicle Speed Sensor Service

The speedometer drive gear is mounted on the output shaft of RWD vehicles, and on the output shaft of the transfer case in four wheel/all wheel drive vehicles. Transaxle speedometer assemblies may be driven by the right side output shaft or the differential carrier assembly.

Late-model vehicles replace the speedometer drive gear with an output shaft speed sensor (OSS) or vehicle speed sensor (VSS), figure 2-33. These sensors send an electrical signal to the Powertrain Control Module (PCM) or Transmission Control Module (TCM). The control module converts the signal into a speed signal for use by other vehicle modules and the speedometer in the instrument cluster.

Diagnosis of these speed sensors is normally accomplished through the use of a scan tool following the procedures outlined in the vehicle Service Manual. Sensor signals can also be tested using an oscilloscope to view the waveform produced.

Refer to the appropriate Service Manual for the proper diagnostic procedures for all switches and sensors.

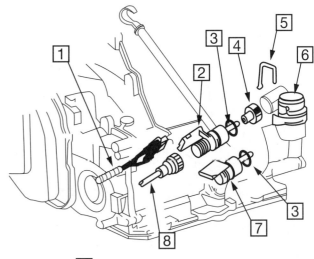

1	V.S.S. LEAD
2	GEAR AND SENSOR ASM.
3	SEAL
4	GEAR
5	RETAINER
6	TRANS. ASM.
7	SENSOR ASM.
8	SPEEDOMETER CABLE

Fig. 2-33. Typical speedometer drive gear assembly.

TRANSMISSION/TRANSAXLE MOUNT INSPECTION AND SERVICE

Mount Inspection

The weight of the transmission or transaxle is supported by the engine and its mounts and the transmission/transaxle mounts. These mounts are critical for the proper operation of the transmission and are important in isolating the powertrain noise from the passenger compartment. The mountings for the engine and transmission/transaxle keep the powertrain in proper alignment with the rest of the drivetrain and help maintain proper adjustment of the linkage attached to the housing.

On FWD vehicles the positioning of the powertrain mounts is critical to ensure proper axle shaft to hub alignment and ensure the front-end geometry is maintained.

Always scribe reference marks on all mounts and crossmembers before removal from the vehicle. Verify these marks are realigned correctly when the transmission or transaxle is reinstalled.

FLUID AND FILTER SERVICE

Automatic transmission fluid (ATF) is a complex lubricant designed to perform four important tasks:

1. Provide a fluid coupling between the engine and the transmission.
2. Work as a heat exchanger by removing heat from the transmission and dissipating it through an oil cooler or into the airstream.
3. Provide pressure to operate servos and clutches.
4. Lubricate all moving transmission parts.

There are a variety of transmission fluids available, and they are not interchangeable. Using the wrong fluid can cause clutch engagement problems or a damaging chemical reaction with system components. Consult the appropriate service literature to determine the proper fluid for each transmission you service. Be sure the fluid you add meets the requirements of the transmission manufacturer.

Operating temperature has a direct effect on how well the transmission fluid can perform its tasks. Under ideal conditions, fluid temperature should be about 175°F and can be expected to perform well for 100,000 miles. As shown in figure 2-34, raising the temperature by 20°F will reduce fluid life by half. Common practice is to change the fluid and filter every 60,000 miles under normal driving conditions. If the vehicle is constantly operated under severe conditions, change the fluid and filter every 15,000 to 20,000 miles.

Checking Fluid Level

Most automatic transmissions are designed to operate with the fluid level between the marks on the dipstick blade, figure 2-35. Fluid level is important, because as little as a pint or ½ liter over or under the specified amount can cause transmission problems.

When the fluid level is low, the oil pump takes in air along with the fluid. Fluid contaminated by air bubbles, or aerated, results in low hydraulic pressure that delays clutch and band applications and slows transmission operation. With a high fluid level,

ATF OPERATING TEMPERATURE		PROJECTED ATF SERVICE LIFE	
F	C	MILES	KM
175	80	100,000	160,000
195	90	50,000	80,000
215	100	25,000	40,000
235	115	12,500	20,000
255	125	6,250	10,000
275	135	3,000	5,000
295	145	1,500	2,500
315	155	750	1,200
335	170	325	500
355	180	160	250
375	190	80	125
390	200	40	65
410	210	20	32

Fig. 2-34. Transmission fluid life expectancy decreases dramatically as operating temperatures increase.

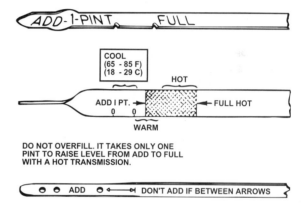

Fig. 2-35. Typical transmission dipstick markings.

meshing of the gears churns the fluid, aerates it, and creates foam. This foaming results in a loss of hydraulic pressure similar to that caused by a low fluid level condition. Aerated fluid can lead to overheating, fluid oxidation, and varnish buildup.

To accurately read the transmission fluid level, both the transmission and engine should be at normal operating temperature. It takes about 10 to 20 miles of city driving to fully warm an automatic transmission to normal operating range. Typically, you can expect to see about a ¾ inch difference on the dipstick between a cold reading and a hot reading. On some transmissions, the dipstick blade is graduated for both hot and cold level checks. However, a reading taken at normal operating temperature is more accurate and is always the preferred method. With an electronically controlled transmission, you can verify ATF temperature by using a scan tool to access the data stream, figure 2-36.

To check transmission fluid correctly, be sure the vehicle is on a level surface. Apply the parking brake, start the engine, and let it idle. If the vehicle has an automatic vacuum-release parking brake, disconnect the vacuum line from the vacuum chamber. Apply the brakes and move the gear selector slowly through all ranges, stopping in each gear range long enough for the transmission to engage. Return the selector to park or neutral, as specified by the manufacturer.

Locate the transmission dipstick, remove it, wipe the dipstick blade clean, then reinstall it into the tube. Make sure the

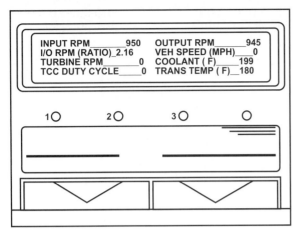

Fig. 2-36. Monitoring the transmission fluid temperature (TFT) parameter on the data stream is an accurate way to determine if the fluid is at normal operating temperature.

dipstick seats completely in the tube. Wait a few seconds, remove the dipstick, and read the fluid level on the blade. To get a correct reading, the fluid level must be equal on both sides of the dipstick blade. If not equal, wipe off the blade and take another reading. A proper fluid level will fall between the marks on the blade that indicate normal operating range. If the level is below the lower mark, top it off using the correct fluid.

Some newer transmissions, such as the Hydra-Matic 4T40-E and the Volkswagen 01M and 01P, do not have a dipstick. A specific procedure that involves removing a threaded plug from the case must be followed to check the fluid level on these units. See the appropriate Service Manual.

Draining Transmission Fluid

The transmission fluid must be hot before it is drained. The vehicle must also be on a level surface, preferably on a hoist or supported by jackstands. Depending on transmission design, the fluid is drained in one of three ways. Remove one of the following:

- The oil pan
- The fluid filler tube
- The drain plug

Oil Pan Removal

Removing the oil pan is the only way to drain some transmissions. This must be done carefully and slowly to prevent hot fluid from gushing out. Place a large drain pan under the transmission. Starting at one end of the pan, remove the attaching bolts in order, working from first one side of the pan to the other. This allows the pan to tilt slowly in one direction for easy draining.

Once the draining fluid has slowed to a trickle, remove the remaining bolts and lift off the oil pan. Then, inspect the inside of the pan carefully for metal or friction material particles. Remove and discard the oil pan gasket and scrape off any remaining gasket material from the transmission case and pan flange. Wash the oil pan in clean solvent and dry with compressed air.

Filler Tube Removal

The fluid filler tube is removed from the side of the oil pan to drain some transmissions. Filler tubes attach in several ways.

Some filler tubes attach to the side of the pan with threaded fittings, while others are press-fit into the pan or transmission case. With either type, have a drain pan in position before loosening the filler tube.

Loosen threaded fittings with a wrench. Use a back-up wrench where applicable to prevent distorting the tube. Back the coupling-nut all the way off, then pull the tube free.

Remove filler tubes that press-fit into the oil pan by pulling the tube straight out. Do not twist the tube; this will cause damage. To reinstall the tube, push it straight into the pan. If the filler tube is pressed into the case, you should not have to remove it to drain the fluid.

With either type, after the transmission has drained, remove the pan for inspection and filter service. If the filler tube has an O-ring seal or a gasket, replace it when reinstalling the filler tube.

Drain Plugs

Most late-model, original-equipment transmissions do not have oil pan drain plugs. However, aftermarket pans and older transmissions do have drain plugs. Remove the drain plug with a wrench and allow the fluid to drain. Some transmission drain plugs are magnetized to attract metal particles. Inspect the plug carefully for such particles as you wipe it clean.

Once the fluid drains, unbolt and remove the pan to service the filter. When reinstalling a drain plug, tighten it to the specified torque.

Older model transmissions may have an additional drain plug on the torque converter. Although most manufacturers discontinued using torque converter drain plugs by about 1980, they are beginning to make a comeback. Some late-model Ford lockup torque converters have a drain plug. Flushing old, contaminated fluid from the converter can effectively eliminate the cause of some clutch shudder problems.

If the converter has a drain plug, there is an access pening at the bottom of the bellhousing. Remove the access cover and rotate the engine until the plug is in position for removal, figure 2-37. After the transmission has drained, place the fluid container under the converter and remove the converter drain plug.

Servicing Filters and Screens

All automatic transmissions use a filtering device to remove foreign or abrasive particles, varnish, and sludge from the fluid, figure 2-38. This filtering device can be either a disposable paper or fabric element or a reusable screen. On transaxles that do not have the valve body mounted to the bottom of the case, the filter is located at the point where fluid leaves the sump rather than at the valve body. The suction side of the pump is

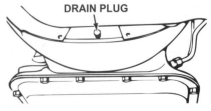

Fig. 2-37. Drain the torque converter during a fluid service if it is fitted with a drain plug.

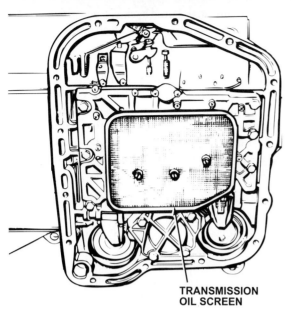

Fig. 2-38. The oil pump draws ATF from the sump through a filter or screen before delivering it to the transmission.

Fig. 2-39. Clean a wire mesh screen using solvent and a brush.

A2

connected to the filter, so the fluid is cleaned before it enters the system. Spin-on canister type filters are used on some of the later transmissions; you could see this in a light truck application and/or some non-domestic vehicles.

Filters and screens are kept in place in various ways. Some screens are retained by attaching screws or by spring steel clips, while others are retained by bolts. Remove the fasteners, then lift off the screen. Many filters and screens fit into the valve body or case with an O-ring. Avoid tearing the O-ring by pulling the filter straight down from the transmission.

Reinstalling most filters and screens is easy, because they fit onto the valve body in only one way. The screen or filter may have an arrow or the word FRONT stamped on them to show how to properly place them on the transmission. Always install new gaskets and O-rings when replacing a filter or screen. Push the screen assembly straight up and into place until fully seated, then tighten the screws or bolts to their recommended torque values.

Transmission filters and screens fall into one of the following categories:

- Metal mesh screen
- Nylon screen
- Paper or synthetic filter

Metal Mesh Screens

The metal screen filter is nothing more than a fine wire mesh designed to trap contaminants. This is an early type of filter usually found on older transmissions. To service a metal screen filter, remove it from the transmission. Clean the screen thoroughly with fresh solvent and a brush, figure 2-39. If the screen has varnish build-up on its mesh surface, soak it in carburetor cleaner, then flush with solvent. If this process does not remove the varnish, replace the screen. Blow the screen dry with low-pressure compressed air. Do not wipe with a cloth, as lint from the cloth can stick to the screen and can cause a transmission malfunction. Inspect the screen closely. Replace the screen if it is torn, broken, or badly clogged.

Nylon Screens

A nylon screen filtering device is similar to a metal screen design, but the mesh is made of glass-reinforced, heat-stabilized nylon, figure 2-40. The nylon mesh is much finer than a metal screen and can filter out smaller particles. You may wash a nylon filter screen with solvent to remove trapped particles, but it cannot be soaked in carburetor cleaner to remove varnish. If a nylon screen filter is broken, torn, or shows any signs of varnish build-up, replace it with a new one.

Paper and Synthetic Filters

Paper and synthetic transmission filters are made of an oil-resistant fabric similar to that in an engine oil filter. Most late-model transmissions use synthetic fabric filters. These filters trap particles within the filter material instead of on the surface, so they trap finer particles and hold more contaminants with less fluid flow restriction than other filters. Whether paper

Fig. 2-40. A nylon screen filter can be washed in solvent and reused if there is no varnish build-up or damage.

or fabric, these filters cannot be cleaned in any way. Replace the filter whenever you service the transmission.

Oil Pan Installation

After replacing the filter, reinstall the oil pan following these general guidelines:

1. Wash the inside of the pan with fresh solvent. If the pan has a magnetic chip collector, remove, inspect, and clean it, as well. Scrape or wire brush any old gasket material off of the flange surface.
2. Dry with low-pressure compressed air; do not wipe the pan with a cloth.
3. Repair dimpled bolt holes by placing the oil pan flange on a flat surface and pounding with a ball-peen hammer to straighten, figure 2-41.
4. Place the gasket on the pan. Do not use gasket cement or sealer. Some pan gaskets are temperature sensitive and form a seal as the transmission warms up. Sealers or lubricants can prevent these gaskets from sealing.
5. Fit the pan to the transmission and install the bolts finger-tight, taking care not to pinch the gasket.
6. Tighten the bolts to specified torque.

Many newer transmissions have a reusable gasket that does not need replacing at every service. If a new gasket is not supplied with the filter kit, and the original one is made from a thick, rubbery material, you can probably reuse it. Thoroughly inspect the gasket before you reinstall it. Watch for signs of tearing, cracking, and dry rot that can cause it to leak.

Refilling the Transmission

Before refilling the transmission, make sure the oil pan is properly installed. If the oil pan has a drain plug, be sure it is installed and properly tightened. If the fluid filler tube was

Fig. 2-41. Flatten dimpled bolt holes before reinstalling the oil pan.

removed, be sure it is secured back in place with a new O-ring or gasket. If the torque converter was drained, be sure the drain plug is installed.

The amount of fluid used initially to refill the transmission depends on whether the torque converter was drained. Typically, two or three quarts is sufficient to refill a transmission. However, if the torque converter was drained, an additional three to five quarts of ATF may be required. The exact amount of fluid needed for an initial refill differs from one transmission model to another. You can use the following general procedure for refilling most transmissions:

1. Add the specified amount of the proper ATF to the transmission through the fluid filler tube.
2. With the gear selector in park, start the engine and run at idle for about two minutes.
3. Firmly apply the brakes, then move the selector through the complete gear range, stopping in each gear to allow the transmission to engage.
4. Check the fluid level. Add the necessary amount of fluid to bring the level up to, but not above, the ADD mark on the dipstick.
5. Operate the engine and transmission to warm them to normal operating temperature, then recheck the fluid level. If necessary, add enough fluid to bring the level to the FULL mark on the dipstick.
6. Inspect the drain plug, oil pan gasket, and fluid filler tube for leakage.

BAND ADJUSTMENT

Some manufacturers specify band adjustment as a part of regular transmission maintenance, while others recommend it only as part of a transmission overhaul. A general industry trend seems to be moving away from using bands that require routine adjustment. The bands in many late-model transmissions adjust by a selective servo piston apply pin that installs during assembly, and no further adjustment is needed once the unit is placed into service.

Band adjustments can often improve transmission operation but will not eliminate the problem. A slipping band is often just a symptom of other internal problems, and an adjustment simply postpones an overhaul. Symptoms of bands that are out of adjustment include:

- Harsh or slipping shifts
- Burnt transmission fluid

Transmission bands require precise adjustment and accurate factory service specifications. The transmission is usually identified by a transmission code that appears on a tag attached to the transmission case or is stamped on the transmission case itself, figure 2-42. Ford Motor Company furnishes code letters on the vehicle identification plate or certification label, figure 2-43. Since transmission operating requirements are different for each vehicle model and engine combination, internal transmission parts are different to provide for this. The transmission model number and part number are the keys you

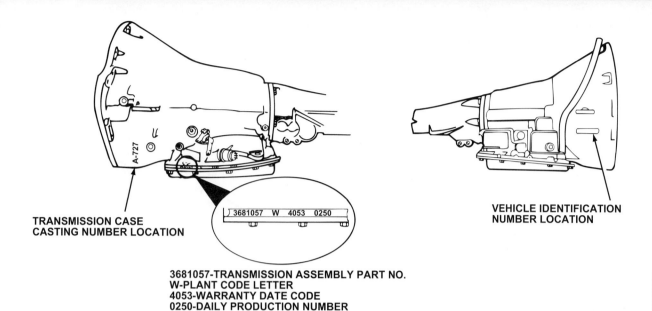

TRANSMISSION CASE CASTING NUMBER LOCATION

3681057   W   4053   0250

VEHICLE IDENTIFICATION NUMBER LOCATION

3681057-TRANSMISSION ASSEMBLY PART NO.
W-PLANT CODE LETTER
4053-WARRANTY DATE CODE
0250-DAILY PRODUCTION NUMBER

Fig. 2-42. Transmission identification numbers are often found on a tag attached to the transmission or stamped directly on the case.

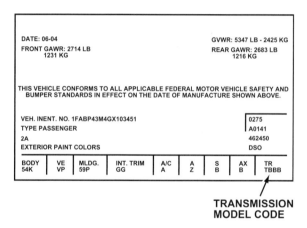

DATE: 06-04
FRONT GAWR: 2714 LB
        1231 KG

GVWR: 5347 LB - 2425 KG
REAR GAWR: 2683 LB
        1216 KG

THIS VEHICLE CONFORMS TO ALL APPLICABLE FEDERAL MOTOR VEHICLE SAFETY AND BUMPER STANDARDS IN EFFECT ON THE DATE OF MANUFACTURE SHOWN ABOVE.

VEH. INENT. NO. 1FABP43M4GX103451
TYPE PASSENGER
2A
EXTERIOR PAINT COLORS

0275
A0141
462450
DSO

BODY 54K	VE VP	MLDG. 59P	INT. TRIM GG	A/C A	A Z	S B	AX B	TR TBBB

TRANSMISSION MODEL CODE

Fig. 2-43. Most transmissions can be identified by a model code on the vehicle certification label.

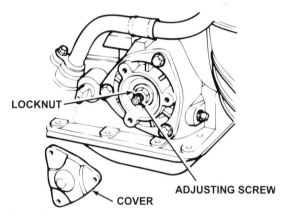

LOCKNUT

ADJUSTING SCREW

COVER

Fig. 2-44. On some transmissions the band adjusting screw is behind a cover plate that bolts to the transmission case.

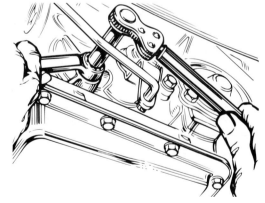

Fig. 2-45. On a typical band adjustment, the locknut is held with a box wrench while the adjusting screw is turned with an inch-pound torque wrench.

use when ordering parts or to identify the transmission for service adjustment procedures.

Adjustment Procedure

Transmission bands can be either externally or internally adjustable. External adjustments are generally made by loosening a locknut, tightening an adjustment screw to a specific torque, then tightening the locknut. Internal adjustments are made only when rebuilding the transmission. Selectively sized **servo** piston apply pins are used to obtain proper clearance.

External Band Adjustment

External band adjustment can be done from outside the case on some transmissions; others require the oil pan be removed. The adjustment screw and locknut are behind a cover plate that bolts to the case on some transmissions, figure 2-44. Generally, you will need an inch-pound torque wrench, with a special 8-point socket or Allen wrench, along with a back-up

wrench to make the adjustment, figure 2-45. A specially sized gauge block is also required to adjust certain bands. Use the identification code stamped on the transmission case to look up the exact adjustment specifications. Watch for special locknuts that contain a fluid seal. These should be replaced after adjusting the bands. To adjust:

1. Loosen the locknut. If the locknut has a fluid seal, remove and discard it. Replace it with a new one when the adjustment is complete.
2. Tighten the adjusting screw to specified torque. The number of turns needed to reach torque will give you an indication of the condition of the friction material on the band.
3. Back off the band adjusting screw the exact number of turns specified by the manufacturer.
4. Hold the adjusting screw securely in place to prevent it from turning while you torque the locknut.

The location of exhaust pipes, shift linkage, or the chassis may block access to the band adjusting screw on some vehicles. Use an adapter or extension on the torque wrench to make the adjustment. Keep in mind that an adapter or extension that adds to the length of the wrench causes applied torque to be greater than the dial reading or calibrated torque value. An extension used in line with the square drive of the torque wrench (at a right angle to the wrench handle) does not affect the torque reading.

Selective Servo Pin Adjustment

On many late-model transmissions, bands are adjusted by means of a selective servo pin. Generally, no adjustment is needed if the correct pin is installed when assembling the transmission. Occasionally, an adjustment will be needed to remedy a poor shift quality complaint, and it can be done without removing the transaxle. However, you are working in tight quarters and removing the unit and making the adjustment on the bench may seem easier.

To choose the correct piston apply pin, follow this general procedure:

1. Assemble and install the servo spring, piston, and available rod.
2. Install a piston selection tool and tighten the tool adjusting screw to specifications.
3. Install a dial indicator so the stem contacts the piston, then zero the dial face, figure 2-46.
4. Back off the piston selection tool screw until the piston stops.
5. Take a dial indicator reading and compare it to specifications.

If the reading does not match factory specifications, remove the tooling, piston, and pin. Select and install a new piston or pin and recheck piston travel.

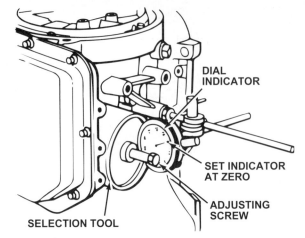

Fig. 2-46. A special selection tool and a dial indicator are used to measure servo piston travel to determine what length piston pin is needed.

ELECTRONIC COMPONENT SERVICE

Many modern transmissions use an onboard computer to control converter clutch application. In addition, computer regulated electronic shift controls are becoming more commonplace. Electronic controls allow for precise regulation of converter lockup and shifting over a wide range of conditions. With computerized shift controls, the mechanical spool-type shift valves in the valve body are replaced with a solenoid ball valve. The solenoids replace many of the valves, springs, check balls, and **orifices** in the valve body that are prone to wear, clogging, and sticking.

A variety of sensors provide input signals to the computer. The computer generates an output signal that is routed to the appropriate solenoid to shift gears or engage or disengage the converter clutch. Some systems use a dedicated transmission computer; others incorporate transmission functions into the engine management computer. A malfunction, lost signal, or improbable signal will generally store a trouble code in the onboard diagnostics. When a problem occurs, access the trouble codes to isolate the offending circuit.

Before testing electrical components, keep in mind that the problem may not be with specific sensors, switches, solenoids, or computers, but with the connectors and wires linking these parts. Check for blown fuses first. Then, look for disconnected, loose, or corroded electrical connectors or wires. Examine the electrical connectors carefully, check proper contact, and correct routing of the wires.

Electronic components do not require adjustment or service. However, adjustment may be necessary when sensors and solenoids are replaced. Adjust to specification following procedures provided by the manufacturer.

CHAPTER QUESTIONS

1. You clean the transmission valve body. Technician A says to remove burrs from valves with a crocus cloth. Technician B says to use carburetor cleaner to remove varnish from valves. Who is right?
   a. A only
   b. B only
   c. Both A and B
   d. Neither A nor B

2. Most externally adjustable bands can be adjusted by using:
   a. An inch-pound torque wrench
   b. A foot-pound torque wrench
   c. A selective servo piston pin
   d. An adjustable wrench

3. The technician is servicing the transmission fluid. Technician A says the fluid should be hot when the transmission is drained. Technician B says the cloth filters can be washed and reused. Who is right?
   a. A only
   b. B only
   c. Both A and B
   d. Neither A nor B

4. The position of the manual valve is controlled by the:
   a. Accelerator linkage
   b. Throttle valve linkage
   c. Kickdown linkage
   d. Gearshift linkage

5. Incorrectly adjusted linkages can cause all of the following problems *EXCEPT*:
   a. Early or late shifts
   b. Burnt transmission fluid
   c. Harsh or slipping shifts
   d. Hunting between gears

6. The proper way to repair a torn CV joint boot is to:
   a. Repack the CV joint and install a split boot.
   b. Repack the CV joint and reseal the boot.
   c. Replace the CV joint and boot.
   d. Replace the axle assembly.

7. O-ring and square-cut seals can be used where there is:
   a. Axial movement
   b. Rotational movement
   c. Axial and rotational movement
   d. Low pressure only

8. The technician is servicing the transmission filter screen. Technician A says to clean varnish from the nylon screen by soaking it in carburetor cleaner. Technician B says dirt should be removed from the screen using a soft, clean cloth. Who is right?
   a. A only
   b. B only
   c. Both A and B
   d. Neither A nor B

9. A defective vacuum modulator can cause all of the following symptoms *EXCEPT*:
   a. Stalling and second gear starts
   b. Harsh upshifts or downshifts
   c. Soft upshifts or downshifts
   d. Slippage and fluid overheating

10. When vacuum testing a modulator diaphragm, it should be able to hold:
    a. 7 to 10 in-Hg for 30 seconds
    b. 10 to 17 in-Hg for 30 seconds
    c. 17 to 20 in-Hg for 30 seconds
    d. 20 to 27 in-Hg for 30 seconds

11. The function of an accumulator is to:
    a. Accumulate hydraulic fluid to prevent overflow
    b. Cushion the effect of band applications
    c. Multiply hydraulic pressure to force faster shifts
    d. Speed the application of the band

12. Governor pressure develops in relation to:
    a. Engine speed
    b. Manifold vacuum
    c. Throttle position
    d. Vehicle speed

A2

CHAPTER THREE

OFF-VEHICLE TRANSMISSION/ TRANSAXLE REPAIR

CHAPTER OBJECTIVES

- The technician will complete the ASE task list for Off-Vehicle Transmission/Transaxle Repair.
- The technician will be able to answer the 13 questions dealing with the Off-Vehicle Transmission/Transaxle Repair sections of the A2 ASE test.

When testing indicates there is internal transmission or torque converter damage, the transmission will have to be removed from the vehicle. This chapter discusses transmission and transaxle removal, teardown and inspection procedures, and common assembly practices. Keep in mind that the information provided here is intended as general guidelines and does not apply to any particular make or model transmission.

TRANSMISSION REMOVAL

Transmission and transaxle removal procedures vary by model application. Whenever you are removing an automatic transmission, it is important to:

- Have accurate service specifications
- Have the necessary tools and equipment
- Follow a logical procedure

Use a transmission jack that attaches securely to the transmission to remove and install the unit, figure 3-1. Always disconnect the battery negative cable to prevent any accidental arcing. Drain the transmission and the fluid cooler. Also drain the torque converter if possible.

Disconnect cooler lines at the transmission and plug the ports to keep contaminants out of the transmission and residual fluid from spilling as you work. Secure the loosened cooler lines out of the way. Reinstall the oil pan if it was removed to drain the fluid. The pan provides a good surface for the transmission jack and prevents damage to the valve body and other internal parts.

Before you remove rotating parts, tag them with index marks so they can be assembled in the same position, figure 3-2. This helps prevent unwanted driveline vibrations. Index the following:

- Torque converter to flexplate
- Rear drive shaft to extension housing
- Rear drive shaft to companion flange
- Front drive shafts to differential housing
- Front drive shafts to wheel hubs

Fig. 3-1. Position and adjust the transmission jack so that it securely supports the unit during removal.

Fig. 3-2. Make index marks on rotating parts before removing them to maintain balance on assembly.

It is impossible to follow a standard removal procedure for all jobs because of the many different transmission and model applications available. The following is a general checklist of items that must be removed or disconnected. Not all items will apply to every vehicle:

- Battery ground cable
- Ignition distributor and cables
- Dipstick filler tube
- Torque converter drain plug
- Transmission oil pan
- Fluid cooler lines
- Vacuum modulator line
- Starter motor
- Shift linkage
- Throttle linkage or kickdown wiring
- Neutral starting switch
- Backup lamp wiring and switch
- Shift control wiring harness and switches
- Speedometer cable
- Drive shaft or axle shafts
- Transmission mounts
- Rear crossmember
- Torque converter-to-flexplate bolts
- Bellhousing-to-engine bolts

An important step is to support the engine to prevent it from shifting as the transmission is removed. Some transaxles require special fixtures to hold the engine in place. With a rear-wheel drive transmission, a jack under the engine oil pan will work for most jobs. Check to make sure all linkages, wiring, hoses, and lines are disconnected and clear of the area.

Once everything is disconnected, move the transmission jack and transmission away from the engine slowly. Grasp the torque converter to make sure it moves as a unit with the transmission as you slowly lower the jack. A C-clamp can be used to hold the converter if room permits.

After the transmission is free of the chassis, remove the torque converter. Pull the converter straight out from the transmission to prevent scoring the front pump or seal.

TORQUE CONVERTER SERVICE

External Component Inspection

While the vehicle is still on the hoist, check for a cracked flexplate, loose or damaged starter ring gear, damaged threads on the converter attaching hardware, or other physical defects. Look for any varnish build-up on the transmission case or metal and friction material in the oil pan. These indicate that the converter needs to be flushed or replaced.

Torque Converter Inspection

Visually inspect the converter housing. Look for signs of ballooning. A converter check valve stuck in the closed position is usually at fault. The closed valve allows pressure to build up inside the converter, and excess pressure expands, or balloons, the converter housing. When the converter balloons to the front, the crankshaft thrust bearing is damaged. If it balloons to the rear, the front pump in the transmission is damaged. In either case, you must replace the converter and other damaged parts. Also check for cracks, especially around welds, and examine the hub for nicks and burrs.

Light scoring on the converter hub can be corrected by carefully polishing with 600-grit crocus cloth. Cover the hub opening to prevent dirt from entering the converter while polishing. Replace the converter if the scoring is deep.

Testing and Measuring

Three quick tests are performed to check the torque converter for:

- Stator-to-impeller interference
- Stator-to-turbine interference
- Stator one-way clutch operation

Interferences are checked using an oil pump. A turbine shaft is also required for stator-to-turbine checking. One-way clutch operation can be checked by hand, but special tools are needed to check for early wear. Special tools are also required to perform a pressure test and friction material coefficient test on a lockup converter.

Stator-to-Impeller Interference Test

This check ensures that there is adequate clearance between the stator and impeller. To test:

1. Place the pump assembly on the workbench facing upward.
2. Fit the converter over the stator support splines and rotate to engage the hub with the pump drive gear or rotor.
3. Hold the pump while rotating the converter counterclockwise.

If the converter binds while rotating, or makes a loud scraping noise, the impeller is contacting the stator, figure 3-3. Replace the converter.

Fig. 3-3. The converter should rotate freely on the pump without binding or scraping when performing a stator-to-impeller test.

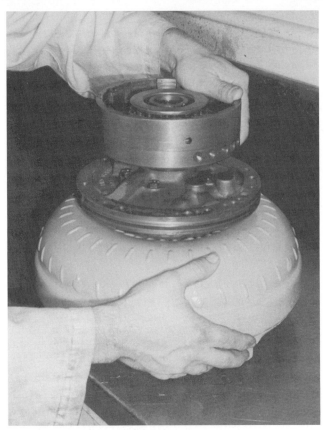

Fig. 3-4. The turbine shaft should turn freely in both directions during a stator-to-turbine interference test.

Stator-to-Turbine Interference Test

Turn the converter and pump assembly over on the bench and make sure the splines remain engaged. Then, insert the **turbine** shaft and test as follows:

1. Rotate the shaft to engage the splines with the turbine hub.
2. Hold both the pump and converter to prevent them from moving.
3. Rotate the turbine shaft. It should turn freely in both directions, figure 3-4.

If you feel any binding while rotating the shaft, replace the converter. Binding results from the stator contacting the turbine and indicates internal damage.

Stator One-Way Clutch Test

A quick way of testing stator clutch action is to insert one finger into the splined inner race and try to turn the inner race in both directions. It should turn clockwise freely but lock up when you try to turn it counterclockwise. This quick check is a go/no-go test only. It does not definitely indicate a failure in its early stages.

A more accurate method of testing is to use a special holding fixture and a torque wrench, figure 3-5. The torque wrench should turn clockwise freely. It should lock up and hold at a specific torque when turned counterclockwise.

Measuring Internal Endplay

A dial indicator and special holding tools are used for checking converter internal endplay, figure 3-6. Tool set-up varies

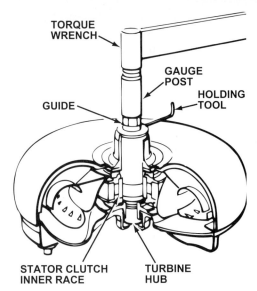

Fig. 3-5. Checking stator one-way clutch operation with a special holding fixture and a torque wrench.

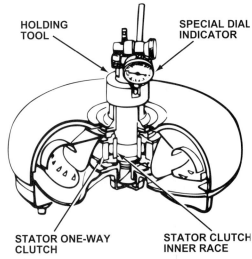

Fig. 3-6. Torque converter internal endplay is checked using a dial indicator and a holding fixture that fits into the converter and attaches to the hub.

for different transmissions, but all are used in essentially the same way:

1. Insert the holding tool in the converter hub until it bottoms. Tighten the tool to lock it in place on the turbine spline.
2. Attach a dial indicator so the plunger rests on the converter hub, then zero the gauge.
3. Lift the tool up as far as it will go and take a dial indicator reading.

If the reading exceeds the specified endplay, replace the converter. In general, lockup converters have a maximum internal endplay of about 0.050 inch.

Pressure Test

A pressure test is used to locate leakage. To perform the test, charge the converter with compressed air and submerge it in a water bath. A special tool with an air fitting is installed in the hub to seal it and allow charging. Check charging pressure specifications for the particular transmission being serviced. Most General Motors and Chrysler converters test at 80 psi. Ford recommends 20 psi of pressure for testing.

Place the pressurized converter in the water tank and watch for bubbles rising to the surface. Look carefully around the hub, seam welds, and drive lugs or studs. Bubbles may not appear immediately, especially if the leak is small or the converter is cold. If no bubbles appear after 10 or 15 minutes, the converter is free of leaks.

Friction Material Coefficient Test

With a lockup converter, determine whether the clutch friction material has enough **coefficient of friction** for use. Do not reuse the converter if the transmission fluid was contaminated by debris, particularly clutch material or metal particles, or overheated.

A bench test fixture is used to test the friction quality of the converter clutch. Insert the fixture test head into the turbine hub and attach a compressed air hose to the air tap. Charge with 25 psi of air pressure to apply the clutch. Use a torque wrench and try to turn the shaft of the test head to check the friction material holding power. If the clutch does not hold at 150 ft-lb, the clutch is defective.

Converter Cleaning and Flushing

Contaminated fluid left in the converter can cause damage. If the converter is to be reinstalled, it should be cleaned. The best cleaning method for conventional converters, and some lockup converters, is flushing.

Solvent is used to flush most converters. However, solvent cannot be used with some friction materials. Bonded linings are especially prone to solvent damage. Check the factory Service Manual for procedures. If in doubt, flush a lockup converter with fresh automatic transmission fluid (ATF) only. Do not use solvent.

Converter flushing can be done either by hand or using a special converter flushing machine.

Hand Flushing

A torque converter must have a drain plug in order to hand flush it. Some converters can be drilled to provide a drain. Consult the Service Manual for drilling position. The drill hole is capped with a plug while flushing and sealed with a special closed-end pop rivet afterwards. To hand flush:

1. Pour at least two quarts of clean solvent into the converter through the hub.
2. Rotate the converter vigorously to slosh the solvent throughout the inside. Turn the turbine and stator with dummy input and stator shafts to dislodge any particles.
3. Stand the converter upright with the drain plug at the bottom. Remove the plug to allow the solvent to drain. Rotate and shake the converter while draining to keep any particles in suspension.

Repeat the procedure until the solvent draining out is clear and free of contamination. To clear out residual solvent, flush the unit in the same manner using fresh transmission fluid.

Machine Flushing

There are several different types of flushing machines available. Most rotate the converter while pumping solvent through it. Some automatically add timed blasts of compressed air to the solvent as it enters the converter. When you use a flushing machine, be sure to follow the instructions specified by the equipment manufacturer to ensure that the converter is properly cleaned.

TRANSMISSION DISASSEMBLY AND INSPECTION

Transmission disassembly varies between models and manufacturers, so there is no standard procedure. However, there are standard practices that apply to any teardown, and standard inspection methods used to recognize potential defects in automatic transmission subassemblies and components.

Transmission Endplay

Every automatic transmission needs a specific amount of **endplay**, and this must be measured before you disassemble the unit. With too little endplay, the geartrain can bind, seize, or lock up. Too much endplay can cause harsh and noisy operation, as well as fast and uneven wear on the geartrain parts.

Automatic transmissions contain several thrust washers and bearings. Manufacturers usually identify these in numerical order from front to rear in the transmission case. At least one of these washers or bearing races is selectively sized to establish endplay. Because the only way to determine the thickness of a selective thrust washer is to measure it with a micrometer, it must be out of the transmission to do this. You measure total endplay now, before disassembly, so you can calculate how much correction is needed when assembling the transmission.

Measuring Endplay

On most transmissions, you measure total endplay at the front end of the input shaft with a dial indicator. The method and location for mounting the dial indicator varies slightly for each transmission model.

General Motors recommends measuring endplay with the transmission vertical and the input shaft facing up, while Chrysler and Ford call for the transmission to be horizontal. Either way is acceptable, as long as the measurements are taken carefully and accurately. To measure endplay:

1. Mount the dial indicator so it is firmly supported and the plunger can contact the nose of the shaft, figure 3-7.
2. Move the shaft and geartrain into the case as far as possible. Center the plunger on the shaft and zero the dial indicator.
3. Move the geartrain and shaft forward in the case as far as possible. Use a large screwdriver behind the input shell or move the entire geartrain by raising the output shaft.
4. Record the dial indicator reading and compare it to specifications. Endplay is corrected by replacing the appropriate selective thrust washer or bearing when you reassemble the unit.

Some transmissions also require measurement of the output shaft endplay at the rear of the transmission, or the transfer shaft

A2

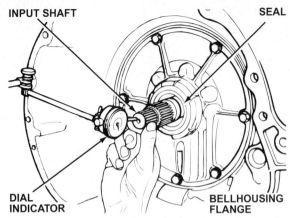

Fig. 3-7. Measure total endplay at the front end of the input shaft with a dial indicator before disassembling the transmission.

endplay at the driven gear of a transaxle drive link assembly. Check the Service Manual to determine how many endplay measurements you need to take and how to take them. Each measurement provides a reference for selecting the correct replacement for one of the thrust washers, bearings, or spacers.

Transmission Disassembly

Once endplay measurements are taken and recorded, disassemble the transmission into its component parts. Due to the diversity of transmission designs, there is not a standard teardown procedure that applies to all units. Follow the recommended procedure for the transmission being serviced.

Disassembly Tips

Organization is the key to a successful transmission overhaul. Keep your work and work area in order to avoid misplacing and incorrectly installing parts. To work more efficiently:

1. Lay out the parts you remove in the same order they are shown in the Service Manual, figure 3-8.
2. Have a tray, or other container, to hold fasteners and small parts.
3. Service subassemblies individually to avoid mixing up the parts.
4. Do not force parts together or apart. Use slide hammers to remove most pumps, seal drivers to press seals and bushings in and out of their bores, and special compressor tools, or presses, to compress return and servo springs. Everything else can be taken apart or put back together with hand pressure. If you cannot separate or install the parts without using force, something is wrong.
5. Never wipe transmission parts with rags or shop towels. Allow parts to air dry or dry them with moisture-free, low-pressure, compressed air after cleaning.

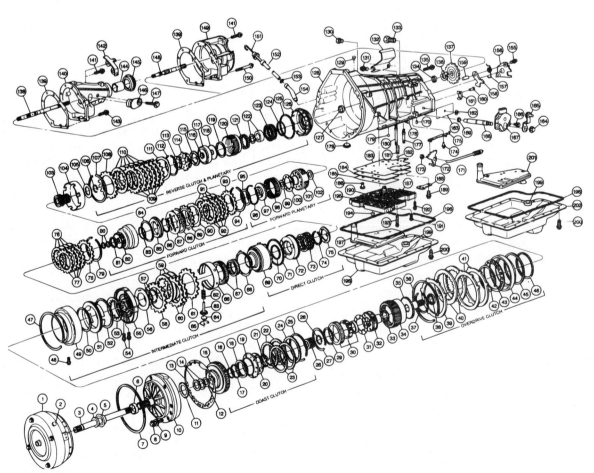

Fig. 3-8. The exploded view diagram in the Service Manual can help you keep track of internal parts during teardown, inspection, and assembly.

Component Cleaning and Inspection

Prepare for inspection by washing metal components in clean solvent and drying with compressed air. Do not allow bearings or planetary gears to spin while drying. Clean band and clutch friction material by wiping with a lint-free rag; do not wash with solvent.

Clean and inspect all of the transmission parts for signs of damage or excessive wear. Due to the number of different transmission designs and component variations, there is no single inspection sequence that applies to every overhaul. Items discussed here are not necessarily presented in the order in which they would be performed when overhauling a transmission.

Oil Pump Inspection

Three types of oil pumps are used for automatic transmissions:

- Gear
- Rotor
- Vane

You will need to disassemble the oil pump and clean all the parts with solvent in order to evaluate it.

If the pump contains a pressure regulator valve, figure 3-9, remove the valve for inspection. Check the valve, springs, spacers, and bore. Look for scoring, corrosion, cracks, and distortion. Check for and clear any restricted fluid passages in the pump housings.

Gear and Rotor Pumps

Gears and rotors must be indexed before you remove them from the pump body. Stamped index marks are often provided by the manufacturer, figure 3-10. If not, make them yourself. Mark indexes with chalk, marking pen, or Prussian blue. Do not use a punch; this can damage the parts.

Disassemble the oil pump and clean all parts and oil passages with solvent, then check the parts for wear. Inspect the condition of the pump housing and stator support. Look for damage on the stator support splines and the metal oil-seal rings. Inspect any bushings for wear and replace them if worn. Check for excessive wear, scoring, and damage on gear and rotor teeth. Also, look for signs of wear on the vanes of a vane-type pump.

If the pump passes a visual inspection, continue by measuring clearances. If any clearance measures out of limits, replace the entire pump assembly.

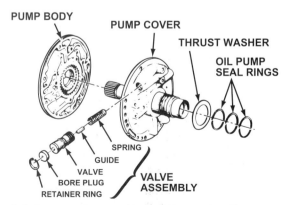

Fig. 3-9. Remove, disassemble, and inspect the oil pump regulator valve.

End clearance

End clearance is the distance between the gear or rotor face and the machined surface of the stator support. Fit the gears or rotors into the pump body. Place a straightedge across the pump body and use a feeler gauge to check the distance between the straightedge and the gear or rotor, figure 3-11.

Fig. 3-10. The factory index marks on these oil pump gears are not for timing, but are a directional indicator to ensure correct installation when the pump is reassembled.

Fig. 3-11. End clearance, the difference betwen the height of the gears or rotors and the pump body, is measured with a straightedge and a feeler gauge.

A2

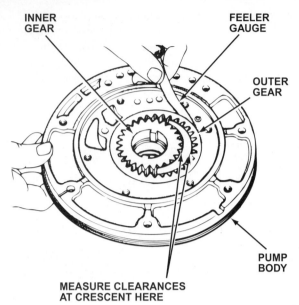

Fig. 3-12. Oil pump side clearance, the distance between the gears or rotors and the pump cavity wall, is measured with a feeler gauge.

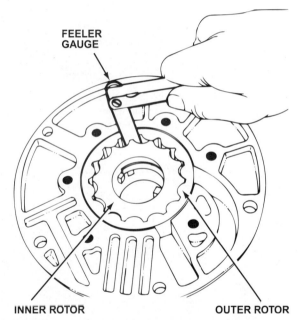

Fig. 3-13. Rotor pump tip clearance, the distance between the high points of two rotor lobes, is measured with a feeler gauge.

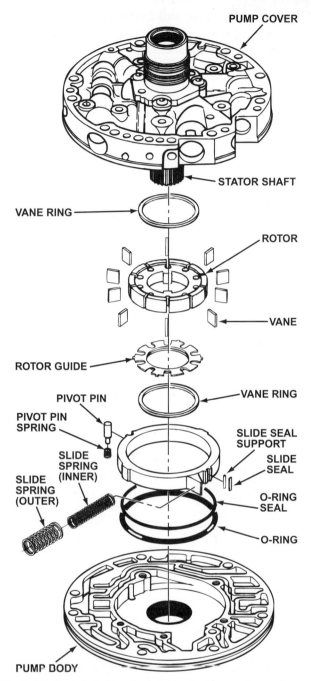

Fig. 3-14. Exploded view of a variable displacement vane-type oil pump.

Side clearance
Side clearance is the distance between the circumference of the outer gear or rotor and the wall of the pump body. Clearance equals the thickest feeler gauge that will fit between the outer gear and pump body, figure 3-12. Check at several locations. If the pump uses a crescent, also check clearance between both the gears and crescent.

Tip clearance
Tip clearance applies only to rotor pumps. Turn the rotors to align a peak on the inner rotor with a peak on the outer rotor. Tip clearance equals the thickest feeler gauge that will fit between the peaks of the inner and outer rotors, figure 3-13. Take readings on several rotor tips to check for variation.

Vane Pumps
Disassemble a vane-type pump and check for wear where the rotating parts of the pump move against the stator support or pump cover, figure 3-14. Also, check the pump pocket for signs of wear.

The two rings that hold the vanes in the rotor are made of a hard material that can crack or break easily; handle them carefully. Inspect the vanes and vane rings for worn areas where they make contact with each other. Inspect the rotor; the part that makes contact with the pump body and the cover must be smooth, with no scratches. Also, look for wear or damage on the oil pump slide and seals.

Bearing Preload

Bearing preload is the measureable drag on tapered roller bearings. This exists when there is no endplay between the bearing rollers and races, causing a drag when a rotating component is turned. The drag is usually measured using an inch-pound torque wrench. The drag measurement is taken while the torque wrench is rotating, not what was required to start the rotation. Preload can be adjusted using shims, thrust washers or adjuster nuts.

Shaft Inspection

Transmission shafts, which are supported in the case by bushings, have splines to mate them with the appropriate gears and other components. Many shafts contain oil passages that distribute lubricating and apply oil to various hydraulic devices.

Inspect shafts for:

*   Cracks or distortion
*   Worn or burred shaft splines
*   Nicks, burrs, scores, or other damage to bearing and thrust washer surfaces
*   Plugged or restricted lubrication passages
*   Worn or damaged oil-seal ring grooves
*   Rough or damaged governor and speedometer drive gear teeth
*   Worn or damaged snapring grooves

Thrust Washer, Thrust Bearing and Bushing Inspection

All moving parts in a transmission rotate around bushings and against thrust washer or thrust bearing surfaces. Bushings carry oil and prevent geartrain wear. Thrust washers and bearings absorb geartrain movement.

Thrust Washers

Inspect thrust washer faces to make sure they are smooth and free of burrs, nicks, and scratches. Also, check the thrust surfaces on gears and other parts to see that they are also smooth. Thrust washers that have hot spots or discoloration due to overheating must be replaced. Measure thickness with a micrometer or vernier caliper; replace if worn, figure 3-15.

Thrust Bearings

Inspect thrust bearings and the surfaces that ride on them. Some caged needle bearings ride directly on the machined surfaces of the parts they separate. Other Torrington bearings have separate races that may be selectively sized, figure 3-16. Inspect bearings for:

*   Missing or damaged rollers
*   Badly worn thrust surfaces
*   Damaged or distorted races

Bushings

Check bushings for scoring and wear. If a bushing requires replacement, inspect the shaft that rides in the bushing for signs of galling, scoring, or wear. In some cases, metal or Teflon® oil-seal rings on the shaft ride inside the bushing. Seal ring wear can

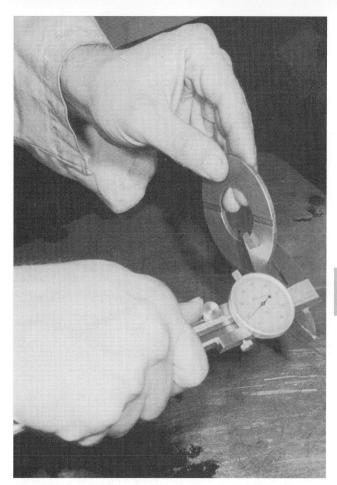

Fig. 3-15. Use a micrometer or caliper to measure thrust washer thickness and evaluate wear.

Fig. 3-16. Inspect the rollers, cage, and races of a Torrington bearing for signs of wear and damage.

damage the bushing. This may lead to wear and damage to the shaft seal ring lands. Replace the seals or shaft as required.

If a bushing needs replacing, remove it by driving or pressing it from the bore. Select the correct driver and install the new bushing, making sure to set it to the proper depth.

A2

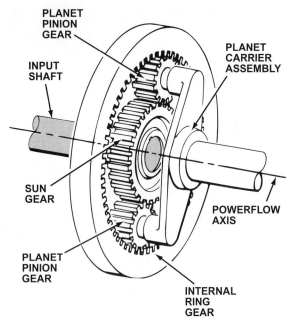

Fig. 3-17. A simple planetary gearset consists of a sun gear, internal ring gear, and planet pinion gears mounted on a planet carrier assembly.

Fig. 3-18. Measuring pinion gear endplay with a feeler gauge.

Planetary Gearset Inspection

Although the individual members of a planetary gearset do not remove from the transmission as an assembly, you must consider them as one during your inspection, figure 3-17. Clean and dry all the planetary gearset pieces to prepare for inspection. Do not allow the compressed air to spin the gears in planetary sets, because this will damage the bearings. Inspect gear teeth and splines for signs of damage and wear. Look for nicks, cracks, rough or sharpened edges, and unusual wear patterns. Replace the gear if any tooth or spline damage is found.

A **sun gear** often rides on a press fit bushing, which is a serviceable item. Check the bushing for wear or scoring. If scoring is evident, check for damage to the shaft. Also, look for distortion on any snaprings and snapring grooves that locate the sun gear.

The **ring gear**, also known as the annulus or internal gear, is often machined into a drum, hub, or shell. Carefully inspect the gear teeth, splines, and other wear areas for signs of damage.

The **planet pinion carrier** assembly is the gearset component most likely to show signs of wear. Replace the carrier assembly if there is obvious damage such as cracked, loose, or broken carriers, pinions, pinion shafts, and lockpins. Planet pinion gears must rotate freely on their shafts without roughness or binding but not have too much gear-to-shaft clearance. Rock each gear back and forth; they should not wobble on the shaft. Use a feeler gauge to measure pinion gear endplay, figure 3-18. Typical pinion endplay clearances range from 0.009 to 0.024 inch (0.24 to 0.60 mm). On some gearsets, you can adjust pinion endplay with thrust washers but, with most, you replace the unit when there is too much end- or sideplay.

Transmission Cases

Inspect the transmission case, bellhousing, and extension housing for the following defects:

- Damage, cracks, and porosity
- Burred or distorted gasket and mating surfaces
- Damaged or stripped bolt holes
- Plugged or restricted vent and fluid passages
- Scored case bushing
- Worn or damaged parking and manual valve linkage parts
- Damaged clutch lugs
- Damaged governor, servo, anchor pin, or speedometer bores
- Damaged snapring grooves

Transaxle Final Drive

Transaxle final drive assemblies can be either chain- or gear-driven by the output shaft. For all designs, the drive components must be disassembled, cleaned, and inspected.

Drive Chain Service

The drive chains used in some transaxles should be inspected for side play and stretch. These checks are made during disassembly and should be repeated as a double-check during reassembly. Chain deflection is measured between the centers of the two sprockets. Typically, very little deflection is allowed. Deflect the chain inward on one side until it is tight, figure 3-19. Mark the housing at the point of maximum deflection. Then deflect the chain outward on the same side until it is tight, figure 3-20. Again mark the housing in line with the outside edge of the chain at the point of maximum deflection. Measure the distance between the two marks. If this distance exceeds specifications, replace the drive chain.

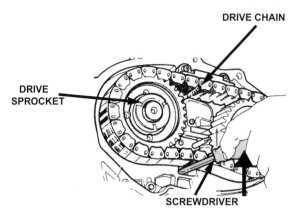

Fig. 3-19. Pry chain inward and mark the position.

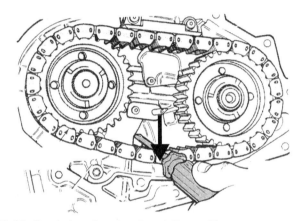

Fig. 3-20. Pry chain outward and mark the position.

Be sure to check for an identification mark on the chain during disassembly. This can be a painted or dark-colored link, and may indicate either the top or the bottom of the chain, so be sure you remember which side was up. The sprockets should be inspected for tooth wear and for wear at the point where they ride. If the chain was found to be too slack, it may have worn the sprockets in the same manner that engine timing gears wear when the timing chain stretches. A slightly polished appearance on the face of the gears is normal.

The removal and installation of the chain drive assembly of some transaxles requires that the sprockets be spread slightly apart. The key to doing this is to spread the sprockets just the right amount. If they are spread too far, they will not be easy to install or remove.

Drive Gear Service
Gear drive systems should be inspected in the same manner as engine timing gears or manual transmission gears. Inspect each gear for:

- Excessive wear
- Damaged or chipped teeth
- Signs of overheating or lack of lubrication

If either of the drive gears fails the inspection replace them as a set, figure 3-21. Check gear backlash during the reassembly process to ensure long and quiet gear set life.

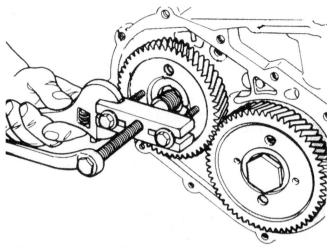

Fig. 3-21. Special puller for removing drive gear from output shaft.

Bearings and Bushing Service
The bearings and bushings used on the sprockets need to be checked for damage. The radial needle thrust bearings must be checked for any deterioration of the needles and cage. The bushings should be checked for any signs of scoring, flaking, or wear. Replace any defective parts.

FINAL ASSEMBLY AND INSTALLATION
Adjusting endplay is part of the final assembly procedure. Use the measurements taken at teardown to determine how much adjustment is needed. Then, choose a selective thrust washer that will bring endplay toward the lower end of the tolerance range specified by the manufacturer.

Follow the procedure in the Service Manual to assemble the transmission. Make sure all clearances and adjustments are within tolerance and tighten all fasteners to specification.

Before installing the valve body, perform an air-pressure test to check the application devices. Apply about 25 psi of air pressure to the appropriate fluid passage and hold the air on for several seconds. Listen for a dull thud or clunk as the clutches and servo apply. Clutch application is not always loud enough to hear. Rest your fingers on the drum and you should be able to feel movement as air pressure is applied. Check bands by watching. You will see them tighten and loosen around the drums as air is applied and released. Governor valve movement will produce a sharp whistling, clicking, or buzzing noise.

Before installing the transmission or transaxle inspect the following for wear and/or damage.

- Converter drive (flex) plate
- Converter attaching bolts
- Converter pilot machining
- Converter pump surfaces
- Crankshaft pilot bore

Replace any components that fail the inspection.

To install the transmission, secure it to the transmission jack and adjust the jack angle to match that of the engine. Fit the torque converter onto the transmission. Make sure it is

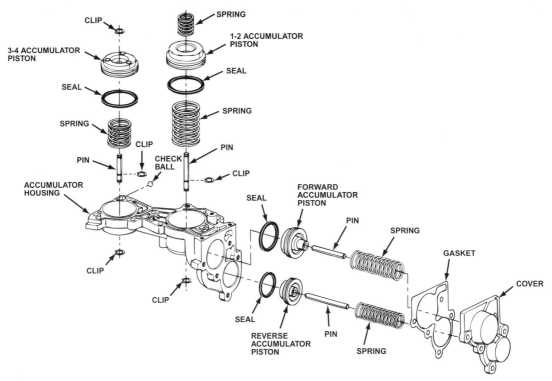

Fig. 3-22. The accumulator assembly, which houses all of the accumulators on this transmission, bolts up to the case as a unit.

fully seated. Rotate the converter or engine so the index marks align. Raise the jack to line up the transmission and engine, then push in to engage the alignment dowels. Install the bell-housing bolts and transmission mounts. Disconnect and remove the jack, then complete the installation.

Align reference marks made during removal of the transmission or transaxle mounts and crossmembers to ensure proper drive train alignment.

Accumulator and Servo Service

Accumulators and servos are simple hydraulic devices that consist of a piston, bore, and return spring. The assembly is held in place by a cover. Integral accumulators incorporate a servo and accumulator into a common bore. Some transmissions have an accumulator assembly that bolts onto the case as a unit, figure 3-22. Remove the piston from the bore and look for the following defects:

- Cracks or scoring in the servo bore
- Nicks, scores, burrs, or signs of wear on the piston and piston rod
- Worn or damaged seals
- Return spring damage, cracking, or distortion
- Faulty spring action
- Fluid passage obstructions or restrictions
- Cover gasket sealing surface distortion or damage
- Burrs or damage to the body-to-case mating surfaces

Also, make sure the piston can move freely in the bore and that check valves function properly. On adjustable units, inspect the adjusting screw, locknut, and actuating lever for thread distortion or other damage.

Band Inspection

Inspect a band and its friction surface, paying close attention to the ends, figure 3-23. Bands wear more at the ends because they apply there first.

Not all transmissions or transaxles utilize bands, but if they are used check them for:

- Distortion
- Cracking
- Excessive or uneven wear
- Burn marks, charring, or **glazing**
- Poor lining bond
- Flaking and pitting
- Chips or particles embedded in the lining

If the band uses apply struts, check them for distortion, figure 3-24. Replace any band that shows signs of any of the above defects.

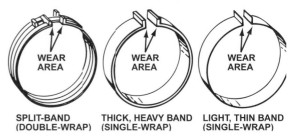

Fig. 3-23. Regardless of design, transmission band wear is usually concentrated near the ends, because this is the area that first contacts the rotating drum.

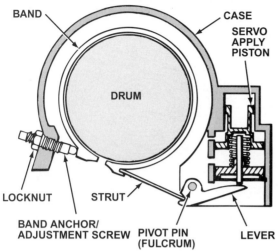

Fig. 3-24. Apply struts, anchor screws, levers, and any other hardware are inspected for wear and damage, along with the band.

Fig. 3-25. Remove the clutch discs from the drum and inspect them individually.

Clutch Pack Service

Disassemble a clutch pack by removing the snapring that holds the discs in the housing. Then, remove the clutch discs and inspect them as described in the following sections, figure 3-25.

Friction Discs

Wipe each friction disc with a dry, lint-free cloth. Inspect for:

- Excessive wear
- Cracks in the lining material
- Charred, burned, or glazed lining surface
- Pitting, flaking, or scoring
- Chips or particles embedded in the lining
- Scoring or burns on disc serrations
- Distortion

If any friction disc shows signs of one or more of the defects above, replace the entire set. Replace the set of friction discs if they do not fit freely in the clutch hub serrations or if there is wear or damage to their splines.

Steel Discs

You also clean steel discs by wiping with a dry, lint-free cloth. Once clean, inspect each disc for:

- Uneven heat discoloration
- Surface scuffing or scoring
- Drive lug damage
- Distortion

You may reuse steel discs that have a uniform pattern of discoloration, as long as the contact surface is smooth. Replace the entire set if you note a rough surface or uneven or spotty discoloration on any of the discs. You should also replace steel discs if they do not fit freely into the clutch drum serrations.

Clutch Piston

To remove the snapring holding the clutch piston in place, you must compress the piston return springs, which is done with a compressor tool. The style of clutch drum will determine which type of compressor tool to use. After removing the snapring, release and remove the spring compressor, then remove and inspect the return springs.

Return Spring Inspection

Clutches use one of two types of piston return springs: a coil or Belleville. Coil springs should be straight and provide proper pressure. Check for broken, distorted, or collapsed springs. If one or more of the springs requires replacement, discard them all and install a complete set of new springs. **Belleville spring** fingers should be free of cracks and other signs of stress, figure 3-26.

Extreme heat or burning in the clutch can cause return springs to take a heat set. Unless this heat set is extreme, the condition is hard to see. When the clutch discs show signs of excessive heat, you should replace the springs as a preventive measure.

Piston Inspection

Remove the clutch piston from the hub. Apply low-pressure, compressed air through the hydraulic apply hole in the housing to force a stuck piston from its bore.

Check the piston for:

- Cracks or scoring in the piston bore
- Nicks, scores, burrs, or signs of wear on the piston
- Seal damage
- Fluid passage obstructions or restrictions

A2

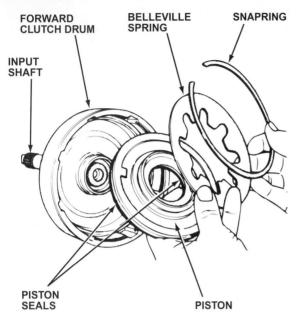

Fig. 3-26. Look for cracks, distortion, wear, and other signs of stress on the fingers of a Belleville spring.

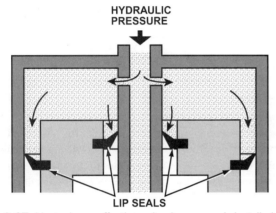

Fig. 3-27. Lip seals are effective only when properly installed. Apply pressure forces the lip of the seal tightly against the cylinder wall.

Clutch Pack Assembly

Begin clutch assembly by installing the piston seals. The lip of a lip-type seal must face in the direction of apply pressure, figure 3-27. Lubricate the seals and carefully fit the piston into its bore. Next, fit the return springs, compress the springs, and install the snapring to hold the assembly together. Check piston operation with air pressure.

Complete the clutch assembly by alternately stacking friction and steel discs on top of the piston, installing the pressure plate, and fitting the snapring. Remember, friction discs must soak in fresh ATF for at least 30 minutes before assembly. After assembling the clutch, measure and adjust clearance as needed.

Clutch Pack Clearance Adjustment

Clutch pack clearance determines whether or not the clutch engages properly and affects shift quality. Depending on the clutch pack design, one of four parts may control clearance:

• Snapring
• Pressure plate or retaining plate
• Steel disc or Washer

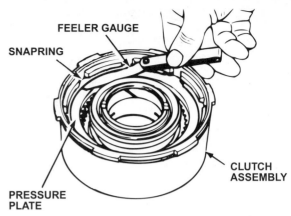

Fig. 3-28. Clutch pack clearance equals the thickest feeler gauge blade that will fit between the pressure plate and the snapring.

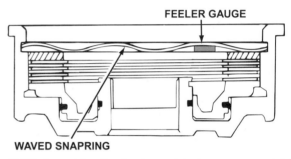

Fig. 3-29. Correct location for measuring clearance on a clutch pack that uses a waved snapring.

Snapring

When a selective snapring is used, check specifications to determine the correct clutch pack clearance. To measure clearance:

1. Depress the pressure plate as far as possible and hold it.
2. Measure the clearance between the pressure plate and snapring with a feeler gauge, figure 3-28.
3. With a waved snapring, measure at a point where the snapring is waved away from the pressure plate, figure 3-29.
4. If clearance is outside specifications, determine how much by inserting the largest feeler gauge blade that will fit. Then, replace the snapring with a new one of the proper thickness.
5. Remeasure the clearance.

Pressure or retaining plate

A selective pressure or retaining plate controls clearance on some clutch packs. When used, there will be both a minimum and maximum clearance listed in the specifications. To measure:

1. Press down on the plate and hold it in position.
2. Insert the minimum-clearance feeler gauge between the plate and snapring. If the blade slips in, you have minimum clearance.
3. Next, try to insert the maximum-clearance feeler gauge. If the blade does not slip in, clearance is within maximum specifications.

If the clearance is not within specifications, replace the pressure or retaining plate with one of the correct thickness, then recheck the clearance.

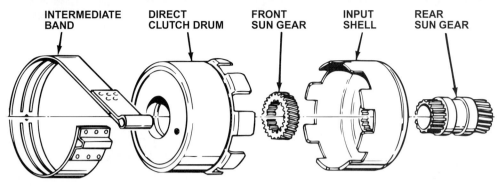

Fig. 3-30. Inspect the load-bearing areas of hard parts, such as drums and shells, for indications of wear and damage.

Steel disc

In some clutches, a selective steel disc controls clearance. Measure clearance using the same procedure as for a selective pressure plate. Always recheck the clearance after making adjustments.

Washer

Some Hydra-Matic transmissions use a selective washer to set clutch pack clearance. A special, selective washer gauge is needed to measure clearance. The gauge installs over the clutch housing with the gauge pin facing toward the housing. Tightening the nut compresses the spring and bottoms the washer on the gauge shoulder. Then, use a feeler gauge to measure the clearance between the gauge pin and the top edge of the housing.

Hub, Drum, and Shell Service

Clutch hubs, drums, and shells have load-bearing areas that must be closely scrutinized, figure 3-30. Wash with solvent, dry with compressed air, then inspect.

Look for any discoloration on the metal surfaces. Overheating tends to turn metal blue, which can be a sign of pending failure. Heat-damaged metal can lose its temper, become soft, and distort, crack, or break if put back in service. Also, look for the following defects:

- Burred, scored, or damaged thrust surfaces
- Obstructions or restrictions in fluid passages
- Worn splines
- Rough or badly worn lug grooves in clutch drums
- Worn or damaged input shell drive lugs
- Nicked or scored band application surfaces on clutch drums
- Nicked or deeply scratched seal ring surfaces inside the clutch drum
- Scored piston bore
- Clutch housing check ball stuck open or closed
- Excessive bushing clearance
- Smooth, flat band application surfaces
- Scored or damaged bushing surfaces

You can remove minor scoring or burrs from band application surfaces by lightly polishing with 320-grit wet or dry sandpaper. Heavy scores or deep scratches cannot be corrected. Replace any parts with such defects. Bushings, which are press fitted, are the only other serviceable item on the above checklist.

Governor Inspection

Whether mounted on a shaft or fitted into a case bore driven by a gear, a governor assembly consists of a shaft, a spool valve or check balls, two weights, two springs, and various snaprings and attaching parts. A governor has several places where sludge and debris may accumulate. This build-up can restrict governor movement and cause erratic shift problems. Disassemble and thoroughly clean the governor, figure 3-31. Inspect for:

- Scoring or rust in the valve bore
- Scores, nicks, or rust on the spool valve
- Damaged or distorted mating surfaces
- Binding, sticking, or damaged weights
- Broken or distorted springs
- Cut, distorted, or loose seals
- Broken snaprings and damaged snapring grooves
- Plugged or restricted fluid passages in the case or output shaft
- Damaged or plugged governor screen
- Damaged gears

Individual governor pieces are generally not available, so you replace the entire governor assembly if there is any damage.

Fig. 3-31. Disassemble the governor, then clean and inspect the individual parts.

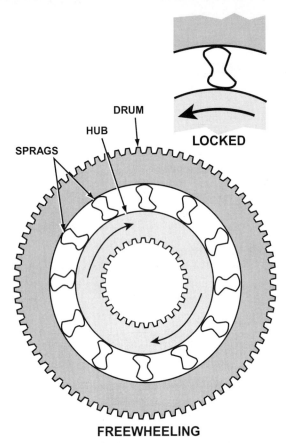

FREEWHEELING

Fig. 3-32. When a one-way sprag clutch hub turns clockwise, the sprags wedge between the drum and hub to lock the unit.

One-Way Clutch Inspection

Most one-way clutches, whether it is a **sprag clutch**, figure 3-32, or a **roller clutch**, figure 3-33, are held together by a snapring. Remove the snapring, then carefully separate the inner race from the outer race and disassemble the unit. Wash all the pieces in solvent, dry with compressed air, and inspect for:

- Wear or damage on rollers or springs
- Bent or damaged spring retainers in sprag clutch assemblies
- Flat spots or chipped edges on clutch rollers

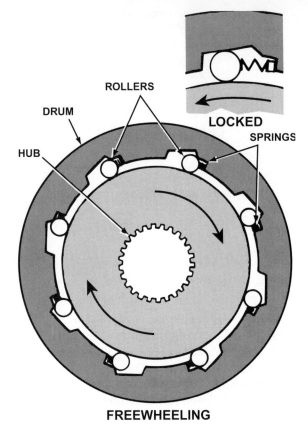

FREEWHEELING

Fig. 3-33. The spring-loaded rollers move toward the narrow end of the cam slots and lock the drum to the hub when a one-way roller clutch hub turns counterclockwise.

- **Brinelling** on roller contact surfaces of clutch races
- Worn, scored, or damaged surfaces on inner and outer clutch races
- Distorted snaprings
- Plugged or restricted lubrication holes in inner clutch races

Replace the complete one-way clutch as an assembly if defects are found. Be sure the sprags or rollers face the right direction when you assemble the unit.

CHAPTER QUESTIONS

1. The first step in removing a transmission is always to:
   a. Disconnect the starter motor
   b. Disconnect the negative battery cable
   c. Drain the torque converter
   d. Lift the vehicle on a hoist

2. Before a geartrain is torn down, a dial indicator should be used to check:
   a. Total endplay
   b. Converter runout
   c. Wear on pump thrust face
   d. Lash between gears in unit

3. Which is true of a transmission oil pump?
   a. Rotary pumps have an internal pressure regulator
   b. Crescent pump tip clearance is measured with a dial indicator
   c. A straightedge is used to check pump end clearance
   d. Pumps should not be disassembled for inspection

4. Rotating the torque converter counterclockwise while holding the pump is a test of the:
   a. Stator-to-turbine interference
   b. Turbine-to-impeller interference
   c. Impeller-to-flexplate interference
   d. Stator-to-impeller interference

5. The converter hub was badly scored. What should the technician replace besides the torque converter and front pump seal?
   a. Transmission input shaft
   b. Torque converter flex plate
   c. Stator support bushing
   d. Pump body bushing

6. The side clearance of a planetary pinion gear measured 0.035 inch. The proper repair would be to:
   a. Install a 0.015 inch thicker thrust washer
   b. Replace the pinion gears
   c. Replace the planetary gearset
   d. Replace the planet carrier

7. Which of the following parts is **NOT** available in selective sizes for adjusting clutch pack clearance?
   a. Snapring
   b. Pressure plate
   c. Washer
   d. Piston

8. Which of the following measurements does **NOT** apply to a gear-type oil pump?
   a. Tip clearance
   b. Side clearance
   c. End clearance
   d. None of the above

9. The servo spring is weaker than the specification. Technician A says this will cause the servo to apply slower. Technician B says this will cause the servo to apply softer. Who is right?
   a. A only
   b. B only
   c. Both A and B
   d. Neither A nor B

10. The automatic transaxle case was broken in an accident. Technician A says because a new case is used there is no need to check endplay. Technician B says good components from the old case may be used on the new case. Who is right?
    a. A only
    b. B only
    c. Both A and B
    d. Neither A nor B

11. Clutch pack clearance can be controlled by:
    a. Snapring
    b. Pressure plate or retaining plate
    c. Steel disc or washer
    d. All of the above

12. When inspecting a clutch band, it will show the greatest amount of wear at the:
    a. Ends
    b. Top
    c. Bottom
    d. Sides

13. As a general rule, the coefficient of friction for a lockup torque converter clutch friction material should be:
    a. 150 inch lbs.
    b. 75 ft. lbs.
    c. 150 ft. lbs.
    d. 15 ft. lbs.

A2

SAMPLE TEST

Test Taking Advice

As soon as you make the decision to schedule an A2 test, begin preparing by including dedicated study time in your weekly schedule. You can improve your test score with just a few hours of study and review per week. Photocopy the practice test included in this study guide so you can use it several times.

The practice test will help you become more comfortable with test taking in general. It will also point out your weak spots and enable you to use your study time more efficiently. When you miss a question, look up the answer and study the subject in the study guide. Take notes on the subject to use for review. After repeated test taking and review, you should have your notes reduced to a single sheet of paper that can be reviewed daily the week before the test, and again on the day of the test.

Arrive at the test site early so parking or unforeseen problems do not cause you stress. Plan to allow time for a last look at your notes before entering the test site. Pay attention to all instructions from the test proctor even if you are a veteran test taker. From time to time ASE adjusts its instructions.

To answer test questions correctly, you must have a clear understanding of what is being asked. Read the question twice to be sure what it is asking. While thinking about the question, recall what you know about the subject. Do this before reading the answers. You are less likely to be influenced into a wrong conclusion by the answers if you recall what you know about the subject first. Since you have recalled your knowledge of the subject, you will be less likely to doubt yourself while reading the answers.

Note all operating conditions stated in the question when considering the answers. However, never assume that conditions exist that are not stated in the question. Treat each answer as a true or false question. Be sure to read all the answers before making your choice. When you conclude that more than one may be correct, reread the question to make sure you haven't missed an important fact, then rely on your knowledge to choose the one that is most correct. There is always one most correct answer. When it seems impossible to decide which answer is correct, it may help to think which item would be more likely to wear out or which things require regular service. These types of items may be the best choice, especially when the question asks, "which is more likely."

Never leave a question unanswered. Unanswered questions are scored as wrong! Guess if you can't make a decision. Guessing gives you a 25% chance of being correct. If you narrow the field to two possibilities, you have a 50% chance. Choose an answer before moving on to the next question in case you run out of time. Make a mark next to the question in the test booklet. Sometimes, other questions contain information that will help answer a question you're not sure of, and you can return to the questions you have marked if you have time. Be cautious when returning to reread a question. If you are still not sure which answer is correct, it's better to leave your original guess than to make a second guess. However, if you are certain that you originally misunderstood the question it's best to change your answer.

---

1. Technician A says that incorrect shift linkage adjustment can cause low mainline pressure and premature clutch and band wear.
   Technician B says that incorrect shift linkage adjustment can cause shifting problems if throttle pressure is mechanically controlled.
   Who is right?
   a. A only
   b. B only
   c. Both A and B
   d. Neither A nor B

2. A clutch and band application chart is needed to interpret results from all of the following tests **EXCEPT**:
   a. Pressure test
   b. Vacuum modulator test
   c. Stall test
   d. Road test

3. Control pressure is another name for:
   a. Governor pressure
   b. Modulator pressure
   c. Throttle pressure
   d. Mainline pressure

4. Technician A says governor pressure is developed from mainline pressure and decreases as road speed increases.
   Technician B says governor pressure works in conjunction with throttle pressure to control shift points.
   Who is right?
   a. A only
   b. B only
   c. Both A and B
   d. Neither A nor B

5. Technician A says that a failed torque converter one-way clutch will cause low-rpm stall test results.
   Technician B says that a failed torque converter one-way clutch can cause poor low-speed acceleration.
   Who is right?
   a. A only
   b. B only
   c. Both A and B
   d. Neither A nor B

6. Technician A says you need to torque the bolts in sequence when installing the oil pan after a fluid maintenance service.

Technician B says an oil pan should be washed in solvent and wiped down with a clean shop towel before reinstalling it.
   Who is right?
   a. A only
   b. B only
   c. Both A and B
   d. Neither A nor B

7. Technician A says that it is normal to find small flakes of aluminum, brass, and bronze in the oil pan when you remove it for service.
   Technician B says that it is normal to find dust-like particles of friction material in the oil pan, but larger pieces indicate a clutch or band problem.
   Who is right?
   a. A only
   b. B only
   c. Both A and B
   d. Neither A nor B

8. Technician A says, when performing a transmission fluid maintenance and the torque converter has a drain

plug, only drain the converter if the fluid was burnt or contaminated. Technician B says that an additional 3 to 5 quarts of ATF may be required if the torque converter is drained. Who is right?
a. A only
b. B only
c. Both A and B
d. Neither A nor B

9. Clutch pack clearance can be adjusted by all of the following **EXCEPT**:
a. Selective snap ring
b. Selective pressure plate or retaining plate
c. Selective friction disc
d. Selective washer

10. Technician A says that you can fix glazed areas on a band by sanding them down with 600-grit sandpaper. Technician B says that a band with glazed areas must be replaced with a new one. Who is right?
a. A only
b. B only
c. Both A and B
d. Neither A nor B

11. The manual valve is connected to the:
a. Accelerator linkage
b. Throttle valve linkage
c. Downshift linkage
d. Gearshift linkage

12. Hunting between gears during a road test might be caused by:
a. Incorrect throttle valve linkage adjustment
b. Defective torque converter clutch
c. Incorrect band adjustment
d. Incorrect shift solenoid adjustment

13. Technician A says a defective vacuum modulator can cause harsh downshifts and harsh or delayed upshifts. Technician B says a defective vacuum modulator can cause soft upshifts and downshifts, as well as overheating and burnt fluid. Who is right?
a. A only
b. B only
c. Both A and B
d. Neither A nor B

14. Inspection of a disassembled valve body reveals shiny areas on the valve lands of a spool valve. Technician A says that this is caused by excess friction, and the valve body should be replaced. Technician B says that the valve can be repaired by polishing with crocus cloth to carefully round the edges of the valve lands. Who is right?
a. A only
b. B only
c. Both A and B
d. Neither A nor B

15. A solenoid that continuously switches on and off a fixed number of times per second is a:
a. Variable force solenoid
b. Pulse-width modulation solenoid
c. On/off solenoid
d. Variable cycling solenoid

16. Technician A says that on a pulse-width modulated solenoid, the total cycle time includes the time the solenoid is switched off as well as the time it is turned on. Technician B says that duty cycle is a comparison of solenoid on time to total cycle time expressed as a percentage. Who is right?
a. A only
b. B only
c. Both A and B
d. Neither A nor B

17. Clutch pack clearance specifications are 0.050 to 0.055 inch. A selective snap ring is used to adjust clearance. The assembled clutch pack measures 0.068 inch, and the installed ring measures 0.045 inch. To correct, the new snap ring should measure:
a. 0.050 inch
b. 0.055 inch
c. 0.060 inch
d. 0.065 inch

18. An air pressure test can check all the following **EXCEPT**:
a. Stator clutch application
b. Servo application
c. Governor valve movement
d. Clutch pack application

19. Technician A says that input shaft endplay should be measured twice:

before teardown and again after assembly. Technician B says selective thrust washers are often used to control transfer shaft endplay on a front-drive transaxle. Who is right?
a. A only
b. B only
c. Both A and B
d. Neither A nor B

20. The pinions of a planetary gearset have a side clearance of 0.032 inch. Technician A says clearance can be corrected by replacing the selective thrust washer. Technician B says the entire planetary gearset should be replaced. Who is right?
a. A only
b. B only
c. Both A and B
d. Neither A nor B

21. A vehicle with an automatic transmission will not start with the shift lever in the PARK or NEUTRAL position. Technician A says a faulty Park/Neutral Position Switch can be the cause. Technician B says a faulty Transmission Range Sensor (TRS) can be the cause. Who is right?
a. A only
b. B only
c. Both A and B
d. Neither A nor B

22. Driveshaft slip yokes are generally lubricated:
a. With grease fittings
b. By the transmission fluid
c. Every 6,000 miles
d. By hand

23. When installing a replacement U-joint that has a grease fitting, the fitting installs facing the:
a. Transmission
b. Differential
c. Front of vehicle
d. Driveshaft

A2

24. Excessive automatic transmission shaft endplay can be caused by any of the following **EXCEPT**:
    a. Thrust washer
    b. Bearing race
    c. Clutch
    d. Transmission case

25. Which of the following is **NOT** a function of the automatic transmission fluid?
    a. Engage clutches or bands
    b. Act as a heat exchanger
    c. Limit torque converter slippage
    d. Lubricate moving parts

26. Some transmissions use manifold vacuum and a vacuum modulator to position the:
    a. Throttle valve
    b. Manual valve
    c. Downshift valve
    d. Governor valve

27. Most late-model domestic transmissions use this type of filter:
    a. Nylon screen
    b. Metal mesh screen
    c. Paper or synthetic filter
    d. Spin-on

28. A vehicle with an automatic transmission shifts early or late. Technician A says this is due to improperly adjusted bands. Technician B says this is due to improperly adjusted linkages. Who is right?
    a. A only
    b. B only
    c. Both A and B
    d. Neither A nor B

29. The most common type of front and rear transmission seals are:
    a. Seal rings
    b. Lip seal
    c. O-rings
    d. Square-cut seals

30. When overhauling a valve body:
    a. Scored valves can be repaired by polishing
    b. The housing must be pried apart
    c. Valve springs can be interchanged
    d. Separator plates and gaskets can be reused

31. Which of the following is **NOT** a type of accumulator?
    a. Integral piston type
    b. Valve type
    c. Check ball type
    d. Independent piston type

32. The lines connecting the transmission to the cooler:
    a. Should be repaired by soldering
    b. Often have double-flare fittings
    c. Can be replaced with aluminum tubing
    d. Are flexible to prevent vibration damage

33. The automatic transmission fluid can be drained by removing any of the following **EXCEPT**:
    a. Filler tube
    b. Oil pan
    c. Drain plug
    d. Filter housing

34. All of the following are types of automatic transmission accumulators **EXCEPT**:
    a. Independent piston type
    b. Integral piston type
    c. Valve type
    d. Spool type

35. Technician A says a solenoid duty cycle of 75 percent means the solenoid is on 25 percent of the cycle. Technician B says a solenoid duty cycle of 75 percent means the solenoid is off 75 percent of the cycle. Who is right?
    a. A only
    b. B only
    c. Both A and B
    d. Neither A nor B

36. Technician A says a stall test is performed to check the torque converter stator one-way clutch operation. Technician B says a stall test is performed to check the holding ability of clutches and bands. Who is right?
    a. A only
    b. B only
    c. Both A and B
    d. Neither A nor B

37. Technician A says when checking governor hydraulic pressure, the pressure increases with vehicle road speed. Technician B says when checking governor hydraulic pressure, the pressure decreases with vehicle road speed. Who is right?
    a. A only
    b. B only
    c. Both A and B
    d. Neither A nor B

38. Which of the following sensors is used to measure changes in pressure?
    a. Potentiometer
    b. Piezoresistive sensor
    c. Optical sensor
    d. Thermistor

39. When performing a voltage drop test at the battery ground terminal, readings over which of the following voltages would indicate high circuit resistance that could cause electronic control problems?
    a. 0.002 volt
    b. 0.02 volt
    c. 0.2 volt
    d. 2.0 volts

40. Which of the following is not used to provide speed inputs to the TCM or PCM?
    a. Hall-effect switch
    b. Optical sensor
    c. Pickup coil
    d. Thermistor

41. Technician A says a two position solenoid can only be in one of two states, opened or closed. Technician B says a two position solenoid can only be closed when at rest. Who is right?
    a. A only
    b. B only
    c. Both A and B
    d. Neither A nor B

42. Which of the following devices is a variable resistor that senses movement or position?
    a. Potentiometer
    b. Piezoresistive sensor
    c. Hall-effect switch
    d. Thermistor

43. Which of the following is the measurement of a pulsing signal at a specific number of cycles per second?
   a. Volts
   b. Ohms
   c. Amps
   d. Hertz

44. An air pressure test is used to:
   a. See how well clutches and bands hold
   b. Check a vacuum modulator
   c. Check for pressure cutback
   d. Pinpoint hydraulic leaks

45. Which of the following devices is used to measure speed?
   a. Potentiometer
   b. Piezoresistive sensor
   c. Hall-effect switch
   d. Thermistor

46. Technician A says burned or overheated automatic transmission fluid will give off a pungent, foul smell.
   Technician B says burnt or overheated automatic transmission fluid is chemically broken down and must be drained and replaced to avoid band and clutch failures.
   Who is right?
   a. A only
   b. B only
   c. Both A and B
   d. Neither A nor B

47. Which of the following sensors is used to measure changes in temperature?
   a. Potentiometer
   b. Piezoresistive sensor
   c. Optical sensor
   d. Thermistor

48. Technician A says mainline hydraulic pressure is also known as control pressure.
   Technician B says mainline hydraulic pressure is also known as modulator pressure.
   Who is right?
   a. A only
   b. B only
   c. Both A and B
   d. Neither A nor B

49. Technician A says torque converter drain back causes delayed initial engagement on start up when the transmission is placed in gear.
   Technician B says torque converter drain back may be caused by a faulty oil pump check valve or bushing.
   Who is right?
   a. A only
   b. B only
   c. Both A and B
   d. Neither A nor B

50. Technician A says the pulse width of a Pulse Width Modulated (PWM) solenoid is the amount of time the solenoid is de-energized during a cycle.
   Technician B says the pulse width of a Pulse Width Modulated (PWM) solenoid is the amount of time the solenoid is energized during a cycle.
   Who is right?
   a. A only
   b. B only
   c. Both A and B
   d. Neither A nor B

51. Technician A says a solenoid duty cycle of 60 percent means the solenoid is on 60 percent of the cycle.
   Technician B says a solenoid duty cycle of 60 percent means the solenoid is off 40 percent of the cycle.
   Who is right?
   a. A only
   b. B only
   c. Both A and B
   d. Neither A nor B

A2

ANSWERS

Chapter 1:
1. c, 2. c, 3. c, 4. b, 5. d, 6. b, 7. c, 8. a, 9. c, 10. a, 11. b, 12. c, 13. b, 14. d, 15. b, 16. a, 17. d, 18. a, 19. b, 20. a, 21. b, 22. d

Chapter 2:
1. c, 2. a, 3. a, 4. d, 5. b, 6. c, 7. a, 8. d, 9. a, 10. c, 11. b, 12. d

Chapter 3:
1. b, 2. a, 3. c, 4. d, 5. d, 6. c, 7 d, 8. a, 9. d, 10. b, 11. d, 12. a, 13. c

Sample Test:
1. c, 2. b, 3. d, 4. d, 5. c, 6. a, 7. c, 8. b, 9. c, 10. b, 11. d, 12. a, 13. c, 14. d, 15. b, 16. c, 17. c, 18. a, 19. c, 20. b, 21. c, 22. b, 23. d, 24. c, 25. c, 26. a, 27. c, 28. b, 29. b, 30. a, 31. c, 32. b, 33. a, 34. d, 35. d, 36. c, 37. a, 38. b, 39. c, 40. d, 41. b, 42. a, 43. d, 44. d, 45. c, 46. c, 47. d, 48. a, 49. c, 50. b, 51. c

GLOSSARY

Accumulator: A device that absorbs the shock of sudden pressure surges within a hydraulic system. Accumulators are used in transmission hydraulic systems to control shift quality.

Actuator: A device that translates the computer output voltage signal into mechanical energy.

Alternating Current (AC): A flow of electricity through a conductor, first in one direction and then in the opposite direction.

Amperage: The amount of current flow through a conductor.

Amplitude: The height or strength of a voltage signal measured from the lowest point to the highest point.

Analog: A voltage signal or processing action that is continuously variable relative to the operation being measured or controlled.

Apply Device: A hydraulically operated band, multi-disc clutch, or mechanically operated one-way clutch that drives or holds the members of a planetary gearset.

Axial Movement: Movement along, or parallel to, the centerline (axis) of a shaft. A dynamic seal is required to contain fluids where axial motion is present.

Backlash: The amount of clearance or play between two mechanical parts.

Band: A strip of flexible steel lined with friction material that is clamped around a circular drum to hold it from turning.

Belleville Spring: A diaphragm-type spring with fingers pointing inward toward a central shaft in a multi-plate transmission clutch.

Brinelling: A condition in which the hard faces of the bearing surfaces pit and wear away. Brinelling results from impact loading and vibration.

Centrifugal Force: The natural tendency of a rotating object to move away from the center and toward the outer edge of the circle in rotation.

Clutch Pack: The assembly of clutch plates and pressure plates that provides the friction surfaces in a multiple-disc clutch.

Coefficient of Friction: A numerical value expressing the amount of friction between two surfaces. The coefficient of friction is obtained by dividing the force required to slide the surfaces across each other by the pressure holding the surfaces together.

Data Parameter: A measured value of control system input or output operation. Parameters include voltage signals, as well as temperature, pressure, speed, and other data.

Data Stream: The electronic data transmitted by the computer to a scan tool.

Diagnostic Trouble Code (DTC): A numeric or alphanumeric sequence relating directly to an abnormal signal from a sensor in the onboard electronic system.

Diaphragm: A flexible membrane used to form a wall and separate two cavities from each other.

Digital: A voltage signal or processing function that has only two levels: on/off or high/low. Also called a discrete signal.

Digital Multimeter (DMM): A hand-held meter capable of measuring voltage, resistance, and current flow then displaying it in digital format on an LCD screen.

Detent: A small depression in a component, typically a shaft or rod, into which a spring-loaded ball or insert drops when the component is moved. This provides a locking effect.

Downshift Valve: An auxiliary shift valve that increases throttle pressure to force a downshift under high driveline loads. Also called a kickdown valve or detent valve.

Duty Cycle: The percentage of the total time that a solenoid is energized during pulse-width modulation as determined by a timed voltage pulse from the computer.

Endplay: The total amount of axial play in an automatic transmission. Endplay is typically measured at the input shaft.

Frequency: The number of periodic voltage oscillations, or waves, occurring in a given unit of time, usually expressed as cycles per second or Hertz.

Glazing: A smooth, shiny, hard appearance on a friction surface that has been subjected to excessive slippage and overheating.

Governor: The valve that converts mainline pressure into governor pressure in relation to vehicle road speed. Governor pressure is one of the principal pressures used to control shift points.

Governor Pressure: The transmission hydraulic pressure that is directly related to vehicle speed. Governor pressure increases with vehicle speed and is one of the principal pressures used to control shift points.

Hertz: A unit of frequency equal to one cycle per second.

Impeller: The finned rotor in a torque converter that is turned by the engine to pump transmission fluid, and thus transmit torque, into the turbine that drives the transmission input shaft.

Limp Home Mode: An operating mode for the transmission that restricts transmission operation to protect internal components while maintaining at least one forward gear range allowing the vehicle to be driven to a service location.

Mainline Pressure: The pressure developed from the fluid output of the pump and controlled by the pressure regulator valve. Mainline pressure operates the apply devices in the transmission and is the source of all other pressures in the hydraulic system.

Manifold Vacuum: The low pressure area, or vacuum, located below throttle plates in the intake manifold of an engine.

Manual Low: Transmission range selected by placing the shift selector in the "L" position. During normal operation the transmission will start in low gear and not upshift.

Manual Second: Transmission range selected by placing the shift selector in the "2" position. During normal operation the transmission will start in low gear and shift to second when speed increases.

Manual Third: Transmission range selected by placing the shift selector in the "3" position. During normal operation the transmission will start in low, shift to second, and then shift to third as speed increases.

Manual Valve: The valve that is moved manually, through the shift linkage, to select the transmission drive range. The manual valve directs and blocks fluid flow to various hydraulic circuits.

One-Way Clutch: A mechanical holding device that prevents rotation in one direction, but overruns to allow it in the other. One-way clutches are either roller or sprag clutches.

Orifices: Small openings or restrictions in a hydraulic circuit that cause a decrease in pressure on the downstream side of the fluid flow.

Pawl: A hinged or pivoted part that fits into a toothed wheel or notched gate to prevent rotation or movement.

Planetary Gearset: A system of gears consisting of a sun gear, internal ring gear, and planet carrier with planet pinion gears.

Planet Pinion Carrier: The bracket in a planetary gear system on which the planet pinion gears are mounted on pins and free to turn.

Planet Pinion Gear: A gear in a planetary gear system that mounts on the carrier and meshes with the ring gear and the sun gear.

Potentiometer: A variable resistor with three terminals. Return signal voltage is taken from a terminal attached to a movable contact that passes over the resistor.

Pulse-Width Modulation: The continuous on/off cycling of a solenoid a fixed number of times per second.

Reference Voltage: A constant voltage signal (below battery voltage) applied to a sensor by the computer. The sensor alters the voltage according to engine operating conditions and returns it as a variable input signal to the computer, which adjusts system operation accordingly.

Resistance: Opposition to electrical current flow.

Ring Gear: The outermost member of the gearset, having teeth in the inside circumference.

Roller Clutch: A one-way, overrunning clutch that uses a series of spring-loaded rollers placed in ramps between two races. A roller clutch locks when turned in one direction, but freewheels when turned in the opposite direction.

Scan Tool: A test instrument that is used to access powertrain control system trouble codes, freeze frame data, and bi-directional control of system actuators.

Sensor: A device that provides an electric signal to a control unit to indicate a certain physical condition.

Serial Data: The stream of computer data transmitted from the vehicle to a scan tool frame by frame.

Servo: A hydraulic piston and cylinder assembly that controls the application and release of a transmission band.

Solenoid: An electromagnetic actuator consisting of a movable iron core with a wire coil surrounding it. When electrical current is applied to the coil, the core moves to convert electrical energy to mechanical energy.

Spool Valve: A sliding valve that uses lands and valleys machined on its surface to control the flow of hydraulic pressure through ports in its bore.

Sprag Clutch: A one-way, overrunning clutch that uses a series of sprags placed in between two races. A sprag clutch locks when turned in one direction, but freewheels when turned in the opposite direction.

Stator: A reaction member of a torque converter mounted on a one-way clutch. The stator multiplies torque by redirecting fluid flow from the turbine back to the impeller.

Sun Gear: The central gear around which other gears revolve in a planetary gear system.

Thermistor: An electronic component whose resistance to electric current changes rapidly and predictably as its temperature changes.

Throttle Pressure: The transmission hydraulic pressure that is directly related to engine load. Throttle pressure, which increases with throttle opening and engine torque output, is one of the principal pressures used to control shift points.

Throttle Valve: The valve that regulates throttle pressure based on throttle butterfly opening or intake manifold vacuum.

Turbine: The finned rotor in a torque converter that is driven by the flow of transmission fluid from the impeller. The turbine connects to the transmission input shaft and provides torque input to the planetary gearset.

Vacuum Modulator: A vacuum motor composed of a housing divided into two chambers by a flexible rubber diaphragm. One chamber is open to atmospheric pressure; the other is connected to intake manifold vacuum and contains a spring. Changes in manifold vacuum cause movement of the diaphragm against spring tension. This movement is used to control the throttle valve.

Valve Body: The casting that contains most of the valves in a transmission hydraulic system. The valve body also has passages for the flow of hydraulic fluid.

Valve Lands: The large, outer circumference of a valve spool that slides against the valve bore. Most spool valves have several lands that are used to block fluid passages.

Voltage Drop: The measurement of the loss of voltage caused by the resistance of a conductor or a circuit device.

A2

A3

MANUAL DRIVETRAINS AND AXLES

CHAPTER ONE

CLUTCH SERVICE

CHAPTER OBJECTIVES

- The technician will complete the ASE task list on Clutch Service.
- The technician will be able to answer 6 questions dealing with the Clutch Service section of the A3 ASE Test.

CLUTCH DIAGNOSIS AND ADJUSTMENT

The number of service operations that can be performed while the clutch assembly is in the vehicle are limited. When you suspect clutch problems, a road test is required to fully evaluate the operation of the clutch assembly. The symptoms of a clutch problem generally fall into four categories:

- Does not release
- Slips
- Grabs or chatters
- Produces excessive noise

Each of these symptoms can result from a variety of problems, figure 1-1. The source of some symptoms can be determined without removing the clutch assembly from the vehicle.

These include:

- **Pilot bearing or bushing** noise
- **Release bearing** noise
- Clutch function
- Clutch release
- Pedal **freeplay**
- Pedal travel

A comprehensive road test allows you to evaluate clutch operation and isolate operating problems.

Bearing or Bushing Noise

Start the engine and begin the road test with a check for pilot bearing or bushing noise. Listen for noise with the engine running, the transmission in gear, and the clutch pedal to the floor. The clutch is released, but the transmission is in gear, which causes the engine crankshaft to spin around the held transmission input shaft. Noise under these conditions indicates a worn pilot bushing or bearing or a worn release bearing, figure 1-2.

Clutch Does Not Release	Clutch Slips	
• Clutch disc has axial runout • Disc hub sticks on splined transmission shaft • Facings rusted onto the flywheel or pressure plate • Defective pilot bearing or bushing • Too much play in release system • Air in the hydraulic system • Clutch improperly bolted down • Diaphragm spring bent during installation • Clutch hub damaged • Clutch disc too thick (incorrect part)	• Clutch facings worn out • Engine or transmission oil leaks • Release bearing lash too tight • Clutch release linkage binding • Slave cylinder binding • Flywheel height out of specification • Wrong clutch installed • Cover or diaphragm spring bent • Clutch overheated • Scoring or nicks on flywheel **Clutch Grabs or Chatters** • Clutch facings contaminated • Wrong clutch facing material (incorrect part)	• Defective clutch linkage • Release bearing improperly positioned • Cover or diaphragm spring bent • Clutch hub damaged • Crank not aligned with transmission shaft • Pressure plate position misadjusted **Clutch Produces Excessive Noise** • Wrong torsion damper • Clutch unbalanced • Defective pilot bearing or bushing • Misaligned release bearing • Defective release bearing • Worn or broken torsion damper

Fig. 1-1. Clutch troubleshooting guide.

Freeplay: The small amount of clearance designed into a mechanical linkage. On a clutch, the portion of clutch pedal travel required before the clutch begins to release.

Pilot Bearing or Bushing: A small roller bearing or solid bronze bushing that is pressed into the end of the crankshaft to support the end of the transmission input shaft.

Release Bearing: The release bearing, also called a throwout bearing, compresses the pressure plate springs to disengage the clutch when the clutch pedal is depressed. The bearing reduces friction between the pressure plate levers and the clutch fork.

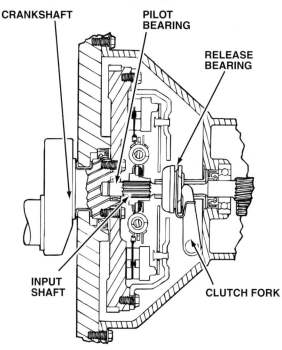

Fig. 1-2. A faulty pilot bearing or bushing or release bearing may be the cause of clutch noise.

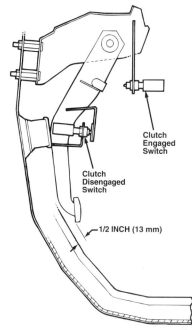

Fig. 1-3. A clutch should fully disengage before the clutch pedal reaches the end of its travel.

A3

To isolate the pilot bushing or bearing from the release bearing, keep the clutch pedal on the floor and shift the transmission into neutral. If the noise persists, the release bearing is bad, since the input shaft is now free to rotate. A bearing noise that occurs if you release the pedal to engage the clutch while in neutral, but goes away when the pedal is depressed, is caused by a defective transmission input shaft bearing.

A bushing that drags or sticks can cause grinding gears during shifts and can lead to misalignment of the clutch disc hub assembly. If the bushing or bearing locks up completely, it is impossible to disengage the clutch. The transmission and clutch assembly must be removed to service the pilot bearing or bushing and the clutch release bearing.

Clutch Function

Clutch function refers to how well the clutch operates during the road test. You should evaluate how smoothly the clutch engages and disengages and how well the clutch transmits engine power. A warped pressure plate may possibly cause a pulsating clutch pedal. This condition may be the result of missing springs or misadjusted counterbalance fingers. A chattering clutch produces a vibration or jerking motion as it engages when the vehicle is accelerated from a stop. A faulty disc, flywheel, or pressure plate causes clutch chatter. Both of these conditions would require the clutch to be disassembled to perform the repairs. A broken engine or transmission mount can also cause these symptoms, so check the mounts before removing the clutch.

An increase in engine RPM should be accompanied by an equal increase in road speed as the vehicle is accelerating.

If the engine seems to "race" without propelling the car forward, check for clutch slippage. Set the emergency brake, place the transmission or transaxle in high gear, hold engine speed at a fast idle, and slowly release the clutch. A clutch that is in good condition should lock up and stall the engine immediately. A partially slipping clutch will allow the engine to run momentarily before stalling. A badly slipping clutch might allow the engine to run with the clutch fully released. Common causes of slipping clutches are wear, oil on the clutch, or improper adjustment.

Clutch Release Check

Make sure the clutch releases fully. With the engine running and the brake on, hold the pedal about 0.5 inch (13 mm) from the floor, figure 1-3. With the pedal fully depressed, move the shift lever between neutral and reverse. If the transmission shifts smoothly without grinding, the clutch is releasing fully. If not, further inspection is necessary, as the cause can be faulty pedal bushings, hydraulic problems, or incorrect adjustment.

Many vehicles are equipped with a clutch engaged and/or a clutch disengaged switch. The switch may be a part of the starter interlock circuit or an input to the **Powertrain Control Module (PCM)**. In either case the switches are designed to prevent the starter from operating unless the clutch pedal is fully depressed. Check to see that the switch is functioning properly.

Check the clutch pedal bushings. Replace those that stick or are excessively worn, figure 1-4. Stiff clutch action may be caused by binding at the pedal pivot point. To check this,

---

Powertrain Control Module (PCM): The PCM is an onboard computer programmed to control the operation of the engine and many transmission functions.

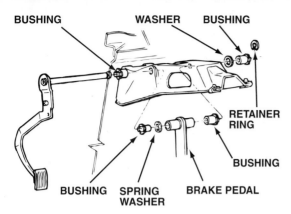

Fig. 1-4. Worn or sticking clutch pedal bushings can cause release problems.

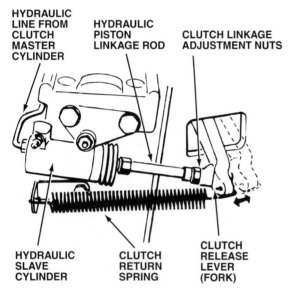

Fig. 1-5. Some external slave cylinders have adjustable pushrods.

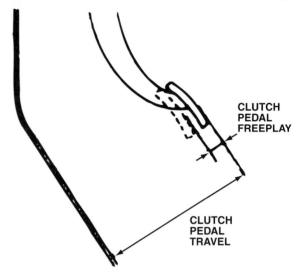

Fig. 1-6. Correct clutch pedal freeplay is 1.0 to 1.5 inches for most vehicles.

Specifications vary between manufacturers, but most are typically between 1.0 and 1.5 inches (25 and 38 mm) of freeplay. If freeplay is not within specifications, adjust it at the clutch cable joint nut, or the release lever rod. The hydraulic clutch release mechanisms on many cars do not require adjustment of the linkage or pedal position.

Pedal Travel Check
Check the clutch pedal to be sure that the travel, or stroke, is within specifications. You can attach a tape measure to the pedal to read the distance traveled as you push down on the pedal.

Clutch Actuation Linkage Inspection and Repair
Before attempting to adjust the clutch several components of the release system must be inspected for wear or damage.

- Linkage pivot points
- Cables
- Bushings
- Shafts
- Mounting brackets
- Automatic or manual adjuster assemblies

Repair or replace any components that do not meet the manufacturer's specifications.

Clutch Adjustment
If the clutch does not meet one or more of the preceding checks, adjust or replace as required. Refer to the appropriate Service Manual for specific adjustment procedures for the vehicle being serviced. Typically, these steps are required to properly adjust a manual release clutch.

1. Loosen the adjustment clevis or rod.
2. Adjust the linkage until the clutch fully releases with the clutch no closer than 0.5 inch (13 mm) from the floor.

disconnect the pedal from the linkage and operate the pedal by hand. If it binds, lubricate the pivot point or replace defective parts. Operate the pedal again. If it no longer binds, reconnect the linkage and perform the clutch release check again.

On hydraulic clutch systems, check the **slave cylinder** and clutch pedal travel. Slave cylinder and clutch pedal travel should be within specifications; typically 0.7 inch (18 mm). Measure it at the clutch fork with the pedal fully depressed, figure 1-5. When you check the slave cylinder travel, inspect for proper lubrication of the clutch fork ball stud pivot.

When a hydraulic clutch system is having release problems, check for air in the system. Pump the pedal several times before performing the clutch release check again. If the clutch will now release properly, the system has air in the lines. System bleeding is covered later in this chapter.

Pedal Freeplay Check
Check the clutch pedal freeplay, figure 1-6. Depress the pedal until you begin to feel resistance, then measure the distance.

Slave Cylinder: A hydraulic cylinder that reacts to hydraulic apply pressure from a master cylinder to perform a mechanical task. On a hydraulic clutch linkage, the slave cylinder causes the clutch fork to move.

Shift the transmission from neutral to reverse. If the gear engages without clashing or grinding, the adjustment is correct.

3. Tighten the locknut on the adjustment yoke or rod securely.

4. Inspect the pedal travel for correct freeplay. If not within specifications inspect all linkage and bushings. Replace as necessary.

5. If proper adjustment cannot be achieved, the clutch will require removal and replacement of defective components.

Oil Leaks

Defective engine crankshaft seals or transmission input shaft seals will allow oil to reach the clutch. If the vehicle has a removable inspection cover, look for traces of oil in the bell-housing or on the clutch assembly. The presence of oil requires removal of the clutch assembly to repair the oil leak and to replace the oil-soaked clutch. Common sources of oil leaks are the rear engine seal, the valve covers, and the front (input shaft) transmission bearing seal, figure 1-7.

Typical Hydraulic Clutch System Bleeding

Most clutch hydraulic systems generally operate on DOT 3 brake fluid, but there are exceptions. Always check the Service Manual to make sure you install the correct fluid. Handle brake fluid with care to avoid spills, as it will damage painted surfaces. If air has entered the clutch hydraulic system, bleed the hydraulic system as follows:

1. Fill the clutch master cylinder reservoir with clean brake fluid.

2. Fit a box end wrench on the slave cylinder bleed screw and attach a hose to the bleeder, figure 1-8. Place the open end of the hose in a container half filled with brake fluid.

3. Slowly depress the clutch pedal. While holding the pedal down, loosen the bleeder screw until fluid starts to run out, and then close the bleeder.

4. Repeat step three until no air bubbles come out with the fluid. Top off the master cylinder with the specified fluid.

Note: Hydraulic clutch systems do not "pump-up" like brake systems. Do not pump the pedal before opening the bleeder screw, as this tends to aerate the fluid.

Pressure Bleeding Procedure

On some late-model systems it will be necessary to use a pressure bleeder and reverse bleed the hydraulic system. To complete the pressure bleeding system:

1. Siphon most of the fluid out of the clutch master cylinder.

2. Connect the pressure bleeder to the slave cylinder bleeder fitting.

3. Apply no more than 10 psi to the pressure bleeder during this operation.

4. Slowly open the bleeder fitting until the fluid level in the master cylinder begins to rise.

5. When the cylinder is ¾ full, close the bleeder screw and remove the fluid again from the master cylinder.

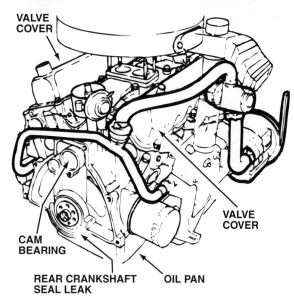

Fig. 1-7. Engine oil leaks are a common source of clutch failures.

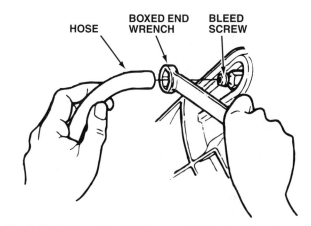

Fig. 1-8. All air must be bled from a clutch hydraulic system to eliminate engagement problems.

6 Repeat this process two or three times until no bubbles appear in the master cylinder and the fluid is clean.

7. Tighten the bleeder screw.

8. Refill the master cylinder to the proper level.

9. Check the system for leaks.

CLUTCH REMOVAL, INSPECTION, AND INSTALLATION

On most vehicles, you must remove the transmission to access the clutch assembly. Refer to the section on transmission removal and installation in Chapter Two of this book for this procedure. Once the transmission is removed, make a reference mark on the flywheel and clutch cover if the clutch is going to be reused. Align the marks on reinstallation to maintain balance.

Loosen the pressure plate assembly bolts evenly, in a "star" pattern, until the spring pressure is released. Remove the bolts, then lift the pressure plate and the clutch disc off the flywheel as an assembly. Inspect each component as described in the following sections.

Flywheel Inspection

Clean the clutch contact surface of the flywheel and inspect it for grooves, hot spots, nicks, and other forms of wear or damage. Next, check the flywheel for runout. Attach a dial indicator to the engine, position the plunger on the center of the clutch contact area, and zero the dial face, figure 1-9. Rotate the crankshaft one complete revolution while observing the dial indicator. Then, compare results to specifications. Also, check crankshaft endplay with the dial indicator. Push the flywheel toward the front of the engine and zero the indicator. Pry evenly on both sides of the flywheel, release, and read endplay on the dial indicator. Compare to specifications and correct as needed on reassembly.

If there is excessive wear or runout, resurface or replace the flywheel before installing the clutch. Before you remove a flywheel, mark its position in relation to the crankshaft to prevent imbalance when the flywheel is reinstalled. When resurfacing a "stepped" flywheel, be sure that equal material is removed from both the friction and pressure plate mounting surfaces.

Dual Mass Flywheel

Some vehicles are equipped with a **dual mass flywheel**, figure 1-10, which requires additional inspection procedures. Some diesel powered vehicles are equipped with a dual mass flywheel to isolate high crankshaft torque spikes prevalent in many diesel engines. These spikes are created under load during the power stroke. Gasoline powered performance engines may also use a dual mass flywheel to prevent transmission damage created by high RPM "speed shifts." Other applications use the dual mass flywheel to help dampen noise from transmission gear operation. Basically, dual mass flywheels separate the flywheel's rotating mass (torque) between the engine and the transmission, preventing more costly damage to transmission and other drivetrain components. The logic here is that clutches are by design "wear components" and are subject to periodic replacement.

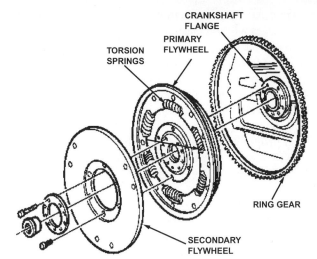

Fig. 1-10. Typical dual-mass clutch components.

Pilot Bearing or Bushing Inspection

The pilot bearing or bushing, which is press fit into the crankshaft flange, centers the transmission input shaft and absorbs loads caused by disengaging the clutch. Some designs are a solid bushing, while others are a sealed ball bearing or caged roller bearing. Often, the pilot bearing is replaced as a precautionary measure whenever the clutch is replaced.

To inspect a bushing, look for signs of galling, scoring, discoloration, or uneven wear along the inside diameter. Replace the bushing if any damage is found. With a sealed ball bearing, slowly rotate the inner race by hand. If the bearing binds or does not rotate smoothly, replace it.

Inspect the rollers of a caged roller bearing for nicks, scores, flaking, or other damage. Replace the bearing if the rollers do not rotate smoothly in the cage.

Remove a pilot bearing or bushing using a slide hammer fitted with a blind bearing puller adapter, figure 1-11. All pilot bearings are installed with an interference fit and can require a considerable amount of force to remove. A snapring generally holds a ball bearing pilot in the crankshaft, and caged bearings may have a lip seal installed on top of them. Remove the snapring or seal to access the bearing.

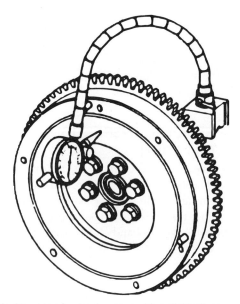

Fig. 1-9. Checking flywheel runout with a dial indicator.

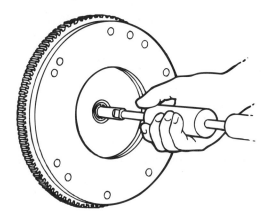

Fig. 1-11. Use a slide hammer with a blind bearing puller to remove a pilot bearing or bushing.

Dual Mass Flywheel: A flywheel that consists of two parts separated by springs used to absorb vibrations in the driveline.

Release Bearing Inspection

It is not possible to accurately test the function of a release bearing. Always replace it whenever the clutch is removed for service, figure 1-12.

Clutch Fork Inspection

Look over the entire clutch fork for signs of cracking, distress, and metal fatigue. Pay close attention to where the release bearing mounts, the ball stud pivots, and the linkage connects, figure 1-13. Look for a binding linkage that tilts the release bearing, causing uneven wear and hindering smooth travel.

Also, inspect the transmission input bearing retainer for wear. If wear is present, the clutch fork is probably bent; if so, replace it.

Clutch Disc Inspection

Inspect the clutch disc for wear or damage. Measure the depth of the rivet heads below the friction material surface using a caliper or depth micrometer, figure 1-14. Replace the disc if the measurement is less than what is specified. Wear limits vary, but 0.012 inch (0.30 mm) can be used as a general guideline. Mount the disc on the transmission input shaft and rotate it to check for **axial runout**. Maximum runout allowed by most clutch manufacturers is approximately 0.020 inch (0.50 mm) on the engine side of the disc.

Axial runout can cause release problems. Always check a new disc for runout because rough handling during shipping can damage the clutch disc.

Pressure Plate Inspection

The pressure plate surface should be smooth and free of **heat checks**, chatter marks, and **hard spots**. Use a straightedge and feeler gauge to detect a warped pressure plate. Also, check the release fingers for wear. If any wear is detected, replace the pressure plate assembly, figure 1-15.

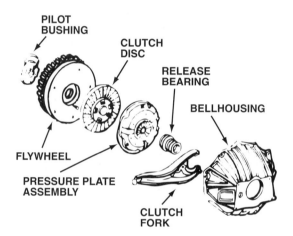

Fig. 1-12. Replace the release bearing whenever the clutch is serviced because there is no method of evaluating its condition.

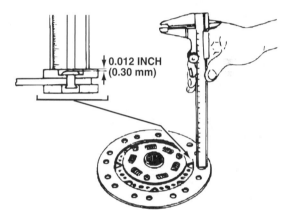

Fig. 1-14. Check clutch disc wear by measuring the distance from the friction material surface to the top of the rivet heads.

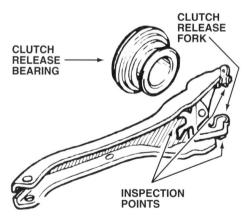

Fig. 1-13. Clutch fork wear areas are the release bearing mounts, ball stud pivot, and linkage connection.

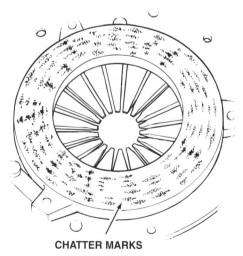

Fig. 1-15. If heat checks, chatter marks, or hard spots are found on the pressure plate contact surface, replace it.

Axial Runout: Total amount of movement away from a centerline, or axis. Also referred to as "wobble" or side-to-side play.
Hard Spots: Circular, bluish/gold, glassy areas on the pressure plate or flywheel friction surfaces where extreme heat has altered the structure of the metal. Hard spots, also called chill spots, usually cannot be successfully machined out.
Heat Checks: Small cracks on the friction surface of a pressure plate or flywheel caused by overheating. Heat checks do not penetrate through the friction surface and can usually be machined out of it.

Clutch Installation

To reinstall a clutch assembly:

1. Install the pilot bushing or bearing. Lightly lubricate the bushing with grease. Some pilot bearings can be packed with grease, but most are sealed units. Make sure the pilot bearing spins freely after it is installed. The bushing should have a press fit in the flywheel and should not rotate.

2. Align the clutch disc to the flywheel and pilot bearing with a clutch alignment tool or spare input shaft, figure 1-16. Slip the pressure plate over the clutch disc, fit it onto the flywheel, and install the bolts finger tight. Be sure to align the index marks when reinstalling a used pressure plate. Tighten the bolts evenly to the specified torque using a "star" pattern. Remove the clutch pilot tool.

3. Lubricate the clutch fork at its pivot point and at the release bearing contact area. Also, lightly lubricate the clutch disc splines on the transmission input shaft. Install the release bearing on the clutch fork, then install the fork in the bellhousing.

4. To install the transmission, align the input shaft precisely with the opening in the center of the clutch disc. Slide the transmission forward to engage the input shaft splines with the clutch disc hub. Then, push the transmission forward so that the end of the input shaft engages with the pilot bushing in the flywheel. Never force the transmission into place or allow its weight to hang on the clutch disc, as this can damage the disc hub, figure 1-17.

5. Once the transmission is installed and properly bolted up, adjust the clutch linkage and pedal freeplay. Freeplay at the clutch fork should be approximately 0.25 inch (6.4 mm) with a mechanical linkage. Most hydraulic systems and those with a self-adjusting cable mechanism should have zero freeplay, figure 1-18.

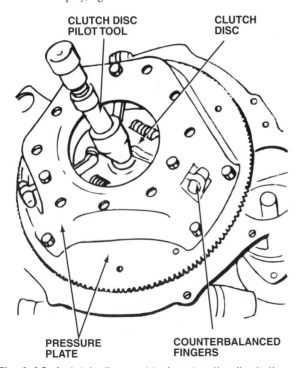

Fig. 1-16. A clutch alignment tool centers the disc to the pilot bearing.

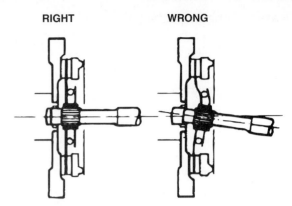

Fig. 1-17. The transmission input shaft must be aligned with the clutch disc splines and the pilot bearing to avoid damage to the disc during installation.

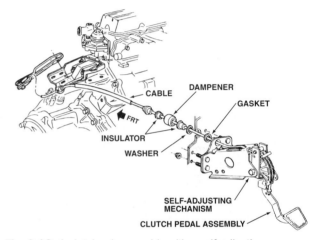

Fig. 1-18. A clutch release cable with a self-adjusting mechanism installs with zero freeplay.

Check the transmission lubricant level and top off as necessary to complete the installation. Test drive the vehicle to make sure the clutch disengages completely and the transmission shifts smoothly.

HYDRAULIC CYLINDER INSPECTION

A hydraulic clutch system consists of a master cylinder and a slave cylinder. The master cylinder is activated by the clutch pedal, and the slave cylinder uses the pressure from the master cylinder to actually operate the clutch fork. Both cylinders must be inspected for leaks and normally replaced if found to be defective. A few cylinders may be rebuilt, but most are no longer designed for this service.

Clutch Master Cylinder Inspection

Inspect the master cylinder for leaks at the pushrod dustboot, figure 1-19. Fluid behind the boot is from a leaking secondary seal and indicates that the master cylinder needs to be replaced. Always inspect and replace the slave cylinder, if necessary, anytime the master cylinder needs service.

Clutch Slave Cylinder Inspection

Inspect the slave cylinder for leaks at the dustboot. If the slave cylinder is mounted in the transmission bellhousing,

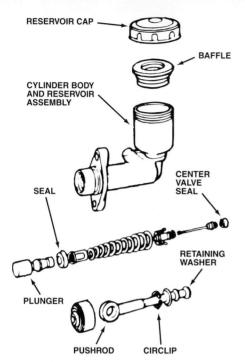

Fig. 1-19. Hydraulic fluid behind the clutch master cylinder dustboot indicates that the unit should be replaced.

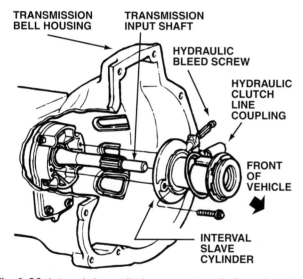

Fig. 1-20. Internal slave cylinders are automatically replaced whenever the clutch is serviced as a preventative measure.

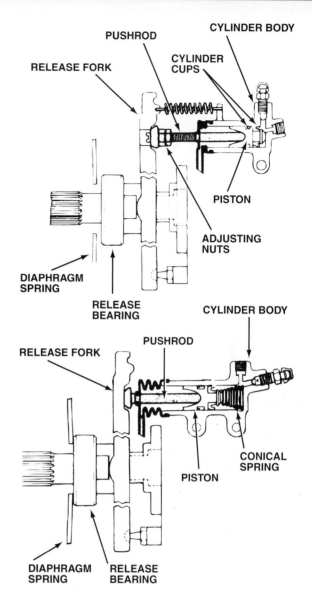

Fig. 1-21. External clutch slave cylinders can be adjustable (top) or self-adjusting (bottom).

replace it anytime the clutch is replaced, figure 1-20. Since the transmission must be removed to gain access to the internally mounted slave cylinder, it is cheap insurance to replace it at this time. Externally mounted units, figure 21, should be replaced when leaks are present.

Bellhousing Alignment
On vehicles that have a separate bellhousing and transmission, the bellhousing must be correctly aligned with the engine and the transmission. Correct alignment ensures proper clutch and transmission operation.

Using a dial indicator and a special tool that attaches to the flywheel or crankshaft, measure the bore runout,

figure 1-22, and the face runout, figure 1-23. Rotate the flywheel or crankshaft to pass the indicator across the surface being measured.

Correct excessive bore runout by using offset alignment dowels on the back of the engine. Correct excessive face runout by machining the transmission mounting surface on the bellhousing or by inserting shim stock between the bellhousing and the engine block. To make a custom shim, you can punch holes in shim stock for bolt holes and cut the remaining shim stock to model the bellhousing shape.

Powertrain Mount Inspection
Broken or deteriorated mounts can cause misalignment and destruction of certain drivetrain components. When a single mount breaks, the remaining mounts are subjected to abnormally high stresses. On front-wheel drive vehicles with transversely mounted engine and transmission, inspect the cradle for cracks and or separations of welds.

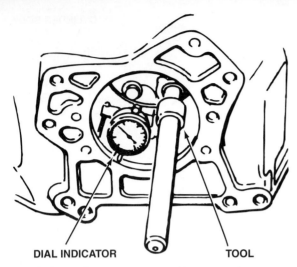

DIAL INDICATOR   **TOOL**

Fig. 1-22. Dial indicator set up to read bore runout on a bellhousing that installs separately from the transmission.

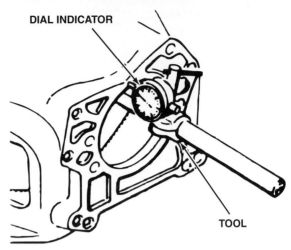

DIAL INDICATOR

TOOL

Fig. 1-23. Dial indicator set up to read face runout on a bellhousing that installs separately from the transmission.

CHAPTER QUESTIONS

1. A sticking pilot bearing can cause all of the following **EXCEPT**:
   a. Clutch not disengaging
   b. Noise
   c. Clutch hub damage
   d. Clutch slippage

2. If noise is heard from the bellhousing area when the transmission is in neutral and the clutch is released, the cause of this noise can be:
   a. The pilot bearing or bushing
   b. The release bearing
   c. The input shaft bearing
   d. All of the above

3. An engine "racing" without a corresponding increase in vehicle speed while accelerating during the road test is caused by:
   a. Clutch slippage
   b. Clutch chatter
   c. Clutch dragging
   d. Clutch not disengaging

4. Upon disassembly, mark the position of the flywheel in relation to the:
   a. Output shaft
   b. Hub
   c. Crankshaft
   d. Pressure plate

5. When replacing a clutch assembly, first check the runout before installing the new:
   a. Pressure plate
   b. Clutch disc
   c. Pressure plate cover
   d. Throwout bearing

6. Leakage observed at the rear dustboot of the clutch master cylinder is an indication that:
   a. The vent is open
   b. A secondary seal is leaking
   c. Too much clutch pedal freeplay exists at the master cylinder
   d. Insufficient clutch pedal freeplay exists at the master cylinder

7. Clean hydraulic cylinder parts with:
   a. Gasoline
   b. Non-petroleum based solvent
   c. Clean rags
   d. Brushes only

8. Which kind of slave cylinder is always replaced?
   a. Self-adjusting
   b. Adjustable
   c. Internally mounted
   d. Cast aluminum

9. The bellhousing transmission bore and the rear face should be checked for:
   a. Endplay
   b. Clearance
   c. Runout
   d. Axial play

10. Correct face runout by:
    a. Machining or installing shims
    b. Using offset dowels
    c. Tightening the mounting bolts
    d. Using an offset transmission mount

A3

MANUAL TRANSMISSION AND TRANSAXLE SERVICE

CHAPTER OBJECTIVES

- The technician will complete the ASE task list on Manual Transmission and Transaxle service.
- The technician will be able to answer 15 questions dealing with the Manual Transmission and Transaxle Service.

TRANSMISSION/TRANSAXLE DIAGNOSIS AND ADJUSTMENT ON VEHICLE

Typically, manual transmission and transaxle problems fall into the following categories:

- Excessive noise
- Oil leaks
- Hard shifting
- Excessive wear
- Failed components

Diagnosis consists of a road test to help you isolate the problem, followed by inspection and adjustment procedures to confirm the diagnosis.

Road Test Diagnosis

Perform a road test and listen carefully for noise. If noise is detected, note the speed, gear range, and driving conditions. During your road test, listen for the following:

1. A whining noise is typical of most gears. However, if the noise seems excessive, it can indicate low transmission oil.
2. A rough growl or grating sound can indicate worn transmission bearings.
3. A noise loudest on corners is usually caused by worn axle bearings, differential gears, or the final drive case bearings.
4. A vibration or growl that continues even when the transmission is in neutral is probably caused by a rough wheel bearing or the final drive case bearings.
5. A gear noise in only one gear generally means that the constant mesh gear combination for that range is damaged or worn.
6. A clunk on acceleration or deceleration indicates a worn differential pinion shaft or side gear, or worn drive axle inner joints.

Oil Leaks

Give the transmission a thorough visual inspection for leaks. Leaks that have been active for a long time are difficult to diagnose. You may have to steam clean the underside of the engine and transmission and then drive the vehicle to determine exactly where the leak is coming from.

Common places to inspect for oil leaks in a manual transmission include the side or top cover gasket and the **output shaft** seal. For transaxles, also check the case halves and the differential seals. Oil leaks may also be caused by a stripped drain or fill plug or a plug missing its gasket.

Other causes of oil leaks include plugged vents, loose fasteners, or damage to the transmission case, housing, or covers. Overfilling the transmission with lubricant can also cause excessive internal pressures, which may cause gaskets to fail and leaks to develop.

When a transmission leaks from one of its seals, check for wear in the shaft, bearing, or bushing. Generally, simply replacing the seal will not fix the problem. The worn part allows the shaft to wobble, which will make the new seal leak also.

Some of the gaskets and seals in a manual transmission can be replaced without removing the gearbox from the vehicle. For example, the rear housing seal and gasket in a rear-wheel drive (RWD) vehicle can usually be installed without removing the transmission. Most gasket and seal replacements require disassembly of the transmission.

Checking and Changing Lubricant

Although a few manual transaxle designs have a dipstick for checking the oil level, most do not. Typically, manual transmission lubricant level is checked by removing a plug from the side of the case.

With the vehicle on a hoist, locate the check/fill plug. Do not remove any fasteners from the outside of the transmission. Doing so can dislodge internal parts, requiring transmission removal and repair. Clean the area around the check/fill plug and remove the plug using the appropriate wrench, figure 2-1. In most cases, the proper fluid level will be at or slightly below the check/fill plug opening. You can usually carefully stick your finger in the fill hole and check the fluid level, figure 2-2.

Output Shaft: The transmission shaft that holds the output gears and the synchronizers. It connects to the driveshaft or propeller shaft to turn the driving wheels. It may also be called the mainshaft.

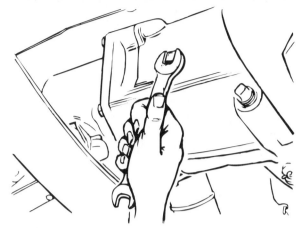

Fig. 2-1. To check the lubricant level, locate and remove the check/fill plug from the transmission case.

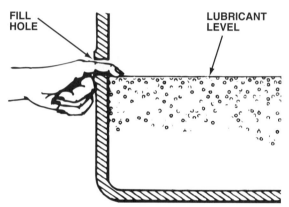

Fig. 2-2. On many manual transmissions, the lubricant level should be at the lower edge of the check/fill plug, and you can check it by inserting a finger into the opening.

Be aware that the correct fluid level on some transmissions is lower than the bottom edge of the check/fill plug opening. Check the Service Manual for the correct lubricant level when working on an unfamiliar transmission. On some, the lubricant will be a certain distance below the opening. To check, insert a bent piece of wire into the hole. Then, remove the wire and use a ruler to measure how far below the opening the oil level is. With other transmissions, there is no method for checking the fluid level. You simply drain the gearbox and refill with the specified amount. Also, watch for units that have more than one check/fill and drain plug.

Leave the dipstick or oil check/fill plug out of the transmission to change the lubricant. To change oil, place a drain pan under the transmission, then remove the drain plug and allow the oil to drain, figure 2-3. Clean and reinstall the drain plug; use a new gasket or apply sealant to the threaded portion of the plug. Tighten the plug to specification. Fill the transmission with the recommended lubricant to the proper level, and reinstall the dipstick or check/fill plug.

Avoid overfilling the transmission. Too high a lubricant level may allow the gears to whip the oil into a foam. This

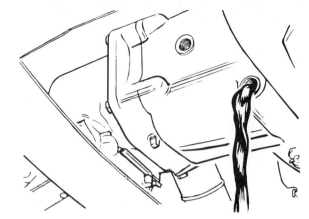

Fig. 2-3. Remove the drain plug to drain the lubricant from a manual transmission.

greatly reduces the lubrication ability of the oil and can cause parts of the transmission to fail.

The transmission and final drive sumps are combined into one common unit on most front-wheel drive (FWD) transaxles. The fill procedure for the common sump design is the same as for conventional transmissions. Transaxles that utilize hypoid gearing in the differential have a separate sump for the final drive. Be sure to check both sumps if the vehicle you are working on is so equipped, keeping in mind that hypoid gear units use gear oil rather than transmission fluid for a lubricant.

Special gear oil is often required for limited-slip differentials. Some vehicle manufacturers recommend that you mix an additive with the gear oil. Always consult the appropriate manuals for service requirements.

Gear Oil Ratings

Gear oils are used in many transmissions and other drivetrain components. As with motor oils, both the American Petroleum Institute (API) and the Society of Automotive Engineers (SAE) have established rating systems for gear oils. The **API Service Classifications** vary from GL-1 through GL-5. The most common gear oils for late-model vehicles are GL-4 and GL-5. These contain extreme pressure (EP) additives to lubricate the final drive hypoid gears. To avoid synchronizer damage, some vehicles use a special GL-4 with non-reactive EP additives. In these cases, standard EP 80-90W oil is not used. In addition, some vehicles require special gear oils that are not classified under the API system. These may be designated HP, EP, and GLS on service charts.

The SAE viscosity grades for gear oils are similar to those for engine oils. Typical gear oil viscosity grades are 75W, 80W, 90W, and 140W. Although higher numbers are assigned to gear oils, they are not necessarily higher in viscosity than engine oils. As with engine oils, gear oil viscosity grades are measured at both high and low temperatures and are available in multigrade designations, such as 75-90W and 80-90W.

A3

API Service Classification: A system of letters that signifies how a lubricant performs. It is assigned by the American Petroleum Institute.

Shift Linkage Adjustment

Many customer complaints deal with shift qualities, such as feel and difficulty in shifting. You should road test the vehicle to verify the complaint and also check clutch release operation. If the clutch is not operating correctly, you will not be able to shift the transmission properly. Verify proper clutch operation as detailed in Chapter One before proceeding.

Shift linkage adjustments for most manual, RWD transmissions are basically the same. With the transmission in neutral, disconnect the shift linkage rods from the side cover levers.

Remove the side cover, figure 2-4, and inspect the following components as required:

- Bushings or bearings
- Levers and shafts
- Sleeves

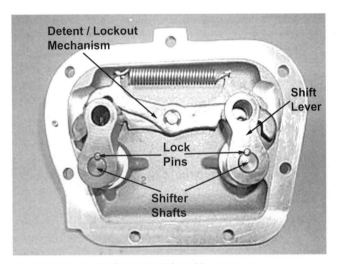

Fig. 2-4. Typical RWD transmission side cover.

- Detent mechanism and interlocks
- Springs

Remove the shift forks from the transmission and inspect for wear, missing inserts, or other damage, figure 2-5.

Replace any defective components before attempting to adjust the shift linkage. Then insert the proper alignment tool into the shifter assembly to lock it in the neutral position, figure 2-6. Loosen the shift rod adjusting nuts and adjust the rods to align with the holes in the shift levers. The rods should enter the levers without drag. Tighten the adjusting nuts.

Shift Lever Adjustment

On some transaxles, the shift control lever is mounted on an extension rod assembly. If the shift strokes become short or the gears do not completely mesh, check the shifter control shaft bushings for wear. Always replace worn shifter control shaft bushings before attempting to adjust the shifter.

Adjust the shift lever position on some floor-mounted units by loosening the guide bolts and adjusting the guide plate until the base of the shift lever is perpendicular to the plate, figure 2-7. Other floor-mounted shifters use shims under the shift lever. Use a feeler gauge to measure the clearance between the shim and the shift lever retainer. Select a shim that allows a clearance from zero to 0.004 inch (0.102 mm).

External Shifter Service

Inspect the transmission or transaxle external shifter for excessive wear or damage. If deficiencies are found it is usually necessary the replace the shifter as an assembly. Refer to the appropriate Service Manual for the proper service procedure. Generally, the shifter is attached to the transmission housing or bracket with several bolts, figure 2-8. Remove the

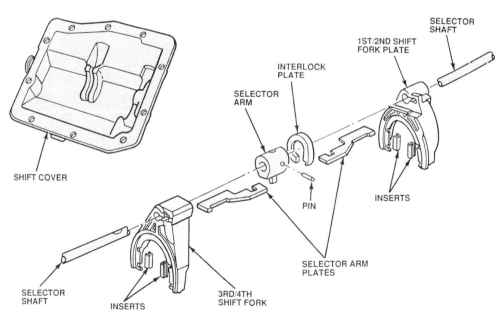

Fig. 2-5. Inspect the shift forks for wear and damage.

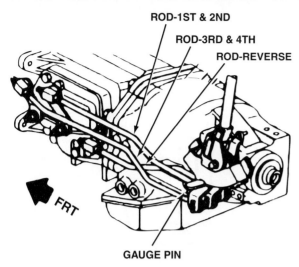

ROD-1ST & 2ND
ROD-3RD & 4TH
ROD-REVERSE
FRT
GAUGE PIN

Fig. 2-6. An alignment tool, or gauge pin, locks the shifter assembly in position so that the shift rods can be adjusted.

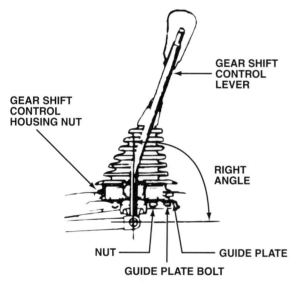

GEAR SHIFT CONTROL LEVER
GEAR SHIFT CONTROL HOUSING NUT
RIGHT ANGLE
NUT
GUIDE PLATE
GUIDE PLATE BOLT

Fig. 2-7. A typical floor-mounted shifter adjusts by loosening the bolts and repositioning the guide plate.

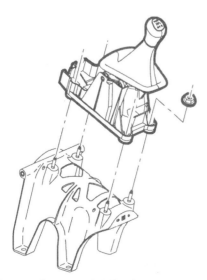

Fig. 2-8. Remove the external shifter from the mounting.

bolts and install the new shifter assembly. Follow the appropriate procedures to adjust the shifter and then verify proper operation in all ranges.

TRANSMISSION AND TRANSAXLE REMOVAL AND INSTALLATION

If repairs cannot be made with the transmission in the vehicle, remove the unit for disassembly and component inspection. The following sections describe general procedures for removing and installing manual transmissions. Separate procedures are provided for transmission removal and installation, as well as transaxle removal and installation. Refer to specifications and service procedures for specific instructions.

Manual Transmission Removal

To remove a RWD transmission, follow these steps:

1. Disconnect the negative battery cable.
2. Remove the distributor cap or distributor, if it is at the back of the engine and can contact the firewall when you remove the transmission.
3. Raise and support the vehicle.
4. Disconnect and remove the exhaust system.
5. Remove any exhaust hangers that attach to the transmission.
6. Support the transmission with a jack, figure 2-9.
7. If a driveline support beam is fitted, remove the bolts that attach it to the axle and the transmission, and remove the beam from the vehicle.
8. Remove the slave cylinder attaching bolts from the clutch housing. For a mechanical clutch, disconnect the cable or other linkage.
9. Drain the fluid from the transmission.

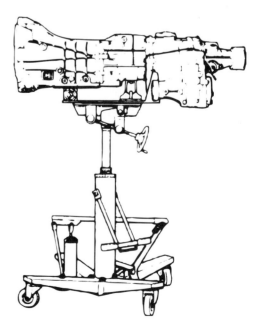

Fig. 2-9. Use a transmission jack to support the gearbox during removal and installation.

A3

10. If you must separate the rear **universal joint** to remove the **driveshaft**, mark the driveshaft rear U-joint and companion flange for proper reinstallation. Remove the bolts attaching the universal joint to the flange. Lower the driveshaft a few inches and tape the U-joint bearing cups to the cross, figure 2-10. Slip the front yoke on the shaft out of the transmission extension housing and off the output shaft.

11. Disconnect the following from the transmission:

   • The electrical connectors at the backup light switch
   • The speedometer cable or electrical sensor connector
   • Special care must be taken when removing connectors that monitor transmission functions through the TCM or PCM, such as input and output speed sensors, gear range sensors, and/or PNP type sensors
   • The shift linkage

12. Unbolt the rear mount and cross member, and inspect the mounts for torn, stretched, or worn rubber. Lower the transmission while supporting the engine.

13. Remove the bellhousing fasteners, and slide the transmission straight back to disengage the **input shaft** from the clutch. Do not allow the weight of the transmission to hang by the input shaft on the clutch disc; this can damage the clutch hub and disc, figure 2-11. Lower the jack and remove the transmission from the vehicle.

Manual Transmission Installation

To install a transmission, follow these steps:

1. Make sure all parts are clean and free of defects.
2. Lubricate the pilot bearing and install the clutch as previously detailed. Use an alignment tool to center the clutch disc splines, figure 2-12.

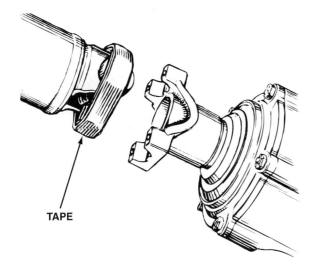

TAPE

Fig. 2-10. Tape U-joint bearing caps to the cross when the joint must be separated to remove the driveshaft.

3. Lubricate the clutch fork ball socket or bushing and the release bearing contact areas of the fork, figure 2-13.
4. Install the clutch fork onto the ball stud.
5. Lubricate the inside of the release bearing collar and the clutch fork groove.

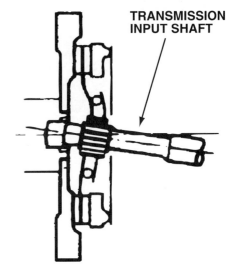

TRANSMISSION INPUT SHAFT

Fig. 2-11. Slide the transmission straight back to clear the input shaft splines and avoid damaging the clutch disc.

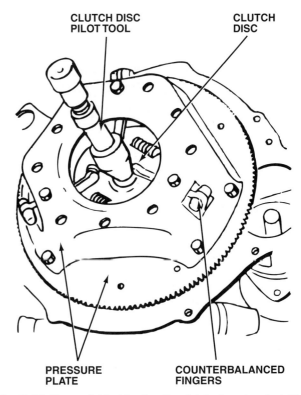

CLUTCH DISC PILOT TOOL

CLUTCH DISC

PRESSURE PLATE

COUNTERBALANCED FINGERS

Fig. 2-12. Use a pilot tool to align the clutch disc when installing the clutch assembly.

Driveshaft: A tubular shaft connecting the power output from the transmission to the pinion of the rear axle in RWD vehicles. Also known as the propeller shaft.

Input Shaft: The transmission shaft that transfers the power from the clutch disc to the countershaft gears. It may also be called the clutch shaft.

Universal Joint: Jointed connections on driveshafts that permit a change in angle. Also referred to as a U-joint.

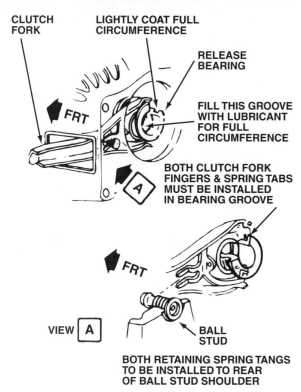

Fig. 2-13. Lubricate the clutch fork and release bearing contact areas.

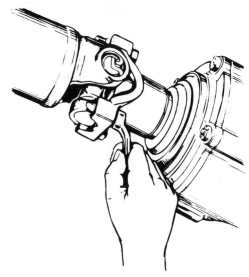

Fig. 2-14. Make sure the reference marks align when you assemble the rear universal joint.

A3

6. Slide the release bearing onto its sleeve, engaging the clutch fork fingers with the groove in the bearing collar.
7. Raise the transmission and align the input shaft with the opening in the center of the clutch disc. Slide the transmission forward to engage the input shaft splines with the clutch disc hub.
8. Then, slide the transmission forward to engage the end of the input shaft with the pilot bushing. To prevent damage, do not force the transmission into place or allow its weight to hang on the clutch disc.
9. Install the bellhousing attaching bolts and tighten them to specifications.
10. Raise the back of the transmission and install the rear mount.
11. Wipe the driveshaft sliding yoke clean. Slide the yoke into the extension housing and onto the output shaft. Return the shaft to its original position to avoid driveshaft runout.
12. Align the driveshaft and companion flange reference marks to maintain driveshaft balance. Assemble the rear U-joint to the flange and tighten the bolts to specifications, figure 2-14.
13. For a hydraulic clutch, install the slave cylinder, making sure the pushrod end engages the clutch fork. For a mechanical clutch, connect and adjust the clutch cable.
14. Install the driveline support beam, if fitted. Tighten the attaching bolts to specification.
15. Reconnect the following:

   • The electrical connectors at the backup light switch
   • The speedometer cable or electrical sensor connector
   • The shift linkage
   • The exhaust system and exhaust hanger at the transmission

16. Fill the transmission with the proper lubricant.
17. Adjust the shift linkage, and then lower the vehicle.
18. Install the distributor or cap, if removed, and attach the negative battery cable.

Manual Transaxle Removal

To remove a transaxle, follow these steps:

1. Disconnect the negative battery cable.
2. Remove the air cleaner assembly and intake air hoses.
3. Disconnect the clutch cable from the clutch release lever, or remove the slave cylinder from the bellhousing.
4. Remove the following:

   • The starter motor
   • The speedometer cable
   • The wiring harness connectors at the transaxle
   • The front and rear torque rod bolts at the transaxle
   • The splash shields, if fitted

5. Install an engine support fixture, if required.
6. Raise the vehicle on a hoist and drain the oil from the transaxle.
7. Remove the exhaust pipe at the exhaust manifold.
8. Remove the lower clutch housing dust cover, figure 2-15.
9. For a rod-type shift mechanism, disconnect the control rod and the extension rod at the transaxle. For a cable-type shift mechanism, disconnect the shift control cable and the select control cable, figure 2-16. Remove the clips and washers, and remove the cable retainers.
10. Remove the left front wheel.
11. Remove the left-side stabilizer bar mounting bolts and left-side ball joint stud bolt. Separate the ball joint from the steering knuckle by prying down the lower control arm.
12. Free the inboard end of the drive axles by gently prying to release the snaprings, figure 2-17.

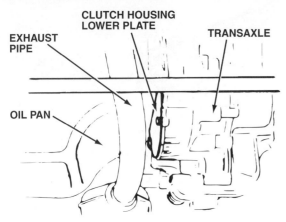

Fig. 2-15. Remove the dust cover at the bottom of the transaxle to expose the flywheel.

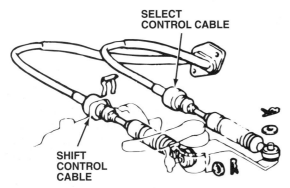

Fig. 2-16. Disconnect the shift control cable and the select control cable at the transaxle.

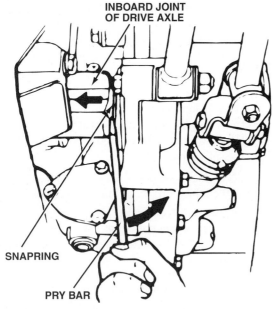

Fig. 2-17. Pry out on the inboard CV joint housing to release the snapring and free the axle.

13. Pull the drive axles out of the differential side gears.
14. Remove the front torque rod.
15. Position a transmission jack under the transaxle case.
16. Scribe reference marks on all mount and crossmembers before loosening the fasteners. These marks must be

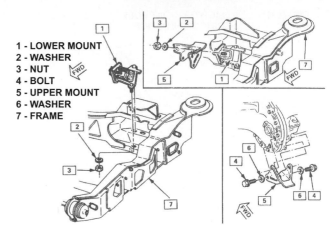

1 - LOWER MOUNT
2 - WASHER
3 - NUT
4 - BOLT
5 - UPPER MOUNT
6 - WASHER
7 - FRAME

Fig. 2-18. Refer to the manufacturer's procedures when removing or installing the transaxle. Using the proper torque and alignment specifications are critical to both the ride and safety of the vehicle.

used to ensure proper drivetrain or subframe/cradle alignment when reinstalling the transaxle.

17. Disconnect and remove any crossmember, transmission mount, or brackets that connect the chassis or engine to the transaxle, figure 2-18.
18. Remove all bolts fastening the transaxle to the engine.
19. Separate the transaxle from the engine by sliding the gearbox toward the left side for transverse engines and back for longitudinal engines. Keep the transaxle straight and level until the input shaft clears the clutch assembly. Then, lower the transmission jack and remove the transaxle.

Manual Transaxle Installation

To install a transaxle, reverse the removal procedure, while noting these important points:

1. When you install the transaxle, guide the right drive axle into the differential side gear as the transaxle is being raised into position.
2. Install the transaxle-to-engine bolts and nuts and tighten them to specification.
3. Align all reference marks applied during transaxle removal. Failure to correctly align the powertrain mounts may result in drivetrain or subframe/cradle misalignment. This misalignment may cause component wear, vibration, or tire wear.
4. Insert the right and left drive axles into the differential side gears until the snaprings on the drive axles engage the differential side gears.
5. With a cable-operated clutch, adjust the clutch pedal freeplay. With a hydraulic clutch, bleed the system to remove trapped air.
6. Refill the transaxle with the recommended oil, allow the fluid to settle, then check for proper level, figure 2-19.
7. Reconnect the negative battery cable.
8. Inspect your work and road test the vehicle, taking steps to ensure all shifts are smooth and without gear clash or grinding.

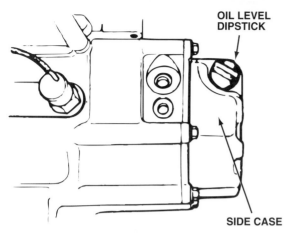

Fig. 2-19. Refill the transaxle with the correct amount of the proper lubricant and recheck the fluid level after filling.

INTERNAL TRANSMISSION/TRANSAXLE PROBLEM DIAGNOSIS

Five types of symptoms are generally associated with internal transmission problems:

- Hard shifting
- Jumping out of gear
- Blockout
- Gear clash
- Noise

Hard Shifting

Hard shifting occurs when the gears engage, but shift effort is excessive. Check the synchronizer hub sleeve for smooth operation. The sleeve should slide freely over the blocking ring and gear teeth. If it will not move easily, disassemble the **synchronizer assembly** and clean and inspect each part. The hub should be free of burrs and other signs of wear. Use a small file to remove burrs from the hub.

Whenever the synchronizers are disassembled, replace the inserts, also known as detents or dogs, and springs, figure 2-20. The sleeve should be cleaned, and internal splines should be inspected for wear. Pay particular attention to the chamfer points at the end of each spline, figure 2-21. Assemble the sleeve and hub, and check for interference between them. If individual parts are not available, replace the entire synchronizer assembly.

Jumping Out of Gear

A transmission jumps out of gear when the lever suddenly slips into neutral while the vehicle is being driven. This problem can be caused by excessive wear in the synchronizer inserts and springs, shift forks or shift rails, or **countershaft**.

Most manual transaxles do not have a side shift cover containing the shift forks and detent mechanisms. The type of construction in manual transaxles uses shift shafts with the shift forks secured to the shafts with roll pins. Detent rollers

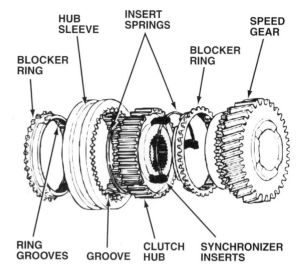

Fig. 2-20. The inserts and springs should be replaced with new ones whenever a synchronizer is disassembled.

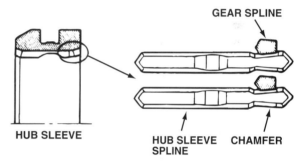

Fig. 2-21. Inspect the chamfer points at the end of each spline on a synchronizer hub closely. These are critical wear areas.

give the feel when shifting and rebuff any attempt to engage two gears at one time. Repair and/or inspection of the shift forks and shift shafts require removal from the vehicle and disassembly of the transaxle.

Blockout

Blockout occurs when the driver moves the shift lever until the synchronizer sleeve is engaged with the blocking ring, and the gear does not immediately engage. When it does engage, the driver feels a double bump at the shift lever. Check the gear cones for worn surfaces, and ensure that the blocking ring is not stuck on the cone. Generally, the gap between the blocking ring and the gear cone should be greater than 0.024 inch (0.61 mm), figure 2-22. Replace the blocking ring if it is worn below specifications.

Gear Clash

Gear clash is a loud grating or buzzing sound. This occurs if the chamfers on the synchronizer sleeve contact those on the gear before the blocking ring has matched the speeds of the two parts. Check the sleeve chamfers for wear, chipping, and burrs. Replace the synchronizer assembly and blocking rings if

Countershaft: The transmission shaft that is gear driven by the input shaft and, in turn, drives the output shaft. Also known as a layshaft.
Synchronizer Assembly: An assembly of sleeves and rings that fits between output gears. The synchronizers aid gear engagement and prevent grinding or clashing.

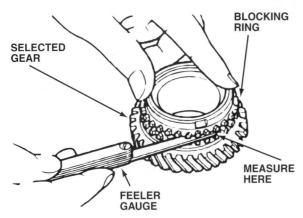

Fig. 2-22. Checking the blocking ring gap with a feeler gauge.

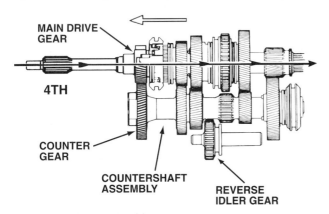

Fig. 2-23. Noise from a worn main drive gear bearing or a countergear bearing is not noticeable in fourth gear because operating in direct drive reduces the load on these bearings.

any damage is present. Also, inspect the clutch gear teeth on the synchronized gear in question. If these teeth are worn, replace the gear.

Noise

Noise can be caused by worn gears or damaged bearings. The rear output shaft bearing usually causes noise during deceleration. Carefully inspect the gear tooth contact pattern. Pay special attention to the contact between the main drive gear and the driven gear on the **countergear**. The main drive gear bearing produces noise similar to the main drive gear and driven countergear.

In a five-speed transmission, this noise disappears in fourth gear. This is because the synchronizer sleeve moves toward the main drive gear and locks the output shaft and main drive gear together, taking the load off of the front bearing. Similarly, the countergear bearing produces noise in all gears but fourth, figure 2-23.

Transmission Shaft Disassembly

Techniques for removing and installing the gears and other parts on the input shaft, output shaft, and countergear vary among manufacturers. This section gives you some general guidelines.

Countergear Inspection and Disassembly

In most RWD transmissions, all the gears on the countershaft are one piece, so each gear cannot be replaced separately. If any gear is bad, the entire assembly must be replaced. Some countergear designs use a countershaft and needle-type roller bearings for support in the transmission case. These bearings should be cleaned and inspected for wear along with the countershaft, figure 2-24. Replace any worn parts. Thrust washers located at each end of the countergear serve two purposes: to prevent transmission case wear and to control countergear endplay. Usually, replacing these washers with new parts will bring the countergear endplay back into specification.

General Specification Guidelines

General guidelines used in this text are as follows. Always refer to the appropriate Service Manual for the exact specification for the vehicle being serviced.

- Gear endplay should be between 0.002 and 0.012 inch (0.05 and 0.30 mm)
- Normal blocker ring clearance should be greater than 0.024 inch (0.61 mm)
- Nominal bearing to snapring clearance should be 0.006 inch (0.15 mm)

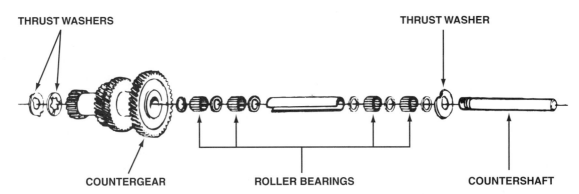

Fig. 2-24. Disassemble, clean, and inspect the needle-type roller bearings and thrust washers used to support the countergear assembly.

Countergear: A gear that meshes with other gears on the input and output shafts of a transmission. Countergears, which assemble on the countershaft, are driven by the input shaft and, in turn, drive the gears on the output shaft. A one-piece set of countergears may be called a cluster gear.

Output Shaft Inspection and Disassembly

Gears and synchronizer assemblies are held in place on the output shaft by snaprings or by press fitting. Prior to disassembly, make the following checks:

- Gear endplay
- Blocking ring to gear clearance
- Output shaft bearing to snapring clearance

To disassemble the output shaft, use a hydraulic press and a bearing separator plate. Be very careful not to damage the gear, the synchronizer assembly, or the output shaft. Generally, second gear and the components behind it are pressed off the rear of the output shaft, figure 2-25. Third gear and the synchronizer assembly come off the front of the output shaft.

Output shaft gear inspection criteria are the same as for the countergear: pay particular attention to the clutch gear teeth at each gear. The synchronizer assembly should be inspected as described in the "hard shifting" symptom listed in the Internal Problem Diagnosis section. Finally, the output shaft should be inspected for shaft diameter using a micrometer and for runout using V-blocks and a dial indicator, figure 2-26.

Clean all disassembled parts with solvent and dry with compressed air. Lubricate sliding surfaces with gear oil or assembly lubricant before reassembly. With the shafts removed from the transmission, clean the case thoroughly and check all mating surfaces to ensure they are absolutely smooth and free of nicks, chips, or gouges.

Transaxle Input Shaft Inspection and Disassembly

Many transaxle designs control input endplay with selective shims. Prior to transaxle disassembly, check for input shaft endplay and record your findings. The following checks should be made:

- Gear endplay
- Blocking ring to gear clearance
- Input shaft bearing to snapring clearance

Disassemble the input shaft by removing the rear bearing snapring and then pressing fourth gear and the rear bearing off the input shaft. Inspect the gears and synchronizer assembly as discussed in the Hard Shifting, Blockout, and Gear Clash sections earlier in the chapter. Measure the input shaft runout and journal diameters, figure 2-27. Replace any worn components and reassemble the input shaft.

Transaxle Output Shaft Inspection

Transaxle output shafts are similar to transaxle input shafts. However, these transaxle shafts have an output gear that drives the final drive ring gear. Inspect the output shaft for:

- Gear endplay
- Blocking ring to gear clearance

Measure the output shaft runout and journal diameters. Replace any worn parts and reassemble the output shaft.

Final Drive Disassembly and Inspection

Transaxle final drive assemblies incorporate the differential and **ring gear** into one assembly. The ring gear is driven by a **pinion gear** on the output shaft. The differential operates in a similar way to the RWD differential assemblies discussed in Chapter Four of this book.

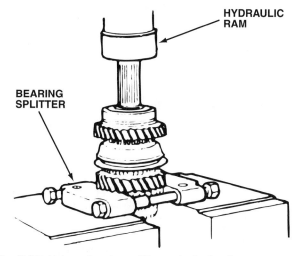

Fig. 2-25. Using a bearing splitter and a hydraulic press to disassemble the output shaft.

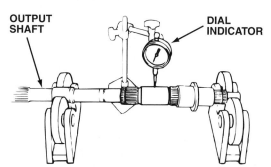

Fig. 2-26. Checking output shaft runout with V-blocks and a dial indicator.

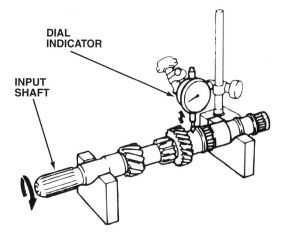

Fig. 2-27. Use V-blocks and a dial indicator to measure transaxle input shaft runout.

Pinion Gear: The driving, and smaller, member of a ring and pinion gearset. In a final drive differential, the pinion gear is driven by the driveshaft and transfers torque to the ring gear.

Ring Gear: The driven, and larger, member of a ring and pinion gearset. The ring gear, which attaches to the differential case, shifts the direction of crankshaft rotation 90 degrees and transfers torque to the drive axles.

Disassemble the differential and inspect it for wear whenever the transaxle is repaired. Inspect the transmission speed and final drive gears, speedometer drive gears, washers, pinion shaft, and case for wear.

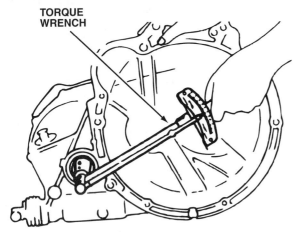

Fig. 2-28. Using a torque wrench to check differential case bearing preload.

After replacing worn components, reassemble the differential and check the differential case bearing preload, figure 2-28. Differential case preload helps maintain ring gear position, allowing proper torque transfer from the output shaft to the drive axles. Preload is usually adjusted using snaprings or selective shims. See Chapter Four of this book for adjustment procedures.

Bearing Inspection

Thoroughly clean the input and output shaft bearings in solvent and air dry them. Do not spin bearings with compressed air; this can damage them. Carefully inspect the bearings for signs of wear or damage, figure 2-29. Lightly coat each bearing with oil and rotate the outer race by hand. Any roughness means the bearing is bad and must be replaced. Inspect the countershaft needle bearings for damage. If any of the bearings or bushings are sealed, do not attempt to clean or lubricate them. You can place sealed bearings in a vise and load them slightly to check for wear.

You can purchase transmission repair kits with everything needed to rebuild a standard transmission. Small parts kits

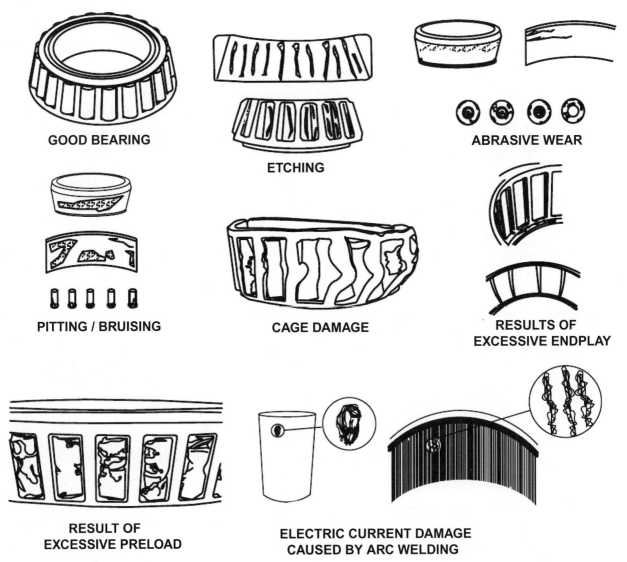

Fig. 2-29. Clean and inspect ball bearings for signs of wear or damage.

contain roller bearings, snaprings, thrust washers, and other special items needed to complete the rebuild process.

Extension Housing, Bushing, and Seal Inspection

Inspect the output shaft bushing and oil seal. If the seal is damaged, the driveshaft **slip yoke** or output shaft bushing may also need to be replaced. Always install the seal with the lip facing inward toward the lubricant. Special tools remove and install seals without damage to the seal or the housing, figure 2-30. Coat the outer edge of the seal with non-hardening gasket sealant to prevent leakage between the output shaft housing and the seal.

Lubrication System Inspection

Transmissions are generally lubricated by oil slung off the rotating gears. In some transmissions, a portion of this oil is recovered in a gutter-type oil receiver that supplies oil to the gears through drilled passages in the transmission shafts, figure 2-31. Remove any sludge or residue from the oil pocket or receiver and make sure all oil passages are clear. During gearbox reassembly, make sure the lubrication grooves in the components on the transmission shafts are properly aligned with the shaft oil holes.

Transmission Mounted Switches and Sensors

Speedometer Drive Gear Service

Speedometer gears and or speedometer sensors are mounted on the output shaft of RWD transmissions, figure 2-32.

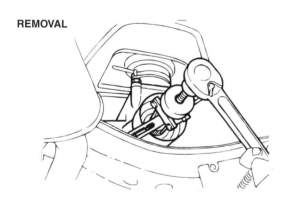

REMOVAL

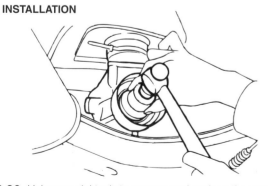

INSTALLATION

Fig. 2-30. Using special tools to remove and replace the rear transmission seal.

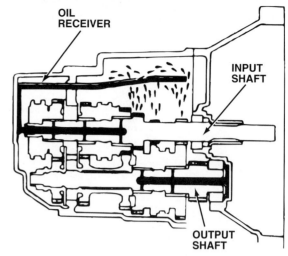

Fig. 2-31. Some transmissions lubricate the gears through oil passages drilled in the shafts.

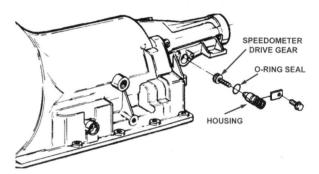

Fig. 2-32. Inspect the speedometer drive gear for excessive wear or damage.

In a transaxle the speedometer drive gear or sensor reluctor is generally mounted on the governor shaft of the RH axle shaft.

Most drive gears are attached to the output shaft with a spring clip or pin. Inspect all components of the drive gear assembly for signs of excessive wear or damage. If the gear requires replacement make sure to use the correct replacement part; otherwise, speedometer calibration will be affected.

Vehicle Speed Sensor Service

The speedometer drive gear is mounted on the output shaft of RWD vehicles, and on the output shaft of the transfer case in four wheel/all wheel drive vehicles. Transaxle speedometer assemblies may be driven by the right side output shaft or the differential carrier assembly.

Late-model vehicles replace the speedometer drive gear with an output shaft speed sensor (OSS) or vehicle speed sensor (VSS), figure 2-33. These sensors send an electrical signal to the Powertrain Control Module (PCM) or Transmission Control Module (TCM). The control module converts the signal into a speed signal for use by other vehicle modules and the speedometer in the instrument cluster.

A3

Slip Yoke: A variable length connection in the driveline that allows the driveshaft to change lengths. Also known as slip joints.

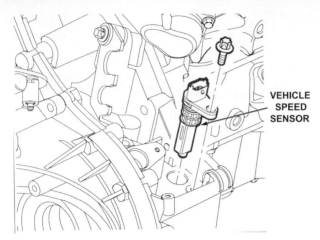

Fig. 2-33. Vehicle Speed Sensor.

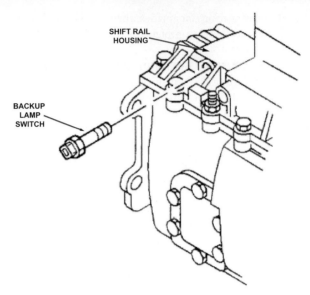

Fig. 2-34. Many manual transmissions and transaxles mount the backup lamp switch on the shift rail or shift fork housing.

Diagnosis of these speed sensors is normally accomplished through the use of a scan tool following the procedures outlined in the vehicle Service Manual. Sensor signals can also be tested using an **oscilloscope** to view the waveform produced.

Refer to the appropriate Service Manual for the proper diagnostic procedures for all switches and sensors.

Range Switches or Sensors

Many transmissions and transaxles are equipped with a multiple contact switch or sensor that sends a signal to the PCM indicating the gear range selected, figure 2-34. The input signals are used for adjusting engine timing and fuel injection parameters, and illuminating the backup lamps when reverse is engaged.

Oscilloscope: An oscilloscope is an instrument commonly used to display and analyze the waveform of electronic signals. In effect, the device draws a graph of the instantaneous signal voltage as a function of time. Also known as a lab scope.

CHAPTER QUESTIONS

1. Worn transmission bearings make
   a. Clunking sound on acceleration
   b. Knock or click on every other wheel revolution
   c. Rough growl or grating sound
   d. Sound loudest on corners

2. A clunk on deceleration can be caused by a worn:
   a. Drive axle inner joint
   b. Drive axle outer joint
   c. 1-2 synchronizer assembly
   d. 3-4 synchronizer assembly

3. Which of the following oils should not be used in transmissions where synchronizer unit wear is a concern?
   a. 75W-90 GLS
   b. 80W-90 EP
   c. 10W-30 SF
   d. ATF

4. When inspecting shift linkage, always replace any worn:
   a. Bushings
   b. Grease fittings
   c. Cross shafts
   d. Spring washers

5. A double bump when shifting a manual transmission is a sign of:
   a. Blockout
   b. Gear clash
   c. Hard shifting
   d. Synchromesh failure

6. A synchronizer hub sleeve that does not slide smoothly over the blocking ring and gear teeth can cause:
   a. Noise
   b. Blockout
   c. Hard shifting
   d. Synchromesh failure

7. A bad rear output shaft bearing will cause noise:
   a. During deceleration
   b. During acceleration
   c. While turning
   d. All the time

8. Most RWD transmissions have a one-piece:
   a. Output gear assembly
   b. Input gear assembly
   c. Countergear assembly
   d. Synchronizer assembly

9. Sealed bearings can be:
   a. Cleaned
   b. Inspected for wear
   c. Lubricated
   d. Disassembled

10. Differential case preload helps maintain:
    a. Ring gear position
    b. Pinion gear position
    c. Ring gear angle
    d. Pinion gear angle

11. While draining a transmission the technician can see brass colored particles in the drain oil. Technician A says the cause is a worn countershaft. Technician B says it is from a worn synchro assembly. Who is right?
    a. A only
    b. B only
    c. Both A and B
    d. Neither A nor B

12. A four-speed transmission has a noise in all forward gears except fourth. Technician A says the countershaft is at fault. Technician B says the noise is in the output shaft. Who is right?
    a. A only
    b. B only
    c. Both A and B
    d. Neither A nor B

13. There is excessive endplay in the countershaft of a four-speed transmission. Technician A says noise will occur in all lower gears. Technician B says excessive backlash will occur in fourth gear. Who is right?
    a. A only
    b. B only
    c. Both A and B
    d. Neither A nor B

14. A manual transaxle shifts fine but jumps out of second gear. Technician A says the problem is a worn input shaft bearing. Technician B says the problem is the second-gear blocking ring. Who is right?
    a. A only
    b. B only
    c. Both A and B
    d. Neither A nor B

15. Technician A says changing tire size can affect speedometer readings. Technician B says changing the rear axle ratio can affect speedometer readings. Who is right?
    a. A only
    b. B only
    c. Both A and B
    d. Neither A nor B

A3

CHAPTER OBJECTIVES

- The technician will complete the ASE task list on Driveline and Axle Service.
- The technician will be able to answer 5 questions dealing with the Driveline and Axle Service section of the A3 ASE Test.

DRIVESHAFT DIAGNOSIS AND REPAIR

Driveshaft service for shafts fitted to rear-wheel drive (RWD) vehicles consists of:

- Visually inspecting the driveshaft
- Balancing the driveshaft
- Checking and adjusting driveshaft angles
- Inspecting the slip yoke and slip joint
- Servicing universal joints (U-joints)
- Removing the driveshaft for further inspection

Driveshaft Inspection

Position the vehicle on a hoist and check the driveshaft for:

- Loose or rusty U-joints
- Dents

Rust found at the bearing cups indicates lubrication failure. Damage to the driveshaft tube can cause excessive vibration. Check driveshaft runout with a dial indicator. Remove surface rust in the area you want to check to give the indicator a smooth surface to ride on. Check the runout specifications for the vehicle you are working on. As a general rule, total runout

should not exceed 0.015 inch (0.38 mm). The ends of the shaft should have less runout, approximately 0.010 inch (0.25 mm).

This is also a good time to look for leaks at the transmission and the rear axle. Usually, the transmission rear seal and bushing cause transmission leaks, and the pinion seal or companion flange causes rear axle leaks. Both can be serviced on the vehicle.

Bent Driveshaft Shafts

A bent driveshaft can cause a vibration in the vehicle. If a bent driveshaft is suspected, the technician will need to perform a runout check on the driveshaft. The dial indicator must be placed at a 90 degree angle from the driveshaft for accurate readings, figure 3-1. Measure the runout 3 inches (76.2 mm) from each yolk weld and verify it is within the specifications in the Service Manual. Then take a second measurement in the center of the driveshaft to verify it is within specifications. If the runout is not within the specifications, the driveshaft must be replaced.

Driveshaft Vibration

Driveshaft vibrations can be classified into four different orders: **first-order**, **second-order**, and **fourth-order**. A first-order vibration may be caused by a bent or out-of-balance driveshaft condition. A second-order vibration may be caused by driveshaft angle, U-joint cancellation, and bad U-joints. A fourth-order vibration may be caused by a bad U-joint. A **third-order** vibration is often caused by a defective tripod joint on a FWD vehicle.

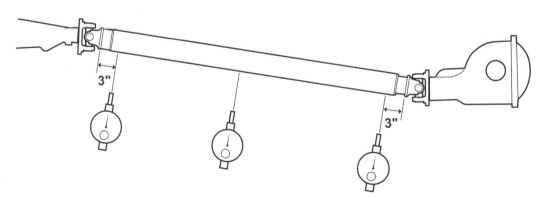

Fig. 3-1. Use a dial indicator to check runout at both ends and near the center of the driveshaft.

First-Order Vibration: A condition that causes one disturbance per revolution of a component.
Fourth-Order Vibration: A condition that causes four disturbances per revolution.
Second-Order Vibration: A condition that causes two disturbances per revolution of a component.
Third-Order Vibration: A condition that causes three disturbances per revolution of a component.

Frequency

Frequency is the number of complete cycles that occur in one second, figure 3-2. Sound and vibration waves are measured in Hz, or Cycles Per Second (CPS). One Hz is equal to one CPS. The sound wave in figure 3-3 has a frequency of 6 Hz because it completes six CPS. The frequency of a sound or vibration can aid in troubleshooting a driveshaft concern.

Vibration Order

Order is the number of disturbances created in one revolution of a component. A single high spot on a tire causes one disturbance per revolution and creates a first-order disturbance. If the wheel rotates 10 times per second, there are 10 disturbances per second. This creates a first-order disturbance of 10 Hz. If the tire developed a second high spot, a second-order disturbance would result. The wheel rotating 10 times per second produces 20 disturbances per second. This creates a second-order disturbance of 20 Hz. Three high spots create a third-order disturbance, and four high spots create a fourth-order disturbance. Higher order disturbances continue to progress in this way.

Order can aid the technician while troubleshooting. For example: a vehicle has an NVH concern that is producing a vibration at 68 Hz. After calculating driveshaft frequency, it is determined the driveshaft has a frequency of 34 Hz. The second-order frequency of the driveshaft is 68 Hz. This matches the frequency of the NVH concern.

By determining that the NVH concern is a possible second-order vibration, you would look at components that could cause a vibration of this type. U-joints would be a good component to check because it is possible they could produce two disturbances with each revolution of the driveshaft. A missing driveshaft weight could be eliminated from the list

of possibilities because this situation would produce a vibration of the first-order.

An unbalanced driveshaft causes a first-order vibration that occurs with changes in road speed but not engine speed. To test for a driveshaft vibration, drive in high gear at the speed where the vibration is most severe. Then, shift to a lower gear but maintain the same speed. If the vibration does not change, suspect the driveshaft.

Driveshaft Balancing Procedures

Balance the wheels and tires first. If wheel and tire balancing do not eliminate a vibration, inspect the driveline. Check the driveshaft for deposits, such as undercoating compounds, and look for dents or other signs of physical damage.

Using an Electronic Vibration Analyzer (EVA)

To balance a driveshaft using an **Electronic Vibration Analyzer (EVA)**, begin by raising the vehicle on the hoist and supporting it by the axle to maintain the driveline angle and prevent the wheels from contacting the ground.

To set up the EVA to balance the driveshaft, place the sensor at the twelve o'clock position on the rear axle input housing and connect it to the input on the EVA. Connect the strobe light to the inductive pickup trigger wire on the EVA and point it at the driveshaft at the six o'clock position, figure 3-4. Also, connect the strobe light to the battery for power. Next, mark the driveshaft at 90 degree intervals and number them from 1 to 4; place a shorter mark halfway between each mark. The procedure to balance the driveshaft is as follows:

1. Have another technician start the vehicle, put it in drive, and run the vehicle at the speed of the vibration.
2. Hold the strobe light at the six o'clock position and determine where the driveshaft is at using the marks on the shaft.
3. Stop the vehicle and place a hose clamp on the driveshaft so the adjustment is at the noted position.
4. Check for the vibration by having another technician repeat step one. If the vibration is gone, add the correct amount of weight at the clamp location and remove the clamp. If the vibration is still present, repeat the procedure and note the new location. The amount of weight may be more or less than the weight of the clamp.

Driveshaft Balance Without Electronic Equipment

Begin by disconnecting the driveshaft from the pinion flange, rotate the shaft 180 degrees, and reinstall it. Road test the vehicle. This procedure frequently solves the problem. If the shaft is still unbalanced, balance it as follows:

1. Support the vehicle on a twin-post hoist with the rear axle housing supported and the wheels free to rotate.
2. Start the engine. Place the transmission in a forward gear and slowly accelerate from zero to 80 MPH. Note the speeds where the vibration is most obvious. Driveline vibrations commonly occur twice: first at approximately 35 MPH (40 kph) and then again at 55 to 60 MPH (90 to 100 kph).

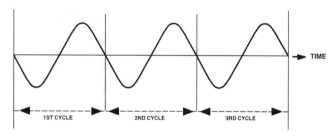

Fig. 3-2. Cycle is the path a wave travels before the wave begins to repeat the path again.

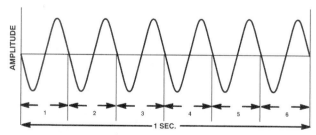

THIS FREQUENCY EQUALS 6 CYCLES PER SECOND (CPS) OR 6 Hz.

Fig. 3-3. Frequency is the number of complete cycles that occur in one second.

Electronic Vibration Analyzer (EVA): A special diagnostic tool capable of reading vibration frequency and amplitude and displaying the results on an LCD screen.

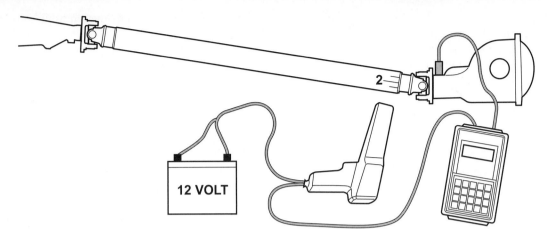

Fig. 3-4. Electronic equipment setup for measuring driveshaft vibration.

3. Brake to a stop, place the transmission in neutral, and switch off the engine.
4. Number the front driveshaft bearing cups from one to four. Attach two screw-type hose clamps to the shaft so their screw ends are opposite the "1" bearing cup, figure 3-5. Repeat steps two and three.
5. If vibration improves, add another weight (hose clamp) and retest. If no improvement is noticed, move the clamps to the "2" bearing cup position and retest. Continue this procedure through the remaining positions to identify the position where vibration diminishes.
6. Repeat the procedure at the remaining U-joint assemblies to remove vibrations.

Driveshaft Angles

Incorrect driveshaft angles can also cause vibration, especially during acceleration. The vibration can often be felt but not heard. Special gauges known as inclinometers are used to measure driveline angles. Several types of inclinometers are available ranging from simple bubble or spirit protractors, figure 3-6, to more elaborate electronic devices. All may be used to measure universal joint angles.

To adjust front U-joint drive angles, add or remove shims under the rear transmission mount. To adjust rear U-joint angles, place tapered shims between the rear leaf springs and the axle housing, or adjust the control arm linkages on coil spring suspensions.

Slip Yoke

A driveshaft slip yoke generally does not require routine service because the yoke splines and outside surface are lubricated by transmission lubricant. However, some do require periodic lubrication with grease to their splines. Check the Service Manual specifications for proper grease type and recommended service intervals. Leaks around the output shaft can be caused by a worn seal or output shaft bushing or by damage to the yoke surface.

Driveshaft Removal

Before removing a driveshaft from the vehicle, mark its position in relation to the transmission and differential, figure 3-7. If **Cardan U-joints** are used at both ends of the shaft, unbolt the joints and remove the shaft. If a single Cardan U-joint is used at the rear of the shaft, unbolt the joint and separate it from the

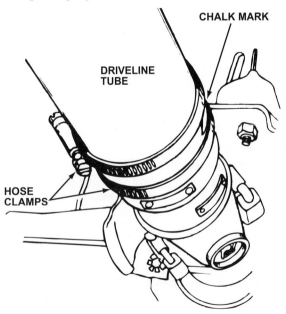

CLAMPS 180 DEGREES FROM CHALK MARK

Fig. 3-5. Hose clamps can be used to check and locate driveshaft imbalance.

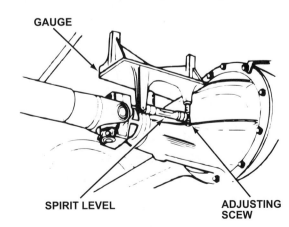

Fig. 3-6. A special level is used to measure driveline angles.

Cardan U-Joint: A U-joint that consists of a metal cross with four needle bearings at each point. This is the most common type of U-joint for a RWD driveshaft. Double Cardan joints have two crosses.

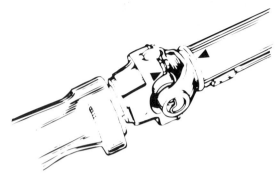

Fig. 3-7. Mark the position of the driveshaft to the transmission and companion flange before you remove it to avoid a balance problem on assembly.

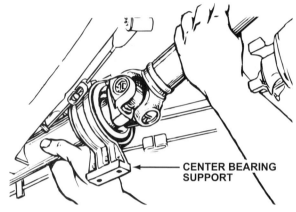

CENTER BEARING SUPPORT

Fig. 3-8. Unbolt the center support and remove it as part of the assembly when working on a two-piece driveshaft.

pinion yoke or companion flange. Slide the shaft rearward off the vehicle, pulling the slip yoke out of the transmission. Look at the rear U-joint and tape the bearing cups together, in order to avoid losing the bearing cups and needle bearings.

For a two-piece driveshaft, use the above procedure to remove the driveshaft from the companion flange, then loosen the center bearing support, figure 3-8. Do not allow the rear shaft to drop or hang from the center bearing.

As you continue to remove the center support bolts, remove the driveshaft assembly as a unit from the rear of the

transmission. Inspect the driveshaft for damage. Then, inspect the slip yoke, universal joints, and center support bearing for wear. Replace any worn parts. Also, check the transmission output shaft seal and replace it if needed.

Driveshaft Installation

Before reinstalling a driveshaft, lubricate all splines and sliding joints. Specially formulated grease is used to reduce friction at the slip yoke.

Driveshaft Phasing

When reinstalling multiple-piece driveshafts, make sure to verify that the universal joints are correctly phased, figure 3-9. Failure to do so will result in vibration and potential damage to bearings and synchronizers from the vibration.

Servicing Universal Joints

Most factory-installed universal joints cannot be lubricated unless they are disassembled. Some factory-installed and most aftermarket U-joints have grease fittings, commonly called zerk fittings, figure 3-10. Grease should be pumped into the joint until fresh lube appears at each cap. If lube does not appear at each cap, disassemble the joint and inspect for damage or contamination.

When replacing universal joints, you may need to know which of two basic types of Cardan U-joint you have. One type is held in place by internal snaprings that fit into grooves at the outer ends of the yokes. The other type is held in place by "C" clips or snaprings that fit into grooves in the bearing cups, figure 3-11.

If you anticipate reinstalling a U-joint when you remove it, mark the position of each bearing, cross, and yoke for proper reassembly. If snaprings are used, loosen them by driving one bearing cup slightly inward. The bearing cups on some universal joints are held in the yokes by molded plastic rings. These will shear when the bearing cup is forced from the yoke. Replacement universal joints will have special bearing cups with internal grooves for snapring installation and bearing cup installation.

If a special removal tool is not available, place the joint in a bench vise with a large socket, bigger in diameter than the

A3

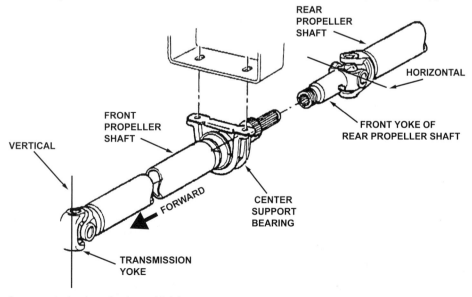

Fig. 3-9. Procedure for correct phasing of universal joints.

Fig. 3-10. Some U-joints have grease fittings to permit periodic lubrication.

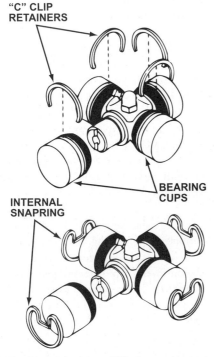

Fig. 3-11. Two types of retainer, "C" clips and snaprings, are used to hold a Cardan U-joint in place.

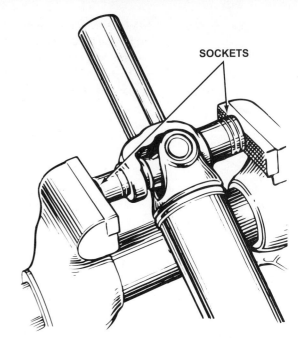

Fig. 3-12. Using sockets and a bench vise to disassemble a Cardan U-joint.

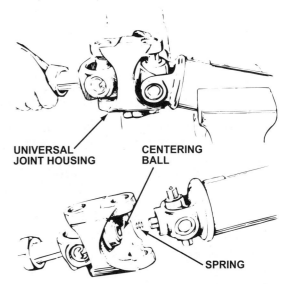

Fig. 3-13. The centering ball and spring must be correctly positioned to maintain alignment on a double Cardan U-joint.

bearing cup, against the yoke and a smaller socket against the opposite bearing, figure 3-12. Closing the vise drives the bearing from the yoke into the larger socket. If this procedure does not force the bearing all the way out, clamp the exposed portion in the vise and drive upward on the yoke with a rubber mallet. Inspect the cross, bearings, and bearing cup assemblies for wear. Replace the entire joint if any wear is found.

To reassemble the joint, insert the cross in its original position inside the yoke. When installing a new universal joint with the zerk fitting, assemble it so that the fitting faces the driveshaft. Make sure all of the needle bearings are in position in the cup and lightly coated with grease. Position the bearing cups in the yoke bores, and press them into position with a bench

vise and suitably sized sockets. Use new snaprings to secure the U-joint in place.

On double Cardan universal joints, figure 3-13, be careful to install the centering ball correctly to maintain U-joint alignment. Also, make sure the spring in the linking yoke is in good condition and properly centered.

FRONT-WHEEL DRIVE AXLE INSPECTION AND REPAIR

Front-wheel drive (FWD) axle inspection and repair involves inspecting and replacing **constant-velocity joints** (CV joints) and removing and replacing axle shafts.

Constant-Velocity Joint: A type of U-joint that transmits torque in a greater range of angles without damage. Commonly known as CV joints, they are used on most FWD axles and on RWD vehicles with independent rear suspension.

Constant-Velocity Joint Inspection

A modern CV joint can be expected to last about 100,000 miles (160, 000 km), but without proper lubrication, it will wear much faster. Most CV joint failures are due to a lack of lubrication and/or contamination caused by a torn boot. Always check CV joint boots for damage to ensure that lubricant remains in the joint.

Outer CV joints, at the wheel end of the axle shaft, usually wear more quickly than the inner joints because they are subject to a variety of axle shaft operating angles. The shaft at the outer CV joint may move as much as 40 degrees to compensate for suspension and steering angles. Normal operating angles at the inner CV joint are only about 10 to 20 degrees.

When checking CV joint boots, raise the vehicle on a hoist and use a trouble light. Wipe grease and dirt from the boot, so that you can see any small tears or punctures. Check that the boot clamps are secure. Also, check to be sure that oil or coolant is not leaking on the boots, since this contaminates the rubber, making the boots weak and prone to tears. Also, look for cracking, flaking, and other signs of rubber deterioration.

Usually, if the boot is damaged, then the CV joint is worn. This is because, as a CV joint turns, centrifugal force pushes grease outward, forcing it through even the tiniest of openings in the boot. This lack of lubrication, coupled with the constant movement of the joint, quickly leads to CV joint failure. In addition, a damaged boot allows dirt, water, and other contaminants into the joint.

If the boot is damaged, remove it. You may have to remove the axle shaft first, which is described in the following section. Place a small amount of grease from inside the boot between your fingertips and rub your fingers together. If the grease feels gritty, replace the CV joint, as described later in this chapter. If the grease feels smooth, you may have caught the problem before any damage was done to the joint. If this is the case, pack the joint with grease and install a new boot, which will be described later in this chapter.

Axle Shaft Removal

Use this procedure as a guide to remove axle shafts and CV joints. Note that after completing step seven, the procedure will vary between manufacturers. On some vehicles, you must disconnect the inner CV joint from the transaxle or differential first, then remove the outer CV joint from the knuckle. However, most vehicle manufacturers suggest that you disconnect the outer CV joint first, which is the method we will cover here.

1. Remove the wheel cover to expose the wheel nuts and spindle or hub nut.
2. With the vehicle on the ground, have an assistant apply the brakes while you loosen the spindle nut with a breaker bar. Do not use an impact wrench. The vibrations from the wrench can damage the CV joint and wheel bearings. Some vehicles have a locking tab that you must pry away from the nut before you can turn it.
3. Loosen the wheel nuts and raise the vehicle on a hoist.
4. Remove the wheels.
5. Drain the fluid from the transaxle or differential using the manufacturer's recommended procedure.

6. Place a drain pan under the differential or transaxle to catch lubricant that leaks out while you are removing the inboard CV joints.
7. Secure suspension springs. Then, disconnect suspension and steering components from the wheel knuckle. The procedures from this point will vary from manufacturer to manufacturer, as discussed earlier.
8. Remove the loosened spindle nut. Then, pull the wheel hub and knuckle to separate the axle shaft and CV joint from the knuckle. For some vehicles, you may need a special tool to press the axle shaft from the knuckle. Do not try to pull the axle shaft from the knuckle because this may cause the joint to break apart. Instead, pull the CV joint housing, if needed. If the vehicle has anti-lock brakes, there may be a toothed gear on the outer CV joint. This gear sends signals to the anti-lock brake system (ABS) controller and must not be damaged, so handle it carefully.
9. Disconnect the inner CV joint from the differential or transaxle. Check the inner CV joint for roll pins, Torx head bolts, or 12-point star bolts that secure the CV joint to the transaxle. If you find these fasteners, remove them. On some automatic transmissions, you must remove the differential cover and remove a C-clip on the end of the axle shaft.
10. Grasp the inner CV joint housing and pull it to separate the axle shaft from the transaxle. Pull the housing gradually so the axle shaft oil seal is not damaged. Use the proper puller to remove the CV joint housing from the transaxle, figure 3-14. If you are working on a vehicle with inner tripod joints, do not pull on the axle shaft, since this may cause the inner CV joint to break apart. Instead, pull the inner CV joint housing while supporting the outer end of the shaft until the shaft releases from the transaxle. Do not use a hammer to separate the CV joint from the transaxle, or you risk damaging the joint.

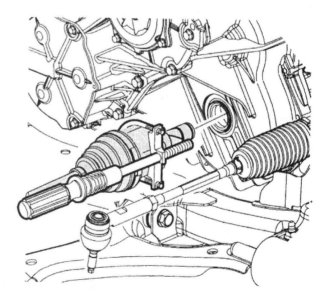

Fig. 3-14. Use the appropriate puller to remove the CV joint housing from the transaxle.

A3

- On some vehicles' automatic transmissions, you must remove only one axle shaft at a time. If you remove both joints, components in the transaxle may rotate slightly and become misaligned.
- Many manufacturers provide special tools that keep transaxle parts aligned while the CV joints are removed. Check the vehicle Service Manual for specific instructions.

Removing and Replacing a CV Joint

If the CV joints are worn and can be separated from the axle shaft, use the following procedure as a guide to remove and replace them. On some vehicles, you must replace the CV joints and axle shaft as a unit.

1. Clamp the axle shaft assembly in a soft-jaw vise.
2. Remove the boot clamps and cut away the boots, figure 3-15. Never reuse old boots.
3. Locate the snapring that holds the CV joint in place and remove it with snapring pliers.
4. Separate the CV joint from the axle shaft. Gently tap the CV joint housing with a soft-face hammer to drive it from the shaft if necessary.
5. Inspect the splines on the end of the axle shaft. If they are chipped or worn, replace the axle shaft.
6. Before installing a new CV joint, match it up to the old one and check the part number to be sure that it is the correct replacement.
7. Wrap tape around the axle shaft splines. This prevents the splines from ripping the new boot as you install it onto the shaft.
8. Slip the new CV joint boot onto the shaft, then remove the tape from the axle shaft splines.
9. Fit the new CV joint onto the axle shaft splines. Tap the joint onto the axle with a soft-face hammer until you hear a click as the snapring drops into the groove. Tug on the joint to make sure the snapring has engaged.
10. Pack the CV joint using the correct amount of recommended grease, figure 3-16. The incorrect grease may contaminate the boot. Often the CV joint boot kit comes with grease. Never mix greases. Use the quantity of grease supplied with the boot; do not overpack the joint.
11. Slip the boot end over the joint housing and install the clamps to secure it to the housing and the axle.

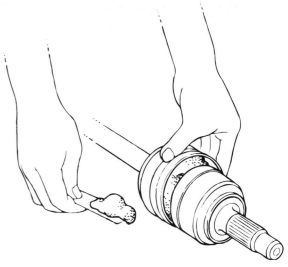

Fig. 3-16. Pack the CV joint with the correct amount of the recommended grease.

12. Install the axle shaft/CV joint assembly in the vehicle.
13. Check wheel alignment after replacing CV joints.

Be aware that some vehicles use boots manufactured of special materials. Special replacement clamps and pliers are required when installing these boots to be sure they seal properly.

There are two-piece or "split" replacement boots available for some CV joint applications. However, these are not recommended by most vehicle manufacturers. Split boots are bolted or glued together, and the glue must cure for two to four hours. Bolt-together boots, if not properly installed, will allow CV joint contamination. Single-piece CV joint boots are the best choice, although you must remove the axle shaft to install this type of boot.

Axle Shaft Installation

To install a transaxle axle shaft, take the following steps:

1. Install a new circlip retainer on the CV joint stub. Align the stub splines with the differential splines and push the CV joint inward until the circlip seats.
2. Install the outboard CV joint by engaging the stub shaft splines with the hub splines. Use a hub tool to seat the stub shaft in the hub. Be careful to avoid damaging the front wheel seals.
3. Attach the lower ball joint nut to the steering knuckle and tighten it to specification.
4. Install the brake hose clip, if used.
5. Install the washer and fit a new nut onto the axle stub hand tight.
6. Install the wheel and tighten the wheel nuts to the specified torque.
7. Lower the vehicle and torque the hub nut to specifications, generally 180 to 200 ft-lbs (240 to 270 Nm). Do not use an impact wrench to tighten the nut; this can damage the CV joints and wheel bearings.
8. On many vehicles, you must stake the nut collar into a slot in the axle shaft. Use a dull or rounded chisel that will not split or crack the nut. If the nut does crack or split, replace it.

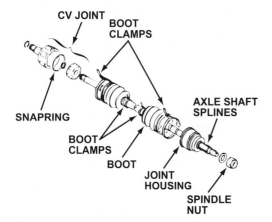

Fig. 3-15. Clamps secure the boot to the axle and the CV joint housing.

REAR-WHEEL DRIVE AXLE AND BEARING REPAIR

The axle shafts on RWD vehicles seldom require repair, but axle bearings and seals are common replacement items. Axles may be semi-floating or full-floating types. Three types of axle bearings are used: the radial ball, the tapered roller, and the straight cylindrical roller, figure 3-17.

In a semi-floating axle, the more common of the two, the axle seal is inside and pressed into the axle housing, figure 3-18. The bearing is pressed onto the axle shaft with a bearing retainer plate on the outside of the bearing and bolted through the backing plate to the axle housing. The axle supports the vehicle weight and drives the wheels. On some semi-floating axles, a flange on the outer end of the axle shaft supports the wheels and brake drum, figure 3-19. Other axle designs use a tapered axle shaft, with a locating key to position the flange and hub assembly, and a retaining nut and washer.

With a full-floating axle, the bearings, which support the vehicle weight, are installed in the wheel hub assembly. This hub assembly rides on the axle housing and is held in place by retaining nuts. The axle only drives the wheel hub and does not support the vehicle weight. Lubricant is sealed into the housing by a seal located on the inside of the wheel hub, and by a gasket between the axle flange and the outer end of the wheel hub.

Typically, C-locks hold the semi-floating axle in the rear housing, figure 3-20. Ball bearing and taper roller bearing axles use a retaining plate to hold the axle in place, figure 3-21.

Wheel Stud Inspection

Never use heat to loosen a tight wheel. It can shorten the life of the wheel, studs, or hub and bearing assemblies. Penetrating oil is not effective in removing tight wheels. However, if used, apply the penetrating oil sparingly to the hub surface only. Excessive force, such as hammering the wheel or the tire, may cause damage. Lightly tap the tire sidewall with a rubber mallet to loosen the wheel.

A torque wrench must be used to ensure that wheel nuts are tightened to specification. Never use lubricants or penetrating fluids on wheel stud, nuts, or mounting surfaces, as this can raise the actual torque on the nut without a corresponding torque reading on the torque wrench. Wheel nuts, studs, and mounting surfaces must be clean and dry. Failure to follow these instructions could result in wheel, nut, and/or stud damage.

A3

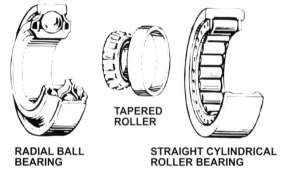

Fig. 3-17. The three types of bearing used on RWD axles.

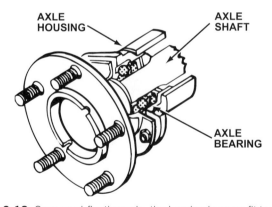

Fig. 3-18. On a semi-floating axle, the bearing is press fit to the shaft and supports the weight of the vehicle.

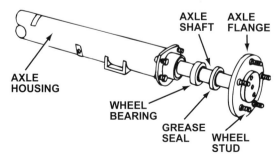

Fig. 3-19. The wheel attaches to a flange that is part of the axle shaft on this semi-floating design.

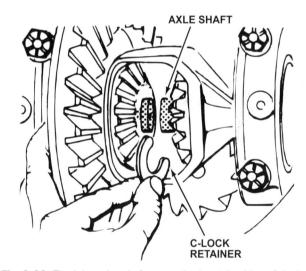

Fig. 3-20. The inboard end of some axles is retained by a C-lock.

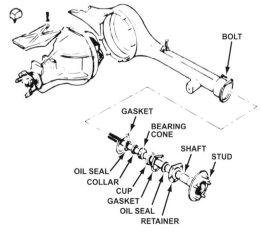

Fig. 3-21. A retainer plate bolts onto the axle housing to hold this semi-floating axle in place.

Axle Bearing Service

Axle bearing service consists of removing and inspecting the axle bearings, replacing the bearing seals, and reinstalling the bearings. The subsections that follow describe these procedures.

Removing Axle Bearings

To repair axle bearings and seals, you need to remove the axle shaft from the housing first. Usually, the wheel and brake drum are removed first, followed by the axle or bearing retainers. Use a slide-hammer puller to remove the axle and bearing from the housing. Once the axle is out of the way, remove the seal from the axle housing with a slide-hammer or seal puller.

Most bearings have a press-fit retaining ring on the inside of the bearing. Strike the retainer with a chisel in several places to distort it enough to remove it. Remove the bearing from the axle shaft with a special tool or in a press using a bearing splitter. When using these tools to remove the axle bearings, direct the force only to the inner race.

On some axle bearings, the bearing must be disassembled before you can press off the inner race. It may be necessary to cut the outer race and cage so that these parts can be removed along with the rollers. After the bearing is apart, remove the inner race as described above.

Inspecting Bearings

Thoroughly inspect the bearings after you remove them from the axle, even if you plan to replace them with new ones. The condition of the bearings can tell you a lot about the condition of the axle components, figure 3-22.

Installing Axle Bearings

Measure the inside diameter, outside diameter, and height of a new bearing to verify that it is the correct replacement. Also, check the axle shaft once more for any signs of damage.

Begin installation by fitting the axle retainer plate on the axle, followed by the bearing. Place a bearing splitter or special tool under the bearing and retaining ring. Make sure the

POOR LUBRICATION

CONTAMINATED LUBRICANT

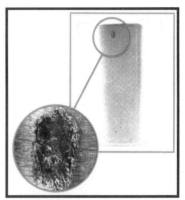

ARC WELDING DAMAGE

LARGE PARTICLE CONTAMINATION

METAL-TO-METAL CONTACT

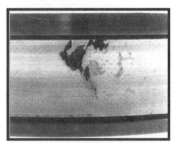

SPALLING FROM DEBRIS

EXCESSIVE PRELOAD

ABRASIVE WEAR

BEARING SEIZURE

Fig. 3-22. Common tapered roller bearing failures.

splitter or tool contacts only the inner bearing race. Place the assembly in a press, and press the bearing firmly into place, figure 3-23. Repeat this procedure for the installation of the bearing retainer.

Installing Axle Seals

Before you reinstall an axle shaft into the axle housing, always replace the axle seal. Be careful not to damage the seal surface around the outside edge of the seal. Coat the outer edge of the new seal with a non-hardening gasket sealant, and coat the inner lip of the seal with grease to retain the inner spring. Be sure the lip of the seal is facing into the axle housing. Use a seal driver to install the seal squarely.

Installing Axles

Reinstalling axles is a simple procedure in most cases. Make sure you have replaced all bearings, seals, and retaining clips before installing the axle. Carefully slide the axle shaft through the new seal to avoid damaging the seal.

After successfully installing the seal and before installing the axle shaft into the housing, check axle shaft and axle flange runout using V blocks and a dial indicator.

Some axles with tapered roller bearings require endplay adjustment. Two oil seals are used, one to the inside and one to the outside of the bearing. An adjuster nut threads into the axle retainer plate to set the axle endplay.

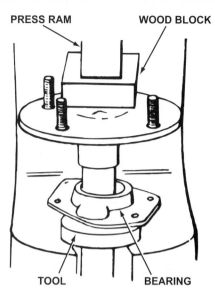

Fig. 3-23. Using a press to install a bearing onto a semi-floating axle.

Make the adjustment by setting a dial indicator against the axle. Turn the adjuster nut until the total endplay, as read on the dial indicator, is within specifications. This adjustment is for the endplay of both axles but is made from one side only.

A3

CHAPTER QUESTIONS

1. An unbalanced driveshaft causes a vibration that:
   a. Increases as vehicle speed increases
   b. Decreases as engine speed increases
   c. Has equal intensity at identical speeds
   d. Decreases with improved road conditions

2. Driveshaft imbalance can sometimes be cured by:
   a. Rotating the shaft half a turn, then reinstalling it
   b. Placing hose clamps on the heavy side
   c. Both a and b
   d. Neither a nor b

3. On a RWD car, front U-joint drive angles can be corrected by:
   a. Placing shims under the rear coil springs
   b. Placing shims under the rear leaf springs
   c. Adjusting control arm linkages
   d. Adding shims under the rear transmission mount

4. Driveshaft slip yokes are generally lubricated:
   a. With grease fittings
   b. By the transmission lubrication system
   c. Every 6,000 miles
   d. By hand

5. The proper way to repair a torn CV joint boot is to:
   a. Repack the CV joint and install a split boot
   b. Repack the CV joint and reseal the boot
   c. Replace the CV joint and boot
   d. Replace the axle assembly

6. In a full-floating axle:
   a. The axle seal is pressed into the inside of the axle housing
   b. The axle supports the weight of the vehicle
   c. The bearings on the axle housing support the weight of the vehicle
   d. A flange on the end of the axle supports the wheels

7. All of the following are used to support the outer ends of axle shafts *EXCEPT*:
   a. Roller bearings
   b. Tapered roller bearings
   c. Ball bearings
   d. Trunnion bearings

8. The best tool for removing a RWD axle and bearing from a housing is:
   a. A hammer
   b. A slide-hammer
   c. A chisel
   d. An arbor

9. Brinelling is a bearing wear condition where:
   a. Metal smears on roller ends due to overheating
   b. The surface appears gray or grayish black
   c. The surface has corroded due to lack of lubrication
   d. The raceway has surface indentations

10. Axles that require endplay adjustments generally use:
    a. Thrust bushings
    b. Thrust washers
    c. Tapered roller bearings
    d. Ball bearings

CHAPTER FOUR

DIFFERENTIAL SERVICE

CHAPTER OBJECTIVES

- The technician will complete the ASE task list on Differential Service.
- The technician will be able to answer 7 questions dealing with the Differential Service section of the A3 ASE Test.

DIFFERENTIAL DIAGNOSIS

Two types of differential assemblies are used on modern vehicles: the removable carrier and the integral housing. The removable carrier must be removed from the vehicle for repair, figure 4-1. The integral housing, sometimes called a Spicer or Salisbury differential, can be repaired on the vehicle and is identified by the presence of an inspection cover, figure 4-2.

Typically, customers complain of noise or lubricant leakage coming from the differential or rear axle assembly. Differential problem diagnosis consists of road testing the vehicle to confirm the customer complaint and a preliminary inspection to isolate the problem area first. This is followed by a mechanical inspection of the differential, which includes disassembly, to confirm the diagnosis.

The Road Test and Preliminary Inspection

In order to get accurate information from a road test, the vehicle must be driven long enough to allow the differential lubricant to reach operating temperature. Once warmed up,

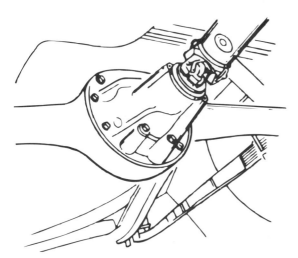

Fig. 4-1. A removable carrier differential cannot be repaired on the vehicle.

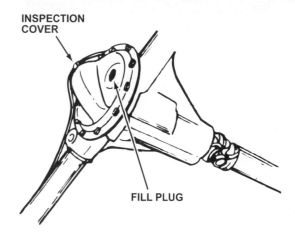

Fig. 4-2. An integral housing differential can be serviced on the vehicle by removing an inspection cover.

the test route should include roads that permit speeds from 25 to 55 MPH (40 to 90 kph) and curves at speeds of 25 to 35 MPH (40 to 60 kph). During the road test, listen for:

- Noise during acceleration
- Noise during deceleration
- Noise at a steady speed
- Intermittent noise
- Noise while turning
- Road speed noise

Noise During Acceleration

Noise heard during acceleration can be caused by a worn rear **pinion bearing** or improper gear tooth contact. As the pinion gear drives the ring gear, the two gears try to move away from each other. This action causes extreme loading of the rear pinion bearing, figure 4-3. If the bearing is worn, noise will be heard during acceleration and will disappear during deceleration or at steady speeds.

Noise During Deceleration

Noise heard while decelerating can be caused by a worn front pinion bearing, figure 4-4. The ring gear drives the pinion gear, causing front bearing load. This noise will disappear during acceleration or at steady speeds.

Pinion Bearing Inspection

If front or rear pinion bearing wear is suspected, disconnect the driveshaft from the differential and rotate the companion

Pinion Bearings: The bearings in a differential assembly that support the pinion gear shaft.

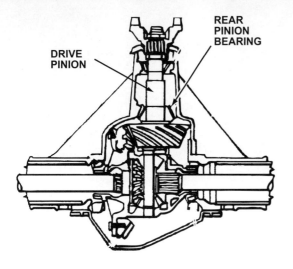

Fig. 4-3. A worn rear pinion bearing is noisy on acceleration, but quiets down at a steady cruise or during deceleration as the load decreases.

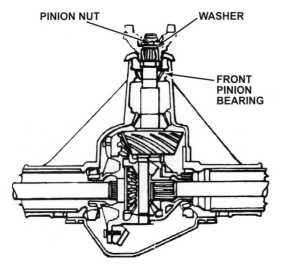

Fig. 4-4. A worn front pinion bearing is noisy only on deceleration because the ring gear is driving the pinion, and the load shifts toward the front of the pinion shaft.

flange by hand. Rotation should be smooth; rough rotation indicates a worn pinion bearing. An alternate method is to rotate the pinion gear with a dial-type, inch-pound torque wrench and observe the needle fluctuations. Large needle fluctuations indicate worn pinion bearings.

Noise at Steady Speed

Noise heard at a specific road speed can be caused by variations in the ring and pinion tooth contact patterns. A gear tooth contact pattern should be taken to identify gear set position. See "Checking Gear Tooth Contact" in the Mechanical Inspection section later in this chapter.

Intermittent Noise

Intermittent noise heard from the differential is often described as chuckle. The differential gears make this noise when differential pinion or side gear damage is present. During your road test, this sound is usually heard as you go around corners but may also be heard during acceleration or deceleration. Remove the differential carrier or inspection cover to inspect for damaged gear teeth.

Noise While Turning

Noise that is heard while turning is commonly called chatter. Chatter is a vibrating or banging noise from the differential assembly. Usually, the cause of chatter is a worn **limited-slip differential** assembly.

Vehicles with chatter problems should have the differential lubricant changed. Limited-slip differentials usually require a friction modifier additive. After changing the lubricant, the customer should be told to drive the vehicle for approximately 100 miles (160 kilometers) to ensure that the limited clutch assembly is fully lubricated. If the chatter persists, remove the differential assembly for further diagnosis.

Road Speed Noise

Road speed noise increases and decreases in proportion to road speed. It can be caused by the various differential components that increase their rotational speed proportional to road speed.

Tires, rear axle bearings, and differential case bearings can cause road speed noise. Inspect tires for proper inflation, irregular wear, and adequate tread. Tire noise does not change as the vehicle travels around a corner.

Rear axle bearings get noisier as road speed increases. Bearing noise increases when the axle bearing is loaded, such as when traveling around a corner.

Left turns cause right bearing noise, while right turns cause left bearing noise. To confirm the diagnosis, remove the axle or bearing assembly and inspect for wear.

Differential case bearing noise also increases with road speed. However, other symptoms are usually not present during a road test. The differential case must be removed to inspect the differential case bearings. Differential repair is discussed later in this chapter.

Mechanical Inspection

After road testing the vehicle to confirm the customer complaint and isolate the problem, you must perform various mechanical inspections to confirm the diagnosis. Mechanical inspection includes:

- Removing the driveshaft
- Checking total preload
- Checking backlash
- Checking ring gear runout
- Checking gear tooth contact

Limited-Slip Differential: A type of final drive differential that supplies a major part of the drive torque to the wheel with the greater traction when one of the wheels is slipping.

Removing the Driveshaft

You will have to get the driveshaft out of the way to perform most of the following mechanical inspections. Mark the driveshaft position in relation to the companion flange. Either remove the driveshaft or tie it to the rear suspension. Tape the U-joint bearing cups in place. Remove the tire and wheel assemblies.

Checking Total Preload

Total preload is measured by turning the pinion shaft with a dial-type, inch-pound torque wrench. Select a socket that properly fits the pinion nut and attach it to the torque wrench. To measure, smoothly rotate the pinion and ring gear assembly with the torque wrench and note the dial reading, figure 4-5. Record your measurement. Typically, differential bearings with normal wear provide a total reading of approximately 10 to 25 inch-pounds (1.13 to 3 Nm). If the dial needle fluctuates during rotation, the pinion or case bearings are probably worn.

Checking Backlash

Depending on the differential type, remove either the carrier assembly or the inspection cover. Drain the remaining lubricant, clean the ring gear teeth with a suitable solvent, and dry with compressed air. Attach a dial indicator to the differential housing, and position the indicator tip to the drive side of the ring gear tooth, figure 4-6. Zero the dial indicator, then gently rock the ring gear without turning the pinion as you observe the dial reading for the **backlash**. Rotate the ring gear 90 degrees at a time and record four readings. Compare these readings to the backlash specified by the manufacturer.

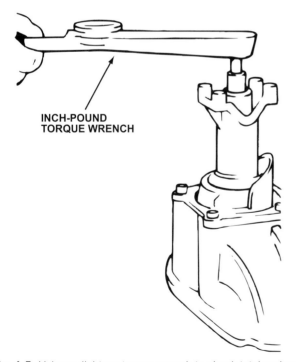

Fig. 4-5. Using a dial-type torque wrench to check total preload.

INCH-POUND TORQUE WRENCH

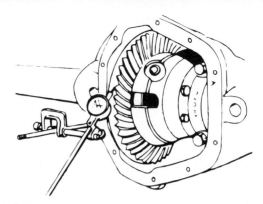

Fig. 4-6. Dial indicator set up to measure ring gear backlash.

Checking Ring Gear Runout

Improper tooth contact patterns can cause differential noise at specific road speeds. To check ring gear runout, position the dial indicator on the back edge of the ring gear and zero the dial face, figure 4-7. Rotate the ring gear one complete revolution, and record the greatest needle movement. Compare your reading with the allowable runout specified by the manufacturer. Worn differential case bearings, a worn differential case, or a worn ring gear can cause excess ring gear runout and tooth contact pattern variations.

Checking Gear Tooth Contact

Apply a thin, even coat of non-drying marking compound to the gear faces around the entire circumference of the ring gear. Then, **preload** the gear set. To preload removable gear sets, wedge a bronze drift or pry bar between the ring gear and differential carrier. For integral gear sets, apply the parking brake three or four clicks to preload the gear set.

Using a socket and ratchet, rotate the ring gear one complete revolution in a counterclockwise direction to generate a coast side pattern. Note both the shape and position of the contact patch on the coast side. Next, rotate the ring gear one

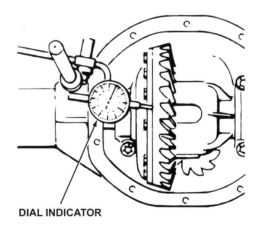

DIAL INDICATOR

Fig. 4-7. Dial indicator set up to measure ring gear runout.

A3

Backlash: Clearance or play between two mechanical parts. In the case of gears, backlash is how far one gear can move without moving the gear it meshes with.

Preload: The resistance one mechanical part exerts against the movement of another part, or the force required to overcome that resistance. Preload, like torque, is measured in inch-pounds, foot-pounds, or Newton meters (Nm).

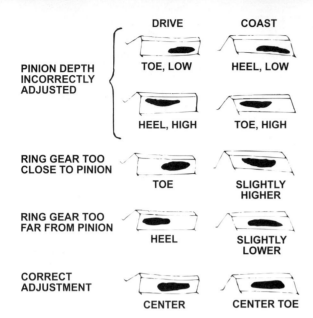

Fig. 4-8. Gear tooth pattern comparison chart.

complete revolution in a clockwise direction to establish a drive side pattern. Compare coast side and drive side results to a contact pattern chart to determine what repairs or adjustments are required, figure 4-8.

DIFFERENTIAL REPAIR

Differential repair includes:

- Pinion seal replacement
- Setting pinion depth
- Setting pinion bearing preload
- Differential case inspection
- Differential case repair and setup
- Tooth pattern adjustments

The sections that follow describe these repair procedures.

Pinion Seal Replacement

Pinion seal replacement requires that the pinion bearing preload be set. To replace a pinion seal:

1. Disconnect the driveshaft from the companion flange as previously described and remove both rear wheels.
2. Measure and record the total bearing preload, as explained previously. Remember, a fluctuating needle on the torque wrench is an indication of worn pinion bearings, which require replacement. If no needle fluctuations are found, proceed to step three.
3. Hold the companion flange with a suitable wrench and tighten the pinion nut to 125 foot-pounds (170 Nm) of torque, figure 4-9. Once again, measure and record the total bearing preload. This ensures that, after you replace the bearing, you can still achieve enough pinion nut torque to hold the pinion position and the bearing preload. A pinion that walks can cause noise on acceleration or deceleration.
4. Use a puller to remove the companion flange. Do not use a hammer, as this can induce runout in the companion flange and can cause driveshaft vibrations. Inspect the sealing surfaces on the companion flange for damage.

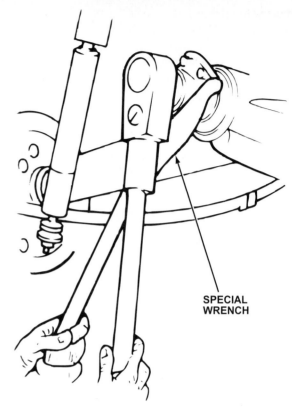

Fig. 4-9. A special wrench holds the companion flange while you tighten the pinion nut with a torque wrench.

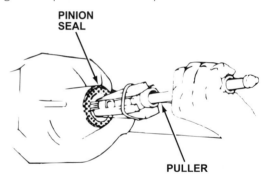

Fig. 4-10. Using a seal puller to remove the pinion seal.

If damage is found and a replacement companion flange is not available, special sleeves can be installed to provide a new sealing surface.

5. Remove the pinion seal. Special tools are available for pinion seal removal, figure 4-10. An alternate removal method is to carefully use a chisel.
6. Coat the inner portion of the replacement seal with grease to retain the tension spring. Next, coat the outer edge of the seal with non-hardening gasket sealant. Install the seal using a seal driver, figure 4-11.
7. Lightly lubricate the sealing surface of the companion flange and install it. Install a new pinion nut and torque it to 125 foot-pounds (170 Nm). Take pinion bearing preload readings. Continue to tighten the pinion nut in small increments until preload is 5 inch-pounds (0.6 Nm) greater than the initial reading taken before teardown. Be careful not to overtighten the pinion nut, or you will damage the crush sleeve.

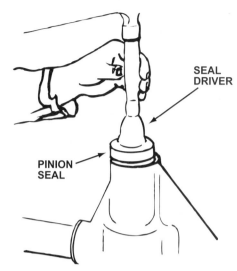

Fig. 4-11. Using a seal drive to install a pinion seal.

Setting Pinion Depth

After replacing the ring and pinion gear set or the pinion bearings, you must set pinion depth to ensure proper gear tooth contact. Vehicle manufacturers specify the base setting as the distance between the nose of the pinion gear and the centerline of the axles or the differential case bearing bores. Pinion depth is generally adjusted by changing the thickness of the shim pack located at some point in the pinion gear mounting, figure 4-12.

In addition to the base depth setting, the pinion gear may also be marked for further adjustment, figure 4-13. In this example, the pinion gear is marked "+2," which means that a 0.002-inch (0.05 mm) shim should be added to or deleted from the standard shim pack in order to move the nose of the pinion gear this distance away from the axle centerline. Conversely, a marking of "−2" means the shim pack thickness should be adjusted to move the nose of the pinion gear 0.002 inch (0.05 mm) closer to the axle centerline. An unmarked pinion gear, or one marked "0," requires no special adjustment.

For some differentials, you need a special fixture and a depth micrometer to set the pinion depth, figure 4-14. These tools are used to determine the difference between the actual depth and the specified depth.

Another method of measuring pinion depth uses a special arbor, gauge block, and a feeler gauge, figure 4-15. Clamp the arbor in the carrier or differential housing bearing bores, and place a gauge block over the pinion gear. Measure the gap between the arbor and the gauge block with the feeler gauge to determine the thickness of the shims required to correct pinion depth.

Setting Pinion Bearing Preload

Depending on the design of the final drive, there are three ways to set pinion bearing preload: the crush sleeve method, the solid spacer method, and the selective shim method. Each method positions the pinion and bearing assembly into the differential housing so that it remains in one position.

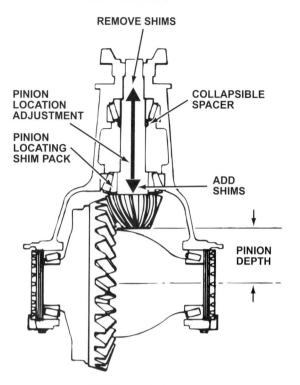

INTEGRAL CARRIER

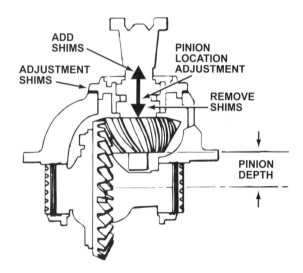

REMOVABLE CARRIER

Fig. 4-12. Pinion depth is adjusted by means of a selective shim pack, which can be located at various locations on the pinion shaft assembly.

Crush Sleeve Method

To set pinion bearing preload with a crush sleeve:

1. Remove the rear pinion bearing from the pinion shaft using a hydraulic press. Clean the pinion gear and shim. Lubricate the bearing and install the shim onto the pinion, then press the bearing onto the pinion. Make sure that you apply force to the inner bearing race only.

2. If new pinion bearings are being installed, remove the outer bearing races from the differential housing and install the new ones.

A3

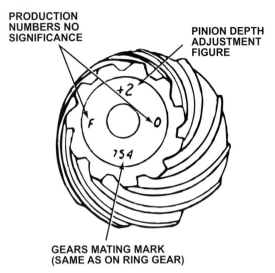

Fig. 4-13. Check for depth reference marks stamped on the end of the pinion gear.

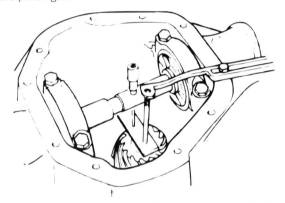

Fig. 4-14. Using a fixture and a depth micrometer to check pinion depth.

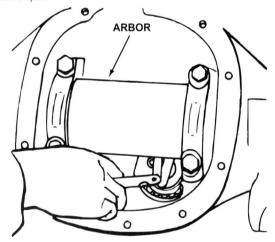

Fig. 4-15. Using an arbor, gauge block, and feeler gauge to measure pinion depth.

3. Install the front bearing and pinion seal into the differential housing, figure 4-16.
4. Slide a new crush sleeve onto the pinion shaft, figure 4-17. Next, assemble the pinion shaft into the front bearing and differential housing. Fit the companion flange onto the pinion and install a new pinion nut. Tighten the nut to draw the pinion and flange together.

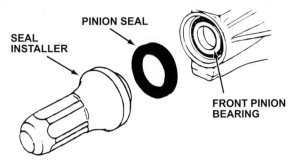

Fig. 4-16. Pinion seal installation.

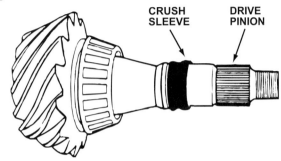

Fig. 4-17. Fit a new crush sleeve onto the pinion shaft, then install the pinion onto the front bearing.

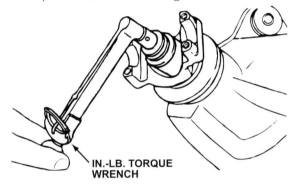

Fig. 4-18. Tighten the pinion nut in small increments to achieve the proper amount of preload.

5. Tighten the pinion nut to 125 foot-pounds (170 Nm) of torque. Continue to tighten the nut in small increments until pinion endplay is removed and preload can be read, figure 4-18. Preload should be adjusted to 10 to 25 inch pounds (1.13 to 3 Nm). Be careful not to overtighten the pinion nut or you will damage the crush sleeve.

Solid Spacer Method

To set pinion bearing preload with a solid spacer:

1. Remove the rear pinion bearing from the pinion shaft using a hydraulic press. Clean the pinion gear and shim. Lubricate the bearing and install the shim onto the pinion, then press the bearing onto the pinion. Make sure that you apply force to the inner bearing race only.
2. If new pinion bearings are being installed, remove the outer bearing races from the differential housing and install the new ones.
3. Install the front bearing and pinion seal into the differential housing.
4. Fit the solid spacer onto the pinion shaft and install the shaft into the front bearing and housing. Assemble the

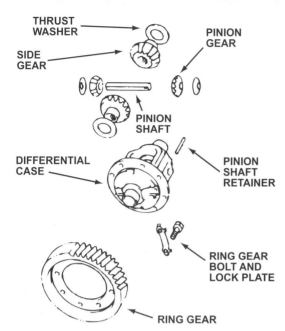

Fig. 4-19. Disassemble the differential case and inspect components for wear and damage.

companion flange onto the pinion along with a new pinion nut. Run the nut in to draw the pinion and flange together and continue tightening to specified torque.

5. Check the pinion bearing preload and compare your findings to the specifications. If there is too much preload, install a thicker spacer. If there is not enough preload, install a thinner spacer. Generally, spacer thickness changes are made in 0.003-inch (0.08 mm) increments.

Selective Shim Method

The selective shim method for setting pinion bearing preload is very similar to the solid spacer method. Shims are selected to set the correct distance between the front and rear pinion bearings.

Check the pinion bearing preload and compare your findings to the specifications. If there is too much preload, increase shim thickness. If there is not enough preload, decrease shim thickness. Like a solid spacer, shim thickness changes are made in 0.003-inch (0.08 mm) increments.

Inspecting the Differential Case

Disassemble the differential case to inspect pinion and side gears, as well as other components, for wear and damage, figure 4-19. Scores, broken gear teeth, or pinion shaft and thrust washer wear requires replacement of the damaged parts. After inspecting and replacing the gears, thrust washers, and pinion shaft, you can replace the case bearings.

REPAIRING LIMITED-SLIP DIFFERENTIALS

Limited-slip differentials use either cone clutch assemblies or friction plates to ensure that one axle continues transmitting differential case torque if the other axle loses traction. Both designs use coil springs to preload the side gears. You can check the preload at the limited-slip differential by holding

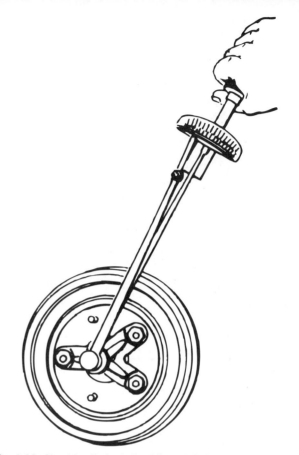

Fig. 4-20. Checking limited-slip differential side gear preload with a torque wrench.

one axle and using a torque wrench to measure how much torque is required to rotate the other axle, figure 4-20. If the torque readings are below specifications, the differential assembly must be rebuilt or replaced. A cone-type differential is not rebuildable, but the friction design is.

To rebuild a friction-type limited-slip differential:

1. Remove the ring gear from the differential case. Then, remove the pinion shaft and preload springs.
2. Insert the pinion shaft into the differential case and wedge a bar between the pinion shaft and one side gear to preload the gear.
3. Use a dial indicator to measure the backlash between the side gear and the pinion gears, figure 4-21. Typically, a reading of 0.001 inch to 0.006 inch (0.03 to 0.16 mm) is acceptable.
4. Measure backlash at the other side gear and correct it by installing selective shims behind the gears. Recheck pinion and side gear backlash after installing shims. Once correct settings have been made, install the preload springs and recheck the clutch pack torque values.

Differential Case Repair and Setup

Once the differential gears have been inspected and assembled in the case, new bearings can be installed. Use a jaw-type bearing puller or a hydraulic press and bearing splitter to remove the old case bearings, figure 4-22. Use a press to fit the new bearings onto the case.

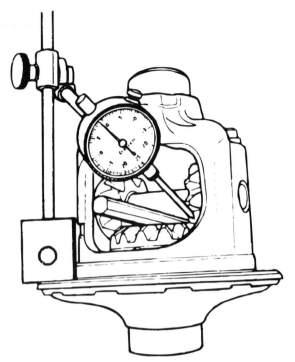

Fig. 4-21. Checking side gear to pinion gear backlash with a dial indicator.

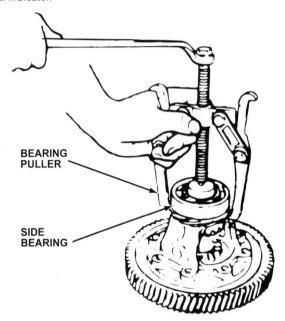

BEARING PULLER

SIDE BEARING

Fig. 4-22. Using a puller to remove differential case bearings.

Differential case bearing preload adjustment is critical to ring and pinion gear setup. The preload adjustment maintains case position and controls backlash between the ring and pinion. This adjustment is made using shims, solid spacers, or threaded adjusters.

Shims

Shims are selected to properly position the differential case in the housing and maintain proper ring and pinion gear contact. Install the original shim packs as a starting point. Several axle models require the use of a case spreader to slightly spread the case for removal and installation of the differential,

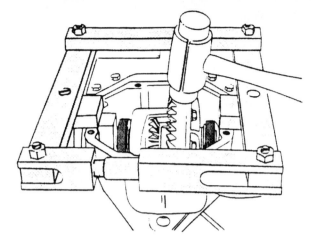

Fig. 4-23. Using a case spreader to install the differential into the case.

figure 4-23. Follow the procedure in the Service Manual and take special care not to spread the case any farther than necessary. To adjust:

1. Place the shim packs against the left and right outer bearing races and install the bearing caps. Tighten the bearing cap bolts to specified torque.

2. Measure the total preload at the companion flange nut and check backlash. The preload reading should have increased 5 to 10 inch-pounds (0.06 to 1.13 Nm) above the pinion preload reading. Use the following guidelines to make further adjustments:

   a. If preload is lower than specified and backlash is correct, increase the thickness of both shim packs to increase bearing preload. Add 0.004 inch (0.10 mm) to each shim pack and recheck the preload.

   b. If preload is higher than specified and backlash is correct, reduce the thickness of both shim packs to decrease bearing preload. Remove 0.004 inch (0.10 mm) from each shim pack and recheck the preload.

   c. If preload is within specifications and there is too much backlash, move the pinion gear closer to the ring gear by removing shims from the right shim pack and adding shims to the left shim pack. As a general rule, a 0.002-inch (0.05 mm) shim change will produce a 0.001-inch change (0.03 mm) in backlash.

   d. If preload is within specifications and there is too little backlash, move the pinion gear away from the ring gear by removing shims from the left shim pack and adding shims to the right shim pack.

   e. If preload is lower than specified and there is too little backlash, increase the thickness of the right shim pack only. This increases backlash as well as total preload.

   f. If preload is higher than specified and there is too much backlash, decrease the thickness of the right shim pack only. This decreases backlash as well as total preload.

3. After establishing correct backlash and preload settings, recheck the ring and pinion gear tooth pattern and correct as needed.

Solid Spacers

Some differential designs use selectively sized solid spacers to position the differential case in the housing. As with shim adjustments, fit the original spacers as a starting point. To adjust:

1. Place the original spacers against the left and right outer bearing races, install the bearing caps, and tighten the bearing cap bolts to specified torque.
2. Measure the total preload at the companion flange nut and check backlash. The preload reading should have increased 5 to 10 inch-pounds (0.06 to 1.13 Nm) above the original pinion preload reading. Use the following guidelines to make further adjustments:

    a. If preload is less than specifications and backlash is correct, increase the spacer thickness on both sides to increase bearing preload. Add 0.004 inch (0.10 mm) to each side and recheck the preload.
    b. If preload exceeds specifications and backlash is correct, decrease the spacer thickness on both sides to decrease bearing preload. Remove 0.004 inch (0.10 mm) from each side and recheck the preload.
    c. If preload is within specifications and there is too much backlash, move the pinion gear closer to the ring gear by reducing the solid spacer thickness on the right side and increasing the solid spacer thickness on the left side by the same amount. Generally, a 0.002-inch (0.05-mm) spacer change results in a 0.001-inch (0.03-mm) change in backlash.
    d. If preload is within specifications and there is too little backlash, move the pinion gear away from the ring gear by reducing the solid spacer thickness on the left side and increasing the solid spacer thickness on the right side an equal amount. Remember, a 0.002-inch (0.05-mm) change in spacer thickness generally produces a 0.001-inch (0.03-mm) change in backlash.
    e. If preload is less than specified and there is too little backlash, increase the right spacer thickness. This will increase backlash as well as total preload.
    f. If preload exceeds specifications and there is too much backlash, decrease the right spacer thickness. This will decrease backlash as well as total preload.

3. Recheck the ring and pinion gear tooth pattern once correct backlash and preload settings have been established.

Threaded Adjusters

Spanner wrenches are used to adjust threaded collars and position the differential case on some designs, figure 4-24. To adjust:

1. Install the differential case, along with the bearings and races, into the differential housing. Thread the adjusters against the bearing races to control differential case sideplay.
2. Adjust backlash to approximately 0.001 to 0.003 inch (0.03 to 0.08 mm). Assemble the bearing caps over the bearings and adjusters, and tighten the cap bolts to

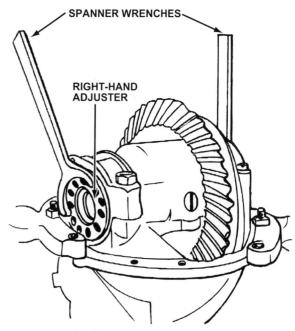

Fig. 4-24. Using spanner wrenches to turn threaded adjusters and position the differential case.

approximately ⅓ of their specified tightening torque. This allows you to tighten the adjusters while maintaining case position.

3. Move the right adjuster two holes to increase case bearing preload and backlash. Measure the total preload and compare your reading to the pinion preload readings. The preload reading should have increased 5 to 10 in-lb (0.6 to 1.1 Nm) above the original preload reading.
4. Use the following guidelines to make further adjustments:

    a. If preload is less than specifications and backlash is correct, move each adjuster inward. This maintains the ring gear position and increases bearing preload.
    b. If preload exceeds specifications and backlash is correct, move each adjuster out. However, be careful not to leave the differential case without any preload. Check for differential case sideplay.
    c. If preload is below specifications and there is too much backlash, move the ring gear toward the pinion by tightening the left adjuster only. This decreases backlash while increasing case bearing preload. Before rechecking your preload and backlash measurements, rotate the pinion several revolutions to stabilize the bearing.
    d. If preload is below specifications and there is too little backlash, move the ring gear away from the pinion by tightening the right adjuster only. This increases both backlash and case bearing preload. Again, rotate the pinion several revolutions to stabilize the bearing before rechecking preload and backlash measurements.

5. Tighten the bearing cap bolts to their specified torque, then recheck backlash and preload. After establishing correct backlash and preload settings, recheck the ring and pinion gear tooth pattern.

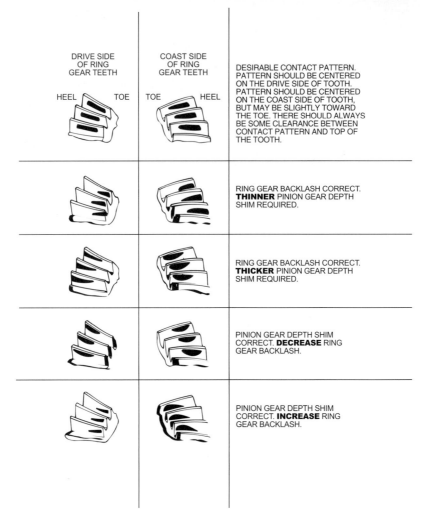

DRIVE SIDE OF RING GEAR TEETH	COAST SIDE OF RING GEAR TEETH	
HEEL · TOE	TOE · HEEL	DESIRABLE CONTACT PATTERN. PATTERN SHOULD BE CENTERED ON THE DRIVE SIDE OF TOOTH. PATTERN SHOULD BE CENTERED ON THE COAST SIDE OF TOOTH, BUT MAY BE SLIGHTLY TOWARD THE TOE. THERE SHOULD ALWAYS BE SOME CLEARANCE BETWEEN CONTACT PATTERN AND TOP OF THE TOOTH.
		RING GEAR BACKLASH CORRECT. **THINNER** PINION GEAR DEPTH SHIM REQUIRED.
		RING GEAR BACKLASH CORRECT. **THICKER** PINION GEAR DEPTH SHIM REQUIRED.
		PINION GEAR DEPTH SHIM CORRECT. **DECREASE** RING GEAR BACKLASH.
		PINION GEAR DEPTH SHIM CORRECT. **INCREASE** RING GEAR BACKLASH.

Fig. 4-25. Check ring and pinion gear tooth pattern after making backlash and preload adjustments.

Tooth Pattern Adjustment

To correct ring gear tooth patterns that are too high or too low, change the pinion shim thickness. For integral design differentials, increase the shim thickness to move the pinion into the ring gear, toward the toe. Decrease shim thickness to move the pinion away from the ring gear and toward the heel of the ring gear tooth, figure 4-25.

Removable carrier design differentials sometimes use a shim in the pinion bearing retainer. Decrease the shim thickness to move the pinion into the ring gear, toward the toe. Increase shim thickness to move the pinion away from the ring gear and toward the heel of the ring gear tooth.

CHAPTER QUESTIONS

1. Noise heard during acceleration can be caused by a worn:
   a. Front pinion bearing
   b. Rear pinion bearing
   c. Differential case bearings
   d. Differential side gears

2. A noise that does not change as the vehicle travels around corners is usually caused by a:
   a. Worn or improperly inflated tire
   b. Worn pinion bearings
   c. Worn axle bearings
   d. Worn differential gears

3. The intermittent noise produced by damaged differential gears is commonly known as:
   a. Chatter
   b. Growl
   c. Whine
   d. Chuckle

4. Differential noise that occurs while turning and can often be cured by a lubricant change and 100 miles (160 kilometers) of normal driving is:
   a. Chuckle noise
   b. Chatter noise
   c. Road speed noise
   d. Gear whine

5. What is indicated by a torque wrench that reads 25 inch-pounds (3 Nm) while the needle is bouncing on the dial when checking total bearing preload?
   a. Normal preload
   b. Excessive preload
   c. Worn pinion bearings
   d. Too little preload exists

6. Backlash is within specifications, but case bearing preload is below specifications in a shim-type differential. To correct:
   a. Remove shims from the left pack, and add shims to the right pack
   b. Remove shims from the right pack, and add shims to the left pack
   c. Add equal shims to both the left and right shim packs
   d. Remove equal shims from both the left and right shim packs

7. Backlash is excessive and case bearing preload is within specifications in a shim-type differential. To correct:
   a. Remove shims from the left pack, and add shims to the right pack
   b. Remove shims from the right pack, and add shims to the left pack
   c. Add equal shims to both the left and right shim packs
   d. Remove equal shims from both the left and right shim packs

8. Both backlash and case bearing preload exceed specifications in a shim-type differential. To correct:
   a. Add shims to the left shim pack
   b. Remove shims from the right pack, and add shims to the left pack
   c. Remove from the right shim pack
   d. Remove equal shims from both shim packs

9. Preload is below specifications and backlash is correct in a threaded adjuster-type differential. To correct:
   a. Move each adjuster out
   b. Move each adjuster in
   c. Move the left adjuster in
   d. Move the right adjuster in

10. Preload is below specifications and backlash is excessive in a threaded adjuster-type differential. To correct:
   a. Move each adjuster out
   b. Move each adjuster in
   c. Move the left adjuster in
   d. Move the right adjuster in

A3

CHAPTER OBJECTIVES

- The technician will complete the ASE task list on Four Wheel Drive Service.
- The technician will be able to answer 7 questions dealing with the Four-Wheel Drive service section of the A3 ASE Test.

TRANSFER CASE DIAGNOSIS AND REPAIR

Transfer case problem diagnosis begins with a road test to confirm the complaint and experience the symptoms. After the road test, various inspection and adjustment procedures are performed to confirm the diagnosis.

The Road Test

The test route should include roads that allow speeds from 25 to 55 MPH (40 to 90 kph). During the road test, check for:

- Shift linkage problems
- Noise
- Gear engagement problems

The sections that follow describe these checks. A troubleshooting chart is a handy reference for analyzing common four-wheel drive (4WD) **transfer case** problems, figure 5-1.

Shift Linkage Problems

An inadequately lubricated or incorrectly adjusted shift linkage can be the cause of many transfer case complaints. Symptoms of shift linkage problems include: hard shifting, not being able to engage a desired gear, or having the transmission jump out of gear. Linkage service and adjustment procedures are discussed later in this chapter.

Noise

A noise complaint is often the result of a lack of lubrication. Check for proper lubricant and fluid levels. Worn transfer case bearings can cause noises similar to those caused by driveline and rear axle problems. If lubricant and fluid levels are correct, you may have to remove and disassemble the transfer case. Transfer case disassembly and repair are detailed later in this chapter.

Gear Engagement Problems

Common customer complaints related to gear engagement include hard shifting and not being able to engage a desired gear.

These symptoms are often caused by shift linkage problems, shift fork wear, or damaged internal gears or bearings. In some cases, shift linkage adjustment may correct these symptoms. If your inspection verifies shift linkage wear or damaged internal gears or bearings, you will have to remove the transfer case for further inspection.

In addition, some transfer cases are shifted electronically or by vacuum-controlled shift mechanisms. Verify that these control systems are functioning properly before removing the transfer case assembly. Inspecting and testing electronic and vacuum control systems are discussed later in this chapter.

TRANSFER CASE INSPECTION AND ADJUSTMENT

Transfer case inspection and adjustment consists of:

- Lubrication checks
- Linkage adjustment
- Front axle preload adjustment

Lubrication Checks

Inadequate or improper lubricant can cause noise as well as transfer case shifting problems. To check the transfer case lubricant:

1. Open the transfer case oil filler plug, and make sure that the oil level is to the bottom of the plug opening, figure 5-2. If not, add the proper lubricant. Many different lubricants are used in transfer cases. Make sure you use the lubricant recommended by the manufacturer.
2. Some 4WD vehicles have a lube fitting on the **steering knuckle**, figure 5-3. Lubricate the fitting with the recommended grease at prescribed service intervals.

Case Oil Change

To change the transfer case oil:

1. Raise the vehicle and place a drain pan under the transfer case.
2. Remove the skid plate, if necessary, and remove the drain and fill plugs. Some drain plugs are magnetic; wipe these plugs clean before reinstalling.

Steering Knuckle: A metal casting that supports the road wheel, joins the suspension to the wheel, and provides pivot points between them.

Transfer Case: A gear case that transfers torque from the transmission to another set of drive wheels. It allows FWD or RWD vehicles to become 4WD. The case contains an input shaft from the transmission or transaxle and output shafts to the drive wheels.

TRANSFER CASE TROUBLESHOOTING GUIDE

CONDITION	POSSIBLE CAUSE	CORRECTION
EXCESSIVE NOISE	1. Lubricant low 2. Bearings worn, damaged, or poorly adjusted 3. Gears worn or damaged 4. Driveshafts or U-joint misaligned	1. Fill with proper amount 2. Adjust bearings. Replace bearings 3. Replace gears 4. Check driveshaft alignment. Check U-joint alignment
SHIFTING LEVER HARD TO MOVE	1. Control lever or stabilizer loose 2. Stabilizer bracket-to-shift lever bolt too tight	1. Tighten bracket bolts 2. Tighten bolt finger-tight
LUBRICANT LEAKAGE	1. Excess lubricant in case 2. Vent clogged 3. Seals or gaskets damaged or improperly installed 4. Driveshaft companion yoke scored at seal 5. Bearings loose or damaged	1. Drain to proper level 2. Clean or replace vent 3. Inspect and replace. Correctly install seals or gaskets 4. Remove scores, nicks on yoke with fine sandpaper. Replace yoke 5. Tighten bearings. Replace bearings
OVERHEATING	1. Too much or too little lubricant 2. Bearings too tight	1. Check lubricant level; adjust as needed 2. Adjust bearings
FRONT AXLE DRIVE DISENGAGES	1. De-clutch lever rod misadjusted 2. Gears or sliding clutch gears worn or damaged 3. Shift rail poppet ball or spring missing 4. Stabilizer or control rods misadjusted	1. Adjust de-clutch rod 2. Replace gears 3. Replace poppet ball or spring 4. Adjust rods
BACKLASH	1. Companion yoke loose 2. Transfer case loose 3. Worn parts	1. Tighten yoke 2. Tighten mounting brackets 3. Replace all worn parts
WILL NOT SHIFT INTO DESIRED RANGE	1. Vehicle speed too high 2. If driving on dry paved road for long time driveline torque load may cause hard shifting 3. Transfer case external linkage binding 4. Lubricant low or wrong type 5. Internal parts binding or worn	1. Stop vehicle; shift into desired range 2. Stop vehicle; shift transmission to Neutral and transfer case to 2H 3. Tighten loose parts. Lubricate, repair or replace parts as needed 4. Add lubricant. Drain and refill with proper lubricant 5. Disassemble unit; repair or replace parts
JUMPS OUT OF 4WD LOW RANGE	1. Transfer case not completely engaged in 4L position 2. Shift linkage loose or binding 3. Range fork cracked, inserts worn, or fork binding on shift rail 4. Annulus gear or lock plate worn or damaged	1. Stop vehicle; shift transfer case into Neutral, then into 4L 2. Tighten, lubricate, or repair linkage as needed 3. Disassemble unit and repair as necessary 4. Disassemble unit and repair as necessary
ELECTRONIC	1. Circuit protection device blown	1. Check fuse or CB; replace if opened
SHIFTING: WILL NOT SHIFT INTO DESIRED RANGE	1. Bad control module 2. Open or short in electrical circuit	1. Perform self-diagnostic tests 2. Test for opens and shorts in circuit; repair or replace wiring, connectors, or motor as needed

Fig. 5-1. Transfer case troubleshooting chart.

3. Allow the old oil to drain completely from the case.
4. Install and tighten the drain plug to specified torque.
5. Fill the transfer case with the proper lubricant to the edge of the fill opening. Install and tighten the fill plug to specified torque.
6. Reinstall the skid plate and lower the vehicle.

Linkage Adjustment

The linkage system should periodically be inspected for free movement, proper engagement, and secure attachment. Adjust, clean, and tighten the linkage system components as necessary.

To adjust the range control linkage for a typical New Process manual shift transfer case, place the range control lever

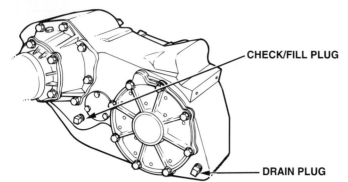

Fig. 5-2. Remove the fill plug to check transfer case fluid level.

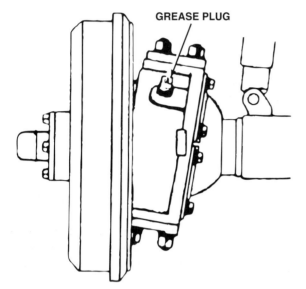

Fig. 5-3. Some 4WD steering knuckles require periodic lubrication.

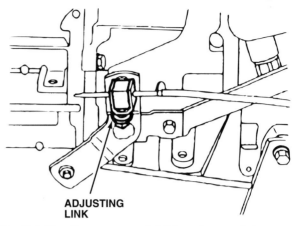

Fig. 5-4. New Process manual shift transfer case linkage adjustment.

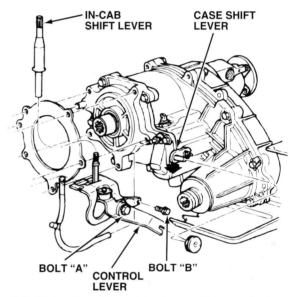

Fig. 5-5. Typical Borg-Warner transfer case linkage adjustment.

in the two-wheel drive (2WD) position. Insert a $^1/_8$-inch (3 mm) spacer between the gate in the console and the lever. Hold the lever in this position and place the outer lever at the transfer case in the 2WD position. Adjust the link to provide a free pin at the transfer case outer lever, figure 5-4.

On Borg-Warner transfer cases, adjust the shift linkage by raising the shift boot to expose the cam plate. Referring to figure 5-5, loosen bolts "A" and "B" two turns. Move the transfer case shift lever to the 4L position. Move the cam plate rearward, until the bottom **chamfered** corner of the neutral lug just contacts the forward right edge of the shift lever. Hold the cam plate in this position and tighten bolt "A" first, then bolt "B." Move the shift lever through all shift positions to check for positive engagement.

FRONT AXLE SERVICE

Front Axle Bearing Preload
Some 4WD vehicles require adjustment to establish front axle bearing preload.

To perform this adjustment:

1. With the vehicle supported on jack stands or a hoist, try to move each front wheel in and out to check for wheel bearing play. There should be none.
2. Make sure the tires rotate smoothly when turned.
3. Remove the wheels and tires. Remove the disc brake caliper and hang it out of the way using a piece of wire; never let the caliper hang by its hose.
4. Remove the locking hub, snapring, and spacer.
5. Remove the wheel setbolts and bearing set plate.
6. Tighten the locknut and turn the hub a few times to seat the bearing. Then, loosen the locknut.
7. Attach a spring scale to a wheel setbolt and measure the frictional force, figure 5-6. Add this reading to the specified amount to obtain the bearing preload.
8. Tighten the locknut until the preload is within specification.

Chamfered: Beveled, tapered, or relieved.

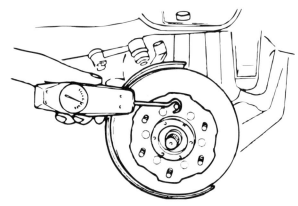

Fig. 5-6. Measuring axle bearing preload with a spring scale.

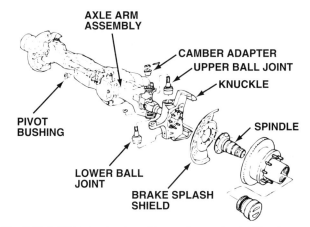

Fig. 5-7. A 4WD steering knuckle can be serviced without removing the axle assembly.

Steering Knuckle Service

Steering knuckle components can often be repaired without removing the front axle assembly from the vehicle, figure 5-7. To remove and replace a 4WD steering knuckle:

1. With the vehicle raised, remove the wheel and tire. Remove the freewheeling hub and disc brake caliper.
2. Disconnect the tie rod from the knuckle. On some vehicles, you must use a gear puller to unbolt and remove the tie rod from the knuckle arm. On other vehicles, remove the cotter pin from the tie rod nut and remove the nut. Other steering or suspension components may also need to be removed.
3. If the vehicle has upper and lower control arm suspension, support the lower arm with a jack and remove the lower arm ball joint nut. Separate the knuckle from the lower arm first, then from the upper arm. Move the lower arm down and remove the knuckle.
4. If the vehicle has independent front suspension, remove the cotter pin from the top ball joint stud. Loosen the nut on the stop stud and the bottom nut inside the knuckle. Remove the top nut. Use a soft-faced hammer to knock out the top stud and free the knuckle from the axle arm.

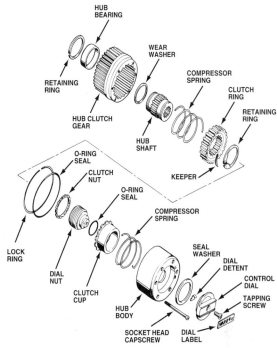

Fig. 5-8. Exploded view of a typical locking hub.

5. Disassemble and inspect the knuckle as follows:
   a. Check the knuckle for damage, wear, or rust on the oil seal friction surface
   b. Remove the oil seal retainer or needle bearing at the back of the steering knuckle and inspect for damage
   c. Remove the nuts or bolts on the top steering knuckle cap along with the cone washers
   d. Using a small drift and hammer, tap the knuckle bearing races out from inside the steering knuckle. Do not tap the bearings

When assembling a steering knuckle, replace all of the bearings and seals, and tighten all bolts to specifications. To test the knuckle bearing preload, attach a spring scale to the end hole in the steering knuckle. The force required to move the knuckle from side to side is the preload. Preload should be within specification. Use shims or spacers to adjust preload.

Locking Hub Service

Inspection procedures and service intervals for **locking hubs** vary by manufacturer. Although all locking hubs perform the same function, there are design variations as well, figure 5-8.

Listed below are the general steps required for this service. Always refer to the appropriate Service Manual for the correct procedures for the vehicle being serviced.

To remove a manual locking, or freewheeling, hub:

1. Set the control handle to the FREE position.
2. Remove the attaching bolts and the hub body.
3. Remove the two retaining rings and the clutch assembly.

Locking Hub: Front wheel hub on a 4WD system that can be manually locked or unlocked to engage and disengage the front drive axle, thereby transmitting engine torque to the front wheels or allowing them to turn freely.

4. Check the hub for smooth turning of the control handle.
5. Check for smooth rotation of the inner hub with the handle in the FREE position. Also, make sure that the inner hub does not rotate when the handle is in the LOCK position.

To disassemble the hub:

1. Remove the control handle screw, the handle, the detent, and seal washer.
2. Remove the clutch nut, dial nut, clutch cup, and compressor spring.
3. Remove the clutch assembly retaining ring and separate the clutch ring, hub shaft, and gear.
4. Remove and discard the O-ring seals; replace with new ones on assembly.
5. Clean all components with solvent and dry with compressed air. Inspect for signs of wear and damage. Replace components as needed.

To reassemble the hub, take the following steps:

1. Apply a light coat of grease to the sliding surfaces on each part.
2. Assemble the clutch assembly and secure with the retaining ring.
3. Fit a new O-ring seal on the dial nut, then assemble the spring, clutch cup, and dial nut into the hub body and secure with the clutch nut.
4. Place the seal washer in the hub body, install the detent and handle, and secure with the screw.
5. Install the clutch hub assembly on the axle and secure with the two retaining rings.
6. Install a new O-ring on the hub body and fit the hub body onto the clutch.
7. Align the hub body bolt holes, install the bolts, and tighten to specified torque.
8. Set the control handle and clutch hub to the FREE position and check that both front wheels rotate freely. Also, check that the hubs lock when the control handle is moved to the engage position.

ELECTRONIC SHIFT CONTROL

Electronic shift control uses an electric motor mounted on the transfer case to engage and disengage 4WD mode, figure 5-9. Diagnostic and service procedures for the electronic shift control can be performed without removing the transfer case from the vehicle. The electronic shift transfer case typically consists of the following items:

- Transfer case
- Panel-mounted switch
- Electronic control module
- Speed sensor
- Shift position sensor
- Electric shift motor

The battery feed circuit provides power to the electronic control module memory circuit. The circuit is generally protected by a circuit breaker. Power for the electronic shift switches and the electric shift motor is supplied through the

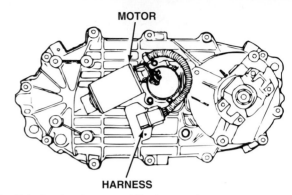

Fig. 5-9. An electric motor shifts the transfer case.

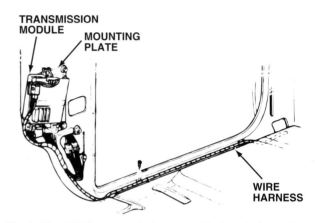

Fig. 5-10. A TCM is generally located behind the kickpanel or under the dash.

ignition switch. These ignition feed circuits are protected by a fuse. The headlamp dimmer circuit or the parking lamp circuit provides power to illuminate the control switches.

Control Module Tests

Most electronic transfer cases are regulated by the transmission control modules (TCM) and have onboard diagnostic capability within their circuitry. A typical self-test procedure is as follows:

1. Access the TCM. These are usually located behind the kickpanel on the passenger side or behind the instrument panel, figure 5-10.
2. Remove all but the main feed harness from the control module.
3. Turn the ignition switch to the run position.
4. Activate the self-test switch. If the indicator lamp flashes steadily, the control module is working properly. If the indicator lamp lights steadily, the module is bad and must be replaced.

The typical control module has three multi-pin connectors attached to it. To test the integrity of these circuits, disconnect the harnesses from the module and do a continuity test using an ohmmeter and a voltmeter. Remember that an ohmmeter should never be connected into a live, powered circuit. Check the Service Manual for procedures, wiring diagrams, and specifications to test each pin in a connector.

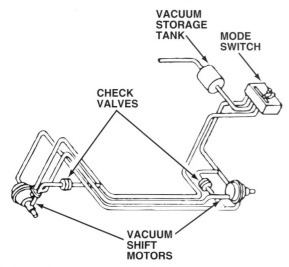

Fig. 5-11. Typical vacuum control system layout.

VACUUM SHIFT CONTROL

A vacuum shift control system switches between 2WD and 4WD on a signal from a dash-mounted or console-mounted switch. This switch controls one or two vacuum motors. If there is one motor, it actuates a front axle disconnect mechanism. When a second motor is used, it disengages the front axle drive chain in the transfer case, figure 5-11.

Front Axle Shift Motor Test

To perform a functional test on a front axle vacuum shift motor:

1. Disconnect the vacuum hoses from the shift motor.
2. Connect a vacuum pump to the shift motor front port and apply 15 in-Hg (50 kPa) of vacuum. Rotate the right, front wheel to fully disengage the axle.
   a. If the shift motor does not retain vacuum for at least 30 seconds, the motor is bad and must be replaced.
   b. If the shift motor does retain vacuum for 30 seconds, go to step three.
3. Disconnect the vacuum pump from the front port on the shift motor. Connect the pump to the rear port on the shift motor and apply 15 in-Hg (50 kPa) of vacuum.
   a. If the shift motor does not retain vacuum for at least 30 seconds, the motor is bad and must be replaced.
   b. If the shift motor does retain vacuum for 30 seconds, go to step four.
4. Remove the cap from the center connecting port on the shift motor and check for vacuum at the port.
   a. If vacuum is present, the motor is good.
   b. If vacuum is not present, slide the boot away from the shift motor stem and measure the distance the stem has extended. It should extend $5/8$ inch (16 mm) as measured from the edge of the shift motor housing to the E-ring on the stem. If not, go to step five.
5. Check the vacuum tubes for leaks or damage and repair as needed.
6. Recheck shift motor operation. If still not operating, replace the motor.

Transfer Case Shift Motor Test

Do a functional test of a transfer case vacuum shift motor as follows:

1. Disconnect the vacuum hoses from the shift motor.
2. Connect a vacuum pump to the front port on the shift motor and apply 15 in-Hg (50 kPa) of vacuum. Turn the rear driveshaft to fully engage the transfer case in the 4WD mode.
   a. If the shift motor does not retain vacuum for at least 30 seconds, the motor is bad and must be replaced.
   b. If the shift motor does retain vacuum for 30 seconds, go to step three.
3. Disconnect the vacuum pump from the front port on the shift motor. Connect the pump to the rear port on the shift motor and apply 15 in-Hg (50 kPa) of vacuum. Shift the transmission into first gear.
   a. If the shift motor does not retain vacuum for at least 30 seconds, the motor is bad and must be replaced.
   b. If the shift motor does retain vacuum for 30 seconds, go to step four.
4. Remove the cap from the center connecting port on the shift motor and check for vacuum at the port. If there is no vacuum at the port, turn the rear driveshaft as necessary to ensure a complete transfer case engagement and check for vacuum again.
   a. If vacuum is present, the motor is good.
   b. If vacuum is not present, slide the boot away from the shift motor stem and measure the distance the stem has extended. It should extend $5/8$ inch (16 mm) as measured from the edge of the shift motor housing to the E-ring on the stem. If not, go to step five.
5. Check the vacuum tubes for leaks or damage and repair as needed.
6. Recheck shift motor operation. If still not operational, replace the motor.

TRANSFER CASE REPAIR

The front and rear yokes, output shaft seals, rear retainer and bearing, oil pump and seal, and speedometer drive gear can all be serviced on most transfer cases without removing the unit from the vehicle.

Transfer Case Seal Replacement

The following steps describe a typical procedure for removing and replacing front or rear transfer case seals:

1. Raise the vehicle and drain the lubricant from the transfer case.
2. Mark the driveshaft and transfer case yoke for reassembly. Disconnect the driveshaft and secure it to the underside of the vehicle.
3. Remove and discard the yoke retaining nut and yoke seal washer from the transfer case. A special tool may be required to hold the yoke while removing the nut. Remove the yoke.
4. Remove the rear output seal using a special tool, figure 5-12. This tool will also enable you to remove the

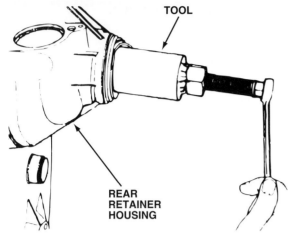

Fig. 5-12. The transfer case output shaft seal is removed with a special seal puller.

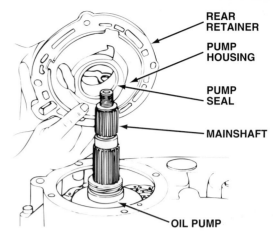

Fig. 5-13. Remove the retainer to access the pump housing and seal.

extension housing bushing. If you do not have this tool, remove the extension housing from the transfer case to service the seal and bushing.

5. Install a new bushing in the extension housing, and then install new seals at the front and rear of the transfer case.

6. Fit the yoke and install a new seal washer and retaining nut. Tighten the nut to specified torque.

7. Align the reference marks and reinstall the driveshaft.

Speedometer Seal Replacement

To replace the speedometer seals, proceed as follows:

1. Remove the speedometer driven gear sleeve and driven gear as an assembly from the rear extension housing.

2. Remove the driven gear from the sleeve, then remove the inner seal and outer O-ring.

3. Install a new seal and O-ring onto the sleeve.

4. Lubricate the seal and O-ring and install the driven gear into the sleeve.

5. Install the assembly into the extension housing.

Rear Retainer and Oil Pump Replacement

The following is a typical procedure for removing and replacing the rear retainer and oil pump assembly.

Disassembly

1. Remove the speedometer driven gear and sleeve.

2. Mark the rear retainer for reassembly. Remove the retainer attaching bolts and remove the retainer. Do not attempt to pry the retainer off the rear case. Instead, tap the retainer loose using a soft-faced hammer.

3. Remove the speedometer drive gear.

4. Separate the pump housing from the retainer and remove the seal from the housing, figure 5-13.

5. If the retainer or bearing need to be replaced, remove the bearing retainer snapring from the rear retainer, then use a bearing driver to remove the bearing, figure 5-14.

6. Clean the retainer with solvent and dry with compressed air. Make sure to completely remove any old gasket sealant from the retainer and the transfer case housing.

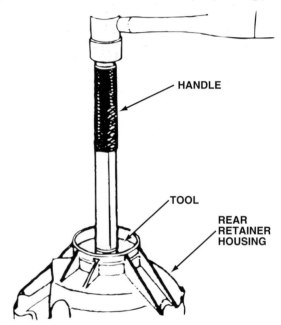

Fig. 5-14. A bearing driver is used to remove and install a rear output bearing.

Assembly

1. Install the oil pump on the mainshaft.

2. Install the seal in the pump housing.

3. Install the speedometer drive gear.

4. Install the rear output bearing in the rear retainer and install the snapring. Be sure the shielded side of the bearing faces the transfer case interior.

5. Install the pump housing in the rear retainer.

6. Apply a bead of RTV sealant to the rear retainer mating surface.

7. Align the retainer and case reference marks and install the retainer on the case.

8. Install and tighten the retainer attaching bolts to specified torque.

9. Install the speedometer driven gear and sleeve.

Transfer Case Removal

To service internal transfer case components, the unit must be removed from the vehicle. Following are typical steps required to remove a transfer case. Always refer to the appropriate

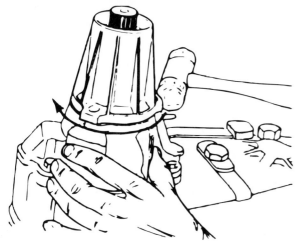

Fig. 5-15. Using a soft-faced hammer to remove an extension housing.

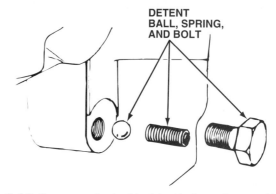

Fig. 5-16. Remove and set aside detent bolts, springs, and balls.

Fig. 5-17. Do not pry on the mating surfaces when separating the case halves.

Service Manual for the correct procedures for the vehicle being serviced:

1. Raise the vehicle on a hoist or jack stands.
2. Drain the lubricant from the transfer case.
3. Mark the transfer case front and rear output shaft yokes and driveshafts for reassembly.
4. Disconnect the speedometer cable and indicator switch wires.
5. Disconnect the shift lever link from the operating lever.
6. Place a jack under the transmission and slightly raise the transmission. If necessary, remove the rear crossmember.
7. Disconnect the front and rear driveshafts at the transfer case. Secure the shafts to the frame rails with rope or wire. Do not allow the shafts to hang.
8. Disconnect or remove any components that are in the way, such as the parking brake cable, vent hose, exhaust pipe, support brackets, or catalytic converter.
9. Remove the transfer case to transmission bolts.
10. Move the transfer case rearward until it is free of the transmission output shaft, then remove the transfer case.
11. Remove all gasket material from the rear of the transmission extension housing.

Transfer Case Disassembly

To disassemble a typical manual transfer case, follow this general procedure:

1. Remove the following small items:

   a. Drain and fill plugs
   b. Front and rear yokes
   c. Any electrical switches

2. If the unit has an extension housing, remove it by removing the bolts and tapping on the housing shoulder with a soft-faced hammer, figure 5-15.
3. Remove the following:

   a. Detent bolts, springs, and balls, figure 5-16
   b. Speedometer driven gear
   c. Snapring

4. Mark the rear retainer for reassembly, then remove the retainer and pump housing. Do not attempt to pry the

retainer off the rear case. Instead, tap the retainer loose using a soft-faced hammer.

5. Remove the following:

   a. Pump housing from the retainer
   b. Pump seal from the housing
   c. Speedometer drive gear from the mainshaft
   d. Oil pump from the mainshaft

6. Remove the bolts attaching the rear case to the front case, then separate the case halves. To separate the case halves, insert a screwdriver or pry bar into the slots cast in the case ends and gently pry upward, figure 5-17. Do not attempt to wedge the case halves apart along the mating surfaces.
7. Remove rear thrust bearing assembly from the front output shaft. Note the thrust position for later reassembly.
8. Remove the following:

   a. Driven sprocket retaining snapring, figure 5-18
   b. Spring retainer, spring, and shift rail, figure 5-19
   c. Drive and driven sprockets, mainshaft, mode fork and bracket, and chain as an assembly
   d. Front output shaft and front thrust bearing assembly
   e. Synchronizer snapring and synchronizer, figure 5-20
   f. Drive sprocket and thrust washer as an assembly; be careful not to lose the needle bearings inside

A3

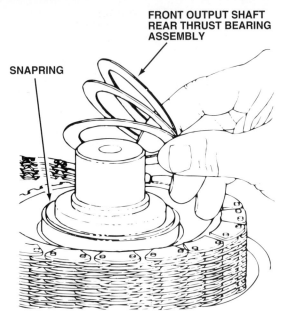

Fig. 5-18. Remove the output shaft rear thrust bearing to access the snapring.

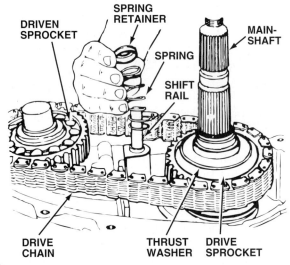

Fig. 5-19. Remove the shift rail, retainer, and spring.

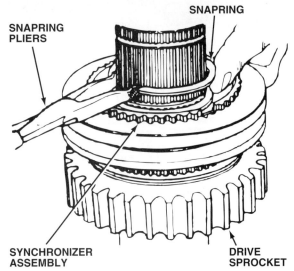

Fig. 5-20. Remove the snapring, then the synchronizer assembly.

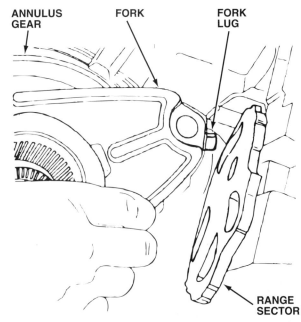

Fig. 5 21. Tilt the range fork to release it from the range sector, then remove it along with the annulus gear.

9. Remove the retaining ring and thrust washer from the annulus gear.
10. Remove the annulus gear and range fork. Turn the fork clockwise to disengage the fork lug from the range sector, then lift the assembly out of the case, figure 5-21.
11. Remove the planetary thrust washer, the planetary assembly, and the mainshaft thrust bearing from the input gear. Then, remove the input gear.
12. Remove the input gear thrust bearing and race. Next, remove the operating lever attaching nut and washer from the range sector. Remove the lever and sector shaft seal, then remove the seal retainer. Now remove the range sector.

13. Remove the output shaft seals from the front and rear case seal bores.

Transfer Case Cleaning and Inspection

Wash all transfer case parts thoroughly in clean solvent. Make sure all lubricant, metallic particles, dirt, and foreign material are removed from every surface. Apply compressed air to all components and to each oil channel. This removes any obstructions or solvent residue. Proceed as follows:

1. Inspect the transfer case and cover for cracks or damaged mating surfaces.
2. Inspect the input shaft gear and output shaft for wear, damaged teeth, or clogged oil passages.

3. Inspect the low gear, 2WD-4WD clutch hub, drive sprocket, and front drive sprocket for wear or damaged teeth.
4. Inspect the hub for worn or damaged sleeve splines or sleeve grooves.
5. Inspect the countergear and speedometer drive gear for wear or damaged teeth.
6. Inspect the needle, roller, and thrust bearings for rough operation or noise during rotation.
7. Inspect the shift forks, the rods, and the springs for wear or improper operation.
8. Inspect the lockplate for damage or signs of wear.

Transfer Case Reassembly

During assembly, lubricate all parts with the recommended transfer case lubricant. Reassemble as follows.

1. Install the following:

    a. Input gear race and the thrust bearing in the front case
    b. Input gear
    c. Mainshaft thrust bearing in the input gear
    d. Range sector shaft seal and the seal retainer
    e. Range sector

2. Fit the operating lever onto the range sector shaft. Then, install and tighten the shaft washer and locknut.
3. Install the planetary assembly over the input gear. Make sure the planetary is fully seated and meshed with the gear.
4. Install the planetary thrust washer on the planetary hub.
5. Install the inserts in the range fork if they were removed. Engage the fork in the annulus gear and install the gear over the planetary assembly. Make sure the range fork mode lug is fully inserted in the range sector slot.
6. Install the annulus gear thrust washer and retainer snapring. The shift rail bore in the case must be completely dry and free of oil. A small amount of oil can prevent the rail from seating completely and can also prevent front case installation.
7. Put the mainshaft in a vise between two wooden blocks, with the small end down. Coat the drive sprocket with plenty of assembly lubricant and position a needle bearing spacer at the center of the drive sprocket bore.
8. Coat the needle bearings with assembly lubricant and install half the needle bearings in each end of the drive sprocket bore.
9. Install a bearing retainer in each end of the drive sprocket bore and position the thrust washer on the bottom of the drive sprocket.
10. Align the assembled drive sprocket and needle bearings with the mainshaft and install the assembly on the mainshaft. Avoid displacing the needle bearings. Make sure the thrust washer is bottomed against the snapring.
11. With the stop ring in its proper position, install the synchronizer assembly onto the mainshaft. Install the synchronizer assembly snapring in the groove on the mainshaft.

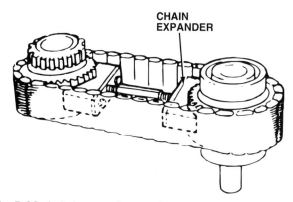

Fig. 5-22. A chain expander must be used when assembling some transfer cases.

12. Install the front thrust bearing assembly in the front case. The correct installation sequence is the thick race, followed by the thrust bearing, and then the thin race.
13. Install the front output shaft.
14. Install the sprockets, mainshaft assembly, mode fork and bracket, and drive chain as an assembly. On some models, you may need to use a chain spreading tool, figure 5-22.
15. Install the following:

    a. Drive sprocket thrust washer and the snapring
    b. Shift rail through the mode fork and bracket
    c. Spring and spring retainer onto the shift rail
    d. Driven sprocket snapring

16. Install the front output shaft rear thrust bearing onto the front output shaft.
17. Install the oil pump and the speedometer drive gear on the mainshaft.
18. Apply a bead of RTV sealant to the mating surfaces and around the holes of the front case. Attach the two halves together. Make sure that the front output shaft rear thrust bearing assembly is seated in the rear case.
19. Align the case bolts and the alignment dowels, then install the bolts. Alternately tighten the bolts to specified torque.
20. Install the rear output bearing in the rear retainer, and install the snapring.
21. Install the seal in the pump housing. Apply assembly lubricant to the pump housing tabs and install the housing in the rear retainer.
22. Apply a bead of RTV sealant to the mating surfaces and around the bolt holes of the rear retainer.
23. Align the rear retainer and case index marks, then install the retainer. Install and tighten the retainer bolts to specified torque.
24. Coat the rear oil seal lip and tension spring with assembly lubricant. Coat the outside of the seal with sealant and install it in the rear retainer bore.
25. Install the washer and the indicator switch.
26. Apply thread sealant to the detent retainer bolt, then install the detent ball, the spring, and the bolt.

A3

27. Install the drain plug and gasket. Coat the front oil seal lip and tension spring with assembly lubricant. Coat the outside of the seal with sealant and install it in the front retainer bore.

28. Install the front and rear yokes, new yoke seal washers, and the yoke nuts.

29. On some models, you can use a screwdriver to check the operation of the transfer case through its range, figure 5-23.

30. Fill the transfer case with the proper amount of the recommended lubricant. Install and tighten the fill plug.

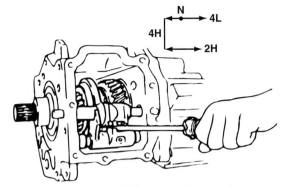

Fig. 5-23. You can check shifting on the bench with some transfer cases.

CHAPTER QUESTIONS

1. A worn or incorrectly adjusted shift linkage can cause all of the following *EXCEPT*:
   a. Hard shifting
   b. Inability to engage a gear
   c. Chatter on turns
   d. Jumping out of gear

2. Transfer case overheating can be caused by all of the following *EXCEPT*:
   a. Too much lubricant
   b. Not enough lubricant
   c. Bearings too tight
   d. Shift linkage binding

3. A likely cause of a transfer case jumping out of 4WD low range is:
   a. A worn lock plate
   b. Low lubricant
   c. A failed control module
   d. Vehicle speed that is too high

4. Front axle preload is measured with a:
   a. Dial indicator
   b. Foot-pound torque wrench
   c. Spring scale
   d. Feeler gauge

5. Control linkage adjustments on a New Process transfer case are made with the range control lever in:
   a. Neutral position
   b. 2WD position
   c. 4WD position
   d. Low position

6. An electronic shift motor usually receives its power from the:
   a. Headlamp circuit
   b. TCM power circuit
   c. Ignition switch circuit
   d. Battery

7. During a module self-test, the module is bad if:
   a. The indicator lamp flashes steadily
   b. The indicator lamp flashes intermittently
   c. The indicator lamp does not flash
   d. The indicator lamp lights steadily

8. To test a vacuum shift motor, how much vacuum is applied to each port?
   a. 5 in-Hg (17 kPa)
   b. 10 in-Hg (34 kPa)
   c. 15 in-Hg (50 kPa)
   d. 25 in-Hg (84 kPa)

9. Once a transfer case is disassembled, inspect for clogged oil passages on the:
   a. Input shaft gear
   b. Ring gear
   c. Countergear
   d. Front drive sprocket

10. Once a transfer case is disassembled, inspect the front drive sprocket for:
    a. Wear or damaged teeth
    b. Heat checking
    c. Chamfered splines
    d. Proper backlash

A3

SAMPLE TEST

This sample test can help you review your knowledge of this entire book. The format of the questions is similar to the certification tests given by the National Institute for Automotive Service Excellence. Generally, the questions here are more difficult than the programmed study questions you answered as you read the technical material in this book.

Read these review questions carefully, then read all the possible answers before making your decision. Always select the **best possible answer**. In some cases, you may think all the answers are partially correct, or you may feel that none is exactly right. But in every case, there is a **best answer** that is the one you should select.

Answers to the questions in this sample test will be found near the end of this book, before the glossary. If you answer at least 20 of these questions correctly, then you can be confident of your knowledge of the subjects covered in this book and in the ASE Certification Test A3, Manual Drive Trains and Axles. If you answer fewer than 20 correctly, you should reread the text and take another look at the illustrations. Also, check the glossary as you review the material.

1. The typical clutch hydraulic system uses:
   a. DOT-3 brake fluid
   b. Dexron-II ATF
   c. GL-5 gear oil
   d. Lithium gear oil

2. Technician A says that worn gear teeth can cause a transmission to jump out of gear.
   Technician B says that worn synchronizing sleeve teeth can cause a transmission to jump out of gear.
   Who is right?
   a. A only
   b. B only
   c. Both A and B
   d. Neither A nor B

3. Technician A says that a common cause of failed clutches is a worn pilot bushing or bearing.
   Technician B says that a defective engine crankshaft seal is a common cause of clutch failure.
   Who is right?
   a. A only
   b. B only
   c. Both A and B
   d. Neither A nor B

4. To isolate pilot bearing or bushing noise from release bearing noise, with the engine running, depress the clutch pedal and shift the transmission into:
   a. First gear
   b. Any gear
   c. Neutral
   d. Reverse

5. During a clutch release check, you should hold the pedal about 0.5 inch (13 mm) from the floor, move the shift lever between first and second gear several times, then:
   a. Slowly release the pedal
   b. Press the pedal all the way to the floor
   c. Shift into neutral
   d. Shift into reverse

6. Whenever the clutch is removed for service, always replace the:
   a. Clutch fork
   b. Clutch disc
   c. Release bearing
   d. Slave cylinder

7. Always check a new clutch disc for:
   a. Endplay
   b. Loose springs
   c. Axial runout
   d. Broken rivets

8. When you remove a flywheel, mark its position in relation to the:
   a. Clutch disc
   b. Crankshaft
   c. Pressure plate
   d. Bellhousing

9. When reassembling a transfer case, the shift rail bore in the case must be:
   a. Lubricated with gear oil
   b. Coated with the recommended lubricant
   c. Honed to oversize
   d. Completely dry and free of oil

10. During transfer case reassembly, when installing the sprockets, mainshaft assembly, mode fork, and drive chain as a complete assembly, you may need to use a:
    a. Hydraulic press
    b. Special puller
    c. Chain spreading tool
    d. Soft-faced hammer

11. Which of the following will **NOT** cause excessive transfer case noise?
    a. Low lubricant
    b. Misaligned driveshaft
    c. Loose control lever
    d. Misaligned U-joints

12. Which of the following will **NOT** cause lubricant leakage?
    a. Clogged vent
    b. Bearings too loose
    c. Driveshaft companion yoke scored at seal
    d. Bearings too tight

13. A removable carrier-type rear axle:
    a. Is identified by an inspection cover
    b. Must be removed from the vehicle for repair
    c. Is also called a Salisbury design axle
    d. Is commonly known as a Spicer axle

14. Rear axle noise heard during deceleration can be caused by:
    a. A worn rear pinion bearing
    b. Improper gear tooth contact
    c. A worn front pinion bearing
    d. Worn U-joints

15. Technician A says that differential case bearing noise will decrease as road speed increases.
Technician B says differential case bearing noise will increase as road speed increases.
Who is right?
    a. A only
    b. B only
    c. Both A and B
    d. Neither A nor B

16. Typically, rear axle bearings with normal wear provide a total bearing preload of:
    a. 5 to 10 in-lb (0.6 to 1.13 Nm)
    b. 10 to 25 in-lb (1.13 to 3 Nm)
    c. 20 to 30 in-lb (2.3 to 3.4 Nm)
    d. 25 to 35 in-lb (3 to 4 Nm)

17. Typically, an acceptable amount of clearance between the side gear and the pinion gear would be:
    a. 0.002 to 0.004 inch (0.05 to 0.10 mm)
    b. 0.005 to 0.010 inch (0.13 to 0.25 mm)
    c. 0.001 to 0.006 inch (0.03 to 0.16 mm)
    d. 0.010 to 0.015 inch (0.25 to 0.38 mm)

18. A likely cause of rear axle noise at a steady speed would be:
    a. Excessive front bearing preload
    b. Ring and pinion tooth contact variations
    c. A worn limited-slip differential
    d. A worn rear pinion bearing

19. Rear axle road speed noise can be caused by all of the following EXCEPT:
    a. Rear axle bearings
    b. Tires
    c. Differential case bearings
    d. Universal joints

20. Technician A says that a noisy left bearing can be heard while making left turns.
Technician B says that the sound of a bad right side bearing is loudest while turning left.
Who is right?
    a. A only
    b. B only
    c. Both A and B
    d. Neither A nor B

21. Check transaxle output shafts for all the following EXCEPT:
    a. Gear endplay
    b. Blocking ring to gear clearance
    c. Bearing to snap ring clearance
    d. Runout

22. During axle shaft installation, do all of the following EXCEPT:
    a. Pack the inner seal lip assembly lubricant
    b. Coat the outer edge of the seal with gasket sealer
    c. Use a seal driver to install the seal
    d. Coat the inner seal lip with gasket sealer

23. Generally, when checking a synchronizer assembly, the gap between the blocking ring and the gear cone should be about:
    a. 0.024 inch (0.61 mm)
    b. Less than 0.024 inch (0.61 mm)
    c. Greater than 0.024 inch (0.61 mm)
    d. None of the above

24. All of the following checks are performed prior to disassembling a transmission output shaft, EXCEPT:
    a. Bearing preload
    b. Blocking ring to gear clearance
    c. Gear endplay
    d. Bearing to snap ring clearance

25. Some axles require endplay adjustments. This adjustment is made:
    a. Within the differential
    b. On one side of the car by an adjuster nut
    c. By both adjuster nuts on both sides of the car
    d. By tightening the axle to the backing plate

26. Technician A says that a dial indicator can be used to check flywheel runout. Technician B says that a dial indicator can be used to check clutch disc wear. Who is right?
    a. A only
    b. B only
    c. Both A and B
    d. Neither A nor B

27. Technician A says that you should always replace an internal slave cylinder whenever you remove the transmission to service the clutch. Technician B says that you should always rebuild or replace the slave cylinder whenever you rebuild or replace the master cylinder. Who is right?
    a. A only
    b. B only
    c. Both A and B
    d. Neither A nor B

28. When installing a replacement U-joint that has a grease fitting, the fitting installs facing:
    a. Transmission
    b. Differential
    c. Front of the vehicle
    d. Driveshaft

29. A ring and pinion gear tooth pattern shows high heel and toe contact. This is caused by:
    a. Incorrect pinion depth
    b. Pinion too close to the ring gear
    c. Pinion too far from the ring gear
    d. Incorrect preload while testing

30. Chuckle is an intermittent noise caused by:
    a. Low differential lubricant level
    b. Worn differential, pinion, or side gears
    c. Worn synchronizer blocking rings
    d. Loose transfer case bearings

A3

ANSWERS

Chapter 1:
1. d, 2. c, 3. a, 4. c, 5. b, 6. b, 7. b, 8. c, 9. c, 10. a

Chapter 2:
1. c, 2. a, 3. b, 4. a, 5. a, 6. c, 7. a, 8. c, 9. b, 10. a, 11. b, 12. a, 13. a, 14. b, 15. c

Chapter 3:
1. a, 2. a, 3. d, 4. b, 5. c, 6. c, 7. d, 8. b, 9. d, 10. c

Chapter 4:
1. b, 2. a, 3. d, 4. b, 5. c, 6. c, 7. b, 8. c, 9. b, 10. c

Chapter 5:
1. c, 2. d, 3. a, 4. c, 5. b, 6. c, 7. d, 8. c, 9. a, 10. a

Sample Test:
1. a, 2. b, 3. c, 4. c, 5. d, 6. c, 7. c, 8. b, 9. d, 10. c, 11. c, 12. d, 13. b, 14. c, 15. b, 16. b, 17. c, 18. b, 19. d, 20. b, 21. c, 22. d, 23. c, 24. a, 25. b, 26. a, 27. c, 28. d, 29. a, 30. b

GLOSSARY

API Service Classification: A system of letters that signifies how a lubricant performs. It is assigned by the American Petroleum Institute.

Axial Runout: Total amount of movement away from a centerline, or axis. Also referred to as "wobble" or side-to-side play.

Backlash: Clearance or play between two mechanical parts. In the case of gears, backlash is how far one gear can move without moving the gear it meshes with.

Cardan U-Joint: A U-joint that consists of a metal cross with four needle bearings at each point. This is the most common type of U-joint for a RWD driveshaft. Double Cardan joints have two crosses.

Chamfered: Beveled, tapered, or relieved.

Constant-Velocity Joint: A type of U-joint that transmits torque in a greater range of angles without damage. Commonly known as CV joints, they are used on most FWD axles and on RWD vehicles with independent rear suspension.

Countergear: A gear that meshes with other gears on the input and output shafts of a transmission. Countergears, which assemble on the countershaft, are driven by the input shaft and, in turn, drive the gears on the output shaft. A one-piece set of countergears may be called a cluster gear.

Countershaft: The transmission shaft that is gear driven by the input shaft and, in turn, drives the output shaft. Also known as a lay shaft.

Driveshaft: A tubular shaft connecting the power output from the transmission to the pinion of the rear axle in RWD vehicles. Also known as the propeller shaft.

Dual Mass Flywheel: A flywheel that consists of two parts separated by springs used to absorb vibrations in the driveline.

Electronic Vibration Analyzer (EVA): A special diagnostic tool capable of reading vibration frequency and amplitude and displaying the results on an LCD screen.

First-Order Vibration: A condition that causes one disturbance per revolution of a component.

Fourth-Order Vibration: A condition that causes four disturbances per revolution.

Freeplay: The small amount of clearance designed into a mechanical linkage. On a clutch, the portion of clutch pedal travel required before the clutch begins to release.

Hard Spots: Circular, bluish/gold, glassy areas on the pressure plate or flywheel friction surfaces where extreme heat has altered the structure of the metal. Hard spots, also called chill spots, usually cannot be successfully machined out.

Heat Checks: Small cracks on the friction surface of a pressure plate or flywheel caused by overheating. Heat checks do not penetrate through the friction surface and can usually be machined out of it.

Input Shaft: The transmission shaft that transfers the power from the clutch disc to the countershaft gears. It may also be called the clutch shaft.

Limited-Slip Differential: A type of final drive differential that supplies a major part of the drive torque to the wheel with the greater traction when one of the wheels is slipping.

Locking Hub: Front wheel hub on a 4WD system that can be manually locked or unlocked to engage and disengage the front drive axle, thereby transmitting engine torque to the front wheels or allowing them to turn freely.

Oscilloscope: An oscilloscope is an instrument commonly used to display and analyze the waveform of electronic signals. In effect, the device draws a graph of the instantaneous signal voltage as a function of time. Also known as a lab scope.

Output Shaft: The transmission shaft that holds the output gears and the synchronizers. It connects to the driveshaft or propeller shaft to turn the driving wheels. It may also be called the mainshaft.

Pilot Bearing or Bushing: A small roller bearing or solid bronze bushing that is pressed into the end of the crankshaft to support the end of the transmission input shaft.

Pinion Bearings: The bearings in a differential assembly that support the pinion gear shaft.

Pinion Gear: The driving, and smaller, member of a ring and pinion gearset. In a final drive differential, the pinion gear is driven by the driveshaft and transfers torque to the ring gear.

Powertrain Control Module (PCM): The PCM is an onboard computer programmed to control the operation of the engine and many transmission functions.

Preload: The resistance one mechanical part exerts against the movement of another part, or the force required to overcome that resistance. Preload, like torque, is measured in inch-pounds, foot-pounds, or Newton meters (Nm).

Release Bearing: The release bearing, also called a throwout bearing, compresses the pressure plate springs to disengage the clutch when the clutch pedal is depressed. The bearing reduces friction between the pressure plate levers and the clutch fork.

Ring Gear: The driven, and larger, member of a ring and pinion gearset. The ring gear, which attaches to the differential case, shifts the direction of crankshaft rotation 90 degrees and transfers torque to the drive axles.

Second-Order Vibration: A condition that causes two disturbances per revolution of a component.

Slave Cylinder: A hydraulic cylinder that reacts to hydraulic apply pressure from a master cylinder to perform a mechanical task. On a hydraulic clutch linkage, the slave cylinder causes the clutch fork to move.

Slip Yoke: A variable length connection in the driveline that allows the driveshaft to change lengths. Also known as slip joints.

Steering Knuckle: A metal casting that supports the road wheel, joins the suspension to the wheel, and provides pivot points between them.

Synchronizer Assembly: An assembly of sleeves and rings that fits between output gears. The synchronizers aid gear engagement and prevent grinding or clashing.

Third-Order Vibration: A condition that causes three disturbances per revolution of a component.

Transfer Case: A gear case that transfers torque from the transmission to another set of drive wheels. It allows FWD or RWD vehicles to become 4WD. The case contains an input shaft from the transmission or transaxle and output shafts to the drive wheels.

Universal Joint: Jointed connections on driveshafts that permit a change in angle. Also referred to as a U-joint.

A3

SUSPENSION AND STEERING

CHAPTER ONE

STEERING SYSTEMS DIAGNOSIS AND REPAIR

CHAPTER OBJECTIVES

- The technician will complete the ASE tasks list on Steering Systems Diagnosis and Repair.
- The technician will be able to answer 10 questions dealing with the Steering Systems Diagnosis and Repair section of the A4 ASE Test.

INSPECTION AND DIAGNOSIS

Owner complaints about the steering system generally fall into four categories:

- Poor handling
- Hard steering
- Fluid leaks
- Noise

The first step in diagnosing a problem is to determine the category into which it fits. This narrows down the number of components to check. The best way to do this is by road testing the vehicle. Next, visually inspect the steering system and related components.

The following is an inspection checklist. Several key elements are introduced here; detailed explanations follow later in this book. To inspect:

1. Check each tire for proper size and inflation. Low pressure in the tires can cause hard steering. Extreme tire wear can increase steering effort.
2. Check **steering wheel freeplay**. Straighten the wheels, then turn the steering wheel left and right, checking how far it turns before the road wheels begin to move. Check specifications; allowable freeplay ranges from 0 to 1.5 inches (0 to 35 mm).
3. Check steering gear lubricant level and top off if necessary. Be aware, lubricant must be at operating temperature ($120°$ to $180°F$, or $50°$ to $80°C$) to get an accurate reading. Manual steering gears use gear oil or grease, while power-assisted units require power steering (PS) fluid or automatic transmission fluid (ATF).
4. Check power steering pump belt tension; adjust if necessary. Inspect the belt for cuts, glazing, or damage, and replace if damaged.

5. Check steering components for:
   - Binding or damaged steering shaft joints
   - Loose or misaligned flexible coupling
   - Steering gear leakage
   - Loose or damaged steering gear mounts
   - Loose or leaking steering rack boots
   - Loose tie rod ends, damaged tie rod end seals, contamination in the seals
   - Looseness or play in the steering linkage, worn linkage ball joints
   - Damage to steering linkage ball joint seals, loss of lubricant or contamination
   - Leaks or loose fittings at the power steering pump or hoses
6. With the vehicle on a frame-contact hoist, try to spread the tires apart from the front while watching the steering linkage. The linkage should not move.
7. Check for looseness or damage to suspension components or bushings.
8. For hard steering, check pinion torque or gear mesh preload; adjust if necessary.
9. For hard steering in a power steering system, pressure test the pump, and repair or replace as necessary. If the pump is okay, check the steering gear control valve.
10. Check wheel runout, balance, and alignment.

Manual Steering Diagnosis

After road testing a vehicle with manual steering, inspect the suspect components based on the symptoms you experience, figure 1-1.

Power Steering Diagnosis

To diagnose problems in a power steering system based on symptoms, refer to figure 1-2.

STEERING WHEEL AND COLUMN SERVICE

Steering wheels do not need much service, but sometimes you must remove them for access to the steering shaft or column. In newer vehicles, removal is complicated by a supplemental inflatable restraint (SIR), or air bag, mounted in the steering wheel. Special steering wheel removal procedures are required

---

Steering Wheel Freeplay: The amount the steering wheel can be turned, using light pressure, before it meets resistance. It is an indicator of steering system responsiveness.

MANUAL STEERING DIAGNOSIS

CONDITION	POSSIBLE CAUSE(S)
Unresponsive steering, excessive play or looseness in system	a. Excessive gear lash in steering gear b. Incorrect worm or pinion bearing preload c. Worn or loose steering shaft couplings, steering gear mounts, or linkage ball joints d. Worn steering gear components e. Excessive front wheel bearing play
Hard steering	a. Low tire pressure b. Insufficient steering or suspension lubrication c. Damaged steering system components d. Incorrect wheel alignment e. Steering gear too tight
Rattling noise in steering system	a. Loose steering gear mounting bolts b. Loose or worn steering shaft bearing
Poor recovery from turns	a. Low tire pressure b. Incorrect wheel alignment c. Insufficient steering or suspension ball joint lubrication d. Binding in strut bearings e. Steering gear too tight f. Binding in steering shaft bearings
Steering wheel vibration, front wheel shimmy	a. Unequal tire inflation b. Unequal tire wear c. Wheel imbalance or runout d. Incorrect wheel alignment e. Worn steering linkage or suspension ball joints f. Worn suspension bushings
Car pulls to one side	a. Unequal tire inflation b. Incorrect wheel alignment c. Loose or worn suspension components
Car wanders, drifts	a. Incorrect tire inflation b. Incorrect wheel alignment c. Binding in steering shaft coupling, steering gear, or upper strut bearing

Fig. 1-1. Manual steering gear system diagnostic chart.

POWER STEERING DIAGNOSIS

CONDITION	POSSIBLE CAUSE(S)
Hard steering	a. Low fluid level b. Loose drive belt c. Low output d. Steering gear problems: • Faulty control valve • External or internal leakage
Car pulls to either side	a. Faulty gear control valve b. Steering gear internal leakage
Temporary increase in steering effort when turning left or right	a. Low fluid level b. Loose drive belt c. Oil on drive belt d. Engine idle too slow e. Steering gear internal leakage f. Malfunctioning steering gear
Chattering, whining, or squealing	a. Loose or worn drive belt b. Loose cylinder mounting or linkage attachment c. Low fluid level d. Loose pump pulley e. Hose-to-car contact f. Dirt or air in system g. High backpressure h. Worn pump bearing i. Defective control or relief valve
Hissing during sharp turns	a. Normal relief valve operation
Lack of assist, one direction	a. Steering gear fluid leakage b. Defective power piston ring
Lack of assist, both directions	a. Loose drive belt b. Low pump output c. Defective power piston ring

Fig. 1-2. Power steering gear system diagnostic chart.

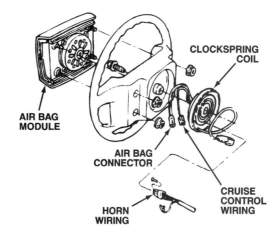

Fig. 1-3. Disable the SIR system before removing the air bag module.

to avoid deploying the air bag. Some vehicles also have controls for the radio and cruise control mounted on the steering wheel, and these must be given special consideration as well.

Steering column service may include working on switches, wiring, and mechanisms for accessory controls, such as the ignition switch, turn signals, and gear shifter. Steering shaft service involves replacing U-joints, flexible couplings, or the entire shaft.

Steering Wheel Removal

Before removing the steering wheel, position it so the front wheels are straight ahead. This will help to ensure that you re-install the steering wheel in the correct position.

When you need to remove a steering wheel on a vehicle that is equipped with an air bag, remove the air bag module first, figure 1-3. Refer to the appropriate vehicle Service Manual for all applicable safety precautions.

A4

CAUTION: If the air bag deploys while you are working on it, you may be seriously injured. Exact procedures vary by manufacturer, but all require the air bag to be disabled before the steering wheel is removed.

Generally, the air bag system is disabled by disconnecting the battery or removing a fuse and waiting about 10 minutes for the stored energy to dissipate. Then, the electrical connectors to the inflator can be safely disconnected, and the air bag module can be removed from the steering wheel as a unit.

CAUTION: Never attempt to disassemble an air bag module. Check the Service Manual for specific requirements on the vehicle you are servicing. Always place the air bag module face up on the work surface when it is removed from the vehicle.

Steering wheels equipped with controls for the radio, cruise control, HVAC system, or other systems require an extra step or two before removal from the column. Generally the switch assembly or assemblies can be removed from the steering wheel by releasing the mounting clips and gently prying them away from the switch housing. Other models require the removal of attachment screws before the switches can be removed. Refer to the appropriate Service Manual for more specific information.

To remove the steering wheel, take off the trim panel, horn pad, or air bag module, then disconnect all wiring between the steering wheel and column. Remove the retaining nut that secures the steering wheel to the steering shaft. Use a steering wheel puller to ease the steering wheel off the shaft, figure 1-4. Never hammer or force the steering wheel loose, or you may damage it or collapse the steering shaft.

Steering Column Service

Manual Tilt Systems

Some steering columns have a mechanism for tilting the steering wheel, figure 1-5. If the tilt mechanism binds, disassemble the steering wheel and column as much as necessary for access to the mechanism, and inspect it for wear, dirt, or damage. Adjust, lubricate, and replace parts as needed.

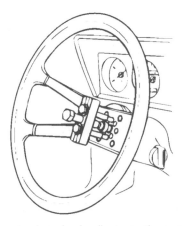

Fig. 1-4. Use a steering wheel puller to gently remove the wheel from the shaft.

Power Tilt and Telescope Systems

Components in the tilt/telescoping steering column system include the following:

- Tilt/Telescoping control switch
- Steering Column Tilt Telescoping Control Module
- Tilt actuator motor with integral position sensor
- Telescope actuator motor with integral position sensor

Motors within the tilt and telescope actuators operate the tilt and telescoping features based on commands from the control module. The driver operates the tilt/telescope switch, which moves the steering wheel to the desired position.

Most systems also allow the driver to program the desired position of the wheel so there is no need to make the adjustment every time the car is driven. The control module stores position information it receives from the telescoping and tilt position sensors. The auto exit function allows the driver to easily enter and exit the vehicle. When the key is turned off and the driver door is opened, the module operates the motor to move the steering wheel out of the driver's way. When the key is turned to the ON position, the Tilt Telescope Control

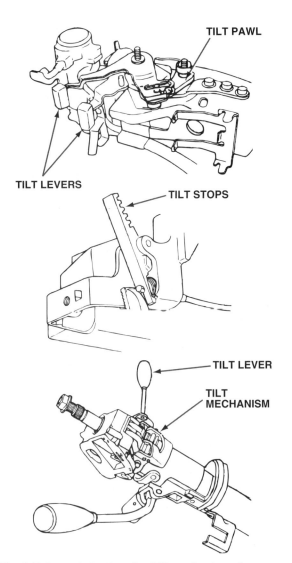

Fig. 1-5. Inspect steering wheel tilt mechanisms for wear and damage.

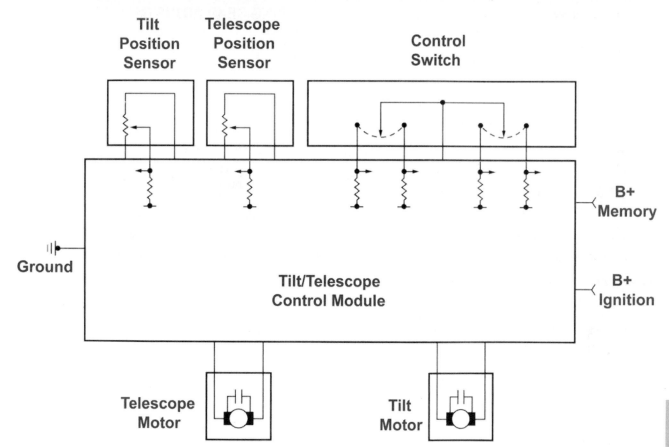

Fig. 1-6. Typical power tilt and telescope steering column schematic.

Module commands the actuator motors to move the column back into the desired driving position, figure 1-6.

Most noises originating from the power tilt and telescope system are the result of dry or binding gear drives. Disassemble the column and lubricate the operating mechanism following the proper steps in the appropriate Service Manual.

Diagnosis of problems with the electronic tilt and telescope functions requires the use of a vehicle specific scan tool. Refer to the appropriate vehicle Service Manual for more information.

Steering Column and Shaft Service

If steering shaft U-joints or flexible couplings are worn, replace them. These often bolt to the shaft, and are replaced by unbolting the old one and bolting the new one in place. Some designs are built into the intermediate shaft, so replacing them requires replacing the shaft, figure 1-7. A pinch bolt is used to connect the coupler to the steering gear input shaft.

Most vehicles are equipped with specially designed sections of the steering shaft which are designed to collapse during a frontal collision, preventing the steering wheel being forced upward and injuring the driver. The **collapsible steering column** sections are not repairable and must be carefully

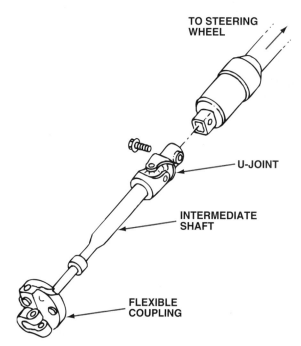

Fig. 1-7. Flexible couplings and U-joints are an integral part of the intermediate shaft on some designs.

Collapsible Steering Column: An energy-absorbing steering column that is designed to collapse if the driver is thrown into it due to a heavy collision.

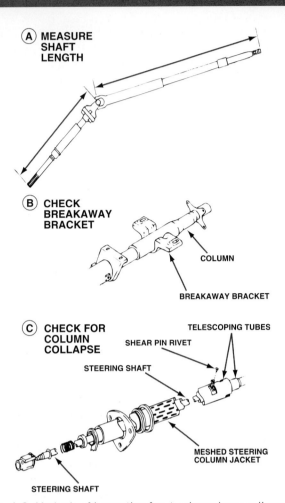

(A) MEASURE SHAFT LENGTH

(B) CHECK BREAKAWAY BRACKET

COLUMN

BREAKAWAY BRACKET

(C) CHECK FOR COLUMN COLLAPSE

TELESCOPING TUBES
SHEAR PIN RIVET
STEERING SHAFT
MESHED STEERING COLUMN JACKET
STEERING SHAFT

Fig. 1-8. Methods of inspecting for steering column collapse.

inspected and replaced if damage is evident. To determine if a steering shaft is collapsed, measure its length and compare to specifications, or examine it for sheared brackets, plastic shards, or crushed mesh sections, figure 1-8. To remove a steering column and shaft:

1. Remove the steering wheel, and disconnect column wiring and mechanical links.
2. Remove steering column and under dash trim panels as needed to access mounting bolts.
3. Remove the bolts of the U-joint or flexible coupling at the steering gear.
4. Remove the fasteners securing the column support brackets to the floor or dash underside, while supporting the steering column.
5. Remove the steering column and shaft.

To install a new steering column and shaft:

1. Position and support the assembly in the vehicle and fasten the column brackets.
2. Connect the U-joint or flexible coupling at the base of the shaft to the steering gear.
3. Reconnect column wiring and mechanisms, fit the trim panels, and install the steering wheel.

STEERING GEAR ADJUSTMENTS

The two most common types of steering gears are:

- Recirculating ball
- Rack and pinion

Both types of steering gear have adjustment methods for ensuring correct operation.

Recirculating Ball Steering Gear

Recirculating ball steering gear adjustments are:

- Worm bearing preload
- Gear mesh preload
- Sector shaft endplay
- Control valve centering

Preload and endplay adjustments take up slack from system wear, and centering the control valve ensures proper direction of hydraulic pressure in a power steering system.

Worm Bearing Preload Adjustment

Worm bearing preload is the resistance offered by the worm shaft bearings. Too much preload makes the steering feel stiff, while too little makes it feel loose. Measure preload at the steering wheel retaining nut, and adjust it at the steering gear. To check:

1. Disconnect the steering linkage from the gear.
2. Remove the horn pad or air bag module from the steering wheel to access to the retaining nut. Observe air bag module removal precautions.
3. Turn the steering wheel to one end of its travel.
4. Turn the steering wheel in the opposite direction until you feel a slight resistance. Stop there.
5. Use a torque wrench and socket on the retaining nut to turn the steering wheel one and a half turns. The torque wrench reading indicates worm bearing preload. If it is incorrect, adjust it as described in one of the following procedures.
6. Reassemble the steering wheel and the linkage.

Depending on the steering gear, adjust worm bearing preload with shims or an adjuster plug. To adjust using shims, figure 1-9:

1. Remove the steering gear and drain its lubricant.
2. Remove the worm cover.

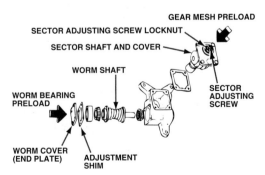

GEAR MESH PRELOAD
SECTOR ADJUSTING SCREW LOCKNUT
SECTOR SHAFT AND COVER
WORM SHAFT
WORM BEARING PRELOAD
SECTOR ADJUSTING SCREW
WORM COVER (END PLATE)
ADJUSTMENT SHIM

Fig. 1-9. Shims set the worm bearing preload, and an adjusting screw sets the gear mesh preload on this steering gear.

Worm Bearing Preload: Worm bearing preload is the resistance to rotation created by the load on the worm shaft bearings.

3. Remove shims to increase worm bearing preload, or add shims to decrease it.
4. Reinstall the worm cover and tighten bolts to specified torque.
5. Refill the steering gear with the correct lubricant and reinstall it.
6. Check and adjust worm bearing preload.
7. Reconnect the linkage to the steering gear.

To adjust worm bearing preload with an adjuster plug, figure 1-10:

1. Loosen the adjuster plug locknut.
2. Turn the plug clockwise to increase preload or counterclockwise to decrease it, until correct.
3. Tighten the locknut onto the adjuster plug.
4. Reconnect the linkage to the steering gear.

Gear Mesh Preload Adjustment

Gear mesh preload is the resistance offered by the meshing of the worm and sector gears. Too much preload makes steering difficult. The opposite of gear mesh preload is gear lash, play between the gears before they mesh. Excessive lash causes too much steering wheel freeplay. Measure gear mesh preload at the steering wheel retaining nut and adjust it at the steering gear:

1. Detach the steering linkage from the steering gear.
2. Remove the steering wheel horn pad or air bag module. Follow air bag precautions.
3. Center the steering gear. Turn the steering wheel to one full stop, then count the turns to the opposite full stop. Return the steering wheel to center, which is half the number of turns from stop to stop.
4. Use a torque wrench and socket on the steering wheel retaining nut to turn it one half turn. The torque wrench reading indicates gear mesh preload. If incorrect, adjust as described in the next section.
5. Reassemble the linkage and the steering wheel.

To adjust gear mesh preload, loosen the locknut on the sector adjusting screw, refer back to figure 1-9. Turn the adjusting screw clockwise to increase preload or counterclockwise to decrease it. Hold the adjusting screw in place while you tighten the locknut.

Sector Shaft Endplay Adjustment

Sector shaft endplay is the distance between the sector shaft adjusting screw and the sector shaft. It is not adjustable in all steering gears, and adjustments can only be made when the steering gear is disassembled, figure 1-11:

1. With the sector shaft removed from the steering gear, use a feeler gauge to check endplay.
2. If it exceeds specifications, install a shim.
3. Hold the adjuster screw between your fingers and turn the sector shaft. It should turn freely. If not, the shim is too thick. Find one that lets the shaft turn freely without excessive endplay.

Centering the Control Valve

If the **control valve** in a power steering gear is not centered, the vehicle may pull, lead, drift, and have poor returnability in one direction. Check control valve centering by raising the vehicle on a lift with the front wheels straight ahead, then starting the engine. If the front wheels turn when the engine starts, the control valve is not centered.

If the steering gear uses a rotary control valve, you cannot center it—rebuild or replace the steering gear to correct. If the steering gear has a spool-type control valve, you can center the control valve by repositioning it in the valve bore, figure 1-12.

To center a control valve:

1. Loosen the screws securing the valve body to the steering gear.

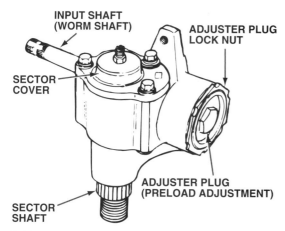

Fig. 1-10. An adjuster plug is used to set worm bearing preload on this steering gear.

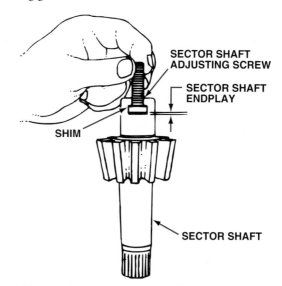

Fig. 1-11. The steering gear must be disassembled to adjust sector shaft endplay.

A4

Control Valve: A power steering system valve that controls the application of pressurized fluid against the power piston.
Gear Mesh Preload: The resistance that the sector gear or roller of a recirculating ball steering gear exerts against worm gear movement, or the force required to move the worm gear against that resistance.
Sector Shaft Endplay: The axial movement of the sector shaft in a standard steering gear.

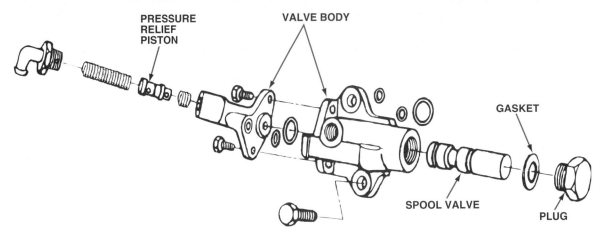

Fig. 1-12. A spool-type control valve can be centered without disassembling the steering gear.

2. Use a soft-faced hammer to tap the end plug, which moves the valve body downward. To move the valve up, tap the screw that secures the valve body to the steering gear.
3. Check for valve centering again. If it is not centered, continue tapping the valve body until the valve is properly positioned.
4. Once the valve is centered, tighten the valve body.

Steering Gear Gaskets and Seal Service

Gasket and seal replacement is possible on some models of steering gears. Refer the the appropriate Service Manual for the correct procedures required for seal and gasket service. Ensure manual gears are refilled with the proper lubricant before placing the vehicle back in service. Follow the procedures detailed in this chapter for refilling and bleeding power steering gears. Always road test the vehicle and check for leaks before returning the vehicle to the customer.

Rack and Pinion Steering Gear

The adjustments you can make on a rack and pinion steering gear are:

- Pinion torque
- Pinion bearing preload

Pinion torque is a measurement of how much force it takes to turn the pinion gear along the rack. It is similar to gear mesh preload in a recirculating ball steering gear. **Pinion bearing preload** indicates how much force the pinion bearings place on the pinion shaft, figure 1-13. Only a few steering gears provide the means to adjust pinion bearing preload.

Pinion Torque Adjustment

Change pinion torque either by adjusting the position of the rack support cover or by adding or removing shims:

1. Remove the rack and pinion assembly from the vehicle and clamp it in the soft jaws of a vise.
2. Using a torque wrench, turn the pinion shaft, taking notice of the torque wrench reading.

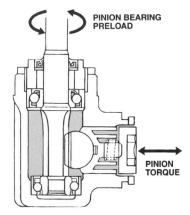

Fig. 1-13. Pinion bearing preload and pinion torque are rack and pinion steering gear adjustments.

3. If the reading does not match specifications, adjust pinion torque in one of the following ways:
   - If the steering gear has an adjustment screw or threaded cover, loosen the locknut and turn the cover or screw clockwise to increase pinion torque or counterclockwise to decrease it
   - If there is no external adjustment mechanism, remove the rack support cover and add or remove shims to adjust pinion torque
4. Once pinion torque is correct, tighten the locknut or rack cover bolts.

Pinion Bearing Preload Adjustment

If the system you are working on has shims under the pinion end cover or an adjuster at the base of the gear, adjust pinion bearing preload as follows:

1. Remove the rack and pinion assembly from the vehicle and clamp it in the soft jaws of a vise.
2. Loosen the rack support cover, so it does not affect pinion movement.

Pinion Bearing Preload: The resistance that the bearings in a rack and pinion steering gear exert against the pinion gear and shaft, or the force required to overcome that resistance.
Pinion Torque: Force required to move the pinion of a rack and pinion steering gear against resistance exerted by the rack.

3. Use a torque wrench to turn the pinion shaft and compare the reading with specifications.
4. Either add or remove shims from under the pinion end cover or turn the adjuster at the base of the gear to adjust preload.
5. Adjust pinion torque.

Bellows Inspection and Replacement

The surface of the tie rods are protected by flexible bellows or boots attached to each end of the steering rack. The bellows should be inspected periodically for cracking, splitting, or other damage. If damage is evident, replace the bellows using the following procedure.

1. Raise the vehicle on a hoist.
2. If necessary, remove the front wheels for access to the steering linkage. Remove the cotter pins and castellated nuts from the outer tie rod ends. Then, separate the tie rod ends from the steering knuckles.
3. Remove the clamps securing the bellows to the tie rod and to the rack housing, then slip the old bellows off the end of the tie rod.

Note: Some rack assemblies utilize a vent tube that connects the left and right bellows. Use care when removing the vent tube as it will be reused upon installation of the new bellows.

4. Clean the tie rod surfaces and inspect for damage before installing the new bellows.
5. Install the new bellows and secure using the clamps provided. Reinstall the vent tube, if equipped
6. Connect the outer tie rod ends to the steering knuckles and install the castellated nuts.
7. Torque the nuts to specifications and install new cotter pins.
8. Steer the vehicle from side to side, ensuring the new bellows move correctly with the tie rods.
9. Lower the vehicle.

REMOVING AND INSTALLING STEERING GEARS

The steering gear bolts to the vehicle frame or underbody and connects to the steering shaft. You must disconnect a recirculating ball steering gear from the steering linkage to remove it, but you remove a rack and pinion steering gear as a unit along with the tie rods.

Manual Steering Gear Replacement

To remove a manual recirculating ball steering gear:

1. Raise the vehicle on a hoist.
2. If the **pitman arm** is secured to the sector shaft by a locknut and cotter pin, remove the nut and pin. Mark the pitman arm and sector shaft before separating them. Inspect the pitman arm for any damage or signs of bending. Replace the pitman arm if any damage is found.

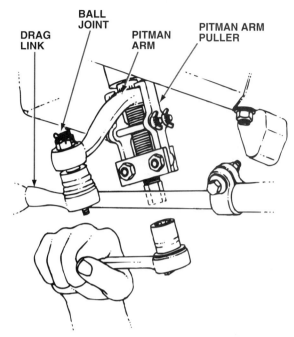

Fig. 1-14. Use a puller to separate the pitman arm from the sector shaft.

3. Use a puller to separate the pitman arm from the sector shaft, figure 1-14. Apply penetrating oil if the parts are difficult to separate. Never hammer on the pitman arm or shaft to loosen them, as this can damage the steering gear.
4. Separate the gear from the steering shaft by disconnecting the U-joint or flexible coupling.
5. Remove the fasteners securing the steering gear housing to the vehicle. Remove the steering gear.

To remove a rack and pinion steering gear, figure 1-15:

1. Raise the vehicle on a hoist.
2. Disconnect the steering shaft by loosening and removing the lower U-joint or pinch bolt.
3. If necessary, remove the front wheels for access to the steering linkage. Remove the cotter pins and castellated nuts from the outer tie rod ends. Then, separate the tie rod ends from the steering knuckles.
4. Remove the rack housing bolts and brackets. If the brackets have rubber bushings, remove them. Remove the rack and pinion assembly.

To install a recirculating ball steering gear:

1. Count the number of turns needed to turn the worm shaft from stop to stop. Then, center the steering gear by turning the worm shaft exactly one half that number of turns from either stop.
2. Use new fasteners and bushings to attach the steering gear housing to the chassis. Tighten bolts to specified torque.
3. Aim the steering wheel straight ahead. Connect the steering shaft U-joint or flexible coupling to the steering gear input shaft.

Pitman Arm: The part of a parallelogram steering linkage that joins the linkage to the steering gear sector shaft and transmits movement from the steering gear to the linkage.

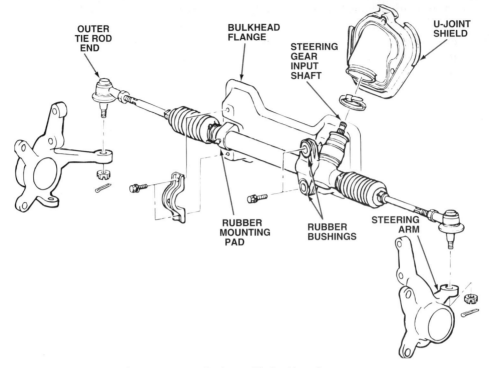

Fig. 1-15. Remove a rack and pinion steering gear as a unit along with the tie rods.

4. Align the splines and reference marks on the sector shaft and pitman arm.
5. Install the sector shaft locknut and tighten to specified torque. Install a new cotter pin, if used.
6. Check steering gear and steering wheel centering. The number of turns from center to lock should be equal on both sides.

To install a rack and pinion steering gear:

1. Replace worn bushings or mounting brackets. Bolt the rack housing, with the bushings and brackets, to the frame or crossmember. Tighten the bolts to specified torque.
2. Count the number of turns needed to turn the pinion shaft from stop to stop. Center the rack by turning the pinion shaft one half the number of turns.

3. Center the steering wheel.
4. Connect the steering gear input shaft to the steering shaft U-joint.
5. Install the outer tie rod ends into the steering knuckles. Tighten the castellated nuts to specifications and secure with new cotter pins.
6. If you removed the wheels, re-install them. Lower the vehicle and torque the wheel nuts to specifications. Check and correct wheel alignment.

Power Steering Gear Replacement

Removing a power-assisted steering gear is similar to removing a manual steering gear. The difference is in disconnecting the steering gear from the hydraulic system, figure 1-16. Use this additional information:

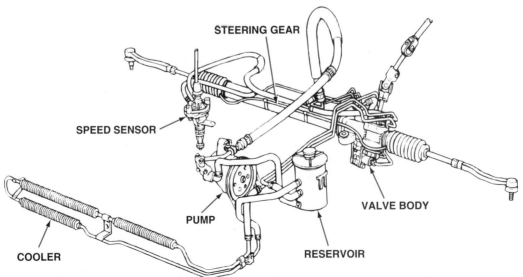

Fig. 1-16. A typical power rack and pinion steering system; hydraulic components are similar for a recirculating ball unit.

1. Steam clean the gear housing, hoses, fittings, and fluid reservoir dry with compressed air.
2. Raise the vehicle on a hoist.
3. Place a drain pan under the steering gear. Disconnect the return hose at the steering gear. Plug the hose and secure it at a point higher than the fluid reservoir. Disconnect, plug, and secure the high-pressure hose. If the system has cooler hoses, disconnect and plug them.
4. Cap off the steering gear hydraulic fittings.
5. Once the hydraulic lines are disconnected, removing a power steering gear is the same as removing a manual unit.
6. Before reinstalling the steering gear, replace any O-ring seals on the pressure and return hose fittings.
7. During installation, connect the pressure, return hoses, and cooler hoses to the steering gear. Tighten the connections with a flare nut wrench.
8. Top off the fluid in the reservoir and bleed the system. Check and correct fluid level again. Some manufacturers recommend flushing the system.
9. Drive the vehicle, then check for fluid leaks.

POWER STEERING HYDRAULIC SERVICE

General power steering hydraulic system service procedures include:

- Checking fluid level and condition
- Replacing the system filter
- Inspecting and replacing system hoses
- Flushing the system
- Bleeding the system

Checking the Power Steering Fluid

Check the power steering fluid level and condition at the fluid reservoir. One of two basic reservoir designs are used:

- Integral
- Remote

Many reservoirs or dipsticks have two level indicators to check the fluid level at normal operating temperature and when cold. For the most accurate results many manufacturers suggest checking the level when the fluid is at operating temperature—about 120° to 180°F (50° to 80°C). Refer to the Service Manual, Owner's Manual, or instructions stamped on the reservoir or cap.

To inspect the fluid:

1. Park the vehicle on level ground, and locate the power steering fluid reservoir.
2. If fluid is leaking from the reservoir cap, the reservoir may be too full or the cap seal may be damaged. Wipe the cap and around the opening with a clean shop rag to keep dirt from entering the system.
3. Depending on the reservoir design:
   - Remove the cap and dipstick assembly, wipe the dipstick with a clean rag, and put the cap back on. Remove it again and see where the fluid level reaches on the dipstick
   - Look where the fluid level reaches on the graduations on the transparent reservoir body

- If there are no level indicators, remove the cap and look inside. Generally the level should be about ⅔ full for proper operation
4. Add or remove fluid as needed to correct the level. Often the power steering fluid specification is stamped on the reservoir or cap. If the level is extremely low raise the front of the vehicle off the ground before adding fluid to prevent an air pocket from forming in the gear or pump. Refer to Bleeding the Power Steering System in this chapter for more information.
5. Once the system is properly filled, wipe up any fluid spilled on the outside of the reservoir, inspect the condition of the cap seal for damage, and if in good condition re-install the cap. If the cap seal is damaged replace as required.
6. Drive the vehicle and check fluid level again. If it is low, look for hydraulic system leaks.

Fluid Condition

While checking the level, also note fluid condition. Dab some on a white paper towel and examine it. The color should be clear and light. If the fluid is brown and thick, and smells like varnish, it may be oxidized. If it contains metal particles, internal damage to the pump or steering gear has occurred.

Black particles indicate deteriorating hoses and seals or other contamination. If the fluid is foamy or cloudy, air is in the system, which reduces hydraulic assist. Repair the problems causing fluid deterioration, flush the entire power steering system, add new fluid, and bleed the system.

Replacing the Power Steering Fluid Filter

A few power steering systems utilize a replaceable fluid filter. Normally this filter is located in the reservoir and is accessed by removing the reservoir cover. If the system shows signs of excessive contamination, drain and flush the system before replacing the filter.

Inspecting Power Steering Hoses and Lines

Most power steering hoses deteriorate from the inside out. As the hoses deteriorate from inside, rubber particles begin to flake off from the interior walls. As deterioration advances, more and more particles are pushed through the system. Rubber particles commonly stick the flow control valve in the pump and can cause accelerated wear of the control valve housing in the steering gear or rack and pinion, leading to complete and expensive system failure.

If any of the following conditions are found, replace the hoses. Remember, if one hose shows signs of wear, always replace all hoses, as all hoses in the system are subjected to the same conditions and wear. Keep the following in mind when inspecting hoses and lines:

- Check tubing for corrosion, abrasion or cracks
- Check the hose to coupling connection for leaks or drips
- Look for small pinholes or cracks in the hose covers
- The brittleness or hardness of the hose is an early sign that the hose has lost its ability to absorb pressure surges

A4

- A soft, spongy hose is a more serious sign of wear, indicating advanced internal deterioration and probable leakage
- Thick fluid in the pump reservoir indicates internal hose deterioration

Replacing Power Steering System Hoses

To replace power steering system hoses:

1. Use a siphon gun to remove all of the fluid from the power steering reservoir.
2. Disconnect one end of the low-pressure hose being replaced and allow the remaining fluid to drain into an approved container.
3. Remove the damaged hose.

> **CAUTION: Disconnect high-pressure flare fittings with a flare nut wrench. Do not use an open-end wrench; it may damage the flare fittings.**

4. Replace the hose, routing it the same way as the original one. Secure the hose with any supports or holddowns as required.

> **CAUTION: Use only hoses designed for power steering systems. Other hose types may fail and result in the loss of vehicle control.**

5. Replace O-rings on the high-pressure fittings.
6. The high-pressure hose may have a stripe running down its length. This provides a visual reference to ensure the hose does not twist as you tighten the fittings.
7. If contamination was present in the power steering fluid flush the system, then refill it. Start the engine, bleed the system, and check for leaks. Recheck fluid level, and top off as required.

Flushing the Power Steering System

If power steering fluid is contaminated, make any needed repairs, then flush the hydraulic system. To flush the system:

1. Raise the vehicle on a hoist.
2. Place a drain pan under the pump. Disconnect the low-pressure return hose from the pump, put the open end of the hose in the drain pan, and plug the pump fitting.
3. With the engine running, have an assistant add fluid to the reservoir as you turn the steering wheel from stop to stop, allowing fluid to circulate through the entire steering gear.
4. Run about 1 quart (1 liter) of fluid through the system, or continue until the fluid runs clear.
5. Stop the engine, reconnect the return hose, and fill the system. Run the engine for about 15 minutes while turning the steering wheel from stop to stop.
6. Bleed the system.

Bleeding the Power Steering System

If there are air bubbles in the power steering fluid, the fluid places uneven pressure against the power piston, and steering feels spongy or jerky. As fluid circulates through the hydraulic system, most air bubbles escape at the fluid reservoir. If air pockets get trapped in the pump or steering gear,

the component makes groaning sounds during operation, and the steering system does not give full assist.

Bleeding the system releases trapped air. You do not have to bleed after a routine reservoir check and refill. But bleeding is required after draining the system to replace parts, or after refilling a fluid reservoir that was extremely low.

To bleed the hydraulic system:

1. If recommended, drive the vehicle onto ramps to elevate the front end.
2. Run the engine for about 10 minutes to bring the fluid to operating temperature.
3. Turn the steering wheel *slowly* from lock to lock several times, which helps release air bubbles in the steering gear. Do not hold the steering wheel in the lock position for more than a few seconds. Have an assistant watch the reservoir, topping it off whenever it runs low.
4. Stop the engine and check fluid condition. If the fluid is foamy or milky, it still has air in it. Wait a few minutes, then bleed the system again.

Many late model power steering pumps have an aluminum housing, a plastic reservoir, and a reservoir cap with an O-ring seal. Generally, you cannot bleed this system using the procedure just described. You must pull vacuum on this system, following a procedure detailed in the Service Manual.

HYDRAULIC PRESSURE CHECKS

Even a small loss of hydraulic pressure causes power steering problems. To check system pressure, pump pressure, and steering gear pressure, you need a pressure gauge. Install the gauge, with the shutoff valve toward the steering gear between the pump outlet fitting and the pressure hose that runs to the steering gear inlet, figure 1-17.

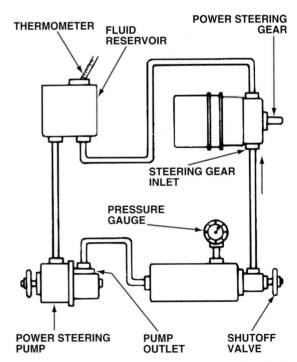

Fig. 1-17. Typical power steering pressure gauge installation.

System Pressure Testing

After installing the pressure gauge, check the power steering system pressure:

1. Fully open the gauge shutoff valve.
2. Start the engine and run to operating temperature.
3. Read the pressure on the gauge and compare it to specifications, typically 1,500 psi (10,500 kPa). If the reading is:

   - Within range, go to the pump pressure test
   - Too high, look for a restriction in the hydraulic system hoses and connectors, eliminate the restrictions, then retest the system
   - Too low, use pump and steering gear pressure tests to find a leak

Pump Pressure Testing

With the pressure gauge still connected, conduct the pump pressure test:

1. Open and close the shutoff valve several times, keeping it closed less than five seconds each time.
2. Record the highest pressure each time you close the valve, then compare the recorded pressures with specifications. If the pressures are:

   - Within range and the difference between readings is less than 50 psi (345 kPa), the pump is okay; go to the steering gear pressure test
   - Within range but the difference between them is greater than 50 psi, the flow control valve in the pump is malfunctioning, and you must repair the valve or replace the pump
   - Too low, but within 50 psi of each other, the pump is malfunctioning, and you must replace the inner seals or the entire pump

Steering Gear Pressure Testing

Still keeping the pressure gauge connected, check steering gear pressure:

1. Turn the steering wheel to one full stop, then to the opposite full stop. Do not keep the steering wheel at full stop for more than a few seconds.
2. Record the pressure reading at each full stop and compare to specifications:

   - Compare the higher pressure reading with the reading from the pump test; if they are the same, the steering gear is okay
   - If one or both full-stop readings are lower than specified, the steering gear is probably leaking internally; remove the steering gear and replace the seals or replace the entire unit

POWER STEERING PUMP SERVICE

Pump Design

The engine drives the power steering pump through a belt and pulleys. There are three major types of pumps in use today:

- Roller
- Vane
- Slipper

Pump Service Procedures

While the internal pumping elements are different, there are no significant external service differences between the different pump designs, figure 1-18.

Servicing a power steering pump consists of:

- Inspecting drive belt alignment
- Checking drive belt tension
- Replacing the drive belt tensioner
- Replacing the drive belt
- Checking for noises, vibration, or leaks
- Removing and replacing the pump

Power Steering Drive Belts

There are two types of belts:

- Drive or V-belts
- Serpentine or Mulit-Rib belts

A single serpentine belt will typically drive all the various accessories on the engine, while a drive belt will usually only drive one or two. Most vehicles that use drive belts have more than one belt. Occasionally, vehicles equipped with serpentine belts will have a separate belt which runs the air conditioning compressor alone. Belts need to be replaced when the inside of the belt is badly cracked, glazed, frayed, or when the rubber begins to harden.

A4

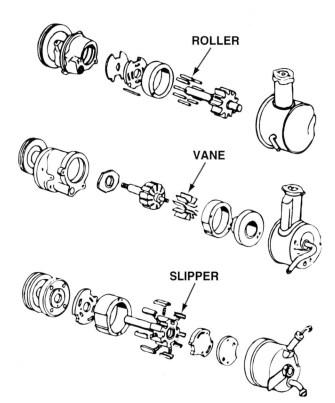

Fig. 1-18. Roller, vane, and slipper are the three common power steering pump designs.

Note: Some applications use multiple V-belts to drive high-load accessories. These belts must be replaced as a **matched set** to ensure even belt tension and long service life.

Checking Drive Belt Pulley Alignment

Check all pulleys and their alignment before installing a new belt. Pulleys should not appear out-of-round, and they should mount squarely on the driveshafts. They should be lined up so the belt lays flat along the pulleys. For more detailed information on pulley alignment refer to the appropriate Service Manual.

Checking Drive Belt Tension

A loose pump drive belt slips under load, and a tight belt wears out quickly and damages accessory bearings. Decreased power assist and a high-pitched squeal from the engine compartment are signs of a slipping power steering pump drive belt.

As part of an inspection and when you replace drive belts, check and adjust belt tension. Tension specifications vary depending on whether belts are new or used. Be sure to use the correct specification. There are two methods for checking belt tension:

- Deflection
- Tension gauge

To check belt tension using the deflection method:

1. Find the longest length of drive belt between two pulleys and locate the midpoint of this length.
2. With your thumb or forefinger, either push the belt away from you or pull it toward you, using moderate pressure.
3. Measure the amount of deflection from the normal belt position and compare it with specifications. Typically, belt deflection will be in the 0.50 to 0.75 inch (13 to 19 mm) range.

A tension gauge provides a more accurate check, figure 1-19. To use the tension gauge:

1. Find the longest length of drive belt between two pulleys and locate the midpoint of this length.
2. Position the tension gauge on the drive belt and press the gauge handle.
3. Measure the force needed to deflect the belt, and compare with specifications. New belt deflection will be about 120 to 150 pounds (530 to 670 Newton), while used belts record about 90 to 120 pounds (400 to 530 Newton) of tension. Belts are considered used after only a few minutes of use. Serpentine belts require more force to deflect.

A serpentine belt usually has a self-adjusting tensioner pulley, figure 1-20. However, tension should be periodically checked to make sure the device is operating properly.

Typically, V-belt tension is adjusted in one of two ways:

- With an adjustable idler pulley
- By repositioning the pump or another accessory on a pivoting bracket

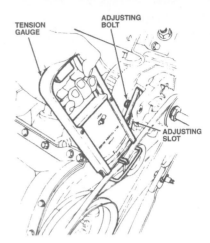

Fig. 1-19. Checking belt tension with a gauge.

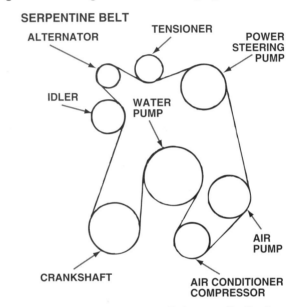

Fig. 1-20. A serpentine belt usually has a self-adjusting tensioner.

To adjust the tension of a belt with an adjustable idler pulley, loosen the pulley adjuster bolt and use an appropriate pry bar or breaker bar to move the idler pulley until it tensions the belt. Tighten the idler pulley bolt and check belt tension. Readjust if needed. Some idler pulleys attach to a threaded shaft, which is used for adjustment. Loosen the pulley center bolt and shaft lock nut. Thread the shaft in or out to reposition the pulley. Tighten the center bolt and lock nut, then recheck belt tension.

To adjust tension using a pivoting bracket, loosen the adjustment bolt, and turn the adjustment screw to move the bracket. If the bracket does not have an adjustment screw, pry it with an appropriate pry bar or breaker bar. Never pry against the accessory that the bracket holds; the housing may bend. Tighten the bolt and recheck belt tension.

After adjusting new belt tension, run the engine for 15 to 20 minutes, then recheck tension using specifications for a used drive belt.

Matched Set: Belts which are made either in the same mold or on the same manufacturing machine have the same exact length and are known as matched sets.

Drive Belt Tensioner Replacement

Always inspect the tensioner for any signs of damage to the belt surface or bearing failure. Check for smooth operation of the tensioner arm on spring-loaded designs. Replace any tensioner that shows signs of damage.

Replacing a Drive Belt

Replacing a drive belt is not difficult, but limited engine compartment space can complicate matters.

To remove a V-belt:

1. Disconnect the battery ground cable as a safety precaution, especially if the engine has an electric cooling fan.
2. Loosen the bolts on the idler pulley or pivoting accessory bracket, or turn a draw bolt on the accessory bracket.
3. Ease tension on the belt by pivoting the accessory or prying the idler pulley away from the belt.

Note: Always apply pressure against the bracket, not the accessory housing, to avoid damaging the housing.

4. Slip the belt off the pulleys.

Before you remove a damaged serpentine belt, locate a diagram of how it is routed around the pulleys. If you do not have a diagram, sketch one. To remove the belt:

1. Disconnect the battery ground cable as a safety precaution, especially if the engine has an electric cooling fan.
2. Most vehicles with serpentine belts use a spring-loaded self-tensioning pulley. Loosen belt tension by rotating the pulley away from the belt with a breaker bar.
3. Slip the belt off the pulleys.

Inspect pulleys for defects that may accelerate belt wear:

- Turn the pulleys with your hands, listening for noise indicating worn bearings. Replace bearings as needed
- Check the pulleys for proper alignment. Adjust the mounting brackets or replace worn components to correct any misalignment
- Check for dirt and grease embedded in the pulley grooves. This is especially important for serpentine belts, where belt ribs ride in the grooves
- Use a soft wire brush to clean the pulleys if needed
- Check pulleys for chips, cracks, or sharp edges that can damage belts. Replace pulleys if needed
- Also, check for oil leaks that may be contaminating belts. Repair any problems

When replacing a drive belt, use the specified size and type of belt:

1. Route the belt over the accessory pulleys. If the drive belt system uses:
   - A self-tensioning pulley, rotate the idler pulley against the spring load far enough to slip the belt over all of the pulleys. Route the belt around the pulleys, placing the belt on the tensioning pulley last. Then, release the self-tensioning pulley slowly to take up belt slack
   - An idler pulley or pivoting accessory bracket, loosen the securing bolts, and move the idler pulley or bracket forward. Slip the belt over the pulleys, then move the pulley or bracket back into place. Tighten the securing bolts

CAUTION: Do not allow the spring-loaded idler to snap back into position with the belt removed as immediate damage to the assembly may result.

2. Reconnect the battery ground cable if you disconnected it earlier.
3. Check and adjust belt tension.
4. After adjusting new belt tension, run the engine for 15 to 20 minutes, then recheck tension using specifications for a used drive belt.

CHECKING FOR NOISE, VIBRATION, OR LEAKS

Power steering system noises usually come from a worn steering pump, degraded fluid, or air getting into the system. The fluid must be air free, or the pump will produce a humming or buzzing noise either all the time or just when turning. Old or contaminated power steering fluid can also cause pump noises, as can restricted hoses or hoses that allow air to be sucked into the return side. A loose belt will make a squeal when turning the steering wheel to full lock.

Most vibration in the steering system does not originate from the power steering pump. However, a bent pulley or loose mounting bracket can create a vibration which may be felt in the steering wheel especially during parking maneuvers when the system pressure is high.

When checking for fluid leaks on systems where the fluid reservoir is not integral with the pump, check for leaks in the supply hose between the pump and reservoir. If the pump and reservoir are one integral unit, look for leaking O-rings and replace as needed. Check the reservoir cap for leaks. If pump fittings leak, but hose fittings are intact, the pump fittings are worn and you must replace the pump. Inspect the pump housing. If it is dented, the pump may leak at the seams and need replacement.

If the power steering fluid level is low, a complete and thorough visual inspection of the entire power steering system should be made to determine the source of the leak.

External Rack Leaks

Power racks typically leak at one or both ends where the rack shaft passes through the end seals, at the pinion input shaft seal, or internally in the spool valve housing. Leaky end seals may or may not leave telltale stains on the outside of the rubber or plastic bellows. If the leak is really bad and the bellows are cracked or loose, the fluid will be dripping from the rack and the bellows will be wet. But if the bellows are still intact and tight, you may not see any obvious signs of leakage.

Power Steering Rack Leak Inspection

The end bellows on a steering rack should be dry with no more than a small amount of power steering fluid present. High mileage vehicles may have some fluid seepage into the boots. If the bellows contain a lot of fluid, the rack is leaking and needs to be repaired or replaced. Loosen the bellows clamp and slide the bellows back to check for fluid inside.

A4

To verify rack seal leaks before beginning a repair follow these steps:

1. Raise the vehicle so the front wheels are off the ground.
2. Loosen and push back both bellows on the ends of the rack so you have a clear view of the seals on both ends of the rack.
3. Wipe off any dirt or oil on the rack bar.
4. Start the engine, and with it idling at approximately 1,200 rpm, turn the steering wheel all the way to the right stop and hold under light pressure for about five seconds. Then repeat the process turning the wheel to the left. Repeat the process six to eight times.
5. Recheck the rack for leaks. If you see fluid dripping from the rack, the end seals are leaking and repairs are needed. If no leaks are found at the end seals, check the pinion input shaft seal and the hoses and pump.

If a hose connection is leaking first check to see if the fitting is tightened properly. It may also be possible to repair the leak by replacing the seals or O-rings.

Internal Rack Leaks

If the seals around the spool valves inside the rack are leaking the steering may feel stiff or tight when a cold vehicle is first started. New seals alone will not repair most internal leaks because the old spool valve seals have usually worn grooves into the inside of the control valve housing. The only repair for this kind of leak is to replace the rack with one that has a new or sleeved control valve housing.

Power Steering Gear Leak Inspection

Power steering gears usually develop leaks at the input shaft or sector shaft seals. Sometimes it is possible to correct the problem by simply replacing the seal. In other cases the internal bearings or bushings are worn to the point that the shaft damages the seal. In this case a complete gear overhaul or replacement will be required.

Follow a procedure similar to the one described previously for checking for rack leaks. Inspect the sealing areas as well as any gear housing for leaks during the test.

REMOVING AND INSTALLING A PUMP

Power steering pump removal and replacement varies by manufacturer and model; the following is a typical procedure, figure 1-21. To remove and replace a pump:

1. Disconnect the battery ground cable.
2. Clean the pump high-pressure and return hose fittings, so dirt will not enter the system.
3. Remove the low-pressure return hose and drain the fluid into a container, then disconnect the high-pressure hose at the pump.
4. Plug hose ends and pump fittings to keep dirt out of the system and pump.
5. Remove the pump drive belt.

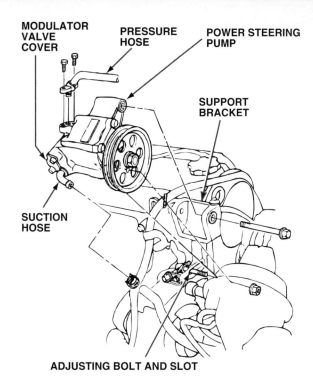

Fig. 1-21. Typical power steering pump installation.

6. Supporting the pump, remove the bolts securing it to the vehicle. Remove the pump.
7. Remove the pulley from the old pump. Reuse it on the new pump if it is in good condition.
8. Replace pump mounts, if damaged.
9. Place the new pump in the engine compartment and install the bolts.
10. Install the drive belt and adjust tension.
11. Remove plugs from hoses and fittings, then connect the hoses to the pump.
12. Fill the fluid reservoir, bleed the system, and top off the reservoir. Check for leaks and readjust belt tension after driving the vehicle.

REBUILDING THE PUMP

Most shops replace the pump with a new one if it is damaged or leaking. However, you may be able to replace some seals, gaskets, or the reservoir to stop leakage. Refer to the appropriate vehicle Service Manual for more information.

STEERING LINKAGE SERVICE

Front Steering Linkage

The two most common types of steering linkage are:

- Parallelogram
- Rack and pinion

Parallelogram steering linkage uses the pitman arm and idler arm to support the center link, forming a parallelogram.

Parallelogram Steering Linkage: A steering linkage configuration consisting of a pitman arm, an idler arm, a center link, and two tie rods, which form three sides of a parallelogram.

Tie rods connect a center link to the steering knuckles. In a rack and pinion steering system, the rack takes the place of the center link. It moves back and forth across the pinion, and tie rods connect it to the steering knuckles, figure 1-22.

Rear Steering Linkage

Vehicles equipped with rear wheel steering capabilities require service on those components very similar to servicing the front steering components. Refer to the appropriate Service Manual and to Chapter Three of this book for more detailed information on rear steering linkage service.

Lubricating Steering Linkage Ball Joints

Many steering linkage ball joints are permanently sealed, so they cannot be lubricated and must be replaced when worn. However, older vehicles and some aftermarket ball joints have grease fittings.

Lubricate at the recommended intervals as follows:

1. Wipe dirt from the grease fitting. If the joint has a grease plug, remove it and install a grease fitting.

2. Using a grease gun, add grease to the joint until the rubber dust cover feels firm. Do not overfill, or the dust cover may break.

3. Wipe excess grease from the fitting.

Separating and Installing Steering Links

Replace steering links if their ball joints are worn, as the wear causes loose steering and wander. Also, replace the link if the joint dust covers are ripped or damaged, allowing abrasive dust to damage the joint and letting the protective lubrication leak out.

To remove a link from the steering linkage, separate the ball joints that connect to other links at each end, figure 1-23. Use this procedure as a guide:

1. Raise the vehicle on a hoist.
2. Remove the ball joint cotter pin and nut.
3. Separate the ball joint from its socket using one of these methods:

   • Place the forked end of a tie rod puller between the ball joint and socket. Be careful not to catch the rubber

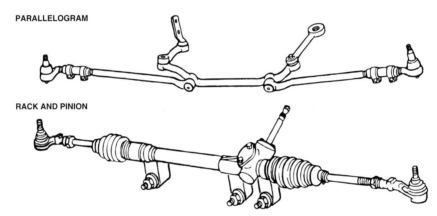

Fig. 1-22. Two common steering linkages are the parallelogram and the rack and pinion.

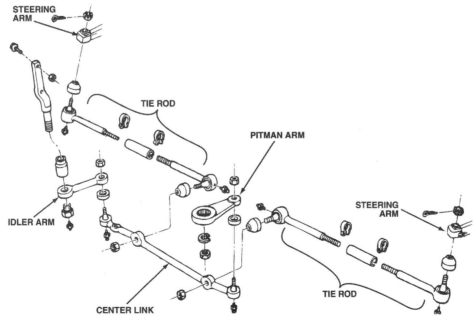

Fig. 1-23. Typical parallelogram steering linkage disassembly.

dust cover between the puller and ball joint, or it will be damaged. Position the other end of the puller on the end of the stud, and tighten the bolt until it presses the ball joint from the socket

- Place a ball joint separator, or "pickle fork," between the ball joint and the socket. Drive the pickle fork with a hammer until the ball joint separates from the socket. This procedure damages the dust cover, so have a new ball joint on hand
- Use an impact wrench with a pickle fork attachment to break the ball joint loose from the socket. This also damages the dust cover

When installing new steering links, always use new castellated nuts and cotter pins.

1. Inspect and clean the ball joint and taper to ensure the ball fits tightly in the inner socket, figure 1-24.
2. Before installing the new joint, check the dust boot for damage.
3. Place the ball in the socket and install the castellated nut. Tighten the nut to specified torque.
4. Install a new cotter pin.
5. Check and correct wheel alignment.

The pitman arm in a parallelogram steering linkage is tightly splined to the steering gear sector shaft. Use a puller to separate them. If they are difficult to separate, apply penetrating oil.

CAUTION: Do not use a torch to loosen them, as heat weakens the metal parts.

Some vehicles have a unique rubber-bonded socket ball joint on the outer tie rod end. These units consist of a rubber-covered ball stud that is pressed into a metal socket, figure 1-25. Position the wheels and steering linkage straight ahead before tightening these joints, or they tend to return to the position in which they were tightened, a condition called "memory steer." Rubber bonded socket joints do not require lubrication. Inspect for wear and replace as needed.

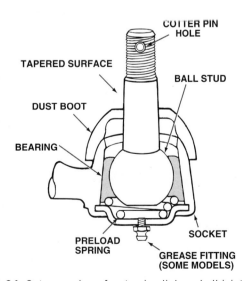

Fig. 1-24. Cut away view of a steering linkage ball joint.

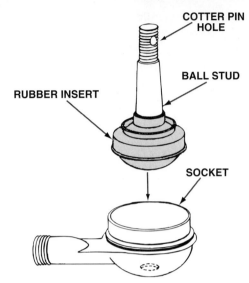

Fig. 1-25. Typical rubber-bonded socket tie rod end.

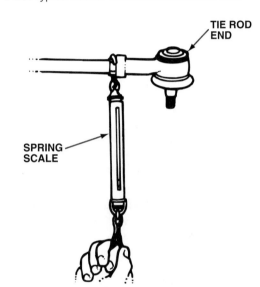

Fig. 1-26. Checking tie rod articulation with a spring scale.

Tie Rod Articulation Effort Test

There should not be excessive play between the inner tie rod end and the rack in a rack and pinion steering system.

Measure the effort required to pivot or articulate the tie rods:

1. Raise the front of the vehicle.
2. Remove the front wheels.
3. Separate the outer tie rod ends from the steering knuckles.
4. Hook a spring scale over the outer tie rod end and pull down, figure 1-26. Check both tie rods and compare the readings to specifications.
5. If articulation effort is not within specifications, replace the inner tie rod end or the entire tie rod.

Servicing the Steering Linkage Damper

Some steering linkages have a damper to help cushion the steering system from road shocks, figure 1-27. If this damper becomes worn and ineffective, or if it leaks oil, replace it.

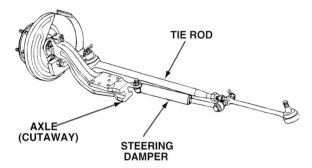

Fig. 1-27. A steering linkage damper cushions the steering system.

STEERING LINKAGE PARALLELISM

In a parallelogram steering linkage, the vehicle steers smoothly when the center link is parallel to the ground. This is called parallelism. If the center link is not parallel, the cause may be a bent or incorrectly positioned idler or pitman arm. This, in turn, affects tie rod position, resulting in bump steer and unequal left and right turning radius.

Check parallelism after you replace parts in the steering linkage. First make sure ride height is equal on each side of the vehicle, tire pressures are correct, and the surface on which the vehicle is parked is level:

1. Position the wheels straight ahead and center the steering gear.
2. Locate the points where the pitman and idler arms connect to the center link and measure the distance from these points to the ground. Some center links have flat machined surfaces for making these measurements.
3. The distance from the pitman arm side and the idler arm side of the center link to the ground should not differ by more than 0.06 inch (1.5 mm).

To adjust parallelism, raise the vehicle on a frame-contact hoist. On some vehicles, loosen the idler arm mounting bolts and reposition the arm in the slots on the frame. Another method is to turn a threaded bushing at the base of the idler arm mounting bracket to change idler arm position.

VARIABLE ASSIST POWER STEERING SYSTEM SERVICE

By design, the **variable assist power steering** system provides more steering assist at slow speeds, making the steering wheel easier to turn such as when parking. At higher speeds, steering assist is reduced and more steering effort is required to steer the car, giving the driver greater feel of the road. Some manufacturers refer to this design as speed-sensitive power steering.

Electronically Controlled Systems

Variable assist power steering is provided by controlling power steering fluid pressure at the power steering gear. A solenoid valve, normally located on the steering gear or on the power steering pump, is used to control power steering pressure by varying the size of an orifice which the power steering fluid must flow through.

The variable assist solenoid control valve is controlled by an electronic solenoid control module which may be remote mounted or directly attached to the steering gear. The control module controls the variable assist solenoid control valve, using a vehicle speed signal from the powertrain control module (PCM).

Problems with electronic variable-assist systems include all of the same things that can go wrong with a conventional power steering system. Conditions such as fluid leaks, worn gear components, and pump and hose failures, etc., plus problems with the control electronics including the vehicle speed sensor circuit, the solenoid valve, and control module, require accurate diagnosis to ensure that the correct repair is carried out. Most of these systems provide diagnostic fault codes that can be accessed with a voltmeter, test light, or scan tool to pinpoint the nature of the fault (if the fault is electronic rather than mechanical or hydraulic).

If power to the solenoid or control valve actuator is lost, the valve keeps the bypass circuit closed so full power assist is provided under all driving conditions. The only indication of trouble, therefore, might be a loss of road feel and/or increased steering sensitivity at highway speeds.

Mechanical Control Systems

A4

The mechanical type of variable assist power steering systems use a variable flow rate power steering pump. The flow rate is proportional to engine speed, allowing for more power assist at lower engine speeds than at higher engine speeds.

The power steering pump has a special flow control valve that allows for variable oil flow to the steering gear. Oil from the pump flows through an orifice in the valve assembly. Oil also flows through a pilot port to one side of the valve. At low engine and pump speeds, the oil flow through the pilot port is not enough to move the valve against spring pressure. This keeps the valve in the fully open position, allowing maximum flow for low-speed parking maneuvers.

As engine speed increases, the pressure in the pilot port also increases. This moves the valve against spring pressure and reduces the size of the flow orifice. Pump oil flow to the steering gear is reduced, which reduces power steering assist at higher speeds.

It is important to remember that variable assist power steering only reduces the amount of pressure that reaches the steering gear at higher road speeds. The only way it could reduce power assist at low speed would be in the unlikely event the actuator or solenoid valve failed in the open position. This could cause a noticeable reduction or loss of power assist.

Diagnosing Variable Assist Systems

Accurate diagnosis of variable assist power steering systems requires following specific steps outlined in the vehicle Service Manual.

Variable Assist Power Steering: A power steering system that uses valves and speed sensors to vary the amount of steering assist according to engine or road speed.

CHAPTER QUESTIONS

1. A vehicle pulls to one side during straight-ahead driving. The cause could be:
   a. Loose steering shaft joints
   b. Misadjusted-manual steering gear
   c. Wheel imbalance
   d. Unequal tire inflation

2. In a vehicle with manual steering, a complaint of "hard steering" can be caused by all of the following *EXCEPT*:
   a. Low tire pressure
   b. Worn steering gear components
   c. Incorrect wheel alignment
   d. Damaged steering system components

3. To pressure test a power steering system, install the pressure gauge between the:
   a. Return hose and reservoir inlet
   b. Sump outlet and suction hose
   c. Pump outlet and pressure hose
   d. Steering gear outlet and return hose

4. In a vehicle with power steering, a buzzing noise is heard at all times when the engine is running. The most likely cause is:
   a. Low pump output
   b. Air in the hydraulic system
   c. Internal steering gear leakage
   d. Normal relief valve operation

5. There is a looseness in the steering column. Technician A says the tie rod ends are loose. Technician B says the steering column universal joints are loose. Who is right?
   a. A only
   b. B only
   c. Both A and B
   d. Neither A nor B

6. If a vehicle has been in a collision, the steering column should be:
   a. Replaced
   b. Inspected
   c. Collapsed
   d. Rebuilt

7. To measure gear mesh preload, you need a:
   a. Dial indicator
   b. Feeler gauge
   c. Torque wrench
   d. Pressure gauge

8. When removing a manual recirculating ball steering gear:
   a. Hammer the pitman arm off the sector shaft
   b. Remove the steering shaft from the vehicle
   c. Mark the pitman arm and sector shaft alignment
   d. Apply penetrating oil to the mounting bolts

9. When removing a manual rack and pinion steering gear:
   a. Disconnect the steering shaft from the pinion shaft
   b. Disconnect the inner tie rod ends from the steering gear
   c. Mark the tie rod to steering arm alignment
   d. Remove the steering wheel from the steering shaft

10. When removing a power assisted steering gear:
    a. Clean the steering gear and hydraulic hoses
    b. Disconnect the return hose from the reservoir
    c. Pull the fluid out of the system with an evacuator
    d. Save the old fluid and reuse if in good condition

11. When bleeding the power steering system:
    a. Elevate the rear axle so the fluid flows better
    b. The fluid should be cold during the procedure
    c. Turn the steering wheel to lock and hold for 30 seconds
    d. Watch the reservoir and top off if it gets low

12. On a vehicle equipped with a power tilt and telescoping steering column system, neither feature operates. Technician A says the power steering pump belt may be loose. Technician B says the tilt and telescope control module may be defective. Who is right?
    a. A only
    b. B only
    c. Both A and B
    d. Neither A nor B

13. The steering wheel spoke is high on the left low on the right. If the toe setting is correct what is required to center the wheelset?
    a. Shorten the right tie rod end.
    b. Lengthen the left tie rod.
    c. Lengthen the left tie rod and shorten the right tie rod.
    d. Shorten the left tie rod and lengthen the right tie rod.

14. Comparing the readings from a pump pressure test, you find that their range is 80 psi (550 kPa). You should:
    a. Repair the pump flow control valve
    b. Replace the pump seals
    c. Adjust pump drive belt tension
    d. Replace the pump pulley

15. To remove a steering wheel from the shaft, use a:
    a. Pry bar
    b. Hammer
    c. Puller
    d. Screwdriver

16. When removing a power steering pump, do all of the following *EXCEPT*:
    a. Run the engine with a hose disconnected to drain the system
    b. Cover or plug the hose ends to prevent system contamination
    c. Remove the pump drive belt before removing the pump
    d. Support the pump while removing the mounting bolts

17. A variable assist power steering system:
    a. Increases pressure to the pump at high vehicle speeds
    b. Increases pressure to the steering gear at high vehicle speeds
    c. Decreases pump speed at low vehicle speeds
    d. Decreases pressure to the gear at high speeds

18. When checking tie rod articulation:
    a. Elevate the rear wheels
    b. Disconnect the inner tie rod ends
    c. Use a pull scale
    d. Disconnect the steering shaft

CHAPTER TWO

SUSPENSION SYSTEMS DIAGNOSIS AND REPAIR

CHAPTER OBJECTIVES

- The technician will complete the ASE task list on Suspension Systems Diagnosis and Repair.
- The technician will be able to answer 13 questions dealing with the Suspension Systems Diagnosis and Repair section of the A4 ASE Test.

FRONT SUSPENSION DIAGNOSIS

The most common wear points on suspensions are bushings and ball joints. As these connections wear, suspension action becomes loose, and steering is affected. Shock absorbers are wear items, as well, and lose their effectiveness as a result of high mileage or extended operation on rough roads, figure 2-1.

When shocks are worn, the vehicle bounces excessively after driving over bumps. Springs typically last longer than bushings, ball joints, and shocks, but after time, they start to sag, causing low ride height, figure 2-2. Worn shocks and springs can cause damage to suspension bumpers and stops as the suspension bottoms out rapidly. Control arms and other suspension links usually do not wear out, but they can be damaged in a collision, from driving over large bumps or deep ruts, or from hitting a curb.

Test drive the vehicle and note unusual noises that occur when crossing pavement joints and other road surface imperfections. Use an open area such as a large parking lot to test the vehicle for excessive sway or body roll.

1. Drive the vehicle in several large figure eights.
2. Note the reaction of the body when exiting a turn in one direction and when beginning a turn back in the opposite direction.
3. Listen for popping or squeaking noises as the body rolls and returns.
4. If excessive roll, sway, or noise is demonstrated continue the inspection in the shop.

Keep in mind that suspension damage and improper ride height generally affects wheel alignment. Therefore, whenever wheels are out of alignment, inspect the suspension system for wear, damage, and correct ride height before performing a wheel alignment.

A4

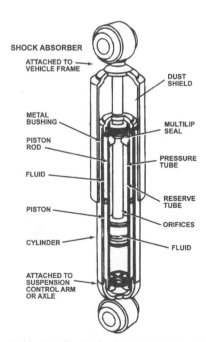

Fig. 2-1. Typical hydraulic shock absorber construction.

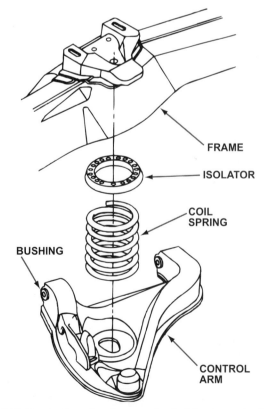

Fig. 2-2. Eventually, coil springs sag due to fatigue, causing low ride height.

Front Suspension Inspection

The suspension interacts with the steering and wheels, so along with examining the suspension, check steering system condition, tire inflation, wheel condition, wheel and tire runout and balance, and wheel alignment. Not all vehicles have all the components listed in this inspection:

1. Bounce the vehicle up and down at each corner, then release it and see how soon it settles. If it bounces more than two or three times, the shocks are worn. Listen for unusual sounds such as squeaks or rattles while bouncing the vehicle.
2. Check ride height. If the vehicle is riding low or one side is lower than the other, the springs are worn. Torsion bars can be adjusted to correct slight ride height problems, but springs must be replaced.
3. Raise the vehicle on an alignment rack and have an assistant turn the steering wheel from lock to lock, while you watch the suspension for binding at the ball joints or struts.
4. Inspect ball joint seals and suspension bushings for damage, cracks, or other signs of deterioration.
5. Check ball joint lubrication. The seal should be full of grease, and the grease should not be hardened.
6. Check ball joint **play**; excess play indicates wear.
7. Push and pull on suspension links to check for looseness, which causes poor handling.
8. Examine coil springs for shiny areas, indicating that the coils clash against each other. Also, examine all types of springs for scratches and damage that can cause metal fatigue and **stress risers**.
9. Inspect the control arm bushings for signs of deterioration or wear. Also check to ensure that control arm mounting shafts are securely fastened to the vehicle frame or body attachment points.
10. Examine shock absorbers. A light film of oil is normal, but dripping oil means they are damaged. Look for dents

in the shock cylinder, which interfere with smooth compression and extension.

11. Examine bump stops for damage and signs of contact showing the suspension bottoms out due to damaged or worn parts, figure 2-3.

Front Suspension Service

Front suspension components that require service are:

- Control arms and bushings
- Strut rods, radius arms, and bushings
- Antiroll bars and bushings
- Coil springs
- Torsion bars
- Shock absorbers
- Struts
- Ball joints
- Steering knuckles
- Axles

INDEPENDENT FRONT SUSPENSION

Front Control Arms and Bushings

Control arms link the axle or wheel hub to the vehicle frame, figure 2-4. A pivoting bushing at the frame allows the wheel to travel up and down, and a ball joint links the control arm to the front wheel. Ball joints allow both vertical wheel travel and wheel turning in response to steering.

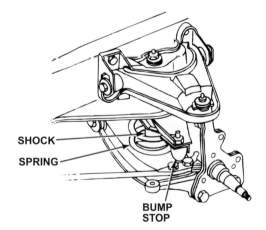

Fig. 2-3. Contact on the bump stops indicates worn suspension components.

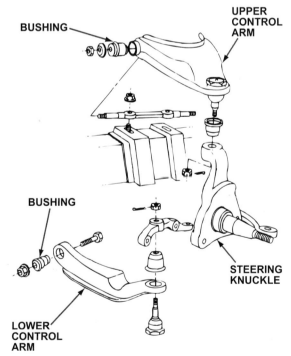

Fig. 2-4. Control arms are isolated from the frame by bushings to allow movement and reduce road shock.

Play: The amount that mechanical parts can move without encountering another part.
Stress Riser: A flaw in the metal of a coil spring or torsion bar that creates extra stress on the metal, causing it to bend more easily at that point.

Removing Front Control Arms

Raise the vehicle on a lift and remove the wheel. If the control arm bears the weight of the suspension spring, remove the spring. Remember that coil springs can spring loose and cause damage and injury if not compressed and handled correctly. Once the load is off the control arm, remove the bolts securing it to the frame.

If a strut rod links the lower control arm to the frame, remove the strut rod before removing the control arm. If the strut rod bolts are adjustable for camber, mark the adjuster position. If shims are used, keep them in order.

Disconnect any other suspension components, such as the shock absorber or antiroll bar, that attach to the control arm. Finally, separate the control arm ball joint to disconnect the arm from the steering knuckle.

Replacing Front Control Arms

To install a control arm:

1. Position the control arm on the vehicle, and reinstall the shims or adjusting bolts.
2. Place the control arm at its normal ride height, and bolt it to the frame.
3. For a weight-bearing control arm, install the spring or torsion bar. Be sure that a coil spring is safely compressed, and be sure to install torsion bars on the correct side of the vehicle. Support the control arm with a jack while you seat the spring.
4. Attach the steering knuckle to the control arm ball joint, and secure it with the castellated nut and a new cotter pin.
5. If there is a strut rod for the lower control arm, install it. Also, attach the shock absorber, antiroll bar, or other items that were disconnected earlier.
6. Remove the jack and spring compressor, if used.
7. Install the wheel and lubricate the suspension.
8. Lower the vehicle. With the weight of the vehicle on the suspension, tighten all fasteners.
9. Check and correct wheel alignment.

Front Control Arm Bumpers and Bushings

After removing the control arm from the vehicle, inspecting or replacing the front **jounce** and **rebound** bumpers and bushings is easy. Bumpers are usually secured by a bracket and one or two bolts. Some bumpers fit over an extension on the frame; pull them off and push new ones in place.

To replace control arm bushings, first remove the control arm from the vehicle. Use a press to push rubber bushings out of the control arm, figure 2-5. Always check new bushings for directional indicators before you install them, and be sure to line them up correctly. Install new metal bushings using a press.

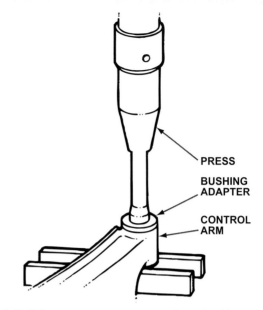

Fig. 2-5. Using a press to remove control arm bushings.

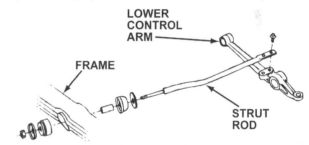

Fig. 2-6. A strut rod braces the control arm to resist deflection due to acceleration and braking forces.

TWIN I-BEAM AXLE

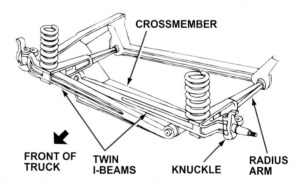

Fig. 2-7. The radius arms brace the suspension against acceleration and braking forces on a twin I-beam suspension.

Strut Rod and Radius Arm Service

Strut rods brace the control arm against the frame to provide resistance to braking and acceleration forces, figure 2-6. The **radius arms** perform the same function on a twin I-beam design, figure 2-7.

A4

Jounce: The inward reaction of the spring and shock absorber when a wheel hits an obstruction.
Radius Arm: A sturdy suspension link that braces a twin I-beam, or sometimes an axle housing, against the frame.
Rebound: The downward movement of a wheel from its normal position when the spring and shock are expanding, as the sudden drop of a wheel into a depression and a weight transfer away from the wheel.
Strut Rod: A suspension link that braces a straight lower control arm against the frame.

To replace strut rods and bushings:

1. Raise the vehicle and remove the strut rod fasteners.
2. Remove the strut rod, then remove the bushings.
3. Clean and inspect the strut rod. If it is reusable, install new bushings.
4. Support the strut rod while installing the fasteners.
5. Lower the vehicle, then tighten the fasteners to specifications.
6. Check and correct wheel alignment.

To replace radius arms and bushings:

1. Raise the vehicle on a frame-contact hoist, and place jack stands under the axle.
2. Remove the front wheels for easier access.
3. Remove the antiroll bar, if any.
4. Secure and remove the suspension spring. Remove the shock absorber, if needed.
5. Remove the lower spring seat, and remove the bolt securing the radius arm to the axle.
6. Remove the nut, washer, and insulator at the end of the radius arm that bolts to the frame. Remove the radius arm.
7. If the radius arm is reusable, install new bushings. If it is damaged, use a new radius arm.
8. Attach the radius arm to the axle with the bolt.
9. Install the other end of the radius arm onto the frame bracket. Torque the nut to specifications.
10. Install the spring seat, spring, and shock absorber.
11. Install the antiroll bar.
12. Install the wheels, lower the vehicle, and tighten the bolt to specified torque.
13. Check and adjust wheel alignment.

Front and Rear Antiroll Bars and Bushings

The **antiroll bar** links the left and right sides of a suspension system to transfer rolling force during cornering, figure 2-8. Also known as a stabilizer bar, roll bar, sway bar, or antisway bar, the antiroll bar reduces body roll. Vehicles may be equipped with antiroll bars on the front, rear, or both ends of the vehicle. Diagnosis of antiroll bar issues are the same for all applications. Anytime excessive body roll is detected when cornering a vehicle inspect the antiroll bar and mounting for damage or missing fasteners.

The antiroll bar is not prone to wear or damage, but its bushings may wear or the brackets come loose. Replace the bushings and brackets:

1. With the vehicle on a hoist and the wheels off, remove the nuts and bolts fastening the antiroll bar brackets in place. Remove the antiroll bar and the spacer bars, if any.
2. If you are replacing the bushings, slide them off the antiroll bar and install new ones.
3. Position the antiroll bar, and spacer bars, if any, and secure the brackets to the vehicle frame and the lower control arms or knuckles. Adjust antiroll bar position while the bolts are loose.
4. Lower the vehicle and tighten bolts to specification.

COIL SPRINGS

The primary cause of coil spring wear is internal friction, resulting from normal operation, which generates heat and weakens the metal. Replace springs in same-axle pairs for even handling.

Compressing Coil Springs

Before replacing coil springs, you must know how to compress them. This is an extremely important safety procedure. Coil springs mounted between a control arm and the vehicle frame support the weight of the vehicle and exert a considerable amount of force, figure 2-9. If you lower the control arm and release the coil spring without compressing it, it will fly out of the

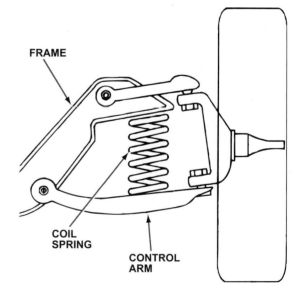

Fig. 2-8. An antiroll bar transfers rolling force from side to side while the vehicle is turning.

Fig. 2-9. A coil spring mounted between the frame and lower control arm is compressed by the weight of the vehicle.

Antiroll Bar: A transverse suspension link that transfers some of the load on one wheel to the opposite wheel. Its main purpose is to prevent body roll during cornering. Also known as a sway bar.

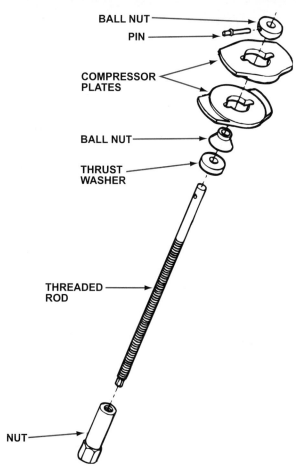

BALL NUT

PIN

COMPRESSOR
PLATES

BALL NUT

THRUST
WASHER

THREADED
ROD

NUT

Fig. 2-10. Spring compressor plates are used when there is clear access to the bottom of a coil spring.

suspension, releasing the force of hundreds of pounds of tension, causing severe injury and damage. There are two methods of compressing coil springs: safety clips and compressor plates.

Check the pressure rating of safety clips to be sure that they can hold the spring you are removing:

1. Disconnect components that may interfere with your work, such as tie rod ends or brake lines.
2. Place a jack under the suspension component that contains the lower spring seat. This may be a lower control arm or a beam axle.
3. Raise the jack to compress the spring.
4. Following instructions from the clip manufacturer, place spring clips around the coils. Generally, a long coil can be secured with five clips, while four clips are sufficient for a short coil. Adjust jack height as needed.
5. Slowly lower the jack, and the clips should tightly hold the coils together to keep the spring compressed. Make sure the clips are secure. Then, lower the jack until the spring is free of its upper seat.
6. Remove the spring. Be sure to handle a compressed spring carefully.
7. To remove the clips, put the spring in a compressor, compress it, remove the clips, and slowly release the compressor.

Spring compressor plates can be used if the lower end of the coil spring is easily accessible from under the vehicle, figure 2-10. The threaded rod must be able to pass through the center of the spring coils. To use:

1. Place the upper and lower compressor plates on the upper and lower spring coils. Be sure the tool is rated to withstand the force of the spring.
2. To install the compressor, slip the threaded rod through the washer, nut, and lower plate. Then, thread the rod through the hole in the upper plate, and install the pin to secure the rod.
3. Check the position of the plates to be sure they are secure on the coils.
4. Use a socket wrench to turn the threaded rod, slowly bringing the plates together. Continue turning the rod until the spring is compressed enough that you can remove it.
5. After removing the spring and tool from the vehicle, slowly unscrew the threaded rod until all tension is released from the spring. Remove the compressor plates from the spring.
6. Compress the new spring to the same length before installing it.

Replacing Coil Springs
To replace coil springs:

1. Raise the vehicle on a hoist and remove the wheels. Disconnect the outer tie rod ends, if necessary, for access.
2. Place a jack under one lower control arm, and lift the control arm until the lower ball joint is unloaded; it moves easily when unloaded.
3. Secure the coil spring with safety clips or compressor plates.
4. Disconnect the ball joints at the lower control arm. Also, disconnect any other suspension components attached to the lower control arm, such as the antiroll bar, shock absorber, or strut rod.
5. Lower the jack and pull the control arm down. Remove the old spring. If the spring insulators are worn or damaged, replace them. Compress a new spring, and secure it with spring clips. Place the new spring in the control arm spring seat.
6. Use the jack to raise the lower control arm. Connect the ball joint.
7. Continue raising the control arm until the spring is compressed enough to remove the clips.
8. Slowly lower the jack to expand on the spring.
9. Connect the shock, antiroll bar, and strut rod.
10. Repeat to replace the opposite spring.
11. Reconnect the outer tie rod ends, if you disconnected them, and install the wheels.
12. Lower the vehicle and bounce it several times to settle the springs. Then, tighten suspension fasteners and wheel lug nuts to specified torque.
13. Check ride height and adjust wheel alignment.

A4

TORSION BARS

A torsion bar is a straight length of spring steel that establishes the ride height of the vehicle. They can be mounted **transversely** or **longitudinally** in the chassis.

Transverse Torsion Bars

To replace a transverse torsion bar, figure 2-11:

1. With the vehicle on a hoist and the wheels removed, remove the torsion bar adjusting bolt.
2. Raise the lower control arm with a jack, and remove any interfering hardware, such as antiroll bar brackets.
3. Remove the bolts securing the torsion bar to the control arm.
4. Remove the bolts securing the torsion bar anchor to the frame crossmember.
5. Remove the torsion bar and anchor from the vehicle, then remove the anchor from the torsion bar.
6. To install the torsion bar, grease the hex end and install the anchor on that end.
7. Double check the mark on the torsion bar that indicates which side of the vehicle the bar should be installed on. Torsion bars are usually marked "left" or "right", or "L" or "R".
8. Position the torsion bar under the vehicle and install the bolts securing it to the control arm.
9. Install the anchor to crossmember bolts.
10. Reattach any hardware removed earlier.
11. Install the adjusting bolt and tighten it slightly. Remove the jack from under the lower control arm.
12. Reinstall the wheels, lower the vehicle, and tighten the fastening bolts and wheel lug nuts to specifications. Use the adjusting bolt to correct ride height.
13. Check and adjust wheel alignment.

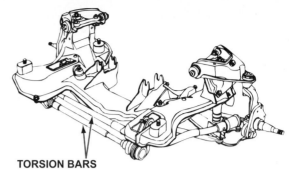

TORSION BARS

Fig. 2-12. Transverse torsion bars fit across the chassis.

Longitudinal Torsion Bars

To replace a longitudinal torsion bar, figure 2-12:

1. With the vehicle on a hoist and the wheels removed, remove the adjuster bolt lock nut, and measure the exposed threads on the adjuster bolt for later reference.
2. Loosen the adjuster bolt until there is no longer tension on the torsion bar.
3. Remove the nuts and bolts securing the torque arm to the lower control arm.
4. Slip the anchor arm off the adjusting bolt. Then, remove the anchor arm, torsion bar, and torque arm as an assembly.
5. Remove the torque arm and anchor arm.
6. To install a torsion bar, grease the torsion bar splines, then press the anchor arm and torque arm into place on the torsion bar.
7. Fit the anchor arm to the adjusting bolt on the frame.
8. Install the bolts that hold the torque arm to the control arm, and tighten them to specified torque.

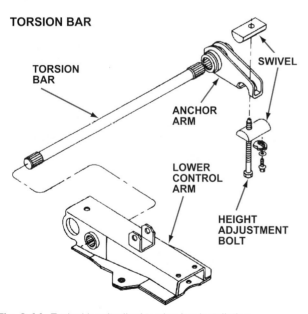

TORSION BAR

Fig. 2-11. Typical longitudinal torsion bar installation.

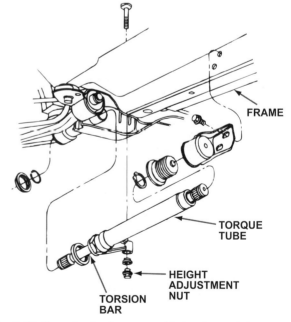

Fig. 2-13. Some torsion bars assemble in a torque tube.

Longitudinal: Oriented from front to rear of the vehicle.
Transverse: Oriented from side to side of the vehicle.

9. Install the bolt and adjusting nut that secure the anchor arm to the frame. Use the measurement taken earlier to adjust the bolt.
10. Install the wheels, lower the vehicle, and tighten suspension bolts and wheel lug nuts.
11. Correct ride height using the adjusting nut, then check and adjust wheel alignment.

A few older vehicles' longitudinal torsion bars are housed inside a torque tube, figure 2-13. Remove the tube and bar as an assembly. Use a hammer to drive the torsion bar free of the torque tube to remove it.

FRONT LEAF SPRINGS

Older vehicles utilized leaf springs to support the front suspension. Today the only applications still using this design are a few heavy duty four-wheel drive trucks. Inspect the leaf spring insulators, shackles, brackets, bushings, and mounts for wear or damage. Refer to the appropriate Service Manual for specific repair instructions.

Front Leaf Spring Service

Leaf springs used on front suspensions are mounted at the front with a hanger and at the rear with a shackle link. Inspect the following components for excessive wear or damage.

- Bushings
- Insulators or silencers
- Shackles
- Mounting brackets
- Axle mounts

Replace any bushing that is loose, physically damaged, or noisy. Replace the hangers, shackles, and other hardware if damage is present.

To remove a front leaf spring:

1. With the vehicle on a hoist, place a jack under the axle or axle housing to support it.
2. Disconnect the lower shock absorber mount.
3. Lower the axle housing slightly, then remove the U-clamps that secure the spring.
4. Remove the shackle nuts and shackle.
5. Lower the rear of the spring.
6. Remove the front bolt and remove the spring.
7. Install new eye bushings in the spring mounts.
8. Clean and inspect all parts before reassembly.
9. Position the front eye in the hanger and install the bolt and nut.
10. Raise the rear of the spring. Install the rear shackle and hardware.
11. Install insulators or silencers.
12. Place the U-bolt over the axle housing, and attach the spring plate to the U-bolt. Install U-bolt nuts.
13. Raise the axle housing and connect the shock absorber.
14. Lower the vehicle, then tighten all fasteners to specified torque.

SHOCK ABSORBERS

Inspect the shock absorbers for damage or signs of leakage. If you determine that shock absorbers are worn, damaged, or leaking replace them. Even if only one shock is worn, replace both shocks on the same axle for even handling.

If the vehicle uses manually filled air shock absorbers, release the air before disconnecting the shock mounts, figure 2-14. If the vehicle has an electronically controlled automatic leveling system, disable the system as directed by the vehicle Service Manual.

There are four types of shock absorber mounts: bayonet, bar, ring, and integral-stud, figure 2-15. To remove shocks, disconnect the upper and lower shock absorber mounts. You may have to apply penetrating oil to the fasteners that secure the shock. If one is available, use a "double square" socket specially designed for removing and installing the nuts on shock absorbers:

- To remove a bayonet mount, hold the stud with locking pliers and loosen the nut with a wrench. Remove the nut, washer, and bushing, then push the stud out of the mounting hole.
- To remove a bar mount, remove the nuts; you may have to hold the bolt head with a wrench. Remove the bolts and set them aside.
- To remove a ring mount, remove the nut and slip the shock off.
- To remove an integral-stud mount, remove the nut on the stud. Slip the stud out of the suspension and remove the shock.

If the shock absorber is inside a coil spring, carefully guide the shock out of the spring. There is usually a hole in the lower control arm through which you can remove the shock.

Compare new shock absorbers with the old ones to be sure you are installing the correct replacement. Pay attention to the type of mounts and the shock absorber extended length, which may be printed on the box or found in the parts manual.

AIR SHOCK ABSORBER

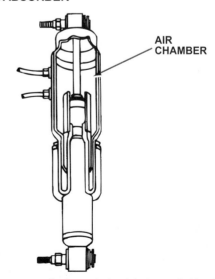

Fig. 2-14. Release pressure from an air shock before unbolting it.

A4

SHOCK ABSORBER MOUNTS

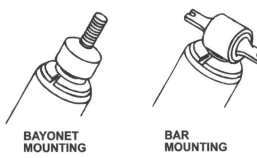
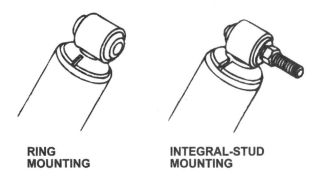

BAYONET MOUNTING   **BAR MOUNTING**   **RING MOUNTING**   **INTEGRAL-STUD MOUNTING**

Fig. 2-15. There are four types of shock absorber mounts.

Before installing a standard hydraulic shock absorber, prime it to remove air bubbles from the fluid. Hold the shock upright as it is installed in the vehicle, and extend it fully. Next, turn it upside down and compress it. Repeat this procedure several times. *Do not* prime gas-charged shock absorbers or coil-over shock absorbers, figure 2-16.

If necessary, support suspension components with jack stands while you are installing the new shocks. Extend non-gas charged shock absorbers and attach the upper and lower mounts. Do not hold the shock housing with vise grips, as you can bend the metal and ruin the shock. Also, never hold the shock absorber piston rod with metal tools. The piston rod moves through the seal while the shock is operating, and any nicks on it will cut the seal. Lower the vehicle and tighten the nuts or bolts to specifications. Bounce the front and rear of the vehicle to ensure that the shocks work properly.

If you are installing gas-charged shocks, there is a wire fastener that keeps the shock absorber compressed. Do not remove this fastener until after you have secured the shock absorber to the vehicle suspension and frame. First, secure one shock absorber mount. Then, position suspension components with a jack until you can secure the other mount. After connecting the upper and lower mounts, remove the fastener on the shock absorber and allow the shock to expand.

Another way to install gas-charged shocks is to secure one shock absorber mount, then loosen the fastener, which allows the shock absorber to expand slightly. When the shock has expanded so that it is even with the other mount, tighten the fastener to keep it from expanding further, and secure the other mount. Remove the fastener and allow the shock to fully extend.

STRUTS

In a MacPherson strut, a coil spring is integral to the strut, figure 2-17. In a modified strut system, the strut and spring are separate components, figure 2-18.

Modified Struts

Before removing the struts, secure suspension springs using the procedures and precautions given earlier. Then, you can safely remove the struts.

COIL-OVER SHOCK ABSORBER

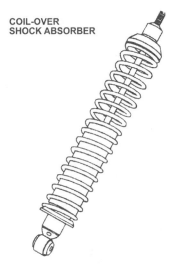

Fig. 2-16. A coil-over shock absorber has a coil spring wound around it.

MACPHERSON STRUT

COIL SPRING

STRUT BASE MOUNTS TO KNUCKLE

LOWER CONTROL ARM

Fig. 2-17. The coil spring is integral to the strut on a MacPherson strut suspension.

MODIFIED STRUT SUSPENSION

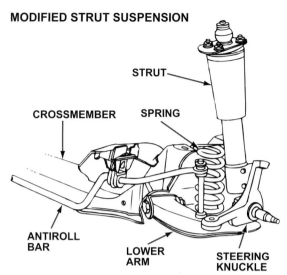

Fig. 2-18. The coil spring is independent on a modified strut suspension.

Integral Spring Struts

Any **axial play**, or up-and-down movement, on a MacPherson strut indicates the upper strut bearing is worn. The procedure varies significantly depending on the vehicle model; however, the following general guidelines can be followed when servicing the strut and/or the upper strut bearing.

To remove struts:

1. Locate the bolts in the engine compartment that secure the upper strut mount to the vehicle body. Remove the dust cap that covers the upper mount. If you are going to reinstall the same strut, mark one of the studs and the corresponding hole, so you can match them.
2. Loosen the nuts securing the upper strut mount to the vehicle body. Remove all but one fastening nut, leaving the remaining nut finger-tight. Do not remove the center nut on the upper strut mount, as it holds the upper spring seat in place and keeps the coil spring compressed.
3. Raise the vehicle and remove the wheels.
4. If brake hoses are fastened to the struts, disconnect them. On some vehicles, the brake caliper prevents access to the lower strut mount; remove it and support it with wire. Do not allow the caliper to hang by the brake line. Disconnect electrical connectors for an electronic suspension.
5. Depending on the suspension design, disconnect the lower strut mount in one of these ways:
   - If the strut base mounts to the steering knuckle, remove the bolts, then pull the knuckle and strut apart, figure 2-19
   - If the strut and knuckle are a single assembly, remove the knuckle along with the strut mount, figure 2-20. Separate the ball joint connecting the knuckle to the lower control arm
   - If the strut lower mount is a pivot bushing attaching it to the lower control arm, hold the pivot bolt with a wrench and remove the nut, figure 2-21. Separate the strut and lower control arm

MACPHERSON STRUT SUSPENSION

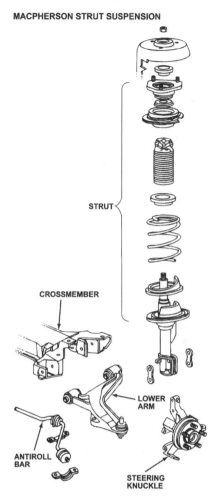

Fig. 2-19. The lower strut mount simply bolts to the steering knuckle on this design.

6. Remove the last fastening nut from the upper strut mount, then remove the strut from the vehicle.
7. After the strut is removed the upper strut bearing can be inspected and replaced if necessary.

Front Strut Cartridge Replacement

Some strut assemblies are designed with replaceable cartridges which can be serviced using the proper procedures. When disassembling an integral-spring strut, use a spring compressor designed for strut springs.

CAUTION: Any improvised methods for strut spring removal are extremely dangerous and are not recommended by vehicle manufacturers or professional technicians.

To disassemble the strut follow this general procedure:

1. Mount the strut in a vise and place spring compressor forks over the coils at each end of the spring. Some shops have a pneumatic strut spring compressor. To use this, mount the strut in the press.

Axial Play: Movement along, or parallel to, the axis of a shaft.

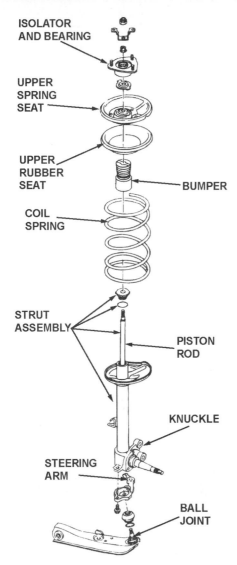

Fig. 2-20. The steering knuckle is integral to the strut, and both are removed to service either one.

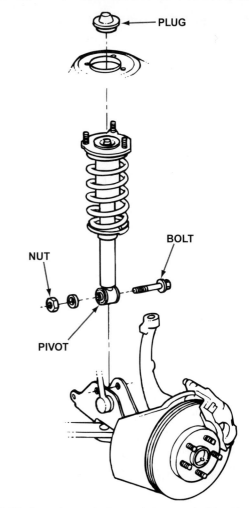

Fig. 2-21. Some lower strut mounts have a pivot bushing that is similar to a ring mount conventional shock absorber.

2. Compress the spring by evenly drawing up the compressor bolts, until there is clearance between the piston rod nut and upper spring seat, figure 2-22. Use a hand wrench, not an impact wrench, to tighten down a manual spring compressor.
3. With the spring compressed and secure, remove the retaining nut at the center of the upper spring seat.
4. Remove the upper spring seat.
5. Gradually release spring tension by loosening the compressor bolts, then remove the spring.

Remove the old cartridge and install the replacement component following the procedures outlined in the vehicle specific Service Manual.

To install an integral-spring strut:

1. Position the upper strut mount on the vehicle body. If you are reinstalling a strut, align the stud and stud hole that you marked earlier. If you are installing a new strut, check the instructions to align the stud with the proper stud hole for correct camber. Hand tighten the nuts securing the upper mount to the vehicle body.

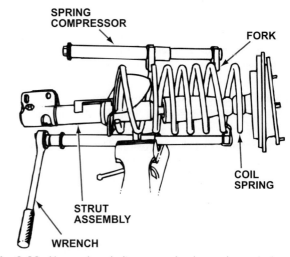

Fig. 2-22. Always draw bolts up evenly when using a strut spring compressor.

2. Connect the lower strut mount:
   • If the strut mounts to the steering knuckle, position the strut and knuckle correctly, install the bolts, and tighten to specifications

- If the strut and wheel knuckle are an integral assembly, connect the ball joint joining the strut and lower control arm
- If the strut mounts to the lower control arm, position the base of the strut on the control arm, install the bushing pivot bolt, and tighten to specification

3. If you disconnected other control arm attachments, reconnect them.
4. Connect any electronically controlled suspension components that were disconnected. If the brake caliper was removed or the brake line unclipped from the strut, reinstall them. If any brake fluid was lost, bleed the brake hydraulic system and add fluid.
5. Install the wheels and lower the vehicle. Tighten the strut mount fasteners, wheel nuts, and suspension fasteners to specified torque. Install the upper strut mount dust caps.
6. Bounce the vehicle several times, then check and adjust wheel alignment.

Front Strut Bearing

Inspect the front strut bearing for excessive wear or damage. Replace any strut bearing that does not meet specifications. The strut bearing may be held in pace with bolts or it may be riveted to the upper support structure. Refer to the vehicle Service Manual for detailed service information.

FRONT SUSPENSION BALL JOINTS

To service suspension ball joints, first check for excess play in the joint, figure 2-23. If play is within specifications, lubricate the joint as needed. If play exceeds specifications, replace the ball joint.

Measuring Ball Joint Wear

To check ball joint wear or play, raise one front wheel at a time off the ground to unload the ball joints on that side. To check for axial play, use a pry bar to move the wheel up and down as you watch for spindle movement. Axial play should be less than 0.06 inch (1.5 mm) for most vehicles. Grasp the top and bottom of the wheel and push it in and out to check for **radial play**. Generally, there should be less than 0.25 inch (6 mm) of radial play. Excessive axial play indicates that the load-carrying ball joint is worn. The **load-carrying ball joint** is installed into the control arm where the suspension spring is seated. Too much radial play may mean the non-load-carrying joint is worn. Be aware, worn wheel bearings can also cause radial play.

Some states require a technician to measure the ball joint wear with a dial indicator and record the amount of play on a work order before replacing the ball joint. To check axial play with a dial indicator, attach it to the weight-bearing control arm and position the plunger on the ball

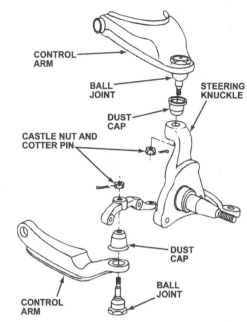

Fig. 2-23. Suspension ball joint installation.

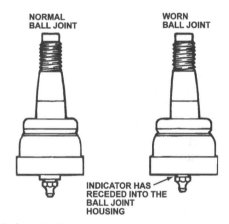

Fig. 2-24. Some ball joints have a wear indicator.

joint. Zero the indicator. Use a pry bar under the tire to lift the tire up. Compare the dial indicator reading to specifications. To check radial play, attach the dial indicator to the control arm, position the plunger against the edge of the wheel, and zero the indicator. Move the wheel in and out, note the dial indicator reading, and compare the reading to specifications.

Some ball joints have wear indicators, figure 2-24. When the joint is new, the indicator shoulder extends from the ball joint socket. As the joint wears, the indicator recedes. Do not unload these ball joints to check for wear. Examine the indicator with the vehicle weight on the ball joint. Unloading the ball joint makes the indicator recede, whether the joint is worn or not.

Load-carrying Ball Joint: A ball joint that links a suspension arm to a knuckle and transfers sprung weight from the arm to the wheel.
Radial Play: Movement along, or parallel to, the radius of a circle.

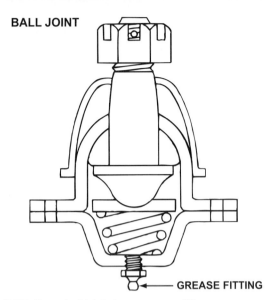

Fig. 2-25. Some ball joints have a grease fitting.

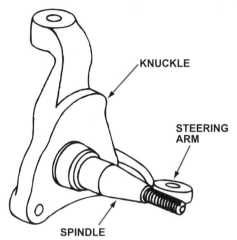

Fig. 2-26. Loose steering knuckle and suspension connections affect steering control and wheel alignment.

Replacing Ball Joints
Replace worn or damaged ball joints as follows:

1. With the vehicle on a lift, remove the wheel and any brake hardware that is in the way.
2. Unload the weight-bearing control arm, compress the suspension spring, and secure it.
3. Remove the ball joint cotter pin and loosen the castellated nut.
4. Separate the ball joint stud from its socket using a spreader tool. Never use heat to free the ball joint. If the ball joint has rivets, carefully drill or chisel them out. Some ball joints are press-fit and require a special tool; others are threaded and can be removed with a socket wrench.
5. Lift the hub and knuckle clear of the ball joint.
6. Install the new ball joint. Clean and inspect the hole in the steering knuckle arm. Replace the steering knuckle if the hole is out-of-round or damaged.
7. Install the castellated nut, tighten it to specified torque, and secure it with a new cotter pin.
8. Reattach any hardware removed earlier.
9. Lubricate the ball joint if it is equipped with a grease fitting, figure 2-25.

STEERING KNUCKLES
Loose connections between the steering knuckle and suspension affect steering control and wheel alignment, figure 2-26. Check for damage and replace the knuckle as needed.

On non-driven wheels, inspect the spindle for bends and wear, especially where the wheel bearings seat. Check for cracks, rust, and other damage. If the spindle is damaged, replace it if it can be separated from the knuckle, or replace the whole steering knuckle if the spindle and knuckle are a cast piece.

If the **steering arms** are bent, wheel alignment will be incorrect. Check for bends, cracks, or other damage and replace

damaged steering arms. On most vehicles, the entire knuckle must be replaced if the steering arm is damaged.

NON-INDEPENDENT FRONT SUSPENSION
Many light trucks and older vehicles utilized non-independent front suspensions. These vehicles were equipped with a solid beam-type axle normally referred to an I-beam axle. Four wheel drive vehicles may also use the non-independent suspension design and be fitted with a solid tube front drive axle. Service for many of the components is similar to the independent suspension designs with a few additional components.

Beam Type Axle Inspection
Solid beam axles generally do not require any service but must be inspected for damage as well as loose mounting fasteners and worn components.

> **CAUTION: Most manufacturers do not support bending an I-beam axle for alignment purposes. Refer to the appropriate Service Manual before attempting to bend the axle.**

Front Drive Axles
Heavy duty pickup trucks may use a solid tube housing on four wheel drive applications, figure 2-27. Inspect the housing and

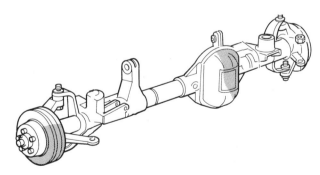

Fig. 2-27. Typical solid tube front drive axle.

Steering Arm: An arm, extending forward or back from the steering knuckle, that links the wheel to the steering linkage.

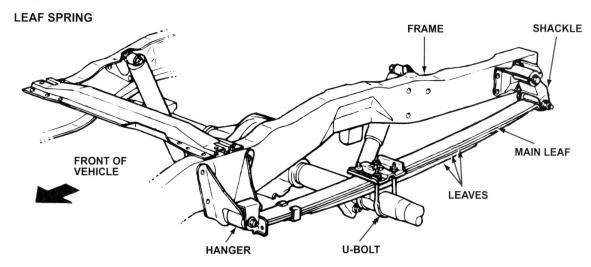

LEAF SPRING

FRAME

SHACKLE

FRONT OF VEHICLE

MAIN LEAF

LEAVES

HANGER

U-BOLT

Fig. 2-28. A rear leaf spring suspension connects the drive axle to the frame.

all mounting hardware for damage or loose fasteners. As with I-beam type axles bent housings should be replaced rather than straightened.

REAR SUSPENSION SERVICE

Worn rear suspension components can cause steering problems, incorrect wheel alignment, and vibration. Many service procedures for rear suspension components are the same as for the front, but some are different. Service of any rear suspension system should begin with an inspection procedure similar to the one given at the beginning of this chapter.

Check all the suspension components, particularly pivot points, bushings, seals, control arms, and mounting or attaching points. Look for damaged parts, cracks or cuts in rubber parts, bent arms, looseness, and noises or squeaking. Use the guidelines under front suspension service for similar parts, as well as the following paragraphs.

Rear Leaf Spring Suspension Service

Rear multileaf springs are mounted at the front with a hanger and at the rear with a shackle link, figure 2-28. Inspect the following components for excessive wear or damage.

- Bushings
- Insulators or silencers
- Shackles
- Mounting brackets
- Axle mounts

Replace any bushing that is loose, physically damaged, or noisy. Replace the hangers, shackles, and other hardware if damage is present.

To remove a rear leaf spring:

1. With the vehicle on a hoist, place a jack under the axle housing to support it.
2. Disconnect the lower shock absorber mount.
3. Lower the rear axle housing slightly, then remove the U-clamps that secure the spring.
4. Remove the shackle nuts and shackle.
5. Lower the rear of the spring.

6. Remove the front bolt and remove the spring.
7. Install new eye bushings in the spring mounts.
8. Clean and inspect all parts before reassembly.
9. Position the front eye in the hanger and install the bolt and nut.
10. Raise the rear of the spring. Install the rear shackle and hardware.
11. Install insulators or silencers.
12. Place the U-bolt over the axle housing, and attach the spring plate to the U-bolt. Install U-bolt nuts.
13. Raise the rear axle housing and connect the shock absorber.
14. Lower the vehicle, then tighten all fasteners to specified torque.

Coil Spring Service

In some rear suspensions, the weight of the vehicle holds the coil springs in place, while the shock absorbers limit suspension downward travel. On these designs, it is extremely important for your safety to support the axle or wheels with jack stands to secure the coil springs before removing the shocks, figure 2-29. Remove and install rear coil springs by compressing them as discussed previously.

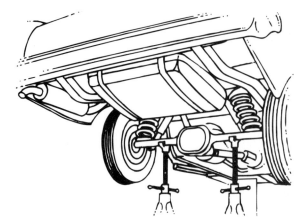

Fig. 2-29. With rear coil springs, support the rear axle with jack stands before disconnecting any suspension components.

A4

INDEPENDENT REAR SUSPENSION SERVICE

Short-Long Arm Rear Suspension

Many newer vehicles use a short-long arm (SLA) rear suspension, figure 2-30. The springs are often located on the shock absorber similar to a strut assembly. They are contained between an upper seat, located just below a rubber isolated mount, and a lower seat, located on the shock absorber.

The top of each shock absorber assembly is bolted to the inner fender or body structure through a rubber isolated mount. The bottom of the shock absorber assembly attaches to the rear knuckle.

Rear Knuckle

Most rear knuckles are made of cast iron and are attached to the upper control arm by a ball joint. Lateral movement is controlled by two lateral arms at the bottom and the upper control arm at the top. Fore and aft movement is controlled by the trailing link. The bottom of the rear shock absorber and spring assembly attaches to the knuckle by a rubber isolated through-bolt.

Upper Control Arm

The rear upper control arm is bolted to the rear suspension crossmember using a pivot bar, which is rubber isolated from the upper control arm. It is connected to the knuckle by a ball joint.

Lateral Arms and Trailing Links

There is no rear lower control arm. Instead, lateral movement of the knuckle is controlled by lateral arms, while fore-and-aft movement is controlled by the trailing link. Rear toe and camber are adjustable by changing the lengths of the lateral arms.

The lateral arms are attached directly to the knuckle. They are bolted to the rear suspension crossmember through two rubber-isolated bushings. The trailing link is mounted between the knuckle and a trailing link bracket, which is connected to the underbody.

Stabilizer Bar

The stabilizer bar connects the forward lateral links. It is mounted to the rear suspension crossmember by rubber isolator bushings. Its function is to control body sway during turns. When one side of the vehicle jounces or rebounds, the sway bar twists to partially send the opposite movement to the other side and keep the body as level as possible.

Chapman Strut Rear Suspension

The **Chapman strut suspension,** figure 2-31, consists of the struts, lateral links, trailing arms, stabilizer bar, and crossmember. Bolted to each strut is a rear knuckle. Generally four lateral links, two per side, are used between the rear crossmember and the knuckle. The lateral links are attached to the crossmember and knuckle at each end. The rearmost lateral link is used to adjust rear toe settings. The trailing arm bolts to the knuckle and to a bracket on the body structure or floor pan. A stabilizer bar attaches to each of the rear struts via link assemblies.

Independent Rear Suspension Service

Follow the precautions and procedures covered in the front suspension system service section when servicing independent rear suspension systems equipped with struts or coil springs. Inspect all bushings, mountings, and fasteners for signs of damage or excessive wear. Replace any components found to be defective.

Rear Strut Replacement

1. Locate the bolts in the passenger compartment or trunk that secure the upper strut mount to the vehicle body.

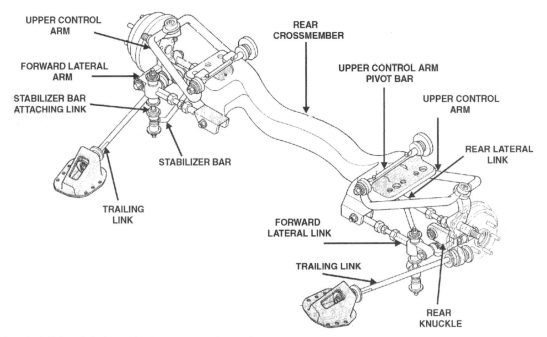

UPPER CONTROL ARM

FORWARD LATERAL ARM

STABILIZER BAR ATTACHING LINK

STABILIZER BAR

TRAILING LINK

REAR CROSSMEMBER

UPPER CONTROL ARM PIVOT BAR

UPPER CONTROL ARM

REAR LATERAL LINK

FORWARD LATERAL LINK

TRAILING LINK

REAR KNUCKLE

Fig. 2-30. A typical SLA style independent rear suspension system.

Chapman Strut Suspension: A type of rear suspension having a telescoping strut that is attached to the chassis at the top and to two links at the bottom, restricting lateral and longitudinal movement.

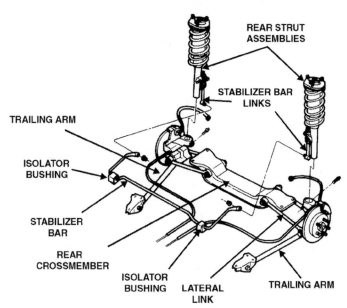

Fig. 2-31. A typical Chapman strut independent rear suspension system.

Remove the dust cap that covers the upper mount. If you are going to reinstall the same strut, mark one of the studs and the corresponding hole, so you can match them.

2. Loosen the nuts securing the upper strut mount to the vehicle body. Remove all but one fastening nut, leaving the remaining nut finger-tight. Do not remove the center nut on the upper strut mount, as it holds the upper spring seat in place and keeps the coil spring compressed.

3. Raise the vehicle and remove the wheels.

4. If brake hoses are fastened to the struts, disconnect them. On some vehicles, the brake caliper prevents access to the lower strut mount; remove it and support it with wire. Do not allow the caliper to hang by the brake line. Disconnect electrical connectors for an electronic suspension.

5. Depending on the suspension design, disconnect the lower strut mount in one of these ways:

   - If the strut base mounts to the rear knuckle, remove the bolts, then pull the knuckle and strut apart
   - If the strut and knuckle are a single assembly, remove the knuckle along with the strut mount. Separate the ball joint connecting the knuckle to the lower control arm
   - If the strut lower mount is a pivot bushing attaching it to the lower control arm, hold the pivot bolt with a wrench and remove the nut. Separate the strut and lower control arm

6. Remove the last fastening nut from the upper strut mount, then remove the strut from the vehicle.

7. After the strut is removed the upper strut bearing can be inspected and replaced if necessary.

Rear Strut Cartridge Replacement

Some strut assemblies are designed with replaceable cartridges that can be serviced using the proper procedures. When disassembling an integral-spring strut, use a spring compressor designed for strut springs.

CAUTION: Any improvised methods for strut spring removal are extremely dangerous and are not recommended by vehicle manufacturers or professional technicians.

To disassemble the strut follow this general procedure:

1. Mount the strut in a vise and place spring compressor forks over the coils at each end of the spring. Some shops have a pneumatic strut spring compressor. To use this, mount the strut in the press.

2. Compress the spring by evenly drawing up the compressor bolts until there is clearance between the piston rod nut and upper spring seat. Use a hand wrench, not an impact wrench, to tighten down a manual spring compressor.

3. With the spring compressed and secure, remove the retaining nut at the center of the upper spring seat.

4. Remove the upper spring seat.

5. Gradually release spring tension by loosening the compressor bolts, then remove the spring.

Remove the old cartridge and install the replacement component following the procedures outlined in the vehicle specific Service Manual.

To install an integral-spring strut:

1. Position the upper strut mount on the vehicle body. If you are reinstalling a strut, align the stud and stud hole that you marked earlier. If you are installing a new strut, check the instructions to align the stud with the proper stud hole for correct positioning. Hand tighten the nuts securing the upper mount to the vehicle body.

2. Connect the lower strut mount:

   - If the strut mounts to the rear knuckle, position the strut and knuckle correctly, install the bolts, and tighten to specifications

A4

- If the strut and rear knuckle are an integral assembly, connect the ball joint joining the strut and lower control arm
- If the strut mounts to the lower control arm, position the base of the strut on the control arm, install the bushing pivot bolt, and tighten to specification

3. If you disconnected other control arm attachments, reconnect them.
4. Connect any electronically controlled suspension components that were disconnected. If the brake caliper was removed or the brake line unclipped from the strut, reinstall them. If any brake fluid was lost, bleed the brake hydraulic system and add fluid.
5. Install the wheels and lower the vehicle. Tighten the strut mount fasteners, wheel nuts, and suspension fasteners to specified torque. Install the upper strut mount dust caps.
6. Bounce the vehicle several times, then check and adjust wheel alignment as required.

Servicing Rear Control or Trailing Arms

Raise the vehicle on a lift and remove the wheel. If the control arm bears the weight of the suspension spring, remove the spring. Remember that coil springs can spring loose and cause damage and injury if not compressed and handled correctly. Once the load is off the control arm, remove the bolts securing it to the frame.

If a strut rod links the lower control arm to the frame, remove the strut rod before removing the control arm. If the strut rod bolts are adjustable, mark the adjuster position. If shims are used, keep them in order.

Disconnect any other suspension components, such as the shock absorber or antiroll bar, that attach to the control arm. Finally, separate the control arm ball joint to disconnect the arm from the rear knuckle.

Replacing Rear Control Arms

To install a rear control arm:

1. Position the control arm on the vehicle, and reinstall the shims or adjusting bolts.
2. Place the control arm at its normal ride height, and bolt it to the frame.
3. For a weight-bearing control arm, install the spring or torsion bar. Be sure that a coil spring is safely compressed, and be sure to install torsion bars on the correct side of the vehicle. Support the control arm with a jack while you seat the spring.
4. Attach the rear knuckle to the control arm ball joint, and secure it with the nut and a new cotter pin.
5. If there is a strut rod for the lower control arm, install it. Also, attach the shock absorber, antiroll bar, or other items that were disconnected earlier.
6. Remove the jack and spring compressor, if used.
7. Install the wheel and lubricate the suspension as required.
8. Lower the vehicle. With the weight of the vehicle on the suspension, tighten all fasteners.
9. Check and correct vehicle alignment as required.

Rear Control or Trailing Arm Bumpers and Bushings

After removing the control or trailing arm from the vehicle, inspecting or replacing the rear jounce and rebound bumpers and bushings is easy. Bumpers are usually secured by a bracket and one or two bolts. Some bumpers fit over an extension on the frame; pull them off and push new ones in place.

To replace control or trailing arm bushings, first remove the control arm from the vehicle. Use a press to push rubber bushings out of the control arm. Always check new bushings for directional indicators before you install them, and be sure to line them up correctly. Install new metal bushings using a press.

REAR SUSPENSION BALL JOINTS

Like the front ball joints, the first step in servicing a rear ball joint is to check for excess play in the joint. If play is within specifications, lubricate the joint as needed. If play exceeds specifications, replace the ball joint.

Measuring Ball Joint Wear

Follow the procedures discussed earlier in this chapter for front ball joints when inspecting rear ball joints.

Replacing Rear Ball Joints

Replace worn or damaged rear ball joints as follows:

1. With the vehicle on a lift, remove the wheel and any brake hardware that is in the way.
2. Unload the weight-bearing control arm, compress the suspension spring, and secure it.
3. Remove the ball joint cotter pin and loosen the castellated nut.
4. Separate the ball joint stud from its socket using a spreader tool. Never use heat to free the ball joint. If the ball joint has rivets, carefully drill or chisel them out. Some ball joints are press-fit and require a special tool; others are threaded and can be removed with a socket wrench.
5. Lift the hub and rear knuckle clear of the ball joint.
6. Install the new ball joint. Clean and inspect the hole in the rear knuckle Replace the rear knuckle if the hole is out-of-round or damaged.
7. Install the castellated nut, tighten it to specified torque, and secure it with a new cotter pin.
8. Reattach any hardware removed earlier.

Rear Knuckle Service

Loose connections between the rear knuckle and suspension may affect wheel alignment and cause vehicle handling issues. Check for damage and replace the knuckle as needed.

Inspect the spindle for bending or excessive wear, especially where the wheel bearings seat. Check for cracks, rust, and other damage. If the spindle is damaged, replace it if it can be separated from the knuckle, or replace the complete knuckle if the spindle and knuckle are a one piece design.

Solid Axle Service

Solid rear axles, unless damaged by a collision or underbody impact, generally last the lifetime of the vehicle, figure 2-32. If the housing of a solid, rear-wheel drive axle is dented, it may interfere with the axle shafts. Examine a solid axle for dents, bends, or leaking fluid. Check rear camber and toe; if the rear wheels cannot be aligned due to axle damage, either replace the axle, or—if damage and misalignment are minor—align the front wheels to the rear-axle thrust line.

SOLID REAR AXLES

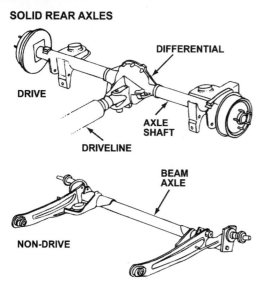

Fig. 2-32. Unless damaged, solid rear axles require minimal service.

ELECTRONICALLY CONTROLLED SUSPENSION SYSTEMS

Electronically controlled suspension systems use **sensors** to gather data about driving and road conditions, an **electronic control unit** (ECU) to process the data and choose the suspension response, and **actuators** to carry out the response through mechanical action. There are two common methods of regulating the suspension:

- Pneumatic
- Hydraulic

A pneumatic system uses a compressor to develop air pressure, which is used to inflate and deflate air springs or air shocks to regulate suspension stiffness and height. Hydraulic systems generally use an electronic motor, or actuator, to position the control rod of the variable hydraulic shock absorbers and regulate suspension stiffness. Some electronic suspension designs use a combination of both air springs and variable shocks, figure 2-33.

AIR SPRING WITH VARIABLE SHOCKS

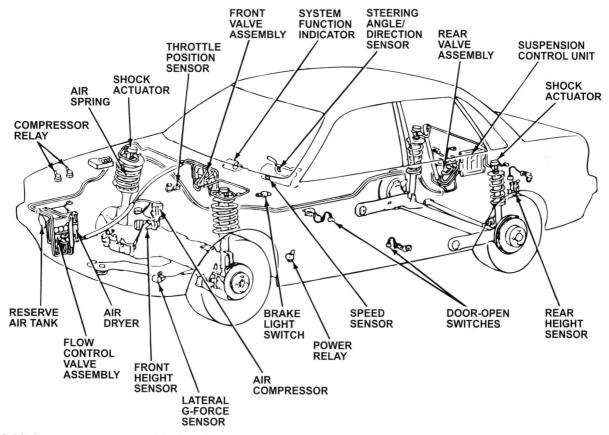

Fig. 2-33. Some systems use a combination of pneumatic and hydraulic controls to regulate the suspension.

Actuator: A device that receives an electronic command from a computer and responds by performing a mechanical action.
Electronic Control Unit (ECU): In an automotive electronic system, a small on-board computer that processes information received from sensors and sends signals to various actuators, so they operate in response to the driving conditions.
Sensor: A device that provides an electric signal to a control unit to indicate a certain physical condition. In an automotive electronic system, sensors monitor such conditions as vehicle speed, suspension height, or steering angle.

If a vehicle has an electronic suspension system, it is important to disable the system before lifting or towing the vehicle. Some systems automatically shut down when the ignition is switched off, others delay shut down for a preset time interval after the ignition is switched off, and still others only shut down when a switch for the electronic system is manually shut off. Always consult the appropriate Service Manual before beginning to service a vehicle with an electronically controlled suspension.

As for repair, the ECU monitors the system for problems during operation. Should a failure occur, the ECU stores a retrievable **diagnostic trouble code (DTC)** to let technicians know what type of malfunction occurred. Usually, a warning lamp in the dashboard flashes to let the driver know when a suspension system fault is electronically detected. Most systems transmit suspension system data to a scan tool, but you must count the number and intervals at which the dashboard warning light flashes on others.

Typically, electronic components must be replaced, rather than repaired, if they fail. However, some sensors and actuators are adjustable. A simple but important check is to make sure that all electrical connections are clean and tight, so nothing prevents the flow of electricity. Because electronic system service is not standardized, always check the appropriate Service Manual for instructions before working on an electronically controlled system.

Suspension Sensor Operation

Sensors used in electronically controlled suspension usually fall into one of two types.

- Potentiometers
- Hall-effect devices

Potentiometers are variable resistors that change their resistance value based on the position to the control lever. Generally the sensor is mounted to the frame or body and the control lever is connected to the suspension via a rubber isolated link, figure 2-34. As the suspension moves up or down the motion is transferred to the sensor, which sends a corresponding voltage signal to the control unit.

Hall-effect sensors are also used to provide the suspension control unit with a voltage signal proportional to the suspension height. Usually the sensor is mounted on the body or frame structure and a small magnet is attached to the suspension system. As the magnet's location varies with suspension movement the sensor's output voltage changes.

The ECU monitors the movement of either sensor and commands suspension height adjustment as required.

Air Spring or Air Shock Suspension

Pneumatic electronically controlled suspensions use air springs or air shocks at the rear wheels, or air springs at all four wheels, to regulate ride height.

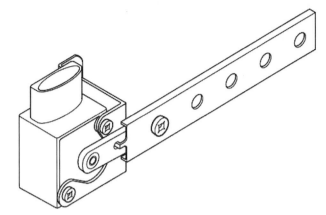

Fig. 2-34. A typical suspension height sensor.

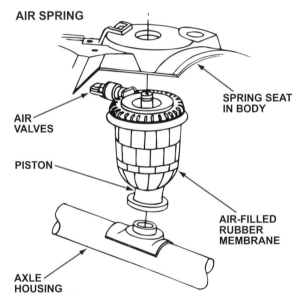

AIR SPRING

SPRING SEAT IN BODY

AIR VALVES

PISTON

AIR-FILLED RUBBER MEMBRANE

AXLE HOUSING

Fig. 2-35. This electronically controlled air spring takes the place of a conventional coil spring.

An air spring takes the place of a coil spring in a suspension. It is a flexible cylinder filled with air, figure 2-35. An electronically controlled air shock is a hydraulic shock absorber with an additional air chamber on the top. Some electronic shocks also have an actuator motor that adjusts damping, figure 2-36. The ECU responds to suspension height-sensor signals, as well as information from other onboard control systems, to control the air pressure in the springs or shocks.

The pneumatic system includes the following:

- Air compressor
- Air dryer
- Airflow control valves
- Air lines and hoses

Diagnostic Trouble Code (DTC): An electronic message, stored in computer memory, indicating the source of a system malfunction.
Hall-effect Sensors: A device that produces a voltage pulse dependent on the presence of a magnetic field. Hall-effect voltage varies as magnetic reactance varies around a current-carrying semiconductor.
Potentiometer: Potentiometers are variable resistors that change their resistance value based on the position of the control lever.

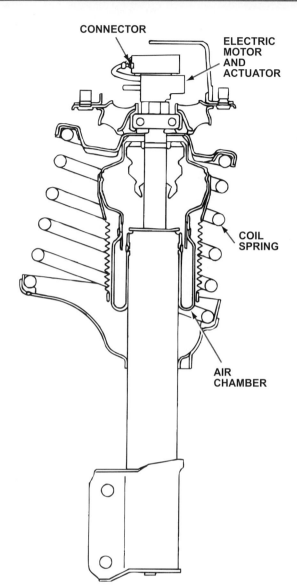

CONNECTOR

ELECTRIC
MOTOR
AND
ACTUATOR

COIL
SPRING

AIR
CHAMBER

Fig. 2-36. This combination shock has an air spring to control height and an actuator to adjust damping.

The motor-driven air compressor draws air into the system and pressurizes it. The air dryer contains a desiccant that draws moisture out of the air to prevent rust or water damage to the system. The ECU controls the airflow solenoid valves to route air to or vent air from the springs and shocks.

To check a pneumatic system for leaks, brush soapy water onto the fittings while the system is pressurized. Air leaking from a fitting will make soap bubbles.

WHEEL BEARING SERVICE

Depending on the individual design, wheel bearings, both front and rear, require periodic inspection, lubrication, adjustment, or replacement.

Bearing Inspection

Many newer vehicles use wheel bearings that are sealed and greased for life and do not require lubrication. If you disassemble, or attempt to repair or lubricate, a sealed bearing you will likely damage the bearing and void the manufacturer's warranty. Basic inspection procedures do not require you to

disassemble a sealed bearing. Sealed bearings are not adjustable. Do not attempt to set or adjust endplay.

Bearing Endplay Inspection

1. Park the vehicle on a level surface. Block the rear wheels to prevent the vehicle from moving.
2. Raise the vehicle so that the front wheels are off the ground. Support the vehicle with safety stands. Do not use a jack to support the vehicle.
3. Visually inspect the hub as you rotate the tire and wheel end assembly. Verify that it rotates smoothly and without noise. While rotating the wheel, grasp the control arm to feel for wheel end hub vibration. If the tire and wheel end assembly does not rotate smoothly, or you hear noise (such as wheel bearing grind) or feel hub vibration during rotation, perform a detailed inspection. If the hub rotates smoothly, proceed to the next step.
4. Grasp the tire and wheel assembly at the nine and three o'clock positions. Check for vertical and horizontal movement. With your hands, apply approximately 50 lb (23 kg) of force to the assembly. You should not feel or see any looseness or movement. If you feel or see any movement or looseness in the tire and wheel end assembly, perform a detailed inspection to determine the cause of the movement, such as worn suspension bushings or pins, wheel-to-hub-mounting endplay, hub endplay, or a combination of them all.

To help determine the cause of hub assembly looseness or movement:

1. Check the wheel-to-hub mounting. Verify that the wheel is mounted correctly and all hub fasteners and hardware are tightened to the correct specification.
2. Have an assistant apply the brake to lock the hub and spindle assembly together. If you detect movement or looseness, the suspension bushings and fasteners should be inspected. If applying the brake eliminates movement or looseness refer to the appropriate Service Manual for detailed instructions and specifications for measuring endplay. If no service information is available the following steps will help you to determine if a problem exists.

Bearing Endplay Measurement

1. Park the vehicle on a level surface. Block the wheels on the opposite end of the vehicle to prevent it from moving.
2. Remove the bearing hub cap, if equipped.
3. Raise the vehicle so that the wheel being serviced is off the ground. Support the vehicle with safety stands. Do not use a jack to support the vehicle.
4. Remove the wheel and drum. Attach the magnetic base of a dial indicator to the end of the spindle. Touch the indicator stem perpendicular against the hub mounting face.
5. Set the dial indicator to ZERO. Do not rotate the hub. Place your hands at the nine and three o'clock positions.
6. Push the hub straight IN. Note the reading. Pull the hub straight OUT. Note the reading. If the total movement of the dial indicator is less than 0.003-inch

A4

(0.08 mm), inspection is complete. No adjustment is required. If the total movement of the dial indicator is 0.003-inch (0.08 mm) or greater, service will be required.

Servicing Conventional Wheel Bearings

1. Park the vehicle on a level surface. Block the wheels on the opposite end of the vehicle to prevent it from moving.
2. Raise the vehicle so that the wheel being serviced is off the ground. Support the vehicle with safety stands. Do not use a jack to support the vehicle.
3. Remove the tire and wheel from the hub.
4. If necessary, remove the brake caliper and caliper mounting bracket. Support the caliper assembly with a wire. Do not allow the caliper to hang by the brake line.
5. Remove the dust cap from the hub.
6. Remove the cotter pin and wheel bearing adjustment nut.
7. Use a clean shop towel to catch the outer bearing as you slide the hub off the spindle.
8. Support the hub and use a brass drift or wooden block to drive the inner bearing and seal from the hub.

To remove grease from the hub, use a stiff fiber brush, not steel, and safety solvent, not gasoline. Allow the clean parts to dry, then wipe with a clean, absorbent cloth. Note that any solvent residue must be completely wiped dry since it may either dilute the grease or prevent it from correctly adhering to the hub components.

CAUTION: Never "spin" a bearing using compressed air to dry it. Personal injury and/or damage to the bearing can occur

Lubricate the wheel bearings with an approved grease as follows.

1. Pack the bearing cones with grease by forcing the grease into the cavities between the rollers and the cage from the large end of the cone. The use of a pressure packer is recommended; otherwise, pack the bearings by hand.
2. Apply a light coat of grease to the spindle-bearing journals.
3. Pack the area of the hub between the two bearings with grease up to the smallest diameter of the bearing cups.
4. Apply a light coat of grease to the interior of the hubcap and wheel retention hardware to indicate what lubricant is installed as well as help prevent corrosion of these parts.

To reinstall the wheel bearings and seal:

1. Place the inner bearing in the hub.
2. Install a new seal using the proper seal driver to prevent damage to the seal, hub, or bearing.
3. Carefully slide the hub onto the spindle and install the outer bearing.
4. Install the washer and bearing adjustment nut.
5. Tighten the adjustment nut following procedures in the appropriate Service Manual.
6. Install a new cotter pin and the hub dust cap.
7. Reinstall any brake components removed earlier.
8. Install the wheel and tire assembly, torquing the lug nuts to the proper specification.

9. Rotate the tire and wheel assembly, checking for free rotation.
10. Lower the vehicle, pump the brake pedal to reseat the brake pads on the rotor, and perform a road test to ensure proper bearing and brake operation.

CRADLE AND CROSSMEMBER INSPECTION

Engine Cradle

Most front wheel drive vehicles mount the engine and transaxle assembly in a structural member known as the engine cradle or simply cradle. Many manufacturers have procedures for checking engine cradle alignment, in order to determine if the frame has suffered collision damage. If the frame is bent, you may not be able to satisfactorily align the wheels. Engine cradle misalignment can also contribute to torque steer. Some vehicles have a sight hole in the frame through which you should be able to see a mark on the engine or engine cradle. Another method is to insert a straight tool, such as a screwdriver, punch, or socket extension, through a hole in the frame, which should line up with another hole in the engine block or cradle. If the engine cradle is out of alignment, the vehicle needs frame work, or the engine must be repositioned before a wheel alignment.

Mark the position of the cradle in respect to the frame or body mounting before removing any of the attaching fasteners. Use these marks to ensure proper alignment is maintained when the cradle is reinstalled. Refer to the appropriate vehicle Service Manual for complete details on cradle alignment procedures.

Crossmembers

As with the cradle many vehicles support the rear suspension on one or more crossmembers that must be correctly positioned to maintain proper vehicle alignment. Even if no precautions are given it is a good idea to mark the position of any crossmember before removing the attaching fasteners. Realigning the marks will help to ensure proper vehicle alignment is maintained upon reassembly.

Inspection Procedures

Inspect engine cradle and crossmember mountings for damage, missing fasteners, or worn bushings or isolators. Replace any components found to be defective before returning the vehicle to service.

ELECTRONICALLY CONTROLLED STEERING SYSTEMS

Some newer vehicles utilize electronic controls in the vehicle steering systems. These systems may control the direction of the front, rear, or both the front and rear wheels of the vehicle. Much of the technology in use is a direct evolution of the variable assist system discussed earlier in this chapter, the main difference being the elimination of the engine driven power steering pump in many new systems.

The disadvantages of the old hydraulic systems are almost too numerous to mention, although no all-around better technology emerged until recently. The hydraulic pumps are a major source of parasitic power losses, often prohibiting their use on smaller engines. That same parasitic power drain also drives down fuel economy. Hydraulic systems are a complicated mix of maintenance-intensive components: they are prone to leaks, use heavy and expensive components, and require large amounts of under-hood space, which is increasingly at a premium. And the pump must always be running when the engine is running for there to be power assist, even when there is no steering input.

The degree of steering support is varied depending on the speed and operating conditions of the vehicle. At a low speed such as when parking, a higher degree of assist supports the driver when maneuvering. At a high speed such as highway driving, a lower degree of assist permits the vehicle to achieve a more stable straight course.

Electro-Hydraulic Steering System Components

Control Module
The steering system control module receives input from several sensors in order to determine the appropriate assist and direction to provide.

- Steering Input Motion Sensor
- Vehicle Speed Sensor or Signal
- Hydraulic Pressure Sensor
- Steering Rack or Linkage Position Sensor
- Vehicle Stability System Input (some systems)

Steering Input Motion Sensor
A sensor records the driver input as to direction of rotation of the steering wheel and the degree of torque applied. The actual sensor may be a Hall-effect sensor or an **optical sensor** located below the instrument panel on the steering column.

Vehicle Speed Sensor or Speed Input
The control module receives a signal either directly from the vehicle speed sensor or from another control module such as the powertrain control module (PCM), the transmission control module (TCM), or the antilock brake control module (ABS).

Hydraulic Pressure Sensor or Transducer
To accurately control directional changes the control module receives input from the hydraulic pressure sensor transducer. The pressure transducer is normally a variable capacitor whose capacitance changes proportionally to the pressure applied. Based on the input the control module will increase or decrease pressure to meet the current system requirements.

Rack or Linkage Position Sensor
To maintain accurate vehicle control and stability the control module needs to know the position of the steered wheels at all times. This information is provided by the rack or linkage position sensor. This sensor is often a Hall-effect sensor similar to the suspension height sensors discussed earlier in this chapter.

Vehicle Stability System Input
Vehicles equipped with stability enhancement systems often integrate the electronically controlled steering system into the stability operation. By effectively preventing excessively fast steering maneuvers vehicle stability can be greatly improved.

Electro-Hydraulic Steering System Outputs
Based on the information provided by the various inputs the steering system control module will command the operation of different actuators:

- Electro-Hydraulic Pump
- Hydraulic Servo
- Related linkages

The electro-mechanical actuator intervenes in the steering system of the hydraulic servo-assisted steering through a steering rack or gear. When a need for steering adjustment is sensed by the control module the electric motor–driven hydraulic pump is activated, providing the required hydraulic pressure to aid the driver in turning the wheels. When the need for assist is no longer required the pump is de-energized, eliminating additional load on the vehicle electrical system.

System Diagnosis
Diagnosis of electronically controlled steering systems requires the use of vehicle specific diagnostic tools. Many of the system control modules are capable of storing diagnostic trouble codes to aid the technician in accurately finding and repairing system problems. Refer to the appropriate Service Manual for the correct diagnostic and repair procedures for the vehicle being serviced.

FULL ELECTRIC STEERING SYSTEMS
A few late-model vehicles are equipped with fully electric steering systems. These systems are often referred to as "steer-by-wire" systems. The operation of the fully electric systems is very similar to the previously discussed electro-hydraulic systems.

The defining difference is that control of the vehicle direction is accomplished through the use of electric motors or servos rather than hydraulic assist to a mechanical steering gear or rack.

Diagnosis of steer-by-wire systems requires the use of vehicle-specific diagnostic tools. Refer to the appropriate Service Manual for more information.

POWER STEERING IDLE SPEED COMPENSATION SYSTEMS
Many smaller vehicles are equipped with systems that automatically increase the engine idle speed when power steering pressure rises. This system serves two purposes.

First, by increasing the idle speed it prevents engine stalling during tight turns such as when parking the vehicle. Second, the increased idle speed provides additional power steering pump speed, increasing pump output, which decreases the effort required to turn the steering wheel.

The idle compensation systems require the addition of one sensor, the power steering pressure (PSP) sensor, to the already electronically controlled engine of all current model vehicles. The PSP sensor is installed either in the high-pressure power steering hose between the pump and the steering gear or rack or directly in the pump outlet housing. Typically the

Optical Sensor: A type of sensor utilizing a light source such as an LED and a phototransistor. Usually used to detect rotation.

sensor is a variable resistor or capacitor that provides a signal to the PCM based on system pressure.

When the PSP sensor input to the PCM indicates that power steering pressure exceeds a predetermined point the PCM will increase idle speed accordingly. When the pressure signal drops back below the set point the PCM reduces idle speed back to normal.

Diagnosis of the power steering idle compensation system requires the use of a vehicle specific diagnostic tool. Refer to the correct Service Manual for more information.

CHAPTER QUESTIONS

1. During a bounce test, the front of a vehicle bounces more than three times before it settles. This in an indication of worn:
   a. Ball joints
   b. Shock absorbers
   c. Springs
   d. Suspension bushings

2. Low ride height is generally caused by:
   a. Worn springs
   b. Leaking shock absorbers
   c. Loose ball joints
   d. Incorrect wheel alignment

3. Bump stop damage is the result of:
   a. Incorrect ride height
   b. Worn control arm bushings
   c. Worn shocks and springs
   d. Worn ball joints and tie rod ends

4. When replacing a weight-bearing control arm, do all of the following *EXCEPT*:
   a. Remove the wheel
   b. Secure the coil spring, if any
   c. Remove the strut rod, if any
   d. Replace the steering knuckle if damaged

5. When securing a coil spring before removing it from the suspension:
   a. Remove the control arm bushings before compressing the spring
   b. Remove the control arm ball joint before compressing the spring
   c. Use a jack to raise the control arm and compress the spring
   d. Use strong wire or rope to secure the compressed spring

6. Torsion bars are:
   a. Interchangeable side-to-side
   b. Adjustable for ride height
   c. Adjustable for spring rate
   d. Used with coil springs

7. Which type of shock absorber should be primed before it is installed?
   a. Conventional hydraulic
   b. Air-type
   c. Gas-charged
   d. Coil-over

8. When the front wheel is pried up and down there is more than 0.5 inch (13 mm) of movement. A possible reason is a worn:
   a. Steering knuckle
   b. Wheel bearings
   c. Load-carrying ball joint
   d. Non-load-carrying ball joint

9. Worn rear suspension components can cause all the following *EXCEPT*:
   a. Steering problems
   b. Vibration problems
   c. Incorrect wheel alignment
   d. Engine cradle misalignment

10. When removing a rear leaf spring, it is important to:
    a. Support the axle housing with a jack before loosening the spring mounts.
    b. Disconnect the control arms from the axle housing to lower the housing.
    c. Compress the springs and lock them in place with clips before unbolting them.
    d. Disconnect the front mounting bolt first, then lower the axle and remove the shackle bolts.

11. Technician A says excessive radial play found during a ball joint wear inspection indicates a worn load-carrying ball joint. Technician B says ball joint wear must be checked with the suspension fully loaded. Who is right?
    a. A only
    b. B only
    c. Both A and B
    d. Neither A nor B

12. Which of the following is *NOT* part of a pneumatic suspension control system?
    a. Compressor
    b. Dryer
    c. Actuator motor
    d. Airflow control valves

13. Technician A says the conventional front wheel bearings must be cleaned and repacked with grease. Technician B says sealed bearings must be opened and repacked with grease. Who is right?
    a. A only
    b. B only
    c. Both A and B
    d. Neither A nor B

14. When checking for worn wheel bearings you should measure:
    a. Endplay
    b. Lateral runout
    c. Radial runout
    d. Rotational torque

15. Before removing the engine cradle you should do which of the following?
    a. Remove the engine cover
    b. Mark the cradle location
    c. Lower the transmission
    d. Align the front wheels

16. Which of the following is *NOT* part of an electronically controlled steering system?
    a. Compressor
    b. Vehicle speed sensor
    c. Steering input motion sensor
    d. Pressure sensor

17. A power steering idle compensation system increases engine speed:
    a. At highway speeds
    b. While parking
    c. When the engine is hot
    d. Only when in Reverse

18. Variable assist power steering systems decrease system pressure:
    a. At low speed
    b. During parking maneuvers
    c. At high speeds
    d. Whenever the engine is running

19. Technician A says excessive axial play of a MacPherson strut indicates that the control arm bushings are worn. Technician B says excessive axial play of a MacPherson strut indicates that the upper strut bearing is worn. Who is right?
    a. A only
    b. B only
    c. Both A and B
    d. Neither A nor B

20. Before towing or lifting a vehicle that has an electronic suspension:
    a. Disable the electronic suspension system.
    b. Remove the fuse for the suspension control system.
    c. Check for diagnostic codes in memory.
    d. Adjust the leveling system to its highest setting.

A4

CHAPTER THREE

WHEEL ALIGNMENT

CHAPTER OBJECTIVES

- The technician will complete the ASE task list on Wheel Alignment.
- The technician will be able to answer 12 questions dealing with the Wheel Alignment section of the A4 ASE Test.

Correct wheel alignment provides good driving characteristics and keeps tire wear to a minimum. For an alignment to have these effects, the vehicle suspension and steering systems must be in good repair, the wheels must be balanced and not have runout, and the tires must be properly and evenly inflated.

Alignment is measured in angles, according to a system of **steering geometry**. Traditionally, five alignment angles at the front wheels were checked:

- Camber
- Caster
- Toe
- Steering axis inclination
- Toe-out on turns

Camber, toe, and toe-out on turns are **tire wear angles**, meaning that if incorrect, the tires wear out quickly. All five traditional angles are **directional control angles**, which means they affect the steering and vehicle control.

Modern suspension geometry demands more precise control to maintain acceptable handling and performance, and two additional measurements are made at the front wheels, figure 3-1:

- Thrust angle
- Setback

Many late-model vehicles require a four-wheel alignment, and rear wheel camber and toe must be checked, as well.

PRELIMINARY INSPECTION

Certain preliminary checks must be performed before the wheel alignment is checked or corrected:

- Check tire inflation. Low air pressure causes steering difficulty and tire squeal; unequal pressure side to side causes pull
- Make sure wheel and tire sizes are within specifications for the vehicle and are the same side to side
- Inspect for wheel or tire damage. Examine the tire sidewall for bulges or indentations
- Check wheel and tire balance and runout
- Check for axial play indicating worn load-carrying ball joints or worn strut upper bearings
- Check for radial play indicating worn non-load-carrying ball joints or worn wheel bearings

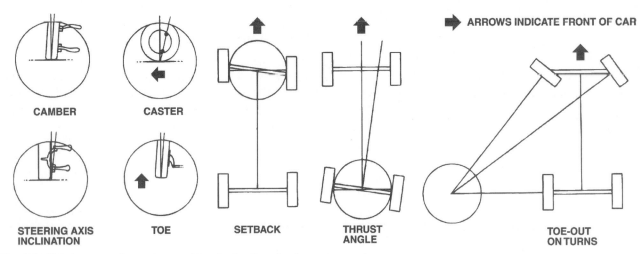

Fig. 3-1. Steering geometry angles used for aligning the wheels.

Directional Control Angle: A wheel alignment angle that affects the steering and handling of the vehicle.
Steering Geometry: A method of measuring wheel alignment using angles measured in degrees of a circle.
Tire Wear Angle: A wheel alignment angle that affects the rate at which tires wear out.

- Inspect the steering and suspension systems for bent links, damaged bushings, excessive play between parts, and bent steering arms
- Check the power steering system for leaks
- Check external bump stops for damage indicating that the suspension is bottoming out
- Bounce the corners of the vehicle to check shock absorber condition
- Inspect the suspension springs for visible damage
- Check ride height. Low or uneven ride height indicates worn springs or bent suspension parts
- Check engine cradle alignment. Incorrect measurements can indicate collision damage to the frame

Make necessary repairs before performing a wheel alignment, or the alignment will be ineffective.

CHECKING RIDE HEIGHT
Measure ride height as follows:

1. Park the vehicle on a level surface. Use a wheel alignment rack if one is available.
2. Bounce the vehicle several times in order to settle the suspension.
3. Use the vehicle Service Manual procedures to locate the points on the suspension or body from which you measure ride height.
4. Use a tape measure or ruler to measure ride height and compare results to specifications.

Typical ride height measurement points are from the:

- Top of the wheel opening on the fender and the ground, figure 3-2A
- Lower edge of the rocker panel and the ground, figure 3-2B
- Axle and the vehicle frame
- Inner and outer control arm pivot and the ground, figure 3-2C
- Center of the spindle and the ground
- Lower spring seat and the axle
- Center of the spindle and the top of the fender

Always make needed suspension repairs before aligning the wheels.

CHECKING ENGINE CRADLE ADJUSTMENT
Many manufacturers have procedures for checking engine cradle alignment, in order to determine if the frame has suffered collision damage. If the frame is bent, you may not be able to satisfactorily align the wheels. Engine cradle misalignment can also contribute to torque steer.

Some vehicles have a sight hole in the frame through which you should be able to see a mark on the engine or engine cradle. Another method is to insert a straight tool, such as a

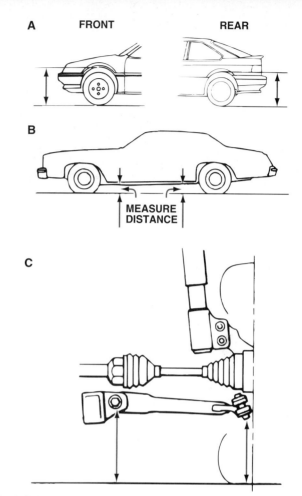

Fig. 3-2. Several methods of measuring ride height.

screwdriver, punch, or socket extension, through a hole in the frame, which should line up with another hole in the engine block or cradle. If the engine cradle is out of alignment, the vehicle needs frame work, or the engine must be repositioned before a wheel alignment.

BASIC ALIGNMENT OVERVIEW
Camber
Camber is the tilt of the wheel from true vertical, as seen from the front of the vehicle, figure 3-3. Zero camber, a vertical wheel and tire, causes the least tire wear. A positive or negative camber angle causes one side of the tire to squirm on the pavement as the tire rolls, and the tire shoulder wears quickly. When camber angles are unequal, the vehicle pulls toward the side with greater camber. Incorrect camber also places stress on the wheel bearings.

Caster
Caster is the tilt of the **steering axis** from true vertical, as seen from the side of the vehicle, figure 3-4. Caster affects

---

Camber: The angle between the centerline of the tire and a line perpendicular to a level surface. More simply, camber is the tilt of a wheel and tire assembly, viewed from the front of the vehicle.
Caster: The angle between the steering axis and a line perpendicular to a level surface, viewed from the side. More simply, caster is the forward or backward tilt of the steering axis.
Steering Axis: The axis on which the steering knuckle pivots. The steering axis runs through the kingpin, the centers of the upper and lower ball joints, or the top pivoting point of the strut and the center of the lower ball joint.

CAMBER

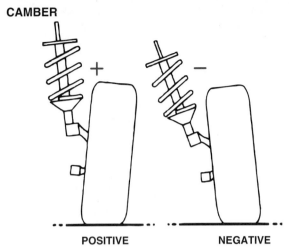

POSITIVE   NEGATIVE

Fig. 3-3. Camber angles can be positive or negative, in relation to a vertical centerline viewed from the front of the vehicle.

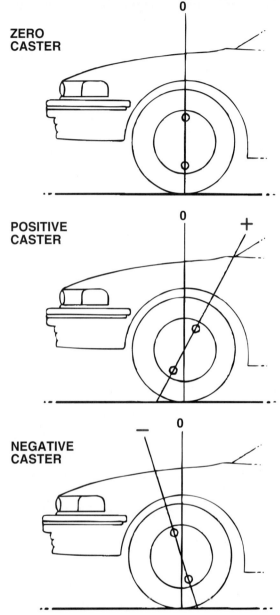

ZERO CASTER

POSITIVE CASTER

NEGATIVE CASTER

Fig. 3-4. The caster angle, which can be positive or negative, is the deviation from a vertical centerline viewed from the side.

straight-ahead stability and steering wheel return. High, positive caster makes the front wheels "want" to go straight, so it gives stability and makes the steering wheel return to center after a turn. However, it also increases the amount of effort needed to turn the steering wheel.

Excessive caster causes hard steering, and too little caster can make steering unstable. This instability can cause wheel shimmy, which eventually results in cup wear on the tires. If caster is unequal side-to-side, the vehicle pulls toward the side with less caster.

Toe

Toe is how the wheels are aimed as seen from above, figure 3-5. Wheels aimed inward have **toe-in**, and wheels aimed outward have **toe-out**. Zero toe—wheels aimed straight ahead—provides the least tire wear. During straight-ahead driving, toe-in or toe-out causes the wheels to move at an angle to the way they are aimed. This scuffs the tire along the pavement, and the tread wears away very quickly.

Toe-in wears out the outside tire edges, while toe-out wears the inner edges. Toe wear is generally more severe than camber wear. On radial tires, toe wear is smooth, but on older, bias-ply tires, it makes a feather-edge wear pattern. Incorrect toe at the rear of a front-wheel drive (FWD) vehicle can wear the tires diagonally. Incorrect toe also causes wander and shimmy.

Toe Change

Toe change, often called **bump steer or toe curve**, occurs during suspension compression and extension when a tie rod is the wrong length or installed at the wrong height, figure 3-6. As the suspension compresses and extends, the outer tie rod end moves

down and up. If its length or installation is incorrect, it pulls or pushes the steering arm and aims the tire in a new direction. The driver notices this condition as the steering wheel jerks to one side when the vehicle drives over a bump or dip.

Toe-out on Turns

Toe-out on turns, sometimes called turning radius, occurs when the outside wheel does not turn as far as the inside wheel

---

Bump Steer or Toe Curve: Other names for toe change.

Toe: The angle between the direction a wheel is aimed and a line parallel to the centerline of the vehicle. When measured linearly, toe is the distance between the front edges of the tires subtracted from the distance between the back edges.

Toe-in: A description of the toe angle when the front edges of the tires point toward each other.

Toe-out: A description of the toe angle when the front edges of the tires point away from each other.

Toe Change: A change in the direction a tire is aimed during suspension compression or extension. Tie rod height and length affect toe change.

Toe-out on Turns: The tendency, during turns, for the outside wheel to travel in a larger arc than the inside wheel.

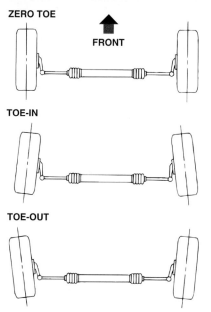

Fig. 3-5. The toe angle is the direction in which wheels point when viewed from above.

while the vehicle is negotiating a turn, figure 3-7. Some degree of toe-out on turns is necessary because the outside wheel has to drive in a wider curve than the inside one. Otherwise, the outside tire would scuff as it tried to turn in a sharper curve than the cornering angle would allow. Engineers design toe-out

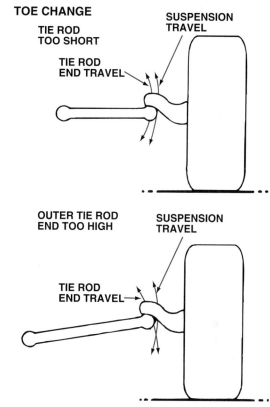

Fig. 3-6. Toe change, or bump steer, is caused by incorrect tie rod length or installation height.

A4

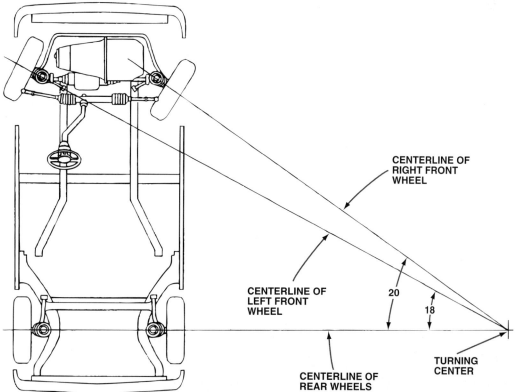

Fig. 3-7. Toe-out on turns is the difference between the centerline of the two front wheels when the vehicle is turning.

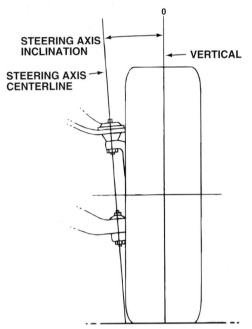

Fig. 3-8. Steering axis inclination is the difference between the steering axis, a line drawn through the upper and lower pivot points, and true vertical.

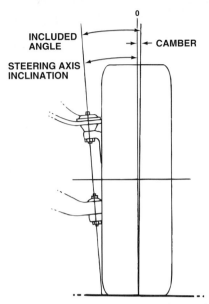

Fig. 3-9. The included angle is the SAI plus the camber angle.

on turns into the steering system. If toe-out on turns is not within specifications, the tires scuff and squeal during turns, and they wear more rapidly.

Steering Axis Inclination

Steering axis inclination (SAI) is the tilt of the steering axis from the vertical, as seen from the front, figure 3-8. Like caster, SAI affects steering feel and stability. In suspension designs that do not allow for much caster, particularly some strut designs, high SAI can provide solid steering feel and stability. Vehicles with low SAI are more prone to wander.

Sometimes SAI is called kingpin inclination (KPI). This dates back to when the suspension pivoted on a kingpin, rather than ball joints. Today, kingpins are found on I-beam front axles, which are used on heavy-duty trucks.

Included Angle

The **included angle** is the SAI plus the camber angle, figure 3-9. If you know the SAI, camber, and included angle measurements, you can diagnose problems in the steering knuckle and suspension, using the chart at the end of this chapter.

Thrust Angle

The **thrust angle** is the angle between the vehicle centerline and the direction the rear wheels are aimed, figure 3-10. If the rear wheels point straight ahead, the **thrust line** is the same as the **geometric centerline** of the vehicle, and there is no thrust angle.

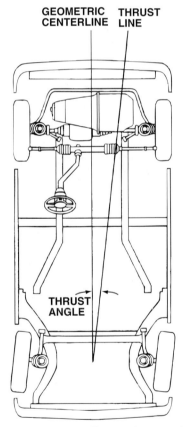

Fig. 3-10. Thrust angle is the difference between the centerline of the rear wheels and the centerline of the vehicle.

Geometric Centerline: An imaginary line that bisects the front and rear axles of a vehicle.
Included Angle: The steering axis inclination angle plus or minus the camber angle.
Steering Axis Inclination (SAI): The angle between the steering axis and a line perpendicular to a level surface, viewed from the front. More simply, steering axis inclination is the inward or outward tilt of the steering axis.
Thrust Angle: The angle between the thrust line and the geometric centerline of a vehicle.
Thrust Line: An imaginary line, running forward from the center of the rear axle, that bisects rear toe.

When a vehicle is driving forward, the rear wheels "steer" it along the thrust line, so zero thrust angle is ideal.

Correcting rear toe should correct the thrust angle, but sometimes the rear axle does not allow for toe corrections. If the thrust angle cannot be eliminated, align the front wheels to the thrust line rather than the vehicle centerline. If the front wheels are aligned to the centerline, but the rear wheels drive along the thrust line, the following problems appear:

- Crooked steering wheel
- Incorrect front camber and toe during driving
- Accelerated tire wear
- Pull

Setback

If one wheel on an axle is positioned further back in the chassis than the opposite wheel, the pushed-back wheel has **setback**, figure 3-11. Occasionally, engineers design a slight amount of setback into a suspension, to compensate for some other problem, but usually setback results from a collision. Replace suspension and steering components that have been bent in an accident. Sometimes, uneven caster can cause setback at the front wheels.

DIAGNOSING ALIGNMENT PROBLEMS

Since incorrect wheel alignment angles cause specific problems, you can get an idea of what needs to be corrected before aligning the wheels. Some problems are revealed by tire wear patterns, while others become apparent during a test drive.

TIRE WEAR PATTERNS

Examine the tire tread wear patterns:

- Both edges worn—underinflation
- Center worn—overinflation
- Inner shoulder wear—negative camber or toe-out
- Outer shoulder wear—positive camber, toe-in, or excessive toe-out on turns
- Diagonal wear on the rear wheels of a FWD vehicle—incorrect rear toe, figure 3-12
- Cupping—imbalance, runout, or suspension damage

Toe and camber cause similar wear patterns, but toe wear, figure 3-12, tends to be more severe than camber wear and also tends to occur on both same-axle tires.

THE TEST DRIVE

Plan a test drive route that includes both left and right turns, straight stretches, and smooth and rough surfaces. If the suspension and steering systems are in good repair, the road test reveals alignment problems.

If the vehicle wanders, or drifts, during straight-ahead driving, suspect negative caster or incorrect toe. Non-alignment problems causing **wander** include incorrect tire inflation, worn wheel bearings, worn suspension bushings or bearings, or a misadjusted steering gear.

Incorrect caster causes the front wheels to shimmy. However, a wheel imbalance and worn suspension, steering bushings, or ball joints can also cause shimmy.

A4

Fig. 3-11. Wheel setback exists when a line drawn between the hubs of two wheels is not square to the vehicle centerline.

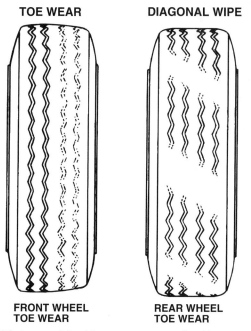

Fig. 3-12. Incorrect front toe causes severe shoulder wear. Incorrect rear toe on a FWD car results in a diagonal tire wear pattern.

Setback: A condition in which one wheel of an axle is located further back than the opposite wheel.
Wander: A driving condition in which the driver must actively steer back and forth to keep the vehicle moving straight.

If the vehicle pulls to one side, excess positive camber or negative caster is likely on that side. **Pull** can also be caused by unequal tire inflation, worn suspension components, a faulty radial tire, an off-center power steering gear control valve, or a dragging brake pad. If switching the tires side to side makes the vehicle pull in the opposite direction, the tire is faulty. If the wheels jerk to one side when you start the engine, suspect the power steering system. If the pull problem changes during braking, suspect the brake system.

Pull can also be caused by high **road crown**. Drive on several different roads to see if the problem changes. In some areas of the country, all the roads have high crowns. In this case, the vehicle may pull during driving, but still have wheel alignment within specifications. To remedy, adjust right wheel camber toward the negative end of the specified range to compensate.

On certain vehicles with rubber-bonded socket (RBS) tie rod ends, **memory steer** can pull the vehicle in one direction. If the steering system was not straight when the RBS joints were torqued down, the rubber pulls the steering system to the position it was in when the joints were tightened. To correct memory steer, loosen the RBS joints, straighten the steering system, and tighten the joints to specified torque.

During cornering, notice whether the steering wheel is hard to turn, and whether it re-centers after the turn. Excessive positive caster causes hard steering; other possible causes include low tire pressure, damage or binding in the steering system, or power steering system problems. If caster is negative, the steering wheel does not return to center without effort.

Tire squeal during turns can mean that toe-out on turns is out of specifications, or that the tires are underinflated. Toe change, or bump steer, makes itself felt over rough road surfaces.

Torque Steer

Torque steer is a drivetrain problem that technicians may mistake for pull. Pull occurs at all speeds, but torque steer is related to acceleration and deceleration and occurs only in FWD vehicles.

Torque steer, probably caused by unequal-length axle shafts, pulls the vehicle in one direction during acceleration and the opposite direction during deceleration. Torque steer is inherent in some FWD designs, but the effect is exaggerated if the engine, transaxle, or engine cradle is at an incorrect angle, or if the engine or transmission mounts are worn.

CORRECTING ALIGNMENT ANGLES

The procedures for measuring wheel alignment angles depend on the alignment equipment used, so we will not detail them here. Some pointers:

- Chock the rear wheels after driving onto the alignment rack; chock the front wheels before raising the rear axle and vice versa

Fig. 3-13. Use a brake pedal depressor to lock the brakes when performing a wheel alignment.

- Lock the wheel turntables and slip plates whenever you are not using them to measure an alignment angle
- Use a brake depressor to hold the brake pedal down when necessary, figure 3-13
- Use a steering wheel lock to keep the steering wheel straight during the toe adjustment

Manufacturers provide a number of methods for adjusting wheel alignment, including:

- Placing shims between suspension components and the vehicle frame
- Turning an eccentric cam bolt
- Changing the position of suspension components
- Adjusting the strut rods
- Adjusting tie rod sleeves
- Moving strut mounts

Computerized alignment equipment generally gives onscreen instructions for aligning specific vehicles. Also, illustrated alignment manuals are published yearly.

Toe-out on turns, SAI, and setback are non-adjustable angles. When they are out of specifications, it means steering or suspension components are damaged and must be replaced. The thrust angle is not adjusted directly, either.

An incorrect thrust angle is a sign of incorrect rear toe. Bringing rear toe into specifications should eliminate the thrust angle.

In a four-wheel alignment, always adjust the rear wheels before adjusting the front wheels. If you cannot bring rear wheel toe within specifications, perform a **thrust alignment**. That is, use the thrust line, instead of the vehicle centerline, as

---

Memory Steer: Steering pull caused by installing rubber bonded socket joints without centering the steering system. The joints try to return to their original position, as if they "remember" it.

Pull: A driving condition in which the driver must actively steer toward one side to keep the vehicle moving straight.

Road Crown: The downward slope of a road from its center to its edge.

Torque Steer: A driving condition in which the vehicle steers to one side during hard acceleration and in the opposite direction during sudden deceleration from high speed. Front wheel drive vehicles with unequal-length axle shafts are prone to torque steer.

Thrust Alignment: A wheel alignment procedure, performed on vehicles when a thrust angle cannot be eliminated, in which the front wheels are aligned to the thrust line instead of the vehicle centerline.

REAR TOE ADJUSTMENT

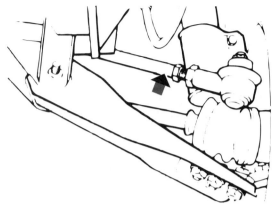

Fig. 3-14. Adjustable tie rod ends set rear toe on some vehicles.

REAR CAMBER & TOE ADJUSTMENT

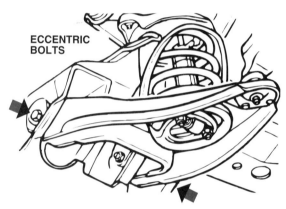

ECCENTRIC BOLTS

Fig. 3-15. Eccentric cam adjusters establish both rear camber and toe.

CAMBER ADJUSTMENT

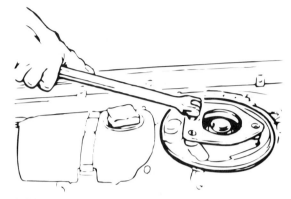

Fig. 3-16. Moving the top strut mount changes the camber angle.

STEERING KNUCKLE   STRUT   OUTER TIE ROD END

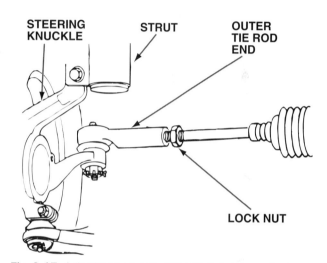

LOCK NUT

Fig. 3-17. Adjusting the length of the tie rod changes the toe angle.

A4

a reference when adjusting the front wheels. Most modern wheel alignment equipment provides for thrust alignments.

When adjusting the front wheels, recheck caster after adjusting camber, and vice versa. The two measurements are related and changing one affects the other. Bring camber and caster within specifications before adjusting toe, because the camber and caster adjustments tend to change toe.

Adjusting Rear Camber and Toe

On many vehicles, rear alignment angles are not adjustable. Others are only adjustable when aftermarket parts are installed. Vehicles with independent rear suspensions normally allow for a rear camber adjustment. On some vehicles, rear toe adjusts by changing the position of tie rod ends, figure 3-14. On vehicles with independent rear suspension, the position of the rear control arms adjusts to set rear-wheel toe. On some vehicles, rear camber and toe are changed by a single adjustment using shims, eccentric bolts, or by repositioning a suspension component, figure 3-15.

Adjusting Front Camber and Caster

Camber and caster are not adjustable on all vehicles. On a strut suspension, camber is often adjusted by repositioning the top of the strut, figure 3-16. Otherwise, the variety of camber and caster adjustment methods includes all those mentioned

earlier. On some vehicles, a single adjustment changes both camber and caster.

Adjusting Front Toe

Before adjusting toe, center and lock the steering wheel to prevent the steering wheel from being off-center after adjustments are made. Adjust front toe by loosening the lock nut and turning the tie rod to lengthen or shorten it, figure 3-17. On most vehicles, lengthening the tie rod increases toe-in, and shortening it increases toe-out.

On a few vehicles, the tie rods are positioned at the front of the wheels, and the steering arms extend forward from the knuckle. In this case, the effects of tie rod length are reversed.

Centering the Steering Wheel

Before beginning to make adjustments to the vehicle alignment, the steering wheel should be locked in the straight-ahead position. Then the toe settings are made, resulting in a steering wheel that is positioned correctly. If the wheel is not locked the result will be a steering wheel that is turned off center when the vehicle is travelling straight ahead. The steering wheel should only be repositioned after the steering rack or gear and tie rods are centered and adjusted. These checks are especially important for some cars with power-assisted steering because the system is sensitive to the centered, straight-ahead steering wheel position.

DIAGNOSING SAI, CAMBER, AND INCLUDED ANGLE

SHORT-LONG ARM SUSPENSIONS

SAI	CAMBER	INCLUDED ANGLE	DIAGNOSIS
CORRECT	LESS THAN SPECS	LESS THAN SPECS	BENT STEERING KNUCKLE OR SPINDLE
LESS THAN SPECS	GREATER THAN SPECS	CORRECT	BENT LOWER CONTROL ARM
LESS THAN SPECS	GREATER THAN SPECS	GREATER THAN SPECS	BENT LOWER CONTROL ARM AND STEERING KNUCKLE OR SPINDLE
GREATER THAN SPECS	LESS THAN SPECS	CORRECT	BENT UPPER CONTROL ARM

STRUT SUSPENSIONS

SAI	CAMBER	INCLUDED ANGLE	DIAGNOSIS
CORRECT	LESS THAN SPECS	LESS THAN SPECS	BENT SPINDLE AND/OR STRUT
CORRECT	GREATER THAN SPECS	GREATER THAN SPECS	BENT SPINDLE AND/OR STRUT
LESS THAN SPECS	GREATER THAN SPECS	CORRECT	BENT CONTROL ARM OR STRUT TOWER OUT AT TOP
LESS THAN SPECS	GREATER THAN SPECS	GREATER THAN SPECS	BENT CONTROL ARM OR STRUT TOWER OUT AT TOP, ALSO BENT SPINDLE AND/OR STRUT
LESS THAN SPECS	LESS THAN SPECS	LESS THAN SPECS	STRUT TOWER OUT AT TOP AND BENT SPINDLE AND/OR BENT STRUT OR CONTROL ARM
GREATER THAN SPECS	LESS THAN SPECS	CORRECT	STRUT TOWER IN AT TOP
GREATER THAN SPECS	GREATER THAN SPECS	GREATER THAN SPECS	STRUT TOWER IN AT TOP AND BENT SPINDLE AND/OR BENT STRUT

KINGPIN TWIN I-BEAM SUSPENSION

SAI (KPI)	CAMBER	INCLUDED ANGLE	DIAGNOSIS
CORRECT	GREATER THAN SPECS	GREATER THAN SPECS	BENT SPINDLE
LESS THAN SPECS	GREATER THAN SPECS	CORRECT	BENT I-BEAM
LESS THAN SPECS	GREATER THAN SPECS	GREATER THAN SPECS	BENT I-BEAM AND SPINDLE
GREATER THAN SPECS	LESS THAN SPECS	CORRECT	BENT I-BEAM

CHAPTER QUESTIONS

1. All of the following are tire wear angles **EXCEPT**:
   a. Camber
   b. Caster
   c. Toe
   d. Toe-out on turns

2. In a four-wheel alignment, check rear-wheel:
   a. Camber and caster
   b. Caster and toe
   c. Caster and SAI
   d. Camber and toe

3. Low tire pressure may cause:
   a. Hard steering
   b. Shimmy
   c. Vibration
   d. Torque steer

4. A vehicle pulls toward the side with more:
   a. Positive caster
   b. Positive camber
   c. Toe-in
   d. SAI

5. Excessive toe-out wears the tires on the:
   a. Inside shoulders
   b. Outside shoulders
   c. Tread edges
   d. Tread center

6. Toe change, or bump steer, is caused by:
   a. Power steering malfunction
   b. Steering gear malfunction
   c. Incorrect toe setting
   d. Wrong tie rod length

7. Incorrect toe-out on turns causes:
   a. Torque steer
   b. Hard steering
   c. Tire squeal
   d. Wander

8. Low SAI contributes to:
   a. Hard steering
   b. Poor steering wheel return
   c. Wander
   d. Tire wear

9. Incorrect thrust angle can cause all the following **EXCEPT**:
   a. Crooked steering wheel
   b. Incorrect front camber
   c. Incorrect front caster
   d. Accelerated tire wear

10. Wear on the inner shoulder of one front tire is most likely caused by:
    a. Toe-in
    b. Toe-out
    c. Positive camber
    d. Negative camber

11. Shimmy is most likely to be caused by incorrect:
    a. Camber
    b. Caster
    c. Toe
    d. Toe-out on turns

12. Technician A says you should check ride height before beginning any alignment work. Technician B says ride height should be checked after camber is set. Who is right?
    a. A only
    b. B only
    c. Both A and B
    d. Neither A nor B

13. Memory steer can be caused by:
    a. Driving over a curb and bending the lower control arm
    b. Tightening outer tie rod ends with the wheels not straightened
    c. Collision damage to the frame and steering linkage
    d. Incorrectly installing wheel alignment shims

14. Use a steering wheel lock to keep the steering wheel straight while adjusting front:
    a. Camber
    b. Caster
    c. Toe
    d. Toe-out on turns

15. During a four-wheel alignment, adjust _____ before _____.
    a. Front camber, rear camber
    b. Rear toe, rear caster
    c. Front toe, front caster
    d. Rear wheels, front wheels

16. A pull to the right can be caused by all of the following **EXCEPT**:
    a. Negative caster on the right, front wheel
    b. A dragging right, front brake pad
    c. Left, front camber greater than right, front camber
    d. High road crown

17. Technician A says you should always align the front suspension before setting any rear angle. Technician B says rear toe angles cannot be set on FWD vehicles. Who is right?
    a. A only
    b. B only
    c. Both A and B
    d. Neither A nor B

18. Front suspension measurements on a vehicle equipped with an SLA suspension indicate that SAI is greater than specs, camber is less than specs, and the included angle is correct. What is the most likely cause?
    a. Incorrect thrust angle
    b. Incorrect toe adjustment
    c. Bent lower control arm
    d. Bent upper control arm

A4

CHAPTER OBJECTIVES

- The technician will complete the ASE task list on Wheels and Tires
- The technician will be able to answer 5 questions dealing with the Wheel and Tires section of the A4 ASE Test

DIAGNOSING WHEEL AND TIRE PROBLEMS

Examine the wheel and tire assembly for obvious damage, such as cracks in the wheel, a damaged tire valve stem, bulges or deep dents in the sidewalls, large cracks in the tread, or missing lug nuts or studs, figure 4-1. Replace damaged wheels or tires.

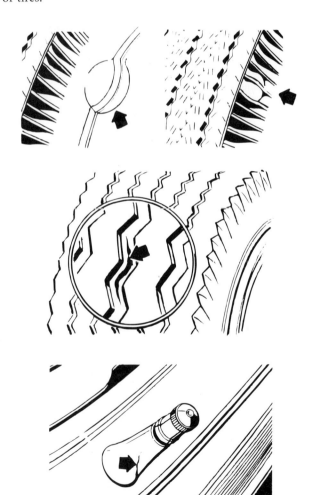

Fig. 4-1. Check tires for signs of sidewall, tread, and valve stem damage.

Tire Sizes and Ratings

Tires are rated based on the following criteria:

- Size
- Load
- Inflation
- Construction
- Maximum Speed

Tire Speed Ratings

The International Organization for Standardization (ISO) utilizes a load/speed index code, which allows you to determine the correct size of tire for the vehicle's intended use. For instance, a tire speed rating will inform you about the weight or load amount a particular set of tires can hold at high speeds. Tires fall into one of the following grade ratings that are used to indicate the top speed at which a tire can safely operate:

- M - up to 81 mph (130 kph)
- N - up to 87 mph (140 kph)
- P - up to 93 mph (150 kph)
- Q - up to 99 mph (160 kph)
- R - up to 106 mph (170 kph)
- S - up to 112 mph (180 kph)
- T - up to 118 mph (190 kph)
- U - up to 124 mph (200 kph)
- H - up to 130 mph (210 kph)
- V - up to 149 mph (240 kph)
- Z - speeds above 149 mph (240 kph)

More recently it was determined that the Z rating turned out to be too vague, and so two more ratings were added:

- W - up to 168 mph (270 kph)
- Y - up to 186 mph (300 kph)

The load/speed index code will usually appear after the size marking on a tire, comprised of two numbers and a letter. For instance, 67H is an example of a load/speed index code. The numbers on this code refer to the maximum load carrying capacity of a particular tire. The letter that is used in conjunction refers to the speed rating, or maximum speed the tire can endure under load and inflation pressure.

Another major aspect of tire ratings is for tread wear, which compares how durable and long lasting a tire actually is. The tread wear rating is calculated with a grade of 100. This means that you may see any grade from 100, 200, 300, to even 600. When the grading is higher this means that the tread will last longer than a tire with a lower number.

Although a tread grading comes in handy, it's always important to consider other elements to maintaining the life of your tread. For instance, inflation pressure is an aspect that greatly contributes to tread life.

Yet another major aspect to a tire's rating is the traction, which allows a tire to stop safely on wet pavement. Traction grading is quite simple; AA, A, B, or C, with the AA rating being the highest and most ideal.

The temperature rating of a tire refers to the heat resistance of the rubber and other materials used in the construction of the tire.

- A - Best
- B - Intermediate
- C - Acceptable

The highest heat resistance or temperature rating for a tire is the Grade A marking. Tires listed as below a Grade C are normally not of high quality and should not be used for sustained periods of high speed driving.

CHECKING TIRE PRESSURE

The tire inflation sticker, found on the door jamb or glove box lid, tells what the cold tire pressure should be. A cold tire is one that has not been driven more than three miles in the past hour. If the tires are hot, the air pressure reading will be higher. Never bleed air out of a hot tire to bring pressure down to specifications; when the tire cools, air pressure will be too low.

Low tire pressure makes steering effort harder and also allows the sidewalls to flex. This weakens the sidewall and wears out the tread edges. Excessive pressure wears the center of the tread and can cause a blowout. Tire pressure must be even side to side to prevent the vehicle from pulling toward the side with less pressure. Add air to a tire slowly, frequently checking the pressure.

> **CAUTION: Do not exceed the maximum pressure stamped on the sidewall.**

If all the tires do not have the same tire pressure, the vehicle will pull or lead to the left or right. You can feel this pull through the steering wheel.

DISMOUNTING AND MOUNTING TIRES

Mounting and dismounting tires improperly can cause personal injury. Always follow all applicable safety precautions when performing tire related service.

Dismounting a Tire

1. Before attempting to dismount a tire from the wheel remove any accumulated mud from the tire and wheel assembly.
2. Place the tire and wheel assembly on the tire service machine.
3. Ensure that the tire valve stem is pointed away from you and others before removing the valve core using a valve core tool.
4. Secure the wheel to the machine using the proper adapter.
5. Follow the machine instructions to break the tire beads free from the wheel rim and remove the tire from the wheel.

Mounting a Tire

1. Lubricate the tire bead and the bead seat on the wheel *before* installing the tire.
2. Follow the machine instructions to install the tire on the wheel.
3. Loosen but do not remove the adapter securing the wheel to the tire machine.
4. Inflate the tire to the correct pressure and reinstall the valve cap.

> **CAUTION: When installing a tire on a wheel rim, do not exceed 30 psi (210 kPa) of air pressure to seat the beads. If the beads fail to seat at 30 psi (210 kPa), lubricate them and try again.**

5. Remove the tire and wheel assembly from the machine.

DIAGNOSING TREAD WEAR

Different wheel and tire problems cause different tread wear patterns, so examining the tread can reveal information about wheel, tire, suspension, steering, and alignment conditions, figure 4-2. If the tread is worn:

- On the outer edges, the tires have been underinflated or the driver is cornering at high speeds
- In the center, the tires have been overinflated
- On the shoulder, the toe or camber is incorrect
- In a feather-edge pattern, it is a bias-ply tire with incorrect toe
- In a cupped pattern, the wheels are out of balance, the shocks are worn, or there is other suspension or steering wear or damage

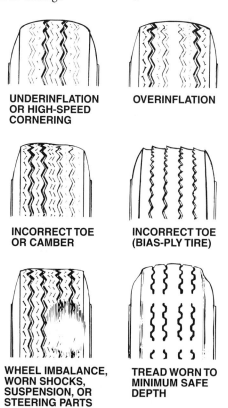

UNDERINFLATION OR HIGH-SPEED CORNERING   **OVERINFLATION**

INCORRECT TOE OR CAMBER   **INCORRECT TOE (BIAS-PLY TIRE)**

WHEEL IMBALANCE, WORN SHOCKS, SUSPENSION, OR STEERING PARTS   **TREAD WORN TO MINIMUM SAFE DEPTH**

Fig. 4-2. Tire wear patterns reveal facts about tire, suspension, steering, and alignment conditions.

A4

- With smooth stripes across the tread, it is worn past its minimum safe depth
- In a diagonal pattern at the rear of a front-wheel drive (FWD) vehicle, rear toe is incorrect
- In heel-toe, or raised tread pattern, the tires are all-season radials that have not been rotated when they should have been

Assessing tire wear can help you decide on service procedures.

WHEEL AND TIRE RUNOUT

If a wheel and tire assembly does not rotate evenly, it has **runout**, figure 4-3. There are two types of runout:

- Radial
- Lateral

Radial runout occurs when the wheel does not rotate in a circle, as viewed from the side; during driving, radial runout causes **hop**. **Lateral runout** occurs when the wheel does not rotate in a single plane, as viewed from the front; it causes wheel **wobble** and **shimmy**. Manufacturers provide specifications for how much runout is allowable on a particular vehicle. There are several possible causes for both types of runout.

Radial runout can result from:

- Off-center wheel lug bolts
- An out-of-round wheel hub
- Axle runout
- Variations in tire sidewall stiffness
- Static wheel imbalance

Possible causes of lateral runout include:

- A bent wheel hub
- A bent wheel mounting flange
- Dynamic wheel imbalance

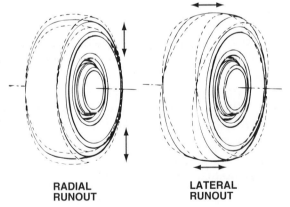

Fig. 4-3. A wheel and tire assembly with runout does not rotate evenly.

RADIAL RUNOUT   LATERAL RUNOUT

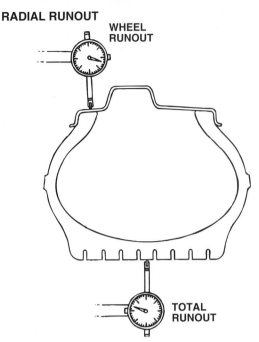

Fig. 4-4. Dial indicator set up for measuring radial runout.

Except for wheel imbalance, these problems require replacing parts to correct the runout.

Checking Wheel and Tire Runout

A dial indicator is used to measure runout, and readings are taken on the wheel and on the tire. Radial runout readings are taken on the wheel bead seat and the tire tread, figure 4-4. To measure radial runout:

1. Park the vehicle with the brake disengaged and the transmission in neutral.
2. Block the front or rear wheels, and use a floor jack to raise the opposite end of the vehicle. Lift the wheels about 2 inches (50 mm) off the ground.
3. Support the dial indicator on a stand near the wheel, and place the indicator tip against the bead seat.
4. Zero the dial indicator.
5. Rotate the tire until the lowest reading shows on the indicator. Zero the indicator at this low point.
6. Rotate the tire again, and read the dial indicator. The highest reading is radial wheel runout.
7. Reposition the indicator tip on the center of the tire tread and zero the indicator.
8. Rotate the tire until the lowest reading shows on the indicator. Zero the indicator at this low point.
9. Rotate the tire again and read the dial indicator. The highest reading is total radial runout.

Hop: A ride problem, resulting from radial runout, that occurs when a tire repeatedly loses contact with the pavement, then lands again harshly.

Lateral Runout: The type of wheel runout that occurs when a wheel and tire do not rotate in a single plane.

Radial Runout: The type of wheel runout that occurs when a wheel and tire do not rotate in a perfect circle around the hub.

Runout: Imperfect movement of a wheel and tire assembly around its axis. A wheel and tire has runout if it does not rotate in a perfect circle around the hub in a single plane.

Shimmy: A side to side shaking of the wheels that is transferred across the axle.

Wobble: A ride problem, resulting from lateral runout, that occurs when the top of a rolling tire constantly moves in and out.

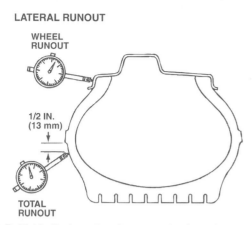

Fig. 4-5. Dial indicator set up for measuring lateral runout.

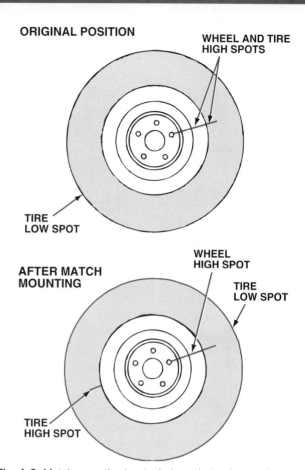

Fig. 4-6. Match mounting is a technique that reduces minor runout.

As a general rule, radial wheel runout should not exceed 0.030 inch (0.75 mm) for alloy wheels or 0.040 inch (1.0 mm) for steel wheels, and total radial runout should not exceed 0.060 inch (1.5 mm) for radial tires. However, actual specifications do vary.

Lateral runout readings are taken on the wheel flange and the tire sidewall, figure 4-5. To measure:

1. With the brake disengaged and the transmission in neutral, block the front or rear wheels, and use a floor jack to raise the opposite end of the vehicle. The tires should be about 2 inches (50 mm) off the ground and rotate freely by hand.
2. Support the dial indicator on a stand near the wheel and tire, position the indicator tip against the wheel flange, and zero the dial face.
3. Slowly rotate the tire so the lowest reading shows on the indicator, then zero the dial face again.
4. Rotate the tire again while watching the dial indicator. Note if there are areas on the wheel where lateral wheel runout exceeds specifications.
5. Reposition the indicator tip on the tire sidewall and zero the indicator.
6. Rotate the tire until the lowest reading shows on the indicator and zero the indicator.
7. Rotate the tire again while monitoring the dial indicator. Note if there are areas on the tire where total lateral runout exceeds the specifications.

In general, wheel lateral runout should not exceed 0.030 inch (0.75 mm) if the vehicle has alloy wheels and 0.045 inch (1.15 mm) if it has steel wheels. Total lateral runout should not exceed 0.080 inch (2.0 mm) for radial tires. If wheel runout is correct, but total runout is out of specifications, the tire is the problem. If both are out of specifications, the problem is most likely the wheel. A technique that sometimes works to eliminate slight runout problems is **match mounting**, figure 4-6. Find the point of highest runout on the wheel and on the tire, then mount the tire on the wheel so that the two high points are opposite each other. The two may cancel each other out during driving.

Checking Hub and Axle Runout

Hub and axle runout are a possible cause of radial runout. Measure at the wheel hub as follows:

1. Remove the wheel and tire assembly.
2. Place a dial indicator on a stand near the hub and position the indicator tip against the hub circumference, figure 4-7.
3. Zero the dial face, rotate the hub until the lowest reading shows on the indicator, then zero the indicator at this low point.
4. Rotate the hub again while monitoring the dial indicator. Note if there are areas on the hub where runout exceeds specifications.

If runout is excessive, either the hub is out of round or the axle shaft is bent. Replace parts as needed.

Checking Mounting Flange Runout

Mounting flange runout is a possible cause of lateral runout. To measure runout at the mounting flange:

1. Remove the wheel and tire assembly from the flange to be checked.
2. Secure the dial indicator on a stand near the hub and position the indicator tip against the face of the mounting flange, figure 4-8.

Match Mounting: A method for minimizing runout of a wheel and tire assembly that consists of mounting the tire with its point of highest runout at the point of lowest wheel runout.

CHECKING HUB RUNOUT

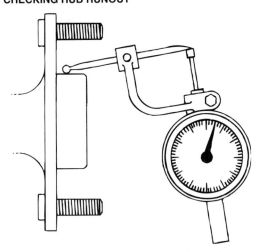

Fig. 4-7. Dial indicator set up to measure hub or axle runout.

CHECKING MOUNTING FLANGE RUNOUT

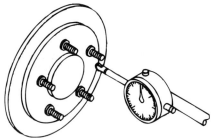

Fig. 4-8. Dial indicator set up to measure mounting flange runout.

3. Zero the dial face, rotate the hub until the lowest reading shows on the indicator, then zero the indicator at this low point.
4. Rotate the hub again while watching the dial indicator. Note if there are areas on the mounting flange where runout exceeds specifications.

If runout is excessive, the flange is bent; replace it.

WHEEL AND TIRE BALANCE

Wheel balance is the weight distribution of the wheel and tire assembly. If the distribution is uneven, the wheels are out of balance. There are two types of wheel and tire balance:

- **Static balance:** weight distribution around the hub
- **Dynamic balance:** weight distribution side to side

When a wheel lacks static balance, it hops, while one lacking dynamic balance wobbles, causing shimmy, figure 4-9. Either condition causes steering problems and accelerated tire wear.

To correct the unequal weight distribution that causes imbalance, small weights are attached to the wheel rim.

STATIC IMBALANCE

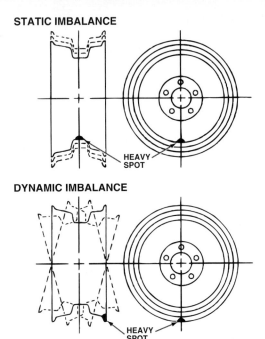

DYNAMIC IMBALANCE

Fig. 4-9. Lack of static balance causes wheel hop, and a dynamic imbalance causes wheel wobble or shimmy.

Wheel Weights

A wheel balancing weight is made of soft lead, with a steel clip or an adhesive to attach it to the wheel rim. Weights are generally sized in 0.25-ounce (7-gram) increments. Attach a clip-on weight by lightly hammering it onto the rim. Adhesive weights often are a number of 0.25-ounce (7-gram) sections on a single strip; break off as many as needed. Remove the paper covering to expose the adhesive, then press the weight to the wheel. Adhesive weights tend to be less true than clip-on weights. That is, their actual weight may vary slightly. Adhesive weights are also less secure, and typically use is limited to aluminum-alloy wheels, which might develop an electrolytic reaction to a steel clip.

If a balancer indicates that several weights are required, consider whether some can be combined to produce the same effect with less total weight added. Too many individual weights begin to act against each other. A computer balancer can usually calculate the most efficient weight placement. Never add more than 6 ounces (170 grams) to the weight of the wheel and tire. If the wheel needs more weight than that to correct balance, it is probably damaged.

Checking and Correcting Balance

There are several methods of balancing the wheel and tire assembly:

- Bubble balancer
- Spin balancer
- On-the-vehicle balancer

Dynamic Balance: The state of a wheel and tire assembly if its weight is evenly distributed side to side.
Static Balance: The state of a wheel and tire assembly if its weight is evenly distributed around the hub.

Bubble Balancer

Bubble balancing only measures static balance, and this method is seldom used on modern vehicles. It works with the wheel and tire removed from the vehicle. To bubble balance a wheel and tire assembly:

1. Remove any old wheel weights and caked-on mud from the wheel.
2. Before placing the wheel on the balancer, check the balancer level indicator to be sure the bubble is centered in the crosshairs. Use the adjusters at the balancer base to center the bubble.
3. Place the tire on the balancer and move the balancer switch to the ON position.
4. Check the bubble. If it has moved out of the crosshairs, the wheel is out of balance.
5. Rotate the tire and wheel until the lightest side, bubble side, is closest to you, then switch the balancer OFF, figure 4-10.
6. Place weights on top of the wheel on the lightest side. Turn the balancer ON to check the position of the bubble. Repeat steps 5 and 6 until the bubble is centered.
7. Switch the balance off and use chalk to mark where to place the weights.
8. Remove the weights, and remove the wheel and tire from the balancer.
9. Mount the weights at the chalk marks, adding half the weight to the outside wheel flange and half to the inner flange.
10. Mount the wheel and tire assembly on the balancer and check bubble position. Adjust the position of the weights if needed.

Spin Balancer

The most typical wheel balancing procedure uses a spin balancer, which also requires removing the wheel and tire assembly from the vehicle, figure 4-11.

To spin balance a wheel and tire:

1. Remove any old wheel weights and caked-on mud from the wheel.
2. Lift the safety cover on the balancer.
3. Choose an adapter that fits the center of the wheel and place it on the balancer driveshaft.
4. Place the wheel on the driveshaft, and secure it with a threaded clamp. The clamp may have reverse threads.
5. Input wheel dimensions so the computer can calculate correctly. Some machines have dials to set wheel dimensions; others have a keypad. Most balancers need to know:
   • Wheel diameter
   • Wheel width
   • Distance between the wheel and balancer

   Wheel diameter is on the tire sidewall. Measure wheel width with the balancer calipers. Use the gauge attached to the balancer to measure the distance between the wheel and balancer cover.
6. Some balancers let you select static or dynamic balance. The dynamic setting checks both.
7. Some balancers have special settings for alloy wheels and steel wheels. Choose the appropriate setting.

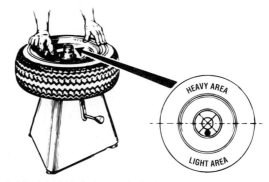

Fig. 4-10. A bubble balancer is the least accurate method of balancing a wheel and tire.

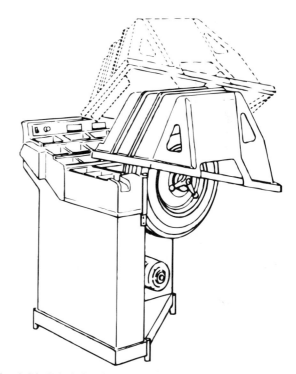

Fig. 4-11. Spin balancing is the most common method of correcting wheel and tire imbalance.

8. Close the balancer safety cover and push the start button. The balancer spins the tire and determines how much weight to add and where.
9. When the wheel stops spinning, open the safety cover and read the display. The computer shows how much weight to add to the outer and inner wheel flanges, figure 4-12.
10. Add the weights, close the safety cover on the balancer, and recheck wheel balance. If needed, add weights as indicated by the computer.

On-Car Balancer

Balancing with the wheel and tire assembly on the vehicle is the most accurate method of obtaining static balance because it balances the hub and axle as well. However, it is a more time consuming process. Since on-vehicle methods balance the wheel and tire to the hub and axle, balance is upset whenever the tires are rotated.

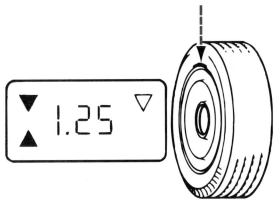

Fig. 4-12. The balancer display indicates how much weight is needed and where to place weights.

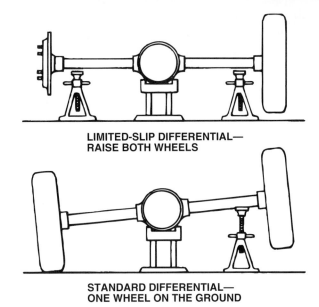

Fig. 4-13. To balance the driven wheels on the vehicle, raise one wheel at a time on a conventional differential and raise both wheels with a limited-slip differential.

Prepare for an on-the-vehicle balancing procedure by removing any old wheel weights and caked-on mud from the wheel. When balancing the driven wheels, determine if the vehicle uses a locking or limited-slip differential as follows:

- With an automatic transmission in park or a manual transmission in gear, raise the vehicle so the wheels clear the floor
- Try to turn one driven wheel by hand. If the wheel does not rotate by itself, it is probably a locking or limited-slip differential. With a FWD vehicle, make sure suspension ride height is correct and the wheels are aimed straight ahead to prevent accidental damage to the constant-velocity (CV) joints and transaxle

Note: *This method does not always determine the differential type; check service literature to be sure.*

With the vehicle on the ground, proceed as follows:

1. When balancing a:
   - Non-driven wheel, raise one wheel with a floor jack, place the motorized balancer drum under it, then lower the wheel until the tire contacts the drum; block the other wheels
   - Driven wheel with a locking or limited-slip differential, raise both driven wheels, remove the wheel from the side you are not balancing, and block the other wheels, figure 4-13
   - Driven wheels with a conventional differential, raise one wheel, keeping the opposite wheel firmly on the ground; block the non-driven wheels
2. Connect the electronic vibration sensor to the chassis on the side of the vehicle that you are balancing. Check the equipment instructions for special procedures.
3. Connect the meter, which tells you approximately how much weight to add, to the electronic vibration sensor. Be sure wires are clear of the wheels and axle.
4. Use the valve stem as a reference point, or place a reference mark on the tire with chalk.
5. Spin the wheel. If you are balancing a:
   - Non-driven wheel, use the motorized drum
   - Driven wheel, use the engine to turn it; have an assistant regulate speed. Never allow the speedometer

reading to exceed 30 mph (48 kph). Be aware, when the engine is driving only one wheel, the wheel spins twice as fast as the speedometer reading

6. Point the meter at the electronic sensor connected to the control arm. The strobe light flashes when the sensor detects vibration, and the heavy part of the tire is at the bottom. Note the position of the reference mark when the light flashes.
7. Stop the wheel. For a:
   - Non-driven wheel, use the brake on the motorized drum
   - Driven wheel, switch the engine off and let the wheel coast to a stop
8. Turn the tire by hand to position the reference mark as you saw it with the strobe light. In this position, the heavy part of the tire is at the bottom.
9. Check the meter for the approximate weight needed and add it to the top of the tire. Add half the weight to the inside and half to the outside of the wheel.
10. Check the balance again and add or reposition the weights as needed.

TIRE ROTATION

Regularly rotating the tires helps keep wear even and prolongs tire life. Use the schedule and rotation pattern suggested by the vehicle manufacturer.

The standard four-tire rotation pattern is to cross non-driven tires to the other axle, and move the driven tires to the other axle on the same side of the vehicle, figure 4-14. For example, on a FWD vehicle, cross the rear tires to the front and move the front tires straight back. For a rear-wheel drive (RWD) vehicle, cross the front tires to the rear and move the rear tires straight forward. In the past, it was believed that crossing radial tires caused tire damage. However, it has been

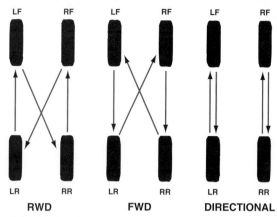

Fig. 4-14. Typical four-wheel tire rotation patterns.

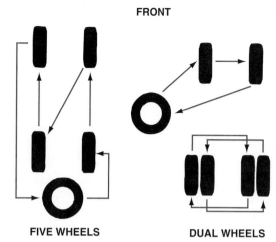

Fig. 4-15. Typical tire rotation patterns for trucks and other vehicles with a full-size spare tire.

determined that this not true and, unless the vehicle has **directional tires**, it is an accepted practice to cross radial tires from side to side.

To rotate directional tires, switch them front to rear on the same side, and only if the same size tires are used at all four wheels. If the front and rear axles use different-size, directional tires, they cannot be rotated.

Most trucks come with a full-size spare and have rotation patterns that include the spare, figure 4-15.

WHEEL FASTENER TORQUE

All wheel fasteners or lug nuts are designed to be tightened to a specific degree of torque. Failure to properly tighten the lug nuts can lead to several problems.

Lug nuts that are not tightened sufficiently may cause:

- Lost wheels
- Cracked wheels
- Damaged lug bolts

Lug nuts that are overtightened may cause:

- Distorted drake rotors
- Stripped threads
- Broken lug bolts

Use a properly calibrated torque wrench or the correct **torque extension bar or torque stick** when installing lug nuts or bolts.

A4

Directional Tire: A tire with a tread pattern that works best rolling in one particular direction. A directional tire should not be switched from one side of the vehicle to the other.
Torque Extension Bar: A specially designed extension bar designed to be used with an air impact wrench when installing wheels on vehicles. The design of the bar limits the amount of torque applied to the fastener to a predetermined level. Also known as a torque stick.

CHAPTER QUESTIONS

1. Technician A says a tire with a speed rating of "Q" is safe up to 120 mph. Technician B says a tire with a speed rating of "Y" is safe up to 186 mph. Who is right?
   a. A only
   b. B only
   c. Both A and B
   d. Neither A nor B

2. Excessive tire pressure can cause:
   a. Weakened sidewalls
   b. A tire blowout
   c. Worn tread edges
   d. Tire overheating

3. All-season, radial tires wear in a heel-toe, or raised tread, pattern due to:
   a. Incorrect wheel balance
   b. Underinflation
   c. Infrequent tire rotation
   d. Incorrect rear toe

4. Radial runout causes:
   a. Pull
   b. Hop
   c. Shimmy
   d. Wobble

5. Possible causes of lateral runout include all of the following **EXCEPT**:
   a. Variations in sidewall stiffness
   b. Bent wheel hub
   c. Bent wheel mounting flange
   d. Dynamic wheel imbalance

6. Check lateral wheel runout by placing a dial indicator tip against the:
   a. Tire sidewall
   b. Wheel flange
   c. Bead seat
   d. Tire tread

7. Incorrect dynamic balance causes:
   a. Pull
   b. Hop
   c. Tramp
   d. Wobble

8. When balancing the wheels and tires on a vehicle with steel wheels, it is advisable to:
   a. Add no more than 6 ounces (170 grams) total to each wheel
   b. Use adhesive-backed wheel weights
   c. Add no more than 6 ounces (170 grams) to each side of the wheel
   d. Add the same amount of weight to each wheel

9. Technician A says maximum alloy wheel lateral runout should not exceed 0.30 inch (0.75 mm). Technician B says excessive lateral runout causes wheel hop. Who is right?
   a. A only
   b. B only
   c. Both A and B
   d. Neither A nor B

10. When performing an on-vehicle wheel balance on the rear wheels of a RWD vehicle with a limited-slip differential, the correct procedure is to:
    a. Raise one wheel and place a motorized drum under it
    b. Raise one wheel and use the engine to run it
    c. Raise both wheels and block the wheel not being balanced
    d. Raise both wheels and remove the wheel not being balanced

11. To rotate the tires on a FWD car:
    a. Cross the front wheels to the rear and move the rear wheels straight forward
    b. Cross the rear wheels to the front and move the front wheels straight back
    c. Cross the front wheels to the rear and cross the rear wheels to the front
    d. Move the front wheels straight back and the rear wheels straight forward

12. When rotating directional tires:
    a. Cross the front wheels to the rear and move the rear wheels straight forward
    b. Cross the rear wheels to the front and move the front wheels straight back
    c. Cross the front wheels to the rear and cross the rear wheels to the front
    d. Move the front wheels straight back and the rear wheels straight forward

13. Technician A says tires should never be rotated on vehicles with radial tires. Technician B says when rotating tires on a vehicle with radial tires they should not be crossed from side to side. Who is right?
    a. A only
    b. B only
    c. Both A and B
    d. Neither A nor B

SAMPLE TEST

This sample test can help you review your knowledge of this entire book. The format of the questions is similar to the certification tests given by the National Institute for Automotive Service Excellence. Generally, the questions here are more difficult than the programmed study questions you answered as you read the technical material in this book.

Read these review questions carefully, then read all the possible answers before making your decision. Always select the **best possible answer.** In some cases, you may think all the answers are partially correct, or you may feel that none is exactly right. But in every case, there is a **best answer** that is the one you should select.

Answers to the questions in this sample test will be found near the end of this book, before the glossary. If you answer at least 20 of these questions correctly, then you can be confident of your knowledge of the subjects covered in this book and in the ASE Certification Test A4, Suspension and Steering. If you answer fewer than 20 correctly, you should reread the text and take another look at the illustrations. Also, check the glossary as you review the material.

1. Excessive pinion torque may cause:
   a. Memory steer
   b. Cocked steering wheel
   c. Steering wheel freeplay
   d. Hard steering

2. On a vehicle equipped with a power tilt and telescoping steering column system, neither feature operates.
   Technician A says the power steering pump belt may be loose.
   Technician B says the tilt and telescope control module may be defective. Who is right?
   a. A only
   b. B only
   c. Both A and B
   d. Neither A nor B

3. Technician A says the cause of hard steering on a vehicle with a manual steering gear could be low tire pressure.
   Technician B says the cause could be incorrect gear mesh preload. Who is right?
   a. A only
   b. B only
   c. Both A and B
   d. Neither A nor B

4. If a vehicle has been in a collision, the steering column should be:
   a. Replaced
   b. Inspected
   c. Collapsed
   d. Rebuilt

5. If power steering pump test readings are within specifications but the difference between the high and low readings is greater than 50 psi, the problem is most likely the:
   a. Steering gear
   b. Flow control valve
   c. Pump seals
   d. Reservoir

6. Technician A says that when power steering fluid is brown colored and smells like varnish, there is air in the system.
   Technician B says to flush the system. Who is right?
   a. A only
   b. B only
   c. Both A and B
   d. Neither A nor B

7. Technician A says that power steering hoses that feel spongy and soft are internally damaged.
   Technician B says to replace them. Who is right?
   a. A only
   b. B only
   c. Both A and B
   d. Neither A nor B

8. Technician A says to lift the front end and turn the steering wheel from stop to stop to check if the power steering control valve is centered.
   Technician B says that if a spool-type control valve is not centered, you cannot center it but must replace the steering gear. Who is right?
   a. A only
   b. B only
   c. Both A and B
   d. Neither A nor B

9. Technician A says to straighten the steering linkage and wheels before removing the steering wheel if the steering wheel contains an air bag.
   Technician B says to remove the air bag module from the steering wheel, then disassemble the column. Who is right?
   a. A only
   b. B only
   c. Both A and B
   d. Neither A nor B

10. Technician A says that there is probably a leak in the hydraulic system if pressures are lower than specified during a power steering system pressure test.
    Technician B says to pressure test the pump and steering gear. Who is right?
    a. A only
    b. B only
    c. Both A and B
    d. Neither A nor B

11. Technician A says to use a puller to separate a pitman arm from a recirculating ball steering gear.
    Technician B says if separation is difficult, you can heat the parts with a torch to help loosen them. Who is right?
    a. A only
    b. B only
    c. Both A and B
    d. Neither A nor B

12. Technician A says to adjust the torsion bars if a truck with a torsion bar front suspension is riding low on the driver's side.
    Technician B says that if ride height cannot be corrected, replace the driver's side torsion bar. Who is right?
    a. A only
    b. B only
    c. Both A and B
    d. Neither A nor B

13. Technician A says that a light film of oil on a front shock absorber indicates the shock is leaking.
    Technician B says to replace front shock absorbers in pairs. Who is right?
    a. A only
    b. B only
    c. Both A and B
    d. Neither A nor B

A4

14. When replacing a coil spring:
    a. Slowly lower the control arm to release spring tension
    b. Disconnect the control arm ball joint
    c. Use pliers to compress the spring
    d. Install spring clips on the compressed spring

15. A rear shock absorber should never be removed without first supporting the wheel on a car with which type of rear suspension?
    a. Torsion bar
    b. Leaf spring
    c. Coil spring
    d. MacPherson strut

16. Technician A says to discharge the air from the shocks before raising a vehicle with an electronically controlled air-shock, rear load-leveling system.
    Technician B says to disable the load-leveling system. Who is right?
    a. A only
    b. B only
    c. Both A and B
    d. Neither A nor B

17. Technician A says that some rack and pinion steering gears have an adjusting screw to set pinion bearing preload.
    Technician B says some steering gears have adjustment shims. Who is right?
    a. A only
    b. B only
    c. Both A and B
    d. Neither A nor B

18. A variable assist power steering system:
    a. Increases pressure to the pump at high vehicle speeds
    b. Increases pressure to the steering gear at high vehicle speeds
    c. Decreases pressure to the gear at high speeds
    d. Decreases pump speed at low vehicle speeds

19. Which can be changed by adjusting the length of the tie rod?
    a. Toe
    b. Camber
    c. Caster
    d. SAI

20. A power steering idle compensation system increases engine speed:
    a. When the engine is cold
    b. While parking
    c. When the engine is hot
    d. At highway speeds

21. Generally, axial play in a ball joint should **NOT** exceed:
    a. 0.06 inch (1.5 mm)
    b. 0.13 inch (2 mm)
    c. 0.25 inch (6 mm)
    d. 0.50 inch (12 mm)

22. Front suspension measurements on a vehicle equipped with a MacPherson strut suspension indicate that SAI is greater than specs, camber is less than specs, and the included angle is correct. What is the most likely cause?
    a. Incorrect thrust angle
    b. Incorrect toe adjustment
    c. Strut tower in at top
    d. Strut tower out at top

23. Technician A says that removing steering linkage with a "pickle fork" may damage the ball joints.
    Technician B says a special puller can prevent damage to the joints. Who is right?
    a. A only
    b. B only
    c. Both A and B
    d. Neither A nor B

24. Which of the following is not a tire wearing angle?
    a. Toe-in
    b. Camber
    c. Caster
    d. Toe-out on turns

25. The left, front tire on a car wears along the outside edge only. The most likely cause is improper:
    a. Caster
    b. Camber
    c. Toe-in
    d. Toe-out

26. An electro-hydraulic steering system eliminates which component?
    a. Clock spring
    b. Power steering pump
    c. Spindle
    d. Air bag module

27. Technician A says to correct ride height by performing a wheel alignment.
    Technician B says to check for bent suspension components if ride height is incorrect. Who is right?
    a. A only
    b. B only
    c. Both A and B
    d. Neither A nor B

28. Technician A says that on a vehicle with an incorrect thrust angle, adjusting rear-wheel toe will eliminate the thrust angle.
    Technician B says to adjust rear-wheel camber to eliminate the thrust angle. Who is right?
    a. A only
    b. B only
    c. Both A and B
    d. Neither A nor B

29. Technician A says that a slight setback of one front wheel is probably caused by suspension damage.
    Technician B says a possible cause is uneven caster side-to-side. Who is right?
    a. A only
    b. B only
    c. Both A and B
    d. Neither A nor B

30. Possible causes of radial runout include all of the following **EXCEPT**:
    a. Out-of-round wheel hub
    b. Off-center wheel lug bolts
    c. Variations in tire sidewall stiffness
    d. Dynamic wheel imbalance

31. Technician A says that a front-wheel shimmy is caused by dynamic imbalance.
    Technician B says a possible cause is a bent wheel hub. Who is right?
    a. A only
    b. B only
    c. Both A and B
    d. Neither A nor B

ANSWERS

Chapter 1:
1. d, 2. b, 3. c, 4. b, 5. b, 6. b, 7. c, 8. c, 9. a,
10. a, 11. d, 12. b, 13. c, 14. a, 15. c, 16. a,
17. d, 18. c

Chapter 2:
1. b, 2. a, 3. c, 4. c, 5. c, 6. b, 7. a, 8. c, 9. d,
10. a, 11. d, 12. c, 13. a, 14. a, 15. b, 16. a,
17. b, 18. b, 19. a

Chapter 3:
1. b, 2. d, 3. a, 4. b, 5. c, 6. d, 7. c, 8. c, 9. c,
10. d, 11. b, 12. a, 13. b, 14. c, 15. d, 16. d,
17. d, 18. d

Chapter 4:
1. b, 2. b, 3. c, 4. b, 5. a, 6. b, 7. d, 8. a, 9. a,
10. d, 11. b, 12. d, 13. d

Sample Test:
1. d, 2. b, 3. c, 4. b, 5. b, 6. b, 7. c, 8. b, 9. c,
10. c, 11. a, 12. c, 13. c, 14. d, 15. c, 16. b,
17. c, 18. c, 19. a, 20. b, 21. a, 22. c, 23. c,
24. c, 25. b, 26. b, 27. b. 28. a, 29. c, 30. c,
31. c

GLOSSARY

Actuator: A device that receives an electronic command from a computer and responds by performing a mechanical action.

Antiroll Bar: A transverse suspension link that transfers some of the load on one wheel to the opposite wheel. Its main purpose is to prevent body roll during cornering. Also known as a sway bar.

Axial Play: Movement along, or parallel to, the axis of a shaft.

Bump Steer or Toe Curve: Another name for toe change.

Camber: The angle between the centerline of the tire and a line perpendicular to a level surface. More simply, camber is the tilt of a wheel and tire assembly, viewed from the front of the vehicle.

Caster: The angle between the steering axis and a line perpendicular to a level surface, viewed from the side. More simply, caster is the forward or backward tilt of the steering axis.

Chapman Strut Suspension: A type of rear suspension having a telescoping strut that is attached to the chassis at the top and to two links at the bottom, restricting lateral and longitudinal movement.

Collapsible Steering Column: An energy-absorbing steering column that is designed to collapse if the driver is thrown into it due to a heavy collision.

Control Valve: The valve in a power steering system that controls the application of pressurized fluid against the power piston.

Diagnostic Trouble Code (DTC): An electronic message, stored in computer memory, indicating the source of a system malfunction.

Directional Control Angle: A wheel alignment angle that affects the steering and handling of the vehicle.

Directional Tire: A tire with a tread pattern that works best rolling in one particular direction. A directional tire should not be switched from one side of the vehicle to the other.

Dynamic Balance: The state of a wheel and tire assembly if its weight is evenly distributed side to side.

Electronic Control Unit (ECU): In an automotive electronic system, a small on-board computer that processes information received from sensors and sends signals to various actuators, so they operate in response to the driving conditions.

Gear Mesh Preload: The resistance that the sector gear or roller of a recirculating ball steering gear exerts against worm gear movement, or the force required to move the worm gear against that resistance.

Geometric Centerline: An imaginary line that bisects the front and rear axles of a vehicle.

Hall-effect Sensors: A device that produces a voltage pulse dependent on the presence of a magnetic field. Hall-effect voltage varies as magnetic reactance varies around a current-carrying semiconductor.

Hop: A ride problem, resulting from radial runout, that occurs when a tire repeatedly loses contact with the pavement, then lands again harshly.

Included Angle: The steering axis inclination angle plus or minus the camber angle.

Jounce: The inward reaction of the spring and shock absorber when a wheel hits an obstruction.

Lateral Runout: The type of wheel runout that occurs when a wheel and tire do not rotate in a single plane.

Load-carrying Ball Joint: A ball joint that links a suspension arm to a knuckle and transfers sprung weight from the arm to the wheel.

Longitudinal: Oriented from front to rear of the vehicle.

Match Mounting: A method for minimizing runout of a wheel and tire assembly that consists of mounting the tire with its point of highest runout at the point of lowest wheel runout.

Matched Set: Belts which are made either in the same mold or on the same manufacturing machine have the same exact length and are known as matched sets.

Memory Steer: Steering pull caused by installing rubber-bonded socket joints without centering the steering system. The joints try to return to their original position, as if they "remember" it.

Optical Sensor: A type of sensor utilizing a light source such as an LED and a phototransistor. Usually used to detect rotation.

Parallelogram Steering Linkage: A steering linkage configuration consisting of a pitman arm, an idler arm, a center link, and two tie rods, which form three sides of a parallelogram.

Pinion Bearing Preload: The resistance that the bearings in a rack and pinion steering gear exert against the pinion gear and shaft, or the force required to overcome that resistance.

Pinion Torque: The force required to move the pinion of a rack and pinion steering gear against the resistance exerted by the rack.

Pitman Arm: The part of a parallelogram steering linkage that joins the linkage to the steering gear sector shaft and transmits movement from the steering gear to the linkage.

Play: The amount that mechanical parts can move without encountering another part.

Potentiometer: Potentiometers are variable resistors that change their resistance value based on the position of the control lever.

Pull: A driving condition in which the driver must actively steer toward one side to keep the vehicle moving straight.

Radial Play: Movement along, or parallel to, the radius of a circle.

Radial Runout: The type of wheel runout that occurs when a wheel and tire do not rotate in a perfect circle around the hub.

Radius Arm: A sturdy suspension link that braces a twin I-beam, or sometimes an axle housing, against the frame.

Rebound: The downward movement of a wheel from its normal position when the spring and shock are expanding, as the sudden drop of a wheel into a depression and a weight transfer away from the wheel.

Road Crown: The downward slope of a road from its center to its edge.

Runout: Imperfect movement of a wheel and tire assembly around its axis. A wheel and tire has runout if it does not rotate in a perfect circle around the hub in a single plane.

Sector Shaft Endplay: The axial movement of the sector shaft in a standard steering gear.

A4

Sensor: A device that provides an electric signal to a control unit to indicate a certain physical condition. In an automotive electronic system, sensors monitor such conditions as vehicle speed, suspension height, or steering angle.

Setback: A condition in which one wheel of an axle is located further back than the opposite wheel.

Shimmy: A side-to-side shaking of the wheels that is transferred across the axle.

Static Balance: The state of a wheel and tire assembly if its weight is evenly distributed around the hub.

Steering Arm: An arm, extending forward or back from the steering knuckle, that links the wheel to the steering linkage.

Steering Axis: The axis on which the steering knuckle pivots. The steering axis runs through the kingpin, the centers of the upper and lower ball joints, or the top pivoting point of the strut and the center of the lower ball joint.

Steering Axis Inclination (SAI): The angle between the steering axis and a line perpendicular to a level surface, viewed from the front. More simply, steering axis inclination is the inward or outward tilt of the steering axis.

Steering Geometry: A method of measuring wheel alignment using angles measured in degrees of a circle.

Steering Wheel Freeplay: The amount the steering wheel can be turned, using light pressure, before it meets resistance. It is an indicator of steering system responsiveness.

Stress Riser: A flaw in the metal of a coil spring or torsion bar that creates extra stress on the metal, causing it to bend more easily at that point.

Strut Rod: A suspension link that braces a straight, lower control arm against the frame.

Thrust Alignment: A wheel alignment procedure, performed on vehicles when a thrust angle cannot be eliminated, in which the front wheels are aligned to the thrust line instead of the vehicle centerline.

Thrust Angle: The angle between the thrust line and the geometric centerline of a vehicle.

Thrust Line: An imaginary line, running forward from the center of the rear axle, that bisects rear toe.

Tire Wear Angle: A wheel alignment angle that affects the rate at which tires wear out.

Toe: The angle between the direction a wheel is aimed and a line parallel to the centerline of the vehicle. When measured linearly, toe is the distance between the front edges of the tires subtracted from the distance between the back edges.

Toe Change: A change in the direction a tire is aimed during suspension compression or extension. Tie rod height and length affect toe change.

Toe-in: A description of the toe angle when the front edges of the tires point toward each other.

Toe-out: A description of the toe angle when the front edges of the tires point away from each other.

Toe-out on Turns: The tendency, during turns, for the outside wheel to travel in a larger arc than the inside wheel.

Torque Extension Bar: A specially designed extension bar designed to be used with an air impact wrench when installing wheels on vehicles. The design of the bar limits the amount of torque applied to the fastener to a predetermined level. Also known as a torque stick.

Torque Steer: A driving condition in which the vehicle steers to one side during hard acceleration from high speed and in the opposite direction during sudden deceleration from high speed. Front-wheel-drive vehicles with unequal-length axle shafts are prone to torque steer.

Transverse: Oriented from side to side of the vehicle.

Variable Assist Power Steering: A power steering system that uses valves and speed sensors to vary the amount of steering assist according to engine or road speed.

Wander: A driving condition in which the driver must actively steer back and forth to keep the vehicle moving straight.

Wobble: A ride problem, resulting from lateral runout, that occurs when the top of a rolling tire constantly moves in and out.

Worm Bearing Preload: Worm bearing preload is the resistance to rotation created by the load on the worm shaft bearings.

BRAKES

CHAPTER OBJECTIVES

- The technician will complete the ASE task list on Hydraulic System Service.
- The technician will be able to answer 12 questions dealing with the Hydraulic System Service section of the A5 ASE Test.

Hydraulic brake system service includes diagnosing and correcting problems that relate to brake fluid condition and level, master cylinder operation, brake warning lamp circuit, brake fluid lines and hoses, and the hydraulic control valves that regulate system pressure. These services, as well as bleeding air from the hydraulic system, are discussed in this chapter.

MASTER CYLINDER SERVICE

Master cylinder service begins with a visual inspection:

1. Ensure fluid is at the proper level.
2. Make sure the reservoir cover vent holes are clean and unrestricted.
3. Look over the master cylinder diaphragm, if there is one, for any cracks, tears, or other damage.
4. Check for external leaks at line connections or at the pushrod.
5. Inspect dust boots, if used; they must be soft and without cracks, and there should be no fluid behind them.

MASTER CYLINDER TESTING

A number of special tests can pinpoint whether a problem is with the master cylinder or elsewhere in the system. First, apply the brake pedal to make sure there is the correct amount of **freeplay**, figure 1-1. Most systems require between 0.13 and 0.50 inch (3 and 13 mm) of freeplay.

Check pedal feel. A spongy pedal with longer than normal travel usually indicates a hydraulic problem, such as a fluidleak or air in the lines. If the brake pedal gradually sinks partway to the floor, then becomes firm, one circuit of the dual-circuit brake hydraulic system is probably at fault. If the pedal gradually sinks all the way to the floor, suspect a master cylinder that is **bypassing** internally.

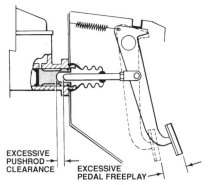

Fig. 1-1. The first step in master cylinder testing is to check for correct brake pedal freeplay.

External Leak Test

A low master cylinder fluid level indicates either normal brake lining wear or a hydraulic system leak. Make sure the cylinder is at least half full, and note the exact level. If the cylinder has run dry, bleed the system first. Apply the brake several times, then check the level again. If the fluid level dropped, there is an external leak. If the external leak is not obvious, have an assistant pump the brakes while you inspect the system for leaks. Be sure to inspect around all fittings and hoses, calipers, wheel cylinders, and master cylinder.

Internal Leak Test

An internal leak test, also called a bypass test, checks the integrity of the primary seals on the master cylinder piston. The cylinder reservoir must be at least half full for testing. To test, watch the fluid in the reservoir as an assistant slowly applies and releases the brake pedal. If the fluid level rises as the pedal is applied and falls as it is released, the seals are leaking. The fluid is bypassing the seals and rising into the reservoir.

Compensating Port Test

If there is no pedal freeplay, the **compensating ports** in the master cylinder may be closed. To test, remove the reservoir cover and watch the fluid in the reservoir as an assistant slowly applies the brakes. A small amount of fluid should be forced

---

Bypassing: In a master cylinder, a condition in which fluid leaks between the piston seals and the bore, which causes the pedal to sink slowly under steady pressure.

Compensating Port: The opening between the master cylinder reservoir and the cylinder bore that allows fluid to enter or exit the hydraulic system to adjust for changes in volume.

Freeplay: The distance a brake pedal can be depressed before the master cylinder starts to displace fluid.

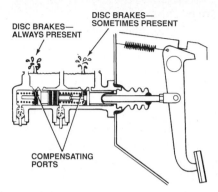

Fig. 1-2. A properly functioning, or open, compensating port creates a small spurt of fluid in the reservoir as the brake pedal is applied.

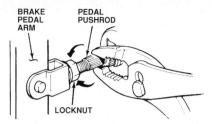

Fig. 1-3. Brake pedal freeplay is usually adjusted by loosening a locknut and turning the pushrod to obtain the proper length.

out of the cylinder bore through the compensating port in each chamber. This causes a small spurt of fluid on the surface, figure 1-2.

When performing the compensating port test on a **quick-take-up (QTU) master cylinder**, the **quick-take-up (QTU) valve** initially restricts fluid flow through the rear compensating port, so a jet of fluid will not appear in the reservoir. However, once the clearance in the brake system is taken up and pressure reaches about 70 to 100 psi (483 to 690 kPa), the QTU valve check ball unseats, and a large quantity of fluid is pumped into the reservoir very rapidly. This can create a safety hazard, so have your assistant apply the brake pedal very lightly. Hand pressure is best, so the opening pressure of the QTU valve is not exceeded.

Quick-Take-Up Valve Test
This valve regulates the flow of fluid between the reservoir and the master cylinder chambers. While it cannot be directly tested, a problem may be indicated if there is excessive pedal travel when the brakes are first applied or if the brake pedal returns slowly when released.

MASTER CYLINDER REPLACEMENT
To remove a master cylinder:

1. Use a flare nut wrench to disconnect the brake lines from the master cylinder fluid outlets. Plug the outlets and cap off the open lines to prevent fluid spillage and system contamination.
2. If there is a fluid level warning switch on the reservoir or a pressure differential switch on the master cylinder body, detach the wiring harness connector.
3. If the vehicle has manual brakes and the brake pedal pushrod is mechanically connected to the master cylinder, disconnect the pushrod from the brake pedal linkage.
4. Remove the bolts that attach the master cylinder to the firewall or power booster, then lift the cylinder from the vehicle. Keep the cylinder upright to prevent fluid spillage.

Once the cylinder is removed from the vehicle, make an internal inspection to determine whether the cylinder can be rebuilt. Internal inspection and rebuild procedures are covered in this chapter. Install the rebuilt or new replacement master cylinder as follows:

1. Bench bleed the master cylinder and cap off the fluid ports.
2. Fit the master cylinder on the firewall or power booster, install the mounting bolts, and tighten them to specified torque.
3. Connect the brake lines to the master cylinder, start the threads by hand, then tighten the fittings with a flare-nut wrench.
4. Attach the wiring harness connector to the fluid level warning switch or pressure differential switch if the cylinder is so equipped.
5. Connect the brake pedal pushrod to the pedal linkage if it was detached when the cylinder was removed.
6. Check and adjust the pedal freeplay and mechanical stoplight switch, then bleed the system. These procedures are detailed in this chapter.

Pedal Linkage Adjustment
It is essential to adjust the pushrod on a new or reconditioned master cylinder to establish the correct brake pedal free play. If correct pushrod adjustment is not obtained, excessive pedal travel or dragging brakes may result. To adjust the pushrod:

1. If the vehicle has a power booster, pump the brake pedal until the reserve is exhausted and the pedal feel hardens.
2. Place a ruler along the axis of brake pedal travel, then slowly apply the pedal by hand until all the slack in the linkage is eliminated. This amount of travel is the freeplay.
3. Adjust the freeplay by shortening or lengthening the brake pedal pushrod. Loosen the locknut on the pushrod, figure 1-3. Rotate the pushrod until you get the specified freeplay, then tighten the locknut.

MASTER CYLINDER OVERHAUL
Overhauling the many and various master cylinders differs, so it is best to consult the vehicle shop manual when overhauling a master cylinder. The following procedures are common practices and general rules that apply to overhauling most master cylinders.

A5

Quick-take-up (QTU) Master Cylinder: A type of master cylinder that applies a large volume of fluid on the initial brake application to take up the clearance designed into low-drag brake calipers.

Quick-take-up (QTU) Valve: The part of the QTU master cylinder that controls the fluid flow between the reservoir and the cylinder bore.

Disassembly

To disassemble a master cylinder:

1. Remove the pushrod and reservoir cap, then drain any remaining fluid from the fluid reservoir.
2. If there is a dust boot on the pushrod end of the cylinder, remove it.
3. Clamp the master cylinder in a vise by its mounting flange. If the fluid reservoir is not part of the cylinder body, remove it.
4. If the cylinder body has tube seat inserts, thread self-tapping screws into the seats, then pry them out using two screwdrivers. Drum brake master cylinders may have residual pressure check valves beneath the seats, which you can now remove.
5. If the pressure differential switch or **proportioning valves** are threaded into the master cylinder body, re-move them. Do not remove the QTU valve unless testing indicates that it needs replacing.
6. Slightly depress the primary piston, then remove the snapring which acts as a piston stop. Some master cylinders have an Allen-head plug that must be removed first.
7. Withdraw the stop washer, primary piston, spring, primary cup, and valve seat from the master cylinder, figure 1-4. If the master cylinder has a stop bolt for the secondary piston, remove it. Use low-pressure compressed air to remove stubborn pistons.
8. Clean the entire cylinder with brake parts cleaner, alcohol, or fresh brake fluid.
9. Inspect the housing casting for cracks, damaged threads, or other signs of damage.
10. Inspect the compensating intake ports; they must be clean and open.

Internal Inspection

Shine a light into the cylinder and inspect the bore. If the unit is made of cast iron and the bore is in good condition or only lightly scratched, pitted, scored, or corroded, the cylinder can probably be honed and rebuilt. Be aware, some manufacturers recommend against honing, and it is advantageous to check the shop manual for specific recommendations.

If the bore is deeply scored, the cylinder must be replaced. Honing to remove deep scores results in an oversized cylinder bore and the new seals cannot withhold pressure, which causes internal leakage.

If an aluminum hydraulic cylinder is scratched, pitted, scored, or corroded in any way, the cylinder must be replaced. Aluminum cylinders cannot be honed because they have a wear-resistant, **anodized finish**, which honing removes.

Honing

Use the following procedure to hone the mildly damaged bore of a cast-iron master cylinder:

1. Clamp the cylinder in a vise by its mounting flange.
2. Select a suitably sized cylinder hone and chuck it in a drill motor.
3. Lubricate the cylinder bore with fresh brake fluid and insert the hone into the bore.
4. Operate the drill motor at approximately 500 rpm, and move the hone back and forth along the entire length of the bore using smooth, even strokes. Never allow the hone stones to come partially out of the end of the bore while honing.
5. Keep the bore lubricated with fresh brake fluid and hone for approximately 10 seconds. Allow the hone to come to a full stop before removing it from the bore.

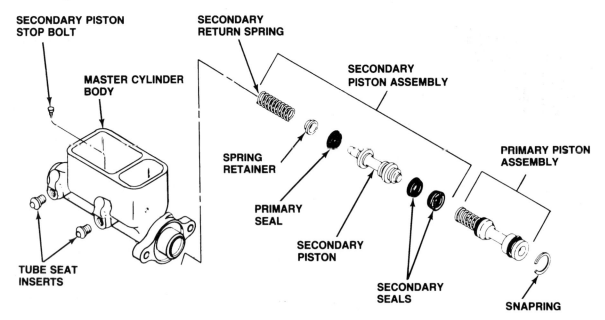

Fig. 1-4. Once the snapring is removed, the pistons can be withdrawn from the master cylinder body.

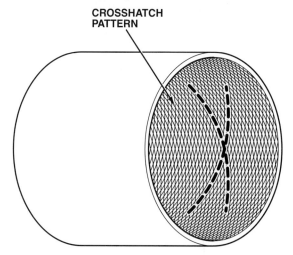

Fig. 1-5. A properly honed cylinder will have an even crosshatch pattern that promotes seal seating.

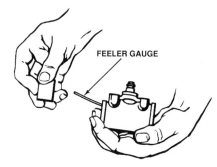

Fig. 1-6. If the piston can be inserted into the bore along with a 0.006-inch (0.15-mm) feeler gauge blade, the bore is oversized and the cylinder must be replaced.

6. Rinse the bore with fresh brake fluid, wipe it clean with a rag, and check the surface finish. It should be free of rust, corrosion, and scratches. The hone should also have created an even crosshatch pattern, figure 1-5.
7. If necessary, repeat the honing process for another 10 seconds. If the bore does not clean up after several repetitions of this procedure, replace the cylinder.
8. After the bore is honed, thoroughly clean the cylinder with a non-petroleum-base brake cleaning solvent to remove all residue and grit.

Cylinder Bore Measurement

After honing a hydraulic cylinder, measure the bore diameter to make sure that too much metal has not been removed. There are two methods of measuring a cylinder bore: One uses a feeler gauge strip, and the other uses a go/no-go gauge.

To check the bore using a feeler gauge, place a narrow, 0.02-inch (6-mm) wide, strip of 0.006-inch (0.15 mm)-feeler gauge inside the bore. Attempt to insert one of the cylinder pistons into the bore with the feeler gauge in place. If the piston fits, the bore is oversized, and the cylinder must be replaced, figure 1-6. Traditionally, most manufacturers have allowed up to 0.006 inch (0.15 mm) of piston clearance. However, many newer cylinders with smaller diameters require tighter clearances. If you are unsure of the proper specification, consult the factory shop manual.

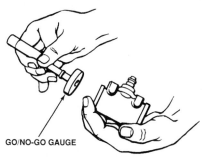

Fig. 1-7. A correct go/no-go gauge is sized to the maximum diameter of the cylinder bore. If the gauge fits into the bore, the bore is oversized and the cylinder must be replaced.

To check the bore with a go/no-go gauge, select the proper sized plug from the gauge kit and attach it to the handle. The correct plug is the same size as the nominal cylinder bore plus 0.006 inch (0.15 mm). Attempt to insert the plug into the bore. If the gauge fits into the cylinder, the bore is oversized, and the cylinder must be replaced, figure 1-7.

Reassembly

To reassemble a master cylinder:

1. Install new residual check valves into the fluid outlet ports, if the cylinder was so equipped. Drive new tubing seats in over the check valves using a brass drift or wooden dowel.
2. Assemble the return spring, spring retainer, and seals onto the secondary piston. Be sure to install seals in the right direction; the seal lip must face toward the hydraulic apply pressure.
3. Lubricate the secondary piston assembly with clean brake fluid and fit it, spring end first, into the bore. If a piston stop bolt is used to hold the piston in place, install it.
4. Assemble the return spring, spring retainer, and seals onto the primary piston. Lubricate the primary piston assembly with fresh brake fluid and install into the bore spring end first.
5. Depress the primary piston and fit the retaining snapring. Install the Allen-head plug, if equipped.
6. Install the fluid reservoir, pressure differential switch, and proportioning valves as required.
7. Bench bleed the master cylinder assembly as described later in this chapter. Then, install the rebuilt cylinder on the vehicle.

BRAKE LINE SERVICE

Brake lines include both the rubber hoses and double-wall steel tubing that transport fluid through the system. Most manufacturers recommend that brake hoses be inspected twice a year or anytime the brakes are serviced. Steel brake tubing should be inspected yearly or anytime the brakes are serviced. Brake lines that are not in perfect condition must be replaced.

Brake Hose Inspection

Flexible brake hoses are used to connect steel tubing to the calipers or cylinders at the wheels. All vehicles have a hose at

A5

Fig. 1-8. Internal leakage, which causes a brake hose to swell or blister, is cause for replacing the hose.

each front wheel to permit the wheels to move freely without damaging the brake lines. Vehicles with independent rear suspension have a hose at each rear wheel as well, while vehicles with a live rear axle generally have a single, rear hose between the axle and the chassis.

Visually inspect brake hoses for swelling, blisters, leaks, stains, cracks, and abrasions. Swelling and blisters are signs of internal fluid leakage that has penetrated to the outer hose covering, figure 1-8. Obvious leaks or stains from leaks may appear on the surface of the hose and around the fittings on the hose ends. Cracks can appear anywhere on the hose, as can signs of abrasion. Finally, check the hose mounting hardware and locating brackets for damage and tightness.

Swelling, which can cause poor braking performance, is not always obvious, and may only be noticeable when the brakes are applied. To check, wrap your hand around the suspect hose and have an assistant slowly depress the brake pedal. If you can feel the hose expand in your hand, it is leaking internally and must be replaced.

Pulling to one side while braking and poor stopping performance may be due to blocked or clogged brake hoses. Also, if one front brake exhibits a blued rotor and has worn out its linings in a short time, suspect a hose clogged with deposits that allows high apply pressure into the caliper, but restricts the flow back up to the master cylinder, thus resulting in drag.

Brake Tubing Inspection

Visually inspect brake lines, beginning where they attach to the master cylinder, and follow them along their paths to the wheels. Look for rust and corrosion along the frame rails, at the mounting clips, or any place where water, dirt, and road salt accumulate. Also, check tubing for kinks, dents, abrasions, and other distortion and damage. Make sure the tubing is properly fastened to the chassis. Loose mounting brackets permit the tubing to vibrate, which results in cracks that lead to fluid leakage. Physical damage is most likely in the areas directly behind the wheels, or where the tubing crosses below an axle or frame member.

Brake Hose Replacement

Brake hoses that fail an inspection are replaced with a new hose. Replacement is the only common form of service because the tools necessary to fabricate new brake hoses are not readily available in the field.

Many brake hoses have a male fitting on one end and a female fitting on the other; these fittings are swaged or crimped onto the hose and do not turn. With this type of hose, the female end must be disconnected first. Other brake hoses have a banjo fitting in place of the male hose end fitting. With this type of hose, it does not matter which end is disconnected first.

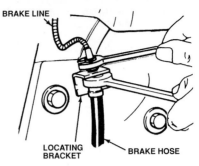

Fig. 1-9. Secure the brake hose fitting with one wrench and loosen the tubing nut with a flare-nut wrench.

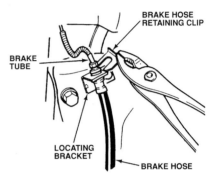

Fig. 1-10. Disconnect the tubing nut, remove the retaining clip with pliers, and separate the hose from the locating bracket.

When removing a hose, clean any dirt from around the fittings at the ends of the hose to prevent it from entering the hydraulic system.

Hold the hose fitting securely with a wrench and use a flare-nut wrench to loosen the tubing nut, figure 1-9. Unscrew the tubing nut from the hose, remove the hose retaining clip with a pair of pliers, and separate the hose from the locating bracket, figure 1-10.

Before you install a new brake hose, make sure it is the proper part for that side of the vehicle; left- and right-side hoses are not always interchangeable. The new hose must also be the proper length, and when the original equipment hose has special armoring and bracket fittings, the replacement part must have them as well.

During installation, carefully route the new hose in the original location. Make sure the hose maintains a distance of at least 0.75 inch (20 mm) from all steering and suspension parts throughout the full range of their movement, so there is no danger of the hose being chafed. Never route brake hoses near exhaust systems, where heat will harm the rubber casing or increase brake fluid temperatures. If copper sealing gaskets are used at either of the hose fittings, use only new parts when installing the hose. Copper gaskets take a set when they are first used, and reusing an old one may cause a leak. Hold the hose fitting steady with a back-up wrench as you tighten the tubing nut to prevent the hose from twisting.

Brake Tubing Replacement

In most cases, custom replacement tubing that is preformed and flared is purchased for a specific application. Rarely does a technician in the field fabricate replacement tubing from raw tubing stock.

Brake tubing is held in place by clips that bolt to the chassis at various points along the line. To replace a section of tubing, you need flare-nut wrenches to loosen the fittings at both ends of the line and suitable sockets, wrenches, or screwdrivers to remove the retaining clip bolts or screws. Make sure to clean any dirt from around the tubing fittings, and use a second wrench where two brake lines connect to prevent twisting the tubing or brake hoses.

HYDRAULIC CONTROL VALVE SERVICE

Hydraulic control valve service includes procedures for testing, adjustment, and replacement. Pressure differential switches and certain height-sensing proportioning valves can be adjusted. However, neither metering valves nor proportioning valves can be repaired or adjusted. Leaking or faulty valves must be replaced. If the defective valve is part of a **combination valve**, the entire valve assembly must be replaced.

Hydraulic Control Valves and Switches

Used in conjunction with the dual master cylinder and the split hydraulic system that has been present on all cars sold in the U.S. since 1967, these valves and switches are essential to the function of a well-engineered and well-balanced system. Metering valves hold off front disc brake application until the lining-to-drum clearance in the rear drum brakes is taken up, thus keeping the front brakes from doing more than their fair share of the work and also preventing front brake lock-up.

Proportioning valves, including the load-sensing type, limit pressure to the rear brakes to prevent lock-up during hard stops. Pressure differential switches sense if one brake circuit is operating at a different pressure from the other, perhaps due to entrapped air or a hydraulic leak, and complete a circuit that illuminates the brake warning light on the dash. Two or more of these functions are often built into one non-serviceable component called a combination valve.

Metering Valve Tests

A faulty metering valve can cause the front brakes to lock up prematurely and may also result in premature wear of the front linings. If you suspect a metering valve failure, begin with a visual inspection. Check around the rubber boot at the valve stem for leakage, figure 1-11. A trace of moisture is normal, but an excessive amount indicates a defective valve. Have an assistant apply the brake pedal while you watch the valve stem. As pressure to the front brakes builds, the valve stem should move. If it does not, replace the valve. More accurate metering valve tests can be performed using pressure gauges.

Pressure Gauge Metering Valve Test

The most precise method of testing a metering valve operation is to check actual closing and opening points of the valve using a pair of pressure gauges. This test requires an assistant to apply the brake pedal, two gauges that register from zero up to a minimum of 500 psi (3450 kPa), and the appropriate fittings to attach the gauges to the hydraulic system. To perform the test:

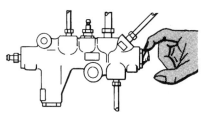

Fig. 1-11. Check behind the valve stem boot of a proportioning valve for signs of leakage.

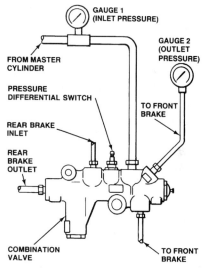

Fig. 1-12. Pressure gauge connections for testing metering valve operation.

1. Tee one of the gauges into the brake line from the master cylinder to the metering valve, figure 1-12. Make sure the gauge does not block the flow of fluid to the metering valve.
2. Connect the second gauge to one of the metering valve outlets that leads to the front brakes.
3. Have an assistant slowly apply the brake pedal while you observe both gauges.
4. If the metering valve is working properly, the gauge readings will rise at the same rate until they reach the valve closing point, figure 1-13A. Closing pressure, which varies by vehicle, typically falls in the 3 to 30 psi (20 to 210 kPa) range.
5. Once the metering valve closes, the reading on the outlet pressure gauge (GAUGE 2) should remain constant, while the inlet pressure gauge (GAUGE 1) reading should continue to increase, figure 1-13B.
6. As inlet pressure (GAUGE 1) reaches approximately 75 to 300 psi (520 to 2070 kPa), the metering valve should open. The outlet pressure gauge (GAUGE 2) reading should then increase until it matches the inlet pressure (GAUGE 1) reading. From that point on, both gauge readings should be identical, figure 1-13C.

A5

Combination Valve: A brake system hydraulic control device that incorporates a pressure differential valve or switch, metering valve, or proportioning valve into one unit.

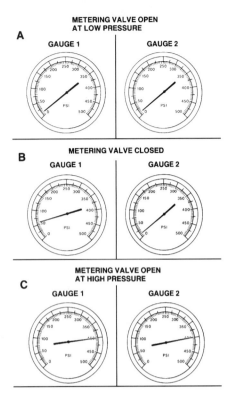

Fig. 1-13. Typical pressure gauge readings during the three phases of a metering valve test.

If the pressures indicated on the gauges do not follow the patterns described above, the metering valve is defective and must be replaced.

Proportioning Valve Tests

A typical proportioning valve failure allows rear brake pressure to increase too rapidly, which causes the rear wheels to lock prematurely during hard stops or on slippery pavement. The proportioning valve can also fail in such a way that no pressure is allowed to the rear brakes, although this is an uncommon type of failure.

Proportioning valve operation can only be tested using pressure gauges. Two pressure gauges that register from 0 to 1000 psi (0 to 6900 kPa), the appropriate fittings to attach the gauges to the hydraulic system, and an assistant are needed to test the proportioning valve. In addition, you need to know the split point of the proportioning valve on the particular make and model of vehicle being tested. Most split points are between 300 and 500 psi (2070 and 3450 kPa), but check the factory shop manual to be sure.

On vehicles where the dual braking system is split front to rear, only a single gauge hookup and test is required, figure 1-14. On vehicles with diagonal-split braking systems and dual proportioning valves, the tests are performed twice, once for each half of the hydraulic system, figure 1-15. To test the proportioning valve:

1. Tee one of the gauges (GAUGE 1) into the brake line from the master cylinder to the proportioning valve, so that the flow of brake fluid to the valve is not restricted.
2. Connect the second gauge (GAUGE 2) to the rear brake outlet of the proportioning valve.

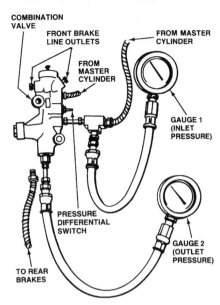

Fig. 1-14. Pressure gauge connections for testing the proportioning valve on a brake system with a front-to-rear split.

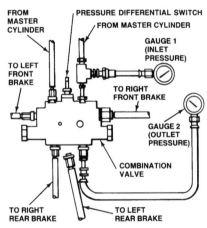

Fig. 1-15. Gauge connections for testing the proportioning valve pressure to the left rear brake assembly on a diagonally split system.

3. Have an assistant slowly apply the brake pedal as you monitor both gauges.
4. The readings on both gauges should rise at an identical rate until the split point pressure is reached, figure 1-16A.
5. Once the split point is reached, the pressure reading on the rear brake outlet (GAUGE 2) should increase at a slower rate than the reading on the inlet pressure gauge (GAUGE 1), figure 1-16B. The proportioning valve delivers less pressure to the rear brakes than that being produced by the master cylinder.

If the pressures indicated on the gauges do not follow the patterns described above, the proportioning valve is defective and must be replaced.

Proportioning Valve Adjustment

In some cases, a height-sensing proportioning valve must be adjusted when it is replaced. The adjustment ensures that the proportioning action takes effect at the correct hydraulic pressure in relation to vehicle loading. There are nearly as many adjustment procedures as there are variable proportioning valves.

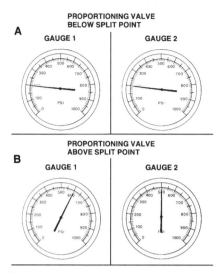

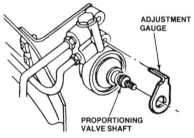

Fig. 1-16. Typical pressure gauge readings during a proportioning valve test.

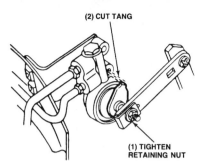

Fig.1-18. After installing the proportioning valve and connecting the operating lever, cut the positioning tang off the plastic adjustment gauge to release the valve.

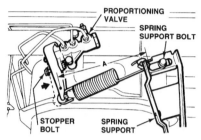

Fig. 1-19. This height-sensing proportioning valve adjusts by loosening the spring support bolt and positioning the support to achieve a specific spring length.

Fig. 1-17. This disposable plastic adjustment gauge holds the proportioning valve in position during installation.

The adjustment procedures are given below for two types of valves in use today. Consult the factory shop manual for the exact procedure on other types of valves.

The height-sensing proportioning valve on some trucks requires a special plastic adjustment gauge. This gauge, which is a one-time use item that is supplied with the replacement part, installs on the valve to hold it in position during installation, figure 1-17. Once the valve operating lever is tightened in place, a tang on the gauge is cut away to allow unrestricted valve operation, figure 1-18.

Other height-sensing proportioning valves require you to set a spring length, figure 1-19. Adjust the distance by loosening the spring support bolt and sliding the spring support until the distance is correct.

Recentering Pressure Differential Switches

After the brake system has been bled, the pressure differential switch may have to be recentered in order to switch off the warning light. Opening a bleeder valve creates a pressure differential between the circuits of the hydraulic system, and the switch interprets this as a fluid loss or partial system failure.

In response, the piston inside the switch body moves to one side and completes the circuit to switch on the warning light. There are three types of pressure differential switches, and each requires a different procedure to recenter it, figure 1-20. To recenter a single-piston pressure differential switch without centering springs, first determine if the brake hydraulic system is split diagonally or front to rear, figure 1-20A. Then, open a bleeder valve in the circuit of the system opposite that which was last bled, slowly depress the brake pedal until the warning light goes out, maintain pedal pressure, and close the bleeder valve.

A5

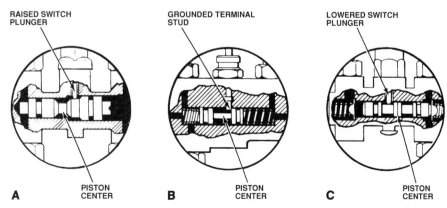

Fig. 1-20. A unique procedure is needed to recenter the piston in each of the three differential switch designs.

Single-piston pressure differential switches equipped with centering springs illuminate the warning light only when the brakes are applied and a pressure difference exists between the two circuits of the brake system, figure 1-20B. The switch recenters itself automatically when the brakes are released, unless the piston sticks in position against the terminal stud. If the warning light remains illuminated after the brake system has been repaired, apply the brake pedal with moderate to hard force. Hydraulic pressure should free the stuck piston and the centering springs will position it properly in the bore. The warning light will then go out.

BRAKE WARNING LAMP SERVICE

The red brake warning lamp can indicate a severe brake system failure. If the brake warning lamp circuit is working correctly, it should prove out by turning on when the ignition switch is turned on, then turning off once the engine is started. When the red brake warning lamp is illuminated, verify proper functioning of the brake system before operating the vehicle. In most cases, the problems you will diagnose will be due to the lamp being illuminated. In some cases though, you may see a lamp that will not work at all. In this section, we will discuss some common ways in which you can diagnose both problems.

On a typical brake system, there are two switches or sensors that can cause the red brake lamp to illuminate. One is located on the master cylinder and the other is located on the parking brake lever. On these systems, application of the parking brake or low brake fluid level will cause the red brake lamp to illuminate. Of course, there are circuit problems that can occur that would cause the lamp to turn on. These include: shorted indicator circuit, ABS system failure (if equipped), or instrument cluster printed circuit board failure.

On some models, the instrument cluster is controlled by an electronic control unit (ECU). If a problem exists on one of these systems, some of the basic principles discussed here can be applied to help diagnose the red brake warning lamp circuit, but more than likely, a factory shop manual along with a wiring diagram manual will have to be consulted. Many factory shop manuals outline very in-depth pinpoint tests that should be followed to quickly lead you to proper diagnosis of the red brake warning lamp. In figure 1-21, an example of a Ford diagnostic test is shown.

BRAKE WARNING LAMP CIRCUIT TESTING

Preliminary Inspection

When diagnosing the brake warning lamp, first check the brake fluid level. If it is low, determine the cause of low fluid level, then fill and recheck the system.

If fluid level is ok, inspect the parking brake system to ensure it is fully released. If the parking brake system does not release inspect all parking brake cables and mechanisms to determine the cause of failure.

Repair and recheck warning lamp operation. If fluid level and parking brake operation are ok, suspect a faulty switch, shorted circuit, or ABS malfunction (if equipped).

Fluid Level Switch Test

To test the fluid level switch, disconnect the switch, then measure the resistance of the switch using a suitable digital volt-ohmmeter. When the fluid level switch is in the full position, the ohmmeter should indicate open circuit, figure 1-22. When the fluid level switch is in the low position, the ohmmeter should indicate continuity.

Parking Brake Switch Test

To test the parking brake switch, disconnect the switch, then measure resistance when parking brake is not applied. The ohmmeter should indicate open circuit. When the parking brake is applied, the ohmmeter should indicate continuity.

Warning Lamp Circuit Wiring Inspection

Unwanted Ground

The wiring diagram shown in figure 1-23 shows three different areas of the circuit where an unwanted ground might occur. If an unwanted ground occurred in any of these areas, the red brake warning lamp would illuminate. In the circuit shown, one way to tell if there is an unwanted ground would be to disconnect the fluid level switch and the parking brake switch. If the lamp is still on, suspect an unwanted ground that exists before the switches.

To check for an unwanted ground in the circuit shown in figure 1-23, first remove the fuse supplying the circuit with power. Next, disconnect both the brake fluid level switch and the parking brake switch. Using a suitable digital volt-ohmmeter, check the resistance of the harness to ground at several points throughout the circuit. If continuity is indicated by the ohmmeter, suspect that portion of the circuit for the unwanted ground.

Open Circuit

The wiring diagram shown in figure 1-24 shows four places where the circuit is open. If an open occurred at point "A" of the circuit, the indicator would not work at all. If an open occurred at points "B" or "C," the brake fluid level indicator portion of the circuit would not work at all. If an open occurred at points "D" or "E," the indicator would not illuminate if the parking brake were applied.

Short Circuit

If the circuit shown in figure 1-24 were grounded at point "A," you would have a short circuit. This condition would cause the fuse supplying the circuit to open. If the fuse were replaced, it would immediately open again if the short were present. To find the short circuit, a careful examination of the wiring harness would be necessary.

Switch Replacement

To replace the parking brake switch, first locate the switch on the parking brake foot pedal or lever. Disconnect the switch, then remove it from its mounting. Install the new switch. Depending on make and model application, the new switch may require adjustment. As a general rule, adjust the switch so the red brake light illuminates as the parking brake is applied. Ensure the lamp goes out after the parking

Test Step	Result/Action To Take
1 CHECK THE BASE BRAKE SYSTEM OPERATION Key In Start Position Operate the base brake system **Does the base brake system operate correctly?**	**Yes** Go To **Step 2** **No** Diagnose Base Brake System
2 CHECK BRAKE WARNING INDICATOR NOTE: Make sure brake fluid is filled to correct level and the parking brake is released. Key in ON position Key In Start Position Observe the instrument cluster brake warning indicator. **Does the brake warning indicator turn on when the ignition switch is in START position and turn off when the ignition switch is in the OFF position?**	**Yes** The system is ok **No** If the brake warning indicator is always on, Go to **Step 3** If the brake warning indicator is never on, Go to **Step 9**
3 CHECK THE PARKING BRAKE SWITCH Key in OFF position Disconnect: Parking Brake Switch Key in ON position **Is the brake warning indicator illuminated?**	**Yes** Go To **Step 4** **No** INSTALL a new parking brake switch
4 CHECK THE ABS MODULE Key in OFF position Disconnect: ABS Module Key in ON position Observe the brake warning indicator **Is the brake warning indicator illuminated?**	**Yes** Go to Step 5 **No** Diagnose ABS/Traction Control System
5 CHECK THE BRAKE LEVEL SWITCH OPERATION NOTE: Prior to running this test step, check the brake fluid level and fill (if necessary) to make sure that the brake fluid level is correct Key in OFF position Disconnect: Brake Fluid Level Switch Key in ON position Observe the instrument cluster brake warning indicator. **Is the brake warning indicator illuminated?**	**Yes** REPAIR the circuit. TEST the system for normal operation **No** Go to **Step 6**
6 CHECK BRAKE FLUID LEVEL SWITCH NOTE: Verify that the brake fluid level is full Measure the resistance between the brake fluid level switch (component side) terminal 1 and the brake fluid level switch (component side) terminal 3; and between the brake fluid level switch (component side) terminal 2 and the brake fluid level switch (component side) terminal 3. **Is the resistance greater than 10,000 ohms between terminals 1 and 3; and less than 5 ohms between terminals 2 and 3 of the brake fluid level switch?**	**Yes** Go to Step 7 **No** INSTALL a new brake fluid level switch. TEST the system for normal operation.
7 CHECK IGNITION SWITCH CIRCUIT Key in OFF position Measure resistance between the brake fluid level switch harness pin 2 and ground Key in START position Measure resistance between the brake fluid level switch harness pin 2 and ground while ignition switch is in the START position **Is the resistance less than 5 ohms with the ignition switch in the START position, and greater than 10,000 ohms with the ignition switch in the OFF position?**	**Yes** Go to Step 10 **No** Go to Step 8
8 CHECK PIN 2 CIRCUIT FOR OPEN Key in OFF position Disconnect ignition switch Measure resistance between the brake fluid level switch harness pin 2 and ignition switch connector circuit 409. **Is the resistance less than 5 ohms?**	**Yes** Diagnose steering column concern **No** REPAIR the circuit. TEST the system for normal operation
9 CHECK PIN 3 CIRCUIT FOR OPEN Key in OFF position Disconnect: Brake Fluid Level Switch Measure the resistance between the instrument cluster harness connector pin (brake fluid level switch) and brake fluid level switch harness pin 3 **Is the resistance less than 5 ohms?**	**Yes** Go to Step 10 **No** REPAIR the circuit. TEST the system for normal operation
10 CHECK FOR CORRECT INSTRUMENT CLUSTER OPERATION Disconnect all instrument cluster connections Check for corrosion and pushed out pins Connect all instrument cluster connectors and make sure they seat correctly Operate the system and verify the concern is still present **Is the concern still present?**	**Yes** INSTALL a new instrument cluster. TEST the system for normal operation. **No** The system is operating correctly at this time. Concern may have been caused by loose or corroded connector. Clear DTC's. Repeat self test.

A5

Fig. 1-21. 2003 Lincoln Town Car brake warning lamp diagnostic test.

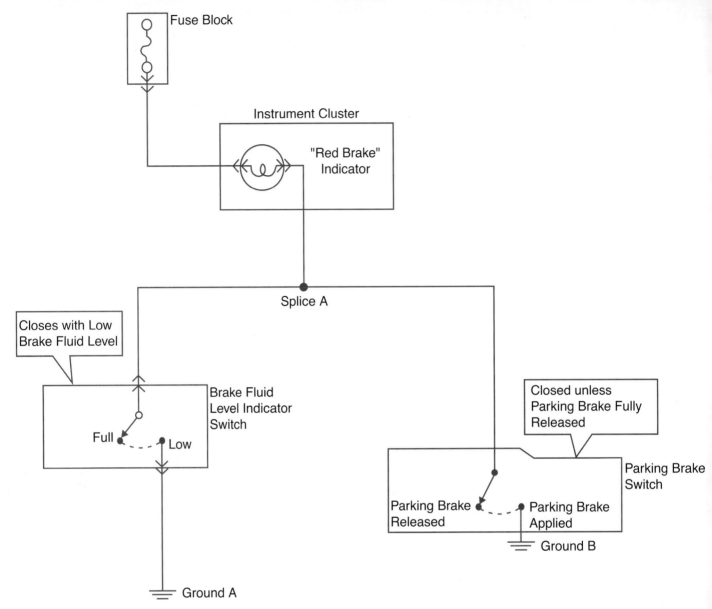

Fig. 1-22. Typical brake warning lamp circuit diagram.

brake is released. Consult a factory shop manual for specific make and model applications.

To replace a brake fluid level switch, first determine if the switch is integral to the master cylinder, or the reservoir. Sometimes the switch may thread into the reservoir and replacing it is just a matter of unscrewing the old one and installing a new one. If it is integral to the cylinder and cannot be replaced separately, the master cylinder should be replaced. On many of these applications, the reservoir can be replaced without replacing the master cylinder. A general replacement procedure is given for one of these applications. As always, consult a factory shop manual if you are not sure which system is found on your specific make and model.

1. Disconnect the brake fluid level switch.
2. Remove fluid from the master cylinder reservoir using a suitable suction device.
3. Carefully pry up on the master cylinder reservoir and remove it from the master cylinder.

4. Remove and discard the reservoir grommets. Lubricate new grommets using new brake fluid and install them to the master cylinder.
5. Install the reservoir until it is fully seated into the master cylinder.
6. Connect the brake fluid level switch, then fill the master cylinder with the recommended fluid. Bleed the system if necessary.

BRAKE FLUID

When topping off the brake fluid, always use the type and DOT grade of brake fluid recommended by the manufacturer. Most vehicles use polyglycol brake fluid, either a DOT 3 or DOT 4 grade fluid. Ford vehicles require a special DOT 3 with an extremely high boiling point. Many import vehicles use DOT 4.

Occasionally, you will run across a vehicle that uses DOT 5 or silicone brake fluid. Some European manufacturers, such as Citroën and Rolls-Royce, use Hydraulic System Mineral Oil

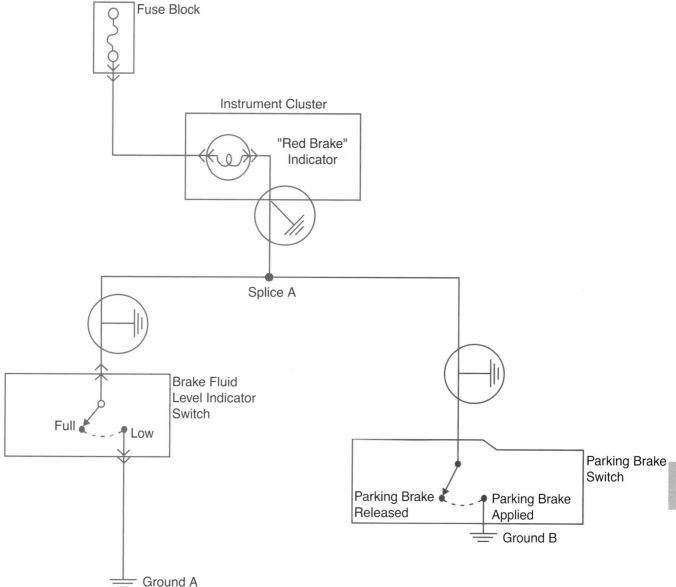

Fuse Block

Instrument Cluster

"Red Brake" Indicator

Splice A

Brake Fluid Level Indicator Switch

Full   Low

Parking Brake Switch

A5

Parking Brake Released   Parking Brake Applied

Ground B

Ground A

Fig. 1-23. This circuit shows several areas where an unwanted ground might occur.

(HSMO) in the brake system, while Audi uses it in the hydraulic brake booster on select models.

To avoid mixing the three types, federal law requires that each be a specific color: polyglycol fluids are clear to amber, silicone fluids are purple, and hydraulic mineral oils are green. Keep in mind that today, many manufacturers recommend routine replacement of brake fluid at specific scheduled intervals. Consult OEM maintenance guides to determine these intervals.

Contamination

Brake fluid that is contaminated with water, rust, dirt, mineral oil, or compounds derived from overheated glycol can cause various system performance problems. For instance, moisture lowers the boiling point, which can allow bubbles to form in the lines that can result in loss of stopping power, especially at high altitudes. Moisture also contributes to corrosion, which may cause caliper or wheel cylinder pistons to seize, resulting

in loss of braking at that wheel and a subsequent pull toward the opposite side. Mineral oil softens and destroys rubber seals, causing catastrophic leaks. Other contaminants can clog valves or the ABS hydraulic control unit. Brake fluid care and maintenance are important for both safety and economy.

Storage and Handling

Storage and handling precautions for brake fluid depend on the type of fluid being used. Polyglycol fluid has a very limited storage life. Once a can of polyglycol fluid has been opened, its entire contents should be used as soon as possible because it immediately begins to absorb moisture that degrades its performance. In contrast, silicone brake fluid and HSMO can be stored almost indefinitely. They are not **hygroscopic**, and there is no limit to the length of time they retain their original properties.

When handling a polyglycol fluid, remember that it is a powerful solvent that can rapidly damage paint. If you spill

---

Hygroscopic: Water absorbing. Polyglycol brake fluids are hygroscopic.

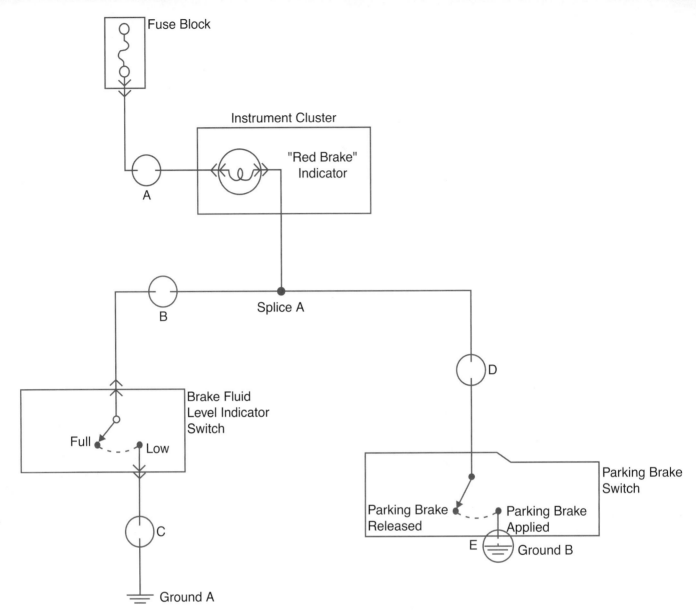

Fig. 1-24. This circuit shows several areas where an open may occur.

any, immediately flush the area with plenty of clean water. Neither silicone nor HSMO brake fluids harm paint.

Brake Fluid Condition

Whenever you check the brake fluid level, also inspect the fluid for dirt, moisture, or oil contamination. Fluid in good condition should be relatively clear. A cloudy appearance indicates moisture contamination, while a dark appearance indicates contamination by rust, dirt, corrosion, or brake dust. A layered appearance can mean a silicone brake fluid was mixed with a polyglycol fluid. The two fluids do not mix, and the entire system should be completely flushed, then refilled with the recommended fluid.

BRAKE BLEEDING

Brake bleeding is a process that pushes new brake fluid through the brake system to force out contaminated fluid and trapped air. Air can enter the brake lines whenever the system

is opened for service. Brake system bleeding must be done in a particular sequence:

1. Master cylinder
2. Combination valve
3. Wheel cylinders and brake calipers
4. Load-sensing proportioning valve
5. Antilock brake system (ABS) hydraulic modulator or pump motor

Combination valves, load-sensing proportioning valves, and ABS hydraulic modulators or pump motors are only bled when present in the system and equipped with bleeder valves. The correct bleeding sequence at the wheels varies from vehicle to vehicle. In some cases, you may have to recenter the pressure differential switch after bleeding the wheel brakes. The centering procedure is detailed in this chapter. Also, some disc brake systems have a metering valve or combination valve that demands special attention if power bleeding the system. Since

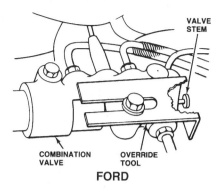

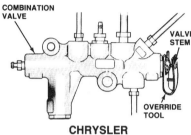

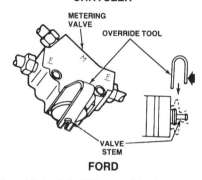

Fig. 1-25. Override tools hold the combination or metering valve open to allow for pressure bleeding the hydraulic system.

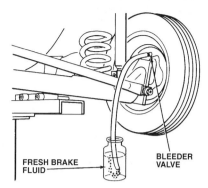

Fig. 1-26. Using clear hose and a partially filled bottle of fresh brake fluid makes it easy to spot air bubbles and prevents spills when bleeding the system.

the operating pressure of power bleeders is within the range where the metering valve blocks fluid flow to the front brakes, you must deactivate the valve. Special override tools are used to hold the valve open for **pressure bleeding**, figure 1-25.

Master Cylinder Bleeding

Bleed new or rebuilt cylinders on the workbench before installing them. This practice eliminates trapped air pockets and greatly speeds bleeding the rest of the brake system.

Master Cylinder Bench Bleeding

1. Clamp the cylinder in a vise.
2. Use a drain pan to catch any fluid leakage from the outlet ports, or fit hoses to the ports to route fluid back to the reservoir. Fill the cylinder with the correct type and grade of new brake fluid.
3. Use the cylinder pushrod, or other round-ended rod, to slowly stroke the cylinder pistons inward until they both bottom.
4. If the fluid outlets are open, plug them with your fingertips. Then, slowly allow both pistons to fully return on the back stroke and remove your fingers from the outlets. If the fluid outlets are connected to the reservoir with hoses, make sure the connections are airtight. Then, slowly allow both pistons to fully return.
5. Repeat steps 3 and 4 until the fluid coming from the outlets is air-free, and bubbles no longer emerge from the compensating and replenishing ports in the reservoir.

Wheel Brake Bleeding

When bleeding the wheel brakes, follow the bleeding sequence recommended by the manufacturer for the particular vehicle being serviced. Sequence can vary not only by manufacturer, but also by year, model, and equipment. Special procedures may be required for vehicles with ABS. Generally, the wheel cylinder or caliper furthest from the master cylinder is bled first, followed by the next closest caliper or cylinder, and so on. Be sure to check the recommendations for the specific vehicle you are working on, as sequences will vary. In all types of wheel brake bleeding, fill the master cylinder with fluid and ensure that it stays at least half full during the entire procedure.

Manual Brake Bleeding

This method requires two people: one person to press the brake pedal, while the other opens and closes the bleeder valves. The brake pedal will sink toward the floor as the valve is opened. Upon signal, the bleeder valve is tightened and the operation repeated until all the air is expelled. To manually bleed a system:

1. If the vehicle has a vacuum or hydraulic power booster, discharge it by pumping the brake pedal with the ignition OFF until the pedal feel hardens.
2. Slip a length of clear plastic hose over the bleeder valve of the first wheel cylinder or caliper in the bleeding sequence, and submerge the open end of the tube in a partially filled container of fresh brake fluid, figure 1-26.
3. Loosen the bleeder valve approximately one-half turn, then have your assistant slowly depress the brake pedal and hold it to the floor. Air bubbles leaving the bleeder valve will be visible in the hose to the container.

A5

Pressure Bleeding: A procedure for removing air from a brake hydraulic system using pressurized fluid and special adapters at the master cylinder.

4. Tighten the bleeder valve, then have your assistant slowly release the brake pedal.

5. Repeat steps 3 and 4 until no more air bubbles emerge from the bleeder valve.

6. Transfer the plastic hose to the bleeder valve of the next wheel cylinder or caliper in the bleeding sequence, and repeat steps 3 and 4. Continue around the vehicle in the specified order until the brakes at all four wheels have been bled.

Pressure Tank Bleeding

Pressure bleeding drum brake systems is a straightforward procedure, but some disc brake systems have a metering valve or combination valve that demands special attention. Since the operating pressure of power bleeders is within the range where the metering valve blocks fluid flow to the front brakes, you must deactivate the valve. An override tool is sometimes used to hold the valve open for pressure bleeding, figure 1-25.

Follow the correct sequence when pressure bleeding a brake system. Be aware, some manufacturers recommend one sequence for manual and another for pressure bleeding. To pressure bleed a system:

1. Make sure the pressure bleeder tank is filled with the proper type and grade of brake fluid. Consult the instructions for the equipment being used.

2. With the bleeder properly sealed and the fluid supply valve closed, use compressed air to charge the bleeder to approximately 30 psi (207 kPa) of pressure.

3. On vehicles with a metering or combination valve, override it with the appropriate tool.

4. Clean the top of the master cylinder, remove the reservoir cover, and clean around the gasket surface. Be careful not to allow any dirt to fall into the reservoir.

5. Select the appropriate pressure bleeder adapter and install it on the master cylinder, figure 1-27.

6. Connect the pressure bleeder fluid supply hose to the adapter, making sure the hose fitting is securely engaged.

7. Open the fluid supply valve on the pressure bleeder to allow pressurized brake fluid to enter the vehicle brake system. Check carefully for fluid leaks that can damage the vehicle finish.

8. Slip the plastic hose over the bleeder valve of the first wheel cylinder or caliper to be bled, and submerge the open end of the tube in a container partially filled with fresh brake fluid.

9. Open the bleeder valve approximately one-half turn, and let the fluid run until air bubbles no longer emerge from the tube. Then, close the bleeder valve.

10. Transfer the plastic hose to the bleeder valve of the next wheel cylinder or caliper in the bleeding sequence. Repeat steps 8 and 9. Continue around the vehicle in the specified order until the brakes at all four wheels have been bled.

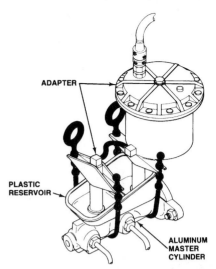

Fig. 1-27. An assortment of adapters are available for connecting a pressure bleeder to a variety of master cylinders.

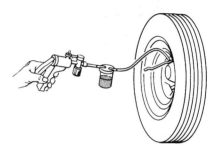

Fig. 1-28. Vacuum bleeding creates a low-pressure zone at the bleeder valve, which draws fluid through the system.

11. Remove the **metering valve** override tool.

12. Close the fluid supply valve on the pressure bleeder.

13. Wrap the end of the fluid supply hose with a rag, then disconnect it from the master cylinder adapter. Be careful not to spill any brake fluid on the vehicle finish.

14. Remove the master cylinder adapter, adjust the fluid level to the full point, and install the fluid reservoir cover.

Vacuum Bleeding

Vacuum bleeding uses a special suction pump that attaches to the bleeder valve. The pump creates a low-pressure area at the bleeder valve, which allows atmospheric pressure to force brake fluid through the system when the valve is opened, figure 1-28. Vacuum bleeding requires only one technician; however, it can only be used on wheel cylinders with cup-type expanders and brake calipers with O-ring seals. On wheel cylinders without cup expanders and calipers with stroking seals, the low pressure can pull the lips of the seals away from the bore and allow air to enter the system. To vacuum bleed a brake system:

1. Attach the open end of the vacuum pump to the bleeder valve of the first wheel cylinder or caliper in the bleeding

---

Metering Valve: A hydraulic system component that keeps the front disc brakes from applying until the space between the shoes and the drum of the rear brakes has been taken up.

Vacuum Bleeding: A procedure for removing air from a brake hydraulic system using a manual vacuum pump or other vacuum source at the bleeder screws of the calipers and wheel cylinders.

sequence. If necessary, use one of the adapters provided with the vacuum bleeding kit to connect to the bleeder valve.

2. Squeeze the pump handle 10 to 15 times to create a partial vacuum in the catch bottle.

3. Loosen the bleeder valve approximately one-half turn. Brake fluid and air bubbles will flow into the bottle.

When the fluid flow stops, tighten the bleeder valve.

4. Repeat steps 3 and 4 until no more air bubbles emerge from the bleeder valve.

5. Transfer the vacuum bleeder to the next wheel cylinder or caliper in the bleeding sequence, and repeat steps 2 and 3. Continue in the specified order until the brakes at all four wheels have been bled.

A5

CHAPTER QUESTIONS

1. Brake pedal reserve that gradually fades under light pressure indicates:
   a. A brake line restriction
   b. Spring tension on the brake pedal is weak
   c. Internal leaks
   d. The system is operating properly

2. Which of the following statements is **NOT** true?
   a. Some imports use HSMO, a green colored oil, as brake fluid
   b. Silicone, or DOT 5 brake fluids, contain a purple dye
   c. Polyglycol brake fluids are amber to clear in color
   d. All DOT approved brake fluids are hygroscopic

3. A bypassing master cylinder can be detected by the:
   a. Internal leak test
   b. External leak test
   c. Compensating port test
   d. QTU test

4. Honing will remove the anodized finish on which type of master cylinder?
   a. Add-on ABS
   b. Aluminum
   c. Cast iron
   d. Composite

5. The first piston installed when rebuilding a master cylinder is the:
   a. Primary piston
   b. Secondary piston
   c. QTU piston
   d. Compensating piston

6. The QTU valve on a master cylinder regulates fluid flow:
   a. Between the master cylinder and the reservoir
   b. Between the two chambers of the reservoir
   c. Between opposite wheels
   d. Between the two channels of the master cylinder

7. The master cylinder should be cleaned with:
   a. Kerosene or carburetor cleaner
   b. Brake parts cleaner or brake fluid
   c. Fresh solvent or hot, soapy water
   d. Motor oil or cutting oil

8. A correctly honed cylinder bore should:
   a. Have a smooth, polished surface
   b. Have a crosshatch pattern
   c. Be larger than the original size by a specified amount
   d. Have scoring no deeper than 0.006 inch (0.15 mm)

9. The first component in a brake system bleeding sequence is the:
   a. Master cylinder
   b. Wheel cylinder
   c. Combination valve
   d. Proportioning valve

10. Generally speaking, which of the wheel brakes should you bleed first?
    a. The one farthest from the master cylinder
    b. The one closest to the master cylinder
    c. The one closest to the driver
    d. The one closest to the passenger

11. What special tool is required to pressure bleed a system equipped with a metering valve?
    a. An adjustment gauge
    b. A torque wrench
    c. A vacuum tool
    d. An override tool

12. On a front brake hose that does not have a banjo fitting, which end do you disconnect first?
    a. Female end
    b. Male end
    c. Caliper end
    d. Either end

13. After bleeding brakes:
    a. The pressure differential switch may need to be recentered
    b. The metering valve may need to be adjusted
    c. The proportioning valve may need to be recentered
    d. The pressure differential switch may need to be adjusted

14. The most precise way to test metering valves is with:
    a. A pressure bleeder
    b. Pressure gauges
    c. An override tool
    d. Vacuum gauge

15. Height-sensing proportioning valves:
    a. Cannot be adjusted
    b. Are used only on FWD vehicles
    c. Can be adjusted in many cases
    d. Are often the cause of brake problems

16. Technician A says a shorted indicator lamp circuit may cause the red brake lamp to illuminate. Technician B says that an ABS system failure could cause the red brake lamp to illuminate. Who is right?
    a. A only
    b. B only
    c. Both A and B
    d. Neither A nor B

17. Technician A says the first thing to do when diagnosing a red brake warning lamp is to check the master cylinder fluid level. Technician B says that the first thing to do is inspect the parking brake system. Who is right?
    a. A only
    b. B only
    c. Both A and B
    d. Neither A nor B

18. True or False? An unwanted ground may cause the red brake warning lamp to illuminate, even if there are no other problems in the system.
    a. True
    b. False

19. Most manufacturers recommend that brake hoses be inspected:
    a. Every 5,000 miles
    b. Once every 6 months or anytime the brakes are serviced
    c. Every 60,000 miles
    d. Twice a year or anytime the brakes are serviced

20. If a brake hose requires replacement:
    a. Cut the hose and splice in a new section
    b. Patch the hose using a suitable patching solution
    c. Replace the hose
    d. Fabricate a new hose and replace the old hose

21. Technician A says that when replacing a metal brake line, flare nut wrenches should be used to loosen the fittings. Technician B states that when replacing a metal brake line, make sure to route it in the original locations that the old line came from. Who is right?
    a. A only
    b. B only
    c. Both A and B
    d. Neither A nor B

22. If an external leak is present, but is not obvious:
    a. The brake fluid evaporated
    b. The fluid was lost internally
    c. Have an assistant pump the brakes and inspect for leaks while the system is under hydraulic pressure
    d. Pump the brakes until the red brake warning indicator illuminates

A5

CHAPTER OBJECTIVES

- The technician will complete the ASE task list on Drum Brake Diagnosis and Repair.
- The technician will be able to answer 5 questions dealing with the Drum Brake Diagnosis and Repair section of the A5 ASE test.

Begin brake drum diagnosis with a road test. When applying the brakes, listen for unusual noises coming from the rear of the vehicle, pay attention to how the brake pedal feels as the brakes activate, and note if the vehicle pulls to one side or shudders as it comes to a stop.

Excessive pedal travel before the brakes apply is often the result of incorrect adjustment, probably due to an inoperative self-adjusting mechanism; the shoes must move too far before contacting the drum. This is a very common cause of low-pedal complaints. A vehicle that pulls to one side is the result of uneven shoe-to-drum clearance from side to side, or a shoe that is hanging up or binding. Pulling due to a drum brake problem is subtle on a vehicle with front disc and rear drum brakes, and the direct cause is often undetectable without removing the drums and inspecting the brake assembly.

DRUM BRAKE HYDRAULIC PROBLEMS

Drum brake wheel cylinder deterioration can result in several braking performance problems. If a wheel cylinder's internal seals are leaking, brake fluid will find its way past the dust boots and eventually contaminate the friction material on the shoes. This will not only reduce stopping power at that wheel, but it often causes grabbing and a grunting or groaning noise when the brakes are applied. Also, hygroscopic brake fluid absorbs moisture when present on the drum brake component (especially the self-adjustment mechanism) and will promote rapid corrosion that will lead to malfunction.

If a wheel cylinder's pistons become seized either from an internal fluid leak, or from the infiltration of salt water from outside, that wheel brake will be inoperative. Obviously, this will reduce stopping power, but it can also cause pulling or even skidding due to uneven braking. If the pistons are seized in the extended apply position, the brake will fail to retract completely, causing a dragging condition, overheating, and premature lining/drum wear.

Equipment exists that can compare the dynamic braking capabilities of all four wheels, but it is not common. So, diagnosis becomes a very straightforward matter.

In cases where your test drive leads you to suspect that there is a problem with the rear drum brakes, raise the rear wheels safely off the ground and spin them by hand. If there is a heavy drag, suspect sluggish or seized wheel cylinder pistons. Have an assistant apply the brakes very gently and slowly while you spin each wheel to make sure that it stops.

The next step is visual inspection. First, look at the outside of the backing plates and the inner side of the tires for evidence of fluid leakage. Next, remove each wheel/tire assembly and drum to see if fluid is present on the hardware and the inside of the backing plate. Next, peel back the wheel cylinder dust boots to see if fluid has collected inside them. If there is any whatsoever, the wheel cylinder must be either reconditioned or replaced.

DRUM BRAKE MECHANICAL PROBLEMS

Lack of self-adjustment, which allows the shoe-to-drum clearance to become excessive, resulting in a low brake pedal and poor stopping performance, is one of the most common drum brake mechanical problems. Others include noise, pedal pulsation, and parking brake malfunctions.

A grinding or scraping noise coming from the rear of the car when the brakes are applied is typically the result of worn-out brake shoe linings. The sound comes from the rivets or the metal shoe surface making contact with the brake drum. Direct inspection is required to determine the cause of the noise.

Pulling to one side during braking is much less an issue with rear brakes than with fronts, but it can still be noticeable and may contribute to skidding. This may occur if the drum brake on one side has a malfunctioning self-adjusting mechanism. Again, drum removal and direct inspection are required.

Pedal pulsation or shudder not due to front disc brake rotor thickness variation is almost always caused by out-of-round drums. The only other possibility is a cracked drum. While coasting at low speed on an uncrowded roadway, apply the parking brake slowly. If you feel pulsation, shudder, or hitching, the problem is in the rear drums and not the front discs. Removal and careful measurement and inspection will be needed in order to detect either an out-of-round or a cracked drum.

A leaking rear axle seal that permits gear lubricant from the differential to contaminate the shoes will reduce stopping power and is likely to cause grabbing and a grunting noise during brake application.

BRAKE DRUM REMOVAL

To service a drum brake, you must first remove the drum to gain access to the friction assembly. The removal procedures differ for **fixed drums** and **floating drums**. With either design, it is sometimes necessary to back off the drum-to-lining adjustment and loosen the parking brake before the drum can be removed. This is because wear at the open edge of the drum or scoring of the brake linings and drum friction surface creates a ridge or several interlocking grooves that hold the drum in place, figure 2-1. If the drums are not going to be machined, mark them with their original location so that they can be returned to the same axle and the same side of the vehicle.

Fixed Drum Removal

Fixed brake drums are usually found at the rear of front-wheel drive (FWD) vehicles (it has been over two decades since drum brakes have been used at the front of any car). In most applications, the nut that retains a fixed brake drum also secures and preloads the wheel bearings in the hub.

To remove a fixed drum, remove the dust cap from the center of the hub. Most designs have either a castellated nut or a castellated retainer that fits over a standard nut. Both are secured by a cotter pin. Remove the cotter pin along with any other locking devices, then remove the nut. Pull outward on the drum to slide it off the spindle.

Take care not to let the thrust washer and outer wheel bearing fall on the ground as they clear the spindle. Also, avoid dragging the inner wheel bearing and grease seal across the retaining nut threads on the spindle.

Once the drum is removed, inspect the grease in the hub and on the wheel bearings. If the grease is relatively fresh and in good condition, set the drum on the bench, open side down, and cover the outer bearing and hub opening so the bearings will not become contaminated. If the grease is old and dirty, repack the wheel bearings before you reinstall the drum. Always repack the wheel bearings when performing a complete brake job. This includes removing all the old grease from the hub.

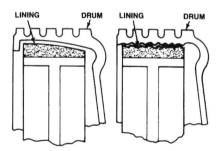

Fig. 2-1. Brake lining and friction surface wear make it difficult to remove a drum unless the parking and service brake adjustments are loosened.

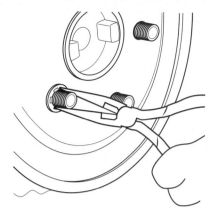

Fig. 2-2. Speed nuts, which hold a floating drum in place on the assembly line, can be removed and discarded during service.

Floating Drum Removal

Most floating brake drums are held in place by the wheel and lug nuts, although some designs have small bolts or screws that fit through a hole on the face of the drum and into a threaded hole on the axle flange. These must be removed before the drum can be removed. Some drums may also be retained by **speed nuts**, which fit over the wheel studs that protrude through the drum from the hub or axle flange. To remove speed nuts, grasp them with a pair of pliers and thread them off the studs, figure 2-2. Once removed, speed nuts can be discarded because their only purpose is to keep the drum in place on the assembly line. Now, the drum should move freely on the hub or axle and slip off over the brake shoes.

BRAKE DRUM INSPECTION

A5

Two inspections are made on a brake drum, a visual inspection followed by careful measurements. After completing a thorough inspection, you will know if the drum is in serviceable condition or is beyond saving and must be replaced. A serviceable drum can be machined to restore the friction surface, then reinstalled in its original position on the vehicle.

Visual Inspection

To inspect a drum, first wash its friction surface with detergent and a scrub brush, and rinse with water. If you see any problems that will require the drum to be machined, immediately measure the drum as described in this chapter. Visually inspect the drum for:

- Scores and grooves
- Cracks
- Heat checks
- Hard spots

Scores and grooves on the drum friction surface increase brake wear and noise. To determine the depth of any scores or

---

Floating Drum: A brake drum that installs on a separate axle flange or hub assembly. Floating drums are commonly found on the drive axle of rear-wheel-drive vehicles.

Fixed Drum: A brake drum that is cast in one piece along with the hub, which contains the wheel bearings. Fixed drums are most often used on non-driven axles, such as at the rear of a front-wheel-drive vehicle.

Speed Nut: A spring-steel clip that threads onto a stud or bolt to position a part. Speed nuts are used to hold floating drums and rotors in place during vehicle assembly.

grooves, use a micrometer with a pointed anvil designed for this purpose. As a general rule, any score or groove deeper than 0.010 inch (0.25 mm) requires **turning** the drum.

Cracks can occur anywhere, but drums usually crack near the bolt circle or web and at the open edge of the friction surface, figure 2-3. Do not confuse small surface checks with cracks that reach deeply into the structure of the drum. If any cracks are visible, replace the drum. Heat checking appears as many small, interlaced cracks on the friction surface.

Heat checks can cause a slight pedal pulsation, increase brake lining wear, and make noise. If the heat checking is minor and the drum checks out in other respects, machine the drum. If heat checking is widespread, replace the drum.

Hard spots are round, bluish/gold, glassy appearing areas that develop on the friction surface, figure 2-4. Hard spots can cause pedal pulsation, brake chatter, and increased lining wear. Since grinding down hard spots requires special equipment and is time-consuming and not always successful, it is common practice to replace drums with hard spots.

Measurement

Brake drums are measured to identify wear and distortion that is not visually apparent. When drums wear, they become oversized, tapered, or barrel-shaped. Distorted drums become bell-mouthed, out-of-round, or eccentric. Most of these problems can be detected using either a drum micrometer or an inside micrometer. However, some forms of drum wear and distortion cannot be identified until the drum is actually turned in a brake lathe.

Drum Inside Diameter

Anytime a brake drum is removed from the vehicle, inside diameter should be measured to check for wear. To measure, first note the discard diameter stamped or cast into the drum, figure 2-5. Then, position the drum so the open side is facing up.

Adjust a drum micrometer to the nominal drum diameter, fit it into the drum, and take measurements at two or three locations, figure 2-6. Compare the largest micrometer reading to the discard diameter stamped on the drum.

If the inside diameter is smaller than the drum discard diameter, the drum may be returned to service. If it has defects that require machining, however, now is the time to determine with careful measurement whether or not the amount of metal that must be removed will put the drum beyond the discard diameter. Also, the amount of additional metal sometimes required to allow for wear in service varies by manufacturer, so check the shop manual for the vehicle in question for the exact value.

Drum Taper Wear, Barrel Wear, and Bellmouth Distortion

Taper wear, barrel wear, and bellmouth distortion are problems that cause variations in brake drum diameter between the open and closed edges of the friction surface. A drum with taper wear has a larger diameter at the closed edge than at the

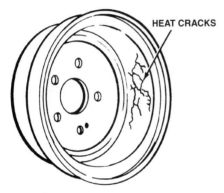

Fig. 2-3. Heat checks, which are a series of small, interlaced cracks on the friction surface of the drum, can be machined out if they are minor and localized.

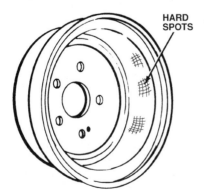

Fig. 2-4. Hard spots, which appear where extreme heat has hardened the iron in the drum, can cause pedal pulsation and chatter, and increase lining wear.

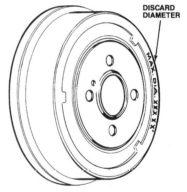

Fig. 2-5. Discard diameter, which is stamped or cast into the face of the drum, shows the machining and wear limits of the drum.

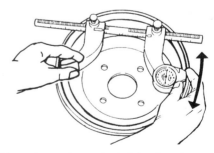

Fig. 2-6. Use a drum micrometer to take diameter measurements at several locations around the drum.

Turning: A machining process that uses a brake lathe to remove metal from drums and rotors to refinish their friction surfaces.

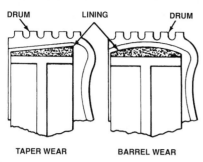

Fig. 2-7. Taper wear, the largest, inside diameter at the closed edge of the friction surface, and barrel wear, the largest, inside diameter at the center of the friction surface, are common in brake drums.

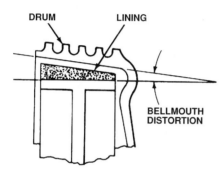

Fig. 2-8. Bellmouth wear, the largest, inside diameter at the open edge of the friction surface, occurs less frequently than other types of brake drum wear patterns.

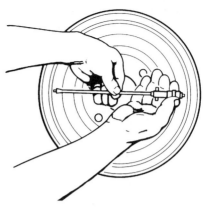

Fig. 2-9. Take three inside micrometer readings, at the closed edge, center, and open edge of the friction surface, to check a drum for taper, barrel, and bellmouth wear.

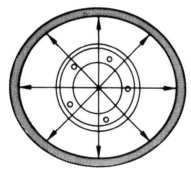

Fig. 2-10. Take four micrometer readings at 45 degree increments around the circumference to check a brake drum for out-of-round distortion.

open edge, while a drum with barrel wear has a larger diameter at the center than at either edge, figure 2-7. A drum with bellmouth distortion has a larger diameter at the open edge than at the closed edge, figure 2-8.

Taper wear can sometimes cause a spongy brake pedal, but barrel wear and bellmouth distortion have no symptoms that are obvious to the driver. These problems can sometimes be spotted by ridges or lips worn into the drum friction surface; other times, unusual wear patterns on the brake linings will reveal the problem.

You can also identify these wear patterns by measuring the drum inside diameter at several points across the friction surface. A drum micrometer cannot reach deeply enough into the drum to make these measurements, so you must use an inside micrometer instead.

Position the inside micrometer in the drum and take three measurements, one at the open edge of the drum, one at the center of the friction surface, and one at the closed edge of the drum, figure 2-9. If the highest and lowest of these measurements vary by more than 0.006 inch (0.15 mm), machine the drum. Replace the drum if machining will not leave the inside diameter at least 0.030 inch (0.75 mm) smaller than the discard diameter.

Out-of-Round Drum Distortion

The diameter of an out-of-round drum varies when measured at several points around its circumference. This causes a pulsating brake pedal, brake vibration, and sometimes, grabby, erratic braking. To check for an out-of-round drum, use a brake drum micrometer to measure the drum inside diameter at four

locations 45 degrees apart from one another, figure 2-10. If the highest and lowest measurements vary by more than 0.006 inch (0.15 mm), correct by machining the drum. Remember, final diameter must be 0.030 inch (0.75 mm) smaller than discard diameter.

Eccentric Drum Distortion

Eccentric brake drum distortion exists when the geometric center of the friction surface is different from that of the hub. This makes the drum rotate with a cam-like motion, which causes the shoe contact pads on the backing plate to wear and creates noise whenever the brakes are applied. Since eccentric drum distortion does not affect inside diameter, it cannot be detected visually or with common measuring tools. This condition is identified while a drum is being turned on a lathe and the tool bit contacts the friction surface on only one side of the drum.

BRAKE DRUM MACHINING

Brake drum machining, also called turning, uses a brake lathe and a carbide tool bit to remove metal from the friction surface of the drum, figure 2-11. Turning can repair most forms of wear, damage, and distortion. When turning a drum, only remove the minimum amount of metal necessary to restore the friction surface. This helps ensure the longest possible service life for the drum.

A5

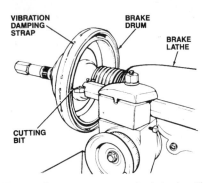

Fig. 2-11. The turning process uses a tool-steel cutting bit to remove metal from the friction surface as the drum rotates on a brake lathe.

In the past when drum brakes were used on the front wheels, it was important to always machine both sides to the same diameter to keep braking force and fade resistance equal from side to side, thus preventing brake pull. Modern vehicles, however, have drums at the rear only, where pulling is much less of a concern. Therefore, it is no longer considered necessary to machine a new drum to the diameter of the worn drum on the other side.

While it is not the function of this study guide to instruct you in the exact procedures required by every brake lathe available, a few guidelines are generally agreed upon within the industry:

- Lathe arbor runout should not exceed .001 in.
- The tool bit should be sharp and properly shaped.
- The feed should be slow.
- Do not take one deep cut. Instead, take enough smaller ones to eliminate the scoring.

BRAKE SHOE REPLACEMENT

The thickness of the lining material is the main factor that determines whether brake shoes should be replaced. The brake shoe friction linings must be at least 0.030 inch (0.75 mm) above the lining table or rivet heads, figure 2-12.

Brake shoes are sold and serviced as axle sets. An axle set consists of four shoes; one pair for the friction assembly at each wheel. Shoes from different manufacturers should never be mixed. Although they will fit and may appear the same, the friction coefficients of the linings may be quite different. Even if only one shoe of an axle set is badly worn, the entire set should be replaced after the problem causing uneven wear has been repaired.

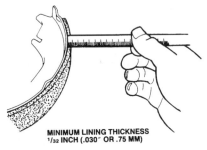

Fig. 2-12. Measure the thickness of the brake shoe friction lining with a machinist scale to determine wear.

The exact procedure used to replace a set of brake shoes varies with the design of the friction assembly and the hardware used to mount and activate shoes. The sections below describe a general procedure that includes the common operations required to disassemble, inspect, and reassemble drum brakes.

Drum Brake Disassembly

The order in which the many parts of the friction assembly are disassembled varies from one brake to another. However, once the drum is removed, removing the shoe return springs is often the next step. Avoid injury by always wearing eye protection when removing and installing springs.

Springs that hook over an anchor post are removed with a special brake spring tool, figure 2-13. Place the tool over the post and hook the flange under the end of the spring. Rotate the tool to lever the spring up and off the anchor. Once the springs are free, remove the anchor plate and adjuster cable or linkage, if fitted, from the anchor post.

Return springs that install between two brake shoes can be removed with a pair of brake spring pliers. However, this is often unnecessary because once the shoes are removed from the anchor, they can be collapsed together by hand to release the tension on the shoe-to-shoe spring.

Once the springs are off, remove the brake shoe holddowns. Although most holddown devices can be removed by hand or with common hand tools, there are special tools available that make the job easier, figure 2-14.

After removing the return springs and shoe holddowns, the friction assembly can be lifted free of the backing plate. In most cases, simply reposition the brake shoes as needed so the shoe-to-shoe return springs, automatic adjusting mechanism, and parking brake linkage can be disconnected.

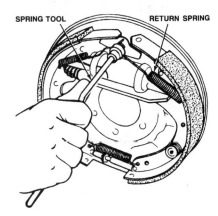

Fig. 2-13. A special brake spring tool is used to lever return springs off the anchor post.

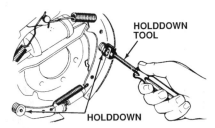

Fig. 2-14. Special tools make removing spring-and-pin brake shoe holddowns easy.

Drum Brake Inspection

Inspect the brake backing plate and its mounting bolts. If the plate is bent or cracked, replace it. If the mounting bolts are loose, tighten them to the torque specification recommended by the manufacturer. Also, check the shoe support pads for grooves, notches, or any other signs of wear. Although minor wear is considered normal, smooth the pads by filing or grinding to provide a good surface for the new shoes to ride on. If the pads are deeply grooved, replace the backing plate. Then, inspect the wheel cylinder as described in the next section.

Most vehicle manufacturers recommend that the shoe return springs, shoe holddown hardware, and automatic adjuster cables be replaced whenever a new set of brake shoes is installed. This is because it is difficult to determine the condition of these parts by inspection.

The automatic adjusting mechanism and parking brake linkage can generally be reused if they pass a visual inspection. To inspect, look for bent components and wear at the points where the parts contact one another. If the brake assembly has **starwheel adjusters**, disassemble the adjuster assembly and clean it thoroughly, figure 2-15. Replace the adjuster if the starwheel teeth are rounded, chipped, or broken. Use a wire brush to clean the adjuster threads, lubricate the threads with brake grease, then assemble the adjuster and thread it through its full range of travel. If the threads bind at any point, repair the problem or replace the adjuster.

Drum Brake Assembly

Drum brake assembly is essentially the reverse of disassembly, making sure that all parts are reinstalled in their proper locations. There are also a few special techniques used to install specific brake components.

To begin, compare the replacement brake shoes to the original equipment parts. They should have the appropriate holes in the **shoe webs**, and the linings should be the same basic size and shape as those on the originals.

Next, determine where the shoes belong on the vehicle. For example, the **primary shoe** on a **dual-servo brake** generally has a smaller lining than the **secondary shoe**, and the friction materials used for the two linings may differ as well.

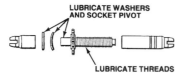

LUBRICATE WASHERS
AND SOCKET PIVOT

LUBRICATE THREADS

Fig. 2-15. Disassemble, clean, and inspect starwheel adjusters. If they pass inspection, they can be lubricated, assembled, and reinstalled.

Always install the primary shoe so it is pulled away from the anchor when the brakes are applied, with the wheel turning in the direction of forward rotation. Some leading-trailing brakes are also designed to use shoes that have different friction characteristics. In these applications, install the replacement shoes in the same relative locations as the original equipment parts.

Remove any parking brake linkage pieces or similar parts from the old shoes. Transfer these parts to the appropriate replacement shoes and install them using new fasteners. Lubricate the shoe support pads on the backing plate with a thin coat of high-temperature brake grease, figure 2-16. Avoid excess lubrication, as grease liquifies at high temperatures. If too much grease is applied, it can run and be absorbed by the friction material, which results in braking problems.

Assemble the shoes onto the backing plate. The procedure varies with the design of the friction assembly; basically, reposition the shoes as needed until the parking brake linkage, brake adjuster, and the shoes themselves are all fitted together in their proper positions.

Once the shoes are assembled in position, install the holddowns to secure the shoes in place. On pin and spring holddowns, insert the pin through the holes in the backing plate and brake shoe web. Then, while holding the pin in place from the backside of the backing plate, use the special tool to compress the spring and retaining washer over the end of the pin. Rotate the washer as needed to lock it onto the flattened end of the pin. Where a spring clip is used with a holddown pin, compress the clip by hand and slip it into position under the flattened end of the pin. To install a coil-spring "beehive" holddown, hold the retaining clip in place from the backside

A5

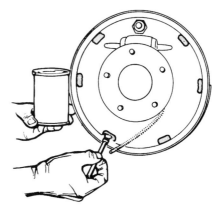

Fig. 2-16. Apply a thin coat of high-temperature brake grease to the shoe contact pads on the backing plate.

Dual-servo Brake: A drum brake that uses servo action to increase apply force. The wheel cylinder pistons push out against the top of both shoes. The primary (leading) shoe moves in the forward direction with the drum, and helps wedge the secondary (trailing) shoe against the drum.
Primary Shoe: The shoe in a servo brake that transfers a portion of its stopping power to the secondary shoe.
Secondary Shoe: The shoe in a servo brake that receives extra application force from the primary shoe. The lining of a secondary shoe is larger than that of the primary shoe because it does most of the braking.
Shoe Web: The portion of the brake shoe below the lining table that receives the application force from the wheel cylinder.
Starwheel Adjuster: In a typical Bendix-style drum brake, a threaded expanding assembly that sets shoe-to-drum clearance when its serrated wheel is turned either manually or by a self-adjusting mechanism.

of the backing plate, then use a Phillips screwdriver to push the spring inward, engaging its hook into the retaining clip.

The final step in drum brake assembly is to install the shoe return springs. It is very important to install the return springs facing in the proper direction and in the correct location.

Some springs can be installed only one way, and their proper position is easy to identify. Different paint colors are often used to distinguish similar springs that have different tensions. Certain springs have a longer straight section and attachment hook at one end than other. These springs must be installed facing a specific direction, or the coiled section of the spring will interfere with another part of the friction assembly. Sometimes, there are several holes in the shoe web where a spring can be attached. If you install a spring in the wrong hole, it will affect the rate at which the brake shoes apply and release.

Return springs are installed in two basic ways, and both methods require a special tool. To install a spring that fits over an anchor post, attach the appropriate end of the spring into the hole in the shoe web. Then, place the notched end of the spring tool on the anchor post, and drape the hook end of the spring over the tool shaft, figure 2-17. Take care not to over-stretch the spring as you lever the tool back, so the spring slides down the shaft and into place on the anchor.

Shoe-to-shoe return springs are installed using brake spring pliers, figure 2-18. Fit one end of the spring into the correct hole in the brake shoe web and place the other end of the spring over the hooked arm of the brake spring pliers. Position the pliers over the shoe the spring is to be attached to so that the pointed arm of the plier contacts the lining at the same level as the hole the spring is to engage. If possible, position the pointed arm on a lining rivet. Otherwise, position it directly on the lining and use extra caution to prevent damage. Squeeze the handle of the pliers to stretch the spring to the appropriate length, then insert the end of the spring into the hole in the web. Remove the plier, and make sure both ends of the spring are fully engaged in the web holes.

Wheel Cylinder Inspection

Grasp the wheel cylinder and attempt to move it. If any movement is detected, make sure all of the mounting hardware is in place and properly tightened. Some import vehicles have wheel cylinders that slide into a slot on the backing plate. These cylinders are designed to move, so simply make sure the mounting clips are present and properly installed. The dust boot that seals the slot must be in good condition.

Inspect the outside of the wheel cylinder for leaks. Minor stains caused by fluid seepage are considered normal. Fold back the cylinder dust boots and look for liquid. If you find more than a slight amount of dampness, rebuild or replace the cylinder.

Next, check for free movement of the wheel cylinder pistons. With the brake drum from only a single wheel removed, have an assistant gently apply and release the brake pedal while you verify that both brake shoes move outward and return smoothly to their stops. On brakes without piston stops, use two large screwdrivers to make sure the pistons are not pushed out of the cylinder bore. Insert the tips of the screwdrivers under the lip at the edge of the backing plate, then lever the screwdriver shafts against the brake shoes to prevent them from moving outward too far.

On some brake designs, a frozen wheel cylinder piston can prevent one or both of the brake shoes from applying. A sticking piston that slows or prevents full return of the brake shoes will cause the brakes to drag, resulting in rapid lining wear and possibly brake fade.

Wheel Cylinder Service

Many wheel cylinders can be taken apart, internally inspected, and rebuilt while they are still mounted on the backing plate. Disassemble a wheel cylinder simply by removing the shoe links and the rubber boots from the ends of the cylinder. Then, press out the pistons, cup seals, spring, and cup expanders, figure 2-19. Inspect, hone, and measure the bore of a wheel cylinder using the same techniques detailed in chapter one for servicing a master cylinder.

Initial Brake Adjustment

Once the brake is assembled, adjust the initial lining-to-drum clearance so the brake pedal travel will be satisfactory. With starwheel brake adjusters, initial adjustment is usually done before the drum is installed.

Both manual and automatic starwheel brake adjusters make their adjustments in very small increments. If you attempt to adjust the brakes manually after the drum is installed, a considerable number of adjuster clicks may be required to get the proper clearance. This is both tiring and time consuming. When you make the initial adjustment before you install the drum, final manual adjustment will be quick and easy, or you

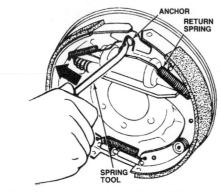

Fig. 2-17. Using a brake spring tool to install a return spring on an anchor post.

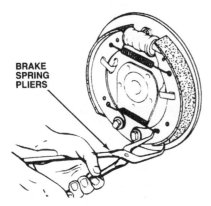

Fig. 2-18. Brake spring pliers are used to install shoe-to-shoe return springs.

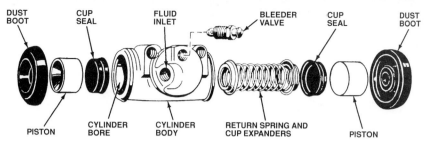

Fig. 2-19. Once the dust boots are removed, most wheel cylinders can be disassembled, inspected, and serviced without removing them from the vehicle.

can use the automatic adjusters to make the final adjustment during the test drive.

To perform the initial adjustment, place a shoe setting caliper inside the brake drum and slide the tool back and forth as you spread the jaws until they span the drum at its widest point, figure 2-20. Then, tighten the lock screw to fix the caliper at this setting. Depending on the brand of tool being used, the opening on the opposite side of the caliper is now set to either equal the drum diameter or at approximately 0.020 inch (0.50 mm) smaller than the drum diameter, providing a clearance of 0.010 inch (0.25 mm) between the drum and each brake shoe.

Remove the caliper from the drum and place the open side over the brake shoes, figure 2-21. If the caliper opening matches the drum diameter, rotate the starwheel adjuster as needed until there is approximately 0.020 inch (0.50 mm) clearance between the caliper opening and the shoes at their widest point. If the caliper setting includes the desired lining-to-drum

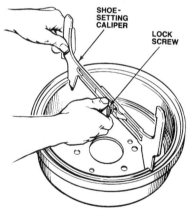

Fig. 2-20. Fit the shoe setting caliper inside the brake drum and adjust it to fit the widest, inside diameter of the drum.

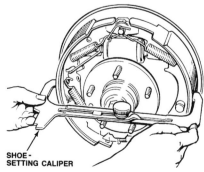

Fig. 2-21. Transfer the drum diameter to the shoes by fitting the opposite jaws of the caliper over the brake friction assembly.

clearance, rotate the starwheel adjuster as needed until the caliper just slides over the shoes at their widest point. Hold the automatic adjuster pawl out of the way while turning the starwheel so it does not become burred. On brakes with dual starwheel adjusters, rotate each starwheel an equal amount.

BRAKE DRUM INSTALLATION

Fixed Drum
The procedure for installing a fixed drum is a very general procedure. Most drum installations are the same, but depending on what vehicle you are working on, the bearing adjustment procedure may be different. In any case, a factory service manual should be consulted for bearing adjustment.

Wheel bearings should be inspected and lubricated as necessary. This is outlined in Chapter 6. Clean the spindle and install a thin coat of wheel bearing grease. Install the brake drum with wheel bearings to the spindle. Install the washer and adjusting nut and tighten finger tight. Tighten the nut while rotating the drum. This will seat the bearings. Loosen the adjusting nut. Tighten the adjusting nut to specifications. Since each application will be different, a factory service manual should be consulted for tightening specifications. Install the adjusting nut retainer, then the cotter pin. Bend ends of the cotter pin around the retainer flange. Ensure the drum rotates freely, then install the grease cap.

Floating Drum
Install the drum to the hub making sure that reference marks made during removal are aligned.

WHEEL SERVICE
Wheel removal and installation are often overlooked aspects of brake service. If wheels are not *removed* and *installed* properly, several problems can result. Some of these include:

- Shortened wheel life
- Premature failure of wheel studs
- Shortened life of wheel hub and bearing
- Warpage of drums and rotors

Never use lubricants or penetrating fluids on wheel studs, nuts, or mounting surfaces. This can raise the actual torque on the nut without a corresponding reading on the torque wrench. Always ensure that wheel studs and nuts are clean and dry. Use of threadlock, sealant, lubricant, paint, or corrosion inhibitor will affect fastener torque and joint clamping force, thereby affecting actual wheel nut torque.

A5

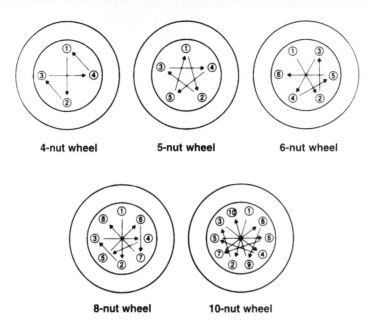

Fig. 2-22. Wheel nut tightening sequence.

Removal

When removing wheels, never use heat to loosen a seized wheel nut. This could damage the wheel and wheel bearings.

1. Raise and support the vehicle.
2. Remove the wheel center cap if equipped.
3. Remove the wheel nut caps if equipped.
4. Place alignment marks on the wheel and hub for installation reference.
5. Remove the wheel nuts. If the wheel is difficult to remove, install two lug nuts, then tap the tire side wall using a suitable mallet.
6. If the wheel is still difficult to remove, perform the following steps:

   a. Install and tighten all wheel nuts.
   b. Loosen each wheel nut two turns on the affected wheel.
   c. Lower the vehicle.
   d. Manually rock the vehicle from side to side.
   e. Drive the vehicle forward slightly, then apply the brakes firmly and quickly.
   f. Drive the vehicle backward slightly, then apply the brakes firmly and quickly.
   g. Repeat procedure if necessary.

7. Repeat from step one after wheels are loose from mounting surface.

Installation

Before installation of the wheels, ensure that no penetrating oil is present on vertical surfaces between the wheel and its mounting surface. Remove any corrosion from wheel mounting surfaces using a suitable wire brush. Also ensure that wheel nuts and studs are clean and dry. Never install anti-seize compound to lug nuts or studs unless directed to do so by OEM service literature. Lastly, always follow the proper tightening sequence and tighten lug nuts to specifications. Failure to follow these guidelines when installing wheels may result in damage to mounting components, poor brake system performance and/or the wheel separating from its mounting surface while the vehicle is being driven.

1. Remove any corrosion or foreign material from wheel and hub mounting surfaces.
2. Clean threads on wheel studs and wheel nuts.
3. Install the wheel, making sure that reference marks made during removal are aligned.
4. Install the wheel nuts. Tighten to specification using a suitable torque wrench in one of the sequences shown in figure 2-22.
5. Install the wheel nut caps if equipped.
6. Install the wheel center cap if equipped.
7. Lower the vehicle.

CHAPTER QUESTIONS

1. Technician A says that a low pedal complaint may be due to inoperative drum brake self-adjusters. Technician B says that a low pedal complaint may be due to weak shoe return springs. Who is right?
   a. A only
   b. B only
   c. Both A and B
   d. Neither A nor B

2. A leaky wheel cylinder can cause:
   a. Grabbing
   b. Loss of stopping power
   c. A grunting or groaning noise when the brakes are applied
   d. All of the above

3. Technician A says that if wheel cylinder pistons are seized in the extend position, the brake will fail to retract completely, causing a dragging condition, overheating, and premature lining/drum wear. Technician B says that seized rear drum brake wheel cylinder pistons will cause a low pedal condition. Who is right?
   a. A only
   b. B only
   c. Both A and B
   d. Neither A nor B

4. Pulsation or shudder during braking may be caused by:
   a. Weak drum brake shoe return springs
   b. A cracked drum
   c. Bellmouthed drum wear
   d. A seized starwheel adjuster

5. Drums should be visually inspected for all of the following **EXCEPT**:
   a. Hard spots
   b. An out-of-round condition
   c. Scoring
   d. Cracks

6. Which of the following is **NOT** used to hold floating drums in place?
   a. Speed nuts
   b. Bolts threaded into the hub
   c. The wheel and lug nuts
   d. A large nut that preloads the wheel bearing

7. Fixed drums are held in place by:
   a. Speed nuts
   b. Bolts threaded into the hub
   c. A large nut that preloads the wheel bearing
   d. The wheel and lug nuts

8. Technician A says that brake drums should always be replaced if they are cracked. Technician B says that brake drums should be reinstalled on the wheel opposite from where they were removed. Who is right?
   a. A only
   b. B only
   c. Both A and B
   d. Neither A nor B

9. Which of the following **CANNOT** be measured with an inside micrometer?
   a. Drum inside diameter
   b. Drum taper, barrel, and bellmouth distortion
   c. Out-of-round distortion
   d. Eccentric drum distortion

10. Technician A says that the shoe with the shorter lining is the primary and should be installed at the rear of the assembly. Technician B says that the shoe with the longer lining is the primary and should be installed at the rear of the assembly. Who is right?
    a. A only
    b. B only
    c. Both A and B
    d. Neither A nor B

11. When assembling a drum brake, apply high-temperature brake grease to the:
    a. Contact pads on the backing plate
    b. Shoe webs
    c. Parking brake cables
    d. Return spring anchors

12. Set the initial brake adjustment with a:
    a. Shoe setting caliper
    b. Brake micrometer
    c. Screw driver after the drum is installed
    d. Torque wrench

A5

CHAPTER OBJECTIVES

- The technician will complete the ASE task list on Disc Brake Diagnosis and Repair.
- The technician will be able to answer 10 questions dealing with the Disc Brake Diagnosis and Repair section of the ASE A5 ASE test.

There are three main categories of disc brake service: pad replacement, caliper overhaul, and rotor machining or replacement. Although it is impossible to determine what repairs are needed until the brake assemblies are inspected, a preliminary road test can help pinpoint problems.

During the road test, listen for noises and note any pedal pulsation or vehicle pulling when applying the brakes. Noises can indicate brake pad problems among other things; pedal pulsation results from rotor damage; and pulling is due to uneven brake application, which can be caused by a number of things.

DISC BRAKE DIAGNOSIS

Brake Drag

Brake drag is a condition that can be caused by several conditions. These include binding or sticking disc brake caliper pistons, binding caliper slides, parking brake not properly adjusted, or hydraulic system concerns. Hydraulic causes of brake drag are described later in this chapter.

Brake Lockup

Brake lockup can occur for a variety of reasons. Some of these include condensation on brake pads, incorrect tire pressure, worn tires, glazed pads, grease or fluid on pads, or a faulty proportioning valve. A thorough inspection of the vehicle is needed in the case of brake lockup.

Brake Noise

Keep in mind that there are some brake noises that are widely considered normal and not a cause for brake service. Such noises include an intermittent squeal or groan when brakes are applied. Sometimes these noises occur only during the first few brake applications in the morning; however, they may be heard at any time while braking. These noises are usually aggravated by different conditions such as cold, heat, moisture, road dust, salt or mud. The following noises *do not* indicate a need for service:

- Clicking noise during ABS stops. This noise is usually heard from the ABS pump motor and valves.
- Morning squeal. This noise is usually caused by low rotor and pad temperatures and goes away once the pads and rotors are warmed up. If the condition cannot be duplicated after warm-up and does not affect brake performance, it does not require service.
- Groan when creeping. If you hear this noise, simply inspect the pads for wear and service as necessary. If pads are not worn out, it does not affect performance or safety. This condition will occur if the vehicle is stopped and the driver slowly releases the brake pedal, allowing the vehicle to move along slowly.
- Wire brush noise. This noise usually occurs with light braking after the brakes have been replaced. It is caused by new rotors and linings not being "broken in." Normally this noise will go away within 100 stops.

If you hear a continuous grinding, pad noise, moaning or continuous squeal coming from the brakes, immediate service is required. Inspect the following components at each wheel for wear, damage, or improper installation:

- Pads and pad insulators
- Anti-rattle springs and clips
- Calipers and slide mechanisms
- Return springs (parking brake)

Some common disc brake noises that require immediate service are outlined as follows:

- Clunking noise. This can be caused from pads that were not properly fitted to the caliper, a loose caliper bracket, or a loose caliper.
- Squealing noise during stopping. This may be the result of an improper disc finish, poor pad isolation, troublesome lining formulations, or the wear indicators contacting the rotor surface, figure 3-1.
- Grinding noise. This could indicate that the pad lining material is worn out. When the rivets or the steel backing of the pad make contact with the rotor, damage to the rotor will occur.

HYDRAULIC SYSTEM DIAGNOSIS

Disc brake hydraulic problems typically involve either leakage or an internal hydraulic problem such as a blockage. Leakage will usually appear as wetness around or under the piston dust boot. Sometimes, leakage may not appear evident unless the brakes are under pressure. Other possible sources are a loose or corroded bleeder screw, a damaged piston seal, or a cracked caliper. Symptoms of leakage will be a low brake pedal, poor stopping, rapidly-falling fluid level in the reservoir, and

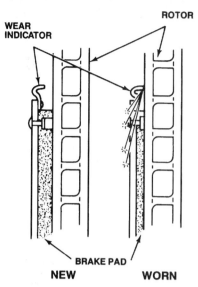

Fig. 3-1. Brake wear indicators make a "chirping" noise to notify the driver when the friction material is worn and the pads need replacement.

possibly pulling to one side during braking caused by fluid contamination of the linings. Identification of the problem will require a careful visual examination.

Another problem that can be caused by the hydraulic system is brake dragging. This could be the result of trapped hydraulic pressure in the system. It is typically caused by crimped lines and hoses or internal deterioration of the hoses. If a crimped line is found, the line should be replaced.

If internal deterioration of a rubber hose is found to be the problem, always replace the hose instead of trying to clear the blockage.

To check for trapped hydraulic pressure, determine which wheel is dragging by raising the vehicle on a hoist and spinning each wheel by hand. Working from the master cylinder to the caliper or wheel cylinder, loosen line and hose connections until the residual pressure is released.

MECHANICAL DIAGNOSIS

Disc brake mechanical problems will usually involve a seized caliper piston, worn parts or calipers that do not move properly on their slides. Each of these problems can be found by doing a thorough visual inspection.

A seized caliper piston will typically show up as hard pulling to the opposite side during brake application. Also, the opposite side brake linings will wear out prematurely. If more than one caliper is seized, poor stopping will result as well. In cases where you suspect such a failure, raise the car and support it safely, then rotate each wheel by hand as you have an assistant slowly apply the brakes. If you can continue to

rotate the wheels while pressure is maintained on the brake pedal, it is likely that the caliper piston on that side is seized. Repair or replace the caliper if you find that the piston is seized.

With typical single-piston calipers, a common mechanical problem is uneven pad wear. Lack of the sliding or floating action that transfers clamping force from the cylinder side of the caliper to the other side results in uneven pad wear and in some cases can result in low or spongy pedal. If the piston is not moving properly on its slides, inspect slides for damage, then disassemble, lubricate, and assemble properly. These procedures are discussed later in this chapter.

Rear disc brakes with integral parking brake mechanisms commonly cause a low-pedal condition when the self-adjustment components become sluggish or seize up altogether, or if the driver does not regularly use the parking brake. This will also result in poor stopping power and accelerated front brake wear, as the rear brakes will not be doing their fair share of the work. If the parking brake mechanism is not functioning properly, repair or replace the caliper as necessary. Often the parking brake mechanism is integral to the caliper and cannot be serviced separately.

BRAKE ROUGHNESS

Pedal pulsation, vibration and brake roughness are common disc brake complaints. Most often, these complaints are due to defects in the disc itself—runout, **rotor thickness variation**, excessive lateral runout, excessive disc thickness variation, **lining material transfer**, rotor corrosion, or cracks. To isolate where the pulsation is coming from, coast at low speed on an uncrowded roadway, hold the steering wheel lightly with your fingers, and apply the brakes gently. If the steering wheel shudders back and forth, the front brakes are at fault.

Rotor lateral runout occurs when the spindle and hub are not parallel to each other, figure 3-2. It is usually not felt in a **sliding caliper** system, and keep in mind that this condition will lead to disc thickness variation. Runout or rotor warpage may be caused by excessive heat, overtorquing lug nuts, or improper mounting of components.

A5

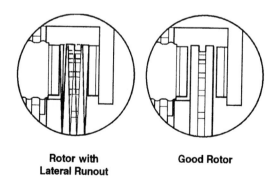

Fig. 3-2. Disc brake rotor lateral runout.

Lining Material Transfer: A condition where lining material becomes attached to the rotor. This is a normally occurring condition, but in some cases, the transfer can be uneven or excessive.
Rotor Lateral Runout: Lateral runout is a side-to-side movement of the rotor as it turns.
Rotor Thickness Variation: Rotor thickness variation is a variance in thickness at different places around the rotor braking surface.
Sliding Caliper: A two-piece brake caliper consisting of a body and anchor plate. The anchor plate rigidly attaches to the vehicle suspension, and the body slides on machined ways to bring the pads into contact with the rotor.

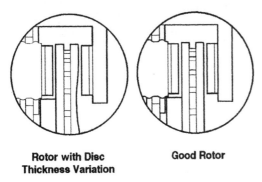

Rotor with Disc Thickness Variation   **Good Rotor**

Fig. 3-3. Comparison between a rotor with excessive disc thickness variation and a normal rotor.

Disc thickness variation occurs when the rotor thickness is not the same all the way around the rotor, figure 3-3. Lateral runout will cause thickness variation when the rotor contacts the brake pad without the brakes being applied as the vehicle is being driven. Eventually the pad will wear the high spot off, causing a thin spot to be worn into the rotor. Other causes of thickness variation are pads that do not move properly on their slides or a sticking caliper. When thickness variation becomes bad enough, it may be felt in both the brake pedal and steering wheel. The condition will usually worsen as the rotor gets hot.

Lining material transfer is a condition where lining material becomes attached to the rotor. This is a normally occurring condition, but in some cases the transfer can be uneven or excessive. This creates an uneven friction surface on the rotor. The brake pads will tend to grab where material has transferred to the rotor, and this is felt in the steering wheel and in the vehicle. If runout and thickness variation are within specifications and roughness complaints are still present, lining material transfer could be the cause.

Rotor corrosion may occur on vehicles that are not driven for long periods of time. The pad material may remove the corrosion when the vehicle is driven; however, some pads may remove corrosion better than others. If all corrosion is not removed, thickness variation or excessive lining material transfer could occur. In this case, thickness variation is caused when the area under the pad is not as corroded as the rest of the rotor.

To correct any of the brake roughness complaints described here, machine or replace rotors as necessary. Rotor service procedures including removal, inspection, machining, and installation are included in this chapter.

ROTOR SERVICE

Removal

Rotors may be of the fixed type made in one piece with the wheel hub, as is found on a typical rear wheel-drive vehicle, or may be of the floating variety, a separate unit that is held against the hub by the wheel and its lugs, and perhaps additional screws or bolts. Many Asian front wheel-drive vehicles have **captive rotors**. These are integral with the hub and require special pullers and procedures for removal. On-car brake lathes provide the most practical means of machining captive rotors. The removal and installation procedures here are for the more common types of rotor, the fixed or floating. Also keep in mind that some rotors are specific to the side of the vehicle that they are installed on. As a general precaution, mark rotors before they are removed to avoid installing them on the wrong side.

1. Inspect fluid in the master cylinder. If the retraction of brake caliper pistons will cause fluid overflow, remove an appropriate amount of fluid using a suitable tool.
2. Raise and support the vehicle, then remove wheels.
3. Retract the caliper piston using a suitable c-clamp or other tool.
4. On models equipped with a caliper bracket, remove the caliper bracket bolts, then the caliper with bracket. Support the caliper and bracket using suitable mechanics wire.
5. On models without a caliper bracket, remove the caliper attaching bolts, then the caliper. Support the caliper using suitable mechanics wire.
6. If the rotor is of the floating variety, remove the rotor hold-down screws (if equipped), place an alignment mark on the rotor and hub for installation reference, then remove the rotor.
7. If the rotor is of the fixed variety, proceed as follows:

   • On most 2-wheel-drive models, you will simply have to remove the dust cap, cotter pin, nut retainer, nut, washer, and outer bearing, then the rotor.

   • On many 4-wheel-drive models, the outer hub will need to be disassembled in order to remove the rotor. This procedure will vary depending on the make and model, so consult a factory shop manual when removing 4-wheel-drive **fixed rotors**.

8. If equipped with serviceable wheel bearings, inspect the grease in the hub and on the wheel bearings. If the grease is relatively fresh and in good condition, set the rotor on the bench and cover the outer bearing and hub opening so the bearings will not become contaminated. If the grease is old and dirty, repack the wheel bearings before you reinstall the rotor/hub. Always repack the wheel bearings when performing a complete brake job. Also, if the rotor is machined, the grease seal must be replaced.

Inspection

Brake rotor inspection consists of two parts, a visual inspection followed by one or more careful measurements. A thorough inspection determines if the rotor is in serviceable condition, must be machined to restore its surface, or is beyond saving and must be replaced.

To begin, wipe the rotor surface clean to make it easier to spot problems. Inspect the rotor for problems on the surface, such as:

• Scoring and grooves
• Cracks
• Heat checking
• Hard spots

Captive Rotors: Rotors that are integral with the hub and require special pullers and procedures for removal, as found on many Asian FWD vehicles. On-car brake lathes provide the most practical means of machining captive rotors.

Fixed Rotor: A fixed rotor is one that installs to a spindle and is held in place by wheel bearings, washer, nut, and cotter pin.

Generally, rotors must be resurfaced if scoring and grooves are deeper than 0.010 inch. If cracks are visible, replace the rotor. Minor, localized heat checks can be machined out, but if heat checking is widespread, replace the rotor. As with drums, hard spots are difficult to remove, and most manufacturers recommend replacing rotors that have hard spots.

Brake Rotor Measurement

Brake rotors are measured to identify wear and distortion that are not visually apparent. All types of rotor wear and distortion can be measured using an outside micrometer and a dial indicator.

Rotor Thickness

The first step is to measure rotor thickness with an outside micrometer to check for wear. To begin, note the discard dimension stamped or cast into the rotor. Then, take a micrometer reading 1 inch in from the outer edge of the rotor to measure thickness, figure 3-4. For best results, use a brake micrometer with a pointed anvil that will measure to the bottom of wear grooves. Compare the measured thickness to the discard dimension.

If the rotor thickness is not at least 0.015 to 0.030 inch larger than the rotor discard dimension, replace the rotor. The amount of additional metal required to allow for wear in service varies depending on the manufacturer. Check the shop manual of the vehicle you are servicing for the exact value. If the rotor needs to be turned, there must be sufficient metal remaining, so the thickness will be at least 0.015 to 0.030 inch larger than the discard dimension after machining. Ford Motor Company rotors, and those from some other manufacturers, are marked differently. Replace one of these rotors whenever its thickness is less than the "minimum thickness" stamped or cast into the outside of the rotor, figure 3-5. If you are unsure of what the measurements on a rotor mean, consult a factory shop manual.

Rotor Taper Variation

Rotor taper variation is a difference in thickness across the friction surface of a rotor, figure 3-6. To check for taper variation, use an outside micrometer with a deep frame to measure the rotor thickness at the outer edge just below the ridge. Take a

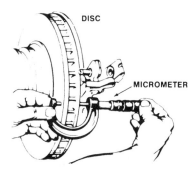

Fig. 3-4. Use an outside micrometer and take a reading approximately 1 inch in from the outer edge to measure rotor thickness.

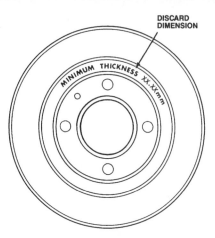

Fig. 3-5. Rotors must be replaced if they measure less than the specified minimum thickness after turning.

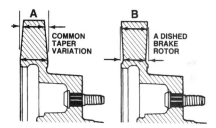

Fig. 3-6. Taper variation is uneven wear across the friction surface of a rotor.

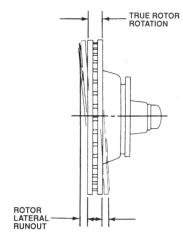

Fig. 3-7. Lateral runout causes a rotor to move from side to side, or wobble, as it rotates.

second measurement at the inner edge of the area swept by the brake pads. Subtract the smaller measurement from the larger one to obtain the taper variation. Repeat these measurements at four points around the rotor. If the variation is greater than 0.003 inch at any point, machine the rotor. A rotor with too much taper will not allow the pads to contact the rotor squarely and can cause the caliper pistons to bind in their bores.

Rotor Lateral Runout

Lateral runout is a side-to-side movement of the rotor as it turns, figure 3-7. Excessive runout can cause brake pedal

---

Rotor Taper Variation: Taper variation is a difference in thickness across the friction surface of a rotor.

pulsations, vibration during braking, and increased brake pedal travel from too much pad knockback. Runout is measured using a dial indicator.

For maximum braking performance, lateral runout should be less than 0.003 inch. However, lateral runout tolerances vary by manufacturer and, depending on the vehicle, anywhere from 0.002 to 0.008 inch may be acceptable. It is only necessary to check lateral runout on one side of the rotor; runout never varies significantly between the two sides.

Check for lateral runout while the rotor is mounted on the vehicle and rotating on the wheel bearings. When making this check, it is very important not to mistake bearing play for lateral runout. Adjustable wheel bearings can be tightened to eliminate play as a factor. With non-adjustable wheel bearings, measure and record bearing play, then subtract it from the final reading on the dial indicator to determine the true runout.

To check the lateral runout of a rotor:

1. Raise and properly support the vehicle so the wheel with the rotor to be checked can turn freely, then remove the wheel.
2. If the vehicle has **floating rotors**, install all the lug nuts and tighten alternately and evenly to specifications in a criss-cross sequence.
3. Either pry the brake pads back, so they do not drag against the rotor, or remove the caliper to access the rotor.
4. Mount a dial indicator so the plunger contacts the rotor at a 90-degree angle about 1 inch from the outer edge, figure 3-8.
5. Rotate the rotor until the lowest reading shows on the indicator dial, then zero the dial.
6. Rotate the rotor until the highest reading shows on the dial; this is the lateral runout with adjustable wheel bearings. With non-adjustable wheel bearings, subtract the bearing play from this figure to find the true lateral runout.

Compare findings to specifications to determine if the rotor can be salvaged or must be replaced. A rotor with runout can be machined and returned to service unless turning reduces it to less than minimum thickness.

Some manufacturers recommend several ways to correct excessive lateral runout. One is to replace the rotor. Other ways include adding correction plates, indexing the rotor, or use of an on-car brake lathe.

The correction plate method involves the addition of a tapered plate between the brake rotor and the hub/axle flange. Correction plates can be used for runout up to .009 inch. The indexing method involves moving the rotor to a different orientation to the hub/axle flange. This method is most effective when runout is out of specifications by a very small amount (.001–.005 inch). The last method involves machining the brake rotors using an on-car brake lathe. An example on-car lathe procedure is described later in this chapter.

Rotor Lack of Parallelism

A rotor that lacks parallelism varies in thickness at different places around its surface, figure 3-9. Often called warpage, lack of parallelism is the most common cause of brake pedal pulsation and also causes braking vibration.

To check for variations in parallelism, use an outside micrometer to measure the rotor thickness at 6 to 12 equally spaced points around the surface. Make all of the measurements at the same distance in from the outer edge of the rotor, so taper variation will not affect the measurements. If the thickness variation between any two points is greater than 0.0005 inch, and there is noticeable brake pedal pulsation, machine the rotor.

Machining

Some carmakers are now recommending that brake rotor machining **not** be done unless there is a pulsation or shudder complaint. During normal pad replacement, the discs should be used as-is providing the rotor meets all specifications. If the rotor does not meet factory specifications, machine or replace as required.

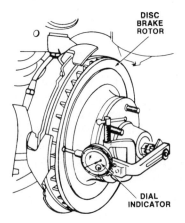

Fig. 3-8. Dial indicator setup to measure rotor lateral runout.

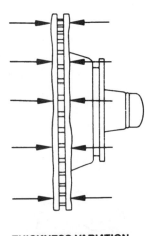

THICKNESS VARIATION AT DIFFERENT POINTS AROUND THE ROTOR

Fig. 3-9. Lack of parallelism, or thickness variation, is the most common cause of brake pedal pulsation.

Floating Rotor: A floating rotor is a separate part that installs onto an axle flange or hub assembly. Floating rotors are generally held in place by the wheel lug nuts or bolts. The rotor does not contain the wheel bearings, which are part of the hub.

It would be impossible to list all instructions for every type of brake lathe in use today, but there are some general guidelines that do apply to all rotor machining:

- Disc brake rotors should only be refinished if they have enough thickness to still be within specifications after refinishing.
- After a rotor has been separated from the hub, clean any rust or contaminants from the hub flange and brake rotor mating surface. Failure to perform this step will result in increased assembled lateral runout.
- Never machine a rotor unless you also machine the rotor at the other side of the same axle an equal amount. This keeps braking force and fade resistance equal from side to side and prevents brake pull.
- Composite rotors, which combine a steel hub "hat" with an iron wear surface, tend to flex during machining, which makes it difficult to hold tolerances and eliminate chatter marks unless heavy lathe adapters that clamp down on the hub are used.
- Even a well-kept lathe may produce a relatively rough directional finish. In the days of asbestos linings, this was acceptable—80–100 RMS was considered fine enough. Today, however, with semi-metallic and ceramic friction material, a very smooth surface on the order of 4060 RMS is required or squealing and rapid wear will result. A non-directional finish should be obtained if machining rotors. Some manufacturers recommend using 120 grit aluminum oxide sandpaper with a lathe finishing tool, or 150 grit aluminum oxide sandpaper with just a sanding block if a lathe finishing tool is not available. If using the lathe finishing tool, always follow the lathe manufacturer's recommended speed setting for applying a non-directional finish.
- Rotors must be washed after machining or hard particles will become embedded in the new linings and cause noise and scoring. Clean the braking surface with denatured alcohol or other approved brake cleaner.

Bench Lathe

When using a bench lathe, first consult the instruction manual that pertains to that particular lathe to ensure proper setup and operation. The following instructions pertain to most lathes and are meant as a general outline as to how to use a bench style lathe.

1. Ensure that rotor mounting surfaces are clean.
2. Mount the rotor to the brake lathe according to the manufacturer's instructions.
3. Attach any necessary vibration dampening attachments to the rotor or lathe.
4. Ensure the bits are not damaged in any way.
5. Replace or rotate bits as necessary.
6. Position cutting bits to the center of the rotor braking surface, ensuring that bits do not contact the rotor surface.
7. If the lathe is equipped to machine drums as well as rotors, ensure that drum feed is not engaged and also ensure that rotor feed is not engaged.
8. Turn the brake lathe on, then adjust the cutting bits until they just contact the rotor.

9. Observe the witness marks made by the bits. If the mark extends approximately ¾ or more around the rotor braking surface, the rotor is mounted properly. If the witness mark is not as just described, remount the rotor to the lathe.
10. Refinish the rotor as outlined under the lathe manufacturer's instructions.
11. After each cut, inspect brake rotor thickness.
12. If the rotor is less than the minimum allowable thickness, replace it.
13. Remove the rotor from the lathe. If it is within specifications, measure the assembled lateral runout as previously described.

On-Car Brake Lathe

In recent years, on-car brake lathes have become a popular alternative to traditional bench-style brake lathes. There are several benefits to using the on-car brake lathe. For one, it allows rotor machining on the vehicle spindle center line, which is the axis of rotation for the rotor. It also stops the stack-up tolerance of related parts from affecting rotor lateral runout. You will find that some bench-style brake lathes may actually induce lateral runout, and instead of machining a rotor to the vehicle spindle center line, it is machined to the centerline of the lathe.

Keep in mind that the cutting bits for the on-car lathe and the bench lathe may not be interchangeable.

There are several brands of on-car brake lathes. The following example will describe use of the Rotunda Pro-Cut On-Car Brake Lathe. Whenever using an on-car lathe, first consult the instruction manual that pertains to that particular lathe to ensure proper setup and operation.

1. Begin setup on the side of the vehicle where the caliper is on the right side of the spindle centerline when facing the vehicle, figure 3-10. This will make lathe setup easier.

A5

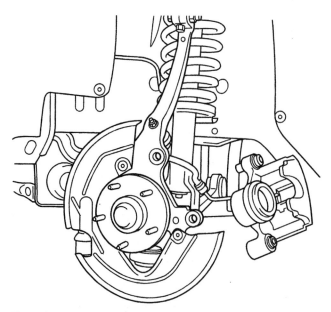

Fig. 3-10. Choosing to setup the on-car brake lathe according to manufacturer's instructions makes setup easier.

2. Select the correct adapter for vehicle application by holding the adapter next to the lug pattern and rotating until one of the predrilled patterns matches the vehicle, figure 3-11. Note that a spacer may be needed.

3. Using the lug nuts supplied with the brake lathe, tighten the adapter to 25–30 ft-lbs. Do not use an impact wrench and do not use the vehicle lug nuts for this procedure.

4. Inspect the cutting bits as follows:

   • Ensure the bits are not damaged in any way.
   • Replace or rotate bits as necessary.
   • Keep in mind that only bits supplied by Rotunda should be used or an improper surface finish could result.

Fig. 3-11. On-car brake lathe adapter selection.

(Rotunda bits are made of a special material and ground to remove chips and provide the proper clearance angle.)

5. Ensure cutting bits are correctly installed.

6. Unscrew all lathe lateral runout screws to ensure that they do not protrude through the lathe plate.

7. Adjust the cutting head back to allow the tool head to clear the rotor when the lathe is being attached to the hub.

8. Attach the lathe to the adapter, figure 3-12:

   • Place lathe so that mounting flange is close to the mating surface on the adapter.
   • The adapter has a dowel pin that must align with one of two holes on the mounting flange.
   • When flange is flush to the adapter, attach shaft of lathe to adapter by rotating large mounting knob.

9. Compensate for lathe runout as follows:

   • Attach a suitable dial indicator to the steering knuckle.
   • Place the dial indicator bit against a flat surface on the outside of the cutting head farthest from the hub, figure 3-13.
   • Tighten the stand handle to prevent lathe from rotating.
   • Pull out feed knob to disengage lathe feed. This will prevent the cutting head from feeding when the motor is in operation.
   • Turn on lathe while observing movement of the dial indicator. Zero the dial indicator.
   • Determine the total needle sweep between the high and low reading on the dial indicator. If the total runout is more than .003 inch, lathe lateral runout must be adjusted. Target range of lathe lateral runout is 0. Maximum is .003 inch.

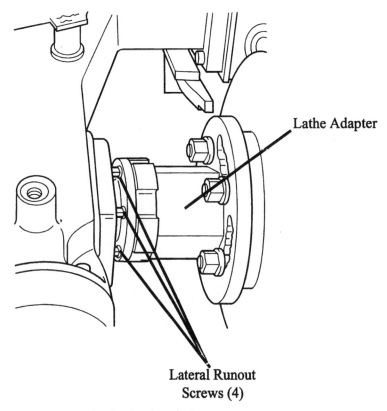

Lathe Adapter

Lateral Runout
Screws (4)

Fig. 3-12. This view shows the brake lathe being fitted to the adapter.

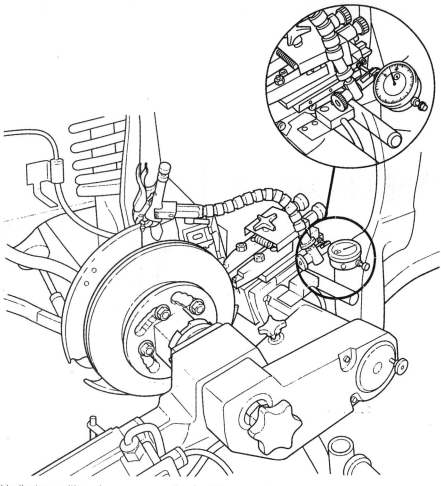

Fig. 3-13. View of dial indicator position when compensating for lathe runout.

- Turn off the lathe. Rotate the mounting flange until the needle reaches its highest point of sweep. (The knob on the back of the motor can be used to manually crank the motor to the highest point.)

- Rotate the lateral runout screw closest to the horizontal position on the side of the hub that is opposite of the cutting head (motor side) so that the needle moves half the distance of the total needle sweep, figure 3-14.

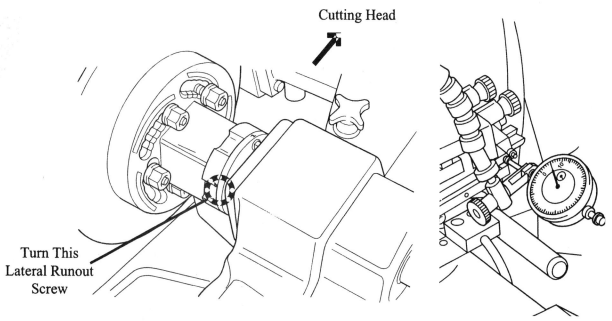

Cutting Head

Turn This Lateral Runout Screw

Fig. 3-14. Lathe lateral runout adjustment.

- If the needle does not move toward the center of the needle sweep as the screw is being turned, you are turning the wrong screw.
- Note the number of lateral runout screws that you turned, then turn on lathe and observe the movement of the dial indicator.
- If runout is still not within specifications, a second lateral runout screw may be adjusted.
- Ensure that the second lateral runout screw is not directly across from the first screw that was turned.

10. Center the cutting head with the brake rotor. Move the cutting head into any of the five holes as necessary. Ensure that metal shavings are cleaned from holes and clean dovetail area when changing the cutting head position.
11. Push the cutting head back into the dovetail until it is square, then tighten the setscrew.
12. Adjust feed knob until the cutting bits clear the edge of the rotor. Loosen the shutoff cam screw, then slide the cam back until it contacts the automatic shutoff switch plunger. Tighten the cam screw.
13. Ensure that the feed knob is in the disengaged position, then turn on lathe.
14. Loosen lock knob on top of the cutting head.
15. Adjust cutting bits until they clear both sides of the rotor.
16. Adjust cutting head until it is at the center of the rotor braking surface.
17. Rotate the adjustment dial until the inner cutting bit touches the rotor. You should be able to hear the bit skimming the rotor.
18. Rotate the adjustment dial until the outer cutting bit touches the rotor.
19. Adjust the feed handle until the cutting bits reach the inner edge of the rotor. Be sure not to contact the rotor hat or damage to the holder plate will result.
20. Adjust bits to desired cutting depth on both sides of the rotor, keeping the following information in mind:
    - Inner side of rotor should be set first, then the outer.
    - The maximum cut depth for each side of the rotor is .008 inch, which would give a total maximum cut of .016 inch for each cut.
    - Do not remove more metal than is needed to clean and true the rotor.
    - The minimum cut for each side is .004 inch for a total maximum cut of .008 inch.
    - A smaller cut causes the bits to get hot and wear out faster. This will result in a poor surface finish.
21. Tighten the lock knob.
22. Install the chip deflector/silencer over the cutting bits.
23. Engage the automatic feed.
24. When the lathe turns off, verify that rotor lateral runout and rotor thickness are within specifications.
25. Clean metal chips before removing the lathe and adapter.
26. Remove lathe and hub adapter from wheel lug nut studs. Clean all remaining metal shavings from adapter and ABS sensor if equipped. Note that special care must be taken to clean metal shavings from exposed 4WD hubs.
27. Repeat procedure on opposite side of the vehicle noting the following:
    - The cutting head is already centered and the automatic stop is already set.
    - Lathe will be turned upside down in order to service opposite side. Remove chip tray, loosen trolley handle and rotate lathe 180 degrees. Reinstall chip tray and tighten handle.
    - Back out lateral runout adjustment screws before attaching hub to adapter.
    - Adjust for lathe runout.

Installation

Some manufacturers recommend applying a high temperature nickel anti-seize lubricant to the inside of the rotor hat to prevent corrosion between the hub and rotor, figure 3-15. If performing this step, be sure to use only factory recommended anti-seize lubricants, apply only a light coat, and ensure that no anti-seize compound comes into contact with stud threads. Keep in mind that if you are installing a new rotor, often you will have to remove a protective coating before installation. Note that some rotors are specific to the side of the vehicle that they are installed on as well.

1. On models with the floating rotor design proceed as follows:
   - Ensure that the rotor mounting surfaces are clean.
   - If rotor retaining bolts or screws are used, consult a factory shop manual to determine if a threadlock is needed.
   - Align reference marks made during removal, then install rotor to hub, then the rotor holddown screws if equipped.
2. On models with the fixed rotor design, proceed as follows:
   - Ensure bearings are properly greased
   - Ensure that a new grease seal is installed.
   - Apply a light coating of grease to the spindle.
   - Install the rotor to the spindle.
   - Consult a factory shop manual for final installation instructions, as installation and adjustment of bearings will vary between manufacturers.
3. Install brake caliper and/or mounting bracket and tighten to factory specifications.
4. Install wheels as outlined later in this chapter.

BRAKE PAD SERVICE

Brake pads are sold and serviced as axle sets, which consist of four pads, the inner and outer pad for the caliper at each wheel. Never mix pads from different manufacturers, as the friction coefficients of the linings may be different, even though they appear the same. If only one pad of an axle set is badly worn, replace the entire set after repairing the problem that caused the uneven wear.

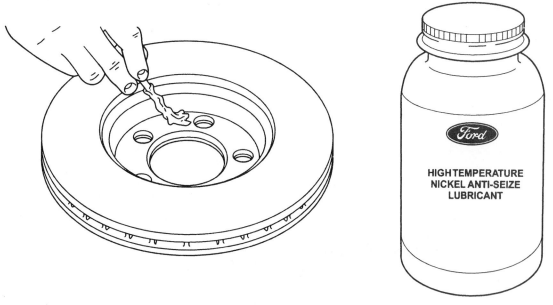

Fig. 3-15. Some manufacturers such as Ford recommend applying anti-seize compound on the rotor to prevent corrosion between the hub and rotor.

Most manufacturers recommend that the bushings, O-rings, retaining bolts, retaining clips, and any other caliper mounting hardware be replaced whenever a new set of brake pads is installed. The exact procedure for replacing a set of brake pads varies with the design of the caliper. However, there are a number of basic steps common to any pad replacement. For caliper removal instructions, refer to the procedures outlined in this chapter.

Keep in mind that on some rear calipers, there are special procedures that need to be followed to retract the piston. Some use an adjusting bolt that will need to be turned in order to retract the piston. On others, a special tool will need to be used to turn the piston back into its bore, figure 3-16. If in doubt, always consult a factory shop manual.

Removal

The first step in replacing brake pads is to remove some of the brake fluid from the master cylinder reservoir with a brake fluid syringe. This makes space for the fluid that will be displaced back into the reservoir when the caliper pistons are bottomed in their bores.

On **fixed calipers**, remove the pad guide pins and retaining spring, then use a pair of pliers to pull the pads straight out of the caliper, figure 3-17. If there is a ridge at the edge of the rotor that prevents a pad from being easily removed, insert a screwdriver between the rotor and pad, and carefully pry the caliper piston back into its bore until there is sufficient clearance to remove the pad.

A5

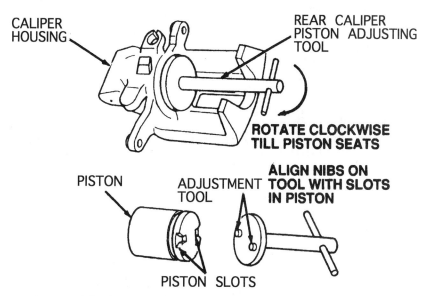

Fig. 3-16. Some calipers require a special tool to retract the piston back into its bore.

Fixed Caliper: A brake caliper that solidly bolts to the vehicle suspension. The caliper does not move when the brakes are applied.

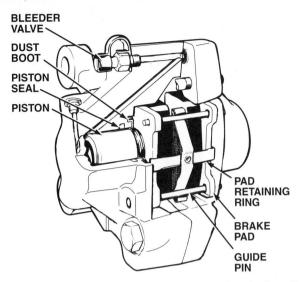

Fig. 3-17. A fixed caliper rigidly mounts to the chassis. Once the guide pins and retaining spring are removed, the pads can be pulled free of the caliper.

Removing the pads from sliding calipers or **floating calipers** generally requires that the movable portion of the caliper be separated or pivoted away from the anchor plate, figure 3-18. Whenever you remove a caliper during brake pad replacement, hang it from the suspension by a wire, so there is no strain on the brake hose that might cause internal or external damage.

Inspection and Cleaning

The thickness of the lining material is the main factor that determines whether the pads should be replaced. The brake pads must be at least 0.030 inch above the pad backing plate or rivet heads, figure 3-19. Measure friction thickness with a machinist scale.

Also, inspect the pads for taper wear, in which the pads are thinner at one end than at the other. Some pad taper wear is normal in floating calipers because the caliper body tends to flex slightly on its mountings. The leading edges of brake pads may also wear faster than the trailing edges because they operate at higher temperatures. However, if there is more than 0.13 inch of taper wear, you should replace the pads and inspect the caliper for possible problems.

Compare the amount of wear on the two pads in each caliper, then compare the amount of pad wear between the two calipers on the same axle. Uneven wear between pads in the same caliper can be caused if the rotor is rough on one side, causing that pad to wear more rapidly. In fixed calipers, a frozen piston will cause uneven wear between the two pads.

All of the pads may not be worn the same amount in sliding or floating calipers because the pad on the piston side usually wears more quickly. However, grossly uneven pad wear occurs in floating and sliding calipers when the mounting hardware rusts or corrodes, causing the caliper to bind as it moves on the guide pins or anchor plate.

Check the friction lining surface for signs of contamination from brake fluid that has leaked past the piston seal and

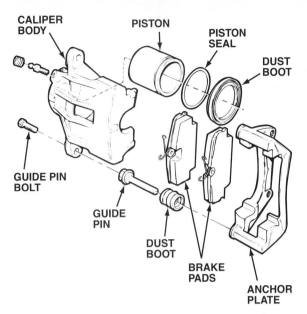

Fig. 3-18. With floating calipers, the anchor plate attaches to the chassis, and the caliper body slides on guide pins connected to the anchor plate as the brakes are applied. To replace the pads, the caliper body must be separated from the anchor plate.

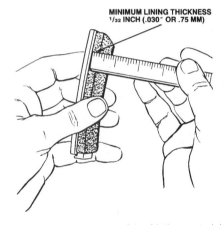

Fig. 3-19. Measure the thickness of the friction material on brake pads to determine if they can be returned to service.

dust boot. Fluid contamination will cause the lining to darken. Brake pads that have been soaked with brake fluid must be replaced.

Inspect the pads for physical damage. Look for large cracks in the lining, loose or missing rivets, a bent backing plate, or a bonded lining that is separating from the backing plate, figure 3-20. If these problems are present, replace the pads.

Installation

Always inspect the brake rotor and the brake caliper, as described in this chapter, before installing new pads. Install the brake pads into the caliper or anchor plate as dictated by the brake design. The pads in fixed calipers slip into place, and a spring retainer on the guide pins prevents the pads from vibrating and causing brake noise. Some designs use shims that

---

Floating Caliper: A two-piece brake caliper consisting of a rigid anchor plate and movable body that compresses the pads as the brakes apply. The caliper body is supported by bushings and O-rings that slide on guide pins and sleeves, which attach to the caliper anchor plate.

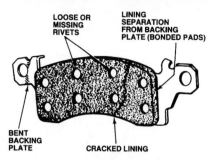

Fig. 3-20. Inspect brake pads for physical damage, such as lining cracks, loose or missing rivets, backing plate distortion, or separation from the backing plate, as well as wear and fluid contamination.

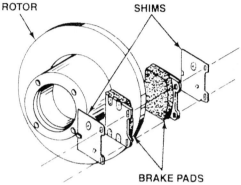

Fig. 3-21. Shims install behind the brake pad backing plates on some vehicles to reduce pad vibration and noise.

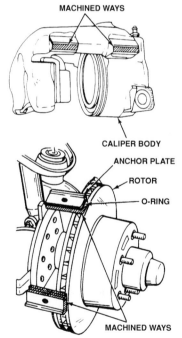

Fig. 3-22. Make sure the machined ways of a sliding caliper are clean and smooth, then lubricate them with a thin coat of high-temperature brake grease.

fit between the caliper pistons and pad backing plates to reduce vibration and noise, figure 3-21. The pads in floating and sliding calipers usually have spring clips or bent tabs on the backing plate that lock them securely into the caliper anchor plate. Antirattle spring clips, of which a number of designs are used, attach to the brake pads or caliper anchor plate to reduce pad vibration and prevent brake noise.

Once the pads are in position, secure them in the appropriate manner. With a fixed caliper, install the guide pins and retaining spring. With a sliding caliper, clean the **ways** and lubricate them using a high-temperature brake grease, figure 3-22. Then, position the caliper body onto the ways over the rotor, and install the retaining hardware. With a floating caliper, lightly coat the caliper bushings and mounting bolts or guide pins with high-temperature brake grease, then position the caliper body over the rotor. Install the mounting bolts and tighten all fasteners to specified torque.

CALIPER SERVICE

Removal

If working on an unfamiliar design, service one side at a time so you can use the other side as a model for reassembly. When removing calipers, make sure that the master cylinder does not run dry. Hoses should be plugged to prevent this from happening. It should also be noted that the procedures given here are meant as a general guide. A factory service manual should always be consulted for specific make and model applications.

1. Inspect fluid in the master cylinder. If the retraction of brake caliper pistons will cause fluid overflow, remove an appropriate amount of fluid using a suitable tool.
2. Raise and support the vehicle, then remove the wheels.
3. Open the caliper bleeder screw to prevent contaminated fluid from being forced up into the hydraulic system when the piston is bottomed (especially important with ABS). Attach a suitable small-diameter hose to the bleeder screw and run it into a jar or bottle to prevent fluid spillage.
4. If the bleeder screw is seized and all attempts to free it fail, the caliper must be replaced. It is sensible to find this out before inspecting the caliper further.
5. Using a C-clamp of sufficient size to span the distance between the back of the outboard pad and the back of the caliper cylinder, compress the piston into its bore all the way, figure 3-23. Alternately, you can pull or pry the caliper outward to compress the piston. Some models require the use of a special tool to turn the piston back into the bore. Other models require you to turn an adjustment screw or bolt to retract the piston.

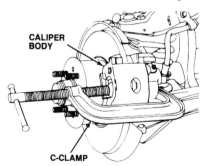

Fig. 3-23. Using a C-clamp to bottom the piston of a single-piston sliding caliper.

Ways: Polished, machined surfaces that permit movement between two metal parts. Ways machined into the anchor plate and caliper body provide a sliding surface for the caliper.

6. Remove the brake hydraulic hose from the caliper and allow any excess fluid to drain into a suitable container. Plug the hose to prevent fluid loss and contamination. Many brake hydraulic hoses use copper washers to seal the connection. Make sure these are removed and discarded.

7. Disconnect any brackets that may be attached to the caliper.

8. Remove the caliper attaching bolts, then the caliper. When removing rear calipers, it may be necessary to disconnect the parking brake cables from the caliper before removal.

9. Remove the old pads and any shims or antirattle springs that are present, carefully noting their position.

10. Check for evidence of fluid leakage around the piston dust boot, then carefully examine the caliper housing for cracks and corrosion or heavy wear on the sliding ways.

11. On rigidly mounted calipers having two or four pistons, pad extraction is usually a matter of prying the pistons away from the rotor, removing guide pins, then pulling the pads out through the open area of the caliper, figure 3-17.

Disassembly

Piston Removal

Various means can be employed to extract caliper pistons. It should be noted that on some rear caliper applications, the piston actually threads into the caliper bore. If this is the case, a special tool will be required to remove the piston, figure 3-16. Other applications require you to turn an adjustment bolt or screw to remove the piston.

If the caliper is still connected to the brake hose, the system's hydraulic pressure can be used. Insert wooden blocks into the calipers between the pistons and caliper bodies to prevent the pistons from coming completely out of their bores. Place drain pans under the calipers to catch brake fluid in the event a piston does come out of its bore. Slowly apply the brake pedal to force the pistons from their bores.

Another common method is to use compressed air. Sufficient pressure is available in most shops to remove all but severely frozen pistons. Use extreme caution when removing caliper pistons in this manner. Clamp the caliper in a vise by its mounting flange. Insert a wooden block or bundle of shop towels between the piston and caliper body to prevent damage to the piston when it comes out of the caliper bore, figure 3-24. Remove the bleeder valve and place a rubber-tipped air nozzle into the caliper fluid inlet. Make sure to keep your fingers clear. Then, slowly apply air pressure to force the piston out of the bore. Use the minimum amount of pressure necessary.

Special tools are available to grip and mechanically remove brake caliper pistons. If, however, neither the hydraulic nor pneumatic methods of removal work on a particular case, chances are that the bore is too corroded to be successfully overhauled.

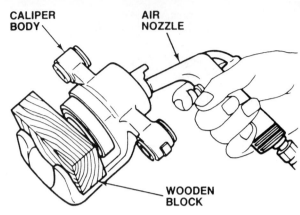

Fig. 3-24. A wooden block helps prevent damage when compressed air is used to remove a caliper piston from its bore.

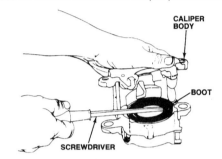

Fig. 3-25. Take care to avoid scratching the bore when using a screwdriver to remove a piston dust boot that is press fit into the caliper body.

Dust Boot and Piston Seal Removal

Once the piston is out of the caliper, remove the dust boot. If the boot is a press fit in the caliper and remains attached to it, use a screwdriver to gently pry the boot out. Take care not to scratch the caliper bore as you remove the boot. If the boot is a stretch fit over the piston and remains attached to that part, simply pull it free and set it aside, figure 3-25.

Next, remove the piston seals. If the caliper has **stroking seals**, insert a pointed wooden or plastic tool under the seals to lever them off of the pistons. If the caliper has **fixed seals** that fit into grooves in the bore, insert the tool under the seals to pry them out of their grooves, figure 3-26.

Once the caliper is disassembled, wash the bore and pistons with clean brake fluid. *Do not use a petroleum-based* solvent. If the parts are particularly dirty, use a soft bristle brush to help remove contamination. *Do not use a wire brush.*

Inspection

Caliper Internal Inspection

Inspect the caliper bore for scoring, rust, corrosion, and wear. This is particularly important on calipers that have stroking seals. Since the bore provides the sealing surface for a stroking

---

Fixed Seal: A rubber seal that fits in a groove machined into the caliper bore. The caliper piston slides through the inside of the seal as the brakes apply and release.

Stroking Seal: A rubber seal that fits into a groove on the caliper piston and strokes, or moves, with the piston as the brakes apply and release.

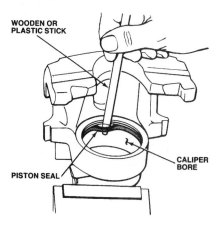

Fig. 3-26. Avoid damaging the caliper bore or piston by using a plastic or wooden probe to remove piston seals.

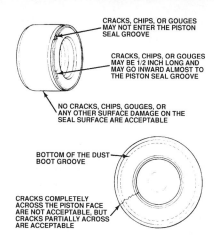

Fig. 3-27. Carefully inspect phenolic caliper pistons for cracks, chips, and gouges.

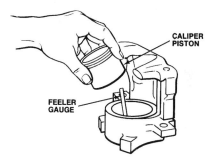

Fig. 3-28. Checking piston-to-bore clearance with a feeler gauge. The feeler gauge equals the maximum allowable clearance.

seal, even a small imperfection in the bore can create a fluid leak. The bore condition of calipers with fixed seals is less critical because the piston provides the sealing surface. Inspect the bores of these calipers for major defects that might prevent the piston from moving freely, and make sure the edges of the seal groove are not rusted or corroded and do not have nicks or burrs that can cut the seal or affect its sealing. As long as the seal groove is in good condition and the bore diameter remains within specifications, *iron calipers* with fixed seals can be honed clean of rust and corrosion. However, if the seal groove is damaged or honing makes the bore oversize, the caliper must be replaced. With *aluminum calipers*, only cleaning with a fiber brush is allowable.

Caliper Piston Inspection

Caliper pistons are made of cast iron, steel, aluminum, or phenolic resin. Pay particular attention when you inspect pistons used in calipers with fixed seals because the outside diameter of the piston provides the sealing surface for the caliper seal. On pistons used with stroking seals, the important area is the groove in which the seal fits. In both cases, the piston must be replaced if the critical surface is not smooth, clean, and entirely free of defects.

Inspect cast-iron, steel, and aluminum pistons for rust, corrosion, nicks, and scoring in their sealing areas. If the piston is chrome plated, make sure the plating is not flaking away. Aluminum pistons are anodized to provide a durable finish, and this surface should not be pitted or damaged in any way. If cast-iron, steel, or aluminum pistons have any of these problems, you should replace them.

Pistons made of phenolic resin are prone to cracking and chipping and must be thoroughly inspected. Minor cracks or chips that extend partially across the piston face are acceptable, as are minor nicks and gouges at the outer edge of the piston, providing they do not extend into the dust boot groove. Replace a piston if cracks extend across the face of the piston or nicks and gouges enter the dust boot groove. Finally, inspect the outer diameter of the piston, figure 3-27. It should be smooth and even. If the surface is scuffed or scored, replace the piston.

Caliper Bore Measurement

There is usually little or no caliper piston and bore wear during normal operation. However, after honing a caliper, the bore must be measured to make sure it has not been honed too far oversize. This step is critical when honing calipers with fixed seals or when a great deal of honing is required to clean up the bore.

Most manufacturers specify between 0.004 and 0.010-inch piston-to-bore clearance for calipers with stroking seals. Consult the factory shop manual for the vehicle you are servicing to get an exact figure.

Too much clearance in a caliper with fixed seals results in seal damage, and the self-adjusting action of the caliper may be affected as well. As a general rule, the maximum piston-to-bore clearance for fixed seal calipers is 0.002 to 0.005 inch for metal pistons and 0.005 to 0.010 inch for phenolic pistons. Consult the factory shop manual for an exact figure.

To measure the caliper piston-to-bore clearance, insert a narrow feeler gauge blade that equals the maximum allowed clearance into the caliper bore, figure 3-28. Then, attempt to insert the piston into the bore alongside the feeler gauge blade. If the piston can enter the bore, repeat the check with a new piston. If a new piston can also enter the bore, the bore is oversized, and the caliper must be replaced.

Caliper Honing

To hone a brake caliper, follow these steps:

1. Mount the caliper in a vise so you have clear access to the bore. Do not clamp on the cylinder body as this can distort the bore.
2. Select the proper size caliper hone and chuck it in a drill. Use fine stones.

A5

3. Lubricate both the bore and hone with clean brake fluid, place the hone into the bore, and operate the drill motor at approximately 500 rpm for about 10 seconds, figure 3-29. If the caliper uses stroking seals, stroke the hone gently in and out of the bore to obtain a crosshatch pattern for good sealing. If the caliper uses fixed seals, you can simply hold the hone steady in the bore because the honing pattern does not matter.

4. Remove the hone, wipe the bore clean, and check the finish. It should be clean, smooth, and free of damage. Repeat the honing sequence as needed. If the bore does not clean up after several attempts, replace the caliper.

5. After you are finished honing, thoroughly clean the caliper bore, seal groove, and fluid inlet passage with clean brake fluid and shop cloths. Make sure all traces of grit and residue are removed. Measure caliper bore as previously outlined.

Assembly

Piston Seal Installation

On calipers with fixed seals, thoroughly lubricate the O-ring seal and the seal groove in the caliper bore with fresh brake fluid. Position one edge of the seal into the groove, then gently work the seal around the bore diameter with your fingers until it is fully seated. Do not twist or roll the seal. Square-cut O-ring seals can be installed facing either way. However, if the seal is a shape other than square-cut, install it facing in the same direction as the original part, figure 3-30.

On calipers with stroking seals, thoroughly lubricate the lip seal and the seal groove in the caliper piston with fresh

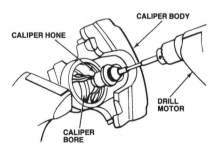

Fig. 3-29. Honing restores the surface of the caliper piston bore.

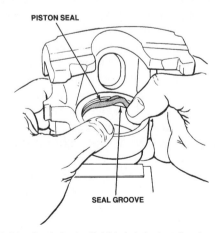

Fig. 3-30. Use fresh brake fluid to lubricate a fixed seal, then install it into the caliper bore groove by hand.

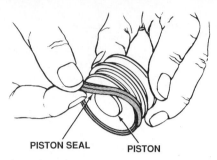

Fig. 3-31. Avoid overstretching a stroking seal as you work it over the piston and into its groove by hand.

brake fluid. Carefully stretch the seal over the end of the piston and into place in the seal groove by hand. Take special care not to cut or damage the seal, particularly the edge of the sealing lip. The sealing lip of a stroking seal must face the bottom of the caliper bore when the piston is installed, figure 3-31.

Dust Boot Installation

Some calipers use a dust boot with a metal reinforcing ring around the outer edge that is a press fit into the caliper body. These boots require a special seal driver for proper installation. To assemble:

1. Lubricate the piston with fresh brake fluid, then slip it into the dust boot until the boot snaps into the groove of the piston.

2. Using only hand pressure, work the piston into the caliper bore past the O-ring seal, and bottom the piston in the bore.

3. Select a dust boot driver of the proper size and use a hammer to seat the metal reinforcing ring at the outer edge of the boot into the groove in the caliper body, figure 3-32.

Other calipers may use a dust boot with a separate metal ring that secures the outer edge of the boot into the caliper body. No special tools are required for assembly. To assemble the piston and dust boot on these calipers:

1. Lubricate the piston with fresh brake fluid and slip it into the dust boot until the boot snaps into the groove in the piston.

2. Work the piston into the caliper bore past the O-ring seal by hand until the piston bottoms in the bore.

3. Using your fingers, position the outer edge of the boot into the groove in the caliper body; the boot must seat properly.

4. Install the metal ring to lock the boot into the groove, figure 3-33.

Another design uses a dust boot with a lip around the outer edge that fits into a groove in the caliper bore. Although special tools are not essential to assemble these calipers, a set of metal or plastic rings about a ½-inch high will make the job easier. To assemble the pistons and dust boots on these calipers:

1. Select the ring that just barely fits over the caliper piston.

2. Lubricate the inner edge of the dust boot with fresh brake fluid, then install it over the assembly ring.

3. Install the lip at the outer edge of the dust boot into the groove in the caliper bore. Reach through the ring with your fingers to make sure the lip is fully seated in the groove.

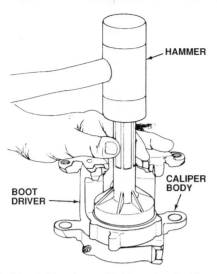

Fig. 3-32. A boot driver is required to seat a dust boot with a metal reinforcing ring into the caliper body.

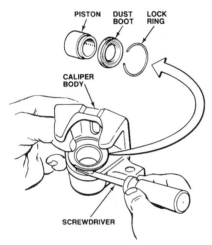

Fig. 3-33. On a caliper boot with a metal lock ring, fit the piston and dust boot by hand, then work the ring over the boot so it snaps into place.

4. Lubricate the piston with fresh brake fluid, then slip it through the ring into the caliper bore. Work the piston past the O-ring seal by hand until it is bottomed in the bore.
5. Carefully remove the ring from the dust boot so that the boot snaps into place on the piston.

Installation

1. Ensure all brake hardware is adequately cleaned before installation.
2. Lubricate caliper slides and/or pad slides as necessary.
3. Install pads to caliper or caliper bracket (depending on vehicle application). Refer to the following information when installing the brake pads:

   - Install the brake pads into the caliper or anchor plate as dictated by the brake design.
   - On some sliding and floating calipers, tabs or "ears" on the pads must be bent (called "clinching") to assure a tight fit in the caliper, thus preventing a clunking noise on application.

- The pads in fixed calipers slip into place, and a spring retainer on the guide pins prevents the pads from vibrating and causing brake noise.
- Some designs use shims that fit between the caliper pistons and pad backing plates to reduce vibration and noise.
- The pads in floating and sliding calipers usually have spring clips or bent tabs on the backing plate that lock them securely into the caliper anchor plate.
- Antirattle spring clips, of which a number of designs are used, attach to the brake pads or caliper anchor plate to reduce pad vibration and prevent brake noise.
- Once the pads are in position, secure them in the appropriate manner.
- With a fixed caliper, install the guide pins and retaining spring.
- With a sliding caliper, clean the ways and lubricate them using a high-temperature brake grease. Then, position the caliper body onto the ways over the rotor and install the retaining hardware, figure 3-32.
- With a floating caliper, lightly coat the caliper bushings and mounting bolts or guide pins with high-temperature brake grease, then position the caliper body over the rotor.

4. Install caliper and tighten to specifications.
5. Install brake hose to caliper using new copper washers. Tighten to specifications.
6. Bleed the brake system as necessary.
7. Apply the brake pedal slowly to pump up the brakes. Continue this until a firm pedal is established.
8. Install wheels as outlined in this chapter, then lower vehicle.
9. Ensure master cylinder is filled to proper level.
10. Inspect calipers for leaks while system is under pressure. Pay particular attention to hose connections and the piston area.

Adjustment

Some rear calipers require an initial adjustment before returning to service. If this adjustment is not performed, damage to the caliper internal parking brake actuator will result when the brakes are first applied.

To adjust the caliper, install the caliper with pads and measure the clearance between the pads and rotor. Typically the clearance should be about .060 inch. If the clearance is not within factory specifications, the caliper piston must be adjusted outward. On some models, this may involve removing the caliper and turning the piston using a special tool like the one shown in figure 3-16. Other designs require you to turn an adjusting nut. Still others require you to remove a plug and turn an allen screw. In any case, consult a factory service manual for the correct procedure. Repeat the adjustment procedure until clearance is within specifications.

When pad clearance has been properly adjusted, apply the parking brake several times until a firm brake pedal is achieved.

A5

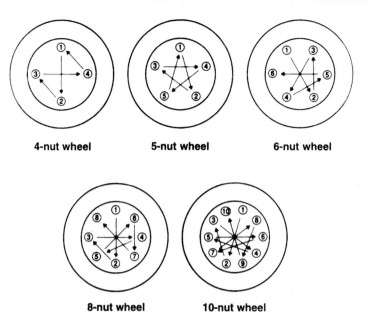

Fig. 3-34. Wheel nut tightening sequence.

WHEEL SERVICE

Wheel removal and installation are often overlooked aspects of brake service. If wheels are not *removed* and *installed* properly, several problems can result. Some of these include:

- Shortened wheel life
- Premature failure of wheel studs
- Shortened life of wheel hub and bearing
- Warpage of drums and rotors

Never use lubricants or penetrating fluids on wheel studs, nuts, or mounting surfaces. This can raise the actual torque on the nut without a corresponding reading on the torque wrench. Always ensure that wheel studs and nuts are clean and dry. Use of threadlock, sealant, lubricant, paint, or corrosion inhibitor will affect fastener torque and joint clamping force, thereby affecting actual wheel nut torque.

Removal

When removing wheels, never use heat to loosen a seized wheel nut. This could damage the wheel and wheel bearings.

1. Raise and support the vehicle.
2. Remove the wheel center cap if equipped.
3. Remove the wheel nut caps if equipped.
4. Place alignment marks on the wheel and hub for installation reference.
5. Remove the wheel nuts. If the wheel is difficult to remove, install two lug nuts, then tap the tire side wall using a suitable mallet.
6. If the wheel is still difficult to remove, perform the following steps:

   a. Install and tighten all wheel nuts.
   b. Loosen each wheel nut two turns on the affected wheel.
   c. Lower the vehicle.
   d. Manually rock the vehicle from side to side.
   e. Drive the vehicle forward slightly, then apply the brakes firmly and quickly.
   f. Drive the vehicle backward slightly, then apply the brakes firmly and quickly.
   g. Repeat procedure if necessary.

7. Repeat from step one after wheels are loose from mounting surface.

Installation

Before installation of the wheels, ensure that no penetrating oil is present on vertical surfaces between the wheel and its mounting surface. Remove any corrosion from wheel mounting surfaces using a suitable wire brush. Also ensure that wheel nuts and studs are clean and dry. Never install anti-seize compound to lug nuts or studs unless directed to do so by OEM service literature. Lastly, always follow the proper tightening sequence and tighten lug nuts to specifications. Failure to follow these guidelines when installing wheels may result in damage to mounting components, poor brake system performance and/or the wheel separating from its mounting surface while the vehicle is being driven.

1. Remove any corrosion or foreign material from wheel and hub mounting surfaces.
2. Clean threads on wheel studs and wheel nuts.
3. Install the wheel, making sure that reference marks made during removal are aligned.
4. Install the wheel nuts. Tighten to specification using a suitable torque wrench in one of the sequences shown in figure 3-34.
5. Install the wheel nut caps if equipped.
6. Install the wheel center cap if equipped.
7. Lower the vehicle.

CHAPTER QUESTIONS

1. Hard pulling to one side during braking may be caused by:
   a. Worn pads
   b. A seized caliper piston on the opposite side to that of the pull
   c. Loose pad mountings
   d. Worn sliding ways

2. Check for pedal pulsation in front disc brakes by:
   a. Applying the brakes in reverse
   b. Braking hard from high speed
   c. Coasting and applying the parking brake
   d. Feeling for steering wheel rocking while braking lightly at low speed

3. Technician A says that scored rotors cause pedal pulsation. Technician B says that pulsation is caused by disc thickness variation. Who is right?
   a. A only
   b. B only
   c. Both A and B
   d. Neither A nor B

4. Brake squeal may be caused by all of the following *EXCEPT*:
   a. A poor rotor friction surface
   b. Missing pad shims
   c. A leaking caliper piston seal
   d. Poor quality linings

5. Technician A says that a low brake pedal may be caused by lack of self adjustment of rear disc calipers with integral parking brake. Technician B says that a low brake pedal may be caused by worn out front disc brake pads. Who is right?
   a. A only
   b. B only
   c. Both A and B
   d. Neither A nor B

6. Pistons may be extracted from caliper bores by means of:
   a. System hydraulic pressure
   b. Shop air pressure
   c. Special tools that grasp the piston
   d. All of the above

7. Slight taper wear on disc brake pads removed from a floating caliper is most likely the result of:
   a. A sticking caliper piston
   b. A lack of caliper guide pin lubrication
   c. Normal wear
   d. A lack of rotor parallelism

8. As a general rule, disc brake pads must be replaced if the friction lining thickness measures less than:
   a. 0.020 inch
   b. 0.030 inch
   c. 0.060 inch
   d. 0.130 inch

9. To avoid causing damage, remove caliper piston seals with a:
   a. Pair of needle-nose pliers
   b. Small screwdriver
   c. Small steel pick
   d. Plastic or wood probe

10. For best results, what drill motor speed should be used when honing a caliper piston bore?
    a. 300 rpm
    b. 500 rpm
    c. 1000 rpm
    d. 1200 rpm

11. Phenolic resin caliper pistons should be replaced if an inspection reveals any of the following *EXCEPT*:
    a. Cracks extending across the piston face
    b. Gouges near the dust boot groove
    c. Scuffed or scored outer diameter surface
    d. Minor nicks or gouges at the outer edge

12. Typically, manufacturers allow rotors to be reused if thickness variation does not exceed:
    a. 0.005 inch
    b. 0.002 inch
    c. 0.001 inch
    d. 0.0005 inch

13. Use a dial indicator to check a rotor for:
    a. Lack of parallelism
    b. Taper variation
    c. Lateral runout
    d. Radial runout

14. Technician A says runout may be caused by overtorquing of lug nuts. Technician B says lateral runout will lead to disc thickness variation. Who is right?
    a. A only
    b. B only
    c. Both A and B
    d. Neither A nor B

15. Technician A says that wheel lug nuts should be tightened in a star pattern with an impact wrench. Technician B says that wheel lug nuts should be tightened in the proper pattern with a torque wrench. Who is right?
    a. A only
    b. B only
    c. Both A and B
    d. Neither A nor B

A5

CHAPTER OBJECTIVES

- The technician will complete the ASE task list on Power Assist Unit Diagnosis and Repair.
- The technician will be able to answer 4 questions dealing with the Power Assist Unit Diagnosis and Repair section of the A5 ASE Test.

VACUUM POWER ASSIST SERVICE

Most late-model vehicles use a vacuum booster to help apply the brakes. The booster is usually located behind the master cylinder on the firewall. Vacuum boosters require three basic tests:

- Operational test
- Vacuum supply test
- Inlet check valve test

Booster Function Test

Check pedal feel and vacuum booster function while test-driving the vehicle. With the engine off, apply the brake pedal repeatedly with medium pressure until the booster reserve is depleted. At least two brake applications should have a power-assisted feel before the pedal hardens noticeably. If the pedal feels hard immediately, or after only one brake application, it may indicate a vacuum leak or a low level of engine vacuum. Inspect the vacuum supply hose to the booster for kinks, cracks, or other damage, figure 4-1. Check engine vacuum at idle with a vacuum gauge.

To test booster function once the reserve is depleted, hold moderate pressure on the brake pedal and start the engine. If the booster is working properly, the pedal will drop slightly.

Booster Vacuum Supply Test

With the ignition OFF, pump the brake pedal to deplete the booster reserve. Disconnect the vacuum supply hose from the booster and connect a vacuum gauge to the hose using a cone-shaped adapter, figure 4-2. Start the engine and allow it to idle while observing the vacuum gauge. Although the amount of vacuum will vary by application, most will register between 15 and 20 in. Hg (50 and 70 kPa) at idle.

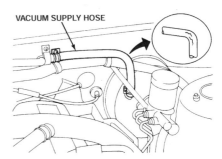

Fig. 4-1. Check vacuum booster supply hoses for cracks and damage.

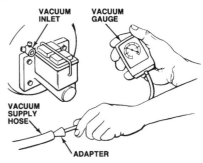

Fig. 4-2. Disconnect the vacuum booster supply hose and check for source vacuum with a gauge.

If the reading is low, check to see if the vacuum hose is kinked, clogged, or cracked. If the hose is not at fault, suspect an engine mechanical problem such as leaky valves, worn rings, an intake manifold vacuum leak, improper cam timing, etc.

Vacuum Inlet Check Valve Test

To test the vacuum **check valve**, disconnect the vacuum supply hose from the intake manifold or vacuum pump, and blow into the hose. If air passes through the valve into the booster, the check valve is defective and should be replaced.

HYDRO-BOOST POWER ASSIST SERVICE

The **Hydro-Boost** power assist system performs the same function as the vacuum assist system. The difference is that it uses hydraulic pressure instead of vacuum to provide power

---

Check Valve: A one-way valve in the hose between the intake manifold and the vacuum brake booster that traps vacuum in the booster.
Hydro-Boost: A mechanical-hydraulic power brake booster using a spool valve to direct hydraulic pressure from the power steering pump to a power piston. The power piston transmits this hydraulic pressure, along with the mechanical force of the driver applying the brake pedal, to the master cylinder.

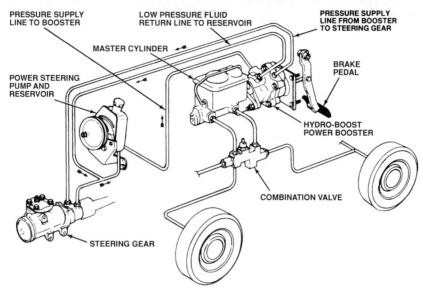

Fig. 4-3. The Bendix Hydro-Boost system uses hydraulic pressure from the power steering pump to provide power brake assist.

assist for the brake system. By using hydraulic pressure, a greater amount of assist can be provided as compared to the vacuum assist system.

The Bendix Hydro-Boost system is used on vehicles, such as those with diesel engines, that produce little or no manifold vacuum. This system is also used on heavy-duty applications, figure 4-3. It uses pressure from the power steering pump to provide braking boost, and includes a high-pressure **accumulator** that has enough capacity to provide several power-assisted stops in the event that the power steering pump belt breaks or a hose ruptures.

When inspecting the Hydro-Boost system, the inspection must include checking the power steering hoses and pump for leaks, power steering fluid level, and drive belt tension. Hydro-Boost operation and accumulator performance must also be tested.

Hydro-Boost Function Test

With the engine OFF, apply the brake pedal five or more times with medium force to discharge the accumulator. The pedal feel will harden noticeably. Next, apply the brake pedal with medium force, and then start the engine. If the booster is working properly, the pedal will drop toward the floor, and then push back upward slightly. If the booster passes this test, perform the accumulator test as described in this chapter. However, if there is no change in the pedal position or feel, the booster is not working. Check the power steering system to determine whether the problem is in the pump or the booster.

Hydro-Boost Accumulator

Many Hydro-Boost systems incorporate an accumulator, which will provide one or more brake applications in the event of hydraulic system failure. This function of the accumulator is usually accomplished by using a pressurized nitrogen gas charge.

Hydro-Boost Accumulator Test

To test the ability of the system to store a short-term high-pressure charge in the accumulator, start the engine and allow it to idle. Charge the accumulator by turning the steering wheel slowly one time from lock to lock; do not hold the steering at full lock for more than five seconds. Switch the engine off, release the steering wheel, and repeatedly apply the brake pedal with medium force. If the accumulator can hold a charge, a Hydro-Boost I unit will provide two or three power-assisted applications, while a Hydro-Boost II unit only provides one or two.

To test the ability of the system to store a long-term charge, start the engine and recharge the accumulator as described above. As the accumulator charges on a Hydro-Boost I system, a slight hissing sound should be heard as fluid rushes through the accumulator-charging orifice. Once the accumulator is charged, switch the engine off and do not apply the brake pedal for one hour. At the end of the hour, repeatedly apply the brake pedal with medium force. Once again, a Hydro-Boost I unit should provide two or three power-assisted applications and a Hydro-Boost II unit should provide one or two.

If the Hydro-Boost unit fails these tests, it usually means the accumulator of a Hydro-Boost I unit, or the accumulator/power-piston assembly of a Hydro-Boost II unit, is leaking. In either case, the booster must be rebuilt or replaced. However, if a Hydro-Boost I system fails the test but does not make the hissing sound to indicate the accumulator is charging, the fluid in the system is probably contaminated. Simply flushing the Hydro-Boost system may cure the problem.

Never begin any work on a Hydro-Boost system until you have discharged the dangerously high pressure stored in the accumulator by pumping the brake pedal numerous times with the engine off.

A5

Accumulator: In Hydro-Boost systems, a gas-charged component that stores hydraulic pressure for emergency use if the power steering belt should break or a hose rupture. Always discharge the accumulator by depressing the pedal numerous times before servicing the system.

CHAPTER QUESTIONS

1. Technician A says that with the engine off you should feel that power assist is present for at least two pedal strokes with a vacuum booster. Technician B says the vacuum in the booster should disappear immediately when the engine is shut down. Who is right?
   a. A only
   b. B only
   c. Both A and B
   d. Neither A nor B

2. If a vacuum power booster is in good condition, starting the engine after the booster has been depleted will cause the brake pedal to:
   a. Sink slightly
   b. Pulse rapidly
   c. Rise slightly
   d. Stay the same

3. When you blow into a vacuum check valve in the direction of the intake manifold:
   a. Air should pass through freely
   b. Air should not pass through
   c. Air should pass through with difficulty
   d. You should feel the check valve vibrate

4. With Hydro-Boost, when you discharge the accumulator, then start the engine, the pedal should:
   a. Push back
   b. Push back, then sink toward the floor
   c. Sink toward the floor, then push back
   d. Sink toward the floor

5. Technician A says that the Hydro-Boost system performs the same function as a vacuum assist system. Technician B says that the Hydro-Boost accumulator can provide one or more brake pedal applications in the event of a power steering system hydraulic failure. Who is correct?
   a. A only
   b. B only
   c. Both A and B
   d. Neither A nor B

ANTILOCK BRAKE SYSTEMS

CHAPTER OBJECTIVES

- The technician will complete the ASE task list on Antilock Brake Systems.
- The Technician will be able to answer 7 questions dealing with the diagnosis section of the A5 ASE Test.

Troubleshooting antilock brake problems can sometimes be done without referring to service literature. More often, it requires detailed diagnostic charts and wiring diagrams found in shop manuals. These charts define the ABS system fault codes and provide step-by-step diagnostic procedures to pinpoint the faulty circuit or component. In addition, ABS testing and service often require a scan tool to access the onboard diagnostic programs, as well as for performing service procedures such as system bleeding.

ANTILOCK SERVICE BASICS

Whether ABS equipped or not, most vehicles use essentially the same brake service procedures. This includes techniques for replacing brake pads and shoes, and refinishing rotors and drums. However, some antilock systems may require special brake bleeding procedures.

On vehicles with non-integral, or **add-on ABS**, the basic brake components are usually identical to those used on the same model without the antilock brake option. For example, between the two vehicles, the brake linings, calipers, wheel cylinders, and brake hoses may share the same replacement part numbers. However, the master cylinder may be different on some, but not all, applications. The brake rotors and drums may also be different, depending on whether the wheel speed sensor tone ring is a part of the assembly, or a separate part.

When working on **integral ABS** that uses a pump and **accumulator** rather than a conventional vacuum booster, be sure to vent all pressure from the accumulator before opening any lines or beginning any brake work, figure 5-1. Pump the brake pedal 25 to 40 times while the ignition is off to relieve pressure.

Some ABS applications create hydraulic pressures as high as 2,700 psi (18,660 kPa). Generally, you can monitor the gradual decrease in pressure remaining in the system by sensing the increasing effort required to depress the brake pedal.

Service Precautions

The following general service precautions apply to all vehicles with ABS:

- Always use the proper brake fluid to refill or top off the reservoir.
- Never connect or disconnect ABS electrical connectors while the ignition is on. Doing so creates momentary high-voltage spikes that can damage delicate electronic components.
- When testing for open or short circuits, do not ground or apply voltage to any circuit unless instructed to do so by the service manual. Test circuits with a high-impedance digital multimeter (DMM) or a special diagnostic tester only. Never use a test lamp.
- Disconnect the wiring harness from the ABS control module before any type of arc, MIG, or TIG welding is done on the vehicle.
- Do not charge the battery in the vehicle with a high amp fast charger unless the battery cables have been disconnected.
- Heat can damage the ABS control module, so it should be removed before a repainted vehicle is put into a bake oven.
- After replacing an ABS component, check the system thoroughly to make sure it functions correctly.
- Use only top-quality replacement parts in the brake system to assure proper ABS operation.
- With integral ABS, always relieve accumulator pressure before servicing the system. Do this by depressing the brake pedal with a steady force 25 to 40 times while the ignition switch is off. Some imports have a special fitting or plug on the modulator that can be opened to relieve accumulator pressure.
- Never disconnect the **wheel speed sensors** with the ignition key on.

A5

Accumulator: The part of the antilock system that supplies the power assist to apply the brakes. The accumulator is usually a nitrogen-charged reservoir that holds a supply of pressurized brake fluid.
Add-on ABS: An antilock brake system that uses a conventional master cylinder and vacuum brake booster unit in the traditional location on the firewall. The ABS hydraulic modulator is added on elsewhere in the vehicle.
Integral ABS: An antilock brake system that has a single, or integral, hydraulic unit that functions as a master cylinder, power booster, and hydraulic ABS modulator. This hydraulic unit mounts on the firewall in the same location as a conventional master cylinder.
Wheel Speed Sensor: An electronic sensing device, generally a permanent-magnet generator, that sends information about wheel rotation to the control module of an antilock system. Generally, one sensor is fitted at each of the four wheels.

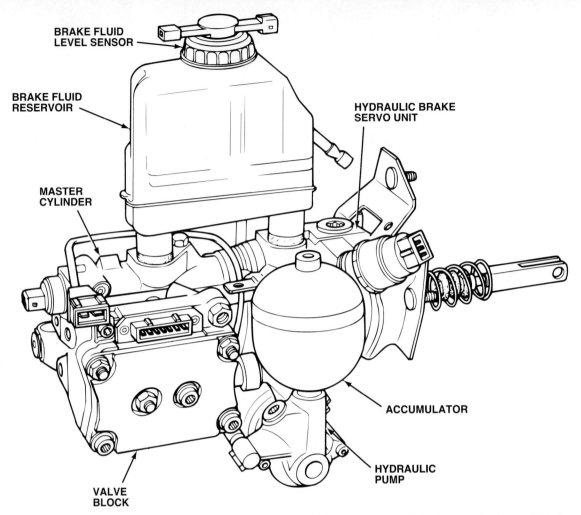

BRAKE FLUID LEVEL SENSOR

BRAKE FLUID RESERVOIR

HYDRAULIC BRAKE SERVO UNIT

MASTER CYLINDER

ACCUMULATOR

HYDRAULIC PUMP

VALVE BLOCK

Fig. 5-1. On an integral ABS with a hydraulic pump and accumulator, discharge the accumulator by pumping the pedal before opening any lines or beginning any brake work.

- If the wheels are raised off the ground, do not turn them when the ignition is on. Doing so will result in a false **diagnostic trouble code (DTC)** being set in the ABS computer.
- When servicing the ABS computer or other ABS electrical components, do not expose these components to electrostatic discharge (ESD) or damage to the component will result. To avoid exposing components to ESD, use a static protection kit when servicing the ABS electrical components, figure 5-2. The table shown in figure 5-2 also shows how much voltage (in the form of ESD) can build up when performing routine tasks.
- Note routing of ABS components during removal. These components are very sensitive to electromagnetic interference (EMI); therefore, careful routing of these components during service is a must.
- Do not hang suspension components from the speed sensor harness.

Detecting ABS Problems

In most cases, an ABS malfunction will not affect normal braking. However, there are exceptions, which are explained later. Typically, an ABS problem only affects the ABS portion of the braking system.

Most ABS problems can be detected by monitoring when the ABS warning lamp, BRAKE warning lamp, or both illuminate. One or both lamps may fail to go out, come on intermittently, or remain on continuously while driving, figure 5-3. Simultaneously, the driver may have noticed a change in the braking characteristics of the vehicle, or a complete loss of ABS function. Typically, the brake warning lamp and the ABS lamp should turn on when the ignition is turned on, then go out once the engine is started.

Avoid blaming the ABS for conventional brake problems. In general, service grabbing, pulling, dragging, or noisy brakes by following the procedures presented in the preceding chapters. Make sure the service brakes are in good working order before searching for an ABS problem. Remember, most ABS

Diagnostic Trouble Code (DTC): Coded letters and/or numbers that correspond to a specific fault in a given system. For example, if you retrieve a code C1194 on a 2002 Ford Escort, it indicates an open or shorted left front dump valve solenoid.

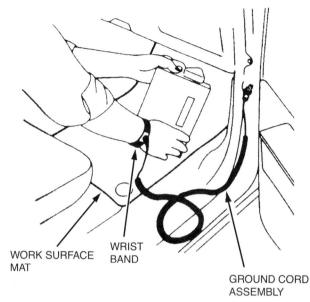

WORK SURFACE MAT

WRIST BAND

GROUND CORD ASSEMBLY

Activity	Relative Humidity	
	Low (10-20%)	High (65-90%)
	Volts	Volts
Walking Across a Carpet	35,000	1,500
Walking Over a Vinyl Floor	12,000	250
Working at a Bench	6,000	100
Sliding Across a Vehicle Seat	25,000	1,000

Fig. 5-2. Electrostatic discharge can damage sensitive electronic components. A static protection kit should be used when servicing these types of components.

SEQUENCE NUMBER	LAMP SEQUENCE	SYMPTOM DESCRIPTION	PERFORM TEST
1		NORMAL LAMP SEQUENCE WITH -EXCESSIVE PEDAL TRAVEL OR SPONGY PEDAL -ANTILOCK BRAKING OPERATION OR VALVE CYCLING DURING NORMAL STOPS ON DRY PAVEMENT -POOR VEHICLE TRACKING DURING ANTILOCK BRAKING	H C D
2		CONTINUOUS "ANTILOCK" LAMP NORMAL "BRAKE" LAMP	A
3		"ANTILOCK" LAMP COMES ON AFTER VEHICLE STARTS MOVING NORMAL BRAKE LAMP	C
4		NO "ANTILOCK" LAMP WHILE CRANKING NORMAL "BRAKE" LAMP	E
5		NO "ANTILOCK" LAMP NORMAL "BRAKE" LAMP	F
6		INTERMITTENT "ANTILOCK" LAMP WHILE DRIVING NORMAL "BRAKE" LAMP	G
7		CONTINUOUS "ANTILOCK" LAMP CONTINUOUS "BRAKE" LAMP	B
8		"ANTILOCK" AND "BRAKE" LAMPS COME ON WHILE BRAKING	B
9		NORMAL "ANTILOCK" LAMP CONTINUOUS "BRAKE" LAMP	B
10		NORMAL OR CONTINUOUS "ANTILOCK" LAMP FLASHING "BRAKE" LAMP	B

Fig. 5-3. This lamp sequence chart, taken from a factory service manual, refers you to a specific troubleshooting procedure based on how the warning lamps illuminate.

only activates when the wheel speed sensors detect a wheel decelerating too quickly, causing an interruption of traction. Integral ABS systems with power assist serve as the exception.

ABS Symptom Diagnosis

This section describes how the diagnosis of some common brake symptoms may be different with ABS.

- Noise—Most ABS makes noise when operating. Typically, the ABS solenoids in the **modulator** assembly buzz and click. Diagnosis for other brake noises is the same as for conventional brake systems.
- Pulling—Faults with ABS usually do not cause brake pull; pulling is most often the result of a conventional brake system problem. Although unlikely, certain ABS failures can cause the brakes to pull. An ABS isolation valve for a front-wheel circuit that remains energized or stuck closed blocks pressure to the affected wheel. This can cause a pull toward the unaffected side when the brakes are applied. Similarly, an ABS dump valve for a front wheel circuit that remains energized or stuck open prevents the affected brake from being applied and results in a pull to the opposite side. A valve that fails to close is often the result of contamination that interferes with the movement of the valve. Look for debris or corrosion within the hydraulic system when you suspect a sticking ABS valve.
- Pedal vibration—The rapid cycling of brake pressure in the hydraulic circuits during an ABS stop pulsates the brake pedal. The amount of pulsation varies with the type of ABS and vehicle application. Pulsation should only occur during a hard, ABS-assisted stop or when braking on a slick surface. It should not occur during normal braking. If it does, especially when accompanied by a shuddering or jerky stop, check the brake rotors for lateral runout or lack of parallelism. An out-of-round drum, loose wheel bearings, or loose brake parts can also cause pedal pulsation during normal braking.
- Grabbing—If the brakes feel jerky or lock up easily during normal braking, check for contaminated linings. Also, examine the drums and rotors for severe scoring. These problems affect ABS operation as well as normal braking. On most antilock systems, low-speed wheel lockup does not indicate a problem. The vehicle must exceed 4 to 6 mph (6 to 10 kph) before the wheel speed sensors provide reliable speed signals and ABS becomes operational.
- Dragging—Although unlikely, ABS with traction control may apply the brake on a drive wheel continuously if current is constantly applied to the traction control solenoids and pump.
- Gradually sinking brake pedal—This problem is often caused by a worn master cylinder. For systems that have a brake fluid level indicator, check for an illuminated ABS or BRAKE warning lamp. On trucks with Kelsey-Hayes rear wheel antilock brakes (RWAL or RABS), dirt in the ABS control valve can prevent the dump valve from fully seating. This allows brake fluid to leak past the valve, causing the pedal to sink.
- Hard Pedal—Increased pedal effort may indicate an ABS problem, but only on integral ABS. The electric pump and accumulator on these systems provide normal power assist. Problems such as a faulty pump, pump relay, or a pressure loss in the accumulator reduce boost, which increases the pedal effort needed to stop the vehicle. Usually, the ABS warning lamp lights, and the ABS control module deactivates itself. With a hard pedal on vehicles with hydro-boost power brakes, look for a loose power steering pump belt, low fluid level, leaky hoses, or faulty valves in the hydro-boost unit.
- ABS Warning Indicator On (No codes or Pass Code)—If the ABS warning indicator is always on and there are no DTCs, the system has been grounded. This could be caused by low brake fluid in the master cylinder (this will also illuminate the RED brake indicator), a shorted ABS warning indicator circuit, or an internally shorted ABS control module.

Preliminary Checks

The following ABS checks are made in addition to the preliminary checks previously recommended for conventional brake components. Before looking for ABS faults, check:

- Battery charge—ABS systems require a fully charged battery; open circuit voltage must be over 10 volts to operate.
- Fuses—Check the ABS control module fuse, main relay fuse, and pump motor fuse. Also, check instrument cluster fuses that could affect the warning lamps.
- Connectors—Check for corroded or loosely installed connections on the following parts: the main relay, pump motor, pump motor relay, pressure switch, main valve, valve block, fluid-level sensor, control module, and wheel speed sensors.
- Grounds—Check for excessive voltage drop across system ground connections, especially those for the control module, pump motor, relay, and hydraulic modulator assembly.
- Inspect vehicle for the installation of aftermarket electronics that could interfere with the ABS system.
- Inspect for aftermarket equipment that can affect curb height or final drive ratio. These items can and will affect ABS operation by causing ABS lamp illumination and/or false cycling of the ABS system.
- Inspect all areas that would indicate leaks. Also inspect all hydraulic lines for cracks, chafing, or leaks.
- Check for external damage to the hydraulic control unit.
- Ensure all wiring is properly connected to the HCU and shows no signs of damage or corrosion.
- Inspect ABS wiring for burnt or missing insulation.
- Ensure that the ABS control unit is properly mounted and secure in its mounts.
- Verify proper operation of the stoplamps, red brake indicator, and amber ABS warning indicator.

Modulator: A device that contains high-speed electric solenoid valves that maintain or reduce pressure in the hydraulic brake circuits that feed the calipers or wheel cylinders. The modulator, which is considered the heart of an antilock system, prevents wheel lockup.

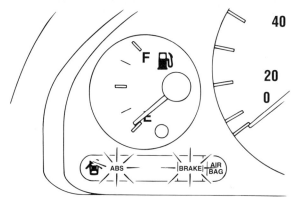

Fig. 5-4. The ABS warning lamp, and the BRAKE warning lamp on some models, should momentarily illuminate when the ignition is switched on.

• Inspect for damaged, loose, or worn suspension and drive components. Wear in these areas can alter speed sensor input signals.

Verifying ABS Operation

When the antilock system is working normally, the ABS warning lamp should illuminate for a few seconds when the ignition is switched on as a bulb check for most vehicles, figure 5-4. During engine cranking, the ABS warning lamp, and possibly the BRAKE warning lamp, will remain on. Once the engine starts, the BRAKE lamp should go out immediately, and the

ABS lamp should switch off after a short delay. On vehicles with traction control, the traction control warning lamp generally functions similarly to the ABS lamp. All of the warning lamps should remain off at all other times.

Test the ABS system by driving on a wet or slick surface at 20 to 25 mph (32 to 48 kph) and stopping suddenly. If ABS works, expect to feel feedback in the brake pedal and hear the buzzing and clicking noises mentioned previously. The vehicle should stop in a straight line without skidding or locking up the wheels.

ABS Monitoring Equipment

A high-impedance, digital multimeter (DMM) is essential for troubleshooting ABS faults. Accurate wiring diagrams and service specifications are needed as well. A scan tool or a dedicated ABS tester is also required for servicing some systems, figure 5-5.

A scan tool can check for diagnostic trouble codes (DTC), as well as display data stream parameters and perform functional tests on some systems, figure 5-6. Functional testing allows you to quickly check the operation of the pump and the modulator solenoids and motors. However, some test functions require bidirectional communication between the scan tool and ABS control module. This allows the scan tool to receive and give commands to the ABS control module. Some manufacturers limit bidirectional communications information and these features are only available with their factory scan tool.

When scan tool testing reveals ABS codes in memory, refer to the appropriate diagnostic chart for troubleshooting. Often,

A5

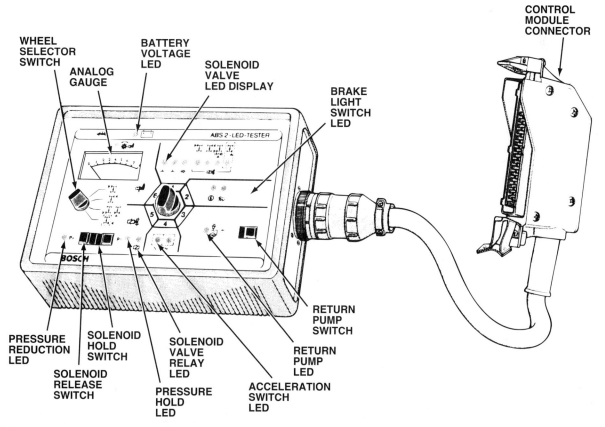

Fig. 5-5. Special equipment, such as this Bosch ABS 2 LED tester, may be required to perform functional tests on specific ABS applications.

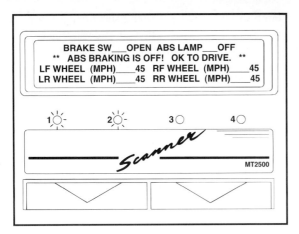

Fig. 5-6. A scan tool can retrieve trouble codes, monitor the data stream, and activate functional tests on some ABS applications.

it is necessary to perform pinpoint tests using a DMM and breakout box to isolate the source of the problem.

Diagnosis with the ABS Warning Lamp

Check bulb operation during the timed bulb check period when the ignition switch is initially turned on. If the bulb illuminates and extinguishes after several seconds, and there are no other brake system complaints, then ABS is probably operational. However, the only way to know for sure is to test the system.

If the ABS warning lamp comes on and remains on, the system has detected a fault that requires further diagnosis. A BRAKE warning lamp that remains on or comes on while driving usually indicates a problem with the hydraulic system, not an ABS failure. Be aware: Some systems use the BRAKE warning lamp to alert the driver of an ABS problem when the ABS lamp or circuit is malfunctioning.

If the ABS lamp comes on and remains on, or flashes, the self-diagnostic program of the ABS control module has detected a system failure. How the warning lamp reacts can provide clues to the nature of the problem.

An ABS warning lamp that lights when the vehicle first begins to move generally indicates a problem with one wheel speed sensor. Speed sensor failures can also cause ABS to engage during normal stops on dry pavement.

Most systems perform a self test to check the integrity of the circuits when the ignition is turned on. Once the vehicle gets underway, a second self-test momentarily energizes solenoids, valves, and motors to check for a dynamic response. Should the system detect a fault during either self-test, the warning lamp illuminates and the control module suspends ABS operation.

On vehicles with integral ABS, if both the BRAKE and ABS warning lamps illuminate and power assist is low, suspect an inoperative pump or an accumulator pressure leak. If power assist is normal and both warning lamps are on, check the fluid level and fluid-level sensor. If the level is normal and the sensor is working, take a brake pressure reading.

When ABS is combined with a traction control system, both systems automatically deactivate when the warning lamp comes on as a failsafe procedure. This should not affect normal braking, and does not pose any danger to the safe operation of the vehicle under normal driving conditions. Vehicles with integral ABS also deactivate power-assisted braking.

If the ABS warning light is on and remains on, first check for obvious problems such as a low fluid level. Next, retrieve diagnostic trouble codes. Refer to a diagnostic chart for the specific vehicle being serviced to conduct circuit voltage, resistance, and continuity tests.

ONBOARD DIAGNOSTICS

Most antilock brake systems have comprehensive self-diagnostic capability; early Bosch systems serve as exceptions.

Typically, the ABS control module generates diagnostic trouble codes. Each DTC represents a specific failure, such as a signal loss from a wheel-speed sensor, erroneous voltage feedback from a modulator solenoid, or an intermittent signal from a pump motor relay circuit. On some applications, a low pressure switch detects pressure loss in the accumulator, and a switch circuit failure will also set a DTC. Be aware: The ABS self-diagnostic routine monitors ABS functions only, and will not recognize problems or set codes for the conventional brake system.

On some vehicles, retrieve codes by grounding the ABS control module diagnostic connector and counting the number of times the ABS warning lamp flashes, figure 5-7. On some others, you access codes by pushing buttons on the control panel of the climate control system in a specified sequence to display results on the vehicle information center or digital speedometer. For some applications, a **scan tool** must be used to retrieve codes from the ABS control module.

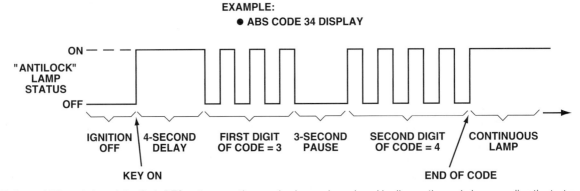

Fig. 5-7. Some ABS control modules flash DTC patterns on the warning lamp when placed in diagnostic mode by grounding the test connector.

Scan Tool: A diagnostic tool that retrieves diagnostic trouble codes and displays the serial data stream, or input and output signals, of an onboard computer to a technician.

Fault Code Diagnosis

Although a DTC pinpoints the specific faulty circuit, it does not tell you the exact nature of the fault, or exactly where the problem is located. The DTC is simply a guide to point you in the right direction. Additional testing is needed to locate the defective component, connection, or wiring. To identify the problem from your list of possibilities, first refer to the diagnostic procedure found in the shop manual. Each step in a troubleshooting sequence eliminates working components and subsystems, which leads to the source of the failure. Often these charts are quite lengthy and involve a number of continuity, resistance, and voltage checks. Carry out each test in the exact order prescribed. Skipping steps, or taking other shortcuts, can lead to false conclusions. Using the factory procedure, you can efficiently identify the problem.

Multiple Diagnostic Trouble Codes

When there are multiple ABS codes in memory, they display either in numerical sequence or the sequence in which you must repair them. Troubleshooting codes in correct order is important, as one code may be responsible for setting other codes. Follow the steps included in the diagnostic chart in sequence to eliminate all possibilities.

When diagnosing with codes, always attempt to make the codes reappear to be sure the problem still exists. First, record and then clear all the codes present. Inspect the wiring for obvious problems such as loose or corroded connectors. Then test drive the vehicle, or perform a wiggle test, or both. Note if the ABS warning lamp comes back on or if the same codes reappear on your scan tool.

When more than three codes appear, the real problem may be a loose or corroded connection shared by multiple circuits. It is extremely rare to have more than one component fail at the same time. Consult a wiring diagram to determine which parts share common circuits on both the power and ground sides.

False Codes

An ABS control module may generate "false" codes, which are a result of the system software design. For example, a wheel speed sensor code may be set if the rear wheels break traction while accelerating on ice or mud. False wheel speed sensor codes can also be triggered on some vehicles if a wheel rotates or spins while the ignition switch is in the on position. In these cases, the ABS control module sets a code because the speed signal from one wheel disagrees with the signals from the other sensors. Changing a tire or working on the brakes with the ignition switch on can set a false DTC.

Changing tire size can trigger wheel speed sensor codes and cause ABS performance problems as well. If replacement tires or wheels have a larger or smaller diameter than the original equipment, rotational speed, and thus wheel speed sensor voltage, will vary. This can be especially critical if there is a difference in tire diameter between the front and rear axles. Keep in mind, the ABS is calibrated for a specific size of tire for a specific size wheel, and most manufacturers recommend against changing tire sizes.

ANTILOCK INSPECTION AND PERFORMANCE CHECKS

The following are typical inspections and performance checks that apply to systems with integral ABS. On these designs, the master cylinder, pump, accumulator, and modulator are combined in an assembly.

Pump and Accumulator Checks

After relieving accumulator pressure, switch the ignition on to check pump operation. If you do not hear the pump engage, check for voltage available at the pump, and take a voltage drop reading across the ground connection at the pump. Normal voltage available at the pump along with a low voltage drop across the ground connection indicates a defective pump assembly. Replace the pump. A low or zero voltage reading at the pump indicates a problem in the power supply; check the relay and wiring harness. A high voltage drop indicates a problem on the ground side of the circuit.

Check accumulator pressure by connecting a high-pressure gauge between the accumulator and modulator assembly, figure 5-8. Switch the ignition on and the accumulator should quickly pressurize the brake fluid to about 600 to

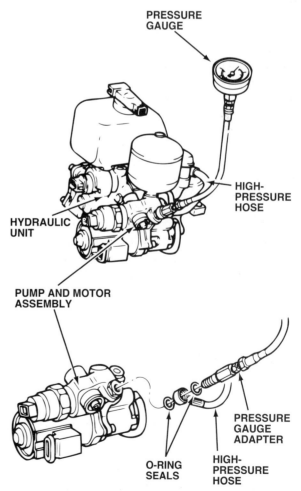

Fig. 5-8. Connect a high pressure gauge between the accumulator and modulator assembly to monitor accumulator pressure on an integral system.

1200 psi (4137 to 8274 kPa). Then, pressure should slowly climb to peak specified pressure, which is sometimes as high as 2700 psi (18,616 kPa). Refer to the appropriate shop manual for exact specifications.

With the gauge connected and the ignition switched on, pump the brake pedal until the pump motor restarts. When the pump stops, switch the ignition off, wait three minutes, and note the pressure. Wait five more minutes, and note the pressure again. Accumulator pressure leakdown should not exceed 20 psi (138 kPa) in five minutes. If the leakdown is greater, check for leakage in the pump, the master cylinder, or the booster assembly.

To locate the pressure leak, switch the ignition on and allow the pump to run for one minute. Then, switch the ignition off and disconnect the return hose from the fluid reservoir. Plug the reservoir outlet and hold the free end of the return hose in a suitable container. Watch the open end of the hose and note what happens during the next five minutes. If there is no fluid flow through the hose, the problem lies in the master cylinder and booster assembly. If fluid flows from the hose, the pump is leaking and the pump and motor assembly should be replaced.

Wheel Speed Sensor Service

Wheel speed sensor circuits are often the cause of ABS problems. These components may suffer from physical damage, buildup of metallic debris on the sensor tip, corrosion, poor electrical connections, damaged wiring, and improper mounting.

With the vehicle on a lift, inspect the wheel speed sensors for damage, figure 5-9. The gear wheels should have all their teeth intact and be free of built-up dirt, and the sensor units must be securely mounted. Check the wiring harness connecting the wheel speed sensors to the main harness. Check the wheel bearings. Wear may allow enough wheel wobble to upset the air gap between the speed sensors and the gear wheel, sending inconsistent speed signals to the ABS control module.

Test a wheel speed sensor by measuring its output voltage and circuit continuity with a DMM. Rotate the wheel by hand at a rate of about one revolution per second. Note the voltage reading from the sensor. A functioning wheel speed sensor generally produces an alternating current (AC) voltage that ranges from about 50 to 700 mV. Refer to the shop manual for the exact specifications.

If voltage readings are low, switch the ignition off and check the resistance across the sensor. Expect the value to be between 800 and 1400 ohms; check the shop manual for the exact specifications. If the resistance is out of range, the sensor is shorted or open; replace it. If sensor resistance meets specifications, test the wiring harness for loose or corroded connections, frayed insulation, or other damage.

Locate grounds or shorts in the wheel speed sensor cables by testing for continuity between the wiring connectors. It is best to simply replace defective wiring, rather than repair it by splicing, soldering, or taping.

An alternate way of testing the wheel speed sensors is with an oscilloscope. When connecting the oscilloscope, connect it as close to the sensor as possible. The oscilloscope reading in figure 5-10 shows a normal speed sensor pattern for low and high speeds. The pattern shown in figure 5-11 shows what a pattern might look like if the vehicle has a damaged sensor

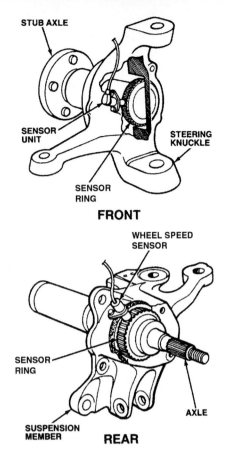

Fig. 5-9. Check wheel speed sensors and their tone rings for signs of physical damage and built-up debris that could affect their operation.

ring. Scope patterns that indicate irregularity can also indicate faulty wiring or interference from other components. Be sure that the vehicle does not have any aftermarket electronic equipment that could interfere with the ABS system.

Wheel Speed Sensor Adjustment

On ABS applications with adjustable wheel speed sensors, always refer to a shop manual for the proper air gap setting. Adjust most sensors by loosening a set screw, then inserting a non-magnetic, plastic or brass, feeler gauge between the tip of the sensor and a high point on the tone ring, figure 5-12. Adjust the position of the sensor so there is a slight drag on the feeler gauge, then tighten the set screw to lock the sensor in place.

When installing new sensors, look for a piece of paper or plastic on the tip end of the unit. This covering must be left in place during installation, as it is the precise thickness to guarantee a correct air gap between the sensor and the tone ring. Adjust the sensor so the tip just touches the tone ring and you can slip the paper or plastic out without ripping it. Tighten the set screw and the air gap is properly set.

Some manufacturers recommend leaving a paper covering in place; the motion of the tone ring removes it after the vehicle is driven for several miles. This is the way sensors are generally installed at the factory, and it is not unusual to find traces of the covering still on the sensor when the vehicle is in for service.

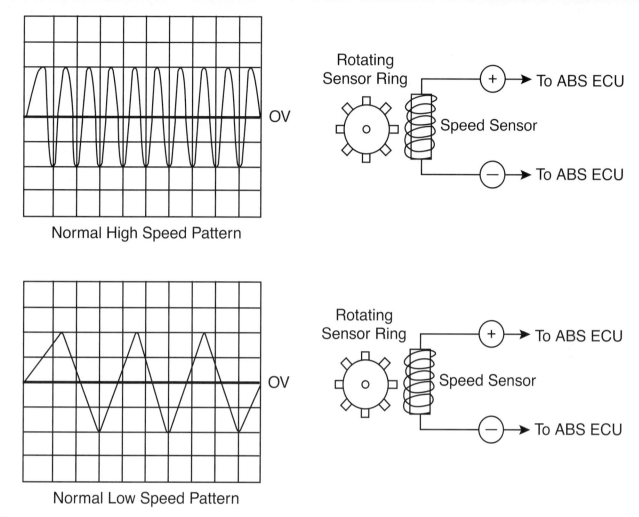

Fig. 5-10. Normal wheel speed sensor readings shown on an oscilloscope.

When reinstalling a used sensor, be sure that there is no trace of the original paper or plastic covering remaining on the tip. If there is, it will be impossible to properly set the air gap with a feeler gauge. Carefully clean the tip of the sensor to avoid damaging the unit.

Wheel Speed Sensor Replacement

Wheel speed sensors are fragile and must be handled with care. Avoid tapping to force the sensor into place; this can fracture the pickup magnet. On some vehicles, the left rear, left front, right front, and right rear wheel sensors may appear

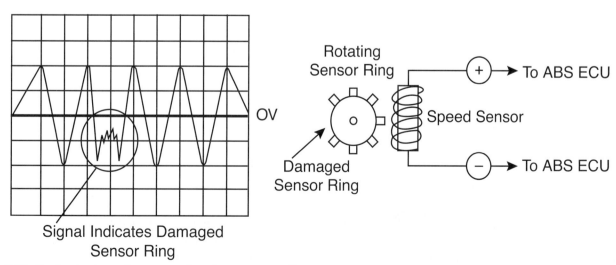

Fig. 5-11. Faulty wheel speed sensor reading shown on an oscilloscope.

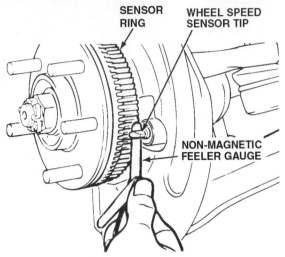

Fig. 5-12. Use a non-magnetic feeler gauge to check and adjust the air gap between the wheel speed sensor and the tone ring.

identical, but each is slightly different. These are a set, and individual sensors are not interchangeable. Installing a sensor in the wrong location will affect ABS function.

Coat steel wheel sensor housings with an anticorrosive high temperature lubricant, such as synthetic grease or silicone brake grease, before installation, figure 5-13. Be sure the lubricant is designed to withstand the high demands of a brake system; do not use ordinary chassis grease. Avoid getting any lubricant on the sensing portion of the assembly; this can result in an erroneous signal to the ABS control module. Also make sure that the sensor wiring is routed correctly to avoid interference from other vehicle systems.

Checking the Fluid Level

Check the master cylinder fluid levels in Add-On ABS as you would any vehicle that is not equipped with ABS. Integral ABS is more complex because you check the fluid level with the hydraulic accumulator either charged or discharged, depending on the type of reservoir fitted by the manufacturer.

On systems that require a charged accumulator, turn the ignition switch ON and pump the brake pedal until the

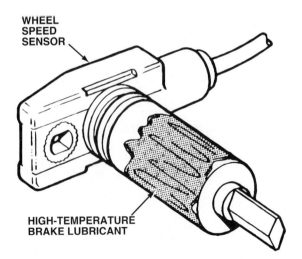

Fig. 5-13. Coat steel wheel speed sensors with high-temperature lubricant before installing them.

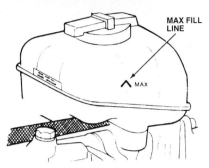

Fig. 5-14. The fluid level of an integral ABS should be at the MAX or FULL mark on the reservoir when the accumulator is fully charged.

hydraulic pump motor begins to run. When the pump stops, the accumulator is fully charged. Check the fluid level against the MAX or FULL mark on the outside wall of the reservoir, figure 5-14.

On systems that require a discharged accumulator to check fluid level, turn the ignition switch OFF. Pump the brake pedal as instructed in the "Antilock Service Basics" section above. Check the fluid levels against the MAX or FULL mark on the outside wall of the reservoir.

ANTILOCK BRAKE BLEEDING

Most Add-On ABS bleeding is identical to that of a conventional brake system, using manual, vacuum, or pressure bleeding. Use the bleeding sequence recommended by the manufacturer. Make sure to include the bleeder valve on the hydraulic modulator or pump if the system is equipped with one. Some modulators have several bleeder valves and a bleeding sequence of their own.

Although some Integral ABS systems can be bled like a conventional system, the majority require special bleeding procedures. If the system has a front/rear split hydraulic system, the front wheels can be bled the same as a normal brake system, manually or with a pressure bleeder. Bleed the rear brakes using either a pressure bleeder or the accumulator pressure of the ABS system.

In most newer ABS systems, the hydraulic control unit does not have to be bled unless it is serviced. Older ABS systems require that the hydraulic control unit be bled whenever the system is bled. Proper hydraulic control unit bleeding procedures can be found in the appropriate factory service manual. The following precautions should be followed when bleeding the system:

- Use a suitable syringe or suction pump to empty the reservoir assembly or hydraulic control unit.
- Do not allow brake fluid to come into contact with the electrical connectors.
- Never reuse brake fluid.
- Ensure that no particles fall into any open ports of the hydraulic control unit or any other hydraulic components.

Pressure Bleeder

1. Charge the pressure bleeder to 35 psi (240 kPa) of pressure.
2. When bleeding the brakes, open one rear bleeder valve for 10 seconds, then close it. Next, open the bleeder valve at the opposite wheel for the same length of time, then close it. Alternate in this way until the fluid from both

bleeders is free of air bubbles. Typically, start at the wheel furthest from the master cylinder and work your way around the vehicle. Always consult the factory shop manual for proper procedures and sequences.

3. When complete, top off the fluid reservoir.

Accumulator Pressure

1. Turn the ignition switch ON. Press the brake pedal repeatedly until the electro-hydraulic pump motor starts. The motor will stop when the accumulator is charged.
2. Attach one end of a length of plastic tubing over the bleeder valve of the right rear caliper, and submerge the open end of the hose in a container of fresh brake fluid.
3. With the ignition switch on, have an assistant lightly press and hold the brake pedal.
4. Alternately open the rear bleeder valves for 10 seconds at a time until the fluid coming from the bleeders is free of air bubbles. Open the bleeder valve slowly and carefully because the accumulator provides much higher pressure than is available from a pressure bleeder.
5. When bleeding is complete, check and correct the fluid level in the reservoir.

WIRING REPAIR

Wiring harness repair procedures will vary from manufacturer to manufacturer. The guidelines for harness repair given here are meant as a general guide. As always, consult a factory Service Manual for specific make and model applications.

If unreliable repair methods are used, the circuit will be unstable, which will result in variable resistance, a short circuit, or an open circuit. These are reasons why proper wiring repair is so important.

Some portions of the ABS wiring harness should not be repaired. They should instead be replaced. For instance, if there is damage to the speed sensor harness pigtail assembly, replace the sensor and harness assembly. Other portions of the harness may be repaired, but only by using the proper techniques outlined here.

When splicing a portion of a circuit together, some manufacturers recommend that the repair be made using shrink tubing that contains a hot melt wax. This will ensure that your repair will be water and air tight. Using this type of shrink tubing will prevent some of the problems with wiring repair previously discussed. In any case, the section that you repair should always be shrink wrapped, not tapped. If electrical tape is used, there is always the potential that the tape could unravel or come off. With shrink wrap, the only way it will come off is if it is improperly installed or if it is tampered with.

The following steps should be used when joining two circuits:

1. Strip 1.5 inches of insulation from one wire, and $3/_4$ of an inch of insulation from the second wire. When stripping the wire, be sure that it is stripped properly or wire strands may be cut off, figure 5-15.
2. Install the heat shrink tubing to one of the wires. Twist the wires together as shown in figure 5-16. Solder the wires using a rosin core mildly activated solder. Do not use acid core solder.
3. Bend the wires as shown in figure 5-17 to shape them for sealing.
4. Position the shrink tubing over the splice, figure 5-18.
5. Heat the shrink tubing until hot melt wax appears from both ends of the tubing, figure 5-19.

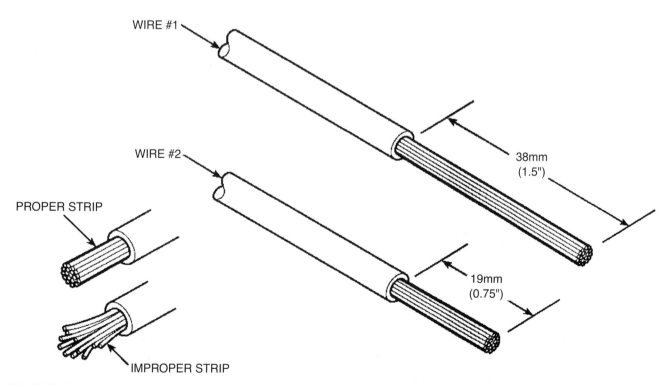

WIRE #1

WIRE #2

PROPER STRIP

IMPROPER STRIP

38mm (1.5")

19mm (0.75")

Fig. 5-15. Strip insulation making sure not to cut any strands of wire.

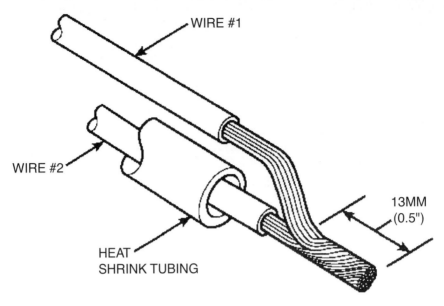

Fig. 5-16. Twist the wires together, then solder them using a rosin core solder.

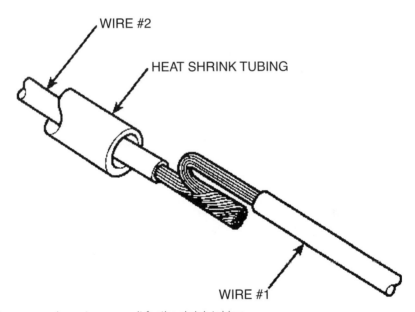

Fig. 5-17. Position the harness as shown to prepare it for the shrink tubing.

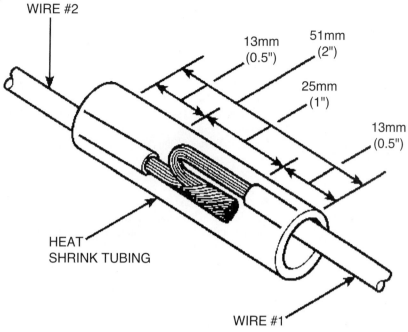

WIRE #2

13mm
(0.5")

51mm
(2")

25mm
(1")

13mm
(0.5")

HEAT
SHRINK TUBING

WIRE #1

Fig. 5-18. Positioning the shrink tubing as shown will provide an airtight and watertight seal.

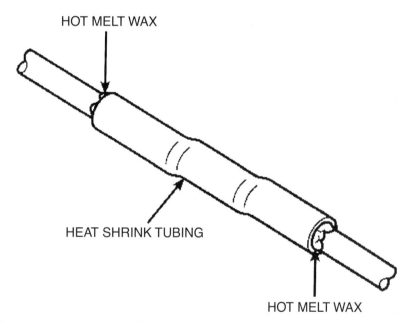

HOT MELT WAX

HEAT SHRINK TUBING

HOT MELT WAX

Fig. 5-19. Hot melt wax should appear at each end of the repair as shown.

A5

CHAPTER QUESTIONS

1. When first testing a car equipped with ABS, it is important to:
   a. Try to lock the brakes
   b. Disconnect the battery ground
   c. Use the parking brake
   d. Note the status of the ABS warning light

2. To avoid spraying the vehicle with brake fluid when removing a hydraulic part from an integral ABS system, it is important to first:
   a. Bleed the system
   b. Wrap the connection with a shop towel
   c. Relieve system pressure
   d. Siphon fluid from the reservoir

3. An ABS warning lamp that comes on when the vehicle first begins to move generally indicates:
   a. A wheel speed sensor problem
   b. A master cylinder problem
   c. An isolation valve problem
   d. An accumulator problem

4. If both the BRAKE and ABS warning lamps illuminate and power assist is low on an integral ABS system, the probable cause is:
   a. A wheel speed sensor or circuit failure
   b. An inoperative pump or an accumulator pressure leak
   c. Dirt in the ABS control valve preventing the dump valve from seating
   d. A malfunctioning isolation valve or a stuck open dump valve

5. When inspecting wheel speed sensors, check for all of the following **EXCEPT**:
   a. Condition of the tone wheel teeth
   b. Secure sensor mounting
   c. Correct input voltage
   d. Proper air gap between the sensor and tone ring

6. To check the fluid level on an integral antilock system when the accumulator must be charged:
   a. Switch the ignition OFF, pump the brake pedal until the pedal feels hard, then check the fluid level
   b. Check fluid level as you would on a vehicle without ABS
   c. Switch the ignition ON, pump the brake pedal to start the pump motor, then check the fluid level after the pump stops
   d. Switch the ignition ON, pump the brake pedal to start the pump motor, then check the fluid level with the pump running

7. When multiple trouble codes are present in an antilock system, look for:
   a. A weak connection at a common ground
   b. An open circuit
   c. Low-voltage signals
   d. Two or more faulty sensors

8. The peak accumulator pressure developed by an ABS hydraulic pump may be as high as:
   a. 600 psi (4137 kPa)
   b. 1,200 psi (8274 kPa)
   c. 1,800 psi (12,573 kPa)
   d. 2,700 psi (18,616 kPa)

9. To pressure-bleed the rear brakes of an integral antilock system, the bleeder should be charged to:
   a. 25 psi (172 kPa)
   b. 35 psi (241 kPa)
   c. 45 psi (310 kPa)
   d. 55 psi (379 kPa)

10. Technician A says that when servicing the ABS computer, care should be taken not to expose it to electrostatic discharge. Technician B says that it is ok to disconnect wheel speed sensors when the ignition switch is on. Who is right?
    a. A only
    b. B only
    c. Both A and B
    d. Neither A nor B

11. A vehicle equipped with ABS exhibits a brake pull when the brakes are moderately applied. The amber ABS indicator on the dash is functioning correctly and proves out when the vehicle is started. The most likely cause of the brake pull is:
    a. A stuck ABS isolation valve
    b. A faulty wheel speed sensor signal
    c. A blown ABS pump motor fuse
    d. A concern not related to the ABS system

12. Technician A says that incorrect tire size could cause a wheel speed sensor code. Technician B says that tire size will not affect the ABS system in any way. Who is right?
    a. A only
    b. B only
    c. Both A and B
    d. Neither A nor B

13. When you encounter multiple ABS DTCs, all of the following are true **EXCEPT**:
    a. The codes can be diagnosed in any order you choose
    b. Multiple codes could indicate a loose or corroded connection
    c. One of the codes may be responsible for setting the other codes
    d. The first step is to record and clear all codes present

14. Which of the following is **NOT** true about wire repairs made to the ABS system?
    a. Wires should be soldered and sealed with shrink tubing that contains a special wax sealant
    b. Solder the wires together using a suitable acid core solder
    c. Damage to the wires can occur if they are improperly stripped
    d. Tape should never be used to hold the wires together

CHAPTER SIX

MISCELLANEOUS BRAKE SYSTEM

CHAPTER OBJECTIVES

- The technician will complete the ASE task list on Miscellaneous Brake System.
- The technician will be able to answer 7 questions dealing with the Miscellaneous Brake System section of the A5 ASE Test.

When diagnosing brake problems or servicing brakes, it is important to consider all the components that can contribute to brake performance deficiencies. For example, the symptoms of worn or incorrectly adjusted wheel bearings may only be noticeable when the brakes are applied, but servicing the brakes will not cure the problem. Or, a malfunctioning parking brake can cause accelerated or uneven brake friction material wear and other brake performance troubles, but while replacing linings may cure the symptoms, it does not address the root cause. A thorough diagnosis and inspection is the only way to ensure a complete repair.

WHEEL BEARING INSPECTION

A body vibration that occurs when the brakes are applied during a road test may be caused by loose wheel bearings. However, a worn wheel bearing makes a growling sound when the vehicle is moving, not only when the brakes are applied. To confirm a wheel bearing problem, swerve the vehicle back and forth to alternately load and unload the bearings on opposite sides of the chassis. The noise from the bad bearing will increase with the load on that side of the vehicle and decrease as the load is reduced. Besides bearing noise, there are three other signs that indicate that a wheel bearing needs attention or replacement: roughness, grease seal leakage, and excessive axial play.

Bearing Roughness

The same wear that causes bearing noise can also be felt as a roughness if the wheel is rotated with the tire off the ground. If the suspect bearing is not on a driven axle, raise and support the vehicle, then slowly rotate the wheels by hand to check bearing condition. Feel for roughness in the bearing as it turns, and listen for a low-frequency rumbling noise. Compare the results on opposite sides of the vehicle to determine where the problem lies.

Bearing Grease Seal Leakage

Grease leaking from the bearing grease seal can be a sign that excessive bearing play has caused seal damage. Always replace leaking grease seals to prevent contamination of the brake linings. Service the wheel bearings at the same time.

Bearing Axial Play

If inward and outward movement of the bearing hub or axle exceeds specifications, the bearings must be serviced. Checking the **axial play**, or endplay, with a dial indicator is the only accurate means of determining the condition of sealed, double-row bearing assemblies.

To check:

1. Raise and properly support the vehicle, then remove the wheel.
2. If the bearings to be checked are on a wheel equipped with a disc brake, push the caliper pistons into their bores just far enough that the brake pads do not drag against the rotor.
3. Mount a dial indicator on the suspension and position the plunger against the edge of the bearing hub, figure 6-1.
4. Push the hub inward toward the suspension until it will move no farther. Hold the hub in position and zero the indicator dial.

A5

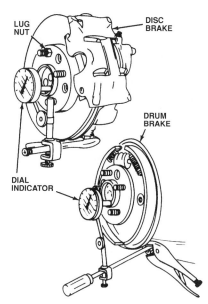

Fig. 6-1. Bearing axial play is measured at the edge of the bearing hub on a dial indicator mounted to the suspension.

Axial Play: Clearance that permits axial motion, or in and out movement of a part.

5. Pull the hub outward away from the suspension until it will move no farther. The dial indicator reading equals the bearing axial play.

Adjustable dual wheel bearings, or **tapered roller bearings**, which are used on the front wheels of most rear-wheel-drive (RWD) vehicles and at the rear wheels of most front-wheel-drive (FWD) vehicles, generally operate with 0.001 to 0.005 inch (0.025 to 0.127 mm) of axial play.

FWD vehicles usually have sealed wheel bearings at the front. Typically, sealed *ball* bearing assemblies are allowed a maximum of 0.002 inch (0.05 mm) of axial play. Consult the factory shop manual to get the proper specifications. If the axial play of a sealed bearing exceeds the amount allowed by the vehicle manufacturer, replace the bearing.

WHEEL BEARING SERVICE

Whenever you replace a tapered roller or ball bearing that has a separate outer **bearing race**, you must replace the race as well. If you install a new bearing in an old race, it will not fit properly, and premature bearing wear and failure will result. Also, install new grease seals whenever wheel bearings are serviced.

Wheel Bearing Cleaning

When an unsealed wheel bearing is removed, wipe as much old grease as possible off of the bearing, using dry rags or paper towels. Then, inspect the grease on the towels for metal chips or other indications of bearing wear or damage. Clean bearings with fresh petroleum-base solvent. Wash each bearing individually and keep bearings with detachable outer bearing races separated, so they can be assembled in the same races from which they were removed.

Once all of the old grease has been washed out, flush the bearings with a non-petroleum-based brake cleaning fluid; this removes any traces of oil and solvent that can contaminate the new grease and lead to premature bearing failure. Finally, hold the bearings by their cages and dry them with unlubricated, low-pressure compressed air. Direct the air through the bearing so it travels across the rollers from side to side. Never spin a bearing with air while drying it. Spinning it at high speed can cause rapid wear and damage.

Wheel Bearing Inspection

Once the bearings are clean and dry, inspect them for signs of wear and damage, figure 6-2. To inspect a bearing, rotate it carefully in a good light so the complete surface of each ball, roller, and race can be fully checked. If any problems are apparent, or its condition appears questionable, replace the bearing.

Wipe the bearing races in the hub clean and examine them under a good light. If they appear pitted or scored, or if the wear surface is flaking off, both the race and bearing must be replaced.

Wheel Bearing Lubrication

Always pack a new or used wheel bearing with the type of grease recommended by the vehicle manufacturer. Several different **thickening agents** are used to formulate greases, and most do not mix. Always clean away every trace of old grease before repacking a wheel bearing, and never add new grease to old.

To pack a wheel bearing, work the grease into the cage and races and between the balls or rollers, so that no air spaces remain. The most effective way to do this is to use a bearing packer, which uses air or hydraulic pressure to force new grease through the entire bearing, figure 6-3.

If a bearing packer is unavailable, pack wheel bearings by hand. To hand pack a tapered roller bearing, fill the palm of one hand with grease. Grasp the bearing in your other hand so the large end faces down. Then, draw the bearing across the grease in your palm to force grease into the cage and rollers until it oozes out the opposite side. Repeat this process all around the bearing until it is completely filled with grease. Finish by spreading a medium coating of grease around the outside circumference of the bearing.

Tapered Roller Wheel Bearing Service

Whenever you replace a tapered roller bearing that has a separate outer bearing race, you must replace the race as well. If you install a new bearing in an old race, it will not fit properly, and premature bearing wear and failure will result. Also, install new grease seals whenever wheel bearings are serviced. Serviceable tapered roller wheel bearings are typically found at the front of RWD vehicles, and at the rear of FWD vehicles.

To service a set of adjustable dual wheel bearings, follow these steps:

1. Raise and support the vehicle so the wheels with the bearings to be serviced hang free, then remove the wheels.
2. Pull the dust cap from the center of the hub to expose the adjusting nut. Remove the cotter pin, retainer, or any other locking devices from the nut. On vehicles that have a split nut with a pinch bolt, loosen the bolt so the adjusting nut can turn freely, figure 6-4.
3. Loosen the adjusting nut by backing it off several turns to allow approximately 0.5 inch (13 mm) of play.
4. Pull the drum or rotor outward to free the thrust washer and outer wheel bearing, then push the drum or rotor inward to reseat it on the spindle.
5. Hold the drum or rotor steady to keep it centered, then remove the adjusting nut, thrust washer, and outer wheel bearing from the hub, and set them aside.
6. Pull the drum or rotor straight outward to slide it off the spindle, taking care not to drag the inner wheel bearing across the adjusting nut threads. The brake adjustment may need to be loosened to remove some drums.

Bearing Race: The portion of a bearing that the rolling elements ride on. Tapered roller bearings usually have a removable outer race that fits into the wheel or brake hub.

Tapered Roller Bearing: A bearing assembly that consists of an inner race, tapered cylindrical rollers, a cage to space the rollers apart, and an outer race.

Thickening Agent: A component of bearing and chassis grease that retains the oils in the mixture.

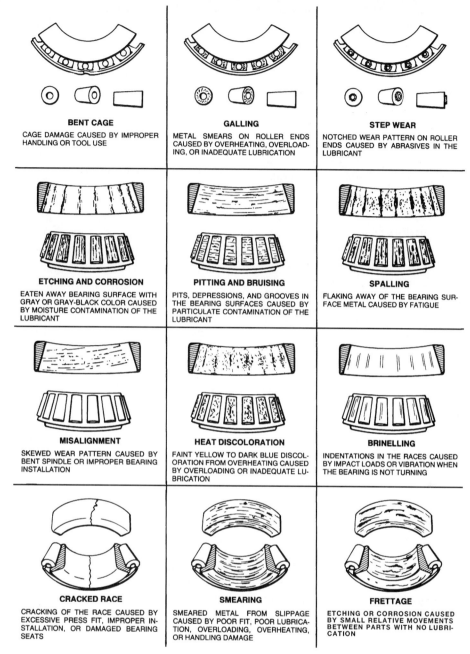

BENT CAGE
CAGE DAMAGE CAUSED BY IMPROPER HANDLING OR TOOL USE

GALLING
METAL SMEARS ON ROLLER ENDS CAUSED BY OVERHEATING, OVERLOADING, OR INADEQUATE LUBRICATION

STEP WEAR
NOTCHED WEAR PATTERN ON ROLLER ENDS CAUSED BY ABRASIVES IN THE LUBRICANT

ETCHING AND CORROSION
EATEN AWAY BEARING SURFACE WITH GRAY OR GRAY-BLACK COLOR CAUSED BY MOISTURE CONTAMINATION OF THE LUBRICANT

PITTING AND BRUISING
PITS, DEPRESSIONS, AND GROOVES IN THE BEARING SURFACES CAUSED BY PARTICULATE CONTAMINATION OF THE LUBRICANT

SPALLING
FLAKING AWAY OF THE BEARING SURFACE METAL CAUSED BY FATIGUE

MISALIGNMENT
SKEWED WEAR PATTERN CAUSED BY BENT SPINDLE OR IMPROPER BEARING INSTALLATION

HEAT DISCOLORATION
FAINT YELLOW TO DARK BLUE DISCOLORATION FROM OVERHEATING CAUSED BY OVERLOADING OR INADEQUATE LUBRICATION

BRINELLING
INDENTATIONS IN THE RACES CAUSED BY IMPACT LOADS OR VIBRATION WHEN THE BEARING IS NOT TURNING

CRACKED RACE
CRACKING OF THE RACE CAUSED BY EXCESSIVE PRESS FIT, IMPROPER INSTALLATION, OR DAMAGED BEARING SEATS

SMEARING
SMEARED METAL FROM SLIPPAGE CAUSED BY POOR FIT, POOR LUBRICATION, OVERLOADING, OVERHEATING, OR HANDLING DAMAGE

FRETTAGE
ETCHING OR CORROSION CAUSED BY SMALL RELATIVE MOVEMENTS BETWEEN PARTS WITH NO LUBRICATION

Fig. 6-2. Tapered roller bearing inspection guide.

A5

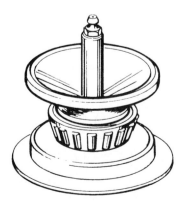

Fig. 6-3. A bearing packer uses air or hydraulic pressure to force grease into the bearing.

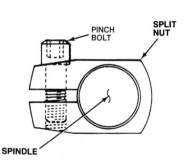

PINCH BOLT

SPLIT NUT

SPINDLE

Fig. 6-4. On a split nut with a pinch bolt, loosen the pinch bolt so the adjusting nut can turn freely.

7. Use a seal puller or a pair of pry bars to carefully remove the grease seal and inner bearing.
8. Clean and inspect the bearings and bearing races as described earlier. Also, clean all old grease from the inside of the drum or rotor hub.
9. If installing new bearings, remove the old outer bearing races from the drum or rotor hub. There are two methods of removing bearing races:
   a. With a bearing race puller, figure 6-5.
   b. With a soft-metal (such as brass) drift. Fit the drift through the hub so it firmly contacts the backside of the race. Strike the drift with a hammer while moving it around the race to drive the race from the hub.
10. New races are pressed or driven into the hub with a bearing race driver or a suitably sized socket, figure 6-6. Support the underside of the hub with a block of wood to prevent damage while installing races.
11. Clean and inspect the spindle for rust, scratches, and discoloration. If the spindle is badly scored, cracked, or discolored from overheating, replace it.
12. Lightly coat the spindle with grease.

13. Pack the wheel bearings with grease as described earlier.
14. Place the drum or rotor outer side down on the workbench and lightly coat the inside of the hub with grease to prevent rust.
15. Put a medium coating of grease on the inner bearing race, then place the inner bearing into the race.
16. Use a seal driver to install the grease seal, then apply a light coating of grease on the seal lip.
17. Turn the drum or rotor over and apply a medium coating of grease to the outer bearing race.
18. Fit the drum or rotor squarely over the spindle and slide it straight back into position. Take care to avoid dragging the bearing races across the spindle threads.
19. Hold the drum or rotor in place, fit the outer bearing over the end of the spindle, and slip it into position in the hub. Install the thrust washer over the bearing and thread the adjusting nut onto the spindle finger-tight.
20. Adjust the wheel bearings as described below.
21. If the axle is equipped with disc brakes, install the anchor plate and brake caliper. If the axle has drum brakes and the brake adjustment was loosened, adjust the brakes.
22. Install the wheel and tighten the lug nuts to specified torque following the correct sequence.

Tapered Roller Bearing Adjustment

There are three ways to adjust tapered roller wheel bearings: by hand, with a torque wrench, or using a dial indicator. Once the axial play is properly set, lock the adjusting nut in place, and install the dust cap with a soft-faced hammer. With a castellated adjusting nut, slots on the nut must align with the hole drilled through the spindle, in order to install the cotter pin. If slots are out of alignment after setting axial play, tighten the nut just enough to insert the cotter pin. Do not loosen the nut. When a locknut is used to secure the adjusting nut, place the locknut over the adjusting nut so the slots in the lock align with the cotter pin hole in the spindle. With either design, insert a new cotter pin and wrap the tabs around the nut lock or adjusting nut to secure it, figure 6-7. To secure a slotted adjusting nut with a pinch bolt, simply tighten the bolt to the specified torque.

Hand Adjustment

To adjust the wheel bearings by hand, rotate the wheel while snugly drawing up the adjusting nut with a wrench to seat the bearings.

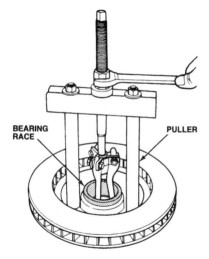

Fig. 6-5. Using a bearing race puller to remove the old race from the hub.

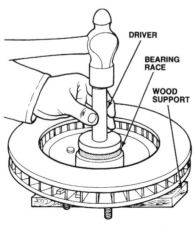

Fig. 6-6. Select a suitably sized driver to install bearing races into the hub.

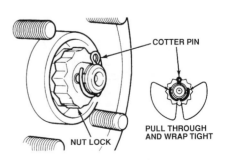

Fig. 6-7. Wrap the tabs of the cotter pin around the nut lock or adjusting nut to secure.

Torque Wrench Adjustment

To adjust the wheel bearings with a torque wrench, rotate the wheel and draw the adjusting nut up to the initial tightening torque value specified by the vehicle manufacturer, figure 6-8. Typically, tapered roller wheel bearings are initially tightened to about 12 to 25 ft-lb (15 to 35 Nm) of torque. Back off the adjusting nut approximately ⅓ turn, then tighten it to the final tightening torque value specified by the vehicle manufacturer. Final torque typically falls in the 10 to 15 in-lb (1 to 1.5 Nm) range. Check axial play and lock the adjusting nut in place.

Dial Indicator Adjustment

To adjust the wheel bearings with a dial indicator, tighten the adjusting nut to 12 to 25 ft-lb (15 to 35 Nm) of torque while rotating the wheel. Back off the adjusting nut ¼ to ½ turn or until it is just loose, then tighten the nut by hand to a snug fit. Mount a dial indicator on the wheel and position it so the plunger rests against the end of the spindle, figure 6-9. Push the wheel back onto the spindle as far as possible, zero the dial indicator, then pull out on the wheel and read axial play on the dial indicator. Tighten the adjusting nut as needed to obtain the clearance specified by the vehicle manufacturer. Typically, axial play tolerance is in the 0.001 to 0.005 inch (0.025 to 0.127 mm) range. Lock the adjusting nut in place to complete the adjustment.

Sealed Wheel Bearing Service

The sealed, double-row wheel bearing assemblies used on the front wheels of most FWD vehicles, as well as the driven and non-driven wheels of many late-model vehicles, are serviced by replacing them when their axial play exceeds the recommended specification.

Some sealed wheel bearing designs combine the bearings with the wheel hub assembly, which makes replacement a relatively easy procedure, figure 6-10. Simply remove the bearing/hub retaining bolts; then, remove the assembly and replace it. Some models require the use of a thread locking compound on the bearing and hub mounting fasteners. The mounting fastener threads should be cleaned with a thread cleaner prior to application of the thread locking compound. Use only the type of thread cleaner and thread locking compound recommended by the vehicle manufacturer.

Replacing a sealed wheel bearing assembly on a driven front axle is more involved. On some designs, the steering knuckle must be removed from the vehicle in order to replace the wheel bearings. A press or special pullers are used to remove the bearings from the steering knuckle, and a press is usually used to install the new bearings, figure 6-11.

Once the new parts are installed and the fasteners are tightened to specified torque, sealed bearings require no adjustment.

Parking Brake Inspection

Check parking brake operation during a road test by applying the parking brake while coasting down a gentle hill. The lever or handle should apply smoothly without binding as it slows the vehicle to a stop. If it does not, suspect cable problems. If more than two-thirds of the parking brake control travel is required to apply the brake, the shoe-to-drum or pad-to-disc

A5

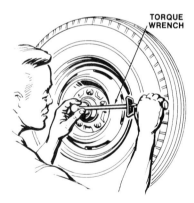

Fig. 6-8. Using a torque wrench to adjust tapered roller wheel bearings.

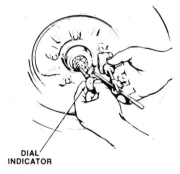

Fig. 6-9. Dial indicator setup for adjusting tapered roller wheel bearings.

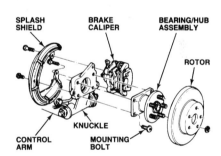

Fig. 6-10. The sealed wheel bearings for the driven axle on some vehicles are an integral part of the bearing/hub assembly.

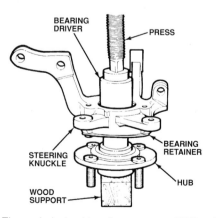

Fig. 6-11. The sealed wheel bearings on some FWD vehicles are press fit to the hub and steering knuckle, so the steering knuckle must be removed from the vehicle to service them.

clearance is probably excessive due to lack of adjustment. If the parking brake cannot hold the vehicle on a grade, inspect the friction assemblies for contaminated or glazed linings, binding cables, and other problems.

Raise the vehicle on a lift to inspect the parking brake cables. Look for rust, corrosion, and fraying. If the cable is in good condition, lubricate the exposed sections with chassis grease for future protection.

Parking Brake Cable Replacement

Parking brake linkages have from one to four cables that can be arranged in a wide variety of configurations. A typical domestic linkage has a control cable that runs from the parking brake control to the equalizer or adjuster, a transfer cable that runs from the equalizer or adjuster to near the rear wheels, and two application cables that run from connectors at the ends of the transfer cable to the parking brake levers at the wheels.

When a parking brake cable needs replacement, check the entire run of all the cables to see if any additional parts need to be replaced. Cable mounting hardware is often badly corroded and will break apart when you remove the old cable. If the mounting hardware is in good condition, transfer it to the new cable. After installing the new cable, adjust it as described in the next section, then apply the parking brake hard three or four times to pre-stretch the cable; readjust the cable if necessary.

Parking Brake Adjustment

A common brake service mistake is to adjust the parking brake cable when the real reason for poor parking brake performance is excessive clearance between the brake linings and the drum or rotor. Make sure the wheel brakes and internal parking brake mechanism are in proper adjustment before shortening the parking brake cable.

When the parking brake is controlled by a foot pedal or under-dash handle, the cable adjuster is generally located under the vehicle at an intermediate lever or equalizer, figure 6-12. If the parking brake is controlled by a floor-mounted lever, the adjustments are usually made inside the passenger compartment where the cables attach to the lever assembly, figure 6-13. On most floor-mounted levers, a rubber boot or plastic cover must be lifted up or removed to access the adjustment mechanism.

Typically, cable adjusters use two jam nuts—an adjusting nut and a locknut—to set the cable length. However, a few cable designs use a single, self-locking adjusting nut. If the nuts

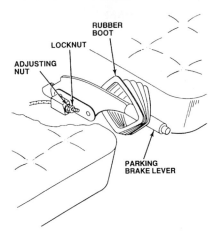

Fig. 6-13. Parking brake cables controlled by a floor-mounted lever generally adjust inside the passenger compartment where the cables connect to the lever.

are seized to the threaded adjuster rod, soak the assembly with penetrating oil before attempting to make the adjustment.

To adjust the cable, hold the adjusting nut in place with an open-end wrench and loosen the locknut with a second wrench, figure 6-14. Rotate the adjusting nut to draw the end of the cable through the lever or equalizer to shorten the working length of the cable. Once the adjustment is complete, hold the adjusting nut in place with an open-end wrench and tighten the locknut against it with a second wrench.

Always use two wrenches to avoid twisting the cables when making an adjustment. Twisting places the cables under additional stress that can lead to premature failure. If necessary, use a pair of locking pliers on an unthreaded section of the threaded rod to hold the cable stationary while tightening the adjusting nut. Some cables have a slot in the end of the threaded rod so a screwdriver can be used to prevent the cable from twisting.

BRAKE WARNING LAMP SERVICE

The red brake warning lamp can indicate a severe brake system failure. If the brake warning lamp circuit is working correctly, it should prove out by turning on when the ignition switch is turned on, then turning off once the engine is started. When the red brake warning lamp is illuminated, verify proper functioning of the brake system before operating the vehicle. In most cases, the problems you will diagnose will be due to the lamp

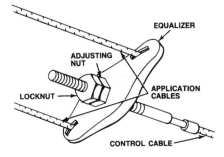

Fig. 6-12. Parking brake cables are adjusted at the equalizer, which is located under the vehicle, on most designs that are activated by a foot pedal or underdash handle.

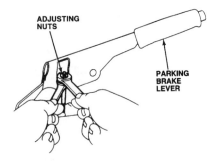

Fig. 6-14. Hold the adjusting nut with one wrench and loosen the locknut with a second wrench, then turn the adjusting nut to obtain the correct cable length.

being illuminated. In some cases though, you may see a lamp that will not work at all. In this section, we will discuss some common ways in which you can diagnose both problems.

On a typical brake system, there are two switches or sensors that can cause the red brake lamp to illuminate. One is located on the master cylinder and the other is located on the parking brake lever. On these systems, application of the parking brake or low brake fluid level will cause the red brake lamp to illuminate. Of course, there are circuit problems that can occur that would cause the lamp to turn on. These include: shorted indicator circuit, ABS system failure (if equipped), or instrument cluster printed circuit board failure.

On some models, the instrument cluster is controlled by an electronic control unit (ECU). If a problem exists on one of these systems, some of the basic principles discussed here can be applied to help diagnose the red brake warning lamp circuit, but more than likely, a factory shop manual along with a wiring diagram manual will have to be consulted. Many factory shop manuals outline very in-depth pinpoint tests that should be followed to quickly lead you to proper diagnosis of the red brake warning lamp. In figure 6-15, an example of a Ford diagnostic test is shown.

BRAKE WARNING LAMP CIRCUIT TESTING

Preliminary Inspection

When diagnosing the brake warning lamp, first check the brake fluid level. If it is low, determine the cause of low fluid level, then fill and recheck the system. If fluid level is ok, inspect the parking brake system to ensure it is fully released. If the parking brake system does not release inspect all parking brake cables and mechanisms to determine the cause of failure. Repair and recheck warning lamp operation. If fluid level and parking brake operation are ok, suspect a faulty switch, shorted circuit, or ABS malfunction (if equipped).

Fluid Level Switch Test

To test the fluid level switch, disconnect the switch, then measure the resistance of the switch using a suitable digital volt-ohmmeter. When the fluid level switch is in the full position, the ohmmeter should indicate open circuit, figure 6-16. When the fluid level switch is in the low position, the ohmmeter should indicate continuity.

Parking Brake Switch Test

To test the parking brake switch, disconnect the switch, then measure resistance when the parking brake is not applied. The ohmmeter should indicate open circuit. When the parking brake is applied, the ohmmeter should indicate continuity.

Warning Lamp Circuit Wiring Inspection

Unwanted Ground

The wiring diagram shown in figure 6-17 shows three different areas of the circuit where an unwanted ground might occur. If an unwanted ground occurred in any of these areas, the red brake warning lamp would illuminate. In the circuit shown, one way to tell if there is an unwanted ground would be to disconnect the fluid level switch and the parking brake switch. If the lamp is still on, suspect an unwanted ground that exists before the switches.

To check for an unwanted ground in the circuit shown in figure 6-17, first remove the fuse supplying the circuit with power. Next, disconnect both the brake fluid level switch and the parking brake switch. Using a suitable digital volt-ohmmeter, check the resistance of the harness to ground at several points throughout the circuit. If continuity is indicated by the ohmmeter, suspect that portion of the circuit for the unwanted ground.

Open Circuit

The wiring diagram shown in figure 6-18 shows four places where the circuit is open. If an open occurred at point "A" of the circuit, the indicator would not work at all. If an open occurred at points "B" or "C," the brake fluid level indicator portion of the circuit would not work at all. If an open occurred at points "D" or "E," the indicator would not illuminate if the parking brake were applied.

Short Circuit

If the circuit shown in figure 6-18 were grounded at point "A," you would have a short circuit. This condition would cause the fuse supplying the circuit to open. If the fuse were replaced, it would immediately open again if the short were present. To find the short circuit, a careful examination of the wiring harness would be necessary.

Stop Light Diagnosis and Adjustment

There are two potential problems in the stop light circuit: Either the stop lights fail to come on when the brakes are applied, or they are always on. Most problems are the result of burned-out fuses or bulbs, a faulty stoplight switch, faulty wiring, or a switch that is out of adjustment.

Virtually all late-model vehicles have mechanical switches on the brake pedal linkage. These require adjustment when they are installed.

Mechanical Stoplight Switch Adjustment

There are two basic methods to adjust stoplight switches. After performing either adjustment, check the brake lights for proper operation.

Stoplight switches for most import vehicles have a threaded shank that screws into place and is secured in position by a locknut. To adjust these switches, loosen the locknut on the threaded shank of the stoplight switch body, figure 6-19. Turn the switch to move it in or out of its mounting bracket and obtain the correct clearance between the brake pedal arm and the switch plunger. When properly adjusted, depressing the brake pedal ½ inch (13 mm) will illuminate the brake lights.

Many domestic vehicles have a semi-automatic adjustment mechanism. To install and adjust, depress the brake pedal and insert the switch to fully seat it into the tubular clip on the brake pedal mounting bracket, figure 6-20. The switch clicks into place when fully seated. Pull up on the brake pedal to adjust the switch position. This causes the switch to ratchet in the tubular clip and emits a series of clicks as it does so. Release the pedal, and repeat the previous step until the clicking of the ratchet stops.

A5

Test Step	Result/Action To Take
1|CHECK THE BASE BRAKE SYSTEM OPERATION Key In Start Position Operate the base brake system **Does the base brake system operate correctly?**	**Yes** Go To **Step 2** **No** Diagnose Base Brake System
2|CHECK BRAKE WARNING INDICATOR NOTE: Make sure brake fluid is filled to correct level and the parking brake is released. Key in ON position Key In Start Position Observe the instrument cluster brake warning indicator. **Does the brake warning indicator turn on when the ignition switch is in START position and turn off when the ignition switch is in the OFF position?**	**Yes** The system is ok **No** If the brake warning indicator is always on, Go to **Step 3** If the brake warning indicator is never on, Go to **Step 9**
3|CHECK THE PARKING BRAKE SWITCH Key in OFF position Disconnect: Parking Brake Switch Key in ON position **Is the brake warning indicator illuminated?**	**Yes** Go To **Step 4** **No** INSTALL a new parking brake switch
4|CHECK THE ABS MODULE Key in OFF position Disconnect: ABS Module Key in ON position Observe the brake warning indicator **Is the brake warning indicator illuminated?**	**Yes** Go to Step 5 **No** Diagnose ABS/Traction Control System
5|CHECK THE BRAKE LEVEL SWITCH OPERATION NOTE: Prior to running this test step, check the brake fluid level and fill (if necessary) to make sure that the brake fluid level is correct Key in OFF position Disconnect: Brake Fluid Level Switch Key in ON position Observe the instrument cluster brake warning indicator. **Is the brake warning indicator illuminated?**	**Yes** REPAIR the circuit. TEST the system for normal operation **No** Go to **Step 6**
6|CHECK BRAKE FLUID LEVEL SWITCH NOTE: Verify that the brake fluid level is full Measure the resistance between the brake fluid level switch (component side) terminal 1 and the brake fluid level switch (component side) terminal 3; and between the brake fluid level switch (component side) terminal 2 and the brake fluid level switch (component side) terminal 3. **Is the resistance greater than 10,000 ohms between terminals 1 and 3; and less than 5 ohms between terminals 2 and 3 of the brake fluid level switch?**	**Yes** Go to Step 7 **No** INSTALL a new brake fluid level switch. TEST the system for normal operation.
7|CHECK IGNITION SWITCH CIRCUIT Key in OFF position Measure resistance between the brake fluid level switch harness pin 2 and ground Key in START position Measure resistance between the brake fluid level switch harness pin 2 and ground while ignition switch is in the START position **Is the resistance less than 5 ohms with the ignition switch in the START position, and greater than 10,000 ohms with the ignition switch in the OFF position?**	**Yes** Go to Step 10 **No** Go to Step 8
8|CHECK PIN 2 CIRCUIT FOR OPEN Key in OFF position Disconnect ignition switch Measure resistance between the brake fluid level switch harness pin 2 and ignition switch connector circuit 409. **Is the resistance less than 5 ohms?**	**Yes** Diagnose steering column concern **No** REPAIR the circuit. TEST the system for normal operation
9|CHECK PIN 3 CIRCUIT FOR OPEN Key in OFF position Disconnect: Brake Fluid Level Switch Measure the resistance between the instrument cluster harness connector pin (brake fluid level switch) and brake fluid level switch harness pin 3 **Is the resistance less than 5 ohms?**	**Yes** Go to Step 10 **No** REPAIR the circuit. TEST the system for normal operation
10|CHECK FOR CORRECT INSTRUMENT CLUSTER OPERATION Disconnect all instrument cluster connections Check for corrosion and pushed out pins Connect all instrument cluster connectors and make sure they seat correctly Operate the system and verify the concern is still present **Is the concern still present?**	**Yes** INSTALL a new instrument cluster. TEST the system for normal operation. **No** The system is operating correctly at this time. Concern may have been caused by loose or corroded connector. Clear DTC's. Repeat self test.

Fig. 6-15. 2003 Lincoln Town Car brake warning lamp diagnostic test.

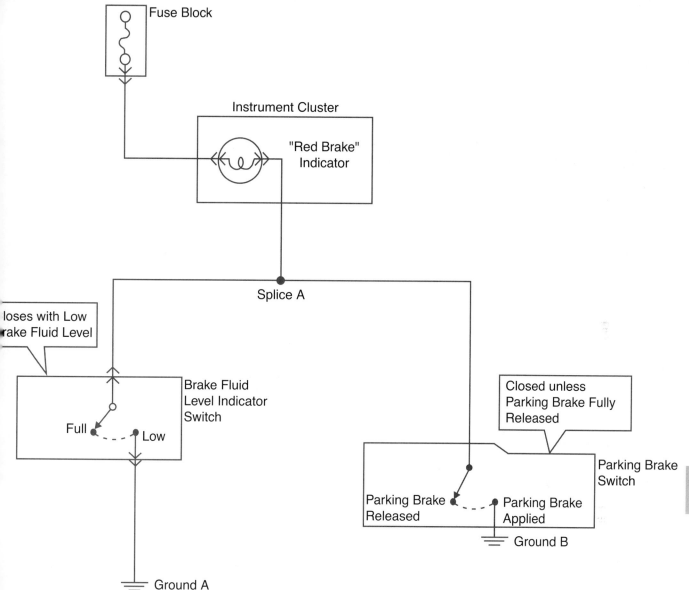

Fig. 6-16. Typical brake warning lamp circuit diagram.

Switch Replacement

To replace the parking brake switch, first locate the switch on the parking brake foot pedal or lever. Disconnect the switch, then remove it from its mounting. Install the new switch. Depending on make and model application, the new switch may require adjustment. As a general rule, adjust the switch so the red brake light illuminates as the parking brake is applied. Ensure the lamp goes out after the parking brake is released. Consult a factory shop manual for specific make and model applications.

To replace a brake fluid level switch, first determine if the switch is integral to the master cylinder, or the reservoir. Sometimes the switch may thread into the reservoir and replacing it is just a mater of unscrewing the old one and installing a new one. If it is integral to the cylinder and cannot be replaced separately, the master cylinder should be replaced. On other applications, the switch is located in the plastic reservoir. On many of these applications, the reservoir can be replaced without replacing the entire master cylinder.

A general replacement procedure is given for one of these applications. As always, consult a factory shop manual if you are not sure of the system found on your specific make and model.

1. Disconnect the brake fluid level switch.
2. Remove fluid from the master cylinder reservoir using a suitable suction device.
3. Carefully pry up on the master cylinder reservoir and remove from master cylinder.
4. Remove and discard the reservoir grommets. Lubricate new grommets using new brake fluid and install them to the master cylinder.
5. Install the reservoir until it is fully seated into the master cylinder.
6. Connect the brake fluid level switch, then fill the master cylinder with the recommended fluid. Bleed the system if necessary.

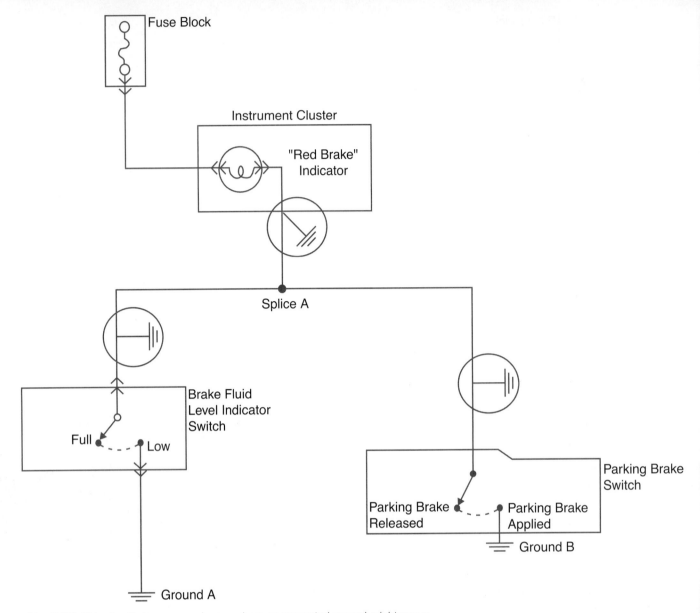

Fig. 6-17. This circuit shows several areas where an unwanted ground might occur.

Brake Pedal Inspection

With the engine running, apply and release the brake pedal several times and check for friction and noise. Brake pedal movement should be smooth and return fast, with no squeaks or noise from the pedal or linkage. Inspect the brake pedal and linkage for proper alignment. Ensure the brake pedal mounting and push rod fasteners are secure and all bushings, washers, and clips are properly installed. Check the brake pedal pushrod floor pan or dash panel grommet for wear and proper installation.

Using light hand pressure, move the brake pedal in the lateral direction to check the bushings for wear. Slight movement is acceptable. If movement is excessive, the brake pedal bushings are worn must be replaced, figure 6-21. Inspect the brake pedal return spring for wear and damage. Friction and binding of brake pedal components or linkages may result in dragging brakes.

Check the brake pedal height and **freeplay** and the stop lamp switch adjustments. Improper brake pedal height and freeplay may result in excessive pedal travel or dragging brakes.

Brake Pedal Linkage Adjustment

It is essential to adjust the pushrod on a new or reconditioned master cylinder to establish the correct brake pedal freeplay. If correct pushrod adjustment is not obtained, excessive pedal travel or dragging brakes may result. To adjust the pushrod:

1. Pedal pushrod. Loosen the locknut on the pushrod, figure 6-22. If the vehicle has a power booster, pump the brake pedal until the reserve is exhausted and the pedal feel hardens.

Freeplay: The distance a brake pedal can be depressed before the master cylinder starts to displace fluid.

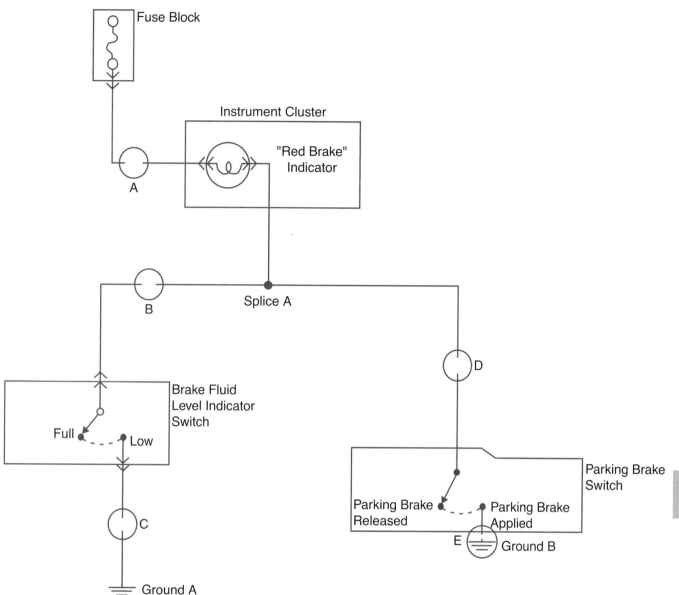

Fig. 6-18. This circuit shows several areas where an open may occur.

2. Place a ruler along the axis of brake pedal travel, then slowly apply the pedal by hand until all the slack in the linkage is eliminated. This amount of travel is the freeplay.

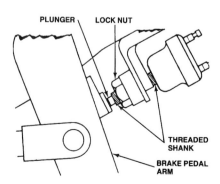

Fig. 6-19. To adjust a stoplight switch with a threaded shank, loosen the locknut, thread the switch in or out to the desired length, then tighten the locknut.

3. Adjust the freeplay by shortening or lengthening the brake, rotating the pushrod until you get the specified freeplay, then tightening the locknut.

Brake Pedal Service

The brake pedal installation method will vary from model to model. Different types of fasteners, brackets, switches, and

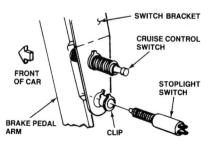

Fig. 6-20. This stoplight switch installs with a tubular clip that semiautomatically adjusts the switch position.

A5

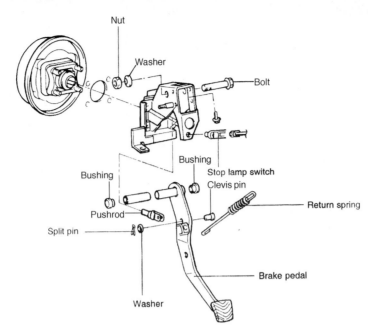

Fig. 6-21. Typical brake pedal components.

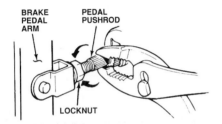

Fig. 6-22. Brake pedal freeplay is usually adjusted by loosening a locknut and turning the pushrod to obtain the proper length.

other components may be used. The following is a basic brake pedal service procedure.

1. Disconnect the brake pedal return spring.
2. Remove the stop lamp switch from the mounting bracket.
3. Remove the push rod split pin and washer from the clevis pin.
4. Remove the clevis pin and detach the push rod from the brake pedal.
5. Remove the brake pedal retaining nut and washer.
6. Remove the bolt securing the brake pedal to the support bracket.
7. Remove the brake pedal sleeve and bushings.

8. Inspect the brake pedal components for wear and damage and replace components as necessary.
9. Install the brake pedal bushings and sleeve to the brake pedal. Some models may require the application of a lubricant to the brake pedal bushings and other components. Follow the vehicle manufacturer's recommendations for lubricant type and application.
10. Position the brake pedal to the support bracket and install the retaining bolt.
11. Install the washer, then install and tighten the retaining nut. Tighten the retaining nut to the specification recommended by the vehicle manufacturer.
12. Position the push rod to the brake pedal and install the clevis pin. Some models may require the application of a lubricant to the clevis pin. Follow the vehicle manufacturer's recommendations for lubricant type and application.
13. Install the clevis pin washer and secure with the split pin.
14. Install the stop lamp switch. Adjust the stop lamp switch as described previously.
15. Connect the brake pedal return spring.
16. Adjust the brake pedal height and freeplay.
17. Check the brake pedal and stop lamps for proper operation.

CHAPTER QUESTIONS

1. All of the following indicate that wheel bearings need service *EXCEPT*:
   a. A growling sound that increases with cornering loads
   b. A body vibration that occurs when the brakes are applied
   c. Roughness, grease seal leakage, and excessive axial play
   d. A growling sound that occurs only when the brakes are applied

2. The axial play of a typical tapered roller wheel bearing assembly should be:
   a. 0.001 to 0.005 inch (0.025 to 0.127 mm)
   b. 0.010 to 0.020 inch (0.050 to 0.100 mm)
   c. 0.010 to 0.050 inch (0.50 to 1.0 mm)
   d. Less than 0.002 inch (0.05 mm)

3. Diagnose the condition of sealed, double-row bearings with:
   a. A dial indicator
   b. A seal inspection
   c. A micrometer
   d. A torque wrench

4. Technician A says that the maximum axial play in a sealed front wheel bearing of a typical FWD car is .0002 inch. Technician B says that the maximum axial play in a sealed front wheel bearing of a typical FWD car is .0005 inch. Who is right?
   a. A only
   b. B only
   c. Both A and B
   d. Neither A nor B

5. Tapered roller wheel bearings can be adjusted by all of the following *EXCEPT*:
   a. Hand method
   b. Torque wrench method
   c. Tension gauge method
   d. Dial indicator method

6. Technician A says that if there is too much travel in the parking brake lever the cables should be shortened. Technician B says that if there is too much travel in the parking brake lever the adjustment of the rear brake lining-to-drum or lining-to-disc clearance should be checked. Who is right?
   a. A only
   b. B only
   c. Both A and B
   d. Neither A nor B

7. If the parking brake will not keep the vehicle from rolling on an incline, the cause may be:
   a. Seized wheel cylinder pistons
   b. Cables shortened excessively at last reline
   c. Seized cables
   d. Out-of-round drums

8. Brake lights should come on when the brake pedal moves down:
   a. 0.005 in.
   b. 0.05 in.
   c. $1/8$ in.
   d. $1/2$ in.

A5

SAMPLE TEST

This sample test will help you review your knowledge of this entire book. The format of the questions is similar to the certification tests given by the National Institute for Automotive Service Excellence. Generally, the questions here are more difficult than the programmed study questions you answered as you read the technical material in this book.

Read these review questions carefully, then read all the possible answers before making your decision. Always select the **best possible answer**. In some cases, you may think all the answers are partially correct, or you may feel that none is exactly right. But in every case, there is a best answer; that is the one you should select.

Answers to the questions in this sample test will be found near the end of this book, before the glossary. If you answer at least 24 of these questions correctly, then you can be confident of your knowledge of the subjects covered in this book and in the ASE Certification Test A5: Brakes. If you answer fewer than 24 correctly, you should reread the text and take another look at the illustrations. Also, check the glossary as you review the material.

1. Technician A says that during a master cylinder overhaul, the primary piston is the first piston installed on assembly. Technician B says that during a master cylinder overhaul, the secondary piston is the first piston installed on assembly. Who is right?
   a. A only
   b. B only
   c. Both A and B
   d. Neither A nor B

2. Technician A says that a feeler gauge and a new piston can be used to check for an oversized master cylinder bore. Technician B says that honing a master cylinder bore should leave the bore wall completely smooth. Who is right?
   a. A only
   b. B only
   c. Neither A nor B
   d. Both A and B

3. A vehicle has the master cylinder mounted next to the steering column in front of the driver. Technician A says that the right front wheel is the first to be bled, followed by the left rear. Technician B says that it takes 3 to 5 strokes of the pedal to bleed each cylinder, and the bleeder valve should be closed prior to the down stroke. Who is right?
   a. A only
   b. B only
   c. Both A and B
   d. Neither A nor B

4. Technician A says the pressure differential switch may need to be recentered after bleeding the brakes. Technician B says there are several types of pressure differential switches, and each requires a different method for recentering. Who is right?
   a. A only
   b. B only
   c. Both A and B
   d. Neither A nor B

5. Technician A says the best way to test a proportioning valve is with a feeler gauge. Technician B says the best way to test a proportioning valve is with a vacuum gauge. Who is right?
   a. A only
   b. B only
   c. Both A and B
   d. Neither A nor B

6. Technician A says a cracked brake hose that is not leaking need not be replaced. Technician B says a brake hose with a blister must be replaced. Who is right?
   a. A only
   b. B only
   c. Both A and B
   d. Neither A nor B

7. Brake pedal reserve that gradually fades under light pressure indicates:
   a. Leaks in the brake lines
   b. Weak brake pedal return spring tension
   c. Internal leaks
   d. The system is operating properly

8. Which of the following is **NOT** a method used to force air and contaminated fluid out of a brake system?
   a. Manual brake bleeding
   b. Pressure tank bleeding
   c. Vacuum bleeding
   d. Bench bleeding

9. The first component in a brake system bleeding sequence is the:
   a. Master cylinder
   b. Wheel cylinder
   c. Combination valve
   d. Proportioning valve

10. The quick-take-up (QTU) valve on a master cylinder regulates fluid flow:
    a. Between the master cylinder and the reservoir
    b. Between the reservoir and the pushrod
    c. Between opposite wheels
    d. Between the two hydraulic circuits of the system

11. Floating drums may be held in place by all of the following **EXCEPT**:
    a. Speed nuts over the wheel studs
    b. Bolts threaded into the hub
    c. The wheel and lug nuts
    d. A castellated spindle nut

12. To detect an out-of-round brake drum, measure it with a:
    a. Drum micrometer
    b. Drum gauge
    c. Drum dial indicator
    d. Shoe setting caliper

13. On calipers with fixed seals, most manufacturers recommend a caliper-to-bore clearance of:
    a. .001–.006 inch for metal pistons; .0005–.0015 for aluminum pistons
    b. .002–.003 inch for aluminum pistons; .003–.007 inch for phenolic pistons
    c. .004–.006 inch for metal pistons; .002–.006 inch for phenolic pistons
    d. .002–.005 inch for metal pistons; .005–.010 inch for phenolic pistons

14. True or False: Some calipers can require special tools to retract the piston.
    a. True
    b. False

15. On calipers with stroking seals, most manufacturers specify a caliper piston-to-bore clearance of:
    a. 0.004 to 0.006 inch
    b. 0.004 to 0.008 inch
    c. 0.004 to 0.010 inch
    d. 0.004 to 0.014 inch

16. A dial indicator can be used to check a brake rotor for:
    a. Radial runout
    b. Parallelism
    c. Taper variation
    d. Lateral runout

17. Technician A says that when turning drums or rotors, both components on the same axle must be machined to the same tolerance. Technician B says that the least amount of metal should be removed during machining. Who is right?
    a. A only
    b. B only
    c. Both A and B
    d. Neither A nor B

18. Technician A says that a new bearing should never be installed in an old bearing race. Technician B says that all wheel bearings are adjustable. Who is right?
    a. A only
    b. B only
    c. Both A and B
    d. Neither A nor B

19. Technician A says that loose wheel bearings can cause a vibration when the brakes are applied. Technician B says that loose wheel bearings can add to rotor lateral runout. Who is right?
    a. A only
    b. B only
    c. Both A and B
    d. Neither A nor B

20. A wheel bearing that needs to be serviced may exhibit all of the following **EXCEPT**:
    a. Roughness
    b. Grease seal leakage
    c. Excessive axial play
    d. Lack of parallelism

21. Technician A says that a basic ABS diagnosis includes checking for a fully charged battery. Technician B says that a basic ABS diagnosis includes checking for blown fuses. Who is right?
    a. A only
    b. B only
    c. Both A and B
    d. Neither A nor B

22. To bleed the rear brakes of an integral ABS, the pressure bleeder should be charged to:
    a. 15 psi (103 kPa)
    b. 25 psi (172 kPa)
    c. 35 psi (241 kPa)
    d. 45 psi (310 kPa)

23. How many power assisted applications should the Hydro-Boost II have in reserve if the accumulator is working properly?
    a. 5 or 6
    b. 4 or 5
    c. 3 or 4
    d. 1 or 2

24. The Hydro-Boost pretest inspection includes:
    a. Pressure testing the power steering pump
    b. Checking accumulator reserve
    c. Checking the power steering pump fluid level
    d. Testing Hydro-Boost function

25. Technician A says that ABS wheel speed sensors are not adjustable. Technician B says that some ABS wheel speed sensors require adjustment upon installation. Who is right?
    a. A only
    b. B only
    c. Both A and B
    d. Neither A nor B

26. True or False: Failure to properly install a vehicle's wheels could result in poor brake system performance.
    a. True
    b. False

27. True or False: A stuck ABS isolation valve could cause a brake pull.
    a. True
    b. False

28. If the ABS and BRAKE warning lamps are on and the power assist is low, the most likely cause would be:
    a. Inoperative ABS control module
    b. A faulty ABS isolation valve
    c. One or more faulty wheel speed sensors
    d. An inoperative pump or an accumulator pressure leak

29. Which of the following statements are not true about on-car brake lathes:
    a. On-car lathes may induce lateral runout
    b. On-car lathes allow rotor machining on the vehicle spindle center line.
    c. The bits used on some on-car lathes cannot be interchanged with those of bench lathes.
    d. You must compensate for lathe runout before the first cut is taken.

30. Which of the following statements are true:
    a. Rotor lateral runout will lead to disc thickness variation
    b. Wheel lug nuts should be tightened with an air impact wrench, as long as the proper tightening sequence is used.
    c. Rotor runout cannot be caused by overtorquing of lug nuts.
    d. Use a dial indicator to measure rotor taper variation

A5

ANSWERS

Chapter 1:
1. c, 2. d, 3. a, 4. b, 5. b, 6. a, 7. b, 8. b, 9. a,
10. a, 11. d, 12. a, 13. a, 14. b, 15. c 16. b,
17. a, 18. a, 19. d, 20. c, 21. d, 22. c

Chapter 2:
1. a, 2. d, 3. a, 4. b, 5. b, 6. d, 7. c, 8. a, 9. d,
10. d, 11. a, 12. a

Chapter 3:
1. b, 2. d, 3. b, 4. c, 5. a, 6. d, 7. c, 8. b, 9. d,
10. b, 11. d, 12. d, 13. c, 14. c, 15. b

Chapter 4:
1. a, 2. a, 3. a, 4. c, 5. c

Chapter 5:
1. d, 2. c, 3. a, 4. b, 5. c, 6. c, 7. a, 8. d, 9. b,
10. a, 11. d, 12. c, 13. a, 14. b

Chapter 6:
1. d, 2. a, 3. a, 4. a, 5. c, 6. b, 7. c, 8. d

Sample Test:
1. b, 2. a, 3. d, 4. c, 5. d, 6. b, 7. c, 8. d, 9. a,
10. a, 11. d, 12. a, 13. d, 14. a, 15. c, 16. d,
17. b, 18. a, 19. c, 20. d, 21. c, 22. c, 23. d,
24. c, 25. b, 26. a, 27. a, 28. d, 29. a, 30. a

GLOSSARY

Accumulator: In Hydro-Boost systems, a gas-charged component that stores hydraulic pressure for emergency use if the power steering belt should break or a hose rupture. Always discharge the accumulator by depressing the pedal numerous times before servicing the system. Also, the part of the antilock system that supplies the power assist to apply the brakes. The accumulator is usually a nitrogen-charged reservoir that holds a supply of pressurized brake fluid.

Add-on ABS: An antilock brake system that uses a conventional master cylinder and vacuum brake booster unit in the traditional location on the firewall. The ABS hydraulic modulator is added on elsewhere in the vehicle.

Anodized Finish: An electrolytically applied coating of a protective oxide. It slows wear.

Axial Play: Clearance that permits axial motion, or in and out movement of a part.

Bearing Race: The portion of a bearing that the rolling elements ride on. Tapered roller bearings usually have a removable outer race that fits into the wheel or brake hub.

Bypassing: In a master cylinder, a condition in which fluid leaks between the piston seals and the bore, which causes the pedal to sink slowly under steady pressure.

Captive Rotors: Rotors that are integral with the hub and require special pullers and procedures for removal, as found on many Asian FWD vehicles. On-car brake lathes provide the most practical means of machining captive rotors.

Check Valve: A one-way valve in the hose between the intake manifold and the vacuum brake booster that traps vacuum in the booster.

Compensating Port: The opening between the master cylinder reservoir and the cylinder bore that allows fluid to enter or exit the hydraulic system to adjust for changes in volume.

Combination Valve: A brake system hydraulic control device that incorporates a pressure differential valve or switch, metering valve, or proportioning valve into one unit.

Diagnostic Trouble Code (DTC): Coded letters and/or numbers that correspond to a specific fault in a given system. For example, if you retrieve a code C1194 on a 2002 Ford Escort, it indicates an open or shorted left front dump valve solenoid.

Dual-Servo Brake: A drum brake that uses servo action to increase apply force. The wheel cylinder pistons push out against the top of both shoes. The primary (leading) shoe moves in the forward direction with the drum, and helps wedge the secondary (trailing) shoe against the drum.

Fixed Caliper: A brake caliper that solidly bolts to the vehicle suspension. The caliper does not move when the brakes are applied.

Fixed Drum: A brake drum that is cast in one piece along with the hub, which contains the wheel bearings. Fixed drums are most often used on non-driven axles, such as at the rear of a front-wheel-drive vehicle.

Fixed Rotor: A fixed rotor is one that installs to a spindle and is held in place by wheel bearings, washer, nut, and cotter pin.

Fixed Seal: A rubber seal that fits in a groove machined into the caliper bore. The caliper piston slides through the inside of the seal as the brakes apply and release.

Floating Caliper: A two-piece brake caliper consisting of a rigid anchor plate and movable body that compresses the pads as the brakes apply. The caliper body is supported by bushings and O-rings that slide on guide pins and sleeves, which attach to the caliper anchor plate.

Floating Drum: A brake drum that installs on a separate axle flange or hub assembly. Floating drums are commonly found on the drive axle of rear-wheel-drive vehicles.

Floating Rotor: A floating rotor is a separate part that installs onto an axle flange or hub assembly. Floating rotors are generally held in place by the wheel lug nuts or bolts. The rotor does not contain the wheel bearings, which are part of the hub.

Freeplay: The distance a brake pedal can be depressed before the master cylinder starts to displace fluid.

Hydro-Boost: A mechanical-hydraulic power brake booster using a spool valve to direct hydraulic pressure from the power steering pump to a power piston. The power piston transmits this hydraulic pressure, along with the mechanical force of the driver applying the brake pedal, to the master cylinder.

Hygroscopic: Water absorbing. Polyglycol brake fluids are hygroscopic.

Integral ABS: An antilock brake system that has a single, or integral, hydraulic unit that functions as a master cylinder, power booster, and hydraulic ABS modulator. This hydraulic unit mounts on the firewall in the same location as a conventional master cylinder.

Lining Material Transfer: A condition where lining material becomes attached to the rotor. This is a normally occurring condition, but in some cases, the transfer can be uneven or excessive.

Metering Valve: A hydraulic system component that keeps the front disc brakes from applying until the space between the shoes and the drum of the rear drum brakes has been taken up.

Modulator: A device that contains high-speed electric solenoid valves that maintain or reduce pressure in the hydraulic brake circuits that feed the calipers or wheel cylinders. The modulator, which is considered the heart of an antilock system, prevents wheel lockup.

Pressure Bleeding: A procedure for removing air from a brake hydraulic system using pressurized fluid and special adapters at the master cylinder.

Primary Shoe: The shoe in a servo brake that transfers a portion of its stopping power to the secondary shoe.

Proportioning Valve: A hydraulic system component that limits the pressure to the rear drum brakes during hard stops to prevent lockup.

Quick-Take-Up (QTU) Master Cylinder: A type of master cylinder that applies a large volume of fluid on the initial brake application to take up the clearance designed into low-drag brake calipers.

Quick-Take-Up (QTU) Valve: The part of the QTU master cylinder that controls the fluid flow between the reservoir and the cylinder bore.

Rotor Lateral Runout: Lateral runout is a side-to-side movement of the rotor as it turns.

Rotor Taper Variation: Taper variation is a difference in thickness across the friction surface of a rotor.

Rotor Thickness Variation: Rotor thickness variation is a variance in thickness at different places around the rotor braking surface.

Secondary Shoe: The shoe in a servo brake that receives extra application force from the primary shoe. The lining of a secondary shoe is larger than that of the primary shoe because it does most of the braking.

Scan Tool: A diagnostic tool that retrieves diagnostic trouble codes and displays the serial data stream, or input and output signals, of an onboard computer to a technician.

Shoe Web: The portion of the brake shoe below the lining table that receives the application force from the wheel cylinder.

Sliding Caliper: A two-piece brake caliper consisting of a body and anchor plate. The anchor plate rigidly attaches to the vehicle suspension, and the body slides on machined ways to bring the pads into contact with the rotor.

Speed Nut: A spring-steel clip that threads onto a stud or bolt to position a part. Speed nuts are used to hold floating drums and rotors in place during vehicle assembly.

Starwheel Adjuster: In a typical Bendix-style drum brake, a threaded expanding assembly that sets shoe-to-drum clearance when its serrated wheel is turned either manually or by a self-adjusting mechanism.

Stroking Seal: A rubber seal that fits into a groove on the caliper piston and strokes, or moves, with the piston as the brakes apply and release.

Tapered Roller Bearing: A bearing assembly that consists of an inner race, tapered cylindrical rollers, a cage to space the rollers apart, and an outer race.

Thickening Agent: A component of bearing and chassis grease that retains the oils in the mixture.

Turning: A machining process that uses a brake lathe to remove metal from drums and rotors to refinish their friction surfaces.

Vacuum Bleeding: A procedure for removing air from a brake hydraulic system using a manual vacuum pump or other vacuum source at the bleeder screws of the calipers and wheel cylinders.

Ways: Polished, machined surfaces that permit movement between two metal parts. Ways machined into the anchor plate and caliper body provide a sliding surface for the caliper.

Wheel Speed Sensor: An electronic sensing device, generally a permanent-magnet generator, that sends information about wheel rotation to the control module of an antilock system. Generally, one sensor is fitted at each of the four wheels.

A5

ELECTRICAL AND ELECTRONIC SYSTEMS

CHAPTER OBJECTIVES

- The technician will complete the ASE task list on General Electrical System Diagnosis.
- The technician will be able to answer 13 questions dealing with the General Electrical System Diagnosis section of the A6 ASE Test.

ELECTRICAL TEST EQUIPMENT

Test Lamps

Test lamps are versatile diagnostic tools for use in answering certain questions about a circuit or a component quickly and easily. Test lamps are available in two types according to their use:

- External-powered
- Self-powered

External-Powered Test Lamps

Often called a 12-volt or probe light, this pointed tool with a bulb in its handle or a bulb connected to two leads and alligator clips is used for voltage-seeking and ground-seeking tests, figure 1-1. It relies on circuit power for operation. To test for an interruption in the insulated side of a circuit, connect the tester lead to a known good ground. Move the probe from point to point along the insulated side of the circuit until an **open circuit** is found. To check for ground, connect the tester lead to a known power source and probe the circuit or component to complete the ground path. If ground is present, the lamp will light.

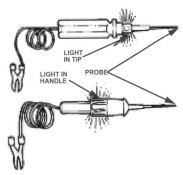

Fig. 1-1. An external-powered test lamp uses the power in the test circuit to check for voltage and ground.

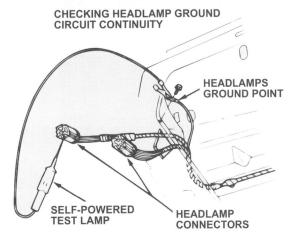

CHECKING HEADLAMP GROUND CIRCUIT CONTINUITY

HEADLAMPS GROUND POINT

SELF-POWERED TEST LAMP

HEADLAMP CONNECTORS

Fig. 1-2. The test circuit must be open to check for continuity with a self-powered test lamp.

Self-Powered Test Lamps

Self-powered test lamps are often called **continuity** lamps and are used to check continuity through a wiring harness or component. Because the self-powered test lamp draws current from its own battery, any circuit or component being tested with the lamp must be disconnected from its voltage source. To use a self-powered test lamp, connect its leads to both ends of the circuit or device, figure 1-2. If the lamp lights, the circuit is complete, or there is electrical continuity through the device. A self-powered test lamp cannot be used to check high-resistance components, such as suppressor-type ignition cables, because of the low **available voltage** of its battery. However, it is ideal for checking fuses, fusible links, bulb filaments, and wiring harnesses or circuits.

Sealing Wires After Probing

Whenever possible, a circuit should be tested by backprobing the connector, not by probing the wire insulation directly. If it is not possible to avoid such damage to the wire insulation, it should be repaired as soon as testing has been completed. The preferred method of repair is the application of **heat shrink tubing** or **heat shrink tape**. Apply the shrink tube or tape and seal in place by heating with a heat gun. Do not use an open flame to apply the heat. If shrink tube is not available use three

---

Available Voltage: The voltage that an electrical device can supply after all losses are taken into account.
Continuity: Continuous, unbroken; used to describe a working electrical circuit or component that is not open.
Heat Shrink Tape: Similar to heat shrink tube but is applied like electrical tape, then heated to seal.
Heat Shrink Tubing: Insulating tubing designed to shrink on wire repairs and seal the connection from moisture and short circuits.
Open Circuit: A circuit that is incomplete; current cannot flow in an open circuit.

turns of electrical tape over the area that was probed, overlapping the tape about ½ inch onto the undamaged insulation at each end of the repair.

Voltmeters

A **voltmeter** measures the electrical pressure differential, in **volts**, between the two points connected by the leads. A voltmeter can be an **analog meter**, figure 1-3, with a needle on a scale, or a **digital meter**, figure 1-4, with a numerical readout. A voltmeter is connected in parallel, or across, a component or circuit. A very small amount of current passes through the meter, while the rest of the current travels through the normal circuit path, figure 1-5. Therefore, the circuit functions normally with the meter connected.

Voltage available at the load is less than that produced by the battery due to circuit **resistance**. A **voltage drop** test is used to calculate the resistance of circuit components while current is flowing in the circuit, figure 1-6. The voltmeter positive lead is connected to the end of the cable that is closest to the power source. The meter negative lead is connected to the cable end that is closest to the circuit ground. The circuit devices must be powered to get a voltage drop reading on the meter. Voltage drop is measured across the device being tested while

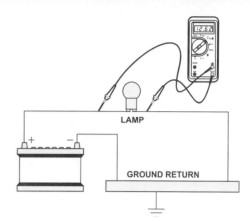

Fig. 1-5. A small amount of current flows through a voltmeter connected in parallel with the test circuit.

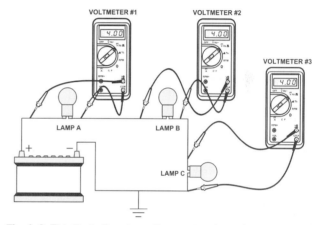

Fig. 1-6. This illustration shows 3 separate voltage drop tests; each meter is reading the voltage drop for a single load in the circuit.

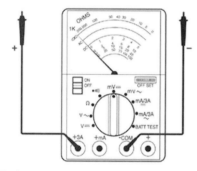

Fig. 1-3. Typical analog multimeter.

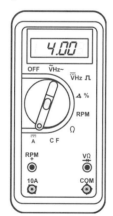

Fig. 1-4. Typical digital multimeter.

current is passing through the circuit. Some Service Manuals provide exact specifications for each application.

Open circuit voltage readings are when there is no load applied to the circuit, figure 1-7. This is a measurement of electrical potential only and not an indication of voltage when the current is flowing.

A voltmeter also can be used to test circuit continuity by connecting it in series with a portion of the circuit and ground, with power applied to the circuit. A meter reading equal to battery voltage shows that there is continuity. This test does not show resistance unless there is current in the circuit.

An analog voltmeter should not be used to test solid-state circuits or components. Analog voltmeters should not be used to test many of the electronic systems used on late-model vehicles because of their low input **impedance**. Such meters may draw too much current, damaging electronic

A6

Analog Meter: A meter displaying values by the movement of a spring loaded needle.

Digital Meter: A meter that provides a numerical readout of the measured value.

Impedance: Impedance is an expression of the opposition that an electronic component, circuit, or system offers to the flow of current.

Open Circuit Voltage: The electrical potential of a circuit when there is no current in it.

Resistance: Opposition to electrical current, usually expressed in ohms.

Volt: A unit of electrical pressure, or electromotive force (EMF).

Voltage Drop: The use or loss of voltage caused by resistance in a conductor, connection, or the circuit load(s).

Voltmeter: A voltmeter is an instrument used for measuring the potential difference, or voltage, between two points in an electrical or electronic circuit. Some voltmeters are intended for use in direct current (DC) circuits; others are designed for alternating current (AC) circuits.

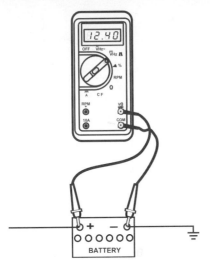

Fig. 1-7. This meter is reading open circuit voltage with no load applied to the battery.

components that work with low current circuitry, or give inaccurate voltage readings because of the additional circuit through the meter.

Conducting a Voltage Drop Test

The voltage that an electrical device uses to do its work is known as the voltage drop. Voltage drop is a normal part of circuit operation, because every load device has resistance; however, an excessive voltage drop can cause a decrease in current and reduce the voltage available to other devices in the circuit. Voltage drops can also be the result of undesired high resistance in a circuit caused by bad connections, malfunctioning components, or wiring problems. *The sum of the individual component, and wiring voltage drops in a series circuit equals the voltage of the source.*

Voltage drop tests can tell you if a device is using too much voltage to do its work. This could mean that the part's resistance is too high or that current flow is too low. If the voltage drop is too low, then some of the part's resistance may be bypassed by a short circuit. Switches, connectors, and conductors normally have no significant voltage drop, but corrosion and loose connections at their junctions often cause a voltage drop, providing less voltage to the rest of the circuit.

You should perform voltage drop tests while current is flowing through the circuit. Voltage drop tests are especially useful for pinpointing faults that occur during operating conditions and might not occur without current flow. You can measure voltage drops directly or calculate them indirectly.

Direct Voltage Drop Test

You can make a voltage drop measurement directly if you can probe both sides of the device with the voltmeter. The voltmeter positive lead is placed on the device side nearest the battery and the negative lead is placed on the side nearest to ground. The voltmeter reading is then the voltage drop across the device. This is because a voltmeter tests the *difference in potential* directly. That is the definition of a voltage drop.

Figure 1-6 shows voltmeter readings for the voltage drops around an entire series circuit. Note that the sum of the voltage drops equals the source voltage applied to the circuit.

Voltage Drop Ground Test

A voltage drop test can also be useful to check for excess resistance on the ground side of a circuit or component. Figure 1-8 shows a voltage drop test performed on the battery cables of a cranking circuit. The voltmeter positive lead is connected to the cable end that is more positive (closer to the battery positive terminal) than the other end. The negative lead is connected to the cable end closest to ground. The voltmeter reading provides a good test of the battery ground connection.

If there is too much resistance, more voltage is dropped across the cables, limiting the voltage available to the circuit. This is often a problem on the ground side of a circuit where a wire or cable is physically attached to the chassis, such as the negative battery cable. Rust, dirt, or corrosion can create enough resistance to cause a substantial voltage drop. Typically a voltage loss (drop) in a ground circuit of approximately 0.2 volts is acceptable in 12 volt electrical circuits. However, this loss can be a major problem with electronic control systems because they operate at low voltage. These systems normally should not have more than a 0.1 volt drop.

Calculated Voltage Drop Test

By conducting pinpoint voltage drop tests and some simple math, you can calculate the voltage drop across any part of a circuit. Sometimes this is a preferable method for determining a voltage drop if you cannot physically reach a portion of the circuit. Figure 1-9 shows a series circuit of lamps being tested in this manner. However, *this method works for **any** circuit as long as **all** measurements are made from the same reference point (usually ground).*

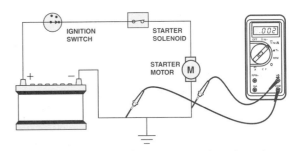

Fig. 1-8. Voltage drop ground tests are a good way to spot ground side electrical problems quickly and easily. Ground problems account for a large percentage of control system problems.

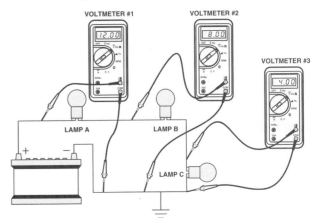

Fig. 1-9. Voltage drops can be calculated from a series of pinpoint voltage tests.

You can find a voltage drop by comparing the voltage available on one side of a load to the voltage available on the other side, and calculating the *difference*. For example:

- Voltmeter 1 in Figure 1-9 shows 12 volts available on one side of lamp A, and 8 volts on the other side. The difference is 12 − 8 = 4 volts; therefore, the voltage drop across lamp A is 4 volts.
- Voltmeter 2 shows the voltage drop across lamp B, 8 − 4 = 4 volts.
- Voltmeter 3 shows the voltage drop across lamp C, 4 − 0 (ground) = 4 volts.

One important fact to remember about ground: *Ground is considered to be at a potential of 0 volts.* It is actually defined that way to make calculations easier, and is one reason it is almost always chosen as the reference point from which voltage measurements are made.

The calculated voltage drop method can also be used effectively in other situations. Assume for a moment that you cannot reach or test lamp C. Using the readings from voltmeters 1 and 2 alone, you can calculate the voltage drop across lamp C. Using voltmeters 1 and 2, you can calculate the voltage drops of lamps A and B as 4 volts each. Since you now know that the total voltage drop is equal to the battery voltage (12 volts), you can reasonably conclude that lamp C is also 4 volts.

Ammeters

An **ammeter**, which measures current in **amperes**, is connected to the circuit in series. This permits the current in the circuit to pass through the meter for measurement, figure 1-10. Unlike a voltmeter, an ammeter has extremely low internal resistance. If connected in parallel, too much current will pass through the meter and damage it.

When current draw specifications for a circuit or component are known, an ammeter reading can determine if a short or grounded circuit is present. A reading greater than that specified indicates a short in the circuit. An ammeter also can detect excessive circuit resistance, which causes a low reading, figure 1-11.

When diagnosing a system to determine why a fuse has blown, knowing the current flow can be helpful. Ammeter testing can determine if the circuit overload is caused by a defective motor, or if two circuits have shorted together.

Ammeters equipped with an inductive pickup measure the magnetic field surrounding any current-carrying conductor. The strength of the magnetic field varies directly with current flow, and the meter translates this into a reading in amperes. Because an inductive pickup is clamped around the conductor, the meter cannot be damaged by connecting it incorrectly.

Ohmmeters

An **ohmmeter**, which measures the resistance to electrical flow in **ohms**, can be used to determine continuity and the amount

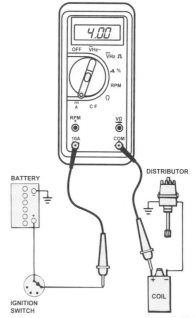

Fig. 1-10. When connected in series, an ammeter measures current in the circuit.

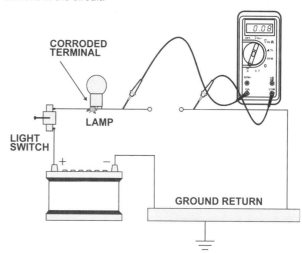

Fig. 1-11. High resistance caused by corrosion at the lamp terminal results in a low current reading on the ammeter.

of circuit resistance. Unlike a voltmeter or ammeter, an ohmmeter contains its own voltage source. An analog ohmmeter can be destroyed if connected to system voltage, and a digital meter will give incorrect readings when connected to any voltage source. For this reason, it is safest to always disconnect the vehicle battery before using an ohmmeter. Since an ohmmeter does not use circuit voltage, either lead can be connected to any test point unless checking diodes or other solid-state devices.

Before using an analog ohmmeter, calibrate, or "zero," it to compensate for its own internal resistance and battery strength. To do this, set the meter control to the desired scale,

A6

Ammeter: An ammeter is an instrument used for measuring the current flow in an electrical or electronic circuit. Some ammeters are intended for use in direct current (DC) circuits; others are designed for alternating current (AC) circuits.
Ampere: The unit for measuring electrical current flow.
Ohm: The unit for measuring electrical resistance.
Ohmmeter: An ohmmeter is an instrument used to measure the resistance to current flow in a circuit or component. Ohmmeters must never be connected to "live" circuits.

touch the leads together, and adjust the calibration control on the meter to get a zero reading. Digital ohmmeters do not require calibration, but the resistance of the leads should be tested when measuring low-resistance circuits.

If a digital meter is not **auto-ranging**, begin testing with the meter at the highest setting, then decrease the setting to get the most accurate reading. Starting with a setting too low results in an open circuit reading. It is important to make sure the reading is displayed correctly; it is easy to misread because of the decimal point settings.

When the ohmmeter leads are connected to the circuit or device being tested, current from the internal power source flows through the circuit or device and back to the meter. Because the internal resistance and source voltage of the meter are known, the current flow through the meter depends on the resistance in the circuit or device being tested.

With the test leads of an analog meter disconnected, the needle will swing to the opposite end of the scale marked infinity. Connect the meter test leads in parallel to the component or circuit to be tested, figure 1-12. Multiply the scale reading by the factor indicated on the meter control to determine the resistance. If the reading is high, switch the meter to a higher scale, if available, and recalibrate the meter before taking a new reading. An infinity reading indicates an open circuit; a low reading indicates a circuit with little resistance.

Since an ohmmeter operates on a low-voltage, low-amperage internal power source, results are not always conclusive when testing circuits designed to carry high current.

A damaged circuit may be able to carry the weak signal of the test meter, but not be able to support the high-current load the circuit normally operates under. For this reason, voltage drop testing is the preferred method of checking circuit continuity.

Oscilloscopes

Another tool used to measure voltage in many applications is the **oscilloscope**. Oscilloscopes or "scopes" are available in either analog or digital styles, figure 1-13. The analog scope incorporates a true live display much like older ignition analyzers. A beam of electrons writes on a phosphorus screen, which is laid out in a grid. The analog scope has the advantage of providing a true live display. The disadvantage lies in the fact that it cannot store signals for future review.

Inputs to the digital scope are digitized, processed, and displayed on the screen for viewing. The digital scope has the advantage of storing the information so that it can be saved, parameters can be calculated, and intermittent glitches can be captured. It also allows for automatic setup and operation. The digital scope does not provide a true live readout and may miss certain short-duration voltage variances. Often the digital scope is known as the digital storage oscilloscope or DSO.

Scan Tools

The diagnostic tools discussed to this point rely on making an actual connection to the circuit or component in question to make a reading. In today's vehicles it is often necessary to access information stored within one of the on-board electronic control modules. For this diagnosis a **scan tool** is used. Scan tools are usually hand-held computers containing programming allowing communication with the control modules, figure 1-14. They connect to the vehicle via the **data link connector**, or DLC, figure 1-15. The scan tool sends requests for information to the control module and displays the results on its screen. Most scan tools can be used to read operating parameters, read and clear **diagnostic trouble codes** (DTCs), and command certain components to operate.

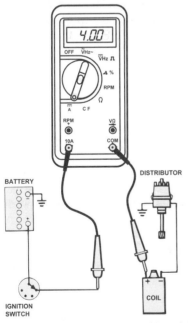

Fig. 1-12. Checking the resistance of an ignition pickup coil with an ohmmeter.

Fig. 1-13. Typical handheld oscilloscopes.

Auto-ranging: A feature of most digital multimeters that automatically selects the appropriate test range without the need for operator input.
Data Link Connector (DLC): A dedicated point for attaching a scan tool to the vehicle communications network.
Diagnostic Trouble Code (DTC): A numeric or alphanumeric code assigned to a particular fault in an onboard electronic system.
Oscilloscope: An oscilloscope is an instrument commonly used to display and analyze the waveform of electronic signals. In effect, the device draws a graph of the instantaneous signal voltage as a function of time.
Scan Tool: Typically a hand-held computer containing programming allowing communication with the control modules.

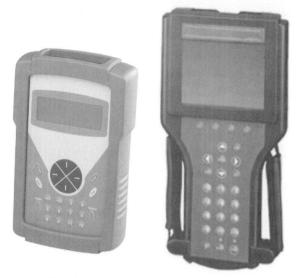

Fig. 1-14. Typical scan tools.

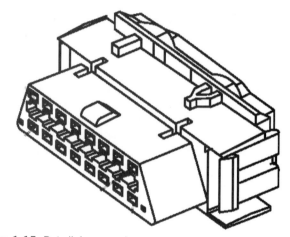

Fig. 1-15. Data link connector.

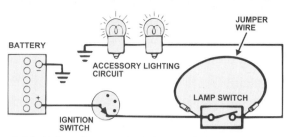

Fig. 1-16. Using a jumper wire to bypass the lamp switch and check circuit integrity.

protection can be connected to a low-rated circuit breaker to prevent circuit damage in case the jumper is accidentally connected incorrectly. The circuit breaker used should have a high enough current rating for testing, but a low enough rating to open quickly if connected incorrectly.

ISOLATING CIRCUIT PROBLEMS

A short circuit can allow current to bypass the intended load, which can increase amperage and damage the electrical circuit. A short circuit can also bypass the control of the circuit so that the circuit cannot operate properly, figure 1-17.

Short circuits can blow the fuse that protects the circuit. A wiring diagram of the fuse involved is an important tool in locating the possible problem areas, and in identifying all of the circuits involved.

A tool for finding short circuits uses a circuit breaker in place of the blown fuse, and an inductive ammeter to follow the circuit wire. As the circuit breaker closes and opens because of the increased current, the inductive meter needle makes a big sweep as it senses the high current. As the meter goes past the short to ground, the meter movement is reduced. These tools work with circuits that are shorted to bypass the load. If the short circuit bypasses the switches that control the operation, it may be necessary to disconnect connectors to find the problem.

A6

The scan tool must always be used in conjunction with the appropriate vehicle service or diagnostic manual. The manuals will provide specific instructions for connecting the tool, reading the information, and interpreting the results. Random use of the scan tool can result in misdiagnosis and wasted diagnostic efforts. Once results are obtained they should be compared to published guidelines and the appropriate repairs completed.

Jumper Wires

A jumper wire is a length of wire with alligator clips at both ends. Although not a true test instrument, it can be very helpful when used in combination with other test instruments. A jumper wire can be used to bypass switches, connectors, and other nonresistive components during a circuit test, figure 1-16. It must never be used to bypass a device that has resistance, or in a way that would ground a hot lead. This will reduce circuit resistance and introduce excessive current, resulting in circuit or component damage, or even a fire. A jumper wire can also be used with a temporary power source to supply current to a remote part of the vehicle for testing.

Many jumper wires include an inline fuse or circuit breaker to protect the circuit. A jumper wire without such

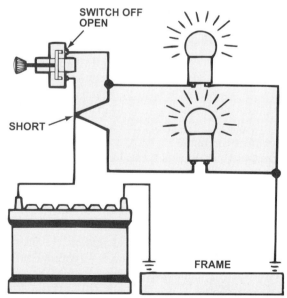

Fig. 1-17. Current in this circuit, which is shorted to power, bypasses the switch so the bulbs remain on regardless of switch position.

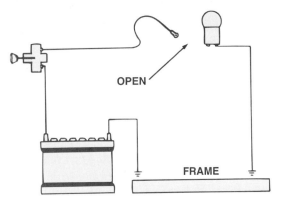

Fig. 1-18. An open circuit creates infinite resistance that prevents current from completing its intended path.

An open circuit is one that prevents current from completing its intended path due to infinite resistance, figure 1-18. Infinite resistance is a result of an air gap in the circuit that prevents current from moving past it. It can be as simple as a disconnected wire or as complicated as a damaged harness from a previous short circuit.

The most important tool for locating an open circuit is a wiring diagram. It is critical to know how the circuit is laid out before testing. When looking for an open circuit, carefully check for voltage at the switches and ground connectors in the suspect circuit. If testing reveals voltage is present at one connection, but not at the next, the open circuit is located between the two test points.

The source of excessive resistance can be confirmed with an ammeter. Locate the problem using an ohmmeter or by performing voltage drop tests.

ABNORMAL OR PHANTOM BATTERY DRAIN PROBLEMS

Phantom battery drain, or parasitic draw, is caused by something in the vehicle constantly drawing current from the battery when the ignition is off. Although a certain amount of discharge is normal and can be expected, a fully charged battery in good condition should not lose its charge when left idle for a few days or even weeks.

Typical causes of battery drain include:

- Acid, moisture, dirt, or corrosion on top of the battery case
- An accessory, such as a trunk light, glove box light, underhood light, or cigarette lighter, remaining on when the vehicle is not in use
- Parasitic drains required to operate systems that continue to work even when the vehicle is parked and the ignition is off

The most serious of these are the parasitic losses resulting from the advent of computer controls. Virtually all late-model vehicles are equipped with computers that control such things as engine operation, radio tuning, suspension leveling, steering assist, antilock brakes, and more. Each of these microprocessors contain random access memory (RAM) that stores information relevant to its job. Remember: RAM requires a constant power supply that puts a continuous drain on the vehicle electrical system. In addition, many electronic control systems conduct a self-diagnostic test after the engine is switched off. The combined drain of several computer memories, or diagnostic test routines, can discharge a battery to the point where there is insufficient cranking power after only a few weeks.

Due to the higher parasitic current drains on late-model vehicles, the old test of removing a battery cable connection and tapping it against the terminal while looking for a spark is both dangerous and no longer a valid check for excessive current drain. Furthermore, every time the power source to computer modules is interrupted, module memories are lost. Information programmed into memory by the vehicle owner, such as radio presets, door lock combinations, seat position memories, and climate controls, all have to be reset when the battery is reconnected. On engine management systems with adaptive learning capability, driveability also may be affected until the computer relearns the engine calibration or transmission shift modifications that were erased from memory.

A clean battery top prevents any drain from the negative to positive battery terminals. Periodically clean the battery top and terminals with a mixture of baking soda and water applied with a brush. Do not allow the solution to enter the battery cells.

To test for abnormal battery drain, disconnect the negative battery cable and connect an ammeter in series between the negative terminal and the cable, figure 1-19. On many late-model vehicles it is necessary to wait up to one hour before taking the reading. Many onboard computers have timer circuits which must time-out before they shut down.

To isolate the source of a draw, disconnect each accessory system one at a time until the meter reading drops into the normal range. This locates the offending circuit. Consult a wiring diagram to determine how power is routed through the circuit, then systematically eliminate components to determine which one was remaining on and draining the battery.

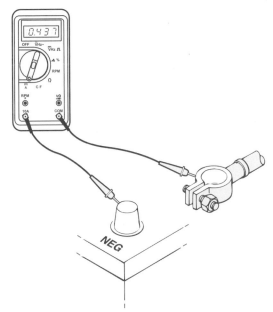

Fig. 1-19. Checking for parasitic draw by connecting an ammeter in series between the negative battery terminal and cable.

CIRCUIT PROTECTION DEVICES

Fuses, circuit breakers, and fusible links are circuit protection devices. Each can carry a specified current without damage, but if this predetermined rating is exceeded, they open to prevent circuit damage. Installing a new device will not solve the problems, as whatever caused the first one to open will quickly do the same to the replacement. Always determine and correct the cause of the blown device before installing a replacement.

Fuses

Although fuses are made in a range of standard sizes and types, most domestic and import manufacturers use only blade-type fuses in late-model applications, figure 1-20. A miniature version, as well as larger maxi and mega versions, of the standard blade-type fuse have gained in popularity in recent years. All fuses are rated by current capacity, and the internal filament burns through to open the circuit when current rating is exceeded.

A fuse generally can be checked while still in place using a test lamp. If the lamp does not light on either side of the fuse, turn the ignition switch to IGN or ACC, or the headlamp switch to the first or second position, whichever applies. A burned fuse will have a hot side and a dead side. Because a fuse is meant to burn out when current is too high, it should never be replaced with one whose rating is higher than the original equipment. A fuse with too high a rating causes circuit or component damage if an overload occurs.

Circuit Breakers

Circuit breakers are mechanical units that operate on the principle of different rates of expansion in heated metals. Unlike fuses that must be replaced after a single overload, circuit breakers are designed to open and close through repeated use. Circuit breakers are used in circuits where temporary overloads can occur frequently and power must be restored rapidly, such as in the headlamp circuit. Three types of circuit breakers are used on motor vehicles.

A cycling or self-resetting circuit breaker, figure 1-21, opens when current through the contacts is excessive, and closes when the points cool a few seconds later. This off/on action continues until the cause of the excessive current is corrected. The second type is the non-cycling breaker, figure 1-22. This type opens like the cycling type but does not reset until power is removed from the circuit, allowing the bimetal element to cool and snap back into position, closing the contacts.

The third and less common type is the manual resetting circuit breaker. It remains open after high current passes through it and must be reset manually. Reset the unit by depressing a button on the case once the source of the problem has been corrected.

Fusible Links

A fusible link is a backup to prevent major harness damage or fire in the event of a serious electrical malfunction, figure 1-23. Fusible links are made of a special smaller wire and are part of the main wiring harness. Fusible links also have a special insulation that is designed to melt but not burn when the wire is overloaded. They react much like a fuse but have higher current ratings. Each fusible link normally protects several smaller circuits with lower rated fuses of their own. Many late-model vehicles have replaced fusible links with a plug-type fuse installed in the underhood fuse box.

When replacing a blown wire-type fusible link, be sure the replacement part is the correct size and rated for the circuit load. If possible, use a replacement fusible link supplied by the vehicle OEM. If one is not available choose a fuse link that is four wire sizes smaller than the circuit it protects. To make the repair, cut out the fusible link at the nearest connector on each side. Attach each end of the replacement fuse link wire to the standard wire with a splice sleeve and solder the connection with rosin-core solder.

PTC Resistors

In the past few years another type of circuit protection device has been developed and is in use in many vehicles today. The device, a positive thermal coefficient resistor, or PTC resistor, is a solid-state current-limiting component. As current exceeds the rated capacity of the PTC the internal crystalline structure

A6

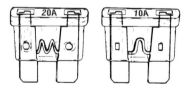

Fig. 1-20. Blade-type fuses of various current ratings are used on most late-model vehicles.

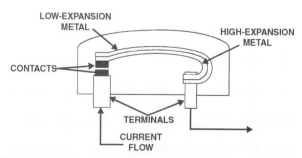

Fig. 1-21. A typical cycling circuit breaker.

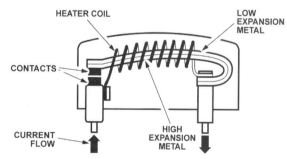

Fig. 1-22. A typical non-cycling circuit breaker.

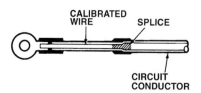

Fig. 1-23. To prevent wiring harness damage, the calibrated wire of a fusible link opens if current exceeds its amperage rating.

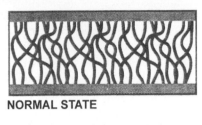

NORMAL STATE

TRIPPED OR OPEN STATE

Fig. 1-24. Normal and open PTC resistor structures.

of the resistor changes and dramatically increases resistance, figure 1-24. This increase in resistance cuts current flow in the circuit, protecting both the wiring and component from damage. The PTC resets only when voltage is removed from the circuit and the internal structure once again assumes its crystalline state. PTCs are not serviceable and must be replaced if defective.

DIODES

Diodes are **semiconductors** used in many electrcial and electronic circuits, figure 1-25. The primary use of a diode is to control the direction of current flow. In simple terms a diode acts as a one-way check valve in the circuit. When the diode is **forward biased** current is allowed to flow though the circuit. When **reversed biased** current flow is blocked in the circuit. Diodes are often used in warning lamp circuits.

Another use of a diode is that of a **clamping diode.** In this application a diode is placed across the terminals of a coil such as the AC compressor clutch. The diode provides a path for the spike current generated when the coil is deenergized and induced voltage is generated. Without the clamping diode this spike current could damage sensitive electronic components in the vehicle.

Light Emitting Diodes

A light emitting diode or LED is used to produce light when current flows in the proper direction. LEDs are commonly

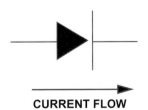

CURRENT FLOW

Fig. 1-25. Schematic symbol for a diode.

used as indicators and for illumination of switches and controls. When several LEDs are placed in a single fixture the assembly can be used to replace lamps such as stop and turn and tail lamps. LEDs used in this application have the advantage of extremely low current draw and long service life.

DATA COMMUNICATIONS BUS

The serial data bus is a high-speed, non-fault tolerant, two-wire twisted pair communications network. It allows communications between various electronic modules, including the engine control module (ECM), transmission control module (TCM), instrument cluster (including MIL), immobilizer control module, and a scan tool connected to the data link connector (DLC).

The Data-High circuit switches between 2.5 volts (rest state) and 3.5 volts (active state), and the Data-Low circuit switches between 2.5 volts (rest state) and 1.5 volts (active state). The data bus has two 120 ohm terminating resistors: one inside the instrument cluster and another one inside the ECM.

Any of the following conditions will cause the data communications bus to fail and result in the storage of network DTCs: either data line shorted to power, to ground, or to the other data line. The data bus will remain operational when one of the two modules containing a terminating resistor is not connected to the network. The data bus will fail when both terminating resistors are not connected to the network. Data communication failures do not prevent the ECM from providing ignition and fuel control.

ELECTRICAL SCHEMATICS

The wiring schematic is the cornerstone of electrical diagnosis, figure 1-26. Schematics break the entire electrical system into individual circuits, and show the electrical current paths and components. Wiring that is not part of the circuit of interest may be referenced to another page where the circuit is shown complete. Most schematics use a top (power) to bottom (ground) sequence to present electrical information, while others are shown in a horizontal format. Because more than one electrical system is located in each subsection, each electrical system's schematics are broken down further into the individual operating system.

Components in the schematic are identified using icons, symbols, or drawings of the internal circuitry. Service publications contain a page identifying the icons and symbols used in that manual. Most service manuals also provide component location information along with connector end-view drawings for reference. Many times a description of the circuit function is also available. Always refer to the correct service manual for the vehicle you are servicing. Using the wrong publication may lead to misdiagnosis and wasted effort.

Use the schematics to trace the path of current flow when diagnosing electrical concerns.

Clamping Diode: A diode installed to eliminate the voltage spike from a collapsing coil from damaging electroinc systems.
Diode: An electrical "check-valve." Diodes allow current flow in one direction only.
Forward Biased: The term applied to a diode when current is allowed to flow in the circuit.
Reversed Biased: The term applied to a diode when it is blocking current flow.
Semiconductors: An electronic component that can either be an insulator or conductor depending on circuit design.

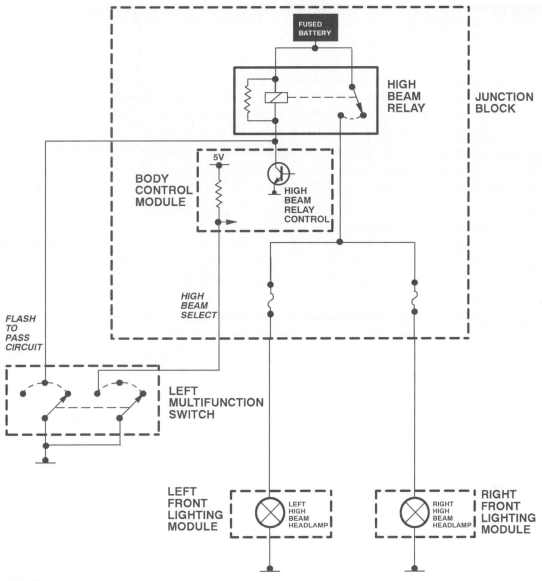

Fig. 1-26. Typical wiring schematic.

CHAPTER QUESTIONS

1. When connecting a voltmeter in the circuit to make a voltage test, Technician A says to connect the meter in series. Technician B says to connect the meter in parallel. Who is right?
   a. A only
   b. B only
   c. Both A and B
   d. Neither A nor B

2. When connecting an ammeter in a circuit to make an amp test, Technician A says to connect the meter in series. Technician B says to connect the meter in parallel. Who is right?
   a. A only
   b. B only
   c. Both A and B
   d. Neither A nor B

3. When testing the battery cable connected from the battery to the starter for resistance, Technician A says an ohmmeter is used. Technician B says to do a voltage drop test. Who is right?
   a. A only
   b. B only
   c. Both A and B
   d. Neither A nor B

4. The ohmmeter does not move when it is connected to the two terminals of a light bulb. This reading indicates the circuit in the bulb is:
   a. Shorted
   b. Grounded
   c. Complete
   d. Open

5. The vehicle's battery is being checked for parasitic draw. Technician A is measuring current in milliamps with a DVOM. Technician B is measuring voltage drop between the battery terminal and cable. Who is right?
   a. A only
   b. B only
   c. Both A and B
   d. Neither A nor B

6. While testing a circuit with an ohmmeter the technician has an infinite reading; when he reverses the meter test leads he has continuity. Technician A says there is a PTC resistor in the circuit. Technician B says there is a diode in the circuit. Who is right?
   a. A only
   b. B only
   c. Both A and B
   d. Neither A nor B

7. When testing computer circuits the DVOM should have an impedance of:
   a. 10k ohms
   b. 100k ohms
   c. 1 megohm
   d. 10 megohms

8. Technician A says 12 gauge wire is smaller then 16 gauge. Technician B says a fusible link is wire that is 4 gauge sizes smaller then the circuit wire. Who is correct?
   a. A only
   b. B only
   c. Both A and B
   d. Neither A nor B

9. While testing a circuit there is 12 volts on both sides of the light bulb and the light is not working. Technician A says the ground is open. Technician B says the bulb is blown. Who is right?
   a. A only
   b. B only
   c. Both A and B
   d. Neither A nor B

10. A corroded ground connector will cause the resistance to: Technician A says increase. Technician B says decrease. Who is right?
    a. A only
    b. B only
    c. Both A and B
    d. Neither A nor B

11. If resistance in the circuit is increased what affect will it have on current flow? Technician A says increase. Technician B says decrease. Who is right?
    a. A only
    b. B only
    c. Both A and B
    d. Neither A nor B

12. A short circuit would cause a drop in resistance, causing the current flow to: Technician A says increase. Technician B says decrease.
    a. A only
    b. B only
    c. Both A and B
    d. Neither A nor B

13. Technician A says when replacing the vehicle battery the negative cable should be disconnected first and reconnected last. Technician B says the battery positive cable should be disconnected first and reconnected last. Who is right?
    a. A only
    b. B only
    c. Both A and B
    d. Neither A nor B

14. When using an ohmmeter all of the following are true *EXCEPT*:
    a. An infinity reading indicates an open circuit.
    b. A low reading indicates a circuit with little resistance.
    c. Results are always conclusive when testing circuits designed to carry high current.
    d. Disconnect the vehicle battery before using an ohmmeter.

BATTERY DIAGNOSIS AND SERVICE

CHAPTER OBJECTIVES

- The technician will complete the ASE task list on Battery Diagnosis and Service.
- The technician will be able to answer 4 questions dealing with the Diagnosis and Service section of the A6 ASE test.

A battery must be restored to a full state-of-charge prior to diagnosis and testing. Once the battery has been charged and tested, a search can be made for the cause of its running down. Batteries do not last forever; all batteries wear out eventually through normal use. However, a weak or discharged battery is most often the symptom of a problem elsewhere in the vehicle.

BATTERY TESTING

State-of-charge and capacity tests are performed to determine the condition of the battery. In addition, a preliminary evaluation on a low-maintenance or maintenance-free battery is required to determine if the battery is capable of accepting a recharge.

Battery State-of-Charge Testing

Until the appearance of sealed, maintenance-free batteries, testing the **specific gravity** of the **electrolyte** with a hydrometer was a universal method of determining battery condition. However, the procedure can be used today only on the minority of batteries that are unsealed and have removable filler caps. When performing a hydrometer test, do not add water to the cells before testing unless the electrolyte level is too low to obtain a sample. If the electrolyte level is low, add water to the correct level in each cell and charge the battery for 5 to 10 minutes before proceeding with the test. When testing in very cold weather, or when using a hydrometer with a built-in thermometer, draw electrolyte into it several times to normalize the temperature of the hydrometer tube or thermometer.

Insert the tube of the hydrometer into one of the end cells and gently draw electrolyte into the hydrometer until the indicator is floating freely without touching the sides or top, figure 2-1. Allowing the float indicator to touch the top or sides of the chamber results in a false reading. Hold the

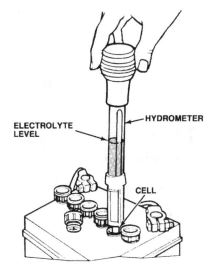

Fig. 2-1. Draw electrolyte into the hydrometer so the indicator floats freely in the tube.

hydrometer at eye level and read the specific gravity. After reading, return the electrolyte to the cell from which it was withdrawn. Repeat to sample the electrolyte in each of the cells.

With an electrolyte temperature of 80°F (27°C), expect a specific gravity of approximately 1.260 on a fully charged battery. The specific gravity of the electrolyte determines the battery state-of-charge, figure 2-2.

If the electrolyte temperature is above or below 80°F (27°C), the specific gravity reading must be corrected. Battery hydrometers often contain a thermometer to make temperature correction quick and easy, figure 2-3. To correct for temperature, add 4 points (0.004) for each 10°F (5.6°C) above 80°F (27°C), or subtract 4 points (0.004) for each 10°F (5.6°C) below 80°F (27°C) from the test results. For example:

If the electrolyte temperature is 10°F (−12°C) and the hydrometer reading is 1.230, the specific gravity must be corrected for a 70°F (39.2°C) temperature variation. Therefore, subtract 28 points (0.004 × 7 = 0.028) from the indicated reading of 1.230 to get a corrected reading of 1.202, which is the true specific gravity.

A6

Electrolyte: The chemical solution, composed of sulfuric acid and water, that conducts electricity and reacts with the plate materials in a battery.
Specific Gravity: The weight of a liquid relative to water, which has an assigned value of 1.0. In an automotive storage battery, the specific gravity is measured with a hydrometer. When corrected to a temperature of 80°F (27°C), the specific gravity of a fully charged battery falls in the 1.260 to 1.280 range.

Hydrometer Specific Gravity Readings

Specific Gravity	State of Charge
1.260-1.280	100 percent
1.230-1.250	75 percent
1.200-1.220	50 percent
1.170-1.190	25 percent
1.140-1.160	Very little useful capacity
1.110-1.130	Discharged

Fig. 2-2. The specific gravity of the electrolyte reflects the state-of-charge of a battery.

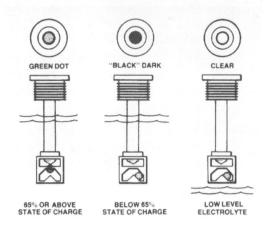

Fig. 2-4. A single ball indicator reflects electrolyte level and the state-of-charge on a maintenance-free battery.

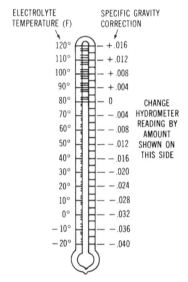

Fig. 2-3. Specific gravity readings must be corrected to the temperature of the electrolyte.

A variation of more than 50 points (0.050) between cells indicates that the battery should be replaced.

Check the battery open circuit voltage to determine if the battery has enough of a charge to be tested. To check, measure voltage across the battery terminals with all of the vehicle electrical circuits switched off. The battery is ready for testing if readings are 12.4 volts or higher.

Sealed maintenance-free batteries are equipped with a built-in state-of-charge indicator in one cell. This indicator has two functions: It shows whether electrolyte has fallen below a minimum level and also serves as a go/no-go hydrometer. The indicator is a plastic rod inserted in the top of the battery and extended into the electrolyte. One design uses a single plastic ball, usually colored green, red, or blue, suspended in a cage from the bottom of the rod, figure 2-4. Depending on the specific gravity of the electrolyte, the ball will float or sink in its cage, changing the appearance of the indicator "eye."

Generally, a green dot in the indicator means the battery is charged enough for testing. If this dot is not visible, the battery must be charged before it is tested. If the indicator eye is

black and color is not visible, the battery is below a 65 percent state-of-charge and must be recharged before testing. If the indicator is clear or light yellow, the electrolyte level has fallen below the bottom of the indicator rod and attached cage. When this clear or light yellow appearance is noted, lightly tap the top of the indicator to dislodge any gas bubbles that might be giving a false indication of low electrolyte level. If the color does not change, replace the battery. Do not attempt to recharge a battery if the electrolyte level is too low.

Some battery indicators contain both a red and a green ball, figure 2-5. This gives the indicator a green, dark, red, and clear appearance, in that order. The red dot indicates the battery is approaching complete discharge and must be charged before being used. Complete indicator information is printed on a label attached to the battery and should be used to make an accurate interpretation of the built-in indicator.

Battery Capacity Testing

A battery capacity, or load, test determines how well a battery can perform when under load. Test results indicate the capacity to furnish adequate starting current while maintaining sufficient voltage to effectively operate the ignition system. An instrument called a charging-battery-starter (CSB) analyzer is

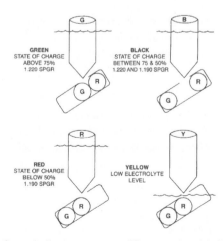

Fig. 2-5. Some indicators use two different colored balls to display state-of-charge information.

used to conduct the test. A CSB analyzer consists of an ammeter, voltmeter, and **carbon pile**, which can be either a fixed or variable resistance.

Exact test procedures vary, so refer to the equipment instructions to perform a load test. For most CSB analyzers, perform a load test as follows:

1. Switch the analyzer off and connect the test leads to the battery. Be sure to observe the correct polarity, and make certain the test clip leads make good contact on the battery posts, figure 2-6. Special adapters may be needed to connect the unit to a battery with side terminals, figure 2-7.
2. If the analyzer has a temperature adjustment, select the setting that matches electrolyte temperature. Use a thermometer in one cell to determine the electrolyte temperature of a battery with vent caps; estimate the temperature on sealed batteries. Minimum capacity test voltages vary significantly with battery temperature, figure 2-8.
3. Refer to specifications for the cold cranking amperage (CCA) rating of the battery. This information should be on a label attached to the battery.

Fig. 2-6. Observe correct polarity when connecting the CSB analyzer to load-test a battery.

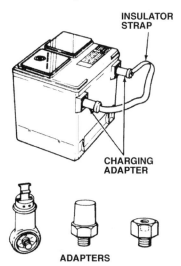

Fig. 2-7. A number of terminal adapters are available for connecting test equipment to a side terminal battery.

BATTERY TEMPERATURE °F (°C)	MINIMUM TEST VOLTAGE
70° (21°) or above	9.6 volts
60° (16°)	9.5 volts
50° (10°)	9.4 volts
40° (4°)	9.3 volts
30° (−1°)	9.1 volts
20° (−7°)	8.9 volts
10° (−12°)	8.7 volts
0° (−18°)	8.5 volts

Fig. 2-8. Electrolyte temperature impacts minimum test voltage during a battery capacity test.

4. On a CSB analyzer with a variable resistor, turn the load control knob to draw battery current at a rate equal to one-half the CCA rating of the battery. On a fixed-load tester, set the battery size indicator to the appropriate position.
5. Maintain this load for 15 seconds while watching the voltmeter. Turn off the control knob immediately after 15 seconds of current draw.
6. On a 12-volt battery, voltage should not fall below 9.6 volts after 15 seconds.

If the battery fails a load test, and the battery had enough of a charge for proper testing, perform a 3-minute charge test to help confirm a faulty battery. This test is also used when load test results are marginal. To test:

1. Connect a battery charger and set the charge rate to 40 amps.
2. After 3 minutes, check the charging voltage. If charging voltage exceeds 15.5 volts, the battery has failed the test.

A battery that passes the 3-minute charge test is able to accept a charge; one that fails is sulfated or severely discharged and must be replaced.

Low-Maintenance Battery Evaluation

To determine if a discharged low-maintenance battery can be recharged or should be replaced, the battery must be charged. If the battery has a very low charge, it will accept a charge at a slow rate. As the battery state-of-charge increases, the rate of the charge increases as well. If the battery cannot be charged, it must be replaced. Once a battery is charged, it can be load-tested.

BATTERY INSPECTION AND SERVICE

Inspection, cleaning, and replacement are the only services a battery normally requires. To inspect:

1. On a battery with vent caps, check to make sure the electrolyte level is above the tops of the plates or at the

A6

Carbon Pile: Fixed or variable resistance load unit which simulates vehicle loads for battery and/or generator testing.

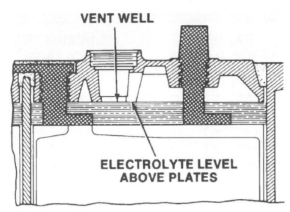

Fig. 2-9. The electrolyte level must be above the tops of the plates in each cell.

indicated level within the cells, figure 2-9. Top off the electrolyte with distilled or mineral-free water as needed.

2. Inspect the battery case, terminals, connectors, holddown, and tray for rust, corrosion, or damage.
3. Inspect the battery case for cracks and check for loose terminal posts. Replace the battery if any of this type of damage is found.
4. Look for accumulated dirt and grease on the battery cover that could cause a voltage draw to ground, and for corrosion buildup on the terminals. Clean and neutralize with baking soda as needed.

Automotive batteries are very heavy and awkward to handle. A dropped battery can seriously injure your foot, spill the electrolyte, and ruin the battery. When removing, carrying, or installing a battery, always use an appropriate battery-carrying strap or carrier to make battery handling easier and safer. Electrolyte can leak from the vent holes at the top of a maintenance-free battery if it is tipped more than 45 degrees in any direction.

When handling batteries, use extreme care to avoid spilling or splashing electrolyte. If spilled, the sulfuric acid in the battery electrolyte can damage paint or corrode metal parts. Battery acid also can destroy clothing, cause severe burns, and permanently injure eyes. Always wear safety glasses and gloves to protect eyes and hands when servicing a battery.

If electrolyte contacts your skin or eyes, flush the area with cold water for several minutes, then flood it with a solution of baking soda and water or a neutralizing eyewash. Never rub the affected area. Get immediate medical attention.

When a battery is charging or discharging, it releases highly explosive hydrogen gas. Hydrogen, which is always present in battery cells, escapes through the flame arrester vent and can form an explosive atmosphere around the battery. Since this explosive gas can remain in or around the battery for several hours after charging, make sure the work area is well-ventilated. Any spark or flame can cause the battery to explode violently, disintegrating its case and showering the vicinity with acid. Follow these important safety precautions to prevent accidents:

- Keep sparks, open flame, and smoking materials far away from batteries at all times
- Operate charging equipment only in a well-ventilated area

- Never short across battery terminals or cable connectors
- Never connect or disconnect charger leads at battery terminals while the charger is running; this always causes sparks
- Never wear a wristwatch or rings when servicing a battery or working on or near electrical systems; this reduces the possibility of arcing and burns

If the battery terminals and cable connectors are corroded, remove the cables from the battery for a thorough cleaning. Disconnect the negative cable first, then the positive cable from the terminals. Use a cable puller to remove terminals that are stuck on a post. Never pry off a terminal with a screwdriver or hit it with a hammer. Use a connector-spreading tool to open the cable terminal. Neutralize corrosion on the cable connectors with a solution of baking soda and water or an ammonia solution. Use a combination wire brush with internal and external bristles, or a battery terminal reamer, for cleaning the battery posts and the inside of the cable connectors. Side terminal batteries should be cleaned between the cable end and the bolt. Posts and terminals must be completely clean to provide good electrical contact.

Disassemble and remove the holddown with any heat shield components, then remove and clean the battery, the battery tray, and the holddown straps with baking soda and water or an ammonia solution to neutralize corrosion, figure 2-10. Be careful to keep corrosion off painted surfaces and rubber parts. Do not let the cleaning solution enter the battery vents. If corrosion is heavy, use a stiff-bristled nonmetallic brush and remove dirt and grease with a detergent solution or with solvent; avoid splashing. Once they are free of corrosion and dirt, rinse the battery, tray, and holddown straps with fresh water and dry with low-pressure compressed air.

Use the battery strap or carrier to reinstall the battery, and assemble the holddown with any heat shield components to secure the battery. Avoid overtightening the holddown, which can damage the case. If necessary, open clamp-type connectors with a spreading tool to fit them onto the posts; never hammer a connector onto a battery post. Connect the positive cable to the battery first; then connect the negative cable.

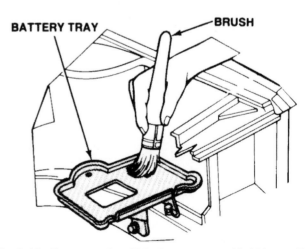

Fig. 2-10. Clean corrosion off the battery tray and holddown with a neutralizing solution.

Install clamp-type connectors flush with or slightly below the tops of the posts. Be aware: Overtightening side terminal bolts can strip the threads out of the battery. To help prevent corrosion on top terminal batteries, apply a light coat of anticorrosion compound to the terminals and connectors after installation.

Battery Charging

Charging a battery replaces energy that was drained during service to restore the battery to its full capacity. The more discharged the battery has become, the greater the charge required to revive it. There are no shortcuts when recharging a battery.

Typically, a battery is either slow charged at a rate of about 3 to 15 amperes, or fast charged at higher rates of up to 50 amperes. Generally, any battery can be charged at any current rate as long as electrolyte **gassing** and spewing does not occur, and the electrolyte temperature remains below 125°F (52°C). When possible, charge at a slow rate of 5 to 15 amperes for best results.

When charging a battery, observe these precautions:

- Charge in a well-ventilated area away from sparks and open flame
- Be sure the charger is off before connecting or disconnecting cables at the battery
- Never try to charge a frozen battery
- Always wear suitable eye protection
- Never fast charge a battery that has failed a 3-minute charge test
- Never fast charge a battery that is sulfated or has plate or separator damage
- Monitor electrolyte temperature closely and stop charging if it rises above 125°F (52°C)

Maintenance-free batteries require special precautions during charging. A battery with a state-of-charge indicator should not be recharged if the eye indicates the electrolyte is below the level of the built-in hydrometer. A high initial charging current heats the electrolyte of a maintenance-free battery and causes it to gas. Since the battery is sealed, venting is minimal and a high charging current can cause internal battery damage and result in an explosion.

A completely discharged battery may not accept a high charging current because the electrolyte is almost pure water and thus a poor conductor of electricity. Since the weak electrolyte solution is highly resistant to the charger current, the amount of current accepted will be very low at first. As the battery is charged, more sulfuric acid forms and the electrolyte will eventually accept the full current from the charger. If a load test indicates that the battery is fully discharged, watch the initial charging rate and terminal voltage carefully. If terminal voltage exceeds 15.5 volts with a high charging current, reduce the current and charge the battery for several hours at a setting low enough to keep terminal voltage under 15.5.

Whenever time permits, a battery should be slow charged using a low charging rate of 5 to 15 amperes. It may require 12 to 24 hours to restore the battery to a full charge. After charging, wash, neutralize, and dry the top of the battery to remove any acid condensation due to gassing.

Make certain that battery cells are filled to the level marks. Cell caps should be left in place during slow charging, but make sure the vent holes in the caps are open. Clean battery posts of any corrosion to ensure good electrical contact. Charge at the recommended rate, checking electrolyte specific gravity with a hydrometer occasionally during the first stage of charging and every hour as the battery approaches full charge. Unless otherwise specified by the battery manufacturer, a battery is fully charged when all cells are gassing, the specific gravity reading is 1.260 to 1.280 when corrected for an electrolyte temperature of 80°F (27°C), and hydrometer readings show no increase during three consecutive hourly readings.

With a maintenance-free battery, follow specifications from the manufacturer for charging rate and time. Determine battery temperature by touch and check the state-of-charge indicator hourly for the green dot. If not visible, gently shake the battery and continue charging. Once the green dot appears and remains visible, the battery is charged and the charger should be switched off and disconnected.

Fast charging a battery delivers a much higher charging rate for a shorter period of time. Normally, fast charging time does not exceed one hour and is usually much less. Equipment operating instructions for charging rate and length of charge should always be followed. However, charge time can generally be estimated based on a preliminary specific gravity reading at an electrolyte temperature of 80°F (27°C), figure 2-11.

During charging, check electrolyte temperature frequently and reduce the charging rate if temperature rises above 125°F (52°C). With a battery tester or voltmeter connected across the battery terminals, check voltage. If it exceeds 15.5 volts for a 12-volt battery or 7.75 volts for a 6-volt battery, lower the charging rate until the voltage reading drops below the specified maximum. Whenever possible, follow a fast charge with a slow charge rate for as long as time permits to bring the specific gravity reading to 1.260 at an electrolyte temperature of 80°F (27°C).

If the battery terminals are removed for cleaning, charging, or any other reason, power is lost to all of the onboard computer modules. This may erase diagnostic trouble code records. The vehicle may have to be driven to restore the adaptive memory for idle speed, fuel trim, and transmission

Specific Gravity Reading	Length of Fast Charge
1.150 or less	Up to 1 hour
1.150 to 1.175	Up to 3/4 hour
1.175 to 1.200	Up to 1/2 hour
1.200 to 1.225	Up to 1/4 hour
Above 1.225	Slow charge only

Fig. 2-11. General guide for fast charging based on the specific gravity of a discharged battery.

Gassing: The emission of hydrogen and oxygen gases from battery cells during charging.

shifting. To allow the PCM to relearn lost values drive the vehicle several miles. Stop 3 or 4 times and accelerate back to road speed. Some engine and transmission computers include programs to enhance the relearn procedure. Refer to the appropriate Service Manual for the correct procedures.

Other accessory settings, such as the radio, clock, memory power seats, steering wheels, and mirrors, can also be lost as well. It is possible to keep these memories alive by providing power into the cigarette lighter or other circuits. Several special tools are available to supply the necessary power to these modules while the battery is disconnected.

Battery Cable Service

The terminals of the two heavy-gauge battery cables that connect the battery to the starter motor and a chassis ground should be cleaned and inspected whenever the battery tray is cleaned.

Because the terminals that connect most cables to the battery can be replaced individually, battery cables seldom require replacement unless their insulation is damaged or corrosion has started to deteriorate the cable strands. Corrosion or other cable damage causes an increase in resistance, which reduces the current carrying capability of the cable.

To replace the battery negative, or ground, cable, disconnect the terminal end from the battery and remove the bolt attaching the other end to the chassis. To replace the positive cable, first disconnect the negative cable at the battery. Then, remove the positive cable terminal at the battery and disconnect the opposite end of the cable from the starter solenoid. In addition to the heavy-gauge cable, many designs include one or more smaller-gauge leads for energizing accessory circuits that must be disconnected before the cable can be removed. Be sure the replacement cable includes all of the necessary leads. Route the new cable along the same path as the old one, making connections in reverse order of removal.

Jump Starting

A booster battery and jumper cables can be used to jump start a vehicle with a dead battery. Unless performed properly, jump starting can damage the charging and electronic control systems, or produce sparks that might cause a battery explosion resulting in personal injury. Wear eye protection when jump starting a vehicle, always properly route the jumper cables, and make connections in the correct order, figure 2-12. To jump start a disabled vehicle:

1. On the disabled vehicle: Switch off the ignition and all accessories, set the parking brake, and place the shift lever in NEUTRAL or PARK.

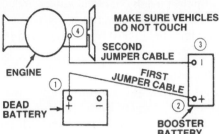

Fig. 2-12. Proper cable routing and connection order for jump starting a vehicle with a discharged battery.

2. First, attach one end of a jumper cable to the positive terminal of the discharged battery. Second, connect the other end of the same cable to the positive terminal of the booster battery.
3. Next, connect one end of the other jumper cable to the negative terminal of the booster battery. Attach the remaining jumper cable end to a good ground on the engine block of the disabled vehicle at least 12 inches from the discharged battery. Some vehicles have a remote jump start terminal for this purpose.
4. Make sure that the two vehicles are not touching each other, and that the clamps from one cable do not accidentally contact the clamps on the other cable.
5. Switch on the ignition of the disabled vehicle and attempt to start it.
6. Once the disabled vehicle starts, remove the cable connection to the engine block or remote terminal first, then disconnect the other end of the same cable from the booster battery. Disconnect and remove the cable linking the two positive battery terminals.

In the past, 24-volt booster chargers or other auxiliary power supplies such as portable welders which would quickly spin the starter motor were sometimes used to jump start vehicles with a dead battery. Never use a 24-volt booster charger or other power supply to jump start a late-model computer-equipped vehicle. Immediate failure of the onboard electronic control modules will result.

Diesel engine glow plug systems may also suffer immediate, severe, and costly damage.

CHAPTER QUESTIONS

1. Before load testing a battery the open circuit voltage test should be above:
   a. 9.5 volts
   b. 10.5 volts
   c. 11.5 volts
   d. 12.5 volts

2. Batteries are load tested to:
   a. 100% CCA
   b. 75% CCA
   c. 50% CCA
   d. 25% CCA

3. A battery load test should be run no longer than:
   a. 15 seconds
   b. 30 seconds
   c. 1 minute
   d. 3 minutes

4. A technician is load testing a battery. After 15 seconds the battery voltage should be above:
   a. 9.5 volts
   b. 10.5 volts
   c. 11.5 volts
   d. 12.5 volts

A6

CHAPTER OBJECTIVES

- The technician will complete the ASE task list on Starting System Diagnosis and Service.
- The technician will be able to answer 5 questions dealing with the Starting System Diagnosis and Service section of the A6 ASE Test.

The starting system includes the battery, ignition switch, safety switch, solenoid, starter motor, and all the circuitry that links these components. Starting circuits often contain relays, fuses, fusible links, circuit breakers, or similar devices to protect the wiring and deliver the required current to the starter motor. For an accurate diagnosis, have a wiring diagram handy during troubleshooting.

SYSTEM TESTING

Almost all starting system tests are performed while the starter motor is cranking the engine. However, if the engine starts and runs during the test, the readings will be inaccurate. Bypass the ignition switch with a remote starter switch to prevent the engine from starting.

On vehicles with the ignition starting bypass in the ignition switch or the starter relay, disable the ignition. Disconnect the wiring harness connector from the distributor or coil pack to disable vehicles with an electronic ignition or engine management system. Be sure any disconnected wires do not contact a ground. When testing, observe the following precautions:

- Be sure the transmission is out of gear during cranking; use the remote starter switch to bypass the safety switch
- Do not crank the starter motor for more than 30 seconds at a time, and allow two minutes between tests for cooling to prevent overheat damage to the motor
- Disconnect the battery ground cable before making or breaking any connections at the starter motor, solenoid, or relay

Cranking Current Draw Test

The cranking current draw test measures the amount of current, in amperes, that the starter circuit requires to crank the engine. This test, which helps isolate the source of a starting problem, is performed with either a charging-starter-battery (CSB) analyzer, or individual voltmeter and inductive ammeter. To test with inductive ammeter:

1. Bypass the ignition with a remote starter switch.
2. Connect the voltmeter leads to the battery terminals, observing correct polarity.

3. Clamp the inductive ammeter pickup around the positive cable.
4. Crank the engine for several seconds and note the voltmeter and ammeter readings, figure 3-1.
5. Compare ammeter readings to specifications. With a CSB analyzer, connect the leads and test according to the equipment instructions. Regardless of method, high current draw is caused by a short in the starter circuit or a binding starter motor or engine. Low current draw often results from high resistance in the starting system circuit, but can also be caused by an undercharged or defective battery.

High resistance in the cranking circuit can cause either high or low current draw. To understand how, it is necessary to know that the starter motor requires high current to get up to speed. Once the starter motor is up to speed, it acts like a generator and produces a counter voltage which limits the current. A motor requires high current when turning slowly. This high

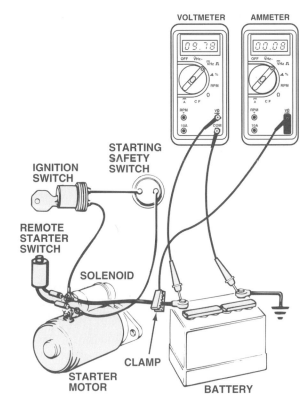

Fig. 3-1. Meter connections to perform a starter current draw test using an ammeter with an inductive pickup.

resistance can prevent the starter from getting enough current to get up to speed. As a result, the motor turns slowly and does not limit the current.

If resistance is high enough, it limits current to the starter. This low current causes the starter motor to turn slowly or not at all. High resistance can be seen on the ammeter when the starter is first engaged. If current momentarily goes high, then settles down to a lower amount, suspect high resistance.

When high resistance is indicated, perform starter circuit resistance tests as described later in the chapter. If testing indicates a starter motor problem, remove the unit for service.

Cranking Voltage Test

This test, which must be performed with a fully charged battery in good condition, measures available voltage at the starter during cranking. Test results are read on a voltmeter. To test:

1. Bypass the ignition switch with a remote starter switch.
2. Connect the negative voltmeter lead to a good ground and connect the positive voltmeter lead to high-current circuit to the starter, figure 3-2. Some manufacturers recommend connecting the voltmeter directly to the starter, while others specify testing at the relay or solenoid. Check the Service Manual for exact procedures and specifications.
3. Crank the engine while monitoring the voltmeter. To interpret test results if the starter motor cranks poorly, and if voltage is:

   • 9.6 or more and the amperage is high, the problem is in the motor, ignition timing is too far advanced, the engine is tight and binding, or there is high circuit resistance. The battery is good and the starter motor is getting enough current to operate
   • 9.6 or more and the amperage is low, the problem is high resistance. The battery is good but there is not enough current through the starter motor
   • 9.6 or less and the amperage is high, the problem is either in the motor, ignition timing is too far advanced, the engine is tight and binding, or there is high circuit

resistance. The high amperage draw pulls down the battery voltage and the battery may be faulty
   • 9.6 or less and the amperage is low. The battery should be tested

Perform a cranking test to check for high resistance in the starter circuit. Starter overloading can result from engine seizing, dragging, or preignition.

CIRCUIT RESISTANCE TESTING

If the current draw and cranking voltage tests indicate that the problem lies in one of the starting system electrical circuits, use the following tests to pinpoint the problem. These tests locate the point of high resistance in the circuit that is causing excessive voltage drop. The resistance usually occurs at one of the connections in the circuits, but internally defective wires and cables may also be at fault. As a general rule, acceptable voltage drop in starting systems is a maximum of 0.1 volt per connection. A greater voltage drop causes starter motor performance problems.

The starting system has three circuits:

• Insulated
• Ground
• Control

The insulated circuit carries the high current needed to operate the starter motor, the ground circuit provides a return path to the battery for power supplied by the insulated circuit, and the control circuit includes all the low-current wiring and devices used to open and close the insulated circuit. To locate the source of high resistance, perform voltage drop tests as described previously in this book at test points recommended by the manufacturer. Take readings while the starter motor is cranking, or use a carbon pile to load the circuit, figure 3-3. Momentarily load the circuit to approximately 150 to 200 amps, and switch the load off quickly to prevent draining the battery. Test the starter ground circuit in a similar manner, figure 3-4. Perform voltage drop tests on the control circuit as needed.

A6

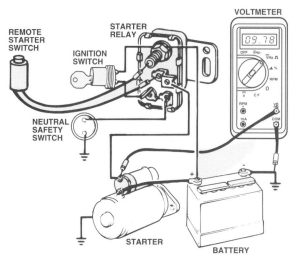

Fig. 3-2. Typical voltmeter connections for performing a cranking voltage test.

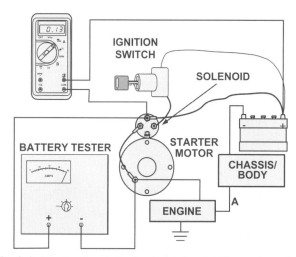

Fig. 3-3. Loading the starter insulated circuit with a carbon pile to locate the source of high resistance by voltage drop testing.

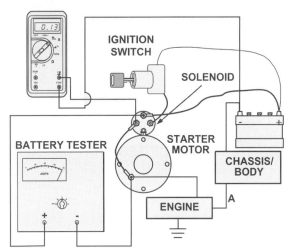

Fig. 3-4. Check for high resistance in the starter ground circuit by voltage drop testing under load.

STARTER RELAYS, SOLENOIDS, AND SAFETY SWITCHES

The starter relay is an electromechanical switch that connects the battery directly to the starter motor when the starter control circuit is closed by turning the ignition key.

A starter solenoid is an electromagnetic device that engages the starter drive with the engine flywheel to crank the engine. The heavy solenoid coil is mounted around a plunger. The plunger connects to a shift lever, which is mechanically attached to the starter drive pinion. Closing the starter control circuit activates the solenoid by energizing the coil. This pulls the plunger in and levers the shift lever out to mesh the gears of the drive pinion with those of the flywheel, figure 3-5. As the plunger continues to move, it closes the starter motor switch to energize the starter.

A starting safety, or neutral safety, switch, which prevents the starter from cranking when the transmission is engaged, is used on all vehicles with automatic transmissions and on some vehicles with manual transmissions, figure 3-6. The safety switch can be mounted on the steering column under the dash panel, on the transmission or transaxle, or on the clutch pedal.

Vehicles with a manual transmission often have a safety switch that is activated by the clutch pedal, so the starter will only operate when the clutch pedal is depressed.

Inspecting, Adjusting, and Replacing Safety Switches

A starting safety switch does not need service during normal use. However, if not correctly adjusted, the switch does not allow power flow in the desired gear position. A simple adjustment may solve an erratic engagement problem, and is important when installing a replacement switch.

A clutch-operated switch is not adjustable. To replace this type of switch, simply remove the defective unit and bolt a new one into the mounting holes of the original switch.

The automatic transmission switch used in some vehicles is threaded into the transmission housing. If a known-good switch is not operating correctly when installed, adjust the internal transmission linkage to correct.

Floor-mounted switches are generally adjustable, figure 3-7. To adjust:

1. Remove the gear selector lever handle.
2. Remove the dial housing.
3. Remove the pointer backup shield.
4. Loosen the screws that hold the switch to the gear selector lever housing.
5. Hold the gear selector lever against the forward stop of the Park position.
6. Move the switch rearward to the end of its travel.
7. Tighten the attaching screws.
8. Check that the engine will start only when the gear selector lever is in Park or Neutral range; readjust the switch if necessary.
9. Reinstall the pointer backup shield, dial housing, and gear selector lever handle.

Some column-mounted switches have alignment holes and are adjusted using a calibrated gauge pin, figure 3-8. To adjust:

1. Disconnect the battery ground cable.
2. Loosen the switch attaching screws.
3. Move the switch until the two alignment holes match.

SOLENOID OFF

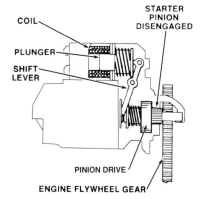

SOLENOID ON

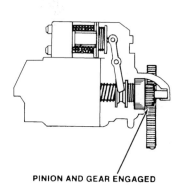

Fig. 3-5. The starter solenoid is an electromagnetic coil that activates a plunger and shift linkage to mesh the drive pinion and flywheel gears.

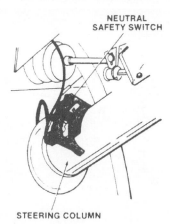

Fig. 3-6. A starting safety switch allows starter engagement only when the transmission is in Park or Neutral range.

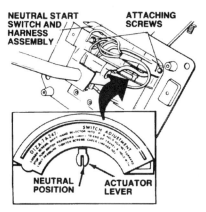

Fig. 3-7. Floor-mounted starting safety switches must be adjusted to operate correctly.

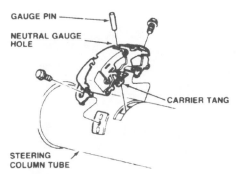

Fig. 3-8. Use a gauge pin to correctly align this column-mounted starting safety switch.

4. Check hole alignment with a gauge pin of the size specified by the manufacturer.
5. Tighten the switch attaching screw.
6. Reconnect the battery ground cable.

7. Check that the engine starts only when the gear selector lever is in Park or Neutral range; readjust the switch if necessary.

Checking and Replacing Relays

Many vehicles use a starting circuit relay. To check relay operation, connect one voltmeter lead to the battery terminal of the relay and the other lead to the relay switch terminal. Then, switch the ignition switch to crank the starter. A voltmeter reading that exceeds 2.5 volts indicates excessive resistance in the control circuit.

If the voltmeter reading is below 2.5 volts and the relay does not close, connect the voltmeter leads to the switch terminal of the relay and ground. Typically, a relay closes whenever the voltage reaches approximately 7.7 volts on a 12 volt system. Confirm the relay ground by connecting the voltmeter leads to the relay case and a chassis ground. The voltmeter reading should be less than 0.1 volt when the starter motor is engaged. A relay that does not operate with a 7.7 or higher voltage and a good ground is faulty and must be replaced.

Replacing most starter relays is simply a matter of locating the relay, labeling and disconnecting its wires, and removing the attachment screws. On older vehicles, the starter relay is often mounted on the firewall or fenderwell. Newer vehicles generally use a relay that simply plugs into a power distribution center in the engine compartment.

Checking and Replacing Solenoids

Starter motor solenoids are a pull-hold type. When the solenoid is first energized, both the **pull-in windings** and the **hold-in windings** are energized to draw in the core. Once the core is pulled in, the pull-in windings are deenergized and the hold-in windings keep the core in position until the cranking circuit is deenergized. Use the same voltmeter test as described for relays to check solenoid operation.

To test starters and solenoids:

1. Confirm there are at least 8 volts available at the solenoid when cranking.
2. If voltage is present, check for battery voltage to the solenoid, then battery voltage to the starter.
3. A starter that fails to crank when battery voltage is available can indicate either a seized engine or starter motor or an open circuit in the starter or ground. A seized engine or motor produces low voltage and high amperage readings, while an open circuit results in high voltage and low amperage readings.

A seized engine, caused by liquid filling the cylinders due to a blown head gasket or leaking fuel injection system, is becoming more common.

In most cases, replacing a starter solenoid involves removing the starter motor and partially disassembling it to disengage the plunger from the starter shift lever.

A6

Hold-In Winding: The coil of small-diameter wire in a solenoid that is used to maintain a magnetic field to hold the solenoid plunger in position once it has been pulled inside the coil.
Pull-In Winding: The coil of large-diameter wire in a solenoid that is used to create a strong magnetic field to pull the solenoid plunger into the coil.

STARTER MOTOR REMOVAL AND REPLACEMENT

Once a system problem is isolated in the starter motor, remove it for further testing or replacement. Starter removal may involve, figure 3-9:

- Loosening, relocating, or removing exhaust heat shields, support brackets, or pipes
- Loosening, relocating, or removing suspension components
- Loosening, relocating, or removing intake air hoses, ducts, pipes, or manifolds
- Loosening or removing engine mounts or loosening and relocating the engine cradle

Label nuts, bolts, and washers removed from the starter motor and other parts to ease reassembly. Also, tag all disconnected wires to prevent circuit failures on assembly.

Starter Removal

The following is a typical starter motor removal sequence. Always consult the repair manual for the vehicle being serviced. To remove the starter:

1. Disconnect the negative battery cable.
2. Raise the vehicle on safety stands or a hoist high enough to access the starter motor.
3. Disconnect tie rods and other suspension links that are likely to interfere with removing the starter from the chassis.
4. Loosen or remove exhaust pipes and other components that interfere with starter motor removal.
5. Disconnect and label all wires and cables to the starter motor or solenoid.
6. Remove any heat shields and brackets covering the starter motor.
7. Remove any mounting bolts and shims securing the starter motor to the engine.
8. Slide the starter free of the bellhousing and guide it out of the chassis.

Pinion Travel Inspection

Incorrect pinion clearance causes pinion damage, stripped flywheel gear teeth, and starter motor failure. Check drive pinion clearance with the starter motor assembled:

1. Disconnect the field coil connector from the solenoid motor terminal, and insulate the connector to prevent accidental arcing.
2. Use jumper cables to connect the positive terminal of a battery to the power input terminal on the solenoid and the negative battery terminal to the starter frame, figure 3-10.
3. Connect a jumper wire from the solenoid switch terminal and momentarily touch the open end of the jumper wire to the starter motor frame. The pinion should snap into position and stay there as long as the jumper wire is completing the circuit.
4. Disconnect the battery and push the pinion back toward the commutator to eliminate slack or endplay on the pinion.
5. Use a feeler gauge to check the pinion-to-pinion stop clearance. Acceptable clearance falls in the 0.010 to 0.140 inch (0.25 to 3.6 mm) range, figure 3-11.

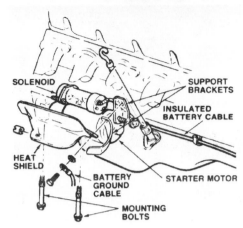

Fig. 3-9. You must remove a number of components to gain clear access to the starter motor.

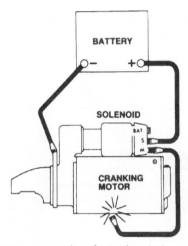

Fig. 3-10. Battery connections for testing starter motor drive pinion clearance.

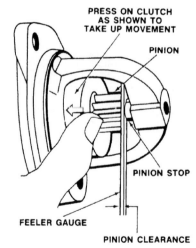

Fig. 3-11. Checking starter motor drive pinion clearance with a feeler gauge.

If pinion clearance is not within specifications, check the shift fork, pivot pin, and starter drive for incorrect installation or wear. Replace the shift fork and pin or the drive, if worn. Pinion clearance cannot be adjusted on motors with an enclosed shift fork.

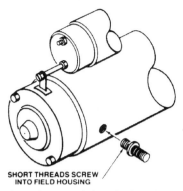

SHORT THREADS SCREW
INTO FIELD HOUSING

Fig. 3-12. Hardware incorrectly installed on the housing can damage the starter motor field windings.

Starter Installation

When replacing a starter motor, make sure the new unit meets the requirements of the vehicle. Some vehicles require a high-temperature starter with an extra field coil, brush lead, and solenoid winding insulation as well as a high-temperature solenoid cap. To install a starter motor:

1. Transfer support brackets or other hardware from the old motor to the replacement motor as required.
2. Fit the starter motor into position on the engine and install the mounting fasteners. Be sure to reconnect any ground cables or brackets that install on the starter mounts.
3. Check flywheel-to-starter engagement. Some vehicles require shims to provide correct starter pinion to-flywheel engagement. These shims are placed between the starter drive housing and the engine block. Remove the flywheel cover and check the starter pinion engagement with the flywheel. Add or remove shims to correct.
4. Connect all wires to the solenoid or starter motor terminals.
5. Connect any suspension or exhaust system parts that were loosened or removed.
6. Connect the negative battery cable.

Test starter motor operation by starting the vehicle. Listen for any unusual sounds and check for correct operation of the starting safety switch. Some late-model starters have a special stud in the motor housing, figure 3-12. Be sure the short end of the stud, with coarser threads, is threaded into the housing. Incorrect installation damages the field coils.

STARTING SYSTEM DIAGNOSIS

If the vehicle starter motor does not turn over or cranks slowly, test the battery as previously described. A discharged battery or one with inadequate reserve capacity can cause these symptoms. If the starter motor does crank, listen carefully. Diagnose starting system problems by sound, figure 3-13.

System Inspection

A simple inspection can uncover many problems within the starting system. Inspection areas include the:

- Battery
- Ignition switch
- **Starting safety switch**
- **Starter solenoid**
- Starter motor

At the battery, check for:

- Loose or corroded terminals
- Loose or corroded ground cable connections
- Frayed or corroded cables
- Damaged insulation

Check the ignition switch for:

- Loose mounting
- Damaged wiring
- Worn or sticking contacts
- Loose connections

If the system has a starting safety switch, check for:

- Improper adjustment
- Loose mounting
- Loose or damaged wiring

If the vehicle has a theft deterrent system it is important to have the information necessary to test it.

    Check starter solenoids for:

- Loose mounting
- Loose connection
- Damaged wiring

Inspect the starter motor for:

- Loose mounting
- Improper pinion adjustment
- Loose wiring and connections
- Damaged wiring and connections

If the system uses a **relay**, check for loose connections and wiring damage. Verify operation using a voltmeter and jump wire.

A6

Relay: An electromagnetic switch that uses a low amperage circuit to open and close a separate contact set that controls current in a high amperage circuit.
Starter Solenoid: An electromagnetic device consisting of an iron core surrounded by a wire coil. The core moves to perform mechanical work when electrical current is applied to the coil.
Starting Safety Switch: A switch in the starting circuit that prevents the starter motor from engaging when the transmission is in a forward or reverse gear. Also known as a neutral start switch.

SYMPTOMS	POSSIBLE CAUSE	CURE
• Nothing happens when ignition switch is turned to Start	1. Battery discharged 2. Open in control circuit 3. Defective starter relay or solenoid 4. Open in motor internal ground connections	1. Recharge or replace 2. Test control circuit for continuity; repair or replace components as necessary 3. Replace relay or solenoid 4. Replace starter motor
• Solenoid contacts click or chatter but starter does not operate OR movable pole shoe starter chatters or disengages before engine has been started	1. Battery discharged 2. Excessive resistance in system 3. Open in solenoid or movable pole shoe hold-in winding 4. Defective starter motor	1. Recharge or replace 2. Make voltage drop tests; replace components as necessary 3. Replace solenoid or movable pole shoe starter 4. Replace starter motor
• Starter motor operates but does not turn car engine	1. Defective starter drive assembly 2. Defective engine flywheel ring gear	1. Replace starter drive 2. Replace engine flywheel ring gear
• Starter motor turns engine slowly or unevenly	1. Battery discharged 2. Excessive resistance in system 3. Defective starter 4. Defective engine flywheel ring gear 5. Poor flywheel/starter engagement	1. Recharge or replace 2. Move voltage drop tests; replace components as necessary 3. Replace starter motor 4. Replace engine flywheel ring gear 5. Adjust starter/flywheel engagement
• Engine starts but motor drive assembly does not disengage	1. Defective drive assembly 2. Poor flywheel/starter engagement 3. Shorted solenoid windings 4. Shorted control circuit	1. Replace starter drive 2. Adjust flywheel/starter engagement, if possible, or replace starter motor 3. Replace solenoid 4. Test control circuit; replace components as necessary

Fig. 3-13. Starting system troubleshooting chart.

CHAPTER QUESTIONS

1. If a starter motor operates but does not turn the engine, the problem may be:
   a. A discharged battery
   b. A defective starter relay
   c. A defective flywheel ring gear
   d. High resistance in system

2. Begin starting system testing by:
   a. Disconnecting the negative battery cable
   b. Measuring the current draw
   c. Bypassing the ignition switch with a remote starter switch
   d. Confirming the complaint

3. High starter motor current draw test results are most likely caused by:
   a. A short in the starter
   b. Excessive resistance in the starter
   c. An undercharged battery
   d. Defective wiring

4. Low voltage readings during a starter motor cranking voltage test with a fully charged battery are most likely caused by:
   a. An open in the starter circuit
   b. High resistance in the starter circuit
   c. A defective starter motor
   d. A defective starter relay

5. To perform an insulated circuit test, connect the positive voltmeter lead to the:
   a. Ignition switch
   b. Positive battery terminal post
   c. Positive battery cable
   d. Starter terminal housing

6. When completing a starter cranking test the battery voltage should not drop below:
   a. 9.5 volts
   b. 10.5 volts
   c. 11.5 volts
   d. 12.5 volts

A6

CHAPTER OBJECTIVES

- The technician will complete the ASE task list on Charging System Diagnosis and Repair.
- The technician will be able to answer 5 questions dealing with the Charging System Diagnosis and Repair section of the A6 ASE Test.

Like all electrical circuits, the charging system, figure 4.1, is subject to four basic electrical failures:

- Short circuits
- Open circuits
- Grounded circuits
- High-resistance circuits

Short circuits are unwanted connections, usually copper-to-copper, in the wiring or components that allow current to bypass part or all of the circuit. An open circuit is one in which a break in the circuit causes extremely high or infinite resistance; usually no current flows through an open circuit. Grounding a circuit creates an unwanted connection between the insulated circuit and the ground circuit. This allows current to bypass part or all of the insulated circuit. High circuit resistance is usually the result of either poor or corroded connections or frayed and damaged wires that impede current.

Insight:

In 1996, SAE J1930 terminology was adopted to standardize component identification. This standard adopted the name "generator" to refer to the component commonly known as an "alternator." This study guide uses the term generator throughout; however, both terms are used interchangeably in the ASE tests.

BASIC DIAGNOSIS

To diagnose charging system problems it is necessary to be familiar with basic system operations. All charging systems operate in a similar manner:

1. The regulator is energized by the ignition system either by battery voltage or a lower regulated voltage. Some systems use the instrument cluster warning light ground to energize the system.
2. The voltage regulator controls current through the generator field windings. With electronic regulators, this is usually done by pulse-width modulation of the ground side circuit. The longer the ON time, voltage low, the higher the output. An external mechanical regulator varies the voltage on the power side of the field circuit. Replacement regulators of this style are now solid-state,

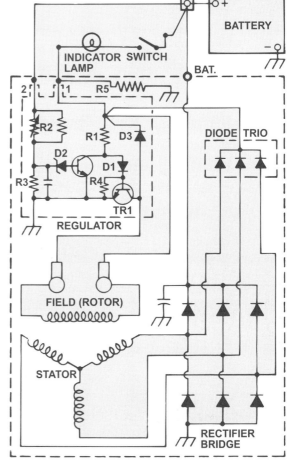

Fig. 4-1. Typical solid-state charging system circuit diagram.

and control the power side, but with a pulse-width modulated signal, rather than a contact point set. On these units, the longer the ON time, voltage high, the higher the output.

3. The regulator is connected to battery voltage to sense charging voltage. This circuit is used to tell the voltage regulator to increase or decrease field current. The regulator also has to have a good ground for reference.

Perhaps the best way to understand how a generator is energized is to look at the charging voltage trace captured on a graphing multimeter as the engine starts, figure 4-2.

The test circuit is fed through the instrument cluster warning lamp, so there is no voltage as the trace begins with

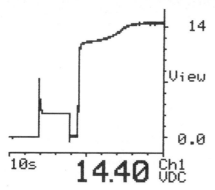

Fig. 4-2. Graphing multimeter trace of the generator being energized at startup.

the ignition switched off. When the ignition is switched on, a 2.8 volt signal energizes the field circuit and turns on the warning lamp. Voltage drops to zero while the starter is cranking, then rises to charging voltage as the engine starts and switches off the warning lamp.

When testing a charging system, use a wiring diagram, and confirm that the regulator and generator are receiving the correct signals, figure 4-1. Basic charging system diagnosis begins with a visual inspection of the system components and wiring. Look for indicators, such as cracked, swollen, or melted wiring insulation, loose or corroded component mounts and ground connections, and signs of tampering, that might create short, open, grounded, and high-resistance circuits.

Most charging system problems can be diagnosed with a digital multimeter (DMM) using ammeter, voltmeter, and ohmmeter functions. Make sure the battery is fully charged before attempting to diagnose charging system problems. Take meter readings to diagnose the charging system, figure 4-3.

Diagnostic Check

Inspecting and testing charging system components on the vehicle helps pinpoint problems. If the problem is with the generator or a **solid-state** regulator, remove the unit from the vehicle for service or replacement. Some common warning signs of charging system failures are:

- Ammeter, voltmeter, or ohmmeter indications and test results
- Low battery state-of-charge
- Generator noise

When working with the charging system, observe these safety precautions:

- Keep the ignition switch off except during actual test procedures
- Disconnect the negative battery cable before removing any leads from the generator or charging the battery
- Remember the output terminal at the generator has voltage present whenever system connections are in place

- Make sure to observe correct polarity when installing battery cables
- Keep the carbon pile off except during test procedures

No Charge or Undercharge

If a charging system has a lower than normal charging rate, or is not charging at all, check for:

- Loose or broken drive belts, pulleys, or supporting brackets
- Defective diodes or stator windings
- Defective voltage regulator
- High resistance or an open circuit in the wiring connecting the generator and the battery
- High resistance in the generator **field circuit**
- Sulfated battery

Overcharging

An excessive charging rate can be caused by a:

- Defective voltage regulator—on some systems, the voltage regulator is part of the powertrain control module (PCM); if defective, replace the PCM
- Shorted field wire—shorted to ground in a system with an externally grounded field, or A-circuit, or shorted to power in a system with an internally grounded field, or B-circuit
- High resistance in the wiring between the battery and main fuse panel—this results in an inaccurate voltage indication to the field circuit from the ignition switch
- Battery with an internal short that accepts a charge with little resistance
- A faulty component drawing excessive current

SYSTEM INSPECTION

Charging system complaints often result from simple and easily corrected problems that become obvious during a quick visual inspection of the system components. To begin:

1. Check the battery electrolyte level, state-of-charge, and capacity. If the battery is worn out or defective, the charging system may not be at fault.
2. Inspect the generator drive belt. Loose belts are a major cause of poor charging system performance. If the belt is loose or damaged remove it for further inspection. Loosen the tension on the belt before attempting to remove it from the engine. Never force or pry a belt over pulley flanges. While the belt is removed, examine the pulleys for damage and misalignment. Replace pulleys as required and install the new belt. Belts must be properly tensioned. A loose belt will slip, and a tight belt can damage bearings. Adjust tension to specifications. Refer to Book A1 in this series for more information on proper belt adjustment procedures. After installing a new drive belt, allow the engine to run for at least 10 to 15 minutes. Switch the engine off, then recheck and adjust belt tension using "used" belt specifications.

A6

Field Circuit: The charging system circuit that delivers current to energize the generator field.
Solid-State: An electronic device consisting chiefly of semiconductors and related components.

SYMPTOMS	POSSIBLE CAUSE	REPAIR
• The meter reading flutters • Warning lamp flickers	1. Loose connections in system wiring 2. Loose or worn brushes 3. Oxidized regulator points	1. Repair system wiring 2. Repair or replace generator 3. Replace regulator
• Ammeter reads discharge • Voltmeter shows low system voltage • Warning lamp stays on • Battery is discharged	1. Faulty generator drive belt 2. Corroded battery cables 3. Loose system wiring 4. Defective field relay 5. Defective battery 6. Wrong battery in car 7. Alternator output low	1. Check and adjust belt 2. Replace battery cables 3. Repair system wiring 4. Replace field relay 5. Replace battery 6. Replace battery 7. Repair or replace generator
• Ammeter reads charge • Voltmeter shows high system voltage • Battery is overcharged	1. Loose system wiring 2. Poor regulator ground 3. Burned regulator points 4. Incorrect regulator setting 5. Defective regulator	1. Repair system wiring 2. Tighten regulator ground 3. Replace regulator 4. Adjust regulator 5. Replace regulator
• Warning lamp stays on when ignition switch is off	1. Shorted positive diode	1. Repair or replace generator
• Generator makes squealing noise	1. Loose or damaged drive belt 2. Worn or defective rotor shaft bearing 3. Defective stator 4. Loose or misaligned pulley	1. Adjust or replace drive belt 2. Repair or replace generator 3. Repair or replace generator 4. Tighten or realign pulley
• Generator makes whining noise	1. Shorted diode	1. Repair or replace generator

Fig. 4-3. Charging system troubleshooting chart.

3. Check all system wiring and connections. Be sure to closely inspect all fusible links. Even when the fusible link looks good it may be damaged internally. If in doubt pull on one end of the fusible link. If the insulation stretches replace the link. Disconnect each connector in the circuit and conduct a visual inspection. Look closely for damaged, corroded, or pushed out pins. Use a new terminal pin to check for a snug fit into the plug, If the socket in the plug is loose replace with a new part. Reconnect and ensure the connector is latched properly. If the circuit is physically sound continue with a voltage drop test described in this chapter.

4. Inspect the generator and regulator mountings for loose or missing bolts. Replace or tighten as needed.

SYSTEM TESTING

On-vehicle generator system tests are essentially the same, regardless of the vehicle. The main differences are meter test points and specifications. This section contains general descriptions of common on-vehicle tests. To check a particular generator or system, use the procedures and specifications from the vehicle manufacturer.

The voltage regulator limits the strength of the magnetic field by changing the current going to the field coil. Therefore, it regulates the generator voltage output according to the electrical system demand. Bypassing a voltage regulator for test purposes is called full-fielding the generator. Bypassing a voltage regulator supplies maximum output to the field coil. Under these conditions, system voltage can increase above 16 volts, which is an unsafe level. Once you determine that

the generator can or cannot produce the required voltage, remove the bypass immediately.

Charging System Output Test

A charging-starting-battery (CSB) analyzer simplifies charging system diagnosis. This test instrument combines the functions of the carbon pile and separate meters needed for various tests. Use the following general procedure to test the charging system output:

1. Connect the analyzer to the vehicle as instructed in the analyzer manual.
2. Set the test selector switch to the charging test position.
3. Switch the ignition on and note the ammeter reading. This is the current required to power the ignition system and accessories; it will not be included in the maximum output reading.
4. Start the engine and run it at 2,000 rpm, or the specified test speed.
5. Adjust the carbon pile to obtain the maximum ammeter reading while keeping the system voltage above 12 volts. Always keep load time to a minimum.
6. Compare the ammeter reading to specifications. If it is:

   • Within 10 percent of specifications, go to step 7
   • Not within 10 percent of specifications, go to step 11

7. Set the test selector switch to the regulator test position.
8. Adjust the engine speed to 2,000 rpm or the specified test speed.
9. Note the voltmeter reading after it stabilizes. The length of time required for the reading to stop rising varies according to battery state-of-charge.

10. Compare the voltmeter reading to specifications. If it is:
   - Within specifications, the voltage regulator is okay
   - Not within specifications, replace the voltage regulator and retest

11. With the engine running at test speed, high rpm, turn on the carbon pile to discharge the battery.

12. As system voltage drops, the voltage regulator should increase generator output.

13. When the amperage output begins to decrease, reduce the carbon pile discharge. Turn the carbon pile off.

14. Add the highest ammeter reading to the readings taken in step 3, using a minimum of 5 amps.

15. Compare the total to specifications. If it is:
   - Within 10 percent of specifications, no problem is found
   - Not within 10 percent of specifications, further testing of the field circuit and regulator is required. With an internal regulator, test other generator inputs for correct voltage

Circuit Resistance Test

Replace or repair any loose or corroded connections or damaged wiring before testing the charging system to prevent inaccurate test results. Isolate high resistance in the positive, or insulated, and negative, or ground, circuits of the charging system by voltage drop testing. Test under load with the engine running at 1,500 to 1,800 rpm and the generator producing a specific current, usually 20 amps applied to the battery. Begin by checking insulated circuit voltage drop by connecting the DMM between the positive battery terminal and the battery, or output, terminal at the generator, figure 4-4. If the voltage drop is higher than specified, move test connections down the circuit to pinpoint the high resistance.

Check voltage drop on the ground circuit of the generator in similar fashion. Connect the DMM between the generator frame and negative battery terminal, figure 4-5.

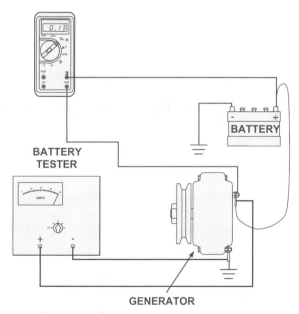

Fig. 4-4. Checking voltage drop on the insulated, or positive, generator circuit.

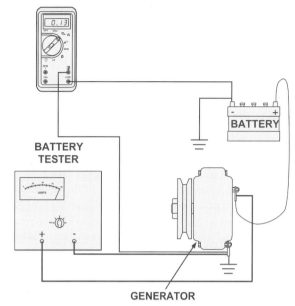

Fig. 4-5. Checking voltage drop on the ground, or negative, generator circuit.

This test is performed when the generator has enough output to charge the battery at a 20 amp rate. It is fairly common to see a negative (-) voltage under these conditions. If voltage drop is excessively high, install an external ground strap between the generator and the engine. This ground strap is always required when the generator is mounted in rubber bushings. The normal limit of voltage drop on this circuit is 0.2 volts.

Current Output Test

There are two stages to a generator current output test, and some manufacturers suggest doing only one stage or the other. Obtain specifications and follow procedures in the Service Manual for the unit being tested.

First Stage

Use a CSB analyzer, or attach a carbon pile across the battery. Connect a voltmeter between the positive battery terminal and ground, and connect an ammeter between the positive battery terminal and the battery terminal at the generator. Start and run the engine at the specified test speed, typically 1,200 rpm, and adjust the carbon pile either to maintain a steady 15-volt level or to get the greatest possible ammeter reading. Compare the ammeter reading to specifications.

This test uses the carbon pile to drop the system voltage and force the voltage regulator to raise the amperage output. This tests the component parts of the existing system for proper operation.

Second Stage

Perform this stage if the ammeter reading does not meet specifications during the first stage. Under the same test conditions, full-field the generator by bypassing the voltage regulator. This provides maximum current through the field windings so that the generator develops maximum output amperage. With a remotely mounted regulator use a jumper wire to provide battery voltage or ground the field wire.

A6

There are two different methods of full-fielding, connecting to power and connecting to ground; it is very important that the right method be used. If the regulator is controlling the ground side of the field windings, the circuit is grounded. If the regulator is controlling the power side of the field, then the circuit should be connected to battery power.

With the generator full-fielded, it is possible for the system voltage to go excessively high. This high voltage can present problems with electronic components. Therefore, full-fielding is often only recommend after it has been determined that the voltage regulator is not functioning properly. This test is used to see if there is an additional problem with the generator.

With an internal voltage regulator that cannot be tested separately, confirm all other voltage inputs to the generator.

Field Current Draw Test

The field current draw test is performed with the engine off. For some vehicles the regulator or warning lamp circuit, or both, may need to be bypassed while testing. Check the Service Manual for specific instructions. To test current draw, connect an ammeter either between the positive battery terminal and the generator field or between the field and ground. Switch the ignition on without starting the engine, or bypass the ignition switch and warning lamp with a jumper wire as directed, and read field current draw on the ammeter. If out of specifications, remove the generator for further testing. If the ammeter reading fluctuates, service the brushes and sliprings.

This test is only performed on charging systems that have an external voltage regulator. Do not attempt this test on the internal regulator.

Voltage Regulator Test

Check the regulated voltage with a voltmeter connected between the generator output terminal and ground, or between the positive battery terminal and ground. Start and run the engine at a fast idle for several minutes to stabilize the charging system. The amperage charge rate into the battery should be low. If voltage readings are too low, confirm the amperage output at the generator before condemning the voltage regulator. High generator amperage output can cause a low voltage reading. If the readings are too high, replace the voltage regulator.

OSCILLOSCOPE TESTING

An oscilloscope can be used to check the generator voltage output and internal operating condition. The generator voltage trace shown on the scope is the result of **wave rectification**, so only the DC portion of the signal is visible, figure 4-6. Look for equally spaced pulses at an equal height from the base line. If any of the diodes or stator windings are bad, it affects the trace. By studying the trace, which is current moving through the circuit, it is possible to determine what is wrong with the generator.

In general, a shorted diode, which tends to break up the trace and disrupt the pattern, has a greater effect on the trace than an open diode, figure 4-7. This is because a shorted diode

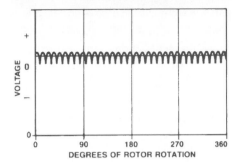

Fig. 4-6. A rectified generator trace produces a repetitive pattern of evenly spaced waves.

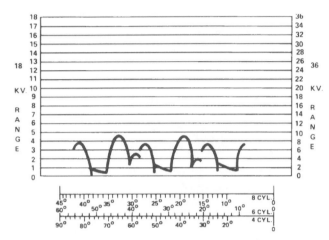

Fig. 4-7. Typical oscilloscope pattern with a shorted generator diode.

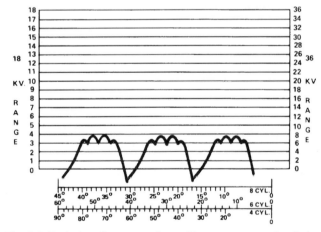

Fig. 4-8. Typical oscilloscope pattern with an open generator diode.

not only reduces the output of its own phase, it also allows current back through the stator to oppose the flow of the next phase. An open diode disrupts current, so the oscilloscope pattern drops out, or spikes down, in a regular pattern, figure 4-8.

VOLTAGE REGULATOR SERVICE

Older electromechanical and most solid-state regulators can be tested as described above. Most digital regulators switch the

---

Wave Rectification: A process by which the alternating current (AC) produced by a generator is converted to the direct current (DC) needed to charge the battery and power electrical devices on the vehicle.

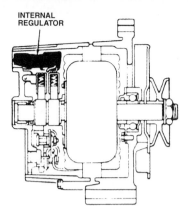

INTERNAL
REGULATOR

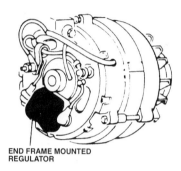

END FRAME MOUNTED
REGULATOR

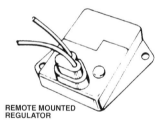

REMOTE MOUNTED
REGULATOR

Fig. 4-9. Typical voltage regulator location and mounting.

field current on and off at a fixed **frequency**, typically about 400 Hz. Generator output voltage is determined by the **duty cycle**, or proportion of on-time to off-time, of the field current signal. Size, shape, and mounting position varies among regulators. Some regulators mount inside the generator housing and include the brush holder. Others attach on the outside of the generator end frame, while still others are remotely mounted away from the generator, figure 4-9.

Replacing external voltage regulators amounts to unplugging the electrical connector and removing one or more fasteners. Integral regulator replacement may require partial disassembly of the generator.

Many late-model vehicles control the output of the generator with a voltage regulator circuit inside the PCM. With this design the PCM is able to ramp up current demands and maintain engine idle speed regardless of the generator load. Direct testing of the voltage regulating circuitry on a computerized system is unnecessary unless the onboard diagnostics

system detects a charging system problem and stores a diagnostic trouble code (DTC) in memory. Computerized regulator replacement requires installing a new PCM.

GENERATOR SERVICE

When a generator tests bad on the vehicle, and it is going to be repaired, remove and bench test the unit. Before removing the generator, test all of the inputs and the output of the unit. Once the generator is removed from the vehicle, check for:

- Rotor continuity
- Rotor ground
- Stator continuity
- Stator ground
- Shorted capacitor
- Diode function

Generator Removal

Remove a generator as follows:

1. Disconnect the negative battery cable.
2. Identify, label, and disconnect all leads from the generator. Some are held by nuts on terminal studs; others are plug-in connections. Be sure to release any clips or springs holding the plugs in the generator.
3. Remove the drive belt.
4. Remove the mounting bolt and adjusting bolts and lift the generator free of the mounting brackets.

Disassembly, Cleaning, and Inspection

Brush any dirt or debris off the outside of the generator housing, then loosen the fasteners adjoining the drive and stator end frames. Mark position of the end frames before separating them so they align easily during assembly. Also, note the location of the brush assembly when separating the end frames. Brushes are generally located in the drive end frame. Check brushes to make sure they slide freely in their holders and are making full contact on the rotor shaft slip rings. Replace the brushes if they are worn to half their original length or less.

Remove the stator and rotor from their end frames. As you disassemble the generator, clean each part and inspect it for excessive wear or damage. As part of the overall inspection during disassembly:

- Check bearings for proper clearance, roughness, or galling
- Remove any oil and dirt from insulation
- Check insulation condition

After inspecting and cleaning the generator, test components and replace any defective parts, then reassemble the unit.

Rotor Tests

Check the rotor winding, or field, for open and short circuits by connecting an ohmmeter between the two slip rings, figure 4-10. Look for high or infinite readings on the ohmmeter. Lower than specified resistance indicates a short; a reading above the specified value indicates an open. If a self-powered test lamp does not light when connected to both slip rings, the winding is open.

A6

Duty Cycle: The percentage of total time in one complete on-off-on cycle during which a solenoid is energized.
Frequency: The number of periodic voltage oscillations, or waves, occurring in one second, usually expressed as Hertz (Hz) or cycles per second.

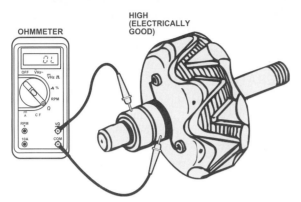

Fig. 4-10. Checking rotor winding continuity with an ohmmeter.

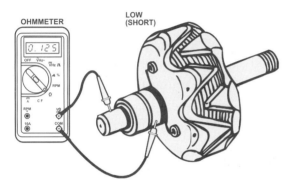

Fig. 4-11. Check for rotor winding continuity by connecting an ohmmeter between the slip ring and shaft.

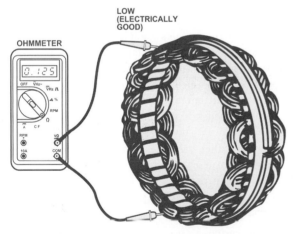

Fig. 4-12. Expect low readings when checking for open stator circuits with an ohmmeter.

To check for grounded rotor winding circuits, connect an ohmmeter or self-powered test lamp from either slip ring to the shaft, figure 4-11. A high ohmmeter reading means the winding is okay; a low reading indicates a short to ground. A self-powered test lamp connected between either slip ring and the shaft lights if the winding is grounded.

Stator Tests

Disconnect stator windings from the end frame and check for open circuits with an ohmmeter or self-powered test lamp. A good winding offers little resistance, so look for low ohmmeter readings or an illuminated test lamp when connected between each pair of stator leads, figure 4-12. A high ohmmeter reading or a test lamp that does not light indicates an open circuit.

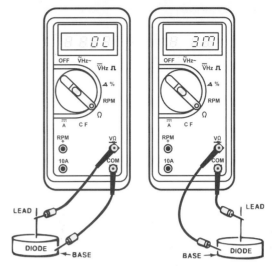

Fig. 4-13. Diodes, which allow current in one direction only, are quickly checked with an ohmmeter.

Shorted Capacitor

A capacitor, located inside the generator, is connected between the positive terminal and ground. Although it is not troublesome, visually inspect it whenever the generator is disassembled. The lead must be attached firmly with its insulation intact. Check with a self-powered test lamp. If the lamp lights, there is continuity because the plates are shorted together. The capacitor is defective; replace it.

Diode Check

Diodes can be checked with a self-powered test lamp. Disconnect each diode from the circuit. The test lamp should light with the probes connected in one direction, and not light with the probes switched, which reverses polarity. When testing with an ohmmeter, a good diode will have high resistance with the test probes connected in one way and an infinite reading with the probes reversed, figure 4-13.

A special diode tester can test a diode that is connected to the circuit. The tester supplies an alternating current and uses it to determine diode condition. The tester meter has a pointer at rest in the center of the scale, and a green zone on both sides of the center indicates a good diode. A red zone at both extremes of the scale indicates a defective diode, positive or negative.

Generator Installation

Before installing the generator, spin the rotor and pulley by hand to be sure there is no drag or binding. Carefully inspect and replace any drive belts that are worn, frayed, or damaged. Then install the generator:

1. Put the generator on its engine mounting brackets and loosely secure the mounting and adjusting bolts.
2. Replace the drive belt and adjust tension.
3. Identify all wiring connections and attach them to their appropriate terminals or sockets.
4. Connect the negative battery cable.
5. Start and run the engine to test the generator. Repeat output tests and listen for noise or vibration coming from the generator or drive belts.

CHAPTER QUESTIONS

1. A generator oscilloscope trace shows a series of equally spaced and equal-size pulses; this indicates:
   a. An open diode
   b. A grounded diode
   c. Good stator and diodes
   d. A weak capacitor

2. There should be battery voltage available at the generator output terminal:
   a. At all times
   b. When the ignition is switched on
   c. When the engine is running
   d. If the regulator is defective

3. Which of the following is **NOT** a typical generator bench test?
   a. Rotor continuity test
   b. Stator ground test
   c. Growler test
   d. Diode test

4. A probable cause of system undercharging is:
   a. Field wire shorted
   b. Sulfated battery
   c. High resistance between battery and fuse block
   d. Low resistance in the generator field circuit

5. If the ohmmeter reading is low when connected between each pair of stator leads, the winding is:
   a. Open
   b. Good
   c. Shorted
   d. Grounded

6. The first step in inspecting the charging system is to:
   a. Replace the generator drive belt
   b. Remove the generator
   c. Check the battery condition
   d. Check system voltage

7. Manufacturers often recommend a voltage output test, rather than a current output test, to prevent:
   a. System overloading
   b. Electronic component damage
   c. Generator damage
   d. Wiring damage

8. If a self-powered test lamp does not light when connected to both slip rings of a rotor, the winding is:
   a. Open
   b. Good
   c. Shorted
   d. Grounded

9. Which of the following is **NOT** a major component of the charging system?
   a. Coil
   b. Generator
   c. Regulator
   d. Field relay

10. Normal charging system voltage at the battery is:
    a. 13.5–14.5
    b. 12.5–13.5
    c. 11.5–12.5
    d. 10.5–11.5

A6

CHAPTER FIVE

LIGHTING SYSTEMS DIAGNOSIS AND REPAIR

CHAPTER OBJECTIVES

- The technician will complete the ASE task list on Lighting Systems Diagnosis and Repair.
- The technician will be able to answer 6 questions dealing with the Lighting Systems Diagnosis and Repair section of the A6 ASE test.

Lighting circuit diagnosis requires the use of standard test meters and instruments to identify the four basic electrical failures:

- Short circuits
- Open circuits
- Grounded circuits
- High-resistance circuits

Late-model vehicles may control many interior and exterior lamps with an electronic control module. Diagnosis of these systems may require the use of the appropriate scan tool. Refer to the proper Service Manual for diagnostic information.

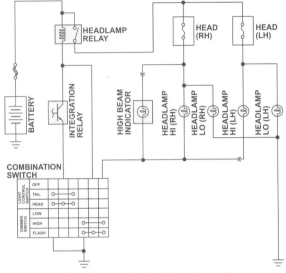

Fig. 5-1. Typical headlamp circuit wiring schematic.

LIGHTING SYSTEM DIAGNOSIS

The vehicle lighting system circuits on a late-model vehicle can be complex, and often there are a number of variations to accommodate different options on the same model vehicle. Accurate specifications, wiring diagrams, and electrical schematics are important to have on hand when servicing the lighting system.

Electrical Schematics

Manufacturers provide electrical wiring diagrams that depict the entire automobile wiring system. An electrical schematic is a portion of the complete wiring diagram that details the operation of an individual circuit. All the electrical information about a complete automotive circuit, including the switches, connectors, loads, and other devices, is included in the schematic, figure 5-1. Interpretation of an electrical schematic is further simplified by circuit numbering, color-coded wires, and representation of components or loads by symbols. The information provided by an electrical schematic makes it easy to trace a circuit during troubleshooting.

Troubleshooting Illumination Problems

There are several symptoms common to all electrical systems. Use the following as a general troubleshooting guideline. With brighter than normal lamps, check for:

- Improper bulb use
- Excessive voltage produced by a voltage regulator set too high, or by a shorted alternator field circuit

With lamps that are dimmer than normal, check for:

- Low charging voltage
- Slipping drive belts
- Dead battery
- High resistance in lamp power circuit
- High resistance in circuit ground connections

If the charging system is not operating, the lamps remain dim regardless of engine speed. A slipping drive belt may cause lamps to decrease brightness as engine speed increases. Lamps that flare or flicker can result from the same problems as dimly lit lamps. However, charging voltage will be high rather than low.

With lamps that operate intermittently or not at all, check for:

- Defective bulb
- Blown fuse or circuit breaker
- Faulty switch or other faulty circuit component
- Loose terminal connection
- Loose ground connection

HEADLAMP SERVICE

Headlamp service may involve replacing sealed-beam headlamps, replacing halogen or Xenon (high intensity discharge [HID]) headlamp bulbs, and aiming the headlamp assembly.

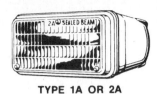

TYPE 1A OR 2A

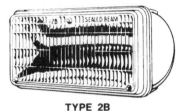

TYPE 2B

**TYPE 2
7" DIAMETER**

**TYPE 1 OR 2
5¾" DIAMETER**

Fig. 5-2. Standard sealed beam headlamp designs.

Headlamp Designs

Vehicles use various types of headlamps, which may be sealed-beam headlamps, halogen, or HID bulb design.

There are five types of conventional sealed-beam head-lamps, figure 5-2:

- Type 1—Single, high beam filament in a circular housing
- Type 1A—Single, high beam filament in a rectangular housing
- Type 2—High and low beam filaments in a circular housing
- Type 2A—High and low beam filaments in a rectangular housing
- Type 2B—High and low beam filaments in a rectangular housing in metric dimensions

Halogen Headlamps

Halogen sealed-beam headlamps are like conventional head-lamps, except for the halogen bulb. There are the same five types of halogen sealed-beam as conventional ones, plus a high and low beam Type 2E. Composite headlamps use a halogen

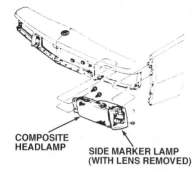

COMPOSITE HEADLAMP   **SIDE MARKER LAMP (WITH LENS REMOVED)**

Fig. 5-3. Composite headlamps use a replaceable halogen bulb behind an aerodynamic lens assembly.

bulb inside an aerodynamic plastic lens, figure 5-3. Composite headlamps also may contain individual halogen bulbs, one for low beam and one for high beam illumination.

Xenon Headlamps

Xenon headlamps are also known as "High Intensity Discharge" (HID) headlamps. HID lighting systems use a special quartz bulb that contains no filament and is filled with xenon gas and a small amount of mercury and other metal salts. Inside the bulb are two electrodes separated by a small gap (about 4 mm or 3/16 inch). When high voltage current is applied to the electrodes, it excites the gases inside the bulb and forms an electrical arc between the electrodes. The hot ionized gas produces a "plasma discharge" that generates an extremely intense, bluish-white light.

Once ignited, the pressure inside an HID bulb builds to more than 30 atmospheres because of heat (up to 1500 degrees F inside the bulb!). This creates a potential explosion hazard, so do not attempt to power an HID bulb outside of the headlamp as-sembly to "test" it. Also, the bulb must be in a horizontal position when it is on, otherwise it may overheat and fail. It typically takes up to 25,000 volts to start a xenon bulb, but only about 80 to 90 volts to keep it operating. The normal 12 volts DC from the ve-hicle's electrical system is stepped up and controlled by an ignit-er module and inverter (ballast), which also converts the voltage to AC (alternating current) necessary to operate the HID head-lamps. The ballast adjusts the voltage and current frequency to 250 to 450 Hz range. Power to the HID system is usually routed through a relay and fused at the power distribution center.

The four basic types of HID headlamp are D1R, D1S, D2R or D2S, which will be displayed on lamp lens:

- D1S and D1R bulbs have a large rectangular igniter mod-ule in the base of the lamp.
- D1R bulbs have black masking for a headlamp system that uses reflectors to direct the beam.
- D1S bulbs are for headlamp systems that use a light shield to direct the beam.
- D2R and D2S bulbs do not have an igniter module in the base.
- D2R bulbs are for reflector systems.
- D2S bulbs are for shielded systems.

Xenon gas has been added to some halogen bulbs to improve light output and the bulbs have been given a blue tinted coating to produce an HID headlamp appearance. These are not high intensity discharge bulbs and do not produce the same intense bluish-white light of HID headlamps.

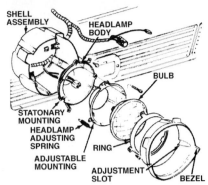

Fig. 5-4. Exploded view of a typical sealed beam headlamp installation.

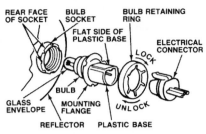

Fig. 5-5. Typical composite headlamp halogen bulb replacement.

Aftermarket HID headlamp conversion kits include the required igniters, ballasts, and HID xenon bulbs.

Headlamp Replacement

Since conventional and halogen sealed-beam headlamp designs are all about the same, the procedures for removal and replacement are similar for all vehicles. Replaceable halogen bulbs in composite headlamps require a different replacement procedure.

To replace a typical sealed-beam headlamp:

1. Make sure the headlamp switch is off. If the vehicle has concealed headlamps, activate the system to expose the bulbs; then switch the ignition and headlamps off.
2. Remove any bezel, grille, or panel that covers the headlamp mounting.
3. Loosen the retaining screws and remove the retaining ring. Do not loosen the aiming bolts by mistake.
4. Slip the retaining ring off, pull the headlamp from its housing, and unplug the connector, figure 5-4.
5. Check the connector for corrosion or damage, and clean or replace it as needed. Some manufacturers recommend using silicone grease on the bulb prongs.
6. Attach the pig-tail connector to the prongs on the new headlamp.
7. Align locating tabs and notches while fitting the headlamp into the housing, then install the retaining ring.
8. Check headlamp operation and aim, adjust if needed, then reinstall any trim previously removed.

Replacing composite halogen headlamp bulbs

To replace the halogen bulb in a typical composite headlamp assembly:

1. Make sure the headlamp switch is turned off.
2. Remove or move aside any trim panels or other items to gain access to the headlamp electrical connector. Then, unplug the electrical connector from the bulb holder.
3. Rotate the plastic retaining ring to align the tabs and notches on the bulb holder and slide the ring off.
4. Remove the bulb from the reflector socket by carefully pulling it straight out, figure 5-5. Do not rotate the bulb during removal.
5. Never touch the glass envelope surrounding the filament of a halogen bulb. Contact with skin causes a chemical reaction in the bulb that leads to premature failure of the new lamp. Holding the bulb assembly by the plastic base,

remove any protective covering from the bulb, carefully align the bulb and socket locating tabs, and insert the bulb holder into the reflector socket until it seats.
6. Slide the retaining ring over the bulb holder and rotate it to lock the assembly in place.
7. Attach the harness connector to the bulb.
8. Switch the headlamps on to check new bulb operation.

Replacing xenon headlamp bulbs

To replace the xenon bulb in a typical composite headlamp assembly:

1. Ensure the headlamp bulb is the problem and not the igniter/ballast, power relay, wiring, fuse, or head-lamp switch.
2. The igniter/ballast and relay can be replaced separately depending on the application.
3. On D1S and D2S bulbs, the igniter is in the base of the bulb and the ballast is a separate component.
4. HID headlamps operate at high voltage so use caution to avoid electrical shock, burns, or electrocution.
5. Ensure headlamps are off and never service the headlamps in wet conditions.
6. Do not touch the ballast when the system is operating.
7. Disconnect battery and use a nine-volt battery backup to keep PCM and other electronic memory settings.
8. Do not touch the quartz bulb because your skin oils can cause the bulb to crack and fail almost immediately. Wear gloves and handle bulb by the base only.

Headlamp Aiming

There are three methods of aiming headlamps:

- Aiming screen
- Mechanical aimer
- Photoelectric aimer

Conventional and halogen sealed-beam headlamps have three aiming pads, which are small glass bumps molded into the lens at specific points. These are used when aiming the headlamps with mechanical aimers.

Aiming Screen

An aiming screen is a fixed screen with guidelines on it. The headlamp beams are projected on the screen and adjusted according to the guidelines. The screen should be in a large room that can be darkened. The screen must be mounted so it is perpendicular to the floor, even if the floor slopes. The screen also must be adjustable, so it can be aligned parallel to the rear axle of the vehicle.

The aiming screen must be 25 feet in front of the headlamps and positioned according to the level of the floor. Aim

HIGH BEAM

HORIZONTAL CENTERLINE OF LAMPS

VERTICAL
CENTERLINE
AHEAD OF
LEFT HEADLAMP

VERTICAL
CENTERLINE
AHEAD OF
RIGHT HEADLAMP

± 4 INCHES
(SETTING OF
HORIZONTAL TAPES)

± 4 INCHES
(SETTING OF
VERTICAL TAPES)

LOW BEAM

HORIZONTAL CENTERLINE OF LAMPS

VERTICAL
CENTERLINE
AHEAD OF
LEFT HEADLAMP

VERTICAL
CENTERLINE
AHEAD OF
RIGHT HEADLAMP

± 4 INCHES
(SETTING OF
HORIZONTAL TAPES)

± 4 INCHES
(SETTING OF
VERTICAL TAPES)

Fig. 5-6. Using an aiming screen from 25 feet to adjust sealed beam headlamps.

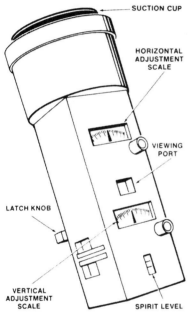

SUCTION CUP

HORIZONTAL
ADJUSTMENT
SCALE

VIEWING
PORT

LATCH KNOB

VERTICAL
ADJUSTMENT
SCALE

SPIRIT LEVEL

Fig. 5-7. Mechanical headlamp aimers are portable units that are set up directly in front of the headlamp.

the headlamps with the lamps on. Check aiming of the low beam and high beam headlamps, figure 5-6.

Mechanical Aiming

Mechanical aimers are a pair of portable devices that are placed on the floor beside the vehicle and calibrated to correct for floor unevenness. They can be used on round or rectangular sealed-beams with aiming pads, as well as on composite headlamps, figure 5-7. However, they cannot be used on headlamps without aiming pads or those covered by a trim panel.

The aimer attaches to the headlamp with a suction cup and rests on three platforms that protrude from the face of the sealed-beam lens. Vertical adjustments are made using the level mounted on top of the aimer. Horizontal adjustments are made using a split image indicator through a viewfinder.

Photoelectric Aiming

Photoelectric, or optical, aiming equipment is mounted on a frame that rides on tracks permanently installed in-floor.

Fig. 5-8. A photoelectric headlamp aimer is positioned directly in front of the headlamp.

The optical aiming head is adjusted to the level of the headlamps on the test vehicle, figure 5-8. Adjust the headlamp so the hot spot of the beam projects against a target in the aimer. A photoelectric device measures beam intensity as well as lamp aim.

HEADLAMP SWITCH, RELAY, AND CIRCUIT SERVICE

In addition to the lamps themselves, headlamp service includes checking, testing, and replacing switches, relays, wiring, and other circuit devices that carry the current through the system.

Testing Headlamp and Dimmer Switches

On most domestic headlamp circuits, the headlamp and dimmer switches are both in series with power to the headlamps, figure 5-9. Power goes through the switches, and the bulbs are grounded. A different method is used on many import circuits. The headlamp switch turns on the power, but the dimmer switch is on the ground side. On newer vehicles the dimmer switch is part of the column-mounted multi-function switch, while older vehicles use a foot-operated dimmer switch.

Most vehicles have a three-position main headlamp switch, figure 5-10:

- First position—off, no current
- Second position—current flows to parking lamps, taillamps, and other circuits
- Third position—current flows to both the second position circuits and to the headlamp circuit

A6

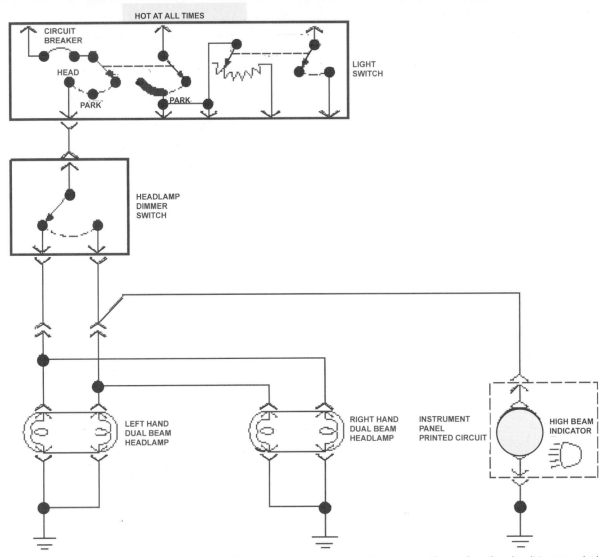

Fig. 5-9. Headlamp and dimmer switches on domestic vehicles typically connect to power and complete the circuit to ground when switched on.

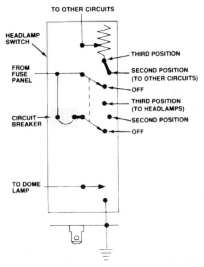

Fig. 5-10. Typical three-position headlamp switch schematic.

There are a number of variations, but all headlamp switches can be checked in a similar way. To test a headlamp switch:

1. Check for voltage at the headlamp switch source terminal. If power is not available, check the power source circuit.
2. If power is available to the switch, turn on the headlamp switch and check for power at the output terminal wire. If power is not coming from the switch, replace the headlamp switch.

To test the dimmer switch:

1. With the headlamps turned on, check for power at the dimmer switch terminals.
2. If either the high or low beams operate, there should be power through the switch.
3. If there is power through the switch to one terminal but not the other, the dimmer switch is defective.

Replacing Headlamp Switches

There are three basic types of headlamp switches:

- Lever-operated, steering column-mounted
- Push-pull, dashboard-mounted
- Rocker-type, dashboard-mounted

Before replacing a headlamp switch, disconnect the negative battery cable. Remember, the switch is connected to the battery at all times, whether the ignition switch is on or off.

Dashboard-Mounted Units

Rocker-type switches are generally either snap-in units or retained by one or more screws behind a snap-in bezel. Replace a snap-in rocker switch by prying the unit from the instrument panel with a small screwdriver. Be careful to avoid breaking any plastic locking tabs. Also, carefully pry off the bezel to access and remove retaining screws, if used. Lift the switch out and unplug the harness connector. Connect the new switch, then snap or screw it in place.

A release button on the switch housing must be depressed to remove most push-pull switches. Press the release button, then pull the knob and shaft from the switch assembly. Removing the mounting nut that holds the switch to the instrument panel, slip the switch clear and unplug the connector. Connect the new switch, fit in place, and install the mounting nut, knob, and shaft.

Column-Mounted Units

To replace a headlamp switch mounted on the steering column, remove shrouding as needed to gain access. Be aware, some designs require steering wheel removal. Unplug the connector from the switch and remove the fasteners holding the switch to the column. Lift the switch up, disengage it from the actuator rod, and remove it from the steering column. Install and check the operation of the new switch.

Replacing Dimmer Switches

The dimmer switch is incorporated into a single multifunction switch assembly that can include the turn signal, horn, cruise control, windshield wiper, and interior light switches as well, figure 5-11. Replacing a multi-function switch requires partial disassembling of the steering column. Install and check the new switch.

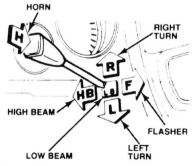

Fig. 5-11. This multi-function switch operates the headlamps, dimmer, turn signals, and horn switches.

Daytime Running Lamps (DRL)

Many vehicles are equipped with Daytime Running Lamps (DRL). Most DRL systems illuminate the high beam headlamps at reduced intensity anytime the ignition switch is in the ON position, the headlamps are switched OFF, and the park brake is released. The circuitry used to reduce the output of the lamps varies by manufacturer. Many OEMs install a special module or controller that sends a reduced voltage signal to the lamps. Others connect both high beam headlamps in series, which cuts the effective voltage to each lamp in half. Vehicles with automatic headlamps generally switch automatically from DRL to regular operation.

Another design illuminates the front park lamps or fog lamps for DRL operation. Most vehicles include an indicator lamp on the instrument panel to inform the driver that the system is activated.

Servicing DRL Systems

Begin your diagnosis by referring to the operational overview in the Service Manual. The DRL system is designed to operate the lamps only when specific conditions are met. For example, if the park brake is applied most systems do not operate. Follow the diagnostic steps in the Service Manual and use the wiring diagrams to trace the circuits of the system. If the headlamps work normally when in the ON position you can rule out the bulbs, circuits, and connectors back to the control switch or module. Check all connectors for damaged, corroded, or pushed out pins. Conduct a voltage drop test across suspect sections of the circuit, keeping in mind that the operating voltage for the DRL system may be less than battery voltage.

Fog Lamps and Driving Lamps

Fog lamps and driving lamps utilize one of two types of bulbs, either sealed-beam or replaceable halogen design. When replacing the halogen lamp take care not to touch the glass portion with your fingers as the oil from your skin will create a hot spot during use, causing the lamp to fail.

Diagnosis of the lighting system follows that of the headlamps and other vehicle electrical system components. Always refer to the appropriate Service Manual when possible.

Fog Lamp and Driving Lamp Aiming

Proper aiming of the fog or driving lamps is as important as the headlamps. The vehicle Service Manual should contain information on the proper method of aiming any factory installed lamp. If the lamps have been added to the vehicle check with the lamp manufacturer for information. If no additional information is available follow these basic guidelines:

- Fog lamps should be aimed just below the low beam headlamps and angled 1-2 degrees toward the right side of the road
- Driving lamps are normally aimed in the same manner as the high beam headlamps. Make sure that no lamp is aimed to project its pattern to left of the vehicle centerline

RETRACTABLE OR CONCEALED HEADLAMPS

Some retractable or concealed headlamps are attached to the vehicle body and have a moving cover; others attach to the

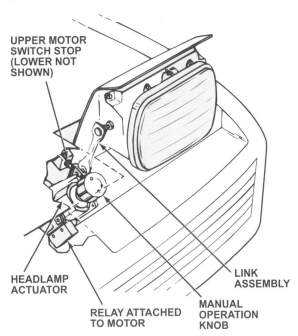

UPPER MOTOR SWITCH STOP (LOWER NOT SHOWN)

HEADLAMP ACTUATOR

RELAY ATTACHED TO MOTOR

MANUAL OPERATION KNOB

LINK ASSEMBLY

Fig. 5-12. Electric motor–driven retractable headlamp assembly.

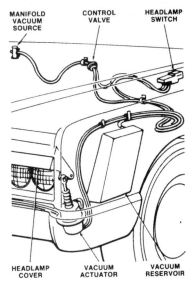

MANIFOLD VACUUM SOURCE

CONTROL VALVE

HEADLAMP SWITCH

HEADLAMP COVER

VACUUM ACTUATOR

VACUUM RESERVOIR

Fig. 5-13. Engine vacuum, routed through tubing and a reservoir, powers the motor that opens and closes the headlamp doors.

cover assembly and move with it. Either an electric or vacuum motor opens or raises the headlamp doors.

Electric systems have a motor-gearbox assembly mounted behind the grille, figure 5-12. Two torsion rods extend outward from the gearbox and attach to the headlamp door. A double contact relay controls motor direction on a typical system. One set of contacts is closed when the relay is at rest and is connected to the door closing circuit. The second contact set closes when the relay is energized and is connected to the door opening circuit. The relay control circuit connects to the headlamp circuit, which directs current to open and close the doors. Limiting contacts in the relay or motor prevent damage when the doors reach the end of their travel.

Electric Actuator Motor and Circuit Diagnosis

If motor-driven doors operate slowly or not at all, check for:

- Rusted hinge points on the doors
- Binding motor bearings
- Defective relays, fuses, and fusible links
- Damaged wires or connectors
- High circuit resistance

Inspect all circuit wiring and components for damage. Ensure that all connectors are clean and tight. Perform a voltage drop test across each side of the circuit to locate defective components, including the switch and any system relays, or high resistance connections.

When a binding motor or linkage overloads the circuit, the circuit breaker or fusible link can open with the doors at mid position. Circuit breakers that cycle open and closed may cause the doors operate erratically.

Older vehicles use vacuum to operate the headlamp doors, figure 5-13. A reservoir and a check valve maintain a vacuum supply while the engine is turned off or under load. A vacuum control valve connected to the headlamp switch directs flow to a vacuum motor attached to the doors. With the

headlamps on, vacuum is blocked and the doors are opened by a spring. When the headlamp switch is off, vacuum is directed to the vacuum motor to close the doors. Air bleeds into the opposing actuator chamber through the vacuum switch. In case of a vacuum failure, the doors go to the open position. If vacuum-operated doors operate slowly or not at all, check for:

- Plugged or restricted hoses
- Faulty vacuum valve at the headlamp switch
- Vacuum leaks in the hoses or diaphragms
- Leaking vacuum reservoir
- Defective vacuum check valve between the reservoir and the engine
- Binding or worn linkage

BULB AND SOCKET DESIGN AND REPLACEMENT

Automotive bulbs and sockets conform to design standards in order to reduce the possibility of installing the wrong bulb. There are different bulb sizes, shapes, and socket connections. Double filament bulbs are used to accommodate two circuits, such as parking and directional, or stop and taillamps that use the same bulb.

Small bulbs used in exterior lighting systems are usually clear and mount behind colored lenses. Some applications call for a red or an amber bulb, which is indicated by an R or NA in the standards. Bulbs have either a brass or glass wedge base, and are generally replaced from the rear of the lamp assembly.

Bulbs with a brass base fit into a matching socket that contains a single or double contact to route current through the filament and complete the insulated circuit, figure 5-14. Double-contact bulbs have an indexed base and fit into the socket in only one way.

Wedge-base bulbs are used in the instrument cluster and other interior lighting applications. The base and optical part of the bulb are a one-piece, formed-glass shell with four

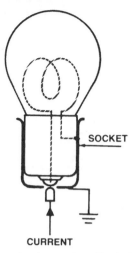

Fig. 5-14. When energized, an automotive bulb filament completes the insulated circuit.

filament wires extending through the base and crimped around it to form the external contacts.

To replace a nonindexed or wedge-base bulb, pull it from the socket and push in the replacement. Push an indexed bulb into the socket and rotate until the bulb is free, then push the replacement into the socket and rotate until it is secure.

If you cannot reach the rear of the lamp assembly, remove the lamp lens to replace the bulb. Screws secure lamp lenses on the outside of the vehicle, nuts on the inside. You may have to remove other trim parts to reach the screws or nuts. When re-installing the lens, correctly position any gaskets and washers.

Replace a socket that is corroded or rusted. In most cases, cut the socket from the wiring harness and splice a new one in place.

PARKING, TAIL, SIDE, DASH, AND COURTESY LAMP SERVICE

The tail, parking, and side marker lamps operate when the headlamp switch is at the park or headlamp position on most vehicles. Typically, the parking and taillamps are on a separate circuit, but share a common switch with the headlamps. Side marker lamps connect in parallel to the parking lamps. Tail-lamp circuits generally share a fuse with another circuit, or have a circuit breaker instead of a fuse. The license plate lamp is on the same circuit as the taillamps, figure 5-15.

Parking Lamp and Taillamp Service

The same general troubleshooting procedures apply for both parking lamps and taillamps. To diagnose problems in either circuit:

1. Make certain the correct bulb type is used in each socket.
2. If neither the taillamps nor the license plate lamp operates, check the power supply and fuse. If the circuit is good at the fuse, check for power between the switch and the last common connector before the lamps. Any open in the circuit, such as a loose connection or a faulty headlamp switch, gets power to the fuse but not to the connector.
3. If only one bulb fails to light, check for a burned-out bulb, a bad ground, or poor connection in the bulb socket.

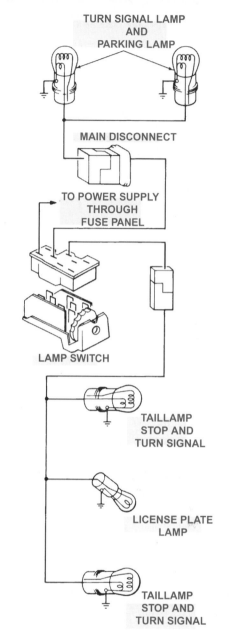

Fig. 5-15. Typical taillamp and parking lamp circuitry.

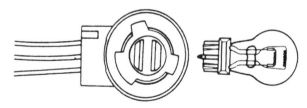

Fig. 5-16. Wedge-type bulbs are often used for side marker lamps.

Side Marker Lamp Service

Side markers generally use wedge-type bulbs mounted in insulated sockets, figure 5-16. Some bulbs are independently grounded and others ground through the turn signal filaments. Side marker lamps that ground through the turn signal filaments are on whenever the parking lamps are lit.

A6

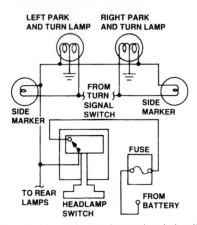

Fig. 5-17. Typical side marker and turn signal circuitry.

However, the side marker goes out each time the turn signal flashes because the ground circuit opens to switch the turn signal off.

The result is parking and side marker lamps that are on at the same time and turn signal and front side markers that flash alternately. With the parking lamps off, the turn signal and side marker lamps flash together. This can make troubleshooting this circuit confusing. For example, a burned-out turn signal filament also prevents the front side marker from operating. However, a burned-out parking lamp filament has no effect on the side marker, figure 5-17.

Dash Lamp Service

Three categories of bulbs are used in instrument panel displays: indicator, warning, and illumination lamps. Dash panel illumination lamps are part of a series parallel circuit where all the bulbs are connected in parallel with each other and in series with a variable resistor, or rheostat. All instrument panel circuits are grounded with a separate ground circuit. An open in the instrument panel ground circuit affects all electrical components mounted in the instrument cluster.

Servicing Switches and Rheostats

Current to the dash lamps is controlled by contacts within the main headlamp switch. They receive current when the parking and taillamps are lit. A rheostat lets the driver control the brightness of the dash lamps. The rheostat may be integral to the headlamp switch or a separate unit mounted in the dash. Intermittent operation of only the instrument lamps may be caused by oxidation buildup on the rheostat coils. Troubleshooting these circuits is similar to that of other lighting circuits, figure 5-18.

Printed Circuit Boards

Printed circuit (PC) boards replaced conventional wiring behind the instrument panel many years ago. A PC board simplifies connections, conserves space and weight, and is inexpensive to manufacture compared to conventional wiring. A conductor plate cut from a sheet of thin copper film is laminated onto an insulator boards, along with the connectors and components that attach to the instrument cluster, to

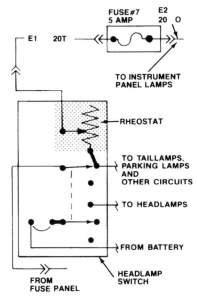

Fig. 5-18. Instrument panel lamp rheostat circuit.

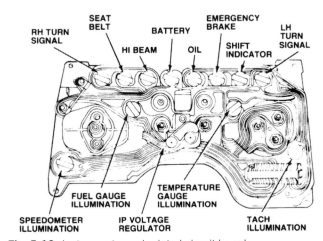

Fig. 5-19. Instrument panel printed circuit board.

manufacture a PC board, figure 5-19. The thin copper conductors cannot tolerate any overload, and a short circuit destroys them. Inspect a PC board by visually following the circuit conductors and testing when needed with a voltmeter. Hairline cracks are difficult to see, but a voltmeter locates them quickly.

Courtesy Lamp Service

Dome and courtesy interior lamps usually have battery voltage at each bulb at all times. Switches installed on the ground side of the circuit regulate current through the bulb, figure 5-20. Switches may be located in the door jambs, headlamp switch, or on the light itself. A short to ground on the insulated, or power, side of the circuit can blow the fuse. A short to ground on the ground, or switch, side does not blow the fuse, but the lamps will stay on.

Check for a defective fuse if none of the dome or courtesy lamps operate. If any of these lamps operate, the fuse is good, so check the individual lamps that do not operate.

Printed Circuit Board: A special circuit board with the electronic circuits encased in a thin film of plastic.

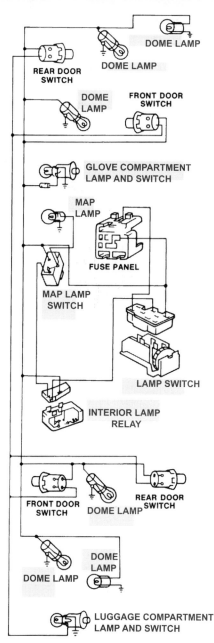

Fig. 5-20. Switches on the ground side of the circuit control most dome and courtesy lamps.

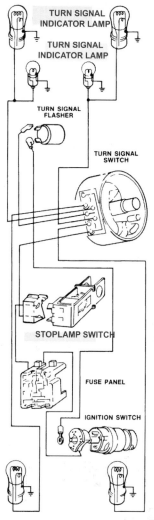

Fig. 5-21. Typical stoplamp and turn signal circuitry.

Test for battery power at the dome lamp socket. If voltage is available at the socket, check for ground when opening doors or turning on the dome lamp at the headlamp switch. A dome lamp that does not turn off can be caused by a faulty door switch or a short to ground, or possibly the dome lamp is turned on at the headlamp switch.

STOPLAMPS, TURN SIGNALS, HAZARD LAMPS, AND BACKUP LAMPS

Stoplamp and turn signal circuits generally are combined because they are connected at the turn signal switch on most vehicles. However, on some vehicles two separate circuits are used. These circuits get voltage from two sources:

- The stoplamp switch is connected to the turn signal switch, so only the stoplamps receive voltage when the brake pedal is depressed and the turn signal is off

- Voltage may also be delivered from the turn signal flasher to the turn signal switch; the flasher connects to the accessory terminal on the ignition switch

Stoplamp and Turn Signal Service

On vehicles where the rear directional and stoplamps share bulb filaments, a circuit is complete to the right and left lamps when the stoplamps are on, figure 5-21. Moving the directional switch to the right or left position removes the corresponding rear lamp from the stoplamp circuit and connects it to the directional circuit.

Since the bulbs on each side are wired in parallel, each bulb can operate independently of the other bulb on the same side. When one bulb is not operating, current is reduced and the flasher is calibrated to operate with a specified amount of current. Inoperative bulbs cause the flasher to stay on or cycle slowly.

A traditional flasher uses a bimetallic strip to open and close contacts and interrupt current through a directional switch. With the switch turned on, resistance in the strip generates heat that causes the strip to bend and opens a contact set. As the strip cools, the contacts close and the cycle starts over again. Many newer vehicles are equipped with electronic flasher devices. These devices time the on and off of the lamps regardless of load.

A6

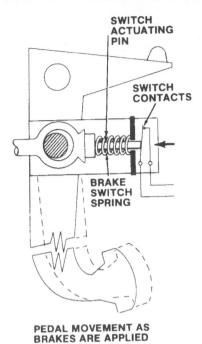

Fig. 5-22. Pedal activated brake lamp switch.

A switch on the brake pedal linkage actuates the stop-lamps when the pedal is depressed slightly, figure 5-22. Some switches are adjustable; others are not and must be replaced if not working properly. Turn signals are controlled by a switch located in the steering column. To replace a turn signal switch, disassemble the steering column as needed to access the unit. Install and check the operation of the new switch.

Stoplamp and Turn Signal Circuit Diagnosis

To diagnose problems in the stoplamp and turn signal circuit, use the following procedure:

1. All signal lamps and indicator lamps are inoperative, check for:
   • Blown fuse
   • Faulty flasher
   • Faulty switch or connector
2. One signal lamp or indicator lamp stays on, check for:
   • Inoperative bulb
3. The signal lamps flash too fast, check for:
   • High voltage in circuit
   • Faulty or wrong type of flasher
   • Wrong type of bulbs
4. The signal lamps flash too slow, check for:
   • Low voltage or high resistance in circuit
   • Faulty or wrong type of flasher
   • Wrong type of bulbs
5. No flashing on either side with lamps on, check for:
   • Faulty or wrong type of flasher
6. Both stoplamps are inoperative, check for:
   • Burned-out bulbs
   • Blown fuse
   • Defective or improperly adjusted stoplamp switch
   • Defective turn signal switch
7. One stoplamp is inoperative, check for:
   • Burned-out bulb, poor ground, or open in circuit

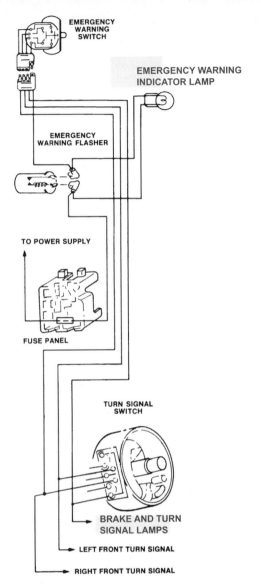

Fig. 5-23. Hazard warning lamp circuitry.

8. Taillamp and stoplamp both work individually, but light will not operate when both are on, check for:
   • Proper ground

Hazard Lamp Service

A separate switch attached to the directional switch enables directional lamps to be operated at the same time as hazard warning lamps. When the hazard lamp switch is applied, the turn signal flasher is disconnected from the circuit and replaced with a hazard flasher, figure 5-23. Unlike the directional lamps, the hazard lamps can be operated with the ignition switch off.

Hazard Lamp Diagnosis

If the hazard lamp flashing rate is too fast or too slow, turn off the hazard lamps and turn on one turn signal. If the rate is:

• Okay, the problem is the flasher in the hazard warning circuit
• Too fast or too slow, follow the troubleshooting procedure for turn signals

If the hazard lamps operate but do not flash, check for:

• Stoplamp switch failure
• Faulty flasher

If the hazard lamps do not operate, but turn signals do, check for:

- Faulty flasher
- Blown fuse
- Open in the insulated circuit to the switch

If one front or both rear hazard lamps do not operate, but all turn signals do, check for:

- Voltage at the hazard warning switch with the switch on; if there is power in but not out, the switch is defective
- If there is voltage on all the switch output leads, check for open or short circuits in the wiring

Backup Lamp Service

Backup lamps receive voltage from the accessory terminal of the ignition switch, and a backup lamp switch connected to the shift linkage or the transmission shift rail controls the ground circuit. The backup lamps switch on when the transmission is in Reverse, figure 5-24. The neutral safety switch is combined in an assembly with the backup lamp switch on some vehicles.

If the lamp does not operate with the ignition switch on and transmission in Reverse, check for:

- Blown fuse
- Improperly adjusted switch
- Faulty bulb

Trailer Wiring

Many vehicles are manufactured with trailer towing capabilities. Others have trailer hitches and wiring installed in the aftermarket. In either case the circuits must be capable of safely carrying the additional load of trailer lamps and electric braking systems. Most OEM systems isolate the trailer lighting on a separate circuit to prevent a short circuit from putting all rear lamps out.

When installing trailer lighting circuits follow the vehicle wiring diagram for the correct connection points. Pay special attention to the high-mounted stoplamp circuit when connecting the brake lamp circuit. Failure to make the connection correctly may result in improper operation of the turn signals.

Trailer brake wiring is usually a heavier gauge than the lighting circuits. All of the trailer brake actuators are connected to the system in parallel. A short circuit anywhere in the brake circuit will cause all of the brakes to be inoperative.

Trailer Wiring Diagnosis and Repair

Trailer wiring is diagnosed in the same manner as other lighting circuits. Corrosion and contamination are usually more

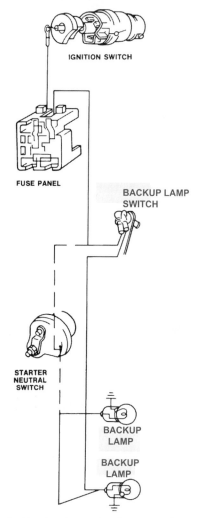

Fig. 5-24. Typical backup lamp circuitry.

A6

prevalent in trailer circuits than in the towing vehicle. Look for signs of rust and corrosion in all trailer wiring components and circuits. If corrosion is present inside the wire insulation, replace the wire.

Use a voltage drop test to locate defective components or high resistance connections. Always use a good grade of shrink tubing when making splices to ensure no moisture can compromise the connection. Clean all ground connections and protect them from the elements with an electrical component sealer.

CHAPTER QUESTIONS

1. When examining a printed circuit board, you:
   a. Cannot follow the conductor path visually
   b. Can locate problems with a voltmeter
   c. Must wear plastic gloves
   d. Need a special test instrument

2. If only one headlamp lights, the problem is probably **NOT** in the:
   a. Bulb
   b. Headlamp switch
   c. Socket
   d. Bulb wiring

3. Headlamps that dim when the engine is idling can be caused by all of the following **EXCEPT**:
   a. Low battery voltage
   b. Poor connections
   c. Faulty circuit breaker
   d. High circuit resistance

4. The only headlamp aiming method that can measure the intensity of the light beam is:
   a. Aiming screen
   b. Mechanical aimer
   c. Electromagnetic aimer
   d. Photoelectric aimer

5. Slow vacuum-operated headlamp door operation could be caused by all of the following **EXCEPT**:
   a. An open headlamp switch circuit
   b. Vacuum leak in the system
   c. Defective actuator motor diaphragm
   d. Plugged or restricted vacuum hose

6. If the hazard lamps do not operate, but turn signals do, the problem may be:
   a. Faulty flasher
   b. Defective stoplamp switch
   c. Burned-out bulb
   d. High voltage

7. The most likely cause of backup lamps not operating with the ignition switch on and the transmission in reverse would be:
   a. Defective ignition switch
   b. Defective brake lamp switch
   c. High circuit voltage
   d. Improper switch adjustment

8. The most likely cause of an inoperative license plate lamp when all the taillamps work normally would be:
   a. Faulty wire or ground
   b. Bad fuse
   c. Faulty switch
   d. Contaminated circuit breaker

9. The most likely cause of the left front turn signal and left front side marker lamps not working would be a:
   a. Burned-out turn signal filament
   b. Burned-out parking lamp filament
   c. Blown parking lamp circuit fuse
   d. Defective flasher unit

10. When all of the signal and indicator lamps in a circuit are inoperative, the problem is likely to be:
    a. Incorrect bulb installation
    b. Low circuit voltage
    c. A blown fuse
    d. A burned-out bulb

11. Xenon headlamps are all the following **EXCEPT**:
    a. High Intensity Discharge (HID) headlamps
    b. Operate at 1500 degrees F
    c. Can be handled with bare hands
    d. Take 25,000 volts to start

CHAPTER SIX

GAUGES, WARNING DEVICES, AND DRIVER INFORMATION SYSTEMS

CHAPTER OBJECTIVES

- The technician will complete the ASE task list on Gauges, Warning Devices, and Driver Information Systems.
- The technician will be able to answer 6 questions dealing with the Gauges, Warning Devices, and Driver Information Systems section of the A6 ASE Test.

Gauges, which indicate various vehicle conditions such as coolant temperature, oil pressure, fuel level, and battery condition, can be analog or digital devices. Gauge and instrument operations on most late-model vehicles are controlled by an onboard computer and are often linked to the engine management system. Diagnostic trouble code (DTC) information is available on some systems to assist in troubleshooting.

DIAGNOSING ANALOG GAUGE PROBLEMS

Before testing any gauge or instrument that appears to be defective, make sure that the condition it monitors is normal. For example, if an engine coolant temperature gauge or warning lamp indicates an engine overheating, test the cooling system before assuming that the gauge or lamp is inaccurate.

Analog gauges operate on one of three principles:

- Mechanical—fluid pressure, fluid temperature, or cables directly operate the gauge
- Thermal—current passing through a bimetallic strip heats one side faster than the other, causing the strip to bend and move a needle
- Electromagnetic—the interaction of magnetic fields causes a gauge needle to move

Thermal or electromagnetic gauges use a signal modified by a sending unit. A sending unit is a **transducer** that changes mechanical, hydraulic, or temperature signals into an electrical signal. Several designs are in use:

- Pressure sending unit—uses a diaphragm to operate a sliding contact against a resistor to change diaphragm deflection into an electrical signal, figure 6-1
- Level sending unit—uses a float in a reservoir to operate a sliding contact against a resistor; a change in fluid level produces a change in gauge circuit resistance, figure 6-2
- Thermal sending unit—uses a heat-sensing element, or thermistor, whose electrical resistance varies along with temperature, figure 6-3

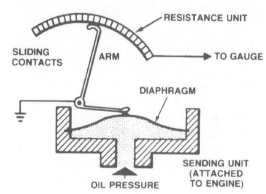

Fig. 6-1. This diaphragm transducer converts oil pressure to an electrical signal.

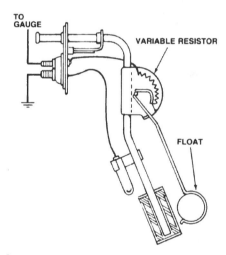

Fig. 6-2. Current across the variable resistor adjusts to the position of the float on this fuel sending unit.

ANALOG GAUGE CIRCUIT VOLTAGE

Intermittent or non-operation of an analog gauge is often caused by an electrical problem in the gauge circuit. High or low gauge readings can result from a defective sending unit, faulty circuitry, or improper voltage supply.

Some mechanical gauges require a continuous, controlled amount of voltage, either the system voltage of 12 volts or a regulated 5 to 6 volts. One type of voltage regulator is a solid-state device with a constant, consistent voltage. The voltage

A6

Transducer: A device that converts, or transduces, one form of energy to another. A sensor is such a device, converting mechanical or hydraulic energy into a voltage signal.

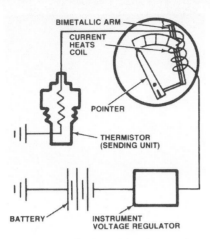

Fig. 6-3. The resistance of a thermistor changes in response to temperature, providing a variable electrical signal to the gauge.

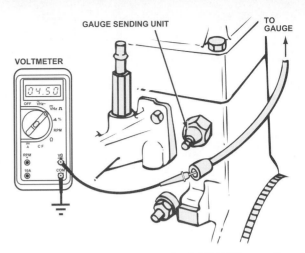

Fig. 6-4. Voltmeter connections to check CVR/ IVR operation at a sending unit.

limiter may be a separate unit on the printed circuit (PC) board, or an integral part of one of the dash units. Another method is the use of a constant voltage regulator (CVR) or an instrument voltage regulator (IVR). One type of CVR/IVR consists of a set of contacts and a bimetallic strip with a heating coil wrapped around it. Its bimetallic strip and vibrating points act like a self-setting circuit breaker to keep gauge voltage at a specific average level. Late-model vehicles utilize solid-state regulators to control voltage to the gauges when required.

Testing Instrument Cluster Voltage

If the proper voltage is not available the gauges may give inaccurate readings. Be aware: Gauges can be damaged by excessive voltage if the CVR/IVR fails. A CVR/IVR fault affects all regulated gauges. Typical symptoms include:

- Gauges fail all at once
- Gauges give inaccurate, all high or all low, readings
- Readings vibrate by more than the width of the needle

Use a voltmeter or test lamp to determine if the CVR/IVR unit is functioning. Never ground or short any of the regulator terminals when testing in order to prevent regulator and instrument panel wiring harness damage.

Since the CVR/IVR is difficult to reach for testing on most vehicles without removing the instrument cluster, make a quick test at one of the gauge sending units in the engine compartment:

1. Check the circuit fuse and replace it, if necessary.
2. Disconnect the wire from one of the gauge sending units.
3. Connect the voltmeter positive lead to the wire and the negative lead to ground, figure 6-4.
4. Switch the ignition on while watching the voltmeter. Voltage should pulsate between zero and a positive voltage. This is normally at about the same rate as that of the turn signal flasher. If the meter is not pulsing, it should hold at a constant lower control voltage.

Replacing the CVR/IVR

Instrument voltage regulators are generally either separate units held to the back of the instrument cluster panel by screws or nuts, or plugged into a printed circuit (PC) board. Remove

the instrument cluster to gain access to the CVR/IVR. If the regulator is built into one gauge, that entire gauge must be replaced if the regulator is defective. Most newer vehicles utilize air core gauges controlled by a pulse-width modulated signal. These systems do not require the use of a CVR/IVR.

ANALOG GAUGE AND SENDING UNIT SERVICE

Except for ammeters and voltmeters, electrical gauges all use a variable resistance sending unit to control current through the gauge.

Testing and Replacing

Analog gauge design is simple. With the low voltage and light current load carried, most gauges are long-lasting. When a gauge appears to work improperly, the cause generally is a problem in the circuit rather than the gauge itself. If a single gauge fails or shows an inaccurate reading, the problem is most likely in the circuit branch or sending unit for that gauge. When all of the gauges fail or show inaccurate readings, the problem is most likely in the CVR/IVR or their shared circuitry.

Most gauges can be tested with a variable resistance gauge tester. By setting the resistance unit to duplicate the resistance of the sending unit, the gauge and wiring can be tested. Gauge testers are adjustable resistors that duplicate the sender values for low and high readings. With the gauge tester set for the correct amount of resistance and the sending unit wiring harness disconnected, connect one test lead to the sending unit wiring harness and the other test to ground. The gauge should register the correct setting.

As with any electrical circuit, the first place to check is the fuse and main power supply. If the fuse is good, work down the circuit from the power source to the gauge, figure 6-5. Switch the ignition on and disconnect the sending unit. Full battery voltage should be available at the CVR/IVR input terminal. If battery voltage is available on the output terminal of the regulator, it is either defective or not properly grounded. Gauges controlled by the PCM or TCM are diagnosed through the control module. Refer to the proper Service Manual for specific testing procedures.

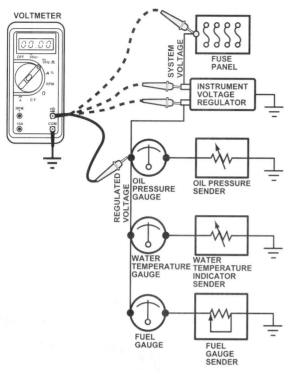

Fig. 6-5. Voltage drop testing a gauge circuit.

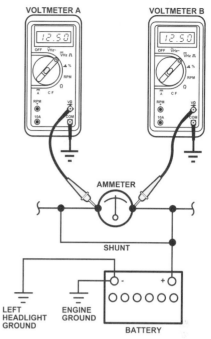

Fig. 6-6. Voltmeter readings on each side of an ammeter should equal battery voltage.

Circuit Testing and Replacement

Troubleshooting a PC board is quick and easy. However, the printed circuit, which is composed of copper foil bonded to a mylar film mounted on a thin composition board, can be easily damaged by improper handling. Any PC defect requires replacement of the entire board. Never use a probe when testing PC board circuits, as this can pierce and damage the circuit or copper conductors. Use an ohmmeter set on its low scale for this procedure:

1. Remove the instrument cluster and visually inspect the printed circuit carefully.
2. Using a schematic, connect the ohmmeter lead to the proper pin plug terminal for the circuit being tested. Trace the circuit between each uncoated position leading to the gauge, indicator, or bulb in that circuit.
3. Check each uncoated position on the other side of the gauge, indicator, or bulb circuit.
4. Connect one test lead to the pin of the circuit being tested. Touch all remaining pin terminals one at a time with the other test leads to check for continuity between circuits.

Ammeters and Voltmeters

Since ammeters and voltmeters measure the performance of the electrical system, they do not require a sending unit to control current passing through them.
Note: Diagnosis of the cause of charging system problems is detailed in Chapter 4 of this book.

Ammeters

A "true" ammeter connects in series or parallel between the generator and the battery. If connected in series, a conductor bar is mounted between the two ammeter connectors. Parallel circuits use two points in the wiring, one close to the battery and the other closer to the generator. When current passes through the conductor bar, or shunt circuit, there is a voltage drop. The direction and amount of the voltage drop is used to determine total current into or out of the battery. Many late-model vehicles place the shunt in the circuit in or near the generator or underhood fuse box. This eliminates the need for heavy gauge circuits attaching directly to the instrument cluster. A loose connection at the ammeter terminal increases resistance and results in intermittent meter operation. Continued operation produces excess heat that damages the wiring and gauge.

To test an ammeter, turn the ignition switch, headlamps, and other accessories on; the gauge should show a discharge. Use a voltmeter or 12-volt test light to check for battery voltage on both sides of the gauge, figure 6-6.

Voltmeters

A voltmeter indicates the system, or battery, voltage using a return spring that keeps the needle in the zero position. The field strength of an electromagnet, which varies according to system voltage, acts on the return spring to move the needle up and down the scale. The balance of the return spring force and field strength is calibrated into volts and displayed on the gauge face. The voltmeter gauge, which connects in parallel to the battery, receives system voltage through the ignition switch.

To test the voltmeter, remove the instrument cluster and disconnect or remove the gauge. Switch the ignition on and check for battery voltage at the gauge connections, figure 6-7. On a combination gauge, there are several connection pins; refer to the Service Manual instructions.

WARNING LAMPS

Some vehicles use warning lamps in the instrument cluster instead of gauges; others use a combination of lamps and gauges.

A6

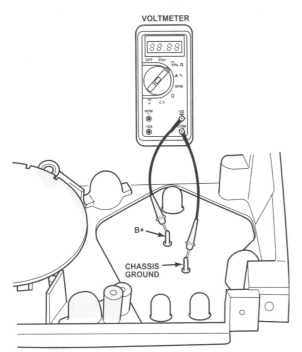

Fig. 6-7. Connect a voltmeter across the gauge circuit to check for battery voltage.

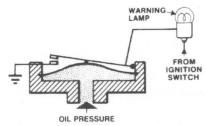

Fig. 6-8. A warning lamp sending unit is an on/off digital switch.

A charging system warning lamp is directly controlled by charging voltage, while a sending unit is used to operate all other warning lamps. Warning lamp sending units are on/off digital switches, rather than variable resistors, figure 6-8.

Late-model vehicles often use one or more of the onboard computers to control the warning lamps. For example, the PCM may monitor the oil pressure switch and send a message to the body control module (BCM) asking it to illuminate the engine warning lamp on the instrument cluster. In another example, the PCM sends a low oil pressure signal directly to the instrument cluster electronic module, which in turn illuminates the warning lamp. Always refer the appropriate Service or Diagnostic Manual before beginning your diagnosis.

Warning lamps controlled directly by the sending unit or switch are diagnosed using the same procedures as for interior lighting circuits.

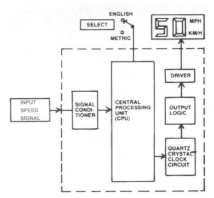

Fig. 6-9. Typical digital speedometer schematic.

Begin with a bulb check by substituting a known-good bulb for the one being tested, especially if only that bulb has failed. Tests from each manufacturer are different; refer to the Service Manual for specific instructions. Before troubleshooting any warning lamp circuit, check the battery and charging systems for proper operation. Conduct voltage drop tests to locate circuit faults.

ELECTRONIC INSTRUMENT CLUSTERS

Late-model vehicles may have fully electronic instrument clusters or a combination of electronic and analog gauges. Electronic instrument clusters and gauges differ considerably in design and display devices used, but all have the same purposes and perform the same functions as analog clusters. The main difference is that these are digital devices controlled by one or more onboard computers. The computer receives input signals from the sending units, processes the signals, and displays them on the instrument cluster.

Figure 6-9 depicts the circuitry required for the operation of the speedometer readout on a digital gauge or cluster. The signal from the vehicle speed sensor is an input to an electronic control module such as the TCM or PCM. After processing the signal the control module sends an output signal to the instrument cluster. The cluster uses the signal to either display the information in digital format or to drive the speedometer to the proper position.

Fully electronic clusters may consist of **light-emitting diodes (LED)**, **liquid crystal displays (LCD)**, **vacuum fluorescent displays (VFD)**, or a **cathode ray tube (CRT)**.

Electronic Digital Gauge Service

The displays in an electronic cluster are part of an electronic system that often contains a self-diagnostic program or test sequence. In most cases, if the computer successfully completes its self-diagnostic test, the problem will be found in the wiring, the connectors, or the sensors and sending units outside the cluster. Often a scan tool can be used in the diagnostic process.

Cathode Ray Tube (CRT): An electron beam tube with a cathode at one end and an anode at the screen end. The "ray" of electrons shot from the cathode to the anode creates a pattern on the luminescent screen.
Light-Emitting Diode (LED): A gallium-arsenide diode that emits energy as light. Often used on automotive indicators.
Liquid Crystal Display (LCD): An indicator consisting of a sandwich of glass containing electrodes and a polarized fluid. Voltage applied to the fluid allows light to pass through it.
Vacuum Florescent Display (VFD): An indicator in which electrons from a heated filament strike a phosphor material that emits light.

Before condemning an electronic gauge or cluster, check the Service Manual for the correct diagnostic procedure. Never ground a circuit to test an electronic gauge unless specifically instructed to do so by the Service Manual, as immediate damage to the gauge and/or circuits may occur. If the gauges all display maximum readings with the engine running, check for loose or damaged connections, poor grounds, or shorted circuits.

Once you have determined the cluster is good, check the other components and circuitry just as you would any other electrical system. You will need the diagnostic charts, specifications, and circuit diagrams in the Service Manual, to properly troubleshoot an electronic instrument problem. Electronic components are subject to damage from electrostatic discharge or ESD. Follow all precautions when handling these components to prevent damage.

DRIVER INFORMATION CENTERS

Many late-model vehicles are equipped with electronic instrumentation that provides a wide variety of information to the driver. These units range from simple trip computers to more complicated electronic message centers that check the level of each fluid, the operation of each lamp, and the opening of doors, the hood, and the trunk. Generally, the module that operates these indicators is fed from the ignition-run circuit and may receive information from one or more of the other onboard computers such as:

- Powertrain Control Module (PCM)
- Transmission Control Module (TCM)
- Body Control Module (BCM)
- Antilock Brake System (ABS)

Most of these modules are capable of storing diagnostic trouble codes (DTC). Accessing the DTCs or signals from these modules requires the use of a scan tool and the proper Service or Diagnostic Manual, diagnostic charts, specifications, and circuit diagrams. In all cases, a problem found to be in the electronic control module or information center requires replacement of the defective component.

AUDIBLE WARNING DEVICES

Audible warning devices, such as buzzers and chimes, are used in many areas:

- Key in switch with door open
- Door ajar
- Excessive speed
- Headlamps on with the door open

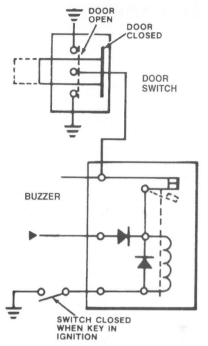

Fig. 6-10. This audible warning device buzzes if the key is in the ignition switch and the door is open.

Some of these may be connected to the key-in-ignition buzzer, figure 6-10. The buzzer connected to the seat belt latch uses a time delay switch to turn off the buzzer after a few seconds.

Diagnosis

Many of the audible warning devices on late-model vehicles are controlled by onboard computers much like the warning lamps or the driver information center. Before beginning your diagnosis check the appropriate Service Manual for the correct procedures. Follow the diagnostic steps required to check for defective components or poor connections. If the audible warning device is controlled directly by the switch or sensor, begin your diagnosis by checking the fuse or power circuit. If power is available connect a jumper wire across the switch terminals or between the circuit and ground on single wire systems. If the warning activates, adjust or replace the switch. If it does not operate, check the continuity of the circuit and repair as necessary. If the circuit and switch are operating properly, replace the warning device.

A6

CHAPTER QUESTIONS

1. The ammeter gauge connects in:
   a. Parallel to the generator and battery
   b. Series with the generator and battery
   c. Parallel to the ignition switch and battery
   d. Series with the ignition switch and battery

2. A warning lamp sending unit uses:
   a. A float
   b. A variable resistor
   c. A diaphragm
   d. An on/off switch

3. A single gauge failure is most likely caused by a:
   a. Faulty gauge
   b. Circuit fault in the gauge wiring
   c. Circuit fault on a shared circuit
   d. Blown fuse

4. The continuous, controlled voltage required by most electromechanical gauges is provided by:
   a. An IVR
   b. A shunt circuit
   c. A transducer
   d. A sending unit

5. A defective IVR can produce all of the following symptoms *EXCEPT:*
   a. Failure of all regulated gauges
   b. Inaccurate readings on all regulated gauges
   c. Excessive needle vibration on all regulated gauges
   d. No needle movement on all regulated gauges with the ignition switch on

6. Which of the following statements is *NOT* true of a printed circuit board?
   a. It is mounted on thin composition board
   b. It is made of copper foil bonded to a mylar base
   c. It can be checked by probing with a test lamp
   d. It is inexpensive to manufacture

7. Diagnosing problems in a driver information center usually requires all of the following *EXCEPT:*
   a. Diagnostic charts
   b. Accurate specifications
   c. A special diagnostic tool
   d. Circuit diagrams

8. An electronic display device using electrodes and polarized fluid to create numbers and characters is called an:
   a. LCD
   b. LED
   c. VFD
   d. CRT

9. Most audible warning devices are activated by:
   a. Time delay switch
   b. Switch to ground
   c. The ignition switch
   d. A fixed resistor

10. When installing a new digital instrument cluster, always:
    a. Replace the odometer memory chip
    b. Replace the printed circuit board
    c. Disconnect the negative battery cable
    d. Disconnect the generator power circuit

CHAPTER SEVEN

HORN, WIPER/WASHER DIAGNOSIS AND REPAIR

CHAPTER OBJECTIVES

- The technician will complete the ASE task list on Horn, Wiper/Washer Diagnosis and Repair.
- The technician will be able to answer 3 questions dealing with the Horn, Wiper/Washer Diagnosis and Repair section of the A6 ASE Test.

The horn, windshield wiper, and windshield washer circuits are diagnosed using standard electrical test procedures and equipment.

HORN SYSTEMS

A vehicle horn operates similar to a warning buzzer, but the armature and contacts are attached to a diaphragm. Sound created by the vibrating diaphragm is magnified by a trumpet attached to the diaphragm chamber. Systems may use one or two horns. A high and low pitch are used in two-horn application; only a high pitch is used in single-horn applications. Each horn is marked with an H or L for identification.

Horn System Diagnosis

There are three types of horn failure:

- No horn operation
- Intermittent operation
- Constant operation

Intermittent or Non-Operation

If a horn operates intermittently, check for:

- Loose contact at the switch
- Loose, frayed, or broken wire
- Defective relay

If a horn does not operate at all, check for:

- Burned fuse or fusible link
- Defective horn
- Faulty relay
- Grounded or defective switch

Constant Operation

When a horn sounds continuously and cannot be shut off, the horn switch contacts are stuck closed. Check for continuity through the horn switch. In systems that use a relay, the relay may also be defective. Check for stuck contacts in the relay.

Horn Service

Typically, a relay supplies voltage to a high-current horn circuit and to a low-current switch and relay circuit on a late-model vehicle, figure 7-1. No relay is used on some older systems and current is supplied through a single switch in the steering column.

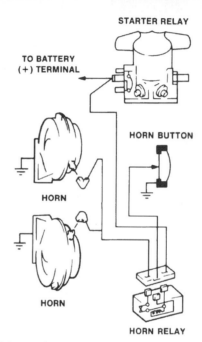

Fig. 7-1. A horn relay protects circuits and components on late-model systems.

A6

Switch and Relay Testing

Switches and relays are circuit control devices. Once a switch has been disconnected from the circuit, it can be diagnosed with a continuity test. Check a relay to determine if the coil is being energized and if current passes through the power circuit. Use a voltmeter to test input, output, and control voltage.

Horn Circuit Testing

Make sure the fuse or fusible link is good before doing any horn or circuit tests. Also, check that the horn ground connections are clean and tight.

On a system with a relay, test the main circuit and the control circuit. Check for current available at the horn, voltage available at the relay, and continuity through the switch. When no relay is used, there are two wires leading to the horn switch and a connection to the steering wheel is made with a double contact slipring. Test points on this system are similar to those on a system with a relay, but there is no control circuit.

Adjusting Horn Pitch

The tone, or pitch, of an electromagnetic horn can be adjusted to clear up the quality of the sound. However, adjustment does not change the horn frequency.

Fig. 7-2. An adjusting screw regulates diaphragm travel to control the pitch of an electromagnetic horn.

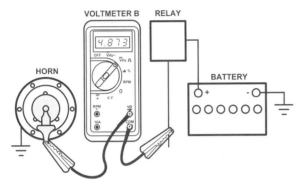

Fig. 7-3. Adjusting horn pitch with an ammeter.

Pitch is controlled by an adjusting screw that extends through the case and changes the diaphragm travel, figure 7-2. If the horn does not work or simply clicks, loosen the adjusting screw about half a turn and try again. If there is no improvement, the horn is defective and must be replaced. If the horn sounds after the last adjustment, attach an ammeter and adjust the screw until the reading is between 4.5 and 5.5 amperes, figure 7-3. If the current draw cannot be adjusted to within these limits, replace the horn.

WINDSHIELD WIPER SYSTEMS

Windshield wiper systems and circuits vary greatly between manufacturers as well as between models. However, basic troubleshooting procedures apply to all electrical parts of the systems. Most modern vehicles combine the windshield wiper and windshield washer functions into a single system. A typical system consists of:

- The wiper motor
- A gearbox
- Wiper arms and linkage
- Washer pump
- Hoses and jets
- Fluid reservoir

The motor and gearbox assembly connects to a switch on the instrument panel or steering column. Some systems have only one or two speeds; others have a variable speed motor. Some may have depressed or concealed parking, a feature that parks the wiper outside of its normal cleaning arc.

Depressed parking is achieved by using an outside arm that becomes longer when turned in the opposite direction to reverse the wiper motor when parking. The park switch reverses armature polarity in the motor to park the wiper arms and linkage, or transmission, figure 7-4. Instead of a depressed park feature, some systems simply extend the cleaning arc below the level of the hood line.

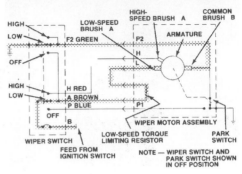

Fig. 7-4. A depressed park windshield wiper circuit uses a park switch to reverse the motor.

Windshield Wiper Diagnosis

Windshield wiper failure can be the result of an electrical problem or a mechanical failure, such as binding linkage. Generally, if the wipers work at one speed setting but not another, the problem is electrical. There is one exception: If the wipers on a depressed or a positive park system do not depress or return properly, the problem can be either mechanical or electrical.

To distinguish between an electrical or mechanical problem, disconnect the wiper arm linkage from the motor and switch the motor on. If the motor operates at all speeds, the problem is mechanical. If the motor still does not operate, the problem is electrical. If the wiper motor does not run at all, check for a:

- Blown circuit breaker
- Grounded or inoperative switch
- Defective motor
- Circuit wiring fault

If the motor operates but the wipers do not, check for:

- Stripped gears in gearbox
- Loose or separated output to gearbox connection
- Loose pivot to arm connection

If the motor operates with the switch in park, or if the motor will not shut off, check for a:

- Defective parking switch inside the motor
- Defective wiper switch
- Good ground connection at the wiper switch

To test the wiper system:

1. Switch the ignition on and set the wiper switch to a speed at which wiper will not work.
2. Check for battery voltage at the appropriate wiper motor terminal:
   - If voltage is present, replace the motor
   - If voltage is not present, continue testing
3. Check for battery voltage at the motor side of the wiper switch:
   - If voltage is present, locate and repair the wiring between the switch and motor
   - If voltage is not present, continue testing
4. Check for battery voltage at the battery side of the wiper switch:
   - If voltage is present, replace the switch
   - If voltage is not present, locate and repair the wiring between the battery and switch

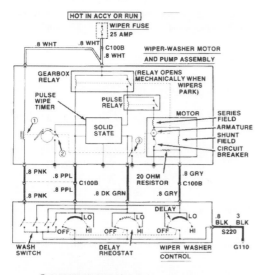

Fig. 7-5. Schematic for a typical rheostat controlled pulse, or interval, wiper.

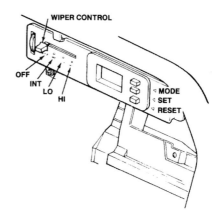

Fig. 7-6. Instrument panel windshield wiper control switch.

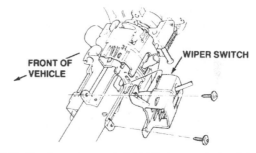

Fig. 7-7. Steering column windshield wiper control switch.

Pulse-Wipe Windshield Wiper Systems

Windshield wipers may also incorporate a delay, or intermittent operation, feature. The length of the delay, or the frequency of the intermittent operation, can be adjusted on some units.

These pulsing, or interval, wipers use either a governor or a solid-state module containing a simple variable **resistor** or **rheostat** and a **capacitor**. The module connects into the electrical circuitry between the wiper switch and wiper motor. While the length of interval is controlled by the variable resistor or rheostat, the interval itself is stopped and started by means of the solid-state pulse wipe timer, figure 7-5.

Troubleshooting is a simple procedure. If the wipers do not run at all:

1. Check the wiper fuse.
2. Use a wiring diagram of the switch in different positions. After studying the diagram duplicate the conditions that the switch should have. If the motor now runs, the problem is in the switch or module. By duplicating the switch conditions and measuring the outputs of the pulse module, diagnosis can be accurate.

If the wipers do not run at all speeds:

1. Check for continuity in the circuit for each speed through the control to ground.

If the washer does not work:

1. Check for damage to hoses and nozzles; also, check the screen inside the reservoir.

2. Ground the washer pump terminal. If the pump works, check continuity through the control wash switch. If the pump does not work, replace the ratchet solenoid in the motor assembly.

Windshield Wiper Service

Wiper motors are replaced if defective. The motor usually mounts in the plenum chamber, or at some point on the bulkhead below the windshield, and is accessible from under the hood. After gaining access to the motor, replacement is simply a matter of disconnecting the linkage, unplugging the electrical connectors, and unbolting the motor.

Rear window wiper motors are generally located inside the rear door panel of station wagons, or the rear hatch panel on vehicles with a hatchback or liftgate. After removing the trim panel covering the motor, replacement is essentially the same as replacing the front motor.

Wiper control switches install either on the steering column or on the instrument panel. Instrument panel switches are either snap-in units or are retained by one or more screws covered by a snap-in bezel, figure 7-6. Steering column wiper switches, which are operated by controls on the end of a switch stalk, require partial disassembly of the steering column for replacement, figure 7-7.

A6

Capacitor: A capacitor is a passive electronic component that stores energy in the form of an electrostatic field. In its simplest form, a capacitor consists of two conducting plates separated by an insulating material called the dielectric.

Resistor: An electric component that resists current flow, used to lower the voltage applied to another device such as a motor.

Rheostat: A continuously variable resistor used to control current through a circuit.

WINDSHIELD WASHER DIAGNOSIS AND SERVICE

Most vehicles use a positive-displacement or centrifugal-type washer pump located in the washer reservoir. However, some older models use a pulse-type pump connected to the wiper motor body.

Windshield Washer Diagnosis

If the washer is inoperative, check for:

- Blown fuse
- Empty reservoir
- Clogged nozzles
- Broken, kinked, or clogged hoses
- Loose or broken wiring
- Blocked reservoir screen
- Leaking reservoir

To quick-check any washer system, make sure the reservoir has sufficient fluid, then disconnect the pump hose and operate the washer switch. If fluid squirts from the pump, the delivery system is at fault. If no fluid squirts from the pump, the pump is defective.

Windshield Washer Service

If the delivery system is at fault, check for blocked or kinked hoses, blocked nozzles, or a blocked washer pump outlet. If the pump motor does not operate, check for voltage at the pump

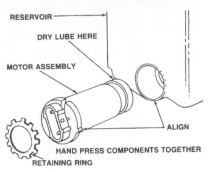

Fig. 7-8. Windshield washer motor pumps cannot be serviced; replace a defective pump.

while operating the washer switch. If voltage is present and the pump does not work, check the pump ground with an ohmmeter. Check for power out of the washer switch and wiper/washer circuit breaker operation. If all are satisfactory, locate and correct the problem in the wiring between the switch and pump.

Washer motors are replaced if defective. Centrifugal or positive-displacement pumps are located on or inside the washer reservoir, figure 7-8. Washer pump switches are installed either on the steering column or on the instrument panel.

CHAPTER QUESTIONS

1. The two circuits in a typical horn system are:
   a. The power and indicator lamp circuits
   b. The low-amperage horn circuit and high-amperage switch circuit
   c. The power and low-amperage switch and relay circuits
   d. The power circuit and a shunt circuit

2. If the windshield washer system is inoperative, but fluid squirts from the pump outlet with the hose disconnected and the switch operating, the problem is likely:
   a. In the pump
   b. In the delivery system
   c. In the circuitry
   d. In the switch

3. Which of the following is **NOT** used to create depressed wiper parking?
   a. Reversing armature polarity
   b. Off-center output arm
   c. Cleaning arc extends below hood line
   d. Variable resistor and capacitor

A6

CHAPTER OBJECTIVES

- The technician will complete the ASE task list on Accessories Diagnosis and Repair.
- The technician will be able to answer 8 questions dealing with the Accessories Diagnosis and Repair section of the A6 ASE Test.

Most modern vehicles are equipped with a number of electric and electronic accessories designed for driver convenience and comfort. The list of available options is long:

- Power windows
- Power seats
- Rear window defroster
- Power door, trunk, and fuel filler latches
- Keyless entry system
- Power convertible top
- Power sunroof
- Heated rear view mirror
- Heated seats
- Heated windshield
- Audio system
- Cigarette lighter
- Clock
- Cruise control
- Anti-theft system
- Airbag system
- Motorized shoulder harnesses

Although some accessories operate on engine vacuum, most are electric or electronically regulated. Troubleshooting follows standard circuit diagnosis and testing techniques. Typical repairs include replacing motors, linkage assemblies, switches, and relays and repairing damaged wiring and connections.

POWER WINDOW SYSTEMS

Vehicle doors and tailgates with power windows contain motors and a regulator assembly to raise and lower the window glass, figure 8-1. The power window circuit consists of the motors and regulators, individual control switches at each door, a master switch assembly, and connecting wiring. The circuit is powered from the accessory terminal of the ignition switch and is generally protected by a circuit breaker located in the main fuse block. The power window circuit has both sides of the motor connected to ground. When the window is operated, one side of the window is disconnected from ground and connected to power; the other side remains connected to ground.

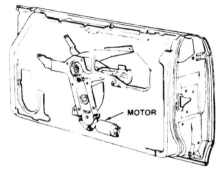

Fig. 8-1. A motor-driven regulator raises and lowers the glass on a power window.

Reversing the polarity reverses the motor and window operation. Power window regulators may be a scissor-type or flex-drive design.

Power Window Diagnosis

If power window operation is slow or intermittent, check for:

- Incorrectly adjusted or aligned regulator
- Motor or regulator gears dry of lubricant
- Motor bushings dry of lubricant
- Defective circuit breaker
- Loose wiring connections
- Window channel runs dry

If a power window is inoperative, check for:

- Defective motor
- Defective switch
- Open wiring circuit

Power Window Testing and Service

Low battery voltage and high circuit resistance are common reasons for slow power window operation. In many late-model vehicles the operation of the power windows is integrated into one or more onboard electronic control modules. Refer to the appropriate Service Manual before beginning diagnosis of a power window malfunction. If the window motor is controlled directly from the switch or through a relay, test power window motor operation:

1. Remove the appropriate door trim panel.
2. Disconnect the electrical connections at the motor terminals and connect the motor terminals to battery voltage with jumper wires. Replace the motor if it does not run.

3. Reverse the jumper connections at the motor terminals. Replace the motor if it does not run in the opposite direction.

Component Replacement

Since power window motors mount inside the door frame, the door panel trim must be removed to replace the motor or regulator. Power window circuit relays are often mounted on a bracket under the instrument panel, inside the door frame, or behind a kick panel. Many of the late-model window motors are riveted to the door frame and the rivets must be drilled out to service the motor. Replacement motors may be riveted or bolted in place.

POWER SEAT SYSTEMS

There are several movement designs for electrically adjustable seats:

- 2-way seats move forward and backward
- 4-way seats move forward, backward, up, and down
- 6-way seats move forward, backward, up and down, and tilt forward and backward

In addition, seats may have inflatable back supports powered by a small pump mounted in the seat frame. Most late-model vehicles use 6-way systems with three reversible motor armatures in one housing, figure 8-2. The motors are the permanent-magnet type and current is regulated through a switch on the ground circuit. An internal circuit breaker is often used to protect the motor. Vertical gear drives and horizontal rack-and-pinion or worm drives provide the seat movement.

Some vehicles with electronic control systems have a memory seat feature allowing the driver to program different seat positions into a control module for later recall. Accurate circuit diagrams are needed to determine how the system components are related and how to organize troubleshooting. Information can be obtained through an onboard diagnostic program on some models.

Power Seat Testing and Service

Troubleshooting power seats is essentially the same as that used for power windows, since the motors generally are the same type. Check for battery voltage available at the circuit breaker and the input connector of the switch. If voltage is available to the switch, remove the switch for continuity testing. Consult the Service Manual circuit diagram to test for correct continuity for all switch positions. If the switch is operational, the seat will have to be removed from the vehicle to check the motor assembly and wiring harness.

With a memory seat system, determine if a discharged or recently disconnected battery is the cause of a preset memory loss. In some systems, all the power seat functions are directed through the control module and will not work if the module is not installed or is not functional. As a first step in troubleshooting this type of system, check voltage and ground to the module.

Component Replacement

The design of most switches installed in a console or armrest allows them to be pried out and pressed back in place. If installed on the side of the seat frame, they are held in place by screws. Power seat motors are located underneath the seat on the track assembly. Since seat removal is necessary for testing, motor replacement can be done at the same time. Before installing the motor ensure that the drive gears will mesh properly to avoid damage. After installation, operate the seat through all directions of travel before reassembling any trim pieces.

REAR WINDOW DEFROSTER SYSTEMS

A heated rear window defroster, like all other electric automotive heaters, uses a high-resistance circuit to produce heat. A grid of electrically conductive lines bonded to the glass surface warms the glass as current is impeded by resistance. Current through the grid is controlled by a relay and switch, figure 8-3. The switch and relay may be separate units or may be combined into a single assembly. A timer relay may automatically switch off the heating element on some models. A warning lamp, which can be an LED or bulb in the switch or on the instrument panel, illuminates when the grid is on. Most late-model systems control the heater through the body control module with a solid-state timer/relay. The grid in these

A6

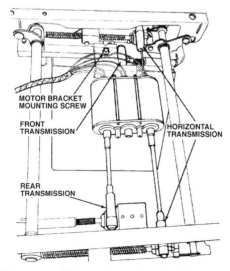

Fig. 8-2. Three reversible armatures in a single housing drive three transmissions to provide six power seat movements.

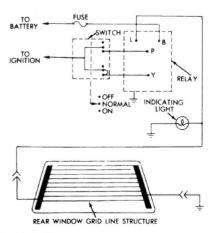

Fig. 8-3. A switch directs current to the rear window defroster through a relay.

systems is typically protected by a fusible link or circuit breaker, while the control circuit is fused.

Rear Window Defroster Testing and Service

To check the operation of a rear window defroster grid:

1. Switch the ignition on without starting the engine, then switch on the defroster while watching the vehicle ammeter or voltmeter. The meter needle should deflect as the switch is turned on. If the vehicle uses an indicator lamp instead of an ammeter or voltmeter, a temperature difference should be felt on the window surface within 2 to 4 minutes.
2. Check for battery voltage available at the grid, figure 8-4.

If voltage to the grid is low, check for a:

- Loose or corroded connection at the grid feed wire
- Faulty ground connection
- Burned fusible link or defective circuit breaker

If battery voltage is available at the grid, look for a defective control switch or relay timer that is defective, or an open ground circuit. A break in one grid wire will cause only the broken wire to malfunction; all of the wires would have to be broken to render the entire grid inoperative.

To check the grid for an open circuit:

1. Turn the system on.
2. Connect a voltmeter negative lead to a good body ground and check the available voltage at the midpoint of each grid line. Readings should be approximately 6 volts.

If no voltage is available, the grid circuit is open between the test point and the insulated, or positive, side of the grid. If the reading equals battery voltage, then the ground side of the grid circuit is open.

Too much resistance results in a grid that operates, but does not produce enough heat. To check, disconnect both grid terminals, check grid resistance with an ohmmeter, and compare the reading to specifications.

Grid lines or **buss bars** can be repaired with a special epoxy conductor. Clean the glass in the area of the broken line with alcohol and mask it, then apply the epoxy.

ELECTRIC DOOR AND TRUNK LOCK SYSTEMS

Electric latches controlled either by solenoids or electric motors are used on doors, rear decks, tailgates, and fuel filler doors. A master control allows the driver to lock or unlock all the doors while seated. Some systems provide switches on each door to operate each lock separately. Individual switches may be overridden by the master control. Each door lock is connected to an electric motor or double-acting solenoid.

The rear deck latch circuit is fed from the ignition run circuit. The rear deck or trunk button is often concealed in the glove compartment or center console. The button activates a solenoid attached to the latch. The circuit consists of a solenoid, switch, wiring, and a fuse.

Electric Door and Trunk Lock Testing and Service

When troubleshooting electric door and trunk latch problems, check for:

- Blown circuit breaker, fuse, or fusible link
- Open circuit to the battery
- Defective switch
- Defective relay
- Defective actuator
- Open wiring harness circuit
- Loose connector
- Disconnected actuator and latch linkage

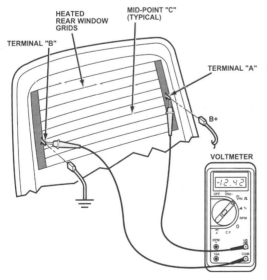

Fig. 8-4. Check for battery voltage available to the grid of a rear window defroster grid.

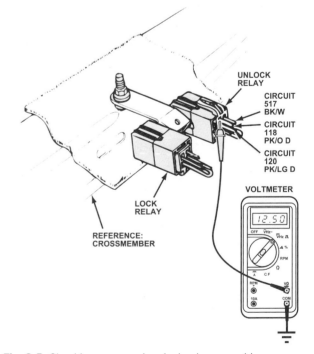

Fig. 8-5. Checking a power door lock relay assembly.

Buss Bar: A solid metal strip used as a conductor and common connection point for wires and devices.

An electrical schematic is essential to troubleshoot and test electric latch system circuits. Check circuitry using standard electrical tests and equipment, figure 8-5.

Component Replacement
Mechanical linkage problems are usually the result of lack of lubrication. The linkage in older vehicles can separate at badly worn connection points.

Motors, solenoids, and relays mount inside the door frame and are retained with screws, pop rivets, or clips. Some motor and solenoid assemblies have slotted brackets to permit adjustment. Door panel trim must be removed to replace these components. Adjust the motor or solenoid to move the lock mechanism to its locked position when its plunger is fully extended.

KEYLESS ENTRY SYSTEMS
The major function of a keyless entry system is to open the vehicle doors without a key. This can be done either with a keypad located on the outside of the door or with a wireless transmitter on the key ring. Both systems use an electronic control module in the trunk or under the instrument panel, figure 8-6. Locking actuators or motors located in the doors are similar to those used with electric locks.

Keyless Entry System Diagnosis
Intermittent operation is often caused by a loose wire or connector. If the system is inoperative, check for:

- Mechanical binding in the door locks
- Low battery voltage
- Blown fuse
- Open circuit to control module
- Defective module
- Defective keypad actuator
- Defective transmitter

Keyless Entry System Testing and Service
Basic keyless entry systems use a relatively simple circuit. However, many systems are wired into corresponding accessories, such as an automatic door lock or anti-theft system, which makes diagnosis appear more complex. Service Manual procedures, circuit diagrams, and specifications are required for effective troubleshooting. Use the circuit diagram to isolate suspect subcircuits and devices for voltage drop testing.

POWER SUNROOF AND CONVERTIBLE TOP SYSTEMS
Electric sunroof panels are opened and closed by a motor moving cables through a tube. The motor generally has a clutch that allows slippage when the motor stalls at the end of the cable travel or the panel is obstructed. The control switch may be located on the instrument panel, in the center console, or on a panel on the headliner. Overload protection is provided by a circuit breaker, which is often located in the fuse block and may also serve the power window circuit.

Electric convertible tops are operated by two double-acting hydraulic cylinders and a pump driven by a reversible electric motor. Two relays, one for raising and one for lowering the top, direct current through the motor, and are controlled by a switch mounted on the instrument panel. A typical convertible top system uses three circuit protection devices: a 20-amp fuse, a fusible link, and a 25-amp circuit breaker. This is important to know when troubleshooting this type of circuit.

Power Sunroof Diagnosis
If the sunroof does not operate properly, check for binding or improper adjustment. Some systems have a clutch adjustment screw that controls slippage, figure 8-7. If the clutch is slipping, tighten the screw and operate the system again. If the clutch slips after adjustment or the motor stalls before opening or closing the sunroof, replace the motor.

Convertible Top Diagnosis
If the convertible top system is inoperative, check for:

- Low battery voltage
- Defective circuit breaker
- Mechanical binding in linkage
- Loose or corroded ground connections

A6

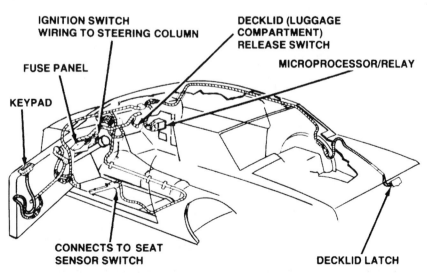

Fig. 8-6. Typical keyless entry system components.

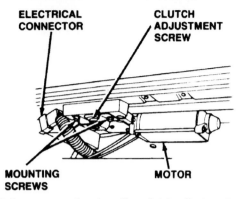

Fig. 8-7. Power sunroof motor with a clutch adjustment screw.

- Lack of hydraulic fluid
- Hydraulic system leakage
- Restrictions in hydraulic system
- Defective cylinder or pump

Power Sunroof and Convertible Testing and Service

These electrical circuits are relatively simple to troubleshoot because they are single circuits that are not integrated with other accessory circuits. However, they may share a circuit breaker with the power windows. Switches, relays, and wiring are checked as in other electrical circuits.

Sunroofs generally are mounted to the roof as a module, with the motor and drive gear assembly attached to the module, and may require headliner removal to service the components.

Convertible top motor and pump units generally mount on the floor behind the rear seat, and are reached by removing the rear seat back and cushion. Hydraulic cylinders are usually located inside each rear quarter panel behind interior trim panels.

POWER SLIDING DOOR & LIFTGATE SYSTEMS

The power sliding doors open and close by a motor moving cables. The motors generally have clutches that allow slippage when the motor stalls at the end of the cable travel or the panel is obstructed. The door(s) can be operated manually or from a switch in the B-pillar and overhead console or from the remote keyless entry system. While the door will not open unless the gear selector is in Park position and the door unlocked, it can be closed when not in Park. Vehicle forward movement adds resistance to the door closing operation. An alarm will sound when the system is enabled and door is open while the vehicle is out of Park. Excessive door movement resistance will cause the system to stop and reverse travel direction. There is a detent switch to determine when the door is latched, ajar, or open. Position sensors monitor the sliding door position at all times.

The power liftgate is opened and closed using a motor with a clutch and gear set through a strut rod connected by a lever. If a fault occurs, the system releases the clutch, allowing manual operation of the liftgate. Liftgate position is determined based on a Hall-effect sensor and open switch. Open and close cycles can only be initiated from the fully closed or open position while the vehicle is in Park and the liftglass ajar

switch is inactive. However, at any time during the cycle the operation can be reversed by pressing any of the open/close switches. The system can be switched to manual operation.

Power Sliding Door Diagnosis

If the power sliding door does not operate properly, inspect for proper mechanical conditions:

1. Manually open and close the door to ensure it moves smoothly and without excessive resistance or binding.
2. Inspect the easily accessible or visible system components for damage or conditions that could cause the condition.
3. Ensure the door also latches and unlatches without the use of excessive force.
4. Inspect for aftermarket devises that can affect operation.

Inspect for faulty electrical connections or wiring that may cause intermittent conditions.

Check for DTCs. Refer to the appropriate Service Manual for the correct diagnostic procedure. Service Manual procedures, circuit diagrams, and specifications are required for effective troubleshooting.

- Inoperative automatic door locks or a power window malfunction
- Door ajar indicator malfunction
- Power door lock inoperative
- Power door lock key cylinder switches inoperative
- Power sliding door closes and reopens
- Power sliding door inoperative
- Power sliding door inoperative from one switch
- Power sliding door opens with gear selector out of Park

Power Liftgate Diagnosis

If the power liftgate does not operate properly, inspect for proper mechanical conditions:

1. Manually open and close the liftgate to ensure it moves smoothly and without excessive resistance or binding.
2. Inspect the easily accessible or visible system components for damage or conditions could cause the condition.
3. Inspect for aftermarket devises that can affect operation.

Inspect for faulty electrical connections or wiring that may cause intermittent conditions.

Check for DTCs. Refer to the appropriate Service Manual for the correct diagnostic procedure. Service Manual procedures, circuit diagrams, and specifications are required for effective troubleshooting.

- Liftgate ajar indicator malfunction
- Door ajar indicator malfunction
- Power door latch system malfunction
- Power door lock key cylinder switches inoperative
- Power liftgate malfunction

Testing and Service

When testing these systems, follow Service Manual procedures.
Service the power sliding door by:

1. Manually open and close the door slowly to ensure it moves smoothly and without excessive resistance or binding.
2. Clean and lubricate or replace the tracks as required.

3. Verify proper power sliding door cable tension
4. Inspect to see that door and latches are aligned and operating properly.
5. Inspect the power door plungers and B-pillar pads for the following conditions:
   - Proper door plunger operating
   - Clean electrical contact from the door plungers to B-pillar pads
   - Proper alignment of the door plungers to the B-pillar pads

HEATED REAR VIEW MIRROR SYSTEMS

A heated rear view mirror is generally incorporated into the rear window defroster circuitry. With the control switch on, the timer-relay contacts close to provide current to both the rear defroster grid and the heated mirror element. A separate fuse, installed between the relay and heating element, is often used to protect the mirror circuit.

Heated Rear View Mirror Testing and Service

If neither the defroster grid nor the heated mirror works, troubleshoot the rear defroster system as described earlier. If the grid works but the heated mirror does not, use a circuit diagram and a DMM to check the mirror fuse and element wiring.

HEATED WINDSHIELD SYSTEMS

Components of an optional heated windshield are quite similar to those of the rear-window electrical grid discussed earlier. A few older model vehicles with heated windshields receive their power from the generator. Always check the charging system thoroughly before troubleshooting a heated windshield problem.

A heated windshield can be activated at any temperature for testing, although some electronic control systems prevent activation above a preset temperature and must be placed in diagnostic mode to test the system. When testing these systems, follow Service Manual procedures. Also, keep a close watch on the windshield surface temperature and turn the system off after two minutes to avoid permanent optical damage to the windshield.

AUDIO SYSTEMS

Always determine the exact nature of the problem before removing audio components for service. Knowing whether the condition is constant or intermittent, occurs with the engine on or off, or only occurs when the vehicle is either parked or moving helps pinpoint the problem.

Radio Diagnosis

The most common causes of poor, intermittent, or no radio reception are:

- Vehicle in a poor reception area
- Antenna trim improperly adjusted
- Defective antenna

Most modern sound systems use a separate ground circuit for the speakers. Some older systems use the vehicle chassis as ground. Any loose connector will affect the operation of part or all of the system.

Servicing Radio Components

Check for voltage available at the radio. Radios are protected by low-amperage fuses located in the interior fuse panel. Older vehicles protected the radio with a fuse either inline on the input circuit or mounted on the back of the radio chassis. If voltage is available, but the radio does not operate, there are internal circuitry problems. Remove the unit and send it to a radio shop for service.

To check a speaker, disconnect both leads at the connector. Next, momentarily connect a fresh 1.5 volt battery across the speaker terminals, then quickly disconnect the battery. Replace the speaker if it does not make a popping noise when the battery is connected and disconnected.

Fixed and Power Antenna Service

Fixed antennas cannot be adjusted up or down. Power antennas automatically rise when the radio is turned on if the ignition switch is in the run or accessory position, and automatically lower when the radio or ignition is switched off.

The antenna lead is a coaxial cable with the signal carried through the center conductor and the outer conductor acting as a shield. For the cable to be effective as a shield, it must be securely grounded at the body connection. A poor ground can cause excess ignition noise in AM reception, or erratic sound. To check antenna ground with a fixed antenna:

1. Tune the radio for a weak AM station or signal.
2. Unscrew and remove the antenna mast.
3. Connect a short jumper wire between the mast mounting stud and the cable lead.
   - If the radio station is not received, the antenna ground is good
   - If the radio station is still received, the ground is poor or open

To check antenna ground with a power antenna:

1. Fully lower the antenna and separate the motor connector.
2. Connect an alligator clip near the top of the antenna.
3. Tune the radio for a weak AM station or signal.
4. Remove the alligator clip and connect a short jumper between the mounting bracket and the top of the mast.
   - If the radio station is not received, the antenna ground is good
   - If the radio station is still received, the ground is poor or open

Noise Suppression Components

Two kinds of noise can affect a radio:

- Radiated
- Conducted

Radiated noise, or **radio frequency interference** (**RFI**), results from an accessory that gives off a signal that is picked up along with the desired radio signal by the antenna. Interference from

Radio Frequency Interference (RFI): A form of electromagnetic interference, created by the ignition secondary circuits, that disrupts radio transmission.

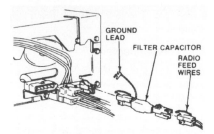

Fig. 8-8. A capacitor used to filter RFI from the radio.

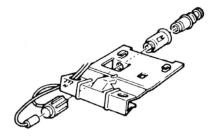

Fig. 8-9. Typical cigarette lighter installation.

radiated noise is controlled by a capacitor or a ground strap, figure 8-8. Radiated noise can be caused by:

- Defective ignition components
- Heater blower, wiper, fan, or A/C system motors
- Electronic components
- Electric fuel pumps
- An overhead compass
- Loose ground strap or loose antenna mount

Operating devices such as turn signals or the cigarette lighter can cause a popping noise on weak or distant AM signals.

Conducted noise is audible at very low volume and results from problems on the insulated circuit. Noise is controlled by an inline filter, or **radio choke**, installed in the input circuit from the ignition switch. Conducted noise can be caused by:

- The generator
- Power modules
- Trim, interior, or opera lights

Radio static also may originate from an outside source, such as high-tension power lines or power tools being used nearby. To determine the cause of excessive radio noise, disconnect the antenna at the back of the radio. If the noise ceases, connect the radio to a known-good antenna. If the noise disappears, replace the antenna. If the noise continues, the problem is in the radio wiring.

Trimming the Antenna

Each time the antenna or radio is repaired or replaced, the antenna must be trimmed to balance reception. Trim adjustment is made with an adjustment screw located either near the antenna lead connector or accessed through the instrument panel trim. Tune the radio to a station as close as possible to 1400 kHz on the AM dial. Then, use a nonmagnetic screwdriver and adjust trim by slowly turning the screw both directions until the radio plays the loudest.

CIGARETTE LIGHTER SERVICE

The cigarette lighter is normally on a dedicated high-amperage circuit protected by a fuse in the interior fuse panel. A cigarette lighter consists of an element and a socket, figure 8-9. The element is a high-resistance heating coil attached to the knob. The socket installs in the ash tray or instrument panel and is held in position with a sleeve that threads onto the socket from the rear. When the heating element is pressed into the socket,

it is held by a bimetallic clip. Current flows through the clip to heat the element. When the element is heated, the clip releases the element, allowing it to return to a ready position. The most common causes of lighter malfunction are:

- Ash accumulation in the socket that burns fuses
- Burned-out or corroded element
- Defective socket

To check the lighter, inspect components and check for voltage available at the socket. Replace the lighter element if voltage is available.

Most newer vehicles also have one or more 12V power outlets for connecting cell phones, radios, etc. The cigarette lighter is not designed to function if inserted into a power outlet socket. The power outlet may be on direct battery power or connected to the ignition circuit.

CLOCK

An automotive clock also connects to constant battery voltage at the main fuse block. A fuse is installed on the rear of the clock on some models. The clock may be a self-contained unit, or a function of the radio. Digital clocks usually combine other functions, such as a timer and a calendar.

Loss of a digital clock display may be caused by an open circuit or poor ground. A clock that burns fuses or does not operate correctly is serviced by replacing the unit. Replacement generally requires dismantling the instrument panel or removing the radio.

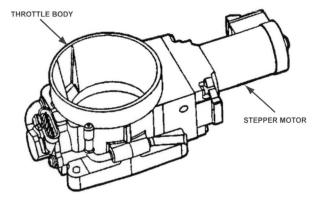

Fig. 8-10. Electromechanical cruise control transducer.

Radio Choke: A coil wound with fine wire and installed in a circuit to absorb oscillations that occur when the circuit is closed or opened.

CRUISE CONTROL SYSTEMS

Cruise control maintains a constant vehicle speed over a variety of highway driving conditions. Older versions, which are electromechanical systems, use a transducer connected to the throttle by mechanical linkage to regulate vacuum based on an electrical signal, figure 8-10. Late-model vehicles control vehicle speed with an output signal from the PCM. **Drive-by-wire** vehicles utilize a small DC **stepper motor** to control the throttle blade. The PCM or throttle control system module utilizes this motor to maintain engine speed during cruise control operation as well.

Cruise Control Diagnosis

All cruise control systems use information, such as the speed of the driveshaft or the speedometer cable, to determine if the vehicle is moving at the set speed. If not, a servo connected to the throttle linkage mechanically increases or decreases throttle opening to maintain the set speed. Perform a thorough visual inspection, then diagnose cruise control problems based on symptoms, figure 8-11.

Cruise Control Testing and Service

Stoplamp switches used on vehicles with a cruise control have two circuits: a stoplamp circuit and a cruise control circuit. The stoplamp circuit switches current on when the brake pedal is depressed, while the cruise control circuit switches current off when the pedal is depressed.

An improperly adjusted servo throttle cable allows vehicle speed to drop several miles per hour below the set speed. Vehicle speed is determined by a speed sensor located on the servo assembly and driven by the speedometer cable, or an electronic sensor mounted on the transmission or other driveline component. Electronic systems generally use an amplifier to operate the actuator.

Any defective component prevents the system from operating. Always check for battery voltage through the fuse. Inspect and repair any poor circuit connections, broken or damaged wires, and vacuum leaks. Further electrical cruise control service consists of checking for ground and insulated circuit continuity by voltage drop testing. Test with a DMM, as current

ELECTRONIC SPEED CONTROL TROUBLESHOOTING	
PROBLEM	**CHECK**
Speed control operates, but does not accelerate or coast down properly	1. Control switch 2. Control switch circuit 3. Servo assembly
Speed changes up or down constantly	1. Throttle linkage adjustment 2. Servo assembly 3. Speedometer cable and sensor 4. Amplifier or reserve
Does not disengage when brakes are applied	1. Brake switch and circuit 2. Vacuum dump valve 3. Servo assembly 4. Amplifier or reserve
Does not disengage when clutch pedal is depressed	1. Clutch switch 2. Clutch switch circuit
Speed does not set in system	1. Throttle linkage adjustment 2. Control switch and circuit 3. Vacuum dump valve 4. Clutch or brake switch 5. Servo assembly 6. Speed sensor
Speed wanders up or down after it is set	1. Actuator cable adjustment 2. Vacuum dump valve 3. Servo assembly
System operates but does not resume properly	1. Control switch and circuit 2. Servo assembly 3. Amplifier or reserve
Speed will resume below 20 mph	1. Control module
Speed engages without operating set button	1. Control switch and circuit

Fig. 8-11. Cruise control system diagnostic chart.

A6

Drive-by-Wire: A method of controlling the vehicle without control cables or rods. The throttle is actuated based on input from a potentiometer attached to the accelerator pedal.
Stepper Motor: A small DC motor that moves or rotates in small increments known as steps.

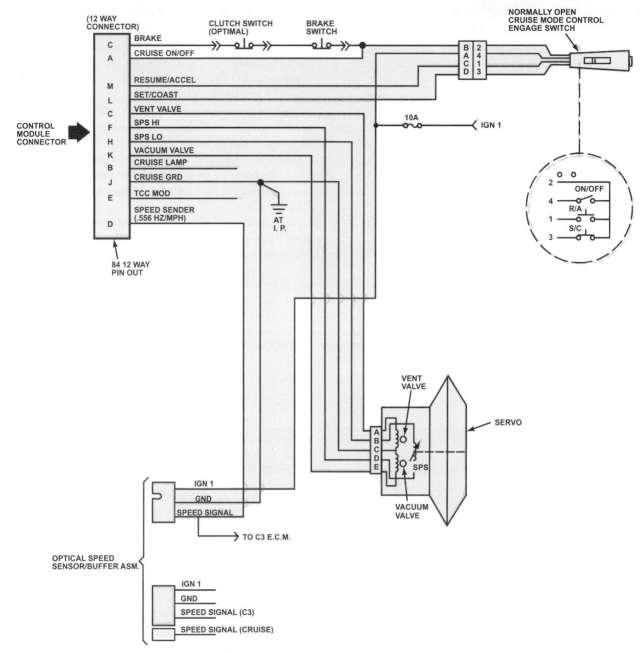

Fig. 8-12. Typical electromechanical cruise control schematic.

draw on a test lamp or analog meter damages electronic components. Troubleshoot cruise control circuitry following an accurate electrical schematic, figure 8-12.

ANTI-THEFT SYSTEMS

Anti-theft devices flash lights, sound an alarm, or both. Some systems prevent the starter or the ignition from operating when activated. Switches in the door jambs, trunk, and hood signal a control unit of any undesirable entry, figure 8-13. Electronic detectors can trigger the alarm if there is a change in battery current draw, a violent vehicle motion, or if glass is broken.

Anti-Theft System Diagnosis

Most factory-installed anti-theft systems are integrated with several other circuits, forming a complex, multiple-circuit system. The easiest way to reduce this circuit complexity is to use the circuit diagram to break the entire circuit into its several

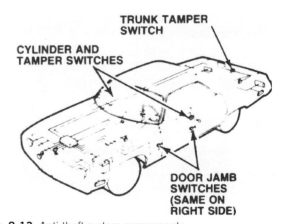

Fig. 8-13. Anti-theft system components.

subcircuits, then check only those related to the problem. If any step indicates that a subcircuit is not complete, check the power source, the components, and the wiring in that subcircuit.

Anti-Theft System Testing and Service

Before doing any diagnostic checks, ensure the following are operational:

- Parking and low-beam headlamps
- Dome and courtesy lamps
- Horn
- Wipers
- Clock
- Electric door locks

Next, check all circuits leading to the controller. Make sure all switches are in their normal, or off, positions. Door jamb switches ground the alarm circuit when a door is opened. Frequently, corrosion builds up on the switch contacts, preventing the switch from operating properly.

Motorized Seatbelt Systems

Motorized seatbelt systems are classified as **passive restraints**. They are designed to automatically move the shoulder belt into position when a front seat passenger enters the vehicle, closes the door, and switches on the ignition. If either front door is opened the respective belt will return to its unlocked position regardless of the position of the ignition switch, allowing the occupant to exit the vehicle. Generally these systems require the occupant to fasten the conventional lap belt for maximum protection.

System Components

The system utilizes a motor, gear reduction system, and a **tape drive** to move the belt into the locked position. Proper operation of the motor is provided by a control module, door position switch, seat cushion switch, motor relay, and a belt travel limit switch. Most systems also include a manual or emergency release to unlock the belt should the electrical operation fail.

System Diagnosis

Most problems with motorized belt systems involve misalignment, wear, or damage to the tape drive or the track. Inspect the entire track and tape for signs of damage or distortion. The track can often be straightened or repaired, while the tape must be replaced if damaged.

Check the electrical system like any other motorized component. Begin diagnosis by verifying that power and ground are available to the control module and the motor. Inspect the fuse, circuit breaker, and relay for damage or open circuits. Perform a voltage drop test on the affected circuit to locate high resistance or corroded connectors. If the electrical system checks out continue diagnosis with the control module. Refer to the appropriate Service Manual for the correct diagnostic procedure.

AIRBAG SYSTEMS

An airbag system consists of two basic subsystems: the airbag modules and the electrical system, which includes the crash sensors, safing sensors and diagnostic module. Some vehicles incorporate seatbelt, pretensioners to enhance the effectiveness of the air bag deployment. The devices tighten and lock the seatbelt, preventing the occupant from moving too far forward during the crash. This allows the airbag to provide maximum safety.

Airbag Control Systems

The control system consists of the diagnostic module crash and safing sensors, and the power and ground circuits. The sensors react to vehicle deceleration according to the direction and force of the impacts, and discriminate between those that require airbag inflation and those that do not. If the deceleration exceeds a preset threshold value the sensors close the circuit and direct power to the igniter, deploying the airbags. The diagnostic module also contains a capacitor that stores an electrical charge that can deploy the airbags in the event the vehicle electrical system is damaged in the crash.

Airbag Modules

The airbag module consists of the airbag itself, the inflator assembly, the housing, and cover. The inflator contains the propellant, which is usually sodium azide combined with either copper oxide or potassium nitrate. Within the inflator is the igniter, which provides the heat necessary to start a chemical reaction causing the sodium azide to decompose explosively, forming harmless nitrogen gas. The gas is forced into the bag and inflates it almost instantaneously. In a properly operating system the bag is fully inflated in less than 40 milliseconds.

Airbag System Diagnosis

The diagnostic module detects system electrical faults, disables the system, and notifies the driver through a system readiness indicator, or airbag warning lamp, in the instrument cluster. Depending on circuit design, a system fault may cause the warning lamp to fail to illuminate, remain lit continuously, or flash. Some systems use a tone generator that produces an audible warning when a system fault occurs if the warning lamp is inoperative.

Airbag Testing and Service

Airbag system components and their location in the vehicle vary according to the system design, but the basic principles of testing are the same as with other electrical circuits. Use an accurate circuit diagram to determine how the circuit is designed and the correct sequence of tests to be followed.

Some airbag systems require the use of special testers. The built-in safety circuits of such testers prevent accidental deployment of the airbag. If you do not have such a tester, follow the recommended test procedures exactly.

All airbag systems require that special precautions be observed when testing or servicing:

- Disconnect the negative battery cable and tape its terminal
- Wait at least 10 minutes after disconnecting the battery to discharge the system capacitor
- Do not use self-powered test equipment unless specified by the Service Manual test procedures and do not probe airbag connectors
- Always wear safety glasses when servicing an airbag system.

A6

Passive Restraint: A passenger restraint system that operates automatically without input from the driver or passengers.
Tape Drive: A flexible nylon or plastic belt equipped with slots to engage the drive motor sprocket.

CHAPTER QUESTIONS

1. Which of the following accessories is powered by the alternator?
   a. Power door locks
   b. Heated windshield
   c. Convertible top
   d. Keyless entry system

2. Which of the following is **NOT** an example of radiated noise picked up by a radio?
   a. Ignition distributor
   b. Heater blower motor
   c. Interior light
   d. Overhead compass

3. All of the following are common causes of cigarette lighter malfunction, **EXCEPT**:
   a. Defective socket
   b. Corroded element
   c. Ash accumulation
   d. Open circuit breaker

4. Most cruise control systems adjust the throttle opening with a/an:
   a. Solenoid
   b. Servo
   c. Switch
   d. Electromagnet

5. Individual power window switches connect to the master window control switch on a:
   a. Series circuit
   b. Shunt circuit
   c. Parallel circuit
   d. Series-parallel circuit

6. Slow or intermittent power window operation can be caused by all of the following **EXCEPT**:
   a. Defective circuit breaker
   b. Gears and bushings dry of lubricant
   c. Misaligned or adjusted regulator
   d. Open motor circuit

7. Airbag systems require that special precautions be observed when testing or servicing, **EXCEPT**:
   a. Disconnect the negative battery cable and tape its terminal
   b. Wait at least 10 minutes after disconnecting the battery to discharge the system capacitor
   c. Use self-powered test equipment to probe airbag connectors
   d. Always wear safety glasses when servicing an airbag system

8. Most modern 6-way power seats use:
   a. Three permanent-magnet armatures
   b. Three electromagnetic armatures
   c. A three-phase motor with an internal circuit breaker
   d. A control module and vacuum motors

9. The best way to test the grid of a rear window defroster is to use a/an:
   a. Ammeter
   b. Ohmmeter
   c. Voltmeter
   d. Self-powered test light

10. Which of the following statements does **NOT** apply to an electric door lock system?
    a. Remove the dashboard to access the motor
    b. Motors may mount on slotted brackets to permit adjustment
    c. Motors, solenoids, and relays mount with screws, pop rivets, or clips
    d. Door panel trim must be removed to replace most components

11. Which of the following would **NOT** prevent the keyless entry system keypad from operating?
    a. Low battery voltage
    b. Blown fuse
    c. Defective transmitter
    d. Open control module circuit

12. A convertible top system generally uses all of the following circuit protection devices **EXCEPT**:
    a. Circuit breaker
    b. Fusible link
    c. 20-amp fuse
    d. Shunt circuit

13. All of the following statements about a heated rearview mirror system are true, **EXCEPT**:
    a. Depressing the control switch opens the timer-relay contacts
    b. The heated mirror is part of the rear window defroster system
    c. The heated mirror shares a fuse with the windshield heater
    d. A separate fuse installs between the relay and heating element

SAMPLE TEST

Test Taking Advice

As soon as you make the decision to schedule an A6 test, begin preparing by including dedicated study time in your weekly schedule. You can improve your test score with just a few hours of study and review per week. Photocopy the practice test included in this study guide so you can use it several times.

The practice test will help you become more comfortable with test taking in general. It will also point out your weak spots and enable you to use your study time more efficiently. When you miss a question, look up the answer and study the subject in the study guide. Take notes on the subject to use for review. After repeated test taking and review, you should have your notes reduced to a single sheet of paper that can be reviewed daily the week before the test, and again on the day of the test. Arrive at the test site early so parking or unforeseen problems do not cause you stress. Plan to allow time for a last look at your notes before entering the test site. Pay attention to all instructions from the test proctor even if you are a veteran test taker. From time to time ASE adjusts its instructions.

To answer test questions correctly, you must have a clear understanding of what is being asked. Read the question twice to be sure what it is asking. While thinking about the question, recall what you know about the subject. Do this before reading the answers. You are less likely to be influenced into a wrong conclusion by the answers if you recall what you know about the subject first. Since you have recalled your knowledge of the subject, you will be less likely to doubt yourself while reading the answers.

Note all operating conditions stated in the question when considering the answers. However, never assume that conditions exist that are not stated in the question. Treat each answer as a true or false question. Be sure to read all the answers before making your choice. When you conclude that more than one may be correct, reread the question to make sure you haven't missed an important fact, then rely on your knowledge to choose the one that is most correct. There is always one most correct answer. When it seems impossible to decide which answer is correct, it may help to think of which item would be more likely to wear out or which things require regular service. These types of items may be the best choice, especially when the question asks, "which is more likely." Never leave a question unanswered. Unanswered questions are scored as wrong! Guess if you can't make a decision. Guessing gives you a 25% chance of being correct. If you narrow the field to two possibilities, you have a 50% chance. Choose an answer before moving on to the next question in case you run out of time. Make a mark next to the question in the test booklet. Sometimes, other questions contain information that will help answer a question you're not sure of, and you can return to the questions you have marked if you have time. Be cautious when returning to reread a question. If you are still not sure which answer is correct, it's better to leave your original guess than to make a second guess. However, if you are certain that you originally misunderstood the question, it's best to change your answer.

---

1. An infinite reading on an auto-ranging digital ohmmeter indicates:
   a. The instrument is set on the incorrect scale
   b. The instrument should be zeroed
   c. A shorted circuit
   d. An open circuit

2. The starter control circuit includes all of the following **EXCEPT**:
   a. The starter switch
   b. The starter motor
   c. The starter relay or solenoid winding
   d. The starting safety switch

3. Which test is performed to determine if a sealed maintenance-free battery can be recharged or if it is too badly sulfated to accept a charge?
   a. Capacity
   b. Hydrometer
   c. Three-minute charge
   d. Load

4. The temperature-corrected figure for a hydrometer reading of 1.240 taken at an electrolyte temperature of 30°F (-1°C) is:
   a. 1.256
   b. 1.260
   c. 1.224
   d. 1.220

5. A dome light that operates off one door switch but not the other can be caused by all of the following **EXCEPT**:
   a. Faulty switch
   b. Faulty bulb
   c. Open connector
   d. Broken wire

6. If lights are dim, the probable cause is:
   a. High ground circuit resistance
   b. Low voltage regulator output
   c. Faulty light switch
   d. Loose terminal connections

7. A fast turn signal flashing rate can be caused by all of the following **EXCEPT**:
   a. Loose terminal connections
   b. The wrong type of flasher
   c. The wrong type of bulbs
   d. High circuit voltage

8. When checking diode resistance by reversing the leads of an ohmmeter, a good diode produces:
   a. Two low readings
   b. Two high readings
   c. One high and one low reading
   d. One high and one infinite reading

9. Connecting a 12-volt battery to a circuit whose total resistance is 0.3 ohms produces a:
   a. 3.6 ampere current
   b. 4.0 ampere current
   c. 36 ampere current
   d. 40 ampere current

A6

10. Which of the following statements about halogen sealed-beam headlights is **NOT** true?
    a. Replace them in the same way as conventional sealed-beam headlights
    b. Install them inside an aerodynamic plastic lens assembly
    c. Size standards are the same as conventional sealed-beam headlights
    d. Three aiming points are used to adjust the beam

11. A battery can be fast-charged for up to one hour if the corrected specific gravity reading is:
    a. 1.150 or less
    b. 1.150 to 1.175
    c. 1.175 to 1.200
    d. 1.200 to 1.250

12. If a probe lamp lights when one lead is connected to ground and the other lead is connected to a point in the circuit:
    a. Voltage is available to where the light is connected
    b. The circuit is shorted to ground beyond the test point
    c. The circuit is open before the test point
    d. The circuit is switched off

13. A self-powered test lamp can damage circuits and components if used to check continuity of:
    a. Complete circuits
    b. High-resistance components
    c. A shunt circuit
    d. A shorted ground circuit

14. A higher than normal ammeter reading when performing a current draw test on a circuit indicates:
    a. An open circuit
    b. Excessive resistance
    c. A short circuit
    d. Infinite resistance

15. Technician A says to replace the shift fork if the starter motor pinion clearance is out of specifications. Technician B says too much starter motor pinion clearance indicates the starter drive is worn.
    a. A only
    b. B only
    c. Both A and B
    d. Neither A nor B

16. All of the following statements about analog gauges are true **EXCEPT**:
    a. They may be mechanical, thermal, or electromagnetic
    b. They use the same sending units that digital gauges do
    c. Readings are displayed with a needle
    d. They require a controlled amount of voltage

17. When the needles on all the regulated voltage gauges vibrate by more than the width of the needle, the most likely cause would be a defective:
    a. Battery
    b. Gauge package
    c. Internal voltage regulator
    d. Instrument cluster wiring connection

18. The only electrical gauges that do **NOT** use a variable-resistance sending unit are:
    a. Ammeters and voltmeters
    b. Fuel gauges
    c. Temperature gauges
    d. Oil pressure gauges

19. Which warning lamp does **NOT** use an on/off switch as a sending unit?
    a. Coolant temperature
    b. Oil pressure
    c. Charging system
    d. Check engine

20. A horn that sounds continuously and cannot be shut off is most likely caused by:
    a. Horn switch contacts stuck closed
    b. Horn switch contacts stuck open
    c. Battery voltage too high
    d. The generator is overcharging

21. Which of the following is a likely cause of a windshield wiper arm **NOT** moving while the motor is running?
    a. Blown circuit breaker
    b. Defective motor or switch
    c. Binding linkage or gears
    d. Wiring problems

22. The most likely source of a rear defroster grid that operates but does not generate enough heat would be:
    a. Low circuit voltage
    b. Circuit current too high
    c. High circuit resistance
    d. Low alternator output

23. Technician A says that with a voltmeter connected to the starter relay battery terminal and the relay switch terminals and the ignition on, a reading of 3.5 indicates high resistance in the relay control circuit. Technician B says this could indicate high resistance in the connections at the battery terminal lead to the ignition switch. Who is right?
    a. A only
    b. B only
    c. Both A and B
    d. Neither A nor B

24. When testing an airbag system, do all of the following **EXCEPT**:
    a. Wear safety glasses
    b. Probe airbag connectors to check voltage
    c. Disconnect the negative battery cable
    d. Allow the system capacitor to discharge prior to testing

25. Which of the following is **NOT** a simple electrical circuit?
    a. Power sunroof
    b. Anti-theft system
    c. Convertible top
    d. Heated mirror

26. A hydrometer reading of 1.240 on a battery with an electrolyte temperature of 70°F (39.2°C) indicates the battery is approximately:
    a. 25 percent charged
    b. 50 percent charged
    c. 75 percent charged
    d. Nearly discharged

27. When checking a horn with an ammeter, readings should be:
    a. 2.5 to 4.5 amperes
    b. 4.5 to 5.5 amperes
    c. 5.4 to 6.4 amperes
    d. Infinite

28. A battery with a state-of-charge indicator should **NOT** be recharged if the eye is:
    a. Black
    b. Red
    c. Green
    d. Light yellow

29. A loose steering column affects grounding and can cause the horn to:
    a. Work only at high pitch
    b. Sound continuously
    c. Not work at all
    d. Work intermittently

30. A 12-volt battery is good if during a battery capacity or load test voltage remains above:
    a. 12 volts
    b. 10.6 volts
    c. 9.6 volts
    d. 8.6 volts

31. Which of the following is **NOT** a pulse or interval wiping system component?
    a. Governor
    b. Solid-state module
    c. Circuit breaker
    d. Pulse relay

32. When servicing a battery, use all of the following **EXCEPT**:
    a. Battery carrier
    b. Safety glasses
    c. Metal brush
    d. Gloves

33. If a wiper motor operates with the switch in park position, check for:
    a. No ground at wiper switch
    b. Stripped gears in gearbox
    c. Loose pivot arm
    d. Pulse relay

34. A battery usually can be charged at any rate as long as the electrolyte temperature remains below:
    a. 150°F (66°C)
    b. 125°F (52°C)
    c. 100°F (38°C)
    d. 75°F (24°C)

35. Windshield wiper arms that do not move but having a motor that runs at all speeds may be caused by all of the following **EXCEPT**:
    a. Stripped gearbox gears
    b. Loose or separated output shaft
    c. Defective motor
    d. Loose pivot arm connection

36. When jump starting a dead battery, which cable should be connected last?
    a. The terminal connected to the positive side of the discharged battery
    b. The terminal connected to the positive side of the booster battery
    c. The terminal connected to the ground terminal on the booster battery
    d. The terminal connected to the ground on the disabled vehicle

37. A Delco-Remy CS voltage regulator:
    a. Requires a special tester
    b. Has a test hole for full-field testing
    c. Switches current at a fixed 800 Hz frequency
    d. Is mounted on the firewall

38. As a general rule, allowable total voltage drop on the starter motor circuits should be less than:
    a. 0.01 volt per connection
    b. 0.10 volt per connection
    c. 1.00 volt per connection
    d. 1.50 volts per connection

39. Generally, a starter motor brush should be replaced when it has worn:
    a. To one-quarter its original length
    b. To one-third its original length
    c. To one-half its original length
    d. Even with the brush holder

40. When rebuilding a starter motor, a growler is used to perform a/an:
    a. Armature short circuit test
    b. Capacity test
    c. Armature field winding test
    d. Pinion clearance test

41. Low no-load speed and low current draw during a starter free running, or no load, test is most likely caused by:
    a. Shorted fields
    b. Open shunt field
    c. Grounded insulated terminal
    d. Broken or weak brush springs

42. High no-load speed and high current draw during a starter free running, or no load, test is most likely caused by:
    a. Shorted fields
    b. Frozen shaft-bearings
    c. Grounded insulated terminal
    d. Broken or weak brush springs

43. Technician A says a self-powered test lamp can be used to check high resistance components, such as suppressor-type ignition cables. Technician B says a self-powered test lamp can be used to check fusible links. Who is right?
    a. A only
    b. B only
    c. Both A and B
    d. Neither A nor B

A6

44. The unit for measuring electrical resistance is called:
    a. Ohm
    b. Ampere
    c. Volt
    d. Circuit

45. Technician A says a battery is slow charged at a rate of about 3 to 15 amperes.
    Technician B says a battery is fast charged at a rate of up to 50 amperes.
    Who is right?
    a. A only
    b. B only
    c. Both A and B
    d. Neither A nor B

46. All of the following are basic electrical failures *EXCEPT*:
    a. Short circuit
    b. Open circuit
    c. Grounded circuit
    d. High circuit

47. Which of the following is the most likely cause of nothing happening when the ignition switch is turned to the Start position?
    a. Defective starter relay or solenoid
    b. Defective starter drive assembly
    c. Defective engine flywheel ring gear
    d. Poor flywheel/starter engagement

48. If a charging system is not charging at all or has a lower than normal charging rate, check for:
    a. Battery with an internal short that accepts a charge with little resistance
    b. Defective voltage regulator
    c. A faulty component drawing excessive current
    d. Defective starter motor

49. With headlamps that are dimmer than normal:
    Technician A says to check for high resistance in the headlamp power circuit.
    Technician B says to check for slipping drive belts.
    Who is right?
    a. A only
    b. B only
    c. Both A and B
    d. Neither A nor B

50. If a power window is inoperative, check for all of the following *EXCEPT*:
    a. Defective voltage regulator
    b. Defective motor
    c. Defective switch
    d. Open wiring circuit

ANSWERS

Chapter 1:
1. b, 2. a, 3. b, 4. d, 5. c, 6. b, 7. d, 8. b, 9. a, 10. a, 11. b, 12. a, 13. a, 14. c

Chapter 2:
1. d, 2. c, 3. a, 4. a

Chapter 3:
1. c, 2. d, 3. a, 4. c, 5. b, 6. a

Chapter 4:
1. c, 2. a, 3. c, 4. b, 5. b, 6. c, 7. b, 8. a, 9. b, 10. a

Chapter 5:
1. b, 2. b, 3. c, 4. d, 5. b, 6. a, 7. d, 8. a, 9. a, 10. c, 11. c

Chapter 6:
1. b, 2. d, 3. a, 4. b, 5. d, 6. c, 7. c, 8. a, 9. b, 10. c

Chapter 7:
1. c, 2. b, 3. d

Chapter 8:
1. b, 2. c, 3. d, 4. b, 5. a, 6. d, 7. c, 8. a, 9. c, 10. a, 11. c, 12. d, 13. c

Sample Test:
1. d, 2. b, 3. c, 4. d, 5. b, 6. a, 7. a, 8. c, 9. d, 10. b, 11. a, 12. a, 13. b, 14. c, 15. b, 16. b, 17. c, 18. a, 19. c, 20. a, 21. c, 22. c, 23. c, 24. b, 25. b, 26. c, 27. b, 28. d, 29. d, 30. c, 31. c, 32. c, 33. a, 34. b, 35. c, 36. d, 37. a, 38. b, 39. c, 40. a, 41. d, 42. a, 43. b, 44. a, 45. c, 46. d, 47. a, 48. b, 49. c, 50. a

GLOSSARY

Ammeter: An ammeter is an instrument used for measuring the current flow in an electrical or electronic circuit. Some ammeters are intended for use in direct current (DC) circuits; others are designed for alternating current (AC) circuits.

Ampere: The unit for measuring electrical current flow.

Analog Meter: A meter displaying values by the movement of a spring loaded needle.

Auto-ranging: A feature of most digital multimeters that automatically selects the appropriate test range without the need for operator input.

Available Voltage: The voltage that an electrical device can supply after all losses are taken into account.

Buss Bar: A solid metal strip used as a conductor and common connection point for wires and devices.

Capacitor: A capacitor is a passive electronic component that stores energy in the form of an electrostatic field. In its simplest form, a capacitor consists of two conducting plates separated by an insulating material called the dielectric.

Carbon Pile: Fixed or variable resistance load unit which simulates vehicle loads for battery and/or generator testing.

Cathode Ray Tube (CRT): An electron beam tube with a cathode at one end and an anode at the screen end. The "ray" of electrons shot from the cathode to the anode creates a pattern on the luminescent screen.

Clamping Diode: A diode installed to eliminate the voltage spike from a collapsing coil from damaging electronic systems.

Continuity: Continuous, unbroken; used to describe a working electrical circuit or component that is not open.

Data Link Connector (DLC): A dedicated point for attaching a scan tool to the vehicle communications network.

Diagnostic Trouble Code (DTC): A numeric or alphanumeric code assigned to a particular fault in an onboard electronic system.

Digital Meter: A meter that provides a numerical readout of the measured value.

Diode: An electrical "check-valve." Diodes allow current flow in one direction only.

Drive-by-Wire: A method of controlling the vehicle without control cables or rods. The throttle is actuated based on input from a potentiometer attached to the accelerator pedal.

Duty Cycle: The percentage of total time in one complete on-off-on cycle during which a solenoid is energized.

Electrolyte: The chemical solution, composed of sulfuric acid and water, that conducts electricity and reacts with the plate materials in a battery.

Field Circuit: The charging system circuit that delivers current to energize the generator field.

Forward Biased: The term applied to a diode when current is allowed to flow in the circuit.

Frequency: The number of periodic voltage oscillations, or waves, occurring in one second, usually expressed as Hertz (Hz) or cycles per second.

Gassing: The emission of hydrogen and oxygen gases from battery cells during charging.

Heat Shrink Tape: Similar to heat shrink tube but is applied like electrical tape then heated to seal.

Heat Shrink Tubing: Insulating tubing designed to shrink on wire repairs and seal the connection from moisture and short circuits.

Hold-In Winding: The coil of small-diameter wire in a solenoid that is used to maintain a magnetic field to hold the solenoid plunger in position once it has been pulled inside the coil.

Impedance: Impedance is an expression of the opposition that an electronic component, circuit, or system offers to the flow of current.

Light-Emitting Diode (LED): A gallium-arsenide diode that emits energy as light. Often used on automotive indicators.

Liquid Crystal Display (LCD): An indicator consisting of a sandwich of glass containing electrodes and a polarized fluid. Voltage applied to the fluid allows light to pass through it.

Ohm: The unit for measuring electrical resistance.

Ohmmeter: An ohmmeter is an instrument used to measure the resistance to current flow in a circuit or component. Ohmmeters must never be connected to "live" circuits.

Open Circuit: A circuit that is incomplete; current cannot flow in an open circuit.

Open Circuit Voltage: The electrical potential of a circuit when there is no current in it.

Oscilloscope: An oscilloscope is an instrument commonly used to display and analyze the waveform of electronic signals. In effect, the device draws a graph of the instantaneous signal voltage as a function of time.

Passive Restraint: A passenger restraint system that operates automatically without input from the driver or passengers.

Printed Circuit Board: A special circuit board with the electronic circuits encased in a thin film of plastic.

Pull-In Winding: The coil of large-diameter wire in a solenoid that is used to create a strong magnetic field to pull the solenoid plunger into the coil.

Radio Choke: A coil wound with fine wire and installed in a circuit to absorb oscillations that occur when the circuit is closed or opened.

Radio Frequency Interference (RFI): A form of electromagnetic interference, created by the ignition secondary circuits, that disrupts radio transmission.

Relay: An electromagnetic switch that uses a low amperage circuit to open and close a separate contact set that controls current in a high amperage circuit.

Resistance: Opposition to electrical current, usually expressed in ohms.

Resistor: An electric component that resists current flow, used to lower the voltage applied to another device such as a motor.

Reversed Biased: The term applied to a diode when it is blocking current flow.

Rheostat: A continuously variable resistor used to control current through a circuit.

Scan Tool: Typically a hand-held computer containing programaming allowing communication with the control modules.

Semiconductors: An electronic component that can either be an insulator or conductor depending on circuit design.

Solid-State: An electronic device consisting chiefly of semiconductors and related components.

Specific Gravity: The weight of a liquid relative to water, which has an assigned value of 1.0. In an automotive storage battery, the specific gravity is measured with a hydrometer. When corrected to a temperature of 80°F (27°C), the specific gravity of a fully charged battery falls in the 1.260 to 1.280 range.

Starting Safety Switch: A switch in the starting circuit that prevents the starter motor from engaging when the transmission is in a forward or reverse gear. Also known as a neutral start switch.

Starter Solenoid: An electromagnetic device consisting of an iron core surrounded by a wire coil. The core moves to perform mechanical work when electrical current is applied to the coil.

Stepper Motor: A small DC motor that moves or rotates in small increments known as steps.

Tape Drive: A flexible nylon or plastic belt equipped with slots to engage the drive motor sprocket.

Transducer: A device that converts, or transduces, one form of energy to another. A sensor is such a device, converting mechanical or hydraulic energy into a voltage signal.

Vacuum Florescent Display (VFD): An indicator in which electrons from a heated filament strike a phosphor material that emits light.

Volt: A unit of electrical pressure, or electromotive force (EMF).

Voltage Drop: The use or loss of voltage caused by resistance in a conductor or connection, or the circuit load(s).

Voltmeter: A voltmeter is an instrument used for measuring the potential difference, or voltage, between two points in an electrical or electronic circuit. Some voltmeters are intended for use in direct current (DC) circuits; others are designed for alternating current (AC) circuits.

Wave Rectification: A process by which the alternating current (AC) produced by a generator is converted to the direct current (DC) needed to charge the battery and power electrical devices on the vehicle.

A6

HEATING AND AIR CONDITIONING

CHAPTER OBJECTIVES

- The technician will complete the ASE task list on Air Conditioning System Diagnosis, Testing, and Service.
- The technician will be able to answer 13 questions dealing with the Air-Conditioning System Diagnosis, Testing, and Service section of the ASE Test.

Air-Conditioning (A/C) diagnosis begins with a preliminary inspection and an evaluation of system performance. Although there are a variety of A/C systems, preliminary inspection procedures are similar for all designs.

PRELIMINARY INSPECTION AND DIAGNOSIS

During a preliminary inspection, system components should be visually checked for proper mounting and signs of damage, modification, or oil leakage. Then, the level of performance is evaluated while testing the operation of the system.

VISUAL CHECK

Examine A/C components for:

- Drive belt deterioration, damage, or incorrect tension
- Loose compressor mounts or brackets and worn bushings
- Jammed or warped clutch hub, or pulley damage
- Loose or damaged compressor clutch wiring or connectors
- Blown or missing fuses or circuit breakers
- Leaking hoses, lines, and fittings
- Blocked or damaged condenser and evaporator fins

If the system passes a visual inspection, switch the A/C on and listen for unusual noises. If any of the visual checks reveal potential problems, correct the concern and then proceed to the performance tests.

Unusual Operating Noises

To diagnose a malfunctioning A/C system by sound, listen for:

- Grinding noise, or roughness when the compressor clutch is engaged—defective clutch bearing
- Heavy knocking sound at the compressor—internal damage
- Clicking at the compressor—internal wear
- Squeal, rubbing noise, accompanied by blower motor vibration, often increasing with fan speed—defective bushings at the blower motor armature shaft
- Squeal upon compressor engagement—defective drive belt
- Thumps, whines, bangs—system blockage or incorrect system pressures
- Honking noise—low refrigerant level

Sight Glass Diagnosis

Some of the **Thermostatic Expansion Valve (TXV)** systems utilize a sight glass to allow for a visual check of the presence of refrigerant, figure 1-1. Sight glass location varies by system design. It may be located in the liquid line between the receiver-drier and the TXV, figure 1-2, or as an integral part of the receiver-drier assembly. The sight glass is always located on the **high-side** of the system. The type of refrigerant used

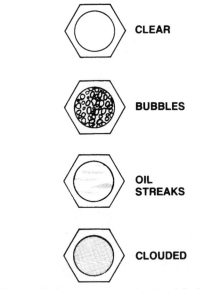

CLEAR

BUBBLES

OIL STREAKS

CLOUDED

Fig. 1-1. A sight glass provides a visual quick check of refrigerant condition.

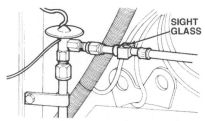

SIGHT GLASS

Fig. 1-2. Sight glass location varies between systems, but is always on the high-side.

High-Side: The portion of the A/C system in which the refrigerant is under high pressure and at high temperature. It includes the compressor outlet, condenser, receiver-drier, and expansion device inlet.

Thermostatic Expansion Valve (TXV): An expansion device that removes pressure from the refrigerant as it flows into the evaporator and also varies the refrigerant flow rate in relation to evaporator temperature.

in the A/C system determines how sight glass readings are evaluated.

Refrigerant-12 (R-12) Sight Glass

Because refrigerant is colorless, the sight glass should be clear. However, it is possible for an empty system to look clear. Looking into the sight glass of an empty system is like looking through an empty glass container. Other signs of an empty system include oil droplets or streaks on the glass.

A low refrigerant level, which allows vapor to enter the system through the pickup tube in the receiver-drier, is indicated by bubbles in the sight glass. As the system loses more refrigerant and takes in more vapor, the bubbles start to look like foam, and oil streaks may form across the glass. Recharge the system.

If refrigerant in the sight glass is a red or yellow color, the system contains leak-detecting dye. As long as the leaks have been repaired and the system is charged to specifications, no service is required.

Refrigerant-134a (R-134a) Sight Glass

Very few R-134a systems use a sight glass. If one is present, certain conditions must be met to get an accurate reading from the sight glass. Typically, a sight glass check is made when:

- Ambient temperature is below 95°F (35°C)
- Humidity is below 70 percent
- Engine speed is at 1,500 rpm
- The A/C switch is on
- Airflow is set to recirculate
- The blower fan is on high
- The temperature control is at the coldest position
- System high-side pressure is below 240 psi (1,670 kPa)

It is normal to see an almost transparent flow of bubbles that disappear at high throttle in an R-134a sight glass. If there are no bubbles, there is too much refrigerant in the system. A constant flow of bubbles, which can be transparent or frothy, indicates a low refrigerant level.

A faint foggy appearance indicates a very low refrigerant level. To repair, add refrigerant as needed.

If the sight glass is heavily fogged, the system may be contaminated by the wrong type of compressor lubricant. Mineral oil, as used in an R-12 system, reacts with R-134a, causing the foggy appearance and resulting in system damage. Repairs can range from a system flush and recharge to replacing the entire system.

Insight

Never diagnose an R-134a system based on sight glass appearance only. It is much less reliable than the R-12 version.

Smells and Temperatures

If condensation cannot drain from the evaporator, the water stagnates, bacteria grows in the water, and a foul odor results. The blower sends air through the evaporator into the passenger compartment and the air becomes contaminated with this smell. Clean the evaporator assembly and repair the evaporator case or drain tube so the condensation can drain.

Insight

There are several OEM Technical Service Bulletins (TSBs) available to aid in diagnosing and repairing evaporator odor issues.

A number of faults can be discovered by touching system parts. High-side components are normally warm or hot to the touch, while **low-side** components are cool or cold. When diagnosing the system by touch, use caution; move the back of your hand near the object, and touch it only if it does not seem extremely hot or cold, figure 1-3. Diagnose by touch as follows:

1. Check for frost on the outside of components, figure 1-4. Frost on the following parts indicates the problems listed:
   - Evaporator outlet could indicate a malfunctioning thermostatic switch
   - Expansion valve stuck shut or clogged with ice
   - Receiver-drier is restricted in the drier pickup tube or **desiccant** sleeve

2. Check the outlet line from the evaporator. It should be cool. If it is warm, the problem may be:
   - Little or no refrigerant in the system
   - No refrigerant pressure
   - The control system not allowing refrigerant release into the evaporator

3. On a TXV system, check the receiver-drier. It should be warm. On an orifice-tube system, the accumulator should be cool or cold.

4. Feel the temperature of the line leading from the condenser to the expansion device. It should be between very

Fig. 1-3. Exercise caution when diagnosing by touch because A/C components can be extremely hot or cold.

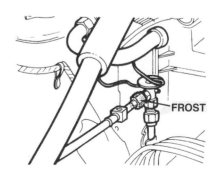

Fig. 1-4. Frost forming on certain components indicates a malfunction.

Desiccant: A chemical agent in the receiver-drier of an A/C system, used to remove moisture.
Low Side: The portion of the A/C system in which the refrigerant is under low pressure and at low temperature. It includes the expansion device outlet, evaporator, accumulator, and compressor inlet.

A7

warm and hot. If it is cold, there may be a restriction in the high-side.

5. Check that the evaporator outlet is the same temperature as or colder than the inlet. If not, check system pressures and refrigerant level.

6. Check the compressor cylinder head. If it is hot or the paint has burned off, the compressor outlet valve may be broken.

SYSTEM PERFORMANCE TESTING

System performance testing, which involves operating the system and evaluating its output, varies by system design. The first step is to determine what type of system is used.

Identifying the Type of System

Some compressors run whenever the A/C is on, while others cycle on and off. Compressors that run continuously are variable displacement units that respond to crankcase suction-pressure differential. Systems in which the compressor cycles on and off are referred to as Cycling Clutch Orifice Tube (CCOT) systems.

Another way to identify a system is by the controls, which may be mechanical, semiautomatic, or fully automatic, figure 1-5. Mechanical systems use hand-operated slide switches or rotary switches. Semiautomatic systems generally use a lever and cable assembly to regulate temperature settings and push-button switches for the other control features. Fully automatic systems often have digital temperature readouts and setting features.

An A/C system can also be identified by the refrigerant control or expansion device used in the system.

Expansion Devices

There are three types of expansion devices:

- Thermostatic expansion valve
- Fixed-orifice **expansion tube**
- **Variable-orifice expansion tube**

TXV Designs

Systems using a TXV are set up as shown in figure 1-6. There are two basic thermostatic expansion valve designs. One TXV design, which resembles the thermostat in the engine cooling system, is located in the evaporator inlet line, figure 1-7. The second TXV design has the valve encased in a thermostatic block valve or H-valve that installs on the inlet line to the evaporator. Regardless of design, a TXV may be mounted either in the engine compartment or on the evaporator case. In some systems, a capillary tube leads from the TXV to the evaporator to sense temperature, figure 1-8. The TXV inlet line, which is smaller than the outlet line, is warmer than the outlet during operation.

Cycling Clutch Orifice Tube (CCOT)

To visually identify a CCOT system, look for an accumulator in the line between the evaporator and the compressor. Also,

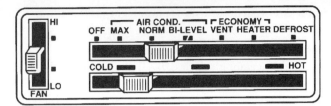
MECHANICAL CONTROLS

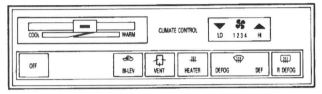
SEMIAUTOMATIC CONTROLS

FULLY AUTOMATIC CONTROLS

Fig. 1-5. Typical A/C control heads.

there is no receiver-drier in the line between the condenser and evaporator on an expansion tube system, figure 1-9.

Fixed Orifice Expansion Tube

The fixed orifice expansion tube, which separates the high- and low-pressure sides of the system, is contained in the inlet line to the evaporator. Typically, the expansion tube is either part of the hose leading to the evaporator or a separate part fitted inside the hose. The size of the fixed orifice is a compromise between system performance at idle and highway speeds, figure 1-10.

Variable Orifice Expansion Tube

The variable orifice expansion tube uses system pressure and refrigerant flow to move a metering piston in the sleeve, figure 1-11. When idling at high ambient temperatures, the piston shifts to a smaller metering area. This compensates for the reduced compressor output and increases the cooling performance.

Older Systems

There were other types of refrigerant control systems built in years past. A few of the systems were:

- Suction Throttling Valve (STV)
- Pilot Operated Absolute Pressure Valve (POA)
- Evaporator Pressure (EVP) Regulator

Expansion Tube: Also known as a fixed-orifice tube, this expansion device removes pressure from the refrigerant as it flows into the evaporator, but does not vary the flow rate.

Variable Orifice Expansion Tube: A type of expansion tube that varies the refrigerant flow rate to compensate for changes in compressor output.

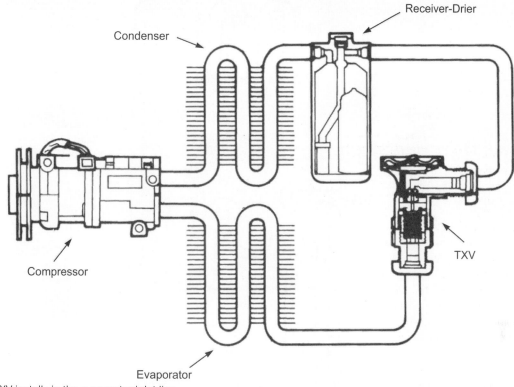

Fig. 1-6. A TXV installs in the evaporator inlet line.

With the phase-out of R-12 refrigerant few of these systems are serviced today. For more information on these systems consult the applicable service manual.

Performance Test

A performance test checks how well the system operates in all the driver selected modes. To conduct the performance test:

1. Make sure the shop area is adequately ventilated before running the engine.
2. With the A/C system operating at the maximum (MAX) setting, verify that all of the plenum air is directed through the evaporator.
3. Install a thermometer in a panel outlet or vent grille.
4. With the A/C set to MAX and the blower fan on high speed, close all the vehicle windows and doors.
5. Allow the engine to run at idle for 10 minutes.
6. Increase engine speed to between 1500 and 2000 rpm and check output temperature. Temperature should be in the 35 to 40°F (2 to 7°C) range.

If the system is not performing satisfactorily, use a manifold gauge set to check system pressures, figure 1-12.

A7

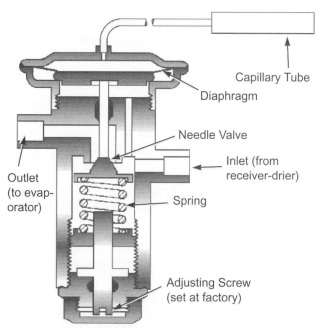

Fig. 1-7. This type of TXV resembles a thermostat in the engine cooling system.

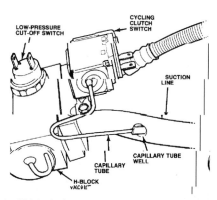

Fig. 1-8. An H-block thermostatic expansion valve with a capillary tube.

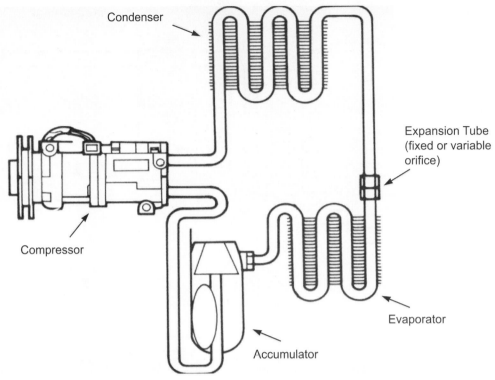

Fig. 1-9. Fixed and variable orifice expansion tubes are located in the inlet line to the evaporator.

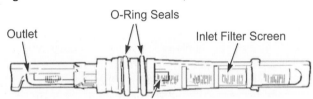

Fig. 1-10. The fixed orifice expansion tube.

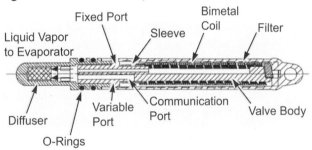

Fig. 1-11. The variable orifice expansion tube offers increased performance at lower speeds.

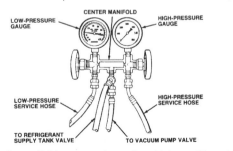

Fig. 1-12. A manifold gauge set monitors high- and low-side pressures.

MANIFOLD GAUGE TESTING

Until recently, all automotive A/C systems operated with R-12. Because R-12 is a **Chlorofluorocarbon** (CFC), it is being phased out and is no longer produced. All newer automotive A/C systems are designed to operate with R-134a. Although there are other refrigerant blends available from the aftermarket, these two (R-12 and R-134a) are the only ones approved by the vehicle manufacturers. Also, the two refrigerants are incompatible, so separate sets of gauges, tools, and supplies are required for each.

Identifying R-12 and R-134a Systems

In a typical R-134a system, each major component—the condenser, compressor, evaporator, pressure switch, expansion valve, and receiver-drier—has a label on it stating that it is designed for use with R-134a, figure 1-13. The hoses and fluid lines have similar labels.

Unique service valves are used for each refrigerant to help prevent contamination. An R-12 system usually has Schrader-type service valves, while metric-thread, quick-connect fittings are used on an R-134a system.

Using Manifold Gauge Sets

A manifold gauge set consists of the center manifold and two or three gauges. The gauge set is used to:

- Monitor the pressure inside an operating system
- Monitor and control the flow of refrigerant into the system during charging
- Access the system for discharging

Chlorofluorocarbon (CFC): A chemical compound containing chlorine, fluorine, and carbon. When released into the atmosphere, the chlorine atoms detach from the CFC molecules, causing a chemical reaction that turns ozone molecules into oxygen. Oxygen does not filter ultraviolet light as ozone does. Refrigerant-12 (CCl2F2) is a CFC.

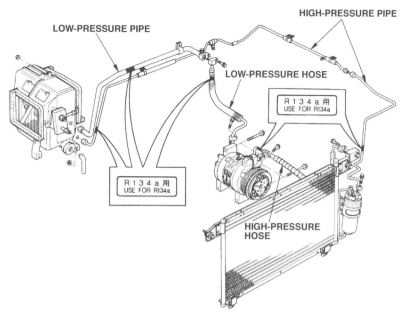

LOW-PRESSURE PIPE

HIGH-PRESSURE PIPE

LOW-PRESSURE HOSE

R 1 3 4 a 用
USE FOR R134a

R 1 3 4 a 用
USE FOR R134a

HIGH-PRESSURE HOSE

Fig. 1-13. Components designed to operate with R-134a are labeled accordingly.

Valves at either end of the gauge manifold control which system pressure, high-side or low-side, is applied to the central manifold area. One hose connects the low-pressure gauge to the low-pressure side of the system, and a second hose connects the high-pressure gauge to the high-pressure side. A third hose connection in the middle of the manifold is used for adding or removing refrigerant. An evacuation pump, refrigerant supply cylinder, or refrigeration oil canister attaches to the center fitting.

With both valves closed, the gauges register the pressure in each side of the system. Opening the low-side valve connects the low-side of the system through the manifold to the center port, so refrigerant can be added or removed. Opening the high-side valve connects the high-side to the central area of the manifold, exposing high-side pressure to the central connection. Typically, a low-pressure gauge registers between about 30 in-Hg (760 mm-Hg) of vacuum and 120 psi (830 kPa) of pressure. The high-side gauge reads pressure only, generally in the 0 to 600 psi (0 to 4,100 kPa) range.

Connecting the Fittings

Service valve locations vary; the easiest way to find them is first to identify the high- and low-sides of the system. Trace the refrigerant line that runs from the condenser to the compressor. This is the high-side of the system and the high-side service port will be somewhere in that line, often near the compressor outlet or on the receiver-drier. The refrigerant line that runs between the compressor suction port and the evaporator is on the low-pressure side, and the service valve is generally located in this line or on the accumulator. To connect a manifold gauge set:

1. Connect the low-pressure gauge hose to the service valve located between the evaporator and the compressor suction port
2. Connect the high-side pressure gauge hose to the high-side fitting between the compressor and orifice tube or TXV
3. The middle hose connection is for system service. Some gauge sets have a tee or splitter valve connection, for con-

necting the refrigerant supply and evacuation pump with separate valves

Threaded Schrader valves are the most common type of service port in R-12 systems, figure 1-14. Larger, metric-thread, quick-connect service valves are used on R-134a systems, figure 1-15. In both types of systems, the high- and low-side connectors are slightly different sizes to prevent attaching the gauges backwards. Follow these guidelines:

- Make sure the shutoff valves are within 12 inches (30 cm) of the service ends of the gauge hoses
- Close shutoff valves before removing them from the system service fittings

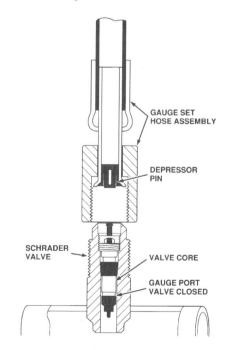

GAUGE SET HOSE ASSEMBLY

DEPRESSOR PIN

SCHRADER VALVE

VALVE CORE

GAUGE PORT VALVE CLOSED

Fig. 1-14. Schrader valve connections are used to service an R-12 system.

- Keep the gauge shutoff valves closed at all times when not in use
- After disconnecting the gauge hoses from a system, connect them to a recovery unit and remove any refrigerant from them

Manifold Gauge Procedures

Manifold gauges let you determine where and at what pressure to deliver refrigerant. The valve opens or closes a passageway to the center service port and hose. Some things to remember when using the valves:

- System testing—keep the valves closed so they read the pressures of each side of the system
- Discharging—connect the center port to a refrigerant recovery and recycling system and open both valves
- Leak-testing—with the engine off, connect the center service hose to a refrigerant supply, close the low-side valve, and open the high-side valve
- Vapor charging—connect a refrigerant supply to the center port, close the high-side valve, and open the low-side valve

Never vent R-12 or R-134a to the air; use a recovery system. When leak-testing, use a minimal amount of refrigerant of about one pound. After leak-testing, recover the refrigerant.

Evaluating Gauge Readings

The pressure read by the manifold gauges varies with refrigerant temperature. The low-side gauge monitors the pressure as the refrigerant enters the compressor, and the high-side gauge measures refrigerant pressure as it leaves the condenser or compressor. If the temperatures of either side are abnormally high or low, the pressure readings will also be abnormal.

Check specifications for normal pressures at various temperatures. Typical high-side readings for an R-12 system at an ambient temperature of about 90°F (32°C) are 180 to 205 psi (1240 to 1415 kPa). High-side pressure is slightly higher for an R-134a system, and typically ranges from about 215 to 240 psi (1470 to 1665 kPa) at the same temperature. On humid days, the high-side pressure will be at the high end of the range.

Gauge Readings and System Condition

When the gauges do not read the specified pressures, there is a system malfunction. Some abnormal readings and possible causes are described next.

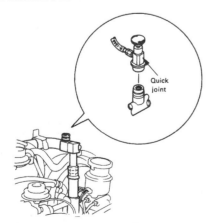

Fig. 1-15. An R-134a system has quick-disconnect type fittings on the service ports.

Low-side low and high-side low, figure 1-16

Condition 1

Low Side:	Low
High Side:	Low
Sight Glass:	Constant stream of bubbles
Evaporator Discharge Air:	Only slightly cool
Diagnosis:	Low refrigerant charge, possible leaks
Remedy:	Locate leaks. Discharge system. Locate and repair leaks. Recharge.

Condition 2

Low Side:	Very low
High Side:	Very low
Sight Glass:	No bubbles, no liquid evident or faint fog
Evaporator Discharge Air:	Warm
Diagnosis:	Refrigerant charge excessively low, possible serious leaks
Remedy:	Add partial refrigerant charge. Locate leaks. Discharge system and repair leaks. Recharge.

Condition 3

Low Side:	Very low pressure, or a vacuum
High Side:	Low
Evaporator Discharge Air:	Only slightly cool
Expansion Valve:	Inlet is cool, possibly frosted, or sweating heavily
Diagnosis:	Restricted TXV or orifice tube
Remedy:	Remove and inspect expansion valve inlet screen. If dirty, replace screen and receiver-drier. An orifice tube clogged with material can indicate a failing compressor.

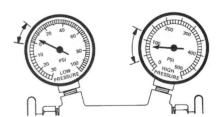

Fig. 1-16. A low refrigerant charge results in low pressure in both the high- and low-side.

Condition 4

Low Side:	Very low
High Side:	Low; may read normal to high if restriction is immediately downstream of the service valve
Evaporator Discharge Air:	Only slightly cool
Liquid Line:	Cool, possibly frosted, or sweating heavily
Receiver-Drier:	Possibly frosted or sweating heavily
Diagnosis:	Restriction in receiver-drier or liquid line
Remedy:	Discharge system, replace receiver-drier, liquid line, or other defective parts. Recharge.

Low-side cycles high and high-side normal, figure 1-17

Condition 5

Low Side:	Compressor cycles off higher than normal; compressor cycles close to normal; reduced cycle range
High Side:	Normal
Compressor:	Cuts in and out too rapidly
Diagnosis:	Defective thermostatic or pressure cycling switch
Remedy:	Replace thermostatic switch.

Condition 6

Low Side:	Compressor cycles off higher than normal; compressor cycles higher than normal
High Side:	Normal
Evaporator Discharge Air:	Warms excessively when compressor is off
Diagnosis:	Misadjusted thermostatic switch or defective pressure-cycling switch
Remedy:	Adjust or replace switch.

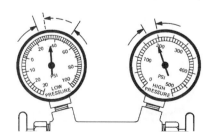

Fig. 1-17. A defective thermostatic switch causes a high low-side pressure with a normal high-side pressure.

Low-side high and high-side high, figure 1-18

Condition 7

Low Side:	High
High Side:	High
Sight Glass:	Possible occasional bubbles
Evaporator Discharge Air:	Warm
Liquid Line:	Very hot
Diagnosis:	Condenser malfunction, overcharge, or refrigerant contamination
Remedy:	Check condenser for obstructions and reduced airflow. Check engine cooling system performance, including clutch-type fan. Discharge, repair, and recharge system.

Condition 8

Low Side:	High
High Side:	High
Sight Glass:	Occasional bubbles
Evaporator Discharge Air:	Warm or only slightly cool
Diagnosis:	Large amount of air in system
Remedy:	Discharge system and replace receiver-drier or accumulator. Recharge.

Condition 9

Low Side:	High
High Side:	Normal to high
Evaporator Discharge Air:	Warm
Evaporator:	Heavy sweating
Suction Line:	Heavy sweating
Diagnosis:	Expansion valve stuck open or temperature-sensing bulb inoperative
Remedy:	Clean contact surfaces of sensing bulb and evaporator outlet pipe. Reinstall sensing bulb, making sure its metal band firmly secures it. If manifold pressures are still high, evacuate system, replace expansion valve and receiver-drier, and recharge. Recheck system for performance and leakage.

A7

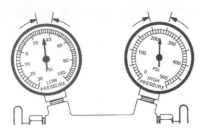

Fig. 1-18. Low-side high and high-side high pressures can be caused by a condenser malfunction, an overcharge, or contaminated refrigerant.

Low-side high and high-side normal, figure 1-19
Condition 10

Low Side:	High
High Side:	Normal
Evaporator Discharge Air:	Warm or only slightly cool
Diagnosis:	Insufficient high-side restriction or too short compressor "on-time"
Remedy:	Replace defective clutch cycling switch or missing O-ring at orifice tube.

Low-side high and high-side low, figure 1-20
Condition 11

Low Side:	High
High Side:	Low
Sight Glass:	Clear
Evaporator Discharge Air:	Warm or only slightly cool
Diagnosis:	Malfunctioning compressor
Remedy:	Verify the control valve is operating properly on a variable-displacement compressor system. Discharge system and

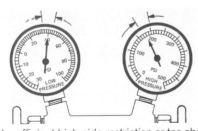

Fig. 1-19. Insufficient high-side restriction or too short compressor "on-time" causes low-side pressure to rise while high-side pressure restriction remains normal.

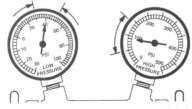

Fig. 1-20. A compressor malfunction causes high low-side pressure and low high-side pressure.

replace the compressor and receiver-drier or accumulator. Recharge.

Condition 12

Low Side:	Low
High Side:	Normal to low
Evaporator Outlet:	Cold or frosted
Diagnosis:	Restricted high-side
Remedy:	Replace restricted expansion device.

Low-side normal, high-side normal, poor cooling, figure 1-21
Condition 13

Low Side:	Normal but constant; does not indicate cycling or modulation
High Side:	Normal; may be slightly high or low
Sight Glass:	Possible occasional bubbles
Evaporator Discharge Air:	Only slightly cool
Diagnosis:	Some air or moisture in the system
Remedy:	Verify the control system is not adding heat to the air. Test for leaks, discharge, and repair as necessary. Replace receiver-drier or accumulator. Check compressor oil level. Recharge.

Condition 14

Low Side:	Normal; may drop into vacuum due to water freezing in the system
High Side:	Normal; will drop if low-side drops
Sight Glass:	Possible tiny bubbles
Evaporator Discharge Air:	Cold but becomes warm when low-side pressure drops into vacuum
Diagnosis:	Excessive moisture in system
Remedy:	Replace receiver-drier or accumulator. Evacuate and recharge.

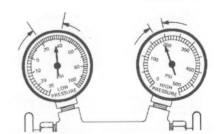

Fig. 1-21. Air or moisture can cause poor cooling, even with normal system pressures.

LEAK DETECTION TESTING

Leaking refrigerant is the main cause of A/C problems. Signs of leaks include:

- Low manifold gauge readings
- Oily deposits on fittings or hoses
- Foam, bubbles, or oil streaks at the sight glass

Always perform a leak test during routine service. Refrigerant leaks are often found where parts join together, especially if they are made of different materials. Parts that move in relation to each other, such as hoses that flex with engine torque, are also vulnerable. Refrigerant is heavier than air, so concentrations of leaking refrigerant are often found underneath components. Always check the entire system in case there is more than one leak, figure 1-22. Common leakage points include:

- Compressor seals
- Refrigerant line connections
- Pinholes in the accumulator, receiver-drier, evaporator, or condenser

A large leak is fairly easy to locate—look for oil on hoses, connections, or seals. If the system has been leaking for quite a while, the oily residue will collect dirt and appear greasy. However, not all leaks are easy to find. Besides a visual inspection, there are several ways to detect leaks:

- Leak detection with fluorescent dye
- Electronic leak detector

Dye Leak Detection

Dye leak detection involves charging the system with fluorescent dye. The dye does not cling to the refrigerant, but it mixes with the system lubricant. To check for leaks, add the dye, then run the air conditioner on high for about 15 minutes. Examine the system for dye leaking out of joints and connectors. An ultraviolet black light is used to find the dye that has leaked from the system. The dye remains in the system until the lubricating oil is changed. If no dye shows up, examine the system again after 24 hours. Once the leak is located, perform the needed repairs. Check the service manual before adding dye; doing so may void the warranty on some systems.

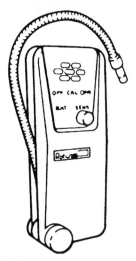

Fig. 1-23. A typical electronic leak detector sounds an alarm and lights a warning lamp when refrigerant is picked up by the sensing probe.

Electronic Leak Detection

Electronic leak detectors are the safest tool for tracking refrigerant leaks. A sensor at the end of a probe reacts to the refrigerant and triggers a light and tone, figure 1-23. Since R-12 and R-134a have different chemical compositions, a separate electronic leak detector is needed for each type of refrigerant. However, dual units that can be switched to sense one refrigerant or the other are available. Electronic detectors are sensitive, so a high concentration of refrigerant in the air may trigger them. To find exactly where the leak is, work in a well-ventilated area moving the probe around all suspect components and connections.

REFRIGERANT AND REFRIGERATION OIL

R-12 and R-134a are incompatible, as are the refrigeration oils used in the two systems. An R-12 system uses mineral oil, while an R-134a system uses a synthetic Polyalkylene Glycol (PAG) or ester oil. Using the wrong type of oil causes compressor failure.

Systems retrofitted for R-134a use usually have an ester oil, while factory installed R-134a systems use one of several PAG oil blends. Ester, mineral, and PAG oils are not compatible, so it is important to identify and top off a system with the correct oil.

Identifying Specified Refrigerant

R-12 is usually sold in white containers, while R-134a comes in a blue container. Recycled R-12 is also in white containers, marked with a Department of Transportation (DOT) code. Only properly trained and certified technicians may perform service procedures involving refrigerant charging, discharging, recovering, and recycling.

Recovering Refrigerant

In past years, technicians vented R-12 into the air when discharging A/C systems. Doing so is now illegal. You may not vent either R-12 or R-134a into the atmosphere. Select the correct recovery and recycling station, for either R-12 or R-134a, to collect refrigerant, figure 1-24. Each type of refrigerant requires a separate recovery and recycling system.

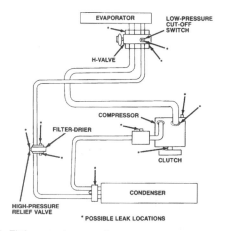

Fig. 1-22. Fittings and connections are common sources of refrigerant leaks; check the entire system for leakage when servicing the air conditioner.

A7

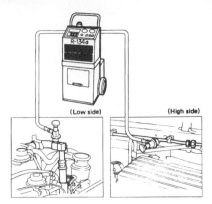

Fig. 1-24. Using a recovery and recycling station to discharge the system.

Due to the incompatibility of refrigerants and lubricants, it is important to determine what the system being serviced is charged with before beginning repairs. Be aware: Mixing refrigerants and oils not only damages the vehicle system, but also contaminates the recycling station, manifold gauge set, and other equipment used to service the system. Electronic refrigerant identifiers are available to reduce the chance of contamination. These units draw a small sample of refrigerant from the vehicle service ports, then analyze the chemical composition of the sample. Typically, an identifier works well for R-12 and R-134a, but will not recognize the aftermarket refrigerant blends.

Refrigeration Oil

Because the lubricating oil circulates with the refrigerant in an A/C system, discharging refrigerant into a recovery station removes oil from the system as well. Recycling equipment separates the oil from the refrigerant. When recharging the system, add the same amount of fresh oil as was removed. The system also loses refrigeration oil during component replacement. Most shop manuals specify how much oil to add after replacing each part. Remember to add mineral oil to an R-12 system and the correct synthetic to an R-134a system, and not to confuse the two. Follow the recommendation of the compressor manufacturer when selecting refrigerant oil.

Refrigerant oil is highly refined and dried to remove almost all water. The purity and dryness of the oil are crucial for proper system operation. When working with refrigerant oil:

- Keep oil containers sealed until use, as they attract moisture
- Store PAG oil in metal, not plastic, containers
- Keep fittings and surrounding areas clean
- Do not return used oil to the system; replace oil with the correct amount of fresh, clean oil
- Use the specified oil

The following steps help maintain the correct amount of oil in the system:

- Measure the amount of oil lost during system discharge, and add that much fresh oil
- Drain and measure the oil from replaced components, and add that amount of fresh oil
- Add the recommended amount of oil that does not drain from the inside of replaced components

SYSTEM SERVICE

An A/C system must be discharged before any fittings are opened for repairs. Once repairs are made, the system must be evacuated and charged to return it to working order.

Discharging and Evacuating the System

Discharge the system before removing or replacing any part. Recover the refrigerant, whether R-12 or R-134a, into a recovery tank and later recycle it. To minimize the amount of refrigerant escaping into the air:

- Use recovery equipment that has shutoff valves within 12 inches (30 cm) of the hose service ends
- Always follow the equipment instructions for using the recovery and recycling station

The following is a general refrigerant discharge and recovery procedure:

1. With the equipment shutoff valves closed, attach the hoses to the system service fittings.
2. Following equipment instructions, recover the refrigerant until the system shows vacuum.
3. Turn off the equipment for five minutes or longer.
4. Check system pressure:

   - If the system has pressure, repeat the recovery process
   - If the system holds a steady vacuum for two minutes, proceed

5. Close the equipment shutoff valves and disconnect them from the system service fittings.

Checking Compressor Oil Level

Inadequate lubrication is the most common cause of compressor failure. Contemporary compressors do not have oil reservoirs, they are lubricated by the refrigerant oil circulating in the system. A system that relies on the oil in the refrigerant as the sole source of lubrication generally contains about 5.5 to 6.5 ounces (160 to 190 ml) of oil. Older compressors with an oil reserve generally contain about 10 to 11 ounces (300 to 325 ml) of oil. Oil is lost from the system when:

- A part is replaced, but the amount of oil it contained is not replaced
- The system is discharged too rapidly
- System pressure is lost through a leak

Traditionally, replacement compressors for an R-12 system are filled with enough oil to charge the system. However, newer compressors are shipped dry so they can be used with either R-12 or R-134a and must be filled with the correct amount of the proper oil for the system being serviced.

Minimize oil loss by discharging the system only when necessary and keeping the discharge rate slow.

Cleaning the System

A/C refrigerant system flushing is normally recommended whenever a compressor fails or a desiccant bag ruptures. Refer to the OEM service manual for additional information when possible. If information is not available, use the following procedure to flush the A/C system:

1. Discharge the A/C system as previously described.
2. Disconnect all A/C refrigerant line fittings and discard O-rings.

3. Remove orifice tube or TXV and discard.

4. Use an approved flushing vessel and flushing liquid. Starting with the evaporator core, slowly force the liquid from the bottom of the core until liquid flows from the top of the core. Continue until only clean, clear liquid flows out of the top. Stop the flow and allow five minutes before draining.

5. Repeat step four to properly flush the condenser.

6. Place caps on one end of the A/C lines. Fill the lines with the flushing liquid and allow five minutes before draining the liquid.

7. Blow the lines, evaporator, and condenser out with pressure regulated dry nitrogen. (Shop air contains moisture and contaminants, which would re-contaminate the A/C system.)

8. Replace the accumulator or receiver-drier.

9. Install a new orifice tube or TXV.

10. If required, replace the compressor with a new or rebuilt unit. (Follow OEM specs for correct quantity of oil to be added.)

11. Before reconnecting the refrigerant lines, add the correct amount of oil to the accumulator, evaporator, and condenser required by the OEM's specifications. Tighten all lines and fasteners to OEM specifications.

12. Evacuate and recharge the A/C system as described in Chapter One.

Charging the System

Before charging a system, consult the factory shop manual for the vehicle you are working on. Determine what type of system it is, its capacity, and if the compressor oil must be filled before charging. There are two charging methods:

- Liquid charging—add liquid refrigerant through the high-side service valve with the compressor off; liquid charge only with the engine off
- Vapor charging—add gaseous refrigerant through the low-side service valve while the compressor is running

Know the system capacity to avoid overfilling it; as little as a quarter-pound overcharge can damage orifice tube systems. Factory systems state the capacity on a sticker located either on or near the compressor, or on the radiator support. An accurate way to monitor how much refrigerant is being added is to place the refrigerant tank on a scale and watch the weight decrease as the refrigerant is drawn into the system, figure 1-25.

Liquid Charging

A small amount of refrigerant can be liquid charged into the high-side of the system after evacuation. To completely liquid charge the system through the high-side, a pump is needed to force the refrigerant in. If the low-side service port is on an accumulator, the system can be liquid charged on the low-side while running the engine. On systems without an accumulator, first liquid charge the high-side, then switch over to the low-side and complete by starting the engine and vapor charging.

Liquid charging is quicker than vapor charging, but the compressor must not be running when the high-side service

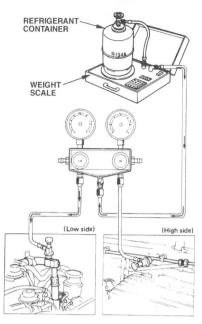

Fig. 1-25. Using a scale to charge a system by weight.

valve is open, as this can rupture the refrigerant container. Follow this procedure:

1. Attach manifold gauges to the system. Connect the service hose to a recovery station and discharge the system. Close both service valves to maintain the vacuum and disconnect the recovery station.

2. After connecting a vacuum pump to the manifold service hose, evacuate the system for at least 30 minutes. Close both valves when finished.

3. Connect the service hose to a refrigerant supply. Open the valve on the refrigerant supply to pressurize the service hose.

4. Open the high-side valve to direct the refrigerant supply into the high-side. The refrigerant container must be turned upside down or the valves on a bulk dispenser or charging station must be set correctly so that liquid refrigerant enters the system.

5. Close the high-side valve before changing refrigerant containers. Connect the new container to the service hose and open the high-side valve.

6. Complete system charging with the specified amount of refrigerant, adding new containers as necessary. Do not overcharge.

7. Turn the refrigerant supply valve off, close the manifold valve, and run the engine for about a minute to stabilize the system.

8. Check system performance.

9. Remove the manifold gauges, and replace all protective caps.

Vapor Charging

Vapor charging is the process of adding refrigerant through the low-side service valve while the compressor is running. Vapor charging can be performed from pound cans, drums, bulk cylinders, and charging stations. Vapor charge a system as follows:

1. Attach manifold gauges to the system. Connect the service hose to a recovery station and discharge the

A7

system. Close both service valves to maintain the vacuum and disconnect the recovery station.

2. After connecting a vacuum pump to the manifold service hose, evacuate the system for at least 30 minutes. Close both valves when finished.

3. Connect the service hose to a refrigerant supply. Open the refrigerant supply valve to pressurize the service hose.

4. Open the high-side valve with the engine off. Observe the low-side gauge to be sure the system is not restricted. Close the valve.

5. Open the low-side valve to direct the refrigerant supply through the low-side service valve. When charging from a bulk source, be sure to position the valves so that only vapor is added. When charging from a canister, it must be upright so liquid does not enter the system.

6. Start and run the engine at about 1,200–1,500 rpm with the A/C control lever OFF.

7. Engage the compressor by setting the control lever to NORM and the blower speed on HIGH. This draws in refrigerant faster. Be sure to add only vapor when the system is running.

8. Add the specified amount of refrigerant. Do not over-charge.

9. Turn the refrigerant supply valve off, close the manifold valves, and run the engine for about a minute to stabilize the system.

10. Check system performance.

11. Remove the manifold gauges and replace all protective caps.

CHAPTER QUESTIONS

1. A clicking noise at the compressor is likely to signal:
   a. Loose compressor mounts
   b. A defective compressor clutch bearing
   c. Liquid refrigerant entering the compressor
   d. Internal damage to the compressor

2. The most likely cause of a thin stream of bubbles visible in the sight glass of an R-12 system with the engine running at idle would be:
   a. Too much refrigerant
   b. Low refrigerant level
   c. Normal operation
   d. Too much oil in the system

3. Frost on the evaporator suction hose indicates a defective:
   a. Expansion valve
   b. Evaporator
   c. Receiver-drier
   d. Compressor

4. Which type of A/C system has an accumulator in the evaporator-to-compressor line but no receiver-drier in the evaporator inlet line?
   a. Externally equalized combination-valve
   b. Valves In Receiver (VIR)
   c. Pilot Operated Absolute (POA)
   d. Cycling Clutch Orifice Tube (CCOT)

5. When running the A/C system to check performance, do all of the following *EXCEPT*:
   a. Put the blower on HIGH
   b. Block all but one vent
   c. Close the car doors and windows
   d. Let the engine idle for 10 minutes

6. The service valves on an R-134a system are:
   a. Twist-on valves
   b. Schrader valves
   c. Stem valves
   d. Quick-connect valves

7. When using manifold gauges to test an A/C system:
   a. Open both valves
   b. Open only the high-side valve
   c. Open only the low-side valve
   d. Keep both valves closed

8. The most likely cause of low pressure on both the high- and low- sides, and frost on the expansion valve inlet of an A/C system would be:
   a. Expansion valve may be starved of refrigerant
   b. Expansion valve stuck closed
   c. Expansion valve stuck open
   d. Condenser malfunction or overcharge

9. The best way to leak check an R-134a system is with a(n):
   a. Leak-detecting dye
   b. Halide torch
   c. Electronic detector
   d. Chlorine torch

10. Leak-checking with dye may:
    a. Void the system warranty
    b. Cause compressor failure
    c. Cause desiccant deterioration
    d. Clog the expansion valve

11. When discharging refrigerant from an A/C system:
    a. Capture escaping refrigeration oil for reuse
    b. Discharge the refrigerant into an empty can
    c. Open only the high-side service valve
    d. Continue until the system shows vacuum

12. The type of oil used in an R-134a system is:
    a. Polyalkylene glycol oil
    b. Mineral oil
    c. Hypoid compressor oil
    d. Type F synthetic oil

13. To minimize refrigerant release into the atmosphere, the length of the hose between the service equipment shutoff valves and the service connections should be less than:
    a. 6 inches (15 cm)
    b. 12 inches (30 cm)
    c. 18 inches (45 cm)
    d. 24 inches (60 cm)

14. The most common cause of compressor failure is:
    a. Liquid refrigerant entering the compressor
    b. Too much refrigerant in the system
    c. Not enough refrigerant in the system
    d. Not enough lubricant circulating through the compressor

15. During liquid charging, the:
    a. Compressor should be running
    b. High-side service valve should be open
    c. Low-side service valve should be open
    d. Engine cooling fan should be running

A7

CHAPTER TWO

REFRIGERATION SYSTEM COMPONENT DIAGNOSIS AND REPAIR

CHAPTER OBJECTIVES

- The technician will complete the ASE task list on Refrigeration System Component Diagnosis and Repair.
- The technician will be able to answer 10 questions dealing with the Refrigeration System Component Diagnosis and Repair section of the A7 ASE Test.

The refrigeration system includes the compressor and clutch, evaporator, condenser, lines and hoses, valves, and other related parts. Since all of these components contain pressurized refrigerant, the system must be discharged and recovered before repairs that involve loosening fittings are made.

COMPRESSOR AND CLUTCH

The compressor and clutch work together to develop and maintain optimum system pressures. When either unit fails, the system cannot operate. The clutch, which drives the compressor, is belt-driven by the engine crankshaft. A worn or incorrectly adjusted drive belt or a slipping clutch reduces compressor efficiency and system performance suffers.

Drive Belt Service

Some engine systems use a single, long serpentine belt to drive accessories while others use several drive belts. With either type, check for:

- Glazing, deterioration, cracking, or fraying—replace as needed, figure 2-1
- Age—replace belts at 48,000 miles (76,000 km), or 4 years, or the recommended interval
- Improper tension—check with a tension gauge, figure 2-2.

To replace a V-type drive belt:

1. Loosen the belt-drive unit and rotate it to relieve belt tension.
2. Slip the belt off of the pulleys.
3. Install the new belt, making sure the V-shape of the belt rests in the pulley groove.
4. Rotate the drive unit to tighten belt tension.
5. Tighten fasteners to specified torque.

To replace a serpentine drive belt:

1. Attach a breaker bar or suitable tool to the adjustment socket on the tensioner, figure 2-3.
2. Swing the breaker bar to move the tensioner pulley and relieve belt tension, and hold it in that position.
3. Slip the belt from the pulleys and release the tensioner.
4. Fit the new belt by routing it around all the accessories, then lever the tensioner down and slip the belt onto the tensioner pulley.

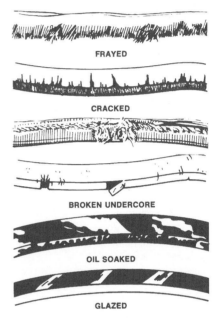

Fig. 2-1. Replace drive belts that are glazed, broken, oil soaked, cracked, or frayed.

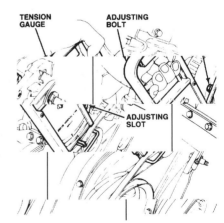

Fig. 2-2. Use a tension gauge to make sure drive belts are correctly adjusted.

5. Once the belt is in place, remove the lever so the tensioner pulley applies the correct tension.

Check specifications for the correct replacement belt. A correctly installed V-belt should ride on the sides of the pulley, not the bottom. The top of the belt should be flush with or not more than about 0.06 inch (1.5 mm) above the top of the pulley grooves, figure 2-4. With dual drive belts, replace both belts

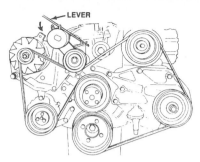

Fig. 2-3. Typical serpentine belt layout with an automatic tensioner.

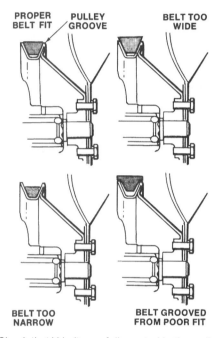

Fig. 2-4. Check that V-belts are fully seated in the pulley grooves.

as a set—if one is bad, the other probably is too, and tension is unequal on mismatched belts. When installing a serpentine belt, be sure its grooves contact all the pulleys correctly.

Compressor Clutch Diagnosis and Service

Common compressor clutch failures include:

- Open field windings
- Slippage due to low supply voltage
- A seized or warped hub assembly
- A damaged or bent pulley
- A defective bearing

Begin troubleshooting at the field windings. Check the power and ground wire connections leading from the field coil. If they are good, the problem may be open windings in the coil preventing clutch operation or shorted field windings drawing excess current and blowing fuses. A field coil receiving a low voltage supply does not engage the clutch properly, resulting in slippage. Check the power supply with a voltmeter.

The clutch seizes if damaged or warped, or if the clutch plate surface is contaminated. Check the pulley to see if it is bent or damaged. Damage to the clutch hub or pulley can cause slippage, failure to engage, or failure to disengage. The clutch bearing should not fail if the drive belt tension is correct

and the bearing dust seal is intact. If the bearing wears due to incorrect belt tension or contamination, replace it and the belt.

Checking Compressor Clutch Operation

The compressor clutch engages to drive the compressor shaft only when there is current through the clutch field winding. If the compressor operates with no current applied to the windings, the clutch is faulty. Another problem that may cause a clutch malfunction is a leaking front compressor seal that allows refrigerant and oil to escape from the system. The oil can contaminate the clutch and cause slippage. To check clutch operation:

1. Switch the engine off and disconnect the compressor clutch power wire.
2. Use a jumper wire with an inline fuse to connect the clutch field winding to the positive battery terminal. The clutch should engage. If it does not:

   - Check the ground connection at the clutch
   - Check the clutch coil winding resistance; if open, replace the coil or clutch assembly

3. Make sure that when the clutch engages, the compressor shaft turns. If it does not, inspect the clutch.
4. With the A/C off, start the engine. If the clutch engages, remove the power wire to the clutch. If the compressor still turns, the clutch is seized and must be replaced.
5. Run the engine at 1,500 rpm with the A/C on MAX. Ensure that the clutch engages and the compressor turns.
6. With the clutch engaged, connect and disconnect the power lead to the clutch. The clutch should engage and disengage without excessive slippage. If it slips, check for:

   - Inadequate voltage or ground at the clutch field coil
   - Excessive air gap between the armature and pulley assembly
   - Excessive friction or binding limiting armature travel
   - Oily or worn clutch surfaces
   - A partially or fully seized compressor

7. Use an ohmmeter to measure coil resistance, figure 2-5. If it is not within specifications, reverse the ohmmeter leads and check again. If resistance is still not within specifications, replace the coil assembly.

Most late model automotive Heating, Ventilation, and Air Conditioning (HVAC) systems rely on the Powertrain Control Module (PCM) to engage or disengage compressor operations in response to the driver's request as well as other conditions. To control the clutch engagement, the PCM uses various inputs such as high or low pressure sensors in the A/C system and engine sensors like the Throttle Position (TP) Sensor, Engine Coolant Temperature (ECT) Sensor, etc.

For instance, when the A/C high-side pressure exceeds a predetermined point, the PCM opens the circuit to the compressor clutch relay. This action disengages the clutch and allows pressure to remain at a safe level. Conversely, when the A/C system pressure is very low, indicating the possible loss of refrigerant, the PCM will not energize the relay control circuit preventing compressor operation. This action prevents compressor damage from the lack of circulating oil.

A7

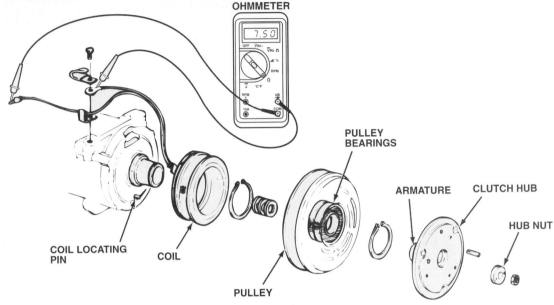

Fig. 2-5. Checking compressor clutch coil winding resistance with an ohmmeter.

Follow the appropriate OEM procedures when diagnosing a PCM controlled compressor clutch. When replacing the PCM because of a compressor clutch failing to engage, the integrity of the compressor clutch diode must be checked. This diode protects the vehicle electronic systems from the voltage spike that occurs when the clutch coil is de-energized. If the diode is defective, the new PCM may be damaged as well.

Servicing Compressor Clutches

Although the clutch mating surfaces eventually scar from normal operation, a badly scarred clutch can slip. If clutch wear is suspected, remove the clutch assembly and inspect the mating surfaces for cracks, heat checks, and scars that are deeper than 0.050 inch (1.3 mm). Replace the clutch if damage is found. Typical service procedures for the compressor clutch include:

- Clutch removal
- Bearing replacement
- Field coil replacement
- Clutch installation

Clutch Removal

Special tools, which are unique to the compressor being serviced, are generally required to remove the clutch for repairs or replacement. Failure to use the proper pulleys and seal removers can damage the compressor. To remove the clutch:

1. Remove the drive belt from the compressor pulley.
2. If there is enough room to work on the compressor clutch while it is on the vehicle, leave it in place. Otherwise, discharge the system, remove and cap the refrigerant lines, and remove the compressor from the vehicle.
3. Disconnect the clutch electrical wiring.
4. Remove the clutch plate and hub, which are held to the compressor shaft with a retaining nut or Torx-head screw. For most clutches, a special hub-retaining tool is used to prevent the clutch plate from rotating while removing the nut, figure 2-6. Never place the hub in a vise.
5. Some compressors have a snapring behind the clutch plate that retains the clutch assembly. If so, remove it, figure 2-7.

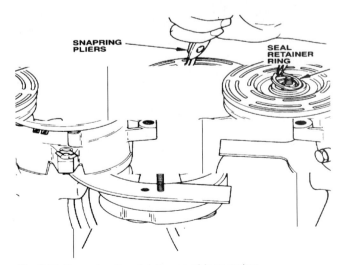

Fig. 2-6. Using a hub retaining tool to remove the clutch hub nut.

Fig. 2-7. Removing the clutch assembly snapring.

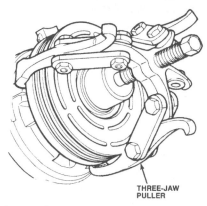

Fig. 2-8. Using a puller to remove the clutch assembly from the compressor.

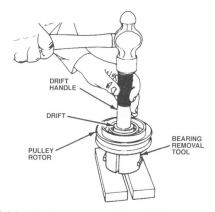

Fig. 2-9. Driving the bearing out of the clutch assembly.

6. Use a special puller to separate the clutch assembly from the compressor shaft, figure 2-8.

When removing a clutch, do not apply pressure to the compressor shaft unless specifically recommended by the manufacturer. Generally, the puller seats on a shaft sleeve to prevent internal compressor damage. Do not attempt to pry the clutch off, as this can damage the assembly, which is often made of aluminum.

Clutch Pulley Bearing Replacement
If the clutch pulley bearing is worn, replace it:

1. Remove the clutch assembly.
2. Most clutch bearings are press-fit in place and also have a snapring. Remove the snapring.
3. Support the clutch on a fixture and use a bearing driver and a soft-faced hammer to remove the old bearing from the housing, figure 2-9.
4. Inspect the old bearing to determine what caused it to fail, and correct any related compressor problems. For example, if the bearing is dirty, check seals for damage, and replace as needed.
5. Press or drive the replacement bearing into the housing using the appropriate tools to prevent damage during installation. Fully seat the bearing against the ridged stop.
6. Install the bearing snapring, if used.
7. Install the clutch assembly on the compressor and return the system to working order.

Field Coil Replacement
When there is a problem with the field coil, the clutch does not work properly. Field coils fail when the:

- Windings are open or shorted
- Connections from the wire harness to the field coil fail

Field coils have a nominal resistance of about 3 to 5 ohms, and carry a current between 2.5 and 3.5 amperes. When checking the field windings, keep the following in mind:

- Shorted windings produce higher current and lower resistance readings
- Open or resistive connections cause lower current and higher resistance readings

Field coils are encased in epoxy. If the problem is in the coil winding itself, replace the entire field coil. Resistive or intermittent connections can be repaired. To replace a field coil on a stationary-field clutch:

1. Remove the compressor clutch assembly.
2. Remove the fasteners holding the field coil in place—some units attach to the compressor housing with screws; others are retained by a snapring.
3. Check field coil resistance, and inspect mounting surfaces and electrical connections. Repair connections as needed and replace the field coil if resistance remains out of specifications.
4. Install the replacement unit by attaching it at the mounting surface with the screws or snapring.
5. Install the clutch assembly. Verify that the armature-to-pulley air gap is within specifications, then connect the electrical circuits and route wiring away from moving parts.

Compressor Clutch Installation
To install the compressor clutch:

1. Reinstall the stationary field coil.
2. Align the clutch with the compressor shaft keyway. Make sure the clutch is squarely aligned with the front of the compressor.
3. Using the correct installation tools, press, or drive with a soft-faced hammer, the clutch assembly onto the shaft until it seats against the locating ridges. Do not use excessive force.
4. Reinstall the snapring, if used.
5. Reinstall the front locking nut or bolt and tighten to specified torque.
6. Check the air gap and compare to specifications.
7. Spin the pulley. It should rotate freely and evenly.
8. Reinstall the compressor onto the vehicle. Reconnect the electrical circuits and install the drive belt.
9. Evacuate and charge the system. Then check compressor clutch and system operation.

Compressor Service
Overhauling a compressor is time-consuming and requires an assortment of special tools, so most shops simply replace a failed unit with a new or rebuilt one.

A7

Compressor Mechanical Failure

Damaged internal parts can also cause compressor failure. Damage to the pistons, cylinder walls, swash-plates, and other parts may be caused by:

- Insufficient refrigerant or lubricant
- Incorrect oil
- Collision damage
- System contamination
- Debris in the cylinder
- Incorrect assembly or disassembly

Inadequate lubrication is the most common cause of compressor failure; lack of lubrication causes excessive friction and overheating, which results in seized parts. Replace a seized compressor.

Compressor Contamination

Damage to A/C system parts can contaminate the compressor. Also, improper evacuation and charging procedures leave moisture in the system, which forms corrosive acids. If the compressor is contaminated, drain the oil to clean it, or replace it.

Removing and Replacing Compressors

Correct removal and replacement procedures for the compressor minimize system contamination and prevent damage to hoses, connectors, and other components. Although exact procedures vary by model, most can be removed using the following general guidelines:

1. Disconnect electrical wiring at the compressor.
2. Discharge the system using a recovery and recycling station. Recycle the refrigerant and measure the oil lost from the system.
3. Remove accessory drive belts as needed.
4. Separate the hose fittings from the compressor and immediately seal or cap all openings to prevent moisture and dirt from entering the system.
5. Remove the fasteners holding the compressor to its mounting brackets, and lift the compressor and clutch assembly from the vehicle as a unit.

Flushing may be recommended to assure there would not be any contaminants remaining in the A/C system from a failed compressor, plugged orifice tube, receiver-drier, or accumulator. At the time of doing an R-12 to R-134a retrofit some manufacturers suggest flushing the system also.

When installing a replacement compressor, make sure the new unit contains the correct amount of the recommended oil, tighten all fasteners to specified torque, and fit a new drive belt and adjust it to the correct tension. If contamination or moisture damage is found in the old compressor, install a new receiver-drier as well. Be aware, receiver-drier or accumulator replacement may be required for warranty by the compressor rebuilder. Then, evacuate and charge the system with the correct amount of the proper refrigerant and operate the system to check performance.

Compressor Testing

Troubleshooting the compressor involves diagnosing the entire A/C system. The following hints are specific to the compressor.

Diagnosing Cycling Clutch Compressors

For a **cycling clutch** compressor, diagnose the cycling pattern. A rapid pattern, when the compressor runs for only a short time then shuts off, indicates a quickly dropping low-side pressure causing the pressure cycling switch to shut the compressor off. Rapid cycling may be caused by:

- Very low refrigerant level
- Restricted fixed-orifice tube

The opposite condition, a slow cycling pattern where the compressor runs longer than normal, occurs when the compressor cannot pull the low-side system pressure down far enough. During a long cycling pattern, the pressure cycling switch stays closed and the compressor continues to run.

Irregular compressor cycling, a combination of cycles that are too long or too short, is often caused by a faulty pressure cycling switch. Irregular cycling results in poor cooling, and possible causes are:

- Pressure cycling switch closing pressure too high—the compressor stays off too long; if the switch sticks open, the compressor does not engage at all
- Closing pressure too high—the compressor switches on too quickly and the off cycle is too short, possibly causing evaporator freeze-up
- Opening pressure too low—the compressor shuts off too quickly, shortening the cooling cycle
- Opening pressure too high—the compressor stays on too long, possibly causing overcooling and evaporator freeze-up

Noise and Vibration

Grinding or banging noises from a running compressor indicate mechanical failure. To diagnose a compressor-related noise or vibration complaint:

1. Listen carefully while operating the system. Some system noise is normal. If in doubt, compare the noise and vibration levels to a similar system.
2. Check for missing or damaged compressor mounting bolts, bushings, and brackets. Tighten and replace as necessary.
3. Check for damaged or worn idler pulley, clutch, or clutch bearings. Check for damaged, loose, or misaligned drive belts. Replace or tension belts as necessary.
4. Check for debris that may be blocking the condenser and causing high system pressures. Check the engine cooling fan; an inoperative fan causes high system pressure.
5. With the engine running at idle, listen to and watch the clutch to make sure it is not hitting or rubbing against other parts.
6. If the noise comes from the front of the compressor, engage and disengage the clutch while the engine is idling to see if the noise stops or gets louder. If the noise gets louder or stops, check the clutch pulley bearing for wear or damage.

Cycling Clutch: A system that maintains refrigerant pressure by engaging and disengaging the electromagnetic compressor clutch.

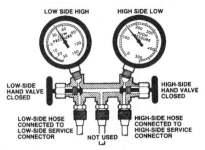

Fig. 2-10. Internal compressor damage often results in high pressure on the low-side and low pressure on the high-side.

7. Perform a system pressure check. If the pressures are abnormally high or low, diagnose and replace components as needed.
8. Run the engine at 1,500 RPM. Listen for excessive rumble or knock that disappears when the clutch engages or disengages. Repair or replace the compressor as necessary.

To check a compressor for seizure:

1. Switch off the engine, and make sure the clutch is not engaged.
2. Remove the drive belt and try to turn the compressor shaft by hand.
3. If you hear grinding or feel resistance, the compressor is likely seized or the bearings are worn.

Checking Compressor Operating Pressures

Characteristic manifold gauge readings from a fully charged but damaged compressor are high on the low-side and low on the high-side, figure 2-10. Typically, these conditions cause the compressor to be noisy with warm or only slightly cool discharge air from the evaporator. Poor compressor performance can be caused by:

- Defective reed valves
- Leaking compressor head gasket
- Worn or scored pistons, rings, or cylinders

EVAPORATOR, CONDENSER, AND RELATED PARTS

Along with the compressor, the evaporator and condenser are major A/C components. Hoses, fluid lines, the receiver-drier, and expansion and suction throttling devices handle and regulate the flow of refrigerant through the major components. Replacing any of these components requires evacuating the system.

Mufflers and Filters

Some systems use mufflers to control refrigerant flow noise, and a filter to purify the refrigerant may be used as well. Inline filters are increasingly important for keeping systems clean. An inline filter can remove up to 90 grams of debris from a system and still allow adequate refrigerant flow, figure 2-11. Mufflers and filters cannot be repaired and are replaced if damaged or clogged.

Hoses and Fluid Lines

If hoses or fluid lines develop leaks, repair the connection or replace the hose, fluid line, or fitting.

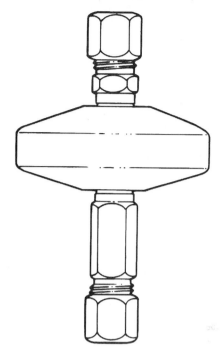

Fig. 2-11. An inline filter removes debris and contaminants.

Repairing Leaking Hoses

To repair a leak at a hose connection:

1. Slightly loosen then retighten the connection. Circulate air around the joint, then recheck it with a leak detector.
2. On O-ring connections, it may be necessary to discharge the system and replace the O-ring. Be sure to clean joint surfaces and lightly lubricate the new O-rings with fresh refrigeration oil. Tighten the connection, recharge the system, and check the joint with a leak detector.
3. If the line has replacement-type hose connections, tighten the hose clamp. Make sure that the clamp is correctly positioned.

If tightening the connection does not stop the leak, replace the hose with one of the same diameter, grade, length, and fittings as the old hose. Too-long or too-short hoses are prone to vibration damage. Also, a barrier-type hose is required for R-134a service and recommended for replacing any refrigerant hose.

Many late-model AC hoses have spring-lock fittings that require a special tool to remove them, figure 2-12. A damaged O-ring, loose or broken garter spring, debris, or corrosion can cause spring-lock fittings to leak. To repair:

1. Separate the coupling.
2. Remove the old O-rings with a plastic tool to prevent damage to the tubing, figure 2-13.
3. If the garter spring is loose, broken, or damaged, use a small wire hook to pull it out of the cage. Install a new spring.
4. If needed, polish the inside of the female coupler with 600-grit emery cloth, then thoroughly clean it.
5. Lubricate new O-rings with the proper refrigeration oil, then install them.
6. Lubricate the inside of the female end, then join the coupler.

A7

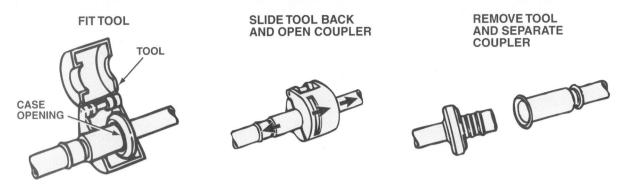

Fig. 2-12. Spring-lock couplings require a special tool that clamps around the fitting and is slid back to expand the garter spring so the coupler can be separated. Fit new O-ring before reconnecting.

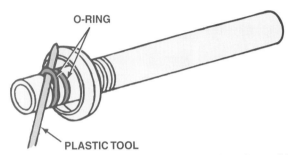

Fig. 2-13. Carefully remove O-rings with a plastic tool to avoid damaging the tubing.

Replacing Refrigeration Lines

Replace rigid refrigeration lines in the case of collision damage, improperly tightened connections, or internal corrosion. Use new lines from the manufacturer for the best results.

Condenser and Evaporator

The condenser and evaporator are particularly susceptible to collision damage and plugging. Both can leak when cracks develop at seams and other stress points.

Condenser and Evaporator Inspection

Replace a condenser or evaporator if it has:

- Collision damage
- Leaks
- Unremovable clogging or debris
- Corrosion from moisture contamination

Symptoms of a defective condenser or evaporator include:

- Excessive high-side pressures, possibly with the pressure relief valve venting excess pressure and frost on the discharge line
- Severe compressor damage, suggesting that debris has contaminated the condenser
- Refrigerant loss, indicating possible leaks at the evaporator or condenser
- Areas of localized frost

Condenser and Evaporator Service

In cases of extreme contamination, collision damage, or irreparable leaks, replace the condenser or evaporator. Use these guidelines:

- Do not remove the replacement part from its sealed bag until just before installation

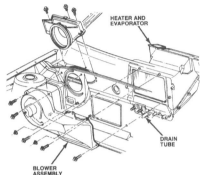

Fig. 2-14. The ventilation system plenum or module may need to be disassembled to remove the evaporator.

- Do not remove the protective plugs from hose connectors prior to installing the hoses
- Make sure all connections are clean
- Lightly lubricate connectors with fresh refrigeration oil before installation
- Tighten connections to specifications

Evaporator Replacement

Procedures for removing and installing an evaporator vary by vehicle. The following general guidelines apply to any installation:

1. Discharge the system using a recovery and recycling station, recycle the refrigerant, and measure how much refrigeration oil was extracted.
2. If the evaporator and heater core are one unit, drain the cooling system.
3. Disconnect any electrical harnesses or thermostatic devices attached to the evaporator.
4. Disconnect, and immediately cap or seal, the refrigerant hoses from the evaporator.
5. Evaporator removal may require disassembling the ventilation system plenum or module, figure 2-14. Follow shop manual procedures.
6. Drain and measure any oil in the old evaporator.
7. Fit the new evaporator in place and connect the hoses using new O-rings. Coat hose connections with clean refrigeration oil to aid installation.
8. Add enough fresh refrigeration oil to replace the amount lost during discharge and evaporator removal, and also add the recommended amount of oil to compensate for what did not drain from the evaporator.

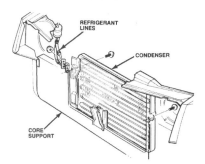

Fig. 2-15. The condenser generally attaches to the radiator core support with sheet-metal screws.

9. Evacuate and recharge the system, then check the system for leaks.

Condenser Replacement

To remove and install a condenser:

1. Discharge the system using a recovery and recycling station, recycle the refrigerant, and measure how much refrigeration oil was extracted.
2. Remove the fan shroud, radiator, grille, trim panels, or other items required to gain access to the condenser, figure 2-15.
3. Disconnect and seal or cap the refrigerant lines at the condenser.
4. Remove fasteners securing the condenser and lift it from the chassis. If the receiver-drier mounts on the condenser, remove both as a unit.
5. Drain and measure the oil in the condenser.
6. Fit the new condenser in place, install new O-rings, coat fitting connections with clean refrigeration oil, then connect the lines.
7. Install the radiator, fan shroud, and other parts removed for disassembly and fill the cooling system.
8. Add enough fresh refrigeration oil to replace the amount lost during discharge and evaporator removal, and also add the recommended amount of oil to compensate for what did not drain from the evaporator.
9. Evacuate and recharge the system, then check the system for leaks.

Evaporator Housing Service

Make sure the evaporator housing is clean so that condensation that forms on the coils can drain properly. Undrained water and debris grow bacteria that can release an unpleasant odor into the passenger compartment when the A/C is running.

Receiver-Drier Service

The receiver-drier is a high-pressure storage device located between the condenser outlet and expansion valve inlet, figure 2-16. A desiccant bag in the receiver-drier removes moisture from the system. The receiver-drier is replaced when there is:

• System or component contamination
• Refrigerant leaks
• Collision damage
• Excessive ambient air entering an open system
• Compressor replacement

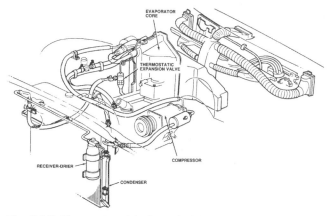

Fig. 2-16. The receiver-drier is on the high side of the system between the condenser and the expansion valve.

The signs of receiver-drier problems include:

• Loss of refrigerant
• Moisture or debris contamination
• Desiccant particles in the system
• Refrigerant starvation due to blocked receiver-drier
• A significant temperature difference between the receiver-drier inlet and outlet
• Frost on the bottom of the receiver-drier

The receiver-drier is not serviceable and must be replaced when defective.

Receiver-Drier Replacement

To remove and replace the receiver-drier:

1. Discharge the system using a recovery and recycling station, recycle the refrigerant, and measure how much refrigeration oil was extracted.
2. Disconnect the receiver-drier inlet and outlet line fittings and cap or seal them. Also, disconnect any electrical wiring to the receiver-drier assembly.
3. Remove the attaching hardware and lift the receiver-drier from the chassis. On some systems, the condenser must be removed before the receiver-drier.
4. Drain and measure any residual oil from the old receiver-drier and transfer any switches or sensors from the old unit to the new one.
5. Install the replacement unit. Tighten the hose connection fittings to specifications before tightening the mounting bracket bolts.
6. Reconnect any electrical connections on the receiver-drier assembly.
7. Add enough fresh refrigeration oil to replace the amount lost during removal, along with the recommended amount of oil to compensate for what did not drain from the receiver-drier.
8. Evacuate and recharge the system, then check the system for leaks.

Accumulator Service

The accumulator is a device on the low-side of an orifice tube system that performs two functions: It serves as a storage

A7

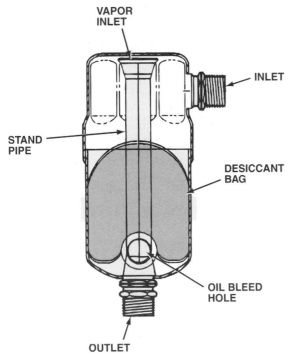

Fig. 2-17. An accumulator stores excess refrigerant and prevents liquid refrigerant from returning to the compressor.

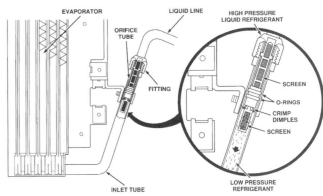

Fig. 2-18. The orifice tube is located in the evaporator inlet line.

container to hold excess refrigerant, and also prevents liquid refrigerant from returning to the compressor. The accumulator, which is located at the evaporator outlet, receives refrigerant in both liquid and vapor form. Refrigerant is stored at the bottom of the unit as a liquid and must be vaporized before it can be picked up at the top of the accumulator and returned to the compressor. The accumulator also contains a desiccant to remove moisture from the system, figure 2-17.

A drain hole at the bottom of the accumulator standpipe allows oil and some refrigerant to return to the compressor. Because of the large desiccant bag and the considerable amount of oil retained by the accumulator, it is important to accurately measure and replace the lost oil when installing a new accumulator. Follow the service manual guidelines.

The accumulator is not serviceable and must be replaced when defective. Also, replace the accumulator whenever a refrigerant hose, compressor, condenser, evaporator, or other major component is replaced.

Accumulator Replacement

To remove and replace the accumulator:

1. Discharge the system, recycle the refrigerant, and measure oil extracted.
2. Disconnect the accumulator inlet and outlet line fittings and cap or seal them.
3. Remove the attaching hardware and lift the accumulator from the chassis.
4. Drain and measure any residual oil in the accumulator.
5. Install the replacement unit.
6. Add the correct amount of fresh refrigeration oil.
7. Evacuate and recharge the system, then check the system for leaks.

Orifice Tube System Service

Fixed-orifice expansion tubes are found on late-model vehicles built by a number of manufacturers. Replace an orifice tube in the case of:

- Orifice clogging
- Inlet or outlet contamination or clogging
- Debris in the system

When an orifice tube fails, the symptoms are similar to those of a clogged expansion valve:

- Airflow through the evaporator warm or only slightly cool
- Very low low-side pressure and low to normal high-side pressure
- Sweating or frost on the line between the expansion tube and evaporator

Test for a defective orifice tube as follows:

1. Connect the manifold gauge set. Start and run the engine at 1,500 RPM for 10 minutes with the A/C on MAX and the blower on HIGH.
2. Check the low-side gauge reading. If it is abnormally low and the high-side gauge indicates that pressurized refrigerant is available, suspect a problem with the orifice tube.

On most systems, the orifice tube is located in the evaporator inlet line, figure 2-18. O-rings on the outside of the tube hold it in place. The orifice tube, which is fragile, often breaks during removal. If this happens, use special extractor tools to remove the pieces. To replace the orifice tube:

1. Discharge the system using a recovery and recycling station, recycle the refrigerant, and measure how much refrigeration oil was extracted.
2. Disconnect the evaporator inlet line.
3. A special tool is used to remove the orifice tube, figure 2-19. Slide the inner sleeve of the tool over the tube until its notch slides over the end of the orifice tube, then engage the notch with a plastic tab on the tube. Rotate the outer sleeve counterclockwise to remove the orifice tube. Do not rotate the tool inner sleeve during removal. The inner sleeve is only to engage the orifice tube.
4. Coat the new orifice tube with clean refrigeration oil.

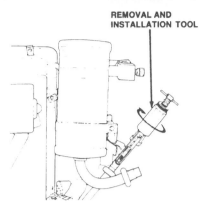

Fig. 2-19. A special tool is used to remove an orifice tube.

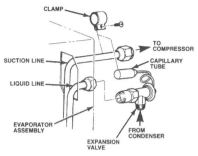

Fig. 2-20. A TXV installs at the evaporator inlet

5. Push the new orifice tube into position until it bottoms against the stop.
6. Install a new top O-ring, and reconnect the evaporator inlet line.
7. Replace oil lost during discharge, then evacuate and charge the system.
8. Test the system for leaks.

On some designs, the orifice tube cannot be removed from the evaporator inlet line. If the orifice tube becomes clogged, install a new line with a built-in orifice tube.

Thermostatic Expansion Valve (TXV) Service

TXV and suction throttling devices regulate refrigerant pressure and flow at the evaporator inlet. A TXV failure can be caused by:

- Debris clogging the valve or inlet screen
- Moisture causing restrictions in the metering valve
- Moisture contamination and corrosion
- Damage to the capillary tube or bulb

The symptoms of a TXV failure depend on the nature of the problem. The most common cause of failure is a restricted TXV. Three major causes of TXV failure and some symptoms they produce are:

1. Valve stuck closed—the evaporator is starved of refrigerant, causing the following symptoms:

   - Airflow through the evaporator warm or only slightly cool
   - Low pressure on both the high- and low-side
   - Sweating or frost on the TXV, which can result from a clogged TXV inlet screen

2. Valve stuck open, capillary and sensing bulb failure—the evaporator floods, causing the following symptoms:

   - Airflow through the evaporator warm or only slightly cool
   - Low-side pressure high

3. Intermittent TXV operation—the A/C works intermittently, causing the following symptoms:

   - Fluctuating output air temperature
   - Intermittent changes in low-side pressure readings
   - System operates normally when first started then stops cooling

Although it may appear to be a TXV problem, a loss of cooling after continued use is often caused by the receiver-drier allowing moisture into the system. In this case, ice forms in the TXV during system operation. When the system warms after shutting down, the ice melts, so the system works normally the next time it is switched on—until the ice re-forms.

Replacing the TXV

When installing or removing a TXV:

- Handle the capillary tube carefully, without bending or kinking it
- Insert the replacement tube fully into the mounting bracket or sleeve
- Make sure the replacement capillary bulb is installed in the same position as the original
- Replace any insulation you removed to gain access to the bulb

The TXV installs at the evaporator inlet, figure 2-20. Following is a typical TXV replacement procedure:

1. Discharge the system using a recovery and recycling station, recycle the refrigerant, and measure how much refrigeration oil was extracted.
2. Disconnect the TXV external equalization line, if used.
3. Remove any insulation that covers the capillary tube and bulb.
4. Remove the bracket holding the capillary bulb in position.
5. Disconnect, and immediately cap or seal, the refrigerant line fittings at the TXV, then remove it from the vehicle.
6. Inspect the TXV inlet screen for debris.
7. Fit the new TXV, install new O-rings if used, lubricate connections with fresh refrigeration oil, and tighten fittings to specification.
8. Replace the equalization line and capillary along with any insulation that was removed. Be sure to replace the capillary in its original position.
9. Replace oil lost during discharge, then evacuate and charge the system.
10. Test the system for leaks.

Service Valves

Service valves are generally welded to a rigid line, the receiver-drier, or the accumulator. The body of the valve is not serviceable. Leaking valve cores can be tightened or replaced. Replacement requires:

1. Discharge the system using a recovery and recycling station, recycle the refrigerant, and measure how much refrigeration oil was extracted.

A7

2. Remove the valve core with a special tool.
3. Inspect the core seating area for burrs, stripped threads, and damage.
4. Install a new valve core.
5. Replace oil lost during discharge, then evacuate and charge the system.
6. Test the system for leaks.

High-Pressure Relief Device Service

A pressure relief valve is a spring-loaded mechanical safety device. If system pressure rises high enough to overcome the force of the relief valve spring, the valve lifts from its seat, allowing refrigerant to escape. The valve remains open only long enough to reduce the system pressure below the setpoint. Pressure relief valves are mounted on the high side of the system. The location varies; look at the discharge port of the compressor, along the high-pressure line, and on the receiver-drier. A high-pressure cutout switch must be added when retrofitting an R-12 system with a pressure relief valve for use with R-134a.

Some systems have a high-pressure cutout switch mounted on the rear of the compressor to protect the compressor. This switch is wired in series with a low-pressure cutout switch and the ambient temperature sensor. When system pressure rises above a preset level, the high-pressure cutout switch opens to interrupt current to the compressor clutch.

When a pressure relief device triggers, diagnose the system to find what is causing the pressure buildup. When a relief valve cycles, both refrigerant and refrigeration oil escape from the system. Replace lost refrigerant and oil after repairing the cause of the high pressure.

CHAPTER QUESTIONS

1. Common compressor clutch failures include all of the following, **EXCEPT**:
   a. Open field windings
   b. A seized or warped hub assembly
   c. Shorted pressure relief switch
   d. A damaged or bent pulley

2. A compressor clutch that remains engaged when the A/C is switched off is most likely caused by:
   a. Open field windings
   b. A seized clutch assembly
   c. Defective pressure sensing device
   d. Shorted field windings

3. Which of the following statements about a compressor front seal is **NOT** true?
   a. Some front seals can be serviced without removing the compressor from the vehicle.
   b. Some manufacturers recommend replacing the entire compressor if the front seal is leaking.
   c. Some front seals can be replaced without discharging the system.
   d. The clutch assembly must be removed from the compressor to access the seal.

4. The most likely cause of a compressor reed valve failure would be:
   a. Gaseous refrigerant entering the compressor
   b. Extremely low system pressure
   c. Insufficient refrigerant or lubricant
   d. Debris circulating in the system

5. The most likely cause of warm evaporator discharge air and manifold gauge readings that show high low-side pressure and low high-side pressure would be:
   a. Internal compressor damage
   b. Low refrigerant level
   c. Ice forming in the expansion valve
   d. An evaporator core restriction

6. After repairing a system that was contaminated by debris, it is advisable to:
   a. Flush the system
   b. Install an inline filter
   c. Overhaul the compressor
   d. Replace the expansion device

7. Which of the following symptoms is **NOT** an indication of a receiver-drier problem?
   a. High low-side pressure and low high-side pressure
   b. A significant temperature difference between the receiver-drier inlet and outlet ports
   c. Frost forming on the bottom of the receiver-drier assembly
   d. Poor system performance as a result of refrigerant starvation due to receiver-drier blockage

8. To find the receiver-drier, look:
   a. Between the condenser outlet and the expansion valve inlet
   b. Between the evaporator inlet and the condenser inlet
   c. Between the compressor inlet and the expansion valve inlet
   d. Between the expansion valve outlet and the evaporator inlet

9. The most likely cause of excessive high-side pressure, the pressure relief valve venting, and frost on the evaporator discharge line would be a(n):
   a. Defective suction throttling device
   b. Contaminated receiver-drier
   c. Defective condenser
   d. Orifice tube failure

10. All of the following are signs of orifice-tube failure **EXCEPT**:
    a. Warm airflow from the evaporator
    b. Frost on the orifice tube-to-evaporator line
    c. Low-side pressure low
    d. High-side pressure high

A7

CHAPTER THREE

HEATING AND ENGINE COOLING SYSTEMS DIAGNOSIS AND REPAIR

CHAPTER OBJECTIVES

- The technician will complete the ASE task list on Heating and Engine Cooling System Diagnosis and Repair.
- The technician will be able to answer 4 questions dealing with the Heating and Engine Cooling System Diagnosis and Repair section of the A7 ASE Test.

Heating problems include output air temperature that is too hot or too cold and incorrect air distribution through the ductwork. Passenger compartment heaters depend on the engine cooling system to provide a steady stream of coolant at normal engine operating temperature. Ensure the engine cooling system is functioning properly before performing any other heating system repairs.

HEATER/VENTILATION CONTROL SYSTEM DIAGNOSIS

An operational check, similar to the one described for A/C systems, is performed to diagnose the heating system.

System Operation Check

To check heating system operation, start and run the engine until it is at operating temperature; the upper radiator hose should feel warm. Select the HEAT mode, turn the temperature control to MAX, and set the blower to HIGH. Check air temperature at the floor vents with a thermometer, and compare with a temperature chart.

System Diagnosis

Diagnose heater system window fogging, heat output, and ventilation problems to determine needed repairs.

Window Fogging

Fogging can result from ventilation system malfunctions or **heater core** problems. Although a sticky residue on the glass often indicates a heater core failure, the ventilation system must be checked as well.

Heating Problems

The heater can have one of three basic problems:

- No heat
- Not enough heat
- Too much heat

Possible causes of a no-heat condition include:

- Blocked coolant flow through the heater core—If the heater hoses are cool with the engine running, the problem may be a plugged heater core, hoses, hose fittings, or a faulty **heater control valve**
- Incorrectly positioned blend doors—If the heater hoses are warm but no heat is delivered to the passenger compartment, check for stuck blend doors, disconnected or broken control cables, or damaged ductwork
- Blocked air inlet ducts—If the airflow improves when the mode selector is changed to the RECIRC position, check for ductwork or cowl air intake blockage
- Defective blower or reduced current to blower—If the blower runs slowly or not at all, refer to blower service instructions

Possible causes of insufficient heat are:

- Faulty heater control valve—Ensure the valve opens and closes smoothly; check the valve controls for correct adjustment, defective control cables, a leak in the vacuum system, or a faulty electrical connection
- Kinked or clogged heater hose—Inspect hoses, especially at the end fittings, and replace as needed
- Contaminated cooling system or low coolant level—Check coolant level and condition, and check for rust or scale around the filler neck
- Blend doors out of position—Check for stuck blend doors, or disconnected or broken control cables
- Defective or incorrectly installed thermostat—Check thermostat type and operation
- Partially blocked heater core—Perform heater core tests

Possible causes of excessive heat are:

- Blend door stuck open—Ensure the linkage moves freely to the full open and closed positions
- Heater control valve stuck open—Check for misadjusted controller, broken valve, defective cable, vacuum system leak, or faulty electrical system

Most present day vehicles use a 195°F (91°C) thermostat. It is critical for the thermostat to function properly. The HVAC system, as well as emission and driveability conditions, depends

---

Heater Control Valve: A cable, vacuum, or electric valve on the heater core inlet that controls the rate of coolant flow into the heater core.

Heater Core: A heat exchanger through which hot coolant passes and releases its heat by conduction into a passing air stream.

on precise control of engine coolant temperatures for satisfactory operation.

Thermostats are designed to open and close at preset temperatures. If a thermostat does not operate properly it should be removed, inspected, and tested. If the thermostat sticks open, the engine will warm up very slowly. If the thermostat sticks closed, the engine will overheat.

Use the following procedure to test the thermostat:

1. Drain the coolant until it is below the level of the thermostat, then remove the water outlet assembly.
2. Remove the thermostat. If visually faulty replace it; if not use the following test to determine correct operation.

   a. Place the thermostat and a thermometer in a container with a 50/50 solution of water and ethylene glycol antifreeze. Place the container over a heater. While heating do not allow the thermostat or thermometer to rest on the bottom of the container; this will cause them to be at a higher temperature than the solution.

   b. Agitate the solution to ensure uniform temperature of the solution, thermostat, and thermometer.

The thermostat valve should start to open at 195°F (91°C). It should be fully opened after the temperature has increased 27°F (15°C). If the thermostat does not operate at the temperature specified, replace it; it cannot be adjusted.

Ventilation System Problems

Many ventilation system problems involve fogged windows and poor air circulation in the vehicle. The three basic ventilation problems are:

- No airflow
- Not enough airflow
- Misdirected airflow

When dealing with complains of no airflow, determine whether there is no airflow in the entire passenger compartment or only at a certain vent. If only one vent is working improperly, check the duct leading to that vent. Also check the condition of the vent door and cables.

Little or no airflow from all vents can be caused by HVAC system air intake or blower problems. To check, set the heater controls to VENT mode, switch on the blower, and operate the fan at each setting. If you cannot hear the blower increase in speed, the problem is probably related to the blower motor, figure 3-1. Refer to the appropriate procedures.

If you can hear the blower increase in speed, but there is little or no airflow, the problem is probably in the HVAC air intake system. Typical HVAC air intake problems are:

- Cowl intake blockage
- Intake air door stuck shut or not operating smoothly

If airflow is insufficient, check for:

- Blocked vent grills
- Partial blockage of the screen covering the cowl intake vent
- Partial or total blockage of the air ducts
- Incorrectly adjusted vent doors

Both inlet and outlet ducts must be clear, since air can enter the vehicle only if there is an outlet for the stale air to exhaust, figure 3-2. Make sure that the flaps in the vent grills open and close easily.

Heater Control Valve

Most heating systems use a heater control valve to regulate coolant flow into the heater core. The valve may be actuated by a cable, vacuum servomotor, or electric solenoid. To check the valve:

1. Determine whether the valve is normally open or normally closed.

A7

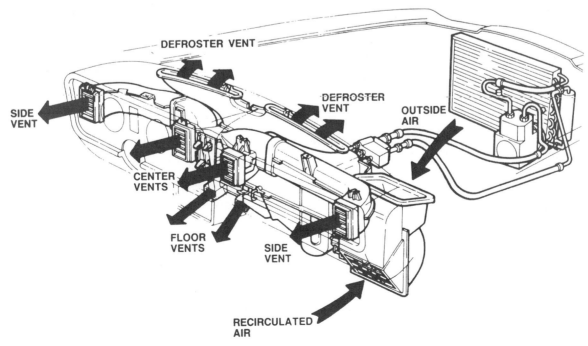

Fig. 3-1. Typical HVAC ventilation system.

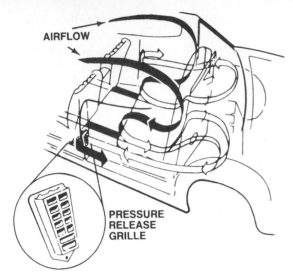

Fig. 3-2. Passenger compartment airflow depends on a clear outlet path for proper circulation.

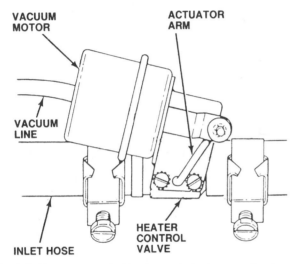

Fig. 3-3. Vacuum-operated heater control valve operation is checked with a hand-operated vacuum pump.

2. Check valve position when it is not actuated, then switch the controls and monitor valve operation. A correctly operating valve opens and closes smoothly and completely.

A vacuum-operated heater control valve on a blend door system is usually open until a vacuum signal closes it, figure 3-3. Use a vacuum pump to check whether the valve opens smoothly and evenly with the correct amount of vacuum applied.

ENGINE COOLING SYSTEM SERVICE

The engine cooling system is the link between engine heat and the passenger compartment heating system. The engine cooling system must work well for the heating system to function properly. The engine water pump, which is belt-driven, provides the coolant circulation; service and adjust drive belts as previously described. Also, inspect cooling system hoses for:

- Hardness, cracks, brittleness
- Sponginess or interior damage
- Loose connections or leakage
- Age, figure 3-4

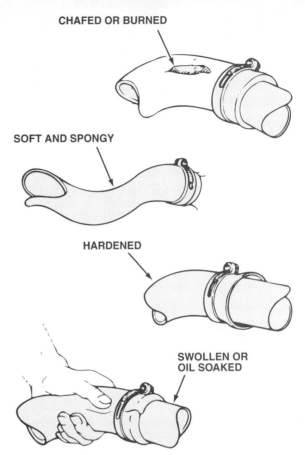

Fig. 3-4. Inspect all coolant hoses for damage.

Hose replacement intervals of about 48,000 to 50,000 miles (76,000 to 80,000 km) as preventive maintenance may be recommended by the vehicle manufacturer. Check the cooling system for seepage and rust damage at the:

- Core plugs
- Water pump shaft seal
- Water pump and thermostat gaskets

Inspect the radiator for:

- Rust or oil in the coolant
- Leaks or corrosion at tank seams
- Kinked or damaged overflow tubes
- Clogged fins or air intake paths
- Loose or missing mounting bolts
- Incorrect coolant level in the overflow tank
- Leaves or other debris blocking the radiator
- Green corrosion on the outside of radiator tubes

Inspect the radiator cap for:

- Looseness at the filler neck
- Brittle or damaged seal
- Sufficient spring action
- Correct pressure rating, figure 3-5

Test the radiator pressure cap using a cooling system pressure tester and an adapter as follows:

1. Attach the cap to one end of the adapter, then connect the opposite end to the tester.

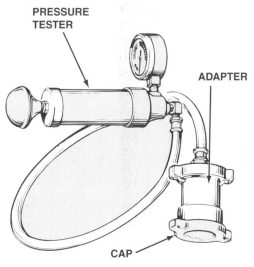

Fig. 3-5. Inspect and test the radiator pressure cap.

2. Pump the tester until the cap vents and observe the gauge reading. The cap should vent when pressure exceeds the rating by one to three pounds. If not, replace the cap.
3. Allow the pressure to stabilize.
4. Observe the gauge; it should hold within one or two psi of the cap rating for one minute. If the gauge reading drops, the cap is bad; replace it.

A pressure cap vacuum valve that is not venting properly causes the upper radiator hose to collapse as the system cools down. Check the vacuum valve by pulling it gently and verifying the slight spring tension.

Check the heater enclosure and plenum for:

- Rust, indicating heater core leakage
- Loose hose connections
- Loose mounting bolts
- Air leaks and missing or detached ducts

An indication of an air leak is a fogged windshield, possibly with an oily film on the inside of the glass.

Check the water pump for:

- Leakage around the pump housing, shaft seal, hose connections, and gasket sealing surfaces
- Misalignment with the drive pulley
- Looseness, sideplay, or endplay in the water pump shaft bearing

If there is a fan clutch, check it for:

- Fluid leakage
- Noisy or rough operation when rotated by hand
- Excessive shaft looseness

If there is an electric fan, check it for:

- Loose electrical connections
- Damaged or poorly routed wiring
- Excessive endplay or sideplay in the motor shaft
- Operation

Check any type of fan for:

- Bent or cracked fan blades
- Binding on its shaft

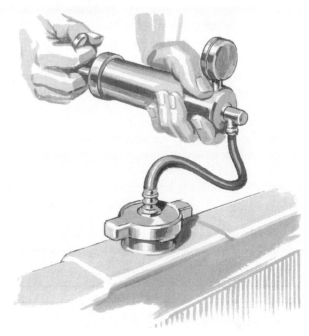

Fig. 3-6. Pressure-test the cooling system to locate leakage.

The radiator fan shroud increases radiator and fan efficiency by forcing the fan airflow through the radiator core, so make sure it is present and securely fastened.

Finally, with the engine running, listen for noises:

- Engine thump at normal operating temperature could indicate a restriction in coolant flow
- Screeching could indicate a loose accessory drive belt or failing water pump bearing
- Buzz or whistle could indicate a poor pressure cap seal or vibrating fan shroud
- Ringing or grinding noise could indicate a worn or damaged water pump bearing, loose drive belt pulley, or defective belt tensioner pulley bearing
- Gurgling from the radiator could indicate a plugged radiator or air in the coolant

System Leak Check

The quickest way to find an external coolant leak is by pressure-testing the cooling system, figure 3-6. Perform the test on a cold engine using a hand pump with a gauge as follows:

1. Remove the pressure cap and attach the tester to the filler neck.
2. Pump the tester until the gauge reading matches the specified system pressure.
3. Ensure the gauge reading remains steady.
4. If the gauge shows a pressure loss, pump the tester to maintain pressure and check for leaks. External leaks should be obvious as pressure in the system forces the coolant out.
5. If no sign of leakage is found, the leak is internal and additional testing is required.

Internal coolant leaks, generally the result of head gasket failure or casting cracks, are more difficult to detect.

Coolant may be seeping into either the combustion chambers or the crankcase. To check for leakage into the crankcase,

A7

remove the dipstick. If the oil on the dipstick looks milky or thickened, it may be contaminated by leaking coolant.

There are several methods to check for coolant in the combustion chambers. Remove the radiator cap, start the engine, and bring it to operating temperature. A major leak reveals itself by creating bubbles in the coolant that rise to the surface at the filler neck. Small leaks can be detected using a chemical test kit or an exhaust gas analyzer.

With chemical testing, vapors directly above the coolant in the radiator are passed through a liquid sensitive to exhaust gases. To use an exhaust gas analyzer, hold the wand over the filler neck. Never allow coolant to be drawn into the machine. Any exhaust gases in the system register on the meters.

Pressure test and inspect the coolant system before draining. Drain the system completely by opening the petcock at the bottom of the radiator and the plugs in the engine block. If the coolant is dirty, or there are deposits in the radiator, flush the cooling system before refilling.

Various methods and equipment may be used to flush the system. If using equipment such as a back flusher, follow the manufacturer's instructions. However, the thermostat should be removed before flushing the system.

Disconnect all hoses from the coolant reservoir. Remove the reservoir and pour out any fluid. Scrub the inside of the reservoir with soap and water. Flush it well with clean water, and then drain it. Install the reservoir and hoses. Install the thermostat, then close the radiator petcock and engine block drains. Refill the cooling system with coolant meeting the OEM's specifications. To ensure sufficient engine cooling, freezing, and engine corrosion protection, maintain a 50/50 solution of water and antifreeze. This will achieve a protection level of -34°F (-37°C). Never use a solution that is more than 70% antifreeze.

Fill the radiator or coolant fill pipe to the base of the filler neck. Fill the coolant reservoir to the "FULL HOT" mark. Before replacing the pressure cap, test it as described earlier in this chapter. Start and run the engine with the pressure cap removed, until the upper radiator hose is hot. With the engine idling, add coolant to the radiator until it reaches the bottom of the filler neck. Install the pressure cap, making sure the cap is secure. Allow the engine to cool to ambient temperature, then check the coolant in the reservoir rank. If not at the "FULL COLD" mark, add coolant.

HEATER CORE SERVICE

Many problems with the heating system are caused by heater core failure. Service procedures include:

- Pressure testing
- Bench testing
- Flushing

Pressure Test

If the engine coolant level is low but the cooling system is not leaking, check the heater core. Coolant may leak from pinholes in the heater core in the form of steam, which enters the passenger compartment along with the heated air. When this air condenses against the cold windows, the coolant deposits

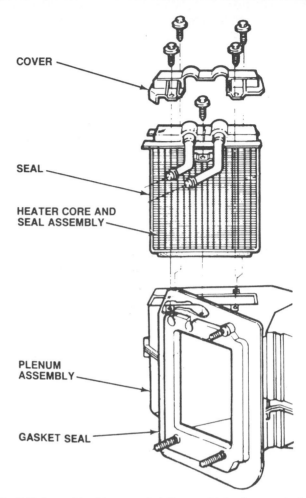

Fig. 3-7. A considerable amount of disassembly is often required to remove the heater core from the plenum assembly.

there, forming a sticky, sweet-smelling residue. To pressure-test the heater core on the vehicle:

1. Drain the coolant.
2. Disconnect the heater hoses from the heater core inlet and outlet tubes.
3. Use adapters to connect a cooling system pressure tester to one heater core tube.
4. Fill the heater core with water and seal off the other tube.
5. Apply specified pressure with the hand pump and watch the gauge for at least three minutes:

   - If pressure holds for three minutes, the heater core is not leaking
   - If the pressure drops, double-check the connection between the tester and heater core; if the leak is not there, remove the heater core for bench testing

Bench Test

Removing the heater core from the vehicle may require considerable disassembly of the heating, ventilation, and air conditioning system plenum or ductwork, figure 3-7. Once removed, bench-test the core to locate the leak:

1. Drain the coolant and plug one heater core tube with a suitable stopper.

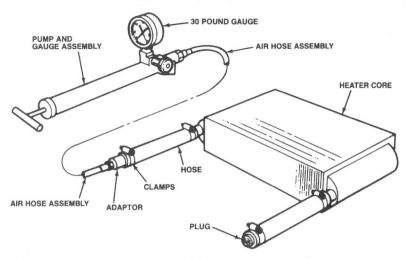

Fig. 3-8. Seal and charge a heater core with air, then submerge it in water to bench-test it.

2. Seal the other tube using a fitting with an air valve.
3. Use a hand pump or low-pressure compressed air and charge the heater core to the recommended pressure, figure 3-8.
4. Submerge the pressurized heater core in a water bath and watch for a stream of bubbles from the leak.

Some heater cores can be repaired by a radiator shop, while others must be replaced if a leak is found.

Flushing

A heater core can collect sediment or scale that insulates the heater core metal from the coolant and reduces the amount of heat available for the passenger compartment. Backflushing, which sends water through the heater core in the opposite direction from the normal coolant flow, removes this sediment without removing the heater core from the vehicle. To backflush:

1. Remove the heater hoses.
2. Connect a drain hose to the inlet tube.
3. Attach a hose and nozzle to the outlet and spray pressurized water through the heater core.

Chemicals such as oxalic acid can also remove deposits. The acid breaks up oily, scaly deposits in the system that water cannot dissolve.

A7

CHAPTER QUESTIONS

1. Possible causes of the heater not providing any heat at all include all of the following *EXCEPT*:
   a. High current flow to blower
   b. Blocked coolant flow through heater core
   c. Blocked air inlet ducts
   d. Clogged heater hoses

2. Very little airflow into the passenger compartment can be caused by all of the following *EXCEPT*:
   a. A partially blocked cowl intake vent
   b. A normal condition at low vehicle speeds
   c. An open circuit to the fan motor
   d. An intake air door jammed shut

3. A heater control valve may be operated by:
   a. Hydraulic pressure
   b. Mechanical crank
   c. Engine-run pulley
   d. Vacuum actuator

4. An upper radiator hose that collapses as the engine cooling system cools down is most likely caused by:
   a. Plugged or damaged radiator fins
   b. A defective radiator cap
   c. Restricted coolant flow
   d. A plugged water pump vent

5. What is the most likely cause of a heating system that fogs the windshield and leaves an oily film on the inside of the glass?
   a. Air or coolant leak in the heater plenum
   b. Debris in the ram air intake system
   c. A leaking heater control valve
   d. Intake air doors stuck closed

6. A grinding noise from the accessory drive belts can be caused by all of the following, *EXCEPT*:
   a. A damaged water pump bearing
   b. A defective belt tensioner pulley bearing
   c. A glazed, cracked, or broken drive belt
   d. A binding A/C belt idler pulley bearing

7. To pressure-test a heater core:
   a. Top off the coolant
   b. Use a special pressure tester
   c. Run the engine
   d. Set the heater control on high

8. A heater core has had sediment buildup; to remove it by backflushing:
   a. Remove the heater core from the plenum
   b. Soak the core in a chemical flush to loosen deposits
   c. Run water through the heater core outlet
   d. Pressurize the heater core with air

CHAPTER FOUR

OPERATING SYSTEMS AND RELATED CONTROLS DIAGNOSIS AND REPAIR

CHAPTER OBJECTIVES

- The technician will complete the ASE task list on Operating Systems and Related Controls Diagnosis and Repair.
- The technician will be able to answer 19 questions dealing with the Operating Systems and Related Controls Diagnosis and Repair section of the A7 ASE Test.

HVAC systems rely on either mechanical, vacuum, electric, electronic controls, or various combinations of these four methods to regulate the temperature and distribution of the airflow into the passenger compartment.

MECHANICAL OPERATING CONTROLS

Mechanical controls are simple, cable-operated devices that move levers or rotary switches to pull **blend doors** and **mode doors** into position, figure 4-1. The blend door determines how much of the intake air is directed through the heater core before entering the passenger compartment. Mode doors direct the airflow to the various ducts. An incorrectly positioned door cannot deliver the proper airflow. Blend and mode door position problems may be caused by the doors themselves binding, being blocked by debris, or by a control cable that is out of adjustment, kinked, loose, or broken. Most newer control cables have a self-adjusting clip, but the self-adjustment range is limited. Adjust control cables before installation:

1. Insert a small screwdriver into the control cable wire loop at the end of the blend door crank arm.

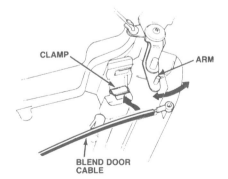

Fig. 4-1. Mechanical controls use a cable assembly to position the blend door.

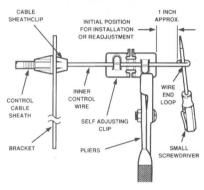

Fig. 4-2. Setting the initial position on a new self-adjusting control cable.

2. Use pliers to slide the self-adjusting clip about one inch (25 mm) down the control cable and away from the end loop, figure 4-2.
3. Set the temperature control lever at maximum cool, then snap the cable housing into the mounting bracket.
4. Attach the self-adjusting clip to the temperature door crank arm.
5. Move the temperature control lever to maximum heat, position the self-adjusting clip, and check cable operation.

VACUUM-OPERATED CONTROLS

Vacuum-operated climate-control systems use intake manifold **vacuum** to operate controls and **actuators**. Many vacuum systems are complex, so it is important to have a vacuum diagram and specifications for the specific vehicle being serviced. In general, take vacuum readings at engine idle speed using a vacuum gauge. Often, components can be tested without removing them from the vehicle using a hand-operated vacuum pump.

Vacuum Component Diagnosis and Replacement

Be aware, moving vacuum-controlled blend doors manually can damage the vacuum motor diaphragm. Disconnect the doors from the actuators before testing door movement. Universal replacement vacuum motors, which have an adjustable

A7

Actuator: A component that converts a vacuum or electrical signal into a physical movement, to operate a part such as a blend door or valve.
Blend Door: A door in an HVAC system that directs air through or around the heater core.
Mode Door: A door in an HVAC system that directs air to the defrost, dash, and heat ducts.
Vacuum: A pressure less than atmospheric pressure.

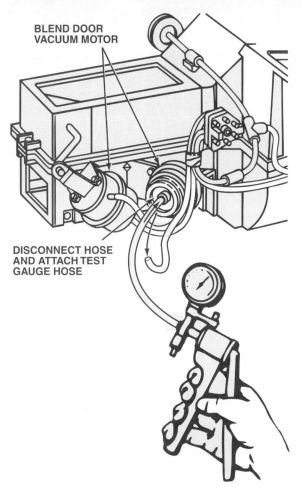

Fig. 4-3. Testing a vacuum operated blend door actuator.

actuating rod allowing them to be used on a number of vehicles, are readily available. To test the vacuum actuator:

1. Connect a vacuum pump to the diaphragm inlet port and apply about 15 to 20 in-Hg (350 to 500 mm-Hg) of vacuum, figure 4-3.
2. Check diaphragm plunger or linkage operation in all positions.
3. Close the pump shutoff valve and watch the gauge. The readings should hold steady for at least one minute if the diaphragm is not leaking.
4. Repeat for each inlet port in the vacuum motor.
5. Be sure the door moves when vacuum is applied.

Troubleshooting the Vacuum System

Begin with a visual inspection:

1. Check vacuum hose routing and connections. Look for and straighten or replace pinched, kinked, or damaged vacuum lines or hoses.
2. Check for blend door interference, disconnect the vacuum servo and check for full travel and free door movement.
3. Check the temperature control cable for kinks, binding, or improper routing.
4. Check all linkages for binding, damage, or loose connections.
5. Connect a vacuum pump to one port of the vacuum reservoir; plug the other port when applicable. Apply

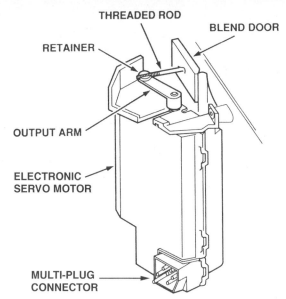

Fig. 4-4. Automatic and semiautomatic temperature control systems often use electronic solenoids to operate the blend door vacuum motors.

15 to 20 in-Hg of vacuum. The reservoir should hold the vacuum for 5 minutes. If it leaks, replace the reservoir.

6. Connect a vacuum pump to one side of a check valve (the valve should hold 15–20 in-Hg of vacuum), then connect the pump to the opposite end of the valve and apply vacuum; the valve should allow a free flow in one direction only.
7. Check restrictor valves by applying vacuum to either side. The valve should bleed down vacuum quickly and smoothly.

Many automatic and semi-automatic temperature control systems use electronically actuated vacuum motors to position blend doors and mode doors. Blend doors maintain a constant temperature in the passenger compartment by mixing fresh or recirculated air with heated or cooled air, figure 4-4. Mode doors direct air flow to the various defrost, dash, and heat ducts. When diagnosing vacuum motors, thoroughly evaluate the vacuum system before attempting to repair the electronic controls. To check blend and mode door operation:

1. Remove the glove box or other obstructions to gain a clear view of the blend door linkage and motor.
2. Start and run the engine until the upper radiator hose feels warm to the touch. Then, move the mode selector to NORM and switch the blower control to HIGH.
3. Move the temperature selection lever from warm to cold while watching the blend door mechanism. Once the blend door moves to the full cold position, move the selector to the full hot setting. Air temperature from the ducts should change as the system adjusts the blend door position.
4. Move the mode selector lever through all available modes. The air should flow from the appropriate heat, defrost, and dash ducts.

If the air temperature or flow does not change, refer to the appropriate section below.

Manual Controls

- Check and adjust the temperature control cable as needed and retest
- Check the vacuum motor linkage and adjust or repair as needed
- If the door moves freely, but only cold air is distributed through the system, check for vacuum at the heater control valve. Vacuum should not be present unless the system is in the MAX A/C setting

Automatic and Semi-Automatic Controls

- Check the blend door movement when the controls are changed from hot to cold. If there is no movement, or it is insufficient, separate the blend door lever or rod from the actuator assembly and check that the door moves freely through its full travel
- If the door moves freely, but is not being moved by the programmer, the problem is in the controls
- If there is sufficient blend door movement, but only cold air is distributed through the system, check for vacuum at the heater control valve. Vacuum should not be present unless the system is in the MAX A/C setting
- If hot coolant is available to the heater core, but only cold air is distributed, either coolant is not circulating through the heater core or air is not flowing through the heater. Feel the heater core return hose to check for circulation

Testing control problems begins with a vacuum and wiring diagram, and a knowledge of how the system is supposed to work. A few basic rules apply to testing manual, automatic, and semi-automatic temperature control systems.

If the discharge air is too cold, check for:

1. Insufficient hot coolant circulating through the heater core.
2. Insufficient airflow through the heater core.

If the discharge air is too hot, check for:

1. Excessive hot coolant circulation through the heater core.
2. Too much airflow being directed through the heater core.

ELECTRICAL AND ELECTRONIC CONTROLS

Electrical and electronic diagnosis is an organized procedure using information and testing to find the cause of a failure. The four basic steps are:

1. Verify the complaint, research the problem, and determine which specific components may be the cause of the complaint.
2. Find the affected circuit on the electrical schematic or wiring diagram.
3. Locate common points of power supply and ground to the branch circuits.
4. Do an area test of the branch circuit using various electrical tests to pinpoint the problem.

This procedure is especially useful in tracing power supply problems to individual components. Electronic control systems use low-voltage signals, so connection quality is even more important. Where possible, use trouble code readouts to localize the problem to specific circuits.

Electrical Circuits and Components

Direct Current (DC) circuits receive current at one end and connect to ground at the other, so the most logical test is to start at one end of the circuit and work your way to the other. Keep in mind:

- If one component, such as an actuator motor, is defective in a circuit with many parts, start the test at the defective part
- If all the parts in the circuit are not operating properly, check ground, then check along the circuit, starting at the power source

In complex, electronically controlled systems, test one sub-system at a time to narrow the problem down to a specific area. Then, perform more detailed tests to isolate the faulty component.

Servicing Electronic Control Systems

Most electronic control systems have a dedicated Electronic Control Module (ECM) for the climate control system. Typically, the climate control ECM is located behind the **control head**, although some may be located alongside, or incorporated into, the Body Control Module (BCM). Consult the service manual to locate the control module.

Most electronic systems have onboard diagnostic programs that are capable of performing self-test routines and storing a Diagnostic Trouble Code (DTC) when a malfunction occurs. Use a scan tool and follow the Service Manual for the exact year, model, and type of climate control system being serviced to access the onboard diagnostic programs.

Self-diagnostic procedures and diagnostic trouble codes seldom reveal the exact nature of a failure. However, they do narrow the problem area and indicate where to begin pinpoint testing. Once the problem has been repaired, rerun the self-diagnostic program to ensure that the fault has been corrected and the system is functioning properly.

Present day vehicles rely on the PCM to command the A/C compressor either on or off. When the PCM receives an HVAC request requiring compressor clutch engagement, the PCM will modify the engine RPM to minimize the impact of compressor clutch operation on engine idle speed.

Some of the PCM inputs are as follows:

- Power steering cutout switch
- Engine Coolant Temperature (ECT)
- Engine RPM
- Ambient Air Temperature (AAT)
- Intake Air Temperature (IAT)
- Vehicle Speed Sensor (VSS)
- Low refrigerant pressure switch
- A/C high-side pressure
- A/C low-side pressure
- Throttle Position (TP) Sensor

A7

Control Head: The dashboard-mounted unit that contains the controls for the HVAC systems.

Because of the PCM's role in most HVAC systems today, testing and repair require the use of the appropriate scan tool as described in this chapter.

Special Testers

Various special electronic testers have been developed to simplify troubleshooting electronic control systems. Although these testers are helpful, they do not repair system failures. A thorough understanding of the test procedures and system operations is required to accurately interpret the results of tests.

Onboard Diagnostic Communication

Most late-model vehicles have a diagnostic connector, or Data Link Connector (DLC), that allows the onboard computer to communicate with a scan tool or other diagnostic test equipment. The DLC may be located in the engine compartment of earlier vehicles, and some models use a dedicated connector that only accesses the A/C or climate control system. Late-model vehicles that comply with OBD-II regulations communicate through the 16-pin DLC located in the passenger compartment.

Scan Tool Capabilities

A scan tool is a hand-held computer that is capable of communicating with the onboard computers of a vehicle, figure 4-5. Scan tools are the only diagnostic tool that will display internal control module information. All other electronic test instruments are limited to accessing the external input and output circuits. A quality scan tool provides:

- DTC retrieval
- Access to the data stream
- The ability to record data during a road test
- A means to actuate onboard tests

The information the vehicle communicates to the scan tool is a function of the onboard computer, not the scan tool. Most vehicle manufacturers market scan tools designed specifically for servicing their systems. Aftermarket scan tools are also available from a number of vendors. Interchangeable software cartridges and cable connectors adapt an aftermarket scan tool to different control system designs, figure 4-6.

A scan tool is essential for diagnosing problems in the electronic control system. The latest units provide a great deal of valuable diagnostic information that is difficult, or impossible, to obtain any other way. Because a scan tool is portable, it can be used while road testing the vehicle. Watching "live" data provides the opportunity to catch an intermittent problem. One of the most useful features of a scan tool is its ability to record data during a road test for playback at a later time. These recordings are called snapshots, movies, or events by the various scan tool manufacturers. When viewing a recording, data appear as if live, but permit viewing of sensor and actuator activity at a relaxed pace.

Electrical and Electronic Component Service

All HVAC systems have an electric blower motor and compressor clutch, and may have control of the engine cooling fan(s) as well. Some systems use electric servo motors to position the blend and mode doors. Any or all of these electric motors may be controlled by the temperature control computer. Automatic and semi-automatic systems use a number of sensors and actuators

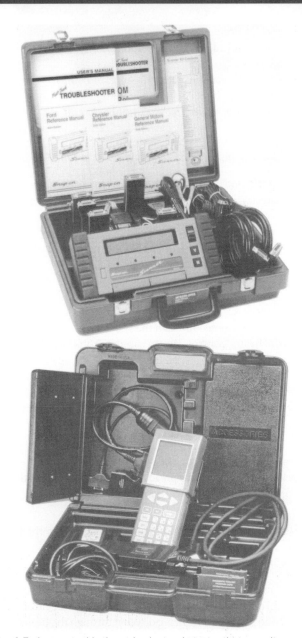

Fig. 4-5. A scan tool is the only electronic tester that permits direct communication with the onboard computer.

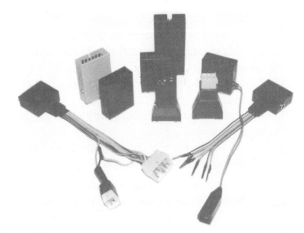

Fig. 4-6. An assortment of cable adapters provides access to a number of onboard control systems.

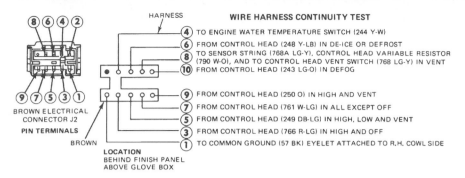

Fig. 4-7. A pin-out chart is needed to check blower switch circuits.

to maintain a preset passenger compartment temperature. As discussed previously, the PCM uses electronic engine data inputs to make decisions when to command A/C clutch operation. The PCM also controls engine RPM during A/C operation. The devices related to the A/C operation also supply inputs used to control engine-cooling fans.

WARNING: Keep hands, tools, and clothing away from the engine cooling fan(s) to help prevent personal injury. The fan can start automatically in response to a PCM command whether or not the engine is running.

Blower Motor

Most ATC HVAC systems utilize a system to control blower operation until the engine reaches operating temperature. Whenever the HVAC system is turned on in any mode, except defog, and the coolant temperature is below approximately 28°F (-2C°), blower operation is disabled. During this time the blower will be commanded off, and any airflow will be directed to the front defrost outlets to keep moisture off the windshield.

Normal blower operation resumes when the defrost function is selected or after the coolant temperature reaches approximately 110°F (43°C).

The blower motor circuit includes the motor, switch, and wiring harness that links them together. Refer to the service manual for specific test information.

Test switch continuity with an ohmmeter, following the procedures outlined in the appropriate Service Manual.

Many vehicles are equipped with a blower motor resistor block, figure 4-7. The resistor block is serviced only as an assembly, if found to be defective.

Many late-model vehicles control blower motor speed with the use of an electronic control module. This control module provides an output voltage to the blower motor proportional to the control switch position.

Diagnosis of the blower motor control module can normally be accomplished with the use of the proper scan tool.

Blend and Mode Door Servomotors

Do not move blend or mode doors manually, as this may cause damage. Blend and mode doors can be repositioned through an onboard diagnostic program with a scan tool on some systems. On other systems, sensors may need to be disconnected or harness terminals jumpered to move the blend doors. Refer to the appropriate Service Manual for moving the blend and mode doors to check alignment in all positions.

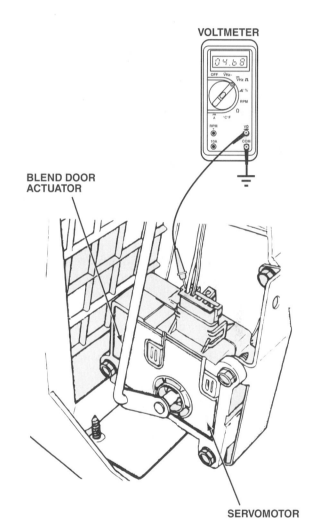

Fig. 4-8. Check for system voltage, usually about 5 volts on an electronic system, available at the servomotor.

An electronically controlled, high-torque servomotor normally produces a low, humming sound as the blend door moves. If the servomotor does not move, check for proper voltage to the servomotor and for proper grounding, figure 4-8. If voltage is available, but the servomotor does not rotate, check for obstructions at the blend or mode door or binding in the linkage before condemning the motor.

Compressor Clutch

The compressor clutch is an electromagnetic device that mechanically connects the compressor pulley to the compressor input shaft. Electrical or component failures that may prevent clutch engagement include:

- Safety switches
  - Refrigerant pressure
  - Coolant temperature
- PCM commands based on inputs from:
  - Power Steering Pressure (PSP) sensor
  - Throttle Position (TP) sensor
  - Engine Coolant Temperature (ECT) sensor
- Time-delay relay
- Blown fuses
- Open electrical connections or wiring
- Defective clutch relay
- Defective A/C module

Check clutch operation by moving the mode selector between the OFF and MAX A/C positions with the engine running. You should hear a click and momentary change in engine speed every time the clutch engages or disengages. If the clutch is not engaging:

1. With the engine running and A/C switched on, test both clutch coil electrical connections with a voltmeter. The possibilities are:
   - Zero volts at either terminal indicates no available voltage to the clutch
   - 12 volts at both terminals indicates the potential of an open ground circuit
   - 12 volts on one terminal and zero volts on the other indicates an open in the compressor clutch coil
2. If a faulty clutch coil is indicated, check coil resistance with an ohmmeter, figure 4-9. Typical clutch coil resistance should be 3–5 ohms.
3. Another possibility is high resistance in either the power or ground circuit. High resistance in the power circuit results in less than required current flow to the clutch coil. Refer to the appropriate service manual for specific circuit tests.
4. Once the fault is isolated to either the power or ground side of the clutch circuit, check the switches by momentarily jumping each switch or connection that may be preventing clutch operation. If clutch operation is restored when you jump a switch, investigate the reason for the open switch.

Caution: Never jump across a sensor, as damage to the PCM or other electronic controls may result.

Never operate the system for more than 60 seconds with a jumper wire installed on a switch. The switch may be functioning properly and opened due to a problem in the system, such as an extremely low refrigerant level, and operating the system can cause compressor damage.

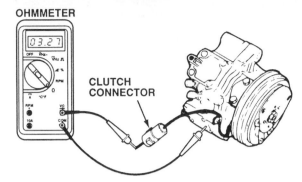

Fig. 4-9. Check compressor clutch coil resistance.

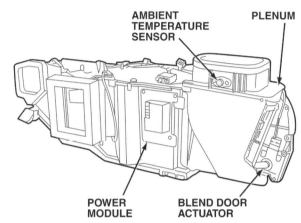

Fig. 4-10. The ambient temperature sensor measures HVAC system intake air temperature.

Temperature Switches and Sensors

Temperature switches such as the **ambient temperature switch** and the engine **coolant temperature switch** are on/off devices that control circuits based on temperature.

Most late-model vehicles have replaced temperature switches with temperature sensors. These sensors are generally thermistors, and are used to provide input to various control modules. A typical system uses thermistors to monitor the **ambient temperature**, evaporator temperature, coolant temperature, and passenger compartment temperature.

An additional coolant temperature switch or sensor may be used to operate an electric cooling fan.

The ambient temperature switch transmits HVAC intake air temperature as a voltage signal to the control module to open and close the compressor clutch circuit, figure 4-10. The switch is generally mounted either in the plenum or near the radiator support. A typical ambient temperature switch opens the compressor clutch circuit to prevent compressor operation below about 35°F (2°C), and closes to allow normal compressor operation at temperatures of about 50°F (10°C) or above.

Ambient Temperature: The temperature of the air surrounding a component.
Ambient Temperature Switch: A digital on/off device that senses ambient temperature and switches off the A/C compressor when the temperature is too cold.
Coolant Temperature Switch: A digital on/off device that senses engine coolant temperature and switches off the A/C compressor when the temperature is too hot, reducing engine load.

| TEMPERATURE | | SENSOR |
F	(C)	VOLTAGE
248	(120)	0.25
212	(100)	0.46
176	(80)	0.84
150	(66)	1.34
140	(60)	1.55
104	(40)	2.27
86	(30)	2.60
68	(20)	2.93
32	(0)	3.59
-4	(-20)	4.24
-40	(-40)	4.90

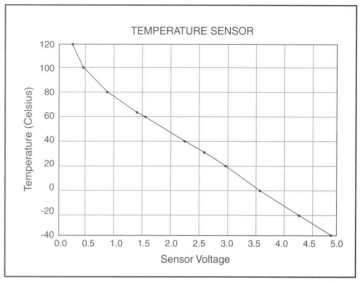

Fig. 4-11. Manufacturers include specifications for temperature sensor voltage drop testing.

An **ambient temperature sensor** is an electronic device that transmits a variable voltage signal to the control unit. The resistance of an ambient sensor varies in proportion to temperature changes. In addition to controlling compressor clutch operation, an ambient temperature sensor signal may also be used by the control unit to compute the correct blend door position.

Whether the system uses a switch or sensor, check the service manual for test conditions and specifications. Either device can be tested with an ohmmeter. To check:

1. With the ignition off, disconnect the A/C control head.
2. Measure the resistance between the two terminals. If it is:

   • Within specifications, the switch is functioning normally

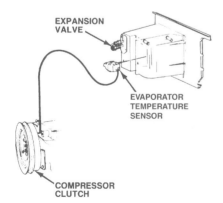

Fig. 4-12. An evaporator temperature sensor is a thermostatic switch that prevents compressor engagement if the evaporator freezes.

   • Infinite, check the wiring for an open circuit between the sensor and the control head
   • If resistance differs considerably from specifications, replace the sensor

A more accurate method of checking a temperature sensor and circuit operation is by voltage drop testing. The resistance of the thermistor, which varies with temperature, determines how much of a reference voltage, usually 5 volts, is dropped by the sensor. Take readings and compare to Service Manual specifications, figure 4-11. Thermistors are typically designed to operate near the mid-point of their range under normal conditions, so expect up to about 2.5 volts on a 5-volt circuit when air temperature is about 86°F (30°C).

An evaporator temperature thermostatic switch, which prevents compressor engagement if the evaporator gets too cold, can be the source of an apparent compressor clutch failure, figure 4-12. If this switch fails, the clutch may:

   • Not engage because the switch does not open
   • Fail to cycle because the switch does not close
   • Cycle erratically

Check the internal resistance of the evaporator temperature switch, and all other thermistors that are used in the system, with an ohmmeter. Check sensor and circuit performance by voltage drop testing. Consult the appropriate Service Manual for procedures and specifications.

Sun Sensor
Automatic and semi-automatic temperature control systems often have a sun sensor, which is used to adjust blend door position depending upon the intensity of the sunlight. A sun sensor generally installs on the top of the dash panel and uses a light-sensitive photo diode to vary circuit resistance through

A7

Ambient Temperature Sensor: An electronic device that transmits a variable voltage signal based on temperature. Sensor resistance varies with temperature changes.

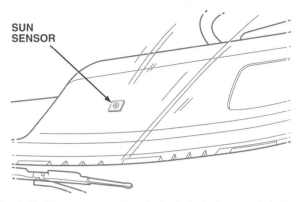

Fig. 4-13. The sun sensor is a photo diode that responds to the intensity of sunlight.

the device, figure 4-13. Perform resistance and voltage drop tests. Replace the sensor if it is defective.

Servicing the Automatic Control Panel

If the control panel of an automatic temperature control system fails, replace it. Some typical control panel failures include sticking or non-functioning push buttons, or lack of display illumination. Another sign is if the computer does not remember comfort settings when the vehicle is turned off and restarted.

CHAPTER QUESTIONS

1. Most cable-type HVAC controls are:
   a. Adjustable
   b. Self-adjusting
   c. Nonadjustable
   d. Obsolete

2. The most likely cause for temperature controller malfunction in a vacuum-operated HVAC system is a problem with the:
   a. Vacuum system
   b. Engine cooling system
   c. Electrical system
   d. Engine manifold

3. The most likely cause of the heater distributing only cold air when hot engine coolant is available at the heater core on a vacuum-operated HVAC system would be:
   a. No vacuum to the programmer checking relay
   b. A defective vacuum servo
   c. An incorrectly adjusted cable
   d. An open blend door actuator circuit

4. Most electronic climate-control modules are located:
   a. In the engine compartment
   b. In the trunk
   c. Under the driver's seat
   d. Behind the control head

5. A thermistor-type sensor can be used on a climate control system for all of the following *EXCEPT*:
   a. Evaporator temperature switch
   b. Ambient temperature switch
   c. Sun sensor
   d. Coolant temperature sensor

6. The onboard diagnostic program of a computer-controlled HVAC system can provide all of the following *EXCEPT*:
   a. Diagnostic trouble codes
   b. Serial data access
   c. Functional tests
   d. Pinpoint test results

7. The only tool capable of displaying internal control module information is a:
   a. Digital Multimeter (DMM)
   b. Scan tool
   c. Special system tester
   d. Lab scope

8. The most accurate method of checking a temperature sensor and circuit is by:
   a. Accessing the data stream
   b. Checking resistance with an ohmmeter
   c. Voltage drop testing
   d. Scan tool testing

9. If clutch coil resistance is within specifications, check engagement by:
   a. Connecting the coil to battery power with jump wires
   b. Installing a jump wire across the relay
   c. Measuring available voltage with the control panel set to maximum cool
   d. Grounding the clutch coil circuit

10. An evaporator temperature thermostatic switch is used to:
    a. Regulate refrigerant flow through the evaporator
    b. Prevent compressor operation above a certain ambient temperature
    c. Prevent compressor operation if refrigerant level is too low
    d. Prevent compressor engagement if the evaporator is too cold

A7

CHAPTER FIVE

REFRIGERANT RECOVERY, RECYCLING, HANDLING, AND RETROFIT

CHAPTER OBJECTIVES

- The technician will complete the ASE task list on Refrigerant Recovery, Recycling, Handling, and Retrofit.
- The technician will be able to answer 4 questions dealing with the Refrigerant Recovery, Recycling, Handling, and Retrofit section of the A7 ASE Test.

RECOVERY AND RECYCLING EQUIPMENT

Recovery and recycling stations capture, filter, and store the refrigerant evacuated from a system for reuse. Typically, recycling salvages about 65 percent of the refrigerant charge. Recovery and recycling stations are available for R-12 and R-134a refrigerants. Dual stations are available that can process both R-12 and R-134a. However, these are two units combined into one cabinet, and a single station cannot process both types of refrigerant. Mixing R-12 with R-134a, or any other refrigerant blend, contaminates the recycling station and results in costly repairs. Use a refrigerant identifier to verify what refrigerant is in the system being serviced before hooking up service equipment.

Maintenance and Certification

The Federal Clean Air Act, Section 609, requires that anyone who performs a service involving refrigerant on an automotive A/C system must be certified to do so. Certification forms can be obtained from the manufacturers of UL-approved refrigerant recovery/recycling equipment. The equipment should have a label saying it is UL-approved and meets SAE standard J1991.

To qualify for certification, a shop must have UL-approved recovery and recycling equipment, and the technician must be able to show proof of training on the use and maintenance of the equipment. The certification form requires the equipment serial number and the signature of the equipment owner or a responsible officer, in addition to the name and address of the technician. Remember that without this certification, it is illegal to perform any refrigerant service.

The Society of Automotive Engineers (SAE) established three standards, J1989, J1990, and J1991, concerning refrigerant recycling, which the U.S. government incorporated into laws. Recycled R-12 is defined by SAE Standard J1991, and manufacturers must make sure their equipment meets this standard, and all applicable recycling equipment standards.

Standard J1990 also applies to equipment manufacture, but contains guidelines that technicians should be aware of, such as the requirement that the tank be tested every five years. This standard also specifies that service hose shutoff valves must be within 12 inches of the hose ends to prevent unnecessary refrigerant release. The equipment must also be able to separate refrigeration oil that comes out of a system during refrigerant discharge and be able to indicate the amount of oil lost, so the technician can replace it in the system. Standard J1989 applies directly to the service technician, establishing guidelines for recovery and recycling equipment use.

Refrigerant Recovery

A recovery and recycling station connects to the vehicle through a manifold gauge set or a charging station, figure 5-1. Once the vehicle system has been serviced, the refrigerant remaining in the manifold gauge set or charging station hoses must be recovered before the service ports are disconnected. Before recovery, connect a manifold gauge set, and verify that there is pressure in the system. Observe all safety precautions and equipment operating procedures detailed in certification training. To recover refrigerant:

1. With the manifold gauge set connected to the vehicle, attach the center hose to the intake side of the recovery and recycling station.
2. Make sure the liquid valves of the recovery station are open, then open both manifold gauge valves.
3. Switch the power on and start the recovery station compressor. The compressor automatically switches off once recovery is complete.
4. Monitor manifold gauges for several minutes; if pressure on either side rises above zero, repeat step 3.
5. Open the recovery station oil drain valve until all oil removed from the system drains from the separator.
6. Note the amount of oil in the catch and add that much fresh oil to the system before recharging.

Refrigerant Recycling

There are two types of recycling equipment: single-pass and multi-pass. Single-pass equipment sends the refrigerant through each recycling stage one time before storing it for use, figure 5-2. A multi-pass system may not complete all the recycling stages before storing the refrigerant, figure 5-3. When refrigerant is needed to charge a system, the equipment cycles the refrigerant until it is clean and dry enough to meet standards for reuse. Either type of system can be used as long as it is UL-approved.

Recycling removes moisture and non-condensable gases from used refrigerant so that it conforms to purity standards established by SAE J1991. For best results and efficiency, the recovery and recycling station recovery tank should be full

Fig. 5-1. A recovery and recycling station processes one type of refrigerant for reuse.

before recycling. Recycling operations vary slightly by equipment; the following is a general procedure:

1. Open both recovery tank valves on the recovery and recycling station.
2. Switch the station power on and activate the switch that starts the recycle operation.
3. Use the station moisture indicator as a sight glass; expect to see a stream of bubbles at start-up that quickly dissipates to no bubbles as the pump reaches peak efficiency.
4. Run the pump at peak efficiency for at least 30 minutes, then check the moisture indicator. Severely contaminated refrigerant can take several hours to recycle. Monitor the moisture indicator and switch the pump off once the refrigerant meets SAE standards.
5. Switch the station power off and close both recovery tank valves.

Disconnect, label, and store the recycled refrigerant tank according to regulations.

REFRIGERANT

In addition to purity standards for recycled refrigerant, SAE standards apply to refrigerant identification, handling, labeling, and storage. Follow all applicable rules as detailed in certification training.

Identification

Read all labels before using a container of refrigerant to make sure it is the correct type for the system being serviced. Use a refrigerant identifier to determine what the vehicle system is charged with; this prevents equipment contamination, figure 5-4. New containers of R-12 are painted white, while R-134a containers are blue. Observe the same color coding when recycling. Remember: Never put R-12 into an R-134a system, or vice versa, or contaminate equipment with another blend of refrigerant.

Handling

Never vent R-12 or R-134a into the air. Always use a recovery and recycling system. Follow the equipment instructions when using recovery and recycling equipment to be within the legal requirements. Separate recovery and recycling equipment,

A7

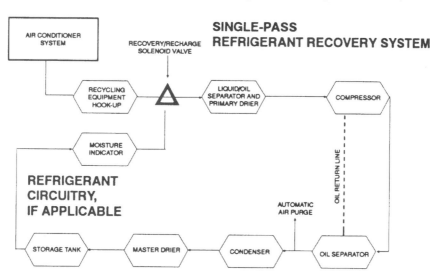

Fig. 5-2. The single-pass refrigerant recycling process.

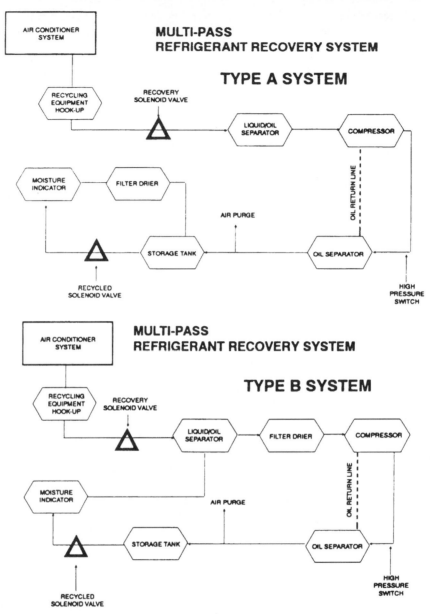

Fig. 5-3. The multi-pass refrigerant recycling process.

manifold gauges, replacement parts, and leak detectors are required for R-12 and R-134a systems.

Labeling and Storage

The storage containers for recycled R-12 must qualify for DOT CFR Title 49. Such a container has "DOT4BA" or "DOT4BW" stamped on it. Never put refrigerant into a disposable container. Before transferring refrigerant into a DOT-approved container, evacuate the tank to at least 17 in-Hg (75 mm-Hg). Find the container gross weight rating and fill it to only 60 percent of that rating. For example, put 30 pounds of refrigerant into a 50-pound container. To dispose of an empty container, evacuate it using approved recovery and recycling equipment until it shows vacuum. Write the word "empty" on the container and dispose of it according to local regulations.

Testing Recycled Refrigerant

Before using recycled refrigerant that has been stored in a portable container, check for non-condensable gases, or air, in

the tank. This is an extremely important step that must not be overlooked. To check for non-condensable gases:

1. Store the container at 65° F (18.3° C), out of direct sunlight, for at least 12 hours before testing. Use a reliable thermometer to monitor ambient temperature within 4 inches (10 cm) of the container.
2. Connect a pressure gauge that measures in 1-psi (0.1 kg/cm^2) increments to the refrigerant container.
3. Compare gauge readings with a pressure and temperature chart, figure 5-5. If the refrigerant pressure is:
   - At or below the specified pressure, the refrigerant can be used
   - Above the specified pressure, continue by purging the tank
4. Attach the recovery and recycling station to the container and slowly vent vapor until the pressure drops below the specified limit. If necessary, recycle the container contents.

Fig. 5-4. A refrigerant identifier determines with what refrigerant a system is charged.

PRESSURE/TEMPERATURE CHART

DEGREES F/C	PRESSURE PSI/Bar	DEGREES F/C	PRESSURE PSI/Bar	DEGREES F/C	PRESSURE PSI/Bar	DEGREES F/C	PRESSURE PSI/Bar	DEGREES F/C	PRESSURE PSI/Bar
65/18.3	74/ 5.20	75/23.9	87/6.11	85/ 29.4	102/ 7.17	95/35.0	118/8.29	105/40.5	136/ 9.56
66/18.8	75/ 5.27	76/24.4	88/6.18	86/ 30.0	103/ 7.24	96/35.5	120/8.43	106/41.1	138/ 9.70
67/19.4	76/ 5.34	77/25.0	90/6.32	87/ 30.5	105/ 7.38	97/36.1	122/8.57	107/41.6	140/ 9.84
68/20.0	78/ 5.48	78/25.5	92/6.46	88/ 31.1	107/ 7.52	98/36.6	124/8.71	108/42.2	142/ 9.98
69/20.5	79/ 5.55	79/26.1	94/6.60	89/ 31.6	108/ 7.59	99/37.2	125/8.78	109/42.7	144/10.12
70/21.1	80/ 5.62	80/26.6	96/6.74	90/ 32.2	110/ 7.73	100/ 37.7	127/8.92	110/43.3	146/10.26
71/21.6	82/ 5.76	81/27.2	98/6.88	91/ 32.7	111/ 7.80	101/ 38.3	129/9.06	111/43.9	148/10.40
72/22.2	83/ 5.83	82/27.7	99/6.95	92/ 33.3	113/ 7.94	102/ 38.8	130/9.13	112/44.4	150/10.54
73/22.7	84/ 5.90	83/28.3	100/ 7.03	93/ 33.9	115/ 8.08	103/ 39.4	132/9.27	113/45.0	152/10.68
74/23.3	86/ 6.04	84/28.9	101/ 7.10	94/ 34.4	116/ 8.15	104/ 40.0	134/9.42	114/45.5	154/10.82

Fig. 5-5. Pressure and temperature chart for checking refrigerant container non-condensable gas content.

A7

R-134a RETROFIT

Retrofit to R-134a should always be considered an option anytime an R-12 A/C system requires major repairs. This includes any R-12 system that needs a replacement compressor, condenser, evaporator, or maybe even hoses. In such situations, you can save your customer much of what it would cost to retrofit later by going ahead and doing the conversion now.

Why? Because the refrigerant (if there's any left) has to be recovered from the system anyway, and the system has to be opened up for repairs. Retrofitting the system to R-134a at this time would be less expensive than doing it later.

A simple retrofit generally should take about an hour and a half to two and a half hours. A more complicated retrofit that involves removing the compressor so it can be drained or replaced might add anywhere from 30 minutes up to 3 hours to the job depending on how difficult the compressor is to remove.

General Retrofit Procedure

The following guidelines are based on the SAE J 1661 standard, which covers the recommended procedure for retrofitting an R-12 system to R-134a. Some vehicles may require more or less work depending on the application. Follow specific retrofit recommendations by the vehicle manufacturer.

Preliminary Inspection

Make sure the A/C system has not already been retrofitted to R-134a or charged with some other refrigerant. Talk to the customer and ask about any previous service that's been performed on the A/C system. Check the service fittings to see if R-134a adapters or some other type of service fittings have been installed. Look for a decal indicating the system has been converted or contains a different refrigerant.

Use a refrigerant identifier to positively establish that the A/C system you are about to convert contains only R-12. If a system is found to contain an unknown refrigerant, DO NOT connect your recovery and recycling machine to the vehicle. Be sure to use an identifier that also detects excessive noncondensable gases (air) in the system. Two to three percent air in a refrigerant charge will cause excessive head pressures and noisy compressor operation.

Recover R-12 Refrigerant

If the system contains no refrigerant, this step is not necessary. If recovery is needed, follow the procedure mentioned previously in this chapter, using a UL-approved recovery and recycling machine to pull any R-12 and refrigerant oil out of the system.

Replace the Desiccant and Add Oil

This step is recommended whether the R-12 system already has a compatible desiccant (such as XH7) or not to restore the system's moisture protection. This is especially important on any retrofit that will use PAG oil.

Replace the accumulator or receiver/drier with one that contains XH7 or XH9 desiccant. Be sure to add the same amount of PAG or POE oil to the new unit as was in the old unit, or as specified by the vehicle manufacturer.

Replace Other Components as Needed

Though additional component replacement is usually not required in most retrofits, it may be necessary in certain applications.

Existing hoses and seals should not need to be replaced unless they are leaking or damaged. If hoses need to be replaced, install nylon barrier style hoses. If seals or O-rings need to be replaced, install ones made of Neoprene W or HNBR.

On some applications, a larger or more efficient condenser may be recommended to improve cooling performance with R-134a. A larger or auxiliary condenser fan may also be recommended. Condensers are expensive to replace, so the cost may only be justified if previous experience shows that a particular vehicle does not cool very well with a stock condenser.

Most compressors are compatible with R-134a and do not have to be replaced. But some do. Some compressors are also not rugged enough to handle the higher operating pressures of R-134a. Check for the manufacturers' specifications.

Install R-134a Service Fittings

Install the high and low-side adapters over the existing service fittings. The larger (16 mm) high-side adapter goes over the 3/8 inch threaded fitting on the liquid line, while the smaller (13 mm) low-side adapter goes over the 7/16 inch threaded fitting on the suction line.

If the adapters are the type that require removal of the **Schrader valve** cores from the original R-12 service fittings (many do not), then do so prior to installing the adapters.

Make sure the threads are clean before screwing the adapters on, and that the adapter threads have been treated with an anaerobic compound to lock them in place.

Install R-134a Retrofit Decal

Label the system so other technicians will know it contains R-134a and not R-12. The R-134a identification label, which is color coded light blue, should go over the old label (or remove the old R-12 label). The label should also be completely filled out (date of retrofit, type and amount of refrigerant, type and amount of lubricant used, etc.).

Also, remove any other decals, tags or references to R-12 on the vehicle.

Evacuate System

Evacuate the system at 29 in-Hg for a minimum of 30 minutes to remove all air and moisture. Dual evaporator systems should be evacuated for one hour.

Recharge with R-134a

Connect your charging equipment to the system, and charge the system to 80% of the original system capacity with R-134a. Then add additional refrigerant in 1/4 pound increments until the system is filled to about 85 to 90% of the original system capacity. Overcharging will reduce cooling efficiency and increase compressor discharge pressures excessively.

Confirm that the system is properly charged by observing the high- and low-side pressure readings with a manifold gauge set. Do not use the sight glass (if one is provided) to determine the level of charge because the glass may appear cloudy even when the system is fully charged with R-134a and PAG oil.

Schrader Valve: A service valve that uses a spring-loaded pin and internal pressure to seal a port; depressing the pin will open the port.

CHAPTER QUESTIONS

1. A technician must be certified to perform all of the following A/C system services **EXCEPT**:
   a. Top off the refrigerant charge
   b. Check compressor clutch operation
   c. Recover and recycle refrigerant
   d. Identify the refrigerant type

2. A refrigerant recovery and recycling station must have a label saying it is:
   a. ASE-approved
   b. DOT-approved
   c. SAE-approved
   d. UL-approved

3. Refrigerant recycling equipment use and maintenance guidelines are defined in SAE Standard:
   a. J1989
   b. J1990
   c. J1991
   d. J1992

4. What color is a new container of R-134a?
   a. White
   b. Pink
   c. Blue
   d. Yellow

5. A container that may be used for recycled R-12 is stamped:
   a. DOT4BW
   b. DOT3BW
   c. DOT2BM
   d. DOT4MW

6. Before use, a container of recycled refrigerant must be tested for:
   a. Water contamination
   b. Non-condensable gases
   c. Chemical purity
   d. Oil contamination

7. Before testing recycled refrigerant, store the container in a warm location out of the sunlight for at least:
   a. 3 hours
   b. 6 hours
   c. 9 hours
   d. 12 hours

8. When recycling refrigerant, run the recycling pump:
   a. For at least one hour
   b. Until there are no bubbles in the sight glass
   c. Until the moisture indicator shows standards are met
   d. Until it automatically shuts off

A7

SAMPLE TEST

This sample test can help you review your knowledge of this entire book. The format of the questions is similar to the certification tests given by the National Institute for Automotive Service Excellence. Generally, the questions here are more difficult than the programmed study questions you answered as you read the technical material in this book.

Read these review questions carefully, then read all the possible answers before making your decision. Always select the **best possible answer**. In some cases, you may think all the answers are partially correct, or you may feel that none is exactly right. But in every case, there is a **best** answer; that is the one you should select.

Answers to the questions in this sample test are found near the end of this book, before the glossary. If you answer at least 17 of these questions correctly, then you can be confident of your knowledge of the subjects covered in this book, and in the ASE Certification Test A7, Heating and Air Conditioning. If you answer fewer than 17 correctly, you should reread the text and take another look at the illustrations. Also, check the glossary as you review the material.

1. The most likely cause of the A/C making a honking noise while operating would be:
   a. Compressor damage
   b. Drive belt wear
   c. Low refrigerant level
   d. Blower motor damage

2. Technician A says bubbles visible in the sight glass of an R-12 system indicate a low refrigerant level. Technician B says it is normal to see bubbles in the sight glass of an R-134a when the engine is running at a high throttle opening. Who is right?
   a. A only
   b. B only
   c. Both A and B
   d. Neither A nor B

3. To locate the source of a foul odor whenever the A/C system is operating, inspect the:
   a. Condenser
   b. Evaporator
   c. Compressor
   d. Receiver-drier

4. During normal operation, the receiver-drier on a TXV system should feel:
   a. Very hot
   b. Warm
   c. Cool
   d. Very cold

5. On a very humid day, you can expect A/C system pressures to be:
   a. Below the normal range
   b. At the low end of the normal range
   c. At the high end of the normal range
   d. Above the normal range

6. Technician A says under normal operating conditions the line leading from the condenser to the expansion device on an A/C system should feel cold. Technician B says a restriction in the A/C system low-side causes the line to feel cold. Who is right?
   a. A only
   b. B only
   c. Both A and B
   d. Neither A nor B

7. When an A/C system uses a suction throttling device, the device is typically located on the:
   a. Accumulator outlet
   b. Compressor outlet
   c. Evaporator outlet
   d. Condenser inlet

8. Which of the following is an expansion device?
   a. Fixed-orifice tube
   b. Pilot Operated Absolute (POA) valve
   c. Evaporator Pressure Regulator (EPR)
   d. Evaporator Temperature Regulator (ETR)

9. Technician A says an A/C system with a low refrigerant level can cause low gauge readings on both the high-side and low-side. Technician B says a defective expansion valve can cause a very low low-side pressure and normal to slightly low high-side pressure. Who is right?
   a. A only
   b. B only
   c. Both A and B
   d. Neither A nor B

10. What tool is used to locate a refrigerant leak in an R-134a A/C system?
    a. Halide torch
    b. Electronic leak detector
    c. Refrigerant identifier
    d. Recovery and recycling station

11. Technician A says Polyalkylene Glycol (PAG) refrigeration oil is used as original equipment on R-134a systems. Technician B says store leftover PAG oil in a tightly sealed metal container for later use. Who is right?
    a. A only
    b. B only
    c. Both A and B
    d. Neither A nor B

12. Technician A says discharging an A/C system slowly minimizes oil loss. Technician B says servicing an air conditioner involves discharging and evacuating the system until it holds a steady vacuum. Who is right?
    a. A only
    b. B only
    c. Both A and B
    d. Neither A nor B

13. The fact that a cycling clutch compressor runs for only a short time, then turns off, is most likely caused by:
    a. A very low refrigerant level
    b. A missing fixed-orifice expansion tube
    c. An open compressor clutch circuit
    d. A stuck over-pressure switch

14. Technician A says a condenser corroded from acids formed by water contamination can be serviced by backflushing.
Technician B says a chemical flush can be used to clean a corroded condenser. Who is right?
   a. A only
   b. B only
   c. Both A and B
   d. Neither A nor B

15. The most likely cause of a heating system delivering too much heat to the passenger compartment would be:
   a. Blocked outlet air ducts
   b. Stuck-open blend door
   c. Partial blockage of the heater core
   d. Reduced current to blower motor

16. A gurgling sound from the radiator could mean:
   a. Defective thermostat
   b. Coolant contamination
   c. Poor pressure cap seal
   d. Radiator blockage

17. Technician A says if there is no pressure drop for three minutes during a heater core pressure test, the heater core is not leaking.
Technician B says the heater core is not contaminated with sediment if there is no pressure drop after three minutes. Who is right?
   a. A only
   b. B only
   c. Both A and B
   d. Neither A nor B

18. Technician A says if the heat level does not change when the temperature selector is moved on a vacuum-operated heating system the vacuum motor linkage may be disconnected.
Technician B says no heat level change when the temperature selector is moved can be caused by a heater control valve malfunction. Who is right?
   a. A only
   b. B only
   c. Both A and B
   d. Neither A nor B

19. When checking blower motor switch continuity:
   a. Test points requiring continuity should read 0 ohms
   b. Refer to a wiring diagram for specified voltage
   c. Jump the blower motor switch to a known-good ground
   d. Check switch amperage in each position

20. During the test for noncondensable gases in recycled R-12, the refrigerant must be:
   a. At or above the specified pressure
   b. Exactly at the specified pressure
   c. At or below the specified pressure
   d. Within 10 psi of the specified pressure

ANSWERS

Chapter 1:
1. c, 2. c, 3. a, 4. d, 5. b, 6. d, 7. d, 8. b, 9. c, 10. a, 11. d, 12. a, 13. b, 14. d, 15. b

Chapter 2:
1. c, 2. b, 3. c, 4. d, 5. a, 6. b, 7. a, 8. a, 9. c, 10. d

Chapter 3:
1. a, 2. c, 3. d, 4. b, 5. a, 6. c, 7. b, 8. c

Chapter 4:
1. b, 2. a, 3. a, 4. d, 5. c, 6. d, 7. b, 8. c, 9. a, 10. d

Chapter 5:
1. b, 2. d, 3. b, 4. c, 5. a, 6. b, 7. d, 8. c

Sample Test:
1. c, 2. a, 3. b, 4. b, 5. c, 6. d, 7. c, 8. a, 9. c, 10. b, 11. a, 12. c, 13. a, 14. d, 15. b, 16. d, 17. a, 18. c, 19. a, 20. c

A7

GLOSSARY

Actuator: A component that converts a vacuum or electrical signal into a physical movement to operate a part such as a blend door or valve.

Ambient Temperature Sensor: An electronic device that transmits a variable voltage signal based on temperature. Sensor resistance varies with temperature changes.

Ambient Temperature: The temperature of the air surrounding a component.

Ambient Temperature Switch: A digital on/off device that senses ambient temperature and switches the compressor off when the temperature is too cold.

Blend Door: A door in a heating, ventilation, and A/C system that directs air through or around the heater core.

Chlorofluorocarbon (CFC): A chemical compound containing chlorine, fluorine, and carbon. When released into the atmosphere, the chlorine atoms detach from the CFC molecules, causing a chemical reaction that turns ozone molecules into oxygen. Oxygen does not filter ultraviolet light as ozone does. R-12 (CCl2F2) is a CFC.

Coolant Temperature Sensor: Often designated as the Engine Coolant Temperature (ECT) Sensor. A variable resistance sensor threaded into the engine coolant passage. Changes resistance as temperature varies.

Coolant Temperature Switch: A digital on/off device that senses engine coolant temperature and switches off the A/C compressor when the temperature is too hot, reducing engine load.

Control Head: The dashboard-mounted unit that contains the controls for the heating, ventilation, and A/C system.

Cycling Clutch: A system that maintains refrigerant pressure by engaging and disengaging the electromagnetic compressor clutch.

Desiccant: A chemical agent in the receiver-drier of an A/C system used to remove moisture.

Expansion Tube: Also known as a fixed-orifice tube, this expansion device removes pressure from the refrigerant as it flows into the evaporator, but does not vary the flow rate.

Heater Control Valve: A cable, vacuum, or electric valve on the heater core inlet that controls the rate of coolant flow into the heater core.

Heater Core: A heat exchanger through which hot coolant flows and releases its heat by conduction into a passing air stream.

High-Side: The portion of the A/C system in which the refrigerant is under high pressure and at high temperature. It includes the compressor outlet, condenser, receiver-drier, and expansion device inlet.

Low-Side: The portion of the A/C system in which the refrigerant is under low pressure and at low temperature. It includes the expansion device outlet, evaporator, accumulator, and compressor inlet.

Mode Door: A door in an HVAC system that directs air to the defrost, dash, and heat ducts.

Schrader Valve: A service valve that uses a spring-loaded pin and internal pressure to seal a port; depressing the pin will open the port.

Thermostatic Bulb: A device that automatically responds to changes in temperature to actuate a damper in the air intake passage.

Thermostatic Expansion Valve (TXV): An expansion device that removes pressure from the refrigerant as it flows into the evaporator and also varies the refrigerant flow rate in relation to evaporator temperature.

Vacuum: A pressure less than atmospheric pressure.

Variable Orifice Expansion Tube: A type of expansion tube that varies the refrigerant flow rate to compensate for changes in compressor output.

A8

ENGINE PERFORMANCE

CHAPTER OBJECTIVES

- The technician will complete the ASE task list on General Engine Diagnosis and Repair.
- The technician will be able to answer 12 questions dealing with the General Engine Diagnosis and Repair section of the A8 ASE Test.

Poor engine performance can be the result of a long list of problems. Performance or driveability problems may be indicated by customer complaints of no starting, hard starting, loss of power, poor fuel mileage, engine knock, or engine misfire. Begin diagnosis by getting specific information from the customer. Find out the exact nature of the problem, under what conditions it occurs, and when the symptoms first started.

CUSTOMER INTERVIEW

This first step in the process is crucial to diagnosing automotive concerns as it helps you get a clear understanding of the situation. Use the following procedures to begin every diagnosis:

- Verify the concern
- Research the history of the concern
- Ask the customer what they think the problem is
- Verify the information you have gathered

One of the most important steps in diagnosis is to verify the customer's concern. Often a driver's description lacks some of the information necessary to begin proper diagnosis. You might misunderstand the driver's description or the symptom may be caused by circumstances that you might not encounter during a typical operation check or test drive.

The best solution is for the driver to demonstrate the problem for you or the service advisor. If that is not practical, question the driver about exactly when the problem occurs. This information can lead you to drive the vehicle under the same conditions, and with an operational check, you can verify the concern and begin to move to the proper subsystem to begin your diagnosis.

A rational diagnostic procedure must be followed to successfully diagnose a customer's complaint. By following logical procedures you can use your time more efficiently and replace or repair the right components. Improper diagnosis leads to come-backs, dissatisfied customers, and a waste of your time and your customer's time.

Before attempting to repair a performance problem, make sure the engine is in sound mechanical condition. In addition to internal engine defects, driveability problems may be caused by a malfunction in the electrical, fuel, ignition, or emission control systems. Accurate troubleshooting information for the vehicle being serviced is essential for testing and evaluating all systems.

After determining that there is a driveability problem, take a systematic approach to solving it. Work in a logical manner to not only repair the problem, but also eliminate any other conditions that may have contributed to the failure. To diagnose performance problems, follow these four steps:

- Preliminary inspection
- Road test
- Review vehicle service history and applicable support materials
- Comprehensive engine testing

PRELIMINARY INSPECTION

Eliminate any obvious problems by performing an underhood inspection. The source of noise or vibration complaints will often be revealed by a visual inspection. Problems such as rough running or stalling may be caused by a broken or disconnected vacuum hose or electrical wire. When performing an inspection, check for the following:

- Drive belts that are properly tensioned and free of cracks, frayed edges, and glazing
- Electrical connections that are secure and clean. Inspect harnesses for signs of brittle insulation, rubbing, and broken or damaged wires
- Engine-mounted accessories that are properly supported; look for loose or missing bolts, worn bushings, and loose or broken support brackets
- Engine mounts, torque struts, and vibration dampers that are in good condition and securely attached
- Hoses, water and vacuum, that are tight and properly routed. Replace any that are loose, brittle, kinked, broken, or otherwise damaged
- Fuel lines, hoses, and fittings that are free of leakage and damage
- Battery, cables, and connections that are tight and free of corrosion. Also, check the battery **electrolyte** level and state-of-charge
- Secondary ignition cables, as well as the distributor cap and coils, that are free of cracks, insulation damage, corrosion, and loose connections
- Air filter element and ductwork that are clear and able to supply a good flow of unrestricted air
- Emission control system components that are properly installed and connected. Repair any brittle, burned, or damaged hoses and loose fittings

Also look the engine over for any signs of leakage. Verify coolant leaks by pressure testing the cooling system. Check the level of the engine oil and coolant, and look for indications of dilution and contamination. Oil dilution is generally caused by raw fuel entering the crankcase. Look for a high fluid level and thin consistency accompanied by the odor of gasoline. Coolant leaking into the crankcase mixes with the oil to create a milky, brown-colored emulsion. Either condition, dilution or coolant contamination, indicates internal engine problems.

Start the engine and allow it to idle while listening for any unusual noises. A stethoscope is a handy tool for isolating top-end and bottom-end engine noises. To isolate difficult noises, connect a timing light and listen. Bottom-end noise will cycle in time with the flashing of the light. Top-end sounds will be audible with every other flash of the light.

While the engine is running, check the exhaust for indications of internal engine problems. Check for:

- Black smoke. This is caused by a rich **air-fuel ratio**, and is often accompanied by the "rotten egg" smell of an over-worked catalytic converter
- Blue smoke. This indicates excessive oil burning and often gives off a pungent odor
- Cloudy white exhaust. This is often the result of engine coolant leaking into the combustion chamber. Burning coolant also produces a distinctive chemical odor. Check the temperature gauge for overheating
- Listen closely to the sound of the exhaust system. Be especially conscious of irregular pulses or whistling sounds that may indicate valve problems or a restricted exhaust

If everything looks good and there are no obvious problems, the vehicle is ready for a road test.

ROAD TEST

Whenever possible, let the customer accompany you on the road test. The customer knows the vehicle and can point out abnormal sounds, vibrations, and other annoyances that might be overlooked or considered normal.

Conduct a thorough road test; one quick lap around the block is not enough. The engine must be brought to normal operating temperature, and the test drive should include a stop-and-go city driving cycle and a period of cruising at highway speed. Proper road testing is extremely important for vehicles equipped with onboard diagnostics. An incomplete test may not record all of the intermittent, or soft, fault codes. A complete road test should take about 15 minutes. If possible, use the same route for all tests so that performance can be compared before and after service, as well as to the performance of similar vehicles. If a **dynamometer** is available, use it to simulate the road test.

When a problem occurs while driving, note the operating conditions. Modulate engine and road speed to help isolate the symptoms. Use the nature of the problem to determine which diagnostic tests to perform. The tests, and the order in which they are performed, depend on if the suspected problem is in the:

- Electrical or electronic system
- Internal engine
- Ignition system
- Fuel system
- Emission control system

VEHICLE SERVICE INFORMATION

Resource materials should be readily available when performing diagnostic procedures. Resource materials and information should include:

- Service History
- Service Manuals
- Diagnostic Manuals
- Wiring Diagrams
- Technical Service Bulletins
- Online Technical Support

The vehicle service history may be found in various ways. Ask the customer if they have copies of repair orders for previous service work. OEM warranty systems track all repairs completed under warranty and provide good details of the problems serviced in the past.

Every vehicle has a specific Service Manual. These manuals contain general service information, and often specific diagnostic and troubleshooting procedures for each system within the vehicle, such as the emission or fuel system.

Most manufacturers also provide some type of Diagnostic Manual for the vehicle or vehicle family. Typically these manuals are for specific automotive systems such as electrical, fuel injection, and emissions/performance.

These manuals are more in-depth than Service Manuals as they provide component descriptions and operation theory along with the applicable troubleshooting procedures.

Some manufacturers dedicate separate publications for wiring diagrams rather than include them in the other manuals. Either way, the wiring diagrams or schematics are required for making most every electrical or electronic repair throughout the vehicle.

Technical Service Bulletins (TSBs) cover information discovered after the Service and/or Diagnostic Manuals were printed, figure 1-1. Always consult TSBs for information about known vehicle concerns or improvements for the most up-to-date information available.

Today there are several online technical support services that compile repair information and TSBs for many vehicles. There is a nominal charge to access these services; however, many times the benefit far outweighs the cost.

SERVICE PRECAUTIONS AND WARNINGS

Cautions and Warnings

The diagnosis and repair procedures in the vehicle Service Manuals generally contain both general and specific cautions and/or warnings. The information is placed at strategic locations throughout most Service Manuals and is designed to prevent the following from occurring:

- Serious bodily injury to the technician
- Serious bodily injury to the driver and/or passenger(s) of the vehicle, if the vehicle has been improperly repaired

A8

Technical
Service
Bulletin

SUBJECT:
Sags/Hesitation/Stumble/Start & Stall

OVERVIEW:
This bulletin involves selectively erasing and reprogramming the Powertrain Control
Module (PCM) with new software (calibration changes).

MODELS:
2003 Minivan and Truck

NOTE: THIS INFORMATION APPLIES TO VEHICLES EQUIPPED WITH A 3.34L ENGINE.

SYMPTOM/CONDITION:
Sags/Hesitation/Stumble or Start & Stall after a cold start in ambient temperatures of -7∞-
30∞ C (20∞ 86∞ F). The sag/hesitation or stumble may persist for up toa minute into a drive cycle
and is attributed to high driveability index (DI) fuel.

DIAGNOSIS:
Using the Diagnostic System and or a Diagnostic Scan Tool with the appropriate Diagnostic
Procedures Manual, verify all engine/transmission systems are functioning as designed. If
Diagnostic Trouble Codes (DTC's) are present, record them on the repair order and repair as
necessary before proceeding further with this bulletin. If no DTC's are present and the customer
has described the above symptoms, perform the Repair Procedure.

NOTE: WHENEVER A POWERTRAIN CONTROL MODULE (PCM) IS REPLACED
DUE TO FAILURE, THE SOFTWARE OF THE REPLACEMENT CONTROLLER
MUST BE VERIFIED FOR THE LATEST REVISION LEVEL. USE THE FLASH
PROCEDURE TO UPDATE REPLACED CONTROLLERS AS NECESSARY.

PARTS REQUIRED:
1   14465020 Label, Authorized Software Update
1   54266086 Label, Authorized Modification

Fig. 1-1. Typical TSB.

Some manuals will contain more cautions and/or warnings, while others may have few included. Following are a few examples of the cautions or warnings you may see.

Battery Disconnect Caution
Before servicing any electrical component, the ignition key must be in the OFF or LOCK position and all electrical loads must be OFF, unless instructed otherwise in these procedures. If a tool or equipment could easily come in contact with a live exposed electrical terminal, also disconnect the negative battery cable. Failure to follow these precautions may cause personal injury and/or damage to the vehicle or its components.

Fuel and EVAP Pipe Caution
In order to reduce the risk of fire and personal injury, observe the following items:

- Replace all nylon fuel pipes that are nicked, scratched, or damaged during installation. Do not attempt to repair the sections of the nylon fuel pipes

- Do not hammer directly on the fuel harness body clips when installing new fuel pipes. Damage to the nylon pipes may result in a fuel leak. Always cover nylon vapor pipes with a wet towel before using a torch near them
- Apply a few drops of clean engine oil to the male pipe ends before connecting fuel pipe fittings. This will ensure proper reconnection and prevent a possible fuel leak

Fuel Gauge Leak Caution

Wrap a shop towel around the fuel pressure connection in order to reduce the risk of fire and personal injury. The towel will absorb any fuel leakage that occurs during the connection of the fuel pressure gauge. Place the towel in an approved container when the connection of the fuel pressure gauge is complete.

Relieving Fuel Pressure Caution

Relieve the fuel **system pressure** before servicing fuel system components in order to reduce the risk of fire and personal injury. After relieving the system pressure, a small amount of fuel may be released when servicing the fuel lines or connections. In order to reduce the chance of personal injury, cover the regulator and the fuel line fittings with a shop towel before disconnecting. This will catch any fuel that may leak out.

Handling ESD Sensitive Parts Notice

Electrostatic discharge (ESD) can damage many solid-state electrical components. ESD susceptible components may or may not be labeled with the ESD symbol. Handle all electrical components carefully. Use the following precautions in order to avoid ESD damage:

- Touch a metal ground point in order to remove your body's static charge before servicing any electronic component
- Do not touch exposed terminals. Terminals may connect to **circuits** susceptible to ESD damage
- Do not allow tools to contact exposed terminals when servicing connectors
- Do not remove components from their protective packaging until necessary

Avoid the following actions unless required by the diagnostic procedure:

- Jumpering or grounding of the components or connectors
- Connecting test equipment probes to components or connectors
- Connect the ground lead first when using test probes
- Ground the protective packaging of any component before opening
- Resting solid-state components on metal workbenches, or on top of TVs, radios, or other electrical devices

Ignition OFF When Disconnecting Battery

Always turn the ignition OFF when connecting or disconnecting battery cables, battery chargers, or jumper cables. Failing to do so may damage the **Powertrain Control Module (PCM)** or other electronic components.

Electric Coolant Fan Caution

An electric fan under the hood can start up even when the engine is not running and can injure you. Keep hands, clothing, and tools away from any underhood electric fan.

COMPREHENSIVE ENGINE TESTING

It is important to follow instructions from both the vehicle and the test equipment manufacturers when performing engine tests. Some tests require the ignition to be disabled while the starter motor cranks the engine.

Others may require bypassing the fuel pump relay, idle speed controller, or some other electrical or electronic component. The proper test equipment, and the knowledge to use it correctly, are essential.

The following are general guidelines for performing comprehensive engine tests. For some tests, more detailed procedures can be found in other books in this series. The tests here are not presented in any specific order. The sequence in which they are performed will vary.

Unusual Engine Noises

Engine noises can be divided into two general catergories: those that originate in the top end of the engine, and those that originate in the bottom end of the engine. Begin engine noise diagnosis by determining where in the engine the noise is coming from. Bottom end, or crankcase, noises occur at crankshaft speed, so they tend to produce a high-frequency knock or rumble. Top end, or valve train, noises occur at a lower frequency because these parts operate at one-half crankshaft speed.

A stethoscope is a handy tool for isolating noises. You can also use a timing light to determine whether a noise is from the top or bottom end of the engine. Connect the timing light and listen. If the engine noise cycles in time with the flashing light, the sound is coming from the bottom end. Sounds that are audible with every other flash of the timing light originate in the top end of the engine.

Top-End Noises

The top end of a healthy engine produces a high pitched, whirring noise with a very rapid and much fainter sewing machine–like clicking coming from the valves. The more valves the engine has and the higher the idle speed, the more the individual clicks will blend into a consistent drone. Any deviation is abnormal and indicates a problem. Listen for:

- An irregular clacking or knocking noise caused by excessive camshaft endplay
- An irregular slapping or thumping at the front of the engine caused by a loose timing belt. A tight belt makes a whirring, whining, hum that rises and falls in pitch with RPM
- A single, clear clack whenever a particular valve opens can be a collapsed lifter or a broken valve spring.
- A loud, cycling, valve rattle that you can hear over the normal valve noise can indicate either worn valve guides or rocker arm pivots

Low pressure or restricted oil flow will produce an excessively loud, rhythmic clatter

Bottom-End Noises

Healthy engines produce an evenly pitched, rapid, whirring sound and nothing else. Knocking or thumping noises are

A8

signs that something is wrong. In general, bottom-end noise can be caused and indicated by:

- An irregular knock at idle that can be made louder or fainter by playing with the clutch pedal indicates too much crankshaft endplay
- A sharp clattering knock that may be continuous at idle or only appear when the throttle closes suddenly can indicate a bad connecting rod bearing. The noise will diminish if the spark plug for the offending cylinder is grounded
- A hollow metallic clatter that is loudest when the engine is cold may be piston slap caused by too much piston-to-cylinder wall clearance. Grounding the spark plug of the affected cylinder will often make piston slap louder because it eliminates the cushioning of the extra gas pressure pushing on the piston
- A sharp knocking that stands out most at idle can indicate a wrist pin that is loose in its bore. Grounding the spark plug of the affected cylinder makes the knock audible at top dead center as well as bottom dead center. Retarding the spark decreases wrist pin noise
- A rapid, steady dull pounding that increases with load is typical of worn main bearings

Spark Knock

Spark knock, which is caused by uncontrolled combustion, sounds like a metallic pinging noise. Spark knock may be heard under a heavy load or on acceleration.

Detonation occurs when combustion of the air/fuel mixture in the cylinder starts off correctly in response to ignition by the spark plug, but one or more pockets of the air/fuel mixture explode outside the envelope of the normal combustion. The collision of the two flames causes a pinging noise. This can be caused by:

- Fuel with too low an octane rating
- Ignition timing that is too far advanced
- High engine operating temperature
- Excessive carbon build-up in the combustion chamber

Preignition occurs when the air/fuel mixture prematurely ignites before the spark plug fires. Then the spark plug ignites the remaining mixture at the normal time. When the two portions of burning mixture meet each other, there is a sudden abnormal rise in cylinder pressure causing engine vibration and a pinging noise. This can be caused by:

- Hot spots in the combustion chamber
- Incorrect heat range spark plug
- Carbon deposits in the combustion chamber

Unusual Exhaust Color and Odor

Although a healthy catalytic converter can do a good job of cleaning up the exhaust, you can tell something about the internal engine condition by checking for unusual smoke or smells:

- Black exhaust smoke. This is caused by a rich air/fuel mixture and is often accompanied by the "rotten egg" smell of an overworked catalytic converter
- Blue exhaust smoke indicates excessive oil burning, which gives off a pungent odor

- Cloudy white exhaust is often the result of engine coolant leaking into the combustion chamber. Burning coolant also produces a distinctive chemical odor. Check the temperature gauge for overheating

Keep in mind that oil vapor odors are not always the result of an internal engine problem. A clogged or malfunctioning positive crankcase ventilation (PCV) system can not only produce a burning oil smell, but can also cause excessive crankcase vapor and increase oil consumption. Always check all external sources before you condemn the engine.

Internal Engine Diagnosis

Specific internal mechanical problems on a running engine can be located by performing several basic tests. To eliminate the possibility of internal engine problems, perform the following tests:

- Intake manifold vacuum
- Cylinder compression
- Cylinder leakage
- Cylinder power balance

A brief description of standard test procedures and interpreting results will be presented here.

Intake Manifold Vacuum Tests

Manifold vacuum tests are performed by connecting a vacuum gauge to the intake manifold downstream of the throttle plates. The gauge records the difference between **atmospheric pressure** and **manifold pressure**. Vacuum gauge readings can pinpoint manifold and vacuum line leaks, valve and valve guide problems, incorrect ignition and valve timing, exhaust restrictions, and poor combustion chamber sealing.

A vacuum gauge is usually calibrated in inches of mercury (in-Hg) or kilopascals (kPa). Normal vacuum at idle is from 15 to 21 in-Hg (50 to 70 kPa) for most engines. Gauge readings should be steady and decrease as the throttle opens. Vacuum decreases as elevation increases, and gauge readings must be corrected accordingly. Manufacturers provide specifications for testing at sea level. To correct for altitude, subtract one in-Hg (3.377 kPa) for every 1,000 feet (305 meters) above sea level.

Some engines, especially if turbocharged or supercharged, require a measure of manifold **boost pressure** test. Boost pressure, also known as positive pressure, specifications are provided by the manufacturer. Gauges for reading **manifold absolute pressure (MAP)** may be calibrated differently than vacuum gauges. Absolute pressure uses a reference point of zero pressure, or total vacuum, regardless of atmospheric pressure.

Refer to Book A1 "Engine Repair" in this series for more detailed information on manifold vacuum test procedures and results.

Cylinder Power Balance Test

The Powertrain Control Module (PCM) in most late-model vehicles incorporates the ability to conduct a power or cylinder balance test utilizing a diagnostic **scan tool**. The scan tool commands the PCM to run the test either automatically or manually at the operator's discretion. Each cylinder is disabled by shutting off the fuel and in some cases the spark to the cylinder being tested. The average RPM drop is displayed on the

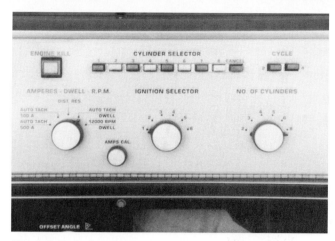

Fig. 1-2. Typical engine analyzer power balance panel.

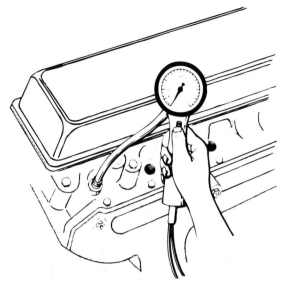

Fig. 1-3. Compression tester gauge installed in the spark plug hole.

scan tool screen and can be related directly to the contribution of that cylinder.

Most older engine analyzers have the capability of performing a power balance test, figure 1-2. The balance test shows if an individual cylinder or a group of cylinders is not producing its share of power. During the test, the spark plug is shorted so there are no power strokes from the cylinder being tested. Results are measured in terms of engine RPM drop, manifold vacuum drop, or a combination of these factors.

If the changes in engine RPM and manifold vacuum are about the same for each cylinder, the engine is in good mechanical condition. If the changes for one or more cylinders are noticeably different, the engine has a problem. The fault may be mechanical, or it may be in the ignition or fuel systems.

A power balance test is not conclusive; further tests are needed to pinpoint the problem. The procedure can be a time saver because it is performed on a running engine. An engine that passes a cylinder balance test will have fairly even compression, so there is usually no need to perform compression and cylinder leakage tests.

Cylinder Compression Tests

The compression test reveals how well each cylinder is sealed by the piston rings, valves, cylinder head gasket, and the spark plug. **Compression pressure** is measured in pounds per square inch (psi), kilopascals (kPa), or bars. The following quantities are equal to each other: 14.5 psi, 100 kPa, and 1 bar. A compression gauge measures the amount of air pressure that a cylinder is capable of producing.

Compression test specifications and procedures for an engine are normally provided in the vehicle Service Manual. Follow the steps in the Service Manual to prepare the engine for a compression test, then install the compression tester, figure 1-3, and run the test.

In general, a compression test is performed with the engine at normal operating temperature, all spark plugs removed, the ignition disabled, the battery fully charged, and the throttle held in wide-open position. Interpret compression gauge readings as follows:

- Compression is normal when the gauge shows a steady rise to the specified value with each compression stroke

- If the compression is low on the first stroke and builds up gradually with each succeeding stroke, but not to specifications, the piston rings or cylinder walls are probably worn
- A low compression reading on the first stroke that builds up only slightly on the following strokes indicates sticking or burned valves
- Two adjacent cylinders with equally low compression indicates a head gasket leak between them
- A higher than normal compression reading usually means excessive carbon deposits have formed on the piston top or in the combustion chamber. Fluid, such as oil, coolant, or fuel in a cylinder, also produces high compression pressure

Cylinder Leakage Test

A cylinder leakage tester, or leak-down tester, gives more detailed results than a compression test. Used as a follow-up to compression testing, a leakage test can reveal:

- The exact location of a compression leak
- How serious the leak is in terms of a percentage of total cylinder compression

The tester forces air into the combustion chamber through the spark plug hole. A gauge installed in the air line indicates how much pressure leaks out of the combustion chamber. The gauge scale is graduated from 0 to 100 percent.

Calibrate the leakage tester according to the equipment instructions before testing. To test a cylinder, the piston must be at TDC of the compression stroke so that both valves are closed. Install the test adapter in the spark plug opening, connect the air hose, and pressurize the cylinder. Note the percentage reading on the scale and interpret as follows:

0-10 percent Good
10-20 percent Fair
20-30 percent Poor
30-100 percent Failed!

For cylinders with more than 20 percent leakage, pinpoint the cause of the leaks as follows:

- Air escaping through the air intake indicates a leaking intake valve

- Air escaping through the exhaust indicates a leaking exhaust valve
- Air escaping through the crankcase and PCV system indicates worn or damaged piston rings, worn cylinder walls, or a worn or cracked piston
- Air bubbles in the coolant indicate a leaking head gasket or a crack in the engine block or cylinder head casting
- High readings on two adjacent cylinders indicate head gasket leakage or a casting crack between cylinders

Ignition System Diagnosis

The automotive ignition system consists of a low-voltage primary circuit and a high-voltage secondary circuit. Voltage varies within these circuits during operation. An **oscilloscope** displays voltage changes during a period of time, and is an ideal instrument for testing ignition system operation.

Traditional automotive oscilloscopes are installed in multifunction engine analyzer units that also contain voltmeters, ammeters, **ohmmeters**, tach-dwell meters, vacuum and pressure gauges, timing lights, and exhaust analyzers. Small handheld oscilloscopes that can also monitor the low-voltage signals of the engine management system are gaining in popularity.

All oscilloscopes work on the same principle: A voltage trace of the system being tested is displayed on a viewing screen. Voltage traces are displayed as a graph of voltage over time. The vertical scale on the screen represents voltage and the horizontal scale indicates time. The voltage range of the scope is generally adjustable. Primary circuits are measured in volts and secondary circuits in kilovolts (kV), or thousands of volts. Time is measured either as a percentage of one complete engine cycle or in milliseconds (mS), thousandths of a second.

An ignition system voltage trace, both primary and secondary, is divided into three sections, firing, intermediate, and **dwell**, figure 1-4. Deviations from a normal pattern indicate a problem. In addition, most scopes will display ignition traces in three different patterns. Each pattern is best used to isolate and identify particular kinds of malfunctions. The three basic patterns are:

- **Superimposed pattern**
- **Parade pattern**
- Stacked or **raster pattern**

In a superimposed pattern, voltage traces for all cylinders are displayed one on top of another to form a single pattern, figure 1-5. This display provides a quick overall view of ignition system operation and can also reveal certain major problems.

The parade pattern displays voltage traces for all cylinders one after another across the screen from left to right in firing order sequence, figure 1-6. This allows easy comparison of voltage levels between cylinders. A parade display is useful for diagnosing problems in the secondary circuit.

A raster pattern shows the voltage traces for all cylinders stacked one above another in firing order sequence, figure 1-7. This display allows you to compare the time periods of the three sections of a voltage trace.

Primary Ignition Patterns

Primary scope patterns are displayed as a low-voltage trace moving from left to right across the screen. Electronic ignition

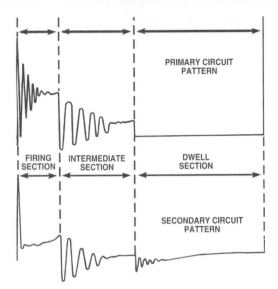

Fig. 1-4. Primary and secondary ignition oscilloscope patterns.

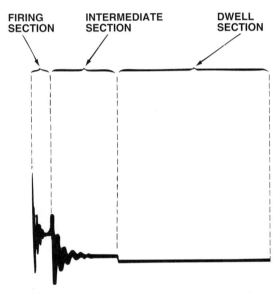

Fig. 1-5. All cylinder traces are displayed one on top of another in a superimposed pattern.

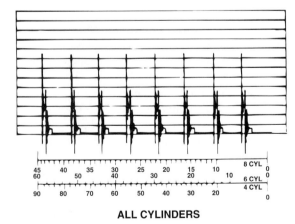

ALL CYLINDERS

Fig. 1-6. Cylinder traces are displayed one after another in a parade pattern.

patterns vary by system, so it is important to know what is normal for the system being tested. Scope manufacturers generally provide sample patterns for comparison.

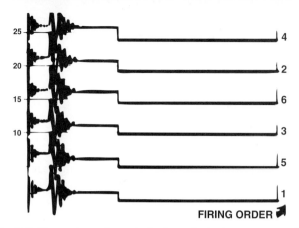

Fig. 1-7. The raster pattern stacks the cylinder traces on top of one another.

Firing Section

The firing section of the pattern corresponds to the amount of time the spark plug is firing. The voltage trace records induced voltage surges in the primary circuit as secondary voltage is being dissipated from the coil. A typical pattern begins with a vertical rise as spark is established, which is followed by a series of diminishing **oscillations** until the spark is extinguished, figure 1-8.

With some electronic ignition systems, there are no oscillations. Firing is displayed as a vertical spike followed by a relatively flat line until the spark ends. In parade display, the height of the oscillations should not vary between cylinders.

Intermediate Section

The intermediate section begins when the spark stops and continues until the primary circuit is switched on by an electronic signal, figure 1-9. Some ignition systems do not have an intermediate section, and the primary circuit is switched on the moment the spark is extinguished.

The voltage trace is created by the dissipation of energy remaining in the coil after firing. A series of diminishing oscillations, similar to the firing section but considerably smaller, is normal.

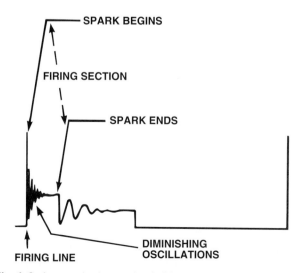

Fig. 1-8. A normal primary circuit firing trace.

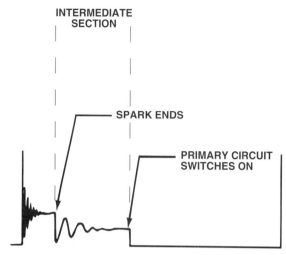

Fig. 1-9. The intermediate section begins as the spark extinguishes and continues until the primary circuit is switched on.

Dwell Section

The dwell section is the time the primary circuit is complete and a low-voltage current flow is building up the magnetic field of the coil. The trace should drop sharply to level off in a relatively flat horizontal line. Dwell ends with the abrupt upward stroke of the first firing oscillation.

Use the raster pattern to compare the dwell period for each cylinder. Dwell sections should not vary by more than four to six degrees between cylinders. Variations can be caused by a worn distributor, timing chain, or faulty **crankshaft position sensor (CKP)**.

Secondary Ignition Patterns

Secondary voltage traces also move left to right across the screen in firing, intermediate, and dwell sequence. Oscillations are displayed on a high-voltage scale. Normal firing voltage with an electronic ignition system can exceed 40 kV.

Firing Section

The firing section of the secondary pattern begins with a straight vertical line that indicates the amount of voltage required to create an arc across the spark plug air gap. This is called the firing line or voltage spike. When the arc is established, less voltage is required to maintain it and the trace drops to about one-quarter the height of the voltage spike, then continues horizontally as the sparkline. The sparkline, which represents continued current across the spark plug gap, may have a series of very small oscillations.

Intermediate Section

The secondary intermediate trace indicates excess coil voltage being dissipated and is similar to that of the primary ignition pattern. Look for a short vertical rise from the sparkline followed by diminishing oscillations. Oscillations should be of relatively even width and taper down gradually to a near horizontal line. The intermediate section ends as the primary circuit is switched on.

Dwell Section

The dwell section begins as the primary circuit is switched on and continues until the firing section begins. A typical trace

A8

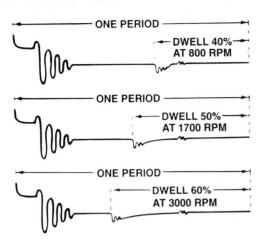

Fig. 1-10. Dwell time increases with engine speed on some electronic control systems.

pattern shows the switching as a sharp downward spike followed by a series of small diminishing oscillations that level off to a nearly flat line. The length of the dwell section and the trace pattern may be engine speed dependent, and varies for different systems, figure 1-10. Some switching signals produce a series of oscillations; others do not. All begin with a sharp vertical drop and continue as a nearly flat horizontal line.

Fuel System Diagnosis

Fuel system malfunctions can cause an assortment of driveability problems, such as engine surging, stalling and misfiring, hard or no starting, and poor fuel mileage. A restriction somewhere in the fuel or air supply is often the cause. Pressure testing is the most effective way to locate fuel supply problems. Test procedures are covered in Chapter Three of this book.

The results of engine diagnostic tests, such as manifold vacuum, cylinder power balance, oscilloscope analysis, exhaust gas analysis, and onboard diagnostics, may indicate fuel system problems.

When checking manifold vacuum, look for an oscillating needle with a reading slightly below normal at idle. This indicates an incorrect fuel mixture. A defective port fuel injector can cause a cylinder with good compression to show poor power balance test results. Onboard diagnostic tests can reveal faults in the electronic circuits. For oscilloscope patterns that indicate fuel problems, refer to Ignition System Diagnosis, discussed previously.

Electrical System Diagnosis

Hard starting, no start, and slow cranking speed can indicate an electrical problem. Check the battery, starting system, and charging system. Specific testing procedures are covered in Chapter Six of this book. Most minor electrical and electronic system malfunctions can be detected by self-diagnostic and scan tool testing. Individual components are tested with a digital multimeter (DMM), or oscilloscope. Component testing is detailed in the subsequent chapters of this book. Accessing and interpreting stored computer codes will be discussed there as well.

Onboard Diagnostic Systems

The computers used in late-model engine control systems are programmed to check their own operation, as well as the operation of each **sensor**, **actuator**, and circuit, figure 1-11. Whenever the computer recognizes a signal that is outside its limits, it records a **diagnostic trouble code (DTC)** in its memory.

Generally, the computer is capable of recognizing the following:

- A particular signal, such as engine speed, is not being furnished
- A signal that is out of limits for too long, such as a too-rich or too-lean oxygen sensor (HO2S) signal
- An improbable signal, such as input from a barometric pressure sensor that indicates the vehicle is being driven at an altitude of 25,000 feet

Some systems have the ability to test sensor or actuator circuit continuity by sending out a test signal and monitoring the voltage of the return signal.

When an out-of-range signal is detected, the computer records it as either a continuous or intermittent fault. A continuous, or hard, failure indicates that the malfunction occurred and is still present. These generally result from the total failure of a component or subsystem. An intermittent, or soft, failure indicates that the malfunction took place momentarily, then disappeared. This type of code usually means that a component or subsystem is functioning erratically, and is often caused by a loose, dirty, or weak connection. Most systems will store an intermittent DTC in the long-term memory for 50 to 60 engine-start cycles.

Retrieving Codes

Most vehicles have a diagnostic connector, or **data link connector (DLC)**, for accessing the computer memory. On older model vehicles, the multi-plug connector can be either under the hood or in the passenger compartment. The DLC is always in the passenger compartment on late-model, Onboard Diagnostic II (OBD-II)–compliant vehicles. The DLC permits connection of a test meter or jumper wire to trigger the diagnostic mode. A DTC is displayed generally in one of four basic ways:

- Numerical display on a scan tool
- Pulsating voltmeter needle
- Pulsating instrument panel lamp
- On a digital instrument cluster display panel

The manner in which the program is activated and the sequence in which codes are displayed vary between manufacturers. The preferred method of DTC retrieval is with a scan tool, figure 1-12. However, not all systems transmit codes to a scan tool, and codes must be read some other way. Each manufacturer publishes a list of trouble codes used with their systems and specific instructions for retrieving codes and clearing the computer memory.

Interpreting Diagnostic Trouble Codes

When properly used, a DTC helps to organize an efficient approach to isolating the source of a problem. Although trouble codes are a valuable diagnostic aid, they will not reveal the precise cause of a problem. However, a DTC does indicate the particular circuit where a malfunction took place. An accurate troubleshooting chart from the manufacturer is required to determine what may have set the code.

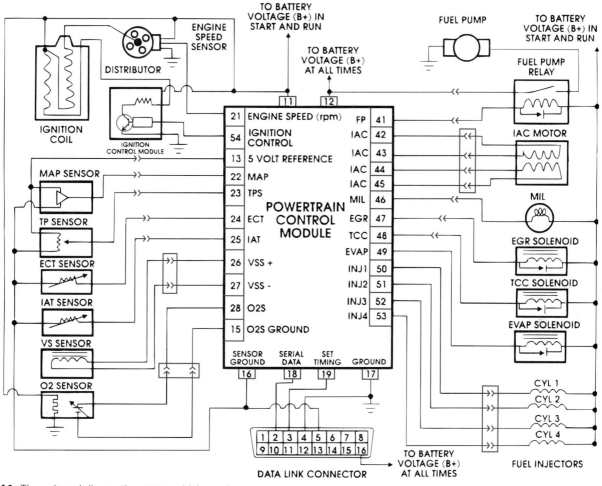

Fig. 1-11. The onboard diagnostic system, which monitors sensor and actuator signals, records a DTC when a circuit abnormality occurs.

Fig. 1-12. Retrieving codes with a scan tool.

Stored codes are often the result of poor circuit connections rather than a component failure. Engine sensor systems operate on low voltage, usually 5.0 volts, and relatively minor changes in resistance will interfere with the signal. Stored codes may be the result of a mechanical problem, and additional engine tests are required to isolate the source. Always check the circuitry and connections before replacing any electronic parts.

Simply disconnecting and reconnecting a multi-plug will often clean the contacts, restore continuity, and eliminate the code. When multiple codes are present, look for a weak

connection at a common grounding point. An open circuit results in either a signal not being generated or received. Low-voltage signals can indicate a shorted circuit.

Individual circuits, sensors, and actuators can be checked by connecting a **breakout box (BOB)** to the computer, figure 1-13. The breakout box allows you to monitor the individual circuit signals with a digital multimeter (DMM) or oscilloscope. Procedures for testing components are discussed in the appropriate chapters of this book.

Exhaust Gas Analyzers

To properly diagnose fuel system concerns an exhaust gas analyzer should be used, figure 1-14. The analyzers are available in many styles and designs. Current models are designed to sample and analyze either four or five gases present in the exhaust from the vehicle. The newest models are designed for five-gas detection and normally provide digital and/or printed results of each test. Either piece of equipment is generally suitable for diagnosing basic fuel system abnormalities and driveability problems. The five-gas units are required in many jurisdictions to permit the technician to verify emissions compliance of a vehicle.

Five-Gas Analyzers

Five-gas analyzers measure the parts per million (ppm) of **hydrocarbons (HC)**, the percentage of carbon monoxide (CO),

A8

Fig. 1-13. Typical breakout box.

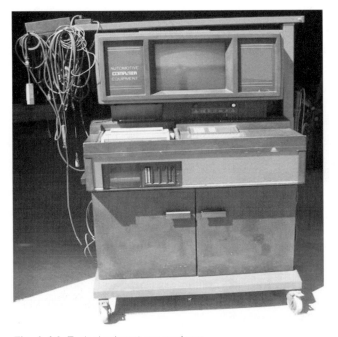

Fig. 1-14. Typical exhaust gas analyzer.

the percentage of oxygen (O2), the percentage of **carbon dioxide (CO2)**, and the percentage of **oxides of nitrogen (NOx)**. Most properly tuned computer-controlled vehicles will produce about 50 ppm of HC, less than 0.5 percent CO, 1.0 to 2.0 percent O2, and 13.8 to 15.0 percent CO2.

Four-Gas Analyzers

Four-gas analyzers measure HC, CO, CO2, and O2. They do not provide data as to the levels of NOx in the exhaust.

Diagnosing Exhaust Gasses

To assist with the discussion that follows, refer to the diagnostic chart for problems that may cause abnormal readings, figure 1-15.

For an accurate analysis of fuel combustion on catalytic converter-equipped vehicles, prevent the air injection system from supplying oxygen into the exhaust stream. This decreases the amount of O2 at the tailpipe, and the efficiency of the converter. The air injection system may be disabled by several means. On some vehicles, disconnecting the air injection pump or plugging the pulse air injection system is effective. For others, the probe of the analyzer can be connected to a port installed upstream of the catalytic converter or to the exhaust opening for the EGR valve. Next, make sure that the engine is at operating temperature, in closed loop, and the HO2S is transmitting a variable signal. Sample the exhaust gases both at idle and at 2,500 RPM. If a dynamometer is used, test under simulated highway load conditions as described by the manufacturer.

Abnormal HC and CO Readings

High HC levels indicate unburned fuel in the exhaust caused by incomplete combustion. The source of high HC emissions can often be traced to the ignition system, but mechanical or fuel system problems also can increase HC emissions, figure 1-16. High levels of HC emissions result from:

- Advanced ignition timing
- Ignition misfire from defective spark plug wires or fouled spark plugs
- An excessively rich or lean air-fuel mixture
- Leaking vacuum hoses, vacuum controls, or seals
- Low engine compression
- Defective valves, valve guides, valve springs, lifters, camshaft, or incorrect valve lash
- Defective rings, pistons, or cylinder walls
- Clogged fuel injectors causing a lean misfire

The amount of CO in the exhaust stream is directly proportional to the amount of O2 contributing to the combustion process. Richer air-fuel mixtures, with lower oxygen content, produce higher CO levels; leaner air-fuel mixtures, with higher oxygen content, produce lower CO levels. High CO emissions may result from one or more of the following abnormal conditions:

- Clogged or dirty intake air passages
- Plugged air filter element
- Throttle body coking
- Rich fuel mixture
- Incorrect idle speed
- Excessive fuel pressure
- Leaking fuel injectors

Both HC and CO levels reading high at the same time may be caused by the following conditions:

- Defective positive crankcase ventilation system
- Defective catalytic converter
- Defective manifold heat control valve
- Defective air pump
- Defective thermostatic air cleaner

Abnormal CO2 and O2 Readings

Since the catalytic converter reduces HC and CO, these emissions are unreliable for determining the air-fuel ratio. However,

	EMISSION	IDLE	OFF IDLE	CRUISE 1800–2000	VAIR-FUEL RATIO	POSSIBLE CAUSES	RELATED SYMPTOMS
1	CO	3%	3%	3%	Rich AFR Below 10:1	Vacuum leak to map sensor Fuel injectors leaking Bad Power Valve (carburetor) Excessive fuel rail pressure Vacuum diaphragm bad	Black smoke or sulfur odor Engine in open loop Surge/hesitation Engine not preconditioned
	HC	250 ppm	280 ppm	300 ppm			
	CO2	7–9%	7–9%	7–9%			
	O2	.2%	.2%	.2%			
2	CO	1.5%	1.5%	1.5%	Rich AFR at low speed 10–12:1	Engine oil diluted w/ fuel Carburetor idle speed Cold engine Idle mixture too rich Choke stuck shut PCV valve defective Fuel injectors leaking	Poor fuel economy Sooty spark/black smoke Rough idle/surge hesitation Vapor canister purge valve bad Vapor canister saturated
	HC	150 ppm	150 ppm	200 ppm			
	CO2	7–9%	7–9%	11–13%			
	O2	.2%	CO	.2%			
3	CO	0.5%	0.5%	1.0%	Lean AFR Over 16:1	Check ignition primary/secondary Vacuum leak Carburetor mixture lean Poor cylinder sealing Fuel injectors restricted Improper timing Exhaust valve leak	Rough idle Misfire–high speed Detonation cruise (2000 rpm) Idle hunting (computer) Overheating
	HC	200 ppm	200 ppm	250 ppm			
	CO2	7–9%	7–9%	7–9%			
	O2	4–5%	4–5%	4–5%			
4	CO	2.5%	1.0%	0.8%	Lean AFR at High Speed Over 16:1	Air cleaner heater door closed Internal carburetor problem (float tuck, wrong jet, metering rod stuck) Fuel injectors restricted Fuel pump pressure low	Rough idle Misfire Surging Hesitation
	HC	100 ppm	80 ppm	50 ppm			
	CO2	7–9%	7–9%	7–9%			
	O2	2–3%	2–3%	2–3%			
5	CO	0.3%	0.3%	0.3%	AFR 13–15:1	Engine not preconditioned Air management system not disabled Converter not warmed	None No driveability symptoms
	HC	100 ppm	80 ppm	50 ppm			
	CO2	10–12%	10–12%	10–12%			
	O2	2.5%	2.5%	2.5%			

Fig. 1-15. Four-gas exhaust emissions failure chart.

CO_2 and O_2 readings can be useful, provided that the air injection system has been disabled.

When air and fuel entering the engine burns with the least amount of wasted energy, at the **stoichiometric** air-fuel ratio, the engine emits the highest amount of CO_2. Look for readings between 13.8 and 15 percent. As the air-fuel ratio of the mixture leans or enriches, the CO_2 level drops. To determine whether a low CO_2 level indicates a lean or rich condition, examine the O_2 reading. Levels of O_2 below approximately 1.0 percent indicate a rich-running engine; above 2.0 percent indicate a lean-running engine.

To perform adequately and operate efficiently, an engine must be in sound mechanical condition. Therefore, it is important to determine the overall mechanical condition of the engine before attempting to isolate or repair the cause of a driveability or performance problem.

Perform a compression or cylinder leakage test to determine the internal sealing capabilities of the engine. When test

A8

Condition	HC	CO	CO_2	O_2	NO_x
Ignition Misfire	Large Increase	Some Decrease	Some Decrease	Some to Large Decrease	Some Decrease
Compression Loss	Some to Large Increase	Some Decrease	Some Decrease	Some Decrease	Some Increase
Rich Mixture	Some to Large Increase	Large Increase	Some Decrease	Some Decrease	Large Decrease
Lean Mixture	Some Increase	Large Decrease	Some Decrease	Some Increase	Large Increase
Minimal Timing Retard	Some Decrease	Possible Increase	No Change	No Change	Possible Decrease
Excessive Timing Retard	Some Increase	No Change	Some to Large Decrease	No Change	Large Decrease
Advanced Timing	Some Increase	Small Decrease Possible	No Change	No Change	Large Increase
EGR Operating	No Change	No Change	Some Decrease	No Change	Large Decrease
EGR Leaking	Some Increase	No Change	No Change	No Change	Possible Increase
AIR Operating	Large Decrease	Large Decrease	Large Decrease	Large Increase	Possible Increase
Converter Operational	Some Decrease	Some Decrease	Some Increase	Some Decrease	Large Decrease
Exhaust Leak	Some Decrease	Some Decrease	Some Decrease	Some Increase	No Change
Worn Engine	Some Increase	Some Increase	Some Decrease	Some Decrease	Large Decrease
Worn Camshaft Lobes	Possible Decrease	Some Decrease	Some Decrease	Some Decrease	Possible Decrease

Fig. 1-16. Effect of engine condition on the formation of exhaust gasses.

results are marginal and indicate valve seating problems, performance can often be restored by adjusting valve lash or servicing hydraulic valve lifters. If test results are below specifications, internal engine repairs are required to restore performance. This chapter focuses on engine repairs that can be performed without disassembling the engine or removing major components.

VALVE LASH ADJUSTMENT

Ideally, an engine should operate with near zero valve lash, or clearance. Under these conditions, valve movement follows the profile of the camshaft lobe exactly to provide efficient operation. Over the life of an engine, valve clearance tends to change as a result of wear on the valve face, valve seat, pushrod, and rocker arm. For many years engines were designed with provisions to make periodic adjustments to correct for this wear. Many late-model engines have no scheduled need for and therefore no provision for making a valve clearance adjustment. These engines require precise machining during overhaul to ensure that the proper clearances are met. If valve clearance problems surface diagnosis will reveal a failed component. Follow the Service Manual procedures for repair or replacement of the component or components involved.

Valve Lifter Designs

With hydraulic lifters, once engine oil pressure is established, the lifters automatically take up all slack in the valve train to maintain zero clearance, figure 1-17. Hydraulic lifters also compensate for metal expansion as the engine warms up. Hydraulic valve lifters do not require routine adjustment.

Mechanical lifters must be set with a precise amount of clearance so that the valves operate with close to zero lash once the engine is at normal operating temperature. Mechanical lifters must be adjusted periodically to compensate for wear in the valve train.

Maintaining the correct clearance is important. Too much clearance prevents the camshaft from opening the valves fully. This shortens effective camshaft duration, causing valves to open late and close early, which reduces engine efficiency and performance. Continued operation stresses valve train parts and can lead to premature failure.

Insufficient clearance causes the valves to open too far. Effective duration is increased so the valves open early and close late. Once the engine warms to operating temperature, the valves might not be able to close completely.

Adjustment Methods

Typical valve clearance specifications range from 0.004 to 0.025 inch (0.10 to 0.64 mm) for intake valves and 0.004 to 0.030 inch (0.10 to 0.76 mm) for exhaust valves. Service Manuals may list valve clearances either as hot or cold specifications, or both. If the valves are to be set cold, check the coolant temperature. It should be about the same as the air temperature, and the valve cover should feel cool to the touch. To use a hot specification, the engine should be warmed to its normal operating temperature. Common adjustment mechanisms include:

- An adjustment locknut holding the rocker arm to the rocker stud

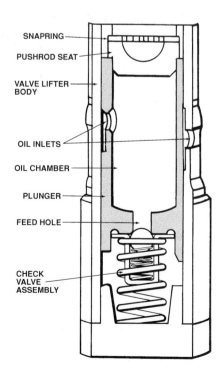

Fig. 1-17. Typical hydraulic lifter.

- Replaceable adjustment shims located between the camshaft lobes and cam followers
- Selective length pushrods

Adjusting Clearance on Overhead Valve Engines

All late-model domestic overhead valve (OHV) engines use hydraulic lifters. Adjustments are required only after high-mileage operation has worn valve train parts beyond the adjustment range of the lifters, or when the rocker arms, pushrods, or lifters were removed for service. Mechanical valve lifters are still used on some import and high-performance engines.

To access the lash adjusters, remove the valve covers. When hot clearance specifications are provided, valves can often be adjusted while the engine is running. Cold clearances are set with the engine off and cooled down. Both procedures are presented here.

Adjusting Clearances with the Engine Running

With many OHV engines, valve lash can easily and accurately be adjusted with the engine running at its normal operating temperature. Remove the valve covers and install a set of oil deflectors on the rocker arms to prevent oil from splashing.

Obtain the proper hot valve clearance specifications and have the necessary feeler gauges and wrenches readily available. Work from one end of the engine to the other and set all of the intake valve clearances first. Then, repeat the sequence to adjust all of the exhaust valves.

Hydraulic Lifters

Stud-mounted adjustable rocker arms used with hydraulic lifters can also be adjusted with the engine running.

Follow this procedure:

1. Starting with any valve, back off the rocker arm locknut until the valve starts to clatter. At this point, the valve has too much clearance.
2. Slowly tighten the nut until the clatter just stops. This removes all lash, but does not compress the plunger into the lifter body so there is no reserve travel left to compensate for wear.
3. Slowly tighten the locknut in 90 degree increments, waiting about 10 seconds between steps to give the lifter time to bleed down. The total amount the locknut is tightened varies between engines. Check the Service Manual for specifications.

Adjusting Clearances with the Engine Off

With the engine not running, the cylinder to be adjusted must be brought up to top dead center (TDC) so that both valves are closed. For engines with mechanical lifters, turn the adjustment screw until there is a slight drag on the feeler gauge blade. Some engines use interference-fit adjustment screws or nuts that retain their position once they are tightened. Others use a locknut to hold an adjustment screw in place once the correct clearance is established. On these engines, always recheck clearance after tightening the locknut.

Two adjustment methods—selective length pushrods and adjustable rocker arms—are used on engines with hydraulic lifters.

A8

Mechanical Lifters

The following general procedure can be used to adjust valve clearance with mechanical lifters on a running engine:

1. Make sure the engine is running at its slowest idle speed and is at normal operating temperature.
2. Insert a feeler gauge of the correct thickness between the rocker arm and valve stem. The feeler gauge should pass through the gap with a slow, steady drag:
   - If force is required to insert the feeler gauge, or if the engine starts missing when the gauge is inserted, the clearance is too tight
   - If the gauge slips through too easily, or if there is a choppy, jerking feel as the gauge passes through, the clearance is too loose
3. Turn the adjusting screw in or out as required.
4. Recheck the clearance after adjustment. If a separate locknut is used, check the clearance once again after tightening the locknut.

Selective Length Pushrods

A few older engines with non-adjustable valve gears use zero-lash hydraulic lifters. However, to allow for valve train wear, the plunger of the lifter must be centered inside the body. This is accomplished by installing shorter or longer pushrods. To check and adjust clearance:

1. Position the cylinder at TDC on its firing stroke.
2. Tighten the rocker arm locknut to the torque value specified by the manufacturer.
3. Depress the pushrod end of the rocker arm with a tappet bleed down wrench, a large screwdriver, or other suitable tool to bottom the plunger in the lifter.
4. Hold the end of the rocker arm down, and measure the clearance between the valve stem tip and the rocker.
5. Compare this value to the specification range for that engine. If the clearance is too great, install a longer pushrod. If it is too little, install a shorter pushrod.

Pushrods for most engines are available in three sizes: standard, 0.060 inch (1.5 mm) oversize, and 0.060 inch (1.5 mm) undersize. In general, pushrods need to be changed only after the head and block mating surfaces have been resurfaced, or the valve seats have been replaced or excessively machined.

Setting Adjustable Rocker Arms

To set adjustable rocker arms with the engine not running, follow this procedure:

1. Position a cylinder at TDC on its power stroke so both valves are closed.
2. Slowly tighten the rocker arm locknut to remove all the slack from the valve train without compressing the hydraulic lifter. The pushrod will no longer rotate freely and the rocker can no longer wiggle from side to side, figure 1-18.
3. Slowly tighten the rocker arm locknut an additional three-quarters to one-and-one-half turns to position the plunger in the center of its travel inside the lifter. How much additional tightening is required varies by engine. Check the Service Manual for exact specifications.

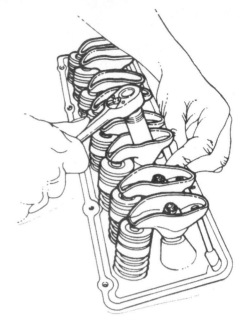

Fig. 1-18. Typical adjustable rocker arm service.

Adjusting Clearance on Overhead Camshaft Engines

Once the valve cover is removed on an overhead cam (OHC) engine, the camshaft contacting the lifter is visible. Rotate the engine by hand while watching the camshaft lobes to bring the cylinder to be adjusted into position. Position the camshaft so that the base circle of a cam lobe is directly in line with its follower or rocker arm pad. Then, that valve is closed and a feeler gauge blade can be inserted to check the clearance. If the engine uses a screw-type adjuster, simply loosen the locknut and reposition the screw until there is a slight drag on the feeler gauge, figure 1-19. Tighten the locknut, recheck clearance, and move on to the next valve. Continue until all the valves are set.

Setting Valve Lash with Replaceable Shims

The replaceable adjustment shims on most engines are located between the camshaft lobe and cam follower. A special tool is used to depress the follower so the shim can be removed,

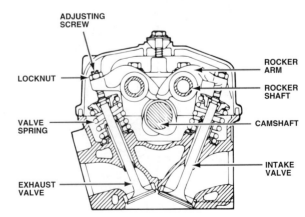

Fig. 1-19. Overhead cam engine with rocker arms and screw-type adjusters.

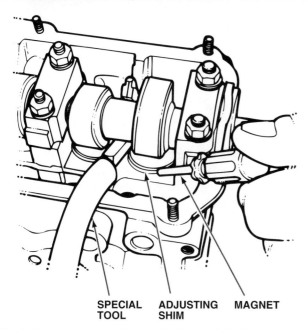

Fig. 1-20. Depress the follower with the special tool to remove/install the adjuster shim.

figure 1-20. To adjust the valve clearance, follow this general procedure:

1. Position the cylinder to be checked at TDC.
2. Measure the clearance with a feeler gauge.
3. Compress the follower and hold it down using the special tool.
4. Pry the shim loose with a small screwdriver, or other suitable tool, and remove it with a magnet or pliers.
5. Measure the thickness of the shim with an outside micrometer.
6. Calculate the thickness of the shim to be installed:
   - Subtract the midpoint of the specified clearance range from the measured clearance
   - Add the result to the thickness of the shim that was removed from the engine
   - The result equals the thickness of the new shim to be installed
7. Install the new shim in the recess in the top of the lifter and firmly seat it into place.
8. Release the follower and recheck the valve lash clearance.

Some engines use a smaller shim that fits directly on top of the valve stem underneath the cam follower. To replace this type of shim, the camshaft and the follower must be removed.

CAMSHAFT AND VALVE TIMING

Camshaft timing can be verified by removing the timing cover and inspecting the timing marks, figure 1-21, or by using a degree wheel and dial indicator. Incorrect valve timing generally results from component wear. Disassemble the camshaft drive, inspect all components, and replace all worn or damaged parts with new ones. Make sure both the crankshaft and camshaft remain in the TDC position and all timing marks are aligned during assembly. Once the camshaft drive is in place, follow the Service Manual procedures for rotating the engine and

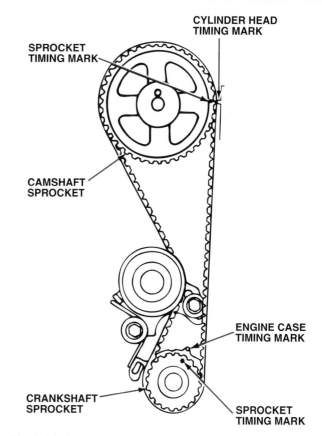

Fig. 1-21. Typical timing belt arrangement for OHC engine.

verifying the alignment of the timing marks. Once you have verified that all timing marks are again in alignment and that the chain or belt is properly tensioned, install the timing cover.

Under normal conditions, the initial valve timing of the engine does not change. However, high-mileage operation can cause both timing chains and belts to stretch or tensioners to weaken to the point where valve timing is altered, figure 1-22. Excess slack in the drive assembly causes the camshaft sprocket to lag behind the crankshaft sprocket as the engine runs. The result is retarded valve timing that can cause a lack of power

A8

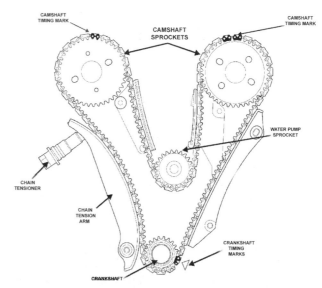

Fig. 1-22. Overhead cam V-type engine timing chain arrangement.

at higher engine speeds and loads. Symptoms are the same as those caused by retarded ignition timing or a lack of timing advance.

Variable Valve Timing

- Intake camshaft timing is continuously variable using a hydraulic actuator attached to the end of each intake camshaft. Engine oil flow to each hydraulic actuator is controlled by a camshaft position actuator control **solenoid**. Exhaust camshaft timing is fixed.
- A single timing chain drives both exhaust camshafts and both intake camshaft hydraulic actuators. While valve overlap is variable, valve lift and duration are fixed.
- Cam timing is determined by the ECM using the crankshaft position (CKP) sensor and camshaft position sensor (CMP 1 and CMP 2) signals. At idle, the intake camshafts are fully retarded and valve overlap is zero degrees. At higher speeds and loads, the intake camshafts can be advanced up to 40 crankshaft degrees.
- Each intake camshaft has a separate camshaft position sensor, hydraulic actuator, and control solenoid. If little or no oil pressure is received by a hydraulic actuator (typically at engine startup, at idle speed or during a fault condition), it is designed to mechanically default to the fully retarded position (zero valve overlap) and is held in that position by a spring loaded locking pin.

COOLING SYSTEM SERVICE

An engine that runs too hot or too cold has poor performance, reduced fuel economy, and increased emission levels. Engine temperatures that are too low or too high are often the result of a cooling system problem. However, other problems, such as incorrect ignition timing, overloading the engine, long periods of idling or slow-speed operation, and other factors, can cause overheating as well.

Check the coolant level and test the concentration using a hydrometer. Look for signs of oil and combustion contamination. Engine oil escaping into the coolant will not mix. The oil will float on top of the coolant. Combustion gases will chemically react with coolant to rapidly break it down, turning it a rust-brown color. The presence of combustion gases cannot be visually verified. Check using a chemical test kit or exhaust gas analyzer; see Book A1 "Engine Repair" of this series.

Cooling System Inspection

Use a pyrometer to monitor actual engine temperature and eliminate the possibility of a faulty gauge, warning lamp, sending unit, or circuitry. Once the problem is verified, inspect the cooling system and make the necessary repairs.

Approach diagnosing an overheating problem by first determining when and at what interval the problem occurs. If the owner adds water, find out how much and how often. Secondly, determine whether the problem can be isolated to a specific driving condition. Visually inspect all cooling system hoses and replace any that are worn or damaged. Also, inspect the water pump drive belt for wear, damage, and correct tension and replace or adjust as needed.

Cooling System Testing

Testing of the cooling system generally consists of testing the coolant and performing system and radiator cap pressure tests. If the system and cap both hold pressure, test the operation of the thermostat.

Testing the Coolant

Coolant concentration and effectiveness are tested with a refractometer or cooling system hydrometer, figure 1-23. For accurate results, the coolant should be hot when tested. Before testing, draw a coolant sample into the hydrometer and return it to the radiator several times to stabilize the internal thermometer of the hydrometer.

Test as follows:

1. Hold the hydrometer straight and draw enough coolant to raise the float. The float should not touch the sides of the hydrometer.
2. With the hydrometer at eye level, take a reading by noting the top of the letter on the float that is touched by the coolant.
3. Find this letter on the hydrometer scale; read down the column under the letter until you are opposite the thermometer reading.
4. The number shown at this point is the degree of protection given by the coolant in the system.

System Pressure Test

Pressure testing the cooling system is a quick and easy way to find an external leak. Perform the test on a cold engine using a hand pump with a gauge:

1. Remove the pressure cap and attach the pressure tester to the filler neck.
2. Pump the tester until the gauge reading matches the specified system pressure, figure 1-24.
3. Observe the gauge; the reading should remain steady.
4. If the gauge shows a pressure loss, pump the tester to maintain pressure and check for leaks.

Radiator Cap Pressure Test

Check the radiator pressure cap using the system pressure tester and an adapter:

1. Attach the cap to the pressure tester.
2. Pump the tester until the gauge reading matches the pressure rating of the cap.

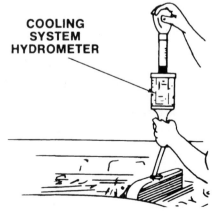

COOLING SYSTEM HYDROMETER

Fig. 1-23. Testing engine coolant with a hydrometer.

Fig. 1-24. Pressure testing the cooling system.

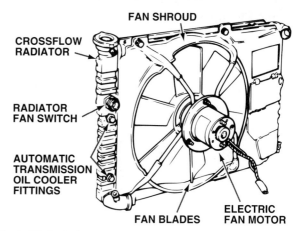

Fig. 1-25. Typical electric cooling fan assembly.

3. Observe the gauge; it should hold steady within one or two psi of the rating for at least 10 seconds, then gradually decrease.
4. If the reading does not drop at all, continue applying pressure until the cap vents. The cap should vent when pressure exceeds the rating by one to three pounds. Replace the cap if it fails either test.

Thermostat Service

A thermostat that opens above or below its temperature rating will cause driveability problems. If the thermostat is stuck open, or there is no thermostat installed in the system, the engine may never reach an efficient operating temperature. In many instances, the thermostat is defective and should be replaced. Thermostat function can be checked on a running engine. Refer to Book A1 "Engine Repair" in this series for more detailed information on thermostat testing.

Fan Clutch Operation Test

A thermometer and an ignition timing light can be used to check the operation of a **viscous fan clutch**. You must know the temperature setting of the drive unit. To test:

1. Attach a thermometer to the engine side of the radiator. Be sure it will clear the fan blades and be visible with the engine running.
2. Connect the timing light and start the engine. Note the thermometer reading on a cold engine.
3. Aim the timing light at the fan blades; they should appear to move slowly.
4. Block the radiator to reduce air flow and raise temperature. Do not allow the engine to overheat.
5. Continue watching the thermometer and keep the timing light on the fan blades.
6. When the thermometer reaches the clutch engagement point, fan speed should increase. The blades will appear to move faster in the timing light beam.

7. Unblock the radiator so that the temperature drops. If the system is working properly, fan speed will decrease when the temperature is below the engagement point of the clutch.

Electric Coolant Fan

Electric coolant fans are designed to operate only when necessary, figure 1-25. Several methods are used to control fan operation:

1. A temperature switch that energizes an electrical relay. This switch is usually mounted in the engine.
2. A temperature switch that closes a set of contacts inside the switch to either complete the power or ground side of the circuit for the fan. This switch can be mounted either in the engine or radiator.
3. An air conditioning, or high discharge pressure, switch to energize an electrical relay to turn on the fan.
4. Computer-controlled relays to energize the fans. This system uses the engine coolant temperature sensor to sense engine temperature.

The coolant fan turns on when engine coolant temperature reaches about 230°F (110°C). Some systems may have either a two-speed fan or two separate fans. These systems control fan use as needed. The fan is also needed to reduce air conditioning high-side pressures. If the fans are computer controlled, they turn on when the coolant temperature is too high or when the computer does not have a coolant temperature sensor reading.

Any diagnosis of the cooling fan begins with an examination of the system wiring diagram. This diagram provides the most accurate and timely understanding of how a particular system should operate.

ELECTRICAL WIRING AND SCHEMATICS

In order to understand and diagnose engine performance it is essential that you have a good understanding of electrical fundamentals and schematics. Generally, schematics can be found in the Service Manual, although a few manufacturers place them in a separate book. In either case ensure that the schematic is for the same year and model of vehicle.

A8

Reading Electrical Schematics

Common Symbols and Icons

Components are shown as symbols or icons rather than actual pictures in the schematic. Most electrical schematics will have a table listing the various symbols or icons used in the manual, figure 1-26.

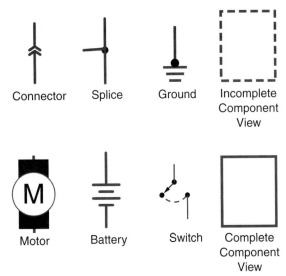

Fig. 1-26. Several common electrical schematic symbols.

Schematic Overview

The schematic does not represent the components and wiring as they physically appear on the vehicle. For example, a 4-foot length of wire is represented no differently in a schematic than one a few inches long, figure 1-27.

The wiring schematic is the cornerstone of electrical diagnosis. Schematics break the entire electrical system into individual circuits, and show the electrical current paths when a circuit is operating properly. Wiring which is not part of the circuit of interest is referenced to another page where the circuit is shown complete. Most schematics use a top (power) to bottom (ground) sequence to present electrical information.

Component Location Tables

The Component Location Table, figure 1-28, shows a list of all the electrical components within a system's electrical schematics and the following information:

- All components
- Grounds
- Pass-through grommets
- Splices

The table consists of four columns labeled as follows:

- Name
- Location

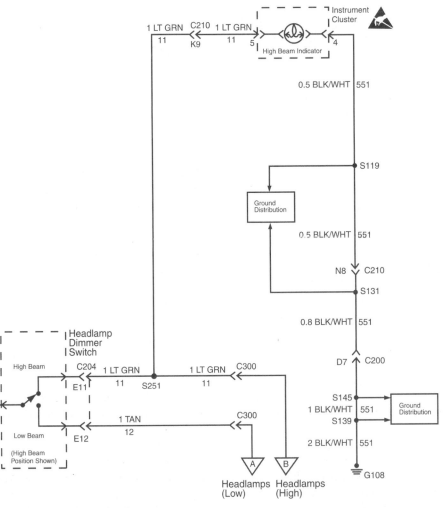

Fig. 1-27. Typical automotive electrical schematic.

Name	Location	Locator View	Connector End View
Auxiliary Engine Coolant Fan Motor	In front of the radiator	*Cooling System Component Views* in Engine Cooling	*Cooling System Connector End Views* in Engine Cooling
Battery	On the RH frame rail to the rear of the engine	*Engine Electrical Component Views* in Engine Electrical	—
Battery Junction Block	On the forward LH side of the engine bulkhead above P200	*Power and Grounding Component Views*	—
Battery, Secondary	On the RH frame rail to the rear of the engine	*Engine Electrical Component Views* in Engine Electrical	—
Brake/Transmission Shift Interlock (BTSI) Solenoid	On the lower portion of the steering column below the column support bracket	*Tilt Wheel/Column Component Views* in Steering Wheel and Column - Tilt	*Tilt Wheel/Column Connector End Views* in Steering Wheel and Column - Tilt

Fig. 1-28. Typical component locator chart.

- Locator View
- Connector End View

Name

The name cells provide the name of the components that are used on the schematic(s). If a connector is listed, the numbers of cavities also are provided.

Location

The location cell provides a written location of where the component is in the vehicle with respect to the vehicle. Most components can be located using the component location view illustrations.

Locator View

This column contains the reference to the appropriate locator view.

Connector End View

This column contains the reference to the appropriate connector end view.

How to Use Connector End Views

Connector end views show the cavity or terminal locations for most connectors shown in the system schematic(s). The drawings show the connector's face as seen after the harness connector has been disconnected from a component or mating connector. Unused cavities are left blank in the table.

In addition, the color and part number of the connector body are provided, along with the family/series name are often included, figure 1-29.

Circuit Descriptions

Most charts also have a circuit description (not shown in Fig. 1-28) that describes how the system works electrically. The circuit description also explains the communication and interaction of all components that affect the operation of the system.

For example: The Wheel Speed Sensor (WSS) coil emits an **electromagnetic** field. A toothed ring on the wheel passes by the WSS and disrupts this electromagnetic field. The disruption in the field causes the WSS to produce a sinusoidal (AC) voltage signal.

BATTERY SERVICE AND TESTING

Battery voltage that is out of specifications can have an adverse effect on the electronic engine control system. If the voltage is too low, actuators such as the fuel injectors may not open far or long enough to deliver the correct amount of fuel. As an opposite effect, when battery voltage is too high the injectors may open too far or too long and deliver more than the designed amount of fuel to the engine. These conditions posed a problem in the early years of electronic controls, but most modern systems feature a voltage correction strategy that corrects for the voltage variations.

Battery Testing

State-of-charge and capacity tests are performed to determine the condition of the battery. In addition, a preliminary evaluation on a low-maintenance or maintenance-free battery is required to determine if the battery is capable of accepting a recharge.

State-of-Charge Testing

Until the appearance of sealed, maintenance-free batteries, testing the **specific gravity** of the electrolyte with a hydrometer was a universal method of determining battery condition. However, the procedure can be used today only on the minority of batteries that are unsealed and have removable filler caps.

Some sealed maintenance-free batteries are equipped with a built-in state-of-charge indicator in one cell. This indicator has two functions: It shows whether electrolyte has fallen below a minimum level and also serves as a go/no-go hydrometer. The indicator is a plastic rod inserted in the top of the battery and extended into the electrolyte. One design uses a single plastic ball, usually colored green, red, or blue, suspended in a cage from the bottom of the rod, figure 1-30. Depending on the specific gravity of the electrolyte, the ball will float or sink in its cage, changing the appearance of the indicator "eye."

Generally, a green dot in the indicator means the battery is charged enough for testing. If this dot is not visible, the battery must be charged before it is tested. If the indicator eye is black and color is not visible, the battery is below a 65 percent

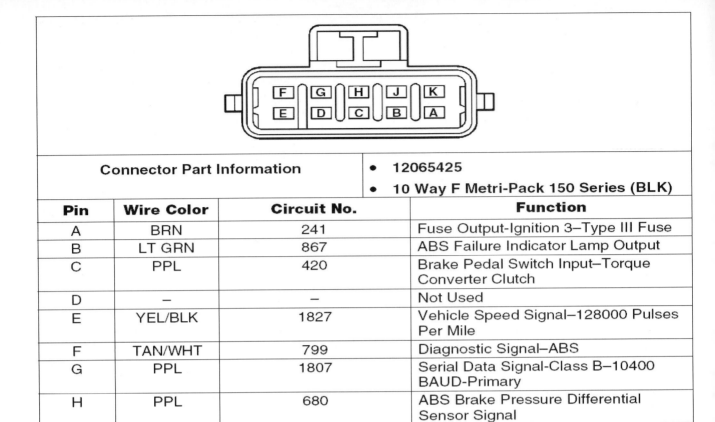

Pin	Wire Color	Circuit No.	Function
Connector Part Information			• 12065425 • 10 Way F Metri-Pack 150 Series (BLK)
A	BRN	241	Fuse Output-Ignition 3–Type III Fuse
B	LT GRN	867	ABS Failure Indicator Lamp Output
C	PPL	420	Brake Pedal Switch Input–Torque Converter Clutch
D	–	–	Not Used
E	YEL/BLK	1827	Vehicle Speed Signal–128000 Pulses Per Mile
F	TAN/WHT	799	Diagnostic Signal–ABS
G	PPL	1807	Serial Data Signal-Class B–10400 BAUD-Primary
H	PPL	680	ABS Brake Pressure Differential Sensor Signal
J	BLK	450	Ground
K	–	–	Not Used
K	BLK	1450	Ground

Fig. 1-29. Typical connector end view chart.

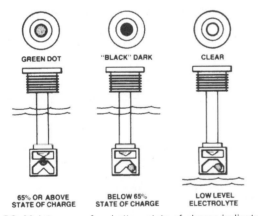

Fig. 1-30. Maintenance-free battery state-of-charge indicator.

state-of-charge and must be recharged before testing. If the indicator is clear or light yellow, the electrolyte level has fallen below the bottom of the indicator rod and attached cage. When this clear or light yellow appearance is noted, lightly tap the top of the indicator to dislodge any gas bubbles that might be giving a false indication of low electrolyte level. If the color does not change, replace the battery. Do not attempt to recharge a battery if the electrolyte level is too low.

Some battery indicators contain both a red and a green ball. This gives the indicator a green, dark, red, and clear appearance, in that order. The red dot indicates the battery is approaching complete discharge and must be charged before being used. Complete indicator information is printed on a label attached to the battery and should be used to make an accurate interpretation of the built-in indicator.

ABNORMAL OR PHANTOM BATTERY DRAIN PROBLEMS

Phantom battery drain, or parasitic draw, is caused by something in the vehicle constantly drawing current from the battery when the ignition is off. Although a certain amount of discharge is normal and can be expected, a fully charged battery in good condition should not lose its charge when left idle for a few days or even weeks. This loss of voltage can cause driveability problems if the draw is enough to cause the PCM to lose stored operational information. The loss of learned values for any of the following systems may cause undesirable performance issues:

- Fuel trim values
- Ignition timing advance information
- Transmission shift points

Typical causes of battery drain include:

- Acid, moisture, dirt, or corrosion on top of the battery case
- An accessory, such as a trunk light, glove box light, underhood light, or cigarette lighter, remaining on when the vehicle is not in use

- Parasitic drains required to operate systems that continue to work even when the vehicle is parked and the ignition is off

The most serious of these are the parasitic losses resulting from the advent of computer controls. Virtually all late-model vehicles are equipped with computers that control such things as engine operation, radio tuning, suspension leveling, steering assist, antilock brakes, and more. Each of these microprocessors contain random access memory (RAM) that stores information relevant to its job. Remember: RAM requires a constant power supply that puts a continuous drain on the vehicle electrical system. In addition, many electronic control systems conduct a self-diagnostic test after the engine is switched off. The combined drain of several computer memories, or diagnostic test routines, can discharge a battery to the point where there is insufficient cranking power after only a few weeks.

Due to the higher parasitic current drains on late model vehicles, the old test of removing a battery cable connection and tapping it against the terminal while looking for a spark is both dangerous and no longer a valid check for excessive current drain. Furthermore, every time the power source to computer modules is interrupted, module memories are lost. Information programmed into memory by the vehicle owner, such as radio presets, door lock combinations, seat position memories, and climate controls, all have to be reset when the battery is reconnected. On engine management systems with adaptive learning capability, driveability also may be affected until the computer relearns the engine calibration or transmission shift modifications that were erased from memory.

A clean battery top prevents any drain from the negative to positive battery terminals. Periodically clean the battery top and terminals with a mixture of baking soda and water applied with a brush. Do not allow the solution to enter the battery cells.

To test for abnormal battery drain, disconnect the negative battery cable and connect an ammeter in series between the negative terminal and the cable, figure 1-31. On many late-model vehicles it is necessary to wait up to one hour before taking the

reading. Many onboard computers have timer circuits which must time out before they shut down.

To isolate the source of a draw, disconnect each accessory system one at a time until the meter reading drops into the normal range. This locates the offending circuit. Consult a wiring diagram to determine how power is routed through the circuit, then systematically eliminate components to determine which one was remaining on and draining the battery.

STARTING SYSTEM SERVICE

The starting system includes the battery, ignition switch, safety switch, starter relay, solenoid, and starter motor, as well as the circuitry that links everything together. A failure at any point of the system can prevent the engine from starting. When an engine fails to crank, perform these preliminary checks:

- Inspect the battery—check for loose, corroded, or damaged terminals and cable connections. Also check the battery state-of-charge
- Inspect the ignition switch—check for loose mounting, damaged wiring, sticking contacts, and loose connections
- Inspect the safety switch—check for proper adjustment, loose mounting and connections, and damaged wiring
- Inspect the solenoid—check for loose mounting, loose connections, and damaged wiring
- Inspect the starter motor—check for loose mounting, proper pinion adjustment, and loose or damaged wiring

If the system passes a visual inspection, perform current draw and cranking voltage tests to determine the general condition of the starter motor. Begin by verifying that the battery is fully charged and in good condition. While testing, the starter motor is cranking the engine; however, the engine must not start and run. To prevent starting, either bypass the ignition switch with a remote starter switch or disable the ignition. Do not crank the starter motor for more than 15 seconds at a time while testing. Allow two minutes between tests for the motor to cool and prevent damage.

Cranking Current Draw Test

The cranking current draw test measures the amount of current, in **amperes**, that the starter circuit requires to crank the engine. This test, which helps isolate the source of a starting problem, is performed with either a charging-starter-battery (CSB) analyzer or individual voltmeter and inductive ammeter. To test with inductive ammeter meter:

1. Bypass the ignition with a remote starter switch.
2. Connect the voltmeter leads to the battery terminals, observing correct polarity.
3. Clamp the inductive ammeter pickup around the positive cable.
4. Crank the engine for several seconds and note the voltmeter and ammeter readings, figure 1-32.
5. Compare ammeter readings to specifications.

With a CSB analyzer, connect the leads and test according to the equipment instructions. Regardless of method, high current draw is caused by a short in the starter circuit or a binding starter motor or engine. Low current draw results from high resistance in the starting system circuit or an undercharged or defective battery.

A8

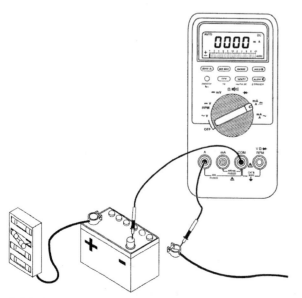

Fig. 1-31. Connection for testing for parasitic draw.

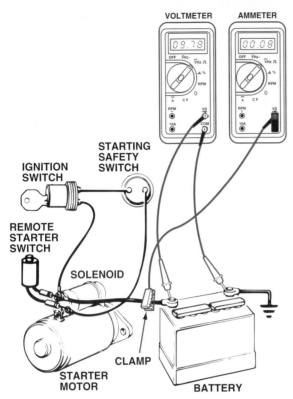

Fig.1-32. Performing a starter motor current draw test with a voltmeter and inductive ammeter.

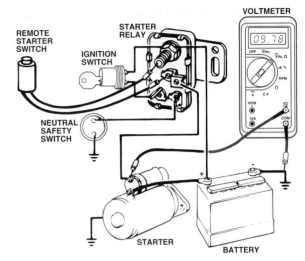

Fig. 1-33 Typical voltmeter connections for performing a starter motor cranking voltage test.

High resistance in the cranking circuit can cause either high or low current draw. This is because the starter motor requires high current to get up to speed. Once up to speed, the starter motor acts like a generator to produce a counter voltage that limits the current. Because the motor requires high current when turning slowly, high resistance can prevent a starter from getting enough current to get up to speed. As a result, the motor turns slowly and does not limit the current.

If resistance is high enough, it limits current to the starter, which causes the starter motor to turn slowly or not at all. High resistance can be seen on the ammeter when the starter is first engaged. If current momentarily goes high, then settles down to a lower amount, suspect high resistance.

When high resistance is indicated, perform starter circuit resistance tests. If testing indicates a starter motor problem, remove the unit for service.

Cranking Voltage Test

This test, which measures **available voltage** at the starter during cranking, is performed to check for high resistance in the starter circuit. Test results are read on a voltmeter. To test:

1. Bypass the ignition switch with a remote starter switch.
2. Connect the negative voltmeter lead to a good ground and connect the positive voltmeter lead to high current circuit (the starter). Some manufacturers recommend connecting the voltmeter directly to the starter, while others specify testing at the relay or solenoid, figure 1-33. Check the Service Manual for exact procedures and specifications.
3. Crank the engine while monitoring the voltmeter.

To interpret test results if the starter motor cranks poorly, and if voltage is:

- 9.6 or more and the amperage is high, the problem is in the motor, ignition timing is too far advanced, the engine is tight and binding, or there is high circuit resistance. The battery is good and the starter motor is getting enough current to operate.
- 9.6 or more and the amperage is low, the problem is high resistance. The battery is good, but there is not enough current through the starter motor.
- 9.6 or less and the amperage is high, the problem is in the motor, ignition timing is too far advanced, the engine is tight and binding, or there is high circuit resistance. The high amperage draw pulls down the battery voltage and the battery may be faulty.
- 9.6 or less and the amperage is low, the battery should be tested.

Circuit Resistance Tests

If the current draw and cranking voltage tests indicate that the problem lies in one of the starting system electrical circuits, perform circuit resistance tests to pinpoint the problem.

These tests locate the point of high resistance in the circuit that is causing excessive **voltage drop**. The resistance usually occurs at one of the connections in the circuits, but internally defective wires and cables may also be at fault. As a general rule, acceptable voltage drop standard in starting systems is a maximum of 0.1 volt per connection. A greater voltage drop causes starter motor performance problems.

The starting system has three circuits:

- Insulated
- Ground
- Control

The insulated circuit carries the high current needed to operate the starter motor, the ground circuit provides a return path to the battery for power supplied by the insulated circuit, and the control circuit includes all the low current wiring and devices used to open and close the insulated circuit. To locate the source of high resistance, perform voltage drop tests recommended by the manufacturer. Take readings while the starter motor is cranking, or use a carbon pile to load the circuit, figure 1-34. Momentarily load the circuit to approximately 150 to 200 amps, and switch the load off quickly to prevent draining the battery. Test the starter ground circuit in a similar manner, figure 1-35. Perform voltage drop tests on the control circuit as needed.

If any of the tests indicate an internal problem, the starter motor must be removed from the vehicle and either repaired or replaced.

Starter Removal

The following is a typical starter motor removal sequence. Always consult the repair manual for the vehicle being serviced. To remove the starter:

1. Disconnect the negative battery cable.
2. Raise the vehicle on safety stands or a hoist high enough to access the starter motor.
3. Disconnect any suspension components that are likely to interfere with removing the starter from the chassis.
4. Loosen or remove exhaust pipes and other components that interfere with starter motor removal.

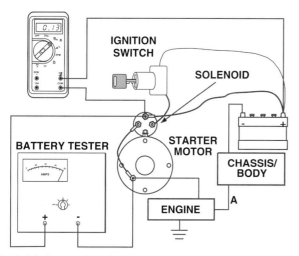

Fig. 1-34. Connections for loading the system and testing for voltage drop on the insulated side of the starting system.

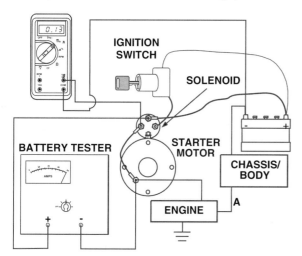

Fig. 1-35. Connections for loading the system and testing for voltage drop on the ground side of the starting system.

5. Disconnect and label all wires and cables to the starter motor or solenoid.
6. Remove any heat shields and brackets covering the starter motor.
7. Remove any mounting bolts and shims securing the starter motor to the engine.
8. Slide the starter free of the bellhousing and guide it out of the chassis.

Starter Installation

When replacing a starter motor, make sure the new unit meets the requirements of the vehicle. Some vehicles require a high-temperature starter with an extra field coil, brush lead, and solenoid winding insulation as well as a high-temperature solenoid cap. To install a starter motor:

1. Transfer support brackets or other hardware from the old motor to the replacement motor as required.
2. Fit the starter motor into position on the engine and install the mounting fasteners. Be sure to reconnect any ground cables or brackets that install on the starter mounts.
3. Check flywheel-to-starter engagement. Some vehicles require shims to provide correct starter pinion-to-flywheel engagement. These shims are placed between the starter drive housing and the engine block. Remove the flywheel cover and check the starter pinion engagement with the flywheel. Add or remove shims to correct.
4. Connect all wires to the solenoid or starter motor terminals.
5. Connect any suspension or exhaust system parts that were loosened or removed.
6. Connect the negative battery cable.

Test starter motor operation by starting the vehicle. Listen for any unusual sounds and check for correct operation of the starting safety switch. Some late-model starters have a special stud in the motor housing. Be sure the short end of the stud, with coarser threads, is threaded into the housing. Incorrect installation damages the field coils.

CHARGING SYSTEM SERVICE

The charging system includes the generator, regulator, and all the wiring and connections in the circuit, figure 1-36. Charging failure symptoms fit into two categories, those that cause the system to:

A8

- Undercharge or not charge
- Overcharge

Systems That Undercharge or Do Not Charge

If a charging system has a lower than normal charging rate, or is not charging at all, check for:

- Loose or broken drive belts, pulleys, or supporting brackets
- Defective **diodes** or stator windings
- Defective voltage regulator
- High resistance or an open circuit in the wiring connecting the generator and the battery
- High resistance in the generator **field circuit**
- Sulfated battery

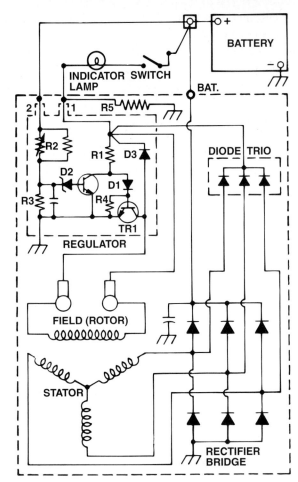

Fig. 1-36. Typical solid-state charging system circuit diagram.

Systems That Overcharge

An excessive charging rate can be caused by a:

- Defective voltage regulator—on some systems, the voltage regulator is part of the powertrain control module (PCM); if defective, replace the PCM
- Shorted field wire—shorted to ground in a system with an externally grounded field, or A-circuit, or shorted to power in a system with an internally grounded field, or B-circuit
- High resistance in the wiring between the battery and main fuse panel—this results in an inaccurate voltage indication to the field circuit from the ignition switch
- Battery with an internal short that accepts a charge with little resistance
- A faulty component drawing excessive current

System Testing

Insight

In 1996, SAE J1930 terminology was adopted to standardize component identification. This standard adopted the name "generator" to refer to the component commonly known as an "alternator." This study guide uses the term generator throughout; however, both terms are used interchangeably in the ASE tests.

On-vehicle generator system tests are essentially the same, regardless of the vehicle. The main differences are meter test points and specifications. This section contains general descriptions of common on-vehicle tests. To check a particular

generator or system, use the procedures and specifications from the vehicle manufacturer.

The voltage regulator limits the strength of the magnetic field by changing the current going to the field coil. Therefore, it regulates the generator voltage output according to the electrical system demand. Bypassing a voltage regulator for test purposes is called full-fielding the generator. Bypassing a voltage regulator supplies maximum output to the field coil. Under these conditions, system voltage can increase above 16 volts, which is an unsafe level. Once you determine that the generator can or cannot produce the required voltage, remove the bypass immediately.

Charging System Output Test

A CSB analyzer simplifies charging system diagnosis. This test instrument combines the functions of the carbon pile and separate meters needed for various tests. Use the following general procedure to test the charging system output:

1. Connect the analyzer to the vehicle as instructed in the analyzer manual.
2. Set the test selector switch to the charging test position.
3. Switch the ignition on and note the ammeter reading. This is the current required to power the ignition system and accessories; it will not be included in the maximum output reading.
4. Start the engine and run it at 2,000 RPM, or the specified test speed.
5. Adjust the carbon pile to obtain the maximum ammeter reading while keeping the system voltage above 12 volts. Always keep load time to a minimum to prevent damage.
6. Compare the ammeter reading to specifications. If it is:
   - Within 10 percent of specifications, go to step 7
   - Not within 10 percent of specifications, go to step 11
7. Set the test selector switch to the regulator test position.
8. Adjust the engine speed to 2,000 RPM or the specified test speed.
9. Note the voltmeter reading after it stabilizes. The length of time required for the reading to stop rising varies according to battery state-of-charge.
10. Compare the voltmeter reading to specifications. If it is:
    - Within specifications, the voltage regulator is okay
    - Not within specifications, replace the voltage regulator and retest
11. With the engine running at test speed, high RPM, turn on the carbon pile to discharge the battery.
12. As system voltage drops, the voltage regulator should increase generator output.
13. When the amperage output begins to decrease, reduce the carbon pile discharge. Turn the carbon pile off.
14. Add the highest ammeter reading to the readings taken in step 3, using a minimum of 5 amps.
15. Compare the total to specifications. If it is:
    - Within 10 percent of specifications, no problem is found
    - Not within 10 percent of specifications, further testing of the field circuit and regulator is required. With an internal regulator, test other generator inputs for correct voltage

Circuit Resistance Test

Replace or repair any loose or corroded connections or damaged wiring before testing the charging system to prevent inaccurate test results. Isolate high resistance in the positive, or insulated, and negative, or ground, circuits of the charging system by voltage drop testing. Test under load with the engine running at 1,500 to 1,800 RPM and the generator producing a specific current, usually 20 amps applied to the battery. Begin by checking insulated circuit voltage drop by connecting the DMM between the positive battery terminal and the battery, or output, terminal at the generator, figure 1-37. If the voltage drop is higher than specified, move test connections down the circuit to pinpoint the high resistance.

Check voltage drop on the ground circuit of the generator in similar fashion. Connect the DMM between the generator frame and negative battery terminal, figure 1-38.

This test is performed when the generator has enough output to charge the battery at a 20 amp rate. It is fairly common to see a negative (-) voltage under these conditions. If voltage drop is excessively high, install an external ground strap between the generator and the engine. This ground strap is always required when the generator is mounted in rubber bushings. The normal limit of voltage drop on this circuit is 0.2 volt.

Current Output Test

There are two stages to a generator current output test, and some manufacturers suggest doing only one stage or the other. Obtain specifications and follow procedures in the Service Manual for the unit being tested.

First Stage

Use a CSB analyzer, or attach a carbon pile across the battery. Connect a voltmeter between the positive battery terminal and ground, and connect an ammeter between the positive battery terminal and the battery terminal at the generator. Start and

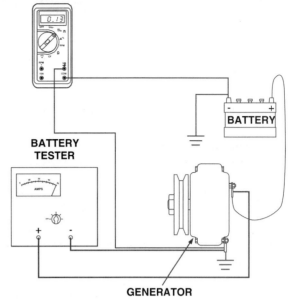

Fig. 1-38. Equipment connections for checking voltage drop in the ground, or negative, generator circuit.

run the engine at the specified test speed, typically 1,200 RPM, and adjust the carbon pile either to maintain a steady 15 volt level or to get the greatest possible ammeter reading. Compare the ammeter reading to specifications.

This test uses the carbon pile to drop the system voltage and force the voltage regulator to raise the amperage output. This tests the component parts of the existing system for proper operation.

Second Stage

Perform this stage if the ammeter reading does not meet specifications during the first stage. Under the same test conditions, full-field the generator by bypassing the voltage regulator. This provides maximum current through the field windings so that the generator develops maximum output amperage. With a remotely mounted regulator, use a jumper wire to provide battery voltage or ground the field wire.

There are two different methods of full-fielding, connecting to power and connecting to ground, and it is important that the right method be used. If the regulator is controlling the ground side of the field windings, the circuit is grounded. If the regulator is controlling the power side of the field, then the circuit should be connected to battery power.

With the generator full-fielded, it is possible for the system voltage to go excessively high. This high voltage can present problems with electronic components. Therefore, full-fielding is often only recommended after it has been determined that the voltage regulator is not functioning properly. This test is used to see if there is an additional problem with the generator.

Field Current Draw Test

The field current draw test is performed with the engine off. For some vehicles, the regulator or warning lamp circuit, or both, may need to be bypassed while testing. Check the Service Manual for specific instructions. To test current draw, connect an ammeter either between the positive battery terminal and the generator field or between the field and ground. Then

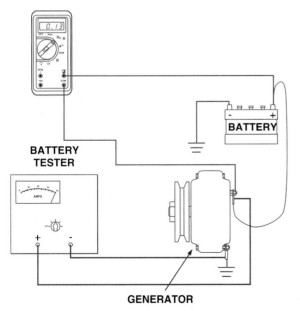

Fig. 1-37. Equipment connections for checking voltage drop in the insulated, or positive, generator circuit.

switch the ignition on without starting the engine, or bypass the ignition switch and warning lamp with a jumper wire as directed, and read field current draw on the ammeter. If out of specifications, remove the generator for further testing. If the ammeter reading fluctuates, service the brushes and windings. This test is performed only on charging systems that have an external voltage regulator. Do not attempt this test on the internal regulator.

Voltage Regulator Test

Check the regulated voltage with a voltmeter connected between the generator output terminal and ground, or between the positive battery terminal and ground. Start and run the engine at a fast idle for several minutes to stabilize the charging system. The amperage charge rate into the battery should be low. If voltage readings are too low, confirm the amperage output at the generator before condemning the voltage regulator. High generator amperage output can cause a low voltage reading. If the readings are too high, replace the voltage regulator.

If any of the above tests indicate a generator problem, the generator must be removed from the vehicle for servicing. For additional information on bench testing and repairing generators, refer to Book A6 "Electrical and Electronic Systems" of this series.

System Inspection

Charging system complaints often result from simple and easily corrected problems that become obvious during a quick visual inspection of the system components.

To begin:

1. Check the battery electrolyte level, state-of charge, and capacity. If the battery is worn out or defective, the charging system may not be at fault.

2. Inspect the generator drive belt. Loose belts are a major cause of poor charging system performance. If the belt is loose or damaged, remove it for further inspection. Loosen the tension on the belt before attempting to remove it from the engine. Never force or pry a belt over pulley flanges. While the belt is removed, examine the pulleys for damage or misalignment. Replace pulleys and install the new belt. Belts must be properly tensioned. A loose belt will slip and a tight belt can damage bearings. Adjust tension to specifications. After installing a new drive belt, allow the engine to run for at least 10 to 15 minutes. Switch the engine off, then recheck and adjust belt tension using "used" belt specifications.

3. Check all system wiring and connections. Be sure to inspect fusible links, and make sure multiple connectors are latched properly. Even when the fusible link looks good it may be damaged internally. If in doubt pull on one end of the fusible link. If the insulation stretches replace the link. Disconnect each connector in the circuit and conduct a visual inspection. Look closely for damaged, corroded, or pushed out pins. Use a new terminal pin to check for a snug fit into the plug. If the socket in the plug is loose replace with a new part. Reconnect and ensure the connector is latched properly. If the circuit is physically sound continue with a voltage drop test.

4. Inspect the generator and regulator mountings for loose or missing bolts. Replace or tighten as needed.

Correct any problems discovered during the inspection. If system performance remains below specifications, isolate the cause by performing system tests.

CHAPTER QUESTIONS

1. The first step in diagnosing a performance or driveability problem is to:
   a. Perform a preliminary inspection
   b. Verify the concern
   c. Get specific information from the customer
   d. Eliminate the possibility of an internal engine problem

2. When using a timing light to isolate an engine noise, expect top-end noises to occur:
   a. With every other flash of the timing light
   b. With every flash of the timing light
   c. Twice for every flash of the timing light
   d. Between each flash of the timing light

3. When performing a manifold vacuum test, raising the engine speed off idle will cause gauge readings to:
   a. Increase slightly
   b. Decrease slightly
   c. Fluctuate rapidly
   d. Remain constant

4. During a compression test, a cylinder reads low on the first stroke, builds up slightly, and levels off below specification. The most likely cause would be:
   a. Sticking or burned valves
   b. Worn piston rings or damaged piston
   c. Leaking head gasket or cracked head
   d. Worn cylinder walls and excessive blowby

5. What would be the sealing ability of a cylinder with a 28 percent loss of air pressure during a leakage test?
   a. Good
   b. Fair
   c. Poor
   d. Bad

6. Which test can be performed on a running engine to quickly detect internal problems?
   a. Cylinder compression
   b. Cylinder leakage
   c. Cylinder power balance
   d. Oscilloscope

7. When scope testing an ignition system with a current limiting module circuit, a hump or small oscillations may appear in the:
   a. Firing section
   b. Sparkline
   c. Intermediate section
   d. Dwell section

8. In the firing section of a secondary circuit scope pattern, the sparkline should level off near:
   a. Half the height of the firing spike
   b. One-third the height of the firing spike
   c. One-quarter the height of the firing spike
   d. The bottom of the firing spike

9. What would be the approximate state-of-charge of a battery whose temperature-corrected specific gravity is 1.225?
   a. 100 percent
   b. 75 percent
   c. 50 percent
   d. 25 percent

10. Which of the following is the most likely cause of high readings during a starter motor current draw test?
    a. A short circuit
    b. An open circuit
    c. High resistance
    d. A weak or discharged battery

11. A charging system that is overcharging can be caused by all of the following *EXCEPT*:
    a. A defective voltage regulator
    b. Shorted field wiring
    c. High generator field circuit resistance
    d. An internal battery short

12. Voltage drop on the alternator ground circuit should be less than:
    a. 0.01 volt
    b. 0.10 volt
    c. 0.02 volt
    d. 0.20 volt

A8

CHAPTER OBJECTIVES

- The technician will complete the ASE task list on Ignition System Diagnosis and Repair.
- The technician will be able to answer 8 questions dealing with the Ignition System Diagnosis and Repair section of the A8 ASE Test.

This chapter discusses testing, repairing, and replacing individual components of the ignition system. Most modern ignition systems contain delicate, and expensive, electronic components that can be destroyed by a voltage surge. The high-voltage surge that results from simply making or breaking a connection can cause damage. When working on the ignition system, take these precautions to avoid damage to the ignition system and personal injury:

1. Unless the procedure specifically states otherwise, switch the ignition off or disconnect the battery ground cable before separating any ignition system wiring connections.
2. Do not touch, or short to ground, any exposed connections while the engine is cranking or running.
3. Do not short the primary circuit to ground without resistance; the high current that results can damage circuits and components.
4. Do not create a secondary voltage arc near the battery or fuel system components. This can cause an explosion.
5. When testing the ignition system, follow the procedure specified by the manufacturer.

SPARK DISTRIBUTION SYSTEMS

Early in the 20th century the first electrical ignition system, the self-starter for the automobile, was invented. This type of ignition system is known as the Kettering system, consisting of points, condenser, and an ignition coil. It became the standard in the automotive industry, replacing magnetos. A gear, chain, or belt from the engine drives the distributor. Inside this distributor is a spring-loaded contact switch known as the points. The points ride on a revolving cam and open and close to fire a single coil, which produces the spark. Inside the distributor is also the rotor, which rotates to direct the spark to the correct spark plug wire.

Distributor Type Ignition Systems (DI)

As vehicle emissions and fuel economy standards became stricter the need for an ignition system that could produce a hotter spark was required. The mechanical points could not handle the required increase in current flow. To solve this problem the first electronic ignition systems replaced breaker points with a transistor. This system uses the distributor to signal the **ignition control module (ICM)** when to fire the spark plug. The ICM uses a power transistor to control the coil primary current flow.

Distributorless Ignition Systems (DIS)

Most late-model vehicles no longer use a distributor to control ignition timing and direct the secondary voltage to the spark plugs. The ignition coil's primary circuit control, originally in the distributor, has been replaced by ignition timing commands from the PCM. The PCM receives input from the crankshaft position sensor (CKP) and uses the information to control ignition timing. The CKP can be a **magnetic pickup** or a Hall-effect sensor; both are discussed later in this chapter. The DIS system design eliminates many moving parts and maintains more accurate control of the ignition timing during the life of the vehicle.

Figure 2-1 provides a sample of ignition related symptoms, definitions, and probable conditions or causes of specific conditions. Always use the appropriate Service Manual when conducting actual diagnostics on a vehicle.

IGNITION SYSTEM DIAGNOSIS

Although most ignition systems are incorporated into the engine management system, ignition failures generally do not set trouble codes and ignition malfunctions cannot be detected on the **serial data stream**. The steps taken to isolate the source of an ignition system failure vary by vehicle and symptom.

Most modern electronic ignition systems are incorporated into the PCM. The ignition, fuel injection, and emission control systems are linked together and all three are diagnosed simultaneously. Proper diagnosis requires the use of a diagnostic scan tool. You may also need to use a breakout box (BOB) and **digital multimeter (DMM)** to complete the diagnostic process. Refer to the appropriate Service or Diagnostic Manual

---

Digital Multimeter: A hand-held meter capable of measuring voltage, resistance, and current flow, then displaying it in digital format on an LCD screen.

Ignition Control Module (ICM): An electronic module designed to control the primary circuit to the ignition coil.

Symptom	Definition	Possible Causes
NO START WITH NORMAL CRANK SPEED	The starter cranks the engine normally but the engine does not start.	Primary ignition circuit failure No RPM signal to ECM / Ignition Module Wet secondary ignition system components
HARD STARTING / LONG CRANKING TIME	The starter cranks the engine normally but requires excessive crank time to start.	Incorrect ignition timing Deficient spark intensity Excessive resistance in primary circuit
STARTS AND STALLS	Engine starts but stalls when the key is released to the RUN position.	Incorrect ignition timing Deficient spark intensity Ignition RUN circuit failure
STALLS AND MAY OR MAY NOT RESTART	Engine stops running under load, usually at idle when the transmission is in gear. Engine may or may not restart quickly.	Incorrect ignition timing Deficient spark intensity Interruption of ignition spark High resistance in the primary circuit
RUNS ROUGH / MISFIRES	Inconsistent production of power. Causes a noticeable vibration.	Inconsistent ignition Deficient spark intensity in one or more cylinders Defective spark plug wires
STUMBLE / SURGE BUCKS / JERKS	A drop off of power between the time the throttle opens and speed increases.	Deficient spark intensity High resistance in the primary circuit Defective spark plug wires
LACK OF POWER	Excessive throttle application is required to maintain cruise. Acceleration is slower than normal.	Incorrect ignition timing Deficient spark intensity
POOR FUEL ECONOMY	Vehicle uses excessive fuel.	Incorrect ignition timing Deficient spark intensity to one or more cylinders Defective spark plug wires
EMISSIONS TEST FAILURE	Vehicle fails one or more emissions tests.	Incorrect ignition timing Deficient spark intensity or duration Excessive resistance in primary circuit Defective spark plug wires

Fig. 2-1. Ignition system driveability diagnostic procedures.

A8

for the correct tools and procedures. Follow the specific instructions of the vehicle and equipment manufacturers when connecting and operating test equipment.

Keep in mind, the scan tool will not reveal the exact nature of the problem, but does help you isolate the circuit or component where the malfunction exists. Scan tools provide the user with many different forms of information. Compare the scan tool readings with the specifications from the service publications to determine if, in fact, a problem exists.

Primary Circuit Testing

Primary circuit voltage has a direct effect on secondary circuit voltage. The loss of a single volt in the primary circuit can reduce secondary circuit voltage by as much as 10 kilovolts (10,000 volts). Common causes of primary circuit voltage loss include: high circuit resistance, insufficient source voltage from the battery, and low charging system output.

Sources of high primary resistance include:

- Loose, corroded, or damaged wiring connections
- An incorrect or defective coil
- A poor ground at the ignition module

Low source voltage can be caused by the following:

- Excessive starter motor current draw
- Low charging voltage
- A discharged battery

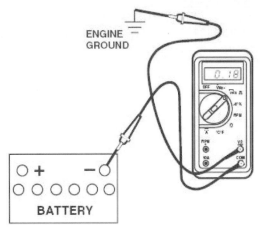

Fig. 2-2. Voltage drop at the battery ground cable should be less than 0.2 volt.

Primary Circuit Voltmeter Tests

First, make sure the battery has the correct performance rating and is fully charged. Then, disable the ignition system following the specific procedures provided by the manufacturer. Next, check for:

- Available voltage while cranking
- Voltage-drop across the battery ground

To test voltage available from the battery while cranking, you can monitor the data stream with a scan tool, or:

1. Connect the **voltmeter** positive lead to the positive battery terminal, not to the cable connector. Connect the voltmeter negative lead to a good ground.
2. Switch the ignition key on and take a voltmeter reading while the engine is cranking.

A reading of ten volts or more indicates the battery is in good condition. Low readings can be caused by a voltage drop across the battery ground cable, excessive starter motor current draw, or incorrect charging system output.

To test voltage drop across the battery ground cable:

1. Connect the voltmeter positive lead to ground and the negative lead to the negative battery terminal, not to the cable connector, figure 2-2.
2. Crank the engine with the starter and take a voltmeter reading.

If the reading is 0.2 volt or less, the battery ground connection and cable are in good condition. When readings exceed 0.2 volt, clean and tighten the battery cable connections and terminals. Repeat the test; replace the ground cable if readings remain high.

Additional ignition test procedures and the equipment used vary by system. Accurate specifications and instructions from the manufacturer are required. The following paragraphs discuss general procedures for testing a variety of electronic components.

Electronic Component Testing

Primary ignition failures often originate from problems in the:

- Primary wiring and connectors
- Distributor signal generator

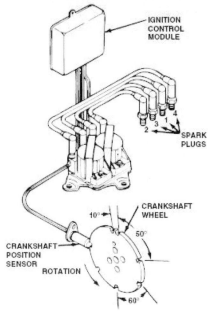

Fig. 2-3. A crankshaft position sensor provides the input used to initiate plug firing on a direct ignition system.

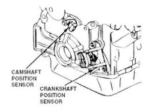

Fig. 2-4. Some systems use an additional sensor on the camshaft to properly phase the firing sequence.

- Ignition control module
- Ignition coil
- Oxygen sensor heater

When voltage drop indicates high or low resistance, disconnect power and verify your findings with an ohmmeter. Most manufacturers provide resistance specifications for components and circuits. Many problems can easily be solved by cleaning connectors and related grounds, or repairing damaged wiring.

In general, an electronic ignition system functions as follows: The distributor signal generator sends a signal to the PCM. The PCM modifies the timing and sends the signal to the ignition control module to toggle the primary coil circuit and fire the spark plugs. Some signals are generated by a pick-up coil or Hall-effect switch mounted in the distributor housing. Direct, or distributorless, ignition systems use a crankshaft position (CKP) sensor to generate an input signal to the ICM, figure 2-3. The ICM provides the output signal to toggle the primary circuit and initiate firing. The system may use an additional camshaft position (CMP) sensor to determine cylinder phasing and achieve more accurate control of plug firing and timing advance, figure 2-4.

Methods to determine whether an ICM is good or defective vary between systems. Procedures outlined by the vehicle manufacturer must be followed. In general, eliminate all other possibilities before condemning the module. Verify power is available to the module, and check for voltage drop across connections on the power and ground circuits. Since modules provide the primary circuit ground connection, many problems can be solved by checking and cleaning the ground.

For any ignition system to operate properly, the following conditions must be met:

- Battery cranking voltage must be over 9 volts
- Primary wiring must be in good condition, and all connections need to be clean and tight
- Spark must be available at the spark plugs while the engine is cranking

The air gap between the pickup coil and trigger wheel is adjustable on some systems. Gap has no effect on the dwell period; dwell is determined by the control module. The air gap must be set to a specific clearance when a new pickup unit is installed. During use, the air gap should not change. However, it should be checked before performing troubleshooting tests.

SECONDARY CIRCUIT DIAGNOSIS AND REPAIR

Often, it is useful when diagnosing a no-start condition to first verify that secondary voltage is available from the coil by performing a spark test. Begin by disconnecting a spark plug cable from the plug. Connect a **spark tester** to the plug wire and attach the ground clip of the tester to a bare metal spot on the engine, figure 2-5. Adjust the spark gap according to Service Manual specifications. If no specifications are available, start with a setting of approximately 1/4" (6mm). Crank the engine while observing the spark tester. A bright blue spark should be clearly visible. Do not crank the engine with the spark plug wires disconnected, as this may create high open-circuit voltage and cause damage to the ignition coil or other electronic systems.

Inspection

Begin your evaluation with a visual inspection of the secondary components. Look for:

- Cracked, burned, or brittle insulation on the ignition cables and boots
- Distributor cap defects, such as a sticking or worn carbon button, cracks, carbon tracks from arcing current, burned or corroded terminals, and corrosion inside the cap towers
- Rotor damage, such as a bent or broken contact strip, burned or eroded tip, cracked or broken positioning lug, and carbon tracks or cracks on the body

Oscilloscope Testing

Oscilloscope testing is the most efficient method of locating secondary circuit malfunctions. Variations in the secondary trace will indicate if parts are malfunctioning or incorrectly adjusted. The following paragraphs describe some common secondary circuit problems that can be detected with an oscilloscope.

Firing Section Abnormalities

Check the firing section of an oscilloscope trace for the following:

- A large firing oscillation with little or no sparkline for one cylinder indicates an open circuit between the distributor rotor and the spark plug, figure 2-6. Use the parade display to isolate the faulty cylinder. Check for a disconnected or broken spark plug cable. This pattern can be created deliberately to check coil output. Remove a cable; the top of the firing line is the maximum available voltage of the coil. Use the kV scale on the side of the screen to read voltage output
- One sparkline that is lower and longer than the rest indicates low-resistance in the circuit between the distributor cap and the spark plug, figure 2-7. Check for carbon tracks in the distributor, poor cable insulation, or a fouled spark plug
- A parade pattern may show a short sparkline still exists even when the spark plug cable has been deliberately disconnected, figure 2-8. This indicates that high-voltage is causing a current leak to ground somewhere, usually through the ignition cable insulation, the distributor cap, or the rotor. Carbon tracks will often accumulate near the leakage

A8

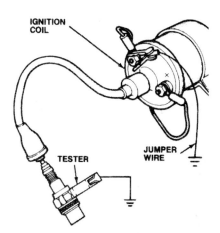

Fig. 2-5. Using a spark tester to check for secondary voltage available from the coil.

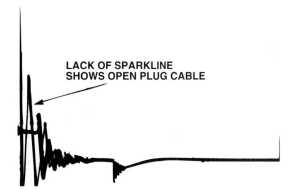

Fig. 2-6. A large firing oscillation without a sparkline on a secondary superimposed pattern indicates an open plug circuit.

Spark Tester: A special tool with an adjustable spark gap used to check spark intensity.

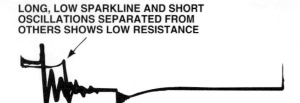

Fig. 2-7. A low, long sparkline on a secondary superimposed pattern indicates low-resistance in one cylinder.

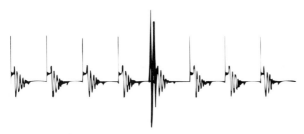

Fig. 2-8. An open plug circuit with a voltage leak in a secondary parade pattern.

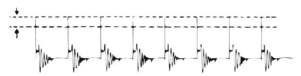

Fig. 2-9. Look for fairly even firing line peaks when viewing a secondary parade pattern.

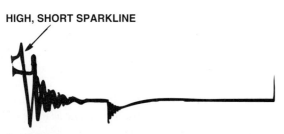

Fig. 2-10. A high, short sparkline on a secondary superimposed pattern indicates high-resistance in one cylinder.

- There should be no more than a 20 percent difference between the highest and lowest firing spikes when comparing cylinders in a parade pattern, figure 2-9. Variations can be caused by fuel or electrical system problems. To separate the two, slowly cover the engine air intake to richen the fuel mixture. If the spikes go down and engine speed increases, the problem is fuel related. If the spikes go down and engine speed remains unchanged, the plug gaps may be too great. If a single spike remains the same height, the cable to that plug may be damaged
- One sparkline that is higher and shorter than the rest indicates high-resistance from an open circuit between the distributor cap and the spark plug, figure 2-10. A damaged or loose cable or a wide plug gap may be at fault.

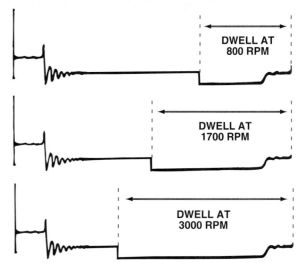

Fig. 2-11. Dwell length increases in proportion to engine speed on some systems.

Corrosion on the cable terminals and in the distributor cap can cause a sparkline for one cylinder to start higher and angle downward more sharply than the others
- A sparkline that jumps erratically or slopes up rather than down is caused by an incorrect fuel mixture in that cylinder. The problem may be mechanical, such as sticking or worn valves, or caused by intake air leaks or fuel **induction** problems

Intermediate Section Abnormalities

Use the intermediate section of the trace to check coil function. A faulty coil, primary circuit, or coil wire between the coil and distributor cap may cause a lack of oscillations.

- Absent coil oscillations with a normal dwell section are the result of a faulty coil or a high-resistance short to ground in the primary circuit
- A pattern displayed upside-down indicates that coil polarity is reversed, usually because of reversed primary connections at the coil
- The entire pattern jumping on the screen results from an intermittent open in the coil secondary winding
- Reduced coil oscillations along with a missing module-on signal are caused by an open between the coil and the distributor cap
- Variation in the firing signals at the end of a raster pattern is caused by worn ignition signal parts or a faulty module. This variation indicates timing differences among cylinders. Note that this is normal for those ignition systems that use computer control of timing to regulate idle speed

Dwell Section Abnormalities

The dwell section of a secondary trace should be a relatively flat line with the possible exception of a current limiting hump. Be aware, dwell length increases with engine speed on some systems, figure 2-11. Dwell variation between cylinders can be checked using the raster display. A dwell variation of more than 4 to 6 degrees between cylinders indicates mechanical wear in the distributor. Use the degree scale at the bottom of the screen to read dwell angles.

SPARK PLUG AND IGNITION CABLE SERVICE

Spark plugs are routinely replaced at specific service intervals as recommended by the vehicle manufacturer. However, these intervals are guidelines and actual spark plug service life will vary. Spark plug life depends upon:

- Engine design
- Type of driving
- Kind of fuel used
- Types of emission control devices

Because the spark plugs are the final component in all secondary circuits, the remainder of the circuit cannot perform properly if they are not in good condition.

Spark Plug Removal

Spark plug access is limited on many late-model engines due to a maze of air conditioning and emission control plumbing and engine-driven accessory mounting. Engine accessories may have to be loosened from their mountings and moved to get to the plugs. Air conditioning compressors, air pumps, and power steering pumps are frequent candidates for relocation during spark plug service. Whenever you must move one of these accessories, be careful of its plumbing and wiring. The spark plugs on some engines are most easily reached from underneath the engine. To remove the spark plugs:

1. Disconnect cables at the plug by grasping the boot and twisting gently while pulling. Do not pull on the cable. Insulated spark plug pliers provide a better grip and are recommended when working near hot manifolds, figure 2-12.
2. Loosen each plug one or two turns with a spark plug socket, then blow dirt away from around the plugs with compressed air.
3. Remove the plugs, keeping them in cylinder number order for inspection.
4. When removing gasketed plugs, be sure the old gasket comes out with the plug.

Spark Plug Inspection

Examining the firing ends of the spark plugs reveals a good deal about general engine conditions and plug operation. The insulator nose of a used plug should have a light brown-to-grayish color, and there should be very little electrode wear. These conditions indicate the correct plug heat range and a healthy engine. Some common spark plug conditions that indicate problems follow.

Oil Fouling

Dark, wet deposits on the plug tip are caused by excessive oil entering the combustion chamber. Piston ring, cylinder wall, and valve guide wear are likely causes in a high-mileage engine. Also, a defective PCV valve can draw oil vapor from the crankcase into the intake and oil foul the plugs.

Carbon Fouling

Soft, black, sooty deposits on the plug end indicate carbon fouling. Carbon results from a plug that is operating too cold. Check for spark plugs with an incorrect heat range, an overly rich air-fuel mixture, weak ignition, inoperative manifold heat control valve or thermostatic air cleaner, retarded timing, low compression, or faulty plug wires or distributor cap. Carbon fouling may also result from overloading due to excessive stop-and-go driving.

Ash Fouling

Certain oil or fuel additives that burn during normal combustion can create ash deposits. Ash deposits are light brownish-white accumulations that form on and around the electrode. Normally, ash deposits are nonconductive, but large amounts may cause misfiring.

Splash Fouling

Small dark patches visible on the insulator indicate splash fouling. Deposits breaking loose from pistons and valves and splashing against hot plug insulators cause splash fouling. The condition often occurs after engine servicing that restores engine power and higher combustion temperatures. Splash-fouled plugs can generally be cleaned and reinstalled.

Gap Bridging

Gap bridging is usually due to conditions similar to those described for splash fouling. The difference is that deposits form a bridge across the electrodes and cause a short. This condition is common in engines with poor oil control.

Insulator Glazing

Shiny, yellow, or tan deposits are a sign of insulator glazing. Frequent hard acceleration with a resulting rise in plug temperature can cause glazing. The high temperature melts normal plug deposits and fuses them into a conductive coating that causes misfiring.

Overheating

Spark plug overheating is indicated by a clean, white insulator tip, excessive electrode wear, or both. The insulator may also be blistered. Incorrect spark plug heat range, incorrect tightening torque, over-advanced timing, a defective cooling system, or lean air-fuel mixture can cause overheating.

Detonation

Detonation causes increased heat and pressure in the combustion chamber that exerts extreme loads on engine parts. Fractured or broken spark plug insulators are a sign of detonation. Over-advanced timing, lean fuel-air mixture, low gasoline octane, and engine lugging are contributing factors. An EGR valve that fails to open can also cause detonation.

A8

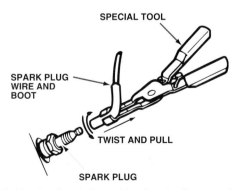

SPECIAL TOOL

SPARK PLUG WIRE AND BOOT

TWIST AND PULL

SPARK PLUG

Fig. 2-12. Use insulated plug cable pliers to disconnect cables from spark plugs.

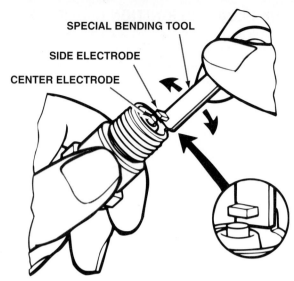

Fig. 2-14. Adjusting spark plug electrode gap.

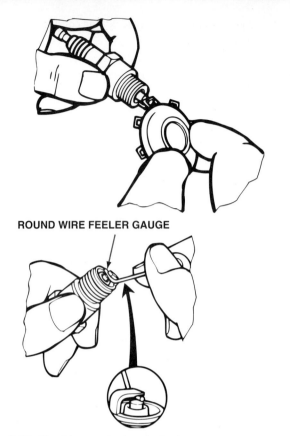

Fig. 2-13. Checking spark plug electrode gap.

Preignition

Preignition, the air-fuel charge igniting before the plug fires, can cause severe damage to the spark plug electrodes. Preignition is usually caused by combustion chamber hot spots or deposits that hold enough heat to prematurely ignite the air-fuel charge. Crossfiring between plug cables or a plug heat range much too hot for the engine can also cause preignition. A loose spark plug may also cause preignition.

Even if the color of the insulator and deposits are normal, rounded and worn electrodes indicate that a plug should be replaced. These plugs are simply worn out. The voltage required to spark across the gap has increased and continues to do so with additional use. Misfiring under load is a clue to worn out plugs. Such plugs also contribute to poor gas mileage, loss of power, and increased emissions.

Also check spark plugs for physical damage caused by a foreign object in the combustion chamber, a plug of the wrong reach being hit by a piston or valve, or by careless installation. Be careful to prevent dirt from falling into spark plug holes during service.

Spark Plug Installation

Spark plugs, both new and used, must be correctly gapped before they are installed. Although a wide variety of gapping tools are available, a round wire feeler gauge is the most efficient for used plugs, figure 2-13.

Adjust the gap by carefully bending the ground electrode, figure 2-14.

- Do not assume that new plugs are correctly gapped
- Do not make gap adjustments by tapping the electrode on a workbench or other solid object

Cleaning the threaded plug holes in the cylinder head with a thread chaser will ensure easy spark plug installation. With aluminum heads, use the tool carefully to avoid damaging the threads.

Some manufacturers recommend using an antiseize compound or thread lubricant on the plug threads. Use thread lubricant only when specified by the manufacturer. Antiseize compound is commonly used when installing plugs in aluminum cylinder heads. Be sure to use the specific compound recommended by the manufacturer, as not all are compatible with aluminum. Whenever thread lubricant or antiseize is used, reduce the tightening torque slightly.

Once the plug gap has been properly set, install as follows:

1. Wipe any dirt and grease from the cylinder head plug seats.
2. Check that gaskets used on the plugs are in good condition and properly installed.
3. Install the plugs in the engine and run them in by hand.
4. Tighten the plugs to specification with a torque wrench following Service Manual specifications.

Ignition Cable Service

Excessive resistance in the secondary circuit can cause driveability problems such as an engine misfire, higher burn voltage, and shorter burn time. Damaged cables are often the cause, and can be tested with an ohmmeter. Typical suppression-type spark plug wires should measure about 4,000 ohms per foot.

Preignition: A premature ignition of the air-fuel mixture before the spark plug fires. It is caused by excessive heat or pressure in the combustion chamber.

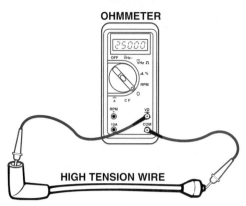

Fig. 2-15. Checking spark plug wire resistance with an ohmmeter.

Excessive resistance can result from:

- Loose or corroded connections at the distributor cap terminal or spark plug
- Damage to the cable conductor from heat, vibration, or mishandling

Test cable resistance as follows:

1. Remove the distributor cap from the housing and disconnect the wire to be tested at the spark plug, or coil, end.
2. Disconnect the other end of the cable to be tested from the distributor cap.
3. Set the ohmmeter on a high scale, then connect a one meter lead to each end of the spark plug cable, figure 2-15. If meter readings are out of specification, replace the cable.

Cable Replacement

Most ignition systems use 7-mm cables. However, others use larger 8-mm cables. The larger cables provide additional **dielectric resistance** in a system where secondary voltages can exceed 40 kV. Use the proper size cables; they are not interchangeable.

Ignition cables generally push-fit into the distributor cap or DIS coil. Twist and pull up on the boot to remove the cable from the cap. Check the cap tower or DIS terminal for dirt, corrosion, or damage. Clean light deposits in the tower with a wire brush. Replace a cap or coil if there is heavy accumulation. Fit the new cable to the cap so the terminal seats firmly on the tower. Fit the rubber boot seal over the tower, or DIS terminal, and squeeze it to remove any trapped air.

Some distributor caps use a male ignition cable terminal that looks much like a spark plug. The cable end snaps onto the terminal instead of fitting down inside the cap tower.

When replacing cables, disconnect only one cable at a time from a spark plug and the distributor cap or DIS coil terminal. For distributors, begin with the cable for cylinder number one and work in firing order sequence. Route each cable in the same location as the one removed and secure it into the cable brackets. To prevent the possibility of crossfiring, do not route cables in firing order sequence next to each other. Make sure that the cables cannot contact the exhaust manifold or interfere with other electrical wiring.

Ignition Coils

Primary wiring and connectors are a potential source of high-resistance, as well as open or grounded circuits. Problems in this area can be found with simple voltmeter and ohmmeter tests. Check for correct supply voltage first. If voltage is present, check for a voltage drop using a voltmeter. When voltage drop indicates high or low resistance, verify with an ohmmeter. Many problems can easily be solved by cleaning connectors or repairing wiring.

Available Voltage

Check available voltage at the coil with a voltmeter by connecting the positive voltmeter lead to the positive (battery) coil terminal and the negative voltmeter lead to ground. Turn the ignition switch on and note the voltmeter reading. On some systems, full battery voltage should be available at the coil. On other systems, a ballast **resistor** provides a low-voltage signal to the coil. Check the Service Manual for the correct specifications.

If voltmeter readings are not within specifications, check the primary circuit. Repair or replace any loose or damaged connections and repeat the test. If available voltage readings are still out of range, check the circuit for a voltage drop.

Voltage Drop

Voltage drop is the amount of voltage that an electrical device normally consumes to perform its task. A small amount of voltage will always be lost due to normal circuit resistance. However, excessive voltage drop can be the result of a high-resistance connection or failed component.

To check voltage drop, the circuit must be powered up and under load. The circuit must also have the maximum amount of current under normal conditions for which the circuit was designed. The amount of voltage drop that is considered acceptable will vary by circuit. Low-current circuits that draw milliamps will be affected by very small voltage drops, while the same amount of voltage drop will have a negligible effect on a high-current circuit.

To measure voltage drop along a circuit, connect the negative voltmeter lead to ground and use the positive meter lead to probe at various points in the circuit. Compute voltage drop by checking available voltage on both sides of a load, then subtracting the voltage reading of the ground side from the reading on the positive side of the load. Take direct voltage drop readings by connecting the positive meter lead to the power side of a load and connecting the negative meter lead to the ground side of the component.

Manufacturers provide voltage drop specifications for various ignition components. Measure the voltage drop across the ignition module ground as follows:

1. Connect the voltmeter positive lead to the negative (distributor) coil terminal; connect the voltmeter negative lead to ground.
2. Switch the ignition on and observe the voltmeter.

Typically, a reading less than 0.5 volt indicates the module ground is in good condition.

High voltage drop can be caused by loose connections, poor ground, or excessive wear. Check and repair wiring, clean the ground circuit, and repeat the test.

Multiple Ignition Coil Designs

The coil packs contain multiple coils, each supplying secondary voltage to two cylinders, figure 2-16. The coils operate on the

A8

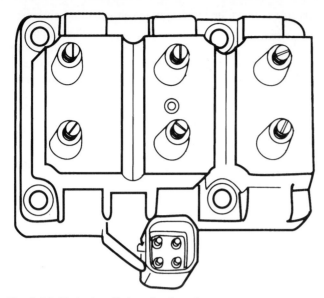

Fig. 2-16. Typical multiple coil coil-pack.

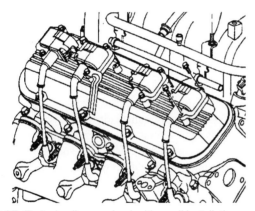

Fig. 2-17. Typical coil-near-plug ignition coil installation.

same basic principal as their predecessors but are configured differently. Generally each coil supplies secondary voltage for a pair of cylinders each time they reach TDC. One cylinder of the pair is on the power stroke while the other is on the exhaust stroke. The spark occurring on the exhaust cylinder is of little value and therefore the system is often called a waste spark system.

Another more recent design provides an individual coil for each cylinder, figure 2-17. This coil is mounted on or near the spark plug it serves. These designs are known as coil-on-plug or coil-near-plug systems.

There are several advantages of multiple ignition coil systems. With coils serving only one or two spark plugs there is much more dwell time available, ensuring a hotter spark than a single coil can provide. The location of the coils reduces or eliminates the need for spark plug wires and the maintenance they require. Finally, the smaller coil operates at a lower temperature, which adds to its expected life. Regardless of the coil design, the diagnostic processes are very similar.

Ignition Coil Diagnosis

The resistance and current draw of the ignition coil can be tested with an ohmmeter or an **ammeter**, respectively. Test a coil at its normal operating temperature.

Resistance will change with temperature. Before testing, make these preliminary checks:

1. Be sure the coil is securely mounted and all electrical connections are clean and tight.
2. Check for a cracked or burned coil tower(s).
3. Check for a dented, cracked, or distorted housing.

Winding Resistance Test

Before attempting to measure the resistance of the primary and secondary windings, disconnect the battery ground cable, primary wiring, and high-tension lead. Use an ohmmeter to measure resistance as follows, figure 2-18:

1. Connect one ohmmeter lead to the positive (battery) primary terminal of the coil.
2. Connect the other ohmmeter lead to the negative (distributor) primary terminal of the coil.

The ohmmeter will display primary winding resistance. If the reading is not within specifications, replace the coil. If primary winding resistance is within range, check the secondary resistance:

1. Connect one ohmmeter lead to a coil tower secondary terminal.
2. For coils serving one cylinder only, touch the second ohmmeter lead to one of the coil primary terminals and note the reading. For coil packs serving a pair of cylinders, touch the other lead to the mating cylinders coil tower secondary terminal.

Current Draw Test

Several manufacturers provide current draw specifications for their ignition coils. Current draw is measured with an ammeter. Test procedures vary; follow the Service Manual recommendations. Some current draw tests are performed on a running engine, others while cranking the engine with the starter, or with the engine stopped, ignition on, and primary circuit complete.

To test current draw, disconnect the positive (battery) primary wire from the coil and connect it to the positive lead of the ammeter. Connect the negative lead of the ammeter to the positive (battery) coil terminal, figure 2-19. When using an inductive ammeter, fit the inductive pickup over the primary wire to the coil positive terminal, leaving the wire connected.

Observe the ammeter reading and compare it to specifications. If there is no reading, the primary circuit is open and the engine will not run. Higher-than-specified current draw can be caused by:

- A short circuit in the coil
- Use of an incorrect coil

Lower-than-specified current draw results from:

- A discharged battery
- Excessive resistance in the coil primary winding

Ammeter: An ammeter is an instrument used for measuring the current flow in an electrical or electronic circuit. Some ammeters are intended for use in direct current (DC) circuits; others are designed for alternating current (AC) circuits.

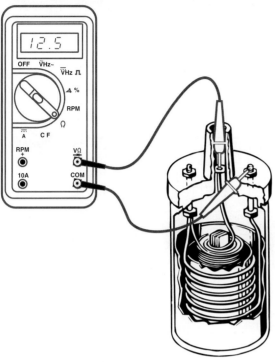

Fig. 2-18. Checking secondary coil winding resistance with an ohmmeter.

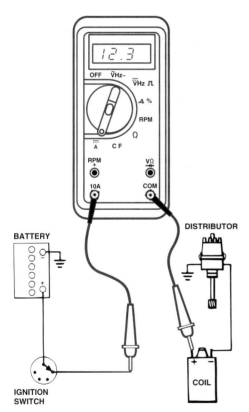

Fig. 2-19. Checking ignition coil current draw with an ammeter.

- Loose or corroded primary connections
- High-resistance in the primary wiring to the coil

Position Sensors

In order to provide the PCM with the correct data regarding engine RPM and cylinder position, one or more sensors are installed to provide input information. The sensor(s) identifies the **top dead center** (**TDC**) point for cylinder number one. Once this position is established the PCM then calculates the position of the remaining cylinders and adjusts ignition timing and control accordingly.

Ignition System Signals

Most electronic ignition systems use an amperage-sensing ignition circuit to limit current through the primary circuit.

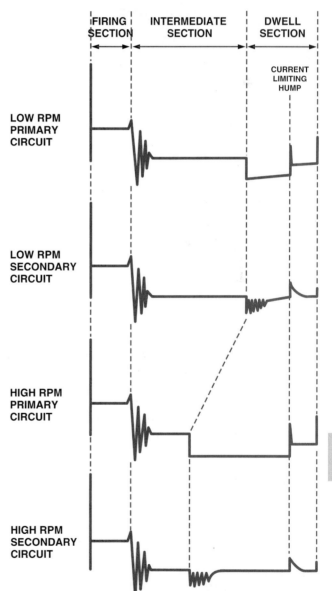

Fig. 2-20. Current limiting produces a hump on an oscilloscope trace at the end of the dwell period.

A8

Top Dead Center (TDC): The point in engine rotation when cylinder number one is at the top of its travel and the valves are closed.

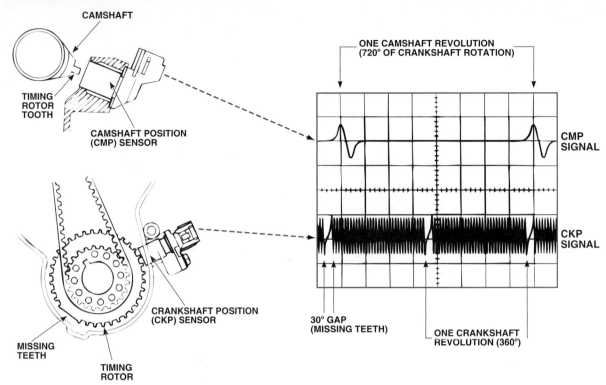

Fig. 2-21. Some systems use both a crankshaft position (CKP) sensor and camshaft position (CMP) sensor to control ignition coil firing.

This current limiting function can be seen on an oscilloscope as a hump during the dwell period just before the module-open signal, figure 2-20. Dwell is short at low engine speed, and increases as RPM increases.

The primary circuit does not energize until the module receives a verifiable engine speed signal from the crankshaft position (CKP) sensor. The CKP sensor provides the ignition module or powertrain control module (PCM) information on crankshaft speed and location. Some systems use an additional camshaft position (CMP) sensor, figure 2-21. A CMP sensor is used to provide the synchronization signal on distributorless ignition and sequential fuel injection systems, and for misfire detection on OBD-II vehicles. There are three basic designs for automotive position or speed sensors:

- Magnetic pickup
- **Hall-effect sensor**
- Optical sensor

The most accurate way to diagnose speed sensor problems is to monitor the signal on an oscilloscope. A magnetic pickup is an analog device that produces a sine wave pattern, while Hall-effect sensors and optical sensors are digital and produce a digital, or square, waveform. For all types, the ignition module or PCM uses the **frequency** of the signal to determine the speed of the sensed component.

Magnetic Pickup Sensor
Whether called a magnetic pickup coil, variable reluctance sensor, or permanent magnet generator, this type of sensor generates voltage as an **analog signal**. These sensors are

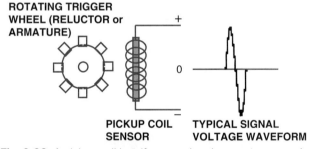

Fig. 2-22. A pickup coil is self-powered and generates an analog AC signal as the magnetic field expands and collapses.

self-contained and do not require an applied voltage to produce a signal. Since these sensors produce their own signal, it is possible to get a waveform with correct amplitude and frequency, even though there are problems on the ground circuits.

The pickup coil is wound around a permanent magnet, whose field expands and collapses as the teeth of a rotating notched or slotted wheel known as the reluctor or trigger wheel pass by it, figure 2-22. The magnetic field generates an alternating current (AC) voltage signal and, as the speed of the engine increases, so do the frequency and amplitude of the signal. The PCM uses the frequency of the signal to determine rotational speed.

The magnetic sensor may be mounted in several locations:

- In the distributor
- Part of the harmonic balancer
- Near the flywheel at the rear of the engine
- In the side of the cylinder block

Depending on the system, the reluctor design varies to meet the design requirements. Refer to the appropriate Service Manual for the exact description of the system used.

Testing a Magnetic Sensor

Regardless of system design, the resistance of a pickup coil can be checked with an ohmmeter. All pickup coils operate at a specific resistance; however, specifications and test points will vary between manufacturers and models.

In general, measurements are taken by connecting the ohmmeter leads to opposite sides of the coil. If the reading is not within specifications, replace the coil. To check for a grounded coil, connect one ohmmeter lead to ground and touch the other ohmmeter lead alternately to each of the pickup coil connectors. The ohmmeter should show **infinite resistance** at all test points. If not, replace the pickup.

The pickup coil can also be tested using an oscilloscope or scope. The coil has a two-wire circuit, a positive lead and a negative lead, connecting the sensor to the PCM. For best results, connect both scope probes directly to the sensor leads as close to the sensor as possible. A good trace generally sweeps up the positive slope and drops on the negative slope. The shape of the trace peak varies for different sensor designs, but most signals must reach a minimum amplitude before the PCM recognizes them. Look for uniformity in the trace cycles.

Air Gap Adjustment

The magnetic sensor is designed to be positioned close to but not touching the reluctor. Most late-model CKP sensors are designed to provide the correct **air gap** between the components and do not require adjustment. Refer to the appropriate Service Manual for the correct installation procedures.

Hall-Effect Sensors

Hall-effect sensors are found in many late-model ignition system, replacing the magnetic pickup type sensor. The mounting and function of the Hall-effect sensor are similar, but the operation and testing are different. A Hall-effect sensor uses a microchip to switch a transistor on and off and generate a digital signal that is transmitted to the PCM. As a slotted or trigger wheel connected to the crankshaft or distributor shaft, figure 2-23, passes between the Hall element and a permanent magnet, the magnetic field expands and collapses to produce an analog signal. The Hall element contains a logic gate that converts the signal into a digital signal, which triggers transistor switching. The transistor transmits a digital square waveform at a variable frequency to the PCM.

Hall-effect operation requires a three-wire circuit power input, signal output, and ground. The Hall element, figure 2-24, receives an input voltage from either the ignition switch or the PCM to power it. As the magnetic field is distorted by the passing of the slotted wheel, the Hall element switches the base of a transistor on and off. This on-off signal is inverted by a transistor, which in turn opens and closes the ground-side of the primary ignition coil circuit.

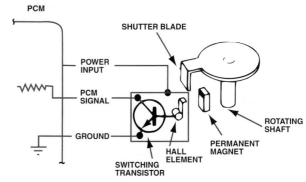

Fig. 2-23. Distributor-mounted Hall-effect sensor.

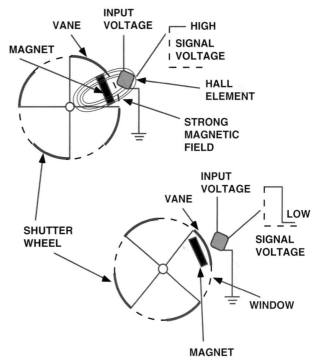

Fig. 2-24. The signal of a distributor-mounted Hall element switches high as the shutter wheel changes the magnetic field from strong to weak.

Hall-effect switches produce a square waveform, figure 2-25, whose frequency varies in proportion to the rotational speed of the crankshaft. A Hall-effect sensor does not generate its own voltage, and power must be provided for the device to work.

When using a scope for diagnosis remember the Hall-effect sensor creates a waveform as the transistor switches on and off. To get a good scope trace, attach the positive scope probe to the transistor output signal and connect the negative probe to the sensor ground. For optimum results, connect both probe leads as close as possible to the sensor.

When a slot in the trigger wheel is aligned with the sensor the signal is low because the magnetic filed is not engulfing the Hall element.

A8

Air Gap: The precise space between a pickup coil and trigger wheel. The correct air gap is critical to proper operation of the sensor.

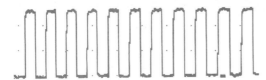

Fig. 2-25. Square-wave pattern from a Hall-effect sensor.

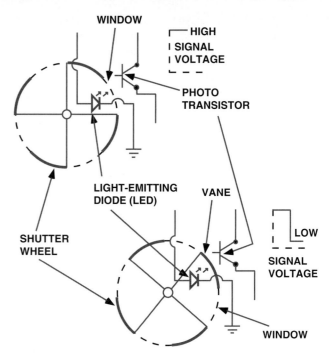

Fig. 2-26. An optical sensor uses an LED and a light-sensitive transistor to transmit a digital square waveform to the PCM at a variable frequency.

When a slot in the trigger wheel is not aligned with the element, the magnetic field saturates the Hall element, causing it to switch on and conduct current. Each time a slot passes the sensor, the signal generated by the Hall element changes state. Depending upon the application, this signal may be amplified or inverted before it is transmitted to the PCM. Therefore, there is no established rule as to whether the signal is high or low with respect to the strength of the magnetic field.

When examining a scope trace, look for sharp, clean state change transitions and a signal that pulls to ground. Amplitude should be even for all waveforms, the pattern should be consistent, and peaks should be at the specified voltage level. The shape and position of the slots on the shutter wheel determine the shape and duty cycle of the waveform. Some Hall-effect sensor patterns have a slight rounding at the top corners of the trace that can generally be overlooked. Remember, the PCM looks for switching at the midpoint of the voltage range, not at the top or bottom. However, rounding at the bottom corners of the trace should sound an alarm. This is often caused by high-resistance on the ground circuit, often from a poor connection, making it difficult for the signal to completely ground. Also, check for the correct voltage on the power circuit to the Hall element. A problem here can cause problems on the signal circuit.

Optical Sensor

An optical sensor uses a light-emitting diode (LED), a shutter wheel, and a phototransistor to produce a digital signal that changes frequency in proportion to rotational speed, figure 2-26. Like a Hall-effect sensor, an optical sensor requires an external power source and uses a three-wire circuit. One wire carries power to operate the LED, one is the signal generated by the transistor, and the third provides a common ground path.

Signal voltage, which is usually 5 volts, switches on and off as the rotating shutter passes between the phototransistor and LED to toggle the ground circuit. When the shutter allows light to shine on the phototransistor, the base of the transistor switches, causing the signal voltage to change state. When the reflector plate blocks the light to the phototransistor, the base of the transistor switches again, and signal voltage changes as well.

Optical sensors are more expensive to manufacture and more delicate than a magnetic pickup or Hall-effect sensor. Therefore, they are the least common of the three types. Typically, optical sensors are used as vehicle speed sensors and engine speed sensors because their high-speed data rate is more accurate than other sensor designs for high RPM applications. When viewed on an oscilloscope, the waveforms will be similar to those produced by a Hall-effect sensor.

Control System Power Flow

In discussing power flow through the electronic control system we will use the composite vehicle as an example. Although this is a basic and simplified system, the principles that apply here also apply to most automotive control systems. The only major differences between most systems are the number of controlled circuits, the design characteristics of individual components, and the arrangement of PCM terminal connections, or pins, figures 2-27 and 2-28.

Internal PCM Functions

Battery, or system, voltage is supplied to the PCM at two points, pins 12 and 13. To understand the need for two power sources, you must be familiar with the basic functions of a computer system, figure 2-29.

All automotive computers perform four functions:

1. **Input**—Information on engine operating conditions provided to the computer, or PCM, as voltage signals from system sensors.
2. **Processing**—The internal function that converts input voltage signals into combinations of **binary** numbers (1's and 0's). The PCM then compares the binary information to instructions and other programmed data to make logical decisions and send output commands to control other devices in the system.
3. **Storage**—All computers have some kind of information storage capacity. This electronic memory stores the computer operating instructions, or program. In addition, some computer systems store certain input signals for later reference. These computers "remember" previous operating conditions and adapt output commands to the "learned" characteristics of vehicle operation. This

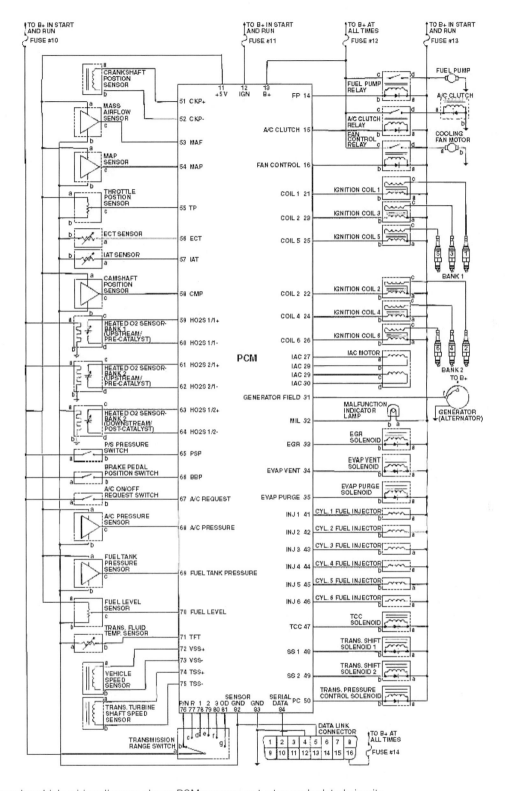

Fig. 2-27. The sample vehicle wiring diagram shows PCM sensors, actuator, and related circuits.

feature, known as adaptive strategy, allows the system to compensate for wear, climatic conditions, driving style, and other variables.

4. **Output**—After receiving an input signal, processing it, and comparing it to information stored in memory, the computer transmits a command to output devices that control engine operation. Output devices, such as sole-

noids and relays, are actuators that convert electrical signals to mechanical motion to obtain a predetermined response and regulate engine operation. The computer may also send output information to display devices such as electronic instrument panels.

On the composite vehicle, pin 13 provides the power supply for the PCM storage circuits. Internal memory circuits can be

A8

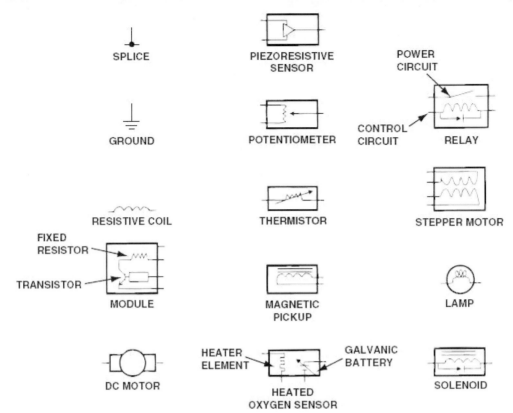

Fig. 2-28. Sample vehicle electrical symbols.

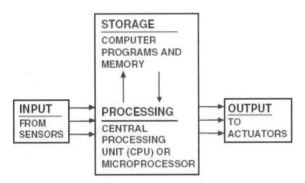

Fig. 2-29. All computers perform 4 basic functions.

further broken down into two categories: volatile and non-volatile. Volatile memory is temporary and requires a constant power supply to retain stored information; information stored here is lost if the battery is disconnected. Information that changes during vehicle operation, such as adaptive strategies and diagnostic trouble codes, are stored in volatile memory. Information in the non-volatile memory is permanent and is not dependent on battery power. Basic operating program information and look-up tables, which are not needed unless the engine is running, are stored in the non-volatile memory, or PROM.

Switching the ignition key to the start or run position directs an additional source of system voltage to pin 12 of the PCM. This provides the necessary power to operate the processing circuits. Power applied here is subsequently directed to the input sensors through a voltage regulator as a low-voltage

reference signal, and as an output voltage signal to the actuators. With the exception of ignition and fuel pump circuits, most input sensors operate on low voltages that seldom exceed 5 volts. However, the internal processor of the PCM requires system voltage. Most control systems will suspend operations and revert to a fail-safe, or limp-home, strategy should supply voltage fall below about 10 volts.

Input Signal Processing

To process information from an input sensor, the PCM applies a low voltage reference signal, usually about 5 volts, to the sensor. Most two-wire sensors have the power source and a fixed resistor inside the PCM. The PCM reads the voltage after the fixed resistor. Current flows through the fixed resistor, then through the variable resistor in the sensor, and back to ground. As the resistance in the sensor changes, the voltage in the PCM changes. As the sensor resistance decreases, the voltage drop decreases, and the read voltage decreases.

A three-wire sensor is usually a **potentiometer**. A 5-volt source is applied to one end of a resistor, and the other end is grounded. The voltage drop is proportional to the position of a sweep arm that sends the signal back to the PCM.

Because the PCM operates on low voltage signals, even small changes in resistance anywhere along a circuit can affect system performance. Many driveability complaints and control system malfunctions are a direct result of excessive resistance on the monitored circuits. Poor (loose, dirty, or corroded) connections and damaged (frayed, pinched, cracked, or broken) wiring and insulation can all be a source of high circuit resistance. The most effective way of locating a source of high resistance on a computer-controlled circuit is voltage drop testing.

Output Signal Processing

The PCM switches output circuits open and closed to command system actuators to turn off and on. Power to most actuators is provided through the ignition switch circuit, and the PCM regulates voltage on the ground side. Actuators respond to PCM commands and, in turn, control other circuits or convert electrical energy into mechanical work. PCM circuits that command actuators are often referred to as driver circuits. Typical output devices include:

- Solenoids
- Relays
- **Stepper motors**

Almost all actuators in engine control systems contain some kind of induction coil.

Every output device controlled by the PCM has a minimum resistance specification, and this is an important consideration when servicing the output side of the system. Internal resistance in an actuator limits the amount of current that is allowed to flow through the output control circuit. If an actuator is shorted, current in excess of the safe maximum limit can flow to the PCM and cause severe damage. Typically, a controlled output will allow no more than 0.75 ampere (750 milliamperes) to flow through the circuit. Shorted actuators are a common cause of PCM failure. If not replaced, a defective actuator can quickly destroy a new PCM. Always check output circuits for shorts and low resistance when replacing a failed PCM.

A8

CHAPTER QUESTIONS

1. Low primary circuit voltage can be caused by all of the following **EXCEPT**:
   a. Excessive starter motor current draw
   b. Incorrect distributor rotor air gap
   c. Low charging voltage
   d. Excessive battery ground cable voltage drop

2. The engine must be running to check for:
   a. Available voltage at the coil
   b. Secondary circuit resistance
   c. Voltage drop across the ignition module ground
   d. Correct rotor air gap

3. A nonmagnetic feeler gauge must be used when checking:
   a. Spark plug gap
   b. Pickup coil air gap
   c. Hall-effect switch operation
   d. Initial timing

4. Spark plug overheating, which is indicated by a clean, white insulator tip and excessive electrode wear, can be caused by all of the following **EXCEPT**:
   a. Incorrect spark plug tightening torque
   b. Over-advanced timing
   c. Rich air-fuel mixture
   d. Lean air-fuel mixture

5. Which of the following spark plug conditions is caused by burning of gasoline additives during normal combustion?
   a. Splash fouling
   b. Insulator glazing
   c. Ash fouling
   d. Excessive electrode wear

6. High secondary circuit resistance can be caused by all of the following **EXCEPT**:
   a. An open circuit between the coil and distributor
   b. Spark plug gap bridging
   c. Excessive spark plug gap
   d. Carbon tracking in the distributor

7. When using an ohmmeter to check an ignition coil, there should be infinite resistance between:
   a. The secondary terminal and negative primary terminal
   b. The secondary terminal and positive primary terminal
   c. The two primary terminals
   d. The primary terminals and the coil case

8. An ammeter is used to check ignition coil:
   a. Polarity
   b. Voltage drop
   c. Current draw
   d. Circuit resistance

CHAPTER OBJECTIVES

- The technician will complete the ASE task list on Fuel, Air Induction, and Exhaust Systems Diagnosis and Repair.
- The technician will be able to answer 9 questions dealing with the Fuel, Air Induction, and Exhaust Systems Diagnosis and Repair section of the A8 ASE Test.

To run efficiently, an engine must be supplied with a constant flow of clean pressurized fuel and filtered air in precisely metered amounts. In addition, the exhaust system must effectively carry combustion gases out of the engine, without excessive **backpressure**. Electronically controlled engines monitor operating conditions through a variety of sensors and adjust the air-fuel mixture for optimum performance.

If the balance of the air-fuel mixture is upset, driveability suffers. Problems of hard starting, no starting, hesitation, surging, power loss, stalling, misfiring, incorrect idle speed, poor idle quality, poor fuel mileage, and dieseling can be caused by a fuel or air induction deficiency. However, mechanical, electrical, electronic, or ignition problems may have similar symptoms. Therefore, it is important to isolate the source of the problem before attempting repairs. To isolate the problem to a specific system, perform the diagnostic tests detailed in the previous chapters of this book.

FUEL SYSTEM SERVICE

When fuel system service is required, observe these safety precautions:

- Keep open flames and sparks away from the vehicle
- Do not smoke near any part of the fuel system
- Work in a well-ventilated area
- Cap or plug all disconnected fuel lines
- Disconnect the battery ground cable before removing or replacing fuel system parts to preven accidental arcing

Inspection

Because of its many parts and connecting lines, the fuel system may develop leaks at several points. Keep in mind any leak, or restriction, will affect operating pressure and can cause a driveability problem. Begin with a thorough inspection of the entire fuel system. To check for damage and safety defects:

1. Inspect the fuel tank for:

   - Physical damage and leakage at fittings, connections, and seams
   - Plugged vents and damaged vent tubes and connecting lines
   - Filler tube and filler tube cap condition and proper venting
   - Leakage at the filler tube, vent line connections, and fuel gauge sending unit
   - Secure mounting; tighten tank hold-down straps if necessary
   - Signs of internal contamination

2. Inspect fuel lines and hoses for:

   - Loose connections and signs of seepage
   - Pinched or crushed lines
   - Weathered, damaged, or deteriorated hoses

3. Inspect fuel filters for:

   - Loose connections and signs of leakage
   - Signs of chafing or other exterior damage
   - Blockage and contamination

4. Check the fuel pump for:

   - Leakage
   - Secure mounting
   - Loose hoses, fittings, and connections

5. Check the intake manifold for:

   - Fuel and air leaks
   - Proper routing of the vacuum lines
   - Deterioration of vacuum lines
   - Loose carburetor, throttle body, or injector mounting

6. Verify that the fuel in the vehicle tank is:

   - Fresh, not stale or old
   - Free from water or other contaminants

7. Refer to the Service or Diagnostic Manual for the correct troubleshooting procedure to follow, figure 3-1.

Fuel Line Replacement

Fuel lines and vapor return lines may be formed of rigid steel tubing, flexible nylon tubing, or neoprene hose. Most lines fasten to the frame of the car with insulated clamps and screws. Replace any damaged insulators and clamps. Rigid lines can be replaced either as preformed units, or be cut and formed to fit the vehicle from bulk stock. Use steel tubing only. Never use copper tubing in place of steel tubing. Hoses must be marked for fuel system use or they rapidly deteriorate when used for

HARD START COLD ENGINE

SECONDARY IGNITION SYSTEM
FUEL PRESSURE
THROTTLE POSITION SENSOR
MAP SENSOR
MINIMUM IDLE AIR FLOW
IDLE AIR CONTROL MOTOR
ENGINE MECHANICAL SYSTEMS
IAT SENSOR

HARD START HOT ENGINE

SECONDARY IGNITION SYSTEM
ENGINE VACUUM
FUEL PRESSURE
THROTTLE POSITION SENSOR
MAP SENSOR
MINIMUM IDLE AIR FLOW
IDLE AIR CONTROL MOTOR
ENGINE MECHANICAL SYSTEMS
EVAP EMISSION SYSTEM
EGR SYSTEM
ECT SENSOR

START AND STALL/ FLOODING

SECONDARY IGNITION SYSTEM
ECM POWER AND GND CKT
FUEL PRESSURE
ECT SENSOR
THROTTLE POSITION SENSOR
MAP SENSOR
THE MINIMUM IDLE AIR FLOW
IDLE AIR CONTROL MOTOR
FUEL INJECTOR(S)

CUTS OUT/MISSES

SECONDARY IGNITION SYSTEM
ECM POWER AND GND CKT
FUEL PRESSURE
IDLE AIR CONTROL MOTOR
EGR SYSTEM
FUEL INJECTOR(S)

LACK OF POWER/SLUGGISH

SECONDARY IGNITION SYSTEM
ECM POWER AND GND CKT
FUEL PRESSURE
ECT SENSOR
THROTTLE POSITION SENSOR
MAP SENSOR
MINIMUM IDLE AIR FLOW
OXYGEN SENSOR SWITCHING
IDLE AIR CONTROL MOTOR
EGR SYSTEM

HESITATION/SAG/STUMBLE

SECONDARY IGNITION SYSTEM
ECM POWER AND GND CKT
ENGINE VACUUM
FUEL PRESSURE
ECT SENSOR
THROTTLE POSITION SENSOR
MAP SENSOR
OXYGEN SENSOR SWITCHING
O2S HEATER
IDLE AIR CONTROL MOTOR
ENGINE MECHANICAL SYSTEMS
EVAP EMISSION SYSTEM
EGR SYSTEM
IAT SENSOR

SURGE/RUNS ROUGH
UNSTABLE/ERRATIC IDLE

SECONDARY IGNITION
ECM POWER AND GND CKT
ENGINE VACUUM
FUEL PRESSURE
COOLANT SENSOR
THROTTLE POSITION SENSOR
MAP SENSOR
MINIMUM IDLE AIR FLOW
OXYGEN SENSOR SWITCHING
O2S HEATER
IDLE AIR CONTROL MOTOR
ENGINE MECHANICAL SYSTEMS
EVAP EMISSION SYSTEM
EGR SYSTEM
IAT SENSOR

POOR FUEL ECONOMY

SECONDARY IGNITION SYSTEM
ECM POWER AND GND CKT
ENGING VACUUM
FUEL PRESSURE
ECT SENSOR
THROTTLE POSITION SENSOR
MAP SENSOR
OXYGEN SENSOR SWITCHING
O2S HEATER
ENGINE MECHANICAL SYSTEMS
EVAP EMISSION SYSTEM
EGR SYSTEM
IAT SENSOR

EMISSION SYSTEM CONCERNS

SECONDARY IGNITION
ENGINE VACUUM
FUEL PRESSURE
THROTTLE POSITION SENSOR
MAP SENSOR
OXYGEN SENSOR(S)
CATALYTIC CONVERTER(S)
ENGINE MECHANICAL SYSTEMS
EVAP EMISSION SYSTEM
EGR SYSTEM
ECT SENSOR
INCORRECT IGNITION TIMING
FUEL INJECTOR(S)

Fig. 3-1. Typical diagnostic table.

gasoline. Do not substitute rubber hoses on vehicles that use nylon fuel tubing. An assortment of fittings are used to join fuel lines:

- Flare type
- Compression type
- Push-connect type
- Spring-lock type, figure 3-2

Some systems use high-pressure fittings with O-ring seals instead of traditional flare connectors. Inspect the O-ring for damage whenever the fitting is disconnected and replace the O-ring if necessary.

Replacement O-rings must be specifically designed for fuel system use. Tighten fittings to the specified torque value to prevent O-ring damage.

Fuel Filter Replacement

The fuel filter is the only item of the system that must be changed at regular service intervals. Replacement recommendations vary by manufacturer, engine, and type of filter used. Always begin by removing the fuel filler cap to relieve any pressure in the tank. After replacing a filter, start and run the engine to check for leaks. There are two common fuel filter designs:

- Inline
- Carburetor or throttle body inlet

Some vehicles use multiple fuel filters. They can be located in the fuel pump, near the fuel tank, and near the carburetor. The filter closest to the fuel tank is the first to become restricted, and to require replacement.

FLARE NUT FITTING

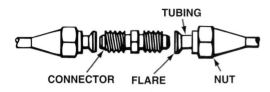

COMPRESSION FITTING

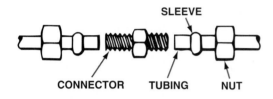

SPRING-LOCK FITTING

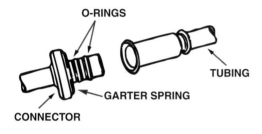

PUSH-LOCK FITTING

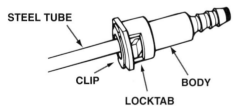

Fig. 3-2. Typical fuel line connections.

Replacing Inline Filters

Disposable inline fuel filters are common and may be used on both carbureted and fuel-injected engines. The filter may be located in the engine compartment or underneath the vehicle near the pump. Inline filters on a low-pressure fuel system generally have a nipple at each end that attaches to a length of hose secured by a clamp. The fuel filter attaches with threaded connections on some high-pressure fuel injection applications; spring-lock connectors are used on others. All filters are designed to allow flow in only one direction. Look for an arrow or other directional indicator on the filter housing, and be sure to properly orient it on installation.

When replacing the filter on a low-pressure system, it is good practice to install new hose clamps along with the new filter to prevent leakage. Always replace spring-type clamps when replacing the fuel filter. To change a low-pressure in-line filter:

1. Place a drain pan under the filter to catch spills.
2. Remove the clamp at one end and pull the hose from the filter fitting.
3. Attach the hose to the new filter, making sure it faces the proper direction. Then, tighten the clamp securely.
4. Remove the clamp at the other end and pull the hose from the filter fitting. Attach this hose to the corresponding fitting on the new filter and tighten the clamp.
5. If the filter has a vapor bypass line, switch the line from the old filter to the new one, figure 3-3.

Replacing Fuel Injection System Filters

Fuel system pressure must be relieved to change the filter on a fuel injected engine. Several methods are used to relieve fuel pressure; follow the Service Manual guidelines. Position a drain pan under the work area to catch spilled fuel. To replace a high-pressure filter with threaded connections, figure 3-4:

1. Disconnect the fuel lines at both ends of the filter canister with an appropriate flare nut wrench. Use a back-up wrench to hold the filter while loosening the fuel line fitting.
2. Loosen the filter canister mounting bracket fasteners, if necessary, and remove the filter from the bracket.
3. Replace any O-rings, gaskets, or sealing washers with new ones.

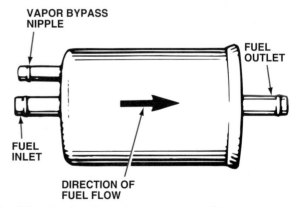

Fig. 3-3. Inline fuel filter with a vapor bypass fitting.

A8

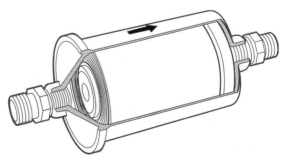

Fig. 3-4. Cutaway of a typical high-pressure fuel injection filter.

4. Start each fuel line by hand to prevent crossthreading of the nut. Check to be sure the filter outlet is facing toward the engine.

5. Install the filter canister in its mounting bracket. Tighten the bracket fasteners, then tighten each fuel line nut securely with a flare nut wrench.

Replacing Carburetor and Throttle Body Inlet Filters

There are two major types of inlet filters, the inlet nut filter and the inlet filter screen assembly, used on domestic carbureted engines.

Inlet Nut Filter or Screen

Remove the air cleaner assembly to access the filter. The fuel line may install to the carburetor with either a flare nut or banjo fitting. Disconnect the fitting, separate the fuel line from the inlet nut, plug or cap the line, and move it out of the way. Remove the fuel inlet nut and lift out the filter and spring, figure 3-5.

Install the spring and new filter element. Some filters contain a **check valve** to shut off fuel flow in case of a rollover accident. The open end of the filter must face toward the nut. Fit a new gasket on the inlet nut, or fit two new sealing washers on the banjo fitting. Install the unit, tighten it to specifications, and reattach the fuel line.

Throttle Body Inlet Screen

To replace the inlet screen on an engine with throttle body fuel injection (TBI), relieve fuel system pressure before disconnecting fittings. To disconnect the fuel line, hold the inlet nut with an open-end wrench and loosen the fuel line with a second open-end wrench.

Plug or cap the line and move it out of the way, then remove the fuel inlet nut. Reach inside the inlet bore with needle nose pliers, grasp the slotted end of the filter-screen assembly, and remove it with a twisting motion. Install a new filter screen assembly in the inlet bore. Thread the inlet nut in place, tighten to specifications, and reinstall the fuel line.

FUEL PUMP AND PRESSURE CONTROLS

To operate efficiently, the engine must be supplied with a constant flow of clean pressurized fuel. Incorrect fuel pressure and low fuel volume can cause starting and driveability problems. The most effective way to check fuel pump operation is by pressure testing the system.

Mechanical Fuel Pump Testing

Two tests, pressure and volume, are performed to check the mechanical fuel pump used on a carbureted engine. A weak pump may produce adequate pressure, but not deliver a sufficient volume of fuel. Both tests are required to get an accurate picture of pump performance.

Pressure Test

A vacuum-pressure gauge is used to test mechanical pump pressure. Prepare for testing by attaching a short length of fuel hose to the gauge, remove the air cleaner, and connect a tachometer to the engine. If the pump has a vapor return line, clamp it closed. Test as follows:

1. Disconnect the fuel inlet line at the carburetor and attach the gauge hose to the fuel line, figure 3-6. The gauge can also be installed using a tee fitting in the fuel inlet line, figure 3-7.

2. Start and run the engine at the test speed specified by the manufacturer. To get an accurate reading, hold the vacuum-pressure gauge at the same height as the carburetor. Compare the gauge reading to specifications. Replace the pump if the pressure reading is low.

3. Stop the engine and leave the gauge connected. The pressure reading should hold for several minutes. If not, the valves are not sealing properly. Replace the pump.

Volume Test

To check fuel pump volume, a length of fuel hose and a graduated container are required. Disconnect and remove the vacuum-pressure gauge, but leave the tachometer attached to the engine.

To check pump volume:

1. Disconnect the fuel outlet hose or line from the pump. Attach the length of fuel hose to the pump outlet.

2. Place the free end of the hose into the graduated container.

3. Start and run the engine at 500 RPM for 15 seconds. Read the fluid level on the scale and multiply by 4, for a 60-second reading.

Compare results to specifications. Most fuel pumps deliver about one quart, or liter, per minute at an engine speed of 500 RPM. Low fuel volume may be caused by either a restriction

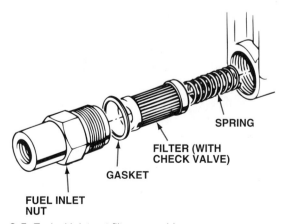

Fig. 3-5. Typical inlet nut filter assembly.

FUEL INLET NUT

GASKET

FILTER (WITH CHECK VALVE)

SPRING

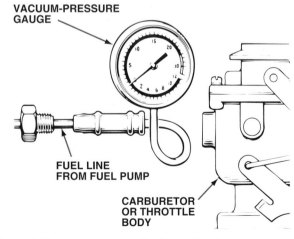

VACUUM-PRESSURE GAUGE

FUEL LINE FROM FUEL PUMP

CARBURETOR OR THROTTLE BODY

Fig. 3-6. Direct gauge connection for performing a mechanical fuel pump pressure test.

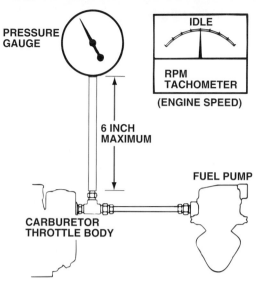

Fig. 3-7. Gauge installation with a tee fitting to test mechanical fuel pump pressure.

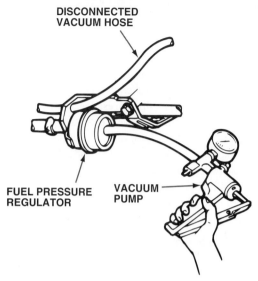

Fig. 3-8. Relieving fuel pressure by applying vacuum to the pressure regulator.

or a mechanical failure. Restrictions may be in the filter, lines, hoses, or tank pickup. Mechanical problems include a worn or broken fuel pump eccentric on the camshaft, pump pushrod, rocker arm, or diaphragm linkage.

Electric Fuel Pump Testing

Tests performed on a low-pressure electric fuel pump used on carbureted engines are similar to those for a mechanical pump. Perform pressure and volume tests and compare results to specifications. If testing the pump with the engine not running, bypass the pump control wiring and supply battery voltage directly to the pump. Also check electric pumps for:

- System voltage
- Good ground connections
- All other electrical connections

Fuel Injection Testing

Pressure testing is the most effective method of troubleshooting a fuel injection problem. Special pressure gauges are required for checking both low-pressure throttle body systems and high-pressure multiport systems. Most throttle body injection systems operate at about 10 to 15 psi (69 to 103 kPa) of pressure. Pressure in a port injection system can vary from about 35 psi (240 kPa) to over 60 psi (414 kPa). Accurate specifications and procedures for the system being tested, along with a test gauge that indicates the proper pressure range, are required.

To provide quick start-up, all injection systems retain pressure when the engine is off. Therefore, fuel system pressure must be relieved before opening fittings to connect the gauge.

Relieving Fuel Pressure

There are several methods of relieving fuel pressure. Follow the Service Manual recommendations for the system being tested. Typical procedures are:

- Apply vacuum to the fuel pressure regulator using a hand-vacuum pump, figure 3-8
- Use a special pressure gauge that has a relief valve, figure 3-9. Attach the gauge to a **Schrader valve** on the throttle body

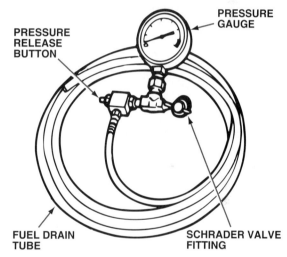

Fig. 3-9. Fuel pressure gauge with relief value for servicing Schrader valve–equipped fuel injection systems.

or fuel rail. Then press the button on the gauge to release pressure.
- Remove the fuel pump fuse and start the engine. Allow the engine to run until it dies

Fuel Injection Pressure Test

The fuel pumps used with fuel injection systems are capable of producing fuel pressure and delivery volume far greater than required by the engine. For this reason, the pressure and volume tests for these pumps measure values other than actual pump output. Typically, specifications are provided for checking the system pressure, which is the regulated pressure supplied to the injectors. System pressure will vary depending upon system design, as well as engine temperature and other operating conditions.

To test system pressure on throttle body injection systems, tee a pressure gauge at the throttle body fuel delivery line, or attach the gauge to the test-port Schrader valve. Some port injection systems also have a Schrader valve on the fuel distribution rail for attaching the gauge. If not, the gauge installs into a fuel line with a tee fitting, banjo fitting, or other adapter.

A8

Install the gauge, start the engine, and allow it to run at idle. Check the gauge reading and make sure the pressure is within specifications. Be sure to check pressure at all speeds, temperatures, and operating conditions specified by the manufacturer. Low system pressure readings may be caused by a faulty pump, a defective pressure relief valve, or a clogged fuel filter.

To check rest, or **residual pressure**, shut the engine off and note the gauge reading. Leave the gauges attached, wait the recommended time, usually 10 to 20 minutes, and take another gauge reading. For most systems, residual pressure should not drop below about 15 psi (103 kPa).

Low residual pressure can be caused by leaking fuel lines, injectors, or cold start valve, a faulty fuel pump check valve, or a defective pressure regulator.

Fuel Injection Volume Test

When a pump volume measure is specified, the sample is taken at the fuel return line rather than at the delivery pipe. Attach a length of hose to the return pipe and route the open end into a graduated container. Operate the fuel pump the recommended period of time and compare the quantity of fuel delivered to specifications. Most systems deliver a quart, or liter, of fuel in less than 30 seconds.

Fuel Pump Replacement

A mechanical fuel pump cannot be repaired and must be replaced if defective. Some electric pumps can be repaired, but most are replaced. Use the following procedures as general guidelines to replace a fuel pump.

Mechanical Fuel Pump

Prepare for pump removal by disconnecting the battery ground cable to prevent accidental arcing, and by loosening the fuel filler cap to relieve any pressure. Also remove or reposition any parts that prevent access to the pump. To replace the pump:

1. Disconnect and plug or cap all fuel and vapor lines from the pump.
2. Loosen the pump mounting bolts.
3. Rotate the engine by hand until the pump pushrod or rocker arm is resting on the low point of the camshaft eccentric.
4. Remove the mounting bolts and lift the pump from the engine.
5. If the pump is driven by a pushrod, remove and inspect it for wear. Use a straightedge to check straightness; replace as needed.
6. Clean all old gasket material from the engine.
7. Install the new pump on the engine and tighten the mounting bolts to the specified torque value.
8. Attach the fuel and vapor lines, reinstall parts removed to gain access, and connect the battery ground cable.
9. Install the filler cap. Start the engine and check the system for leaks.

Electric Fuel Pump

Electric fuel pumps are usually located either under the vehicle or inside the fuel tank. Some systems use two pumps, one of each type. The in-tank pump provides a constant stream of fuel to supply the main external pump. The main pump delivers a

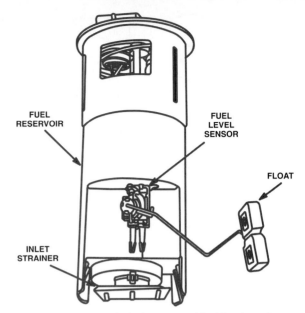

Fig. 3-10. In-tank electric fuel pump and fuel level sender assembly.

high-pressure fuel charge to the injectors. For all systems, be sure to relieve fuel injection system pressure and disconnect the negative battery cable before opening fuel lines. The following procedures are provided as general guidelines only. Refer to the Service Manual for specific instructions.

In-Tank Electric Pump

Most late-model vehicles have an in-tank electric fuel pump, figure 3-10. To access an in-tank fuel pump, the fuel tank may need to be removed from the vehicle. Typically, the fuel pump is incorporated with the gauge sending unit and is replaced by removing the sending unit retaining cam ring. Loosen the cam ring with a spanner wrench and lift out the assembly. Some pumps are a separate unit, but it will also be installed with a retaining cam ring.

Before removing the retaining cam ring, clean the area around it to remove any dirt that might fall into the tank. Remove the pump and level sender assembly from the fuel tank. In most cases, the entire pump, filter, and gauge sending unit is replaced with a new assembly. If the pump is a separate unit, be sure the hoses connecting the pump to mounting flange fittings are in good condition. Some manufacturers recommend that the rubber hoses and clamps be replaced whenever the pump unit is removed from the tank, and that the pickup strainer be replaced as well. Always install new gaskets, seals, or O-rings when replacing an in-tank pump.

External Electric Pump

Older fuel injected vehicles use an external electric fuel pump located underneath the vehicle on a frame rail near the fuel tank. Most vehicles have a protective cover over the pump housing that must be removed to access the pump fittings and fasteners. To remove the pump, disconnect the electrical wiring and fuel lines, then unbolt the pump and lift it from the frame rail. To install the pump, loosely fit the fuel lines, bolt the pump to the frame rail, then tighten the fuel lines and make the electrical connections.

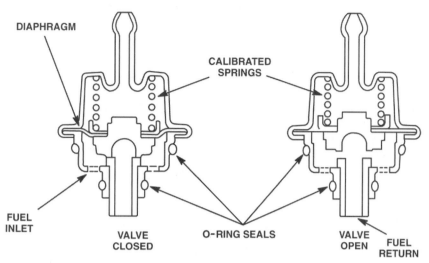

Fig. 3-11. Fuel pressure regulator operation.

Fuel Pressure Regulator Service

Fuel injection systems all use some form of pressure regulator to maintain uniform fuel pressure at the injectors. A pressure regulator that is out of specifications can cause hard starting and numerous performance problems. Make sure there are no fuel supply problems or line restrictions before replacing the pressure regulator.

Return-Type Fuel Systems

The fuel pressure regulator contains a pressure chamber separated by a diaphragm relief valve assembly with a calibrated spring in the vacuum chamber side, figure 3-11. Fuel pressure is regulated when pump pressure, acting on the bottom side of the diaphragm, overcomes the force of the spring action on the top side. The diaphragm relief valve moves, opening or closing an orifice in the fuel chamber to control the amount of fuel returned to the fuel tank.

Vacuum acting on the top side of the diaphragm along with spring pressure controls fuel pressure. A decrease in vacuum creates an increase in fuel pressure. An increase in vacuum creates a decrease in fuel pressure.

Example: Under heavy load conditions, the engine requires more fuel flow. Vacuum decreases under heavy load conditions because of throttle opening. A decrease in vacuum allows more pressure to the top side of the pressure relief valve, thus increasing fuel pressure.

Returnless Fuel Systems

Many late-model vehicles use a returnless fuel system. This system regulates fuel pressure utilizing a mechanical regulator without the vacuum assist. The regulator can be mounted anywhere in the fuel pressure line and many are located in the fuel tank connected to the in-tank pump housing, figure 3-12.

These systems rely on the PCM to control fuel flow from the injectors into the engine based on the input from engine sensors. See Chapter Five of this book for more information on computer controlled engine management systems.

FUEL INJECTION CONTROL SYSTEMS

Electronic fuel injection systems use sensors to monitor operating conditions and actuators to adjust the air-fuel ratio to

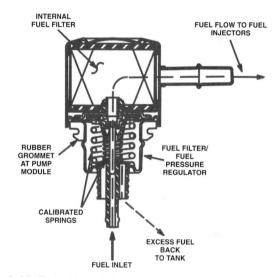

Fig. 3-12. Typical in-tank fuel pressure regulator.

provide cold enrichment, acceleration enrichment, deceleration fuel shut-off, and idle speed stabilization. Most of the sensors are resistors. Voltage signals from the sensors to the computer change according to resistance changes. Three factors can change resistance:

- Air or fuel pressure
- Air or coolant temperature
- Physical motion

Determine the operation and condition of a sensor or actuator by measuring resistance through the unit and the resistance between the sensor and ground with an ohmmeter. Do not overlook the circuit. Electronic problems are often caused by poor connections or damaged wiring. Always test the circuit first.

A **high-impedance** digital multimeter (DMM) or oscilloscope can be used to measure supply and ground voltage at a sensor, as well as voltage drop across the sensor. An oscilloscope measures voltage as a function of time and thus displays signal interference. The average voltage over the span of a few milliseconds is displayed as a trace on the screen.

A8

Component Testing

Before testing individual components on a fuel injected engine perform a diagnostic test using a scan tool. Check the PCM for any active or stored codes. If one or more diagnostic trouble codes are present refer to the appropriate Service Manual for the correct diagnostic procedure. Most Service Manuals include information on diagnosing fuel system problems when no codes are present.

Two types of sensors, **thermistor** and potentiometer, are commonly used on electronic fuel injection systems. Actuators are generally either a switch, a relay, or a solenoid. Both sensors and actuators can be tested using a DMM or oscilloscope.

A thermistor is a sensor that measures resistance changes in proportion to temperature, figure 3-13.

These sensors have a 2-wire connector: One wire provides the signal voltage and the other is the return ground. To check for an internal open or short, connect the ohmmeter across the 2-wire connector, figure 3-14.

Manufacturers provide specific resistance values for specific temperatures, as well as voltages, for testing sensors. Test temperature sensors by immersing them in water or engine coolant and heating or cooling as required to determine resistance at specific temperatures.

A potentiometer is a sensor that provides variable resistance across an operational range. It is most often used as a voltage regulating device. These sensors use a 3-wire connector to maintain a uniform temperature and current level across the resistor. One wire supplies the reference voltage, a second wire provides the signal voltage, and the third wire is the ground side of the sensor and carries the return current. The

sensor signal is proportional to the movement of the potentiometer and is unaffected by changes in temperature. Two ohmmeter connections are required to check the operation of a potentiometer, figure 3-15. To check, connect the ohmmeter:

- Across the signal voltage and return current pins
- Across the signal and reference voltage pins

Both tests should show continuity, and resistance should change with the movement of the sensor lever or rod. However, a more precise way to evaluate a potentiometer is to perform a sweep test. During a sweep test, signal voltage is monitored on a DMM as the device is moved through its full range of travel, figure 3-16. A sweep test can also be performed while monitoring signal voltage with an oscilloscope.

A sensor that measures motion, such as a throttle position (TP) sensor or exhaust gas recirculation (EGR) valve position sensor (EVP), can be hand-operated while checking

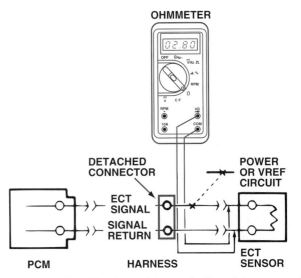

Fig. 3-14. Checking the resistance of a thermistor sensor with an ohmmeter.

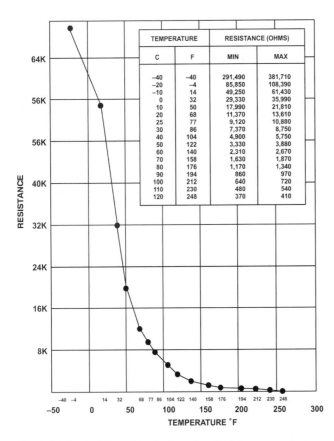

TEMPERATURE		RESISTANCE (OHMS)	
C	F	MIN	MAX
–40	–40	291,490	381,710
–20	–4	85,850	108,390
–10	14	49,250	61,430
0	32	29,330	35,990
10	50	17,990	21,810
20	68	11,370	13,610
25	77	9,120	10,880
30	86	7,370	8,750
40	104	4,900	5,750
50	122	3,330	3,880
60	140	2,310	2,670
70	158	1,630	1,870
80	176	1,170	1,340
90	194	860	970
100	212	640	720
110	230	480	540
120	248	370	410

Fig. 3-13. Typical thermistor temperature/resistance comparison.

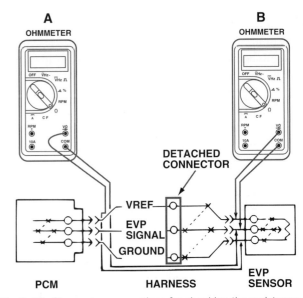

Fig. 3-15. Ohmmeter connections for checking the resistance of a potentiometer.

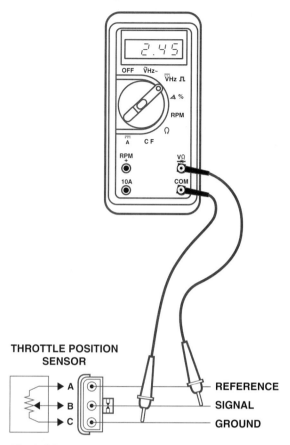

THROTTLE POSITION SENSOR

A ▶ REFERENCE
B ▶ SIGNAL
C ▶ GROUND

Fig. 3-16. Meter connections for performing a sweep test on a potentiometer sensor.

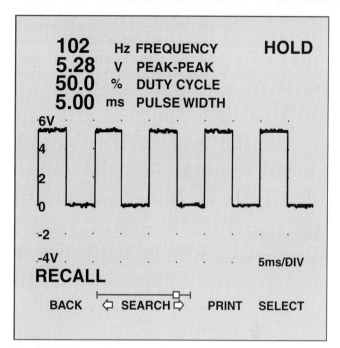

Fig. 3-17. The on (low-voltage) time and off (high-voltage) time of a solenoid operating at a 50 percent duty cycle are equal.

its resistance. A sensor that measures pressure, such as a manifold absolute pressure (MAP) sensor, can be operated with a hand vacuum or pressure pump while testing.

A solenoid used as an output actuator can be checked for circuit problems with a DMM or oscilloscope much the same as a sensor. On actuators that use a multiplug connector, refer to the Service Manual for test points and values.

Many automotive solenoids are controlled by a pulsing on and off signal. Since most solenoids are digital, they can be only on or off. However, by changing the ratio of on-time to total cycle time, the powertrain control module (PCM) can control how much work the solenoid performs. Work can be performed only when there is current available. On a solenoid that is switched to ground by the PCM, current is available when the signal voltage is low. More or less work can be performed by varying the amount of time the solenoid is switched on during each cycle. This practice of varying the on-time ratio is called **pulse width modulation (PWM)**. The pulse width is the amount of time a solenoid is energized, or on, during one cycle and is usually measured in milliseconds (ms).

The duty cycle of a solenoid is the percentage of the cycle during which the solenoid is energized, or performing work. Duty cycle is the ratio of the pulse width to a complete cycle

expressed as a percentage. A solenoid operating at a zero percent duty cycle is never on and is not performing any work. A solenoid operating at a 100 percent duty cycle is always on and working constantly. A 50 percent duty cycle means the solenoid is energized for 50 percent of the total cycle and off the other 50 percent of the time, figure 3-17. A solenoid operating at a 75 percent duty cycle is on 75 percent of the time and off during 25 percent of each cycle.

An electronic fuel injector is a good example of a variable pulse width actuator. A fuel injector also operates at a variable **frequency**. The computer changes injector pulse width, in relation to the amount of fuel needed by the engine, based on input from system sensors. A short pulse width delivers little fuel; a longer pulse width delivers more fuel. However, fuel injectors do not operate at a fixed frequency, and their cycle varies with engine speed. When the injector opens is determined by the frequency of the signal, and how long it stays on is determined by the pulse width of the signal.

Oxygen Sensor Service

All current fuel injection systems utilize at least one oxygen sensor. Originally referred to as an "O2S," now it is known as a heated oxygen sensor or "HO2S". This book will refer to the sensor as the HO2S or simply the oxygen sensor, figure 3-18. in the amount of oxygen in the exhaust vs. the outside air.

The most common HO2S is made of zirconium dioxide or zirconia. A zirconia HO2S generates a maximum output voltage of approximately 1 volt and produces a signal range of about 0.1 to 0.9 volt (100 to 900 mV).

A8

Frequency: The number of periodic voltage oscillations, or waves, occurring in a given unit of time, usually expressed as cycles per second or Hertz.

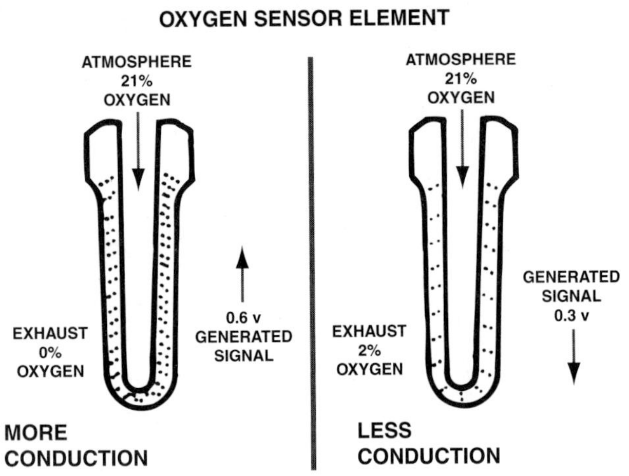

OXYGEN SENSOR ELEMENT

Fig. 3-18. The HO$_2$S generates a voltage based on the difference in the amount of oxygen in the exhaust vs. the outside air.

The amount of oxygen in the exhaust, compared to the amount of oxygen in the outside air, determines how much voltage the HO2S generates. A zirconia oxygen sensor must warm to at least 300° C (572° F) before it can generate a valid signal.

When working on vehicles with an oxygen sensor, observe these precautions:

- Do not obstruct the vent holes on the sensor
- Use only a high-impedance digital voltmeter to test sensor output
- Do not use silicone sprays near an oxygen sensor
- Use only HO2S-safe RTV

Oxygen Sensor Testing

To determine the voltages the oxygen sensor produces, use a DMM capable of displaying minimum, maximum, and average voltage readings, or an oscilloscope. To test with a DMM, connect the positive meter lead to the HO2S signal wire and connect the negative lead to a reliable ground. Be careful not to pull at the sensor wire or to allow it to make contact with a hot exhaust manifold. Also, beware of puncturing a grouping of signal wires with a common grounding shield. Doing so may ground out the sensor.

Next, run the engine until the HO2S reaches operating temperature and the control system switches from **open-loop** to **closed-loop** operation. Once the system is in closed-loop, the DMM should sample a range of oxygen sensor voltages similar to that produced during a real-life duty cycle. Select the "minimum-maximum" feature on the DMM, then raise engine speed to 2,000 rpm for 30 seconds. Return engine speed to idle, then quickly snap open and release the throttle once. Switch off the minimum-maximum feature.

For a properly functioning engine, the DMM should display a minimum voltage below 200 mV, a maximum voltage of at least 700 mV, and an average of approximately 450 mV. If voltages differ, refer to an HO2S diagnostic chart, figure 3-19. Please note that this procedure tests a system, not an individual component. Incorrect voltages do not always indicate a faulty oxygen sensor.

For more accurate HO2S test results, monitor sensor voltage with an oscilloscope. The PCM looks for the oxygen sensor voltage signal to change direction near the 450 mV midpoint of the range. Ideally, the signal is evenly split and stays above and below 450 mV equal amounts of time. This indicates an oxygen content that is equivalent to the ideal stoichiometric air-fuel ratio of 14.7:1, figure 3-20. When exhaust oxygen content is high, a zirconia HO2S generates a low-voltage signal. A low exhaust oxygen content causes the HO2S to produce a high-voltage signal. An HO2S signal that remains below longer than it stays above 450 mV indicates a lean condition, and a waveform that spends more time above 450 mV indicates a rich running condition. The farther from the voltage midpoint the switch occurs, the more severe the mixture deviation.

Oxygen Sensor Replacement

To replace an HO2S, disconnect the sensor output lead from the wiring harness. Spray manifold heat valve solvent around the sensor threads and allow it to soak for several minutes. Then use a special socket to unscrew the sensor from the manifold. In some cases, it may be easier to remove the sensor if the manifold is slightly warmed. Clean any rust, residue, or corrosion from the sensor hole threads with a thread-chasing tap. Most new sensors come with the antisieze compound already applied to the threads. When installing a used sensor, coat the threads only with a compound specifically designed for oxygen sensor use and recommended by the manufacturer. Thread the sensor into the manifold and torque to specifications, generally in the 20 to 35 ft-lb. (15 to 25 Nm) range.

FUEL INJECTOR SERVICE

Most automotive fuel injectors are electronically actuated solenoids controlled by the PCM, figure 3-21. Some older vehicles utilize, hydraulic injectors, but these are rarely seen on gasoline engines today.

Injector Testing

Electronic injectors are solenoid-operated actuators and can be checked with a DMM or oscilloscope.

Before testing the injectors, make sure that:

- The fuel pump delivery pressure is correct
- The pressure regulator is functioning properly
- The battery is fully charged
- The charging system is working properly
- The PCM is receiving the supply voltage it requires

Current flow in an injector circuit varies by manufacturer and model year. Refer to the appropriate Service Manual for the correct specifications. Many late-model systems use a low-resistance injector in conjunction with the PCM's ability to limit the current flow in the circuit. The initial current flow is high to rapidly energize the solenoid, and then once the injector opens, the PCM ramps down the current. This design is sometimes called "peak and hold" injection. The PCM regulates injector activity by controlling the ground side of the circuit.

A weak or defective injector can often be detected by performing a cylinder balance test. See Chapter One of this book. Uneven balance may be caused by the injector or an ignition or mechanical problem. Eliminate all other possibilities before replacing the injector.

An injector flow balance test can be performed while the injectors are installed in the engine. A special balance tester

VOLTAGE READINGS			COURSE OF ACTION
Minimum	Maximum	Average	
Under 200 mV	Over 700 mV	400-500 mV	None—System operating properly.
Over 200 mV	Not applicable	400-500 mV	Replace oxygen sensor.
Not applicable	Under 700 mV	400-500 mV	Replace oxygen sensor.
Under 200 mV	Over 700 mV	Under 400 mV	Check for cause of lean air-fuel ratio.
Under 200 mV	Under 700 mV	Under 400 mV	Check the oxygen sensor by enriching the air-fuel mixture. If the sensor responds, investigate for a lean running engine. If the sensor does not respond, replace the sensor.
Under 200 mV	Over 700 mV	Over 500 mV	Investigate cause of rich running engine.
Over 200 mV	Over 700 mV	Over 500 mV	Check the sensor by leaning out the air-fuel mixture. If the sensor responds, investigate for a rich running engine. If it does not respond, replace it.

Fig. 3-19. Oxygen sensor diagnostic chart.

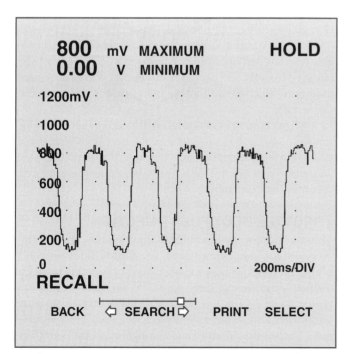

Fig. 3-20. Oscilloscope trace of a good HO2S that is switching normally.

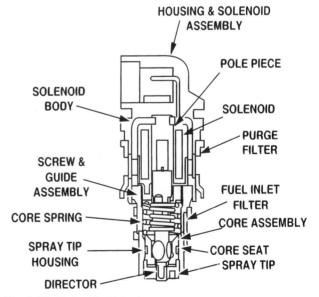

Fig. 3-21. Typical fuel injector.

is required to turn the injector on for a precise time period without running the engine, figure 3-22. The test allows the injector to spray a measured amount of fuel into the manifold, causing a drop in fuel rail pressure that can be recorded and compared to specifications. Any injector whose pressure drop exceeds specifications should be replaced.

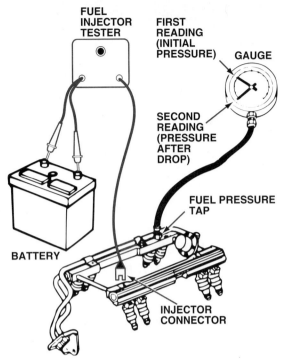

Fig. 3-22. Equipment setup for performing an injector flow balance test.

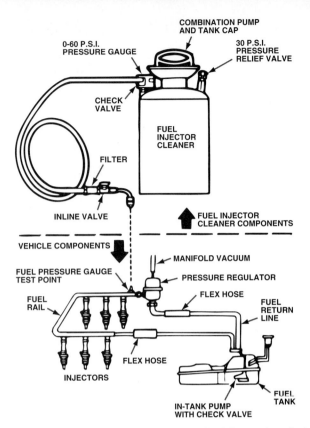

Fig. 3-23. Fuel injector cleaner used with the injectors installed on the fuel rail.

One or more of the following checks may be specified by the manufacturer to determine if the injectors are functioning properly:

- Check multipoint injectors by listening to each one with a stethoscope while the engine is running at slow idle. If you do not hear a steady clicking as the solenoid switches on and off, the injector is defective
- Observe throttle body injector action by removing the air cleaner cover or air intake duct. With the engine idling, the spray pattern from the injector tip should be steady, uniform, and conical in shape. The spray pattern can easily be examined by connecting a timing light and aiming it at the injector tip. This will "freeze" injector operation for more detailed study
- Measure the injector solenoid coil resistance with an ohmmeter. Unplug the injector electrical connector, connect the ohmmeter leads across the injector pins, and note the meter reading. Then move one test lead to the side of the injector or to the engine block to check for a short. Replace injectors that are not within specifications
- Check the injector harness by unplugging it from the computer and connecting an ohmmeter between the supply and return terminals for each injector or group of injectors. When the injectors are energized in groups, the resistance of the harness and injector group will be less than that of a single injector. A high-resistance reading indicates an open in one or more injectors or circuits. Low-resistance readings are caused by a short circuit
- The injector pulse width and duty cycle can be checked with an oscilloscope. Be aware, with grouped injectors the scope pattern reflects activity for all injectors in the group simultaneously

Cleaning Fuel Injectors

Electronic fuel injectors cannot be repaired. If they do not work within the limits specified by the manufacturer, they are replaced with new or rebuilt units. However, they can be cleaned if varnish or carbon builds up on the injector tip.

Various cleaning devices and special solutions are available to clean fuel injectors. Some require the injectors to be removed from the fuel rail or throttle body. Others can be used to clean the injectors without removing them from the vehicle, figure 3-23.

When cleaning injectors, follow the equipment directions exactly. The cleaning solvents used are very powerful, and if allowed to remain in the system, they can corrode plated parts. Some injectors are not designed to be cleaned and may be damaged in the attempt.

THROTTLE BODY FUEL INJECTION

Throttle body, or single point, fuel injection is a common feature on many domestic engines. The throttle body assembly houses the throttle plates and provides the mounting point for the fuel injectors, idle speed controller, and throttle position sensor, figure 3-24. A fuel pressure regulator and temperature sensor may also be incorporated into the unit. Most of these items can be serviced without removing the throttle body from the vehicle.

If the internal passages become gummed up, the throttle body can be removed, disassembled, cleaned, and resealed. Remove the unit from the vehicle and disassemble it. Once the components have been removed from the casting, it can be cleaned with a soft-bristle brush and an aerosol cleaner, or

FUEL PRESSURE REGULATOR

INJECTOR

AIR INTAKE

FUEL SUPPLY FROM TANK

INJECTION

FUEL RETURN TO TANK

THROTTLE BODY (FUEL CHARGING ASSEMBLY)

THROTTLE PLATE

Fig. 3-24. Throttle body fuel injection assembly.

submerged in carburetor cleaner if necessary. Reassemble using new gaskets and O-rings, then reinstall it on the intake manifold. There are no adjustments to make during reassembly. Adjusting the throttle position sensor, idle speed, and fuel mixture are covered later in this book.

AIR INTAKE SYSTEM SERVICE

The air intake system consists of:

- Air intake ductwork
- Air cleaner and filter element
- Intake manifold

Air Intake Ductwork

A typical late-model air intake system is a complex system of ducts, filters, meters, valves, and tubes, figure 3-25. When servicing, make sure the intake ductwork is properly installed and all connections are airtight. Any air leakage downstream of the **airflow sensor** can create a lean condition and affect engine performance.

Air Filter Service

The air filter element is the only part of the intake air system that requires periodic replacement. Although change intervals vary by manufacturer, the air filter element on most late-model engines is replaced every 30,000 miles. In particularly dusty areas, or when operated under severe service, the filters should be checked and changed more frequently. An accumulation of engine oil on the element or in the housing indicates mechanical problems. Oil entering the air filter is the result of a crankcase ventilation system malfunction or excessive blow-by. A paper element cannot be cleaned, and must be replaced if it is dirty or torn.

Carbureted and throttle body injected engines have the air filter mounted directly to the carburetor or throttle body. To replace the filter element, remove the fasteners holding the housing cover, lift off the cover, and take out the element. Check top and bottom seals for dust leakage and check the filter material for breaks.

Most fuel injected engines use a flat filter element installed in a remote air cleaner housing. Some of the ductwork may have to be disconnected and moved aside or removed to access the filter housing. Unfasten the clips holding the housing together, then lift out the filter element.

Intake Manifold

During service, the intake manifold should be checked for secure mounting and vacuum leaks. Be aware, a vacuum leak

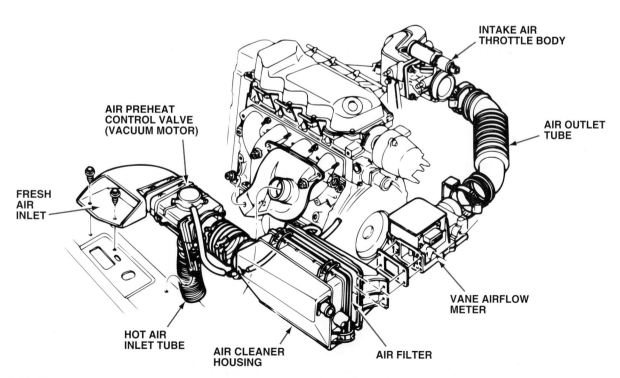

INTAKE AIR THROTTLE BODY

AIR PREHEAT CONTROL VALVE (VACUUM MOTOR)

AIR OUTLET TUBE

FRESH AIR INLET

VANE AIRFLOW METER

HOT AIR INLET TUBE

AIR CLEANER HOUSING

AIR FILTER

Fig. 3-25. The intake ductwork delivers fresh air to the combustion chambers.

A8

normally influences the engine more at idle because of higher intake vacuum than at higher engine speeds when the percentage of air entering is less. Diagnostic time can be decreased by understanding what to expect of the fuel system when there is a vacuum leak.

Carbureted engines with a vacuum leak affecting one cylinder will typically lean the fuel mixture only of that one cylinder, causing the engine to run worse at idle. The same engine with a centrally located leak will lean the fuel mixture for all cylinders. Note that a "feedback" carbureted system may be able to compensate for the leak after entering the closed loop operational mode.

Most TBI engines react differently than carbureted engines because they use a speed density method of fuel injection. A vacuum leak into one cylinder may also lean the fuel mixture for that one cylinder. A centrally located vacuum leak will not influence the fuel delivery, but will raise idle RPM. Vacuum leaks at the vacuum signal to the MAP sensor will enrich the fuel mixture.

Multiport fuel injected (MFI) engines of the speed density type will raise idle RPM when a leak occurs, except if the leak appears at the MAP sensor itself. MAP signal leaks will enrich the mixture.

Multiport fuel injected engines that use the mass air flow (MAF) or volume airflow methods of fuel injection lean the fuel mixture to all cylinders with any type of vacuum leak. This is because the air induced through the leak is not being metered by the airflow sensor.

EXHAUST SYSTEM SERVICE

Servicing the exhaust system consists of inspecting the pipes, brackets, mufflers, and catalytic converters, as well as inspecting and testing the manifold heat control valves. Check each component for damage, exhaust leakage, loose connections, and loose mounting. Tighten where required. The converter or muffler generally is not repaired if damaged, but is replaced with a new one. The replacement procedure is essentially the same for both.

Exhaust Manifold Service

Inspect the exhaust manifold to cylinder head area. If signs of leaking exist remove the manifold for further inspection.

Check the manifold and head sealing surfaces for:

- Warping or distortion
- Erosion
- Cracks
- Pitting

If any problems are found, refer to the Service Manual for applicable repair procedures. Also inspect the seal between the manifolds and the exhaust pipe. Replace or repair as necessary.

Exhaust System Inspection

Inspect the following components for signs of damage, leaking, corrosion, or other abnormalities:

- All exhaust piping
- Muffler(s)
- Resonator(s)
- Heat shields

Repair or replace any components that are defective, figure 3-26, following procedures outlined in the appropriate Service Manual.

Catalytic Converter Service

Catalytic converters are required by law to give at least 50,000 miles of service. However, if the car is properly tuned and still cannot meet the emissions specifications, perform a vacuum test or backpressure test. These tests indicate only that a restriction exists somewhere in the exhaust system. Check the rest of the system before removing and replacing the converter.

Vacuum Test

Connect a vacuum gauge to a manifold vacuum source to perform the test.

To check for a restriction:

1. Run the engine at idle; vacuum should remain steady and within specifications. If it drops toward zero, a restriction is indicated. Continue the test.
2. Slowly increase engine speed to 2,000 RPM. Vacuum should remain as high as at idle.
3. Quickly close the throttle. Vacuum should rise rapidly to above idle level. If the reading is 5 in-Hg or more below normal, and returns slowly and unevenly, the exhaust system is restricted.

Backpressure Test

Use this test only on vehicles with dual-bed bead-type converters:

1. Disconnect the hose at the secondary air manifold and remove the check valve.
2. Use an adapter to connect a fuel pressure gauge to the air manifold.
3. With the engine at normal operating temperature and running at 2,500 RPM, check the backpressure reading on the gauge. If it is above 1.75 psi (12.06 kpa), the exhaust system is restricted.

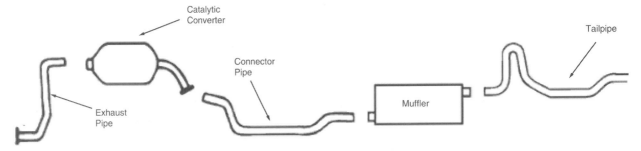

Fig. 3-26. Typical exhaust system components.

For vehicles with other styles of converters, you can purchase a special tool kit to check backpressure. The tool requires that a small hole be drilled in the exhaust pipe upstream from the converter. A gauge is attached to the hole and the test is performed. When completed a small rivet is driven into the hole to seal the system.

Temperature Test

Before testing, repair any known problems that may cause high emissions, as well as any exhaust leaks. Then, disable the air injection system and connect an exhaust gas analyzer. Next, precondition the engine by running it at 2,500 RPM for three minutes. Check the exhaust gas analyzer gauges. If CO exceeds 0.3 percent, O2 exceeds 0.4 percent, and HC falls between 120 ppm and 400 ppm, expect a faulty converter.

TURBOCHARGER SYSTEMS

A turbocharger is an exhaust driven compressor used to increase the power output of an engine. The system requires no maintenance other than more frequent engine oil and filter changes. Turbocharger malfunctions usually fall into one of the following categories:

1. Lack of proper lubrication—which is caused by the wrong type of oil, a restricted oil supply line, or a worn engine that develops low oil pressure.
2. Dirty or contaminated oil system—which is caused by infrequent oil changes, failure of an engine bearing, piston ring, or other internal component, or an oil filter bypass valve stuck open.
3. Contamination in the air intake or exhaust systems—which is caused by a leaking air duct or missing air cleaner, or a damaged catalytic converter if it is installed between the turbocharger and the exhaust manifold.

Turbocharger Troubleshooting

Turbocharger problems are generally revealed by:

- Lack of power from the engine
- Heavy black smoke from the exhaust
- Blue smoke from the exhaust
- High engine oil consumption
- Abnormal sounds

Use the troubleshooting charts, figure 3-27, figure 3-28, and figure 3-29, to isolate the cause of turbocharger malfunctions.

Turbocharger Inspection

Perform a preliminary inspection as follows:

1. Make sure the air cleaner is in place and that there are no loose connections, leaks, restrictions, or broken ductwork.
2. Check the exhaust system for burned areas, leakage, and loose connections.
3. Disconnect the turbocharger air inlet and exhaust outlet, then inspect the turbine and compressor with a flashlight and a mirror. Look for bent or broken blades and wear marks on the blades or housing.
4. Turn the turbine wheel by hand. Listen and feel for binding or rubbing. Check for freeplay by moving both

LACK OF POWER OR EMITS BLACK EXHAUST SMOKE

POSSIBLE CAUSE	CORRECTION
Damaged or disconnected air cleaner ducting	Inspect and correct
Restricted air filter element	Replace air filter
Intake or exhaust manifold leak	Check turbocharger installation for air or exhaust leak
Turbocharger damage	Check turbocharger rotating assembly for binding or dragging
Exhaust system restriction	Check exhaust system; check manifold heat control valve
Carburetor or fuel injection problem	Inspect and correct
Incorrect ignition timing, advance–or other ignition problem	Inspect and correct
EGR problem	Inspect and correct
Lack of compression or other engine wear	Inspect and correct
Low boost pressure	Check boost pressure and wastegate operation; adjust or replace as required

Fig. 3-27. Turbocharger diagnosis lack of power or black exhaust smoke.

HIGH OIL CONSUMPTION OR EMITS BLUE EXHAUST SMOKE

POSSIBLE CAUSE	CORRECTION
Excessive blowby or PCV problem	Check for engine wear; service PCV system
Engine oil leakage	Inspect and correct
Worn engine rings, cylinders, valves, valve guides	Check for engine wear; check for low compression and cylinder leakage
Leaking turbocharger oil seals*	Replace turbocharger
Restricted turbocharger oil return or too much oil in center housing	Check oil return line for restrictions and blow out with compressed air; check center housing for sludge; clean as required
Carburetor or fuel injection problem	Inspect and correct
Incorrect ignition timing, advance or other ignition problem	Inspect and correct
EGR problem	Inspect and correct

*Smoke and detonation indicates a leak on the compressor side; smoke alone indicates a leak on the turbine side.

Fig. 3-28. Turbocharger diagnosis for high oil consumption or blue exhaust smoke.

ends of the shaft up and down. There should be little if any movement.

5. Check the shaft seal areas for signs of oil leakage, figure 3-30.

Turbocharger Service

Turbocharger service consists of testing the boost pressure and checking the **wastegate** operation. A turbocharger can be disassembled, internal components replaced, and clearances set with a dial indicator. However, common practice is to simply replace a defective unit.

A8

TURBOCHARGER PROBLEMS

SOUND	CAUSE
Louder than normal noise that includes hissing	Exhaust leak
Uneven sound that changes in pitch	Restricted air intake from a clogged air cleaner filter, bent air ducting, or dirt on the compressor blades
Higher than normal pitch sound	Intake air leak
Sudden noise reduction, with smoke and oil leakage	Turbocharger failure
Uneven noise and vibration	Possible shaft damage, damaged compressor or turbine wheel blades
Grinding or rubbing sounds	Shaft or bearing damage, misaligned compressor or turbine wheel
Rattling sound	Loose exhaust pipe or outlet elbow, damaged wastegate

Fig. 3-29. Turbocharger diagnosis for unusual noises.

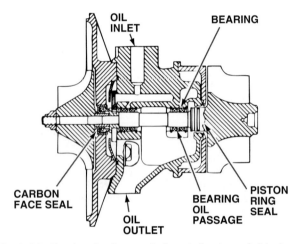

Fig. 3-30. Check turbocharger shaft seals for signs of oil leakage.

Testing Boost Pressure

Boost pressure can be checked during a road test, or on a chassis dynamometer, using a pressure gauge. Connect the gauge to a pressure port on the compressor side of the turbo, or tee it into the line running to the warning lamp pressure switch. Use a long enough hose so the gauge is inside the passenger compartment during testing. A turbocharger will not develop normal boost unless the engine is under load. Start and warm the engine to normal operating temperature. Accelerate from zero to 40 or 50 mph and note the gauge reading under load. Compare results to Service Manual specifications.

Testing the Wastegate Actuator

The wastegate is a pressure relief device that protects the system from overcharging, figure 3-31. Test the wastegate actuator as follows:

1. Connect a hand-operated pump and pressure gauge to the actuator.
2. Apply about 5 psi (34 kPa) of pressure. If pressure drops below 2 psi (14 kPa) after one minute, the actuator diaphragm is leaking.

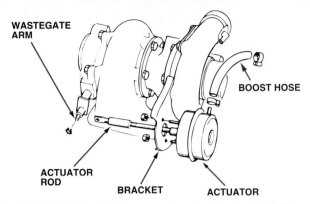

Fig. 3-31. Typical turbocharger wastegate actuator installation.

3. Clamp or mount a dial indicator on the turbocharger housing so that the plunger contacts the actuator rod.
4. Apply the specified boost pressure to the actuator diaphragm and note the amount of rod movement shown on the indicator. If not within specifications, generally less than 0.015 inch (0.38 mm), repair or replace the actuator.
5. Remove the fastener that holds the rod to the wastegate arm or link, then move the arm. It should travel freely through a 45-degree arc. If not, replace the wastegate.

SUPERCHARGER SERVICE

A supercharger is a crankshaft-driven positive displacement pump that supplies an excess volume of intake air to the engine. The supercharger boosts the pressure and density of the intake air charge to increase engine output, figure 3-32. A typical supercharger consists of two lobed rotor shafts supported by bearings in a cast housing. The two shafts are geared together so they rotate in opposite directions. One of the shafts is driven off the crankshaft by a belt. The supercharger supplies boost whenever the engine is running. Most units use a vacuum-operated

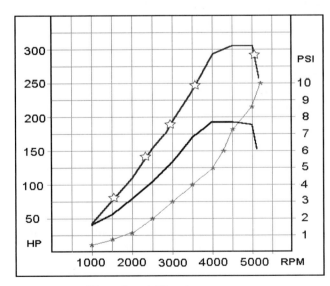

Fig. 3-32. Typical horsepower comparison of supercharged to naturally aspirate engine.

bypass valve to bleed off excess boost pressure during idle and low-speed operation.

With the exception of belt inspection and adjustment, a supercharger does not require routine maintenance. Bearings are lubricated by a self-contained oiling system. Some systems allow the oil level to be checked. However, a low oil level indicates an internal problem.

Typical problems include:

- Incorrect boost
- Poor response and fuel economy
- Excessive noise
- Oil leakage

Many problems are a result of a malfunctioning boost control or bypass valve. Valve operation can quickly be checked using a hand-operated vacuum pump. On some systems, boost can be checked with a pressure gauge. Boost pressure, which depends on test speed, varies from about 3.5 to 11 psi (24 to 75 kPa) for most units. Internal components are typically not serviceable. If a problem is detected, replace the assembly.

A8

CHAPTER QUESTIONS

1. All of the following may be used for a fuel line **EXCEPT**:
   a. Copper tubing
   b. Neoprene hose
   c. Nylon tubing
   d. Steel tubing

2. On a carbureted engine, the fuel filter usually attaches to the lines with:
   a. Spring-lock fittings
   b. Flare nut fittings
   c. Compression fittings
   d. Hose clamps

3. A good mechanical fuel pump operating at 500 RPM will deliver one quart or liter of fuel in about:
   a. 15 seconds
   b. 30 seconds
   c. 45 seconds
   d. One minute

4. Which of the following is the typical operating pressure range of a throttle body injection system?
   a. 5 to 10 psi
   b. 10 to 15 psi
   c. 15 to 25 psi
   d. 25 to 35 psi

5. With the fuel pump running and a pressure gauge installed, applying vacuum to the fuel pressure regulator should cause gauge readings to:
   a. Increase about 5 to 7 psi
   b. Increase about 10 to 15 psi
   c. Decrease about 5 to 7 psi
   d. Decrease about 10 to 15 psi

6. The primary purpose of the pressure regulator in a fuel injection system is to:
   a. Limit pressure produced by the pump
   b. Maintain uniform pressure at the injectors
   c. Control the air-fuel ratio
   d. Maintain residual pressure for quick startup

7. The signal carried by the ground wire on a potentiometer is also known as:
   a. Signal voltage
   b. Reference voltage
   c. Return voltage
   d. System voltage

8. An oscilloscope can be used to monitor electronic injector:
   a. Opening pressure and delivery volume
   b. Solenoid coil resistance
   c. Flow balance
   d. Pulse width and duty cycle

9. To check the boost pressure of a turbocharger, a pressure gauge is installed in the:
   a. Compressor side of the turbo
   b. Turbine side of the turbo
   c. Wastegate of the turbo
   d. Intake manifold

CHAPTER OBJECTIVES

- The technician will complete the ASE task list on Emission Control Systems Diagnosis and Repair.
- The technician will be able to answer 8 questions dealing with the Emission Control Systems Diagnosis and Repair section of the A8 ASE Test.

Reducing the exhaust emissions of a modern internal combustion engine to an acceptable legal level is a complex task. A number of engine subsystems are used to break down and reduce exhaust pollutants. These may include:

- Positive crankcase ventilation
- Idle speed control
- Exhaust gas recirculation
- Exhaust gas treatment
- Catalytic converter
- Inlet air temperature control
- Intake manifold temperature control
- Fuel vapor control

Emission control system use and design vary by engine, manufacturer, and model year. Not every vehicle uses all of the subsystems listed above. However, all of the subsystems that are used on a particular engine are designed to interact with each other to lower exhaust emissions. Most emission control devices are electronically regulated by the engine management system. Before attempting to diagnose what appears to be an emission control problem, make sure the engine is in sound mechanical condition and good running order. Isolating a faulty component is a process of elimination that may include electronic and dynamic troubleshooting.

POSITIVE CRANKCASE VENTILATION (PCV) SYSTEMS

A flow restriction in the PCV system can result in driveability problems. Improper venting, or scavenging, of the crankcase can result in oil dilution and sludge formation. In extreme cases, oil collects in the air cleaner and eventually clogs the filter element. Symptoms of a clogged or damaged PCV system include:

- Increased oil consumption
- Diluted or contaminated oil
- Escaping blowby vapors
- Unstable engine operation at idle and low speed

PCV service includes inspection, testing, and component replacement. There are no adjustments possible.

System Inspection

Conduct a thorough visual examination. Be sure to:

1. Inspect hoses for proper routing and tight connections. Also, check hoses for signs of cracking, deformation, and clogging.
2. Check the air filter element for signs of excessive blowby deposits.
3. Check the crankcase inlet air filter, if equipped, for blockage.
4. Check for deposits that may restrict passages in the intake manifold.
5. Check the PCV valve for deposits or clogging.

The plunger inside a PCV valve must move freely to open and close the vent port, figure 4-1. A quick way to check a typical PCV valve is to shake it and listen. Expect to hear the plunger move inside the valve. A valve that does not rattle is probably clogged and should be replaced. A good valve can be cleaned with carburetor cleaner spray. Drain the cleaner from the valve and let it air dry.

System Testing

Use the following method to test the PCV system:

1. Connect a tachometer and start the engine.
2. Disconnect the PCV valve and the vent line from the crankcase. Engine speed should increase slightly.
3. Listen for a hissing noise from the valve.
4. Place a finger over the end of the valve. A strong vacuum should be felt and engine speed should drop by 40 RPM or more if the system is working properly.

A8

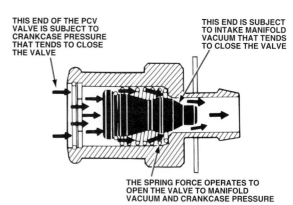

THIS END OF THE PCV VALVE IS SUBJECT TO CRANKCASE PRESSURE THAT TENDS TO CLOSE THE VALVE

THIS END IS SUBJECT TO INTAKE MANIFOLD VACUUM THAT TENDS TO CLOSE THE VALVE

THE SPRING FORCE OPERATES TO OPEN THE VALVE TO MANIFOLD VACUUM AND CRANKCASE PRESSURE

Fig. 4-1. Cross section of a typical PCV valve.

If engine speed does not increase when the valve is disconnected, or does not drop at least 40 RPM when the valve is blocked, the system is not working properly. Check the valve, hoses, and manifold passages for tight connections and blockage. Insufficient engine speed drop can also be caused by the wrong PCV valve being installed.

On some engines, the evaporative emission control (EVAP) vapor canister purges through the PCV line. Leakage in the purge hose will cause poor test results. Disconnect and plug the canister purge hose, then repeat the tests. If the PCV system passes the second test, the problem is in the purge system.

PCV SYSTEM SERVICE

Service of the PCV system usually consists of cleaning or replacing the filter, or replacing the connecting hoses or the valve itself.

Filter Replacement

The PCV inlet air is filtered through the engine air filter on some engines. Simply replace the element at the recommended interval. Other designs have a separate PCV filter element that mounts in the air cleaner housing, figure 4-2. This may be a foam filter or a wire mesh screen, which unless torn or otherwise damaged can be cleaned and reinstalled. To service, remove the filter, wash with solvent, air dry, then reinstall. Lightly oil a foam type filter with clean motor oil before installation.

Filters installed in the oil filler cap are usually made of wire mesh. Remove the filler cap and soak the complete cap and filter in solvent. Allow it to drain and dry in the air. Do not dry with compressed air; this will damage the wire mesh.

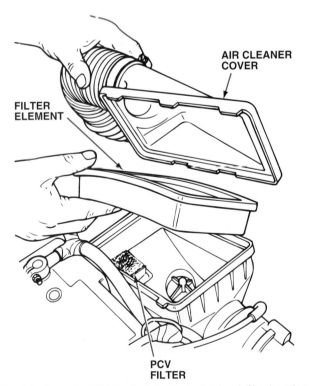

Fig. 4-2. Separate PCV filter installed in the intake air filter housing.

Hose Replacement

Any damaged or deteriorated hose must be replaced to ensure proper system operation. Use only hose designed for PCV and fuel system applications. Standard heater hose cannot withstand the blowby vapors and will quickly fail.

PCV VALVE REPLACEMENT

A PCV valve cannot be distinguished by its appearance; internal valve characteristics are specifically calibrated for each application. Always refer to the part number when replacing a valve. When installing a valve, make sure to fit it with the arrow indicating direction of flow pointing toward the intake manifold. If the valve is mounted in a rubber grommet, it must provide a snug fit. If the grommet is hardened or cracked, replace it.

THERMOSTATIC VACUUM SWITCH TEST

A **thermostatic vacuum switch** is normally activated by engine coolant or air temperature. The vacuum switch may be opened or closed by high or low temperatures, depending upon its use and the system design.

Coolant-controlled switches are tested with the engine cold, and at normal operating temperature. In some cases, a third check is made at higher than normal temperature. Do not allow the engine to overheat. A typical test procedure for a three-port switch is shown in figure 4-3.

SPARK DELAY VALVE TESTS

In many older model vehicles spark delay valves were used to slow the vacuum advance signal to the distributor. Some of theses valves delayed vacuum by means of a restricted **orifice** in the vacuum line, figure 4-4.

Test a delay valve by attaching a vacuum gauge to the distributor side of the valve. Use a vacuum pump to apply 10 to 15 in-Hg (69 to 103 kPa) of vacuum to the valve inlet side. The gauge reading should rise slowly to a steady reading after vacuum is applied. Note the time required for the vacuum gauge to level off to a steady reading and compare it to specifications.

To check the release operation of the valve, reverse the pump and gauge connections. When vacuum is applied, the gauge reading should rise quickly and immediately. For further testing, refer to the appropriate Service or Diagnostic Manual.

EXHAUST GAS RECIRCULATION (EGR) SYSTEM

Exhaust gas recirculation systems meter a small amount of exhaust gas into the intake system, where it dilutes the air-fuel mixture going to the cylinders. This lowers the peak combustion temperature to reduce the formation of oxides of nitrogen (NO_x).

Original design EGR valves used a spring-loaded diaphragm that is activated by a vacuum signal to open or close an exhaust passage, figure 4-5. Most late-model systems use a PWM solenoid or stepper motor to actuate the pintle and control the

---

Orifice: A small opening or restriction in a line or passage that is used to regulate pressure and flow.

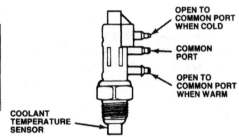

Fig. 4-3. Typical 3-port vacuum switch test procedure.

COLOR CODE	SWITCHING TEMPERATURE	
	CLOSED BELOW	OPEN ABOVE
BROWN	27°C (80°F)	35°C (95°F)
GREEN	39°C (103°F)	53°C (128°F)
YELLOW	57°C (135°F)	71°C (160°F)
RED	93°C (200°F)	107°C (225°F)

flow of exhaust gasses, figure 4-6. If the EGR valve fails to open when it should, expect:

- Increases in NO_x formation
- Pinging and detonation
- Reduced fuel mileage

If the EGR valve leaks, expect:

- Rough idling
- Stalling
- Hesitation

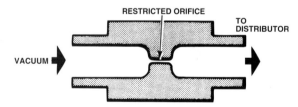

Fig. 4-4. Restricted orifice vacuum delay valve.

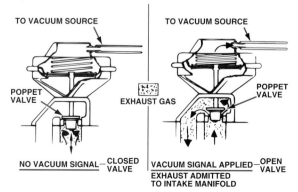

Fig. 4-5. Simple vacuum-operated, spring-loaded diaphragm type EGR valve.

On a speed density system, an EGR leak may cause a rich fuel mixture because it lowers manifold vacuum.

System Testing

Although each manufacturer has features unique to its systems, the function of any EGR vacuum diaphragm valve can be quickly checked as follows:

1. Start and run the engine until it is at normal operating temperature.
2. Connect a tachometer to the engine.
3. Disconnect the EGR valve vacuum hose. Connect a vacuum gauge to the hose and a vacuum pump to the valve.
4. Accelerate the engine to 2000 RPM and read the gauge to verify that vacuum is available to the EGR valve.

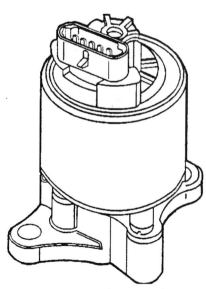

A8

Fig. 4-6. Typical stepper motor controlled EGR valve.

5. With the engine running at 2000 RPM, apply 8 to 10 in-Hg (55 to 69 kPa) of vacuum to the valve. The engine RPM should drop from 1500 RPM to 1350 RPM. This tests flow through the valve. Some EGR systems operate only when there is a slight positive pressure in the exhaust system. These have an integral or external backpressure transducer. It may be necessary to restrict the exhaust pipe when applying vacuum to the EGR valve to make it operate.

If there was no vacuum signal to the valve, test the vacuum circuit back to the source. If the vacuum is controlled by the PCM, certain conditions need to be met before the EGR valve is activated. Typically, these include most or all of the following:

- Engine coolant is at or above a minimum temperature
- Engine speed is above idle and below a maximum specified RPM
- The vehicle is moving at a minimum speed
- The control system is in closed-loop operation
- The throttle is open, but not wide open
- There is backpressure in the exhaust

Exact test conditions and specifications vary. Follow the Service Manual procedure for the particular system.

EGR Valve Replacement
Most EGR valves bolt to the intake manifold or cylinder head. Simply remove the bolts and lift off the valve. Inspect the valve and manifold passages for combustion deposits. These deposits are a normal result of continued operation. Excessive buildup can clog exhaust gas passages in the intake manifold and cause a new valve to fail.

Some EGR valve assemblies can be cleaned and reinstalled. Other valve designs cannot be cleaned and must be replaced. When cleaning a valve, be careful not to damage the diaphragm.

Install the EGR valve using a new gasket, and tighten the fasteners to the specified torque value to prevent exhaust gas leaks.

EGR Vacuum Controls
The vacuum signal to the EGR valve may be regulated by one or more of the following:

- Vacuum amplifier
- Temperature control valve
- Thermal vacuum switch
- Time delay solenoid
- Backpressure transducer
- Pulse width modulated (PWM) solenoid

Many components of vacuum operated systems are tested using a vacuum pump, while electronically controlled systems require the use of a scan tool and digital mulitmeter. Test procedures vary; accurate service information is required. Make sure all EGR connections are properly routed and tight. Replace any hoses that are pinched, cracked, broken, or otherwise damaged.

Not all vehicles rely on an EGR valve to control NO_x emissions. Many late-model vehicles do not require the valve or external systems to keep the emissions within acceptable limits.

EXHAUST GAS TREATMENT
In addition to exhaust gas recirculation, many engines use secondary air injection reaction (AIR) to reduce tailpipe pollutants. Pumping fresh air into the exhaust as it leaves the engine helps to complete combustion. Air injection helps to **oxidize** any unburnt fuel in the exhaust to reduce HC and CO emissions. Two AIR system designs are used:

- Pump-type
- Pulse-type

PUMP-TYPE SYSTEMS
An air pump delivers a stream of fresh air to the exhaust, figure 4-7. Although a few engines use an electric motor to drive the air pump, figure 4-8, most are driven by a belt off of

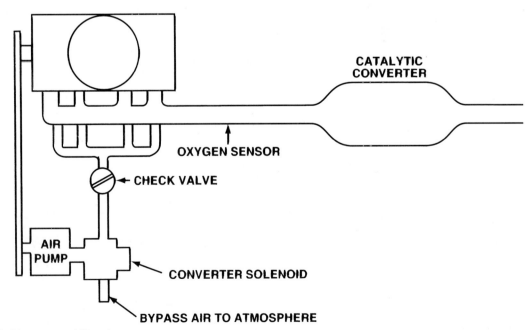

CATALYTIC CONVERTER

OXYGEN SENSOR

CHECK VALVE

AIR PUMP

CONVERTER SOLENOID

BYPASS AIR TO ATMOSPHERE

Fig. 4-7. Belt-driven pump AIR system.

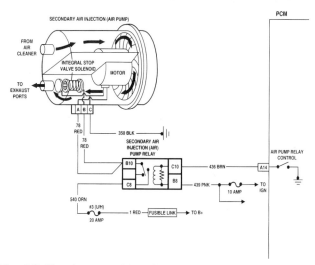

Fig. 4-8. Electric motor–driven AIR pump.

the crankshaft. With the exception of belt adjustment, there are no routine adjustments. However, manufacturers do recommend periodic inspections to ensure exhaust emissions are kept within legal limits.

Inspection
Inspect a pump-type AIR system as follows:

1. Check drive belt condition and tension.
2. Inspect all hoses and lines for loose connections, cracking, brittleness, or burning.
3. Inspect the check valve for exhaust leakage. Look for changes in the color of the metal that indicate excessive heat.
4. Disconnect the pump hose at the check valve. Start the engine and check for airflow from the open end of the hose.
5. Raise engine speed to 1500 RPM and check for an airflow increase.

6. With the engine running at fast idle, momentarily pinch off the pump outlet hose and listen for the relief valve to open.
7. If a filter is used, remove it and check for clogging.

Component Testing
Correct operation of the air pump and the various valves and switching devices is essential for proper system operation. Use the following procedures to test these parts.

Electronic System Controls
Many vehicles are equipped with secondary air systems controlled by the PCM, figure 4-9. Generally these systems utilize electrically operated solenoids to control the flow of air in the system. Begin diagnosis of these systems by checking for diagnostic trouble codes. If DTCs are present, refer to the appropriate Service or Diagnostic Manual for the correct repair procedures.

Gulp Valve
A **gulp valve** is used on early AIR systems to control backfiring, figure 4-10. With the engine running at idle, disconnect the vacuum line at the valve and check for vacuum. If there is no vacuum to the valve, look for a restricted hose. Reconnect the vacuum line, increase engine speed to 2000 RPM, then quickly close the throttle. Engine speed should stay high for a moment before returning to idle. If not, or if the engine backfires, replace the valve.

Next, disconnect the gulp valve discharge hose and place a finger over the end to seal it off. Increase engine speed to 2000 RPM, then quickly close the throttle. You should hear a momentary blast of air from the valve. If not, replace the valve.

Check Valve
A one-way check valve is used to prevent the reverse flow of exhaust gases through the system, figure 4-11. To test a check valve, remove it and blow air through the inlet end, then

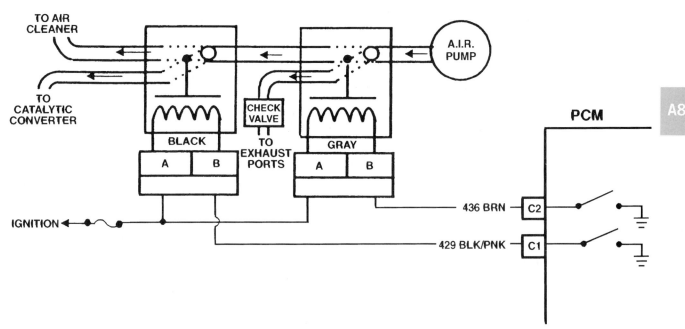

Fig. 4-9. AIR control solenoid outputs from the PCM.

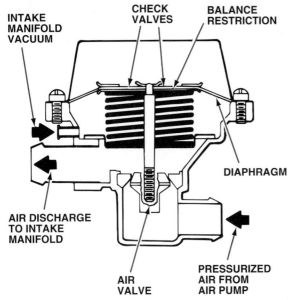

Fig. 4-10. A gulp valve directs pump air to the intake manifold during deceleration to prevent backfiring.

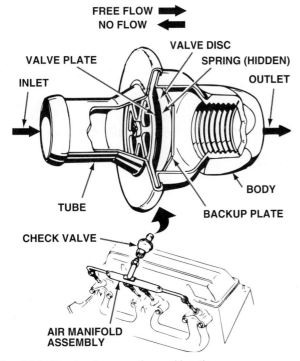

Fig. 4-11. Check valve operation and location.

through the outlet end of the valve. The valve should permit free movement of air through the inlet, but no air movement in the reverse direction.

PULSE-TYPE SYSTEMS

Pulse-type, or aspirator, AIR systems use the natural low-pressure pulses in the exhaust system to draw fresh air in through a reed-type check valve. Some systems use a valve assembly that has a separate check valve for each cylinder.

Other designs direct fresh air into the exhaust through a single aspirator valve.

Single Aspirator Systems

If an aspirator valve fails, noise from the exhaust system will increase at idle. Hot exhaust gases traveling back through the valve may cause the valve-to-air cleaner hose to harden and crack.

Check the aspirator air system as follows:

1. Inspect hose connections for leaks.
2. Check the aspirator tube and exhaust manifold connection for leaks.
3. Start the engine and stabilize the idle speed.
4. Disconnect the aspirator inlet hose.
5. Intake air pulses should be felt at the aspirator inlet, air cleaner side of the valve. If hot exhaust gas is felt, replace the valve.

Pulse Air Valve Systems

Diagnose a pulse air valve assembly which contains individual check valves as follows:

1. Listen for a brief hissing noise at the valve assembly. A noise indicates either the connections are loose at the manifold or the valve assembly is defective. Check the connections first, then the valve assembly.
2. Poor engine performance and surging can result if one or more of the check valves has failed. This allows exhaust gas to enter through the air cleaner.
3. Burned paint on the pulse air valve assembly, or a charred or cracked rubber hose to the air cleaner, indicates the valve is allowing hot exhaust gas to flow through the valve.
4. Poor driveability may indicate that the rubber hose has chipped inside and that some of the chips have been drawn into the intake air charge. To repair, clean the carburetor or throttle body, then replace both the hose and the pulse air valve assembly.

CATALYTIC CONVERTER SYSTEMS

The harmful emissions can be processed in a three-way catalytic converter to help ensure compliance with government mandated standards, figure 4-12. Like the engine, the three-way catalytic converter is sensitive to the air-fuel ratio. Maximum conversion efficiency is obtained when the stoichiometric air-fuel ratio is supplied to the engine.

Converter Operation

The purpose of the three-way converter is to help clean the NO_x, HC and CO emissions in the engine exhaust (hence the term "three-way"). Three metals (platinum, palladium, and rhodium) are used as **catalysts** to promote the conversion of the emissions. The process occurs in two stages. In the first stage, the catalyst encourages NO_x to break down into free nitrogen (N2) and free oxygen, with the oxygen portion encouraged to further oxidize CO into harmless carbon dioxide (CO2).

Catalyst: Specific compounds that enhance a chemical reaction without being consumed by the reaction.

Fig. 4-12. Three-way converter operation.

In the second stage, the oxygen-enriched emissions pass over a second catalyst that encourages further oxidation of HC and CO into water vapor and carbon dioxide. Some earlier systems used a "mini Ox" converter upstream of the main catalyst.

Effective catalytic control of all three pollutants is possible only if the exhaust gas contains a very small amount of oxygen.

Converter Testing

Onboard Diagnostics II (OBD II) regulations require monitoring the functionality of the catalyst in the catalytic converter. When the catalyst system has deteriorated to the point that vehicle emissions increase by more than 1.5 times the standard, OBD II requires **malfunction indicator lamp (MIL)** illumination.

The oxygen content in a catalyst is important for efficient conversion of exhaust gases. When a lean air-fuel ratio is present for an extended period, oxygen content in a catalyst can reach a maximum. When a rich air-fuel ratio is present for an extended period, the oxygen content in the catalyst can become totally depleted. When this occurs, the catalyst fails to convert the gases. This is known as catalyst "punch through."

Catalyst operation is dependent on its ability to store and release the oxygen needed to complete the emissions-reducing chemical reactions. As a catalyst deteriorates, its ability to store oxygen is reduced. Since the catalyst's ability to store oxygen is somewhat related to proper operation, oxygen storage can be used as an indicator of catalyst performance. To accomplish this, two oxygen sensors are required, figure 4-13. By utilizing an oxygen sensor upstream from the catalytic converter, and a second sensor located downstream, oxygen storage can be determined by comparing the two voltage signals.

As the PCM constantly adjusts the air-fuel mixture to maintain a stoichiometric ratio, the change in oxygen content is less noticeable downstream from the converter. The upstream sensor switches voltage more rapidly than the downstream sensor. Due to the effects of the converter, the oxygen content at the downstream sensor should be stable. Hence the voltage output from the downstream sensor changes less rapidly.

To monitor catalyst efficiency, the PCM expands the rich and lean switch points of the HO2S. With extended switch points, the air-fuel mixture runs richer and leaner to overburden the catalytic converter. Once the test is started, the air-fuel mixture runs rich and lean and the HO2S switches are counted. A switch is counted when an oxygen sensor signal goes from below the lean threshold to above the rich threshold. The number of rear sensor switches is divided by the number of front sensor switches to determine the switching ratio.

As catalyst efficiency deteriorates over the life of the vehicle, the switch rate at the downstream sensor approaches that of the upstream sensor. If at any point during the test period the switch ratio reaches a predetermined value, a DTC may be set and the MIL is illuminated. If the test passes the first time, no further testing is conducted during that trip.

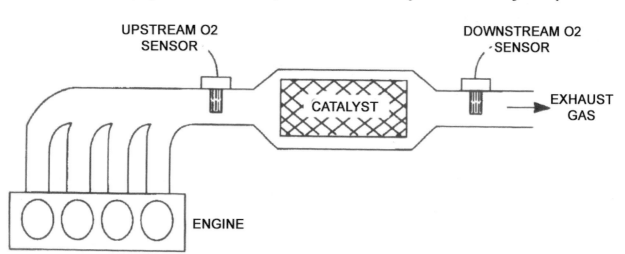

Fig. 4-13. In order to monitor catalyst operation HO$_2$S sensors are mounted before and after the converter.

There are several factors that can adversely affect the monitoring of catalyst efficiency. They are:

- Exhaust leaks. Allowing excess amounts of oxygen to enter the exhaust system can mask a faulty converter
- Fuel contaminants such as engine oil, coolant, phosphorus, lead, silica, and sulfur can interfere with the converter's chemical reaction, affecting the catalyst's oxygen storage capacity

EVAPORATIVE EMISSION CONTROLS

The evaporative (EVAP) control system prevents fuel tank vapors from entering the atmosphere. Fuel evaporation emits hydrocarbons (HC) directly into the atmosphere. As fuel evaporates in the fuel tank, vapors are routed into a charcoal canister. Through the use of a purge solenoid, manifold vacuum draws these vapors into the combustion chamber.

- OBD II regulations require that the diagnostic system:
- Verify airflow from the canister to the engine
- Monitor for HC loss to the atmosphere
- Regulations also require that "the MIL shall illuminate and a fault code shall be stored. Manufacturers may employ a second warning indicator (other than the MIL) for a leak caused by a missing or loose fuel cap"

Purge Tests

On late-model vehicles the PCM controls purging of the stored vapor with a duty cycle purge solenoid, figure 4-14.

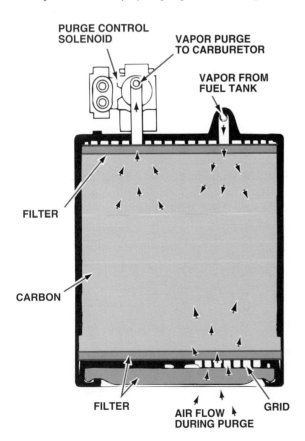

ELECTRIC PURGE VALVE CANISTER

Fig. 4-14. A PCM-controlled solenoid operates the canister purge valve on late-model applications.

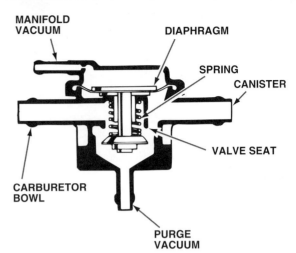

Fig. 4-15. A simple vacuum-activated canister purge valve for a carburetor equipped engine.

The PCM does not allow purge during the cold start warm-up period or during hot restart time delay. Once the vehicle enters closed-loop operation and delay times have elapsed, the PCM energizes the solenoid. The solenoid is energized approximately five to ten times per second, depending upon the throttle position, engine speed, and engine load. The PCM varies the pulse width signal to the solenoid to control the quantity of vapor drawn into the intake manifold.

When the purge is in process the resulting air-fuel ratio enrichens. The PCM monitors HO2S signals during canister purge and sets a DTC if no change is seen in the values. Use a scan tool to check for DTCs. If present, refer to the appropriate Service or Diagnostic Manual for further information about service procedures.

Older systems, those without PCM control, use a vacuum-operated purge valve to open and close the purge line, figure 4-15. The purge valve also may shut off the vapor vent line to the canister whenever the engine is running. Check valve operation with a vacuum gauge and pump.

Whether an electronic solenoid or a vacuum valve is used, a canister that does not purge properly can cause:

- Incorrect air-fuel ratio
- An increase in exhaust emissions
- Loss of fuel economy
- Driveability complaints

EVAP SYSTEM LEAK DETECTION

Inspection

Check all EVAP system hoses for damage or deterioration and replace as needed. Replacement hose must be designed for fuel system use. Securely tighten all connections.

Check that the vapor vent hose leading to the canister is properly routed and positioned. Normally, the hose is routed in a downhill position to prevent liquid gasoline from accumulating in the hose and seeping into the canister. If there is liquid in the line, the canister cannot purge properly. This also creates a potential fire hazard.

If you find liquid gasoline in the canister, follow the procedure in the Service Manual to remove and replace the canister.

Leak Detection Pump (LDP) Systems

The Leak Detection Pump must perform two primary functions:

- Pressurize the EVAP system
- Seal the charcoal canister

The LDP system, figure 4-16, contains the following components:

- Three-port solenoid that activates the two primary functions of the system
- Vacuum-driven pump that contains a reed switch, check valves, and a spring loaded diaphragm
- Canister vent valve that contains a spring loaded vent seal valve

When the outside ambient air temperature is within predetermined parameters, the leak detection portion of the monitor is run immediately after a cold start. The three-port solenoid is energized, allowing vacuum to pull the pump diaphragm up. This draws air from the atmosphere into the pump. When the solenoid is deenergized, the pump is sealed, spring pressure drives the diaphragm down, and air is pumped into the system.

Insight

In order for the monitor to run, the fuel tank must be 15%–85% full. If the tank is too empty or too full, the LDP will not run.

The solenoid and diaphragm pump cycles to pressurize the EVAP system. The spring on the diaphragm is calibrated to 7.5 inches of water. If no leaks are present, pressure equalizes and the pump cycle rate falls to zero.

Insight

If a DTC is present, check the fuel filler cap. A primary cause of an LDP failure is a loose or incorrect fuel filler cap.

Non-LDP Systems

On a vehicle without an EVAP leak detection pump system, changes in **short term memory** and movement in target IAC at idle or idle speed change are used to monitor the system. There are two steps for this test.

Step One

Step one is a non-intrusive test. The PCM compares adaptive memory values between purge and purge-free cells. The PCM

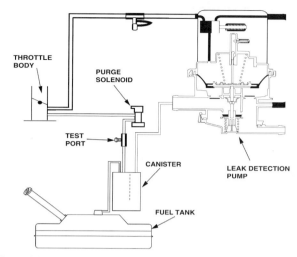

Fig. 4-16. Typical EVAP system equipped with a leak detection pump.

uses these values to determine the amount of fuel vapors entering the system. If the differences between the cells exceeds a predetermined value, the test passes. If not, then the monitor advances to stage two.

Step Two

Once the enabling conditions are met, the PCM de-energizes the canister purge solenoid. The PCM then waits until engine RPM and idle air control have stabilized. Once stable, the PCM increments the purge solenoid cycle rate approximately 6% every eight engine revolutions. If during the test any one of three conditions occur before the purge solenoid cycle reaches 100%, the EVAP system is considered to be operational and the test passes. These conditions are as follows:

- RPM rises by a predetermined amount
- Short term drops by a predetermined amount
- Idle air control closes by a predetermined amount

When neither of the previous conditions occur, the test fails and the PCM will store a DTC for the failure.

Canister Filter Replacement

A few older vehicles had provisions for servicing the filter in the canister. Late-model vehicles do not require maintenance of the charcoal canister.

A8

CHAPTER QUESTIONS

1. A defect in the PCV system can cause all of the following **EXCEPT**:
   a. Increased oil consumption
   b. Diluted or contaminated oil
   c. Unstable engine operation at idle and low speed
   d. Overheating

2. The primary purpose of an EGR system is to slow combustion and lower peak temperatures in order to reduce:
   a. Hydrocarbons
   b. Oxides of nitrogen
   c. Carbon dioxide
   d. Carbon monoxide

3. If the EGR valve leaks, expect all of the following **EXCEPT**:
   a. Rough idling
   b. Stalling
   c. Pinging and detonation
   d. Hesitation

4. The downstream HO2S is used PRIMARILY to:
   a. Verify proper operation of the catalytic converter
   b. Prevent engine surging
   c. Adjust the air-fuel ratio
   d. Control NO_x emissions

5. Air injection helps to oxidize any unburnt fuel in the exhaust to reduce:
   a. Hydrocarbons
   b. Oxides of nitrogen
   c. Carbon dioxide
   d. Carbon monoxide

6. The LDP is designed to:
   a. Transfer fuel from the tank to the injectors
   b. Stabilize engine speed under load
   c. Pressurize the EVAP system to check for leaks
   d. Control idle speed

7. On a vehicle without an EVAP leak detection pump system, the system test passes if:
   a. Fuel vapors entering the system exceed a predetermined value.
   b. RPM drops by a predetermined amount
   c. Short term raises by a predetermined amount
   d. Idle air control opens by a predetermined amount

8. A canister that does not purge properly can cause all of the following **EXCEPT**:
   a. Incorrect air-fuel ratio
   b. An increase in exhaust emissions
   c. Loss of fuel economy
   d. Increased blowby

CHAPTER FIVE

COMPUTERIZED ENGINE CONTROL DIAGNOSIS AND REPAIR (INCLUDING OBD II)

CHAPTER OBJECTIVES

- The technician will complete the ASE task list on Computerized Engine Control Diagnosis and Repair (including OBD II).
- The technician will be able to answer 13 questions dealing with the Computerized Engine Control Diagnosis and Repair (including OBD II) section of the A8 ASE Test.

Modern automotive engine management systems use a complex network of electronic components to keep the engine operating at peak efficiency with minimal emissions, while at the same time delivering an acceptable level of performance and driveability. Precise, rapid electronic communications between the system components is the key to maintaining this delicate balance.

Troubleshooting electronic engine control systems requires a familiarity with automotive electrical and electronic systems and the use of computer control systems on late-model vehicles. Following is a short review of these principles to illustrate that there are more similarities than differences among the different control systems.

The components used in an electronic control system are extremely delicate and can easily be damaged by improper handling or testing. Be aware, your body is a conductor that is capable of producing a static electrical charge that can destroy a sensor designed to operate on a low voltage signal. Wear a ground strap or discharge any static electricity by touching a ground before picking up an electronic component. Also, use only equipment designed for electronic testing. Avoid using analog test meters, which are typically designed for working with high current circuits, to troubleshoot electronic systems and components.

COMPUTER CONTROL PRINCIPLES

The operation of any computer system is divided into four basic functions: input, processing, storage, and output. A computer operates by converting input voltage signals to other voltage signals that represent combinations of numbers. The numbers represent information about quantities measured by sensors. These include temperature, speed, distance, position, pressure, and other factors of engine and vehicle operation. The computer processes the voltage signals by computing the numbers they represent and then delivering output commands to actuators that control engine and vehicle operation. Additionally, a computer stores processed information and its own operating instructions in the form of other numerical information. There are four basic functions of any computer system, figure 5-1.

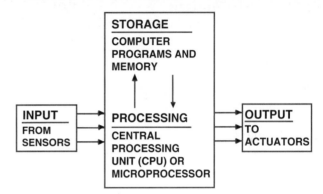

Fig. 5-1. All computers perform four basic functions: input, processing, storage, and output.

1. Input—Input information provided as voltage signals from system sensors is received by the computer, or powertrain control module (PCM).
2. Processing—The PCM processes, or computes, the input voltage signals into combinations of binary numbers (1 and 0), or bits. It then compares the processed information to instructions and other data in its program to make logical decisions and send output commands to other devices in the system.
3. Storage—Every computer has an electronic memory to store its operating instructions, or program. Some computer systems also require that some input signals be stored for later reference. Many systems can "remember" previous operating conditions and adapt their output commands to "learned" characteristics of vehicle operation. All systems have some kind of information storage capability, or memory.
4. Output—After receiving and processing input information, the computer sends output commands to other devices to control engine operation. The output devices are actuators such as solenoids and relays. The computer may also send output information to display devices such as electronic instrument panels.

COMPUTER CONTROLLED ENGINE FUNCTIONS

The output commands of an engine control system regulate most, or all, of the following operations:

- Fuel metering, fuel injection, or a carburetor
- Ignition timing advance

A8

- Idle speed
- Electric fuel pump control
- Exhaust gas recirculation (EGR)
- Secondary air injection (AIR)
- Evaporative emissions vapor (EVAP) canister purging
- Intake mixture preheating, or early fuel evaporation (EFE)
- Automatic transmission torque converter clutch (TCC) lockup, and transmission shifting
- Air conditioning (A/C) compressor clutch engagement
- Electric cooling fan operation

Self-Diagnostic Programs

Most engine control systems have a self-diagnostic program that monitors operating signals and records a diagnostic trouble code (DTC) in the event of a communicated failure. Although a DTC does not identify the exact source of a failure, it does isolate the offending circuit and can save a considerable amount of diagnostic time.

To retrieve codes from memory, the powertrain control module (PCM) must be placed in diagnostic mode. Although codes are often displayed as sequential flashes of the MIL, the most accurate method of code retrieval is with a scan tool. In addition to stored codes, a scan tool can display **data parameters or parameter identifiers (PIDs)** transmitted by the PCM on the serial data stream. What information is available to the scan tool varies by the system being tested and the tool itself. Follow procedures from the vehicle and equipment manufacturers.

System Diagnosis

The electronic control system does not monitor or control all functions of the engine. Mechanical systems and components, such as vacuum and coolant lines, wiring and connections, fuel delivery, ignition operation, and cooling system condition, must be inspected before troubleshooting the electronic control system. Also check for body damage, mechanical damage, tampering, and newly installed accessories that might compromise system operation. Conducting a thorough preliminary evaluation often reveals the cause of, or conditions that contribute to, common driveability complaints.

Prepare the Engine for Testing

To test an engine control system thoroughly, the engine should be warmed to normal operating temperature. However, some initial tests, such as troubleshooting a no-start problem, are performed on a cold engine. Other instances would include problems that only occur when the engine is cold, or operating in open-loop. In many cases, it is advantageous to check engine operation immediately after a cold start, then watch the data readings as the engine warms and goes into closed-loop.

Many driveability complaints and system trouble codes relate to warm, closed-loop operation. One basic test of any engine control system is to verify that it goes into closed-loop operation. As a minimum, the engine should be run for two to three minutes above 2000 RPM. This allows the oxygen sensor, catalytic converter, and coolant temperature to come up to operating range and permits the system to enter closed-loop. Even when warm, many systems require several minutes of engine

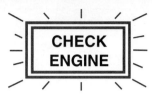

Fig. 5-2. The MIL, which lights or flashes when a DTC sets, should come on as a bulb check when the ignition is switched on.

operation to let the open-loop timer in the PCM expire and before they will enter closed-loop. To warm the engine completely, you may have to run it for 10 to 15 minutes or drive the vehicle for several miles.

Check MIL Function

All OBD II vehicles are required to have a malfunction indicator lamp (MIL) on the instrument panel that lights to indicate major system problems. The lamp may be labeled:

- ENGINE
- CHECK ENGINE
- SERVICE ENGINE SOON
- Some other term that indicates a system problem

Any MIL should illuminate when the ignition key is turned on without starting the engine, figure 5-2. This is a basic bulb check similar to the bulb check for generator or brake system warning lamps.

If the MIL does not light with the key on, the PCM probably will not go into the diagnostic mode. The problem may be as simple as a burned out bulb, it may be a faulty circuit, or it could be an internal PCM fault. Refer to the appropriate Service or Diagnostic Manual for complete test procedures.

If the MIL lights steadily with the engine running, it indicates that a system problem exists and a DTC has been recorded. Not all system faults light the MIL. With some faults, the MIL may flash briefly when the code is recorded, then go out.

A flashing MIL while driving an OBD II vehicle indicates a serious misfire condition which will damage the catalytic converter. Vehicles exhibiting this symptom should not be driven. Converter overheating may occur.

Other problems may set a trouble code in memory but not light the MIL at all. Code setting conditions vary by manufacturer, year, and model. Accurate service information for the vehicle being tested is required for troubleshooting.

Diagnostic Trouble Codes

DTCs identify faults in ECM system sensors and circuits or indicate individual system conditions. An OBD II DTC is a five-character, alphanumeric fault identifier, figure 5-3. Since a letter is included in every DTC, the only way to retrieve codes is with a scan tool.

The first character of an OBD II DTC is a letter. Refer to figure 5-3 for an explanation of other letter codes.

The second character is a number that indicates if the code is common to all OBD II vehicles (0) or specific to one vehicle manufacturer (1). Remember, only emissions related, P0 codes will activate the MIL.

The third character is a number used by all manufacturers to identify which system has a fault. This designation will

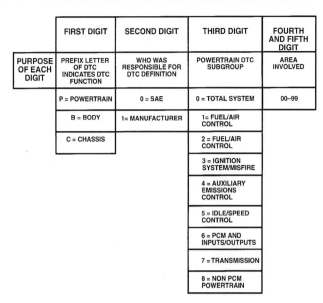

PURPOSE OF EACH DIGIT	FIRST DIGIT	SECOND DIGIT	THIRD DIGIT	FOURTH AND FIFTH DIGIT
	PREFIX LETTER OF DTC INDICATES DTC FUNCTION	WHO WAS RESPONSIBLE FOR DTC DEFINITION	POWERTRAIN DTC SUBGROUP	AREA INVOLVED
	P = POWERTRAIN	0 = SAE	0 = TOTAL SYSTEM	00–99
	B = BODY	1= MANUFACTURER	1= FUEL/AIR CONTROL	
	C = CHASSIS		2 = FUEL/AIR CONTROL	
			3 = IGNITION SYSTEM/MISFIRE	
			4 = AUXILIARY EMISSIONS CONTROL	
			5 = IDLE/SPEED CONTROL	
			6 = PCM AND INPUTS/OUTPUTS	
			7 = TRANSMISSION	
			8 = NON PCM POWERTRAIN	

Fig. 5-3. OBD II DTC code components.

be the same for P0 (OBD II) or P1 (manufacturer's) codes. Following is the established numbering system:

- 1 - Air/Fuel metering system input faults
- 2 - Air/Fuel metering output faults
- 3 - Ignition system or misfire faults
- 4 - Auxiliary emission controls
- 5 - Vehicle speed control and idle control system
- 6 - Computer output circuit faults
- 7 - Transmission
- 8 - Transmission

The fourth and fifth characters indicate the actual problem associated with the code, (e.g., signal voltage low, system always lean, etc.)

The intent of OBD II code designation is to help the technician identify the system at fault, then pinpoint the actual problem or specific circuit causing the fault.

Once a problem is identified by code, the technician must use appropriate Service Manuals to complete the diagnosis and repair.

Diagnostic Strategy

The most valuable aspect of diagnosis with a scan tool is the ability to compare data from many sensors and actuators. However, scan tool data should not be used alone. Vehicle symptoms, driving conditions, and an understanding of operational principles are also important diagnostic tools.

Today's vehicles require today's technicians to be aware of the ways traditional technology blends with newer, more complex system-based technologies. Vehicles manufactured before the 1970s controlled fuel and ignition timing through vacuum and mechanical weights and springs. Exhaust emissions were not seriously considered until the early 1970s. Modern vehicles use computerized controls to control fuel and ignition timing precisely. The tradeoff, however, for this technological advancement is that today's drivetrain problems can result in repeated and multiple component failures that require a system-based approach. For example, a late-model vehicle has

the following symptoms: hard starting when cold, an engine miss, and a failed emission test. The initial diagnosis finds a fouled spark plug. Replacing the spark plug and retesting emissions results in a passing report and a smoothly running engine. While this approach addresses the immediate symptom, it does not deal with the underlying cause of the fouled spark plug.

The Result?

The customer returns the next day with the same symptoms. Only then does the technician examine further to determine that a faulty injector is leaking when the engine is turned off. This leak floods a cylinder. The flooded cylinder causes its associated spark plug to fail. This would also drain the fuel rail, causing extended cranking on a cold start.

This example clearly illustrates that a systems-based approach to the diagnostic process is vital to help eliminate multiple and repeated component failures that result in dissatisfied customers.

When approaching any diagnostic problem, take the time to define vehicle symptoms. How is the vehicle running? Does it have rich symptoms like poor gas mileage or a failed emissions test? Does it surge or idle rough? Is it hard to start? Next, do a thorough inspection for obvious problems such as vacuum leaks and damaged electrical connections. Don't forget to consider the basics such as low fuel pressure, incorrect ignition timing, low or uneven engine compression, and fuel quality. If possible, a review of recent vehicle service may yield valuable diagnostic clues. For recent vehicle service information, check dealership resources and communicate with the vehicle owner.

Connect the scan tool and retrieve stored DTCs and freeze frame data. Record your findings, then check the Service Manual to learn the specific conditions that cause the DTC. Take the time to thoroughly understand what caused the DTC.

Check the readiness status of system monitors. If the readiness status is "NO" for all monitors, review recent service history; the battery may have been changed or the vehicle may have been in another shop where DTCs were erased. The vehicle must be driven through the complete drive cycle to ensure all monitors run. If readiness status is "NO" for only one or two sensors, check sensors, actuators, and related circuitry for problems that would prevent the monitor from running. Again, the vehicle may have to complete an entire drive cycle to provide the time and conditions to run the remaining monitors.

When there is more than one DTC in memory, diagnose and correct component-related DTCs before diagnosing system failure DTCs. A sensor or actuator problem may prevent a monitor from running or cause a system to fail the monitor. Once a component failure is repaired, drive the vehicle through the specified drive cycle to be sure the system is fully repaired. For example, when discovering a code P0125, "excessive time to enter closed loop," and a code P0155, "HO2S/1, Bank 2 Heater Malfunction," the best procedure is to diagnose and repair the HO2S/1 heater malfunction first, even though its DTC is a higher number.

Next, clear codes and drive the vehicle as directed in the Service Manual. In this example, it is probable that the failed oxygen sensor heater caused the system to be slow entering

A8

closed loop. Misfire and fuel control DTCs are considered priority codes and should always be diagnosed first.

When using the drive cycle to confirm repairs, review freeze frame data for the driving conditions present at the time the DTC was recorded. It is especially important when confirming misfire and fuel control repairs to closely match the engine rpm, calculated load, and engine temperature values recorded in the freeze frame.

How close is close? Before the PCM will deactivate the MIL for misfire and fuel control codes, engine speed must be within 375 rpm of the engine speed when the code was set, and the calculated load value must be within ±10% of the load present when the code was set. Be aware that some manufacturers may direct you to drive a portion of the drive cycle to confirm a particular repair. Drive cycles vary between manufacturers and must always be followed exactly. Freeze frame and scan tool data must be analyzed with care. Use service manuals to learn the normal parameters for each sensor and actuator. Review freeze frame data to identify all sensors and actuators that are out of range. Many times a sensor will be out of range and not set a DTC, especially when the out-of-range sensor is responding to an unusual condition. Try to determine if the suspect sensor is reporting an unusual vehicle condition or sending a signal that doesn't match the actual symptoms or other sensor data. When you have gathered all necessary information—vehicle symptoms, driving conditions, DTCs, and sensor/actuator data—use your knowledge and experience to pick out the most probable cause of the symptom. Always refer to appropriate service manuals for proper test procedures when testing sensors, actuators, and related circuits.

Once all of the preliminary checks have been made, check for codes stored in memory. To access PCM memory, the system must be placed in diagnostic mode. Procedures for entering diagnostics vary by manufacturer and system. Most systems display codes as a series of flashes on the MIL, or on the display screen of a scan tool. The following paragraphs outline the common features and principles of trouble code diagnosis.

When the PCM recognizes a signal or condition that is absent or out of range, a DTC is stored in memory. A DTC can indicate a problem in a particular circuit or subsystem, but does not pinpoint the exact cause of the problem. Checking codes can direct you to where to start your troubleshooting. In general, trouble codes fall into one of two categories: those that indicate a fault that exists at the time of testing, and those that indicate a fault that occurred in the past but is no longer present. Although manufacturers use different terminology to describe the types of codes, common usage refers to codes for faults present during testing as "hard" codes, and codes for faults not present during testing as **intermittent or "soft" codes**. This book will use the term "intermittent" for all codes of that type. As a rule, OBD II vehicles store all codes relating to emission system components as hard codes or faults. The PCM stores information as to the number of starts or warm-up cycles since the code was set.

Code Formats

Pre-OBD II vehicles generated DTCs based on two or three digits. Each code indicated a particular component or circuit that was at fault. These codes are not necessarily specific to the exact nature of the problem and can lead to extensive diagnosis to resolve the problem. OBD II DTCs are composed of a five digit alphanumeric sequence, figure 5-3. The OBD II DTC is much more definitive as to the area of the problem and the circumstance under which it was set into memory.

Hard Codes

A **hard code** indicates a failure that is present at the time of testing and remains permanently in the system until the cause has been repaired. If the PCM memory is erased, a hard code will reappear immediately or within a few minutes after start up because the problem that set the code still exists in the system. Hard codes indicate a full-time problem that requires immediate attention. These are top priority problems, and must be repaired first, before any other code repairs are made. Hard codes are generally easy to diagnose because the conditions that caused the code to set are present at the time of testing.

A hard code enables you to go right to a certain area, or areas, and begin pinpoint testing to isolate the defective component. Most diagnostic charts are designed to troubleshoot hard codes, figure 5-4. The procedures assume that the problem is present at the time of testing.

Intermittent Codes

The term intermittent code indicates an intermittent problem: one that comes and goes. The PCM records most intermittent codes when they occur, then maintains a record of the fault in memory. An intermittent code represents a problem that occurred sometime in the past, before testing, but is not present now. The problem, and the DTC, may not reappear if PCM memory is cleared and the system retested. The conditions to set the code may happen only at a certain speed, temperature, or other condition that cannot be recreated in the shop.

Because intermittent codes indicate sporadic problems, diagnostic charts usually do not isolate the problem immediately. Generally, special intermittent, or symptom diagnostic, test procedures must be followed to troubleshoot intermittent codes accurately. Do not open or disconnect electrical connectors when intermittent codes are present. This may temporarily solve a problem without revealing the basic cause.

Checking codes at this point is a preliminary step; it does not provide a definitive answer as to the source of the problem. Write down any codes in memory now for future reference. Then start and run the engine, if possible, to verify that the system is operational and the PCM is controlling engine functions.

Separating Hard and Intermittent Codes

When diagnosing pre-OBD II vehicles first determine whether codes are hard or intermittent. Some systems specify the type of code on the scan tool display, but most do not. To distinguish between a hard and an intermittent code, record all codes, and then clear the PCM memory. Codes can be cleared from all OBD II and most late-model vehicles using a scan tool.

On pre-OBD II vehicles codes can be cleared by momentarily disconnecting the battery or removing the fuse for the PCM power circuit. OBD II systems store the DTCs in a

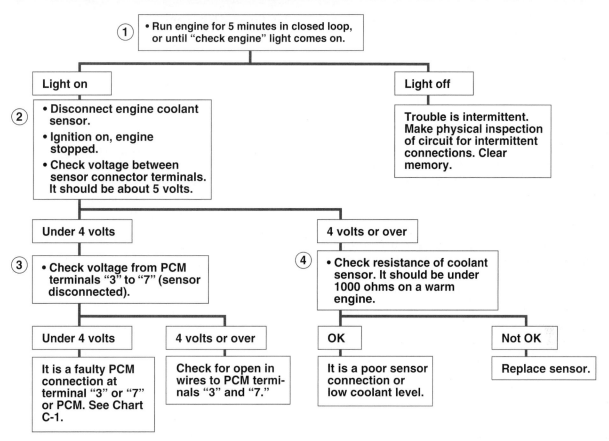

Fig. 5-4. Diagnostic charts, such as this one for an open engine coolant temperature (ECT) circuit, are designed for troubleshooting a hard code failure.

memory known as **EEPROM** and will not erase when power is removed. In either case, refer to the Service or Diagnostic Manual for the correct procedure.

After clearing the codes, drive the vehicle and watch for the MIL to light, an indication that the code has reset. If a code reappears immediately or soon, a hard fault is indicated. If the code does not reappear quickly, it was most likely an intermittent code. To diagnose any DTC, go to the test or troubleshooting chart for that particular code.

Pre-OBD II vehicles' trouble codes should be diagnosed and serviced in a basic order: hard codes first, followed by intermittent codes. Most of those vehicles transmit codes in numerical order from the lowest to the highest, and this is usually the order in which they should be serviced. Exceptions would be codes that indicate communications and internal PCM problems. These are priority situations that should be serviced first, before any other codes.

OBD II vehicles generate codes based on a much more complex basis. Start your diagnosis of multiple code situations by diagnosing the first code in memory. If other DTCs should be serviced first, the Service or Diagnostic Manual will direct you to do so.

OBD II System Operation

Comprehensive Component Monitor
The OBD II diagnostic system continuously monitors all engine and transmission sensors and actuators for shorts, opens,

and out-of-range values, as well as values that do not logically fit with other powertrain data (rationality). On the first trip during which the comprehensive component monitor detects a failure that will result in emissions exceeding a predetermined level, the ECM will store a DTC, illuminate the MIL, and store a freeze frame.

System Monitors
The OBD II diagnostic system also actively tests some systems for proper operation. While the vehicle is being driven fuel control and engine misfire are checked continuously. Oxygen sensor response, oxygen sensor heater operation, catalyst efficiency, EGR operation, EVAP integrity, variable valve timing, and thermostat operation are tested once or more per trip. When any of the System Monitors detects a failure that will result in emissions exceeding a predetermined level on two consecutive trips, the ECM will store a diagnostic trouble code (DTC) and illuminate the malfunction indicator lamp (MIL). Freeze frame data captured during the first of the two consecutive failures is also stored.

FUEL CONTROL—For many vehicles the monitor will set a DTC if the system fails to enter Closed Loop mode within a few minutes of startup, or the Long Term Fuel Trim is excessively high or low anytime after the engine is warmed up, indicating the loss of fuel control. This is always the case when the Long Term Fuel Trim reaches its limits.

ENGINE MISFIRE—For many vehicles, the monitor uses the CKP sensor signal to continuously detect engine misfires,

A8

both severe and non-severe. If the misfire is severe enough to cause catalytic converter damage, the MIL will blink as long the severe misfire is detected.

CATALYTIC CONVERTER—For many vehicles the monitor compares the signals of the upstream heated oxygen sensors to the signal from the downstream heated oxygen to determine the ability of the catalyst to store free oxygen. If the converter's oxygen storage capacity is sufficiently degraded, a DTC is set.

EGR SYSTEM—For many vehicles the monitor uses the MAP sensor signal to detect changes in intake manifold pressure as the EGR valve is commanded to open and close. If the pressure changes too little or too much, a DTC is set.

EVAP SYSTEM—For many vehicles the monitor first turns on the EVAP vent solenoid to block the fresh air supply to the EVAP canister. Next, the EVAP purge solenoid is turned on to draw a slight vacuum on the entire EVAP system, including the fuel tank. Then the EVAP purge solenoid is turned off to seal the system. The monitor uses the fuel tank (EVAP) pressure sensor signal to determine if the EVAP system has any leaks. If the vacuum decays too rapidly, a DTC is set. In order to run this monitor, the engine must be cold and the fuel level must be between ¼ and ¾ full.

VARIABLE VALVE TIMING—For many vehicles the monitor compares the desired valve timing with the actual timing indicated by the CMP sensors. If the timing is in error, or takes too long to reach the desired value, a DTC is set.

ENGINE THERMOSTAT—This monitor confirms that the engine warms up fully within a reasonable amount of time. If the coolant temperature remains too low for too long, a DTC is set.

OXYGEN SENSORS—This monitor checks the maximum and minimum output voltage, as well as switching and response times for all oxygen sensors. If an oxygen sensor signal remains too low or too high, or switches too slowly or not at all, a DTC is set.

OXYGEN SENSOR HEATERS—This monitor checks the time from cold start until the oxygen sensors begin to operate. If the time is too long, a DTC is set. Battery voltage is continuously supplied to the oxygen sensor heaters whenever the ignition switch is on.

Comprehensive Component Monitors

Comprehensive component monitors are most like the OBD I monitoring system that watches engine and transmission sensor inputs and actuator outputs for shorts, opens, and out-of-range values. OBD II computer (ECM) programs are enhanced to include identification of sensor values that don't logically fit with other powertrain data. For instance, if the Throttle Position Sensor (TPS) is reporting wide-open, but other sensors are reporting idle speed values, the ECM will set a DTC for the TPS.

Remember, comprehensive component monitors are one trip monitors. The ECM will activate the MIL and store DTC and freeze frame data the first time an emissions related fault is detected. If a misfire or fuel control problem is detected after the original DTC was recorded, freeze frame date for the misfire or fuel control code will replace the original data.

Readiness Status and System Monitors

You will recall that the monitor readiness status tells the technician if a particular diagnostic monitor (test) has been completed since the last time DTCs were cleared from memory. There are two important concepts to understand when viewing monitor readiness status: First, the vehicle must be driven under specific conditions for some monitors to run, and second, the emissions system being monitored must be operational. If battery power is disconnected and the vehicle isn't driven through an entire drive cycle, the readiness status will be "NO." If there is an electrical problem or component failure in a monitored system, the monitor will not run. A DTC may be recorded that points to the electrical or component failure, but the system cannot be tested by the monitor, so the readiness status will be "NO." A readiness status of "NO" for any of the five monitored systems, catalyst, EGR, EVAP, Oxygen sensors, and Oxygen sensor heaters, does not mean a failed monitor, only that the monitor has not been completed. At the same time, a "YES" status does not mean the system passed the monitor, only that the test was completed. In both cases, you must check for codes to investigate further.

Fuel Control Monitor

The fuel control monitor is designed to constantly check the ability of the ECM to control the air/fuel ratio. For many vehicles the ECM program that fine tunes the air/fuel ratio is called Fuel Trim. It is divided into a short term program and a long term program. Both trim programs are presented as diagnostic data when a freeze frame is recorded. Separate short term and long term data are displayed for cylinder bank 1 and cylinder bank 2.

The oxygen sensor (HO2S) drives the fuel trim program anytime the vehicle is in closed loop. The starting point for fuel trim is 0% correction, figure 5-5. When the ECM sees a lean (low voltage) signal from an upstream HO2S, the fuel trim program adds fuel to compensate for the detected leanness. The short term fuel trim display on the scan tool will move to the positive (+) side of 0% to indicate more fuel is being added. When the ECM sees a rich (high voltage) signal from the HO2S, the fuel trim program subtracts fuel to lean the mixture. The scan tool will display a percentage on the negative (-) side of 0%. If short term fuel trim is necessary in one direction (rich or lean correction) for a period of time, the ECM will command a correction of long term fuel trim. When A/F control is out of acceptable range for too long a time, a DTC will set. Long term fuel trim represents correction to fuel delivery over time. If the oxygen sensor voltage is fluctuating, but is mainly below 450 mV, indicating a lean A/F ratio, long

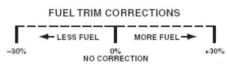

Fig. 5-5. Fuel trim corrections may be displayed on the scan tool as percentage of correction.

term fuel trim will increase and the ECM will command longer injector pulse width. If oxygen sensor voltage is fluctuating, but remains mostly above 450 mV, indicating a rich mixture, long term fuel trim will decrease and the ECM will command shorter injection pulse width to adjust fuel delivery.

Short term fuel trim is useful when confirming fuel control. Observe short term fuel trim on the scan tool while adding propane through the intake system. The additional fuel will cause a rich mixture. If the fuel system is in closed loop, short term fuel trim will move in a negative direction as the fuel trim program shortens fuel injector pulse width in response to a higher HO2S voltage signal. Driving the system lean by pulling a vacuum line will cause short term fuel trim to increase injector pulse width. The scan tool display will move in a positive direction.

During diagnosis, be sure to look at both short and long term fuel trim. A problem that has existed for some time will cause long term fuel trim to record high or low. Once the problem is repaired, long term fuel trim will not change for a while, but short term fuel trim will begin immediately to move in the opposite direction. A restricted fuel filter for instance will cause a lean mixture. Long term fuel trim will eventually show a positive percentage (more fuel) as the system compensates for the lean mixture. Once the fuel filter is replaced, the A/F ratio is suddenly too rich. Comparing short and long term fuel trim immediately after the filter is replaced will reveal opposite readings: a negative percentage reading in short term fuel trim because the ECM is attempting to return the A/F ratio to normal by subtracting fuel, and a positive percentage reading in long term fuel trim because the long term program still "remembers" the lean correction and is waiting to see what happens.

Misfire Monitor

Engine misfire monitoring uses the CKP signal as the primary sensor. When a misfire occurs, whether due to engine compression, ignition, or fuel, crankshaft speed is affected. The ECM is programmed to notice the intermittent change in CKP pulses, figure 5-6.

Camshaft position is used to identify which cylinder misfired. Because outside factors such as electrical interference and rough roads can mimic a misfire, most ECM programs keep track of how many times a cylinder misfires in a given number of engine rotations. The ECM activates the MIL when misfire reaches a predetermined percentage of rpm.

Remember, misfire monitoring, like fuel trim monitoring, is a two trip monitor. The MIL will glow steadily once a misfire

is detected. If misfiring becomes severe enough to damage the catalytic converter, the MIL will blink continuously until the misfire becomes less severe.

Catalytic Converter Monitor

As mentioned earlier, the catalytic converter monitor checks converter efficiency by comparing upstream HO2S signals with the downstream HO2S signal. In normal operation the upstream HO2S signals will switch frequently between 200 mV and 900 mV and the downstream HO2S signal will show very little fluctuation and a voltage that tends to stay above the 450 mV threshold, figure 5-7. As catalyst performance begins to degrade, less oxygen is used in the converter and so less ends up in the exhaust, causing voltage fluctuations and a lower voltage bias, figure 5-8. When the downstream HO2S voltage signal begins to fluctuate within about 70% of the upstream HO2S signal on two consecutive trips, the ECM will record freeze frame data, set a DTC, and actuate the MIL.

EVAP Monitor

A vehicle will fail the EVAP monitor if the ECM, using information from the fuel tank pressure sensor, sees vacuum decrease too quickly after the EVAP vent and EVAP purge solenoids have been closed. Keep in mind that simple problems like a loose, damaged, or missing gas cap will cause this code to set. Be careful when making quick repairs. For example, after replacing a damaged gas cap on a vehicle brought in for a lit MIL, you may be tempted to clear the DTC and return the car to the customer after a short road test. However, the EVAP monitor won't run if the engine is warm (above 86°F) or if the fuel level is not between ¼ and ¾ full. If the EVAP system has other problems and the EVAP monitor doesn't run during the

CATALYST MONITOR EFFICIENCY TEST

PRE-CATALYST HO2S1

POST-CATALYST HO2S2

GOOD CATALYST

MONITOR TEST PASSED

Fig. 5-7. When the catalyst is working efficiently most oxygen is used for oxidation and reduction, so post-converter voltage fluctuations are minimal.

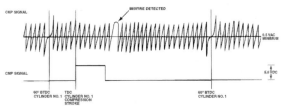

Fig. 5-6. The ECM is programmed to notice the sudden change in CKP sensor pulses.

CATALYST MONITOR EFFICIENCY TEST

PRE-CATALYST HO2S1

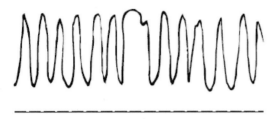

POST-CATALYST HO2S2

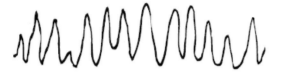

DEGRADED CATALYST

MONITOR TEST FAILED

Fig. 5-8. As catalyst performance becomes less efficient, less oxygen is used and voltage fluctuations from the post-converter begin to increase.

road test, the MIL will come on after you return the vehicle to the customer.

Some technicians use a sensor simulator to simulate a cold start so the monitor will run. A scan tool can be used to check EVAP system integrity, even with a full tank of gas. First, idle the engine. Then, using a scan tool, close the EVAP vent solenoid and open the EVAP purge solenoid. Intake manifold vacuum will draw a vacuum into the EVAP system.

Now close the EVAP purge solenoid to trap vacuum in the system. Observe the fuel tank pressure sensor reading on the scan tool. If the system is leaking, voltage will climb as pressure increases. As always, test and repair procedures must be followed exactly. Some test procedures, the IM 240 for example, specify testing EVAP system integrity with pressure instead of vacuum.

Freeze Frame Data

A freeze frame is a miniature "snapshot" (one frame of data) that is automatically stored in the ECM/TCM memory when an emissions-related DTC is first stored. If a DTC for fuel control or engine misfire is stored at a later time, the newest data are stored and the earlier data are lost. All parameter ID (PID) values listed under "Scan Tool Data" are stored in freeze frame data. The ECM/TCM stores only one single freeze frame record.

Scan Tool Data

Figure 5-9 shows the different types of information that can be displayed on the OBD II scan tool.

Checking Open-Loop and Closed-Loop Operation

Electronic engine control systems have two basic operating modes: open-loop and closed-loop. In open-loop, the PCM ignores the heated oxygen sensor (HO2S) and controls fuel metering based on engine speed, load, and temperature signals and its own program. In closed-loop, the PCM responds to the rich and lean signals of the HO2S as well as signals from other sensors. The PCM then controls fuel delivery to maintain the air-fuel ratio in relation to overall engine requirements. In most conditions, except high-power operation, the ratio is 14.7:1.

A cold engine starts in open-loop and goes to closed-loop as soon as the HO2S is warm enough to send an accurate

ECT: 248 to –40 °F / 120 to –40°C / 0 to 5.0 volts	EGR: 0 to 100%
IAT: 248 to –40 °F / 120 to –40°C / 0 to 5.0 volts	Evap Purge: 0 to 100%
MAP: 20 to 101 kPa pressure / 24 to 0 in. Hg. vacuum / 0 to 5.0 volts	Evap Vent: On / Off
	Fuel Tank (EVAP) Pressure: –14.0 to +14.0 in. H₂O / –0.5 psi to +0.5 psi / 0 to 5.0 volts
MAF: 0 to 175 gm/sec / 0 to 5.0 volts	
TP: 0 to 100%	Fuel Tank Level: 0 to 100% / 0 to 5.0 volts
Tach: 0 to 6000 rpm	P/S Switch: On / Off
VSS: 0 to 110 mph	Brake Switch: On / Off
Calculated Load Value: 0 to 100%	AC Request: On / Off
HO2S 1/1: 0 to 1.0 volts	AC Pressure: 25 to 450 psi / 0 to 5.0 volts
HO2S 2/1: 0 to 1.0 volts	AC Clutch: On / Off
HO2S 1/2: 0 to 1.0 volts	Fan Control: On / Off
Loop: Open / Closed	Fuel Pump: On / Off
Bank 1 Injector Pulse Width: 0 to 15 milliseconds (ms)	TR: P/N, R, 1, 2, 3, OD
Bank 2 Injector Pulse Width: 0 to 15 milliseconds (ms)	TFT: 248 to –40°F / 120 to –40°C / 0 to 5.0 volts
Bank 1 Long Term Fuel Trim: –30% to +30%	TSS: 0 to 6000 rpm
Bank 1 Short Term Fuel Trim: –30% to +30%	SS1: On / Off
Bank 2 Long Term Fuel Trim: –30% to +30%	SS2: On / Off
Bank 2 Short Term Fuel Trim: –30% to +30%	TCC: 0 to 100%
Timing Advance: 0 to 60° BTDC	PC: 0 to 100%
IAC: 0 to 100%	MIL: On / Off / Flashing
Battery: 0 to 18 volts	DTCs: P0###
Generator Field: 0 to 100%	Misfire Cylinder #: 1, 2, 3, 4, 5, 6

Fig. 5-9. The above data can be accessed by the technician using the OBD II scan tool and the Data Link Connector (DLC).

voltage signal to the PCM. Some systems also have a timer circuit that keeps the engine in open-loop for several minutes after any start-up regardless of HO2S and engine temperatures. In addition, some systems return to open-loop at idle and during full-throttle acceleration. For accurate diagnosis, it is important to know the open-loop and closed-loop characteristics of the particular engine being serviced. Along with checking trouble codes, verifying open-loop and closed-loop operation is a primary point in diagnosing most driveability problems.

Use a scan tool to determine if an engine is operating in open-loop or closed-loop. Most systems transmit a digital parameter that displays what strategy the PCM is operating in. When a loop control parameter is not available, simply monitor HO2S feedback signal voltage. If HO2S voltage fluctuates rapidly above and below the midpoint of its operating range (generally, 450 millivolts), it is sending a reliable feedback signal and the system should be in closed-loop. If HO2S voltage does not move from the midpoint, the PCM considers the signal unreliable and maintains open-loop control.

Driveability Symptom Tests

Many engine control system problems produce clear and recognizable driveability symptoms but will not set a code.

Typical driver complaints or symptoms include:

- Rough or high idle
- Surging or hesitation
- Stalls at idle or during deceleration
- Pinging, or detonation
- Poor fuel mileage

Test procedures or troubleshooting charts for these and other common symptoms are usually available in the factory Service Manuals. However, in order to use these tests, the symptom must occur or be present at the time of testing. Symptomatic tests are not designed for use on intermittent problems.

When using a symptomatic test, be sure to follow the one for the specific vehicle year, model, and engine. The tests are often different for cold and for warm engines.

Computer Controlled Timing Service

As discussed in Chapter Two, many late-model vehicles utilize the PCM to monitor and control the ignition timing. Timing adjustments are made based on several factors:

- Engine coolant temperature
- Intake air temperature
- Engine load
- Throttle position
- PCM operating strategies
- Knock sensor input

When one or more of these inputs is out of range the PCM may not be able to accurately control the timing. When the PCM determines an input is invalid it will substitute a value in an attempt to get the best possible performance and emission output from the engine. Some of the driveability symptoms include:

- Poor fuel economy
- Emissions failure
- Detonation or pinging on acceleration
- Hard starting

Inches of Mercury Absolute	Inches of Mercury Vacuum	MAP Sensor Signal Voltage (volts)
31.00	0.5 psi	4.80
29.92	0.00	4.60
27.00	2.92	4.10
25.00	4.92	3.80
23.00	6.92	3.45
20.00	9.92	2.92
15.00	14.92	2.09
10.00	19.92	1.24
5.00	24.92	0.24

Fig. 5-10. Sample MAP sensor voltage chart.

As with any computer-controlled system, use a scan tool to check for DTCs before attempting any repair.

Operating Range Tests

The analog signal from a sensor can drift out of range as the sensor ages or wears. Some sensors can develop an erratic signal, or dropout, at one point in the signal range. A loose or corroded ground connection for a sensor can also force the signal out of range, but not far enough to set a code.

These and similar problems can cause driveability problems without setting a code. The operation of many sensors can be checked using the operating range charts provided by the manufacturer. These charts list signal range specifications for voltage, resistance, frequency, or temperature that the sensor provides under varying conditions, figure 5-10.

Use a DMM or scope to test the sensor signal. Take initial readings at the sensor connector, then, if necessary, at the main connector to the PCM. If possible, operate the sensor through its full range and check the signal at several points.

Road Test and Record Data

If the vehicle transmits computer data in a road test or normal operating condition, drive it and try to duplicate the problem. A quality scan tool can electronically record the data stream when the problem occurs while driving. Analyzing the recorded data can help locate the faulty circuit or component. Look for unusual circuit activity, such as high or low signals, voltage dropout, and lack of switching. When a problem is indicated on one circuit, be sure to check for unusual activity on all of the related circuits.

Diagnosis of Emissions and Driveability Problems

No Start Diagnosis

To run, an engine requires four things: air, fuel, compression, and ignition, all at the right time. Perform the following tests to find what the problem is:

- Observe the engine's cranking speed; if it is too slow check the battery and starting system.
- Check fuel pressure and volume
- Verify the electrical signal to the injector with a 12V test light, depending on the OEM's recommendation
- Use a properly gapped spark tester to check for spark
- Check compression by performing a cranking vacuum or compression test

A8

- Check the ignition timing
- Verify camshaft drive integrity and valve timing

Hard Start Diagnosis

A variety of sensor or physical conditions may result in a hard start condition without setting a diagnostic trouble code (DTC). In order to determine if any of these conditions exist, perform the following actions:

- Inspect for an engine coolant temperature (ECT) sensor that has shifted in value.
- Inspect the mass air flow (MAF) sensor for proper installation.
- Inspect the camshaft position (CMP) sensor for proper mounting and/or a bad connection. An extended crank occurs if the engine control module (ECM) does not receive a CMP signal.
- Verify proper operation of the manifold absolute pressure (MAP) sensor.
- Inspect the exhaust gas recirculation (EGR) system for proper sealing/connections and operation.

Engine Misfire Diagnosis

- Inspect the engine control module (ECM) grounds for being clean, tight, and in the proper locations.
- Inspect the heated oxygen sensors (HO2S). The HO2S should respond quickly to different throttle positions. If they do not, inspect the HO2S for silicon or other contaminants from fuel or the use of improper RTV sealant. The sensors may have a white, powdery coating and result in a high but false signal voltage rich exhaust indication. The ECM will then reduce the amount of fuel delivered to the engine, causing a severe driveability problem.
- Inspect the air intake ducts for being collapsed, damaged, loose, improperly installed, or leaking, especially between the mass air flow (MAF) sensor and the throttle body.
- Test the exhaust gas recirculation (EGR) system for proper operation.
- Inspect for proper operation of the manifold absolute pressure (MAP) sensor.
- Inspect for an engine coolant temperature (ECT) sensor that has shifted in value.
- Inspect the MAF sensor and intake air system for proper operation.

Engine Hesitation Diagnosis

Momentary lack of response as the accelerator is pushed down. Can occur at any vehicle speed. Usually more pronounced when first trying to make the vehicle move, as from a stop. May cause the engine to stall if severe enough.

- Inspect the engine control module (ECM) grounds for being clean, tight, and in the proper locations.
- Inspect the heated oxygen sensors (HO2S). The HO2S should respond quickly to different throttle positions. If they do not, inspect the HO2S for silicon or other contaminants from fuel or the use of improper RTV sealant. The sensors may have a white, powdery coating and result in a high but false signal voltage rich exhaust indication.

The PCM will then reduce the amount of fuel delivered to the engine, causing a severe driveability problem.

- Inspect the air intake ducts for being collapsed, damaged, loose, improperly installed, or leaking, especially between the mass air flow (MAF) sensor and the throttle body.
- Test the exhaust gas recirculation (EGR) system for proper operation.
- Inspect for proper operation of the manifold absolute pressure (MAP) sensor.
- Inspect for an engine coolant temperature (ECT) sensor that has shifted in value.
- Inspect the MAF sensor and intake air system for proper operation.

Poor Fuel Economy Diagnosis

Fuel economy, as measured by an actual road test, is noticeably lower than expected. Also, fuel economy is noticeably lower than the economy was on this vehicle at one time, as previously shown by an actual road test.

- Inspect the engine control module (ECM) grounds for being clean, tight, and in the proper locations.
- Discuss driving habits with the owner.
- Is the A/C ON or the Defroster mode ON full time?
- Are the tires at the correct pressure?
- Are the wheels and tires the correct size?
- Are there excessively heavy loads being carried?
- Is the acceleration rate too much, too often?
- Remove the air filter element and inspect for dirt or for restrictions.
- Inspect the air intake system and crankcase for air leaks.
- Inspect the crankcase ventilation valve for proper operation.
- Inspect for an inaccurate speedometer.

Engine Surges Diagnosis

Engine power variation under steady throttle or cruise. Feels like the vehicle speeds up and slows down with no change in the accelerator pedal position.

- Inspect the engine control module (ECM) grounds for being clean, tight, and in the proper locations.
- Inspect the heated oxygen sensors (HO2S). The HO2S should respond quickly to different throttle positions. If it does not, inspect the HO2S for silicon or other contaminants from fuel or the use of improper RTV sealant. The sensors may have a white, powdery coating and result in a high but false signal voltage rich exhaust indication. The ECM will then reduce the amount of fuel delivered to the engine, causing a severe driveability problem.
- Inspect the mass air flow (MAF) sensor for any contamination on the sensing element.
- Inspect the air intake ducts for being collapsed, damaged, loose, improperly installed, or leaking, especially between the MAF sensor and the throttle body.
- Test the exhaust gas recirculation (EGR) system for proper operation.
- Inspect for proper operation of the manifold absolute pressure (MAP) sensor.
- Inspect for an engine coolant temperature (ECT) sensor that has shifted in value.

*Rough, Unstable or Incorrect Idling
and Stalling Diagnosis*

Engine runs unevenly at idle. If severe, the engine or vehicle may shake. Engine idle speed may vary in RPM. Either condition may be severe enough to stall the engine.

- Inspect the engine control module (ECM) grounds for being clean, tight, and in the proper locations.
- Remove and inspect the air filter element for dirt or for restrictions.
- Inspect the air intake ducts for being collapsed, damaged areas, looseness, improper installation, or leaking, especially between the MAF sensor and the throttle body.
- Inspect the Transaxle Range Switch input with the vehicle in drive and the gear selector in drive or overdrive.

INPUT SENSORS

An assortment of sensing devices used throughout the vehicle electronically transmit operating information to the PCM. Sensor signals can describe the state, temperature, position, or operating status of the system or component they monitor. Automotive sensors are classified as:

- Speed sensor
- Oxygen sensor
- Position sensor
- Pressure sensor
- Temperature sensor

The crankshaft position (CKP) signal is the primary input and the foundation upon which all other PCM functions are based. Manufacturers refer to this input as the distributor, tach, engine speed, RPM, or reference signal, depending upon the system. The purpose of this signal is to let the PCM know the engine is turning over and how fast it is turning. If there is no signal, the PCM will not initiate ignition or fuel delivery. An erratic signal on a running engine results in incorrect operation of the ignition system and the fuel injectors. Systems use Hall-effect sensors, magnetic pickups, and optical sensors to provide a CKP signal.

Different electronic control systems assign different priorities to the other sensors once the engine is running. Often, a system can operate without any noticeable driveability problems when only a few of the high priority sensors are functioning. Begin troubleshooting by checking the signal of these high-priority sensors. Typically, the list includes the throttle position (TPS), manifold absolute pressure (MAP), or mass airflow (MAF), and engine coolant temperature (ECT) sensors. These components, as well as other sensing devices in the system, fit one of the categories mentioned above.

Regardless of how a sensor is used, you need to know the following to analyze its performance:

- What type of signal it transmits
- How it provides information to the PCM
- What its specific application is
- How it connects to the circuitry

The type of signal can be analog or digital, DC or AC. The signal may provide information to the PCM as a variable voltage, a digital step signal, or a pulse train. The specific application is

what the unit is sensing. A wiring schematic will show how the unit connects to the circuitry.

Speed Sensor

Vehicles use a number of speed sensors. Speed sensors can monitor the crankshaft, camshaft, distributor shaft, transmission components, driveshaft, axle shafts, or wheels to determine how fast they are rotating.

There are three basic designs for automotive speed sensors:

- Magnetic pickup
- Hall-effect switch
- Optical sensor

A magnetic pickup is an analog device that produces an AC voltage, while Hall-effect switches and optical sensors are digital and produce a DC signal. For all types, the PCM uses the frequency of the signal to determine the speed of the sensed component. Refer back to Chapter Two for further details of the operation of these sensors.

Oxygen Sensor

As discussed in Chapter Three a heated oxygen sensor (HO2S) is an analog voltage generating device that produces a linear voltage signal based on the oxygen content of the exhaust, figure 5-11. An HO2S provides feedback information to the PCM on how well the electronic control system is responding to changing demands for fuel.

Although there are several HO2S types, most are galvanic batteries. The HO2S produces a signal whose frequency, amplitude, voltage levels, duty cycle, and peak-to-peak voltages provide combustion efficiency information to the PCM, which is used to regulate fuel injector pulse width. An OBD II system uses two sensors, an upstream HO2S before the catalytic converter and downstream HO2S after it. The PCM can gauge

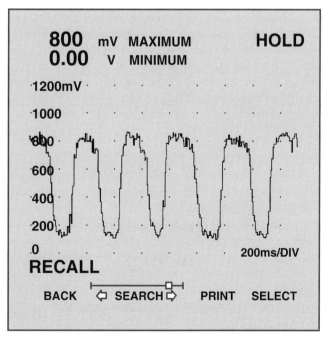

Fig. 5-11. A good HO2S scope trace features rounded peaks and even amplitude.

A8

converter operating efficiency by comparing the two signals. The following discussion applies to upstream units.

An HO2S can have one, two, three, or four wires linking it to the PCM. Single wire circuits deliver a signal only, and the circuit grounds through the sensor housing. With these, a loose mounting or dirt and corrosion on the sensor threads creates resistance on the ground circuit. With a two wire HO2S, one wire carries the signal and the other grounds the sensor through the PCM. A heated oxygen sensor (HO2S) has a three or four wire circuit: three if the sensor and heater have a common ground and four if each has a separate ground circuit.

A simple procedure for HO2S diagnosis is to remember the phrase "lean and low." When the exhaust oxygen content is high, there is somewhat less difference between the oxygen in the air and the oxygen in the exhaust. Therefore, the sensor will produce a lower voltage (100mv to 420mv), which indicates a lean condition to the PCM.

When exhaust oxygen content is low, there is a large difference between the oxygen in the air and the oxygen in the exhaust. Therefore, the sensor will produce a higher voltage (460 mV to 900 mV), which indicates a rich condition to the PCM.

The sensor continually switches between high and low voltage, signaling the PCM to maintain the ideal air-fuel ratio. An HO2S voltage of 440 to 550mv is equivalent to about a 14.7 to 1 air-fuel ratio. An HO2S must be at 572°F (300°C) before it generates a valid signal.

An HO2S produces a low voltage, low current analog signal that is very susceptible to induced voltage interference. Since signal voltage is rapidly changing, it is difficult to get an accurate reading on a DMM. Most control systems provide HO$_2$S information on the data stream, but this is not always a reliable diagnostic aid. The best way to evaluate HO$_2$S operation is to monitor circuit activity with a lab scope.

When viewing an HO$_2$S trace on a lab scope look for even amplitude with rounded peaks; the rising slope tends to be slightly steeper than the trailing slope. Frequency of the signal increases with engine speed. The midpoint of the wave moves up on the screen when the mixture is rich and down when it is lean. Some noise on the trace is normal and is exaggerated if scope leads are too close to secondary ignition leads. A short or clipped peak can indicate a cylinder firing, EGR flow, or other problem that affects combustion, figure 5-12.

Position Sensor

On an automotive control system, position information is generally provided to the PCM by a potentiometer sensor. A potentiometer is a variable resistor that provides an analog voltage signal to the PCM based on the motion or position of the monitored component. Most automotive systems use a potentiometer as a TP sensor, to provide a driver demand signal based on accelerator pedal position. Systems may also use a potentiometer to measure EGR valve opening, canister purge valve condition, and vane airflow sensor position information to the PCM. A potentiometer requires three wires:

- Reference
- Signal
- Ground

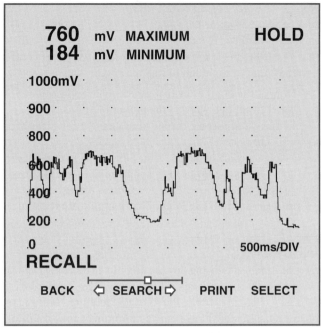

Fig. 5-12. Short or clipped peaks on an HO2S trace indicate combustion or fuel mixture problems.

All potentiometers work in a similar fashion to convert mechanical movement into a variable voltage. The voltage supplies input information to the PCM as an analog signal. The PCM applies a reference voltage, usually 5 volts, to one end of a variable resistor. A terminal at the opposite end of the resistor connects to the PCM ground path. The third terminal, which attaches to a movable wiper that sweeps across the resistor, sends the variable signal voltage back to the PCM. Internal PCM circuits digitize the analog potentiometer signal for processing.

Signal voltage is high or low, depending on whether the movable wiper is near the supply end or the ground end of the resistor, figure 5-13. Most automotive potentiometer sensors transmit a low signal voltage when the mechanical device they attach to is at rest. For example, when the throttle or EGR valve is closed, the potentiometer signal voltage is at its lowest, which is slightly above zero. As the linkage moves to its fully open position, signal voltage rises to its highest, which is slightly below reference voltage.

Check potentiometer operation by connecting a DMM to the signal and ground wires and operating the device through its full range of travel, figure 5-14. Look for correct minimum and maximum voltages and a smooth transition as the device moves from closed to open. Signal voltage that is too high in the closed position indicates either a ground circuit problem or an incorrectly adjusted sensor.

A common potentiometer failure is signal dropout, where the signal is lost as the wiper moves through a worn area on the resistor contact. Although difficult to isolate with a DMM, signal dropout is easily spotted when performing a sweep test with a lab scope, figure 5-15. A regular, reoccurring dropout indicates wear, while an irregular dropout indicates problems on the power, or reference voltage, side of the circuit. This can be caused by a circuit or PCM failure; troubleshoot the circuit to find the source of the problem.

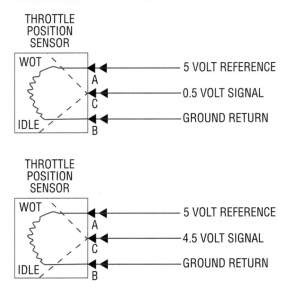

THROTTLE
POSITION
SENSOR

WOT
A ——— 5 VOLT REFERENCE
C ——— 0.5 VOLT SIGNAL
——— GROUND RETURN
IDLE
B

THROTTLE
POSITION
SENSOR

WOT
A ——— 5 VOLT REFERENCE
C ——— 4.5 VOLT SIGNAL
——— GROUND RETURN
IDLE
B

Fig. 5-13. The position of the variable wiper on a potentiometer determines whether the signal voltage will be high or low.

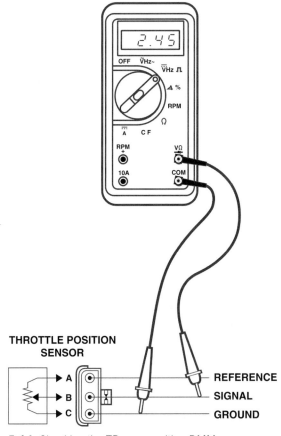

THROTTLE POSITION
SENSOR

A ——— REFERENCE
B ——— SIGNAL
C ——— GROUND

Fig. 5-14. Checking the TP sensor with a DMM.

Pressure Sensor

Automotive control systems measure MAP or barometric pressure (BARO) with a pressure-sensing device to determine the load on the engine. These sensors generally use either a piezoresistive crystal or a capacitive-ceramic device to generate an input signal to the PCM. The resistance of a piezoresistive crystal changes when pressure is applied to it, causing it to produce an

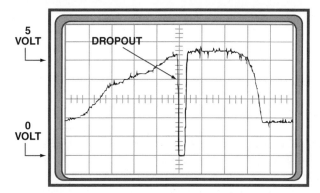

5
VOLT ——→   DROPOUT

0
VOLT ——→

Fig. 5-15. Scope trace showing signal dropout during a potentiometer sweep test.

analog signal. Capacitive-ceramic units use manifold vacuum to vary the distance between two plates and transmit a digital signal.

The PCM applies a reference voltage, usually 5 volts, to a piezoresistive crystal. On a typical MAP sensor, one side of the piezoresistive crystal is inside a sealed reference chamber, and the other side is in a chamber connected to intake manifold vacuum. Changes in manifold vacuum provide a variable pressure, which acts on the crystal to vary its resistance. The resistance of the crystal determines how much of the reference voltage drops before returning to the PCM as signal voltage.

Piezoresistive sensors require a three wire circuit: reference, signal, and ground, figure 5-16. Typically, signal voltage is low, about 0.5 volt, when manifold vacuum is high, such as at idle. As manifold vacuum decreases, the signal voltage increases. Signal should be about 4.75 volts, with the key on and the engine off. To check an analog piezoresistive sensor, monitor signal voltage on a DMM while applying vacuum with a hand pump.

Some MAP sensors work under the same principle but produce a digital signal with variable frequency instead of an analog voltage. Operation of this type of sensor is best analyzed with a lab scope, figure 5-17. Use a hand vacuum pump to perform an operating range test. Expect frequency to be high with low manifold vacuum and low at high vacuum. Be aware, the frequency of a pressure sensor signal varies with atmospheric pressure, so it changes with altitude. A unit that is out of calibration can produce a waveform that looks good but is operating at the wrong frequency. Check the service manual for correct specifications.

Temperature Sensor

Temperature measurement is critical for an automotive control system because most operating parameters adjust to compensate for changes in operating temperature. Most control systems use a negative temperature coefficient (NTC) thermistor as an ECT sensor. If an intake air temperature (IAT) sensor is used, it will be a thermistor as well. An NTC thermistor is a variable resistor, which transmits an analog voltage signal that decreases as temperature increases.

The PCM applies a reference voltage, usually 5 volts, through a **pull-up resistor** to the thermistor directly on the signal wire. As the thermistor heats up, it pulls the reference voltage closer to ground. By monitoring the reference signal, the PCM determines temperature based on how much of the signal voltage is dropped across the thermistor, figure 5-18. Some sen-

A8

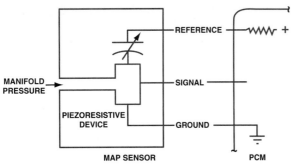

Fig. 5-16. Manifold vacuum acts on a piezoresistive crystal to provide a variable analog signal to the PCM based on engine load.

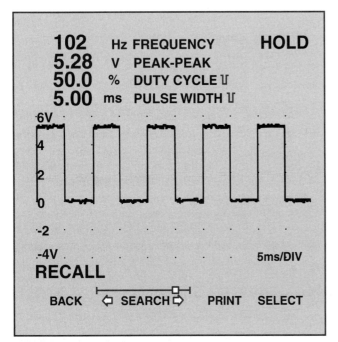

Fig. 5-17. A digital MAP sensor transmits a variable frequency signal to the PCM.

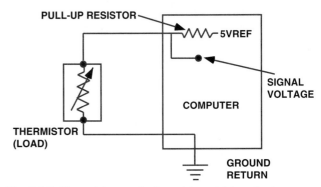

Fig. 5-18. The resistance of a thermistor, which varies in proportion to temperature, determines how much of the signal voltage is dropped to ground.

sors use an internal shunt circuit to increase their operating range. Thermistors have a two wire circuit: reference and ground.

Most thermistor failures are due to an open or short circuit, which can be detected with a digital multimeter (DMM). However, voltage dropout and drift can also cause problems with this type of sensor. Expect signal voltage to change slowly because it responds to changing temperature. The best way to isolate signal dropout and drift is to make a timed data recording. Use a **graphing multimeter (GMM)** to record signal voltage from a cold start until the engine reaches normal operating temperature.

OUTPUT ACTUATORS

The actuators are the output devices activated by the PCM to control vehicle operation. These devices convert electrical energy into mechanical work. Actuators usually contain some kind of induction coil and operate at current levels that are much higher than input sensor circuits, which only carry information. A feature of most automotive actuators is that the

PCM regulates the device by controlling on the ground side of the circuit. One side of the actuator coil receives system voltage, and the ground side circuit connects to the PCM.

Most of the system voltage is dropped across an actuator, which reduces the current applied to the output driver transistors in the PCM. To regulate this voltage drop, the coil windings of an actuator must meet a minimum resistance specification. If coil resistance is too low, higher voltage and current on the ground circuit can overheat and destroy the transistors in the PCM driver circuit.

Common actuators used on an electronic engine management system include solenoids, relays, and stepper motors.

Solenoid

A solenoid is an electromechanical device that uses magnetism to move an iron core. The core provides mechanical motion to some other system part. A solenoid thus changes electrical voltage and current into mechanical movement. Solenoids operate fuel injectors, carburetor metering rods and air bleeds, vacuum control valves, transmission hydraulic circuits, and other devices in an engine control system. There are two types of solenoids used in automotive systems:

- On/off
- Pulse width modulated

All solenoids are digital devices, which can only be switched on or off. However, by regulating the amount of time the induction coil is switched on in relation to the amount of time that it is switched off, the PCM can vary the movement of the core. This type of solenoid control is known as pulse width modulation.

On/Off Solenoid

An on/off solenoid is used to regulate the flow of air or fluid, or to move a mechanical linkage. Solenoids use a two wire circuit: power and ground. On a typical automotive application, voltage is applied to one solenoid terminal, and the PCM switches the other circuit to ground. Most solenoids are energized for varying lengths of time as determined by PCM programming, switch inputs from the driver, or input sensor signals.

The operation of an on/off solenoid can be checked by monitoring voltage on the power circuit with a DMM. On a

---

Graphing Multimeter (GMM): A multimeter displays signals in conventional digital format or in a value over time relationship.

solenoid that switches to ground, full voltage, which may be either system voltage or a lower regulated voltage, should be available when the solenoid is switched off because the circuit is open. When the solenoid energizes, or switches on, the circuit is complete and the measured voltage should drop to ground. Resistance specifications are available for most solenoids, and this check can also be made with a DMM.

A more accurate way to check a solenoid is to measure the amperage draw through the driver circuit. For this test, the circuit must be under power and loaded so that current is applied to the device. To test with a DMM, set the meter to the amperage scale and connect it in series between the solenoid negative terminal and ground, or the actual driver circuit if it can be energized. Leave the circuit energized for one to two minutes to check the draw. Compare results to specifications.

Pulse Width Modulation
Many automotive solenoids are pulsed on and off rapidly at a specific number of cycles per second, or **Hertz (Hz)**. The operating cycle of a pulsed solenoid is the sequence from off to on and back to off again. An actuator solenoid can operate at any fixed number of cycles per second, or fixed frequency: 10 Hz, 20 Hz, 60 Hz, and so on.

The pulse width, which is usually measured in milliseconds (ms), is the amount of time a solenoid is energized, or the "on" part of the cycle. Although the operating frequency of a solenoid may be fixed, the ratio of "on-time" to "total cycle time" can be varied. This PWM control allows a digital output signal to provide varied or analog control of a mechanical device.

The duty cycle of a PWM solenoid is the percentage of the complete off-on-off cycle during which the solenoid is energized, or on. It is the ratio of pulse width to complete cycle width, figure 5-19. Duty cycle is usually expressed as a percentage. A 25 percent duty cycle means that the solenoid is energized for 25 percent of the total off-on-off cycle time; a 75 percent duty cycle means that the solenoid is energized for

75 percent of the cycle. A zero percent or a 100 percent duty cycle indicates that the solenoid is fully off or fully on, respectively.

Attempting to read voltage on a PWM solenoid with a DMM can be misleading because of the way the meter samples the signal and the rapid speed at which the pulses occur. For example, a DMM set to the voltage scale and connected to a 5 volt PWM solenoid operating at a 50 percent duty cycle would read 2.5 volts. However, a DMM designed for automotive use generally has a duty cycle setting. In this mode, the meter displays the duty cycle of the signal as a percentage.

Pulse width and duty cycle can also be measured on a lab scope trace. When viewing a trace, look for a good, clean transition as the solenoid energizes. The slope should be a vertical line between system voltage and ground. The collapsing coil creates a spike, or inductive kick, which can go either up or down, depending upon how the unit switches. Resistance on the ground circuit may cause a trace to not pull to the baseline.

Relay
A relay is a digital device that uses a low current circuit to open and close a switch and control current on another circuit, figure 5-20. The PCM switches the relay control circuit to energize and de-energize the relay coil. An electromagnet in the coil closes the power circuit contacts to allow a high current signal through the power circuit. Typically, relays used in electronic engine control systems include the fuel pump relay, lamp driver relays, and system power relays. Relays can be switched on either the power or ground side of the circuit, and both types can be used on the same vehicle. Two common relay failures are defective coil windings and insufficient contact between the points.

Stepper Motor
A stepper motor operates by moving its armature in small increments in one direction or the other. A pintel, which does not rotate, is threaded onto the end of the armature shaft. As

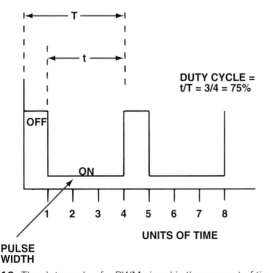
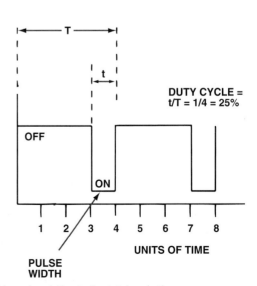

Fig. 5-19. The duty cycle of a PWM signal is the amount of time the solenoid is on in relation to the total cycle time.

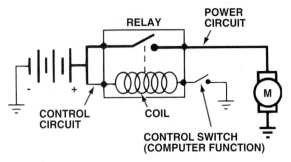

Fig. 5-20. Applying power to the low current control circuit of a relay closes the contacts to allow high current through the power circuit.

the armature rotates, the pintel moves in or out on the threads depending upon the direction of the armature. These motors contain either two or four coils. When two coils are used, the PCM controls the polarity of each coil, as well as the sequence of energizing them. The PCM can apply a positive charge at one end of the coil and negative at the other, then switch to reverse the polarity and magnetic pull on a part of the armature. By pulsing these two coils in sequence, the PCM commands the armature to move in small increments or steps. Stepper motors commonly operate idle air control valves and fuel or air bleed controls in some feedback carburetors.

Diagnostic Tools

Accurate diagnosis of computer controlled systems relies on the use of the proper tools. Several different tools are required for the various tests that must be performed.

Among those are:

- Digital multimeter (DMM)
- Diagnostic scan tool
- Oscilloscope
- Breakout box (BOB)

Voltmeter

A voltmeter measures the electrical pressure differential, in volts, between the two points connected by the leads, figure 5-21. A voltmeter is connected in parallel, or across, a component or circuit. A very small amount of current passes through the meter, while the rest of the current travels through the normal

circuit path. Therefore, the circuit functions normally with the meter connected.

Ohmmeter

An ohmmeter, which measures the resistance to electrical flow in ohms, can be used to determine continuity and the amount of circuit resistance, figure 5-22. Unlike a voltmeter or ammeter, an ohmmeter contains its own voltage source. Since an ohmmeter does not use circuit voltage, either lead can be connected to any test point unless checking diodes or other solid-state devices.

Ammeter

An ammeter, which measures current in amperes, is connected to the circuit in series, figure 5-23. This permits the current in the circuit to pass through the meter for measurement.

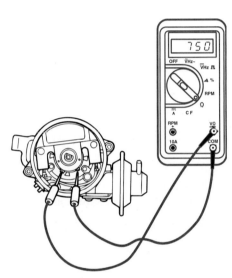

Fig. 5-22. Ohmmeter connection testing the resistance of a pickup coil.

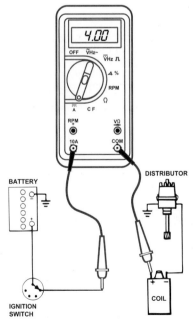

Fig. 5-23. Using an ammeter to check coil primary circuit current draw.

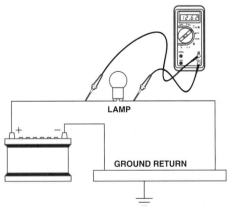

Fig. 5-21. Voltmeters are connected in parallel to the circuit being tested.

Unlike a voltmeter, an ammeter has extremely low internal resistance. If connected in parallel, too much current will pass through the meter and damage it.

When current draw specifications for a circuit or component are known, an ammeter reading can determine if a short or grounded circuit is present. A reading greater than that specified indicates a short in the circuit. An ammeter also can detect excessive circuit resistance, which causes a low reading.

Oscilloscope

Another tool used to measure voltage in many applications is the oscilloscope. Oscilloscopes, or "scopes," are available in either analog or digital styles. The analog scope incorporates a true live display, much like older ignition analyzers. A beam of electrons writes on a phosphorus screen, which is laid out in a grid. The analog scope has the advantage of providing a true live display. The disadvantage lies in the fact that it cannot store signals for future review.

Technically, the digital scope is known as the **digital storage oscilloscope**, or **DSO**. Inputs to the digital scope are digitized, processed, and displayed on the screen for viewing. The digital scope has the advantage, storing the information so that in can be saved, parameters can be calculated, and intermittent glitches can be captured. It also allows for automatic setup and operation. The digital scope does not provide a true live readout and may miss certain short-duration voltage variances.

Diagnostic Scan Tool

The diagnostic tools discussed to this point rely on making an actual connection to the circuit or component in question to make a reading. In today's vehicles it is often necessary to access information stored within one of the onboard electronic control modules. Scan tools are usually hand-held computers containing programming allowing communication with the control modules. They connect to the vehicle via the data link connector, or DLC, figure 5-24. The scan tool sends requests for information to the control module and displays the results on its screen.

Most scan tools can be used to read operating parameters, read and clear DTCs, and command certain components to operate.

The scan tool must always be used in conjunction with the appropriate vehicle service or diagnostic manual. The manuals will provide specific instructions for connecting the tool, reading the information, and interpreting the results. Random use of the scan tool can result in misdiagnosis and wasted diagnostic efforts. Once results are obtained they should be compared to published guidelines and the appropriate repairs completed.

Circuit Testing Using Serial Data

Using serial data to test ECM circuits can be of great value during driveability diagnosis; however, there are some items to remember. The data that are being read on the scan tool could actually be default values that the ECM substitutes to compensate for possible circuit failures. Also, serial data transmitted by the ECM to the scan tool are an interpretation of what the ECM thinks it is seeing. The true readings may be different. You can confirm actual signal values by testing the circuit

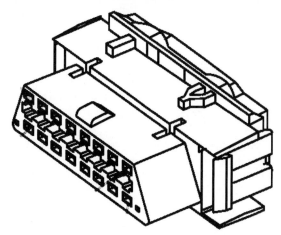

Fig. 5-24. Data Link Connector for all OBD II vehicles.

live with a DVOM, breakout box, or lab scope, depending on what you need to test. False data stream values may be caused by an internal ECM fault or ECM ground circuit problem. The following are examples of using serial data to test and diagnose driveability and intermittent problems:

- Thermistors: disconnect or short across thermistor circuit to check the maximum range of the sensor. For example, disconnect the ECT to create an open circuit. The temperature reading should drop to - 40°F (-40°C). Install a jumper wire across the connector to create a short circuit. Temperature should go to a maximum reading, about 266°F (130°C)
- Create the opposite circuit problem to see if a DTC sets. For example, a P0117 code in memory tells you an ECT sensor circuit voltage went low, indicating a short. To create an open circuit, disconnect the ECT sensor and see if the ECM sets a P0118 (circuit high). If it does, then the circuit and ECM are operational and the problem is probably in the sensor
- Intermittent problem testing: Wiggle, tap, heat up, or cool down a component or circuit to see if the serial data for that circuit change
- Testing the effect of one circuit on another by manipulating the input signal. Manipulate the signal by disconnecting circuits or substituting values. Here are some examples:

  - IAT, ECT, TP sensor, MAP, MAF, and HO2S signals' effect on injector pulse width.
  - ECT, ACT, TP sensor signals' effect on idle speed control.
  - IAT, ECT, TP, MAP, and MAF signals' effect on ignition timing control.
  - ECT, TP sensor, and EVP signals' effect on EGR control
  - ECT and TP sensor signals' effect on canister purge
  - VSS, TP sensor, ECT, and MAP signals' effect on torque convert clutch operation.

Circuit Testing Operations

While scan tools are an important part of any diagnosis, once you locate a problem you must use either a DVOM or lab scope to accurately check a circuit. The following section covers circuit testing procedures and guidelines for using the proper test equipment.

A8

Voltage

When using a DVOM to check voltage in and out of sensors, always check the voltage using the signal ground return at the sensor, rather than using an engine or battery ground, figure 5-14. Sensors are grounded directly through the ECM, rather than being connected directly to a chassis ground. This way sensors avoid noise interference. Sensors need a "clean" ground for reliable operation.

An open signal ground return will cause the ECM to see a high voltage on the sensor signal line. An example would be a TP sensor that always sends a wide open throttle (high voltage) signal to the ECM.

Resistance

Ohms law says that even very low resistance in an automotive computer circuit will cause sensors and actuators to work improperly because of low voltage. For example, an on-board ECM ignition feed circuit drawing 365 milliamps with a resistance in the ignition feed wire of 2.5 ohms will cause a voltage supply drop of 1.5 volts. This voltage drop will cause severe driveability problems. One example of this may be a car that idles too high because the ECM monitors the battery voltage. If the supply voltage is low the ECM may raise the idle speed so the charging system could charge what the ECM thinks is a low battery.

To check resistance, make sure that the circuit to be tested is not under power. Place the leads across the circuit or component to be tested, figure 5-25. To read ohms, place the meter on auto-ranging or start at the higher scales and work down.

Voltage Drop

Checking voltage drop is one of the most important tests that a technician can perform on a circuit. A voltage drop test measures the difference in electrical pressure between two points in a live circuit. Voltage drops can cause major driveability symptoms in on-board computer systems. A voltage drop on an ECM power ground can cause sensor voltage references to be higher than normal, throwing off the overall sensor calibration of the entire engine control system, figure 5-26.

Another example of a driveability symptom might be a car with an idle speed that continuously hunts. To start diagnosis, you connect the scan tool to check trouble codes and the idle smoothes out. This is usually caused by a poor ground.

To check voltage drop, the circuit must be powered up and have current flowing. The circuit also must have the maximum amount of current flowing under normal conditions by which the circuit was designed.

Although there is no exact amount of voltage drop that is considered acceptable, you should remember that low current circuits that draw milliamps will be affected by very small voltage drops. A good rule of thumb would be a drop of 0.2 volt or less. However, even this is too much for some circuits. A power ground circuit should have a voltage drop of no more than 0.1 volt. A computer ground circuit should have a voltage drop of no more than 0.05 volt.

Amperage

Too much amperage flow through an ECM actuator driver circuit can partially damage that circuit and cause severe driveability problems. Most ECM actuator components carry milliamps through their circuits. Using an ohmmeter and calculating amperage draw from resistance and voltage readings is not always accurate because the device under test does not carry the actual load it was designed to carry. Most actuator devices carry about 180 ma (12.6 volts at 70 ohms) to 500 ma (12.6 volts at 25 ohms), but there are always exceptions to the rule. Fuel injectors may carry much more amperage

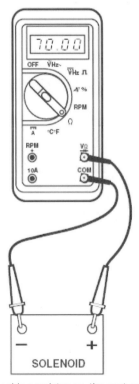

Fig. 5-25. When checking resistance, the part must not be under power or you will probably destroy your meter.

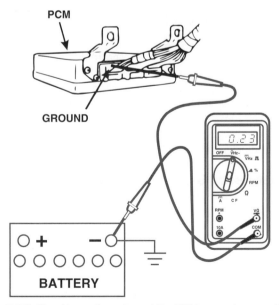

Fig. 5-26. Checking voltage drop at the PCM ground connection.

through their circuits (as much as 8 amps depending on the type of injector). To check amperage draw, the circuit must be powered up and have current flowing. Set your meter for amperage draw and connect it in series between the solenoid negative terminal and ground, or the actual driver circuit if you can energize it, figure 5-27. Start by checking amps first, then move down to milliamp scale. Leave the circuit energized for 1 to 2 minutes to check draw.

Remember, this test is for solenoids such as Canister Purge, EGR, and Air Management only. Do not check fuel injectors in this manner. Holding an injector on for any length of time destroys it.

AC Ripple

On-board automotive computers do not like to see AC ripples pass through the internal components. This effect can cause logic problems as well as many other types of driveability problems. For example, a bad alternator with a dropped diode can severely affect an automotive computer system. To check for AC ripple voltage, switch your DVOM to AC and connect the black lead to a good ground and the red lead to the "BAT," or power, terminal on the back of the alternator (not the battery), figure 5-28. A good alternator should measure less than 0.5 volts AC with the engine running and the headlights on. A higher reading indicates damaged alternator diodes.

Frequency

Frequency is the number of times a signal repeats itself in one second. Frequency is measured in hertz. A signal that repeats itself 10 times a second is operating at a frequency of 10 hertz.

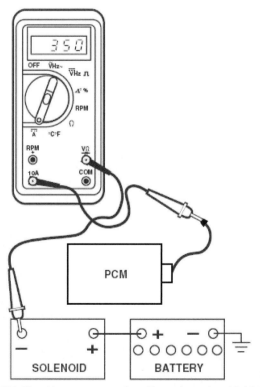

Fig. 5-27. Checking amperage draw through a solenoid driver circuit.

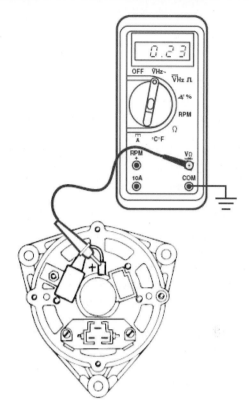

Fig. 5-28. Checking for voltage ripple from an AC generator.

Many automotive computer systems read the frequency of a signal instead of the voltage. Ford MAP sensors and AC Delco Mass Airflow Sensors are examples of sensors that produce this type of signal. For example, a Ford EEC-IV MAP sensor has a 5 volt reference voltage applied to it. At a duty cycle of 50 percent (half of the time on and half of the time off), the DVOM will average the reading so you would see 2.5 volts. However, the number of times the signal switches on and off in one second will change depending on manifold vacuum. To accurately diagnose these signals, you must have a meter that can read frequency, figure 5-29.

Duty Cycle

Duty cycle is the percentage of time a digital signal is high versus low. When measuring duty cycle, one complete cycle is considered 100 percent. For a 5 volt signal at a 50 percent duty cycle, the voltage would read 2.5 volts.

For automotive applications, when dealing with digital waves, and especially with ECM outputs, we are concerned with the amount of time the signal is low, rather than high. This is because the low time is when the driving transistor is on, completing the circuit to ground.

You can measure duty cycle with a DVOM that has a duty cycle setting. Attach the red lead to the signal wire and the black lead to a good engine ground, figure 5-30.

PCM Pin Voltage Charts

A PCM pin voltage chart, figure 5-31, identifies all the connector terminals at the main harness connector by number, circuit name, and the voltage levels that should be present

A8

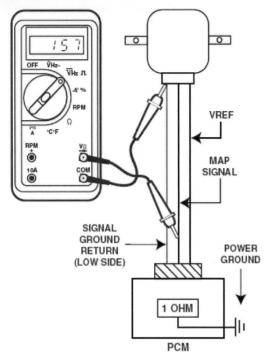

Fig. 5-29. Checking the frequency of a MAP sensor.

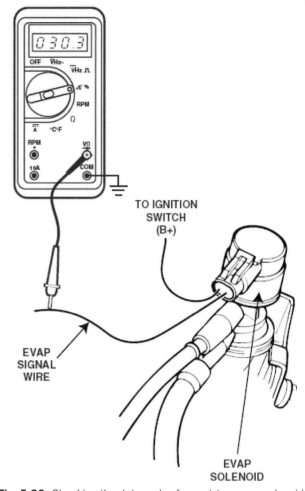

Fig. 5-30. Checking the duty cycle of a canister purge solenoid.

under various conditions. Some circuits have different voltage specifications with the key on and the engine off, during cranking, and when the engine is running. Use the pin voltage charts to check input signals to the PCM and output signals from the PCM. Checking signals at the PCM harness connector is closely related to sensor operating range tests.

Check Ground Continuity

Use a DMM to check the voltage drop across the main PCM ground connection, figure 5-26. Also, check voltage drop across the ground connection of any sensor that may be causing the problem. Refer to the Service Manual for the correct pin locations to conduct the tests. Low resistance ground connections are critical for electronic control circuits.

With the ignition on, voltage drop across the ground connection for an electronic circuit should be 0.1 volt or less. The voltage drop across a high resistance ground connection in series with a sensor circuit increases the signal voltage of the sensor. This ground resistance can offset the signal voltage enough to cause serious driveability problems. For example, on a throttle position sensor that operates on a 5 volt reference, a 0.5 volt drop across the ground connection equals a 10 percent error in throttle angle measurement.

Troubleshooting Intermittent Problems

Intermittent driveability problems can often be extremely difficult to diagnose and repair. A soft code in memory provides a clue as to the general area in which to start testing. Remember, however, that if a soft code is erased, the problem that set it may not recur right away. To reset a soft code, simulate the conditions that cause the problem during a road test to catch the intermittent fault. The following paragraphs

outline some basic points that can help troubleshoot intermittent problems.

Diagnostic Tools

Intermittent problems require the use of various tools to pinpoint the actual cause. Both the DMM and the scan tool are valuable in most cases; however, occasionally the need for more enhanced signal information may be required. For these instances the use of a DSO may be necessary. The DSO allows the technician to view voltage signals over time while storing the information for later retrieval and review. Most oscilloscopes in use today in the automotive market are of the DSO design.

Simulate the Problem

Try to recreate the conditions that the customer describes. It may not always be possible to duplicate the conditions exactly. Generally, driving conditions described by the customer can be recreated during a road test. For cold starting problems, the vehicle may have to stand overnight to recreate the conditions. If the problem caused a soft code, try to get the code to reoccur during testing.

Wiggle Tests and Output Cycling Tests

Most control systems have long term memory that records soft codes for intermittent problems. In a wiggle test, tap or wiggle

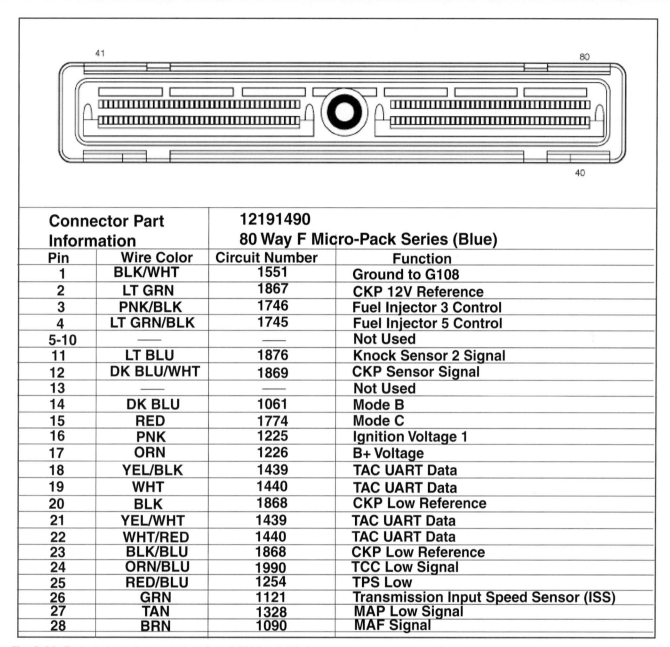

Connector Part Information		12191490 80 Way F Micro-Pack Series (Blue)	
Pin	Wire Color	Circuit Number	Function
1	BLK/WHT	1551	Ground to G108
2	LT GRN	1867	CKP 12V Reference
3	PNK/BLK	1746	Fuel Injector 3 Control
4	LT GRN/BLK	1745	Fuel Injector 5 Control
5-10	—	—	Not Used
11	LT BLU	1876	Knock Sensor 2 Signal
12	DK BLU/WHT	1869	CKP Sensor Signal
13	—	—	Not Used
14	DK BLU	1061	Mode B
15	RED	1774	Mode C
16	PNK	1225	Ignition Voltage 1
17	ORN	1226	B+ Voltage
18	YEL/BLK	1439	TAC UART Data
19	WHT	1440	TAC UART Data
20	BLK	1868	CKP Low Reference
21	YEL/WHT	1439	TAC UART Data
22	WHT/RED	1440	TAC UART Data
23	BLK/BLU	1868	CKP Low Reference
24	ORN/BLU	1990	TCC Low Signal
25	RED/BLU	1254	TPS Low
26	GRN	1121	Transmission Input Speed Sensor (ISS)
27	TAN	1328	MAP Low Signal
28	BRN	1090	MAF Signal

Fig. 5-31. Typical pin assignment chart for a PCM (partial list).

wiring, connectors, and components to try to get the problem to occur and reset the code. Wiggle tests can be done with the key on and the engine off or with the engine running. Usually, a wiggle test can be conducted with a scan tool connected. This allows you to monitor the data stream and watch for parameters to suddenly change. Be aware, some systems will not set codes with a scan tool connected and operating in the diagnostic mode. For these vehicles, either monitor the data stream, or simply perform the test without the scan tool. If the problem occurs during the wiggle test, remember what you did to cause it. After wiggle testing, check for codes in memory once again to verify the fault.

Some vehicles have output cycling tests as part of their diagnostic capabilities. These systems have a bidirectional PCM that accepts commands from a scan tool. When in the test mode, the PCM generates a signal to switch an actuator on and off in a controlled condition. While the actuator is being switched, perform a wiggle test and take voltmeter readings to pinpoint an intermittent fault.

Check Connectors for Damage

Intermittent problems are often caused by damaged wiring connectors and terminals. Poor connections create high resistance that interrupts the signal. Unplug the connectors in the problem circuit and inspect them carefully.

Look for:

- Bent or broken terminals
- Corrosion
- Terminals that have been forced back into the connector shell, causing an intermittent connection
- Loose, frayed, or broken wires inside the connector shell.

A8

Most connectors are repairable, and often spraying a small amount of electronic contact cleaner on the terminals will help to remove dirt, corrosion, and moisture. If damage is severe, replace the connector.

PCM/ECM Replacement

Vehicle computers do fail, but not with great frequency or regularity. Too often the PCM or ECM is replaced simply because someone thought it might be the problem. However, from time to time, manufacturers release revised computers to correct specific vehicle problems. Most newer control modules can be "flash" programmed to electronically update the internal programming, rather than physically replacing the PCM or ECM.

Check these items before replacing the PCM or ECM:

1. Battery voltage supply to the PCM or ECM and main system ground—Be sure the battery is fully charged and provides at least 9.6 to 10 volts during cranking. Be sure the charging system is maintaining correct battery charge. Most control systems receive battery voltage through a fuse, fusible link, or both. Be sure that battery voltage is available at the specified terminal of the main harness connector. Most systems are grounded remotely through a wire in the harness. Trace and check the ground connection to ensure good continuity.
2. Operation of a system power relay—The power to the PCM or ECM may be supplied through a system power relay. If so, check the relay.
3. Sensor reference voltage and ground circuits—Many sensors share a common reference voltage supply from the PCM or ECM and a common ground. Incorrect or erratic reference voltage or bad common ground can affect operation of several sensors simultaneously. The system may appear as if the PCM or ECM has a major internal problem.
4. Resistance and current flow through all controlled solenoids and relays—Every output device controlled by the PCM or ECM has a minimum resistance specification, Actuator resistance limits the current through the PCM or ECM output control circuit. If the actuator is shorted, current can exceed the maximum safe resistance and internally damage the PCM or ECM. Before replacing a PCM or ECM, check all output circuits for shorts or low resistance that could cause internal damage to the computer.

As a general rule, the PCM or ECM should be at the bottom of the list of things to replace. It can fail, but a sensor, actuator, faulty wiring, poor connection, or mechanical failure is more likely the cause of the problem.

Interrelated Systems

There are many systems on a late-model vehicle that directly or indirectly interface with the PCM. When diagnosing any driveability concern check for any of the following systems and verify they are operating properly before condemning the PCM or its inputs and outputs:

- Cruise control system
- Security alarm or other anti-theft device
- Traction and/or torque control systems
- Climate control systems
- Aftermarket components of any type

Begin your diagnosis by disabling or monitoring the interfacing system that may be causing the concern. Cruise control systems directly or indirectly control the throttle opening and may be the root cause of a throttle control problem.

Keep in mind that most anti-theft devices shut off the fuel to the engine and may also disable the starter circuit. A system that is not operating correctly may cause the engine to fail to start or start and then stall. If the starter circuit is affected generally a failure in the theft deterrent system will result in a no-crank concern. Traction and torque control systems send a message to the PCM requesting a reduction in engine torque to help reduce wheel spin or reduce transmission wear during upshifts.

Many vehicles adjust engine idle based on load from the air conditioner compressor. If the signal from the climate control system is flawed the PCM may either not increase idle or increase it too much. In either case the driver will report idle concerns and/or stalling. Aftermarket accessories when properly installed usually do not cause significant driveability concerns. However, many accessories are not properly installed and may cause a multitude of driveability or emission problems.

Clearing DTCs & Turning the MIL Off

ONE TRIP MONITORS: A failure on the first trip of a "one trip" emissions diagnostic monitor causes the ECM to immediately store a DTC and freeze frame, and turn on the MIL. All comprehensive component monitor faults require only one trip.

TWO TRIP MONITORS: A failure on the first trip of a "two trip" emissions diagnostic monitor causes the ECM to store a temporary DTC. If the failure does not recur on the next trip, the temporary DTC is cleared from memory. If the failure does recur on the next trip, the ECM will store a DTC and freeze frame, and turn on the MIL. All the system monitors are two trip monitors. Engine misfire that is severe enough to damage the catalytic converter is a two trip monitor, with the additional condition that the MIL will blink while the severe misfire is occurring.

AUTOMATIC CLEARING: If the vehicle completes three consecutive "good trips" (three consecutive trips in which the monitor that set the DTC is run and passes), the MIL will be turned off, but the DTC and freeze frame will remain stored in ECM memory. If the vehicle completes 40 warm-up cycles without the same fault recurring, the DTC and freeze frame are automatically cleared from the ECM memory.

MANUAL CLEARING: Any stored DTCs and freeze frame data can be erased using the scan tool, and the MIL (if lit) will be turned off. Although it is not the recommended method, DTCs and freeze frame data will also be cleared if the ECM power supply of the battery is disconnected.

Monitor Readiness Status

The monitor readiness status indicates whether or not a particular OBD II diagnostic monitor has been run since the last time that DTCs were cleared from ECM and TCM memory. If the monitor has not yet run, the status will display on the Scan Tool as "Not Complete." If the monitor has been run, the status will display on the scan tool as "Complete." This does not mean that no faults were found, only that the diagnostic monitor has been run. Whenever DTCs are cleared from memory or the battery is disconnected, all monitor readiness status indicators are reset to "Not Complete." Monitor readiness status indicators are not needed for the Comprehensive Component, Fuel Control, and Engine Misfire monitors because they run continuously. The readiness status of the following system monitors can be read on the scan tool:

Oxygen Sensors	Oxygen Sensor Heaters
Catalytic Converter	EGR System
EVAP System	Variable Valve Timing
Engine Thermostat	

Warm-Up Cycle

Warm-up cycles are used by the ECM for automatic clearing of DTCs and freeze frame data. To complete one warm up cycle, the engine coolant temperature must rise at least 40°F (22°C) and reach a minimum of 160°F (71°C).

Trip

A trip is a key-on cycle in which all enable criteria for a particular diagnostic monitor are met and the diagnostic monitor is run. The trip is completed when the ignition switch is turned off.

Drive Cycle

Most OBD II diagnostic monitors will run at some time during normal operation of the vehicle. However, to satisfy all of the different trip enable criteria and run all of the OBD II diagnostic monitors, the vehicle must be driven under a variety of conditions. As an example, the following drive cycle will meet the enable criteria to allow all monitors to run.

1. Ensure that the fuel tank is between ¼ and ¾ full
2. Start cold (below 86°F/30°C) and warm up until engine temperature is at least 160°F (71°C)—one minute minimum
3. Accelerate to 40–55 mph at 25% throttle and maintain speed for five minutes
4. Decelerate without using the brake (coast down) to 20 mph or less, then stop the vehicle. Allow the engine to idle for 10 seconds, turn the key off, and wait one minute
5. Restart and accelerate to 40–50 mph at 25% throttle and maintain speed for two minutes
6. Decelerate without using the brake (coast down) to 20 mph or less, then stop the vehicle. Allow the engine to idle for 10 seconds, turn the key off, and wait one minute.

A8

CHAPTER QUESTIONS

1. The cause of a MIL not lighting during a bulb check when the ignition is switched on can be all of the following **EXCEPT**:
   a. A faulty circuit
   b. A DTC in memory
   c. A burned out bulb
   d. An internal PCM failure

2. The analog voltage signal of an NTC thermistor will:
   a. Decrease as temperature increases
   b. Increase as temperature decreases
   c. Be about 5 volts on most applications
   d. Be high if the sensor is shorted to ground

3. A failure that sets a soft code in PCM memory is one that:
   a. Exists at the time of testing
   b. Indicates a top priority problem
   c. Occurred in the past but no longer exists
   d. Can be located with a diagnostic chart

4. During open-loop operation, the PCM controls fuel metering based on:
   a. Engine speed, load, temperature, and its own program
   b. Feedback information from the HO2S
   c. The stoichiometric air-fuel ratio
   d. Learned information in adaptive memory

5. When measured with a DMM, the voltage drop across the main PCM ground connection should be:
   a. 1.0 volt or less
   b. 0.1 volt or less
   c. 0.01 volt or less
   d. 0.001 volt or less

6. Excessive voltage drop across a high resistance ground connection in series with a sensor will cause:
   a. Sensor reference voltage to decrease
   b. Sensor reference voltage to increase
   c. Sensor signal voltage to decrease
   d. Sensor signal voltage to increase

7. Regardless of sensor design, what attribute of a speed sensor signal does the PCM process to determine speed?
   a. Frequency
   b. Amplitude
   c. Voltage
   d. Duty cycle

8. With the engine operating in closed loop the HO2S signal displayed on a lab scope is evenly cycling between about 460 mV and 900 mV with even amplitude and rounded peaks. This indicates:
   a. Normal operation
   b. A lean fuel mixture
   c. A rich fuel mixture
   d. A poor ground connection

9. What type of sensor is a variable resistor that provides an analog voltage signal to the PCM based on motion or position?
   a. Thermistor
   b. Potentiometer
   c. Piezoresistive
   d. Hall-effect switch

10. If total cycle time of a PWM signal is 5ms and the solenoid is energized for 2ms during each cycle, the duty cycle of the solenoid would be:
    a. 20%
    b. 40%
    c. 60%
    d. 80%

11. An assortment of sensing devices used throughout the vehicle electronically transmit operating information to the PCM. What is the the primary input upon which all others PCM functions are based?
    a. Crankshaft position (CKP)
    b. Camshaft position (CMP)
    c. Map sensor
    d. Oxygen sensor

12. Which of the following DTCs are considered priority codes and should be diagnosed first?
    a. Auxilary emission controls
    b. Misfire and fuel control
    c. Transmission
    d. Vehicle speed control

13. Technician A says when viewing monitor readiness, the vehicle must be driven under certain conditions for some monitors to run.
    Technician B says the emission system being monitored must be operational.
    Who is right?
    a. A only
    b. B only
    c. Both A and B
    d. Neither A nor B

SAMPLE TEST

Test Taking Advice

As soon as you make the decision to schedule an A8 test, begin preparing by including dedicated study time in your weekly schedule. You can improve your test score with just a few hours of study and review per week. Photocopy the practice test included in this study guide so you can use it several times.

The practice test will help you become more comfortable with test taking in general. It will also point out your weak spots and enable you to use your study time more efficiently. When you miss a question, look up the answer and study the subject in the study guide. Take notes on the subject to use for review. After repeated test taking and review, you should have your notes reduced to a single sheet of paper that can be reviewed daily the week before the test, and again on the day of the test.

Arrive at the test site early so parking or unforeseen problems do not cause you stress. Plan to allow time for a last look at your notes before entering the test site. Pay attention to all instructions from the test proctor even if you are a veteran test taker. From time to time ASE adjusts its instructions.

To answer test questions correctly, you must have a clear understanding of what is being asked. Read the question twice to be sure what it is asking. While thinking about the question, recall what you know about the subject. Do this before reading the answers. You are less likely to be influenced into a wrong conclusion by the answers if you recall what you know about the subject first. Since you have recalled your knowledge of the subject, you will be less likely to doubt yourself while reading the answers.

Note all operating conditions stated in the question when considering the answers. However, never assume that conditions exist that are not stated in the question. Treat each answer as a true or false question. Be sure to read all the answers before making your choice. When you conclude that more than one may be correct, reread the question to make sure you haven't missed an important fact, then rely on your knowledge to choose the one that is most correct. There is always one most correct answer When it seems impossible to decide which answer is correct, it may help to think of which item would be more likely to wear out or which things require regular service. These types of items may be the best choice, especially when the question asks, "which is more likely."

Never leave a question unanswered. Unanswered questions are scored as wrong! Guess if you can't make a decision. Guessing gives you a 25% chance of being correct. If you narrow the field to two possibilities, you have a 50% chance. Choose an answer before moving on to the next question in case you run out of time. Make a mark next to the question in the test booklet. Sometimes, other questions contain information that will help answer a question you're not sure of, and you can return to the questions you have marked if you have time. Be cautious when returning to reread a question. If you are still not sure which answer is correct, it's better to leave your original guess than to make a second guess. However, if you are certain that you originally misunderstood the question, it's best to change your answer.

1. Most on-board diagnostic systems will recognize and store a hard code for all of the following **EXCEPT**:
   a. An absent signal
   b. An intermittent signal
   c. An improbable signal
   d. An out-of-range signal

2. Technician A says that absolute pressure uses a reference point of zero pressure, or total vacuum, regardless of atmospheric pressure or altitude.
   Technician B says that to correct intake manifold vacuum readings for altitude, add one in-Hg (3.377 kPa) for every 1000 feet (305 meters) above sea level.
   Who is right?
   a. A only
   b. B only
   c. Both A and B
   d. Neither A nor B

3. The most accurate method of detecting severely worn piston rings would be to perform a:
   a. Manifold vacuum test
   b. Cylinder power balance test
   c. Compression test
   d. Cylinder leakage test

4. Which oscilloscope pattern allows you to display the voltage traces for all cylinders one after the other from left to right across the screen in firing order?
   a. Raster
   b. Parade
   c. Stacked
   d. Superimposed

5. Technician A says that a high, short firing line on a secondary oscilloscope trace is the result of low resistance from a short circuit.
   Technician B says that a damaged plug wire, worn distributor cap, or excessive plug gap results in a high, short firing line on a secondary oscilloscope trace.
   Who is right?
   a. A only
   b. B only
   c. Both A and B
   d. Neither A nor B

6. High levels of hydrocarbon (HC) emissions are often the result of a malfunction in the:
   a. Ignition system
   b. Fuel system
   c. PCV system
   d. Emission control system

A8

7. When the positive voltmeter lead of a voltmeter is connected to the positive (battery) coil terminal and the negative voltmeter lead is connected to ground, the voltmeter displays:
   a. Coil primary voltage drop
   b. Coil primary resistance
   c. Coil primary available voltage
   d. Coil potential voltage

8. Technician A says that an excessively high secondary voltage discharge can be caused by high primary circuit resistance.
   Technician B says a loss of secondary voltage will cause a greater loss of primary voltage.
   Who is right?
   a. A only
   b. B only
   c. Both A and B
   d. Neither A nor B

9. Technician A says that the battery must be able to provide at least 9.6 volts while cranking the engine.
   Technician B says a voltage drop of more than 0.2 volt across the battery ground cable can result in low cranking voltage.
   Who is right?
   a. A only
   b. B only
   c. Both A and B
   d. Neither A nor B

10. The current draw of an ignition coil is checked with:
    a. A voltmeter
    b. An ammeter
    c. An ohmmeter
    d. An oscilloscope

11. Technician A says that some electronic ignition distributors have an adjustable air gap between pick-up and reluctor.
    Technician B says that most air gaps can be adjusted with a standard 0.008-inch steel feeler gauge and a screwdriver.
    Who is right?
    a. A only
    b. B only
    c. Both A and B
    d. Neither A nor B

12. On an oscilloscope raster display of the secondary ignition system, the most likely cause of an 8 to 10 degree dwell variation between cylinders would be:
    a. Worn spark plugs
    b. Worn distributor bushings
    c. Defective ignition coil
    d. Incorrect ignition timing

13. Technician A says to check the primary winding resistance of an ignition coil by connecting one ohmmeter lead to the battery primary terminal and the other ohmmeter lead to the distributor terminal of the coil.
    Technician B says to check for a shorted coil winding, connect one ohmmeter lead to either coil primary terminal and touch the other ohmmeter lead to the metal case of the coil.
    Who is right?
    a. A only
    b. B only
    c. Both A and B
    d. Neither A nor B

14. To check total, centrifugal, and vacuum advance on a conventional distributor, all of the following instruments are used *EXCEPT*:
    a. Tachometer
    b. Vacuum pump
    c. Dwell meter
    d. Timing light

15. A magnetic timing meter pickup operates on the same principle as a(n):
    a. Magnetic pickup in a distributor
    b. Hall-effect sensor
    c. Stroboscopic timing light
    d. LED pickup coil

16. Which of the following materials should *NOT* be used for fuel lines?
    a. Rigid steel tubing
    b. Flexible nylon tubing
    c. Double-wall copper tubing
    d. Neoprene hose

17. Technician A says that a good mechanical fuel pump will deliver about a quart, or liter, of fuel per minute at an engine speed of 500 RPM.
    Technician B says that most fuel-injection pumps will deliver a quart, or liter, of fuel in less than 30 seconds.
    Who is right?
    a. A only
    b. B only
    c. Both A and B
    d. Neither A nor B

18. An electronic input device that provides a signal voltage based on the position of a movable wiper on a variable resistor is called a:
    a. Thermistor
    b. Motion detector
    c. Potentiometer
    d. Piezoelectric generator

19. Technician A says that a solenoid that operates with a varying duty cycle can be checked with a good DMM designed for automotive use.
    Technician B says the only way to check the variable duty cycle of a solenoid is with an oscilloscope.
    Who is right?
    a. A only
    b. B only
    c. Both A and B
    d. Neither A nor B

20. All of the following problems affect manifold vacuum gauge readings *EXCEPT*:
    a. Worn valves and valve guides
    b. Poor combustion chamber sealing
    c. Unmetered air leakage
    d. Exhaust restrictions

21. On a fuel injected engine, system pressure would be:
    a. The fuel pressure the pump is capable of producing
    b. The fuel pressure held in the lines with the pump off
    c. The fuel pressure used as a counterforce to regulate air-fuel mixture
    d. The regulated fuel pressure supplied to the injectors

22. An unmetered air leak downstream of the airflow sensor can cause:
    a. A lean condition and poor engine performance
    b. The PCM to provide additional fuel to compensate for the excess air during open-loop operation
    c. The needle of a vacuum gauge to fluctuate between 20 and 23 in-Hg with the engine running at idle
    d. The electronic control system to remain in the closed loop mode

23. Most turbocharger failures are caused by:
    a. Excessive high-speed operation
    b. Exhaust temperatures too high
    c. Dirt and contamination
    d. Operation with leaded gasoline

24. A turbocharger that makes a light, steady whistling sound that rises in pitch as the engine accelerates is an indication of:
    a. A loose exhaust pipe or outlet elbow
    b. An intake air leak
    c. Normal operation
    d. Damaged bearings

25. Technician A says that if you disconnect the hose from the PCV valve on a running engine, there should be a hissing noise from the valve and engine speed should drop slightly.
    Technician B says that with the engine at idle and the PCV hose disconnected from the PCV valve, you should feel a strong vacuum if you plug the valve with your finger and engine speed will drop if the system is working properly.
    Who is right?
    a. A only
    b. B only
    c. Both A and B
    d. Neither A nor B

26. Technician A says that the idle air control (IAC) valve may have to be disconnected to perform a cylinder balance test on an engine with a DIS system.
    Technician B says that the secondary wires are shorted to ground for each cylinder to perform a cylinder balance.
    Who is right?
    a. A only
    b. B only
    c. Both A and B
    d. Neither A nor B

27. A high idle speed and high step count on a speed density control system can be caused by all of the following *EXCEPT*:
    a. Stuck open IAC pintle
    b. IAC valve stuck closed
    c. A misadjusted throttle
    d. Vacuum leaks

28. The exhaust gas recirculation (EGR) system does all of the following *EXCEPT*:
    a. Reduce oxides of nitrogen emissions
    b. Slow down the combustion process
    c. Dilute the fuel mixture
    d. Raise peak combustion temperatures

29. An air injection system used to control emissions may use all of the following components *EXCEPT*:
    a. A wastegate
    b. A gulp valve
    c. An aspirator
    d. A check valve

30. Technician A says that a malfunction in the canister purge system can result in driveability problems and a loss of fuel economy.
    Technician B says that incorrect canister purging can change the air-fuel ratio and result in increased exhaust emissions.
    Who is right?
    a. A only
    b. B only
    c. Both A and B
    d. Neither A nor B

31. Technician A says that too much valve lash clearance can increase the effective camshaft duration and cause a rough idle.
    Technician B says that too much valve lash clearance will prevent the valves from seating properly and cause poor performance that can lead to burnt valves.
    Who is right?
    a. A only
    b. B only
    c. Both A and B
    d. Neither A nor B

32. Technician A says that high resistance in an electronic control circuit can cause problems because these systems use low voltage components.
    Technician B says that low resistance in an electronic actuator can cause PCM failure because it allows too much current to pass through it.
    Who is right?
    a. A only
    b. B only
    c. Both A and B
    d. Neither A nor B

33. A feeler gauge is not required to adjust the valves on a running engine that is equipped with:
    a. Stud-mounted adjustable rocker arms and hydraulic lifters
    b. Selective length pushrods and hydraulic lifters
    c. Overhead camshafts with shim-type adjusters
    d. Overhead camshafts with screw-type adjusters

34. Technician A says that a hard code failure is easy to troubleshoot because the problem that set the code still exists.
    Technician B says that to find the cause of an intermittent code failure, simply follow all the steps in the diagnostic chart for that code.
    Who is right?
    a. A only
    b. B only
    c. Both A and B
    d. Neither A nor B

A8

35. Problems in the cooling system can cause all of the following **EXCEPT**:
    a. Increased emission levels
    b. Reduced fuel economy
    c. Engine overloading
    d. Poor engine performance

36. An oxygen sensor signal voltage that remains below 450 mV indicates:
    a. A rich fuel mixture
    b. A lean fuel mixture
    c. Closed-loop operation
    d. The stoichiometric mixture

37. Technician A says that the operation of a fluid drive fan clutch can be checked using a timing light. Technician B says that the operation of an electric cooling fan may be controlled by the PCM.
    Who is right?
    a. A only
    b. B only
    c. Both A and B
    d. Neither A nor B

38. The most accurate way to check a PCM controlled solenoid is to:
    a. Measure the voltage drop to ground
    b. Measure the amperage draw through the driver circuit
    c. Measure voltage on the power circuit
    d. Measure solenoid resistance with an ohmmeter

39. Technician A says that the LDP is used to check for leaks in the intake manifold. Technician B says the LDP is part of the AIR system.
    Who is right?
    a. A only
    b. B only
    c. Both A and B
    d. Neither A nor B

40. A charging system oscilloscope trace that regularly drops out or spikes down is most likely caused by:
    a. An open diode
    b. A shorted diode
    c. High diode resistance
    d. A shorted stator winding

41. The starter control circuits include all of the following **EXCEPT**:
    a. The starter switch
    b. The starter motor
    c. The starter relay or solenoid winding
    d. The starting safety switch

42. Technician A says that with a voltmeter connected to the starter relay battery terminal and the relay switch terminals and the ignition on, a reading of 3.5 indicates high resistance in the relay control circuit. Technician B says this could indicate high resistance in the connections at the battery terminal lead to the ignition switch.
    Who is right?
    a. A only
    b. B only
    c. Both A and B
    d. Neither A nor B

43. An open in the circuit between the coil and distributor cap causes which of the following oscilloscope patterns?
    a. Reduced oscillations in the intermediate section
    b. An erratic jumping of the trace on the screen
    c. A high firing peak and short sparkline in the firing section
    d. Different firing spike heights between cylinders in parade display.

44. When all of the following methods of checking base timing are available, the most accurate would be:
    a. Static timing with a test light
    b. Dynamic timing with a magnetic probe
    c. Dynamic timing with a stroboscopic light
    d. Static timing with a magnetic probe

45. On a fuel injection system, all of the following can cause low residual pressure **EXCEPT**:
    a. Faulty fuel pump check valve
    b. Leaking injectors
    c. Defective pressure regulator
    d. A clogged fuel filter

46. All of the following are methods to relieve fuel pressure **EXCEPT**:
    a. Apply vacuum to the fuel pressure regulator using a hand-vacuum pump
    b. Use a special pressure gauge that has a relief valve.
    c. Remove the fuel pump fuse and start the engine
    d. Open fuel tank gas cap

47. If an LDP DTC is present, the primary cause of failure is:
    a. Non-functioning three-port solenoid
    b. Open or closed vacuum-driven pump reed switch
    c. A loose or incorrect fuel filler cap
    d. Stuck canister vent valve

48. Which of the following is the typical operating pressure range of a port injection system?
    a. May vary from about 35 psi to more than 60 psi
    b. 10 to 15 psi
    c. 15 to 25 psi
    d. 25 to 35 psi

49. When inspecting a spark plug, which of the following conditions would indicate detonation?
    a. A clean white insulator tip
    b. Soft, black, sooty deposits on insulator tip
    c. Dark wet deposits on insulator tip
    d. Fractured or broken insulator tip

50. An electronic ignition system primary circuit will not energize until the module receives a verifiable engine speed signal from which of the following sensors?
    a. Engine Coolant Temperature (ECT)
    b. Camshaft Position (CMP)
    c. Crankshaft Position (CKP)
    d. Throttle Position (TP)

51. The dwell section of an ignition system oscilloscope display corresponds to:
    a. The time the primary circuit is closed
    b. The time the primary circuit is open
    c. The time the coil is discharging excess enrgy
    d. The time secondary voltage is flowing to the spark plug

52. Technician A says a four-gas exhaust analyzer is not used to measure oxides of nitrogen (NO_x).
Technician B says a four-gas exhaust analyzer is used to measure oxides of nitrogen (NO_x).
Who is right?
a. A only
b. B only
c. Both A and B
d. Neither A nor B

53. Which test is the most effective for determining the condition of a battery?
a. Visual
b. Specific gravity
c. State-of-charge
d. Open circuit voltage

54. High levels of hydrocarbons (HC) in the exhaust are a result of:
a. A rich air-fuel mixture
b. Unburned fuel
c. A lean air fuel mixture
d. A defective catalytic converter

55. All of the following are types of position or speed sensors *EXCEPT*:
a. Magnetic pickup
b. Hall-effect
c. Optical
d. Thermistor

56. Technician A says a thermistor is a sensor that provides variable resistance across an operating range. Technician B says a potentionmeter is a sensor that measures resistance changes in proportion to temperature.
Who is right?
a. A only
b. B only
c. Both A and B
d. Neither A nor B

57. The purpose of the fuel pressure regulator in a fuel injection system is to?
a. Limit pressure produced by the fuel pump
b. Maintain uniform pressure at the injectors
c. Maintain residual pressure for quick startup
d. Control air-fuel ratio

58. The oxygen sensor voltage readings are minimum 190 mV, maximum 750 mV, with an average of 380 mV. Technician A says this indicates a lean engine running condition. Technician B says this indicates a rich engine running condition.
Who is right?
a. A only
b. B only
c. Both A and B
d. Neither A nor B

59. Which of the following sensor signals is *NOT* used during open loop engine operation?
a. MAF sensor
b. HO2 sensor
c. CKP sensor
d. TPS

60. During a cranking voltage test, a starter motor should crank freely and voltmeter readings should remain above:
a. 12.0 volts
b. 10.2 volts
c. 9.6 volts
d. 8.7 volts

ANSWERS

Chapter 1:
1. c, 2. a, 3. b, 4. a, 5. c, 6. c, 7. d, 8. c, 9. b, 10. a, 11. c, 12. d

Chapter 2:
1. b, 2. c, 3. b, 4. c, 5. c, 6. d, 7. d, 8. c

Chapter 3:
1. a, 2. d, 3. d, 4. b, 5. c, 6. b, 7. c, 8. d, 9. a

Chapter 4:
1. d, 2. b, 3. c, 4. a, 5. a, 6. c, 7. d, 8. d

Chapter 5:
1. b, 2. a, 3. c, 4. a, 5. b, 6. d, 7. a, 8. c, 9. b, 10. b, 11. b, 12. b, 13. c

Sample Test:
1. b, 2. a, 3. d, 4. b, 5. b, 6. a, 7. c, 8. d, 9. c, 10. b, 11. a, 12. b, 13. c, 14. c, 15. a, 16. c, 17. c, 18. c, 19. a, 20. c, 21. d, 22. a, 23. c, 24. c, 25. d, 26. c, 27. b, 28. d, 29. a, 30. c, 31. d, 32. c, 33. a, 34. a, 35. c, 36. b, 37. c, 38. b, 39. a, 40. a, 41. b, 42. c, 43. a, 44. b, 45. d, 46. d, 47. c, 48. a, 49. d, 50. c, 51. a, 52. a, 53. c, 54. b, 55. d, 56. d, 57. b, 58. a, 59. b, 60. c

A8

GLOSSARY

Actuator: A device that receives a voltage signal or command from a computer and responds by performing a mechanical action.

Air-Fuel Ratio: The ratio of air to fuel by weight of the air and fuel mixture drawn into the engine.

Airflow Sensor: A sensor used to measure the rate, density, temperature, or volume of air entering the engine.

Air Gap: The precise space between a pickup coil and trigger wheel. The correct air gap is critical to proper operation of the sensor.

Ammeter: An ammeter is an instrument used for measuring the current flow in an electrical or electronic circuit. Some ammeters are intended for use in direct current (DC) circuits; others are designed for alternating current (AC) circuits.

Ampere: The unit for measuring electrical current flow.

Analog Signal: A voltage signal or processing action that varies continuously with the variable being measured or controlled.

Atmospheric Pressure: Weight of air at sea level, about 14.7 pounds per square inch, decreasing at higher altitudes.

Available Voltage: The voltage present at a given point within the electrical system.

Backpressure: A pressure created by restrictions in the exhaust system that tends to slow the exit of exhaust gases from the combustion chamber.

Binary: A mathematical system containing only two digits (0 and 1), used by digital computers to process information, make calculations, and develop output commands.

Boost Pressure: The amount of air pressure increase above atmospheric pressure provided by a turbocharger.

Breakout Box (BOB): A breakout box is a service tool that tees-in between the computer and the multi-pin harness connector. Once connected in series with the computer and the harness, it permits measurements of computer signals.

Carbon Dioxide (CO_2): A colorless, odorless, incombustible gas formed as a byproduct of combustion in a gasoline engine. Although not considered a pollutant, carbon dioxide percentage in the exhaust can be used to determine combustion efficiency.

Carbon Monoxide (CO) An odorless, colorless, tasteless, poisonous gas. A major pollutant from an internal combustion engine.

Catalyst: Specific compounds that enhance a chemical reaction without being consumed by the reaction.

Centrifugal Advance: A method of advancing the ignition spark using weights in the distributor that react to centrifugal force generated by engine speed.

Check Valve: A valve that permits flow in one direction but prevents it in the opposite direction.

Circuit: A circle or unbroken path of conductors composed of wiring, switches, and other electrical components that leads to and from a power source through the component operated by the electric current.

Closed-Loop: An operational mode in which the PCM reads and responds to feedback signals from its sensors and adjusts system operation accordingly.

Compression Pressure: The total amount of air pressure developed by a piston moving to TDC with both valves closed.

Crankshaft Position Sensor (CKP): An electronic device designed to supply engine RPM and position to the PCM.

Data Link Connector (DLC): A dedicated point for attaching a scan tool to the vehicle communications network.

Data Parameter or Parameter Identifiers: A measured value of control system input or output operation. Parameters include voltage signals, as well as temperature, pressure, speed, and other data.

Detonation: An unwanted explosion of an air-fuel mixture caused by high heat and compression. Also called knocking or spark knock.

Diagnostic Trouble Code (DTC): A numeric or alphanumeric sequence relating directly to an abnormal signal from a sensor in the onboard electronic system.

Dielectric Resistance: A poor conductor of electrical current or a high resistance.

Digital Multimeter: A hand-held meter capable of measuring voltage, resistance, and current flow, then displaying it in digital format on an LCD screen.

Digital Storage Oscilloscope (DSO): A digital style oscilloscope with the ability to store data for review at a later time.

Diode: An electronic semiconductor device that acts as an electrical gate to allow current in one direction but not the other. Diodes are used to rectify alternating current produced by a generator into direct current.

Drive-by-Wire: A throttle control system that relies on electronic signals from the accelerator pedal position sensor to direct the PCM or throttle actuator control module to operate the throttle blade(s).

Duty Cycle: The percentage of total time in one complete on-off-on cycle during which an output device is energized.

Dwell or Dwell Angle: Also called cam angle. The measurement in degrees of how far the distributor cam rotates while the primary circuit is closed.

Dynamometer: A machine used to measure mechanical power, such as the power of an engine.

EEPROM: Electronically Eraseable Programmable Read Only Memory—memory that does not erase when voltage is removed. A scan tool is required to erase DTCs stored in EEPROM.

Electrolyte: The chemical solution composed of sulfuric acid and water that conducts electricity and reacts with the plate materials in a battery.

Electromagnet: A soft iron core wrapped in a coil of a current-carrying conductor. Current in the coil induces a magnetic field around the core.

Electrostatic Discharge (ESD): The passage of a static electrical charge from a component to ground. Generally associated with the potential for damage to electronic components.

Field Circuit: The charging system circuit that delivers current to energize the generator field.

Frequency: The number of periodic voltage oscillations, or waves, occurring in a given unit of time, usually expressed as cycles per second or Hertz.

Graphing Multimeter (GMM): A multimeter displays signals in conventional digital format or in a value-over-time relationship.

Gulp Valve: A valve used in an air injection system to prevent backfire. During deceleration it redirects air from the air pump to the intake manifold to lean out the air-fuel mixture.

Hall-Effect Sensor: A signal-generating switch that develops a transverse voltage across a current-carrying semiconductor when subjected to a magnetic field.

Hard Code: A diagnostic trouble code that comes back within one cycle of the ignition key is a "hard" code. This means that the defect is there every time the powertrain control module checks that circuit or function.

Hertz (Hz): A unit of frequency measurement equal to one cycle per second.

High-Impedance: A high level of opposition to current created by the combined forces of resistance, capacitance, and inductance in a circuit.

Hydrocarbon (HC): A chemical compound made up of hydrogen and carbon, which is major pollutant given off by an internal combustion engine. Gasoline itself is a hydrocarbon compound.

Ignition Control Module (ICM): An electronic module designed to control the primary circuit to the ignition coil.

Induction: The creation of an electrical current as a conductor moves through a magnetic field or when a magnetic field moves across a conductor.

Infinite Resistance: A condition caused by an incomplete or open circuit that prevents current through the circuit.

Intermittent or Soft Code: A diagnostic trouble code that is not there every time the PCM checks the circuit.

Magnetic Pickup: A signal-generating device that uses a permanent magnet to create a voltage pulse. The trigger wheel movement creates magnetic flux changes in the pickup coil to induce a varying-strength voltage.

Malfunction Indicator Lamp (MIL): A lamp mounted on the instrument cluster to alert the driver that an emission system component is operating out of its specified range.

Manifold Absolute Pressure: Combination of atmospheric and manifold pressure or boost pressure.

Manifold Pressure: Vacuum, or low air pressure, in the intake manifold of a running engine, caused by the descending pistons creating empty space in the cylinders faster than the entering air can fill it.

Ohmmeter: A meter designed to measure the resistance of a circuit or component. DMMs can be set to an ohmmeter function.

Onboard Diagnostics II (OBD II): Regulations governing the tailpipe emissions from motor vehicles. Most light-duty vehicles built after 1995 must comply with OBD II standards.

Open-Loop: An operational mode in which the PCM adjusts a system to function according to predetermined instructions and does not always respond to feedback signals from its sensors.

Orifice: A small opening or restriction in a line or passage that is used to regulate pressure and flow.

Oscillations: Steady, uninterrupted up-and-down swings, or waveforms.

Oscilloscope: An oscilloscope is an instrument commonly used to display and analyze the waveform of electronic signals. In effect, the device draws a graph of the instantaneous signal voltage as a function of time. Also known as a lab scope.

Oxides of Nitrogen (NOx): Various combinations of nitrogen and oxygen that form when exposed to high cylinder temperatures. NO_x is responsible for the formation of photochemical smog.

Oxidize: To combine an element with oxygen, or convert it into its oxide. For example, when carbon burns, it combines with oxygen to form carbon dioxide or carbon monoxide.

Parade Pattern: Oscilloscope display that shows voltage traces for all cylinders displayed one after another in firing order from left to right across the screen.

Potentiometer: A variable resistor with three terminals. Return signal voltage is taken from a terminal attached to a movable contact that passes over the resistor.

Powertrain Control Module (PCM): The PCM is an onboard computer programmed to control the operation of the engine and many transmission functions.

Preignition: A premature ignition of the air-fuel mixture before the spark plug fires. It is caused by excessive heat or pressure in the combustion chamber.

Pull-Up Resistor: A resistor installed in the PCM in series with the sensor thermistor to protect the electronic components from a short to ground.

Pulse Width Modulation (PWM): A signal with a variable on-time to off-time ratio. Usually used to control solenoid-type actuators.

Raster Pattern: Oscilloscope display that shows voltage traces for all cylinders stacked top to bottom or bottom to top on the screen in firing order sequence.

Residual Pressure: A constant pressure held in the fuel system when the pump is not operating.

Resistor: An electronic component that impedes current flow. Resistors are used to lower the voltage applied to another device.

Scan Tool: A test instrument that is used to access powertrain control system trouble codes and freeze frame data, and has bi-directional control of system actuators.

Schrader Valve: A service valve that uses a spring-loaded pin and internal pressure to seal a port.

Sensor: A device that provides an electric signal to a computer to indicate a certain physical condition. In an automotive electronic system, sensors monitor such conditions as vehicle speed, throttle opening, or steering angle.

Serial Data Stream: The electronic data transmitted by an onboard computer to a scan tool frame by frame.

Short Term Memory: Values stored in the PCM pertaining to the air-fuel ratio at specific engine RPM and load conditions. Short term memory is constantly updated during engine operation.

Signal Voltage: The variable input voltage a sensor transmits to the PCM. Signal voltage equals reference voltage minus the voltage dropped to ground by the sensor.

Solenoid: An electromagnetic actuator consisting of a movable iron core with an induction coil surrounding it. When electrical current is applied to the coil, the core moves to convert electrical energy to mechanical energy.

Spark Tester: A special tool with an adjustable spark gap used to check spark intensity.

Specific Gravity: The weight of a liquid relative to water, which has an assigned value of 1.0. In an automotive storage battery, the specific gravity is measured with a hydrometer. When corrected to a temperature of 80°F (27°C), the specific gravity of a fully charged battery falls in the 1.260 to 1.280 range.

Stepper Motor: A direct current motor whose armature moves in small increments, or steps, as different coils are energized in sequence. As the armature moves, a threaded pintel moves in and out along with it.

Stoichiometric: The air-fuel ratio of approximately 14.7:1 that provides the most complete combustion and combination of oxygen and hydrocarbon molecules.

Superimposed Pattern: Oscilloscope display that shows voltage traces for all cylinders one on top of, or superimposed upon, another to form a single pattern.

System Pressure: Fuel injection operating pressure created by the fuel pump.

Thermistor: An electronic component whose resistance to electric current changes rapidly and predictably as its temperature changes.

Thermostatic Bulb: A device that automatically responds to changes in temperature to actuate a damper in the air intake.

Thermostatic Vacuum Switch: A device that automatically responds to changes in temperature to operate a switch that opens or closes a vacuum port.

Top Dead Center (TDC): The point in engine rotation when cylinder number one is at the top of its travel and the valves are closed.

Vehicle Emissions Control Information (VECI): An underhood label containing specific emissions and idle speed information.

Viscous Fan Clutch: A temperature-sensing fan drive filled with a silicone fluid. As the temperature of the air passing the clutch increases, the internal valving in the clutch allows the fluid to flow into the coupling and increases the speed of the fan blade.

Voltage Drop: The measurement of the loss of voltage caused by the resistance of a conductor or a circuit device.

Voltmeter: A voltmeter is an instrument used for measuring the potential difference, or voltage, between two points in an electrical or electronic circuit. Some voltmeters are intended for use in direct current (DC) circuits; others are designed for alternating current (AC) circuits.

Wastegate: A diaphragm-actuated bypass valve used to limit turbocharger boost pressure by limiting the speed of the exhaust turbine.

Wave Rectification: A process by which the alternating current (AC) produced by a generator is converted to the direct current (DC) needed to charge the battery and power electrical devices on the vehicle.

A8

L1

ADVANCED ENGINE PERFORMANCE SPECIALIST

TEST BACKGROUND INFORMATION

The purpose of the L1 test is to evaluate your knowledge of diagnosing powertrain driveability problems and emission failures on electronically controlled systems. The ASE changed some of the test questions and updated the composite vehicle.

Test Content

Diagnostic area	Number of questions
General Powertrain Diagnosis	5
Computerized Powertrain Control Diagnosis (Including OBD II)	13
Ignition System Diagnosis	7
Fuel System and Air Induction Systems Diagnosis	7
Emission Control Systems Diagnosis	10
IM Failure Diagnosis	8
Total	50

Note:

The test may contain up to 15 additional questions for ASE research purposes. Your answers to these questions do not affect your score. However, since you do not know which questions they are, you must answer all to the best of your ability and plan time for up to 65 questions. At press time, according to ASE, the L1 certification and re-certification tests have the same content.

Summary of the ASE L1 Test

You are expected to be certified in A8 engine performance and have skill diagnosing problems or failures in the following areas:

- General powertrain
- Computerized powertrain controls
- Ignition systems
- Fuel systems and air induction systems
- Emission control systems
- State emission inspection and maintenance programs

To test your ability to read and understand shop manuals, the ASE designed a composite vehicle reference book that you must reference for some test questions. For those technicians that are re-certifying, note the following:

The new type 3 composite vehicle has a generic four cycle V6 engine. The engine has four chain driven overhead camshafts and 24 valves. The sequential multi-port fuel injection system uses a mass airflow sensor. The ignition system is distributorless and uses one coil over each spark plug. The system uses no spark plug wires.

The major additions from the previous composite vehicle engine include VVT (Variable Valve Timing), TAC (Electronic Throttle Control Actuator), data communications bus, anti-theft immobilizer system, electronically controlled EGR (Exhaust Gas Recirculation) and ORVR (Onboard Refueling Vapor Recovery) evaporative emission control system components.

Scan tool data includes on board diagnostic (OBD) II system monitors, and readiness status.

The test may include engine cooling and exhaust system problems. The use of the word "powertrain" means the technician must expect questions on electronic control of the transmission, and the effect of modifications on electronically controlled systems. Diagnosis includes scope waveform analysis of crankshaft and camshaft sensors.

Fuel system diagnosis is strictly of fuel injection systems, and the subject of fuel quality has been added. Emission failure diagnostic questions include: State emission inspection and maintenance (IM) 240, acceleration simulation mode (ASM), and two speed idle (TSI) emissions tests results.

ASE L1 TASK LIST

Carefully read the Task List, noting the areas in which your skills are strong or weak. You can do this by checking off each task that you do not perform often or do not understand completely.

A. General Powertrain Diagnosis (5 questions)

1. Inspect and test for missing, modified, inoperative, or tampered powertrain mechanical components.
2. Locate relevant service information.
3. Research system operation using technical information to determine diagnostic procedure.
4. Use appropriate diagnostic procedures based on available vehicle data and service information; determine if available information is adequate to proceed with effective diagnosis.
5. Establish relative importance of observed vehicle data.
6. Differentiate between powertrain mechanical and electrical/electronic problems, including variable valve timing (VVT) systems.
7. Diagnose engine mechanical condition using an exhaust gas analyzer.
8. Diagnose driveability problems and emission failures caused by cooling system problems.

9. Diagnose driveability problems and emission failures caused by engine mechanical problems.
10. Diagnose driveability problems and emission failures caused by problems or modifications in the transmission and final drive, or by incorrect tire size.
11. Diagnose driveability problems and emission failures caused by exhaust system problems or modifications.
12. Determine root cause of failures.
13. Determine root cause of multiple component failures.
14. Determine root cause of repeated component failures.

B. Computerized Powertrain Controls Diagnosis Including OBD II (13 questions)

1. Inspect and test for missing, modified, inoperative, or tampered computerized powertrain control components.
2. Locate relevant service information.
3. Research system operation using technical information to determine diagnostic procedure.
4. Use appropriate diagnostic procedures based on available vehicle data and service information; determine if available information is adequate to proceed with effective diagnosis.
5. Determine current version of computerized powertrain control system software and updates; perform reprogramming procedures.
6. Research OBD II system operation to determine the enable criteria for setting and clearing diagnostic trouble codes (DTCs) and malfunction indicator lamp (MIL) operation.
7. Interpret OBD II scan tool data stream, diagnostic trouble codes (DTCs), freeze frame data, system monitors, monitor readiness indicators, and trip and drive cycle information to determine system condition and verify repair effectiveness.
8. Establish relative importance of displayed scan tool data.
9. Differentiate between electronic powertrain control problems and mechanical problems.
10. Diagnose no-starting, hard starting, stalling, engine misfire, poor driveability, incorrect idle speed, poor idle, hesitation, surging, spark knock, power loss, poor mileage, illuminated MIL, and emission problems caused by failures of computerized powertrain controls.
11. Diagnose failures in the data communications bus network; determine needed repairs.
12. Diagnose failures in the anti-theft/immobilizer system; determine needed repairs.
13. Perform voltage drop tests on power circuits and ground circuits.
14. Perform current flow tests on system circuits.
15. Perform continuity/resistance tests on system circuits and components.
16. Test input sensor/sensor circuit using scan tool data and/or waveform analysis.
17. Test output actuator/output circuit using scan tool, scan tool data, and /or waveform analysis.
18. Confirm the accuracy of observed scan tool data by directly measuring a system, circuit, or component for the actual value.
19. Test and confirm operation of electrical/electronic circuits not displayed in scan tool data.

20. Determine root cause of failures.
21. Determine root cause of multiple component failures.
22. Determine root cause of repeated component failures.
23. Verify effectiveness of repairs.

C. Ignition System Diagnosis (7 questions)

1. Inspect and test for missing, modified, inoperative, or tampered components.
2. Locate relevant service information.
3. Research system operation using technical information to determine diagnostic procedure.
4. Use appropriate diagnostic procedures based on available vehicle data and service information; determine if available information is adequate to proceed with effective diagnosis.
5. Establish relative importance of displayed scan tool data.
6. Differentiate between ignition electrical/electronic and ignition mechanical problems.
7. Diagnose no-starting, hard starting, stalling, engine misfire, poor driveability, spark knock, power loss, poor mileage, illuminated MIL, and emission problems on vehicles equipped with distributorless ignition (DI) systems; determine needed repairs.
8. Diagnose no-starting, hard starting, stalling, engine misfire, poor driveability, spark knock, power loss, poor mileage, illuminated MIL, and emission problems on vehicles equipped with distributor ignition (DI) systems; determine needed repairs.
9. Test for ignition system failures under various engine load conditions.
10. Test ignition system component operation using waveform analysis.
11. Confirm base ignition timing and/or spark timing control.
12. Determine root cause of failures.
13. Determine root cause of multiple component failures.
14. Determine root cause of repeated component failures.

D. Fuel Systems and Air Induction Systems Diagnosis (7 questions)

1. Inspect and test for missing, modified, inoperative, or tampered components.
2. Locate relevant service information.
3. Research system operation using technical to determine diagnostic procedure.
4. Evaluate the relationships between fuel trim values, oxygen sensor readings, and other sensor data to determine fuel system control performance.
5. Use appropriate diagnostic procedures based on available vehicle data and service information; determine if available information is adequate to proceed with effective diagnosis.
6. Establish relative importance of displayed scan tool data.
7. Differentiate between fuel system mechanical and fuel system/electronic problems.
8. Differentiate between air induction system mechanical and air induction system electrical/electronic problems, including electronic throttle actuator control (TAC) systems.
9. Diagnose hot or cold no-starting, hard starting, stalling, engine misfire, poor driveability, spark knock, incorrect

L1

idle speed, poor idle, flooding, hesitation, surging power loss, poor mileage, dieseling, illuminated MIL, and emission problems on vehicles equipped with fuel injection fuel systems; determine needed action.

10. Verify fuel quality, fuel system pressure, and fuel system volume.
11. Evaluate fuel injector and fuel pump performance (mechanical and electrical operation).
12. Determine root cause of failures.
13. Determine root cause of multiple component failures.
14. Determine root cause of repeated component failures.

E. Emission Control Systems Diagnosis (10 questions)

1. Inspect and test for missing, modified, inoperative, or tampered components.
2. Locate relevant service information.
3. Research system operation using technical information to determine diagnostic procedure.
4. Use appropriate diagnostic procedures based on available vehicle data and service information; determine if available information is adequate to proceed with effective diagnosis.
5. Establish relative importance of displayed scan tool data.
6. Differentiate between emission control systems mechanical and electrical/electronic problems.
   Note: Tasks 7 though 11 refer to the following emission control subsystems: Positive crankcase ventilation, ignition timing control, idle and deceleration speed control, exhaust gas recirculation, catalytic converter system, secondary air injection system, intake air temperature control, early fuel evaporation control, and evaporative emission control (including ORVR).
7. Determine need to diagnose emission control subsystems.
8. Perform functional tests on emission control subsystems; determine needed repairs.
9. Determine the effect on exhaust emissions caused by a failure of an emission control component or subsystem.
10. Use exhaust gas analyzer readings to diagnose the failure of an emission control component or subsystem.
11. Diagnose hot or cold no-starting, hard starting, stalling, engine misfire, poor driveability, spark knock, incorrect idle speed, poor idle, flooding, hesitation, surging, power loss, poor mileage, dieseling, illuminated MIL, and emission problems caused by a failure of emission control components or subsystems.
12. Determine root cause of failures.
13. Determine root cause of multiple component failures.
14. Determine root cause of repeated component failures.
15. Verify effectiveness of repairs.

F. I/M Failure Diagnosis (8 questions)

1. Inspect and test for missing, modified, inoperative, or tampered components.
2. Locate relevant service information.
3. Evaluate emission readings obtained during an I/M test to assist in emission failure diagnosis and repair.
4. Evaluate HC, CO, NOx, CO2, and O2 gas readings; determine the failure relationships.

5. Use test instruments to observe, recognize and interpret electrical/electronic signals.
6. Analyze HC, CO, NOx, CO2, and O2 readings; determine diagnostic test sequence.
7. Diagnose the cause of no-load I/M test HC emission failures,
8. Diagnose the cause of no-load I/M test CO emission failures.
9. Diagnose the cause of loaded-mode I/M test HC emission failures.
10. Diagnose the cause of loaded-mode I/M test CO emission failures.
11. Diagnose the cause of loaded-mode I/M test NOx emission failures.
12. Evaluate the MIL operation for onboard diagnostic I/M testing.
13. Evaluate monitor readiness status for onboard diagnostic I/M testing.
14. Diagnose communication failures with the vehicle during onboard diagnostic I/M testing.
15. Perform functional I/M tests (including fuel cap tests).
16. Verify effectiveness of repairs.

ABOUT THIS STUDY GUIDE

This study guide does not attempt to instruct you in ASE A8 level subjects. If you need a review of those subjects, we recommend the Chek-Chart ASE A8 Study Guide. The Chek-Chart ASE A6 Study Guide should also be helpful if you need brushing up in the electrical area. The Chek-Chart Scan Tool and Lab Scope Guide would make an excellent companion to this study guide.

This guide begins by presenting a diagnostic path and thought process. This path describes a slightly different diagnostic approach for driveability problems than it does for emission failure problems. The guide gives a review of diagnostic tests and values used in testing basic engine systems. Emission control systems in the ASE task list are discussed by comparing symptoms to problems. In addition, there are chapters on the ASE composite vehicle and OBD II system diagnosis, and the I/M failure diagnosis, ignition systems, and fuel and air induction systems. In the back of the guide, you will find a helpful glossary and sample test and discussion.

RECOMMENDED TEST PREPARATION

Study and review the diagnosis of defects in the following subject areas:

- Engine: mechanical, air intake, cylinder sealing, valve train, cooling, and exhaust systems.
- Transmission: torque converter lock up and electronic shift control.
- Ignition system: distributor and distributorless types.
- Fuel injection system: fuel quality, fuel delivery, and fuel control.
- Emission systems: PCV, electronic timing control, deceleration emission controls, idle speed controls, EGR, exhaust catalysts, secondary air injection, intake air temperature controls, early fuel evaporation systems, and evaporative systems.
- IM: visual, functional, and tailpipe test failures

CHAPTER OBJECTIVES

- The technician will complete the ASE task list on Basic Powertrain Diagnosis.
- The technician will be able to answer 5 questions dealing with the Basic Powertrain Diagnosis section of the L1 ASE Test.

DIAGNOSTIC PATH AND THOUGHT PROCESS

To diagnose powertrain driveability or emission problems and determine the root cause of a symptom, you must use your knowledge of the following systems:

- Engine mechanical: Air intake, **cylinder sealing**, valvetrain, and exhaust
- Ignition: Triggering, primary, and secondary
- Fuel injection: Pump, regulator, lines, hoses, injectors, idle air control, cranking, and open loop **fuel control**
- Emission controls: Positive crankcase ventilation (PCV), ignition timing control, deceleration **enleanment**, exhaust gas re-circulation (EGR), **catalyst**, closed loop fuel control, secondary air injection, intake air temperature control, and evaporative emission control (EVAP)
- Transmission and **final drive**: Electronic control of torque converter lock-up and shift control

Keep the driveability or tailpipe emission symptom in mind. Begin with a visual inspection, looking for obvious flaws such as missing, modified, disconnected, or defective components. The term visual inspection may be misleading; moving things out of your way, flexing and wiggling wire and vacuum connections, and tapping on components are an important part of visual inspections. Also take the time to verify that all ECM and sensor grounds are clean and tight. Perform a ground circuit **voltage drop** test if necessary.

Don't waste time looking for the solution to a problem for which the **original equipment manufacturer (OEM)** already has a proven cure. Check the technical service bulletins (TSBs) for the vehicle in your shop's reference library or electronic files.

In some cases, you will want to look up OEM system operation to know correct OEM system operation prior to testing it. Before performing a test on a device or system, note the specifications and any OEM special pre-test requirements or procedures.

Locating electrical parts can be difficult and time consuming. An electrical component locator manual can sometimes indicate where to begin the search.

To find this or other information, you will need to properly identify the vehicle application. You will need to use the following information:

- Vehicle year
- Make
- Model
- Production date
- VIN
- Engine size
- **Emissions certification type**

Since the symptom has to do with engine performance or tailpipe emission, you should check the engine's mechanical condition first, then make the customer aware of any expensive problems. At this point, it is the customer's choice whether or not to proceed.

The right approach to the diagnosis depends on the symptom and the amount of preliminary information available to you. Think of the problem as existing somewhere in a pyramid of systems, figure 1-1.

Depending on the information already at hand, you could start the search for the cause of the symptom using a tailpipe gas analysis. Check any emissions-related trouble code. Then work from the top of the pyramid down.

Catalyst: A substance that speeds or aids in a chemical reaction.
Cylinder Sealing Parts: Engine parts that contain compression or combustion in the cylinder, piston rings, valves, and headgasket.
Emissions Certification Type: A reference to whether the vehicle has a Federal or California emissions system configuration.
Enleanment: To make leaner, as in adding less fuel to the mixture.
Final Drive: Usually refers to the driveshaft, differential gears, and drive axles.
Fuel Control: A statement of whether or not the PCM is able to deliver the correct, and quickly varying, fuel mixture to satisfy the needs of a three-way catalytic converter.
Original Equipment Manufacturer (OEM): The manufacturer that made the component for its original assembly when new.
Voltage Drop: The measurement of the loss of voltage caused by unwanted resistance in a circuit connection, conductor, or device.

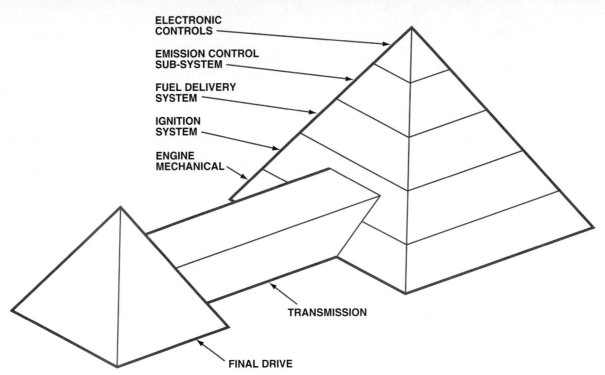

ELECTRONIC
CONTROLS

EMISSION CONTROL
SUB-SYSTEM

FUEL DELIVERY
SYSTEM

IGNITION
SYSTEM

ENGINE
MECHANICAL

TRANSMISSION

FINAL DRIVE

Fig. 1-1. The pyramid of powertrain systems is made up of vehicle systems that can cause engine performance or emissions symptoms.

In Chapter 5, Emission Control System Failures, you will be guided to the next step of this diagnostic path, to uncover the causes of emission failures.

Your actual diagnostic path may be guided by:

- State emissions test failure flow charts
- Original equipment manufacturer (OEM) no-code driveability flow charts
- OEM trouble code diagnostic flow charts
- Company policies

Insight
Remember, some flow charts do not tell you to check the basics, or the obvious; they take it for granted it has been done!

Verifying the Driveability Symptom

Knowing the symptom helps organize your approach. The operator of the vehicle is a good source for this information. Get the driver to describe the symptom in as much detail as possible. It is important to know what the complaint is, the conditions under which it occurs, and the severity of the symptoms. Typically, you want to know:

- Whether it occurs regularly or at random, and if it is happening now
- If certain conditions, such as accelerating or climbing hills, cause or contribute to the symptom
- If the problem exists all the time or some of the time

- If the problem occurs at certain temperatures, such as on cold starts or after a **hot soak**
- What all the symptoms are, noises, vibrations, smells, performance, or any combination
- Whether the problem has occurred before, and what was done to repair it
- When the vehicle was last serviced and what work was performed

The actual symptom may be different from the customer's description of it, or your understanding of it may be different from the customer's. Having the customer accompany you on a test drive to pinpoint symptoms as they occur would be ideal. There is nothing better than your own observation of the symptom. Just make sure you are working on the right one.

Verifying the Emission Symptom

The customer's description of a symptom may, or may not, be relevant to the emission failure. In this case, the customer's description of an unrelated symptom may mislead you from the true cause of the emissions test failure. Use your best judgment.

Begin with the **vehicle inspection report (VIR)** or perform your own inspection.

Verify the type of failure first:

- Visual
- Functional
- Tailpipe emission

Then compare your inspection results to the VIR.

Hot Soak: A period of time after shutting down a warm engine where heat saturates the combustion chambers, valvetrain, intake, and residual fuel.
Vehicle Inspection Report (VIR): Reports the results of a state emissions inspection.

Intuitive Diagnosis

At this point, you may be tempted to use an intuitive approach. This approach relies on working knowledge and experience, based on past successes fixing problems. You are counting on the high likelihood that the cause is the same as previous experience has shown.

Use this method to guide you only to systems that need testing. Do not let this method lead you to replace parts until the proper testing is done. Make sure the success of this repair is verified with care. The intuitive method can be a valuable addition to your diagnostic skill.

ELECTRICAL REVIEW

To help you make better diagnoses, this section begins with a brief refresher on electrical behavior and explains measuring the different aspects of an electrical charge using common test equipment. It is important to understand the fundamental behavior of electricity before you attempt to troubleshoot an electrical or electronic problem. There is no mystery to electricity, and how it behaves under any given circumstance is entirely predictable. The section concludes with a short discussion of **Ohm's Law** and how to apply it to diagnostic situations.

Electrical Current

Electricity is a form of energy that results when electrons, which are negatively charged atomic particles, transfer from one atom to another. This **electron** transfer occurs most readily in materials known as conductors and can be activated by an external force, such as heat, friction, or a magnetic field. Electrons tend to move at random but can be organized and directed. Electric **current** is the controlled flow of electrons from atom to atom within a **conductor**.

To control the flow of electrical power a path must be provided for the current to follow. These pathways, or circuits, route the electrical charge to various points, where it is used to perform work. In order to function, a circuit must form a complete loop so that electron transfer remains uninterrupted, figure 1-2. Automotive circuitry begins at one battery terminal, travels through the wiring harnesses, and returns to the other battery terminal. If there is a break, or open, in the circuit, current cannot flow since the electrons have nowhere to go, and no work can be performed, figure 1-3.

Amperage

The amount of current flowing through a circuit, conductor, or electrical device is rated in **amperage** or amps. Amperage is determined by counting the number of electrons that move past a certain point in the circuit in a given amount of time.

The ampere is the unit that indicates the rate of electric current flowing through a circuit.

Ammeter

An **ammeter** is a gauge that is used to measure the current flow in a circuit. Typical ammeters are connected in series with the circuit or component to be tested. The meter bridges the gap in an open circuit so that all the current flows through the meter, figure 1-4. The second type of ammeter uses an **inductive pickup** clamp around the circuit being tested. The meter reads the strength of the electromagnetic field created by the current passing through the inductive clamp. **Digital** ammeters have high input **impedance** that results in an extremely low amount of current being drawn off the circuit when connected in series. Since all ammeters have low resistance, they will act as a **jumper wire** to short a circuit if connected in parallel.

Observing correct polarity is important when using an ammeter with an inductive pickup. Most inductive clamps are marked with an arrow, which points in the direction of current flow when properly connected, figure 1-5.

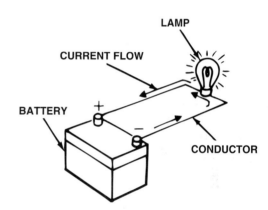

Fig. 1-2. No matter how simple or complex, an electrical circuit must form a complete loop in order for current to flow.

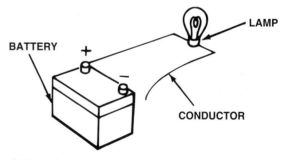

Fig. 1-3. Any break or open in a circuit prevents current flow.

L1

Ampere (AMP): The unit of measure for electric current.
Ammeter: A test instrument which measures current flow in a circuit.
Conductor: A material that readily allows current flow.
Current: The flow of electrons through a conductor.
Electron: Negatively charged atomic particles.
Impedance: Resistance to current flow often used in rating test meters.
Jumper Wire: A length of wire with probes or clips at each end used to bypass a portion of a circuit.
Ohm's Law: A series of formulas that are used to determine the values in an electrical circuit. Any two of the values can be multiplied or divided to determine the third unknown value.

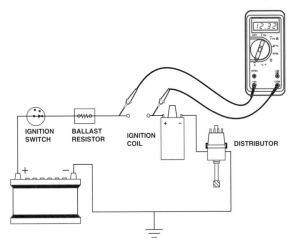

Fig. 1-4. A traditional ammeter is always connected in series to measure the current flow of a circuit.

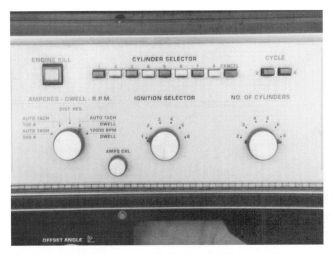

Fig. 1-5. Observing correct polarity is critical for ammeter testing; inductive pickup clamps usually have an arrow to indicate their polarity.

Once you get an accurate reading on the ammeter, compare the reading to the current specifications provided by the vehicle manufacturer. Current specifications are not always available, so you may need to use Ohm's law and calculate the proper amount of current flow for a particular circuit. In general:

- If the ammeter shows no current flow, the circuit is open at some point. This indicates no continuity
- If the ammeter shows less current flow than is normal, the circuit is complete but contains too much resistance. This can be caused by improper or defective components or by loose or corroded connections

- If the current flow is greater than normal, some of the normal circuit resistance is being bypassed by a short. This can be caused by faulty components or defective wire insulation

Electromotive Force

To flow current through a circuit requires an action that organizes all of the randomly drifting electrons and pushes them in one direction. This action is known as **electromotive force (EMF)**, or voltage. Voltage can be measured as the potential difference that exists between two points in a circuit, such as the two terminals of a battery. One of these points must have a negative charge, and the other must have a positive charge. The strength of the force depends upon the strength of the charges at each point.

Voltage

Voltage is a force that is applied to a circuit and can exist even when there is no current flowing. In automotive applications, voltage is supplied by the battery and the **generator**. Chemical reaction creates a difference in electromotive force between the positive and negative terminals of a battery, while mechanical energy is converted to electrical energy in a generator to keep the battery charged. A **voltmeter** is used to measure voltage and results are recorded in units called volts. The actual value of a **volt** is the amount of energy required to move one amp from the point of lower potential to the point of higher potential. In practical terms, one volt is the amount of force required to move one ampere of current through one **ohm** of resistance.

Voltmeter

A voltmeter can be either a digital or analog instrument. It is normally connected in parallel with a circuit or across a voltage source. As with ammeters, digital voltmeters have high impedance, which prevents high current from damaging the meter and limits the load the meter places on the circuit. An internal resistor protects an analog voltmeter from too much current flow. Digital voltmeters also have an internal resistor that is in parallel to the circuit being tested. This resistor must be at least 1 megaohm, and a good digital meter will use a 10 megaohm resistor. Meters used on electronic circuits should have a minimum impedance of 10 megaohms. The high internal resistance of a digital voltmeter draws very little current from a circuit and, when connected in parallel, the effect of the voltmeter on circuit voltage drop is insignificant.

Testing with a Voltmeter

Typically, a voltmeter is used to:

- Measure the source voltage of a circuit
- Measure the voltage drop caused by a load
- Check for circuit continuity
- Measure voltage at any point in a circuit

Electromotive Force (EMF): The force that causes the electrons to move from atom to another atom. More commonly known as voltage.

Generator: A device that produces electrical energy by passing a magnetic field through a coil of wire. Known for many years as an alternator due to the fact that alternating current is produced in the stator assembly; J1930 (OBD II) term for alternator (generating device that uses a diode rectifier).

Ohm: The unit of measure for resistance to current flow.

Volt: The unit of measure for electrical pressure or electromotive force.

Voltmeter: An electrical test meter that measures electrical pressure (EMF).

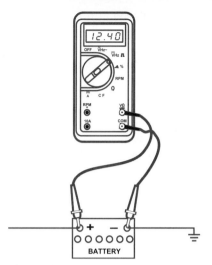

Fig. 1-6. A voltmeter is connected in parallel across a voltage source. This meter is displaying open-circuit battery voltage.

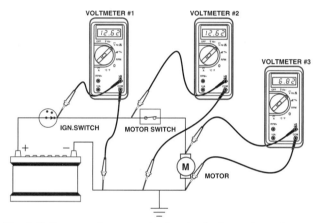

Fig. 1-7. Source voltage can also be checked anywhere along a circuit by grounding the negative meter lead and probing the circuit with the positive meter lead.

To measure voltage or voltage drop, connect the voltmeter in parallel. To perform a continuity check, connect the voltmeter in series with the portion of the circuit being tested.

Checking Source Voltage
The source, or available, voltage within a circuit can be measured with or without current flowing through the circuit. The battery is the voltage source for all DC automotive circuits. It is checked by connecting the positive lead of the voltmeter to the positive battery (B+) terminal and the negative lead to the negative battery (ground) terminal, figure 1-6. This measures no-load, or open-circuit, battery voltage, which should be about 12.2 volts with the engine not running.

Source voltage can be checked in a similar fashion, at any point along a circuit, by grounding the negative meter lead and probing the supply wire with the positive meter lead, figure 1-7. Low source voltage in a circuit is the result of high resistance, and loose or corroded connections are often at fault. A loss of source voltage indicates an open in the circuit.

Checking Voltage Drop
Voltage drop is the amount of voltage that an electrical device normally consumes to perform its task. However, excessive

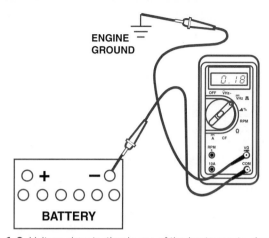

Fig. 1-8. Voltage drop testing is one of the best ways to check the integrity of a circuit or electrical device. This meter is displaying 0.18 voltage drop across the engine ground and the battery.

voltage drop can be the result of a high-resistance connection or failed component.

Checking voltage drop is one of the most important tests you can perform on a circuit. Voltage drops can cause major driveability symptoms in onboard computer systems. A voltage drop on an engine control module (ECM) power ground can cause sensor voltage references to be higher than normal, throwing off the overall sensor calibration of the entire control system.

To check voltage drop, the circuit must be powered up and have current flowing. The circuit must also have the maximum amount of current flowing under normal conditions for which the circuit was designed. The amount of voltage drop that is considered acceptable will vary by circuit. Low-current circuits that draw milliamps will be affected by very small voltage drops, while the same amount of voltage drop will have a negligible affect on a high-current circuit. In general, voltage drop on a power ground circuit should be less than 0.1 volt.

To measure voltage drop, connect the meter in the same fashion used to take system voltage readings. Leave the negative meter lead attached to the negative battery terminal, and use the positive meter lead to probe at various points in the circuit to check a power ground, figure 1-8. You can compute voltage drop by checking available voltage on both sides of a load, then subtracting the voltage reading of the ground side from the reading on the positive side of the load. You can take direct voltage drop readings by connecting the positive meter lead to the power side of a load and connecting the negative meter lead to the ground side of the component. Check electronic sensor voltage drop in a similar way. Connect the digital multimeter (DMM) negative lead to the sensor ground terminal and probe the signal line with the positive meter lead. Remember, the sum of all the voltage drops in a circuit will equal the source voltage.

Checking Continuity
Continuity testing is similar to no-load voltage testing, since both procedures tell you if system voltage is being applied to a part of the circuit. However, for a continuity check, the voltmeter is connected in series with the circuit rather than in parallel.

L1

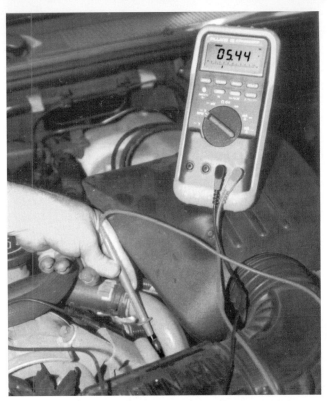

Fig. 1-9. Check continuity with a voltmeter by connecting it in series with the device being tested and energizing the circuit.

To check continuity with a voltmeter, open the circuit at the test point by disconnecting the power wire. Then, attach the positive voltmeter lead to the source voltage side of the open circuit and connect the negative voltmeter lead to the ground side of the test point. Next, energize the circuit and note the voltmeter reading, figure 1-9. If the voltmeter reads system voltage, the circuit is complete. If the voltmeter reads near zero voltage, the circuit is open. Due to the high resistance of the DMM, the circuit cannot carry current so the meter reads source voltage.

Resistance

Voltage forces current through a conductor, but all conductive materials oppose current flow to some extent. This opposition, known as resistance, exists in some degree in all electrical devices. If you know how much resistance a circuit should have, you can quickly determine the overall condition of the circuit by measuring its resistance. There are five factors, or characteristics, that determine how much resistance is present in an electrical circuit. These are:

1. The atomic structure of the material. All conductors have some resistance, but the low resistance in a good conductor will flow current when a fraction of a volt is induced
2. The length of the conductor. The longer a piece of wire or cable, the higher its resistance
3. The cross-sectional area of the conductor. The thinner a piece of wire or cable, the higher its resistance
4. The temperature of the conductor. In most cases, the higher the temperature of the conducting material, the higher its resistance. However, some sensors are designed to operate exactly the opposite

5. The condition of the conductor. Broken strands of a cable or a partially cut wire reduces the cross-sectional area of the conductor and raises resistance. Loose, dirty, or corroded connections have the same effect and are a major cause of electrical problems

Ohms

An ohm is the unit established to measure electrical resistance. One ohm is equal to the amount of resistance present when one volt of electromotive force pushes one ampere of current through a circuit. The resistance of any electrical device or circuit can be measured two ways:

- Directly with an ohmmeter measuring the resistance offered by the device or circuit in ohms
- Indirectly with a voltmeter, measuring the voltage drop across the device or circuit

Since every electrical device, or load, in a circuit offers some resistance, voltage is reduced as it pushes current through each load. Voltage drop testing was detailed earlier in this chapter.

Tips for Using an Ohmmeter

An ohmmeter is a self-powered test instrument that can only be used when there is no voltage applied to the circuit device being tested. Any current flow from an outside source will damage the meter. Before testing with an ohmmeter, make sure the circuit is not under power, or remove the component to be tested from the circuit, figure 1-10.

Ohmmeters, whether analog or digital, operate on the voltage drop principle. When you connect the leads of an ohmmeter to a device for testing, the meter directs a low-voltage current from its power source through the device. Since the source voltage and the internal resistance of the meter are known, the resistance of the test device can be determined by the amount of voltage dropped as current flows through it. The ohmmeter makes this calculation and directly displays the resistance of the test device in ohms.

Be aware, ohmmeter testing may not always be conclusive. Resistance faults in wiring and connections often generate heat, which further increases the resistance of an operating circuit. In these cases, the fault may not be apparent unless the circuit is under power. The device may be able to relay the low-voltage signal of an ohmmeter, but not be able to carry the signal when system voltage is applied to it. Another consideration is the fact that most ohmmeters will only read as low as 0.1 ohm, yet smaller amounts of resistance can cause problems, especially on electronic circuits. These low-resistance faults can only be determined through voltage drop testing. However, an ohmmeter has definite advantages for many test situations and is particularly useful to:

- Measure the resistance of parts that have specific resistance values that fall within the usable range of the meter
- Measure high-resistance items, such as secondary ignition cables and electronic pickup coils
- Test internal parts of components that require disassembly to reach the test points
- Bench test parts such as switches, circuit breakers, and relays before assembly or installation
- Check circuit continuity of components

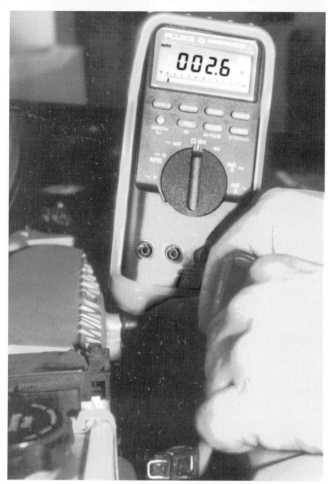

Fig. 1-10. Using an ohmmeter to measure the resistance of an electronic fuel injector. Note, the multi-plug has been disconnected to prevent current flow through the injector.

Ohm's Law

The relationship between current flow, electromotive force, and resistance is predictable for any electrical, or electronic, circuit or device. This relationship was first stated as a theory by George Ohm in 1827 and has since become known as Ohm's Law. Ohm determined that there are three characteristics at work in an electrical device: voltage, amperage, and resistance. If you know two of them you can always calculate the third, since the relationship of these three never changes, figure 1-11.

According to Ohm's Law, when a force of one volt pushes one ampere of current through a circuit, the resistance present is 1 ohm. This establishes and gives a value to the ohm, the unit with which resistance is measured. Now, you can use one of three simple mathematic equations to calculate the missing factor:

- To calculate voltage, multiply amperes by resistance
  $V = A \times R$
- To calculate amperage, divide voltage by resistance
  $A = V \div R$
- To calculate resistance, divide voltage by amperage
  $R = V \div A$

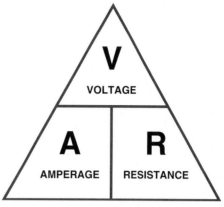

Fig. 1-11. This diagram is an easy way to remember the relationship of the three elements of Ohm's Law; when one is missing you can calculate it based on the other two.

Even though you may never need to use one of these equations to figure out the missing characteristic, it is important to understand the logic behind them.

Suppose you are dealing with a fused circuit operating on system voltage that keeps blowing the fuse after a short period of time. A quick check tells you 12 volts are available on either end of the circuit, and you know the fuse is rated at 10 amps. Therefore, Ohm's Law tells you there is low resistance in the circuit because amperage is equal to voltage divided by resistance. So, if voltage is constant, a drop in resistance is the only condition that will allow enough current to flow through the circuit to overload the fuse.

Very few, if any, automotive problems will require you to actually calculate Ohm's Law equations to repair them. However, you will find it much easier to locate faults in electric and electronic circuitry once you understand the relationships of current, voltage, and resistance expressed in Ohm's Law.

In an automotive electrical system, DC voltage originates at the battery, and the open-circuit, or no-load, voltage of a good battery will be about 12.6 volts. With the engine running, a typical charging system regulates output between 13.5 and 14 volts. This is the source, or system, voltage that provides power to all of the circuits on the vehicle. Therefore, voltage should remain fairly stable, unless there is an unexpected change in resistance. Low voltage in a vehicle electrical system is often the result of either a charging system problem or a bad battery. If resistance is unchanged, a drop in system voltage results in less current flow, and a rise in system voltage will increase amperage, or current flow, as well. Ohm's Law says:

- Voltage and amperage are directly proportional to each other as long as resistance remains the same. Both must move in the same direction, figure 1-12

Resistance in an electrical circuit should only be that of the load devices specified by the engineer. This includes all switches, relays, motors, solenoids, lamps, and other parts that create resistance to perform usable work. The resistance of all the loads determines the circuit amperage. Remember, system voltage should remain stable and within its designed range unless there is a battery or charging system problem. Therefore, the circuit with the greatest total resistive load will flow the least amount of

L1

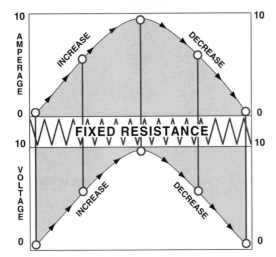

Fig. 1-12. Voltage and amperage increase or decrease directly in proportion to each other as long as resistance remains constant.

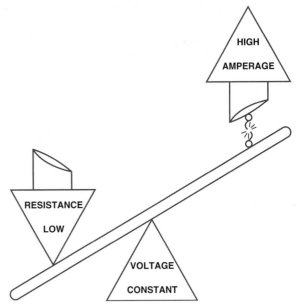

Fig. 1-14. High amperage overloading a fuse is often the effect of low resistance allowing too much current to flow.

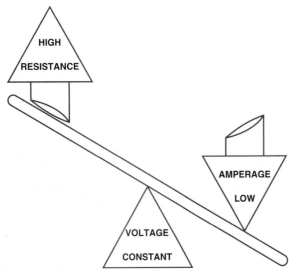

Fig. 1-13. Amperage and resistance are inversely proportional when voltage is constant, so if either one increases the other must decrease.

current, and the circuit with the least resistance will allow the greatest amperage flow. According to Ohm's Law.

- Amperage and resistance are inversely proportional to each other as long as voltage remains the same. They move in opposite directions, figure 1-13

Under normal circumstances, you will not see a situation where amperage is held constant while voltage and resistance change. Amperage is the strength of the electrical charge moving through a conductor, and it responds to changes in voltage or resistance. Although high amperage is the cause of many blown fuses, it is most often the effect of low circuit resistance rather than the cause of the problem, figure 1-14.

Understanding the inverse relationship of amperage to resistance at a steady voltage is an important diagnostic aid. Any circuit damage, whether an open or short, poor or corroded connection, frayed wire, broken insulation, or a defective component, will change the designed resistance of the circuit. When the battery and charging system are in good condition, a change in resistance will increase or decrease amperage in the circuit. Excessive amperage will cause blown fuses, while reduced amperage can cause slow motor operation, dim bulbs, sluggish solenoid or relay response, and less than peak performance from other circuit devices.

Diodes

Diodes serve as one-way check valves in an electrical system. They allow current to flow in one direction, but prevent current flow in the other. A **diode** is used to direct current flow and protects solid state devices from voltage spikes. Each diode has two halves, an anode and a cathode. The diode allows current flow through the cathode to the anode. Diodes are used in circuits to re-direct current flow. A good example of diodes being used is in an **alternator**, where they modify current from alternating current to direct. A standard silicon diode causes a voltage drop of approximately 0.6V.

Clamping Diodes

Clamping diodes are diodes placed in a circuit in parallel with a magnetic coil. When the magnetic field produced by the coil collapses because power is removed, it produces a voltage spike with polarity opposite that of normal current flow. The diode is wired in parallel with the coil so when the field collapses, the spike is blocked from flowing in the circuit. The diode prevents the spike from reaching a computer or other solid state component.

For example, when a relay is de-energized, the resulting voltage spike can exceed 40 volts. A starter relay can produce a voltage spike of nearly 200 volts. Clamping diodes protect the vehicle computers from these spikes.

Alternator: See Generator.

Diode: An electronic component designed to allow current flow in one direction only. Used in control circuits and in rectifier assemblies in the generator.

Series Circuits

In a **series circuit**, the current has only one path to follow. In figure 1-15, using conventional current flow theory, you see that the current must flow from the battery through the resistor, and back to the battery. The circuit must be continuous, or have continuity. If one wire is disconnected from the battery, the circuit is broken and there is no current. If electrical loads are wired in series, they must all be switched on and working or the circuit is broken and none of them work. A simplified example of a series circuit is shown in figure 1-16. Current flows from the battery through the horn switch, through the horn, and then back to the battery.

Series Circuits and Ohm's Law

Ohm's law can easily be applied to a series circuit. If any two of the values are known, the third can be calculated using Ohm's Law. Some characteristics of a series circuit are:

- Current is the same everywhere in the circuit. Since there is only one path for current, the same amount of current must be available at all points of the circuit
- Voltage drops may vary from load to load if the individual resistances vary, but the sum of all voltage drops in the series is equal to source voltage
- The total resistance is the sum of all individual resistances in the series

In figure 1-15, the circuit consists of a 3 ohm resistor connected to a 12 volt battery. The amperage is found by using Ohm's Law:

$$E \div R = I$$
$$12 \div 3 = 4 \text{ amperes}$$

When you know the current and the individual resistances of a series circuit, you can calculate the voltage drop across each load. The sum of these drops equals the source voltage. For the 2 ohm resistor in figure 1-17:

$$I \times R = E$$
$$2 \times 2 = 4 \text{ volts}$$

For the 4 ohm resistor in figure 1-17:

$$I \times R = E$$
$$2 \times 4 = 8 \text{ volts}$$

The sum of the volts is 4 volts + 8 volts = 12 volts, which is the source voltage.

Parallel Circuits

When current can follow more than one path to complete a circuit, that circuit is called a **parallel circuit**. The points where current paths split and rejoin are called junction points. The separate paths that split and meet at junction points are called branch circuits or **shunt** circuits. A parallel circuit is shown in figure 1-18. In an automobile, the headlamps are wired in parallel with each other, figure 1-19.

Parallel Circuits and Ohm's Law

The features of a parallel circuit are:

- The voltage applied to, or measured across, each branch of the circuit is the same
- The total current in a parallel circuit is the sum of the current in each branch
- The total resistance of a parallel circuit is always less than the lowest individual resistance. The reason is that when you add resistors in parallel, you are actually adding more conductors, or paths in which current can flow, which reduces the total resistance

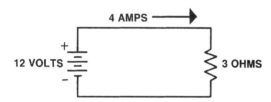

Fig. 1-15. A simple series circuit.

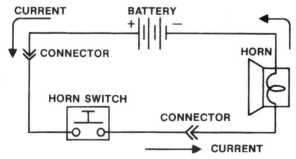

Fig. 1-16. This horn circuit diagram illustrates a simple series circuit.

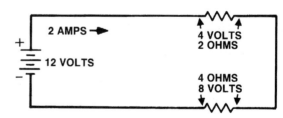

Fig. 1-17. A series circuit with more than 1 resistor.

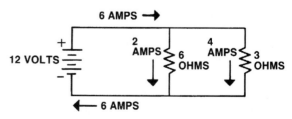

Fig. 1-18. A parallel circuit.

L1

Parallel Circuit: An arrangement that provides separate power supplies and ground paths to several loads.
Series Circuit: An arrangement in which current must flow through one load before another. Each load shares the power supply with the other loads in the circuit.
Shunt: A parallel electrical connection or branch circuit, in parallel with another branch circuit or connection.

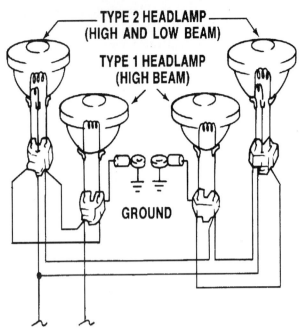

Fig. 1-19. The headlamps are wired in parallel with each other in all headlamp circuits.

There are two ways to calculate the total resistance, or equivalent resistance, in a parallel circuit. One formula for any number of resistors is:

Rt = 1 ÷ (1 ÷ R1 + 1 ÷ R2 + 1 ÷ R3)

Note: Rt = Total circuit resistance.

For the circuit illustrated in figure 1-18:

R = 1 ÷ (1 ÷ 6 + 1 ÷ 3) = 2 ohms

Another way to calculate total resistance is the product-over-the-sum method:

R1 = (R1 × R2) ÷ (R1+R2)

This formula can be used for only two resistances at a time. If more than two are wired in parallel, you must calculate their values in pairs until you determine one total resistance for the circuit. For the circuit in figure 1-18:

R1 = (6 × 3) ÷ (6 + 3) = 2 ohms

To apply Ohm's Law to a parallel circuit, sometimes you must treat branches as independent circuits and sometimes you must deal with the entire circuit, depending upon which values are unknown. To find current, you must treat each branch separately because of the different current in each branch. Voltage is applied equally across all branches, so the source voltage is divided by the branch resistance to determine the current through that branch. Adding the current in all the branches gives the total current in the circuit. In the circuit shown, figure 1-18, current through the 6 ohm resistor is:

E ÷ R = I
12 volts ÷ 6 ohms = 2 amps

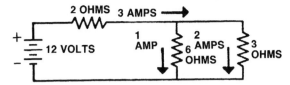

Fig. 1-20. A series-parallel circuit.

Through the 3 ohm resistor, it is:

E ÷ R = I
12 volts ÷ 3 ohms = 4 amps

Total circuit current is 2 amps + 4 amps = 6 amps.

If the resistance of a branch is unknown, dividing the source voltage by the branch current gives the branch resistance. In figure 1-18, for the first branch:

R1 = 12 volts ÷ 2 amps = 6 ohms

For the second branch:

R2 = 12 volts ÷ 4 amps = 3 ohms

Total resistance of the circuit can be calculated using the product-over-the-sum method:

Rt = (6 ohms × 3 ohms) (6 ohms + 3 ohms) = 2 ohms

Or, if all you need is the equivalent circuit resistance, divide the source voltage by the total circuit amperage as follows:

Rt = 12 volts ÷ 6 amps = 2 ohms

To determine source voltage, multiply the total circuit current by the total circuit resistance. Or, since the voltage is the same across all branches, multiply one branch current by the same branch resistance. In figure 1-18:

I × R = E
6 amps × 2 ohms = 12 volts

Or, (branch I) × (branch R) = E:

Branch 1: 2 × 6 = 12 volts

Branch 2: 4 × 3 = 12 volts

Series-Parallel Circuits

As the name suggests, series-parallel circuits combine the two types of circuits already discussed. Some of the loads are wired in series, but there are also some loads wired in parallel, figure 1-20. The entire headlamp circuit of an automobile is a **series-parallel circuit**, figure 1-21. The headlamps are in parallel with each other, but the switches are in series with the battery and with each lamp. Both lamps are controlled by the switches, but one lamp still lights if the other is burned out. Most of the circuits in an automobile electrical system are series-parallel.

Series-Parallel Circuits and Ohm's Law

Values in a series-parallel circuit are figured by reducing the parallel branches to equivalent values for single loads in series. Then the equivalent values and any actual series loads are combined.

To calculate total resistance, first find the resistance of all loads wired in parallel. If the circuit is complex, it may be

---

Series-Parallel Circuit: An arrangement that combines two or more loads in parallel with one or more loads in series.

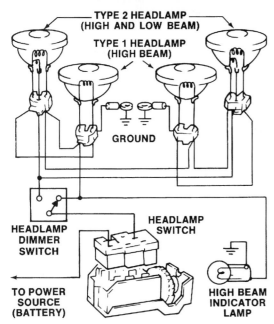

TYPE 2 HEADLAMP
(HIGH AND LOW BEAM)

TYPE 1 HEADLAMP
(HIGH BEAM)

GROUND

HEADLAMP
DIMMER
SWITCH

HEADLAMP
SWITCH

TO POWER
SOURCE
(BATTERY)

HIGH BEAM
INDICATOR
LAMP

Fig. 1-21. A complete headlamp circuit, with all bulbs and switches, is a series-parallel circuit.

handy to group the parallel branches into pairs and treat each pair separately. Then add the values of all loads wired in series to the equivalent resistance of all the loads wired in parallel. In the circuit shown in figure 1-20:

$$Rt = (6 \times 3) \div (6 + 3) + 2 = 4 \text{ ohms}$$

In the illustration, the equivalent resistance of the loads in parallel is:

$$(6 \times 3) \div (6 + 3) = 2 \text{ ohms}$$

The total of the branch currents is $1 + 2 = 3$ amps, so the voltage drop is:

$$I \times R = E$$
$$3 \times 2 = 6$$

The voltage drop across the load in series is 2 [×] 3 = 6 volts. Add these voltage drops to find the source voltage:

$$6 + 6 = 12 \text{ volts}$$

To determine the source voltage in a series-parallel circuit, you must first find the equivalent resistance of the loads in parallel, and the total current through this equivalent resistance. Figure out the voltage drop across this equivalent resistance and add it to the voltage drops across all loads wired in series.

To determine total current, find the currents in all parallel branches and add them together. This total is equal to the current at any point in the series circuit. In figure 1-20:

$$I = (E \div R1) + (E \div R2) = (6 \div 6) + (6 \div 3) = 1 + 2 = 3 \text{ amps}$$

Notice that there are only 6 volts across each of the branch circuits because another 6 volts have already been "dropped" across the 2 ohm series resistor.

With this summary of electrical theory, you can perform more accurate diagnoses, resulting in more efficient repairs, and a higher percentage of satisfied customers.

MORE DIAGNOSTICS

Check the Basics

Some mechanical and electrical systems are not monitored by the electronic powertrain control system. Failures here can cause driveability or emission problems without setting codes. Other problems may not be detected by a scan tool or **lab scope**. Some problems may be the root cause of a code or a sensor that is out of range, even though it is on a system that is not monitored by the electronic powertrain control system.

The following tests, described over the next several pages, may be performed to detect these types of problems. The tests are not necessarily in the order they should be performed. This is a reminder list. The list does not have a specific order or specific procedures.

No-Start Diagnosis

To run, an engine requires four things: air, fuel, compression and ignition, all at the right time. Perform the following tests to find what the problem is:

- Observe the engine's cranking speed; if it is too slow, check the battery and starting system
- Check fuel pressure and volume
- Verify the electrical signal to the injector with a 12V test light, figure 1-22, depending on the OEM's recommendation
- Use a properly gapped spark tester to check for spark
- Check compression by performing a cranking vacuum or compression test
- Check the ignition timing
- Verify camshaft drive **integrity** and valve timing

Battery

Perform a preliminary visual inspection and check the **electrolyte** level. The battery should measure 12.6V or higher, if it is fully charged. The minimum state of charge needed to perform a load or capacity test is 12.4V.

If the state of charge is too low, perform a "3 minute (sulfation) test" while charging. To do this, connect the charger and set it on high. In three minutes, check the charging voltage. If at the end of three minutes, the charging voltage is above 15.8V, the battery may be considered sulfated. It should be replaced because it may never accept a full charge. If the battery passes, continue charging at a normal rate until it is fully charged. A capacity test should be performed with a load of half the cold cranking amperes applied for 15 seconds. By the end of this time, the battery should not have dropped below 9.6V. If it does, replace it.

Sometimes, a battery's state of charge is low because of a key OFF drain. To test for a key OFF drain, disconnect the negative battery cable connection. Connect a (known good)

L1

Electrolyte: The chemical solution in a battery that conducts electricity and reacts with the plate materials.
Integrity: Soundness, intactness of a component, or a person's adherence to a code of values.
Lab Scope: An oscilloscope used to observe electronic sensor and actuator waveforms, usually not capable of reading high secondary ignition voltage.

Fig. 1-22. Using a 12V test light to verify electrical signal to an injector.

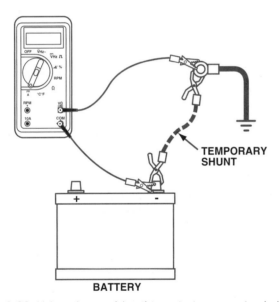

Fig. 1-23. Using a jumper (shunt) to protect an ammeter during a battery drain test.

12-volt test light in series with the battery post and the battery cable terminal connector. If the light illuminates, there is a large drain. If the test light does not illuminate, remove it and proceed to the next test.

Temporarily connect a jumper (shunt) in series between the negative battery post and the disconnected cable's battery terminal connector. Connect an ammeter across the battery post and the battery terminal connector, figure 1-23. The shunt will protect your meter from a current increase while the vehicle's capacitors are charging up. Wait 3–4 minutes, then disconnect the jumper before measuring. Use the highest meter range first, usually 10 or 20 amps. Then scale down to milliamps to check

for a small (parasitic) drain. If you measure zero, check the ammeter's circuit protection. There are electronic control devices that need power even with the key OFF. You will need to look up their normal parasitic drain, to know if there is an abnormal drain on the system.

Starting

Disable both ignition and fuel, or just the fuel system. This not only prevents startup, but also prevents crankcase oil dilution caused by gasoline washing past the rings while performing cranking tests. Limit cranking tests to 15 seconds to protect the starter from overheating. The starter should crank the engine at normal speed and not draw more current than specified. Battery voltage during a "15-second starter draw test" should not drop below 9.6V and the amperes should stay within OEM specifications. Keep in mind that some electronic engine control systems require at least 10.5V during normal startup. Voltage lower than 10.5V may cause a no-start.

When the starter cranks too slowly and draws high current, the problem may be caused by:

*   A short in the starter
*   Excessive mechanical load

When the starter cranks too slowly and draws low current, the problem may be caused by:

*   Poor battery capacity
*   Excessive resistance in the circuit
*   Excessive resistance in the starter

When the starter cranks too fast and draws low current, the problem is probably a low compression problem—often a camshaft drive defect.

If the starter engages the flywheel but does not release, or makes unusual noise during cranking, the problem may be caused by:

*   Improper pinion to flywheel clearance
*   Bad starter drive
*   Shorted starter solenoid or relay
*   Starter not aligned properly

When the starter spins but does not engage the flywheel, the cause may be:

*   Defective starter drive
*   Starter mounting bolts loose

When the solenoid clicks but the starter does not spin, the problem may be caused by:

*   A defective solenoid switch
*   Excessive resistance in the starter control circuit

Charging

Begin by checking the alternator belt condition and tension. Check battery voltage with the ignition key in the OFF position. Test the charging system voltage at the battery, with the engine running at idle speed and accessories turned on. If there is no OEM specification available, it should maintain a minimum of at least 0.5V above the battery's key OFF voltage with the accessory loads on.

If the system voltage is low, first be sure engine idle speed is correct, then look for high resistance in a wire or connection.

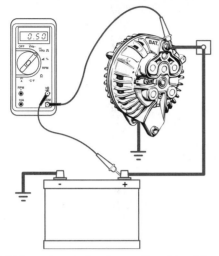

Fig. 1-24. Voltage drop testing the positive side of the charging circuit.

To do this, perform a voltage drop test on the charging circuit, figure 1-24. Check both the positive and ground side of the circuit. It is important to turn on enough accessories to cause a load of at least 20 amperes on the alternator. This will ensure that the flaw in the circuit is revealed. If this does not uncover the problem, verify that the field circuit voltage or amperage is at specification.

Check for overcharging. Measure the voltage at the battery with the engine running at 2000 rpm and the accessories turned off. It should not be above the OEM's specified charging system voltage limit.

Other tests include performing:

- An oscilloscope alternator diode **ripple test**
- Alternating Current (AC) volt leakage test. AC voltage above 0.5V is the rule of thumb for a failed alternator
- Current leakage test using an ammeter in the charging circuit

Insight

Think of the powertrain systems affected by a weak battery or defective charging system: starting, ignition, fuel delivery, fuel control, emission controls, and transmission controls. Low or high system voltage will affect tailpipe emissions. When a engine control module (ECM) goes into a "limited operation strategy" because of low system voltage, it may disable the EGR, causing higher emission of Nitrogen Oxides (NOx).

Cooling

Check the coolant condition and the level with a coolant tester (hydrometer). Most manufacturers recommend a 50/50 mix of antifreeze/water in all but the coldest climates. A 70/30 mix is the maximum ratio allowed for all but a few vehicle applications. Look for corrosion or contamination in the system. Use the radiator cap pressure specification when pressurizing the system to perform a leak check.

Proper engine temperature is critical for clean emissions and optimal engine operation. Use a scan tool to accurately determine and confirm thermostat operation. A lower temperature, stuck-open thermostat, or no thermostat may cause a long warmup time, or in cool weather no warmup. This in turn may cause:

- Extended high idle speed
- High **Carbon Monoxide** (CO) tailpipe emission

Left uncorrected, other symptoms may be:

- **Fouled** spark plugs
- High hydrocarbon (HC) tailpipe emission
- High fuel consumption
- Abnormal **fuel trim** readings
- Carbon build up
- Oxygen (O2) sensor carbon contamination
- Catalyst damage

Engine cooling fan systems are often controlled by the ECM. The ECM uses the coolant temperature signal to know when to activate a relay to control the cooling fan. A system that is bypassed to make the fan run constantly may cause the same high CO symptoms as a thermostat that is stuck open.

Overheating problems are caused by:

- Low coolant level
- Poor or no coolant circulation
- Inoperable auxiliary fan
- Lack of airflow

An engine overheating during an emissions test may cause the test to be aborted. However, an engine running hotter than normal, but not overheating, may cause a NOx emission test failure.

Engine Cylinder Power Contribution Test

A cylinder power contribution test tells you which cylinder or cylinders' combustion is not as efficient as the others. It does not tell you which system is at fault, figure 1-25.

A low power contribution by one or more cylinders may be caused by:

- A vacuum leak
- Compression loss
- Poor valve lift
- Weak spark
- Fuel injector defect
- Primary ignition wiring fault

L1

Carbon Monoxide: An odorless, colorless, tasteless poisonous gas. A pollutant produced by the internal combustion engine.
Fouled: Contaminated, like a spark plug contaminated (fouled) with carbon.
Fuel Trim (FT): Fuel delivery adjustments based on closed-loop feedback. Values above the central value (0%) indicate increased injector pulse width. Values below the central value indicate decreased injector pulse width. Short Term Fuel Trim is based on rapidly switching oxygen sensor values. Long Term Fuel Trim is a learned value used to compensate for continual deviation of the Short Term Fuel Trim from its central value. (Term means time. Short Term Fuel Trim makes an immediate correction for O2 sensor bias. Long Term Fuel Trim makes a correction for Short Term Fuel Trim bias).
Ripple Test: A test that checks for unwanted A/C. voltage leaking from an alternator rectifier bridge.

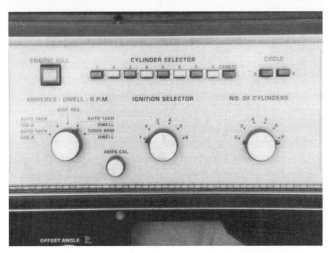

Fig. 1-25. Oscilloscope power balance test control panel.

- ECM failure
- Fuel injector electrical circuit defect

Do not forget that on a multiport system, a fuel injector with a bad intake O-ring seal can cause a vacuum leak that has more effect on its own cylinder. So use your favorite vacuum leak detection method and include injector O-ring seals in your search. Exhaust gas leaking into the intake from an Exhaust Gas Recirculation (EGR) valve has an unequal effect on cylinder power loss. The cylinders closest to the EGR are affected most.

This effect is more severe at low rpm than at high rpm.

Diagnosing Different Configurations

Since there are so many different valvetrain, fuel system, and ignition system configurations, seriously consider system **configuration** when analyzing test results. To understand this better, look at the following example:

Configuration
Inline 4-cylinder engine
Distributor ignition
Throttle-body fuel injection

Power Contribution

CYLINDER NUMBER	RPM DROP
1	110
2	30
3	115
4	105

Compression Test Results
All cylinders within specification

Ignition Scope Check
All cylinders appear O.K.

The above engines' symptoms are: runs rough, has poor idle quality, and HC emission is high. The cylinder power contribution test result shows number 2 does not contribute its share of power because the drop in engine speed is only 30 rpm. The fuel system configuration dictates that it cannot be a fuel

distribution problem, since fuel is delivered by a TBI system. It would be a good idea, at this point, to perform a running compression test. It may show low-running compression on cylinder number 2. A worn camshaft lobe should be suspect, but any part of the valvetrain that is causing this cylinder's valve to not open enough would reduce its power contribution.

However, if this engine in the example had a multiport fuel-injection system, a fuel injector problem would have to be considered a possible cause. The O-ring seal on number 2 injector should be checked for a vacuum leak. A fuel-injector volume or pressure drop test should be performed, to see if number 2 injector delivers a proper amount of fuel.

As this example illustrates, you must consider system configuration in your analysis, or you will not be aware of all the possible causes of a symptom.

Insight
Most problems that affect engine power contribution cause a rise in HC emission. Only those problems that cause a rich condition cause a proportional rise in CO emission. The more effect the problem has on power contribution, the higher the HC emission will be.

Engine Mechanical Condition Tests
A cranking compression test will reveal a cylinder with a sealing problem. Testing dry and then wet with a few squirts of oil will indicate whether you have ring or valve problems. The fastest compression test is an automated relative compression test performed on an engine analyzer.

Use a leak down test to locate the cause of a compression leak. A leak of 20 psi or greater during a leak down test is serious. Listen to find where the air is escaping. You will hear it coming from the:

- Tailpipe when the exhaust valve is leaking
- Intake if an intake valve is leaking
- Crankcase if the rings are bad or the piston is damaged
- Cooling system filler if the block is cracked, the head is cracked, or the head is warped and the head gasket is leaking

But none of these tests will disclose an engine breathing problem, such as a worn camshaft lobe or a valvetrain problem that prevents the proper amount of air from entering the cylinder. However, a running compression test will uncover this problem and you should perform it when other tests are inconclusive.

Carbon deposits on intake valves can be a difficult problem to diagnose. Intake valve deposits can cause an engine to run lean while cruising and accelerating, and rich during deceleration.

During lean conditions, NOx emission is high. During rich conditions, CO emission is high. Intake valve deposits can also cause driveability problems such as a rough idle, stumble, **hesitation**, and loss of power under load.

Often, an engine that displays a rough idle problem runs smooth after a fuel-injector cleaning service is performed. Intake valve deposits that were also removed by the fuel-injector service

---

Configuration: The organization of related components in a specific order.
Hesitation: A sudden loss of power or forward motion.

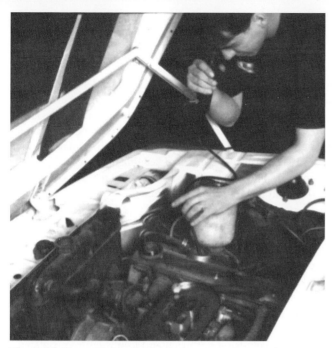

Fig. 1-26. Use a flexible fiber optic borescope to see where you normally cannot see.

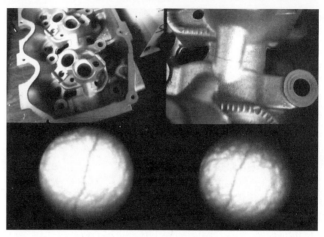

Fig. 1-27. A borescope can help spot defects even after a tear down.

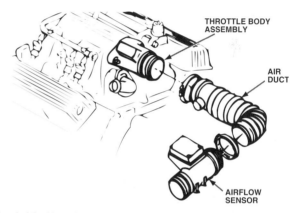

Fig. 1-28. Air leaks at the air duct connections or breaks in the air duct would cause a lean condition.

could have been the reason performance improved. All that was really needed was a carbon clean solution administered through the intake manifold, by way of a manifold vacuum port.

A **borescope** inspection is one way to know for sure if there are excessive deposits on the intake valves. By inserting it through the intake, you can see the back sides of the valves.

Try a borescope inspection to actually see some problems such as intake valve deposits, or to check for a cracked head or block before condemning the head gasket, figure 1-26. A borescope can eliminate some tear down inspections and improve on others, figure 1-27. This can be a real time-saver for you and a great value for the customer.

Insight
A final thought to remember that will aid your diagnosis: Most mechanical engine problems that cause engine performance symptoms do so by affecting combustion efficiency, which increases HC emission.

Air Intake System Problems

Remember to check for vacuum leaks. Keep in mind that a vacuum leak does not cause a power imbalance but increases engine speed. If the system uses an airflow sensor, any leak, even in an intake air duct, is air that was not measured, figure 1-28. Whether it's an air duct leak or vacuum leak, if too large, the system cannot compensate, resulting in a lean combustion problem. Lean combustion will cause HC and NOx emissions to increase. When the lean combustion problem is severe

enough to cause a **misfire**, NOx emission will fall and HC emission will increase dramatically.

On systems that use a **Manifold Absolute Pressure (MAP)** sensor, a vacuum leak will cause the engine speed to increase. The faster speed of the engine produces more total mass or volume of emissions. However, the emissions remain proportionally the same. HC emission will increase if the vacuum leak causes a power imbalance.

Dirty air filters, unless extremely restricted, are usually compensated for by today's modern fuel injection systems. However, air filters must still be changed when needed because they do protect an expensive airflow sensor and engine.

Insight
Carbureted vehicles built in the '80s experiencing an air intake problem could cause a power imbalance and an rpm decrease at idle.

L1

Borescope: A device used to look inside areas of the engine that usually cannot be seen without disassembly.
Misfire: Incomplete combustion resulting in increased emissions and the possibility of catalyst damage.
Manifold Absolute Pressure (MAP): The pressure in the intake manifold referenced to a perfect vacuum. Since manifold vacuum is the difference between manifold absolute pressure and atmospheric pressure, all the vacuum readings in the Composite Vehicle Preparation/Reference Booklet are taken at sea level (where standard atmospheric pressure equals 101 kPa or 0 in. Hg).

Idle System Problems

Curb idle is usually controlled by the ECM on most late-model vehicles. However, most have what is called a minimum air rate, minimum throttle angle, or minimum idle speed adjustment. Check the tune-up procedure section of your shop manual for the proper procedure. If the minimum air rate is incorrect, the vehicle may suffer from:

- Off-idle hesitation
- Idle load **compensation** problems
- Low or high idle speed
- Rough idle quality
- Stall on deceleration

If the Throttle Position (TP) sensor is adjustable, adjustment usually accompanies a minimum idle adjustment.

Inspect behind the throttle plate for carbon build-up. Look in the throttle bore and the bypass port, figure 1-29. This build-up of carbon will affect the minimum air rate. Check the OEM recommendations before cleaning. Some throttle bores have a special coating that may be removed by cleaner, exposing it to corrosion and carbon build-up. Carbon build-up in the throttle bore or bypass port may cause:

- Low idle speed
- Rough idle quality
- Off-idle hesitation

Fuel Quality

Check for fuel quality problems such as water contamination or alcohol content. Too much alcohol not only decreases engine power, it also damages fuel delivery system components. Test kits are available to check for fuel contamination.

Stale or old gasoline that has been stored for a long time may cause hard starting. Old gas can also increase HC due to misfires, but seldom prevents starting.

Low octane gasoline can cause spark knock or engine ping and increase NOx emission.

Refineries control seasonal gasoline volatility. Higher **fuel volatility** on an unseasonably warm day can increase NOx production. It can also vaporize in the fuel delivery system, causing a leaner fuel mixture. The leaner mixture will cause an increase of HC emission. When the vaporization problem is severe enough, **fuel starvation** from **vapor lock** occurs. Lower gasoline volatility in cold weather can cause hard starting and driveability problems during cold engine operation.

When in doubt about the fuel, it is best to test it or replace it with fresh fuel of the proper octane.

Fuel System Tests

Visual inspection for fuel leaks is a first step when there is a lean combustion problem, or a fuel odor complaint. In tight places where there is poor visibility, the gas analyzer can help you search for a leak. Watch the HC reading on the analyzer and use the sample probe to sniff out the leak.

Do not neglect to perform fuel pressure and volume tests, figure 1-30. Even if access is difficult, they are absolutely necessary for diagnosing both rich and lean mixture problems. Use pressure and volume tests to help diagnose defects of the:

- Fuel pump
- Rest or static pressure **check valve**
- Fuel pressure regulator
- Fuel injector

Fuel injectors can fail in many different ways. Most defects affect a pressure drop or volume flow test. Refer to OEM specifications. Some shops try injector cleaning first, replacing injectors only if cleaning does not solve the problem. Be sure to check the OEM's recommendations because cleaning damages some types of injectors. In this case, the only safe alternative is replacement.

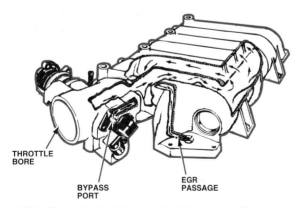

Fig. 1-29. Check the throttle bore, throttle plate, and bypass port for carbon build-up.

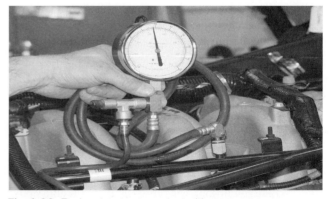

Fig. 1-30. Fuel system pressure test with pressure gauge.

Check Valve: A valve that permits flow in only one direction.
Compensation: To correct for too much or too little of something.
Fuel Starvation: The lack of fuel available for efficient combustion.
Fuel Volatility: The lower the temperature at which a fuel vaporizes, the higher the volatility.
Vapor Lock: When fuel vaporizes in a line or device and blocks the flow of liquid fuel, usually causes engine stall.

An increase of CO emission, caused by the fuel delivery system, is usually one of the following high-pressure problems:

- Defective pressure regulator
- Pinched return hose
- Crushed return line
- Fuel injector **nozzle** leak

If the system is allowed to continue with these rich conditions, it may foul the spark plugs, causing a misfire, resulting in increased HC emission.

If a high CO emission, rich condition is so severe it causes all available combustion O2 to be used up, HC emission will also increase.

An increase of HC and NOx emissions caused by the fuel-injection system is usually due to one of the following low pressure or volume problems:

- Weak fuel pump
- Restricted fuel filter
- Restricted fuel line
- Pinched fuel delivery hose
- External fuel leak
- Dirty fuel injector or poor spray pattern
- Punctured fuel pressure regulator **diaphragm**

If the lean condition is so severe it causes a misfire, NOx emission will decrease and HC emission will increase dramatically.

Ignition System Problems

First, let's clear up some **OBD** II ignition terms: EI is an **Electronic Ignition** system that is a direct ignition system using either two spark plugs per coil, or a direct ignition system with one coil per spark plug. DI is an ignition system that uses a distributor.

Unless you have an engine that is a no-start or an obvious ignition wire problem to repair, start by checking the ignition timing first. Regardless of whether it is an EI type, or not, if it has a specification and a procedure available, be sure to check it. Few crank sensors are adjustable and will change initial timing if not adjusted properly. You should verify the timing advance capability of most models.

Acceptable type spark testers, like a High Energy Ignition Tester (HEI), are great for a no-start diagnosis. However, it is difficult to say for certain that the spark is adequate, just by watching it jump the gap of a spark tester. Oscilloscope checks of secondary voltage are best for showing a spark plug, spark plug wire, distributor cap, or rotor problem.

EI systems give some problems with scope hook-up, but most manufacturers now have methods for connecting, even on EI systems that have no plug wires.

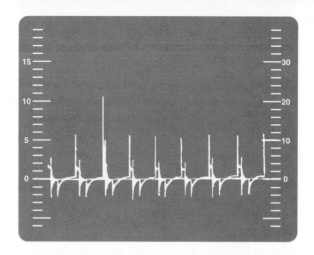

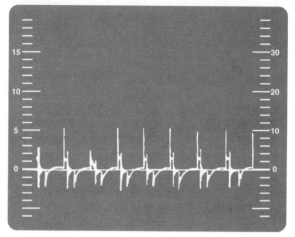

Fig. 1-31. Examples of common ignition secondary problems displayed on an oscilloscope.

Remember, two things will not change: High voltage on the scope means high resistance in the circuit. Low voltage on the scope means low resistance, or **short circuit** problems, figure 1-31.

Any ignition problem that affects combustion increases HC emission.

Insight

When any type of misfire occurs, it may cause the O2 sensor to send a low voltage signal to the ECM. The ECM interprets this to mean the system is lean, when in reality it is not. Unless the ECM recognizes this as a fault, the ECM will adjust the

L1

Diaphragm: A thin flexible wall, separating two cavities, used to turn a change of vacuum or pressure into mechanical movement, such as the diaphragm in a vacuum advance.
Electronic Ignition (EI): An ignition system that has coils dedicated to specific spark plugs (one or two spark plugs) and does not use a distributor; often referred to as distributorless ignition.
On Board Diagnostics (OBD): A diagnostic program contained in the PCM that monitors computer inputs and outputs for failures. OBD II is an industry-standard, second generation OBD system that monitors emissions control systems for degradation as well as failures.
Nozzle: The opening through which a substance flows.
Short Circuit: A condition in which a path is provided around the circuit load to another circuit or ground.

injector **on time** and fuel trim to increase fuel delivery. However, no amount of fuel will lower the amount of oxygen passing the O2 sensor from the misfire. During this time, the system will be rich and CO emission will be higher.

If the ECM recognizes the signal is false, it will set a code and remain in open-loop mode. This mode does not necessarily mean the system will be rich because some systems actually default lean.

Exhaust System Problems

Sometimes, a loss of power can be caused by a restricted or clogged exhaust system. A first step to check for a restricted exhaust is a vacuum test. To perform this test, warm the engine and attach a vacuum gauge to the manifold vacuum. Run the engine to at least 1500 rpm. Vacuum should be steady at 17 to 21 inches of mercury (in-hg), depending on engine condition. If the exhaust is restricted severely enough, the vacuum may never reach this value. The vacuum will drop as the exhaust backpressure builds.

Be aware, some other engine performance problems can cause the same vacuum test results. These include a loss of fuel pressure or volume, weak spark, or low charging voltage.

The next step is exhaust backpressure testing. Use a pounds per square inch (psi) pressure gauge in the O2 sensor threaded mounting hole, figure 1-32, in the EGR backpressure transducer exhaust port hose, an OEM gas analyzer exhaust gas test port (if you are lucky), or an aftermarket exhaust gas backpressure test kit. If you cannot find an OEM specification, use a specification of 3psi maximum backpressure at 1500 rpm. Another option is to disassemble and visually inspect to find the restriction.

Exhaust system air leaks can cause a safety problem for passengers. Poisonous emissions from the leak could reach the passenger compartment. Exhaust leaks can cause annoying popping sounds in the exhaust and cause your gas analyzer to give some

pretty strange readings. The problem with an exhaust leak is that it lets air into the exhaust, as well as letting exhaust gas out.

The extra air can cause sudden combustion of hot exhaust gas. The extra air also dilutes the exhaust stream, causing unreliable gas analyzer readings.

To check for the location of an exhaust leak, have a helper cover the tailpipe outlet to cause backpressure. Listen for a hissing sound, at the site of a leak, along the length of the exhaust system.

Transmission and Final Drive Problems

State emission inspections performed on dynamometers have created another reason for periodic **drivetrain** inspection and repair.

A drivetrain problem can be the cause of an aborted or failed emission test. It is important to realize during your drivetrain inspection that any modification of tire circumference, or final gear ratio, will change the ratio of engine speed to vehicle speed. A simple change of tire size now has an effect on emissions.

One example would be certain OEM's ECM strategies for EGR system operation. Some systems **monitor** a ratio of engine speed to vehicle speed for decisions about opening and

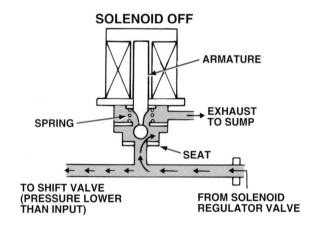

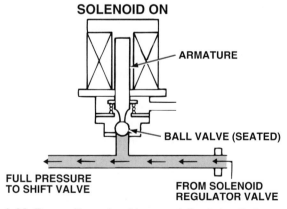

Fig. 1-33. Two position solenoids are on/off switches that open and close passages to regulate fluid flow in the transmission.

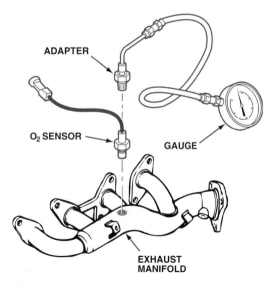

Fig. 1-32. Using a pressure gauge to test exhaust system backpressure.

Drivetrain: A reference that describes the parts from the engine to the drive axle(s).
Monitor: To watch, observe, or check something.
On time: The time when an actuator is energized, as when a fuel injector is signaled to allow fuel to flow.

modulating the EGR valve. A modification here could cause a state emission test failure.

A drivetrain problem can create an unsafe condition that would cause an emissions test to be aborted. Diagnosing drivetrain safety problems requires much the same approach as engine problems. Visual inspection of **CV boots**, U-joints, or axle vibration dampers requires grasping, pushing, and pulling to check for worn joints. Listen while test driving to see if you hear that telltale clicking noise on turns, indicating a bad CV joint.

Some defects can affect emissions by adding or changing engine load conditions. Check levels and condition of fluids. Use pressure tests to help diagnose automatic transmission problems. Perform electrical checks of transmission fluid temperature (TFT), transmission turbine speed (TSS), and the transmission range (TR) switch, as well as engine and vehicle speed (VSS) sensors. Electrically check the torque converter clutch lock-up and shift control solenoids, figure 1-33.

EXHAUST GAS ANALYZERS

To properly diagnose fuel system concerns an exhaust gas analyzer should be used. The analyzers are available in many styles and designs. Current models are designed to sample and analyze either four or five gasses present in the exhaust from the vehicle. The newest models are designed for five gas detection and normally provide digital and/or printed results of each test. Either piece of equipment is generally suitable for diagnosing basic fuel system abnormalities and driveability problems.

Five-Gas Analyzers

Five-gas analyzers measure the parts per million (ppm) of **hydrocarbons** (HC), the percentage of **carbon monoxide** (CO), the percentage of oxygen (O2), the percentage of carbon dioxide (CO2) and the percentage of oxides of nitrogen (NOx). Most properly tuned computer-controlled vehicles will produce about 50 ppm of HC, less than 0.5 percent CO, 1.0 to 2.0 percent O2 and 13.8 to 15.0 percent CO2.

Four-Gas Analyzers

Four-gas analyzers measure HC, CO, CO2 and O2. They do not provide data as to the levels of NOx in the exhaust.

Diagnosing Exhaust Gasses

For an accurate analysis of fuel combustion on catalytic converter-equipped vehicles, prevent the air injection system from supplying oxygen into the exhaust stream. This decreases the amount of O2 at the tailpipe and the efficiency of the converter. The air injection system may be disabled by several means. On some vehicles, disconnecting the air injection pump or plugging the pulse air injection system is effective. For others, the probe of the analyzer can be connected to a port installed upstream of the catalytic converter or to the exhaust opening for the EGR valve. Next, make sure that the engine is at operating temperature, in closed loop, and the HO2S is transmitting a variable signal. Sample the exhaust gases both at idle and at 2,500 RPM. If a dynamometer is used, test under simulated highway load conditions as described by the manufacturer.

Refer to Chapter 6 for additional information.

Abnormal HC and CO Readings

High HC levels indicate unburned fuel in the exhaust caused by incomplete combustion. The source of high HC emissions can often be traced to the ignition system, but mechanical or fuel system problems also can increase HC emissions. High levels of HC emissions result from:

- Advanced ignition timing
- Ignition misfire from defective spark plug wires or fouled spark plugs
- An excessively rich or lean air-fuel mixture
- Leaking vacuum hoses, vacuum controls, or seals
- Low engine compression
- Defective valves, valve guides, valve springs, lifters, camshaft, or incorrect valve lash
- Defective rings, pistons, or cylinder walls
- Clogged fuel injectors causing a lean misfire

The amount of CO in the exhaust stream is directly proportional to the amount of O2 contributing to the combustion process. Richer air-fuel mixtures, with lower oxygen content, produce higher CO levels; leaner air-fuel mixtures, with higher oxygen content, produce lower CO levels. High CO emissions may result from one or more of the following abnormal conditions:

- Clogged or dirty intake air passages
- Plugged air filter element
- Throttle body coking
- Rich fuel mixture
- Incorrect idle speed
- Excessive fuel pressure
- Leaking fuel injectors

Both HC and CO levels reading high at the same time may be caused by the following conditions:

- Defective positive crankcase ventilation system
- Defective catalytic converter
- Defective manifold heat control valve
- Defective air pump
- Defective thermostatic air cleaner

Abnormal CO2 and O2 Readings

Since the catalytic converter reduces HC and CO, these emissions are unreliable for determining the air fuel ratio. However, CO2 and O2 readings can be useful, provided that the air injection system has been disabled.

When air and fuel entering the engine burns with the least amount of wasted energy, at the stoichiometric air-fuel ratio, the engine emits the highest amount of CO2. Look for readings

Carbon Monoxide: An odorless, colorless, tasteless poisonous gas. A pollutant produced by the internal combustion engine.
CV Boot: The flexible cover used to prevent road dirt contamination of a CV joint.
Hydrocarbons: Chemical compounds in various combinations of hydrogen and carbon. A major pollutant from an internal combustion engine. Gasoline, itself, is a mixture of hydrocarbons.

between 13.8 and 15 percent. As the air-fuel ratio of the mixture leans or enriches, the CO_2 level drops. To determine whether a low CO_2 level indicates a lean or rich condition, examine the O_2 reading. Levels of O_2 below approximately 1.0 percent indicate a rich running engine; above 2.0 percent indicates a lean running engine.

To perform adequately and operate efficiently, an engine must be in sound mechanical condition. Therefore it is important to determine the overall mechanical condition of the engine before attempting to isolate or repair the cause of a driveability or performance problem.

Perform a compression or cylinder leakage test to determine the internal sealing capabilities of the engine. When test results are marginal and indicate valve seating problems, performance can often be restored by adjusting lash or servicing hydraulic valve lifters. If test results are below specifications, internal engine repairs are required to restore performance.

Variable Valve Timing

The variable valve timing system advances or retards camshaft timing to increase engine output, improve fuel efficiency and decrease emissions. A hydraulic actuator on the cam drive uses oil pressure to rotate the cam's position slightly, increasing valve duration. Cam timing is determined by the engine control module (ECM) using the crankshaft position (CKP) sensor and camshaft position sensor (CMP 1 and CMP 2) signals.

Each intake camshaft has a separate camshaft position sensor, hydraulic actuator, and control solenoid. If little or no oil pressure is received by a hydraulic actuator, it is designed to mechanically default to the fully retarded position.

CHAPTER QUESTIONS

1. Voltage drop in a circuit always equals:
   a. The resistance of each component
   b. The current flow through the ground circuit
   c. The source voltage
   d. None of the above

2. A diode is designed to:
   a. Allow current flow in both directions
   b. Prevent current flow in both directions
   c. Add extra resistance to control circuits
   d. Allow current flow in one direction only

3. When diagnosing a starting problem, disabling the ignition and fuel or just the fuel system prevents start up. What else is prevented while performing cranking tests?
   a. Crankcase oil dilution
   b. Excessive fuel backwash
   c. False scan tool readings
   d. Parasitic drains

4. In a series circuit with three 4 ohm bulbs and 12 volts applied, the total circuit voltage drop will be:
   a. 12 volts
   b. 4 volts
   c. 8 volts
   d. 1 volt

5. The unit of measure for current flow in a circuit is:
   a. Amps
   b. Volts
   c. Ohms
   d. Watts

6. The unit of measurement for resistance in a circuit is:
   a. Volts
   b. Ohms
   c. Watts
   d. Amps

7. A circuit that has one path for current flow is called a:
   a. Complex circuit
   b. Series circuit
   c. Parallel circuit
   d. Bias circuit

8. The voltage drop across an electrical component depends on the voltage applied and the _____ of the component.
   a. Size
   b. Resistance
   c. Electron
   d. Weight

9. When performing a no-start diagnosis, if fully charged, a battery should measure:
   a. 12.3V
   b. 12.4V
   c. 12.5V
   d. 12.6V

10. A long warm-up time may be caused by:
    a. Low ambient temperature
    b. Stuck-open thermostat
    c. No thermostat
    d. All of the above

11. An engine breathing problem, such as a worn camshaft lobe or valvetrain problem that prevents the proper amount of air entering the cylinder, may be diagnosed by running which test?
    a. Compression test
    b. Running compression test
    c. Engine mechanical test
    d. Standing rhinostatic test

12. Technician A says that watching a spark jump a gap of a spark tester is adequate to determine whether there is a spark problem. Technician B says it's important to run an oscilloscope check of secondary voltage to determine whether the problem exists in a spark plug wire. Who is right?
    a. A only
    b. B only
    c. Both A and B
    d. Neither A nor B

13. True of false? When you believe a loss of power is being caused by a restricted or clogged exhaust system, the first step to check for a restricted exhaust system is to perform an exhaust backpressure test.
    a. True
    b. False

14. Technician A says a five-gas exhaust gas analyzer is used to measure HC, CO, O2, CO2, and NOx. Technician B says a five-gas analyzer is used to measure HC, CO, O2, CO2, and N2. Who is right?
    a. A only
    b. B only
    c. Both A and B
    d. Neither A nor B

15. While diagnosing a starting problem, it is determined that the solenoid clicks but does not spin. Technician A says that a defective solenoid may be causing the problem. Technician B says it might be due to excessive resistance in the starter control circuit. Who is right?
    a. A only
    b. B only
    c. Both A and B
    d. Neither A nor B

16. In a series circuit containing three 4 ohm bulbs with 12 volts applied, resistance total is:
    a. 3 ohms
    b. 12 ohms
    c. 4 ohms
    d. 1 ohm

17. In a series circuit with three 4 ohm bulbs and 12 volts applied, current flow is:
    a. 1 amp
    b. 12 amps
    c. 4 amps
    d. 8 amps

L1

CHAPTER OBJECTIVES

- The technician will complete the ASE task list on Computerized Powertrain Controls Diagnosis Including OBD II.
- The technician will be able to answer 13 questions dealing with the Computerized Powertrain Controls Diagnosis Including OBD II section of the L1 ASE Test.

This chapter focuses on the operation and diagnosis of computerized powertrain control systems. The industry is placing more emphasis on the technician's ability to diagnose these complex control system defects and failures. If you need additional information on engine control systems refer to the A8 study guide.

As with any diagnostic routine once you have verified the customer's concern, begin your diagnosis by checking for missing, modified, inoperative, or tampered computerized powertrain control components. If any are found, repair or replace and retest the system before continuing.

Most OEMs provide diagnostic information for the computerized powertrain control systems either in the Service Manual or in a separate Diagnostic Manual. Locate the correct diagnostic information for the vehicle being serviced. Keep in mind that it is very important to take into account the following when looking up information:

- Model year
- Manufacturer/Make
- Model
- Production date
- VIN
- Engine size
- Emissions certification type

Most service and diagnostic procedures begin with a short description of system operation to familiarize you with the designed operating strategies for the system. Make it a habit to always read this information before jumping into the diagnostic routine.

COMPOSITE VEHICLE TYPE 3 INFORMATION

General Description

This generic four cycle, V6 engine has four overhead chain-driven camshafts, 24 valves, distributorless ignition, and a mass airflow-type closed-loop **sequential multiport fuel injection** system. The Engine Control Module (ECM) receives input from sensors, calculates ignition and fuel requirements, and controls engine actuators to provide the desired driveability, fuel economy, and emissions control, figure 2-1. The ECM also controls the vehicle's charging system. The powertrain control system has OBD II-compatible sensors and diagnostic capabilities. The ECM receives power from the battery and ignition switch and provides a regulated 5 volt supply for most of the engine sensors. The engine is equipped with a single exhaust system and a three-way catalytic converter, without any secondary air injection. Engine control features include variable valve timing, electronic throttle actuator control (TAC), a data communications bus, a vehicle anti-theft immobilizer system, and onboard refueling vapor recovery (ORVR) EVAP components. The control system software and OBD II diagnostic procedures stored in the ECM can be updated using factory supplied calibration files and PC-based interface software, along with a reprogramming device or scan tool that connects the PC to the vehicle's data link connector (DLC).

Fuel System

- Sequential Multiport Fuel Injection (SFI)
- Returnless Fuel Supply with electric fuel pump mounted inside the fuel tank
- Fuel pressure is regulated to a constant 50 psi (345 kPa) by a mechanical regulator in the tank. Minimum acceptable fuel pressure is 45 psi (310 kPa). The fuel system should maintain a minimum of 45 psi (310 kPa) for two minutes after the engine is turned off.

Ignition System

- Electronic (Distributorless) Ignition (EI) with six ignition coils (coil-over-plug)
- Firing order: 1-2-3-4-5-6
- Cylinders 1, 3, and 5 are on Bank 1; cylinders 2, 4, and 6 are on Bank 2
- Ignition timing is not adjustable
- Timing is determined by the ECM using the Crankshaft Position (CKP) sensor signal
- The ignition control module is integrated into the ECM

Sequential Multiport Fuel Injection (SFI): A fuel injection system that uses one electronic fuel injector for each cylinder. The injectors are pulsed in the sequence of each cylinder's intake stroke.

Electrical Diagram 1 of 3

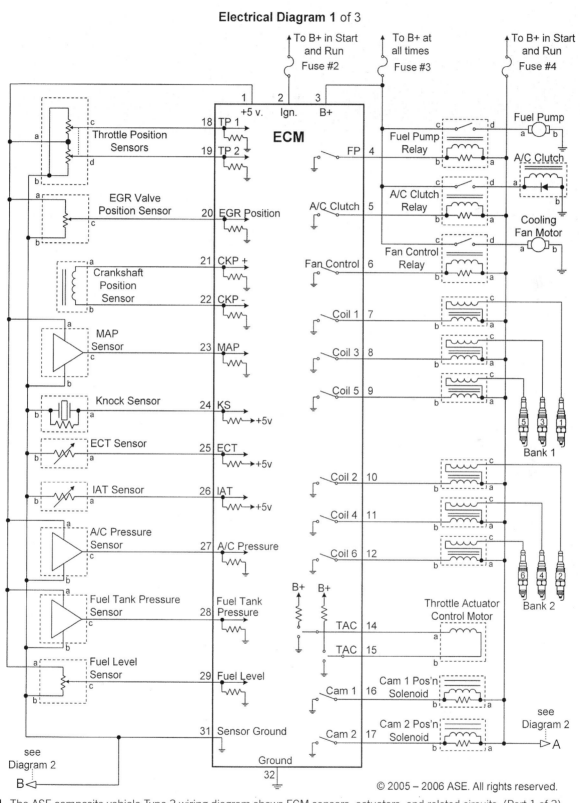

Fig. 2-1. The ASE composite vehicle Type 3 wiring diagram shows ECM sensors, actuators, and related circuits. (Part 1 of 3)

Electrical Diagram 2 of 3

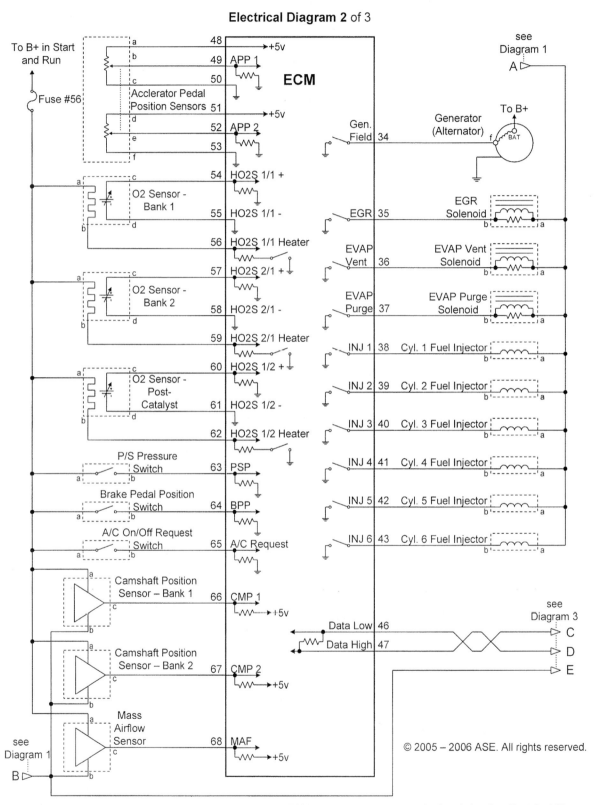

Fig. 2-1. The ASE composite vehicle Type 3 wiring diagram shows ECM sensors, actuators, and related circuits. (Part 2 of 3)

Electrical Diagram 3 of 3

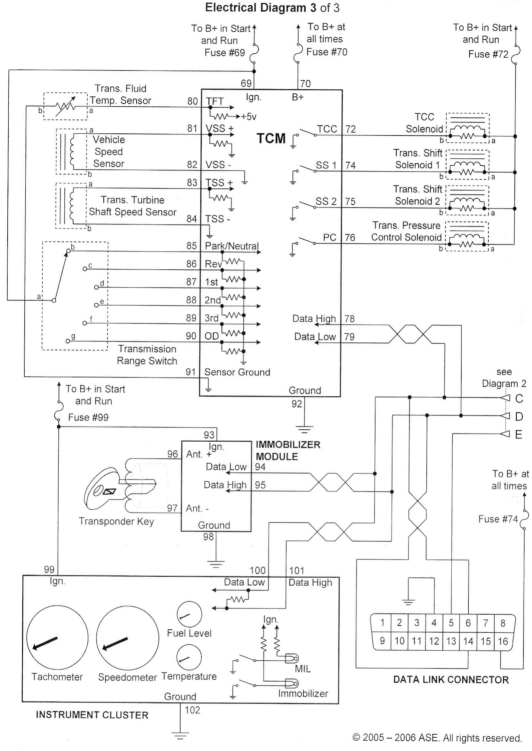

Fig. 2-1. The ASE composite vehicle Type 3 wiring diagram shows ECM sensors, actuators, and related circuits. (Part 3 of 3)

L1

Idle Speed

- Non-adjustable closed throttle stop (minimum air rate)
- Normal no-load idle range is 850 to 900 rpm with an idle air control value of 15% to 25%

Automatic Transmission

- Four-speed automatic **overdrive transaxle**, with shifting controlled by a transmission control module (TCM). The TCM communicates with the ECM and other modules through the data bus.

Overdrive: A condition in which the drive gear rotates slower than the driven gear. Output speed of the driven gear is increased, while output torque is reduced. A gear ratio of 0.70:1 is an overdrive gear ratio.

Transaxle: The combination of a transmission and differential gears, used in front wheel drive and rear engine vehicles.

- The TCM provides its own regulated 5 volt supply, performs all OBD II transaxle diagnostic routines, and stores transaxle diagnostic trouble codes (DTCs). The control system software and OBD II diagnostic procedures stored in the TCM can be updated in the same way as the ECM.
- Failures that result in a pending or confirmed DTC related to any of the following components will cause the TCM to default to fail-safe mode: range switch, shift solenoids, turbine shaft speed sensor, and the vehicle speed sensor. The TCM will also default to fail-safe mode if it is unable to communicate with the ECM.
- When in fail-safe mode, maximum line pressure will be commanded, the transmission will default to 2nd gear and the torque converter clutch will be disabled.

Variable Valve Timing

- Intake camshaft timing is continuously variable using a hydraulic actuator attached to the end of each intake camshaft. Engine oil flow to each hydraulic actuator is controlled by a camshaft position actuator control solenoid. Exhaust camshaft timing is fixed.
- A single timing chain drives both exhaust camshafts and both intake camshaft hydraulic actuators. While valve overlap is variable, valve lift and duration are fixed.
- Cam timing is determined by the ECM using the crankshaft position (CKP) sensor and camshaft position sensor (CMP 1 and CMP 2) signals. At idle, the intake camshafts are fully retarded and valve overlap is zero degrees. At higher speeds and loads, the intake camshafts can be advanced up to 40 crankshaft degrees.
- Each intake camshaft has a separate camshaft position sensor, hydraulic actuator, and control solenoid. If little or no oil pressure is received by a hydraulic actuator (typically at engine startup, at idle speed, or during a fault condition), it is designed to mechanically default to the fully retarded position (zero valve overlap), and is held in that position by a spring-loaded locking pin.

Electronic Throttle Control

- The vehicle does not have a mechanical throttle cable, a cruise control throttle actuator, or an idle air control (IAC) valve. Throttle opening at all engine speeds and loads is controlled directly by a throttle actuator control (TAC) motor mounted on the throttle body housing.
- Dual accelerator pedal position (APP) sensors provide input from the vehicle operator, while the actual throttle angle is determined using dual throttle position (TP) sensors.
- If one APP sensor or one TP sensor fails, the ECM will turn on the malfunction indicator lamp (MIL) and limit the maximum throttle opening to 35%. If any two (or more) of the four sensors fail, the ECM will turn on the MIL and disable the electronic throttle control.
- In case of failure of the electronic throttle control system, the system will default to limp-in operation. In limp-in mode, the spring-loaded throttle plate will return to a default position of 15% throttle opening, and the TAC value on the scan tool will indicate 15%. This default position will provide a fast idle speed of 1400 to 1500 rpm, with no load and all accessories off.
- Normal no-load idle range is 850 to 900 rpm at 5% to 10% throttle opening.
- No idle relearn procedure is required after component replacement or a dead battery.

Data Communications Bus

- The serial data bus is a high-speed, non-fault tolerant, two wire twisted pair communications network. It allows peer-to-peer communications between various electronic modules, including the engine control module (ECM), transmission control module (TCM), instrument cluster (including the MIL), immobilizer control module, and a scan tool connected to the data link connector (DLC).
- The Data-High circuit switches between 2.5 (rest state) and 3.5 volts (active state), and the Data-Low circuit switches between 2.5 (rest state) and 1.5 volts (active state). The data bus has two 120 ohm terminating resistors: one inside the instrument cluster, and another one inside the ECM.
- Any of the following conditions will cause the data communications bus to fail and result in the storage of network DTCs: either data line shorted to power, to ground, or to the other data line.
- The data bus will remain operational when one of the two modules containing a terminating resistor is not connected to the network. The data bus will fail when both terminating resistors are not connected to the network.
- Data communication failures do not prevent the ECM from providing ignition and fuel control.

Immobilizer Anti-Theft System

- When the ignition switch is turned on, the immobilizer control module sends a challenge signal through the antenna around the ignition switch to the transponder chip in the ignition key. The transponder key responds with an encrypted key code. The immobilizer control module then decodes the key code and compares it to the list of registered keys.
- When the engine is started, the ECM sends a request to the immobilizer control module over the data bus to verify the key validity. If the key is valid, the immobilizer control module responds with a "valid key" message to the ECM to continue normal engine operation.
- If an attempt is made to start the vehicle with an invalid ignition key, the immobilizer control module sends a message over the data bus to the instrument cluster to flash the anti-theft indicator lamp. If the ECM does not receive a "valid key" message from the immobilizer control module within 2 seconds of engine startup, the ECM will disable the fuel injectors to kill the engine. Cycling the key off and cranking the engine again will result in engine restart and stall.
- The immobilizer control module and ECM each have their own unique internal ID numbers used to encrypt their messages, and are programmed at the factory to recognize each other. If either module is replaced, the scan tool must

be used to program the replacement module, using the VIN, the date, and a factory-assigned PIN number.

- Up to eight keys can be registered in the immobilizer control module. Each key has its own unique internal key code. If only one valid key is available, or if all keys have been lost, the scan tool can be used to delete lost keys and register new keys. This procedure also requires the VIN, the date, and a factory-assigned PIN number.

- The ECM, TCM, and the immobilizer control module do not prevent operation of the starter motor for anti-theft purposes.

On-Board Refueling Vapor Recovery (ORVR) EVAP System

- The on-board refueling vapor recovery EVAP system causes fuel tank vapors to be directed to the EVAP charcoal canister during refueling, so that HC vapors do not escape into the atmosphere

- The following components have been added to the traditional EVAP system for QRVR capability: a one inch I.D. fill pipe, a one-way check valve at the bottom of the fill pipe, a fuel vapor control valve inside the fuel tank, and a ½ inch I.D. vent hose from the vapor control valve to the canister.

- The fuel vapor control valve has a float that rises to seal the vent hose when the fuel tank is full. It also prevents liquid fuel from reaching the canister and blocks fuel from leaking in the event of a vehicle roll-over.

SENSORS

Crankshaft Position (CKP) Sensor

A **magnetic-type sensor** that generates 35 pulses for each crankshaft revolution. It is located on the front engine cover, with a 35-tooth iron wheel mounted on the crankshaft just behind the balancer pulley. Each tooth is ten crankshaft degrees apart, with one space for a "missing tooth" located 60 degrees before top dead center of cylinder number 1, figure 2-2.

Camshaft Position (CMP 1 and CMP 2) Sensors

A pair of three-wire solid state (**Hall-effect** or **optical-type**) **sensors** that generate a signal once per intake camshaft revolution. The leading edge of the bank 1 CMP signal occurs on the cylinder 1 compression stroke, and the leading edge of the bank 2 CMP signal occurs on the cylinder 4 compression stroke, figure 2-2. When the intake camshafts are fully retarded (zero valve overlap), the signals switch at top dead center of cylinders 1 and 4. When the intake camshafts are fully advanced (maximum valve overlap), the signals switch at 40 crankshaft degrees before top dead center. These signals allow the ECM to determine fuel injector and ignition coil sequence, as well as actual intake valve timing. Loss of one CMP signal will set a DTC, and valve timing will be held at the fully retarded position (zero valve overlap). If neither CMP signal is detected during cranking, the ECM will store a DTC and disable the fuel injectors, resulting in a no-start condition. Located at the rear of each valve cover, with an interrupter mounted on the intake camshafts to generate the signal.

Mass Airflow (MAF) Sensor

Senses airflow into the intake manifold. The sensor reading varies from 0.2 volt (0 gm/sec) at key-on, engine-off, to 4.8 volts (175 gm/sec) at maximum airflow, figure 2-3. At sea level, no-load idle (850 rpm), the sensor reading is 0.7 volt (2.0 gm/sec). Located on the air cleaner housing.

Manifold Absolute Pressure (MAP) Sensor

Senses intake manifold absolute pressure. The MAP sensor signal is used by the ECM for OBD II diagnostics only. The sensor reading varies from 4.5 volts at 0 in. Hg vacuum I 101 kPa

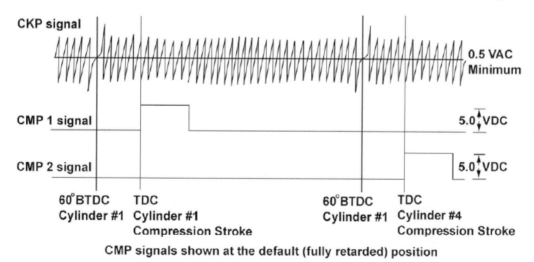

Fig. 2-2. CKP and CMP sensor waveforms.

Hall-Effect Sensor: A signal-generating switch that develops a transverse voltage across a current-carrying semiconductor when subjected to a magnetic field.

Magnetic Type Sensor: Magnetic pulse generator, a signal-generating device that creates a voltage pulse as magnetic flux changes around a pickup coil.

Optical Sensor: Uses a light-emitting diode and shutter blade to trigger the switching of a photo-sensitive transistor, sends a square wave signal used for engine rpm and/or piston position.

MASS AIRFLOW (gm/sec)	SENSOR VOLTAGE
0	0.2
2	0.7
4	1.0
8	1.5
15	2.0
30	2.5
50	3.0
80	3.5
110	4.0
150	4.5
175	4.8

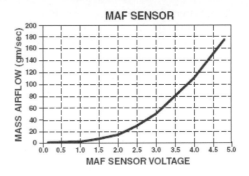

Fig. 2-3. MAF signal voltage increases as airflow increases.

VACUUM AT SEA LEVEL (in. Hg.)	MANIFOLD ABSOLUTE PRESSURE (kPa)	SENSOR VOLTAGE
0	101.3	4.5
3	91.2	4.0
6	81.0	3.5
9	70.8	3.0
12	60.7	2.5
15	50.5	2.0
18	40.4	1.5
21	30.2	1.0
24	20.1	0.5

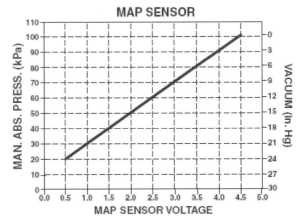

Fig. 2-4. MAP sensor signal voltage increases as intake manifold vacuum decreases and manifold absolute pressure increases.

pressure (key on. engine off, at sea level) to 0.5 volts at 24 in. Hg vacuum /20.1 kPa pressure, figure 2-4. At sea level, no-load idle with 18 in. Hg vacuum (40.4 kPa absolute pressure); the sensor reading is 1.5 volts. Located on the intake manifold.

Throttle Position (TP 1 and TP 2) Sensors

A pair of redundant non-adjustable **potentiometers** that sense throttle position The TP 1 sensor signal varies from 4.5 volts at closed throttle to 0.5 volts at maximum throttle opening (decreasing voltage with increasing throttle position), figure 2-5. The TP 2 sensor signal varies from 0.5 volts at closed throttle to 4.5 volts at maximum throttle opening (increasing voltage with increasing throttle position). Failure

of one TP sensor will set a DTC and the ECM will limit the maximum throttle opening to 35%. Failure of both TP sensors will set a DTC and cause the throttle actuator control to be disabled, and the spring-loaded throttle plate will return to the default 15% position (fast idle). Located on the throttle body.

Engine Coolant (ECT) Sensor

A negative temperature coefficient (NTC) thermistor that senses engine coolant temperature. The sensor values range from -40°F to 248°F (-40°C to 120°C). At 212°F (100°C), the sensor reading is 0.46 volt, figure 2-6. Located in the engine block water jacket.

Throttle Position (% open)	TP 1 Sensor Voltage	TP 2 Sensor Voltage
0	4.50	0.50
5	4.30	0.70
10	4.10	0.90
15	3.90	1.10
20	3.70	1.30
25	3.50	1.50
40	2.90	2.10
50	2.50	2.50
60	2.10	2.90
75	1.50	3.50
80	1.30	3.70
100	0.50	4.50

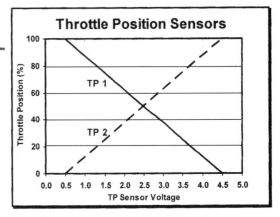

Fig. 2-5. TPS signal voltage increases as the throttle is opened.

Potentiometer: A variable resistor with three terminals. Signal voltage comes from a terminal attached to a movable contact that passes over the resistor.

TEMPERATURE °F	TEMPERATURE °C	SENSOR VOLTAGE
248	120	0.25
212	100	0.46
176	80	0.84
150	66	1.34
140	60	1.55
104	40	2.27
86	30	2.60
68	20	2.93
32	0	3.59
−4	−20	4.24
−40	−40	4.90

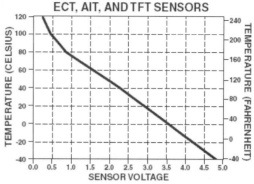

ECT, AIT, AND TFT SENSORS

NOTE: ALL THREE SENSORS HAVE THE SAME TEMPERATURE / VOLTAGE RELATIONSHIP

Fig. 2-6. ECT, IAT, and TFT sensors signal voltage decreases as temperature increases.

Accelerator Pedal Position (APP 1 and APP 2) Sensors

A pair of redundant non-adjustable potentiometers that sense accelerator pedal position. The APP 1 sensor signal varies from 0.5 volts at the released pedal position to 3.5 volts at maximum pedal depression (increasing voltage with increasing pedal position), figure 2-7. The APP 2 sensor signal varies from 1.5 volts at the released pedal position to 4.5 volts at maximum pedal depression (increasing voltage with increasing pedal position, offset from the APP 1 sensor signal by 1.0 volt). The ECM interprets an accelerator pedal position of 80% or greater as a request for wide open throttle. Failure of one APP sensor will set a DTC and the ECM will limit the maximum throttle opening to 35%. Failure of both APP sensors will set a DTC and cause the throttle actuator control to be disabled, and the spring-loaded throttle plate will return to the default 15% position (fast idle). Located on the accelerator pedal assembly.

EGR Valve Position Sensor

A three-wire non-adjustable potentiometer that senses the position of the EGR valve pintle. The sensor reading varies from 0.50 volts when the valve is fully closed to 4.50 volts when the valve is fully opened, figure 2-8. Located on top of the EGR valve.

Knock Sensor

A two-wire piezoelectric sensor that generates an AC voltage spike when engine vibrations within a specified frequency range are present, indicating spark knock. The signal is used by the ECM to retard ignition timing when spark knock is detected. The sensor signal circuit normally measures 2.5 volts DC with the sensor connected. Located in the engine block.

Intake Air Temperature (IAT) Sensor

A negative temperature coefficient (NTC) sensor that senses air temperature. The sensor values range from -40°F to 248°F (-40°C to 120°C). At 86°F (30°C), the sensor reading is 2.6 volts, figure 2-6. Located in the air cleaner housing.

Vehicle Speed Sensor (VSS)

A magnetic-type sensor mat senses rotation of the final drive and generates a signal that increases in **frequency** as vehicle speed increases. The TCM uses the VSS signal to control **upshifts, downshifts**, and the torque converter clutch. The

Accelerator Pedal Pos'n (% depressed)	APP 1 Sensor Voltage	APP 2 Sensor Voltage
0	0.50	1.50
5	0.65	1.65
10	0.80	1.80
15	0.95	1.95
20	1.10	2.10
25	1.25	2.25
40	1.70	2.70
50	2.00	3.00
60	2.30	3.30
75	2.75	3.75
80	2.90	3.90
100	3.50	4.50

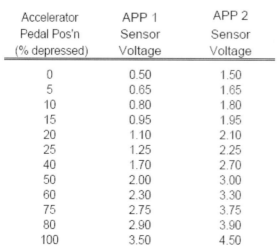

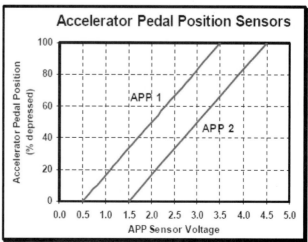

Accelerator Pedal Position Sensors

Fig. 2-7. APP sensors signal voltage increases as the accelerator pedal is depressed.

Downshift: To shift into a lower gear ratio.
Frequency: A measurement in Hertz (cycles per second) of how often something occurs in a specific amount of time.
Upshift: To shift into a higher gear ratio.

L1

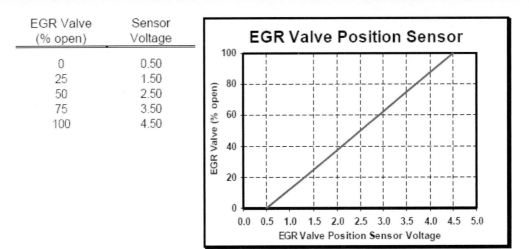

EGR Valve (% open)	Sensor Voltage
0	0.50
25	1.50
50	2.50
75	3.50
100	4.50

Fig. 2-8. EGR valve position sensor signal voltage increases as sensor is opened.

TCM communicates the VSS signal over the data communications bus to the ECM to control high-speed fuel cutoff, and to the Instrument Cluster for speedometer operation The signal is displayed on the scan tool in miles per hour and kilometers per hour. Located on the transaxle housing.

Heated Oxygen Sensors (HO2S ⅓, HO2S ⅔ and HO2S ½)

Electrically heated zirconia sensors that measure oxygen content in the exhaust stream. Sensor ⅓ is located on the Bank 1 exhaust manifold (cylinders 1, 3, and 5). Sensor ⅔ is located on the Bank 2 exhaust manifold (cylinders 2, 4, and 6). Both up-

stream sensor signals are used for closed loop fuel control and OBD II monitoring. Sensor ½ is mounted in the exhaust pipe after the catalytic converter (downstream). See figure 2-9 to view the relative locations of upstream and downstream HO2S sensors. The HO2S sensor signal is used for OBD II monitoring of catalytic converter operation. The sensor outputs vary from 0.0 to 1.0 volt. When a sensor reading is less than 0.45 volt, oxygen content around the sensor is high; when a sensor reading is more than 0.45 volt, oxygen content around the sensor is low. No bias voltage is applied to the sensor signal circuit by the ECM. With the key on and engine off, the sensor readings are zero volts. Battery voltage is continuously supplied to the oxygen sensor heaters whenever the ignition switch is on.

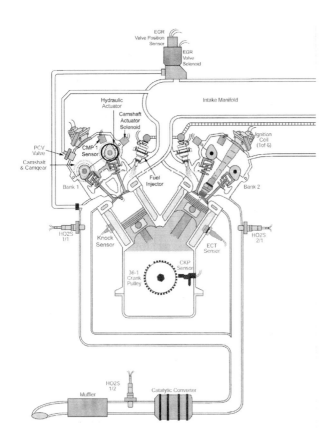

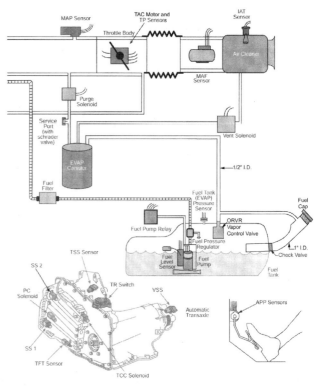

Fig. 2-9. ASE Composite Type 3 vehicle. (Part 1 of 2).   **Fig. 2-9.** ASE Composite Type 3 vehicle. (Part 2 of 2).

Power Steering Pressure (PSP) Switch

A switch that closes when high pressure is detected in the power steering system. The signal is used by the ECM to adjust idle airflow to compensate for the added engine load from the power steering pump. Located on the P/S high pressure hose.

Brake Pedal Position (BPP) Switch

A switch that closes when the brake pedal is depressed (brakes applied). The signal is used by the ECM to release the torque converter clutch. Located on the brake pedal.

A/C On/Off Request Switch

A switch that is closed by the vehicle operator to request A/C compressor operation. Located in the climate control unit on the instrument panel.

A/C Pressure Sensor

A three-wire solid-state sensor for A/C system high-side pressure, figure 2-10. The sensor reading varies from 0.25 volt at 25 psi to 4.50 volts at 450 psi. The signal is used by the ECM to control the **A/C compressor clutch** and radiator fan, and to adjust idle air flow to compensate for the added engine load from the A/C compressor. The ECM will also interrupt compressor operation if the pressure is below 40 psi or above 420 psi. Located on the A/C high side vapor line.

Fuel Level Sensor

A potentiometer that is used to determine the fuel level. The reading varies from 0.5 volt/0% with an empty tank to 4.5 volts/100% with a full tank. When the fuel tank is ¼ full, the sensor reading is 1.5 volts. When the fuel tank is ¾ full,

the sensor reading is 3.5 volts. Used by the ECM when testing the evaporative emission (EVAP) system. Located in the fuel tank.

Fuel Tank (EVAP) Pressure Sensor

Senses vapor pressure or vacuum in the evaporative emission (EVAP) system compared to **atmospheric pressure**, figure 2-11. The sensor reading varies from 0.5 volt at 1/2 psi (14 in. H2O) vacuum to 4.5 volts at 1/2 psi (14 in. H20) pressure. With no pressure or vacuum in the fuel tank (gas cap removed), the sensor output is 2.5 volts. Used by the ECM for OBD II evaporative emission system diagnostics only. Located on top of the fuel tank.

Transmission Fluid Temperature (TFT) Sensor

A negative temperature coefficient (NTC) thermistor that senses transmission fluid temperature. The sensor values range from -40°F to 248°F (-40°C to 120°C). At 212°F (100°C), the sensor reading is 0.46 volts. This signal is used by the TCM to delay shifting when the fluid is cold, and control torque converter clutch operation when the fluid is hot. Located in the transaxle oil pan.

Transmission Turbine Shaft Speed (TSS) Sensor

A magnetic-type sensor that senses rotation of the torque converter turbine shaft (input/mainshaft) and generates a signal that increases in frequency as transmission input speed increases. Used by the ECM to control torque converter clutch operation and sense transmission slippage. Located on the transaxle housing.

A/C HIGH SIDE PRESSURE (psi)	SENSOR VOLTAGE
25	0.25
50	0.50
100	1.0
150	1.5
200	2.0
250	2.5
300	3.0
350	3.5
400	4.0
450	4.5

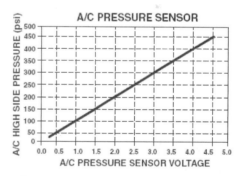

Fig. 2-10. A/C pressure sensor signal voltage increases as high-side pressure increases.

FUEL TANK (EVAP) (in. H₂O)	PRESSURE (psi)	SENSOR VOLTAGE
− 14.0	− 0.50	0.5
− 10.5	− 0.375	1.0
− 7.0	− 0.25	1.5
− 3.5	− 0.125	2.0
0	0	2.5
3.5	0.125	3.0
7.0	0.25	3.5
10.5	0.375	4.0
14.0	0.50	4.5

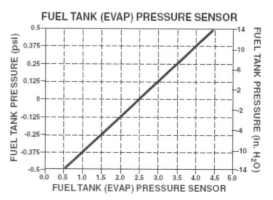

Fig. 2-11. Fuel Tank (EVAP) pressure sensor signal voltage increases as pressure increases.

L1

A/C Compressor Clutch: An electromagnetic device that engages the otherwise freewheeling A/C pulley.
Atmospheric Pressure: The pressure caused by the weight of the earth's atmosphere. At sea level, this pressure is 14.7 psi (101 kPa).

Transmission Range (TR) Switch

A six-position switch that indicates the position of the transaxle manual select lever: Park/Neutral, Reverse, Manual Low (1), Second (2), Drive (3), or Overdrive (OD). Used by the PCM to control transmission line pressure, upshifting, and downshifting. Located on the transaxle housing.

ACTUATORS

All coils, injectors, solenoids, and relays receive a constant battery positive voltage feed from the ignition switch and are controlled by the ECM providing a ground connection.

Fuel Pump Relay

When energized, this relay supplies battery voltage (B+) to the fuel pump. The relay coil resistance spec is 48 ± 6 ohms.

Fan Control (FC) Relay

When energized, this relay provides battery voltage (B+) to the radiator/condenser fan motor. The ECM will turn the fan on when engine coolant temperature reaches 210°F (99°C) and off when coolant temperature drops to 195°F (90°). The fan also runs whenever the A/C compressor clutch is engaged. The relay coil resistance spec is 48 ± 6 ohms.

A/C Clutch Relay

When energized, this relay provides battery voltage (B+) to the A/C compressor clutch coil. The relay coil resistance spec is 48 ± ohms.

Throttle Actuator Control (TAC) Motor

A bidirectional pulse-width modulated DC motor that controls the position of the throttle plate. A scan tool data value of 0% indicates an ECM command to fully close the throttle plate, and a value of 100% indicates an ECM command to fully open the throttle plate (wide open throttle). Any throttle control actuator motor circuit fault will set a DTC and cause the throttle actuator control to be disabled, and the spring-loaded throttle plate will return to the default 15% position (fast idle). When disabled, the TAC value on the scan tool will indicate 15%.

Malfunction Indicator Lamp (MIL)

The MIL is part of the instrument cluster and receives commands from the ECM and TCM over the data communications bus. If the instrument cluster fails to communicate with the ECM and TCM, the MIL is continuously lit by default. Under normal conditions, when the ignition switch is turned on the lamp remains lit for 15 seconds for a bulb check. Afterward, the MIL will light only for emissions related concerns. Whenever an engine misfire severe enough to damage the catalytic converter is detected, the MIL will flash on and off.

Camshaft Position Actuator Control Solenoids

A pair of duty cycle–controlled solenoid valves that increase or decrease timing advance of the intake camshafts by controlling engine oil flow to the camshaft position actuators. When the duty cycle is greater than 50%, the oil flow from the solenoid causes the actuator to advance the camshaft position. When the duty cycle is less than 50%, the oil flow from the solenoid causes the actuator to retard the camshaft position. When the ECM determines that the desired camshaft position has been achieved, the duty cycle is commanded to 50% to hold the actuator so that the adjusted camshaft position is maintained. The solenoid winding resistance spec is 12 ± 2 ohms.

Exhaust Gas Recirculation (EGR) Valve

A **duty cycle**–controlled solenoid that, when energized, lifts the spring-loaded EGR valve pintle to open the valve. A value of 0% indicates an ECM command to fully close the EGR valve, and a value of 100% indicates an ECM command to fully open the EGR valve The solenoid is enabled when the engine coolant temperature reaches 150°F (66°C) and the throttle is not closed or wide open. The solenoid winding resistance spec is 12 ± 2 ohms.

Fuel Injectors

Electro-mechanical devices used to deliver fuel to the intake manifold at each cylinder. Each injector is individually energized once per camshaft revolution timed to its cylinder's intake stroke. The injector winding spec is 12 ± 2 ohms.

Ignition Coils

These six coils, mounted above the spark plugs, generate a high voltage to create a spark at each cylinder individually. Timing and dwell are controlled by the ECM directly, without the use of a separate ignition module. The coil primary resistance spec is 1 ± .5 ohms. The coil secondary resistance spec is 10K ± 2K.

Generator Field

The ECM supplies this variable-duty cycle signal to ground the field winding of the generator (alternator), without the use of a separate voltage regulator. Increasing the duty cycle results in a higher field current and greater generator (alternator) output.

Evaporator Emission (EVAP) Canister Purge

A duty cycle-controlled solenoid that regulates the flow of vapors stored in the canister to the intake manifold. The solenoid is enabled when the engine coolant temperature reaches 150°F (66°C) and the throttle is not closed. A duty cycle of 0% blocks vapor flow, and a duty cycle of 100% allows maximum vapor flow. The duty cycle is determined by the ECM, based on engine speed and load. The solenoid is also used for OBD II testing of the evaporative emission (EVAP) system. The solenoid winding resistance spec is 48 ± 6 ohms. There is also a service port with a Schrader valve and cap installed on the hose between the purge solenoid and the canister.

Evaporative Emission (EVAP) Canister Vent Solenoid

When energized, the fresh air supply hose to the canister is blocked. The solenoid is energized only for OBD II testing of the evaporative emission (EVAP) system. The solenoid winding resistance spec is 48 ± 6 ohms.

Torque Converter Clutch (TCC) Solenoid Valve

A duty cycle–controlled solenoid valve that applies the torque converter clutch by redirecting hydraulic pressure in the

---

Duty Cycle: Describes the time of a complete cycle of action, including both the on (energized) and off (deenergized) time of a solenoid.

transaxle. With a duty cycle of 0%, the TCC is released. When torque converter clutch application is desired, the pulse width is increased until the clutch is fully applied. The solenoid will then maintain a 100% duty cycle until clutch disengagement is commanded. Then the pulse width is decreased back to 0%. If the brake pedal position switch closes, the duty cycle is cut to 0% immediately. The solenoid is enabled when the engine coolant temperature reaches 150°F (66°C), the brake switch is open, the transmission is in 3rd or 4th gear, and the vehicle is at cruise (steady throttle) above 40 mph. In addition, whenever the transmission fluid temperature is 248°F (120°C) or more, the ECM will command TCC lockup. The solenoid winding resistance is 48 ± 6 ohms.

Transmission Pressure Control (PC) Solenoid

This pulse width modulated solenoid controls fluid in the transmission valve body that is routed to the pressure regulator valve. By varying the duty cycle of the solenoid, the ECM can vary the line pressure of the transmission to control shift feel and slippage. When the duty cycle is minimum (10%), the line pressure will be maximized. When the duty cycle is maximum (90%) the line pressure will be minimized. The solenoid winding resistance spec is 6 ± 1 ohms.

Transmission Shift Solenoids (SS1 and SS2)

These solenoids control fluid in the transmission valve body that is routed to the 1-2, 2-3, and 3-4 shift valves. By energizing or de-energizing the solenoids, the ECM can enable a gear change, figure 2-12. The solenoid winding resistance is 12 ± 4 ohms.

SFI SYSTEM OPERATION AND COMPONENT FUNCTIONS

Starting Mode

When the ignition switch is turned on, the ECM energizes the fuel pump relay for 2 seconds, allowing the fuel pump to build up pressure in the fuel system. Unless the engine is cranked within this two-second period, the fuel pump relay is de-energized to turn off the pump. The fuel pump relay will remain energized as long as the engine speed (CKP) signal to the ECM is 100 rpm or more.

GEAR	SS 1	SS 2
P,N,R, or 1	ON	OFF
2	OFF	OFF
3	OFF	ON
4	ON	ON

Fig. 2-12. This chart shows transmission solenoid applications for the complete vehicle.

Clear Flood Mode

When the throttle is wide open (throttle opening of 80% or greater) and the engine speed is below 400 rpm, the ECM turns off the fuel injectors.

Run Mode: Open and Closed Loop

Open Loop

When the engine is first started and running above 400 rpm, the system operates in open loop. In open loop, the ECM does not use the oxygen sensor signal. Instead, it calculates the fuel injector pulse width from the throttle position sensor, the coolant and intake air temperature sensors, the MAF sensor, and the CKP sensor. The system will stay in open loop until all of these conditions are met:

- Both upstream heated oxygen sensors are sending varying signals to the ECM
- The engine coolant temperature is above 150°F (66°C)
- Ten seconds has elapsed since startup
- Throttle position is less than 80%

Closed Loop

When the oxygen sensor, engine coolant temperature sensor, and time conditions are met, and the throttle opening is less than 80%, the system goes into closed loop. Closed loop means that the ECM adjusts the fuel injector pulse widths for Bank 1 and Bank 2 based on the varying voltage signals from the upstream oxygen sensors. An oxygen sensor signal below 0.45 volt causes the ECM to increase injector pulse width. When the oxygen sensor signal rises above 0.45 volt in response to the richer mixture, the ECM reduces injector pulse width. This feedback trims the fuel control program that is based on the other sensor signals.

Acceleration Enrichment Mode

During acceleration, the ECM uses the increase in mass airflow and the rate of change in throttle position to calculate increased fuel injector pulse width. During wide open throttle operation, the control system goes into open loop mode.

Deceleration Enleanment Mode

During deceleration, the ECM uses the decrease in mass airflow, the vehicle speed value, and the rate of change in throttle position to calculate decreased fuel injector pulse width.

Fuel Cut-Off Mode

The ECM will turn off the fuel injectors, for safety reasons, when the vehicle speed reaches 110 mph, or if the engine speed exceeds 6000 rpm.

OBD II SYSTEM OPERATION

Comprehensive Component Monitor

The OBD II diagnostic system continuously monitors all engine and transmission sensors and actuators for shorts, opens, and out-of-range values, as well as values that do not logically fit with other powertrain data (rationality).

L1

Comprehensive: Inclusive or complete.
Freeze Frame: Operating conditions that are stored in the memory of the PCM at the instant a diagnostic trouble code is set. (The current stored PCM data of what was sensed and what commands were being given at the instant in time the most current trouble was set).

On the first trip during which the **comprehensive** component monitor detects a failure that will result in emissions exceeding a predetermined level, the ECM will store a DTC, illuminate the MIL, and store a **freeze** frame.

System Monitors

The OBD II diagnostic system also actively tests some systems for proper operation while the vehicle is being driven; fuel control and engine misfire are checked continuously. Oxygen sensor response, oxygen sensor heater operation, catalyst efficiency, EGR operation, EVAP integrity, variable valve timing, and thermostat operation are tested once or more per trip. When any of the System Monitors detects a failure that will result in emissions exceeding a predetermined level on two consecutive trips, the ECM will store a diagnostic trouble code (DTC) and illuminate the malfunction indicator lamp (MIL). Freeze frame data captured during the first of the two consecutive failures are also stored.

FUEL CONTROL — This monitor will set a DTC if the system fails to enter Closed Loop mode within 5 minutes of startup, or the Long Term Fuel Trim is excessively high or low anytime after the engine is warmed up, indicating the loss of fuel control. This is always the case when the Long Term Fuel Trim reaches its limit (+30% or -30%).

ENGINE MISFIRE — This monitor uses the CKP sensor signal to continuously detect engine misfires both severe and non-severe. If the misfire is severe enough to cause catalytic converter damage, the MIL will blink as long as the severe misfire is detected.

CATALYTIC CONVERTER — This monitor compares the signals of the two upstream heated oxygen sensors to the signal from the downstream heated oxygen to determine the ability of the catalyst to store free oxygen. If the converter's oxygen storage capacity is sufficiently **degraded**, a DTC is set.

EGR SYSTEM — This monitor uses the MAP sensor signal to detect changes in intake manifold pressure as the EGR valve is commanded to open and close. If the pressure changes too little or too much, a DTC is set.

EVAP SYSTEM — This monitor first turns on the EVAP vent solenoid to block the fresh air supply to the EVAP canister. Next, the EVAP purge solenoid is turned on to draw a slight vacuum on the entire EVAP system, including the fuel tank. Then the EVAP purge solenoid is turned off to seal the system. The monitor uses the fuel tank (EVAP) pressure sensor signal to determine if the EVAP system has any leaks. If the vacuum **decays** too rapidly, a DTC is set. In order to run this monitor, the engine must be cold (below 86°F/30°C) and the fuel level must be between ¼ and ¾ full.

VARIABLE VALVE TIMING — This monitor compares the desired valve timing with the actual timing indicated by the CMP sensors. If the timing is in error, or takes too long to reach the desired value, a DTC is set.

ENGINE THERMOSTAT — This monitor confirms that the engine warms up fully within a reasonable amount of time. If the coolant temperature remains too low for too long, a DTC is set.

OXYGEN SENSORS — This monitor checks the maximum and minimum output voltage, as well as switching and response times for all oxygen sensors. If an oxygen sensor signal remains too low or too high or switches too slowly or not at all, a DTC is set.

OXYGEN SENSOR HEATERS — This monitor checks the time from cold start until the oxygen sensors begin to operate. If the time is too long, a DTC is set. Battery voltage is continuously supplied to the oxygen sensor heaters whenever the ignition switch is on.

Monitor Readiness Status

The monitor readiness status indicates whether or not a particular OBD II diagnostic monitor has been run since the last time that DTCs were cleared from ECM and TCM memory. If the monitor has not yet run, the status will display on the Scan Tool as "Not Complete." If the monitor has been run, the status will display on the scan tool as "Complete." This does not mean that no faults were found, only that the diagnostic monitor has been run. Whenever DTCs are cleared from memory or the battery is disconnected, all monitor readiness status indicators are reset to "Not Complete." Monitor readiness status indicators are not needed for the Comprehensive Component, Fuel Control, and Engine Misfire monitors because they run continuously. The readiness status of the following system monitors can be read on the scan tool:

Oxygen Sensors
Oxygen Sensor Heaters
Catalytic Converter
EGR System
EVAP System
Variable Valve Timing
Engine Thermostat

Warm-Up Cycle

Warm-up cycles are used by the ECM for automatic clearing of DTCs and Freeze Frame data. To complete one warm up cycle, the engine coolant temperature must rise at least 40°F (22°C) and reach a minimum of 160°F (71°C).

Trip

A trip is a key-on cycle in which all enable criteria for a particular diagnostic monitor are met and the diagnostic monitor is run. The trip is completed when the ignition switch is turned off.

Drive Cycle

Most OBD II diagnostic monitors will run at some time during normal operation of the vehicle. However, to satisfy all of the different trip enable criteria and run all of the OBD II diagnostic monitors, the vehicle must be driven under a variety of conditions. The following drive cycle will meet the enable criteria to allow all monitors to run on the composite vehicle.

Decay: To decline or decrease gradually in activity, strength, or performance.
Degraded: Worn down, performing at less than usual standards.

1. Ensure that the fuel tank is between ¼ and ¾ full
2. Start cold (below 86°F/30°C) and warm up until engine temperature is at least 160°F (71°C) — one minute minimum
3. Accelerate to 40–55 mph at 25% throttle and maintain speed for five minutes
4. Decelerate without using the brake (coast down) to 20 mph or less, then stop the vehicle. Allow the engine to idle for 10 seconds, turn the key off, and wait one minute
5. Restart and accelerate to 40–50 mph at 25% throttle and maintain speed for two minutes
6. Decelerate without using the brake (coast down) to 20 mph or less, then stop the vehicle. Allow the engine to idle for 10 seconds, turn the key off, and wait one minute

Freeze Frame Data

A Freeze Frame is a miniature "**snapshot**" (one frame of data) that is automatically stored in the ECM/TCM memory when an emissions-related DTC is first stored. If a DTC for fuel control or engine misfire is stored at a later time, the newest data are stored and the earlier data are lost. All parameter ID (PID) values listed under "Scan Tool Data" are stored in freeze frame data. The ECM/TCM stores only one single freeze frame record.

Storing and Clearing DTCs & Freeze Frame Data, Turning the MIL On & Off

ONE TRIP MONITORS: A failure on the first trip of a "one trip" emissions diagnostic monitor causes the ECM to immediately store a DTC and freeze frame, and turn on the MIL. All comprehensive component monitor faults require only one trip.

TWO TRIP MONITORS: A failure on the first trip of a "two trip" emissions diagnostic monitor causes the ECM to store a temporary DTC. If the failure does not recur on the next trip, the temporary DTC is cleared from memory. If the failure does recur on the next trip, the ECM will store a DTC and freeze frame, and turn on the MIL. All the system monitors are two trip monitors. Engine misfire that is severe enough to damage the catalytic converter is a two trip monitor, with the additional condition that the MIL will blink while the severe misfire is occurring.

AUTOMATIC CLEARING: If the vehicle completes three consecutive "good trips" (three consecutive trips in which the monitor that set the DTC is run and passes), the MIL will be turned off, but the DTC and freeze frame will remain stored in ECM memory. If the vehicle completes 40 warm-up cycles without the same fault recurring, the DTC and freeze frame are automatically cleared from the ECM memory.

MANUAL CLEARING: Any stored DTCs and Freeze Frame data can be erased using the scan tool, and the MIL (if lit) will be turned off. Although it is not the recommended method, DTCs and Freeze Frame data will also be cleared if the ECM power supply of the battery is disconnected.

Scan Tool Data

Figure 2-13 shows the different types of information that can be displayed on the OBD II scan tool.

OBD II SYSTEM DIAGNOSTICS

OBD II General Description

On-board Diagnostics Second Generation (OBD II) is a government-mandated system designed to monitor fuel system performance, engine misfire, and emission systems operation during normal vehicle operation.

The system includes industry-wide standardization intended to improve the diagnostic process by allowing all technicians (dealership and aftermarket) equal access to on-board computer information using a Generic Scan Tool (GST). Important features common to all OBD II vehicles include:

- A common Data Link Connector (DLC)
- Access to on-board vehicle information using a GST
- Standardized Diagnostic Trouble Codes (DTCs)
- MIL operation
- Standardized terminology for fuel, ignition, and emission systems components
- Expanded emissions related on-board testing (readiness tests and system monitors)
- New emission related diagnostic procedures
- Performance feedback from selected actuators (bi-directional actuator control)

Data Link Connector (DLC)

OBD II standards establish guidelines for the DLC. It is a 16-pin connector, figure 2-14, used to access on-board computer information through a GST. The DLC must be located in a standard position, in plain view under the driver's side dash, and be easily accessed by the technician. Between 1994 and 1996, locations varied slightly because manufacturers were allowed a grace period to make production changes.

Generic Scan Tool (GST)

The GST connects to the 16 pin DLC connector and relays specific OBD II information used in enhanced diagnosis. The technician can also use the GST to activate selected actuators when performing a system diagnosis. Although manufactured by numerous companies, the GST has the following features that are required by OBD II regulation:

- Record and display the OBD II alphanumeric, five digit DTCs
- Display the status of on-board computer "readiness tests"
- Record and display freeze frame data
- Display sensor and actuator information when requested by technician
- Clear DTCs and freeze frame data from vehicle computer memory

Diagnostic Trouble Codes (DTCs)

DTCs identify faults in ECM system sensors and circuits or indicate individual system conditions. An OBD II DTC is a five-character, alphanumeric fault identifier, figure 2-15. Since a letter is included in every DTC, the only way to retrieve codes is with a scan tool. The first character of an OBD II DTC is a letter. Composite vehicle questions in the L1 test will refer to

L1

Snapshot: A technician-recorded scan tool record or "movie" of PCM data during an event, so that the data can be played back.

ECT: 248 to –40 °F / 120 to –40°C / 0 to 5.0 volts	EGR: 0 to 100%
IAT: 248 to –40 °F / 120 to –40°C / 0 to 5.0 volts	Evap Purge: 0 to 100%
MAP: 20 to 101 kPa pressure / 24 to 0 in. Hg. vacuum / 0 to 5.0 volts	Evap Vent: On / Off
	Fuel Tank (EVAP) Pressure: –14.0 to +14.0 in. H_2O / –0.5 psi to +0.5 psi / 0 to 5.0 volts
MAF: 0 to 175 gm/sec / 0 to 5.0 volts	Fuel Tank Level: 0 to 100% / 0 to 5.0 volts
TP: 0 to 100%	P/S Switch: On / Off
Tach: 0 to 6000 rpm	Brake Switch: On / Off
VSS: 0 to 110 mph	AC Request: On / Off
Calculated Load Value: 0 to 100%	AC Pressure: 25 to 450 psi / 0 to 5.0 volts
HO2S 1/1: 0 to 1.0 volts	AC Clutch: On / Off
HO2S 2/1: 0 to 1.0 volts	Fan Control: On / Off
HO2S 1/2: 0 to 1.0 volts	Fuel Pump: On / Off
Loop: Open / Closed	TR: P/N, R, 1, 2, 3, OD
Bank 1 Injector Pulse Width: 0 to 15 milliseconds (ms)	TFT: 248 to –40°F / 120 to –40°C / 0 to 5.0 volts
Bank 2 Injector Pulse Width: 0 to 15 milliseconds (ms)	TSS: 0 to 6000 rpm
Bank 1 Long Term Fuel Trim: –30% to +30%	SS1: On / Off
Bank 1 Short Term Fuel Trim: –30% to +30%	SS2: On / Off
Bank 2 Long Term Fuel Trim: –30% to +30%	TCC: 0 to 100%
Bank 2 Short Term Fuel Trim: –30% to +30%	PC: 0 to 100%
Timing Advance: 0 to 60° BTDC	MIL: On / Off / Flashing
IAC: 0 to 100%	DTCs: P0###
Battery: 0 to 18 volts	Misfire Cylinder #: 1, 2, 3, 4, 5, 6
Generator Field: 0 to 100%	

Fig. 2-13. The above data can be accessed by the technician using the OBD II scan tool and the Data Link Connector (DLC).

DATA LINK CONNECTOR

VIEW IS LOOKING

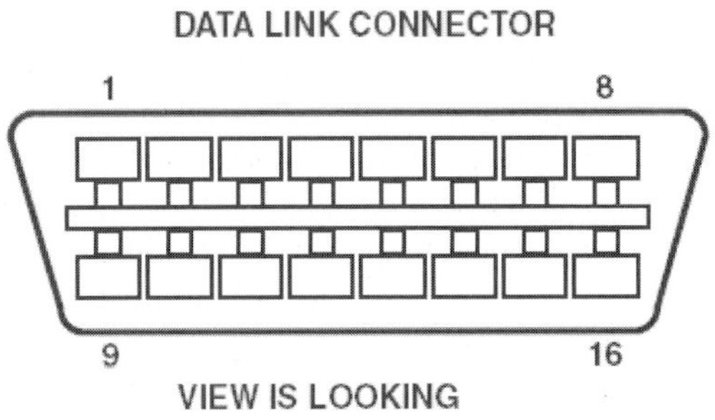

Fig. 2-14. The Data Link Connector (DLC) has the same shape and pin designations for all OBD II vehicles.

powertrain codes, designated by a capital "P." Powertrain codes tell the technician there is a problem in the fuel, air metering, ignition, or an emission control system. Refer to figure 2-15 for an explanation of other letter codes. The second character is a number that indicates if the code is common to all OBD II vehicles (0) or specific to one vehicle manufacturer (1). Remember, only emissions related, P0 codes will activate the MIL. The third character is a number used by all manufacturers to identify which system has a fault. This designation will be the same for P0 (OBD II) or P1 (manufacturer's) codes. Following is the established numbering system:

- 1 - Air/Fuel metering system input faults
- 2 - Air/Fuel metering output faults

- 3 - Ignition system or misfire faults
- 4 - Auxiliary emission controls
- 5 - Vehicle speed control and idle control system
- 6 - Computer output circuit faults
- 7 - Transmission
- 8 - Transmission

The fourth and fifth characters indicate the actual problem associated with the code, (e.g., signal voltage low, system always lean, etc.) The intent of OBD II code designation is to help the technician identify the system at fault, then pinpoint the actual problem or specific circuit causing the fault. Once a problem is identified by code, the technician must use appropriate service manuals to complete the diagnosis and repair.

MIL Operation

The most significant difference to remember when using the MIL to begin diagnosis on an OBD II vehicle is that there are no soft codes. If the MIL is on, a DTC and freeze frame data are recorded in computer memory and there is definitely a problem. The OBD I practice of clearing codes and driving the vehicle to see if codes reset must not be used on OBD II vehicles. All system monitor codes and many comprehensive component monitor codes require specific driving conditions before they will test a system or set a DTC. A quick trip around the block to confirm repairs often will not set a DTC, so the

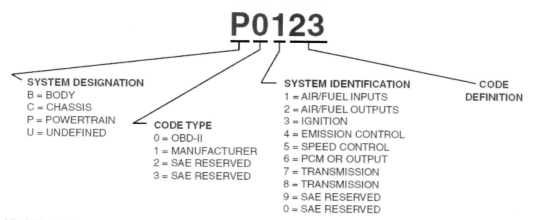

Fig. 2-15. OBD II DTCs use a standard format to help all technicians interpret problems more easily.

technician has no way of knowing if the problem still exists. It is best to clear DTCs only when instructed to do so by the manufacturer's diagnostic procedure, because freeze frame data and readiness test status are also erased when DTCs are cleared. Instead, use the stored freeze frame data to see what driving conditions were present when the code was set. Look for unusual readings from other sensors that may give a clue to the cause of the problem. Try to develop a "total picture" of vehicle operating conditions at the time the DTC was recorded. The same information is useful to help simulate driving conditions on a test drive as you verify the symptoms.

Remember, the MIL will be activated only for failures that cause excessive emissions. Problems in related systems or components may be recorded in ECM memory as OBD II (P0) or manufacturer-designated (P1) DTCs. All powertrain codes should be reviewed and investigated as part of the diagnostic process for driveabilty complaints.

Comprehensive Component Monitors

Comprehensive component monitors are most like the OBD I monitoring system that watches engine and transmission sensor inputs and actuator outputs for shorts, opens, and out-of-range values. OBD II computer (ECM) programs are enhanced to include identification of sensor values that don't logically fit with other powertrain data. For instance, if the Throttle Position Sensor (TPS) is reporting wide-open throttle (4.5 volts on the composite vehicle), but other sensors are reporting idle speed values, the ECM will set a DTC for the TPS.

Remember, comprehensive component monitors are one trip monitors. The ECM will activate the MIL and store DTC and freeze frame data the first time an emissions-related fault is detected. If a misfire or fuel control problem is detected after the original DTC was recorded, freeze frame date for the misfire or fuel control code will replace the original data.

Readiness Status and System Monitors

You will recall that the monitor readiness status tells the technician if a particular diagnostic monitor (test) has been completed since the last time DTCs were cleared from memory. There are two important concepts to understand when viewing monitor readiness status: First, the vehicle must be driven under specific conditions for some monitors to run, and second, the emissions system being monitored must be operational. If battery power is disconnected and the vehicle isn't driven through an entire drive

cycle, the readiness status will be "NO." If there is an electrical problem or component failure in a monitored system, the monitor will not run. A DTC may be recorded that points to the electrical or component failure, but the system cannot be tested by the monitor, so the readiness status will be "NO." A readiness status of "NO" for any of the five monitored systems, catalyst, EGR, EVAP, Oxygen sensors, and Oxygen sensor heaters, does not mean a failed monitor, only that the monitor has not been completed. At the same time, a "YES" status does not mean the system passed the monitor, only that the test was completed. In both cases, you must check for codes to investigate further.

Fuel Control Monitor

The fuel control monitor is designed to constantly check the ability of the ECM to control the air/fuel ratio. On the composite vehicle, the ECM program that fine tunes the air/fuel ratio is called Fuel Trim. It is divided into a short term program and a long term program. Both trim programs are presented as diagnostic data when a freeze frame is recorded. Separate short term and long term data are displayed for cylinder bank 1 and cylinder bank 2.

The oxygen sensor (HO2S) drives the fuel trim program anytime the vehicle is in closed loop. The starting point for fuel trim is 0% correction, figure 2-16. When the ECM sees a lean (low voltage) signal from an upstream HO2S, the fuel trim program adds fuel to compensate for the detected leaness. The short term fuel trim display on the scan tool will move to the positive (+) side of 0% to indicate more fuel is being added. When the ECM sees a rich (high voltage) signal from the HO2S, the fuel trim program subtracts fuel to lean the mixture. The scan tool will display a percentage on the negative (-) side of 0%. If short term fuel trim is necessary in one direction (rich or lean correction) for a period of time, the ECM will command a correction of long term fuel trim. When A/F control is out of acceptable range for too long a time, a DTC will set. On the composite vehicle, if long term fuel trim reaches +30% (lean correction) or -30% (rich correction) on two

L1

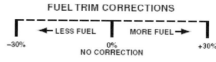

Fig. 2-16. On the composite vehicle, fuel trim corrections are displayed on the scan tool as percentage of correction.

consecutive trips, the ECM will activate the MIL and record a DTC and freeze frame data.

Long term fuel trim represents correction to fuel delivery over time. If the oxygen sensor voltage is fluctuating, but is mainly below 450 mV, indicating a lean A/F ratio, long term fuel trim will increase and the ECM will command longer injector pulse width. If oxygen sensor voltage is fluctuating, but remains mostly above 450 mV, indicating a rich mixture, long term fuel trim will decrease and the ECM will command shorter injection pulse width to adjust fuel delivery.

Short term fuel trim is useful when confirming fuel control. Observe short term fuel trim on the scan tool while adding propane through the intake system. The additional fuel will cause a rich mixture. If the fuel system is in closed loop, short term fuel trim will move in a negative direction as the fuel trim program shortens fuel injector pulse width in response to a higher HO2S voltage signal. Driving the system lean by pulling a vacuum line will cause short term fuel trim to increase injector pulse width. The scan tool display will move in a positive direction.

During diagnosis, be sure to look at both short and long term fuel trim. A problem that has existed for some time will cause long term fuel trim to record high or low. Once the problem is repaired, long term fuel trim will not change for a while, but short term fuel trim will begin immediately to move in the opposite direction. A restricted fuel filter, for instance, will cause a lean mixture. Long term fuel trim will eventually show a positive percentage (more fuel) as the system compensates for the lean mixture. Once the fuel filter is replaced, the A/F ratio is suddenly too rich. Comparing short and long term fuel trim immediately after the filter is replaced will reveal opposite readings: a negative percentage reading in short term fuel trim because the ECM is attempting to return the A/F ratio to normal by subtracting fuel, and a positive percentage reading in long term fuel trim because the long term program still "remembers" the lean correction and is waiting to see what happens.

Misfire Monitor

Engine misfire monitoring uses the CKP signal as the primary sensor. When a misfire occurs, whether due to engine compression, ignition, or fuel, crankshaft speed is affected. The ECM is programmed to notice the **intermittent** change in CKP pulses, figure 2-17.

Camshaft position is used to identify which cylinder misfired. Because outside factors such as electrical interference and rough roads can mimic a misfire, most ECM programs keep track of how many times a cylinder misfires in a given number of engine rotations. The ECM activates the MIL when misfire reaches a predetermined percentage of rpm.

Remember, misfire monitoring, like fuel trim monitoring, is a two trip monitor. The MIL will glow steadily once a misfire is detected. If misfiring becomes severe enough to damage the catalytic converter, the MIL will blink continuously until the misfire becomes less severe.

Catalytic Converter Monitor

As mentioned earlier, the catalytic converter monitor checks converter efficiency by comparing upstream HO2S signals with the downstream HO2S signal. In normal operation the upstream HO2S signals will switch frequently between 200 mV and 900 mV and the downstream HO2S signal will show very little fluctuation and a voltage that tends to stay above the 450 mV **threshold**, figure 2-18. As catalyst performance begins to degrade, less oxygen is used in the converter and so less ends up in the exhaust, causing voltage fluctuations and a lower voltage bias, figure 2-19. When the downstream HO2S voltage signal begins to fluctuate within about 70% of the upstream HO2S signal on two consecutive trips, the ECM will record freeze frame data, set a DTC, and actuate the MIL.

EVAP Monitor

A vehicle will fail the EVAP monitor if the ECM, using information from the fuel tank pressure sensor, sees vacuum decrease too quickly after the EVAP vent and EVAP purge solenoids have been closed. Keep in mind that simple problems like a loose, damaged, or missing gas cap will cause this code to set.

Be careful when making quick repairs. For example, after replacing a damaged gas cap on a vehicle brought in for a lit MIL, you may be tempted to clear the DTC and return the car

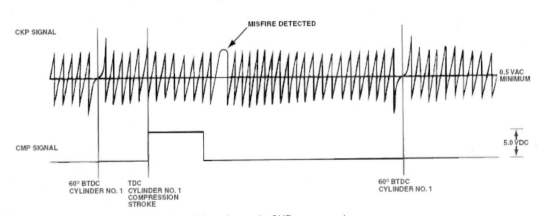

Fig. 2-17. The ECM is programmed to notice the sudden change in CKP sensor pulses.

Intermittent: Occurring infrequently, not often, or rarely.
Threshold: The upper limit of or beginning of something.

CATALYST MONITOR EFFICIENCY TEST

PRE-CATALYST HO2S1

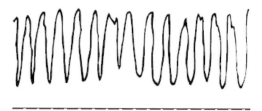

POST-CATALYST HO2S2

GOOD CATALYST

MONITOR TEST PASSED

Fig. 2-18. When the catalyst is working efficiently, most oxygen is used for oxidation and reduction, so post converter voltage fluctuations are minimal.

CATALYST MONITOR EFFICIENCY TEST

PRE-CATALYST HO2S1

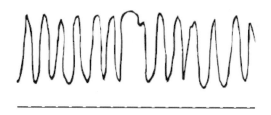

POST-CATALYST HO2S2

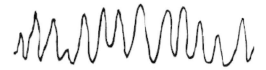

DEGRADED CATALYST

MONITOR TEST FAILED

Fig. 2-19. As catalyst performance becomes less efficient, less oxygen is used and voltage fluctuations from the post converter begin to increase.

to the customer after a short road test. However, the EVAP monitor won't run if the engine is warm (above 86°F) or if the fuel level is not between ¼ and ¾ full. If the EVAP system has other problems and the EVAP monitor doesn't run during the road test, the MIL will come on after you return the vehicle to the customer.

Some technicians use a sensor simulator to simulate a cold start so the monitor will run. A scan tool can be used to check EVAP system integrity, even with a full tank of gas. Refer to figure 2-9 to trace the following test procedure on the composite vehicle. First, idle the engine. Then, using a scan tool, close the EVAP vent solenoid and open the EVAP purge solenoid. Intake manifold vacuum will draw a vacuum in the EVAP system. Now close the EVAP purge solenoid to trap vacuum in the system. Observe the fuel tank pressure sensor reading on the scan tool. The composite vehicle will show 0.5 volt at ½ psi vacuum. If the system is leaking, voltage will climb toward 2.5 volts as pressure increases. As always, test and repair procedures must be followed exactly. Some test procedures, the IM 240 for example, specify testing EVAP system integrity with pressure instead of vacuum.

Diagnostic Strategy

The most valuable aspect of diagnosis with a scan tool is the ability to compare data from many sensors and actuators. However, **scan tool data** should not be used alone. Vehicle symptoms, driving conditions, and an understanding of operational principles are also important diagnostic tools.

Today's vehicles require today's technicians to be aware of the ways traditional technology blends with newer, more complex system-based technologies. Vehicles manufactured before the 1970s controlled fuel and ignition timing through vacuum and mechanical weights and springs. Exhaust emissions were not seriously considered until the early 1970s. Modern vehicles use computerized controls to control fuel and ignition timing precisely. The tradeoff, however, for this technological advancement is that today's drivetrain problems can result in repeated and multiple component failures that require a system-based approach. For example, a late-model vehicle has the following symptoms: hard starting when cold, an engine miss, and a failed emission test. The initial diagnosis finds a fouled spark plug. Replacing the spark plug and retesting emissions results in a passing report and a smoothly running engine. While this approach addresses the immediate symptom, it does not deal with the underlying cause of the fouled spark plug.

The result?

The customer returns the next day with the same symptoms. Only then does the technician examine further to determine that a faulty injector is leaking when the engine is turned off. This leak floods a cylinder. The flooded cylinder causes its associated spark plug to fail. This would also drain the fuel rail, causing extended cranking on a cold start.

This example clearly illustrates that a systems-based approach to the diagnostic process is vital to help eliminate multiple and repeated component failures that result in dissatisfied customers.

When approaching any diagnostic problem, take the time to define vehicle symptoms. How is the vehicle running? Does it have rich symptoms like poor gas mileage or a failed emissions test? Does it surge or idle rough? Is it hard to start? Next, do a thorough inspection for obvious problems such as

L1

Scan Tool Data: Information from the computer that is displayed on the scan tool, including data stream, DTCs, freeze frame, and system monitor readiness status.

vacuum leaks and damaged electrical connections. Don't forget to consider the basics such as low fuel pressure, incorrect ignition timing, low or uneven engine compression, and fuel quality. If possible, a review of recent vehicle service may yield valuable diagnostic clues. For recent vehicle service information, check dealership resources and communicate with the vehicle owner.

Connect the scan tool and retrieve stored DTCs and freeze frame data. Record your findings, then check the service manual to learn the specific conditions that cause the DTC. Take the time to thoroughly understand what caused the DTC.

Check the readiness status of system monitors. If the readiness status is "NO" for all monitors, review recent service history; the battery may have been changed or the vehicle may have been in another shop where DTCs were erased. The vehicle must be driven through the complete drive cycle to ensure all monitors run. If readiness status is "NO" for only one or two sensors, check sensors, actuators, and related circuitry for problems that would prevent the monitor from running. Again, the vehicle may have to complete an entire drive cycle to provide the time and conditions to run the remaining monitors.

When there is more than one DTC in memory, diagnose and correct component-related DTCs before diagnosing system failure DTCs. A sensor or actuator problem may prevent a monitor from running or cause a system to fail the monitor. Once a component failure is repaired, drive the vehicle through the specified drive cycle to be sure the system is fully repaired. For example, when discovering a code P0125, "excessive time to enter closed loop," and a code P0155, "HO2S/1, Bank 2 Heater Malfunction", the best procedure is to diagnose and repair the HO2S/1 heater malfunction first, even though its DTC is a higher number.

Next, clear codes and drive the vehicle as directed in the service manual. In this example, it is probable that the failed oxygen sensor heater caused the system to be slow entering closed loop. Misfire and fuel control DTCs are considered **priority codes** and should always be diagnosed first.

When using the drive cycle to confirm repairs, review freeze frame data for the driving conditions present at the time the DTC was recorded. It is especially important when confirming misfire and fuel control repairs to closely match the engine rpm, calculated load, and engine temperature values recorded in the freeze frame.

How close is close? Before the PCM will deactivate the MIL for misfire and fuel control codes, engine speed must be within 375 rpm of the engine speed when the code was set, and the calculated load value must be within ±10% of the load present when the code was set. Be aware that some manufacturers may direct you to drive a portion of the drive cycle to confirm a particular repair. Drive cycles vary between manufacturers and must always be followed exactly. Freeze frame and scan tool data must be analyzed with care. Use service manuals to learn the normal parameters for each sensor and actuator.

Review **freeze frame** data to identify all sensors and actuators that are out of range. Many times a sensor will be out of range and not set a DTC, especially when the out-of-range sensor is responding to an unusual condition. Try to determine if the suspect sensor is reporting an unusual vehicle condition or sending a signal that doesn't match the actual symptoms or other sensor data. When you have gathered all necessary information—vehicle symptoms, driving conditions, DTCs, and sensor/actuator data—use your knowledge and experience to pick out the most probable cause of the symptom. Always refer to appropriate service manuals for proper test procedures when testing sensors, actuators, and related circuits.

Insight

The following section will present some examples of ECM inputs and explain how unusual readings might affect vehicle operation. Tips for testing various components are also included.

Battery Voltage

The ECM uses battery voltage as an input for the computer-controlled charging system. A low voltage signal may cause the ECM to increase both idle speed and alternator field current to generate higher alternator output. When idle speed is above specification and fuel system control based on HO2S and fuel trim data appears normal, check battery voltage, generator, and idle air control (IAC) data. If battery voltage is low and generator field and IAC percentages are higher than normal, test the battery and charging system for defects. Also, check accessory load sensors for false signals. A power steering pressure switch that sticks closed, for example, will cause the ECM to raise idle speed.

Brake Pedal Position (BPP) Switch

The BPP switch is used on the composite vehicle as an input to control the torque converter clutch. On some systems, however, the BPP switch is also part of the ABS (anti lock brake) system. Many of these vehicles use information from the ABS wheel speed sensors as an input for the misfire monitor. When traveling over rough roads, tire slip and driveline torque affect the smooth rotation of the crankshaft, simulating engine misfire. At the same time, wheel speed sensors send erratic signals to the ECM. When the ECM sees the erratic signals, it suspends the misfire monitor. If the BPP switch fails to close or open as expected, the ECM disables ABS braking and ignores wheel speed data. The misfire monitor is again suspended because the ECM has incomplete information.

Idle Air Control (IAC) Valve

The IAC valve regulates idle speed by controlling the amount of air that bypasses the throttle plate. Lower than-normal IAC percentage means the ECM is trying to reduce idle speed; higher percentage means the ECM is trying to increase idle speed. For example, a vacuum leak will cause idle speed to increase. The ECM will command a lower percentage opening from the IAC

Priority Codes: Codes that are more important than, and take precedence over, others.

to compensate. An EGR that doesn't fully close at idle will reduce idle speed and quality. The ECM will command a larger IAC opening, in an attempt to maintain specified idle speed.

A quick way to test IAC performance is to view IAC percentage on the scan tool while increasing engine load at idle. If the IAC percentage increases when the A/C is turned on (or the steering wheel is turned) and the idle speed remains steady, the system is working normally. If the IAC doesn't respond or idle speed decreases with increased load, physically check the IAC valve for damage or passages clogged with carbon.

Intake Air Temperature (IAT) Sensor

The IAT sensor measures the temperature of air in the intake system. IAT data are used as the air density input for air/fuel ratio calculations. In the composite vehicle, the IAT sensor has the same temperature/voltage signal relationship as the Engine Coolant Temperature (ECT) and Transmission Fluid Temperature (TFT) sensors. To confirm IAT sensor accuracy, measure air temperature near the sensor and compare with the temperature reading on the scan tool. After turning off the engine and waiting for 10 minutes with the hood down, the measured temperature should be within 5°F of the IAT temperature on the scan tool. Compare IAT with ECT temperature readings after turning off the engine and waiting for 15–20 minutes. The two readings should be almost identical. When the vehicle is cold, before being started in the morning, IAT signal voltage should be the same as voltage signals from the ECT and TFT sensors.

Manifold Absolute Pressure (MAP) Sensor

The MAP sensor is used on the composite vehicle to monitor EGR operation. It senses changes in manifold pressure as the EGR valve opens and closes. Typical MAP sensor problems like a cracked vacuum hose or a poor electrical connection will lead to EGR trouble codes. It is important to remember that manifold pressure can be described two ways, as pressure or vacuum. When the EGR valve opens, the intake manifold fills more quickly. Intake manifold vacuum drops toward 0 in. Hg, but manifold absolute pressure rises toward 100 kPa. Pay attention to your scan tool displays and read all MAP sensor questions carefully.

Mass Airflow (MAF) Sensor

The MAF sensor measures the volume of air flowing into the intake manifold. The voltage values of the composite vehicle sensor range from 0.2 volt with no flow (0 gm/sec) to 4.8 volts at maximum air flow (175 gm/sec). The sensor is located in the air intake system before the throttle plate, usually near the air cleaner. When diagnosing driveability problems, observe MAF and RPM on the scan tool as the engine is accelerated. MAF signal voltage (or gm/sec value) will increase at about the same rate as engine RPM. Don't forget, the ECM is capable of computing a **default MAF value** based on engine speed and throttle position signals. The only sure way to check the MAF signal is to verify the signal at the sensor, not on the scan tool. If the MAF signal increases more slowly than engine RPM and there is a low power complaint, suspect a restricted air filter. If there are lean symptoms, suspect air leaks between the MAF sensor and the throttle plate usually caused by cracked air ducts. When the complaint is hesitation on acceleration, check that cracks in the air ducting aren't opening as the engine torques on the motor mounts.

When faced with a no-start problem, unplug the MAF sensor. If the vehicle starts, check the electrical circuit for a shorted 5-volt reference wire. Some systems will shut down ignition and fuel injection if the 5-volt reference is lost. Unplugging the sensor restores the signal. Also, check for a lean system. Some vehicles will default to a rich mixture when the MAF signal is lost. The vehicle will start because added fuel compensates for the lean problem.

No Start Diagnosis

To run, an engine requires four things: air, fuel, compression and ignition, all at the right time. Perform the following tests to find what the problem is:

- Observe the engine's cranking speed; if it is too slow check the battery and starting system.
- Check fuel pressure and volume
- Verify the electrical signal to the injector with a 12V test light, depending on the OEM's recommendation
- Use a properly gapped spark tester to check for spark
- Check compression by performing a cranking vacuum or compression test
- Check the ignition timing
- Verify camshaft drive integrity and valve timing

Hard Start Diagnosis

A variety of sensor or physical conditions may result in a hard start condition without setting a diagnostic trouble code (DTC). In order to determine if any of these conditions exist, perform the following actions:

- Inspect for an engine coolant temperature (ECT) sensor that has shifted in value.
- Inspect the mass air flow (MAF) sensor for proper installation.
- Inspect the camshaft position (CMP) sensor for proper mounting and/or a bad connection. An extended crank occurs if the engine control module (ECM) does not receive a CMP signal.
- Verify proper operation of the manifold absolute pressure (MAP) sensor.
- Inspect the exhaust gas recirculation (EGR) system for proper sealing/connections and operation.

Engine Misfire Diagnosis

- Inspect the engine control module (ECM) grounds for being clean, tight, and in the proper locations.
- Inspect the heated oxygen sensors (HO2S). The HO2S should respond quickly to different throttle positions. If they do not, inspect the HO2S for silicon or other contaminants from fuel or the use of improper RTV sealant.

L1

Default Value: A value used in place of another value known to be unreliable.

The sensors may have a white, powdery coating and result in a high but false signal voltage rich exhaust indication. The ECM will then reduce the amount of fuel delivered to the engine, causing a severe driveability problem.
- Inspect the air intake ducts for being collapsed, damaged, loose, improperly installed, or leaking, especially between the mass air flow (MAF) sensor and the throttle body.
- Test the exhaust gas recirculation (EGR) system for proper operation.
- Inspect for proper operation of the manifold absolute pressure (MAP) sensor.
- Inspect for an engine coolant temperature (ECT) sensor that has shifted in value.
- Inspect the MAF sensor and intake air system for proper operation.

Engine Hesitation Diagnosis
Momentary lack of response as the accelerator is pushed down. Can occur at any vehicle speed. Usually more pronounced when first trying to make the vehicle move, as from a stop. May cause the engine to stall if severe enough.

- Inspect the engine control module (ECM) grounds for being clean, tight, and in the proper locations.
- Inspect the heated oxygen sensors (HO2S). The HO2S should respond quickly to different throttle positions. If they do not, inspect the HO2S for silicon or other contaminants from fuel or the use of improper RTV sealant. The sensors may have a white, powdery coating and result in a high but false signal voltage rich exhaust indication. The PCM will then reduce the amount of fuel delivered to the engine, causing a severe driveability problem.
- Inspect the air intake ducts for being collapsed, damaged, loose, improperly installed, or leaking, especially between the mass air flow (MAF) sensor and the throttle body.
- Test the exhaust gas recirculation (EGR) system for proper operation.
- Inspect for proper operation of the manifold absolute pressure (MAP) sensor.
- Inspect for an engine coolant temperature (ECT) sensor that has shifted in value.
- Inspect the MAF sensor and intake air system for proper operation.

Poor Fuel Economy Diagnosis
Fuel economy, as measured by an actual road test, is noticeably lower than expected. Also, fuel economy is noticeably lower than the economy was on this vehicle at one time, as previously shown by an actual road test.

- Inspect the engine control module (ECM) grounds for being clean, tight, and in the proper locations.
- Discuss driving habits with the owner.
- Is the A/C on or the defroster mode on full time?
- Are the tires at the correct pressure?
- Are the wheels and tires the correct size?
- Are there excessively heavy loads being carried?
- Is the acceleration rate too much, too often?
- Remove the air filter element and inspect for dirt or for restrictions.

- Inspect the air intake system and crankcase for air leaks.
- Inspect the crankcase ventilation valve for proper operation.
- Inspect for an inaccurate speedometer.

Engine Surges Diagnosis
Engine power variation under steady throttle or cruise. Feels like the vehicle speeds up and slows down with no change in the accelerator pedal position.

- Inspect the engine control module (ECM) grounds for being clean, tight, and in the proper locations.
- Inspect the heated oxygen sensors (HO2S). The HO2S should respond quickly to different throttle positions. If it does not, inspect the HO2S for silicon or other contaminants from fuel or the use of improper RTV sealant. The sensors may have a white, powdery coating and result in a high but false signal voltage rich exhaust indication. The ECM will then reduce the amount of fuel delivered to the engine, causing a severe driveability problem.
- Inspect the mass air flow (MAF) sensor for any contamination on the sensing element.
- Inspect the air intake ducts for being collapsed, damaged, loose, improperly installed, or leaking, especially between the MAF sensor and the throttle body.
- Test the exhaust gas recirculation (EGR) system for proper operation.
- Inspect for proper operation of the manifold absolute pressure (MAP) sensor.
- Inspect for an engine coolant temperature (ECT) sensor that has shifted in value.

Rough, Unstable, or Incorrect and Stalling Diagnosis
Engine runs unevenly at idle. If severe, the engine or vehicle may shake. Engine idle speed may vary in RPM. Either condition may be severe enough to stall the engine.

- Inspect the engine control module (ECM) grounds for being clean, tight, and in the proper locations.
- Remove and inspect the air filter element for dirt or for restrictions.
- Inspect the air intake ducts for being collapsed, damaged areas, looseness, improper installation, or leaking, especially between the MAF sensor and the throttle body.
- Inspect the Transaxle Range Switch input with the vehicle in drive and the gear selector in drive or overdrive.

Circuit Testing Using Serial Data
Using serial data to test ECM circuits can be of great value during driveability diagnosis; however, there are some items to remember. The data that are being read on the scan tool could actually be a default value that the ECM substitutes to compensate for possible circuit failures. Also, serial data transmitted by the ECM to the scan tool is an interpretation of what the ECM thinks it is seeing. The true readings may be different. You can confirm actual signal values by testing the circuit live with a DVOM, breakout box, or lab scope, depending on what you need to test. False data stream values may be caused by an internal ECM fault or an ECM ground circuit problem. The

following are examples of using serial data to test and diagnosis driveability and intermittent problems:

- Thermistors: disconnect or short across thermistor circuit to check the maximum range of the sensor. For example, disconnect the ECT to create an open circuit. Temperature reading should drop to -40°F (-40°C). Install a jumper wire across the connector to create a short circuit. Temperature should go to a maximum reading, about 266°F (130°C)
- Create the opposite circuit problem to see if a DTC sets. For example, a P0117 code in memory tells you an ECT sensor circuit voltage went low, indicating a short. To create an open circuit, disconnect the ECT sensor and see if the ECM sets a P0118 (circuit high). If it does, then the circuit and ECM are operational and the problem is probably in the sensor
- Intermittent problem testing: Wiggle, tap, heat up, or cool down a component or circuit to see if the serial data for that circuit changes
- Testing the effect of one circuit on another by manipulating the input signal. Manipulate the signal by disconnecting circuits or substituting values. Here are some examples:
  - IAT, ECT, TP sensor, MAP, MAF, and HO2S signals' effect on injector pulse width.
  - ECT, ACT, TP sensor signals' effect on Idle speed control.
  - IAT, ECT, TP, MAP, and MAF signals' effect on ignition timing control.
  - ECT, TP sensor, and EVP signals' effect on EGR control
  - ECT and TP sensor signals' effect on canister Purge
  - VSS, TP sensor, ECT, and MAP signals' effect on torque convert clutch operation.

Circuit Testing Operations

While scan tools are an important part of any diagnosis, once you locate a problem you must use either a DVOM or lab scope to accurately check a circuit. The following section covers circuit testing procedures and guidelines for using the proper test equipment.

Voltage

When using a DVOM to check voltage in and out of sensors, always check the voltage using the signal ground return at the sensor, rather than using an engine or battery ground, figure 2-20. Sensors are grounded directly through the ECM, rather than being connected directly to a chassis ground. This way sensors avoid noise interference. Sensors need a "clean" ground for reliable operation.

An open signal ground return will cause the ECM to see a high voltage on the sensor signal line. An example would be a TP sensor that always sends a wide open throttle (high voltage) signal to the ECM.

Resistance

Ohm's law says that even very low resistance in an automotive computer circuit will cause sensors and actuators to work improperly because of low voltage. For example, an on-board ECM ignition feed circuit drawing 365 milliamps with a resistance in the ignition feed wire of 2.5 ohms will cause a voltage supply drop of 1.5 volts. This voltage drop will cause

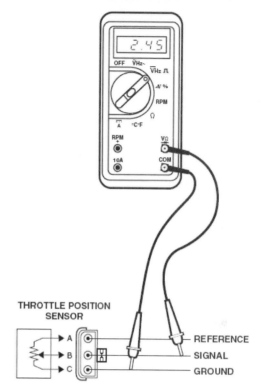

Fig. 2-20. Checking voltage to a throttle position sensor.

severe driveability problems. One example of this may be a car that idles too high because the ECM monitors the battery voltage. If the supply voltage is low the ECM may raise the idle speed so the charging system could charge what the ECM thinks is a low battery.

To check resistance, make sure that the circuit to be tested is not under power. Place the leads across the circuit or component to be tested, figure 2-21. To read ohms, place the

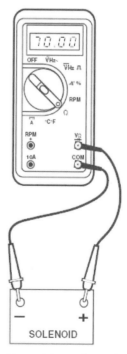

Fig. 2-21. When checking resistance, the part must not be under power or you will probably destroy your meter.

meter on auto-ranging or start at the higher scales and work down.

Voltage Drop

Checking voltage drop is one of the most important tests that a technician can perform on a circuit. A voltage drop test measures the difference in electrical pressure between two points in a live circuit. Voltage drops can cause major driveability symptoms in on-board computer systems. A voltage drop on a ECM power ground can cause sensor voltage references to be higher than normal, throwing off the overall sensor calibration of the entire engine control system, figure 2-22.

Another example of a driveability symptom might be a car with an idle speed that continuously hunts. To start diagnosis, you connect the scan tool to check trouble codes and the idle smooths out. This is usually caused by a poor ground.

To check voltage drop, the circuit must be powered up and have current flowing. The circuit also must have the maximum amount of current flowing under normal conditions by which the circuit was designed.

Although there is no exact amount voltage drop that is considered acceptable, you should remember that low current circuits that draw milliamps will be affected by very small voltage drops. A good rule of thumb would be a drop of 0.2 volt or less. However, even this is too much for some circuits. A power ground circuit should have a voltage drop of no more than 0.1 volt. A computer ground circuit should have a voltage drop of no more than 0.05 volt.

Amperage

Too much amperage flow through a ECM actuator driver circuit can partially damage that circuit and cause severe driveability problems. Most ECM actuator components carry milliamps through their circuits. Using a ohmmeter and calculating amperage draw from resistance and voltage readings is not always accurate because the device under test does not carry the actual load it was designed to carry. Most actuator devices carry about 180 ma (12.6 volts at 70 ohms) to 500 ma (12.6 volts at 25 ohms), but there are always exceptions to the rule. Fuel injectors may carry much more amperage through their circuit (as much as 8 amps depending on the type of injector).

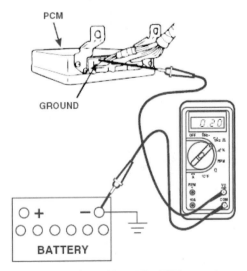

Fig. 2-22. Checking voltage drop at the ECM ground connection.

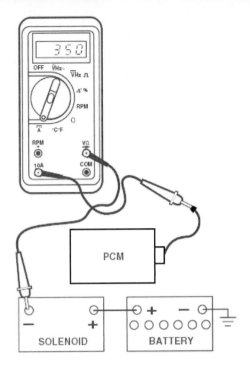

Fig. 2-23. Checking amperage draw through a solenoid driver circuit.

To check amperage draw, the circuit must be powered up and have current flowing. Set your meter for amperage draw and connect it in series between the solenoid negative terminal and ground, or the actual driver circuit if you can energize it, figure 2-23. Start by checking amps first, then move down to milliamp scale. Leave the circuit energized for 1 to 2 minutes to check draw.

Remember, this test is for solenoids such as Canister Purge, EGR, and Air Management only. Do not check fuel injectors in this manner. Holding an injector on for any length of time destroys it.

AC Ripple

On-board automotive computers do not like to see AC ripples pass through the internal components. This effect can cause logic problems as well as many other types of driveability problems. For example, a bad alternator with a dropped diode can severely affect an automotive computer system.

To check for AC ripple voltage, switch your DVOM to AC and connect the black lead to a good ground and the red lead to the "BAT," or power, terminal on the back of the alternator (not the battery), figure 2-24. A good alternator should measure less than 0.5 volts AC with the engine running and the headlights on. A higher reading indicates damaged alternator diodes.

Frequency

Frequency is the number of times a signal repeats itself in one second. Frequency is measured in hertz.

A signal that repeats itself 10 times a second is operating at a frequency of 10 hertz. Many automotive computer systems read the frequency of a signal instead of the voltage. Ford MAP sensors and AC Delco Mass Airflow Sensors are examples of sensors that produce this type of signal.

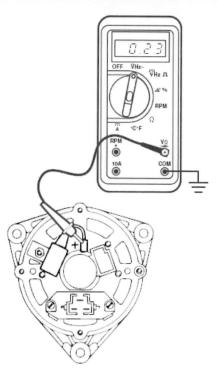

Fig. 2-24. Checking for voltage ripple from an AC generator.

For example, a Ford EEC-IV MAP sensor has a 5 volt reference voltage applied to it. At a duty cycle of 50 percent (half of the time on and half of the time off), the DVOM will average the reading so you would see 2.5 volts. However, the number of times the signal switches on and off in one second will change depending on manifold vacuum. To accurately diagnose these signals, you must have a meter that can read frequency, figure 2-25.

Duty Cycle

Duty cycle is the percentage of time a digital signal is high verses low. When measuring duty cycle, one complete cycle is

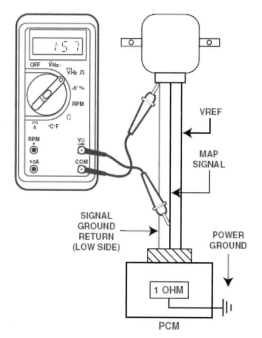

Fig. 2-25. Checking the frequency of a MAP sensor.

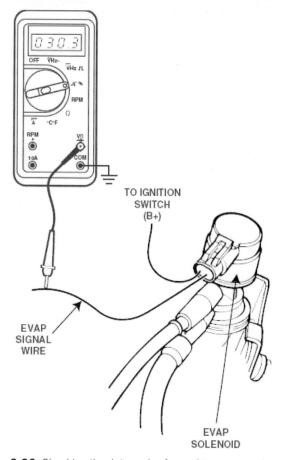

Fig. 2-26. Checking the duty cycle of a canister purge solenoid.

considered 100 percent. For a 5 volt signal at a 50 percent duty cycle, the voltage would read 2.5 volts.

For automotive applications, when dealing with digital waves, and especially with ECM outputs, we are concerned with the amount of time the signal is low, rather then high. This is because the low time is when the driving transistor is on, completing the circuit to ground.

You can measure duty cycle with a DVOM that has a duty cycle setting. Attach the red lead to the signal wire and the black lead to a good engine ground, figure 2-26.

IMMOBILIZER ANTI-THEFT SYSTEM DIAGNOSIS

The following are possible causes for Immobilizer Anti-Theft System failures:

- The ignition key is not registered with the immobilizer unit
- Poor communication between the immobilizer antenna and ignition key caused by low battery voltage or interference from a metal key chain
- Immobilizer unit failure
- ECM failure
- Ignition key failure
- Incorrect ignition key used
- Poor communication between the ECM and immobilizer unit caused by low battery voltage or noise interference
- Open or short in wiring harness
- Blown fuse

CHAPTER QUESTIONS

1. True or false? The type 3 composite vehicle has a four cycle, V6 engine with four overhead chain-driven camshafts, 24 valves, distributorless ignition, and a speed density type closed loop sequential multiport fuel injection system.
   a. True
   b. False

2. Which of the following statements is **NOT** true? The ECM on the composite vehicle:
   a. Controls the vehicle's charging system.
   b. Receives power from the battery and ignition switch and provides a regulated 5 volt supply for most of the engine sensors.
   c. Controls the shifting of the composite vehicle's four speed automatic overdrive transmission.
   d. Receives input from sensors, calculates ignition and fuel requirements, and controls engine actuators to provide the desired driveability, fuel economy, and emissions control.

3. Which of the following sensor signals is **NOT** used during open loop engine operation?
   a. MAF sensor
   b. O2 sensor
   c. CKP sensor
   d. TPS

4. True or false? OBD II is a government-mandated system designed to monitor fuel system performance, engine misfire, and emission systems during normal vehicle operation. It includes industry-wide standardization intended to improve the diagnostic process by allowing all technicians equal access to on-board computer information using a GST.
   a. True
   b. False

5. On U.S designed vehicles built after 1996, where would you find the DLC?
   a. In plain view under the passenger's side dash
   b. In plain view under the exact center of the dash
   c. In plain view under the driver's side of the dash
   d. Location varies, depending on manufacturer and/or model.

6. Technician A is diagnosing an OBD II vehicle and is about to clear the DTCs and take the vehicle for a short drive to see if the DTCs reset. Technician B says that a quick trip around the block may not set a DTC so it may not be possible to confirm whether a problem has actually been corrected.
   Who is right?
   a. A only
   b. B only
   c. Both A and B
   d. Neither A nor B

7. True or false? Since a scan tool has the ability to compare data from many sensors and actuators, its data, used alone, provide sufficient diagnostic information to diagnose all problems.
   a. True
   b. False

8. Technician A says when viewing monitor readiness, the vehicle must be driven under certain specific conditions for some monitors to run. Technician B says the emissions system being monitored must be operational.
   Who is right?
   a. A only
   b. B only
   c. Both A and B
   d. Neither A nor B

9. The engine misfire monitor uses the signal of which of the following primary sensors?
   a. ECT
   b. IAT
   c. CKP
   d. MAP

10. Which of the following DTCs are considered priority codes and should be diagnosed first?
    a. Auxiliary emission controls
    b. Misfire and fuel control
    c. Transmission
    d. Vehicle speed control

11. True or false? The MAP sensor is used on the composite vehicle to monitor EGR operation.
    a. True
    b. False

12. When using a DVOM to check voltage in and out of a sensor: Technician A says to always use an engine or battery ground. Technician B says to always use the ground return at the sensor.
    Who is right?
    a. A only
    b. B only
    c. Both A and B
    d. Neither A nor B

13. A computer ground circuit should have a voltage drop of no more than:
    a. 0.1 volt
    b. 1.0 volt
    c. 0.5 volt
    d. 0.05 volt

CHAPTER OBJECTIVES

- The technician will complete the ASE task list on Ignition System Diagnosis and Repair.
- The technician will be able to answer 7 questions dealing with the Ignition System Diagnosis and Repair section of the L1 ASE Test.

This chapter discusses testing, repairing, and replacing individual components of the ignition system. Most modern ignition systems contain delicate, and expensive, electronic components that can be destroyed by a voltage surge. The high-voltage surge that results from simply making or breaking a connection can cause damage. When working on the ignition system, take these precautions to avoid damage to the ignition system and personal injury:

1. Unless the procedure specifically states otherwise, switch the ignition off or disconnect the battery ground cable before separating any ignition system wiring connections.
2. Do not touch, or short to ground, any exposed connections while the engine is cranking or running.
3. Do not short the primary circuit to ground without resistance; the high current that results can damage circuits and components.
4. Do not create a secondary voltage arc near the battery or fuel system components. This can cause an explosion.
5. When testing the ignition system, follow the procedure specified by the manufacturer.

Most modern electronic ignition systems are incorporated into the ECM. The ignition, fuel injection, and emission control systems are linked together and all three are diagnosed simultaneously. Certain components of the electronic ignition system are monitored by the ECM. When a problem in one of these circuits is detected, the ECM will illuminate the Malfunction Indicator Lamp (MIL). Proper diagnosis requires the use of a diagnostic scan tool. You may also need to use a breakout box (BOB), figure 3-1, and **digital multimeter** (DMM) to complete the diagnostic process. Refer to the appropriate Service or Diagnostic Manual for the correct tools and procedures. Follow the specific instructions of the vehicle and equipment manufacturers when connecting and operating test equipment.

Keep in mind, the scan tool will not reveal the exact nature of the problem, but does help you isolate the circuit or

Fig. 3-1. Typical breakout box.

component where the malfunction exists. Scan tools provide the user with many different forms of information. Compare the scan tool readings with the specifications from the service publications to determine if, in fact, a problem exists.

Figure 3-2 provides a sample of ignition related symptoms, definitions, and probable conditions or causes of specific conditions. Always use the appropriate Service Manual when conducting actual diagnostics on a vehicle.

SPARK DISTRIBUTION SYSTEMS

Early in the 20th century the first electrical ignition system, the self-starter for the automobile, was invented. This type of ignition system is known as the Kettering system, consisting of points, condenser, and an ignition coil. It became the standard in the automotive industry, replacing magnetos. A gear, chain, or belt from the engine drives the distributor. Inside this distributor is a spring loaded contact switch known as the points. The points ride on a revolving cam and open and close to fire a single coil, which produces the spark. Inside the distributor is also the rotor, which rotates to direct the spark to the correct spark plug wire.

L1

Digital Multimeter: A hand-held meter capable of measuring voltage, resistance, and current flow, then displaying it in digital format on an LCD screen.

Symptom	Definition	Possible Causes
NO START WITH NORMAL CRANK SPEED	The starter cranks the engine normally but the engine does not start.	Primary ignition circuit failure No RPM signal to ECM / Ignition Module Wet secondary ignition system components
HARD STARTING / LONG CRANKING TIME	The starter cranks the engine normally but requires excessive crank time to start.	Incorrect ignition timing Deficient spark intensity Excessive resistance in primary circuit
STARTS AND STALLS	Engine starts but stalls when the key is released to the RUN position.	Incorrect ignition timing Deficient spark intensity Ignition RUN circuit failure
STALLS AND MAY OR MAY NOT RESTART	Engine stops running under load, usually at idle when the transmission is in gear. Engine may or may not restart quickly.	Incorrect ignition timing Deficient spark intensity Interruption of ignition spark High resistance in the primary circuit
RUNS ROUGH / MISFIRES	Inconsistent production of power. Causes a noticeable vibration.	Inconsistent ignition Deficient spark intensity in one or more cylinders Defective spark plug wires
STUMBLE / SURGE BUCKS / JERKS	A drop off of power between the time the throttle opens and speed increases.	Deficient spark intensity High resistance in the primary circuit Defective spark plug wires
LACK OF POWER	Excessive throttle application is required to maintain cruise. Acceleration is slower than normal.	Incorrect ignition timing Deficient spark intensity
POOR FUEL ECONOMY	Vehicle uses excessive fuel.	Incorrect ignition timing Deficient spark intensity to one or more cylinders Defective spark plug wires
EMISSIONS TEST FAILURE	Vehicle fails one or more emissions tests.	Incorrect ignition timing Deficient spark intensity or duration Excessive resistance in primary circuit Defective spark plug wires

Fig. 3-2. Ignition system driveability diagnostic procedures.

Distributor Type Ignition Systems (DI)

As vehicle emissions and fuel economy standards became stricter the need for an ignition system that could produce a hotter spark was required. The mechanical points could not handle the required increase in current flow. To solve this problem the first electronic ignition systems replaced breaker points with a transistor. This system uses the distributor to signal the **ignition control module** (ICM) when to fire the spark plug. The ICM uses a power transistor to control the coil primary current flow.

Distributorless Ignition Systems (DIS)

Most late-model vehicles no longer use a distributor to control ignition timing and direct the secondary voltage to the spark plugs. The ignition coil's primary circuit control, originally in the distributor, has been replaced by ignition timing commands from the ECM. The ECM receives input from the

---

Ignition Control Module (ICM): An electronic module designed to control the primary circuit to the ignition coil.

crankshaft position sensor (CKP) and uses the information to control ignition timing. The CKP can be a **magnetic pickup** or a **Hall-effect sensor**; both are discussed later in this chapter. The DIS system design eliminates many moving parts and maintains more accurate control of the ignition timing during the life of the vehicle.

Position Sensors

In order to provide the ECM with the correct data regarding engine RPM and cylinder position, one or more sensors are installed to provide input information. The sensor(s) identifies the **top dead center** (TDC) point for cylinder number one. Once this position is established the ECM then calculates the position of the remaining cylinders and adjusts ignition timing and control accordingly.

Ignition System Signals

Most electronic ignition systems generally use an amperage-sensing ignition circuit to limit current through the primary circuit. This current limiting function can be seen on an oscilloscope as a hump during the dwell period just before the module-open signal, figure 3-3. Dwell is short at low engine speed, and increases as RPM increases.

The primary circuit does not energize until the module receives a verifiable engine speed signal from the crankshaft position (CKP) sensor. The CKP sensor provides the ignition module or engine control module (ECM) information on crankshaft speed and location. Some systems use an additional camshaft position (CMP) sensor, figure 3-4. A CMP sensor is used to provide the synchronization signal on distributorless ignition and sequential fuel injection systems, and for misfire detection on OBD-II vehicles. There are three basic designs for automotive position or speed sensors:

- Magnetic pickup
- Hall-effect sensor
- Optical sensor

The most accurate way to diagnose speed sensor problems is to monitor the signal on an oscilloscope. A magnetic pickup is an analog device that produces a sine wave pattern, while Hall-effect sensors and optical sensors are digital and produce a digital, or square, waveform. For all types, the ignition module or ECM uses the frequency of the signal to determine the speed of the sensed component.

Magnetic Pickup Sensor

Whether called a magnetic pickup coil, variable reluctance sensor, or permanent magnet generator, this type of sensor generates voltage as an analog signal. These sensors are self-contained and do not require an applied voltage to produce a signal. Since these sensors produce their own signal, it is

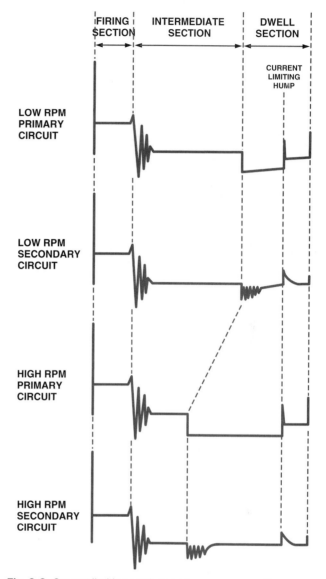

Fig. 3-3. Current limiting produces a hump on an oscilloscope trace at the end of the dwell period.

possible to get a waveform with correct amplitude and frequency, even though there are problems on the ground circuits.

The pickup coil is wound around a permanent magnet, whose field expands and collapses as the teeth of a rotating notched or slotted wheel known as the reluctor or trigger wheel pass by it, figure 3-5. The magnetic field generates an alternating current (AC) voltage signal and, as the speed of the engine increases, so does the frequency and amplitude of the signal. The ECM uses the frequency of the signal to determine rotational speed.

Crankshaft Position Sensor (CKP): An electronic device designed to supply engine RPM and position to the ECM.
Hall-Effect Sensor: A signal-generating switch that develops a transverse voltage across a current-carrying semiconductor when subjected to a magnetic field.
Magnetic Pickup: A signal-generating device that uses a permanent magnet to create a voltage pulse. The trigger wheel movement creates magnetic flux changes in the pickup coil to induce a varying strength voltage.
Top Dead Center (TDC): The point in engine rotation when cylinder number one is at the top of its travel and the valves are closed.

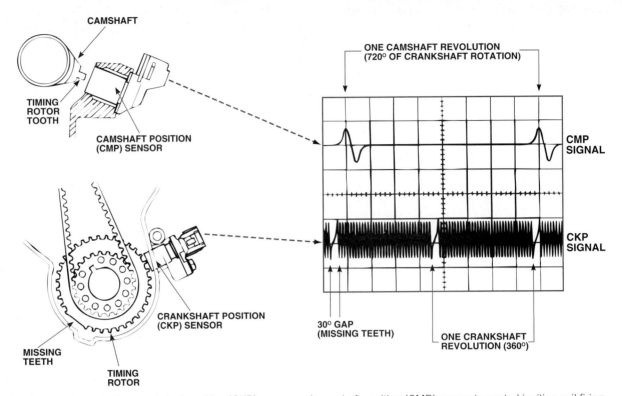

Fig. 3-4. Some systems use both a crankshaft position (CKP) sensor and camshaft position (CMP) sensor to control ignition coil firing.

The magnetic sensor may be mounted in several locations:

- In the distributor
- Part of the harmonic balancer
- Near the flywheel at the rear of the engine
- In the side of the cylinder block

Depending on the system, the reluctor design varies to meet the design requirements. Refer to the appropriate Service Manual for the exact description of the system used.

Testing a Magnetic Sensor

Regardless of system design, the resistance of a pickup coil can be checked with an ohmmeter. All pickup coils operate at a specific resistance; however, specifications and test points will vary between manufacturers and models.

In general, measurements are taken by connecting the ohmmeter leads to opposite sides of the coil. If the reading is not within specifications, replace the coil. To check for a grounded coil, connect one ohmmeter lead to ground and touch the other ohmmeter lead alternately to each of the pickup coil connectors. The ohmmeter should show **infinite resistance** at all test points. If not, replace the pickup.

The pickup coil can also be tested using an oscilloscope or scope. The coil has a two-wire circuit, a positive lead and a negative lead, connecting the sensor to the ECM. For best results, connect both scope probes directly to the sensor leads as close to the sensor as possible. A good trace generally sweeps up the positive slope and drops on the negative slope. The shape of the trace peak varies for different sensor designs, but most signals must reach a minimum amplitude before the ECM recognizes them. Look for uniformity in the trace cycles.

Air Gap Adjustment

The magnetic sensor is designed to be positioned close to but not touching the reluctor. A non-magnetic type feeler gauge must be used to check the gap. Most late-model CKP sensors are designed to provide the correct air gap between the components and do not require adjustment. Refer to the appropriate Service Manual for the correct installation procedures.

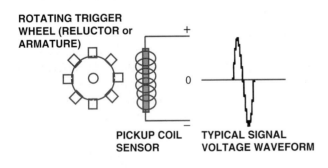

Fig. 3-5. A pickup coil is self-powered and generates an analog AC signal as the magnetic field expands and collapses.

Infinite Resistance: A condition caused by an incomplete or open circuit that prevents current through the circuit.

Hall-Effect Sensors

Hall-effect sensors are found in many late-model ignition systems, replacing the magnetic pickup type sensor. The mounting and function of the Hall-effect sensor is similar, but the operation and testing are different. A Hall-effect sensor uses a microchip to switch a transistor on and off and generate a digital signal that is transmitted to the ECM. As a slotted or trigger wheel connected to the crankshaft or distributor shaft, figure 3-6, passes between the Hall element and a permanent magnet, the magnetic field expands and collapses to produce an analog signal. The Hall element contains a logic gate that converts the signal into a digital signal, which triggers transistor switching. The transistor transmits a digital square waveform at a variable frequency to the ECM.

Hall-effect operation requires a three-wire circuit-power input, signal output, and ground. The Hall element, figure 3-7, receives an input voltage from either the ignition switch or the ECM to power it. As the magnetic field is distorted by the passing of the slotted wheel, the Hall element switches the base of a transistor on and off. This on-off signal is inverted by a transistor, which in turn opens and closes the ground-side of the primary ignition coil circuit.

Hall-effect switches produce a square waveform, figure 3-8, whose frequency varies in proportion to the rotational speed of the crankshaft. A Hall-effect sensor does not generate its own voltage, and power must be provided for the device to work.

When using a scope for diagnosis remember the Hall-effect sensor creates a waveform as the transistor switches on and off. To get a good scope trace, attach the positive scope probe to the transistor output signal and connect the negative probe to the sensor ground. For optimum results, connect both probe leads as close as possible to the sensor.

When a slot in the trigger wheel is aligned with the sensor the signal is low because the magnetic field is not engulfing the Hall element.

When a slot in the trigger wheel is not aligned with the element, the magnetic field saturates the Hall element, causing it to switch on and conduct current. Each time a slot passes the sensor, the signal generated by the Hall element changes state. Depending upon the application, this signal may be amplified or inverted before it is transmitted to the ECM. Therefore, there is no established rule as to whether the signal is high or low with respect to the strength of the magnetic field.

When examining a scope trace, look for sharp, clean state change transitions and a signal that pulls to ground. Amplitude should be even for all waveforms, the pattern should be consistent, and peaks should be at the specified voltage level. The shape and position of the slots on the shutter wheel determine the shape and duty cycle of the waveform. Some Hall-effect sensor patterns have a slight rounding at the top corners of the trace that can generally be overlooked. Remember, the ECM looks for switching at the midpoint of the voltage range, not at the top or bottom. However, rounding at the bottom corners of the trace should sound an alarm. This is often caused by high-resistance on the ground circuit, often from a poor connection, making it difficult for the signal to completely ground. Also, check for the correct voltage on the power circuit to the Hall element. A problem here can cause problems on the signal circuit.

Optical Sensor

An optical sensor uses a light-emitting diode (LED), a shutter wheel, and a phototransistor to produce a digital signal that changes frequency in proportion to rotational speed, figure 3-9. Like a Hall-effect sensor, an optical sensor requires an external power source and uses a three-wire circuit. One wire carries

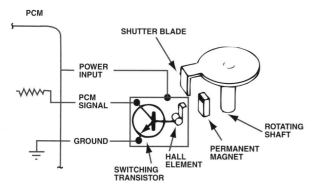

Fig. 3-6. Distributor-mounted Hall-effect sensor.

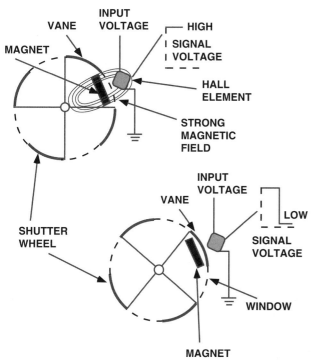

Fig. 3-7. The signal of a distributor-mounted Hall element switches high as the shutter wheel changes the magnetic field from strong to weak.

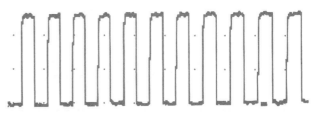

Fig. 3-8. Square-wave pattern from a Hall-effect sensor.

L1

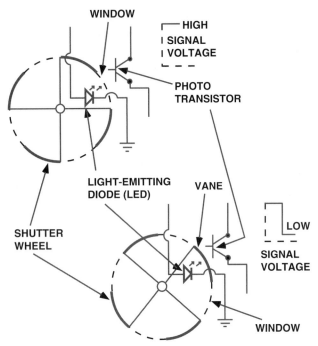

Fig. 3-9. An optical sensor uses an LED and a light-sensitive transistor to transmit a digital square waveform to the PCM at a variable frequency.

power to operate the LED, one is the signal generated by the transistor, and the third provides a common ground path.

Signal voltage, which is usually 5 volts, switches on and off as the rotating shutter passes between the phototransistor and LED to toggle the ground circuit. When the shutter allows light to shine on the phototransistor, the base of the transistor switches, causing the signal voltage to change state. When the reflector plate blocks the light to the phototransistor, the base of the transistor switches again, and signal voltage changes as well.

Optical sensors are more expensive to manufacture and more delicate than a magnetic pickup or Hall-effect sensor. Therefore, they are the least common of the three types. Typically, optical sensors are used as vehicle speed sensors and engine speed sensors because their high-speed data rate is more accurate than other sensor designs for high RPM applications. When viewed on an oscilloscope, the waveforms will be similar to those produced by a Hall-effect sensor.

Ignition Coils

Primary wiring and connectors are a potential source of high-resistance, as well as open or grounded circuits. Problems in this area can be found with simple voltmeter and ohmmeter tests. Check for correct supply voltage first. If voltage is present, check for a voltage drop using a **voltmeter**. When **voltage drop** indicates high or low resistance, verify with an **ohmmeter**. Many problems can easily be solved by cleaning connectors or repairing wiring.

Available Voltage

Check **available voltage** at the coil with a voltmeter by connecting the positive voltmeter lead to the positive (battery) coil terminal and the negative voltmeter lead to ground. Turn the ignition switch on and note the voltmeter reading. On some systems, full battery voltage should be available at the coil. On other systems, a ballast resistor provides a low-voltage signal to the coil. Check the Vehicle Service Information for the correct specifications.

If voltmeter readings are not within specifications, check the primary circuit. Repair or replace any loose or damaged connections and repeat the test. If available voltage readings are still out of range, check the circuit for a voltage drop.

Voltage Drop

Voltage drop is the amount of voltage that an electrical device normally consumes to perform its task. A small amount of voltage will always be lost due to normal circuit resistance. However, excessive voltage drop can be the result of a high-resistance connection or failed component.

To check voltage drop, the circuit must be powered up and under load. The circuit must also have the maximum amount of current under normal conditions for which the circuit was designed. The amount of voltage drop that is considered acceptable will vary by circuit. Low-current circuits that draw milliamps will be affected by very small voltage drops, while the same amount of voltage drop will have a negligible effect on a high-current circuit.

To measure voltage drop along a circuit, connect the negative voltmeter lead to ground and use the positive meter lead to probe at various points in the circuit. Compute voltage drop by checking available voltage on both sides of a load, then subtracting the voltage reading of the ground side from the reading on the positive side of the load. Take direct voltage drop readings by connecting the positive meter lead to the power side of a load and connecting the negative meter lead to the ground side of the component.

Manufacturers provide voltage drop specifications for various ignition components. Measure the voltage drop across the ignition module ground as follows:

1. Connect the voltmeter positive lead to the negative (distributor) coil terminal; connect the voltmeter negative lead to ground.
2. Switch the ignition on and observe the voltmeter.

Typically, a reading less than 0.5 volt indicates the module ground is in good condition.

High voltage drop can be caused by loose connections, poor ground, or excessive wear. Check and repair wiring, clean the ground circuit, and repeat the test.

Multiple Ignition Coil Designs

The coil packs contain multiple coils each supplying secondary voltage to two cylinders, figure 3-10. The coils operate on the

---

Available Voltage: The voltage present at a given point within the electrical system.
Ohmmeter: A meter designed to measure the resistance of a circuit of component. DMMs can be set to an ohmmeter function.
Voltage Drop: The measurement of the loss of voltage caused by unwanted resistance in a circuit connection, conductor, or device.
Voltmeter: An electrical test meter that measures electrical pressure (EMF).

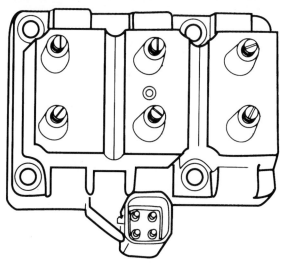

Fig. 3-10. Typical multiple coil coil-pack.

same basic principal as their predecessors but are configured differently. Generally each coil supplies secondary voltage for a pair of cylinders each time they reach TDC. One cylinder of the pair is on the power stroke, while the other is on the exhaust stroke. The spark occurring on the exhaust cylinder is of little value and therefore the system is often called a waste spark system.

Another more recent design provides an individual coil for each cylinder, figure 3-11. This coil is mounted on or near the spark plug is serves. These designs are known as coil-on-plug or coil-near-plug systems.

There are several advantages of multiple ignition coil systems. With coils serving only one or two spark plugs there is much more dwell time available, ensuring a hotter spark than a single coil can provide. The location of the coils reduces or eliminates the need for spark plug wires and the maintenance they require. Finally, the smaller coil operates at a lower temperature, which adds to its expected life. Regardless of the coil design, the diagnostic processes are very similar.

Ignition Coil Diagnosis

The resistance and current draw of the ignition coil can be tested with an ohmmeter or an **ammeter**, respectively. Test a coil

at its normal operating temperature. Resistance will change with temperature. Before testing, make these preliminary checks:

1. Be sure the coil is securely mounted and all electrical connections are clean and tight.
2. Check for a cracked or burned coil tower(s).
3. Check for a dented, cracked, or distorted housing.

Winding Resistance Test

Before attempting to measure the resistance of the primary and secondary windings, disconnect the battery ground cable, primary wiring, and high-tension lead. Use an ohmmeter to measure resistance as follows, figure 3-12:

1. Connect one ohmmeter lead to the positive (battery) primary terminal of the coil.
2. Connect the other ohmmeter lead to the negative (distributor) primary terminal of the coil.

The ohmmeter will display primary winding resistance. If the reading is not within specifications, replace the coil. If primary winding resistance is within range, check the secondary resistance, figure 3-13:

1. Connect one ohmmeter lead to a coil tower secondary terminal.
2. For coils serving one cylinder only, touch the second ohmmeter lead to one of the coil primary terminals and note the reading. For coil packs serving a pair of cylinders, touch the other lead to the mating cylinders coil tower secondary terminal.

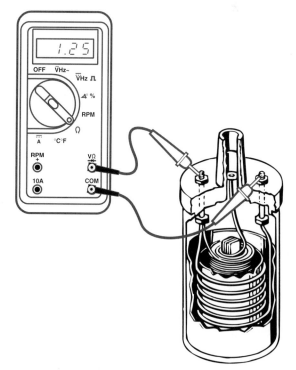

Figure 3-12. Checking resistance in the primary coil winding.

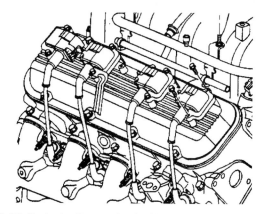

Fig. 3-11. Typical coil-near-plug ignition coil installation.

Ammeter: A test instrument that measures current flow in a circuit.

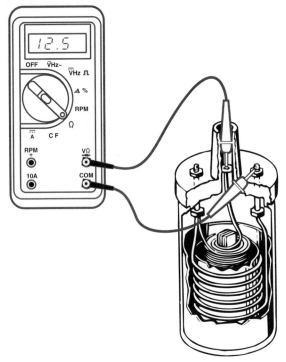

Fig. 3-13. Checking secondary coil winding resistance with an ohmmeter.

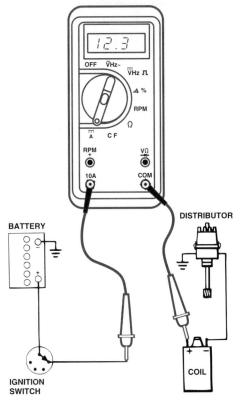

Fig. 3-14. Checking ignition coil current draw with an ammeter.

Current Draw Test

Several manufacturers provide current draw specifications for their ignition coils. Current draw is measured with an ammeter. Test procedures vary; follow the Service Manual recommendations. Some current draw tests are performed on a running engine, others while cranking the engine with the starter, or with the engine stopped, ignition on, and primary circuit complete.

To test current draw, disconnect the positive (battery) primary wire from the coil and connect it to the positive lead of the ammeter. Connect the negative lead of the ammeter to the positive (battery) coil terminal, figure 3-14. When using an inductive ammeter, fit the inductive pickup over the primary wire to the coil positive terminal, leaving the wire connected.

Observe the ammeter reading and compare it to specifications. If there is no reading, the primary circuit is open and the engine will not run. Higher-than-specified current draw can be caused by:

*   A short circuit in the coil
*   Use of an incorrect coil

Lower-than-specified current draw results from:

*   A discharged battery
*   Excessive resistance in the coil primary winding
*   Loose or corroded primary connections
*   High-resistance in the primary wiring to the coil

SECONDARY CIRCUIT DIAGNOSIS AND REPAIR

Often, it is useful when diagnosing a no-start condition to first verify that secondary voltage is available from the coil by performing a spark test. Begin by disconnecting a spark plug cable from the plug. Connect a **spark tester** to the plug wire and attach the ground clip of the tester to a bare metal spot on the engine, figure 3-15. Adjust the spark gap according to Service Manual specifications. If no specifications are available, start with a setting of approximately 1/4" (6mm). Crank the engine while observing the spark tester. A bright blue spark should be clearly visible. Do not crank the engine with the spark plug wires disconnected, as this may create high open-circuit voltage and cause damage to the ignition coil or other electronic systems.

Inspection

Begin your evaluation with a visual inspection of the secondary components. Look for:

*   Cracked, burned, or brittle insulation on the ignition cables and boots
*   Distributor cap defects, such as a sticking or worn carbon button, cracks, carbon tracks from arcing current, burned or corroded terminals, and corrosion inside the cap towers
*   Rotor damage, such as a bent or broken contact strip, burned or eroded tip, cracked or broken positioning lug, and carbon tracks or cracks on the body

---

Spark Tester: A special tool with an adjustable spark gap used to check spark intensity.

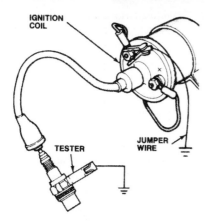

Fig. 3-15. Using a spark tester to check for secondary voltage available from the coil.

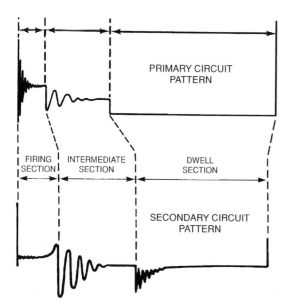

Fig. 3-16. Ignition oscilloscope patterns, both primary and secondary, can be divided into three distinct sections.

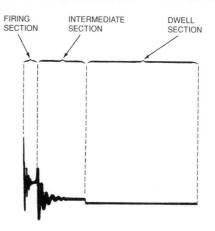

Fig. 3-17. A superimposed pattern displays cylinder traces on top of each other.

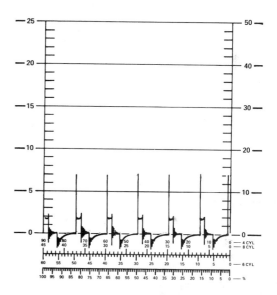

Fig. 3-18. Parade pattern displays cylinder traces horizontally across the screen.

Oscilloscope Testing

Because an oscilloscope displays voltage changes during a period of time, it is an ideal instrument for examining the variable voltages produced in both the primary and secondary ignition circuits. Oscilloscopes display a voltage trace on a viewing screen as a graph of voltage versus time. The vertical scale on the screen represents voltage and the horizontal scale represents time.

Both primary and secondary ignition system voltage traces can be divided into three sections: firing, intermediate, and dwell, figure 3-16. Deviations from a normal pattern indicate a problem. In addition, most scopes display ignition traces in three different patterns. You can use each pattern to isolate and identify particular kinds of malfunctions. The three basic patterns are:

- Superimposed
- Parade, or display
- Stacked, or raster

In a superimposed pattern, voltage traces for all cylinders are displayed on top of each other to form a single pattern, figure 3-17. This display provides a quick overall view of ignition system operation and can also reveal certain major problems.

The parade pattern displays voltage traces for all cylinders one after the other from left to right across the screen in firing order sequence, figure 3-18. This allows easy comparison of voltage levels between cylinders. A parade display is useful for diagnosing problems in the secondary circuit.

A raster pattern shows the voltage traces for all cylinders stacked one above the other in firing order sequence, figure 3-19. This display allows you to compare the time periods of the three sections of a voltage trace.

Oscilloscope testing is the most efficient method of locating secondary circuit malfunctions. Variations in the secondary trace will indicate if parts are malfunctioning or incorrectly adjusted. The following paragraphs describe some common secondary circuit problems that can be detected with an oscilloscope.

L1

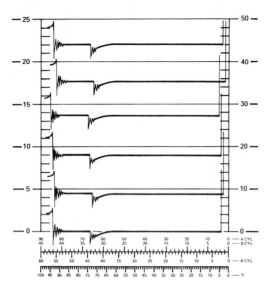

Fig. 3-19. Raster pattern stacks cylinder traces vertically on the screen.

Firing Section Abnormalities

Check the firing section of an oscilloscope trace for the following:

- A large firing oscillation with little or no sparkline for one cylinder indicates an open circuit between the distributor rotor and the spark plug, figure 3-20. Use the parade display to isolate the faulty cylinder. Check for a disconnected or broken spark plug cable. This pattern can be created deliberately to check coil output. Remove a cable; the top of the firing line is the maximum available voltage of the coil. Use the kV scale on the side of the screen to read voltage output
- One sparkline that is lower and longer than the rest indicates low resistance in the circuit between the distributor cap and the spark plug, figure 3-21. Check for carbon tracks in the distributor, poor cable insulation, or a fouled spark plug
- A parade pattern may show a short sparkline still exists even when the spark plug cable has been deliberately disconnected, figure 3-22. This indicates that high voltage is causing a current leak to ground somewhere, usually through

the ignition cable insulation, the distributor cap, or the rotor. Carbon tracks will often accumulate near the leakage

- There should be no more than a 20 percent difference between the highest and lowest firing spikes when comparing cylinders in a parade pattern, figure 3-23. Variations can be caused by fuel or electrical system problems. To separate the two, slowly cover the engine air intake to richen the fuel mixture. If the spikes go down and engine speed increases, the problem is fuel related. If the spikes go down and engine speed remains unchanged, the plug gaps may be too great. If a single spike remains the same height, the cable to that plug may be damaged
- One sparkline that is higher and shorter than the rest indicates high resistance from an open circuit between the distributor cap and the spark plug, figure 3-24. A damaged

LONG, LOW SPARKLINE AND SHORT OSCILLATIONS SEPARATED FROM OTHERS SHOWS LOW RESISTANCE

Fig. 3-21. A low, long sparkline on a secondary superimposed pattern indicates low resistance in one cylinder.

Fig. 3-22. An open plug circuit with a voltage leak in a secondary parade pattern.

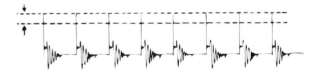

Fig. 3-23. Look for fairly even firing line peaks when viewing a secondary parade pattern.

LACK OF SPARKLINE SHOWS OPEN PLUG CABLE

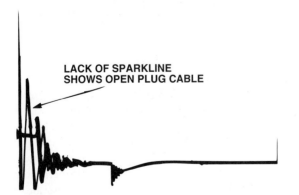

Fig. 3-20. A large firing oscillation without a sparkline on a secondary superimposed pattern indicates an open plug circuit.

HIGH, SHORT SPARKLINE

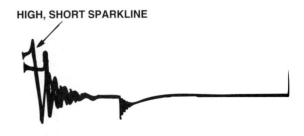

Fig. 3-24. A high, short sparkline on a secondary superimposed pattern indicates high-resistance in one cylinder.

or loose cable or a wide plug gap may be at fault. Corrosion on the cable terminals and in the distributor cap can cause a sparkline for one cylinder to start higher and angle downward more sharply than the others

- A sparkline that jumps erratically or slopes up rather than down is caused by an incorrect fuel mixture in that cylinder. The problem may be mechanical, such as sticking or worn valves, or caused by intake air leaks or fuel induction problems

Intermediate Section Abnormalities

Use the intermediate section of the trace to check coil function. A faulty coil, primary circuit, or coil wire between the coil and distributor cap may cause a lack of oscillations.

- Absent coil oscillations with a normal dwell section are the result of a faulty coil or a high-resistance short to ground in the primary circuit
- A pattern displayed upside-down indicates that coil polarity is reversed, usually because of reversed primary connections at the coil
- The entire pattern jumping on the screen results from an intermittent open in the coil secondary winding
- Reduced coil oscillations along with a missing module-on signal are caused by an open between the coil and the distributor cap
- Variation in the firing signals at the end of a raster pattern is caused by worn ignition signal parts or a faulty module. This variation indicates timing differences among cylinders. Note that this is normal for those ignition systems that use computer control of timing to regulate idle speed

Dwell Section Abnormalities

The dwell section of a secondary trace should be a relatively flat line with the possible exception of a current limiting hump. Be aware, dwell length increases with engine speed on some systems, figure 3-25. Dwell variation between cylinders can be checked using the raster display. A dwell variation of more than 4 to 6 degrees between cylinders indicates mechanical wear in the distributor. Use the degree scale at the bottom of the screen to read dwell angles.

Ignition Coil Service

Ignition coils for a distributor system are very similar to the procedure described previously in this chapter. Refer to the appropriate Service Manual for the correct diagnostic steps.

Distributor Service

Rust, dirt, grease, and varnish tend to collect inside a distributor while it is operating. Accumulated dirt and grime can affect centrifugal advance operation, cause crossfiring, and short circuit electrical connections. In addition, high-mileage operation, as well as mechanical defects, can cause bushing and drive gear wear.

Distributor overhauls, once a common practice for breaker point ignition, are seldom performed on electronic distributors. Electronic distributors have fewer movable parts and are less prone to wear. However, the electronic distributor must be removed to replace the pickup coil on some engines. Once out, the distributor can be cleaned, inspected, tested, and repaired.

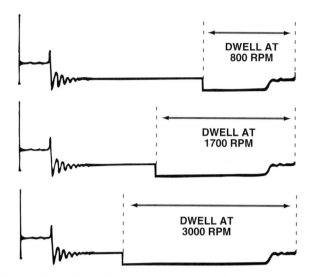

Fig. 3-25. Dwell length increases in proportion to engine speed on some systems.

Distributor Removal

Removal principles for all distributors are similar, although the exact details will vary somewhat by manufacturer and engine. Typically, the air cleaner, intake duct work, or other engine accessories must be removed or loosened and relocated. It is always advisable to disconnect the battery ground cable to prevent accidental arcing.

The distributors used on some late-model engines couple directly to the end of the camshaft by an offset tang on the distributor shaft, figure 3-26. Cylinder positioning has no effect on distributor removal or installation because the drive will connect to the camshaft in only one position. These distributors usually have a pair of slotted ears that fit over two studs and are retained by nuts. Remove the distributor from the engine simply by removing the two nuts.

Most distributors are driven by a helical gear, or bevel gear, that engages a spiral gear on the camshaft or auxiliary shaft in the engine. These are generally held in the engine with

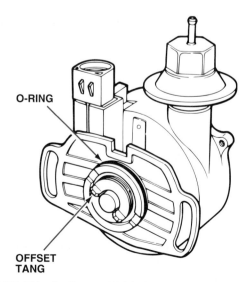

Fig. 3-26. This distributor, which bolts to the cylinder head, is driven directly by the camshaft.

a holddown clamp and a bolt, figure 3-27. The clamp rides over a mounting flange on the distributor base. After the bolt and clamp have been removed, the distributor should come free easily. Most distributors can be removed using the following procedure:

1. Disconnect and remove the distributor cap. Ignition cables can usually be left attached to the cap; simply position the cap and wires out of the way.
2. Rotate the engine to bring number one cylinder to top dead center on the compression stroke.
3. Mark a reference point on the distributor housing in line with the position of the rotor tip.
4. Also mark reference points on the distributor housing and engine so the distributor can be installed in the same position.
5. Disconnect the primary circuit wiring to the distributor.
6. Disconnect any vacuum lines attached to the distributor.
7. Loosen the distributor holddown fastener, then lift off the holddown bracket. Some units require an offset wrench.
8. Carefully loosen and remove the distributor from the engine. It may be necessary to twist the distributor gently to loosen it from the engine; do not use force.
9. With gear-driven distributors, the rotor will move as the gears disengage. Note how far the rotor rotates off the reference mark as the distributor is removed.

Clean all oil, grease, dirt, and rust from the distributor shaft and housing with solvent and a brush. Keep solvent away from vacuum advance units, bushings, and electronic components.

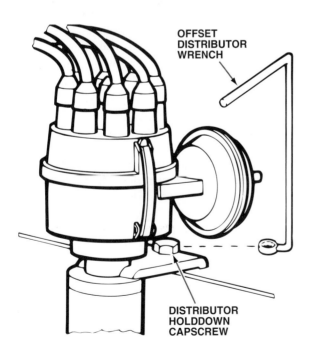

Fig. 3-27. An offset wrench may be needed to remove the distributor holddown bolt and clamp.

Dry the distributor with low-pressure compressed air and perform a preliminary inspection. Look for:

- Binding or excessive shaft movement; check endplay and side play
- Worn or chipped drive gear teeth, or dog lugs
- Loose or damaged electrical leads and connections
- Loose or damaged breaker plate and vacuum advance unit mounting
- Worn or binding breaker plate bearings
- Signs of inadequate lubrication

Disassembly and Assembly

There are a wide variety of distributor designs. Disassembly procedures will vary for each. Most distributors share these common characteristics:

- Drive gears and dogs generally attach to the shaft with a roll pin
- Machine screws attach vacuum units to the distributor housing; an eye on the diaphragm stem slips over a post on the breaker plate
- Springs hold the **centrifugal advance** weights in place
- The breaker plate is attached to the housing with screws

Follow Service Manual procedures and disassemble the distributor into component pieces, figure 3-28. Clean the inside of the distributor and all the moving parts, except vacuum units, with solvent and a small brush. Dry parts with low-pressure compressed air. Make sure that all dirt and solvent residue are removed, especially from electrical connections. Wipe dirt off with a clean, lint-free cloth.

Inspect all components for signs of damage or wear, replace parts as needed, and assemble the distributor. Always replace any O-rings or gaskets that seal the housing to the engine. Lightly lubricate all moving parts during assembly. Keep in mind, proper lubrication is essential, but too much lubrication is as bad as not enough. Distributor rotation will spray excess lubricant around the inside of the distributor, where it collects dirt and can cause short circuits.

Many solid-state distributors require that a silicone lubricant be applied to specific locations within the distributor. Typical points are at the ignition module primary connections, on the rotor contact tip, and at the distributor connections. The silicone lubricant prevents corrosion and moisture that might interfere with voltage signals. Some distributors require a film of silicone lubricant between the module and its mounting base to help dissipate heat.

Distributor Installation

After the distributor has been serviced, follow these general directions to install the distributor:

1. Make sure the ignition switch is off or the battery ground cable is disconnected.
2. Rotate the distributor shaft to align the rotor with the reference mark on the housing. Turn an additional amount to compensate for gear engagement.

Centrifugal Advance: A method of advancing the ignition spark using weights in the distributor that react to centrifugal force generated by engine speed.

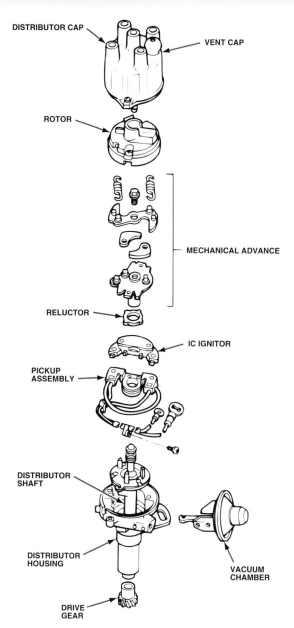

DISTRIBUTOR CAP
VENT CAP
ROTOR
MECHANICAL ADVANCE
RELUCTOR
IC IGNITOR
PICKUP ASSEMBLY
DISTRIBUTOR SHAFT
DISTRIBUTOR HOUSING
VACUUM CHAMBER
DRIVE GEAR

Fig. 3-28. Disassemble the distributor, then clean, inspect, and test the components.

3. Align the distributor housing mark with the reference point on the engine.
4. If an O-ring or gasket is used, make sure it is in position. Lubricate O-rings to ease installation.
5. Insert the distributor into the engine, turn the rotor to engage the drive gears, and push lightly to seat the distributor.
6. Make sure the distributor is fully seated in the engine and engaged with the camshaft and oil pump drive. If necessary, wiggle the shaft or rotate the engine slightly to engage the oil pump.
7. Check that the rotor and reference mark are aligned. If out of position, note the amount and raise the distributor up. Reposition the rotor the same amount and lower the distributor back into place.

8. When installing a distributor that couples directly to the camshaft end, align the tangs on the distributor shaft with the slots in the end of the camshaft. Seat the distributor against the cylinder head and install the fasteners.
9. Fit the distributor holddown clamp. Install the bolt and draw it up snug.
10. Connect distributor primary wiring and attach the vacuum lines to the advance unit, if so equipped.
11. Install the distributor cap and any other items removed during disassembly.
12. Reconnect the battery ground cable, start the engine, check and adjust timing.

Distributor Cap and Rotor Replacement

Never clean cap electrodes or the rotor terminal by filing. If electrodes are burned or damaged, replace the part. Filing changes the rotor air gap and increases resistance. Most caps are replaced by simply undoing spring-type clips, L-shaped lug hooks, or holddown screws. Lift the old cap off and install a new one. When replacing the cap, be sure to install the spark plug cables in correct firing sequence.

Rotors may be retained by holddown screws or may simply slip-fit onto the shaft. Rotors also use one or more locating lugs to correctly position them on the distributor shaft. Make sure the rotor is fully seated. If not, it can strike the cap when the engine is started.

Ignition Timing Methods

Ignition advance on most late-model vehicles is not adjustable, and in most cases, no provisions are made for verification. Some vehicles do have a provision for retarding ignition timing if excessive **detonation** is present. This adjustment requires the use of a scan tool.

Mechanically Controlled Timing

Ignition timing can be advanced within the distributor centrifugally and with vacuum. The speed of the engine governs centrifugal advance and engine load determines vacuum advance. As speed increases, so does the timing advance. Also, light load operating conditions will advance timing to decrease fuel consumption.

A few older model vehicles use dual diaphragm distributor units. Depending on their design they can either use one diaphragm for advance and the other for retard, or use one for low advance and the other for high advance. The advance/retard unit uses ported vacuum to advance the timing, and manifold vacuum to allow the timing to retard further in the absence of ported vacuum.

The dual advance unit use manifold vacuum through a thermal vacuum switch to advance the timing on cold engines for better driveability.

Static Timing Procedure

The following procedure can be used to statically time an electronic ignition system:

1. Rotate the engine until the crankshaft timing mark aligns with the proper timing specification, and #1 cylinder is on the compression stroke.

Detonation: Also called ping, or spark knock. An unwanted explosion of an air-fuel mixture caused by high heat and compression.

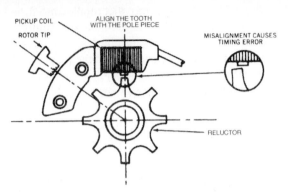

Fig. 3-29. To static time a distributor, align a trigger wheel tooth with the pole piece and the rotor with the secondary lead for the first plug in the firing order.

2. Loosen the distributor holddown clamp and bolt.
3. Rotate the distributor housing in the direction of rotor rotation until the trigger wheel tooth is aligned with the pole piece, and the rotor is pointed toward #1 plug wire in the distributor cap, figure 3-29.
4. Tighten the holddown bolt.
5. Check and adjust the dynamic timing.

Dynamic Timing

Dynamic timing is adjusted by rotating the distributor housing with the engine idling at normal operating temperature. Most manufacturers specify that the distributor vacuum lines be disconnected and plugged, or that the computer control of timing be disabled. See the underhood service decal for instructions. Precise spark timing is important to ensure correct engine performance and to reduce vehicle emissions.

1. Connect a timing light and tachometer.
2. Disconnect and plug distributor vacuum lines or disable computer control to prevent unwanted vacuum advance.
3. Slightly loosen the distributor holddown bolt.
4. Start the engine. Adjust idle speed to specifications to prevent unwanted centrifugal or ignition module RPM advance.
5. Point the timing light toward the timing marks. Carefully sight the marks at a right angle, figure 3-30. Looking at the marks from an incorrect position can result in an initial timing error of as much as two degrees.
6. Rotate the distributor housing until the proper marks are aligned.
7. When the timing is set to specifications, carefully tighten the distributor holddown bolt. Recheck the timing.

Magnetic Timing

On some engines the initial timing can be set using either a timing light or a magnetic timing meter. Magnetic timing is more accurate than a timing light because it eliminates the optical viewing error, and the timing signal comes directly from the crankshaft dampener.

A magnetic timing meter operates on the same principle as a magnetic pickup. The meter probe is a pickup coil which is inserted into a socket on the engine, figure 3-31. A notch, tab, or magnetic particle in the crankshaft, flywheel, or vibration damper generates a pulse signal every time it passes the

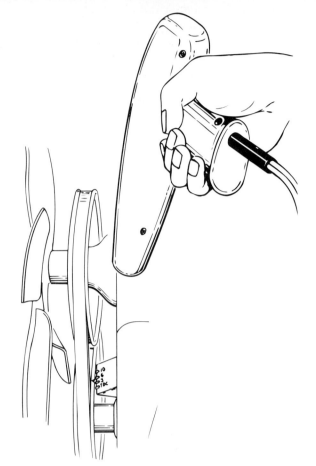

Fig. 3-30. Using a timing light to check timing on a running engine.

end of the probe. On many engines, the notch, tab, or particle is offset from top dead center by a specific number of degrees. The other connection is on the number one spark plug wire. The timing meter calculates the amount to advance or retard based on the two signals received.

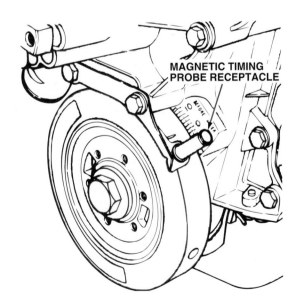

Fig. 3-31. Some engines have a receptacle for attaching a magnetic timing meter.

Centrifugal and Vacuum Advance Tests

Initial timing and idle speed must be adjusted before spark advance is tested. A stroboscopic timing light, preferably with an adjustable advance meter, a tachometer, and a vacuum pump, are used to check advance. Three advance checks can quickly be made with an adjustable timing light:

- Total advance
- Centrifugal advance
- Vacuum advance

To check total advance:

1. Connect a tachometer and an adjustable timing light to the engine.
2. Start the engine and verify that initial timing and idle speed are correct.
3. Increase engine speed to the specified RPM for checking total advance.
4. Hold engine speed and adjust the timing light advance meter to bring the timing marks back into proper alignment.
5. Read the degrees of total advance recorded on the timing light meter and compare to specifications.

If the reading is within specifications, centrifugal and vacuum mechanisms are both functioning properly. For readings not within specifications, test the individual advance devices to determine which is at fault following the procedures in the appropriate Service Manual.

Computer-Controlled Timing

The ignition module or ECM calculates ignition timing on most late-model vehicles. The ECM receives inputs from sensors giving engine temperature, RPM, load, vehicle speed, throttle position, amount of EGR, barometric pressure, and possible detonation.

Typically, setting base timing involves disabling the computer from controlling timing. Follow the procedure on the engine decal, or check other sources if the decal does not specify. This operation can be done by disconnecting a wire or coolant sensor, jumping between two wires, or jumping the connectors in the data link connector (DLC).

Distributorless Ignition Testing and Service

Distributorless ignition systems (DIS) rely on a crankshaft, or a camshaft sensor, or both, to relay engine speed and crankshaft position to the ECM. Also, these systems use multiple ignition coils. As described earlier in this chapter, some systems use one coil for each cylinder; others use the "waste spark method" where one coil fires two cylinders.

Each pairing of spark plugs is in cylinders where the pistons are at top dead center at the same time: the first at the top of the compression stroke, the second at the top of the exhaust stroke. When the coil fires, the spark going to the cylinder on compression ignites the mixture, figure 3-32. The spark to the other cylinder is "wasted" at the top of the exhaust stroke. The plug firing on the compression stroke requires higher voltage than the plug firing on the exhaust stroke.

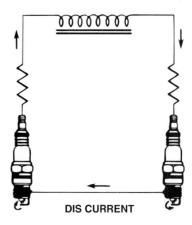

Fig. 3-32. A waste-spark system fires two plugs simultaneously.

SPARK PLUG AND IGNITION CABLE SERVICE

Spark plugs are routinely replaced at specific service intervals as recommended by the vehicle manufacturer. However, these intervals are guidelines and actual spark plug service life will vary. Spark plug life depends upon:

- Engine design
- Type of driving
- Kind of fuel used
- Types of emission control devices

Because the spark plugs are the final component in all secondary circuits, the remainder of the circuit cannot perform properly if they are not in good condition.

Spark Plug Removal

Spark plug access is limited on many late-model engines due to a maze of air conditioning and emission control plumbing and engine-driven accessory mounting. Engine accessories may have to be loosened from their mountings and moved to get to the plugs. Air conditioning compressors, air pumps, and power steering pumps are frequent candidates for relocation during spark plug service. Whenever you must move one of these accessories, be careful of its plumbing and wiring. The spark plugs on some engines are most easily reached from underneath the engine. To remove the spark plugs:

1. Disconnect cables at the plug by grasping the boot and twisting gently while pulling. Do not pull on the cable. Insulated spark plug pliers provide a better grip and are recommended when working near hot manifolds, figure 3-33.
2. Loosen each plug one or two turns with a spark plug socket, then blow dirt away from around the plugs with compressed air.
3. Remove the plugs, keeping them in cylinder number order for inspection.
4. When removing gasketed plugs, be sure the old gasket comes out with the plug.

L1

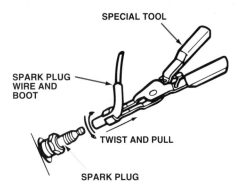

Fig. 3-33. Use insulated plug cable pliers to disconnect cables from spark plugs.

Spark Plug Inspection

Examining the firing ends of the spark plugs reveals a good deal about general engine conditions and plug operation. The insulator nose of a used plug should have a light brown-to-grayish color, and there should be very little electrode wear. These conditions indicate the correct plug heat range and a healthy engine. Some common spark plug conditions, figure 3-34, that indicate problems follow.

Oil Fouling

Dark, wet deposits on the plug tip are caused by excessive oil entering the combustion chamber. Piston ring, cylinder wall, and valve guide wear are likely causes in a high-mileage engine. Also, a defective PCV valve can draw oil vapor from the crankcase into the intake and oil foul the plugs.

Carbon Fouling

Soft, black, sooty deposits on the plug end indicate carbon fouling. Carbon results from a plug that is operating too cold. Check for spark plugs with an incorrect heat range, an overly rich air-fuel mixture, weak ignition, inoperative manifold heat control valve or thermostatic air cleaner, retarded timing, low compression, or faulty plug wires or distributor cap. Carbon fouling may also result from overloading due to excessive stop-and-go driving.

Ash Fouling

Certain oil or fuel additives that burn during normal combustion can create ash deposits. Ash deposits are light brownish-white accumulations that form on and around the electrode. Normally, ash deposits are nonconductive, but large amounts may cause misfiring.

Splash Fouling

Small dark patches visible on the insulator indicate splash fouling. Deposits breaking loose from pistons and valves and splashing against hot plug insulators cause splash fouling. The condition often occurs after engine servicing that restores engine power and higher combustion temperatures. Splash-fouled plugs can generally be cleaned and reinstalled.

Gap Bridging

Gap bridging is usually due to conditions similar to those described for splash fouling. The difference is that deposits form a bridge across the electrodes and cause a short. This condition is common in engines with poor oil control.

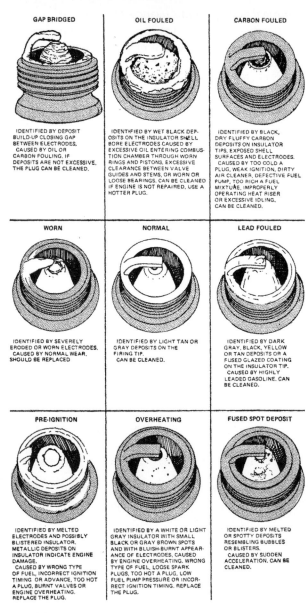

Fig. 3-34. Spark plug condition chart.

Insulator Glazing

Shiny, yellow, or tan deposits are a sign of insulator glazing. Frequent hard acceleration with a resulting rise in plug temperature can cause glazing. The high temperature melts normal plug deposits and fuses them into a conductive coating that causes misfiring.

Overheating

Spark plug overheating is indicated by a clean, white insulator tip, excessive electrode wear, or both. The insulator may also be blistered. Incorrect spark plug heat range, incorrect tightening torque, over-advanced timing, a defective cooling system, or lean air-fuel mixture can cause overheating.

Detonation

Detonation causes increased heat and pressure in the combustion chamber that exerts extreme loads on engine parts. Fractured or broken spark plug insulators are a sign of detonation. Over-advanced timing, lean fuel-air mixture, low gasoline octane, and engine lugging are contributing factors. An EGR valve that fails to open can also cause detonation.

Preignition

Preignition, the air-fuel charge igniting before the plug fires, can cause severe damage to the spark plug electrodes. Preignition is usually caused by combustion chamber hot spots or deposits that hold enough heat to prematurely ignite the air-fuel charge. Crossfiring between plug cables or a plug heat range much too hot for the engine can also cause preignition. A loose spark plug may also cause preignition.

Even if the color of the insulator and deposits are normal, rounded and worn electrodes indicate that a plug should be replaced. These plugs are simply worn out. The voltage required to spark across the gap has increased and continues to do so with additional use. Misfiring under load is a clue to worn out plugs. Such plugs also contribute to poor gas mileage, loss of power, and increased emissions.

Also check spark plugs for physical damage caused by a foreign object in the combustion chamber, a plug of the wrong reach being hit by a piston or valve, or by careless installation. Be careful to prevent dirt from falling into spark plug holes during service.

Spark Plug Installation

Spark plugs, both new and used, must be correctly gapped before they are installed. Although a wide variety of gapping tools are available, a round wire feeler gauge is the most efficient for used plugs, figure 3-35. Adjust the gap by carefully bending the ground electrode, figure 3-36.

- Do not assume that new plugs are correctly gapped
- Do not make gap adjustments by tapping the electrode on a workbench or other solid object

Cleaning the threaded plug holes in the cylinder head with a thread chaser will ensure easy spark plug installation. With aluminum heads, use the tool carefully to avoid damaging the threads.

Some manufacturers recommend using an antiseize compound or thread lubricant on the plug threads. Use thread lubricant only when specified by the manufacturer. Antiseize compound is commonly used when installing plugs in aluminum cylinder heads. Be sure to use the specific compound recommended by the manufacturer, as not all are compatible with aluminum. Whenever thread lubricant or antiseize is used, reduce the tightening torque slightly.

Once the plug gap has been properly set, install as follows:

1. Wipe any dirt and grease from the cylinder head plug seats.
2. Check that gaskets used on the plugs are in good condition and properly installed.
3. Install the plugs in the engine and run them in by hand.
4. Tighten the plugs to specification with a torque wrench following Service Manual specifications.

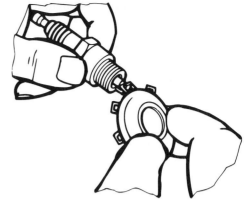

ROUND WIRE FEELER GAUGE

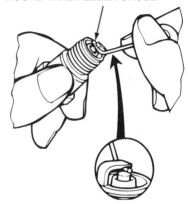

Fig. 3-35. Checking spark plug electrode gap.

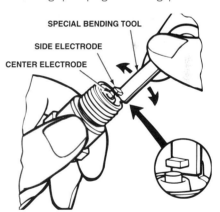

SPECIAL BENDING TOOL

SIDE ELECTRODE

CENTER ELECTRODE

Fig. 3-36. Adjusting spark plug electrode gap.

Ignition Cable Service

Excessive resistance in the secondary circuit can cause driveability problems such as an engine misfire, higher burn voltage, and shorter burn time. Damaged cables are often the cause, and can be tested with an ohmmeter. Typical suppression-type spark plug wires should measure about 4,000 ohms per foot.

Excessive resistance can result from:

- Loose or corroded connections at the distributor cap terminal or spark plug

---

Preignition: A premature ignition of the air-fuel mixture before the spark plug fires. It is caused by excessive heat or pressure in the combustion chamber.

- Damage to the cable conductor from heat, vibration, or mishandling

Test cable resistance as follows:

1. Remove the distributor cap from the housing and disconnect the wire to be tested at the spark plug, or coil, end.
2. Disconnect the other end of the cable to be tested from the distributor cap.
3. Set the ohmmeter on a high scale, then connect a one meter lead to each end of the spark plug cable, figure 3-37. If meter readings are out of specification, replace the cable.

Cable Replacement

Most ignition systems use 7-mm cables. However, others use larger 8-mm cables. The larger cables provide additional **dielectric resistance** in a system where secondary voltages can exceed 40 kV. Use the proper size cables; they are not interchangeable.

Ignition cables generally push-fit into the distributor cap or DIS coil. Twist and pull up on the boot to remove the cable from the cap. Check the cap tower or DIS terminal for dirt, corrosion, or damage. Clean light deposits in the tower with a wire brush. Replace a cap or coil if there is heavy accumulation. Fit the new cable to the cap so the terminal seats firmly on the tower. Fit the rubber boot seal over the tower, or DIS terminal, and squeeze it to remove any trapped air.

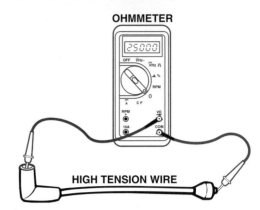

Fig. 3-37. Checking spark plug wire resistance with an ohmmeter.

Some distributor caps use a male ignition cable terminal that looks much like a spark plug. The cable end snaps onto the terminal instead of fitting down inside the cap tower.

When replacing cables, disconnect only one cable at a time from a spark plug and the distributor cap or DIS coil terminal. For distributors, begin with the cable for cylinder number one and work in firing order sequence. Route each cable in the same location as the one removed and secure it into the cable brackets. To prevent the possibility of crossfiring, do not route cables in firing order sequence next to each other. Make sure that the cables cannot contact the exhaust manifold or interfere with other electrical wiring.

Dielectric Resistance: A poor conductor of electrical current or a high resistance.

CHAPTER QUESTIONS

1. The current draw of an ignition coil is measured with which of the following instruments?
   a. A voltmeter
   b. An ammeter
   c. An ohmmeter
   d. An oscilloscope

2. A fouled spark plug may cause which of the following ignition oscilloscope patterns?
   a. A large firing oscillation with little or no spark line
   b. One spark line that is higher and shorter than the rest
   c. A spark line that jumps erratically or slopes up rather than down
   d. One spark line that is lower and longer than the rest

3. During an oscilloscope test of the secondary ignition system, the intermediate section of the trace pattern is displayed upside down. This would most likely indicate which of the following?
   a. Reversed primary connections at the ignition coil
   b. An open circuit between the coil and the distributor cap
   c. An intermittent open in the coil secondary winding
   d. A high resistance short to ground in the primary circuit

4. An electronic ignition system primary circuit will not energize until the module receives a verifiable engine speed signal from which of the following sensors?
   a. Engine Coolant Temperature (ECT)
   b. Camshaft Position (CMP)
   c. Crankshaft Position (CKP)
   d. Throttle Position (TP)

5. When inspecting a spark plug, which of the following conditions would indicate detonation?
   a. A clean white insulator tip
   b. Soft, black, sooty deposits on insulator tip
   c. Dark wet deposits on insulator tip
   d. Fractured or broken insulator tip

6. When performing an ignition coil current draw test, higher than specified current draw may be caused by which of the following?
   a. A short circuit in the coil
   b. Discharged battery
   c. High resistance in primary wiring to the ignition coil
   d. Loose or corroded primary connections

7. Spark plug overheating, which is indicated by a clean white insulator tip and excessive electrode wear, can be caused by all of the following *EXCEPT*:
   a. Incorrect spark plug tightening
   b. Over-advanced ignition timing
   c. Rich air-fuel mixture
   d. Lean air-fuel mixture

L1

CHAPTER OBJECTIVES

- The technician will complete the ASE task list on Fuel and Air Induction System Diagnosis and Repair.
- The technician will be able to answer 7 questions dealing with the Fuel and Air Induction System Diagnosis and Repair section of the L1 ASE Test.

To run efficiently, an engine must be supplied with a constant flow of clean pressurized fuel and filtered air in precisely metered amounts. In addition, the exhaust system must effectively carry combustion gases out of the engine, without excessive **backpressure**. Electronically controlled engines monitor operating conditions through a variety of sensors and adjust the air-fuel mixture for optimum performance.

If the balance of the air-fuel mixture is upset, driveability suffers. Problems of hard starting, no starting, hesitation, surging, power loss, stalling, misfiring, incorrect idle speed, poor idle quality, poor fuel mileage, and dieseling can be caused by a fuel or air induction deficiency. However, mechanical, electrical, electronic, or ignition problems may have similar symptoms. Therefore, it is important to isolate the source of the problem before attempting repairs. To isolate the problem to a specific system, perform the diagnostic tests detailed in the other chapters of this book and the vehicle service information.

FUEL SYSTEM SERVICE

When fuel system service is required, observe these safety precautions:

- Keep open flames and sparks away from the vehicle
- Do not smoke near any part of the fuel system
- Work in a well-ventilated area
- Cap or plug all disconnected fuel lines
- Disconnect the battery ground cable before removing or replacing fuel system parts to prevent accidental arcing

Inspection

Because of its many parts and connecting lines, the fuel system may develop leaks at several points. Keep in mind any leak, or restriction, will affect operating pressure and can cause a driveability problem. Begin with a thorough inspection of the entire fuel system. To check for damage and safety defects:

1. Inspect the fuel tank for:
   - Physical damage and leakage at fittings, connections, and seams
   - Plugged vents and damaged vent tubes and connecting lines
   - Filler tube and filler tube cap condition and proper venting
   - Leakage at the filler tube, vent line connections, and fuel gauge sending unit
   - Secure mounting; tighten tank holddown straps if necessary
   - Signs of internal contamination

2. Inspect fuel lines and hoses for:
   - Loose connections and signs of seepage
   - Pinched or crushed lines
   - Weathered, damaged, or deteriorated hoses

3. Inspect fuel filters for:
   - Loose connections and signs of leakage
   - Signs of chafing or other exterior damage
   - Blockage and contamination

4. Check the fuel pump for:
   - Leakage
   - Secure mounting
   - Loose hoses, fittings, and connections

5. Check the intake manifold for:
   - Fuel and air leaks
   - Proper routing of the vacuum lines
   - Deterioration of vacuum lines
   - Loose carburetor, throttle body, or injector mounting

6. Verify that the fuel in the vehicle tank is:
   - Fresh, not stale or old
   - Free from water or other contaminants

7. Refer to the Service or Diagnostic Manual for the correct troubleshooting procedure to follow, figure 4-1.

Backpressure: A pressure created by restrictions in the exhaust system that tends to slow the exit of exhaust gases from the combustion chamber.

HARD START COLD ENGINE
- SECONDARY IGNITION SYSTEM
- FUEL PRESSURE
- THROTTLE POSITION SENSOR
- MAP SENSOR
- MINIMUM IDLE AIR FLOW
- IDLE AIR CONTROL MOTOR
- ENGINE MECHANICAL SYSTEMS
- IAT SENSOR

HARD START HOT ENGINE
- SECONDARY IGNITION SYSTEM
- ENGINE VACUUM
- FUEL PRESSURE
- THROTTLE POSITION SENSOR
- MAP SENSOR
- MINIMUM IDLE AIR FLOW
- IDLE AIR CONTROL MOTOR
- ENGINE MECHANICAL SYSTEMS
- EVAP EMISSION SYSTEM
- EGR SYSTEM
- ECT SENSOR

START AND STALL/ FLOODING
- SECONDARY IGNITION SYSTEM
- ECM POWER AND GND CKT
- FUEL PRESSURE
- ECT SENSOR
- THROTTLE POSITION SENSOR
- MAP SENSOR
- THE MINIMUM IDLE AIR FLOW
- IDLE AIR CONTROL MOTOR
- FUEL INJECTOR(S)

CUTS OUT/MISSES
- SECONDARY IGNITION SYSTEM
- ECM POWER AND GND CKT
- FUEL PRESSURE
- IDLE AIR CONTROL MOTOR
- EGR SYSTEM
- FUEL INJECTOR(S)

LACK OF POWER/SLUGGISH
- SECONDARY IGNITION SYSTEM
- ECM POWER AND GND CKT
- FUEL PRESSURE
- ECT SENSOR
- THROTTLE POSITION SENSOR
- MAP SENSOR
- MINIMUM IDLE AIR FLOW
- OXYGEN SENSOR SWITCHING
- IDLE AIR CONTROL MOTOR
- EGR SYSTEM

HESITATION/SAG/STUMBLE
- SECONDARY IGNITION SYSTEM
- ECM POWER AND GND CKT
- ENGINE VACUUM
- FUEL PRESSURE
- ECT SENSOR
- THROTTLE POSITION SENSOR
- MAP SENSOR
- OXYGEN SENSOR SWITCHING
- O2S HEATER
- IDLE AIR CONTROL MOTOR
- ENGINE MECHANICAL SYSTEMS
- EVAP EMISSION SYSTEM
- EGR SYSTEM
- IAT SENSOR

**SURGE/RUNS ROUGH
UNSTABLE/ERRATIC IDLE**
- SECONDARY IGNITION
- ECM POWER AND GND CKT
- ENGINE VACUUM
- FUEL PRESSURE
- COOLANT SENSOR
- THROTTLE POSITION SENSOR
- MAP SENSOR
- MINIMUM IDLE AIR FLOW
- OXYGEN SENSOR SWITCHING
- O2S HEATER
- IDLE AIR CONTROL MOTOR
- ENGINE MECHANICAL SYSTEMS
- EVAP EMISSION SYSTEM
- EGR SYSTEM
- IAT SENSOR

POOR FUEL ECONOMY
- SECONDARY IGNITION SYSTEM
- ECM POWER AND GND CKT
- ENGING VACUUM
- FUEL PRESSURE
- ECT SENSOR
- THROTTLE POSITION SENSOR
- MAP SENSOR
- OXYGEN SENSOR SWITCHING
- O2S HEATER
- ENGINE MECHANICAL SYSTEMS
- EVAP EMISSION SYSTEM
- EGR SYSTEM
- IAT SENSOR

EMISSION SYSTEM CONCERNS
- SECONDARY IGNITION
- ENGINE VACUUM
- FUEL PRESSURE
- THROTTLE POSITION SENSOR
- MAP SENSOR
- OXYGEN SENSOR(S)
- CATALYTIC CONVERTER(S)
- ENGINE MECHANICAL SYSTEMS
- EVAP EMISSION SYSTEM
- EGR SYSTEM
- ECT SENSOR
- INCORRECT IGNITION TIMING
- FUEL INJECTOR(S)

Fig. 4-1. Typical diagnostic table.

FUEL QUALITY

Check for fuel quality problems such as water contamination or alcohol content. Too much alcohol not only decreases engine power, but also damages fuel delivery system components. Test kits are available to check for fuel contamination.

Stale or old gasoline that has been stored for a long time may cause hard starting. Old gas can also increase HC due to misfires, but seldom prevents starting.

Low octane gasoline can cause spark knock or engine ping and increases NOx emission.

Refineries control seasonal gasoline volatility. Higher fuel volatility on an unseasonably warm day can increase NOx production. It can also vaporize in the fuel delivery system,

causing a leaner fuel mixture. The leaner fuel mixture will increase HC emissions. When the vaporization problem is severe enough, fuel starvation from vapor lock occurs. Lower gasoline volatility in cold weather can cause hard starting and driveability problems during cold engine operation.

When in doubt about fuel, it is best to test it or replace it with fresh fuel of the proper octane.

Water Contamination

A fuel system contaminated with water may cause driveability concerns such as:

- Misfire for one or more cylinders
- Hesitation

L1

- Stalling
- No start condition

The components of a fuel system that has been contaminated with water should be inspected for:

- Rust
- Deterioration
- Fuel filter restriction

To check for fuel system contaminants, a sample should be drawn from the bottom of the fuel tank. If the sample is clear and bright, the fuel is satisfactory. If the sample is cloudy or a water layer is present at the bottom of the sample, check for particulate contaminants as follows:

1. Using an approved fuel container, draw approximately 1 pint or 0.5 liter of fuel from the fuel tank.
2. Place the container on a level surface and wait 5 minutes for the contaminants to settle.
3. Sand contaminants will typically be identified by light brown or white crystals.
4. Rubber will typically be identified by black irregular particles.
5. If any contaminants or water is present, clean the fuel system.

Alcohol Content

For gasoline powered vehicles that are not E85 compliant, concentrations of ethanol greater than 10 percent may cause driveability concerns such as:

- Lack of power
- Hesitation
- Stalling
- No start condition

Severe ethanol contamination may also cause:

- Deterioration of rubber components
- Fuel filter restriction
- Fuel system corrosion

If alcohol contamination is suspected, perform the alcohol in fuel test as follows:

1. Using an approved 100 ml cylinder with 1 ml graduation markings and a stopper, fill the cylinder with 90 ml of fuel.
2. Add 10 ml of water to bring the level to 100 ml.
3. Install the stopper on the cylinder and shake vigorously for 15 seconds.
4. Carefully loosen the stopper to release pressure from the cylinder.
5. Re-install the stopper and shake the cylinder vigorously for another 15 seconds.
6. Place the cylinder on a level surface and wait 5 minutes to allow the liquids to separate.
7. The bottom layer of liquid will contain the alcohol and water.
8. The water and alcohol content will have more than 10 ml of water placed in the cylinder.
9. If the bottom layer of liquid is at the 15 ml mark on the cylinder, this would indicate approximately 5 percent alcohol content in the fuel. The actual amount of alcohol may be slightly higher, as this is not an exact test.

Fuel Line Replacement

Fuel lines and vapor return lines may be formed of rigid steel tubing, flexible nylon tubing, or neoprene hose. Most lines fasten to the frame of the car with insulated clamps and screws. Replace any damaged insulators and clamps. Rigid lines can be replaced either as preformed units, or be cut and formed to fit the vehicle from bulk stock. Use steel tubing only. Never use copper tubing in place of steel tubing. Hoses must be marked for fuel system use or they rapidly deteriorate when used for gasoline. Do not substitute rubber hoses on vehicles that use nylon fuel tubing. An assortment of fittings are used to join fuel lines:

- Flare type
- Compression type
- Push-connect type
- Spring-lock type, figure 4-2

Some systems use high-pressure fittings with O-ring seals instead of traditional flare connectors. Inspect the O-ring for

FLARE NUT FITTING

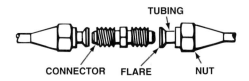

COMPRESSION FITTING

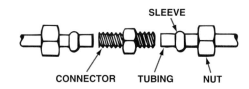

SPRING-LOCK FITTING

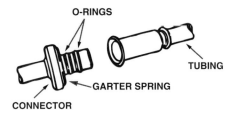

PUSH-LOCK FITTING

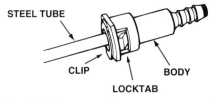

Fig. 4-2. Typical fuel line connections.

damage whenever the fitting is disconnected and replace the O-ring if necessary.

Replacement O-rings must be specifically designed for fuel system use. Tighten fittings to the specified torque value to prevent O-ring damage.

Fuel Filter Replacement

The fuel filter is the only item of the system that must be changed at regular service intervals. Replacement recommendations vary by manufacturer, engine, and type of filter used. Always begin by removing the fuel filler cap to relieve any pressure in the tank. After replacing a filter, start and run the engine to check for leaks. There are two common fuel filter designs:

- Inline
- Carburetor or throttle body inlet

Some vehicles use multiple fuel filters. They can be located in the fuel pump, near the fuel tank, and near the carburetor. The filter closest to the fuel tank is the first to become restricted, and to require replacement.

Replacing Inline Filters

Disposable inline fuel filters are common and may be used on both carbureted and fuel-injected engines. The filter may be located in the engine compartment or underneath the vehicle near the pump. Inline filters on a low-pressure fuel system generally have a nipple at each end that attaches to a length of hose secured by a clamp. The fuel filter attaches with threaded connections on some high-pressure fuel injection applications; spring-lock connectors are used on others. All filters are designed to allow flow in only one direction. Look for an arrow or other directional indicator on the filter housing, and be sure to properly orient it on installation.

When replacing the filter on a low-pressure system, it is good practice to install new hose clamps along with the new filter to prevent leakage. Always replace spring-type clamps when replacing the fuel filter. To change a low-pressure inline filter:

1. Place a drain pan under the filter to catch spills.
2. Remove the clamp at one end and pull the hose from the filter fitting.
3. Attach the hose to the new filter, making sure it faces the proper direction. Then, tighten the clamp securely.
4. Remove the clamp at the other end and pull the hose from the filter fitting. Attach this hose to the corresponding fitting on the new filter and tighten the clamp.

5. If the filter has a vapor bypass line, switch the line from the old filter to the new one, figure 4-3.

Replacing Fuel Injection System Filters

Fuel system pressure must be relieved to change the filter on a fuel injected engine. Several methods are used to relieve fuel pressure; follow the Service Manual guidelines. Position a drain pan under the work area to catch spilled fuel. To replace a high-pressure filter with threaded connections, figure 4-4:

1. Disconnect the fuel lines at both ends of the filter canister with an appropriate flare nut wrench. Use a back-up wrench to hold the filter while loosening the fuel line fitting.
2. Loosen the filter canister mounting bracket fasteners, if necessary, and remove the filter from the bracket.
3. Replace any O-rings, gaskets, or sealing washers with new ones.
4. Start each fuel line by hand to prevent cross-threading of the nut. Check to be sure the filter outlet is facing toward the engine.
5. Install the filter canister in its mounting bracket. Tighten the bracket fasteners, then tighten each fuel line nut securely with a flare nut wrench.

Replacing Carburetor and Throttle Body Inlet Filters

There are two major types of inlet filters, the inlet nut filter and the inlet filter screen assembly, used on domestic carbureted engines.

Inlet Nut Filter or Screen

Remove the air cleaner assembly to access the filter. The fuel line may install to the carburetor with either a flare nut or banjo fitting.

Disconnect the fitting, separate the fuel line from the inlet nut, plug or cap the line, and move it out of the way. Remove the fuel inlet nut and lift out the filter and spring, figure 4-5.

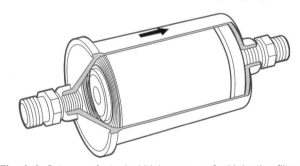

Fig. 4-4. Cutaway of a typical high-pressure fuel injection filter.

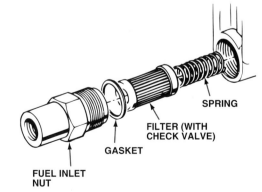

Fig. 4-5. Typical inlet nut filter assembly.

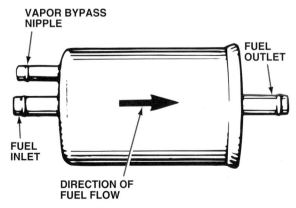

Fig. 4-3. Inline fuel filter with a vapor bypass fitting.

Install the spring and new filter element. Some filters contain a check valve to shut off fuel flow in case of a rollover accident. The open end of the filter must face toward the nut. Fit a new gasket on the inlet nut, or fit two new sealing washers on the banjo fitting. Install the unit, tighten it to specifications, and reattach the fuel line.

Throttle Body Inlet Screen

To replace the inlet screen on an engine with throttle body fuel injection (TBI), relieve fuel system pressure before disconnecting fittings. To disconnect the fuel line, hold the inlet nut with an open-end wrench and loosen the fuel line with a second open-end wrench.

Plug or cap the line and move it out of the way, then remove the fuel inlet nut. Reach inside the inlet bore with needle nose pliers, grasp the slotted end of the filter screen assembly, and remove it with a twisting motion. Install a new filter screen assembly in the inlet bore. Thread the inlet nut in place, tighten to specifications, and reinstall the fuel line.

FUEL PUMP AND PRESSURE CONTROLS

To operate efficiently, the engine must be supplied with a constant flow of clean pressurized fuel. Incorrect fuel pressure and low fuel volume can cause starting and driveability problems. The most effective way to check fuel pump operation is by pressure testing the system.

Mechanical Fuel Pump Testing

Two tests, pressure and volume, are performed to check the mechanical fuel pump used on a carbureted engine. A weak pump may produce adequate pressure, but not deliver a sufficient volume of fuel. Both tests are required to get an accurate picture of pump performance.

Pressure Test

A vacuum-pressure gauge is used to test mechanical pump pressure. Prepare for testing by attaching a short length of fuel hose to the gauge, remove the air cleaner, and connect a tachometer to the engine. If the pump has a vapor return line, clamp it closed. Test as follows:

1. Disconnect the fuel inlet line at the carburetor and attach the gauge hose to the fuel line, figure 4-6.
   The gauge can also be installed using a tee fitting in the fuel inlet line, figure 4-7.
2. Start and run the engine at the test speed specified by the manufacturer. To get an accurate reading, hold the vacuum-pressure gauge at the same height as the carburetor. Compare the gauge reading to specifications. Replace the pump if pressure reading is low.
3. Stop the engine and leave the gauge connected. The pressure reading should hold for several minutes. If not, the valves are not sealing properly. Replace the pump.

Volume Test

To check fuel pump volume, a length of fuel hose and a graduated container are required. Disconnect and remove the vacuum-pressure gauge, but leave the tachometer attached to the engine.

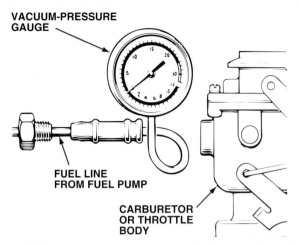

Fig. 4-6. Direct gauge connection for performing a mechanical fuel pump pressure test.

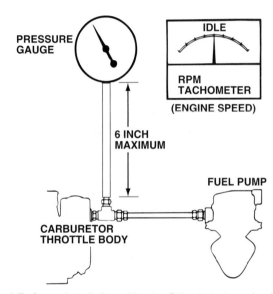

Fig. 4-7. Gauge installation with a tee fitting to test mechanical fuel pump pressure.

To check pump volume:

1. Disconnect the fuel outlet hose or line from the pump. Attach the length of fuel hose to the pump outlet.
2. Place the free end of the hose into the graduated container.
3. Start and run the engine at 500 RPM for 15 seconds. Read the fluid level on the scale and multiply by 4 for a 60-second reading.

Compare results to specifications. Most fuel pumps deliver about one quart, or liter, per minute at an engine speed of 500 RPM. Low fuel volume may be caused by either a restriction or a mechanical failure. Restrictions may be in the filter, lines, hoses, or tank pickup. Mechanical problems include a worn or broken fuel pump eccentric on the camshaft, pump pushrod, rocker arm, or diaphragm linkage.

Electric Fuel Pump Testing

Tests performed on a low-pressure electric fuel pump used on a carbureted engine are similar to those for a mechanical pump. Perform pressure and volume tests and compare results to specifications. If testing the pump with the engine not running, bypass the pump control wiring and supply battery voltage directly to the pump. Also check electric pumps for:

- System voltage
- Good ground connections
- All other electrical connections

Fuel Injection Testing

Pressure testing is the most effective method of troubleshooting a fuel injection problem. Special pressure gauges are required for checking both low-pressure throttle body systems and high-pressure multiport systems. Most throttle body injection systems operate at about 10 to 15 psi (69 to 103 kPa) of pressure. Pressure in a port injection system can vary from about 35 psi (240 kPa) to over 60 psi (414 kPa). Accurate specifications and procedures for the system being tested, along with a test gauge that indicates the proper pressure range, are required.

To provide quick start-up, all injection systems retain pressure when the engine is off. Therefore, fuel system pressure must be relieved before opening fittings to connect the gauge.

Relieving Fuel Pressure

There are several methods of relieving fuel pressure. Follow the Service Manual recommendations for the system being tested. Typical procedures are:

- Apply vacuum to the fuel pressure regulator using a hand-vacuum pump, figure 4-8
- Use a special pressure gauge that has a relief valve, figure 4-9. Attach the gauge to a **Schrader valve** on the throttle body or fuel rail. Then press the button on the gauge to release pressure
- Remove the fuel pump fuse and start the engine. Allow the engine to run until it dies

Fuel Injection Pressure Test

The fuel pumps used with fuel injection systems are capable of producing fuel pressure and delivery volume far greater than required by the engine. For this reason, the pressure and volume tests for these pumps measure values other than actual pump output. Typically, specifications are provided for checking the system pressure, which is the regulated pressure supplied to the injectors. System pressure will vary depending upon system design, as well as engine temperature and other operating conditions.

To test system pressure on throttle body injection systems, tee a pressure gauge at the throttle body fuel delivery line, or attach the gauge to the test-port Schrader valve. Some port injection systems also have a Schrader valve on the fuel distribution rail for attaching the gauge. If not, the gauge installs into a fuel line with a tee fitting, banjo fitting, or other adapter. Install the gauge, start the engine, and allow it to run at idle. Check the gauge reading and make sure the pressure is within specifications. Be sure to check pressure at all speeds, temperatures, and operating conditions specified by the manufacturer. Low system

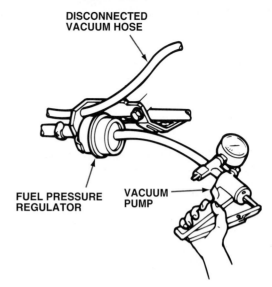

Fig. 4-8. Relieving fuel pressure by applying vacuum to the pressure regulator.

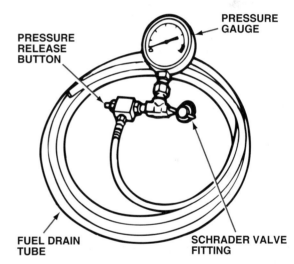

Fig. 4-9. Fuel pressure gauge with relief valve for servicing Schrader valve-equipped fuel injection systems.

pressure readings may be caused by a faulty pump, a defective pressure relief valve, or a clogged fuel filter.

To check rest, or residual pressure, shut the engine off and note the gauge reading. Leave the gauges attached, wait the recommended time, usually 10 to 20 minutes, and take another gauge reading. For most systems, residual pressure should not drop below about 15 psi (103 kPa).

Low residual pressure can be caused by leaking fuel lines, injectors, or cold start valve, a faulty fuel pump check valve, or a defective pressure regulator.

Fuel Injection Volume Test

When a pump volume measure is specified, the sample is taken at the fuel return line rather than at the delivery pipe. Attach a

L1

Schrader Valve: A valve that is depressed to open and closes automatically when released. Used to fill and hold air in tires and tubes, refrigerant in A/C systems, and as a service (test) port on OBD II evaporative systems.

length of hose to the return pipe and route the open end into a graduated container. Operate the fuel pump the recommended period of time and compare the quantity of fuel delivered to specifications. Most systems deliver a quart, or liter, of fuel in less than 30 seconds.

Fuel Pump Replacement

A mechanical fuel pump cannot be repaired and must be replaced if defective. Some electric pumps can be repaired, but most are replaced. Use the following procedures as general guidelines to replace a fuel pump.

Mechanical Fuel Pump

Prepare for pump removal by disconnecting the battery ground cable to prevent accidental arcing, and by loosening the fuel filler cap to relieve any pressure. Also remove or reposition any parts that prevent access to the pump. To replace the pump:

1. Disconnect and plug or cap all fuel and vapor lines from the pump.
2. Loosen the pump mounting bolts.
3. Rotate the engine by hand until the pump pushrod or rocker arm is resting on the low point of the camshaft eccentric.
4. Remove the mounting bolts and lift the pump from the engine.
5. If the pump is driven by a pushrod, remove and inspect it for wear. Use a straightedge to check straightness; replace as needed.
6. Clean all old gasket material from the engine.
7. Install the new pump on the engine and tighten the mounting bolts to the specified torque value.
8. Attach the fuel and vapor lines, reinstall parts removed to gain access, and connect the battery ground cable.
9. Install the filler cap. Start the engine and check the system for leaks.

Electric Fuel Pump

Electric fuel pumps are usually located either under the vehicle or inside the fuel tank. Some systems use two pumps, one of each type. The in-tank pump provides a constant stream of fuel to supply the main external pump. The main pump delivers a high-pressure fuel charge to the injectors. For all systems, be sure to relieve fuel injection system pressure and disconnect the negative battery cable before opening fuel lines. The following procedures are provided as general guidelines only. Refer to the Service Manual for specific instructions.

In-Tank Electric Pump

Most late-model vehicles have an in-tank electric fuel pump, figure 4-10. To access an in-tank fuel pump, the fuel tank may need to be removed from the vehicle. Typically, the fuel pump is incorporated with the gauge sending unit and is replaced by removing the sending unit retaining cam ring. Loosen the cam ring with a spanner wrench and lift out the assembly. Some pumps are a separate unit, but it will also be installed with a retaining cam ring.

Before removing the retaining cam ring, clean the area around it to remove any dirt that might fall into the tank.

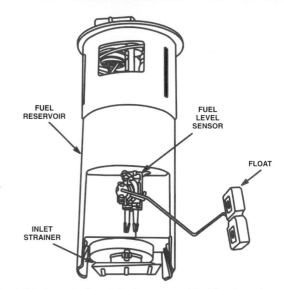

Fig. 4-10. In-tank electric fuel pump and fuel level sender assembly.

Remove the pump and level sender assembly from the fuel tank. In most cases, the entire pump, filter, and gauge sending unit is replaced with a new assembly. If the pump is a separate unit, be sure the hoses connecting the pump to mounting flange fittings are in good condition. Some manufacturers recommend that the rubber hoses and clamps be replaced whenever the pump unit is removed from the tank, and that the pickup strainer be replaced as well. Always install new gaskets, seals, or O-rings when replacing an in-tank pump.

External Electric Pump

Older fuel injected vehicles use an external electric fuel pump located underneath the vehicle on a frame rail near the fuel tank. Most vehicles have a protective cover over the pump housing that must be removed to access the pump fittings and fasteners. To remove the pump, disconnect the electrical wiring and fuel lines, then unbolt the pump and lift it from the frame rail. To install the pump, loosely fit the fuel lines, bolt the pump to the frame rail, then tighten the fuel lines and make the electrical connections.

Fuel Pressure Regulator Service

Fuel injection systems all use some form of pressure regulator to maintain uniform fuel pressure at the injectors. A pressure regulator that is out of specifications can cause hard starting and numerous performance problems. Make sure there are no fuel supply problems or line restrictions before replacing the pressure regulator.

Return-Type Fuel Systems

The fuel pressure regulator contains a pressure chamber separated by a diaphragm relief valve assembly with a calibrated spring in the vacuum chamber side, figure 4-11. Fuel pressure is regulated when pump pressure, acting on the bottom side of the diaphragm, overcomes the force of the spring action on the top side. The diaphragm relief valve moves, opening or closing an orifice in the fuel chamber to control the amount of fuel returned to the fuel tank.

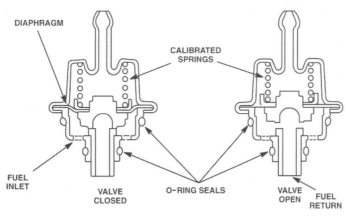

Fig. 4-11. Fuel pressure regulator operation.

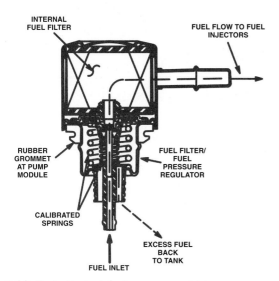

Fig. 4-12. Typical in-tank fuel pressure regulator.

Vacuum acting on the top side of the diaphragm along with spring pressure controls fuel pressure. A decrease in vacuum creates an increase in fuel pressure. An increase in vacuum creates a decrease in fuel pressure.

Example: Under heavy load conditions, the engine requires more fuel flow. Vacuum decreases under heavy load conditions because of throttle opening. A decrease in vacuum allows more pressure to the top side of the pressure relief valve, thus increasing fuel pressure.

Returnless Fuel Systems

Many late-model vehicles use a returnless fuel system. This system regulates fuel pressure utilizing a mechanical regulator without the vacuum assist. The regulator can be mounted anywhere in the fuel pressure line and many are located in the fuel tank connected to the in-tank pump housing, figure 4-12.

These systems rely on the ECM to control fuel flow from the injectors into the engine based on the input from engine sensors. See Chapter Two of this book for more information on computer controlled engine management systems.

FUEL INJECTION CONTROL SYSTEMS

Electronic fuel injection systems use sensors to monitor operating conditions and actuators to adjust the air-fuel ratio to provide cold enrichment, acceleration enrichment, deceleration fuel shut-off, and idle speed stabilization. Most of the sensors are resistors. Voltage signals from the sensors to the computer change according to resistance changes. Three factors can change resistance:

- Air or fuel pressure
- Air or coolant temperature
- Physical motion

Determine the operation and condition of a sensor or actuator by measuring resistance through the unit and the resistance between the sensor and ground with an ohmmeter. Do not overlook the circuit. Electronic problems are often caused by poor connections or damaged wiring. Always test the circuit first.

A **high-impedance** digital multimeter (DMM) or oscilloscope can be used to measure supply and ground voltage at a sensor, as well as voltage drop across the sensor. An oscilloscope measures voltage as a function of time and thus displays signal interference. The average voltage over the span of a few milliseconds is displayed as a trace on the screen.

Component Testing

Before testing individual components on a fuel injected engine perform a diagnostic test using a scan tool. Check the ECM for any active or stored codes. If one or more diagnostic trouble codes are present refer to the appropriate Service Manual for the correct diagnostic procedure. Most Service Manuals include information on diagnosing fuel system problems when no codes are present.

L1

High Impedance: A high level of opposition to current created by the combined forces of resistance, capacitance, and inductance in a circuit.

Two types of sensors, **thermistor** and **potentiometer**, are commonly used on electronic fuel injection systems. Actuators are generally either a switch, a relay, or a **solenoid**. Both sensors and actuators can be tested using a DMM or oscilloscope.

A thermistor is a sensor that measures resistance changes in proportion to temperature, figure 4-13. These sensors have a 2-wire connector: One wire provides the signal voltage and the other is the return ground. To check for an internal open or short, connect the ohmmeter across the 2-wire connector, figure 4-14.

Manufacturers provide specific resistance values for specific temperatures, as well as voltages, for testing sensors. Test temperature sensors by immersing them in water or engine coolant and heating or cooling as required to determine resistance at specific temperatures.

A potentiometer is a sensor that provides variable resistance across an operational range. It is most often used as a voltage regulating device. These sensors use a 3-wire connector to maintain a uniform temperature and current level across the resistor. One wire supplies the reference voltage, a second wire provides the signal voltage, and the third wire is the ground side of the sensor and carries the return current. The sensor signal is proportional to the movement of the potentiometer and is unaffected by changes in temperature. Two ohmmeter connections are required to check the operation of a potentiometer, figure 4-15. To check, connect the ohmmeter:

• Across the signal voltage and return current pins
• Across the signal and reference voltage pins

Both tests should show continuity, and resistance should change with the movement of the sensor lever or rod. However, a more

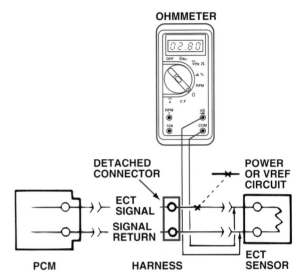

Fig. 4-14. Checking the resistance of a thermistor sensor with an ohmmeter.

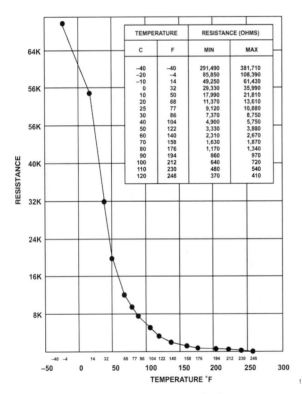

Fig. 4-13. Typical thermistor temperature/resistance comparison.

TEMPERATURE		RESISTANCE (OHMS)	
C	F	MIN	MAX
–40	–40	291,490	381,710
–20	–4	85,850	108,390
–10	14	49,250	61,430
0	32	29,330	35,990
10	50	17,990	21,810
20	68	11,370	13,610
25	77	9,120	10,880
30	86	7,370	8,750
40	104	4,900	5,750
50	122	3,330	3,880
60	140	2,310	2,670
70	158	1,630	1,870
80	176	1,170	1,340
90	194	860	970
100	212	640	720
110	230	480	540
120	248	370	410

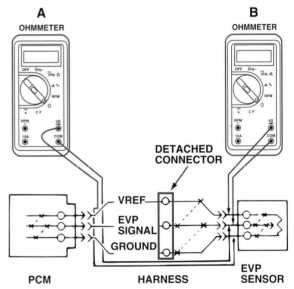

Fig. 4-15. Ohmmeter connections for checking the resistance of a potentiometer.

Potentiometer: A variable resistor with three terminals. Signal voltage comes from a terminal attached to a movable contact that passes over the resistor.
Solenoid: An electromagnetic actuator consisting of a movable iron core with an induction coil surrounding it. When electrical current is applied to the coil, the core moves to convert electrical energy to mechanical energy.
Thermistor (Thermal Resistor): A resistor made from a substance that changes electrical resistance as its temperature increases. See Negative Temperature Coefficient (NTC) thermistor.

precise way to evaluate a potentiometer is to perform a sweep test. During a sweep test, signal voltage is monitored on a DMM as the device is moved through its full range of travel, figure 4-16. A sweep test can also be performed while monitoring signal voltage with an oscilloscope.

A sensor that measures motion, such as a throttle position (TP) sensor or exhaust gas recirculation (EGR) valve position sensor (EVP), can be hand-operated while checking its resistance. A sensor that measures pressure, such as a manifold absolute pressure (MAP) sensor, can be operated with a hand vacuum or pressure pump while testing.

A solenoid used as an output actuator can be checked for circuit problems with a DMM or oscilloscope much the same as a sensor. On actuators that use a multi-plug connector, refer to the Service Manual for test points and values.

Many automotive solenoids are controlled by a pulsing on and off signal. Since most solenoids are digital, they can be only on or off. However, by changing the ratio of on-time to total cycle time, the powertrain control module (ECM) can control how much work the solenoid performs. Work can be performed only when there is current available. On a solenoid that is switched to ground by the ECM, current is available when the signal voltage is low. More or less work can be performed by varying the amount of time the

solenoid is switched on during each cycle. This practice of varying the on-time ratio is called **pulse width modulation** (PWM). The pulse width is the amount of time a solenoid is energized, or on, during one cycle and is usually measured in milliseconds (ms).

The **duty cycle** of a solenoid is the percentage of the cycle during which the solenoid is energized, or performing work. Duty cycle is the ratio of the pulse width to a complete cycle expressed as a percentage. A solenoid operating at a zero percent duty cycle is never on and is not performing any work. A solenoid operating at a 100 percent duty cycle is always on and working constantly. A 50 percent duty cycle means the solenoid is energized for 50 percent of the total cycle and off the other 50 percent of the time, figure 4-17. A solenoid operating at a 75 percent duty cycle is on 75 percent of the time and off during 25 percent of each cycle.

An electronic fuel injector is a good example of a variable pulse width actuator. A fuel injector also operates at a variable **frequency**. The computer changes injector pulse width, in relation to the amount of fuel needed by the engine, based on input from system sensors. A short pulse width delivers little fuel; a longer pulse width delivers more fuel. However, fuel injectors do not operate at a fixed frequency, and their cycle varies with engine speed. When the injector opens is determined by the frequency of the signal, and how long it stays on is determined by the pulse width of the signal.

Oxygen Sensor Service

All current fuel injection systems utilize at least one oxygen sensor. Originally referred to as an "O2S," now it is known as

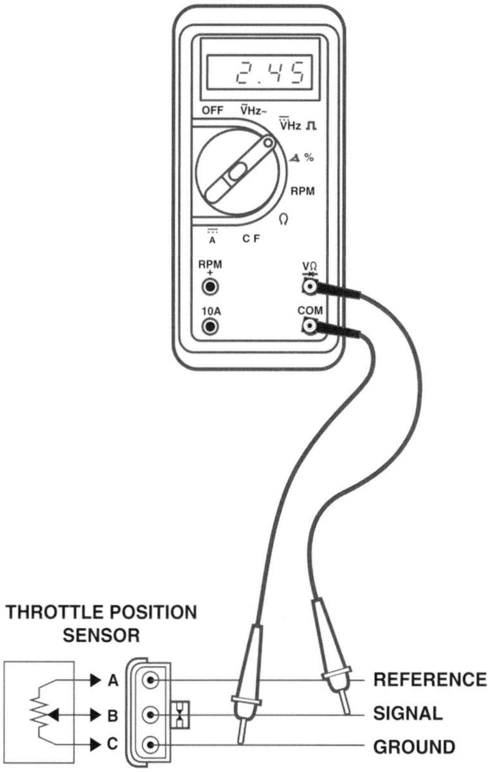

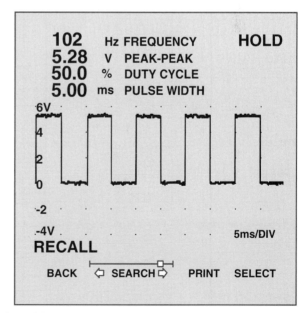

Fig. 4-16. Meter connections for performing a sweep test on a potentiometer sensor.

Fig. 4-17. The on (low-voltage) time and off (high-voltage) time of a solenoid operating at a 50 percent duty cycle are equal.

L1

Duty Cycle: Describes the time of a complete cycle of action, including both on (energized) and off (de-energized) time of a solenoid.
Frequency: A measurement in Hertz (cycles per second) of how often something occurs in a specific amount of time.
Pulse Width Modulation (PWM): A signal with a variable on-time to off-time ratio. Usually used to control solenoid-type actuators.

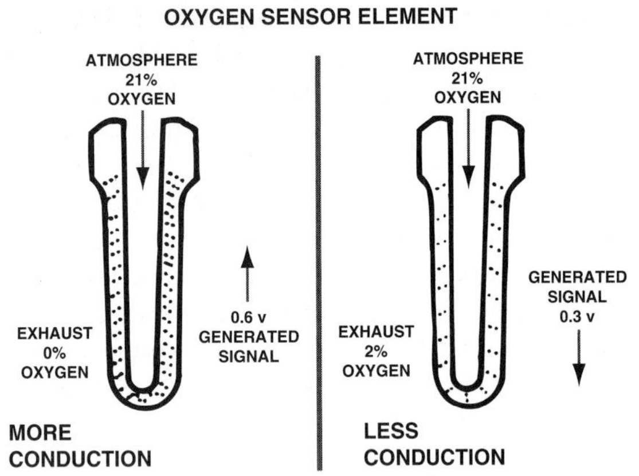

OXYGEN SENSOR ELEMENT

Fig. 4-18. The HO2S generates a voltage based on the difference in the amount of oxygen in the exhaust vs. the outside air.

a heated oxygen sensor or "HO2S." This book will refer to the sensor as the HO2S or simply the oxygen sensor, figure 4-18.

The most common HO2S is made of zirconium dioxide or zirconia. A zirconia HO2S generates a maximum output voltage of approximately 1 volt and produces a signal range of about 0.1 to 0.9 volt (100 to 900 mV). The amount of oxygen in the exhaust, compared to the amount of oxygen in the outside air,

determines how much voltage the HO2S generates. A zirconia oxygen sensor must warm to at least 300° C (572° F), before it can generate a valid signal.

When working on vehicles with an oxygen sensor, observe these precautions:

- Do not obstruct the vent holes on the sensor
- Use only a high-impedance digital voltmeter to test sensor output
- Do not use silicone sprays near an oxygen sensor
- Use only HO$_2$S-safe RTV

Oxygen Sensor Testing

To determine the voltages the oxygen sensor produces, use a DMM capable of displaying minimum, maximum, and average voltage readings, or an oscilloscope. To test with a DMM, connect the positive meter lead to the HO2S signal wire and connect the negative lead to a reliable ground. Be careful not to pull at the sensor wire or to allow it to make contact with a hot exhaust manifold. Also, beware of puncturing a grouping of signal wires with a common grounding shield. Doing so may ground out the sensor.

Next, run the engine until the HO$_2$S reaches operating temperature and the control system switches from **open-loop**

VOLTAGE READINGS			COURSE OF ACTION
Minimum	**Maximum**	**Average**	
Under 200 mV	Over 700 mV	400-500 mV	**None—System operating properly.**
Over 200 mV	Not applicable	400-500 mV	**Replace oxygen sensor.**
Not applicable	Under 700 mV	400-500 mV	**Replace oxygen sensor.**
Under 200 mV	Over 700 mV	Under 400 mV	**Check for cause of lean air-fuel ratio.**
Under 200 mV	Under 700 mV	Under 400 mV	**Check the oxygen sensor by enriching the air-fuel mixture. If the sensor responds, investigate for a lean running engine. If the sensor does not respond, replace the sensor.**
Under 200 mV	Over 700 mV	Over 500 mV	**Investigate cause or rich running engine.**
Over 200 mV	Over 700 mV	Over 500 mV	**Check the sensor by leaning out the air-fuel mixture. If the sensor responds, investigate for a rich running engine. If it does not respond, replace it.**

Fig. 4-19. Oxygen sensor diagnostic chart.

Open-Loop: An operational mode in which the ECM adjusts a system to function according to predetermined instructions and does not always respond to feedback signals from its sensors.

to **closed-loop** operation. Once the system is in closed-loop, the DMM should sample a range of oxygen sensor voltages similar to that produced during a real-life duty cycle. Select the "minimum-maximum" feature on the DMM, then raise engine speed to 2,000 rpm for 30 seconds. Return engine speed to idle, then quickly snap open and release the throttle once. Switch off the minimum-maximum feature.

For a properly functioning engine, the DMM should display a minimum voltage below 200 mV, a maximum voltage of at least 700 mV, and an average of approximately 450 mV. If voltages differ, refer to an HO$_2$S diagnostic chart, figure 4-19. Please note that this procedure tests a system, not an individual component. Incorrect voltages do not always indicate a faulty oxygen sensor.

For more accurate HO$_2$S test results, monitor sensor voltage with an oscilloscope. The ECM looks for the oxygen sensor voltage signal to change direction near the 450 mV midpoint of the range. Ideally, the signal is evenly split and stays above and below 450 mV equal amounts of time. This indicates an oxygen content that is equivalent to the ideal stoichiometric air-fuel ratio of 14.7:1, figure 4-20. When exhaust oxygen content is high, a zirconia HO$_2$S generates a low-voltage signal. A low exhaust oxygen content causes the HO$_2$S to produce a high-voltage signal. An HO$_2$S signal that remains below longer than it stays above 450 mV indicates a lean condition, and a waveform that spends more time above 450 mV indicates a rich running condition. The farther from the voltage midpoint the switch occurs, the more severe the mixture deviation.

Oxygen Sensor Replacement

To replace an HO$_2$S, disconnect the sensor output lead from the wiring harness. Spray manifold heat valve solvent around the sensor threads and allow it to soak for several minutes. Then use a special socket to unscrew the sensor from the manifold. In some cases, it may be easier to remove the sensor if the manifold is slightly warmed. Clean any rust, residue, or corrosion from the sensor hole threads with a thread-chasing tap.

Most new sensors come with the antisieze compound already applied to the threads. When installing a used sensor, coat the threads only with a compound specifically designed for oxygen sensor use and recommended by the manufacturer. Thread the sensor into the manifold and torque to specifications, generally in the 20 to 35 ft-lb. (15 to 25 Nm) range.

FUEL INJECTOR SERVICE

Most automotive fuel injectors are electronically actuated solenoids controlled by the ECM, figure 4-21. Some older vehicles utilize hydraulic injectors, but these are rarely seen on gasoline engines today.

Injector Testing

Electronic injectors are solenoid-operated actuators and can be checked with a DMM or oscilloscope.

Before testing the injectors, make sure that:

- The fuel pump delivery pressure is correct
- The pressure regulator is functioning properly
- The battery is fully charged
- The charging system is working properly
- The ECM is receiving the supply voltage it requires

Current flow in an injector circuit varies by manufacturer and model year. Refer to the appropriate Service Manual for the correct specifications. Many late-model systems use a low-resistance injector in conjunction with the ECM's ability to limit the current flow in the circuit. The initial current flow is high to rapidly energize the solenoid, and then once the injector opens, the ECM ramps down the current. This design is sometimes called "peak and hold" injection.

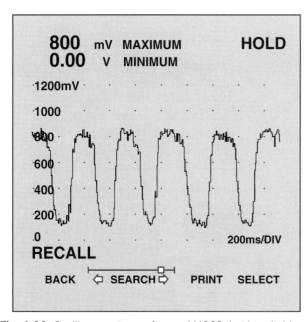

Fig. 4-20. Oscilloscope trace of a good HO2S that is switching normally.

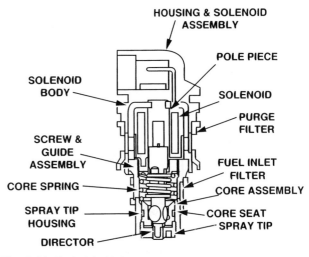

Fig. 4-21. Typical fuel injector.

L1

Closed-Loop: An operational mode in which the ECM reads and responds to feedback signals from its sensors and adjusts system operation accordingly.

The ECM regulates injector activity by controlling the ground side of the circuit.

A weak or defective injector can often be detected by performing a cylinder balance test. See Chapter One of this book. Uneven balance may be caused by the injector or an ignition or mechanical problem. Eliminate all other possibilities before replacing the injector.

An injector flow balance test can be performed while the injectors are installed in the engine. A special balance tester is required to turn the injector on for a precise time period without running the engine, figure 4-22. The test allows the injector to spray a measured amount of fuel into the manifold, causing a drop in fuel rail pressure that can be recorded and compared to specifications. Any injector whose pressure drop exceeds specifications should be replaced.

One or more of the following checks may be specified by the manufacturer to determine if the injectors are functioning properly:

- Check multipoint injectors by listening to each one with a stethoscope while the engine is running at slow idle. If you do not hear a steady clicking as the solenoid switches on and off, the injector is defective
- Observe throttle body injector action by removing the air cleaner cover or air intake duct. With the engine idling, the spray pattern from the injector tip should be steady, uniform, and conical in shape. The spray pattern can easily be examined by connecting a timing light and aiming it at the injector tip. This will "freeze" injector operation for more detailed study
- Measure the injector solenoid coil resistance with an ohmmeter. Unplug the injector electrical connector, connect the ohmmeter leads across the injector pins, and note the meter reading. Then move one test lead to the side of the injector or to the engine block to check for a short. Replace injectors that are not within specifications
- Check the injector harness by unplugging it from the computer and connecting an ohmmeter between the supply and return terminals for each injector or group of injectors. When the injectors are energized in groups, the resistance of the harness and injector group will be less than that of a single injector. A high-resistance reading indicates an open in one or more injectors or circuits. Low-resistance readings are caused by a short circuit
- The injector pulse width and duty cycle can be checked with an oscilloscope. Be aware, with grouped injectors the scope pattern reflects activity for all injectors in the group simultaneously

Cleaning Fuel Injectors

Electronic fuel injectors cannot be repaired. If they do not work within the limits specified by the manufacturer, they are replaced with new or rebuilt units. However, they can be cleaned if varnish or carbon builds up on the injector tip.

Various cleaning devices and special solutions are available to clean fuel injectors. Some require the injectors to be removed from the fuel rail or throttle body. Others can be used to clean the injectors without removing them from the vehicle, figure 4-23.

When cleaning injectors, follow the equipment directions exactly. The cleaning solvents used are very powerful, and if allowed to remain in the system, they can corrode plated parts. Some injectors are not designed to be cleaned and may be damaged in the attempt.

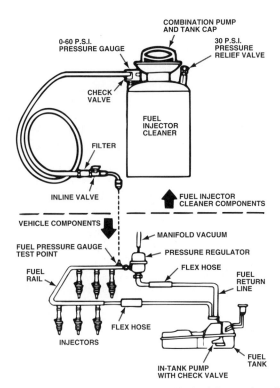

Fig. 4-22. Equipment setup for performing an injector flow balance test.

Fig. 4-23. Fuel injector cleaner used with the injectors installed on the fuel rail.

THROTTLE BODY FUEL INJECTION

Throttle body, or single point, fuel injection is a common feature on many domestic engines. The throttle body assembly houses the throttle plates and provides the mounting point for the fuel injectors, idle speed controller, and throttle position sensor, figure 4-24. A fuel pressure regulator and temperature sensor may also be incorporated into the unit. Most of these items can be serviced without removing the throttle body from the vehicle.

If the internal passages become gummed up, the throttle body can be removed, disassembled, cleaned, and resealed. Remove the unit from the vehicle and disassemble it. Once the components have been removed from the casting, it can be cleaned with a soft-bristle brush and an aerosol cleaner, or submerged in carburetor cleaner if necessary. Reassemble using new gaskets and O-rings, then reinstall it on the intake manifold. There are no adjustments to make during reassembly. Adjusting the throttle position sensor, idle speed, and fuel mixture are covered later in this book.

ELECTRONIC THROTTLE CONTROL SYSTEMS

The electronic throttle control system, which is also known as a drive-by- or fly-by-wire system, eliminates the need for a mechanical cable or linkage. It also allows other systems such as the cruise control system to be managed by the ECM. Stability and traction control systems can also be integrated. The system includes the following components:

- Accelerator Pedal Position (APP) sensors
- Throttle Position (TP) sensor
- TAC electric motor
- Engine Control Module (ECM)

The system performs the following functions:

- Accelerator pedal position sensing
- Throttle position sensing
- Throttle positioning to meet driver and engine demands
- Internal diagnosis

The APP sensor is used to determine the accelerator pedal angle, figure 4-25.

The TP sensor is used to determine the throttle angle, figure 4-26.

The TAC electric motor opens and closes the throttle valve, figure 4-26.

The control center for the Electronic Throttle Control System is the ECM. The ECM determines the driver's intent by the position of the APP sensors and then calculates the proper throttle positioning response. Throttle position response is achieved by the ECM providing a pulse width modulated voltage to the TAC motor.

In the case of the ASE L1 composite vehicle type 3, the throttle opening at all engine speeds and loads is controlled directly by a throttle actuator control (TAC) motor mounted on the throttle body housing. Dual accelerator pedal position (APP) sensors provide input from the vehicle operator, while the actual throttle angle is determined using dual throttle position (TP) sensors. If one APP sensor or one TP sensor fails, the ECM will turn on the malfunction indicator lamp (MIL) and limit the maximum throttle opening to 35%. If any two (or more) of the four sensors fail, the ECM will turn on the MIL and disable the electronic throttle control.

In case of failure of the electronic throttle control system, the system will default to limp-in operation. In limp-in mode, the spring-loaded throttle plate will return to a default position of 15% throttle opening. This default position will provide a fast idle speed of 1400 to 1500 rpm, with no load and all accessories off.

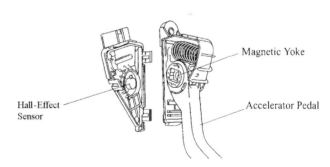

Fig. 4-25. Typical accelerator pedal (AP) position sensor.

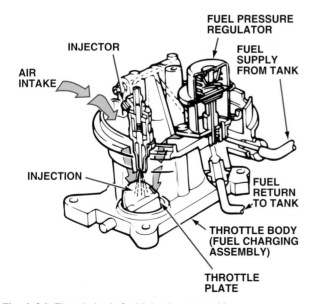

Fig. 4-24. Throttle body fuel injection assembly.

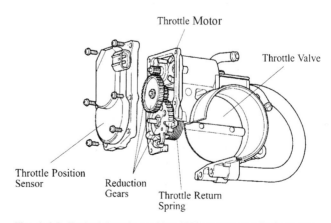

Fig. 4-26. Typical throttle position (TP) sensor and TAC electric motor.

L1

Accelerator Pedal Pos'n (% depressed)	APP 1 Sensor Voltage	APP 2 Sensor Voltage
0	0.50	1.50
5	0.65	1.65
10	0.80	1.80
15	0.95	1.95
20	1.10	2.10
25	1.25	2.25
40	1.70	2.70
50	2.00	3.00
60	2.30	3.30
75	2.75	3.75
80	2.90	3.90
100	3.50	4.50

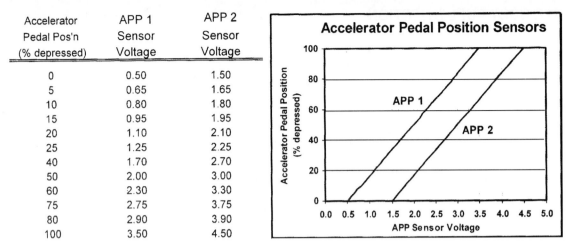

Fig. 4-27. Composite vehicle type 3 accelerator pedal position 1 and 2 sensor voltage chart.

Throttle Position (% open)	TP 1 Sensor Voltage	TP 2 Sensor Voltage
0	4.50	0.50
5	4.30	0.70
10	4.10	0.90
15	3.90	1.10
20	3.70	1.30
25	3.50	1.50
40	2.90	2.10
50	2.50	2.50
60	2.10	2.90
75	1.50	3.50
80	1.30	3.70
100	0.50	4.50

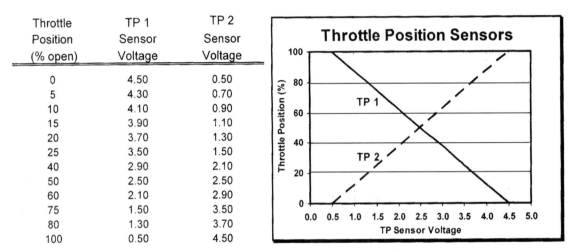

Fig. 4-28. Composite vehicle type 3 throttle position sensor 1 and 2 voltage chart.

- Normal no-load idle range is 850 to 900 rpm at 5% to 10% throttle opening.
- No idle relearn procedure is required after component replacement or a dead battery.

A pair of redundant non-adjustable potentiometers located on the accelerator pedal assembly sense the accelerator pedal position. The APP 1 sensor signal varies from 0.5 volts at the released pedal position to 3.5 volts at maximum pedal depression (increasing voltage with increasing pedal position), figure 4-27. The APP 2 sensor signal varies from 1.5 volts at the released pedal position to 4.5 volts at maximum pedal depression (increasing voltage with increasing pedal position, offset from the APP 1 sensor signal by 1.0 volt). The ECM interprets an accelerator pedal position of 80% or greater as a request for wide open throttle. Failure of one APP sensor will set a DTC and the ECM will limit the maximum throttle opening to 35%. Failure of both APP sensors will set a DTC and disable the throttle actuator control allowing the spring-loaded throttle plate to return to the default 15% position (fast idle).

A pair of redundant non-adjustable potentiometers located on the throttle body sense the throttle position. The TP 1 sensor signal varies from 4.5 volts at closed throttle to 0.5 volts at maximum throttle opening (decreasing voltage with increasing throttle position), figure 4-28. The TP 2 sensor signal varies from 0.5 volts at closed throttle to 4.5 volts at maximum throttle opening (increasing voltage with increasing throttle position). Failure of one TP sensor will set a DTC and the ECM will limit the maximum throttle opening to 35%. Failure of both TP sensors will set a DTC and cause the throttle actuator control to be disabled, and the spring-loaded throttle plate will return to the default 15% position (fast idle).

AIR INDUCTION SYSTEM

A running engine demands a constant supply of fresh intake air. On electronic injection systems, intake air must be precisely measured for the ECM to calculate the correct amount of fuel needed to meet the demands of the engine, figure 4-29. The intake air system can be divided into two sections, upstream and downstream. Upstream would be anything installed before the airflow sensing device, such as the air filter, thermostatic control valve, and ductwork. The downstream section includes the intake manifold, throttle body, ductwork, and any other components that connect

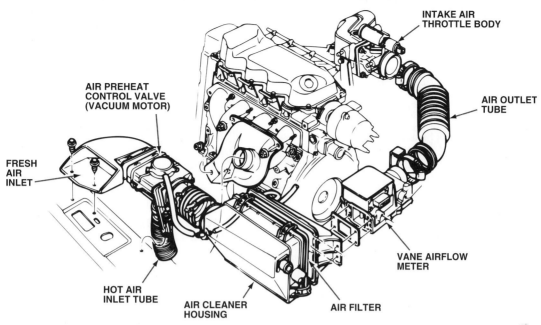

Fig. 4-29. The intake ductwork delivers fresh air to the combustion chambers.

the airflow meter to the engine. Each section presents unique concerns.

Upstream Intake Air

For the ECM to control fuel delivery for efficient combustion, intake air must be provided in sufficient quantity, and at the correct temperature. Problems in the upstream airflow can generally be traced to a restriction or a malfunctioning thermostatic control valve. Either condition can cause driveability concerns, but will seldom set a diagnostic trouble code.

Air Flow Problems

A clogged air filter element is the most common source of an upstream air restriction. Since a restriction limits the amount of air allowed into the engine, it can result in a rich running condition for a carbureted engine or a lack of power for carbureted or fuel-injected engines. Inspect and replace the filter element as needed. Oily deposits on the element or sludge build-up in the filter housing indicate a problem in the PCV system. Inspect the housing and ductwork. Repair or replace parts that are broken, collapsed, or otherwise damaged.

Typical symptoms of restricted air flow include: hard starting, surging, misfire, lack of power, and poor fuel economy. Restrictions that create a rich running condition will cause abnormal activity on the serial data stream. Look for an oxygen sensor signal that stays high and switches slowly. Injector pulse width and fuel correction parameters should be low as the ECM attempts to lean out the mixture.

Air Temperature Problems

Engine operation is upset when the intake air thermostatic control does not work correctly. A cold engine requires warm intake air for efficient combustion. When intake air temperature is too low, engine performance is erratic. Typically, the engine tends to stall easily and will not accelerate properly.

Once the engine is up to temperature, the air control valve must close off the preheated air to maintain operating efficiency. High intake air temperature can cause a power loss, and possibly detonation. Typical complaints are an engine that seems to be running out of fuel, and rough or erratic automatic transmission shifting.

On the composite vehicle, and many other systems, the ECM calculates intake air temperature (IAT) using the variable voltage signal from a thermistor-type sensor. The data stream may include parameters for temperature, voltage, or both. Only the IAT sensor signal voltage is available when scanning the composite vehicle. This is a typical 5-volt circuit, so 2.5 volts is the midpoint; readings should be near this point under normal operating conditions. When intake air temperature is 86°F (30°C), IAT signal voltage is 2.6 volts on the composite vehicle. Signal voltage is high when temperature is low, and goes down as temperature comes up.

Intake Air Control Valves

A blend door is used to regulate cold and preheated air. Vacuum diaphragms, temperature sensors, and thermostatic bulbs are used to move and position the blend door. The primary purpose of the air control valve is to reduce hydrocarbon (HC) and carbon monoxide (CO) emissions from cold engines. Malfunctions can cause emission test failure.

Vacuum Diaphragm Problems

Generally, applying vacuum will open the preheated air passage. So, cold driveability suffers because there is no warm air available when the unit fails.

Temperature Sensor Problems

Sensor specifications for when the blend door starts to open and for when it is fully open are generally provided by the manufacturer. Sensors often incorporate a switch used to regulate vacuum flow to a diaphragm, figure 4-30. Use a thermometer to check temperature as you start and run the

L1

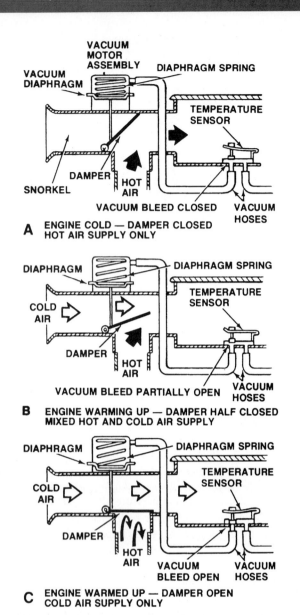

Fig. 4-30. A temperature sensitive switch used to activate a blend door diaphragm.

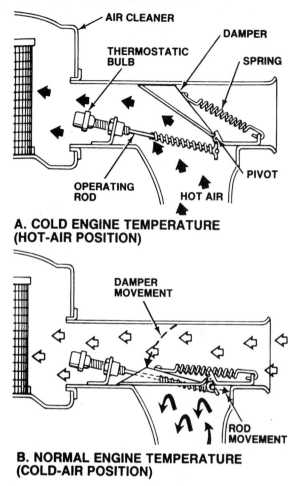

Fig. 4-31. Thermostatic bulb assembly requires a bench test.

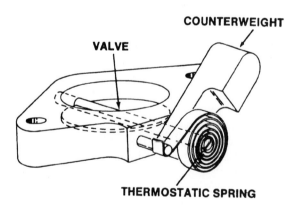

Fig. 4-32. Mechanical spring-tension thermostatic heat control valve.

engine. As with a diaphragm, preheated air is unavailable when the unit fails. Poor cold driveability and high emissions are typical symptoms.

Thermostatic Bulb Problems

Checking the function of a thermostatic bulb, figure 4-31, requires a bench test. The hot air inlet should close off as the unit soaks in a hot water bath. Typically, it will take water temperature of about 130° to 150°F (53° to 65°C) to fully close the preheat damper.

Manifold Heat Control Valves

On some vehicles, intake air is preheated by circulating warm air off the exhaust or coolant through intake manifold passages. Spring pressure, figure 4-32, or vacuum, figure 4-33, can be used to regulate preheat airflow. A thermostat is used to control flow on systems that operate with coolant. With any design, a valve stuck open can cause increased fuel consumption, poor performance during warmup, and increased exhaust emissions.

A valve stuck closed can cause poor acceleration, a lack of power, and poor high-speed performance.

Downstream Intake Air

On a mass airflow system, any air leaking into the engine downstream bypasses the airflow meter and cannot be detected by the ECM. There is no fuel correction to compensate for the additional air since the ECM does not see it. As a result, the air-fuel mixture goes lean. This sort of leakage is known as unmetered air.

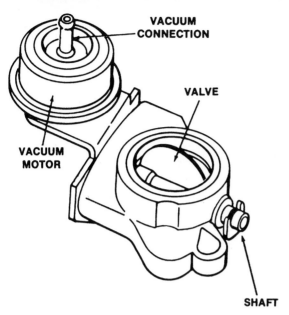

Fig. 4-33. Vacuum actuated thermostatic heat control valve.

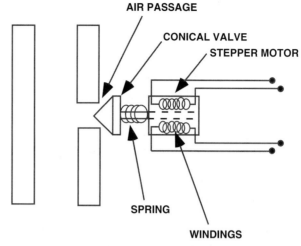

Fig. 4-34. A stepper motor maintains a constant idle with incremental adjustments to bypass air flow.

Injector pulse width may increase after the fact in response to a low oxygen sensor signal. However, the mixture is usually unstable and driveability is affected. Severe leaks can exceed the correction capability of the system, prevent O2S switching, and cause the system to remain in open loop.

On a speed density system, any air leaks affecting vacuum to the map sensor cause lower than expected vacuum readings on the sensor. This causes the map sensor to send an incorrect signal to the ECM, indicating a heavier load than is actually on the engine. This false signal causes the fuel system to run richer than is actually needed.

Symptoms of an unmetered air leak are usually a high or unstable idle speed and possibly stalling. Inspect intake air ductwork for leaks, and also check the condition and routing of all vacuum, breather, and bypass hoses. Most leaks can be detected through manifold vacuum testing as previously described in this chapter.

Idle Air Control (IAC) Valve Diagnosis

The idle air control (IAC) valve on most systems is a variable position stepper motor. The motor regulates the flow of air that bypasses the throttle plate with a pintle valve to maintain a constant idle speed, figure 4-34. Malfunctions in the idle speed control system may or may not set a diagnostic trouble code. Check for loose connections and damaged wiring to the idle control motor and all of the input sensor circuits. Input sensors that affect idle speed can include some or all of the following:

- Throttle position
- Coolant temperature
- Airflow
- Manifold absolute pressure
- Engine speed
- Vehicle speed
- Exhaust gas oxygen
- Exhaust gas recirculation
- Canister purge

- Air conditioner on/off
- Cooling fan on/off

Some IAC motors are basically pulse-width modulated solenoids, so the signal on a running engine can be checked with an oscilloscope or voltmeter. Check continuity of the solenoid windings with an ohmmeter. Many systems, like the composite vehicle, transmit IAC position information as a data stream parameter. Data may be presented as a percentage or a numerical count. Zero percent or a low count indicates the bypass is closed, and a high count or a 100 percent reading indicates the bypass passage is fully open.

Symptoms of an IAC failure include a high, low, or erratic idle speed, and possibly a tip-in sag, hesitation, and deceleration stalls.

Throttle Body Diagnosis

Throttle body problems include air leakage from worn throttle shaft bores or poor base gasket sealing, and an unstable air supply due to sludge deposit build-up on the throttle plates, housing bore, and IAC valve. Both conditions can cause driveability complaints and emissions test failures.

Air leaking at the throttle body base or throttle shafts will lower manifold vacuum. Expect vacuum gauge readings to be below normal with a fluctuating needle. Idle speed and quality may be affected as well.

Detecting sludge deposits, or throttle body coking, may require a visual inspection. However, data stream parameters can point you in the right direction. IAC values will tend to be high as the system attempts to let in more air to compensate for the restriction caused by the deposits. Symptoms of throttle body coking are most noticeable at idle, off-idle acceleration, and deceleration. Complaints include erratic or unstable idle speed, tip-in sag, hesitation, stalls, and poor performance.

AIR INTAKE SYSTEM SERVICE

The air intake system consists of:

- Air intake ductwork
- Air cleaner and filter element
- Intake manifold

L1

Air Intake Ductwork

A typical late-model air intake system is a complex system of ducts, filters, meters, valves, and tubes. When servicing, make sure the intake ductwork is properly installed and all connections are airtight. Any air leakage downstream of the **airflow sensor** can create a lean condition and affect engine performance.

Air Filter Service

The air filter element is the only part of the intake air system that requires periodic replacement. Although change intervals vary by manufacturer, the air filter element on most late-model engines is replaced every 30,000 miles. In particularly dusty areas, or when operated under severe service, the filters should be checked and changed more frequently. An accumulation of engine oil on the element or in the housing indicates mechanical problems. Oil entering the air filter is the result of a crankcase ventilation system malfunction or excessive blow-by. A paper element cannot be cleaned, and must be replaced if it is dirty or torn.

Carbureted and throttle body injected engines have the air filter mounted directly to the carburetor or throttle body. To replace the filter element, remove the fasteners holding the housing cover, lift off the cover, and take out the element. Check top and bottom seals for dust leakage and check the filter material for breaks.

Most fuel injected engines use a flat filter element installed in a remote air cleaner housing. Some of the ductwork may have to be disconnected and moved aside or removed to access the filter housing. Unfasten the clips holding the housing together, then lift out the filter element.

Intake Manifold

During service, the intake manifold should be checked for secure mounting and vacuum leaks. Be aware, a vacuum leak normally influences the engine more at idle because of higher intake vacuum than at higher engine speeds when the percentage of air entering is less. Diagnostic time can be decreased by understanding what to expect of the fuel system when there is a vacuum leak.

Carbureted engines with a vacuum leak affecting one cylinder will typically lean the fuel mixture only of that one cylinder, causing the engine to run worse at idle. The same engine with a centrally located leak will lean the fuel mixture for all cylinders. Note that a "feedback" carbureted system may be able to compensate for the leak after entering the closed loop operational mode.

Most TBI engines react differently than carbureted engines because they use a speed density method of fuel injection. A vacuum leak into one cylinder may also lean the fuel mixture for that one cylinder. A centrally located vacuum leak will not influence the fuel delivery, but will raise idle RPM. Vacuum leaks at the vacuum signal to the MAP sensor will enrich the fuel mixture.

Multiport fuel injected (MFI) engines of the speed density type will raise idle RPM when a leak occurs, except if the leak appears at the MAP sensor itself. MAP signal leaks will enrich the mixture.

Multiport fuel injected engines that use the mass air flow (MAF) or volume airflow methods of fuel injection lean the fuel mixture to all cylinders with any type of vacuum leak. This is because the air induced through the leak is not being metered by the airflow sensor.

Airflow Sensor: A sensor used to measure the rate, density, temperature, or volume of air entering the engine.

CHAPTER QUESTIONS

1. The oxygen sensor voltage readings are minimum 190 mV and maximum 750 mV, with an average of 380 mV. Technician A says this indicates a lean engine running condition. Technician B says this indicates a rich engine running condition. Who is right?
   a. A only
   b. B only
   c. Both A and B
   d. Neither A or B

2. All of the following may be used for a fuel line **EXCEPT**:
   a. Steel tubing
   b. Neoprene hose
   c. Copper tubing
   d. Nylon tubing

3. The purpose of the fuel pressure regulator in a fuel injection system is to?
   a. Limit pressure produced by the fuel pump
   b. Maintain uniform pressure at the injectors
   c. Maintain residual pressure for quick startup
   d. Control air-fuel ratio

4. Technician A says a returnless fuel system regulates fuel pressure using a vacuum type fuel pressure regulator. Technician B says a returnless fuel system regulates fuel pressure using a mechanical type fuel pressure regulator. Who is right?
   a. A only
   b. B only
   c. Both A and B
   d. Neither A or B

5. Technician A says a thermistor is a sensor that provides variable resistance across an operating range. Technician B says a potentiometer is a sensor that measures resistance changes in proportion to temperature. Who is right?
   a. A only
   b. B only
   c. Both A and B
   d. Neither A or B

6. The oxygen sensor voltage readings are minimum 190 mV and maximum 600 mV, with an average of 350 mV. Technician A says this indicates a lean engine running condition. Technician B says this indicates the system is operating properly. Who is right?
   a. A only
   b. B only
   c. Both A and B
   d. Neither A or B

7. Technician A says that pulse width modulation is the amount of time a solenoid is de-energized during one duty cycle. Technician B says that pulse width modulation is the amount of time a solenoid is energized during one duty cycle. Who is right?
   a. A only
   b. B only
   c. Both A and B
   d. Neither A or B

L1

CHAPTER OBJECTIVES

- The technician will complete the ASE task list on Emission Control System Failures.
- The technician will be able to answer 10 questions dealing with the Emission Control System Failures section of the L1 ASE Test.

This chapter focuses on the effect of emissions control system failures on tailpipe emissions and driveability, to help you in the diagnostic process and the ASE L1 test. Emission control system failures are a common cause of engine performance and emissions problems. The industry is placing more emphasis on the technician's ability to diagnose emission failures and emission control system defects. The A8 study guide is available if you require more information regarding theory, operation, and testing of emission control systems.

Manufacturers have installed a variety of systems to control pollution from two main sources of vehicle emissions, figure 5-1. The sources are:

- **Hydrocarbon (HC)** evaporation
- HC, **Carbon monoxide (CO)**, and nitrogen oxides (NOx) emissions from the tailpipe

Hydrocarbon evaporation pollution can come from fuel leaks or from evaporative system failures, mentioned in this chapter. However, this chapter focuses on the effect of emission control system defects on the tailpipe gases and driveability. Analysis of tailpipe gases is usually an early step in the diagnosis of both emissions failures and engine performance problems. The effect on the tailpipe gases is a symptom that provides you with evidence of what type of problem exists.

The next important step in the diagnosis is to think of the powertrain systems, the emission control systems among them, that can cause this symptom and in what way they can fail to cause the type of symptom evident. This chapter provides information on the systems listed in the ASE L1 task list. The task list does not include emissions systems used exclusively on the carburetor. It does include those that are used on fuel injected systems. Also, because of the space it would require to describe all of these original equipment manufacturer (OEM) systems and the many variations of them, this chapter discusses each system generically. However, this generic approach will achieve the main purpose.

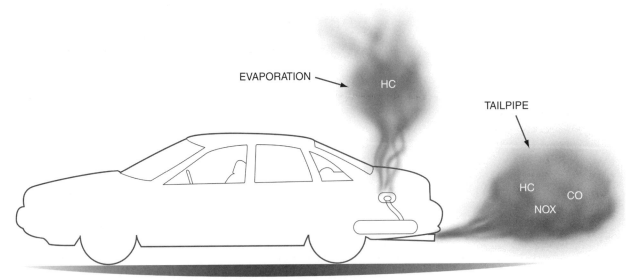

Fig. 5-1. The two main sources of vehicle emissions are HC evaporation and tailpipe HC, CO, and NOx.

Carbon Monoxide: An odorless, colorless, tasteless poisonous gas. A pollutant produced by the internal combustion engine.
Hydrocarbons (HC): Chemical compounds in various combinations of hydrogen and carbon. A major pollutant from an internal combustion engine. Gasoline, itself, is a mixture of hydrocarbons.

Together with Chapters 1, 2, 3, and 4, this chapter helps prepare you for information in Chapter 6. Chapter 6 has information on diagnosing I/M failures using five-gas analysis. This chapter includes O2 sensor waveform analysis, for both emissions and engine performance problems, and methods for testing catalytic converters.

TAILPIPE EMISSIONS AND THE ASE TEST

Electronic fuel-injection systems, when in closed loop, are capable of compensating for minor mixture problems, such as a small vacuum leak or oil that is slightly contaminated with gasoline. Some of the following emission control system problems, when minor, may be hardly noticeable when analyzing tailpipe emissions from a vehicle's engine that is not under load. The effects may be more noticeable on a scan tool as fuel trim data biased rich or lean.

When it is beyond the ability of a system to compensate for a problem, the final effect on tailpipe emissions is minimized by the catalyst and secondary air injection, as long as they are functioning properly.

The statements in the following emission control system list, regarding emission increases, are assumptions. There is no way to know the actual capacity of the catalyst or secondary air injection to further reduce the emission before it exits the tailpipe. However, for the purpose of the ASE test, we must assume the condition is severe enough to have a noticeable effect on the tailpipe emissions and treat the tailpipe emission failure as a symptom of a particular type of problem.

Most emissions problems can be placed into one of five categories as follows:

- Rich mixture
- Lean mixture
- Misfire (partial or no combustion)
- NOx problems
- Catalytic converter failure

To make sure these problem categories are clearly understood, consider the following circumstances.

When a rich mixture is the problem, clearly, it should be categorized as rich mixture. But what if the rich mixture has fouled a spark plug, causing the problem to be both a rich mixture and a misfire? Two problems now exist and must be treated separately. The rich mixture is in the rich problem category, the fouled plug in the misfire problem category, since even if the rich mixture problem is repaired, the misfire would remain until the fouled plug is cleaned or replaced. Also, replacing the fouled plug does not necessarily solve the rich condition.

When there is an ignition or mechanically caused misfire, there is no doubt it should be in the misfire problem category. What if a lean mixture causes a misfire? The basic problem is still a lean mixture. Once the lean mixture is repaired, the misfire will cease. A lean mixture can cause a NOx problem, but when the lean mixture problem is repaired, the NOx problem ceases. Because the basic problem is a lean mixture, it must be thought of as in the lean mixture problem category.

When an Exhaust Gas Recirculation (EGR) leaks exhaust into the intake (or opens too much), allowing too much exhaust gas to flow on acceleration or **cruise**, the effect is a misfire. The exhaust leak or extra flow into the intake does not contain enough O_2 to lean out the mixture. In fact, because it **displaces** more O_2 than HC, the resulting reaction of the O_2 sensor signal is a voltage increase or richer signal. In either case, it does not truly change the mixture. It dilutes the mixture and causes a misfire and should be in the misfire problem category.

Your first goal is to establish which of the above categories the problem is in. Methods for establishing which type of problem exists can be found in this chapter under the headings "Five-gas Analysis" and "O2 Sensor Waveform Analysis."

Each of these problems can be caused by a variety of emissions control system defects. To use the information in this chapter to help decide which emissions systems to check and what type of defect or defects to check it for, you must be able to recall what system or system defects can have that effect. This requires some study and memorization of the following information. This way, for each type of problem you will know what emission control system or systems to test and know what type of defect or defects to check it for.

Memorizing the following items from this text about the emission controls will help you, whether you are trying to diagnose an emissions failure or taking a test with emission questions:

- The emission or emissions the system was installed on the vehicle to control
- The tailpipe emission or emissions that will increase as a result of a particular system defect

Insight
The emission that increases as a result of an emission system defect is not necessarily the emission or emissions it was installed to control. Often, an emission control system failure causes the increase of an emission that is unrelated to the purpose of the system.

MALFUNCTION INDICATOR LIGHT

The MIL lights for ECM-monitored component failures. The MIL also lights when the ECM detects exhaust gas oxygen levels that could indicate that catalytic converter problems may allow hydrocarbon emissions to increase to greater than 1.5 times the Federal Test Procedure (FTP) standard. The MIL flashes whenever an engine misfire is severe enough to damage the catalytic converter. Problems in related systems or components are recorded in ECM memory as OBD II (P0) or manufacturer-designated (P1) DTCs. All powertrain codes should be reviewed and investigated as part of the diagnostic process for either driveability complaints or emission problems.

Using the MIL to begin diagnosis highlights a very important difference between OBD II and I. On OBD II vehicles, do not use the OBD I practice of clearing codes and driving the vehicle to see if the code is hard or soft. Valuable data that can help you find the problem and verify the repair is lost if the

L1

Cruise: To maintain a steady rate of vehicle speed.
Displace: Take the place of something.

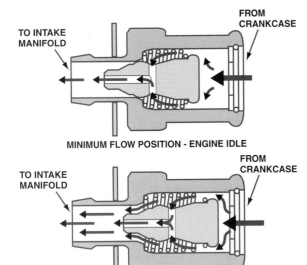

MINIMUM FLOW POSITION - ENGINE IDLE

MAXIMUM FLOW POSITION - CRUISING SPEED

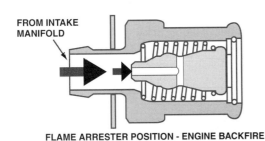

FLAME ARRESTER POSITION - ENGINE BACKFIRE

Fig. 5-2. A variable orifice PCV valve has three operating positions.

codes are cleared. If the MIL is on, it means a DTC and freeze-frame data are recorded in computer memory. Consider any code on an OBD II vehicle a hard code.

Remember that a quick test drive is not enough to confirm repairs. All monitors require the enabling criteria (specific operating conditions) exist before the test will run to pass or fail that component or system. The repair cannot be verified by the OBD II system until these enabling criteria exist.

POSITIVE CRANKCASE VENTILATION (PCV) SYSTEM

The PCV system reduces the amount of HC vapor that escapes to the atmosphere from the engine crank-case. Generally there are two types of PCV metering systems in use, a fixed **orifice** and a variable orifice. The variable orifice is the more common type, figure 5-2. The PCV system can cause either rich or lean problems. When a lean problem is severe enough, it can result in a misfire problem, or in a fuel injection system, a high idle problem.

A rich mixture problem can occur from two different types of failure.

The first type of failure is from gasoline contamination in the crankcase oil. A greater amount of HC vapor is drawn into the PCV system and causes the mixture to be richer.

This can cause the CO emission to be higher, carbon build-up in the combustion chamber, and may affect idle speed.

The contamination could be caused by:

- A leaking injector
- A hard starting problem
- Short driving distances
- A stuck-open coolant thermostat
- Infrequent oil changes

The second type of problem is reduced airflow through the vacuum side of the PCV system. The lower rate of airflow could decrease or increase engine idle speed and affect combustion efficiency adversely.

This causes the HC and/or CO emission to be higher and may affect idle speed and quality.

The defect could be:

- A collapsed PCV vacuum hose
- A leaking PCV vacuum hose
- A clogged orifice
- A plugged vacuum port
- The wrong PCV valve for the application

A lean problem can be caused by too much airflow from the PCV system.

This causes both HC and NOx emissions to increase. If there is enough extra airflow, a lean misfire will occur, causing HC to increase dramatically. The problem has a greater effect at low speed and can affect idle speed and idle quality, and cause off-idle hesitation, or stalling at low speed.

The defect could be:

- A leaking PCV vacuum hose or connection
- A variable orifice stuck in the full flow position
- The wrong PCV valve for the application

Insight

On some systems, the right PCV valve for the application is critical. Some aftermarket manufacturers try to fit too many applications with the same valve. In some cases, using the OEM PCV valve is the only way to avoid incorrect, rough idle, or off-idle hesitation symptoms. A damaged PCV valve allowing oil to be pulled into the intake system could foul spark plugs and cause excessive exhaust and smoke.

EVAPORATIVE EMISSION (EVAP) SYSTEM

Vapor from the evaporation of raw fuel in the gas tank and other fuel system components is a major source of HC emissions. It has been estimated that 20 percent of all vehicle hydrocarbon emissions came from unregulated fuel evaporation. The evaporative emission (EVAP) system traps, stores, and then burns evaporated fuel to reduce these passive emissions.

Fuel evaporation controls are fairly simple, figure 5-3, but often ignored by service technicians unless there is a major driveability problem. However, EVAP function is very important to overall emission control.

Orifice: A small opening or restriction in a line or passage that is used to regulate pressure and flow.

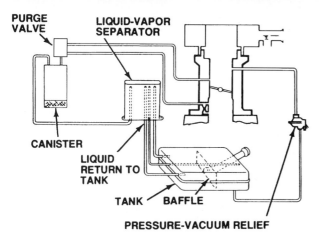

Fig. 5-3. Typical evaporative emission control system.

While EVAP systems vary from manufacturer to manufacturer, most use common components, such as:

* Sealed fuel filler cap
* Fuel tank that allows for expansion
* Vapor storage canister
* Liquid separator
* Purge control device

Most filler caps have a pop-off valve that vents pressure over about 1 psi. A reed valve allows fresh air in to equalize tank and atmospheric pressures when atmospheric pressure is greater. All fuel tanks have a dead space that allows for normal expansion of fuel, and many incorporate a limiter to prevent overfilling.

Vapor storage canisters are simply containers filled with activated charcoal that store fuel vapor until it can be drawn into the engine and burned. The canister is designed to store vapor only, and the bottom of the canister is open to atmospheric pressure. Liquid separators prevent liquid fuel from reaching the canister by allowing only vapor to pass.

The EVAP system lowers the amount of HC vapor that escapes to the atmosphere from the gas tank There are many types in use, some with variable or constant **purge** rates. Some systems have both variable and constant purge features. A few older systems use the crankcase for storage.

Older systems were designed to purge under a variety of conditions. Most modern evaporative systems are prevented from purging unless the engine is up to **normal operating temperature** and the vehicle is being driven at cruising speed. Modern systems are controlled and monitored by electronic circuits, figure 5-4. The following statements would apply to most systems built since the late 1980s:

A rich problem can occur from two different types of failures.

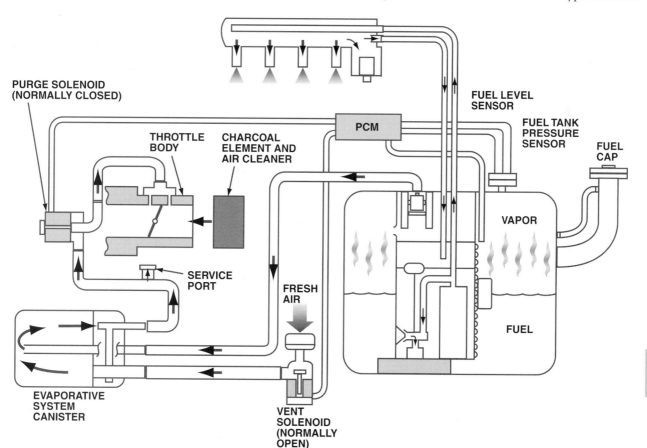

Fig. 5-4. A modern evaporative emission control system.

Normal Operating Temperature: A temperature within the factory-specified operating range of the engine when fully warmed up. Sometimes abbreviated as N.O.T.
Purge: To get rid of or evacuate.

The first type of failure can cause a rich problem from an increase of vapor or even liquid fuel to flow to the intake when the system purges.

This can cause an increase of CO emission, carbon build-up in the intake manifold and combustion chambers, and gasoline odor from the canister vent.

The canister saturation could have occurred as a result of a defective purge system that was not functioning for a long time; a canister on a system that has not been purged in a long time should be checked for saturation. A driver that severely and repeatedly tops off the fuel tank when filling it could also cause the canister saturation.

The defect could be:

- Canister saturation
- Failed liquid protection device

The second type of failure can cause a rich mixture problem because of vapor constantly purging, or purging at an inappropriate time.

This can cause an increase of CO emission at times when the system was not meant to purge and carbon build-up in the engine.

The defect could be a:

- Misrouted vapor or vacuum hose
- Defective purge control system
- Defective electrical control circuit
- Faulty ECM

Two different types of failures can cause a lean mixture problem.

The first type of failure is a vacuum leak causing extra ambient air without the usual HC vapor content to flow to the intake manifold.

This can cause an increase of both HC and NOx emissions. If there is enough extra airflow, a lean misfire will occur, causing HC to increase dramatically. The problem has more effect at low speed and can cause rough idle quality or off-idle hesitation.

The defect could be:

- A leaking manifold vacuum hose or line
- An open vapor line to the fuel tank

The second type of failure is inadequate tank ventilation, causing fuel starvation. This can lead to increased HC and NOx emissions and, if severe enough, a misfire will occur. Other accompanying symptoms can be a lack of power on acceleration and **surge** while cruising. If severe, the problem can cause stalling. A clogged canister vent or a defective gas cap vacuum relief valve could be the defect.

EVAP Canister Purge Control

Vehicle manufacturers have used a wide variety of purge control devices over the years. Early canisters were simply connected to manifold vacuum. Manifold vacuum draws off the vapor to purge the canister as soon as the engine starts. Later systems use ported vacuum. This way vapor is only drawn in when engine speed is above idle. At this point, the

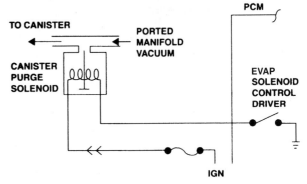

Fig. 5-5. Late-model systems use a PCM output signal to regulate canister purging.

engine is better able to burn the additional fuel. Some systems use a temperature control valve that allows purging only when the engine is warm.

On current vehicles, canister purging is a PCM controlled function. Operation is similar to that of EGR solenoids mentioned earlier. The PCM controlled EVAP solenoid switches a vacuum signal to allow or prevent purging based on engine speed, temperature, and other inputs, figure 5-5. The composite vehicle's system allows purge whenever the engine coolant temperature is over 150°F (66°C) and the throttle is open. When energized, engine vacuum purges fuel vapors (HC) from the charcoal canister.

Purge Control Problems

Problems with the purge system often result in a rich air-fuel mixture due to the high hydrocarbon content of the vapors. Some control systems may set a diagnostic trouble code (DTC), such as P0440 used on the composite vehicle, when an EVAP malfunction is detected. Failure can also set related fuel correction codes and affect serial data as well. The integrity of the EVAP system must be monitored by the on-board control system to comply with OBD-II regulations. When available, canister purge information usually shows up in a data stream as: EVAP on/off.

Purge Tests

On late-model vehicles the PCM controls purging of the stored vapor with a duty cycle purge solenoid, figure 5-6. The PCM does not allow purge during the cold start warm-up period or during hot restart time delay. Once the vehicle enters closed-loop operation and delay times have elapsed, the PCM energizes the solenoid. The solenoid is energized approximately five to ten times per second, depending upon the throttle position, engine speed, and engine load. The PCM varies the pulse width signal to the solenoid to control the quantity of vapor drawn into the intake manifold.

When the purge is in process the resulting air-fuel ratio enrichens. The PCM monitors HO2S signals during canister purge and sets a DTC if no change is seen in the values. Use a scan tool to check for DTCs. If present, refer to the appropriate Service or Diagnostic Manual for further information about service procedures.

Surge: A gain, then loss, of power that comes in repeating waves.

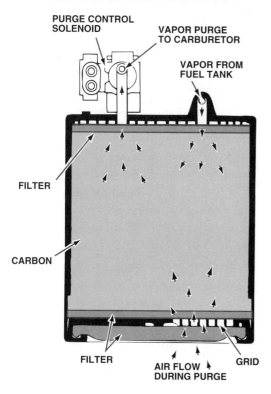

PURGE CONTROL
SOLENOID

VAPOR PURGE
TO CARBURETOR

VAPOR FROM
FUEL TANK

FILTER

CARBON

FILTER   AIR FLOW   GRID
          DURING PURGE

ELECTRIC PURGE VALVE CANISTER

Fig. 5-6. A PCM-controlled solenoid operates the canister purge valve on late-model applications.

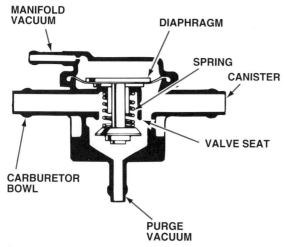

MANIFOLD
VACUUM   DIAPHRAGM

              SPRING

              CANISTER

              VALVE SEAT

CARBURETOR
BOWL

PURGE
VACUUM

Fig. 5-7. A simple vacuum-activated canister purge valve for a carburetor equipped engine.

Older systems, those without PCM control, use a vacuum-operated purge valve to open and close the purge line, figure 5-7. The purge valve also may shut off the vapor vent line to the canister whenever the engine is running. Check valve operation with a vacuum gauge and pump.

Whether an electronic solenoid or a vacuum valve is used, a canister that does not purge properly can cause:

- Incorrect air-fuel ratio
- An increase in exhaust emissions
- Loss of fuel economy
- Driveability complaints

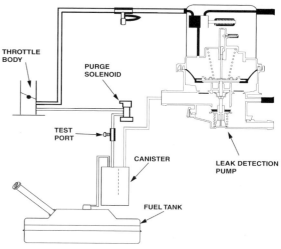

THROTTLE
BODY

PURGE
SOLENOID

TEST
PORT

              CANISTER

              LEAK DETECTION
              PUMP

FUEL TANK

Fig. 5-8. Typical EVAP system equipped with a leak detection pump.

EVAP System Leak Detection

Inspection

Check all EVAP system hoses for damage or deterioration and replace as needed. Replacement hose must be designed for fuel system use. Securely tighten all connections.

Check that the vapor vent hose leading to the canister is properly routed and positioned. Normally, the hose is routed in a downhill position to prevent liquid gasoline from accumulating in the hose and seeping into the canister. If there is liquid in the line, the canister cannot purge properly. This also creates a potential fire hazard.

If you find liquid gasoline in the canister, follow the procedure in the Service Manual to remove and replace the canister.

Leak Detection Pump (LDP) Systems

The Leak Detection Pump must perform two primary functions:

- Pressurize the EVAP system
- Seal the charcoal canister

The LDP system, figure 5-8, contains the following components:

- Three-port solenoid that activates the two primary functions of the system
- Vacuum-driven pump that contains a reed switch, check valves, and a spring-loaded diaphragm
- Canister vent valve that contains a spring-loaded vent seal valve

When the outside ambient air temperature is within predetermined parameters, the leak detection portion of the monitor is run immediately after a cold start. The three-port solenoid is energized, allowing vacuum to pull the pump diaphragm up. This draws air from the atmosphere into the pump. When the solenoid is deenergized, the pump is sealed, spring pressure drives the diaphragm down, and air is pumped into the system.

Insight

In order for the monitor to run, the fuel tank must be 15%–85% full. If the tank is too empty or too full, the LDP will not run.

L1

The solenoid and diagram pump cycles to pressurize the EVAP system. The spring on the diaphragm is calibrated to 7.5 inches of water. If no leaks are present, pressure equalizes and the pump cycle rate falls to zero.

Insight

If a DTC is present, check the fuel filler cap. A primary cause of an LDP failure is a loose or incorrect fuel filler cap.

Non-LDP Systems

On a vehicle without an EVAP leak detection pump system, changes in short term memory and movement in target IAC at idle or idle speed change are used to monitor the system. There are two steps for this test.

Step One

Step one is a non-intrusive test. The PCM compares adaptive memory values between purge and purge-free cells. The PCM uses these values to determine the amount of fuel vapors entering the system. If the differences between the cells exceeds a predetermined value, the test passes. If not, then the monitor advances to stage two.

Step Two

Once the enabling conditions are met, the PCM de-energizes the canister purge solenoid. The PCM then waits until engine RPM and idle air control have stabilized. Once stable, the PCM increments the purge solenoid cycle rate approximately 6% every eight engine revolutions. If during the test any one of three conditions occur before the purge solenoid cycle reaches 100%, the EVAP system is considered to be operational and the test passes. These conditions are as follows:

- RPM rises by a predetermined amount
- Short term drops by a predetermined amount
- Idle air control closes by a predetermined amount

When neither of the previous conditions occur, the test fails and the PCM will store a DTC for the failure.

INTAKE AIR TEMPERATURE CONTROLS

The intake air temperature controls lower HC and CO emissions. They also improve cold engine and cold weather driveability. Additionally, they speed engine warm-up by sometimes providing heated air when the ambient air temperature is cold. This improves combustion efficiency and allows leaner air fuel mixtures to be sufficient when the ambient air temperature is lower than **optimum**.

Intake air temperature controls are sometimes both a thermostatic air cleaner (TAC) and an early fuel evaporation (EFE) device. Two types of TACs are in use, an air temperature controlled **thermostatic bulb** type and an air temperature controlled vacuum type, figure 5-9. Early fuel evaporation systems can be an EFE valve type:

- Controlled by a thermostatic coil
- Vacuum controlled with a coolant temperature sensitive valve
- Vacuum controlled with an electrical solenoid

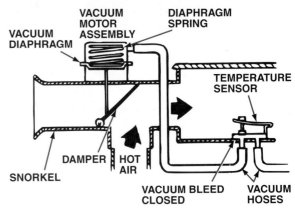

ENGINE COLD - DAMPER CLOSED
HOT AIR SUPPLY ONLY

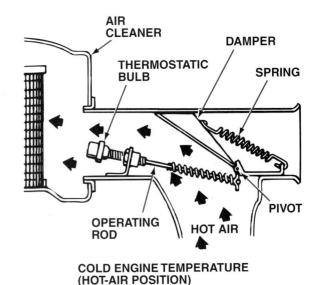

COLD ENGINE TEMPERATURE
(HOT-AIR POSITION)

Fig. 5-9. Vacuum-operated and thermostatic bulb type TAC emission controls.

It could also be an electrically heated grid type controlled with a relay and an electronic control circuit.

Neither the TAC nor the EFE is commonly subject to failures that cause rich mixture problems. However, vacuum operated TAC and EFE systems are both subject to lean problems due to vacuum leaks.

Insight

A sticking EFE valve could cause excessively high temperatures and possibly damage the exhaust valves.

A vacuum leak can cause HC and NOx to increase. If the leak is severe, a misfire can cause HC to increase dramatically.

The defect can be a leaking:

- Vacuum hose or line
- Vacuum motor

Optimum: The best, highest, peak, or most favorable condition.
Thermostatic Bulb: Uses a wax pellet that expands and contracts in reaction to temperature to create a mechanical movement, as in a coolant thermostat or thermostatic air cleaner.

A NOx failure can also occur from either a TAC or EFE system defect.

If either the TAC or EFE heat the intake air above the optimum temperature, they can cause a NOx failure because of the increase of combustion temperature. This can also cause engine pinging or spark knock and dieseling.

The defect causing the failure of either the thermostatic bulb type or the vacuum type TAC could be a:

- Stuck air door
- Binding linkage

The defect causing the failure of a vacuum-operated TAC could be a:

- Defective temperature sensitive vacuum control
- Pinched vacuum hose
- Bad check valve
- Weak vacuum motor return-spring

The failure of the **heat riser** type EFE system could be caused by a:

- Binding heat valve
- Defective coolant temperature operated vacuum valve
- Pinched system vacuum hose
- Defective electronic controlled vacuum solenoid
- Defective control circuit

The failure of the electric grid type could be caused by a:

- Shorted relay
- Defective control circuit

Insight

If extreme overheating of the intake air occurs, it may cause the fuel to vaporize in the fuel rail or line, resulting in a fuel vapor lock.

Cold Temperature Driveability Problems

When these devices do not supply heated air during cold engine and cold ambient air temperature, combustion is less efficient. This causes higher HC emission, rough idle quality, or off-idle hesitation during the warm-up period. Not relating these symptoms to these devices often causes these failures to go undiagnosed.

The problem can be a failure of either the TAC or the EFE not supplying heat during cold engine operation.

The failure of either the thermostatic bulb or the vacuum-controlled type TAC could be caused by a:

- Stuck air door
- Binding linkage
- Damaged, disconnected, or missing hot air duct
- Defective or missing heat stove
- Missing or defective air cleaner

The failure of the vacuum controlled type TAC can be caused by a/an:

- Air temperature sensitive vacuum control device
- Pinched vacuum hose or line
- Leaking vacuum hose or line
- Defective vacuum motor
- Removed or misrouted hot air duct

A heat riser type EFE that is controlled by a temperature-sensitive coil or is a vacuum type can fail because of a:

- Heat riser valve stuck open
- Clogged heat riser exhaust passage

The vacuum type heat riser EFE can fail due to a:

- Defective vacuum motor
- Leaking vacuum hose or line
- Defective coolant temperature vacuum control valve

The electrically controlled vacuum type EFE can fail because of a defective:

- Electronic solenoid
- Relay
- Vacuum hose
- Control circuit

The electric waffle type grid EFE could fail due to a defective:

- Grid
- Relay
- Control circuit

Insight

Problems with inoperative intake air temperature controls often go unnoticed. They are usually only visually inspected during a state emissions inspection test. The systems must look as though they can operate to pass the inspection, but unseen problems go undetected. TAC and EFE emission control systems are not functionally tested during most state emission inspections, and the tailpipe is always tested with the engine warmed up.

THROTTLE BODY WARMER

The throttle body warmer is not considered an official emission device even though it is similar to an EFE system. Its purpose is really to prevent a driveability problem. It is included here because when defective, it can have an effect on emissions similar to a failed emissions device. Coolant passages in the throttle body allow engine coolant to warm the throttle area, figure 5-10.

The warmer prevents the throttle from icing in cool and humid conditions. It also reduces the rate of carbon build-up in the throttle area during all weather conditions.

Carbon build-up in the throttle area is created by condensation of excess crankcase **blowby** gases. When **crankcase pressure** is high, the gases flow through the fresh air side of the PCV system. The build-up in the throttle area occurs because

L1

Blowby: Combustion gases that get past the piston rings into the crankcase; these include water vapor, acids, and unburned fuel.
Crankcase Pressure: The pressure created inside the crankcase by the blowby of a running engine.
Heat Riser: A valve used to redirect exhaust through special passages heating the intake manifold so less fuel condenses in the intake manifold during cold engine operation.

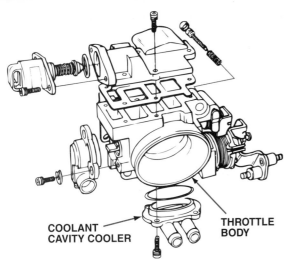

Fig. 5-10. The throttle body warmer consists of coolant passages in the throttle body.

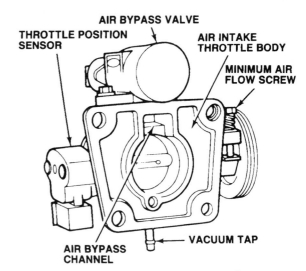

Fig. 5-11. Idle air bypass type idle control device.

the low-pressure area behind the throttle is colder than the ambient temperature. This causes the crankcase gases to **condense** on the back of the throttle plate and bore.

The throttle warmer increases the time it takes to develop a troublesome deposit. Some throttle bores have a special coating to retard carbon build-up. Extra care to prevent damaging the coating is required when cleaning these.

Even when the throttle body warmer is operating correctly, carbon build-up on the backside of the throttle plate and bore is unavoidable. When this occurs, it reduces airflow to the intake manifold at idle speed. The engine operates with less efficiency at speeds below the manufacturer's planned idle speed.

This can cause an increase of HC emissions at idle speed, reduced idle speed, a rough idle quality, and possible stalling at idle, especially under accessory loads.

Cold Weather Problems
When the throttle body warmer is not functioning, rapid carbon build-up and even icing on the throttle plate and bore can occur. This can cause increased HC emission at idle speed, stalling at low speed (especially under accessory loads), and off-idle hesitation or surge.

The system could fail due to a:

- Clogged coolant passage
- Disconnected or collapsed coolant hose
- Bypassed coolant hose missed during an inspection

IDLE SPEED CONTROLS
The idle speed control's purpose is to maintain the idle speed at the OEM's specification. This specific speed maintains idle quality while keeping the total volume of emissions as low as possible. Several different types of controls are used. Some control the throttle angle and others control an air channel that bypasses the throttle, figure 5-11.

Idle speed controls can have a high or low idle problem.

When there is an increase of airflow to the engine during idle, it can often cause a driveability problem at idle and the abort or failure of an emissions test. The cause is the increase of engine idle speed. This increased engine idle speed can cause slamming when the transmission is placed into gear and a **lurching** problem when the brake is released.

When the idle speed is high, it can cause the vehicle to fail an emissions test because the increased engine speed produces a higher volume of emissions.

The total volume of idle speed HC, CO, and NOx emissions will be greater. An IM 240 test will be affected most because it measures the emissions by volume and includes testing at idle speed. When the idle speed is higher than allowed, the vehicle test is aborted.

The failure could be due to:

- The wrong minimum air rate or throttle angle adjustment
- A defective idle control device
- Compromised electric circuitry and connections
- A leaking throttle body gasket

The decrease in airflow causes a lower idle speed. This can cause HC emissions at idle to increase, a rough idle quality, and possibly, off-idle hesitation and stalling.

The failure can be due to:

- An improper minimum air rate or throttle angle adjustment
- A defective idle control device
- Carbon build-up on the throttle bore or the idle air bypass port
- Compromised ECM and/or wiring

DECELERATION EMISSION CONTROLS
The purpose of these deceleration emission control systems is to control the increase of CO and HC tailpipe emissions

---

Condense: A change of state from a vapor to a liquid.
Lurch: The action of a vehicle to jump into motion when placed into gear even though the brake is applied.

during deceleration. Deceleration emission controls are made up of a variety of different systems, such as ignition timing controls, deceleration enleanment fuel control, idle air control, or throttle angle control.

Each of these systems works differently to control the exhaust emissions during deceleration.

The ignition timing control advances the spark timing during deceleration to provide more complete **oxidation** in the combustion chamber. The electronic fuel injection system's deceleration fuel enleanment mode decreases the fuel delivery. The system may even cut off the fuel, depending on how rapid the deceleration is. This leaner mixture provides less fuel to escape to the exhaust. A throttle angle control or a dashpot works similarly, slowing the time it takes the throttle to close when it is released during deceleration. The result decreases the severity of the **enrichment**. Idle air control devices open during deceleration to allow more airflow into the intake, making the air-fuel ratio leaner.

Since the IM 240 emissions test measures the emissions during deceleration, these devices, if defective, can be the cause of a high CO failure. When defective, they can also cause a sulfur smell from the exhaust caused by the catalyst overheating during deceleration, carbon build-up in the exhaust, or O2 sensor carbon contamination.

A failure can be due to:

- The electronic control system entering a "**limited operational strategy** mode" because of a recognized system defect, disabling the "deceleration enleanment mode," and/or deceleration timing advance
- The timing advance system disabled by defective wiring or module
- A defective idle speed control device or circuit
- A defective or misadjusted dashpot

IGNITION TIMING CONTROL

Precise spark timing control during all engine operating conditions is critical for maintaining acceptable exhaust emission levels. Therefore, the timing control system must be considered when diagnosing emission control problems as explained in Chapter 3.

With ECM controlled spark-timing, manufacturers generally provide specifications for checking base timing, as well as timing advance. You may have to disconnect the engine coolant sensor lead wire connector jumper across two terminals of the diagnostic connector or perform some other task in order to put the ECM in diagnostic mode.

To obtain optimum driveability, emissions levels, and fuel economy, ignition timing must vary in response to engine speed and load. The control system advances or retards timing as follows:

- Timing must advance as engine speed increases, and retard as engine speed decreases
- Timing must retard as engine load increases, and advance as load decreases

When ignition timing does not respond to engine speed and load, combustion efficiency suffers. This results in a loss of performance and an increase in exhaust emissions. Incorrect timing will be reflected on manifold vacuum gauge readings and exhaust gas analysis results.

Timing Control Driveability Problems and Emission Failures

Ignition takes place too early when timing is over-advanced.

Piston speed slows down because the piston is still on its compression stroke during combustion. This causes high combustion pressure and inefficient burning, which leads to detonation and high exhaust emissions. Incomplete combustion causes a high hydrocarbon (HC) level with all other exhaust gases within specification.

With retarded timing, the piston is already well into its power stroke when ignition takes place. As a result, the effect of combustion on the piston is reduced. The fuel mixture burns slowly, but completely, and the engine suffers from a lack of power. Expect hydrocarbon (HC) readings to be below normal when all other exhaust gases are within specification.

SECONDARY AIR INJECTION SYSTEMS

The purpose of air injection into the exhaust stream is to oxidize (burn) HC and CO emissions before they exit the tailpipe. Most of today's systems inject air **upstream** to clean up the exhaust emissions only during cold engine operation prior to closed-loop operation. The injection of air upstream also speeds the warm-up of the O2 sensor and catalytic converter.

The system may be of the belt-driven pump type, figure 5-12, belt-driven magnetic clutch pump type, electrically powered pump type, figure 5-13, or pulse aspirator type. Some of these exhaust aspirator systems have either an upstream or downstream exhaust connection, figure 5-13. Some older systems have both upstream and **downstream** connections.

Air injection systems can fail in three basic ways: no air injected, air injected at the wrong time, or air injected in the wrong place.

When no **ambient** air is being injected into the exhaust, the O2 sensor and the catalytic converter take longer to warm up. There can be additional carbon build-up in the exhaust

L1

Ambient: Surrounding or all around, such as ambient air temperature.
Downstream: Further toward the direction of flow, toward the tailpipe when referenced to exhaust.
Enrichment: To make richer, as in adding more fuel to the mixture.
Limited Operational Strategy: A mode of computer operation that limits or prevents the operation of some systems when a fault is detected.
Oxidation: The combining of an element with oxygen in a chemical process that requires heat.
Upstream: Toward the origination of flow, toward the engine in the exhaust stream.

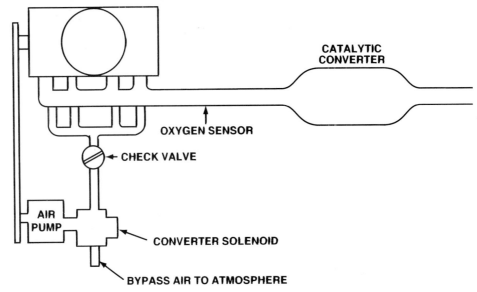

Fig. 5-12. Belt-driven pump AIR system.

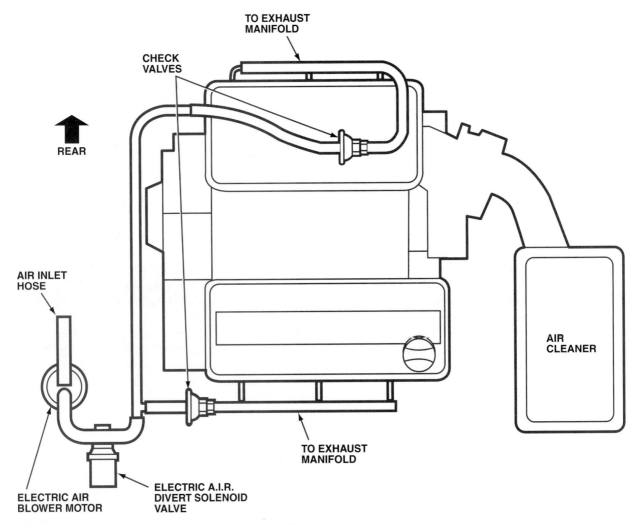

Fig. 5-13. Electrically powered pump type secondary air injection system.

contaminating the O2 sensor and catalyst, causing premature catalytic converter replacement.

If the system is meant to direct air downstream to a dual bed converter, HC and CO will be higher.

The failure can be due to a(n):

- Missing or broken air pump belt
- Inoperative electric air pump
- Defective electric air pump control circuit

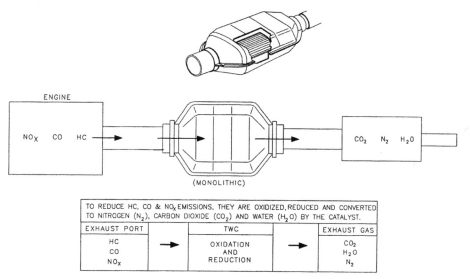

EXHAUST PORT		TWC		EXHAUST GAS
HC CO NO_x	→	OXIDATION AND REDUCTION	→	CO_2 H_2O N_2

TO REDUCE HC, CO & NO_x EMISSIONS, THEY ARE OXIDIZED, REDUCED AND CONVERTED TO NITROGEN (N_2), CARBON DIOXIDE (CO_2) AND WATER (H_2O) BY THE CATALYST.

Fig. 5-14. The purpose of the three-way catalytic converter is to oxidize HC and CO into CO2 and H2O, and to reduce NOx into N2 and CO2.

- Inoperative air pump magnetic clutch
- Defective air pump magnetic clutch electrical control circuit
- Defective diverter or control valve
- Pinched air hose
- Collapsed air pipe
- "Limited operation strategy mode" due to a detected system defect
- Defective or missing tubing

If the secondary air is entering the exhaust during deceleration or heavy acceleration, it can cause an exhaust system backfire, an unusually strong sulfur smell during deceleration and heavy acceleration, and possible exhaust system damage.

The air entering the exhaust can be caused by a defective:

- Air hose or pipe
- Check valve
- **Diverter valve**
- Diverter valve vacuum control circuit
- Diverter valve electrical control circuit
- Routing of vacuum or supply hoses

If the secondary air has not been diverted from the exhaust manifold upstream of the O2 sensor after warm-up, it can cause the O2 sensor to be biased lean. If the electronic control system recognizes the **bias**, a "System lean" trouble code may be set. If it does not recognize the bias, the fuel command will be rich.

This can be caused by a defective/wrong:

- Leaking air hose or air pipe
- Check valve
- Diverter valve
- Diverter valve vacuum control circuit
- Diverter valve electrical control circuit
- Missing vacuum or supply hose

When secondary air is injected upstream of a three-way catalytic converter, it prevents the catalyst from reducing NOx. This can cause the vehicle to fail an **ASM** or IM240 emissions test for high NOx emission. The extra air in the exhaust can also cause the test to be aborted because the air in the exhaust dilutes the CO2 to a level below the acceptable levels required for the automated emissions test analyzer to accept the exhaust sample.

THE THREE-WAY CATALYTIC CONVERTER SYSTEM

The purpose of the three-way catalytic converter is to oxidize HC and CO into CO2 and H2O, and to reduce NOx into N2 and CO2, figure 5-14. The three-way catalytic converter is really part of a system. The system consists of the ECM, the O2 sensor, and the converter. The goal of the system is to provide the catalyst with the correct chemical mixture of exhaust gases so it can control all three harmful tailpipe emissions.

Either palladium (Pd) or platinum (Pt) can be used as the catalyst to promote a reaction in an oxidation converter. Oxidation affects two exhaust gases, hydrocarbons (HC) and carbon monoxide (CO). The addition of oxygen combines with HC and CO to form harmless carbon dioxide (CO2) and water (H2O). Rhodium (Rh) is used as a catalyst in a reduction converter. Reduction lowers levels of oxides of nitrogen (NO_X) in the exhaust. The rhodium strips oxygen from NO_X and releases nitrogen and oxygen in its place. Newer converters combine both an oxidation and reduction catalyst in a single housing.

The catalytic converter has a **light off temperature** of approximately 500°F. Normal operating temperature range of the catalytic converter is 930 to 1600°F. Damage to a Pt + Pd washcoat catalytic converter may occur at 1300°F. At temperatures of 1700 to 2500°F, the substrate will melt.

L1

Acceleration Simulation Mode (ASM): A method of emissions testing that simulates a constant vehicle acceleration load.
Bias: To spend more or less time in one direction, or have a greater or lesser value in one direction than another.
Light Off Temperature: The temperature at which a catalytic converter begins to be effective.

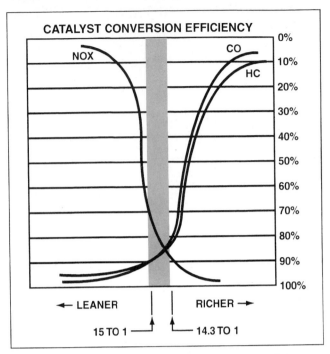

Fig. 5-15. The shaded area in this catalytic converter efficiency chart shows the best air-fuel mixture range to reduce all three harmful emissions.

The converter functions two different ways. To oxidize HC and CO, it needs heat and O2. To reduce (separate the oxygen from) NOx it needs CO. Since the mixture cannot be both lean and rich at the same time, it must be switched back and forth. The catalyst stores O2 when the mixture is lean to oxidize HC, and uses CO to reduce NOx when the mixture is rich.

The O2 sensor reports to the ECM the O2 content in the exhaust. The ECM uses this information to decide what mixture command will be given. This is called closed-loop operation and provides an air-fuel mixture that is not constant or fixed. The mixture is purposely varied so it switches back and forth across a 14.7 to 1 mixture range in a fairly tight band, figure 5-15. The switching makes the exhaust O2 and CO vary. When the exhaust is a little lean, O2 increases. When it is a little rich, CO increases. At idle speed, the complete lean to rich switching cycle must be completed between once every two seconds and five times per second.

Since efficiency of the converter depends on closed loop fuel control and the accuracy and response of the O2 sensor, verifying closed loop fuel control and O2 sensor testing should be performed prior to testing the converter.

Limited Analysis of Catalyzed Emissions

The effect of closed loop fuel control and the catalytic converter on exhaust emissions hides combustion problems. The levels of individual gases still depend on the same variables as previously mentioned; however, an added variable is the capacity of the converter to decrease HC, CO, and O2 created by combustion problems. The gases, when sampled after the converter, are useful only to diagnose extreme mixture or misfire problems the converter cannot clean up.

The engine loads applied during ASM and IM240 tests have a tendency to increase the effect of most defects. The

results of these tests often show a more dramatic change in gases than TSI test results. In this respect, the result of ASM and IM240 tests can be easier to diagnose. In the case of the IM240 test, gases are reported in grams per mile on a trace or graph and there is no correlation between the grams per mile and the shop analyzer's readings in percent and parts per million.

The fact that the converter itself could be the cause of a failure adds to the complexity of the diagnosis. A bad converter can cause high levels of HC, CO, O2, and NOx. High NOx levels can also be caused by a defective air injection system or leaks in the exhaust that add unwanted air to the exhaust, upstream of the converter, after warm-up. The extra O2 prevents the converter from reducing NOx.

Since most technicians feel that taking exhaust samples upstream of the converter is impractical and fuel control verification is so important to accurate diagnosis, the O2 sensor waveform becomes the best window to check both fuel control and combustion problems. By comparing the O2 sensor waveform to the gas results, valuable information is added to help with diagnosis. However, this comparison is helpful only if the O2 sensor is working properly. A check of its accuracy and response should be performed first.

O2 SENSOR ACCURACY AND RESPONSE

To check the response of the O2 sensor, the engine and sensor must be warm. A digital storage oscilloscope (DSO) is connected to the O2 sensor signal wire and engine ground. DSO set-up varies by make and type. Refer to the DSO manufacturer's instructions. The scope should be set to a 1-second-per-division sweep and 200 millivolts (.2v) DC per division screen for O2 sensor tests. Since most DSOs have ten divisions horizontally, this provides a ten-second view of the waveform.

Bias the O2 sensor fully rich by metering propane into the intake. Watch the voltage response. It should immediately climb above 900 millivolts (.9v) within one tenth of a second, figure 5-16. Then shut off the propane and observe the voltage response. It should fall to 100 millivolts (.1v) or lower within 1 second, figure 5-17. The fuel control system, in closed loop, is trying to compensate for the propane. When the propane is turned off, the command is still lean. Repeat the test to confirm the O2 sensor response.

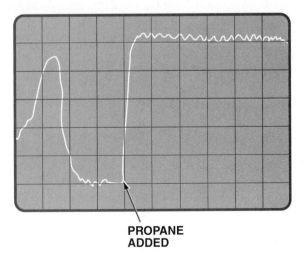

PROPANE ADDED

Fig. 5-16. A good O2 sensor responds within 1 tenth of a second to propane enrichment.

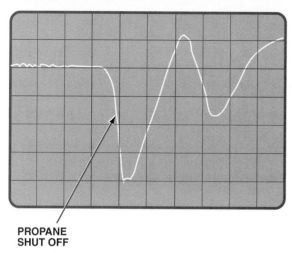

**PROPANE
SHUT OFF**

Fig. 5-17. A good O2 sensor responds within 1 second of shutting off the propane enrichment.

If the vehicle is equipped with two O2 sensors upstream of the converter, both must be checked. When the O2 sensor voltage is fixed or does not respond as expected, it must be replaced before proceeding. However, prior to condemning an O2 sensor for being biased low, check for secondary air injection defects or an exhaust leak, upstream of the O2 sensor.

Now that O2 sensor response has been determined good or the sensor has been replaced, the next step will reveal what direction diagnosis should take.

O2 SENSOR WAVEFORM ANALYSIS

O2 sensor waveform analysis is probably the quickest way to know what kind of an emission or engine performance problem exists. With the DSO hooked up to the O2 sensor, analyzing the waveform can disclose what type of problem to search for. On some vehicles, a scanner will report if the system is in closed loop. However, to check if the electronic system truly has control over the air-fuel mixture, you need to monitor the O2 sensor signal with a DSO.

The O2 sensor's average voltage should be approximately 450 millivolts (.45v) and should range between 200 and 800 millivolts (.2 and .8v). Late-model fuel injected vehicles, with the engine and O2 sensor warmed up, at **curb idle speed** should complete 2 to 4 cycles on the scope screen, figure 5-18. Open the throttle slightly and the O2 sensor pattern should immediately increase above 700 millivolts (.7v), then continue switching as it did previously. At a steady 2500 rpm there should be 8 to 10 complete patterns on the scope screen, figure 5-19.

When fuel control problems occur, as in the following illustrations, a comparison of the condition to the fuel command tells us if the system is fooled by a faulty sensor signal or if the problem is outside the electronic control system. The actual fuel command from the ECM is compared to the expected fuel command.

This can be done by using a scanner to monitor injector on time (pulse width in milliseconds) and fuel trim or by

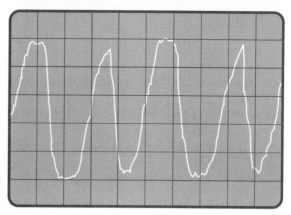

Fig. 5-18. The O2 sensor pattern should show 2 to 4 complete cycles at curb idle speed.

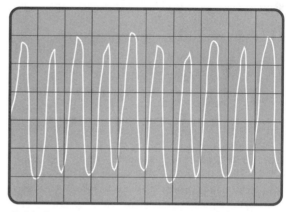

Fig. 5-19. The O2 sensor pattern should show 8 to 10 complete cycles on the screen at 2500 rpm.

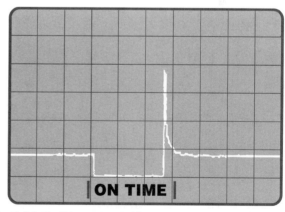

|ON TIME|

Fig. 5-20. On this saturated driver type injector pattern you measure the on time across the falling edge to the rising edge of the waveform.

measuring the injector on time with a DSO. There are three types of injector waveform patterns: **saturated driver**, peak and hold, and pulse width modulated. Examples of good waveforms are illustrated for each type; each caption explains how to measure the on time, figures 5-20, 5-21, and 5-22.

Curb Idle Speed: Factory-specified idle speed in drive.
Saturated Driver: An injector driver that uses no special methods other than to conduct the current required to open the injector, and withstands the resulting voltage spike.

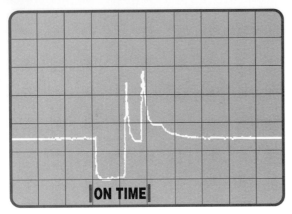

Fig. 5-21. On this peak and hold type injector pattern you measure the on time from the falling edge to the second rising edge of the waveform.

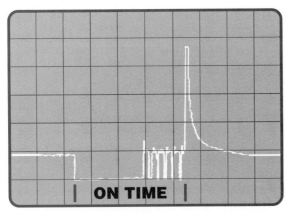

Fig. 5-22. On this pulse width modulated type injector pattern you measure from the falling edge to the last and highest edge.

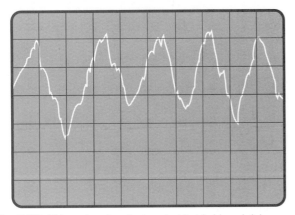

Fig. 5-23. This system has fuel control but is biased rich.

The illustrations of O2 sensor waveforms, figures 5-23 through figure 5-26, show fuel control problems.

Figure 5-23 shows the system has fuel control because it is switching but it is biased rich. The fuel command should be leaner; look for a sensor signal that would cause the command from the ECM to be richer than normal.

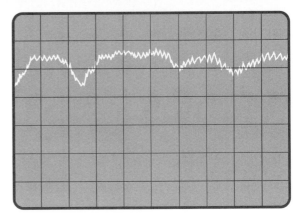

Fig. 5-24. This system is fixed rich.

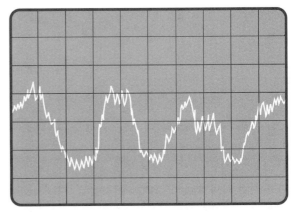

Fig. 5-25. This system has fuel control but is biased lean.

Figure 5-24 shows the O2 sensor signal fixed at nearly 1 volt. This system is biased rich and is not in fuel control because it is not switching. The fuel command should be lean. If the fuel command is lean, look for a defect for which the fuel control system can not compensate, like high fuel pressure. If the fuel command is rich, look for a faulty sensor signal or a defect that would cause the system to think the engine is under a load or needs the extra fuel for a cold engine or cold air.

Figure 5-25 shows the system has fuel control because it is switching but it is biased lean. The fuel command should be richer. Look for a faulty sensor signal that would cause the command from the ECM to be leaner than normal.

Figure 5-26 shows the O2 sensor signal fixed at nearly 0 volts. This system is biased lean and is not in fuel control because it is not switching. The fuel command should be richer. If the fuel command is rich, look for defects in another system that the fuel control system cannot compensate for, like low fuel pressure or volume. If the fuel command is lean, look for a faulty sensor signal or an engine operating hotter than normal.

Figure 5-27 shows a consistent misfire or what is called a **combustion event**. A quick disturbance of the trace of more than 100 millivolts (.1v) is an event. The following illustrations of O2 sensor waveforms, figure 5-27 to figure 5-33, show variations of these combustion events or misfires.

Combustion Event: Refers to a misfire as observed by a deviation in the O2 sensor oscilloscope waveform.

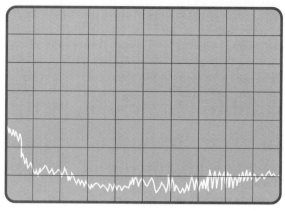

Fig. 5-26. This system is fixed lean

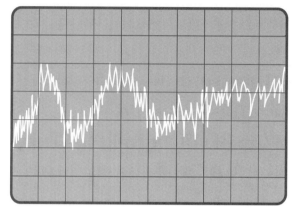

Fig. 5-27. This waveform indicates a constant misfire is occurring.

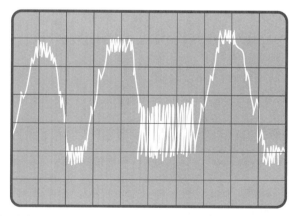

Fig. 5-28. This waveform shows an intermittent misfire is occurring.

In figure 5-27 the symptom is the vehicle has a rough idle. It is only in partial fuel control because it has a consistent ignition or mechanical misfire. The waveform is being observed at idle speed.

Figure 5-28 shows a vehicle that has an intermittent rough idle; it is only in partial fuel control because it has an intermittent ignition misfire observed at idle speed.

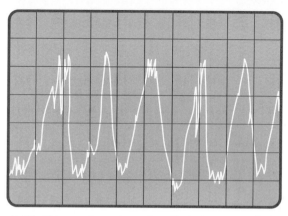

Fig. 5-29. This waveform shows the effect of a vacuum leak on combustion.

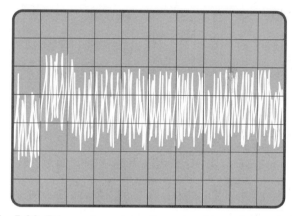

Fig. 5-30. This waveform shows the system has no fuel control.

Figure 5-29 shows a vehicle that idles fast and stumbles **off idle**. The fuel system is only in partial fuel control and has numerous combustion events because it has a vacuum leak.

Figure 5-30 shows a vehicle that has a constant misfire and poor acceleration. The events occur too fast to be fuel control. One of its two TBI injectors is not delivering any fuel.

Figure 5-31 shows a vehicle with a stumble during acceleration; it loses fuel control during acceleration because it has a bad throttle position TP sensor.

Figure 5-32 shows a vehicle that stumbles as it accelerates and surges at steady throttle because it has an EGR that is opening too much and a bad multiport injector driver.

Figure 5-33 shows a vehicle that bogs down when accelerating. The engine speed actually declines. It has proper fuel enrichment during acceleration, but does not achieve fuel control because it has a fuel pressure regulator that sticks closed.

If the scope trace shows the vehicle has fuel control, and there are no misfires and the vehicle still has an emission problem, it is time to check the secondary air injection (if equipped), and catalytic converter.

CATALYTIC CONVERTER TESTING

The converter functions two different ways. To oxidize HC and CO, it needs heat and O2. To reduce (separate the oxygen

Off Idle: Just above idle speed.

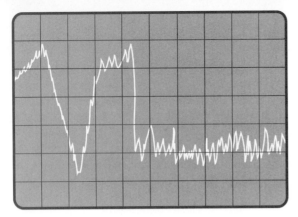

Fig. 5-31. This waveform shows the effect of a bad throttle position sensor on acceleration enrichment.

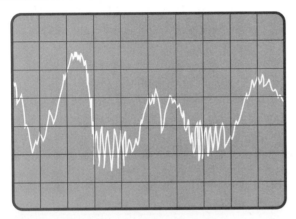

Fig. 5-32. This waveform shows the effect of two combustion problems on acceleration and at cruising speed.

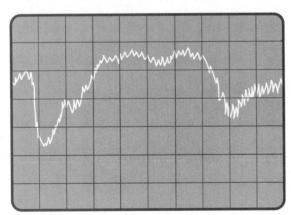

Fig. 5-33. This waveform shows the effect of a bad fuel pressure regulator causing high fuel pressure.

from) NOx it needs CO. Since the mixture cannot be both lean and rich at the same time, it must be switched back and forth. The catalyst stores O2 when the mixture is lean to oxidize HC, and uses CO to reduce NOx when the mixture is rich.

At present, there is no EPA-approved method for testing catalytic converters. It is recommended that more than one of the following test methods be used prior to condemning or replacing a catalytic converter.

The only accurate way to diagnose a catalytic converter is by comparing actual engine out gases (pre-cat) to post-cat gases. Kits are available to drill a small hole in front of the converter, attach a sampling probe to a 5-gas analyzer, and analyze the readings.

Visual Inspection

Begin with a visual inspection. Look for large dents, tears, or punctures. Look for signs of overheating such as discoloration or scorching on the converter or under the vehicle.

Also check for exhaust leaks in the upstream exhaust pipes and connections; air leaks can prevent the catalyst's reduction of NOx.

Check Secondary Air Injection

Follow the OEM system performance test to make sure the secondary air injection system is operating as designed. Check the system for any unwanted air leaks to the converter.

Tap Test

Tap on the converter with a rubber mallet and listen for a rattle or a hollow sound. If it rattles or sounds hollow, the catalyst may be broken or missing. Remove the converter and inspect to confirm. Replace the converter if necessary.

Temperature Test

This test is pretty much a **go/no-go test** and is not to be relied upon by itself. For this test, you need an accurate **digital pyrometer** that can read temperatures over 500° F, figure 5-34.

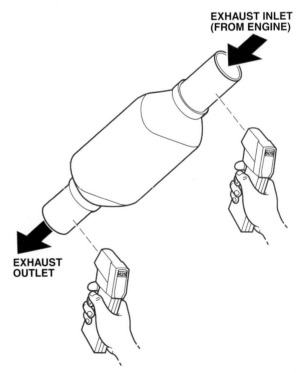

EXHAUST INLET
(FROM ENGINE)

EXHAUST
OUTLET

Fig. 5-34. Performing the catalytic converter temperature test with a digital pyrometer. Temperature should be 5% higher at outlet than inlet.

Digital Pyrometer: A non-contact thermometer that displays temperature digitally.
Go/No-Go Test: A test to check whether or not something works, not how well it functions.

Drive the vehicle on the road or a dynamometer with a load applied to warm up the combustion chamber, the O2 sensor, and the converter.

While running the engine at 2000 rpm with no load, measure the temperature as close to the converter inlet as possible. Abort the test if the surface temperature is not 300° F or higher, because the results will not be reliable. Now check the exhaust temperature just past the converter outlet. The temperature at the outlet should be at least 5% hotter than the inlet temperature. As an example, if inlet is 600°F, then outlet temperature should be 30°F hotter, or 630°F. This test is not 100% accurate. There have been experiments that show the converter actually cools down when all it is converting is NOx and sometimes there is no change in temperatures when it is only converting CO.

If the result is 5% or more above the inlet temperature, you know the converter is working but not how efficiently. If the outlet temperature is 200°F more than the inlet, it is probable that the converter is overheating. Recheck for misfire, rich mixture, or secondary air injection defects. If the result is not 5% hotter, the converter fails. Remember to confirm your diagnosis using other converter tests before replacing the converter.

Catalytic Converter Monitor

The catalytic converter monitor checks the converter's efficiency by observing the upstream and downstream HO2S signals. In closed loop operation the upstream HO2S signal switches frequently between 200 mV and 900 mV. If the converter is efficient the downstream HO2S signal voltage should have little fluctuation and tend to stay above the 450 mV threshold, figure 5-35.

When the catalyst performance becomes inefficient, less oxygen is used in the converter and flows past the downstream HO2S. When this happens it causes voltage fluctuations and a lower voltage bias in the downstream HO2S, figure 5-36. On

CATALYST MONITOR EFFICIENCY TEST

PRE-CATALYST HO2S1

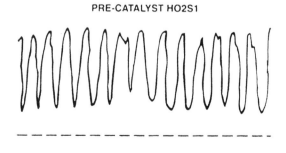

POST-CATALYST HO2S2

GOOD CATALYST

MONITOR TEST PASSED

Fig. 5-35. When the catalyst is working correctly, oxygen is used for both oxidation and reduction in the converter. Fluctuation of the remaining post-converter oxygen is minimal.

CATALYST MONITOR EFFICIENCY TEST

PRE-CATALYST HO2S1

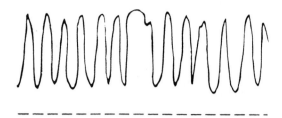

POST-CATALYST HO2S2

DEGRADED CATALYST

MONITOR TEST FAILED

Fig. 5-36. As the catalyst performance degrades, less oxygen is used. The amount of post-converter oxygen begins to fluctuate and, consequently, the post-converter HO2S voltage fluctuation increases.

the composite vehicle, when the downstream HO2S voltage signal begins to fluctuate within about 70% of the upstream HO2S signal on two consecutive trips, the ECM records freeze frame data, sets a trouble code, and actuates the MIL.

HC and CO2 Converter Test

This test is based on the concept that a warmed-up converter will produce more than 12% CO2, when supplied with enough raw fuel. Since we do not actually know the volume of fuel delivered to the converter, HC must be monitored during the test.

To begin the test, run the vehicle until it reaches normal operating temperature. Then place the analyzer sample probe in the tailpipe. Cruise the engine at 2000 rpm for two minutes. This ensures the converter is fully warmed. Turn the ignition key OFF and immediately disable the ignition. It is a good idea to plan ahead so the converter doesn't cool down while you find a way to disable the ignition.

Keep in mind, raw fuel must be delivered to the exhaust. Disabling the ignition by disconnecting primary wires may prevent the injectors from delivering fuel and defeat the test. Check a service manual as necessary. Crank the engine for 10 seconds and record the highest HC and CO2 readings.

If the recorded HC reading is below 500 ppm, the converter passes. If the recorded HC is higher than 500 ppm, it may be due to excess fuel. Look at the recorded CO2 reading. If the recorded CO2 reading is above 12%, the converter still passes. If the recorded CO2 reading is below 12%, the converter fails.

Tailpipe O2 Converter Test for Feedback Vehicles

This test uses the exhaust oxygen reading to verify converter operation. An analyzer that has a BAR 90 or higher specification and has a fast screen refresh rate is necessary. Analyzers that do not meet these requirements will give inaccurate test results. Be sure the analyzer is calibrated properly before performing the O2 test.

The vehicle must have no combustion or fuel control problems. There must be no leaks in the exhaust system. Any leaks letting air into the exhaust will dilute the exhaust sample with ambient O2 and make the test results false.

Start by disabling the secondary air injection (if equipped), making sure there are no air leaks into the exhaust. Warm the engine to normal operating temperature and verify closed loop. Run the engine at 2000 rpm, and observe the exhaust gas readings on the analyzer. When the converter reaches light-off temperature the gases will clean up. Continue to wait until the gases stabilize.

With the gases stabilized, the O2 should be at or near 0%. If it is higher, check the CO%. If there is CO, the converter is not operating properly. Confirm your finding with the snap portion of the test. If the CO is 0% the mixture may be too lean to test the converter; meter propane into the intake until the CO is about .5%. If the O2 drops to 0%, the converter is not operating properly.

Once stabilized, snap the throttle, snapping it open wide and immediately allowing it to return to idle. Record a movie of the snap on the analyzer and play it back or observe the CO on an analyzer. The reading will increase momentarily after the snap. When it peaks, freeze the screen and/or immediately look at the O2. It should not be above 1.2% when CO peaks. If the O2 remains below 1.2%, the converter passes. If the O2 rises to about 1.2%, the converter is weak. If the O2 rises above 1.2%, the converter is bad.

Although this test is most often reliable, one test alone is not acceptable to the EPA; use another test to confirm these results.

Tear-Down Inspection

One sure way to know a converter is defective is a tear down inspection. This means removing the pipes from the converter and looking inside. If you see the converter is clogged, broken, or empty, you know without doubt it is defective.

If you find the converter is empty, be sure to check downstream in the pipes and muffler for pieces of the burnt monolith. If it is not yet a problem, it may be later. The piece downstream may cause high exhaust backpressure, when it is dislodged or somehow moves and blocks exhaust flow.

REPLACING A BAD CONVERTER

Keep in mind that if the converter failed, unless it was **damaged** by a **road hazard**, a combustion problem probably caused it to fail. Be sure the problem is repaired prior to replacing the converter. Check the vehicle's factory emissions warranty; models 1995 and later have an 8-year 80,000-mile warranty. If you replace the converter be sure to follow the EPA guidelines for documenting the reason for replacement. The installer must retain the documentation for six months. The old converter must be labeled and kept for 15 days from the date of installation.

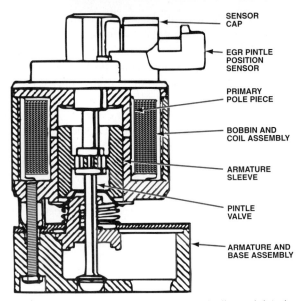

Fig. 5-37. GM's linear EGR valve is electronically modulated.

SENSOR CAP

EGR PINTLE POSITION SENSOR

PRIMARY POLE PIECE

BOBBIN AND COIL ASSEMBLY

ARMATURE SLEEVE

PINTLE VALVE

ARMATURE AND BASE ASSEMBLY

EXHAUST GAS RECIRCULATION (EGR) SYSTEM

The EGR system reduces the amount of NOx produced in the combustion chamber. The EGR does this by letting a controlled amount of exhaust gas into the intake to dilute the air-fuel mixture. The dilution lowers the combustion temperature and thereby lowers NOx production.

There are many types of systems and all are different in some way: vacuum-operated coolant temperature controlled, vacuum with exhaust backpressure control and modulation, and vacuum electronically controlled and **modulated**, electronic digital and linear computer controlled, figure 5-37. All require just three things to operate correctly: The correct signal arrives to open the valve, the valve itself operates correctly, and the ports are not clogged with carbon.

All EGR valve systems are subject to some type of vacuum leak.

This can be caused by the:

- EGR valve itself
- Valve gasket
- Vacuum diaphragm
- Vacuum hose or line
- Vacuum control device

All of the above leaks can cause a leaner mixture. See Chapter 1 for checking vacuum leaks.

When the EGR fails or operates only partially, engine pings or knock on mild acceleration can occur. NOx emission will also increase from the increased combustion temperature.

This can be caused by a(n):

- Inoperative EGR valve
- Carbon-restricted EGR port

Modulated: A more sophisticated method of controlling an actuator, not just an off and on signal, controls how much work is done.
Road Hazard Damage: Damage to a component caused by rocks, curbs, speed bumps, etc.

Fuel Control Problem Diagnosis

Exhaust condition:	Fuel command:	Path:
Rich	Rich	Verify sensor signals using the appropriate response chart specifications.
Rich	Lean	Check for gasoline-contaminated oil, defective EVAP system, fuel pressure regulator leaking gasoline into the vacuum line, high fuel pressure, too much EGR flow.
Lean	Lean	Verify sensor signals using the appropriate response chart specifications.
Lean	Rich	Check for an unmeasured intake air leak, vacuum leak, low fuel pressure or volume, restricted injectors.

- Defective vacuum supply
- Defective vacuum control device
- Defective electrical control circuit
- Inoperative solenoid

If the EGR opens too soon or too much, the result is mixture dilution and misfire during acceleration and cruise. The stumble and surging can be worse on acceleration, particularly under a load. The misfire can raise the HC emissions high enough to fail an emissions test.

The problem can be caused by:

- Increased exhaust system backpressure
- A defective EGR backpressure transducer or modulator
- A restricted system vacuum vent
- Installation of the wrong EGR
- Installation of the wrong calibration orifice
- The wrong EGR for the application

When the EGR valve is allowing exhaust gas to leak into the intake at idle speed, the result can be rough idle quality and stalling as well as increased HC emission from the misfire, but without the usual accompanying increase of O_2 emissions. These problems do not have as much effect as speed increases.

The cause can be a:

- Defective EGR valve
- Plugged vacuum vent

- Defective vacuum control solenoid
- Defective vacuum control vent solenoid
- Pinched vacuum hose
- Misrouted vacuum hose
- Control circuit electrical short
- Defective backpressure transducer
- Missing vacuum restrictor
- Manifold vacuum supply connected to a ported system

Insight

Theory says tailpipe O_2 emission does not increase as much in this circumstance as it does during other types of misfire problems. Because of the EGR's exhaust gas dilution of the air-fuel mixture, there is not as much increase in exhaust O_2.

However, the theory does not take into account the existing O_2 that enters the exhaust from the misfiring cylinders. Nor does it take into account the effect of the catalyst to use any extra O_2 to oxidize the exhaust HC coming from the misfire. The result is that the gases sampled at the tailpipe are masked into a nearly indefinable state.

When you are confronted by a test question that has a gas analyzer test result showing a higher than normal HC reading without the normal O_2 rise from the misfire, the current pat answer seems to be "the EGR did it."

L1

CHAPTER QUESTIONS

1. Technician A says the purpose of air injection into the exhaust stream is to oxidize HC and CO emissions before they exit the tailpipe.
Technician B says injection of air upstream will speed the warm up of the catalytic converter.
Who is right?
   a. A only
   b. B only
   c. Both A and B
   d. Neither A nor B

2. The purpose of an EGR system is to slow combustion and lower peak temperature in order to reduce:
   a. Carbon dioxide (CO2)
   b. Oxides of Nitrogen (NOx)
   c. Hydrocarbons (HC)
   d. Carbon monoxide (CO)

3. A vehicle is in the shop with a lean fuel mixture problem.
Technician A says the problem can be caused by a leaking vacuum PCV hose allowing too much air flow through the PCV system.
Technician B says the problem may be caused by gasoline contamination in the crankcase oil.
Who is right?
   a. A only
   b. B only
   c. Both A and B
   d. Neither A nor B

4. The purpose of the three-way catalytic converter is to reduce which of the following emissions?
   a. HC, CO, and O2
   b. HC, CO, and CO2
   c. HC, CO, and NOx
   d. HC, CO2, and NOx

5. Technician A says an LDP (Leak Detection Pump) pressurizes the EVAP system and seals the charcoal canister.
Technician B says the LDP de-pressurizes the EVAP system and seals the charcoal canister.
Who is right?
   a. A only
   b. B only
   c. Both A and B
   d. Neither A nor B

6. A pulse type AIR system is driven by a/an?
   a. Drive belt
   b. Electric motor
   c. Low pressure pulses in the exhaust system
   d. Hydraulically

7. The catalytic converter has a light-off temperature of approximately?
   a. 5°F
   b. 50°F
   c. 500°F
   d. 5000°F

8. Technician A says the purpose of deceleration emission control devices is to control the increase of carbon dioxide (CO2) and hydrocarbon (HC) tailpipe emissions during deceleration.
Technician B says the purpose of deceleration emission control devices is to control the increase of carbon monoxide (CO) and hydrocarbon (HC) tailpipe emissions during deceleration.
Who is right?
   a. A only
   b. B only
   c. Both A and B
   d. Neither A nor B

9. Technician A says the throttle body warmer reduces the rate of carbon build-up in the throttle areas.
Technician B says the throttle body warmer prevents the throttle from icing under cool and humid conditions.
Who is right?
   a. A only
   b. B only
   c. Both A and B
   d. Neither A nor B

10. A vehicle's engine hesitates on acceleration and surges at cruising speeds. The problem does not occur with the vacuum hose disconnected from the EGR valve. Which of the following is right?
   a. Inoperative EGR
   b. Clogged EGR ports
   c. Stuck open EGR vent solenoid
   d. Weak EGR valve spring

CHAPTER OBJECTIVES

- The technician will complete the ASE task list on I/M Failure Diagnosis.
- The technician will be able to answer 8 questions dealing with the I/M Failure Diagnosis section of the ASE L1 Test.

As explained in Chapter One, when beginning an emissions failure diagnosis, find out if the driver has any driveability symptoms or concerns, other than the emissions failure. Keep in mind that any driveability symptoms the operator describes may or may not be related to the emission failure. Some emission failures have very little effect on driveability and go unnoticed by the driver. However, any customer **driveability complaints**, noted now, may help reinforce the validity of your diagnosis later.

Read the **vehicle inspection report** (VIR) to find what type of failure was recorded. The format and information contained in the report will depend on where the vehicle was tested. Most states provide a pamphlet or flyer to explain to the consumer how to read the report; these can be very helpful and informative for you as well. For help with IM240 inspection reports, see the explanation under the heading "Reading the IM240 **Emissions Trace**."

Check the inspection report to see if the failure was in the visual, functional, or tailpipe portion of the inspection. Visual or functional failures may require further diagnosis. In fact, some states require visual failures to be functionally repaired prior to certification.

Refer to the vehicle service information and technical service bulletins to diagnose and determine the required repairs.

If the vehicle has a combination of visual and tailpipe failures or functional and tailpipe failures, decide if the visual or functional failure could be the cause of the tailpipe failure. After a repair of this type, be sure to verify the tailpipe emission improvement under similar conditions as the state emissions test before you release the vehicle back to the **test lane**. The vehicle may be tested for the five exhaust gases in the shop using a portable exhaust gas analyzer.

Here are some examples of this type of **redundant** failure:

A vehicle has a visual failure for a broken vacuum hose to the fuel pressure regulator, combined with an ASM tailpipe failure for high CO emission. It is highly probable that when the vacuum line to the pressure regulator is repaired, the high CO emission problem will be solved too.

This seems like an obviously easy diagnosis and a quick repair. However, be sure to verify this "quick" repair before releasing the vehicle. You might repair the vacuum hose and think it safe for the customer to return to the test lane. Don't; you are asking for a test lane "come back."

Check the tailpipe emissions under the same conditions as the ASM test prior to releasing the vehicle to the test lane. It might surprise you to find that, although the CO problem is solved, the NOx level is now above the **emission cut point**. The rich mixture may have masked the high NOx problem because rich mixture ratios tend to lower combustion temperature. Or, the engine may have higher combustion pressure because carbon deposits have built up in the combustion chambers as a result of the rich mixture.

In this example, a vehicle failed a two speed idle (TSI) test at idle for high CO. The technician repairs the cause of the rich condition. The vehicle returns to the test lane and fails this time for high HC. Carbon deposited on the valves while the condition was rich is now causing a misfire.

Even after discovering an obvious cause of the original failure, you need to verify the result of the repair to prevent a "come back" from the emissions inspection test lane. Keep in mind, you and your shop may be graded for the "comeback rate" on the mandatory state report card.

In 1993, the California Bureau of Automotive Repair conducted an undercover investigation. An undercover vehicle was bugged with a bad spark plug so it would fail an emissions test for high HC. The investigation revealed a sad fact: Of the licensed repair stations visited, 54% could not accurately diagnose the bad spark plug.

In some states that have ASM or IM240 tests, a high number of customers' vehicles are failing emissions retest after being improperly diagnosed and repaired.

L1

Driveability Complaint: The expressed dissatisfaction of a customer with a vehicle's driving performance.

Emission Cut Point: The point at which a tailpipe emission exceeds state mandated limit.

Emissions Trace: An IM 240 emissions inspection report showing emissions, in grams per mile, during a specific drive cycle.

Redundant: Needlessly repeated.

Test Lane: Garage stall or bay, used for emissions inspections.

Vehicle Inspection Report (VIR): Reports the results of a state emissions inspection.

This chapter focuses on diagnosing emission test tailpipe failures, since this has proved to be an area of difficulty in the shop and on ASE tests. A discussion of all five gases and new methods for diagnosis, such as O2 sensor tests, waveform analysis, and catalytic converter testing, follows.

INSPECTION AND MAINTENANCE PROGRAMS

Inspection and Maintenance (IM) programs are intended to promote regular vehicle maintenance, figure 6-1. Mandatory IM programs force the public to find and repair the causes of increased vehicle emissions. Inspections include visual, functional and tailpipe testing. The maintenance portion of any IM program is most important of all. Maintenance includes scheduled service as well as repairs to defective systems that lower levels of HC, CO, and NOx produced by the vehicle.

The success of IM programs relies on technicians with a high level of personal integrity and knowledge.

- Integrity to perform an honest inspection and repair
- Knowledge to perform an accurate diagnosis and a reliable repair

Hopefully, your efforts to learn the material presented in this study guide will help in the latter category.

In an effort to prevent customers from making repeat trips for testing due to inaccurate diagnosis and ineffective repairs, many states issue "report cards." The report cards document the performance of repair stations and technicians when making emissions related diagnosis and repairs.

Basic to All State Inspections

Most state vehicle emission inspections have six parts:

1. PRELIMINARY SAFETY CHECKS. The vehicle is checked for conditions that endanger the vehicle during testing and problems that make it unsafe for the technician to perform the test

2. VEHICLE IDENTIFICATION. This includes verifying the customer's need for an emissions inspection. It also includes gathering necessary information to properly identify the emission control equipment for the visual portion of the inspection. In most states, the following information is gathered:

- Geographic area of vehicle registration
- Vehicle Identification Number (VIN)
- Year, Make, Model, Model type designation (passenger car, truck, etc.)
- Gross Vehicle Weight Rating (GVWR)
- Engine size and type
- Certification type Federal (FED), California (CA), or 50 state
- EPA underhood label's list of emissions equipment

3. VISUAL INSPECTION. Individual state inspection regulations prescribe what equipment must be visually inspected. The visual inspection may require use of an emission control system applications manual, vacuum diagram, electrical component locator, or electrical wiring diagram to verify:

- All emissions-related equipment is present
- The equipment appears able to function
- System vacuum hoses, lines, and wiring are intact and routed correctly

4. FUNCTIONAL TESTING. Some states include functional tests of all or some of the following systems:

- Ignition initial timing
- EVAP system
- Gas tank fillpipe restrictor
- EGR system
- MIL test

Insight
Scanner checks of OBD II systems for emissions-related trouble codes are part of some states' functional tests.

5. TAILPIPE TESTING. The cut points for tailpipe emission failures are set by individual state regulation. They must meet or exceed EPA standards. Generally, states use one of the following three test types

- Two-Speed Idle (TSI)
- Acceleration Simulation Mode (ASM)
- Inspection and Maintenance 240 second test (IM240)

6. VEHICLE INSPECTION REPORT (VIR), a printed report explaining results of the inspection to the consumer and/or repair facility

TAILPIPE TESTS EXPLAINED

Two Speed Idle Test

The purpose of the TSI test is to identify vehicles that have high HC and CO emissions. It cannot identify vehicles with high HC and CO emissions under a load, during cruise, or during **transient** loaded acceleration and deceleration.

Fig. 6-1. The purpose of vehicle emission inspection is to ensure that polluting vehicles are repaired.

NOx cannot be measured because a load is not applied to the vehicle to show its true NOx production. To help control NOx emission, functional checks of the EGR system and ignition initial timing are included in the test procedure. The two speed idle test is incapable of detecting other defects that cause high NOx emission, such as engine cooling system and carbon deposit problems.

The vehicle must be fully warmed up prior to testing. Normal operating temperature increases the probability that the system is in closed loop and that the catalytic converter is operating efficiently.

The TSI tailpipe test is performed with the vehicle in park or neutral at two engine speeds. During the first part, the technician runs the engine at cruise between 2200 and 2700 rpm. During the second part, the engine is run at factory curb idle with a maximum speed of approximately 1100 rpm. Lights, air conditioning, and other accessories must be off while testing. During the entire test, the engine is idle, meaning it has no load on it while the tailpipe is tested.

When a vehicle fails the test on the first try, the BAR 90 specification provides for a second chance test with an automated preconditioning sequence. The technician is prompted to run the engine for three minutes between 2200 and 2700 rpm. The analyzer then automatically proceeds to the second chance test. Preconditioning ensures the vehicle is warmed up prior to performing the second chance test.

The tailpipe is tested using an automated, partial sample, four-gas analyzer, figure 6-2. HC is measured in parts per million. CO, CO_2, and O_2 are measured as a percentage of the exhaust sample.

During the test, the analyzer measures and calculates the sum of carbon dioxide (CO_2) and CO percentages to monitor exhaust sample dilution. Exhaust system leaks that allow outside (ambient) air to mix with exhaust gas create sample dilution. When the sum of CO_2 and CO drop below the 7% or 8% threshold, the analyzer will automatically abort the test.

Severe engine performance problems can lower the CO_2 and CO sum to a level below the threshold and cause the analyzer to falsely abort the test.

Acceleration Simulation Mode (ASM)
The purpose of the ASM test is to identify high HC, CO, and NOx emissions while the engine is at a steady cruising speed under a steady load. ASM testing is sometimes referred to as steady state testing because there is no variation of engine speed or load during the test. This test will not identify vehicles that emit high HC, CO, and NOx during transient (varying) acceleration and deceleration. Nor does it identify high HC or CO emissions at idle, unless an idle test is included.

ASM tailpipe testing requires the use of a state-approved, automated dynamometer, figure 6-3. A dynamometer works like a treadmill for the vehicle. The dynamometer must be able to calculate and provide a fixed load according to the weight of the vehicle being tested. To do this, the dynamometer is equipped with an automatic scale to weigh the vehicle prior to testing. The calculated load is applied to the drive wheels continuously during the test. ASM testing simulates driving under a light, constant acceleration.

The most common steady states used in conjunction with each other for **ASM** tests are **50/15** and **25/25**. The term 50/15 means a load of 50% of vehicle weight is applied by the dynamometer while the technician drives the vehicle at 15 miles per hour. The term 25/25 indicates a load of 25% of vehicle weight is applied by the dynamometer while the technician drives the vehicle at 25 miles per hour, figure 6-4.

All wheel drive, full-time four wheel drive vehicles that cannot be disengaged and traction control vehicles that cannot be disengaged cannot be tested on two-wheel dynamometers.

The vehicle is safety checked prior to testing for adequate braking, oil level, coolant level, fluid leaks, tire condition, and pressure. During the emissions test, if there is an unsafe condition for the vehicle, equipment, or the technician, the test can be aborted. The cause might be one of the previously mentioned safety items or a drivetrain problem.

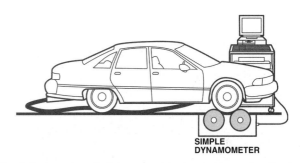

Fig. 6-3. An automated dynamometer is used to apply a fixed load to the drive wheels during the ASM test.

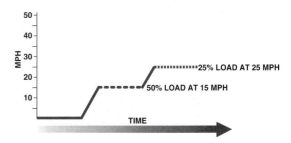

Fig. 6-4. Two portions of the ASM test are 50/15 and 25/25.

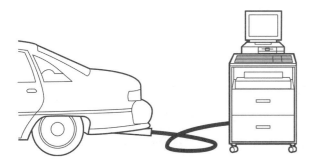

Fig. 6-2. An automated four-gas analyzer is used for two speed idle tailpipe testing.

ASM 25/25: A load of 25 percent of vehicle weight applied at 25 mph.
ASM 50/15: A load of 50 percent of vehicle weight applied at 15 mph.

To perform the test, the vehicle is driven onto the dynamometer. It is restrained with tie-down straps or chains. To prevent overheating, a cooling fan is positioned in front of the vehicle to provide radiator airflow during the test.

On rainy days, the technician must drive the vehicle without a load until the tires are dry to prevent tire slippage on the rollers when the dynamometer load is applied.

The vehicle is accelerated to the target speed with no more than a 1-mile-per-hour variation above or below the state prescribed MPH. Both the 25/25 and 50/15 steady states are used for most ASM tests.

An automated, partial sampling, five-gas analyzer is used for the tailpipe test. The unit of measurement for HC and NOx is parts per million. CO, CO_2, and O_2 are measured as a percentage of the exhaust sample. The sampling is done after the tailpipe gases are allowed a short time to stabilize at each of the target test speeds.

As in the TSI test, exhaust leaks that create gas sample dilution above a predetermined level will cause the analyzer to abort the test.

Insight
Both TSI and ASM tests are steady state. The TSI test is steady state because the tailpipe is tested while the engine is at a steady speed and no load. The ASM is steady state because both vehicle speed and engine load are steady during the tailpipe test. Some states require that an idle speed tailpipe test be included with the ASM test.

IM240

The IM240 test is the most accurate of the three tests because it most nearly simulates city driving. Unlike the two previous tests, the IM240 measures the total mass of HC, CO, and NOx emissions by weight in grams per mile. This test uses a more expensive dynamometer that imitates the inertial weight of a vehicle in motion, figure 6-5. That is, besides simulating a load on acceleration, it simulates the force that keeps the car in motion during highway deceleration.

The technician must check the same safety items that are required for the ASM test. The vehicle is restrained on the dynamometer. A cooling fan is used to provide airflow through the radiator.

The IM240 test simulates idle, acceleration, cruise, deceleration, and braking during the drive cycle, figure 6-6. This is called transient emission testing because the test constantly measures all emissions during the varying speed and load drive cycle.

If vehicle emissions are above the state specified cut points during the first 100 seconds (phase 1) portion of the test, the analyzer will automatically continue to test through phase 2, using the full 240 seconds of the test. If vehicle emissions drop below the cut points during the phase 2 portion of the test, the vehicle may still pass depending on the final calculated values.

If the vehicle passes during the first 100 seconds of the tailpipe test, the analyzer will automatically end the test, skipping the phase 2 portion of the test.

The same unsafe conditions as the ASM test can cause the technician to abort during the IM240 test.

Insight
Some state programs may differ from the descriptions in this text. If you will be diagnosing and repairing emission failures,

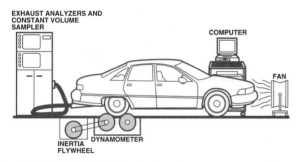

Fig. 6-5. The IM 240 tailpipe test requires a more expensive dynamometer, capable of simulating acceleration load and deceleration force.

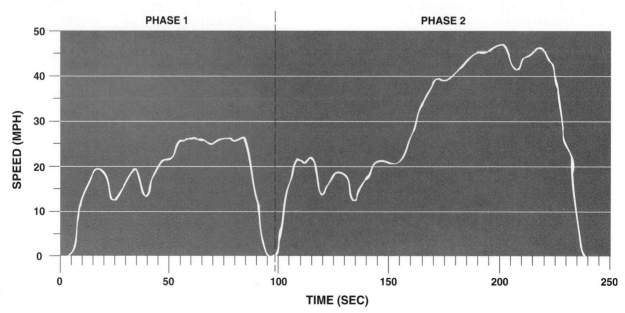

Fig. 6-6. The IM240 tailpipe test drive cycle has two phases.

it is important you learn the specific details of your state's emission inspection program.

CHEMISTRY OF COMBUSTION

Air and gasoline mix as they enter the combustion chamber. They are made up of the following chemicals:

- Air contains approximately, 78% N_2 (nitrogen), 21% O_2 (oxygen) and 1% other gases
- Fuel contains, for our purposes, 100% HC (hydrocarbons)

The total volume of these chemicals entering the intake of the engine as air and fuel exits through the exhaust system. However, the combustion process changes them into other chemicals.

Combustion causes the separation of HC into H (hydrogen) and C (carbon) and O_2 into O oxide. The combustion or burning process also causes oxidation (bonding with oxygen). If combustion were ideal, H+H+O bonding would occur to create H_2O (water vapor). C+O+O bonding would occur to create CO_2 (carbon dioxide). CO_2 is considered by some to be involved in the global warming process. However, CO_2 is a desirable result of the combustion process. N_2 would be heated but not separated or bonded. The results of this theoretically perfect combustion would be vehicle exhaust containing no harmful gasses.

Combustion Formula Equation

Perfect: $HC + O_2 = H_2O + CO_2$
Real World: $HC + O_2 + N = H_2O + CO_2 + HC + O_2 + NOx$

Unfortunately, real-world combustion is not perfect and produces harmful gases. Under all operating conditions, the combustion flame is quenched to some degree by cooler surface areas of the combustion chamber, causing some HC to be left over. In oxygen-poor areas of the combustion chamber, some C is bonded to only one O, creating CO, even when the mixture is best for the operating condition. Even in a cool engine, combustion flame front temperatures are hot enough to separate N_2 into N and bond it with O, creating combinations of N+O, N+O+O, and rarer N+O+O+O. This group of nitric oxides is called NOx. NOx occurs during all phases of combustion but is highest when temperatures rise above 2500° F.

The stoichiometric air-fuel ratio of approximately 14.7 lbs. of air to 1 lb. of fuel is chemically the best air-fuel ratio to keep catalytic converter efficiency high, figures 6-7 and 6-8. An air-fuel ratio of 14.7 to 1 produces lower levels of pollutants and is a compromise between power and efficiency, figure 6-9.

The five gases used for analysis are: HC, CO, CO_2, O_2, and NOx. The following statements are true of the relationship of the five gases to the stoichiometric air-fuel ratio:

- CO_2 peaks at approximately 14 to 1, slightly richer than 14.7 to 1
- CO rises sharply on the rich side of 14.7 to 1 and remains level on the lean side
- HC rises on both the rich and lean sides of 14.7 to 1
- O_2 rises sharply on the lean side of 14.7 to 1 but drops quickly and stays low on the rich side
- CO and O_2 are equal at 14.7 to 1

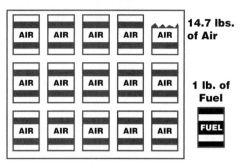

Fig. 6-7. Example of 14.7 lbs. of air and 1 lb. of fuel.

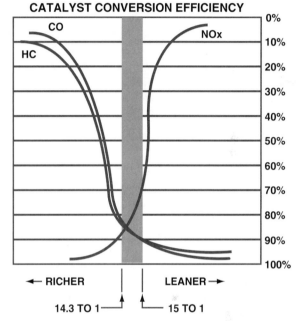

Fig. 6-8. The three-way catalytic converter's capacity to convert harmful emissions is highest in the shaded area of the above illustration.

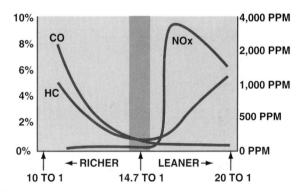

Fig. 6-9. The 14.7 to 1 mixture ratio is best to lower all three harmful emissions.

NOx is low on the rich side of 14.7 to 1 and rises on the lean side of 14.7 to1. When air-fuel ratios approach approximately 16 to 1, NOx production decreases. When a lean misfire occurs, NOx drops dramatically.

Carbon Monoxide

By chemical composition, gasoline is a complex structure built on a compound hydrocarbon base. Hydrocarbons are simply molecules of hydrogen and carbon that are chemically bonded together. During the combustion process, chemical

L1

bonds break down to release free carbon, which combines, or bonds to, free oxygen. This bonding results in the formation of either CO or CO2, or both. CO is a highly toxic, unwanted by-product of incomplete hydrocarbon combustion and a major pollutant. On the other hand, CO2 is a relatively harmless substance that forms during complete combustion and as a result of catalytic conversion.

Some CO will always be present in the exhaust, at least as long as engines continue to be less than 100 percent efficient. While CO is a product of incomplete combustion, it is not the best indicator of combustion efficiency.

Carbon monoxide is a colorless, odorless, and tasteless toxic gas. When carbon monoxide is inhaled, it will inhibit the blood's ability to carry oxygen to body tissue and vital organs such as the heart and brain. Excessive amounts of CO can overcome you within minutes without warning, causing loss of consciousness and suffocation. Symptoms and exposure to CO measured in ppm (parts per million) are as follows:

CO ppm:	Symptoms:
50	Maximum allowable concentration for continuous exposure for healthy adults in any 8 hour period allowed by OHSA.
200	Mild headache, dizziness, fatigue, and nausea after 2 to 3 hours.
400	Severe headache within 1 to 2 hours with other symptoms intensifying. Life threatening after 3 hours.
800	Dizziness, nausea, and convolutions within 45 minutes. Unconsciousness within 2 hours. Death within 2 to 3 hours.
1600	Headache, dizziness, and nausea within 20 minutes. Death within 1 hour.
3200	Headache, dizziness, and nausea within 5 to 10 minutes. Death within 25 to 30 minutes.
6400	Headache, dizziness, and nausea within 1 to 2 minutes. Death within 10 to 15 minutes.
12,800	Death within 1 to 3 minutes.

Hydrocarbons

Since unburned fuel is a hydrocarbon, this makes hydrocarbon emissions quite different from CO emissions, which only occur as a by-product of combustion. This is important, since a five-gas analyzer will detect the presence of hydrocarbons when placed near an open gasoline fuel filler neck or even near a windshield washer bottle filled with a washer fluid that contains a hydrocarbon-based additive, even though no combustion is taking place. Hydrocarbons are measured in ppm, or parts per million of sampled exhaust.

Hydrocarbon emissions are raw fuel. When sensed by an emission analyzer they are in vapor form, but they are raw fuel nonetheless. The inherent inefficiencies of the internal combustion engine will produce some HC. This is especially problematic when "cool" spots in the combustion chamber away from the spark plug quench the combustion process. When the flame goes out completely, we no longer get CO, but unburned HC still exits. The engine expels these hydrocarbons either through the exhaust, or by condensing them back into a liquid that leaks past the rings and into the crankcase.

Unburned fuel that condenses on the cylinder walls and runs back into the crankcase will eventually contaminate the crankcase to the point where the PCV system draws the raw fuel directly from the crankcase into the intake manifold. This will cause high CO and may result in high HC if the mixture gets too rich to burn, resulting in a misfire.

Oxygen

Oxygen is a very important part of combustion that reduces emission levels by improving the efficiency of the catalyst. Oxygen is also a good diagnostic tool for evaluating how rich or lean the air-fuel mixture is. Because this gas is such an effective mixture indicator, the O2 sensor of an electronic control system uses information about oxygen levels in the exhaust as a way to signal whether the fuel mixture is rich or lean. Remember lean is low.

High levels of oxygen in the exhaust cause the O2 sensor to generate a low voltage signal to the ECM. The ECM interprets a low voltage signal as an indication of a lean condition and a request for additional fuel in the mixture. Remember, lean is low.

Carbon Dioxide (CO2)

CO2 is formed during complete combustion; it is an indicator of combustion efficiency. During good combustion, the carbon in the fuel combines with a molecule of oxygen to form the harmless CO2 instead of the dangerous CO. The higher the CO2 level, the better.

Oxides of Nitrogen (NOx)

Our atmosphere is 78 percent nitrogen, 21 percent oxygen, and 1 percent other gases. This mix enters the combustion chamber as part of the air-fuel mixture. When combustion temperatures reach 2500°F, the nitrogen combines with oxygen to form oxides of nitrogen, or NOx.

There are several contributing factors to the formation of NOx, but all are related to high combustion temperatures. It is possible for cylinder temperatures to reach as high as 4500°F. Anything that raises combustion temperature to 2500°F or higher results in NOx formation.

When NOx mixes with hydrocarbons (unburned fuel) in the lower atmosphere a brown haze known as smog is formed.

OPERATING CONDITIONS AND AIR-FUEL RATIOS

When operating under cold engine or heavy load conditions, it is not possible to use a 14.7 to 1 mixture or driveability problems will occur. Starting a cold engine in cold weather may require a ratio as rich as 1 to 1. During warm-up, the mixture may need to be a rich 6 to 1. After the engine has reached operating temperature, heavy acceleration or climbing steep hills may still require mixtures as rich as 12 or 10 to 1. At cruising speeds with a light engine load, leaner mixtures of 18 or 19 to 1 are possible and provide better fuel economy. To use a 14.7 to 1 air-fuel ratio engine operating conditions must be:

- Near normal operating temperature
- Light or no engine load
- Steady speed or gradual changes

COMBUSTION PROBLEMS

Rich

Not enough air or too much fuel causes a mixture too rich for the operating condition. The following are some common causes of not enough air:

- Clogged air filter
- Clogged PCV valve
- Collapsed air intake duct
- Restricted turbocharger
- Faulty choke thermostat
- Defective supercharger

The following are some common causes of too much fuel:

- Oil diluted with gasoline contamination
- Defective evaporative system
- High fuel pressure
- O2 sensor voltage biased low by exhaust leak or contamination
- Defective ECM sensor or circuit

Lean

Too much air or not enough fuel causes a mixture too lean for the operating condition. The following are some common causes of a lean mixture:

- A vacuum leak in the intake manifold
- Leaking vacuum hose or a vacuum operated device
- Unmeasured air entering the intake of systems using an airflow or mass air sensor

The following are some common causes of not enough fuel:

- Low fuel pressure
- Dirty fuel injectors
- A defective computer sensor or circuit

Misfire

A misfire is incomplete or no combustion. The following are some common causes of misfire:

- Partial or complete loss of compression
- Valvetrain problems
- Camshaft drive problem
- Poor spark
- Wrong spark timing
- EGR mixture dilution
- Extreme mixture problems

HC Emissions Failure

High HC emissions are caused by incomplete burning of the fuel. The following are some common causes of high HC emission:

- Improper ignition timing
- Ignition misfire
- Leaking or sticking fuel injector
- Faulty fuel pressure regulator
- Improper fuel pressure
- Improperly installed fuel cap
- Head gasket leakage
- Low cylinder compression
- EGR valve open
- Oxygen sensor contaminated or responding to a false lean or rich condition
- Faulty ECM
- Faulty input sensor
- Faulty output device

CO Emissions Failure

High CO emissions (rich fuel mixture) are usually caused by insufficient air or too much fuel reaching the cylinder. The following are some common causes of high CO emission:

- Dirty or plugged air filter
- Leaking or sticking fuel injector
- High fuel pressure
- Faulty fuel pressure regulator
- Oxygen sensor contaminated or responding to a false lean condition
- Faulty ECM
- Faulty input sensor
- Faulty output device
- PCV valve clogged or wrong size orifice

HC and CO Emissions Failure

The following are some common causes of high HC and CO (rich fuel mixture) emissions:

- Improper ignition timing
- Ignition misfire
- Leaking or sticking fuel injector
- Faulty fuel pressure regulator
- Improper fuel pressure
- Improperly installed fuel cap
- Head gasket leakage
- Low cylinder compression
- EGR valve open

L1

- Oxygen sensor contaminated or responding to a false lean or rich condition
- Faulty ECM
- Faulty input sensor
- Faulty output device
- Dirty or plugged air filter

NOx Emission Failure

Combustion temperatures within the normal range but higher than usual may cause NOx emission failures. NOx increases are caused by problems that either directly affect combustion temperature or indirectly affect it by raising combustion pressure. Keep in mind that a lean air/fuel mix will cause NOx problems. The following are some common causes of high NOx emission:

- Over-advanced initial ignition timing
- Over-advancing or prematurely advancing ignition timing
- Decreased or no EGR flow
- Combustion chamber carbon deposits
- Inefficient engine cooling
- Lean mixture
- Lower octane fuel
- Low fuel pressure
- Fuel contaminated with water
- Faulty fuel injector
- Carburetor set too lean
- Oxygen sensor contaminated or responding to a false rich condition or lazy switching
- Higher intake air temperature
- Vacuum leak
- Head gasket leak
- Timing belt slippage
- Faulty input sensor
- Faulty output device
- Restricted exhaust system
- Low engine oil level
- Brake drag
- Drag from drivetrain excessive
- Faulty wheel bearings
- Faulty catalytic converter

Excessively Low CO2 Reading

An excessively low CO2 reading is caused by a rich air-fuel mixture. The following are some common causes of an excessively low CO2 reading:

- Exhaust system leak
- Leaking or sticking fuel injector
- Faulty fuel pressure regulator
- High fuel pressure
- Faulty ECM
- Faulty input sensor
- Faulty output device
- Defective PCV

Low O2 Reading

An excessively low O2 reading is caused by a lack of air or rich air-fuel mixture. The following are some common causes of a low O2 reading:

- Dirty or plugged air filter
- Combustion chamber carbon deposits
- Leaking or sticking fuel injector
- Faulty fuel pressure regulator
- High fuel pressure
- Faulty ECM
- Faulty input sensor
- Faulty output device
- Oxygen sensor contaminated or responding to a false lean
- Faulty EVAP system

High O2 Reading

An excessively low O2 reading is caused by a lean air-fuel mixture. The following are some common causes of a high O2 reading:

- Vacuum leak
- Low fuel pressure
- Faulty input sensor
- Exhaust system leak

FIVE-GAS ANALYSIS

Except for a few vehicles that have CO specifications for mixture adjustment, there are no factory specifications to guide you in analyzing exhaust gases. State emissions test failure cut points are above the amount of harmful gases the vehicle should normally produce. Trying to diagnose defects by memorizing every possible combination of exhaust gas readings is impossible and memorizing some can be misleading. It is more important to know how the gases react as a group to a particular defect. Most engine performance or emission deficiencies are caused by the following five basic problems:

- Air-fuel mixture too rich or too lean
- Misfire caused by an ignition, mechanical, carbon deposit, or EGR dilution
- Combustion temperature too high or too low
- Incorrect timing
- O2 sensor failure

Gas analysis reveals the effect of the above problems on tailpipe emissions. Think of five-gas readings as a symptom of the problem, not the actual problem. Gas readings show the symptom, in terms of the result of its effect on tailpipe emissions. Gas readings will show you what type of problem exists (misfire, rich mixture, etc.); they will not identify the specific cause. Now that you are aware of the goal of gas analysis, let's begin with some basics. The five gases and measurement for analysis are:

- HC, in ppm (parts per million)
- CO, in % (percent)
- CO2, in % (percent)
- O2, in % (percent)
- NOx, in ppm (parts per million)

The exhaust gases, sampled upstream of the catalytic converter, without secondary air injection, give a very accurate picture of combustion efficiency. However, there must be no exhaust leaks upstream to allow dilution of the exhaust gas sample.

When diagnosing a combustion problem, each of the gases gives a hint as to what the problem is, figure 6-10. Some

Condition	HC	CO	CO2	O2	NOx
Ignition Misfire	Large Increase	Some Decrease	Some Decrease	Some to Large Decrease	Some Decrease
Compression Loss	Some to Large Increase	Some Decrease	Some Decrease	Some Decrease	Some Increase
Rich Mixture	Some to Large Increase	Large Increase	Some Decrease	Some Decrease	Large Decrease
Lean Mixture	Some Increase	Large Decrease	Some Decrease	Some Increase	Large Increase
Minimal Timing Retard	Some Decrease	Possible Increase	No Change	No Change	Possible Decrease
Excessive Timing Retard	Some Increase	No Change	Some to Large Decrease	No Change	Large Decrease
Advanced Timing	Some Increase	Small Decrease Possible	No Change	No Change	Large Increase
EGR Operating	No Change	No Change	Some Decrease	No Change	Large Decrease
EGR Leaking	Some Increase	No Change	No Change	No Change	Possible Increase
AIR Operating	Large Decrease	Large Decrease	Large Decrease	Large Increase	Possible Increase
Converter Operational	Some Decrease	Some Decrease	Some Increase	Some Decrease	Large Decrease
Exhaust Leak	Some Decrease	Some Decrease	Some Decrease	Some Increase	No Change
Worn Engine	Some Increase	Some Increase	Some Decrease	Some Decrease	Large Decrease
Worn Camshaft Lobes	Possible Decrease	Some Decrease	Some Decrease	Some Decrease	Possible Decrease

Fig. 6-10. Effect of engine condition on the formation of exhaust gases.

are better than others at indicating a particular type of problem. The key is to use them together to reach a conclusion.

CO is good for indicating a rich condition, figure 6-11. The graph illustrates that on the rich side of 14.7 to 1, CO rises proportionately. However, on the lean side of 15 to1, CO stays level. This means CO is not useful for indicating a very lean condition.

O2 is good for indicating a lean condition, figure 6-12. The graph illustrates that on the lean side of 14 to 1, O2 rises proportionately. However, on the rich side of 14 to 1, it remains the same. This means O2 is not good for indicating very rich conditions. If a misfire occurs, O2 is higher than normal

no matter what the mixture is. By itself, O2 is not a good misfire indicator.

CO and O2, used together, are good mixture indicators, figure 6-13. The illustration shows they are at equal concentrations at 14.7 to 1. If CO is higher than O2, the mixture is rich. If O2 is higher than CO, the mixture is lean.

HC is a good misfire indicator, figure 6-14. The illustration shows that when a misfire occurs, HC is higher, regardless of mixture. It will be higher proportionate to the severity of the misfire. HC is not a good indicator of mixture because it rises when the mixture is very rich or even a little lean.

L1

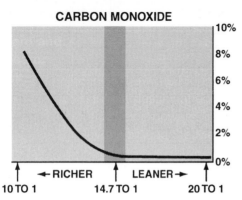

Fig. 6-11. The level of the carbon monoxide (CO) emission sample increases in proportion to mixture richness.

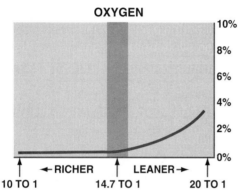

Fig. 6-12. The level of the oxygen (O2) emission sample increases in proportion to mixture leanness.

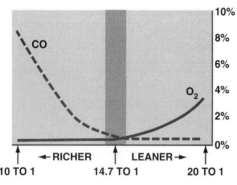

Fig. 6-13. Used together, the CO and O2 emission samples are the best indicators of mixture condition.

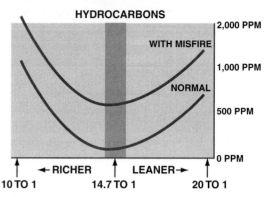

Fig. 6-14. The hydrocarbon (HC) emission sample is the best indicator of a misfire.

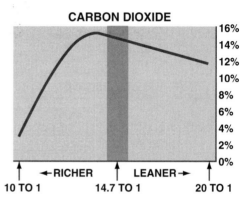

Fig. 6-15. The carbon dioxide (CO2) emission sample is a good indicator of combustion efficiency.

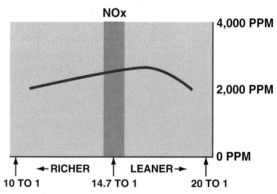

Fig. 6-16. The amount of the NOx emission sample increases as the mixture gets leaner until the mixture approaches a 16 to 1 mixture ratio.

CO2 is an indicator of efficient combustion, figure 6-15. The illustration shows that CO2 is actually at its highest at 14 to 1, just a little richer than 14.7 to 1. However, we can say that if CO2 is high, combustion is efficient and should be free of serious mixture or misfire problems.

NOx is produced in the high flame front temperatures of combustion and increases as flame front temperature increases. NOx is caused by timing, temperature, pressures, and a lean air/fuel mix. NOx is an indicator of the temperature of combustion, figure 6-16. The illustration shows that NOx is highest just before 16 to 1 and drops on either side of 16 to 1. It rises on the lean side of 14.7 to 1 because the combustion

temperature becomes hotter as the mixture becomes leaner until the fuel mixture reaches approximately 16 to 1. When the mixture is leaner than 16 to 1, combustion efficiency becomes poor and NOx production decreases. The level of NOx also drops when a misfire occurs. Defects that increase combustion temperature increase NOx at any mixture ratio, unless a misfire condition occurs. There is a dramatic increase of NOx during detonation because there is more than one flame front.

Exactly what the normal amount of each of the five gases should be at the tailpipe is impossible to say. So many variables make it difficult to predict. Factors such as combustion chamber design, planned ignition and valve timing, combustion temperature, ambient air temperature, fuel qualities, etc. all have an effect on what comes out of the tailpipe. What is normal also depends on the operating conditions of the test you are performing, such as trying to match a TSI (no load), ASM (steady state), or IM240 (transient) test. Experience is the best teacher of what is normal when it comes to tailpipe gas analysis. Refer to figure 6-17 for typical exhaust gas output.

Most combustion problems have enough effect on gases to be noticeable even if you use one of the many published approximate ranges for normal readings. Problems that have only a minor effect on combustion will have a minor effect on the gases. They are more difficult to diagnose. Diagnosing these types of problems requires using alternative testing methods to verify the cause before proceeding to parts replacement.

The following statements describe the reaction of the gases as a group to combustion problems. The gas that is the best indicator of the problem is listed first.

RICH: CO will increase in proportion to the severity of the problem. O2 will be at a minimum. CO2 will decrease. HC will increase with severity. NOx will decrease.

LEAN: O2 will increase in proportion to the severity of the problem. CO will be at a minimum. CO2 will decrease. HC will increase. NOx will increase unless the lean condition is beyond 16 to 1, at which point it will decrease. When the lean condition reaches the misfire point, see MISFIRE below.

MISFIRE: HC will increase in proportion to the severity of the problem. O2 will increase in proportion to the severity of the problem. CO2 will decrease. CO and NOx will decrease.

COMBUSTION IN THE WARMER RANGE OF NORMAL: NOx will increase in proportion to the temperature increase. CO, HC, and O2 will decrease slightly, and CO2 will increase slightly.

COMBUSTION IN THE COOLER RANGE OF NORMAL: NOx will decrease in proportion to the temperature decrease. CO and HC will increase. O2 and CO2 will decrease slightly.

Keep in mind that in the two examples of temperature, the difference in temperature affects both combustion efficiency and the ECM fuel decision. Cooler is less efficient, warmer is more efficient. Cooler means a richer and warmer means a leaner ECM fuel decision.

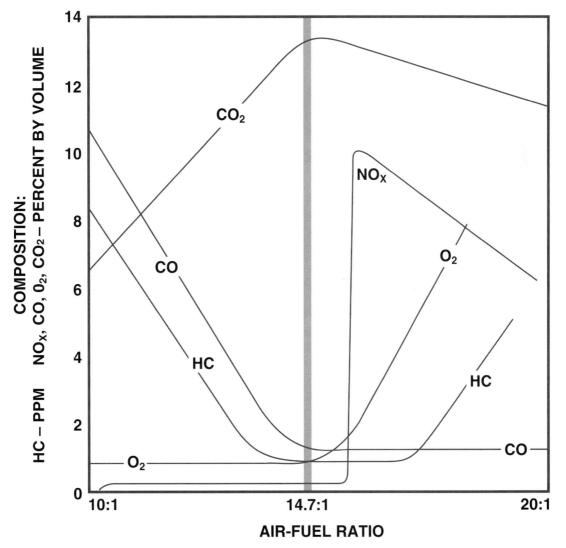

Fig. 6-17. At a 14.7:1 air-fuel ratio, emission is optimum. The "bad" gases (HC and CO) are lowest and CO2, the indicator of combustion efficiency, is at its highest level.

Now look at two of the above statements: LEAN and MISFIRE; both cause a similar reaction. It seems difficult to analyze which may be the problem. However, a simple mixture bias test provides an answer. Get out your propane kit and slowly meter propane into the intake. The HC should decrease and the CO_2 should increase if there is a lean problem. If the problem is a misfire, HC will increase from the additional fuel. If the closed loop fuel control system is defeating the bias, disconnect the O_2 sensor(s) and repeat the test. If the problem disappears with the O_2 sensor disconnected and no added propane, the problem is a lean bias of the closed loop fuel control.

Once the type of problem is established, you should begin to think what systems may be involved and in what way the system must fail to cause this type of problem. Keep in mind, the objective of gas analysis is to analyze whether there is a mixture (rich or lean), misfire, or possibly a combination of problems. Do not expect to diagnose precisely what defect is the cause of the gas readings. Diagnosing it will require testing individual systems to find the defect that is the cause of the problem.

Reading the IM240 Emissions Trace

A useful feature of the IM240 test for diagnosing a failure is the actual results of the test. The emissions trace, captured during the drive cycle, figure 6-6, provides you with:

- What emission increased or decreased
- The operating conditions under which it occurred
- A comparison of three emissions to the drive cycle at any moment during the test

A trace is a graph of the emissions readings during the drive cycle. There are four graphs: one for each of three emissions measured, HC, CO, and NOx, and one for the evaporative purge test, figure 6-18.

The horizontal scale at the bottom of the graph is measured in seconds. From left to right, it measures 240 seconds in eight 30-second intervals. It is the same on all five graphs. This makes it possible to compare an event on one graph to events on another graph.

The vertical scale on the left of the emissions graph measures the amount of emission in grams per mile. The HC scale measures 6 grams per mile and is divided into 6 parts, 1 gram per mile each. The CO scale measures 60 grams per mile and is divided into 4 parts, 15 grams per mile each. The NOx scale measures 12 grams per mile and is divided into 12 parts, 1 gram per mile each.

The cut point for pass or fail is the average of the total emission during the entire drive cycle. So, even though an emission may spike way up the scale or is higher during one phase of the cycle than the other, the vehicle can still pass, as long as its average for both phases is below the cut point, figure 6-19.

The evaporative system canister purge graph is different from the other graphs. It measures the amount purged in liters and is actually the total of just the peaks of the graph during the drive cycle, figure 6-20. The evaporative purge graph can indicate whether or not the evaporative system is involved in a CO problem. Or it may help you diagnose the cause of an evaporative system failure.

Analyzing the Trace

The trace shows what the emissions levels were during the test. To be more useful for diagnosis, the drive cycle should be superimposed on the trace. Comparing the emissions graphs to each other, superimposed on the drive cycle, allows you to compare the reaction of all the gases to the operating condition.

Your knowledge of how the gases relate to each other, how they should react to operating conditions, and what problems cause them to change is valuable diagnostic information.

By comparing how tailpipe emissions readings reacted to an operating condition, and recalling what underlying problems may have created the readings it becomes possible to choose which systems to test and what defect or defects to test for. You can also eliminate other problems as possibilities. This procedure reduces diagnostic time.

The information you need from the trace is:

- The emission or emissions that failed
- Severity of the emission failure
- The levels of the other emissions at the time of the failure
- Is there a pattern in the trace and does it repeat?

Observing the level of the failed emission and comparing it to the level of other emissions at the same moment in time will point to the problem area. For example, a vehicle fails for high CO and HC. CO is very high but HC is only a little high. It's possible this may be a rich mixture causing a misfire. But if CO is a little high and HC is very high, besides being rich, there is probably another problem like an ignition or mechanical misfire.

Diagnostic Hint

The CO% will increase first, up to 2.5% before HC. After CO% has reached 2.5%, HC will increase dramatically.

Another clue can be obtained from the trace by noticing what the driving condition is during the emission increase. For example, a vehicle that fails for high HC with a trace that shows HC very high during acceleration may have a weak ignition system causing a misfire as cylinder pressure rises. What if you also notice the CO level is real low during acceleration? A lean misfire may be causing the high emission. Another example might be a vehicle that failed for high NOx displays a low CO and higher than normal, but not a failing HC level. Readings such as these probably point to a lean mixture problem.

Watch for a correlation between the driving condition and the emission levels. Know what to expect, like higher NOx and HC under load or CO levels lower at cruise. If levels are different than expected, they are hints as to the cause of the problem.

Also remember this, the IM240 is the only test that can show a deceleration failure. Watch the drive cycle and look to the deceleration emission controls for defects causing these problems. Even if the vehicle didn't fail for CO, if the CO is above normal during the entire trace, chances are it will be very high during deceleration. Look for causes of constant enrichment and loss of fuel control, such as a fuel pressure regulator diaphragm leaking fuel into the intake or crankcase oil contaminated with gasoline.

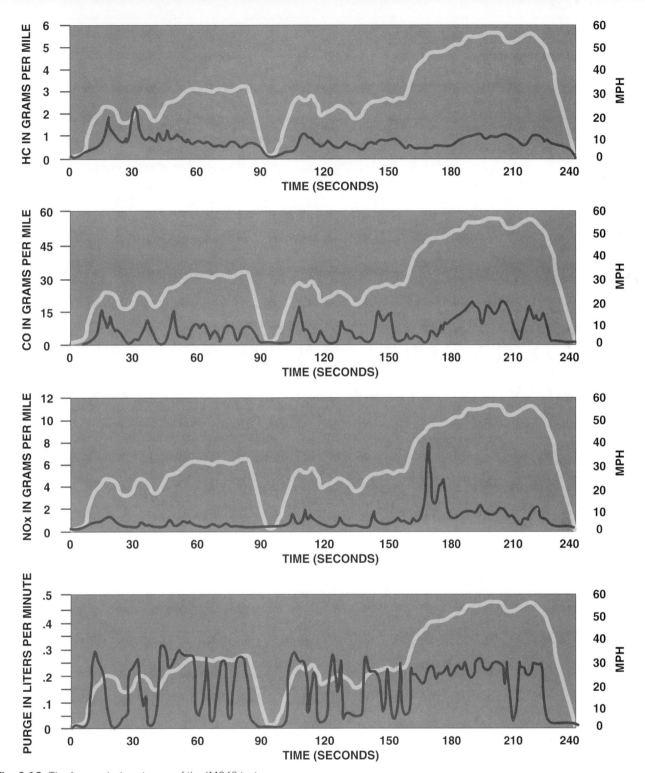

Fig. 6-18. The four emissions traces of the IM240 test.

DIAGNOSIS OF EMISSION TEST FAILURES

The following steps are useful for diagnosing any type of emission tailpipe test failure:

Read the repair order and vehicle inspection report. Talk with the driver of the vehicle.

Recreate the conditions under which the car failed.

Baseline the emissions with a gas analyzer while using the O2 sensor for a misfire monitor.

Perform a visual inspection and repair defects related to the emission failure.

Diagnose and repair any ECM codes that are emissions related. On OBD II vehicles, record codes and freeze frame data. Use the appropriate manufacturer's DTC flow chart. Complete the repair. Put the vehicle through the necessary conditions for that system monitor to run. Recheck the vehicle for a DTC. Verify sensor values with a scan tool. Some manufacturers

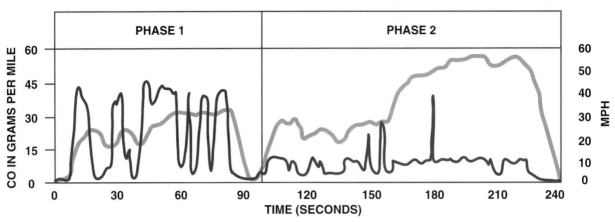

Fig. 6-19. When the vehicle fails phase 1, Phase 2 of the test provides another chance for the vehicle to pass.

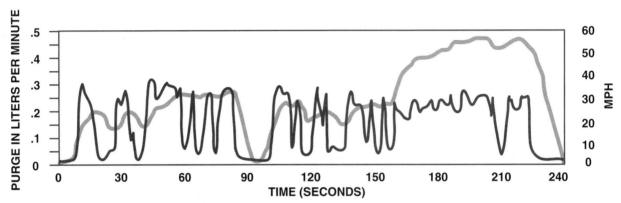

Fig. 6-20. The evaporative purge graph trace shows the amount of HC vapor that was purged from the evaporative emission system during the test.

require the use of a scan tool to perform an ECM reset after the repair has been performed.

Check the accuracy and response of the O2 sensor.

Verify that the vehicle has fuel control and detect misfires in the O2 sensor waveform.

Once the type of problem is known, refer to the correct diagnostic path to find the defect.

Re-Creating Two Speed Idle Tailpipe Test Failures

The TSI test tailpipe test emission results are reported in percent and parts per million, just like a shop analyzer. There is a direct correlation between your re-created test and the official test. TSI test conditions are easy to re-create because no load is applied. However it is a good idea to check the inspection report to see what the actual speeds were on the original test.

If the report shows idle speed was higher during the emissions test than it is during your test, you should suspect the vehicle might not have been properly warmed up. Another possibility is the vehicle takes an unreasonable amount of time to warm up because of a defective thermostat. An electrical radiator-cooling fan that runs all the time (because the control system has been bypassed) can also cause a long warm-up. Be sure the high speed also matches the original test.

The function of some systems like fuel delivery, airflow, EGR, and EVAP may be affected by a different test speed, figure 6-21. EGR flow and EVAP purge are not likely to occur on newer vehicles because there are no vehicle speed or correct gear shift signals. The idea is to re-create the same conditions

during the diagnosis. Check the coolant and oil level prior to testing. Be sure your analyzer is as accurate as the test center's analyzer, that it is in proper calibration, and the sampling system has no leaks. Use a DSO to monitor the O2 sensor during the test.

Re-Creating Acceleration Simulation Tailpipe Test Failures

The ASM tailpipe test is probably the most difficult to re-create unless your shop is equipped with a dynamometer. The vehicle is put under conditions that simulate climbing two different, precise grades for 30 seconds each. If your shop does not have a dynamometer to reproduce these conditions, you are at a disadvantage. However, a road test in the correct gearshift position at the vehicle speed of the original test at least provides a baseline to start the analysis.

Check the coolant and oil level before simulating the ASM test. Automatics are tested using drive, not overdrive. Manual transmissions are usually tested using second gear, but not always. Look carefully at the inspection report to compare engine speed to vehicle speed; these two factors are the most important to match during your test. Be sure to use an accurate analyzer that is calibrated and has no sampling system leaks. Use a DSO to monitor the O2 sensor during the test.

Re-Creating IM240 & ASM II Tailpipe Test Failures

Check the coolant and crankcase oil levels prior to performing a simulation test drive. If you are fortunate, use the shop's

	EMISSION	IDLE	OFF IDLE	CRUISE 1800–2000	AIR-FUEL RATIO	POSSIBLE CAUSES	RELATED SYMPTOMS
1	CO	3%	3%	3%	Rich AFR Below 10:1	Vacuum leak to map sensor Fuel injectors leaking Bad Power Valve (carburetor) Excessive fuel rail pressure Vacuum diaphragm bad	Black smoke or sulfur odor Engine in open loop Surge/hesitation Engine not preconditioned
	HC	250 ppm	280 ppm	300 ppm			
	CO2	7–9%	7–9%	7–9%			
	O2	.2%	.2%	.2%			
2	CO	1.5%	1.5%	1.5%	Rich AFR at low speed 10–12:1	Engine oil diluted w/ fuel Carburetor idle speed Cold engine Idle mixture too rich Choke stuck shut PCV valve defective Fuel injectors leaking	Poor fuel economy Sooty spark/black smoke Rough idle/surge hesitation Vapor canister purge valve bad Vapor canister saturated
	HC	150 ppm	150 ppm	200 ppm			
	CO2	7–9%	7–9%	11–13%			
	O2	.2%	CO	.2%			
3	CO	0.5%	0.5%	1.0%	Lean AFR Over 16:1	Check ignition primary/secondary Vacuum leak Carburetor mixture lean Poor cylinder sealing Fuel injectors restricted Improper timing Exhaust valve leak	Rough idle Misfire—high speed Detonation cruise (2000 rpm) Idle hunting (computer) Overheating
	HC	200 ppm	200 ppm	250 ppm			
	CO2	7–9%	7–9%	7–9%			
	O2	4–5%	4–5%	4–5%			
4	CO	2.5%	1.0%	0.8%	Lean AFR at High Speed Over 16:1	Air cleaner heater door closed Internal carburetor problem (float tuck, wrong jet, metering rod stuck) Fuel injectors restricted Fuel pump pressure low	Rough idle Misfire Surging hesitation
	HC	100 ppm	80 ppm	50 ppm			
	CO2	7–9%	7–9%	7–9%			
	O2	2–3%	2–3%	2–3%			
5	CO	0.3%	0.3%	0.3%	AFR 13–15:1	Engine not preconditioned Air management system not disabled Converter not warmed	None No driveability symptoms
	HC	100 ppm	80 ppm	50 ppm			
	CO2	10–12%	10–12%	10–12%			
	O2	2.5%	2.5%	2.5%			

Fig. 6-21. Four-gas exhaust emissions failure chart.

repair grade RG 240 dynamometer to simulate the drive cycle. Otherwise, choose a 4-minute route through the neighborhood, simulating the drive cycle, figure 6-6. Use a portable five-gas analyzer while on the test drive. A portable five-gas analyzer will prove the failure is repeatable and give you emissions measurements in percent and parts per million. It provides a baseline to measure the success of your diagnosis and repairs. Use a digital storage oscilloscope to monitor the O2 sensor during the test drive. This will provide a misfire monitor during the simulation.

You don't need to drive hills; just be as accurate as reasonably possible on the gas pedal to imitate the drive cycle. The imitation does not have to be perfect, but don't hit the gas pedal too hard; 80% throttle will cause open loop mode on most vehicles. Open loop operation will defeat the accuracy of the test drive to simulate the IM240. Note any driveability symptoms you observe during the simulation such as noises, pings, or smoke.

The Diagnostic Path

Now observe the results of the simulation. Did the failure recur? When? What happened to the other gases when it occurred? These are clues to keep in mind as the diagnosis continues.

Visually inspect the engine systems and emissions systems for any defective, disconnected, missing, or modified parts. Repair these obvious defects first.

Check: idle speed, initial timing and advance capability, valve lash. Adjust as necessary.

Interrogate the ECM for emission trouble codes. If there are any emission-related codes present, diagnose and repair them as necessary.

Test the O2 sensor calibration and response. Replace it if necessary. Use the O2 sensor waveform to tell if the system is in fuel control. Look for misfire events in the waveform.

Now, on the basis of the O2 sensor pattern, it's time to choose one of four paths:

- Misfire diagnosis
- Fuel control problem diagnosis
- NOx failure (no fuel control problem evident) diagnosis
- Catalytic converter testing

Misfire Diagnosis

Use an Ignition Oscilloscope to check the ignition secondary and primary systems. Use a lab scope to check the quality of ignition trigger signals. Repair as necessary and recheck.

Test manifold vacuum at idle speed for a clue to an air leak, vacuum leak, or EGR leak, figure 6-22. Test manifold vacuum at 3000 rpm for clues to a restricted exhaust, low fuel pressure or volume, or too much EGR flow. When too much EGR flow is the problem, verify that the backpressure transducer or modulator is operating correctly (if applicable), that the EGR valve is the correct one for the application, and if

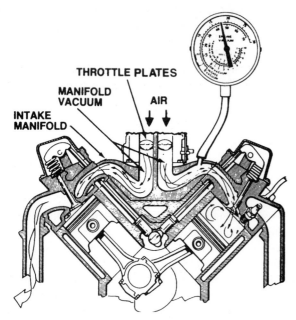

Fig. 6-22. Testing manifold vacuum.

applicable, that the installed orifice size is correct. Use the manufacturer's test method to prove the defect, then repair as necessary and retest.

Perform a cylinder power balance test. Check for a defective fuel injector using the pressure drop or volume method. Repair as necessary and retest.

Check for carbon deposits on intake valves. Use a solution designed specifically for the removal of carbon deposits from valves to perform the cleaning.

Recheck the O2 sensor waveform for misfire events and fuel control to verify the repair.

NOx Failure Diagnosis

Verify the initial timing and timing advance capability as well as knock retard system operation (if equipped).

Test EGR function for: proper vacuum or electrical signal, valve operation, and open EGR/manifold ports.

Verify engine cooling system efficiency and radiator cooling fan operation. Ensure thermostat is operating normally.

Inspect the TAC and EFE to see if either is stuck in the hot air position. Check IAT readings and duct routing for fresh air.

Check for possible machine work to the cylinder head or decking block. This will cause a higher compression ratio, which could lead to more pressure and heat.

Check the O2 sensor for overly lean readings.

Check for carbon buildup in the combustion chamber with a bore scope.

Check the secondary air injection system to see if it is allowing or causing ambient air to enter the exhaust upstream of the TWC. The extra O2 present in the exhaust stream prevents the TWC from reducing NOx.

Finish the Job

Always check the catalytic converter prior to retesting the vehicle. Most if not all of the above problems will at some point cause a catalytic converter failure. At minimum, do a tap test and listen for a rattle or a hollow sound. No single test of the converter is foolproof, so perform at least two types. The cranking HC and CO2 test and the snap CO versus O2 test are good indicators.

Test the secondary air injection system to make sure it is performing correctly. Use the OEM performance test in the shop manual.

FUNCTIONAL TESTING

Initial Ignition Timing

In some states, ignition timing is checked, even on EI (distributorless) ignition systems, when there is a specification and adjustment procedure. Ignition timing functional tests may include both initial timing and timing advance verification as explained in Chapter 3.

EVAP System

A pressure test is used to check the entire evaporative system for leaks, figure 6-23. The system is tested by electronic equipment that pressurizes the system with nitrogen to 14 inches of water (about 0.5 psi). If the system remains above 8 inches of water after two minutes, the EVAP system passes. In some

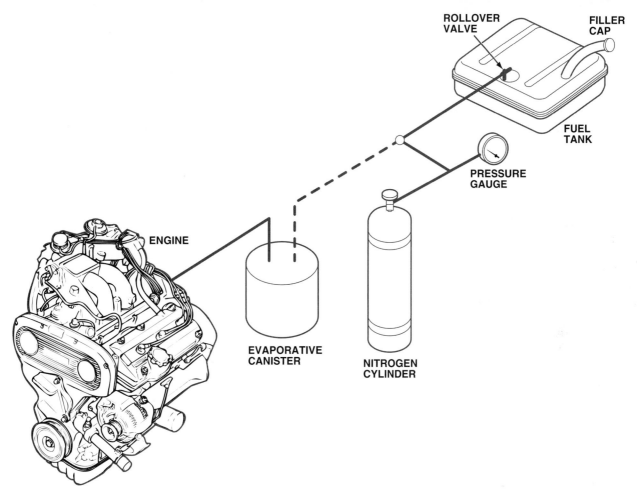

Fig. 6-23. The evaporative system is checked for leaks by pressurizing it with nitrogen.

states, instead of a system pressure test, a gas cap test is performed much like a radiator pressure cap test. The cap is installed on test equipment that electronically tests the gas cap for leaks. If the cap leaks, it will fail.

A purge test is used to determine whether fuel vapor stored in the canister flows to the engine when the vehicle is driven, figure 6-24. After the technician connects the test equipment, a purge test is performed electronically while the vehicle is driven on a dynamometer, a type of vehicle treadmill. Canister purge flow is measured by a flow meter and must be a minimum of 1 liter during the test to pass.

Gas Tank Fillpipe Restrictor

The fillpipe restrictor test is performed with a dowel gauge to check the diameter of the restrictor. Oversized fillpipe restrictors allow the use of larger fuel nozzles used to dispense fuel containing more sulfur or phosphorus than allowed by law. The substandard fuel causes higher emissions and possible damage to the catalytic converter.

EGR System

The EGR system is functionally tested to check for clogged ports, proper vacuum or electrical signal to the valve, and actual valve operation, as explained in Chapter 5.

Malfunction Indicator Lamp Test

The Malfunction Indicator Lamp (MIL) is checked to see if the MIL lights with the ignition key ON and turns off when the engine is running. If the MIL is lit when the engine is running, diagnostic codes must be retrieved and interpreted.

Insight
Scanner checks of OBD II systems for emissions-related trouble codes are part of some states' functional tests.

I/M OBD DIAGNOSIS

MIL Operation
The most significant difference to remember when using the MIL to begin diagnosis on an OBD II vehicle is that there are no soft codes. If the MIL is on, a DTC and freeze frame data are recorded in computer memory and there is definitely a problem. The OBD I practice of clearing codes and driving the vehicle to see if codes reset must not be used on OBD II vehicles. All system monitor codes and many comprehensive component monitor codes require specific driving conditions before they will test a system or set a DTC. A quick trip around the block to confirm repairs often will not set a DTC, so the technician has no way of knowing if the problem still exists.

L1

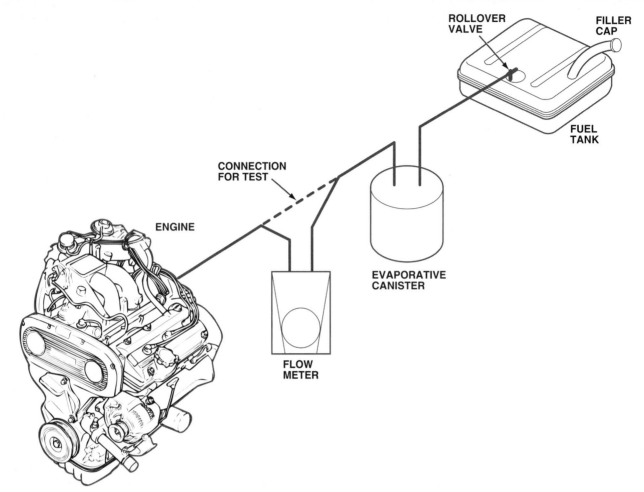

Fig. 6-24. A flow meter monitors the amount of vapor purged by the evaporative system.

It is best to clear DTCs only when instructed to do so by the manufacturer's diagnostic procedure, because freeze frame data and readiness test status are also erased when DTCs are cleared. Instead, use the stored freeze frame data to see what driving conditions were present when the code was set. Look for unusual readings from other sensors that may give a clue to the cause of the problem. Try to develop a "total picture" of vehicle operating conditions at the time the DTC was recorded. The same information is useful to help simulate driving conditions on a test drive as you verify the symptoms.

Remember, the MIL will be activated only for failures that cause excessive emissions. Problems in related systems or components may be recorded in ECM memory as OBD II (P0) or manufacturer-designated (P1) DTCs. All powertrain codes should be reviewed and investigated as part of the diagnostic process for driveabilty complaints.

Comprehensive Component Monitors

Comprehensive component monitors are most like the OBD I monitoring system that watches engine and transmission sensor inputs and actuator outputs for shorts, opens, and out-of-range values. OBD II computer (ECM) programs are enhanced to include identification of sensor values that don't logically fit with other powertrain data. For instance, if the Throttle Position Sensor (TPS) is reporting wide-open

throttle (4.5 volts on the composite vehicle), but other sensors are reporting idle speed values, the ECM will set a DTC for the TPS.

Remember, comprehensive component monitors are one trip monitors. The ECM will activate the MIL and store DTC and freeze frame data the first time an emissions related fault is detected. If a misfire or fuel control problem is detected after the original DTC was recorded, freeze frame date for the misfire or fuel control code will replace the original data.

Readiness Status and System Monitors

You will recall that the monitor readiness status tells the technician if a particular diagnostic monitor (test) has been completed since the last time DTCs were cleared from memory. There are two important concepts to understand when viewing monitor readiness status: First, the vehicle must be driven under specific conditions for some monitors to run, and second, the emissions system being monitored must be operational. If battery power is disconnected and the vehicle isn't driven through an entire drive cycle, the readiness status will be "NO." If there is an electrical problem or component failure in a monitored system, the monitor will not run. A DTC may be recorded that points to the electrical or component failure, but the system cannot be tested by the monitor, so the readiness status will be "NO." A readiness status of "NO" for any of the five monitored systems, catalyst, EGR, EVAP, Oxygen sensors, and Oxygen sensor heaters, does not mean a failed monitor, only that the monitor test has not been completed. At the same time, a "YES" status does not mean the system passed the monitor, only that the test was completed. In both cases, you must check for codes to investigate further.

Fuel Control Monitor

The fuel control monitor is designed to constantly check the ability of the ECM to control the air/fuel ratio. On the composite vehicle, the ECM program that fine tunes the air/fuel ratio is called Fuel Trim. It is divided into a short term program and a long term program. Both trim programs are presented as diagnostic data when a freeze frame is recorded. Separate short term and long term data are displayed for cylinder bank 1 and cylinder bank 2.

The oxygen sensor (HO2S) drives the fuel trim program anytime the vehicle is in closed loop. The starting point for fuel trim is 0% correction, figure 6-25. When the ECM sees a lean (low voltage) signal from an upstream HO2S, the fuel trim program adds fuel to compensate for the detected leaness. The short term fuel trim display on the scan tool will move to the positive (+) side of 0% to indicate more fuel is being added. When the ECM sees a rich (high voltage) signal from the HO2S, the fuel trim program subtracts fuel to lean the mixture. The scan tool will display a percentage on the negative (-) side of 0%. If short term fuel trim is necessary in one direction (rich or lean correction) for a period of time, the ECM will command a correction of long term fuel trim. When A/F control is out of acceptable range for too long a time, a DTC will set. On the composite vehicle, if long term fuel trim reaches +30% (lean correction) or -30% (rich correction) on two consecutive trips, the ECM will activate the MIL and record a DTC and freeze frame data.

FUEL TRIM CORRECTIONS

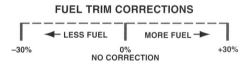

Fig. 6-25. On the composite vehicle, fuel trim corrections are displayed on the scan tool as a percentage of correction.

Long term fuel trim represents correction to fuel delivery over time. If the oxygen sensor voltage is fluctuating, but is mainly below 450 mV, indicating a lean A/F ratio, long term fuel trim will increase and the ECM will command longer injector pulse width. If oxygen sensor voltage is fluctuating, but remains mostly above 450 mV, indicating a rich mixture, long term fuel trim will decrease and the ECM will command shorter injection pulse width to adjust fuel delivery.

Short term fuel trim is useful when confirming fuel control. Observe short term fuel trim on the scan tool while adding propane through the intake system. The additional fuel will cause a rich mixture. If the fuel system is in closed loop, short term fuel trim will move in a negative direction as the fuel trim program shortens fuel injector pulse width in response to a higher HO2S voltage signal. Driving the system lean by pulling a vacuum line will cause short term fuel trim to increase injector pulse width. The scan tool display will move in a positive direction.

During diagnosis, be sure to look at both short and long term fuel trim. A problem that has existed for some time will cause long term fuel trim to record high or low. Once the problem is repaired, long term fuel trim will not change for a while, but short term fuel trim will begin immediately to move in the opposite direction. A restricted fuel filter, for instance, will cause a lean mixture. Long term fuel trim will eventually show a positive percentage (more fuel) as the system compensates for the lean mixture. Once the fuel filter is replaced, the A/F ratio is suddenly too rich. Comparing short and long term fuel trim immediately after the filter is replaced will reveal opposite readings: a negative percentage reading in short term fuel trim because the ECM is attempting to return the A/F ratio to normal by subtracting fuel, and a positive percentage reading in long term fuel trim because the long term program still "remembers" the lean correction and is waiting to see what happens.

Misfire Monitor

Engine misfire monitoring uses the CKP signal as the primary sensor. When a misfire occurs, whether due to engine compression, ignition, or fuel, crankshaft speed is affected. The ECM is programmed to notice the intermittent change in CKP pulses, figure 6-26. Camshaft position is used to identify which cylinder misfired. Because outside factors such as electrical

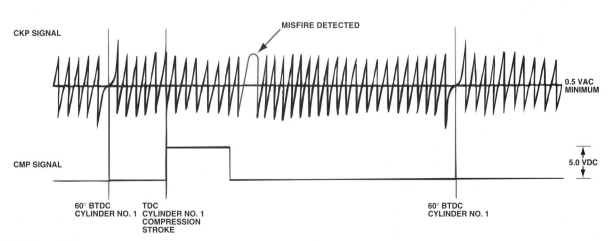

Fig. 6-26. The PCM is programmed to notice the sudden change in CKP sensor pulses.

interference and rough roads can mimic a misfire, most ECM programs keep track of how many times a cylinder misfires in a given number of engine rotations. The ECM activates the MIL when misfire reaches a predetermined percentage of rpm.

Remember, misfire monitoring, like fuel trim monitoring, is a two trip monitor. The MIL will glow steadily once a misfire is detected. If misfiring becomes severe enough to damage the catalytic converter, the MIL will blink continuously until the misfire becomes less severe.

Catalytic Converter Monitor

As mentioned earlier, the catalytic converter monitor checks converter efficiency by comparing upstream HO2S signals with the downstream HO2S signal. In normal operation the upstream HO2S signals will switch frequently between 200 mV and 900 mV and the downstream HO2S signal will show very little fluctuation and a voltage that tends to stay above the 450 mV threshold, figure 6-27. As catalyst performance begins to degrade, less oxygen is used in the converter and so less ends up in the exhaust, causing voltage fluctuations and a lower voltage bias, figure 6-28. When the downstream HO2S voltage signal begins to fluctuate within about 70% of the upstream HO2S signal on two consecutive trips, the ECM will record freeze frame data, set a DTC, and actuate the MIL.

EVAP Monitor

A vehicle will fail the EVAP monitor if the ECM, using information from the fuel tank pressure sensor, sees vacuum decrease too quickly after the EVAP vent and EVAP purge solenoids have been closed. Keep in mind that simple problems like a loose, damaged, or missing gas cap will cause this code to set.

Be careful when making quick repairs. For example, after replacing a damaged gas cap on a vehicle brought in for a lit MIL, you may be tempted to clear the DTC and return the car to the customer after a short road test. However, the EVAP monitor won't run if the engine is warm (above 86°F) or if the fuel level is not between ¼ and ¾ full. If the EVAP system has other problems and the EVAP monitor doesn't run during the road test, the MIL will come on after you return the vehicle to the customer.

Verify the Repair

Repeat the test drive and then compare the five-gases and O2 sensor waveform to the original test drive results. There should be a significant improvement, even in the gases that originally passed the emission test. Let the customer know there will be a direct benefit in gas mileage from any improved combustion efficiency.

As with anything new, the first time takes longer, but you'll be surprised. The more you use the diagnostic routine, the faster you will find defects and fix problems. If you think this takes too long or try short cuts, you become part of a problem that causes a high comeback rate of vehicle repair and retest.

CATALYST MONITOR EFFICIENCY TEST

PRE-CATALYST HO2S1

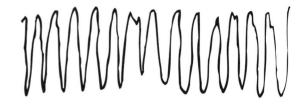

POST-CATALYST HO2S2

GOOD CATALYST

MONITOR TEST PASSED

Fig. 6-27. When the catalyst is working efficiently, most oxygen is used for oxidation and reduction, so post-converter voltage fluctuations are minimal.

CATALYST MONITOR EFFICIENCY TEST

PRE-CATALYST HO2S1

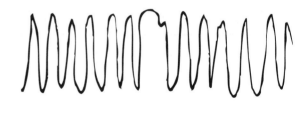

POST-CATALYST HO2S2

DEGRADED CATALYST

MONITOR TEST FAILED

Fig. 6-28. As catalyst performance becomes less efficient, less oxygen is used and voltage fluctuations from the post-converter begin to increase.

CHAPTER QUESTIONS

1. Technician A says a five-gas exhaust gas analyzer is used to measure HC, CO, O2, CO2, and NOx.
   Technician B says a five-gas exhaust gas analyzer is used to measure HC, CO, O2, CO2, and N2.
   Who is right?
   a. A only
   b. B only
   c. Both A and B
   d. Neither A nor B

2. Which of the following emissions is not measured during a two speed idle test?
   a. Carbon monoxide (CO)
   b. Carbon dioxide (CO2)
   c. Hydrocarbons (HC)
   d. Oxides of nitrogen (NOx)

3. When diagnosing a combustion problem, each of the gases gives a hint as to what the problem is. Which of the following gases is considered a good indicator for rich condition?
   a. Carbon dioxide (CO2)
   b. Carbon monoxide (CO)
   c. Hydrocarbons (HC)
   d. Oxygen (O2)

4. An ignition misfire will cause a large increase in which of the following exhaust gas readings?
   a. Carbon monoxide (CO)
   b. Carbon dioxide (CO2)
   c. Hydrocarbons (HC)
   d. Oxygen (O2)

5. Technician A says when viewing monitor readiness, the vehicle must be driven under certain specific conditions for some monitors to run. Technician B says the system being monitored must be operational.
   Who is right?
   a. A only
   b. B only
   c. Both A and B
   d. Neither A nor B

6. The IM240 test measures the total mass of HC, CO, and NOx emissions by weight in:
   a. Liters per kilometer
   b. Grams per mile
   c. Ounces per mile
   d. None of the above

7. Which of the following is NOT a common cause of "too lean" combustion problems?
   a. High fuel pressure
   b. Vacuum leak in the intake manifold
   c. Unmeasured air entering the intake of systems using a mass airflow sensor
   d. Dirty fuel injectors

8. Technician A says the MIL (Malfunction Indicator Lamp) should light when the ignition switch is turned on.
   Technician B says if the MIL is lit with the engine running, diagnostic trouble codes must be retrieved and interpreted.
   Who is right?
   a. A only
   b. B only
   c. Both A and B
   d. Neither A nor B

SAMPLE TEST

As soon as you make the decision to schedule an L1 test, begin preparing by including dedicated study time in your weekly schedule. You can improve your test score with just a few hours of study and review per week.

Photocopy the practice test included in this study guide so you can use it several times.

The practice test will help you become more comfortable with test taking in general. It will also point out your weak spots and enable you to use your study time more efficiently.

When you miss a question, look up the answer and study the subject in the study guide. Take notes on the subject to use for review. After repeated test taking and review, you should have your notes reduced to a single sheet of paper that can be reviewed daily the week before the test, and again on the day of the test.

Arrive at the test site early so parking or unforeseen problems do not cause you stress. Plan to allow time for a last look at your notes before entering the test site. Pay attention to all instructions from the test proctor even if you are a veteran test taker. From time to time ASE adjusts its instructions.

To answer test questions correctly, you must have a clear understanding of what is being asked. Read the question twice to be sure what it is asking. While thinking about the question, recall what you know about the subject. Do this before reading the answers. You are less likely to be influenced into a wrong conclusion by the answers if you recall what you know about the subject first. Since you have recalled your knowledge of the subject, you will be less likely to doubt yourself while reading the answers.

Note all operating conditions stated in the question when considering the answers. However, never assume that conditions exist that are not stated in the question. Treat each answer as a true or false question. Be sure to read all the answers before making your choice. When you conclude that more than one may be correct, reread the question to make sure you haven't missed an important fact, then rely on your knowledge to choose the one that is most correct. There is always one most correct answer.

When it seems impossible to decide which answer is correct, it may help to think of which item would be more likely to wear out or which things require regular service. These types of items may be the best choice, especially when the question asks, "which is more likely?"

Never leave a question unanswered. Unanswered questions are scored as wrong! Guess if you can't make a decision. Guessing gives you a 25% chance of being correct. If you narrow the field to two possibilities, you have a 50% chance. Choose an answer before moving on to the next question in case you run out of time. Make a mark next to the question in the test booklet.

Sometimes, other questions contain information that will help answer a question you're not sure of, and you can return to the questions you have marked if you have time. Be cautious when returning to reread a question. If you are still not sure which answer is correct, it's better to leave your original guess than to make a second guess. However, if you are certain that you originally misunderstood the question, it's best to change your answer.

Scan tool data and freeze frame data for composite vehicle questions will appear as shown in the following table, with four boxes per horizontal row. Not all rows shown in the illustration will appear for each question. You can expect to see anywhere from two to six horizontal rows containing data for each question.

When faced with a question that has a large amount of scan tool freeze frame data, limit the time it takes to answer the question by reading only the data that applies to or verifies an available answer. For example, an answer says the throttle position (TP) sensor is bad. To check if this is a true or false answer, look at the TP throttle opening value and compare it to the crankshaft (CKP) sensor rpm. The answer is false if the engine rpm indicates the throttle opening value is correct. It verifies that the TP sensor is good. The answer is true if the engine rpm doesn't agree with the throttle opening.

You can use this method of comparison verification to compare other engine operating conditions stated in the question like engine load, temperature, etc., to the scan tool data. This way, instead of checking all the freeze frame data, you will spend time checking only data that contains information to help decide which answer is best.

The scan tool data used on composite vehicle questions will appear in the following format:

SCAN TOOL DATA			
ENGINE COOLANT TEMP. ECT) SENSOR 0	INTAKE AIR TEMP. (IAT) SENSOR 0	MANIFOLD ABSOLUTE PRESSURE (MAP) SENSOR 0	MASS AIRFLOW (MAF) SENSOR 0
THROTTLE POSITION 1 (TP1) SENSOR 0	THROTTLE POSITION 2 (TP2) SENSOR 0	ACCELERATOR POSITION 1 (APP1) SENSOR 0	ACCELERATOR POSITION 2 (APP2) SENSOR 0
CRANKSHAFT POSITION SENSOR CKP 0	CALCULATED LOAD VALUE	KNOCK SENSOR (KS) 0	HEATED OXYGEN SENSOR 1/1 (HO2S1/1) 0
HEATED OXYGEN SENSOR 2/1 (HO2S2/1) 0	HEATED OXYGEN SENSOR 1/2 (HO2S1/2) 0	VALID IGNITION KEY YES/NO	FUEL ENABLE YES/NO
INJECTOR PULSE WIDTH BANK 1 0	INJECTOR PULSE WIDTH BANK 2	BANK 1 SHORT TERM/LONG TERM FUEL TRIM 0/0	BANK 2 LONG TERM/SHORT TERM FUEL TRIM 0/0
LOOP OPE/CLOSED	MONITOR STATUS DISABLED/NOT COMPLETE/ COMPLETE	IGNITION TIMING ADVANCE 0	KNOCK SENSOR DETECTED YES/NO
THROTTLE ACTUATOR CONTROL (TAC) 0	BATTERY VOLTAGE 0	GENERATOR FIELD 0	INTAKE CAM 1 DESIRED ADVANCE 0
INTAKE CAM 2 DESIRED ADVANCE 0	CAMSHAFT POSITIION SENSOR 1 (CMP1) 0	CAMSHAFT POSITIION SENSOR 2 (CMP2) 0	EGR VALVE OPENING DESIRED 0
EGR POSITION SENSOR 0	EVAP PURGHE SOLENOID 0	EVAP CANISTER VENT SOLENOID 0	FUEL TANK (EVAP) SOLENOID ON/OFF
FUEL TANK EVAP PRESSURE 0	FUEL TANL LEVEL 0	POWER STEERING SWITCH (PS) ON/OFF	BRAKE SWITCH ON/OFF
A/C REQUEST SWITCH ON/OFF	A/C PFRESSURE 0	A/C CLUTCH ON/OFF	FAN CONTROL ON/OFF
FUEL PUMP ON/OFF	TRANSMISSION RANGE (TR) P/N, 1, 2, 3, OD	TRANSMISSION FLUID TEMPERATURE (TFT) 0	VEHICLE SPEED SENSOR (VSS) 0
TRANSMISSION TURBINE SHAFT SPEED (TSS)	SHIFT SOLENOID 1 (SS1) ON/OFF	SHIFT SOLENOID 2 (SS2) ON/OFF	TORQUE CONVERTER CLUTCH (TCC)

SAMPLE TEST

1. Technician A says voltage and amperage are inversely proportional to each other as long as resistance remains the same.
   Technician B says amperage and resistance are directly proportional to each other as long as voltage remains the same.
   Who is right?
   a. A only
   b. B only
   c. Both A and B
   d. Neither A nor B

2. A circuit that has one path for current flow is called a:
   a. Complex circuit
   b. Series circuit
   c. Parallel circuit
   d. Bias circuit

3. Technician A says when testing a circuit, the ammeter should be connected to the circuit in parallel. Technician B says connecting an ammeter to the circuit in parallel will allow too much current to pass through the meter, which may result in damage to the meter.
   Who is right?
   a. A only
   b. B only
   c. Both A and B
   d. Neither A nor B

4. A diode is designed to:
   a. Allow current flow in both directions
   b. Prevent current flow in both directions
   c. Add extra resistance to control circuits
   d. Allow current flow in one direction only

5. Technician A says an engine breathing problem, such as a worn camshaft lobe or valve train problem that prevents the proper amount of air entering the cylinder, may be diagnosed by running a compression test.
   Technician B says an engine breathing problem, such as a worn camshaft lobe or valve train problem that prevents the proper amount of air entering the cylinder, may be diagnosed by a cranking compression test.
   Who is right?
   a. A only
   b. B only
   c. Both A and B
   d. Neither A nor B

6. During a cylinder leak down test, a cylinder has more than 20 percent leakage with air escaping though the tailpipe. The most likely cause would be:
   a. Damaged piston rings
   b. Leaking exhaust valve
   c. Leaking intake valve
   d. Cracked piston

7. A long warm-up time may be caused by all of the following *EXCEPT*:
   a. Low ambient temperatures
   b. No thermostat
   c. Stuck open thermostat
   d. Stuck closed thermostat

8. Technician A says that watching a spark jump a gap of a spark tester is adequate to determine whether there is a spark problem.
   Technician B says it's important to run an oscilloscope check of the secondary voltage to determine if the problem exists in the spark plug, spark plug wire, or motor.
   Who is right?
   a. A only
   b. B only
   c. Both A and B
   d. Neither A nor B

9. Technician A says voltage and amperage are inversely proportional to each other as long as resistance remains the same.
   Technician B says amperage and resistance are inversely proportional to each other as long as voltage remains the same.
   Who is right?
   a. A only
   b. B only
   c. Both A and B
   d. Neither A nor B

10. In a series circuit with a 3 Ohm resistor and 12 volts applied, the current flow is:
    a. 1 amp
    b. 12 amps
    c. 4 amps
    d. 8 amps

11. When diagnosing a starter problem, it is determined that the solenoid clicks but the starter does not spin.
    Technician A says that a defective solenoid may be causing the problem.
    Technician B says it might be due to low resistance in the starter control circuit.
    Who is right?
    a. A only
    b. B only
    c. Both A and B
    d. Neither A nor B

12. When diagnosing a starting problem, disabling the ignition and fuel or just the fuel system prevents start up. What else is prevented when performing cranking tests?
    a. False scan tool readings
    b. Crankcase oil dilution
    c. Excessive fuel backwash
    d. Parasitic drains

L1

13. When performing a no-start diagnosis, if fully charged, a battery should measure:
    a. 12.3 volts
    b. 12.4 volts
    c. 12.5 volts
    d. 12.6 volts

14. Technician A says intake valve deposits can cause an engine to run rich while cruising or accelerating.
    Technician B says intake valve deposits will cause an engine to run rich during deceleration.
    Who is right?
    a. A only
    b. B only
    c. Both A and B
    d. Neither A nor B

15. A vehicle has a delayed start problem when the engine is cold. It has an extended cranking time before starts, but runs OK after it is started.
    Which of these is the cause?
    a. Defective electronic fuel injector
    b. Restricted exhaust
    c. No CKP sensor signal
    d. Defective fuel pump check valve

16. A vehicle that otherwise runs fine, stalls when the driver attempts to parallel park.
    Which of these is correct?
    a. Bad power steering switch
    b. High power steering pump pressure
    c. Bad TCC solenoid or circuit
    d. Defective TP circuit

17. A vehicle in for repair runs rough and the MIL is flashing.
    Technician A says check for a severe misfire condition.
    Technician B says clear the codes and test drive the vehicle.
    Who is right?
    a. A only
    b. B only
    c. Both A and B
    d. Neither A nor B

18. Technician A says the catalytic converter monitor compares upstream HO2S signals to downstream HO2S signals.
    Technician B says in normal operation the downstream HO2S signal will switch frequently between 200mV and 900mV and upstream HO2S will show very little fluctuation and a voltage that tends to stay above the 450mV threshold.
    Who is right?
    a. A only
    b. B only
    c. Both A and B
    d. Neither A nor B

19. With the ignition key on, the engine off, and the connector unplugged from the IAT sensor, the technician inserts a jumper between the terminals of the connector. The scanned data reads 140°F or 60°C. Which of these is correct?
    a. The circuit passes the test
    b. Low circuit resistance
    c. This is not a valid test
    d. High circuit resistance

20. This TP sensor signal shown below was observed with a scope while the throttle was being opened and then closed. Which of these are **NOT** correct?
    a. This can cause the PCM to go into a clear flood mode
    b. This can cause erratic shifting on an electronic transmission
    c. This could cause a hesitation on acceleration
    d. This is a typical TP fault

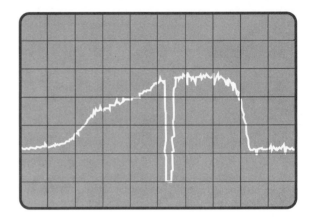

21. Which of the following conditions is most likely to cause the gas analyzer results shown below?
    a. EGR valve stuck open
    b. Restricted fuel return
    c. Ignition misfire
    d. Brake booster vacuum leak

ENGINE SPEED	IDLE	2500 RPM
HC (ppm)	1353	1456
CO (percent)	0.56	0.51
CO_2 (percent)	10.1	10.3
O_2 (percent)	5.1	5.2

22. A technician is measuring the voltage drop on the sensor ground circuit. With the ignition key on, measuring between the sensor ground and engine ground, the technician observes 0.651 volt. Which of these is correct?
    a. Low primary voltage
    b. Low reference voltage
    c. Low circuit resistance
    d. High circuit resistance

23. A vehicle failed its Acceleration Simulation Mode (ASM) emissions test for high NOx emission with the emissions levels shown below. Which of these is the most likely cause?
    a. EGR ports clogged
    b. EGR stuck open
    c. Plugged EGR solenoid vacuum vent
    d. Retarded ignition timing

LOAD/SPEED	50/15	25/25
HC (ppm)	33	22
CO (percent)	0.2	0.1
CO₂ (percent)	14.8	14.9
O₂ (percent)	0.3	0.2
NOx (ppm)	1231	1469

24. Use the gas analyzer measurements shown below to decide what type of problem this vehicle has. Which of these is correct?
    a. Flat camshaft lobe
    b. Leaking fuel injector
    c. Ignition misfire
    d. EGR not opening

ENGINE SPEED	IDLE	2500 RPM
HC (ppm)	410	251
CO (percent)	2.3	1.9
CO₂ (percent)	11.8	12.5
O₂ (percent)	0	0.3

25. During a visual inspection, the technician notices a burned and brittle secondary air injection hose, connected between the check valve and diverter valve. Which of these is correct?
    a. Hose has aged and needs to be replaced
    b. Too much pressure from the air pump
    c. Hose condition indicates a bad check valve
    d. Replace the failed diverter valve

26. A vehicle's engine runs smooth at idle but misfires when accelerated. Which of these is correct?
    a. Open plug wire
    b. Burned valve
    c. Broken wire in injector harness
    d. Low primary ignition voltage

27. If the air-fuel mixture is too rich, which of the following will increase?
    a. Hydrocarbons (HC) and oxygen (O2) emission levels
    b. Hydrocarbons (HC) and carbon monoxide (CO) emission levels
    c. Carbon monoxide (CO) and carbon dioxide (CO2) emission levels
    d. Hydrocarbons (HC) and carbon dioxide (CO2) emission levels

28. The gas analyzer readings shown below caused a vehicle to fail its emissions test. Which of the following problems could be the cause?
    a. Restricted fuel return line
    b. Secondary air injection downstream
    c. Shorted coolant temperature circuit
    d. Brake booster has a vacuum leak

ENGINE SPEED	IDLE	2500 RPM
HC (ppm)	640	534
CO (percent)	4.2	3.6
CO₂ (percent)	11.2	12.8
O₂ (percent)	0.1	0.6

29. A vehicle is being tested on a dynamometer with a vacuum gauge connected to the manifold vacuum. The vehicle is accelerated and driven at 25 mph. During the test, the vacuum drops to 8" hg and the vehicle loses power and speed. Which of the following answers is the most likely reason?
    a. Disconnected fuel pressure regulator vacuum hose
    b. Pinched fuel return line
    c. Burned exhaust valve
    d. Restricted exhaust

30. A vehicle intermittently misfires and loses power when run with a load on a dynamometer. However, it runs smoothly without the load applied. Which of these is correct?
    a. Cracked piston ring or rings
    b. Fouled spark plugs
    c. Defective spark plug boot insulator
    d. Broken wire in the injector harness

31. A vehicle is in the shop with a lean fuel mixture problem at idle and low speeds.
    Technician A says the problem can be caused by a leaking vacuum hose allowing too much air flow through the PCV system.
    Technician B says the problem may be caused by gasoline contamination in the crankcase oil.
    Who is right?
    a. A only
    b. B only
    c. Both A and B
    d. Neither A nor B

32. A vehicle has failed the I/M 240 emissions test for high CO and HC. NOx emission is lower than expected. The O2 sensor waveform shows it is fixed high.
    Technician A says the cause could be an intermittent open in an injector driver circuit.
    Technician B says the cause could be a ruptured fuel pressure regulator diaphragm.
    Who is right?
    a. A only
    b. B only
    c. Both A and B
    d. Neither A nor B

L1

33. An evaporative system pressure test is being performed. Air can be heard escaping from the gas tank filler neck. Which of these is **NOT** correct?
    a. Defective gas cap seal
    b. Wrong gas cap is installed
    c. Missing EVAP service port cap
    d. Damaged tank filler neck

34. You are examining a secondary superimposed ignition waveform from an electronic ignition as illustrated below.
    Technician A says that the ignition system generates waveform A, with shorter dwell period, while the engine runs at a high RPM.
    Technician B says that the ignition system generates waveform B, with longer dwell period, while the engine runs at a low RPM.
    Who is right?
    a. A only
    b. B only
    c. Both A and B
    d. Neither A nor B

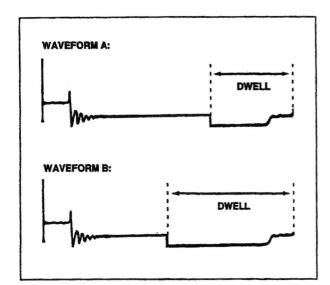

35. The injector wave form shown below was recorded at 1800 rpm.
    Technician A says the pattern is normal.
    Technician B says there is a bad driver or ground.
    Who is right?
    a. A only
    b. B only
    c. Both A and B
    d. Neither A nor B

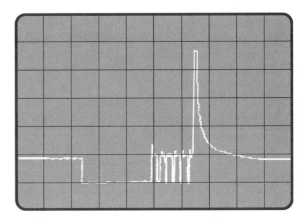

36. The wave forms shown below are for the pre-catalyst and post-catalyst O2 sensors. They were observed on a fully compliant OBD II vehicle at normal operating temperature. Which of these is correct?
    a. Too much oxygen in the exhaust
    b. O2 sensor waveforms are normal
    c. Downstream O2 sensor is lazy
    d. Waveform shows there is no fuel control

PRE-CATALYST HO2S1

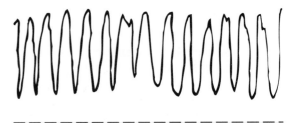

POST-CATALYST HO2S2

37. A vehicle has high HC emission at idle. The initial ignition timing is correct. The O2 sensor voltage is biased low. The CO2 level is a little lower and O2 level is a little higher than expected. The technician meters propane through the intake while monitoring the tailpipe gasses with an analyzer and notices that the CO2 increases while the HC drops. Which of these is correct?
    a. Defective spark plug wire
    b. Fouled spark plug
    c. Leaking brake booster
    d. Restricted air filter

38. A vehicle that runs rough above idle speed produced the gas readings on the analyzer shown below. Which of the following reasons is the most likely cause of the symptom?
   a. Higher than normal fuel pressure
   b. An exhaust valve leak
   c. Resistance high in the ignition coil primary circuit
   d. Dilution from a stuck-open EGR valve

CKP SIGNAL

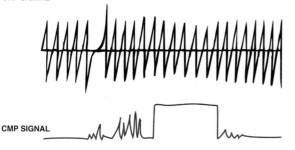

CMP SIGNAL

39. A vehicle that seems to run fine at cruising speed idles fast, surges, and sometimes stalls at idle, especially when the engine is cold.
   Technician A says the idle air bypass is clogged with carbon.
   Technician B says the problem is an air or vacuum leak.
   Who is right?
   a. A only
   b. B only
   c. Both A and B
   d. Neither A nor B

40. Technician A says a LDP (Leak Detection Pump) pressurizes the EVAP system and seals the charcoal canister.
   Technician B says the LDP depressurizes the EVAP system and seals the charcoal canister.
   Who is right?
   a. A only
   b. B only
   c. Both A and B
   d. Neither A nor B

41. A vehicle runs rough and has a misfiring problem. While checking the ignition primary circuit, the technician observes the waveform shown below of the crankshaft (CKP) and camshaft (CMP) sensor signals at idle. Which of these is correct?
   a. Intermittent ground connection
   b. Broken tooth on the reluctor
   c. High resistance in the pickup coil
   d. Reference voltage is too high

ENGINE SPEED	IDLE	2500 RPM
HC (ppm)	68	1156
CO (percent)	0.31	0.22
CO₂ (percent)	14.1	11.3
O₂ (percent)	0.8	4.6

42. A vehicle is towed to the shop because the engine will not crank.
   Technician A says the problem could be a bad crankshaft (CKP) sensor.
   Technician B says the problem could be the PRNDL switch.
   Who is right?
   a. A only
   b. B only
   c. Both A and B
   d. Neither A nor B

43. A vehicle has failed its Acceleration Simulation Mode (ASM) test for high NOx emission. Which of these could NOT be the cause?
   a. Coolant thermostat stuck closed
   b. Restricted radiator
   c. Carbon deposits
   d. EGR is stuck open

44. Which exhaust gases are good mixture indicators?
   a. Carbon dioxide (CO2) and oxygen (O2)
   b. Hydrocarbons (HC) and carbon monoxide (CO)
   c. Carbon monoxide (CO) and oxygen (O2)
   d. Oxygen (O2) and carbon dioxide (CO2)

45. The O2 sensor waveforms shown below of the pre- and post-catalyst sensors were observed at 2000 rpm. The vehicle was fully preconditioned. Which of these is right?
   a. The catalyst is defective
   b. These are normal waveforms
   c. The catalyst is defective
   d. The mixture is too lean

PRE-CATALYST HO2S1

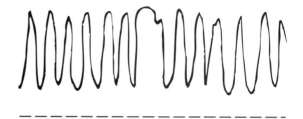

POST-CATALYST HO2S2

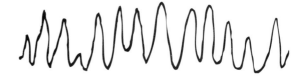

L1

46. A vehicle has a lack of power when climbing uphill. The sensor values shown below were observed driving uphill. Which of these is correct?
    a. High resistance TP ground circuit
    b. Bad MAP sensor or circuit
    c. High fuel pressure
    d. Restricted fuel filter

SENSOR	VOLTAGE
TP	3.2
MAP	2.8
O2	0.170

47. While checking a fuel pump circuit, the technician connects his meter leads across the two connections as shown below. At idle, the meter displays 1.12 volts. Which of these is correct?
    a. High resistance in the fuel pump relay control circuit
    b. The voltage drop is too low
    c. High resistance in the fuel pump relay power circuit
    d. The circuit passes the test

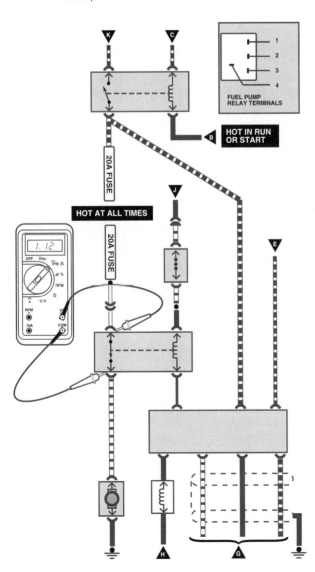

48. A vehicle with the wiring diagram shown below will not run. The vehicle cranks OK but will not start. With a jumper across the fuel pump check connector the engine will start. Once running it will continue to run with the jumper removed, but will not restart after it is shut off. Using the diagram above, which of these is correct?
    a. Bad main relay control circuit
    b. Bad cranking position control circuit
    c. Faulty ignition switch run circuit
    d. Blown # 5 fuse

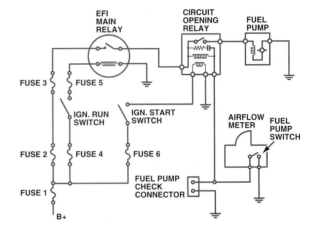

49. The oxygen sensor voltage readings are minimum 190 mV, maximum 600 mV, with an average of 350mV.
    Technician A says this indicates a lean engine running condition.
    Technician B says this indicates the system is operating properly.
    Who is right?
    a. A only
    b. B only
    c. Both A and B
    d. Neither A nor B

50. A vehicle has a fast idle and creeps forward in drive. The curb idle is 1100 rpm. This is way above the target 850 rpm specified. The scan data show the IAC command at 0% opening. Which of these is the cause?
    a. Bad VSS sensor signal
    b. Carbon in idle bypass port
    c. Damaged PCM
    d. Air (vacuum) leak

COMPOSITE VEHICLE QUESTIONS

Answering these questions may require you to refer to the composite vehicle reference section.

51. The composite vehicle will not start. There is no spark from the ignition system and no signal to the fuel injectors.
Technician A says a short at connector (a) of the CKP sensor caused damage to the ECM.
Technician B says a short at connector (a) of the VSS caused damage to the ECM.
Who is right?
   a. A only
   b. B only
   c. Both A and B
   d. Neither A nor B

52. The composite vehicle will not start. It has no spark and no signal to the injectors. The "snap shot" below was taken during cranking. Which of these is correct?
   a. Bad CKP sensor
   b. Open circuit at pin # 91
   c. Open circuit at pin # 32
   d. Open circuit at pin #1

SCAN TOOL DATA			
ENGINE COOLANT TEMP. ECT) SENSOR -40ºF/-40ºC/5.0V	INTAKE AIR TEMP. (IAT) SENSOR -40ºF/-40ºC/5.0V	MASS AIRFLOW (MAF) SENSOR 175 gm/sec/ 5.0V	THROTTLE POSITION 1 (TP1) SENSOR 100%/5.0V
CRANKSHAFT POSITION SENSOR CKP 193 RPM	HEATED OXYGEN SENSOR 1/1 (HO2S1/1) 0V	HEATED OXYGEN SENSOR 2/1 (HO2S2/1) 0V	HEATED OXYGEN SENSOR 1/2 (HO2S1/2) 0V
BANK 1 LONG/SHORT TERM FUEL TRIM 0%/0%	INJECTOR PULSE WIDTH BANK 1 0 ms	INJECTOR PULSE WIDTH BANK 2 0 ms	BANK 2 LONG/SHORT TERM FUEL TRIM 0%/0%
THROTTLE ACTUATOR CONTROL (TAC) 25%	EVAP CANISTER PURGE SOLENOID 0%	EVAP CANISTER VENT SOLENOID OFF	MANIFOLD ABSOLUTE PRESSURE (MAP) SENSOR 101.3 kpa/ 0 in. Hg/ 5.0V
BATTERY VOLTAGE 10.8	GENERATOR FIELD 0%	EGR VALVE CONTROL SOLENOID 0%	FUEL PUMP RELAY (FP) ON

53. The composite vehicle MIL is lit. A DTC P0141 (HO2 1/2 heater problem) and the freeze frame below are stored. Which of these is correct?
   a. Vehicle's fuel mixture is lean and vehicle will hesitate
   b. Vehicle is running rich and may fail an emissions test
   c. No driveability problems, but the HO2 1/2 sensor heater may be bad
   d. The vehicle has a misfire that may cause damage to the converter

SCAN TOOL DATA			
ENGINE COOLANT TEMP. ECT) SENSOR 212ºF/100ºC/0.46V	INTAKE AIR TEMP. (IAT) SENSOR 86ºF/30ºC/2.6V	MASS AIRFLOW (MAF) SENSOR 80 gm/sec/ 3.5V	THROTTLE POSITION 1 (TP1) SENSOR 25%/1.5V
CRANKSHAFT POSITION SENSOR CKP 2014 RPM	HEATED OXYGEN SENSOR 1/1 (HO2S1/1) 0.2 to 0.7V	HEATED OXYGEN SENSOR 2/1 (HO2S2/1) 0.2 to 0.8V	HEATED OXYGEN SENSOR 1/2 (HO2S1/2) 0V
BANK 1 LONG/SHORT TERM FUEL TRIM -1%/+2%	INJECTOR PULSE WIDTH BANK 1 2.3 ms	INJECTOR PULSE WIDTH BANK 2 2.2 ms	BANK 2 LONG/SHORT TERM FUEL TRIM +2%/-1%
BATTERY VOLTAGE 14.1	GENERATOR FIELD 40%	EGR VALVE CONTROL SOLENOID 0%	FUEL PUMP RELAY (FP) ON

54. The composite vehicle MIL is on steady and a DTC P0131 (HO2S 1/1, voltage low, and freeze frame below, has been recorded. Which of these is correct?
   a. Defective HO2S 1/1 circuit
   b. High ECT circuit resistance
   c. Shorted ECT circuit
   d. Bad fuel pressure regulator

SCAN TOOL DATA			
ENGINE COOLANT TEMP. ECT) SENSOR 176ºF/80ºC/0.84V	INTAKE AIR TEMP. (IAT) SENSOR 95ºF/35ºC/2.45V	MASS AIRFLOW (MAF) SENSOR 2 gm/sec/ 0.7V	THROTTLE POSITION 1 (TP1) SENSOR 0%/0.5V
CRANKSHAFT POSITION SENSOR CKP 850 RPM	HEATED OXYGEN SENSOR 1/1 (HO2S1/1) 0.17V	HEATED OXYGEN SENSOR 2/1 (HO2S2/1) 0.2 to 0.8V	HEATED OXYGEN SENSOR 1/2 (HO2S1/2) 0.7 to 0.8V
BANK 1 LONG/SHORT TERM FUEL TRIM +30%/+30%	INJECTOR PULSE WIDTH BANK 1 15.0 ms	INJECTOR PULSE WIDTH BANK 2 2.1 ms	BANK 2 LONG/SHORT TERM FUEL TRIM -3%/+2%
BATTERY VOLTAGE 13.9	GENERATOR FIELD 40%	EGR VALVE CONTROL SOLENOID 0%	FUEL PUMP RELAY (FP) ON
MALFUNCTION INDICATOR LAMP (ON)	DIAGNOSTIC TROUBLE CODES P0131	LOOP Closed	IGNITION TIMING ADVANCE +30º BTDC

55. A technician is checking the scan data on the composite vehicle. The brake booster was just replaced to repair a vacuum leak. The data show the long term fuel trim at +30 and short term at -10.
Technician A says this is normal.
Technician B says further diagnosis is necessary.
Who is right?
   a. A only
   b. B only
   c. Both A and B
   d. Neither A nor B

56. While diagnosing a DTC P0300 (bank 1 misfire) a technician has an ohmmeter connected across the #1 fuel injector terminals. The technician observes a reading of 20 ohms. Which of these is correct?
   a. Circuit passes the test
   b. Resistance below specification
   c. Not a valid test
   d. Resistance above specification

57. The composite vehicle failed an emissions test due to high NOx emissions. The MIL is on and there is a DTC P0401 (EGR system problem). Which of these is the cause?
    a. Grounded EGR circuit pin #35
    b. Restricted EGR port
    c. EGR solenoid stuck on
    d. Advanced timing

SCAN TOOL DATA			
ENGINE COOLANT TEMP. ECT) SENSOR 212°F/100°C/0.46V	INTAKE AIR TEMP. (IAT) SENSOR 104°F/40°C/2.27V	MASS AIRFLOW (MAF) SENSOR 60 gm/sec/ 3.2V	THROTTLE POSITION 1 (TP1) SENSOR 20%/1.3V
CRANKSHAFT POSITION SENSOR CKP 1800 RPM	HEATED OXYGEN SENSOR 1/1 (HO2S1/1) 0.2 to 0.8V	HEATED OXYGEN SENSOR 2/1 (HO2S2/1) 0.2 to 0.8V	HEATED OXYGEN SENSOR 1/2 (HO2S1/2) 0.6 to 0.7V
BANK 1 LONG/SHORT TERM FUEL TRIM -2%/+3%	INJECTOR PULSE WIDTH BANK 1 2.3 ms	INJECTOR PULSE WIDTH BANK 2 2.3 ms	BANK 2 LONG/SHORT TERM FUEL TRIM +1%/-4%
THROTTLE ACTUATOR MOTOR (TAC) 15%	EVAP CANISTER PURGE SOLENOID 50%	EVAP CANISTER VENT SOLENOID OFF	MANIFOLD ABSOLUTE PRESSURE (MAP) SENSOR 303 kpa/ 21 in. Hg/ 1.0V
BATTERY VOLTAGE 13.9	GENERATOR FIELD 40%	EGR VALVE CONTROL SOLENOID 60%	FUEL PUMP RELAY (FP) ON
MALFUNCTION INDICATOR LAMP (ON)	DIAGNOSTIC TROUBLE CODES P0401	LOOP Closed	IGNITION TIMING ADVANCE +30° BTDC

58. A technician is testing the composite vehicle fuel injector circuits. With the key on and the engine off, the technician places a voltmeter between the cylinder #1 fuel injector terminal (b) and engine ground. The meter reads 12.57 volts. Which of these is correct?
    a. Injector circuit is not grounded
    b. Injector winding is open
    c. Injector circuit is grounded
    d. ECM has been damaged

59. The composite vehicle's engine has a constant misfire at all speeds. The ignition system, cylinder compression, and fuel pressure check OK. The technician is checking the injector circuits with key on and the engine off. A voltmeter is connected to terminal (b) of the cylinder #1 injector and engine ground. The meter reads 0 volts; all others in that bank read 12.58 volts. Which of the following answers correctly describes the test results?
    a. ECM pin #38 circuit open
    b. Injector winding open
    c. ECM pin #38 circuit shorted to pin #39
    d. Fuse #4 blown

60. On the composite vehicle, if neither of the Camshaft Position (CMP-1 or CMP-2) sensor signals are detected, the ECM will store a DTC.
    Technician A says the ECM will also disable the ignition coils.
    Technician B says the ECM will also disable the fuel injectors.
    Who is right?
    a. A only
    b. B only
    c. Both A and B
    d. Neither A nor B

61. On the composite vehicle, if one of the Accelerator Pedal Position (APP) sensors fails, the ECM will turn on the MIL and limit the maximum throttle opening to which of the following percentages?
    a. 15 percent
    b. 25 percent
    c. 35 percent
    d. 45 percent

62. The evaporative system of the composite vehicle has failed an I/M 240 emissions test. While checking the system, the technician measures the resistance of the purge valve solenoid. It is 12 ohms.
    Technician A says the solenoid resistance is too low.
    Technician B says the ECM may have been damaged.
    Who is right?
    a. A only
    b. B only
    c. Both A and B
    d. Neither A nor B

63. The composite vehicle has failed an I/M 240 test because of high NOx emission. The cooling system and thermostat are working correctly. Technician A says a broken vacuum hose to the EGR could be the cause.
    Technician B says an open circuit at pin #35 could be the cause.
    Who is right?
    a. A only
    b. B only
    c. Both A and B
    d. Neither A nor B

64. The composite vehicle's engine has a constant misfire at all engine speeds. The MIL is flashing, and a DTC P0301 (cylinder 1 misfire) is stored. While checking the primary ignition voltage, with the key on and engine off, the technician notices that the meter reads 0.00 volts at ECM pin #7. Which of these is the problem?
    a. Fuse #4 (B+) blown
    b. Short to battery voltage at pin (a) on coil #1
    c. Open secondary winding in cylinder #1 coil
    d. Broken connection at (b) on cylinder #1 coil

65. On the composite vehicle, pin #23 MAP sensor and pin #18 TP #1 sensor are both shorted to ground.
    Technician A says this will cause the MAF sensor signal voltage at pin #68 to be low.
    Technician B says this will cause the 5-volt reference supply to be lower.
    Who is right?
    a. A only
    b. B only
    c. Both A and B
    d. Neither A nor B

SAMPLE TEST ANSWER DISCUSSION

1. (D) is correct. Voltage and amperage are directly proportional to each other as long as resistance remains the same. Amperage and resistance are inversely proportional to each other as long as voltage remains the same. (A), (B), and (C) are wrong due to both technicians being wrong.

2. (B) is correct. A series circuit only has one path through which current can flow. (A) is wrong. A complex circuit has more than one parallel circuit. (C) is wrong. A parallel circuit has more than one path through which current can flow. (D) is wrong. Bias refers to voltage applied to the same point in a circuit.

3. (B) is correct. Ammeters act as a jumper wire if connected in parallel. (A) is wrong. Ammeters are connected in series with the component being tested. (C) and (D) are wrong because only technician B is correct.

4. (D) is correct. A diode only allows current to flow in one direction; thus (A), (B), and (C) are wrong.

5. (A) is correct. A running compression test checks cylinder breathing by measuring the amount of air entering a cylinder. (B) is wrong. A cranking compression test only checks for cylinder sealing. Since only technician A is correct, (C) and (D) are wrong.

6. (B) is correct. A leaking exhaust valve will cause air to escape through the tailpipe. (A) and (D) are wrong. Damaged piston rings or a cracked cylinder will cause air to leak into the crankcase. (C) is wrong. A leaking intake valve will cause air to leak into the intake manifold.

7. (D) is correct. A stuck closed thermostat will restrict coolant flow and cause a quicker warm-up time and possible engine overheating. (A) is wrong. Low ambient temperatures can cause longer warm-up times. (C) and (D) are wrong. A stuck thermostat or no thermostat at all can cause longer warm-up times due to the coolant flow not being restricted.

8. (B) is correct. Oscilloscope checks of secondary voltage are best for showing a spark plug, spark plug wire, distributor cap, or rotor problem. (A) is wrong. It is difficult to say for certain that the spark is adequate just by watching it jump the gap of a spark tester. Since only technician A is correct, (C) and (D) are wrong.

9. (B) is correct. Ohm's law says amperage and resistance are inversely proportional to each other as long as voltage remains the same. (A) is wrong. Ohm's law says voltage and amperage are directly proportional to each other as long as resistance remains the same. Since only technician B is correct, (C) and (D) are wrong.

10. (C) is correct. Ohm's law says to calculate amperage, divide voltage (12) 1. (B) is wrong. 1 divided by 3 does not equal 12. (D) is wrong. 12 divided by 3 does not by resistance (3) equals 4 amps. (A) is wrong. 12 divided by 4 does not equal 8.

11. (A) is correct. A defective solenoid will keep the starter motor from spinning. (B) is wrong. Excessive resistance, not low resistance, will cause the solenoid to click. Since only technician A is correct, (C) and (D) are wrong.

12. (B) is correct. Crankcase oil dilution is caused by gasoline washing past the rings while performing cranking tests. (A), (C), and (D) are wrong. Disabling ignition will not cause false scan tool readings, excessive fuel backwash, or parasitic drains.

13. (D) is correct. A fully charged battery should measure 12.6V or higher. (A), (B), and (C) are wrong. 12.5V and below is too low for a fully charged battery.

14. (B) is correct. Intake valve deposits effect engine breathing and can cause a rich condition while decelerating. (A) is wrong. Intake valve deposits can cause an engine to run lean while cruising or accelerating. Since only technician B is correct, (C) and (D) are wrong.

15. (D) is correct. A defective fuel pump check valve can cause the system to leak residual pressure. This causes longer cranking time while pressure builds. (A) is wrong. A defective fuel injector, if leaking, causes hard starting when warm. An inoperative injector causes a problem under all conditions. (B) is wrong. A restricted exhaust has a greater effect on a warm engine and causes a problem at high speeds. (C) is wrong. No CKP signal will prevent start up.

16. (A) is correct. A bad power steering pressure switch will not signal the ECM to increase engine idle speed to compensate for the extra load from higher power steering pump pressure during parallel parking. (B) is wrong. Higher pump pressure would be idle speed compensated if the power steering pressure switch is working. (C) is wrong. A bad TCC solenoid, if engaged, will cause a stalling problem under all idle conditions. (D) is wrong. A defective TP circuit, unless intermittent, would have a constant effect under all operating conditions.

17. (A) is correct. The MIL is flashing because the ECM has detected a misfire that may damage the converter. (B) is wrong. Clearing codes will lose valuable stored data. Since only technician A is correct, (C) and (D) are wrong.

18. (A) is correct. The catalytic converter monitor checks converter efficiency by comparing upstream HO2S signals with the downstream HO2S signal. (B) is wrong. In normal operation the upstream HO2S signals will switch frequently between 200mV and 900 mV and the downstream HO2S signal will show very little fluctuation and a voltage that tends to stay above the 450mV threshold. Since only technician A is correct, (C) and (D) are wrong.

19. (D) is correct. The jumper in the IAT simulates the lowest circuit resistance possible. This should cause the ECM to believe the engine is very hot and report the maximum temperature in the scan data. The fact that the ECM is reporting 140°F or 60°C indicates there is additional resistance somewhere in the circuit. (A) and (B) are both wrong. There is additional resistance somewhere in the circuit. (C) is wrong. This is a valid test; in fact, the opposite check for this circuit is to check the IAT unplugged (open circuit) without a jumper. The ECM should report the

L1

minimum temperature. If not, there is a short somewhere in the circuit.

20. (A) is correct. The PCM requires a minimum voltage to activate its clear flood mode. This is the only choice that is not correct. The waveform clearly shows a drop of voltage during the fault. (B), (C), and (D) are wrong because they are true statements.

21. (C) is correct. An ignition misfire causes HC emission to increase at all speeds. (A) is wrong. A stuck-open EGR valve will cause a misfire at low speed. O2 would not increase as much. (B) is wrong. A restricted fuel return causes a very rich condition and a large increase of CO emission. (D) is wrong. A vacuum leak in the brake booster will cause a lean condition, causing CO emission to decrease.

22. (D) is correct. The voltage drop of 0.651 volt is way above the standard allowable and indicates high sensor ground circuit resistance. (A) and (B) are wrong. A low primary voltage supply or reference voltage will not increase the ground circuit voltage drop. (C) is wrong. Low circuit resistance causes less voltage drop than normal.

23. (A) is correct. Restricted EGR ports, causing inadequate flow, are a cause of high NOx emission. (B) and (C) are both wrong. If the EGR is stuck open or a plugged vacuum vent caused it to remain open, it cannot be the cause of the NOx increase. (D) is wrong. Retarded ignition timing reduces the production of NOx.

24. (B) is correct. The analyzer readings indicate a rich mixture that is even richer at idle speed. A leaking fuel injector can have this effect on the mixture and is worse at idle than cruising speeds. (A) and (C) are wrong. An ignition misfire or a flat camshaft lobe causes an increase of HC emission because of cylinder inefficiency. CO emission is not directly affected. (D) is wrong. The inoperative EGR will not cause an increase of CO emission. If the test isn't performed on a dynamometer or during a test drive, the EGR valve will probably not open anyway.

25. (C) is correct. A bad secondary air injection check valve allows exhaust to burn the attached air hose and possibly damage the diverter valve. (A) is wrong. The description of burned and brittle is typical of a bad check valve, not an old hose. (B) is wrong. The additional pressure from the air pump will force more air into the exhaust. A good check valve will still prevent exhaust flow toward the air injection system. (D) is wrong. There is no evidence presented that the diverter valve is damaged, although it is possible if the check valve is bad.

26. (D) is correct. Low primary ignition voltage causes the ignition system to have less reserve voltage capacity. This causes misfires during acceleration and high rpm operation when cylinder pressures are high, because voltage requirements are high. (A), (B), and (C) are wrong. An open spark plug wire, a burned valve, or a broken wire in the injector harness would cause a constant misfire.

27. (B) is correct. CO and HC will increase with an air-fuel mixture that is too rich. (A) is wrong because O2 will remain

the same with a too-rich air-fuel mixture. (C) and (D) are wrong, as CO2 will decrease as the air-fuel mixture richens.

28. (A) is correct. The analyzer readings indicate a rich condition. A restricted fuel return line causes high fuel pressure, resulting in a rich condition. (B) is wrong. Secondary air injection downstream will not cause a rich condition. (C) is wrong. A shorted coolant temperature circuit sends (low voltage) a hot signal causing a lean mixture. (D) is wrong. A leaking brake booster causes a lean condition.

29. (D) is correct. By a process of elimination, a restricted exhaust is the only problem listed that could be the cause. (A) is wrong. Lack of vacuum to the regulator raises fuel pressure and causes more trouble at low-speed light load. Under load on the dynamometer, an increase of fuel pressure is needed. (B) is wrong. A pinched fuel system return line causes increased fuel pressure. (C) is wrong. A burned exhaust valve causes a constant misfire, not just a loss of power under load.

30. (C) is correct. The higher the required voltage, the more a defective spark plug boot insulator will have a tendency to leak spark to ground. The conditions described in the question are typical of this problem. (A) is wrong. A cracked piston ring or piston rings will cause a misfire that is constant, not just under load. (B) and (D) are both wrong. Fouled spark plugs or a broken wire in the injector harness cause a constant misfire.

31. (A) is correct. A leaking PCV vacuum hose will cause a lean fuel mixture at idle and low speed. (B) is wrong. Gasoline contaminated engine oil will cause a rich fuel mixture condition. (C) is wrong because technician B is wrong. (D) is wrong because technician A is right.

32. (B) is correct. A ruptured fuel pressure regulator diaphragm allows fuel to enter the intake through the manifold vacuum connection. This causes a rich condition as indicated by both the gas readings and the O2 sensor waveform. (A) is wrong. An intermittent open injector driver will cause a misfire, not a rich condition. (C) and (D) are both wrong because only technician B is correct.

33. (C) is correct. The EVAP system service cap is present only to prevent dirt from entering the service port. A missing cap cannot cause a leak because a Schrader valve seals the port. (A), (B), and (D) are wrong. All of these can cause a leak from the system.

34. (D) is correct. Dwell increases with engine speed. Both technicians A and B are wrong.

35. (A) is correct. The injector scope pattern shown is an injector that has a pulse width modulated driver. The waveform is normal. (B) is wrong. The illustration shows a normal pulse width modulated injector waveform. (C) and (D) are both wrong because only technician A is correct.

36. (B) is correct. The illustration for this question shows the HO2S waveform of a good converter. (A) and (D) are both wrong. The upstream HO2S shows good fuel control with no bias. (C) is wrong. The downstream HO2S waveform shows

the results of a good converter storing oxygen and using it to oxidize HC and CO into H_2O and CO_2.

37. (C) is correct. The propane test proves the cause of the high HC emission is a lean mixture. A leaking brake booster is the cause. (A) and (B) are both wrong. A fouled spark plug or a defective spark plug wire will continue to cause high HC emission during the test. (D) is wrong. A restricted air filter causes a rich mixture, increasing CO emission, unless the system is equipped with an air flow sensor.

38. (C) is correct. High resistance in the ignition coil primary circuit will make the secondary ignition system unable to produce the higher voltage, causing the engine to misfire at higher speeds. (A) is wrong. Higher than normal fuel pressure will cause CO emission to increase. (B) is wrong. A leaking exhaust valve will cause HC emission to increase due to poor combustion efficiency. (D) is wrong. A stuck-open EGR valve will cause HC emission to increase at idle.

39. (B) is correct. Fast idle speed is caused by a vacuum or air leak. (A) is wrong. Carbon in the idle air bypass port decreases idle speed. (C) and (D) are both wrong because only technician B is correct.

40. (A) is correct. LDP must perform two functions, pressurize the EVAP system and seal the charcoal canister. (B) is wrong because technician B says LDP depressurizes the EVAP system. (C) is wrong because technician B is wrong. (D) is wrong because technician A is right.

41. (A) is correct. The waveform is typical of an intermittent ground circuit. (B) is wrong. The CMP sensor pattern shown is of a Hall-effect, not an A/C. generator (pickup coil). It has no reluctor. (C) is wrong. This sensor does not use a pickup coil. (D) is wrong. The top of the square wave will be taller if the reference voltage is too high, but it is pulled down by a good ground.

42. (B) is correct. If the PRNDL switch is bad, it will cause an open starter control circuit. (A) is wrong. A bad CKP sensor will not prevent engine cranking. (C) and (D) are both wrong because only technician B is correct.

43. (D) is correct. A stuck-open EGR will cause a misfire at low speeds, but will NOT cause high NOx emission. (A) and (B) are both wrong. A coolant thermostat stuck closed or a restricted radiator will cause hotter combustion temperatures and result in increased NOx emission. (C) is wrong. Carbon deposits can increase combustion pressure, which will increase combustion temperatures.

44. (C) CO and O_2 is the correct answer. If CO is higher than O_2 the mixture is rich. If O_2 is higher than CO the mixture is lean. (A), (B), and (D) are wrong. CO_2 is actually at its highest at an air-fuel ratio of 14 to 1, slightly richer than 14.7 to 1 (stoichiometric air fuel ratio). HC is a bad indicator of mixture because it rises when the mixture is very rich or even a little lean.

45. (A) is correct. The activity of the post-converter HO2S indicates the converter is degraded and is no longer storing O_2 or properly oxidizing HC and CO.

46. (D) is correct. A restricted fuel filter limits fuel delivery during times when additional fuel is required, causing a lack of power when climbing hills. (A) is wrong. The TP sensor signal is normal for the operating conditions. High resistance in the TP ground circuit will cause higher TP signal voltage and result in increased fuel delivery. (B) is wrong. The MAP signal is normal for the heavier engine load indicated by the question. (C) is wrong. High fuel pressure causes more of a problem at light load and lower engine speeds.

47. (C) is correct. A 1.12 volt drop across the fuel pump relay power circuit is too high. (A) is wrong. The meter leads are connected to show the voltage drop across the relay power circuit, not the control circuit. (B) is wrong. The amount of voltage drop is too high. (D) is wrong. The circuit fails.

48. (B) is correct. A bad crank position circuit causes a no start by preventing the fuel pump from operating while cranking. The jumper in the fuel pump check connector overcomes this problem because it activates both the crank and run control circuits to engage the fuel pump relay. The engine stays running when the jumper is removed because the run circuit is O.K. (A) is wrong. If the main relay is bad, the jumper in the fuel pump check connector would not engage the fuel pump. (C) and (D) are wrong. The vehicle would not continue to run with the jumper removed if the ignition switch run circuit or fuse # 5 is bad.

49. (A) is correct. O2 sensor readings of minimum under 200mV, maximum under 700mV, and average under 400mV indicate a lean running condition. (B) is wrong. O2 sensor readings of minimum over 200mV, maximum over 700mV, and average 400–500mV would indicate the system is operating properly. (C) is wrong because technician B is wrong. (D) is wrong because technician A is right.

50. (D) is correct. To gain this much rpm, the engine must be getting additional air from a vacuum leak. (A) is wrong. A bad VSS will not have an effect on engine idle speed. (B) is wrong. Carbon deposits in the idle bypass port will lower, not increase, idle speed. (C) is wrong. There is no evidence of a damaged PCM.

51. (D) is correct. Neither technician is correct. It is unlikely a CKP sensor or VSS could do damage to the ECM. Both circuits use very low current.

52. (B) is correct. The high scan tool readings of 5 volts on the ECT, IAT, MAF, and TP data are a result of no voltage drop occurring, due to an open ground circuit at ECM pin #91. (A) is wrong, because there is a CKP engine speed signal of 193 RPM. (C) is wrong. If there is an open circuit at pin #32, the ECM will not have a ground. It won't be able to communicate with the scan tool, nor will it be able to supply the 5-volt reference voltage. (D) is wrong. If there is an open at ECM pin #1, there will be no reference voltage. The reading on the ECT, IAT, MAF, and TP data will be 9 volts.

53. (C) is correct. The post-catalyst HO2S 1/2 is not used for making fuel decisions. A bad heater or heater circuit will prevent if from producing a signal. (A) and (B) are wrong. The voltage values the HO2S 1/1 and HO2S 2/1 are showing do not indicate a lean or rich bias and appear to be

L1

switching, indicating fuel control. (D) is also wrong. There is no evidence of a misfire. To test for a misfire, the HO2S 1/1 and HO2S 2/1 signals need to be observed with a DSO.

54. (A) is correct. By process of elimination, a bad HO2S 1/1 circuit is the only possibility. (B) is wrong. High resistance in the ECT circuit causes the ECM to think the engine is cold. The resulting fuel decision will cause both oxygen sensor voltage signals to be biased high and perhaps prevent closed loop operation. (C) is wrong. A short in the ECT circuit will make the ECM think the engine is hot. The fuel decision will be lean and perhaps prevent closed loop operation. (D) is also wrong. A fuel pressure regulator problem will cause a rich or lean problem common to both engine banks.

55. (A) is correct. Because the system had a vacuum leak, the ECM has been correcting for a lean condition. This is evidenced by the +30 long term fuel trim. Because the problem has just been repaired, the short term fuel trim is beginning to indicate the need to adjust the system leaner than it has been, evidenced by the -10 correction. The long term correction has not yet had enough time to adjust back to normal. (B) is wrong. The technician is not correct because there is no evidence that there is a need for further diagnosis. (C) and (D) are both incorrect because only technician A is right.

56. (D) is correct. 20 ohms is too much resistance. The maximum allowable injector resistance is 16 ohms. The resistance specification is 12 ± 4 ohms. (A) is wrong. The resistance is not within spec. (B) is wrong. The resistance is not too low. (C) is wrong. The test is valid.

57. (B) is correct. A restricted EGR port will cause higher NOx because without EGR flow the combustion temperature will be higher. (A) is wrong. A grounded circuit to pin #33 will hold the EGR solenoid on. This opens the EGR, causing a low speed misfire but not a NOx problem. (C) is wrong. A stuck open EGR would cause the same symptom as (A). (D) is wrong. This is a tempting answer, but it's incorrect. While it is true advanced timing causes high NOx emission, 30° advanced timing is normal advance at cruising speed.

58. (A) is correct. The meter reading of 12.57 volts at connector (b) of the injector indicates that power is available, but the driver is not grounding the injector solenoid. Since the key is on, power should be available. However, because the engine is not cranked, nor is it running, the ECM injector driver is not turning the injector on. (B) is wrong. If the injector winding is open, a meter reading of 0 volts will occur between the engine ground and (b). (C) is wrong. A reading of close to 0 volts will occur if the injector circuit is grounded at (b). (D) is wrong. For reasons explained in answer (A), there is no reason to suspect ECM damage.

59. (B) is correct. The meter reading of 0 volts at terminal (b) of the #1 injector indicates that the power is interrupted somewhere. The fact that other injector (b) terminals read

12.58 volts indicates that this is not a problem common to all injectors. The conclusion can be made that the #1 injector winding has an open circuit because the power supply is common to all. (A) is wrong. The circuit to pin #38 is the ground circuit from the #1 injector driver. It does not supply power and it should be open with the key on and engine off. (C) is wrong. Both circuit pins #38 and #39 are injector driver circuits and even if shorted to each other will not supply a ground with the key on and engine off, unless they are both shorted to ground. (D) is wrong. If fuse #4 is blown, no injector will receive power.

60. (B) is correct. When neither of the camshaft position sensor signals are detected, the ECM will disable the fuel injectors. (A) is wrong. When neither of the camshaft position sensor signals are detected, the ECM will not disable the ignition coils. (C) is wrong because technician A is wrong. (D) is wrong because technician B is right.

61. (C) is correct. When one of the composite vehicle's APP sensors fails, the ECM will limit the maximum throttle opening to 35 percent. (A) and (B) are wrong. The percentage is less than the composite vehicle's ECM maximum throttle opening percentage. (D) is wrong. The percentage is more than the composite vehicle's ECM maximum throttle opening percentage.

62. (C) is correct. Both technicians are correct. The purge valve resistance of 12 ohms is too low. The resistance specification is 48 ± 6 ohms; minimum resistance is 42 ohms. The extra current flow through the purge valve solenoid, caused by the low resistance, can damage the ECM. (A), (B), and (D) are wrong because both technicians are correct.

63. (C) is correct. Both technicians are correct because a broken vacuum hose or an open circuit at pin #35 will prevent the EGR from opening. The EGR needs vacuum to open and pin #35 provides ground for the EGR solenoid to open so vacuum can reach the EGR valve. (A), (B), and (C) are wrong because both technicians are correct.

64. (D) is correct. The meter reading of 0 volts at connection (b) of cylinder #1 coil indicates an open circuit (the primary coil winding). With the key on, there should be 12 volts available because when the engine is off, no ground is supplied to the coil. (A) is wrong. If fuse #4 is blown, the vehicle will not run because there would be no power to any coil or injector. (B) is wrong. Since all the ignition coils are supposed to have system voltage at pin (a), short to battery voltage will not cause a problem. (C) is wrong. Since the secondary winding is a completely separate circuit, an open circuit in its winding would not cause the meter to read) volts on pin (b) of the #1 primary coil winding connection.

65. (D) is correct. Neither technician is correct because a short to ground on both the MAP and TP circuits cannot affect the MAF signal nor the 5-volt reference voltage. (A), (B), and (C) are wrong because neither technician is correct.

ANSWERS

Chapter 1:
1. c, 2. d., 3. a, 4. a, 5. a, 6. b, 7. b, 8. b, 9. d, 10. d, 11. b, 12. b, 13. b, 14. a, 15. a, 16. b, 17. a

Chapter 2:
1. b, 2. b, 3. b, 4. a, 5. c, 6. b, 7. b, 8. c, 9. c, 10. b, 11. b, 12. b, 13. d

Chapter 3:
1. b, 2. d, 3. a, 4. c, 5. d, 6. a, 7. c

Chapter 4:
1. a, 2. c, 3. b, 4. b, 5. d, 6. a, 7. b

Chapter 5:
1. c, 2. b, 3. a, 4. c, 5. a, 6. c, 7. c, 8. b, 9. c, 10. d

Chapter 6:
1. a, 2. d, 3. b, 4. c, 5. c, 6. b, 7. a, 8. c

L1

GLOSSARY

Abort: To stop prematurely.

A/C: Air Conditioning.

A/C Compressor Clutch: An electromagnetic device that engages the otherwise freewheeling A/C pulley.

Acceleration Simulation Mode (ASM): A method of emissions testing that simulates a constant vehicle acceleration load.

Acceleration Simulation Mode (ASM) Test: A method of vehicle emissions testing that uses a dynamometer to simulate constant acceleration. HC and NOx are measured in parts per million; CO is measured as a percentage during testing.

Airflow Sensor: A sensor used to measure the rate, density, temperature, or volume of air entering the engine.

Air Gap: The precise space between a pickup coil and trigger wheel. The correct air gap is critical to proper operation of the sensor.

Alphanumeric: A combination of letters and numbers.

Alternator: See Generator.

Ambient: Surrounding or all around, such as ambient air temperature.

Ammeter: A test instrument that measures current flow in a circuit.

Ampere (AMP): The unit of measure for electric current.

Analog Meter: An electrical test meter that uses a spring-loaded needle and a magnetic field to indicate a circuit value on the meter scale.

ASM 25/25: A load of 25 percent of vehicle weight applied at 25 mph.

ASM 50/15: A load of 50 percent of vehicle weight applied at 15 mph.

Atmospheric Pressure: The pressure caused by the weight of the earth's atmosphere. At sea level, this pressure is 14.7 psi (101 kPa).

Available Voltage: The voltage present at a given point within the electrical system.

Backpressure: A pressure created by restrictions in the exhaust system that tends to slow the exit of exhaust gases from the combustion chamber.

Baseline: To establish a starting point so that any improvement made is measurable.

Bias: To spend more or less time in one direction, or have a greater or lesser value in one direction than another.

Bi-directional control: A feature of OBD II that enables a scan tool to give a command to a computer actuator.

Blink: The on-off-on-off cycle of a light. A light may blink regularly, like a turn signal, or intermittently.

Blowby: Combustion gases that get past the piston rings into the crankcase; these include water vapor, acids, and unburned fuel.

Blown: A blown fuse is an open circuit, a blown head gasket is one that is damaged in such a way as to leak compression and combustion from the chamber it seals.

Borescope: A device used to look inside areas of the engine that usually cannot be seen without disassembly.

Calculated Load Value: The percentage of engine capacity being used based on current airflow divided by maximum airflow.

Calibration: A procedure to ensure the accuracy of a test instrument.

Capacitor: A device that can store voltage without affecting the voltage in any way. Formed by bringing two conductive surfaces close together, separated only by an insulator. Also called a condenser.

Carbon Monoxide: An odorless, colorless, tasteless poisonous gas. A pollutant produced by the internal combustion engine.

Catalyst: A substance that speeds or aids in a chemical reaction.

Centrifugal Advance: A method of advancing the ignition spark using weights in the distributor that react to centrifugal force generated by engine speed.

Cease: To stop immediately.

Certificate: A document used to verify that a vehicle has officially passed an emissions test.

Check Valve: A valve that permits flow in only one direction.

Circuit: A path for current flow.

Closed-Loop: An operational mode in which the ECM reads and responds to feedback signals from its sensors and adjusts system operation accordingly.

Combustion Event: Refers to a misfire as observed by a deviation in the O_2 sensor oscilloscope waveform.

Come Back: A returning, dissatisfied customer.

Compensation: To correct for too much or too little of something.

Comprehensive: Inclusive or complete.

Condense: A change of state from a vapor to a liquid.

Conductor: A material that readily allows current flow.

Configuration: The organization of related components in a specific order.

Constant Velocity (CV) Joint: A shaft coupling, consisting either of a ball and cage assembly or a tripod and tulip, that allows changes in the angle between two rotating shafts without affecting the rate of rotation.

Correlate: To bear a mutual, corresponding, or reciprocal relationship.

Crankcase Pressure: The pressure created inside the crankcase by the blowby of a running engine.

Creep: The tendency of a vehicle equipped with an automatic transmission to move in gear, without depressing the accelerator.

Crankshaft Position Sensor (CKP): An electronic device designed to supply engine RPM and position to the ECM.

Criteria: Standards on which to base a judgment.

Cruise: To maintain a steady rate of vehicle speed.

Curb Idle Speed: Factory-specified idle speed in drive.

Current: The flow of electrons through a conductor.

CV Boot: The flexible cover used to prevent road dirt contamination of a CV joint.

Cylinder or Engine "Bank": One side of a V-type engine.

Cylinder Sealing Parts: Engine parts that contain compression or combustion in the cylinder, piston rings, valves, and headgasket.

Data Link Connector (DLC): The standardized vehicle plug used to connect the scan tool to the vehicle's computer.

Decay: To decline or decrease gradually in activity, strength, or performance.

Default Value: A value used in place of another value known to be unreliable.

Degraded: Worn down, performing at less than usual standards.

Detonation: Also called ping, or spark knock. An unwanted explosion of an air-fuel mixture caused by high heat and compression.

Diagnostic Trouble Code (DTC): Code stored by the computer when a problem is detected. Read using a scan tool, each code corresponds to a particular problem. (When a DTC is referred to in the ASE L1 test question, the number and description of the code will both be given. For instance, P0114 = Intake Air Temperature Circuit, intermittent.)

Diaphragm: A thin flexible wall, separating two cavities, used to turn a change of vacuum or pressure into mechanical movement, such as the diaphragm in a vacuum advance.

Dielectric Resistance: A poor conductor of electrical current or a high resistance.

Digital KV: An oscilloscope report, digitally displayed (given in numbers) instead of a waveform or secondary ignition pattern.

Digital Meter: An electrical test meter that displays the measured value in numeric form.

Digital Multimeter: A hand-held meter capable of measuring voltage, resistance, and current flow, then displaying it in digital format on an LCD screen.

Digital Pyrometer: A non-contact thermometer that displays temperature digitally.

Dilution: To diminish the purity or strength of a mixture.

Diode: An electronic component designed to allow current flow in one direction only. Used in control circuits and in rectifier assemblies in the generator.

Displace: Take the place of something.

Distributor Ignition (DI): An ignition system that uses a distributor.

Diverter Valve: Also called a dump valve. A valve used in the air injection system to prevent backfire. During deceleration it "dumps" air from the air pump into the atmosphere.

Dowel Gauge: A round rod used to judge the diameter of the gas tank fillpipe restrictor.

Downshift: To shift into a lower gear ratio.

Downstream: Further toward the direction of flow, toward the tailpipe when referenced to exhaust.

Driveability Complaint: The expressed dissatisfaction of a customer with a vehicle's driving performance.

Drive Cycle: A set of parameters that must be met in order for OBD II monitors to properly run and complete.

Driveline: Refers to the parts from the transmission output to the drive axle(s).

Drivetrain: A reference that describes the parts from the engine to the drive axle(s).

Duty Cycle: Describes the time of a complete cycle of action, including both on (energized) and off (de-energized) time of a solenoid.

Dynamometer: A device to simulate driving a vehicle, similar to a treadmill.

e.g.: For example.

EGR Vacuum Modulator: See: Exhaust Backpressure Transducer.

Exhaust Gas Recirculation (EGR): A system to introduce metered amounts of inert gas (exhaust) into the combustion process to cool the flame temperature.

Electrolyte: The chemical solution in a battery that conducts electricity and reacts with the plate materials.

Electromotive Force (EMF): The force that causes the electrons to move from atom to another atom. More commonly known as voltage.

Electron: Negatively charged atomic particles.

Electronic Ignition (EI): An ignition system that has coils dedicated to specific spark plugs (one or two spark plugs) and does not use a distributor; often referred to as distributorless ignition.

Emissions Certification Type: A reference to whether the vehicle has a Federal or California emissions system configuration.

Emission Cut Point: The point at which a tailpipe emission exceeds state mandated limit.

Emissions Trace: An IM 240 emissions inspection report showing emissions, in grams per mile, during a specific drive cycle.

Emit: To send out or release.

Enable: To make able or possible.

Enleanment: To make leaner, as in adding less fuel to the mixture.

Enrichment: To make richer, as in adding more fuel to the mixture.

Environmental Protection Agency (EPA): An agency of the federal government that is responsible for regulating pollution control.

EPA Under Hood Label: A label required by the EPA to be placed under the vehicle's hood. Gives basic emissions application and configuration information.

EVAP Evaporative Emissions System: Containment of HC vapors within the fuel system utilizing charcoal charged canisters to absorb fuel vapors that are drawn into the intake system during cruise.

Evaporation: The change of state of a liquid to a vapor.

Evaporative Liquid Protection Device: A check valve or other device that prevents liquid gasoline from reaching the evaporative system canister.

Evaporative Purge Graph: An IM 240 report of the amount of HC vapor, measured in liters, purged to the engine from the evaporative system.

Exhaust Backpressure Transducer: A device that uses the exhaust backpressure to control the flow of vacuum to an EGR.

Feedback: Generally referring to any system that provides information to the PCM regarding the effect of system controls. The O2 sensors' feedback informs the PCM of the results of fuel control commands.

Final Drive: Usually refers to the driveshaft, differential gears, and drive axles.

Flame Front: Refers to the combustion flame started by spark that propagates out as part of the combustion process.

Flow Chart: A step-by-step instruction, in chart form, leading to the diagnosis of a DTC or symptom.

Fouled: Contaminated, like a spark plug contaminated (fouled) with carbon.

Freeze Frame: Operating conditions that are stored in the memory of the PCM at the instant a diagnostic trouble code is set. (The current stored PCM data of what was sensed and what commands were being given at the instant in time the most current trouble was set).

Frequency: A measurement in Hertz (cycles per second) of how often something occurs in a specific amount of time.

Fuel Control: A statement of whether or not the PCM is able to deliver the correct, and quickly varying, fuel mixture to satisfy the needs of a three-way catalytic converter.

Fuel Starvation: The lack of fuel available for efficient combustion.

Fuel Trim (FT): Fuel delivery adjustments based on closed-loop feedback. Values above the central value (0%) indicate increased injector pulse width. Values below the central value indicate decreased injector pulse width. Short Term Fuel Trim is based on rapidly switching oxygen sensor values. Long Term Fuel Trim is a learned value used to compensate for continual deviation of the Short Term Fuel Trim from its central value. (Term means time. Short Term Fuel Trim makes an immediate correction for O_2 sensor bias. Long Term Fuel Trim makes a correction for Short Term Fuel Trim bias).

Fuel Volatility: The lower the temperature at which a fuel vaporizes, the higher the volatility.

Functional Test: A test that actually causes a device to operate. Used to prove the device works.

Generator: A device that produces electrical energy by passing a magnetic field through a coil of wire. Known for many years as an alternator due to the fact that alternating current is produced in the stator assembly; J1930 (OBD II) term for alternator (generating device that uses a diode rectifier).

Generic: Universal (all the same).

Go/No-Go Test: A test to check whether or not something works, not how well it functions.

Gross Vehicle Weight Rating (GVWR): The manufacturer's specified maximum weight for a vehicle including passengers and cargo.

Hall-Effect Sensor: A signal-generating switch that develops a transverse voltage across a current-carrying semiconductor when subjected to a magnetic field.

Hall Effect (Switch): An electronic triggering and signaling device that produces a square wave signal. The frequency of the signal increases with the speed of the engine. Used to communicate engine rpm and on some applications piston position.

L1

Heat Riser: A valve used to redirect exhaust through special passages heating the intake manifold so less fuel condenses in the intake manifold during cold engine operation.

Hesitation: A sudden loss of power or forward motion.

High Impedance: A high level of opposition to current created by the combined forces of resistance, capacitance, and inductance in a circuit.

Hot Soak: A period of time after shutting down a warm engine where heat saturates the combustion chambers, valvetrain, intake, and residual fuel.

Hydrocarbons (HC): Chemical compounds in various combinations of hydrogen and carbon. A major pollutant from an internal combustion engine. Gasoline, itself, is a mixture of hydrocarbons.

Ignition Control Module (ICM): An electronic module designed to control the primary circuit to the ignition coil.

IM 240: A method of vehicle emissions testing that uses a dynamometer to simulate transient (varying) acceleration and deceleration forces of motion under specific driving conditions. HC, CO, and NOx tailpipe emissions are measured during testing in grams per mile. The evaporative system is checked for leaks and purge is measured in liters of vapor.

Impedance: Resistance to current flow often used in rating test meters.

IM Test: Inspection and Maintenance Test; vehicle emissions test and repair required by state governments.

Inductive Ammeter: An ammeter that uses the principle of magnetic induction to measure current flow in an electrical circuit. This type of meter is typically used for measuring large currents such as starting and charging systems.

Inductive Ammeter Pickup: A tool used to sense the magnetic field surrounding a conductor indicating the strength of the current flow.

Inertia: The tendency of a body at rest to remain at rest, and a body in motion to remain in motion, unless acted upon by an outside force.

Inertia Switch: A switch that interrupts power to the fuel pump upon impact.

Infinite Resistance: A condition caused by an incomplete or open circuit that prevents current through the circuit.

Infrequent: Seldom happening or occurring, not often, or rare.

Integrity: Soundness, intactness of a component, or a person's adherence to a code of values.

Intermittent: Occurring infrequently, not often, or rarely.

Jumper Wire: A length of wire with probes or clips at each end used to bypass a portion of a circuit.

Knock Retard System: A system that senses detonation and retards timing until detonation ceases.

Lab Scope: An oscilloscope used to observe electronic sensor and actuator waveforms, usually not capable of reading high secondary ignition voltage.

Light-Off Temperature: The temperature at which a catalytic converter begins to be effective.

Limited Operational Strategy: A mode of computer operation that limits or prevents the operation of some systems when a fault is detected.

Lurch: The action of a vehicle to jump into motion when placed into gear even though the brake is applied.

Magnetic Pickup: A signal-generating device that uses a permanent magnet to create a voltage pulse. The trigger wheel movement creates magnetic flux changes in the pickup coil to induce a varying strength voltage.

Magnetic Type Sensor: Magnetic pulse generator, a signal-generating device that creates a voltage pulse as magnetic flux changes around a pickup coil.

Malfunction Indicator Lamp (MIL): A lamp on the instrument panel that lights when the PCM detects an emissions-related problem. Similar to a "CHECK ENGINE" Light.

Mandated: Ordered by law.

Manifold Absolute Pressure (MAP): The pressure in the intake manifold referenced to a perfect vacuum. Since manifold vacuum is the difference between manifold absolute pressure and atmospheric pressure, all the vacuum readings in the Composite Vehicle Preparation/Reference Booklet are taken at sea level (where standard atmospheric pressure equals 101 kPa or 0 in. Hg).

Mass Airflow (MAF) System: A fuel injection system that uses a mass airflow (MAF) sensor to measure the mass (weight) of the air drawn into an engine, measured in grams per second.

Misfire: Incomplete combustion resulting in increased emissions and the possibility of catalyst damage.

Modulated: A more sophisticated method of controlling an actuator, not just an off and on signal, controls how much work is done.

Monitor: To watch, observe, or check something.

Negative Temperature Coefficient (NTC) Thermistor: A type of resistor, often used in automobiles to sense engine or air temperature. Its resistance decreases as temperature increases.

Nitrogen Oxides (NOx): Chemical compounds of nitrogen and oxygen. Combines with HC in the atmosphere when exposed to sunlight to produce smog.

Noid Light: A light specifically designed to test the signal to a fuel injector.

No-Load Testing: A method of vehicle emissions testing while the vehicle is in neutral or park. It measures tailpipe emissions in parts per million and CO emissions in percent. Sometimes called idle testing because no load is on the engine. Examples include testing at factory idle speed and No-Load and Two-Speed Idle (TSI) tests at idle speed and 2500 rpm.

Normal Operating Temperature: A temperature within the factory-specified operating range of the engine when fully warmed up. Sometimes abbreviated as N.O.T.

Nozzle: The opening through which a substance flows.

Octane Rating: A measurement of the ability of a fuel to resist detonation.

Off Idle: Just above idle speed.

Ohm: The unit of measure for resistance to current flow.

Ohm's Law: A series of formulas that are used to determine the values in an electrical circuit. Any two of the values can be multiplied or divided to determine the third unknown value.

Ohmmeter: A meter designed to measure the resistance of a circuit or component. DMMs can be set to an ohmmeter function.

On Board Diagnostics (OBD): A diagnostic program contained in the PCM that monitors computer inputs and outputs for failures. OBD II is an industry-standard, second generation OBD system that monitors emissions control systems for degradation as well as failures.

On time: The time when an actuator is energized, as when a fuel injector is signaled to allow fuel to flow.

Open-Loop: An operational mode in which the ECM adjusts a system to function according to predetermined instructions and does not always respond to feedback signals from its sensors.

Optical Sensor: Uses a light-emitting diode and shutter blade to trigger the switching of a photo-sensitive transistor; sends a square wave signal used for engine rpm and/or piston position.

Optimum: The best, highest, peak, or most favorable condition.

Orifice: A small opening or restriction in a line or passage that is used to regulate pressure and flow.

Original Equipment Manufacturer (OEM): The manufacturer that made the component for its original assembly when new.

Overdrive: A condition in which the drive gear rotates slower than the driven gear. Output speed of the driven gear is increased, while output torque is reduced. A gear ratio of 0.70:1 is an overdrive gear ratio.

Oxidation: The combining of an element with oxygen in a chemical process that requires heat.

Parallel Circuit: An arrangement that provides separate power supplies and ground paths to several loads.

Parameters: A specified range of operative values.

Partial Sampling: A method of exhaust emissions measurement that continuously captures a small amount as a sample to judge the content of the whole.

Parts Per Million: A measurement of how many parts of HC are found in a sample of one million parts of exhaust gas.

Peak and Hold Driver: A PCM fuel injector control circuit that switches to a current limiting circuit once the initial, higher current circuit has opened the injector.

Photochemical Smog: A combination of pollutants that, when acted upon by sunlight, forms chemical compounds that are harmful to human, animal, and plant life.

Ping: See Detonation.

Ping Pong Rate: A statistic of how many failed and "repaired" vehicles return more than once to the emissions inspection lane for a retest. Statistics are kept for individual technicians, shops, and the industry as a whole.

Pinion Gear: A smaller gear that meshes with a larger gearwheel or toothed rack.

Potentiometer: A variable resistor with three terminals. Signal voltage comes from a terminal attached to a movable contact that passes over the resistor.

PRNDL Switch: An electrical gearshift position indicator used on automatic transmissions.

Post Cat: After the catalytic converter (downstream) in the exhaust.

Powertrain Control Module (PCM): An OBD II term for the electronic computer that controls the engine and transmission. Similar to an ECM, VCM, ECA, ECU, or SBEC.

Pre-Cat: Before the catalytic converter (upstream) in the exhaust system.

Precondition: The act of preparing a vehicle prior to testing.

Preignition: A premature ignition of the air-fuel mixture before the spark plug fires. It is caused by excessive heat or pressure in the combustion chamber.

Preliminary: Before, to precede, to come before, or in preparation for something.

Priority Codes: Codes that are more important than, and take precedence over, others.

Proportionate: The constant, but unequal, relationship between two related items.

P/S: Power Steering.

Pulse Width: A measurement, usually in milliseconds, of actuator on time.

Pulse Width Modulation (PWM): A signal with a variable on-time to off-time ratio. Usually used to control solenoid-type actuators.

Pulse Width Modulated Driver: An injector driver that turns the injector on and keeps it on while turning off and on so rapidly the injector doesn't have time to mechanically close. This lowers the amount of current required to keep the injector open.

Purge: To get rid of or evacuate.

Rationality: Acceptable to reason.

Reduced: The chemical separation of a compound.

Redundant: Needlessly repeated.

Relative: Having a relationship to, or connection with, something.

Reluctor: The iron or steel trigger or armature in a magnetic pulse generator that excites the pickup coil.

Residual Pressure: A constant pressure held in the fuel system when the pump is not operating.

Rest Pressure: Sometimes called static pressure. Maintained after shutdown in a fuel delivery system to prevent vapor lock and aid in quick restart.

Restrained: Prevented or limited movement as in tying down a vehicle so it cannot jump off a dynamometer.

Ripple Test: A test that checks for unwanted A.C. voltage leaking from an alternator rectifier bridge.

Road Hazard Damage: Damage to a component caused by rocks, curbs, speed bumps, etc.

Root Cause of Failure: A component or system failure that, if not repaired, can cause other failures. If the secondary failure is repaired, but the root cause is not repaired, the secondary failure will reoccur. For example, a plugged PCV passage can cause high crank-case pressure, resulting in oil leaks from gaskets and seals. Replacing the gaskets and seals may stop the oil leak, but if the root cause (the PCV restriction) is not diagnosed and repaired, the oil leaks will eventually return.

Rough Idle or Running: A misfire problem that causes the engine not to run smoothly.

Rule of Thumb: A judgment based on practical experience rather than specification.

Saturated: To the point where no more can be absorbed.

Saturated Driver: An injector driver that uses no special methods other than to conduct the current required to open the injector, and withstands the resulting voltage spike.

Scan Tool: A test instrument that is used to access powertrain control system trouble codes, freeze frame data, and bi-directional control of system actuators.

Scan Tool Data: Information from the computer that is displayed on the scan tool, including data stream, DTCs, freeze frame, and system monitor readiness status.

Schrader Valve: A valve that is depressed to open and closes automatically when released. Used to fill and hold air in tires and tubes, refrigerant in A/C systems, and as a service (test) port on OBD II evaporative systems.

Secondary Air Injection: A system that provides air to the exhaust system under controlled conditions to reduce emissions; can be either pulse or air-pump type.

Secondary Air Injection Check Valve: A one-way valve that prevents exhaust from damaging system components.

Secondary Air Injection Pressure Regulator: Limits air pump pressure.

Sequential Multiport Fuel Injection (SFI): A fuel injection system that uses one electronic fuel injector for each cylinder. The injectors are pulsed in the sequence of each cylinder's intake stroke.

Series Circuit: An arrangement in which current must flow through one load before another. Each load shares the power supply with the other loads in the circuit.

Series-Parallel Circuit: An arrangement that combines two or more loads in parallel with one or more loads in series.

Short Circuit: A condition in which a path is provided around the circuit load to another circuit or ground.

Shunt: A parallel electrical connection or branch circuit, in parallel with another branch circuit or connection.

Simulation: To reproduce operating conditions or their effect by other means.

Snapshot: A technician-recorded scan tool record or "movie" of PCM data during an event, so that the data can be played back.

Solenoid: An electromagnetic actuator consisting of a movable iron core with an induction coil surrounding it. When electrical current is applied to the coil, the core moves to convert electrical energy to mechanical energy.

Spark Knock: See Detonation.

Spark Tester: A special tool with an adjustable spark gap used to check spark intensity.

Speed-Density System: A fuel-injection system that calculates the amount of air drawn into the engine using engine rpm, air temperature, manifold vacuum, and volumetric efficiency, rather than measuring the mass or volume of air directly with an airflow meter.

L1

Stoichiometric mixture: A mixture of the best proportion to burn efficiently, typically 14.7 to 1.

Stumble: A sudden lack of power as if the vehicle coughs or chokes before finally accelerating.

Sulfate: The crystallization of lead sulfate on the plates of a constantly discharged battery.

Surge: A gain, then loss, of power that comes in repeating waves.

Supercharger: An accessory belt-driven device used to force a greater volume of air into the cylinders.

System Pressure: Fuel injection operating pressure created by the fuel pump.

Technical Service Bulletin (TSB): Contains factory advice for dealership technicians to repair defects and/or to notify them of changes in repair procedures.

Temperature Sensitive Vacuum Control Valve: A device for regulating control vacuum by air or coolant temperature.

Test Lane: Garage stall or bay, used for emissions inspections.

Thermostatic Bulb: Uses a wax pellet that expands and contracts in reaction to temperature to create a mechanical movement, as in coolant thermostat or thermostatic air cleaner.

Thermistor (Thermal Resistor): A resistor made from a substance that changes electrical resistance as its temperature increases. See Negative Temperature Coefficient (NTC) thermistor.

Three Way Catalyst (TWC): A catalytic converter system that oxidizes HC and CO, and reduces NOx.

Threshold: The upper limit or beginning of something.

Timing Advance Capability: The ability of a timing advance system to advance ignition timing proportionate to engine speed.

Top Dead Center (TDC): The point in engine rotation when cylinder number one is at the top of its travel and the valves are closed.

Torque Converter: A type of fluid coupling used to connect the engine crankshaft to an automatic transmission input shaft.

Torque Converter Clutch (TCC): An electronically controlled clutch mechanism that locks the torque converter to eliminate fluid power loss under light load cruising conditions.

Transaxle: The combination of a transmission and differential gears, used in front wheel drive and rear engine vehicles.

Transducer: A device that transforms or controls one type of energy with another.

Transient: Coming and going, temporary or changing amounts of something.

Transmission Turbine: A part of the torque converter that hydraulically transmits the output power of the engine to the transmission.

Transmission Valve Body: Contains hydraulic shift valves.

Trigger signal: An electronic signal used to switch (trigger) an electronic device like a transistor.

Trip: A drive cycle that meets operating condition requirements for OBD II monitors (diagnostic tests) to run.

Turbocharger: A device that uses exhaust gases to turn a turbine that forces a greater volume of air into the cylinders.

Two Speed Idle (TSI) Testing: (See No-Load Testing).

Universal Joint (U-Joint): A shaft coupling, consisting of two yokes joined by a steel crosspiece, that allows changes in the angle between two rotating shafts. Also called a "Cardan joint."

Upshift: To shift into a higher gear ratio.

Upstream: Toward the origination of flow, toward the engine in the exhaust stream.

Valve Body: The casting that contains most of the valves in a transmission hydraulic system. The valve body also has passages for the flow of hydraulic fluid.

Vapor Lock: When fuel vaporizes in a line or device and blocks the flow of liquid fuel; usually causes engine stall.

Vaporization: The change of state process of a liquid into a vapor.

Variation: Not constant, changing.

Vehicle Identification Number (VIN): A number assigned to the vehicle by the manufacturer used to identify it. Contains coded information on body type, original engine size and type, etc.

Vehicle Inspection Report (VIR): Reports the results of a state emissions inspection.

Vibration Damper: A device used to counteract the affect of a dynamic imbalance.

Volatility: The boiling point or temperature at which a liquid changes to a vapor.

Volt: The unit of measure for electrical pressure or electromotive force.

Voltage Drop: The measurement of the loss of voltage caused by unwanted resistance in a circuit connection, conductor, or device.

Voltmeter: An electrical test meter that measures electrical pressure (EMF).

Volumetric Efficiency: A comparison of the actual volume of air-fuel mixture drawn into an engine to the theoretical maximum volume.

Wastegate: A vacuum diaphragm-actuated bypass valve, used to control exhaust flow to limit turbocharger boost pressure by limiting the speed of the exhaust turbine.

Waveform: The pattern traced by voltage over a specific time on an oscilloscope display.

Zirconia (O2) Sensor: A type of oxygen sensor that acts like a chemical battery because it requires no supplied power.

GLOSSARY OF OBD II POWERTRAIN DIAGNOSTIC TROUBLE CODES

P01-FUEL AND AIR METERING

P0100	Mass (MAF) or Volume (VAF) Air Flow Circuit Malfunction
P0101	MAF or VAF Circuit Range/Performance Problem
P0102	MAF or VAF Circuit Low Input
P0103	MAF or VAF Circuit High Input
P0104	MAF or VAF Circuit Intermittent
P0105	Manifold Absolute Pressure (MAP)/Barometric (BARO) Pressure Circuit Malfunction
P0106	MAP or BARO Circuit Range/Performance Problem
P0107	MAP or BARO Circuit Low Input
P0108	MAP or BARO Circuit High Input
P0109	MAP or BARO Circuit Intermittent
P0109	Intake Air Temperature (IAT) Circuit Malfunction
P0111	IAT Circuit Range/Performance Problem
P0112	IAT Circuit Low Input
P0113	IAT Circuit High Input
P0114	IAT Circuit Intermittent
P0115	Engine Coolant Temperature (ECT) Circuit Malfunction
P0116	ECT Circuit Range/Performance Problem
P0117	ECT Circuit Low Input
P0118	ECT Circuit High Input
P0119	ECT Circuit Intermittent
P0120	Throttle Position (TP) Sensor/Switch A Circuit Malfunction
P0121	TP Sensor/Switch A Circuit Range/Performance Problem
P0122	TP Sensor/Switch A Circuit Low Input
P0123	TP Sensor/Switch A Circuit High Input
P0124	TP Sensor/Switch A Circuit Intermittent
P0125	Insufficient Coolant Temperature for Closed Loop Fuel Control
P0126	Insufficient Coolant Temperature for Stable Operation
P0130	O2 Sensor Circuit Malfunction (Bank 1 Sensor 1)
P0131	O2 Sensor Circuit Low Voltage (Bank 1 Sensor 1)
P0132	O2 Sensor Circuit High Voltage (Bank 1 Sensor 1)
P0133	O2 Sensor Circuit Slow Response (Bank 1 Sensor 1)
P0134	O2 Sensor Circuit No Activity Detected (Bank 1 Sensor 1)
P0135	O2 Sensor Heater Circuit Malfunction (Bank 1 Sensor 1)
P0136	O2 Sensor Circuit Malfunction (Bank 1 Sensor 2)
P0137	O2 Sensor Circuit Low Voltage (Bank 1 Sensor 2)
P0138	O2 Sensor Circuit High Voltage (Bank 1 Sensor 2)
P0139	O2 Sensor Circuit Slow Response (Bank 1 Sensor 2)
P0140	O2 Sensor Circuit No Activity Detected (Bank 1 Sensor 2)
P0141	O2 Sensor Heater Circuit Malfunction (Bank 1 Sensor 2)
P0142	O2 Sensor Circuit Malfunction (Bank 1 Sensor 3)
P0143	O2 Sensor Circuit Low Voltage (Bank 1 Sensor 3)
P0144	O2 Sensor Circuit High Voltage (Bank 1 Sensor 3)
P0145	O2 Sensor Circuit Slow Response (Bank 1 Sensor 3)
P0146	O2 Sensor Circuit No Activity Detected (Bank 1 Sensor 3)
P0147	O2 Sensor Heater Circuit Malfunction (Bank 1 Sensor 3)
P0150	O2 Sensor Circuit Malfunction (Bank 2 Sensor 1)
P0151	O2 Sensor Circuit Low Voltage (Bank 2 Sensor 1)
P0152	O2 Sensor Circuit High Voltage (Bank 2 Sensor 1)
P0153	O2 Sensor Circuit Slow Response (Bank 2 Sensor 1)
P0154	O2 Sensor Circuit No Activity Detected (Bank 2 Sensor 1)
P0155	O2 Sensor Heater Circuit Malfunction (Bank 2 Sensor 1)
P0156	O2 Sensor Circuit Malfunction (Bank 2 Sensor 2)
P0157	O2 Sensor Circuit Low Voltage (Bank 2 Sensor 2)
P0158	O2 Sensor Circuit High Voltage (Bank 2 Sensor 2)
P0159	O2 Sensor Circuit Slow Response (Bank 2 Sensor 2)
P0160	O2 Sensor Circuit No Activity Detected (Bank 2 Sensor 2)
P0161	O2 Sensor Heater Circuit Malfunction (Bank 2 Sensor 2)
P0162	O2 Sensor Circuit Malfunction (Bank 2 Sensor 3)
P0163	O2 Sensor Circuit Low Voltage (Bank 2 Sensor 3)
P0164	O2 Sensor Circuit High Voltage (Bank 2 Sensor 3)
P0165	O2 Sensor Circuit Slow Response (Bank 2 Sensor 3)
P0166	O2 Sensor Circuit No Activity Detected (Bank 2 Sensor 3)
P0167	O2 Sensor Heater Circuit Malfunction (Bank 2 Sensor 3)
P0170	Fuel Trim Malfunction (Bank 1)
P0171	System Too Lean (Bank 1)
P0172	System Too Rich (Bank 1)
P0173	Fuel Trim Malfunction (Bank 2)
P0174	System Too Lean (Bank 2)
P0175	System Too Rich (Bank 2)
P0176	Fuel Composition Sensor Circuit Malfunction
P0177	Fuel Composition Sensor Circuit Range/Performance
P0178	Fuel Composition Sensor Circuit Low Input
P0179	Fuel Composition Sensor Circuit High Input
P0180	Fuel Temperature Sensor A Circuit Malfunction
P0181	Fuel Temperature Sensor A Circuit Range/Performance
P0182	Fuel Temperature Sensor A Circuit Low Input
P0183	Fuel Temperature Sensor A Circuit High Input
P0184	Fuel Temperature Sensor A Circuit Intermittent
P0185	Fuel Temperature Sensor B Circuit Malfunction
P0186	Fuel Temperature Sensor B Circuit Range/Performance
P0187	Fuel Temperature Sensor B Circuit Low Input
P0188	Fuel Temperature Sensor B Circuit High Input
P0189	Fuel Temperature Sensor B Circuit Intermittent
P0190	Fuel Rail Pressure Sensor Circuit Malfunction
P0191	Fuel Rail Pressure Sensor Circuit Range/Performance
P0192	Fuel Rail Pressure Sensor Circuit Low Input
P0193	Fuel Rail Pressure Sensor Circuit High Input
P0194	Fuel Rail Pressure Sensor Circuit Intermittent
P0195	Engine Oil Temperature Sensor Malfunction
P0196	Engine Oil Temperature Sensor Range/Performance
P0197	Engine Oil Temperature Sensor Low
P0198	Engine Oil Temperature Sensor High
P0199	Engine Oil Temperature Sensor Intermittent

P02-FUEL AND AIR METERING

P0200	Injector Circuit Malfunction
P0201	Injector Circuit Malfunction - Cylinder 1
P0202	Injector Circuit Malfunction - Cylinder 2
P0203	Injector Circuit Malfunction - Cylinder 3
P0204	Injector Circuit Malfunction - Cylinder 4
P0205	Injector Circuit Malfunction - Cylinder 5

L1

P0206	Injector Circuit Malfunction - Cylinder 6
P0207	Injector Circuit Malfunction - Cylinder 7
P0208	Injector Circuit Malfunction - Cylinder 8
P0209	Injector Circuit Malfunction - Cylinder 9
P0210	Injector Circuit Malfunction - Cylinder 10
P0211	Injector Circuit Malfunction - Cylinder 11
P0212	Injector Circuit Malfunction - Cylinder 12
P0213	Cold Start Injector 1 Malfunction
P0214	Cold Start Injector 2 Malfunction
P0215	Engine Shutoff Solenoid Malfunction
P0216	Injection Timing Control Circuit Malfunction
P0217	Engine Overtemp Condition
P0218	Transmission Over Temperature Condition
P0219	Engine Overspeed Condition
P0220	TP Sensor/Switch B Circuit Malfunction
P0221	TP Sensor/Switch B Circuit Range/Performance Problem
P0222	TP Sensor/Switch B Circuit Low Input
P0223	TP Sensor/Switch B Circuit High Input
P0224	TP Sensor/Switch B Circuit Intermittent
P0225	TP Sensor/Switch C Circuit Malfunction
P0226	TP Sensor/Switch C Circuit Range/Performance Problem
P0227	TP Sensor/Switch C Circuit Low Input
P0228	TP Sensor/Switch C Circuit High Input
P0229	TP Sensor/Switch C Circuit Intermittent
P0230	Fuel Pump Primary Circuit Malfunction
P0231	Fuel Pump Secondary Circuit Low
P0232	Fuel Pump Secondary Circuit High
P0233	Fuel Pump Secondary Circuit Intermittent
P0234	Engine Overboost Condition
P0235	Turbocharger Boost Sensor A Circuit Malfunction
P0236	Turbocharger Boost Sensor A Circuit Range/Performance
P0237	Turbocharger Boost Sensor A Circuit Low
P0238	Turbocharger Boost Sensor A Circuit High
P0239	Turbocharger Boost Sensor B Malfunction
P0240	Turbocharger Boost Sensor B Circuit Range/Performance
P0241	Turbocharger Boost Sensor B Circuit Low
P0242	Turbocharger Boost Sensor B Circuit High
P0243	Turbocharger Wastegate Solenoid A Malfunction
P0244	Turbocharger Wastegate Solenoid A Range/Performance
P0245	Turbocharger Wastegate Solenoid A Low
P0246	Turbocharger Wastegate Solenoid A High
P0247	Turbocharger Wastegate Solenoid B Malfunction
P0248	Turbocharger Wastegate Solenoid B Range/Performance
P0249	Turbocharger Wastegate Solenoid B Low
P0250	Turbocharger Wastegate Solenoid B High
P0251	Injection Pump Fuel Metering Control "A" Malfunction (Cam/Rotor/Injector)
P0252	Injection Pump Fuel Metering Control "A" Range/Performance (Cam/Rotor/Injector)
P0253	Injection Pump Fuel Metering Control "A" Low (Cam/Rotor/Injector)
P0254	Injection Pump Fuel Metering Control "A" High (Cam/Rotor/Injector)
P0255	Injection Pump Fuel Metering Control "A" Intermittent (Cam/Rotor/Injector)

P0256	Injection Pump Fuel Metering Control "B" Malfunction (Cam/Rotor/Injector)
P0257	Injection Pump Fuel Metering Control "B" Range/Performance (Cam/Rotor/Injector)
P0258	Injection Pump Fuel Metering Control "B" Low (Cam/Rotor/Injector)
P0259	Injection Pump Fuel Metering Control "B" High (Cam/Rotor/Injector)
P0260	Injection Pump Fuel Metering Control "B" Intermittent (Cam/Rotor/Injector)
P0261	Cylinder 1 Injector Circuit Low
P0262	Cylinder 1 Injector Circuit High
P0263	Cylinder 1 Contribution/Balance Fault
P0264	Cylinder 2 Injector Circuit Low
P0265	Cylinder 2 Injector Circuit High
P0266	Cylinder 2 Contribution/Balance Fault
P0267	Cylinder 3 Injector Circuit Low
P0268	Cylinder 3 Injector Circuit High
P0269	Cylinder 3 Contribution/Balance Fault
P0270	Cylinder 4 Injector Circuit Low
P0271	Cylinder 4 Injector Circuit High
P0272	Cylinder 4 Contribution/Balance Fault
P0273	Cylinder 5 Injector Circuit Low
P0274	Cylinder 5 Injector Circuit High
P0275	Cylinder 5 Contribution/Balance Fault
P0276	Cylinder 6 Injector Circuit Low
P0277	Cylinder 6 Injector Circuit High
P0278	Cylinder 6 Contribution/Balance Fault
P0279	Cylinder 7 Injector Circuit Low
P0280	Cylinder 7 Injector Circuit High
P0281	Cylinder 7 Contribution/Balance Fault
P0282	Cylinder 8 Injector Circuit Low
P0283	Cylinder 8 Injector Circuit High
P0284	Cylinder 8 Contribution/Balance Fault
P0285	Cylinder 9 Injector Circuit Low
P0286	Cylinder 9 Injector Circuit High
P0287	Cylinder 9 Contribution/Balance Fault
P0288	Cylinder 10 Injector Circuit Low
P0289	Cylinder 10 Injector Circuit High
P0290	Cylinder 10 Contribution/Balance Fault
P0291	Cylinder 11 Injector Circuit Low
P0292	Cylinder 11 Injector Circuit High
P0293	Cylinder 11 Contribution/Balance Fault
P0294	Cylinder 12 Injector Circuit Low
P0295	Cylinder 12 Injector Circuit High
P0296	Cylinder 12 Contribution/Range Fault

P03-IGNITION SYSTEM OR MISFIRE

P0300	Random/Multiple Cylinder Misfire Detected
P0301	Cylinder 1 Misfire Detected
P0302	Cylinder 2 Misfire Detected
P0303	Cylinder 3 Misfire Detected
P0304	Cylinder 4 Misfire Detected
P0305	Cylinder 5 Misfire Detected
P0306	Cylinder 6 Misfire Detected

P0307	Cylinder 7 Misfire Detected
P0308	Cylinder 8 Misfire Detected
P0309	Cylinder 9 Misfire Detected
P0311	Cylinder 11 Misfire Detected
P0312	Cylinder 12 Misfire Detected
P0320	Ignition/Distributor Engine Speed Input Circuit Malfunction
P0321	Ignition/Distributor Engine Speed Input Circuit Range/Performance
P0322	Ignition/Distributor Engine Speed Input Circuit No Signal
P0323	Ignition/Distributor Engine Speed Input Circuit Intermittent
P0325	Knock Sensor (KS) 1 Circuit Malfunction (Bank 1 or Single Sensor)
P0326	KS 1 Circuit Range/Performance (Bank 1 or Single Sensor)
P0327	KS 1 Circuit Low Input (Bank 1 or Single Sensor)
P0328	KS 1 Circuit High Input (Bank 1 or Single Sensor)
P0329	KS 1 Circuit Intermittent (Bank 1 or Single Sensor)
P0330	KS 2 Circuit Malfunction (Bank 2)
P0331	KS 2 Circuit Range/Performance (Bank 2)
P0332	KS 2 Circuit Low Input (Bank 2)
P0333	KS 2 Circuit High Input (Bank 2)
P0334	KS 2 Circuit Intermittent (Bank 2)
P0335	Crankshaft Position (CKP) Sensor A Circuit Malfunction
P0336	CKP Sensor A Circuit Range/Performance
P0337	CKP Sensor A Circuit Low Input
P0338	CKP Sensor A Circuit High Input
P0339	CKP Sensor A Circuit Intermittent
P0340	Camshaft Position (CMP) Sensor Circuit Malfunction
P0341	CMP Sensor Circuit Range/Performance
P0342	CMP Sensor Circuit Low Input
P0343	CMP Sensor Circuit High Input
P0344	CMP Sensor Circuit Intermittent
P0350	Ignition Coil Primary/Secondary Circuit Malfunction
P0351	Ignition Coil A Primary/Secondary Circuit Malfunction
P0352	Ignition Coil B Primary/Secondary Circuit Malfunction
P0353	Ignition Coil C Primary/Secondary Circuit Malfunction
P0354	Ignition Coil D Primary/Secondary Circuit Malfunction
P0355	Ignition Coil E Primary/Secondary Circuit Malfunction
P0356	Ignition Coil F Primary/Secondary Circuit Malfunction
P0357	Ignition Coil G Primary/Secondary Circuit Malfunction
P0358	Ignition Coil H Primary/Secondary Circuit Malfunction
P0359	Ignition Coil I Primary/Secondary Circuit Malfunction
P0360	Ignition Coil J Primary/Secondary Circuit Malfunction
P0361	Ignition Coil K Primary/Secondary Circuit Malfunction
P0362	Ignition Coil L Primary/Secondary Circuit Malfunction
P0370	Timing Reference High Resolution Signal A Malfunction
P0371	Timing Reference High Resolution Signal A Too Many Pulses
P0372	Timing Reference High Resolution Signal A Too Few Pulses
P0373	Timing Reference High Resolution Signal A Intermittent/Erratic Pulses
P0374	Timing Reference High Resolution Signal A No Pulses
P0375	Timing Reference High Resolution Signal B Malfunction
P0376	Timing Reference High Resolution Signal B Too Many Pulses

P0377	Timing Reference High Resolution Signal B Too Few Pulses
P0378	Timing Reference High Resolution Signal B Intermittent/Erratic Pulses
P0379	Timing Reference High Resolution Signal B No Pulses
P0380	Glow Plug/Heater Circuit "A" Malfunction
P0381	Glow Plug/Heater Indicator Circuit Malfunction
P0382	Exhaust Gas Recirculation Flow Malfunction
P0385	CKP Sensor B Circuit Malfunction
P0386	CKP Sensor B Circuit Range/Performance
P0387	CKP Sensor B Circuit Low Input
P0388	CKP Sensor B Circuit High Input
P0389	CKP Sensor B Circuit Intermittent

P04-AUXILIARY EMISSION CONTROLS

P0400	Exhaust Gas Recirculation (EGR) Flow Malfunction
P0401	EGR Flow Insufficient Detected
P0402	EGR Flow Excessive Detected
P0403	EGR Circuit Malfunction
P0404	EGR Circuit Range/Performance
P0405	EGR Sensor A Circuit Low
P0406	EGR Sensor A Circuit High
P0407	EGR Sensor B Circuit Low
P0408	EGR Sensor B Circuit High
P0410	Secondary Air Injection System Malfunction
P0411	Secondary Air Injection System Incorrect Flow Detected
P0412	Secondary Air Injection System Switching Valve A Circuit Malfunction
P0413	Secondary Air Injection System Switching Valve A Circuit Open
P0414	Secondary Air Injection System Switching Valve A Circuit Shorted
P0415	Secondary Air Injection System Switching Valve B Circuit Malfunction
P0416	Secondary Air Injection System Switching Valve B Circuit Open
P0417	Secondary Air Injection System Switching Valve B Circuit Shorted
P0418	Secondary Air Injection System Relay "A" Circuit Malfunction
P0419	Secondary Air Injection System Relay "B" Circuit Malfunction
P0420	Catalyst System Efficiency Below Threshold (Bank 1)
P0421	Warm Up Catalyst Efficiency Below Threshold (Bank 1)
P0422	Main Catalyst Efficiency Below Threshold (Bank 1)
P0423	Heated Catalyst Efficiency Below Threshold (Bank 1)
P0424	Heated Catalyst Temperature Below Threshold (Bank 1)
P0430	Catalyst System Efficiency Below Threshold (Bank 2)
P0431	Warm Up Catalyst Efficiency Below Threshold (Bank 2)
P0432	Main Catalyst Efficiency Below Threshold (Bank 2)
P0433	Heated Catalyst Efficiency Below Threshold (Bank 2)
P0434	Heated Catalyst Temperature Below Threshold (Bank 2)
P0440	Evaporative Emission (EVAP) Control System Malfunction
P0441	EVAP Control System Incorrect Purge Flow
P0442	EVAP Control System Leak Detected (small leak)
P0443	EVAP Control System Purge Control Valve Circuit Malfunction

L1

P0444	EVAP Control System Purge Control Valve Circuit Open
P0445	EVAP Control System Purge Control Valve Circuit Shorted
P0446	EVAP Control System Vent Control Circuit Malfunction
P0447	EVAP Control System Vent Control Circuit Open
P0448	EVAP Control System Vent Control Circuit Shorted
P0449	EVAP Control System Vent Valve/Solenoid Circuit Malfunction
P0450	EVAP Control System Pressure Sensor Malfunction
P0451	EVAP Control System Pressure Sensor Range/Performance
P0452	EVAP Control System Pressure Sensor Low Input
P0453	EVAP Control System Pressure Sensor High Input
P0454	EVAP Control System Pressure Sensor Intermittent
P0455	EVAP Control System Leak Detected (gross leak)
P0460	Fuel Level Sensor Circuit Malfunction
P0461	Fuel Level Sensor Circuit Range/Performance
P0462	Fuel Level Sensor Circuit Low Input
P0463	Fuel Level Sensor Circuit High Input
P0464	Fuel Level Sensor Circuit Intermittent
P0465	Purge Flow Sensor Circuit Malfunction
P0466	Purge Flow Sensor Circuit Range/Performance
P0467	Purge Flow Sensor Circuit Low Input
P0468	Purge Flow Sensor Circuit High Input
P0469	Purge Flow Sensor Circuit Intermittent
P0470	Exhaust Pressure Sensor Malfunction
P0471	Exhaust Pressure Sensor Range/Performance
P0472	Exhaust Pressure Sensor Low
P0473	Exhaust Pressure Sensor High
P0474	Exhaust Pressure Sensor Intermittent
P0475	Exhaust Pressure Control Valve Malfunction
P0476	Exhaust Pressure Control Valve Range/Performance
P0477	Exhaust Pressure Control Valve Low
P0478	Exhaust Pressure Control Valve High
P0479	Exhaust Pressure Control Valve Intermittent
P0480	Cooling Fan 1 Control Circuit Malfunction
P0481	Cooling Fan 2 Control Circuit Malfunction
P0482	Cooling Fan 3 Control Circuit Malfunction
P0483	Cooling Fan Rationality Check Malfunction
P0484	Cooling Fan Circuit Over Current
P0485	Cooling Fan Power/Ground Circuit Malfunction

P05-VEHICLE SPEED CONTROL AND IDLE CONTROL SYSTEMS

P0500	Vehicle Speed Sensor (VSS) Malfunction
P0501	VSS Range/Performance
P0502	VSS Low Input
P0503	VSS Intermittent/Erratic/High
P0505	Idle Control System Malfunction
P0506	Idle Control System RPM Lower Than Expected
P0507	Idle Control System RPM Higher Than Expected
P0510	Closed Throttle Position Switch Malfunction
P0520	Engine Oil Pressure Sensor/Switch Circuit Malfunction
P0521	Engine Oil Pressure Sensor/Switch Circuit Range/Performance
P0522	Engine Oil Pressure Sensor/Switch Circuit Low Voltage

P0523	Engine Oil Pressure Sensor/Switch Circuit High Voltage
P0530	A/C Refrigerant Pressure Sensor Circuit Malfunction
P0531	A/C Refrigerant Pressure Sensor Circuit Range/Performance
P0532	A/C Refrigerant Pressure Sensor Circuit Low Input
P0533	A/C Refrigerant Pressure Sensor Circuit High Input
P0534	Air Conditioner Refrigerant Charge Loss
P0550	Power Steering Pressure Sensor Circuit Malfunction
P0551	Power Steering Pressure Sensor Circuit Range/Performance
P0552	Power Steering Pressure Sensor Circuit Low Input
P0553	Power Steering Pressure Sensor Circuit High Input
P0554	Power Steering Pressure Sensor Circuit Intermittent
P0560	System Voltage Malfunction
P0561	System Voltage Unstable
P0562	System Voltage Low
P0563	System Voltage High
P0565	Cruise Control On Signal Malfunction
P0566	Cruise Control Off Signal Malfunction
P0567	Cruise Control Resume Signal Malfunction
P0568	Cruise Control Set Signal Malfunction
P0569	Cruise Control Coast Signal Malfunction
P0570	Cruise Control Accel Signal Malfunction
P0571	Cruise Control/Brake Switch A Circuit Malfunction
P0572	Cruise Control/Brake Switch A Circuit Low
P0573	Cruise Control/Brake Switch A Circuit High
P0574	Cruise Control Related Malfunction
P0575	Cruise Control Related Malfunction
P0576	Cruise Control Related Malfunction
P0576	Cruise Control Related Malfunction
P0578	Cruise Control Related Malfunction
P0579	Cruise Control Related Malfunction
P0580	Cruise Control Related Malfunction

P06-COMPUTER AND OUTPUT CIRCUITS

P0600	Serial Communication Link Malfunction
P0601	Internal Control Module Memory Check Sum Error
P0602	Control Module Programming Error
P0603	Internal Control Module Keep Alive Memory (KAM) Error
P0604	Internal Control Module Random Access Memory (RAM) Error
P0605	Internal Control Module Read Only Memory (ROM) Error
P0606	PCM Processor Fault
P0608	Control Module VSS Output "A" Malfunction
P0609	Control Module VSS Output "B" Malfunction
P0620	Generator Control Circuit Malfunction
P0621	Generator Lamp "L" Control Circuit Malfunction
P0622	Generator Field "F" Control Circuit Malfunction
P0650	Malfunction Indicator Lamp (MIL) Control Circuit Malfunction
P0654	Engine RPM Output Circuit Malfunction
P0655	Engine Hot Lamp Output Control Circuit Malfucntion
P0656	Fuel Level Output Circuit Malfunction

P07-TRANSMISSION

P0700	Transmission Control System Malfunction
P0701	Transmission Control System Range/Performance

P0702	Transmission Control System Electrical
P0703	Torque Converter/Brake Switch B Circuit Malfunction
P0704	Clutch Switch Input Circuit Malfunction
P0705	Transmission Range Sensor Circuit Malfunction (PRNDL Input)
P0706	Transmission Range Sensor Circuit Range/Performance
P0707	Transmission Range Sensor Circuit Low Input
P0708	Transmission Range Sensor Circuit High Input
P0709	Transmission Range Sensor Circuit Intermittent
P0710	Transmission Fluid Temperature Sensor Circuit Malfunction
P0711	Transmission Fluid Temperature Sensor Circuit Range/Performance
P0712	Transmission Fluid Temperature Sensor Circuit Low Input
P0713	Transmission Fluid Temperature Sensor Circuit High Input
P0714	Transmission Fluid Temperature Sensor Circuit Intermittent
P0715	Input/Turbine Speed Sensor Circuit Malfunction
P0716	Input/Turbine Speed Sensor Circuit Range/Performance
P0717	Input/Turbine Speed Sensor Circuit No Signal
P0718	Input/Turbine Speed Sensor Circuit Intermittent
P0719	Torque Converter/Brake Switch B Circuit Low
P0720	Output Speed Sensor Circuit Malfunction
P0721	Output Speed Sensor Range/Performance
P0722	Output Speed Sensor No Signal
P0723	Output Speed Sensor Intermittent
P0724	Torque Converter/Brake Switch B Circuit High
P0725	Engine Speed input Circuit Malfunction
P0726	Engine Speed Input Circuit Range/Performance
P0727	Engine Speed Input Circuit No Signal
P0728	Engine Speed Input Circuit Intermittent
P0730	Incorrect Gear Ratio
P0731	Gear 1 Incorrect Ratio
P0732	Gear 2 Incorrect Ratio
P0733	Gear 3 Incorrect Ratio
P0734	Gear 4 Incorrect Ratio
P0735	Gear 5 Incorrect Ratio
P0736	Reverse Incorrect Gear Ratio
P0740	Torque Converter Clutch (TCC) Circuit Malfuction
P0741	TCC Circuit Performance or Stuck Off
P0742	TCC Circuit Stuck On
P0743	TCC Circuit Electrical
P0744	TCC Circuit Intermittent
P0745	Pressure Control Solenoid Malfunction
P0746	Pressure Control Solenoid Performance or Stuck Off
P0747	Pressure Control Solenoid Stuck On
P0748	Pressure Control Solenoid Electrical
P0749	Pressure Control Solenoid Intermittent
P0750	Shift Solenoid A Malfunction
P0751	Shift Solenoid A Performance or Stuck Off
P0752	Shift Solenoid A Stuck On
P0753	Shift Solenoid A Electrical
P0754	Shift Solenoid A Intermittent
P0755	Shift Solenoid B Malfunction
P0756	Shift Solenoid B Performance or Stuck Off

P0757	Shift Solenoid B Stuck On
P0758	Shift Solenoid B Electrical
P0759	Shift Solenoid B Intermittent
P0760	Shift Solenoid C Malfunction
P0761	Shift Solenoid C Performance or Stuck Off
P0762	Shift Solenoid C Stuck On
P0763	Shift Solenoid C Electrical
P0764	Shift Solenoid C Intermittent
P0765	Shift Solenoid D Malfunction
P0766	Shift Solenoid D Performance or Stuck Off
P0767	Shift Solenoid D Stuck On
P0768	Shift Solenoid D Electrical
P0769	Shift Solenoid D Intermittent
P0770	Shift Solenoid E Malfunction
P0771	Shift Solenoid E Performance or Stuck Off
P0772	Shift Solenoid E Stuck On
P0773	Shift Solenoid E Electrical
P0774	Shift Solenoid E Intermittent
P0780	Shift Malfunction
P0781	1-2 Shift Malfunction
P0782	2-3 Shift Malfunction
P0783	3-4 Shift Malfunction
P0784	4-5 Shift Malfunction
P0785	Shift/Timing Solenoid Malfunction
P0786	Shift/Timing Solenoid Range/Performance
P0787	Shift/Timing Solenoid Low
P0788	Shift/Timing Solenoid High
P0789	Shift/Timing Solenoid Intermittent
P0790	Normal/Performance Switch Circuit Malfunction

P08-TRANSMISSION

P0801	Reverse Inhibit Control Circuit Malfunction
P0803	1-4 Upshift (Skip Shift) Solenoid Control Circuit Malfunction
P0804	1-4 Upshift (Skip Shift) Lamp Control Circuit Malfunction
P0805	Clutch Position Sensor Circuit
P0806	Clutch Position Sensor Circuit Range/Performance
P0807	Clutch Position Sensor Circuit Low
P0808	Clutch Position Sensor Circuit High
P0809	Clutch Position Sensor Circuit Intermittent
P0810	Clutch Position Control Error
P0811	Excessive Clutch Slippage
P0812	Reverse Input Circuit
P0813	Reverse Output Circuit
P0814	Transmission Range Display Circuit
P0815	Upshift Switch Circuit
P0816	Downshift Switch Circuit
P0817	Starter Disable Circuit
P0818	Driveline Disconnect Switch Input Circuit
P0819	Up and Down Shift Switch to Transmission Range Correlation
P0820	Gear Lever X-Y Position Sensor Circuit
P0821	Gear Lever X Position Circuit
P0822	Gear Lever Y Position Circuit
P0823	Gear Lever X Position Circuit Intermittent

P0824	Gear Lever Y Position Circuit Intermittent
P0825	Gear Lever Push-Pull Switch (Shift Anticipate)
P0826	Up and Down Shift Switch Circuit
P0827	Up and Down Shift Switch Circuit Low
P0828	Up and Down Shift Switch Circuit High
P0829	5-6 Shift
P0830	Clutch Pedal Switch A Circuit
P0831	Clutch Pedal Switch A Circuit Low
P0832	Clutch Pedal Switch A Circuit High
P0833	Clutch Pedal Switch B Circuit
P0834	Clutch Pedal Switch B Circuit Low
P0835	Clutch Pedal Switch B Circuit High
P0836	Four Wheel Drive Switch Circuit
P0837	Four Wheel Drive Switch Circuit Range/Performance
P0838	Four Wheel Drive Switch Circuit Low
P0839	Four Wheel Drive Switch Circuit High
P0840	Transmission Fluid Pressure Sensor/Switch A Circuit Malfunction
P0841	Transmission Fluid Pressure Sensor/Switch A Circuit Range/Performance
P0842	Transmission Fluid Pressure Sensor/Switch A Circuit Low
P0843	Transmission Fluid Pressure Sensor/Switch A Circuit High
P0844	Transmission Fluid Pressure Sensor/Switch A Circuit Intermittent
P0845	Transmission Fluid Pressure Sensor/Switch B Circuit Malfunction
P0846	Transmission Fluid Pressure Sensor/Switch B Circuit Range/Performance
P0847	Transmission Fluid Pressure Sensor/Switch B Circuit Low
P0848	Transmission Fluid Pressure Sensor/Switch B Circuit High
P0849	Transmission Fluid Pressure Sensor/Switch B Circuit Intermittent
P0850	Park/Neutral Switch Input Circuit
P0851	Park/Neutral Switch Input Circuit Low
P0852	Park/Neutral Switch Input Circuit High
P0853	Drive Switch Input Circuit
P0854	Drive Switch Input Circuit Low
P0855	Drive Switch Input Circuit High
P0856	Traction Control Input Signal
P0857	Traction Control Input Signal Range/Performance
P0858	Traction Control Input Signal Low
P0859	Traction Control Input Signal High
P0860	Gear Shift Module Communication Circuit
P0861	Gear Shift Module Communication Circuit Low
P0862	Gear Shift Module Communication Circuit High
P0863	Transmission Control Module (TCM) Communication Circuit
P0864	TCM Communication Circuit Range/Performance
P0865	TCM Communication Circuit Low
P0866	TCM Communication Circuit High
P0867	Transmission Fluid Pressure
P0868	Transmission Fluid Pressure Low
P0869	Transmission Fluid Pressure High
P0870	Transmission Fluid Pressure Sensor/Switch C Circuit
P0871	Transmission Fluid Pressure Sensor/Switch C Circuit Range/Performance

P0872	Transmission Fluid Pressure Sensor/Switch C Circuit Low
P0873	Transmission Fluid Pressure Sensor/Switch C Circuit High
P0874	Transmission Fluid Pressure Sensor/Switch C Circuit Intermittent
P0875	Transmission Fluid Pressure Sensor/Switch D Circuit
P0876	Transmission Fluid Pressure Sensor/Switch D Circuit Range/Performance
P0877	Transmission Fluid Pressure Sensor/Switch D Circuit Low
P0878	Transmission Fluid Pressure Sensor/Switch D Circuit High
P0879	Transmission Fluid Pressure Sensor/Switch D Circuit Intermittent
P0880	TCM Power Input Signal
P0881	TCM Power Input Signal Range/Performance
P0882	TCM Power Input Signal Low
P0883	TCM Power Input Signal High
P0884	TCM Power Input Signal Intermittent
P0885	TCM Power Relay Control Circuit/Open
P0886	TCM Power Relay Control Circuit Low
P0887	TCM Power Relay Control Circuit High
P0888	TCM Power Relay Sense Circuit
P0889	TCM Power Relay Sense Circuit Range/Performance
P0890	TCM Power Relay Sense Circuit Low
P0891	TCM Power Relay Sense Circuit High
P0892	TCM Power Relay Sense Circuit Intermittent
P0893	Multiple Gears Engaged
P0894	Transmission Component Slipping
P0895	Shift Time Too Short
P0896	Shift Time Too Long
P0897	Transmission Fluid Deteriorated
P0898	Transmission Control System Malfunction Indicator Lamp Request Circuit Low
P0899	Transmission Control System Malfunction Indicator Lamp Request Circuit High

P09-TRANSMISSION

P0900	Clutch Actuator Circuit/Open
P0901	Clutch Actuator Circuit Range/Performance
P0902	Clutch Actuator Circuit Low
P0903	Clutch Actuator Circuit High
P0904	Gate Select Position Circuit
P0905	Gate Select Position Circuit Range/Performance
P0906	Gate Select Position Circuit Low
P0907	Gate Select Position Circuit High
P0908	Gate Select Position Circuit Intermittent
P0909	Gate Select Control Error
P0910	Gate Select Actuator Circuit/Open
P0911	Gate Select Actuator Circuit Range/Performance
P0912	Gate Select Actuator Circuit Low
P0913	Gate Select Actuator Circuit High
P0914	Gear Shift Position Circuit
P0915	Gear Shift Position Circuit Range/Performance
P0916	Gear Shift Position Circuit Low
P0917	Gear Shift Position Circuit High
P0918	Gear Shift Position Circuit Intermittent
P0919	Gear Shift Position Control Error

P0920	Gear Shift Forward Actuator Circuit/Open
P0921	Gear Shift Forward Actuator Circuit Range/Performance
P0922	Gear Shift Forward Actuator Circuit Low
P0923	Gear Shift Forward Actuator Circuit High
P0924	Gear Shift Reverse Actuator Circuit/Open
P0925	Gear Shift Reverse Actuator Circuit Range/Performance
P0926	Gear Shift Reverse Actuator Circuit Low
P0927	Gear Shift Reverse Actuator Circuit High
P0928	Gear Shift Lock Solenoid Control Circuit/Open
P0929	Gear Shift Lock Solenoid Control Circuit Range/Performance
P0930	Gear Shift Lock Solenoid Control Circuit Low
P0931	Gear Shift Lock Solenoid Control Circuit High
P0932	Hydraulic Pressure Sensor Circuit
P0933	Hydraulic Pressure Sensor Range/Performance
P0934	Hydraulic Pressure Sensor Circuit Low
P0935	Hydraulic Pressure Sensor Circuit High
P0936	Hydraulic Pressure Sensor Circuit Intermittent
P0937	Hydraulic Oil Temperature Sensor Circuit
P0938	Hydraulic Oil Temperature Sensor Range/Performance
P0939	Hydraulic Oil Temperature Sensor Circuit Low
P0940	Hydraulic Oil Temperature Sensor Circuit High
P0941	Hydraulic Oil Temperature Sensor Circuit Intermittent
P0942	Hydraulic Pressure Unit
P0943	Hydraulic Pressure Unit Cycling Period Too Short
P0944	Hydraulic Pressure Unit Loss of Pressure
P0945	Hydraulic Pump Relay Circuit/Open
P0946	Hydraulic Pump Relay Circuit Range/Performance
P0947	Hydraulic Pump Relay Circuit Low
P0948	Hydraulic Pump Relay Circuit High
P0949	Auto Shift Manual Adaptive Learning Not Complete
P0950	Auto Shift Manual Control Circuit
P0951	Auto Shift Manual Control Circuit Range/Performance
P0952	Auto Shift Manual Control Circuit Low
P0953	Auto Shift Manual Control Circuit High
P0954	Auto Shift Manual Control Circuit Intermittent
P0955	Auto Shift Manual Mode Circuit
P0956	Auto Shift Manual Mode Circuit Range/Performance
P0957	Auto Shift Manual Mode Circuit Low
P0958	Auto Shift Manual Mode Circuit High
P0959	Auto Shift Manual Mode Circuit Intermittent
P0960	Pressure Control Solenoid A Control Circuit/Open
P0961	Pressure Control Solenoid A Control Circuit Range/Performance
P0962	Pressure Control Solenoid A Control Circuit Low
P0963	Pressure Control Solenoid A Control Circuit High
P0964	Pressure Control Solenoid B Control Circuit/Open
P0965	Pressure Control Solenoid B Control Circuit Range/Performance
P0966	Pressure Control Solenoid B Control Circuit Low
P0967	Pressure Control Solenoid B Control Circuit High
P0968	Pressure Control Solenoid C Control Circuit/Open
P0969	Pressure Control Solenoid C Control Circuit Range/Performance
P0970	Pressure Control Solenoid C Control Circuit Low
P0971	Pressure Control Solenoid C Control Circuit High
P0972	Shift Solenoid A Control Circuit Range/Performance
P0973	Shift Solenoid A Control Circuit Low
P0974	Shift Solenoid A Control Circuit High
P0975	Shift Solenoid B Control Circuit Range/Performance
P0976	Shift Solenoid B Control Circuit Low
P0977	Shift Solenoid B Control Circuit High
P0978	Shift Solenoid C Control Circuit Range/Performance
P0979	Shift Solenoid C Control Circuit Low
P0980	Shift Solenoid C Control Circuit High
P0981	Shift Solenoid D Control Circuit Range/Performance
P0982	Shift Solenoid D Control Circuit Low
P0983	Shift Solenoid D Control Circuit High
P0984	Shift Solenoid E Control Circuit Range/Performance
P0985	Shift Solenoid E Control Circuit Low
P0986	Shift Solenoid E Control Circuit High
P0987	Transmission Fluid Pressure Sensor/Switch E Circuit
P0988	Transmission Fluid Pressure Sensor/Switch E Circuit Range/Performance
P0989	Transmission Fluid Pressure Sensor/Switch E Circuit Low
P0990	Transmission Fluid Pressure Sensor/Switch E Circuit High
P0991	Transmission Fluid Pressure Sensor/Switch E Circuit Intermittent
P0992	Transmission Fluid Pressure Sensor/Switch F Circuit
P0993	Transmission Fluid Pressure Sensor/Switch F Circuit Range/Performance
P0994	Transmission Fluid Pressure Sensor/Switch F Circuit Low
P0995	Transmission Fluid Pressure Sensor/Switch F Circuit High
P0996	Transmission Fluid Pressure Sensor/Switch F Circuit Intermittent
P0997	Shift Solenoid F Control Circuit Range/Performance
P0998	Shift Solenoid F Control Circuit Low
P0999	Shift Solenoid F Control Circuit High